Catching the Wind: Edward Kennedy and the Liberal Hour

An Empire of Their Own: How the Jews Invented Hollywood

Winchell: Gossip, Power, and the Culture of Celebrity

Life, the Movie: How Entertainment Conquered Reality

Walt Disney: The Triumph of the American Imagination

Barbra Streisand: Redefining Beauty, Femininity, and Power

CATCHING

THE WIND

CATCHING

THE WIND

Edward Kennedy and the Liberal Hour

NEAL GABLER

CROWN
NEW YORK

Published in the United States by Crown, an imprint of Random House,
a division of Penguin Random House LLC, New York.

CROWN and the Crown colophon are registered trademarks of
Penguin Random House LLC.

LIBRARY OF CONGRESS CATALOGING-IN-PUBLICATION DATA
Names: Gabler, Neal, author.
Title: Catching the wind / Neal Gabler.
Description: First edition. | New York : Crown, 2020. | Includes
bibliographical references and index.
Identifiers: LCCN 2020019328 (print) | LCCN 2020019329 (ebook) |
ISBN 9780307405449 (hardcover) | ISBN 9780804137027 (ebook)
Subjects: LCSH: Kennedy, Edward M. (Edward Moore), 1932–2009. |
Legislators—United States—Biography. | United States. Congress.
Senate—Biography. | United States—Politics and government—
1945–1989. | United States—Politics and government—1989–
Classification: LCC E840.8.K35 G34 2020 (print) |
LCC E840.8.K35 (ebook) | DDC 973.92092 [B]—dc23
LC record available at https://lccn.loc.gov/2020019328
LC ebook record available at https://lccn.loc.gov/2020019329

Printed in the United States of America on acid-free paper

randomhousebooks.com

2 4 6 8 9 7 5 3 1

First Edition

Book design by Fritz Metsch

Once again, to my beloved daughters,
Laurel and Tänne,
and to my equally beloved son-in-law,
Braden, and daughter-in-law, Shoshanna,
all of whom have devoted their lives
to serving others,

And to my granddaughter, Sadie, the joy of my life.

No man is more fortunate.
May they live in a gentler, kinder, and more moral world,
and may they continue to help make it so.

"And He will set the sheep on His right side, but the goats on His left. Then the King will say to those on His right hand, 'Come, you blessed of my Father, inherit the kingdom, for I was hungry and you gave me something to eat, I was thirsty and you gave me something to drink, I was a stranger and you invited me in, I needed clothes and you clothed me, I was sick and you looked after me, I was in prison and you came to visit me.'

"Then the righteous will answer Him, 'Lord, when did we see you hungry and feed you, or thirsty and give you something to drink? When did we see you a stranger and invite you in, or needing clothes and clothe you? When did we see you sick or in prison and go to visit you?'

"The King will reply, 'Truly I tell you, whatever you did for one of the least of these brothers and sisters of mine, you did for me.'

"Then He will say to those on his left, 'Depart from me, you who are cursed, into the eternal fire prepared for the devil and his angels. For I was hungry and you gave me nothing to eat, I was thirsty and you gave me nothing to drink, I was a stranger and you did not invite me in, I needed clothes and you did not clothe me, I was sick and in prison and you did not look after me.'

"They also will answer, 'Lord, when did we see you hungry or thirsty or a stranger or needing clothes or sick or in prison, and did not help you?'

"He will reply, 'Truly I tell you, whatever you did not do for one of the least of these, you did not do for me.'"

—MATTHEW 25:35–45

CONTENTS

Introduction: They Came   xiii

ONE: *The Youngest*   3

TWO: *The Least*   54

THREE: *The Succession*   94

FOUR: *"If His Name Was Edward Moore . . ."*   143

FIVE: *The Lowest Expectations*   179

SIX: *"Do a Little Suffering"*   228

SEVEN: *"A Heightened Sense of Purpose"*   251

EIGHT: *A Dying Wind*   307

NINE: *All Hell Fell*   355

TEN: *A Fallen Standard*   399

ELEVEN: *A Shadow President*   440

TWELVE: *"The Wrong Side of Destiny"*   471

THIRTEEN: *Starting from Scratch*   519

FOURTEEN: *"People Do Not Want to Be Improved"*   573

FIFTEEN: *"Awesome Power with No Discipline"*   613

SIXTEEN: *S.3*   641

SEVENTEEN: *"Our Long National Nightmare Is Over"*   690

Acknowledgments   737

Notes   743

Bibliography   827

Index   843

They Came

ON A BRISK, bright, cool August morning in Hyannis Port, they came. First the Barnstable motorcycle police, their bikes parked near the DO NOT ENTER sign, standing guard on Marchant Avenue a few hundred yards outside the famous Kennedy compound to keep onlookers at bay. Then the newsmen milling on Marchant, waiting to deliver their stand-ups while their white transmission vans lined Irving Avenue, bumper to bumper, satellite dishes tilted skyward between the trees, and the thick cables running down Scudder Avenue, perpendicular to Irving. And then the family: Ethel Kennedy, Robert Kennedy's widow; and Jean Kennedy Smith, the senator's sole surviving sibling, gaunt in oversized sunglasses and wearing a large straw hat; and Sargent Shriver, his brother-in-law, whose wife, Eunice, had died just two weeks before; and Kennedy cousins, dozens of them; and grandchildren, four of them. Then friends came, like John Kerry and his wife, Teresa Heinz—Kerry, who had been Massachusetts's junior senator and later a Democratic presidential candidate. And others, neither family nor dignitaries, came to pay respects outside the compound, ordinary admirers like Anne Griswold of Centerville, who brought flowers and a balloon and a thank-you note—"not a condolence card"—to the senator "for all he's done"; and April Thomas of Marston Mills, whose two-year-old daughter, in a red sundress and red hat, held a sign written in blue marker: "Teddy, you are a true gift of love, a work of art, signed by God! May his angels embrace you in love."

They came.

And they came again the next morning, among them Caroline Kennedy, the late president's daughter, and Patrick Kennedy, Senator Kennedy's youngest son, who had been traveling at the time of his father's death, as the family—eighty-five of them—attended mass in the rambling white clapboard house on the lip of Nantucket Sound, the house where the Kennedys had summered since 1926. Then they filed out onto the porch, some holding hands, others speaking quietly, a few laughing, and strolled down the driveway to watch the honor guard carry the flag-draped casket to a hearse. After the doors of the hearse closed, many of them touched the car reverently before scattering to their own vehicles in the motorcade for the seventy-mile journey to Boston—a journey that Ted had planned, as he had planned every event of his funeral.

He had planned not just the route but the scale of the observance— drawn to what he saw as his proportions. There was to be no riderless horse pulling a caisson through Washington's streets as at John Kennedy's funeral, no train like the one that carried Robert Kennedy's body from New York to Washington, echoing Lincoln's funeral train, which bore him from Washington to his resting place in Springfield, Illinois. Ted's motorcade was long but modest, informal, democratic, less solemn than celebratory: Ted's scale, Ted's mood.

As the caravan crept through Hyannis Port and down Main Street, they came. "I remember where I was when President Kennedy died, and I'll remember where I was when the senator left Hyannis Port," said Virginia Cain, who had walked two miles to see the cortege pass. And past the local John F. Kennedy Museum, where an admirer had written across an old Ted Kennedy campaign poster: "God bless Ted. The last was first," and where someone had draped a rosary over a photograph of Ted. And along the course north to Route 6, as gulls circled in the sky, they came, lining the streets, hundreds of them, many in shorts and shirtsleeves. Some applauded as the hearse passed, while Patrick, sitting in the passenger seat of the hearse, his eyes wet, mouthed thanks. Some saluted. Some waved flags or held signs: THANK YOU, TEDDY. Two women put their hands over their hearts as tears coursed down their cheeks. At Sagamore Bridge, connecting Cape Cod to the mainland, a bagpiper blew a dirge.

As the cortege moved down the flat highway, they came, some standing along the road, others stopping their cars on the overpasses, and they came as it snaked into Boston, at 4 P.M. that afternoon, up Summer Street in South Boston, holding signs—FOREVER OURS; FAIR WINDS AND CALM SEAS—past construction workers in hardhats and members of the carpenters' union lifting more signs in tribute, and past landmarks and points of significance to Kennedy: St. Stephen's, where his mother had been baptized almost a hundred twenty years earlier and where her funeral was held nearly fifteen years earlier; past his office in the federal building named for his late brother John, where Kennedy once had to escape angry crowds protesting his support for school busing to racially integrate Boston's public schools; past Faneuil Hall, where Mayor Thomas Menino had the bell rung forty-seven times for each year of Kennedy's Senate service; past Boston Common, where, as *The Boston Globe* reported, there were "women in wheelchairs, girls in strollers, and men wearing Red Sox T-shirts." And as the caravan crawled up Park Street, the *Globe* also reported, the crowd began applauding, the applause building into a crescendo, with "whoops and hollers," and some of the more boisterous even climbed lampposts and waved flags. And as it moved past the Rose Fitzgerald Kennedy Greenway into Dorchester and to the JFK Library, where the casket would lie, thousands were waiting there in line to file past. They came.

And not just in Boston. Several dozen homeless men held hands, bowed their heads, and sang "We Shall Overcome" in the basement of a Washington church. And in Washington's Dupont Circle, people gathered at twilight, many of them on their way home from work, holding a sheet of paper they had been handed with the closing lines from Kennedy's famous 1980 address at the Democratic Convention: "The work goes on, the cause endures, the hope still lives, and the dream shall never die." A vigil was held in Plaza Park in Las Vegas. At Tanglewood in the Berkshires of Massachusetts, singer James Taylor delivered his own eulogy to Kennedy and sang "Shed a Little Light," which he had composed for Martin Luther King Jr. The previous night, the Boston Red Sox had an Air Force bugler play "Taps" before their game. But there was one place they didn't come, couldn't come, that summer day: the Senate chamber, where Kennedy's desk, the desk in the last row of the Senate, which had been Daniel Webster's desk and, by some accounts, John Kennedy's desk, was draped in black, a vase of white roses on top, the customary way to honor a fallen senator. And someone had placed something else on the desk—a copy of Robert Frost's poem "The Road Not Taken," which concludes: "Two roads diverged in a wood, and I— / I took the one less traveled by, / And that has made all the difference."

Of senators' funerals, only those of Daniel Webster, Henry Clay, Robert Taft, and, of course, Robert Kennedy, could be compared to Edward Kennedy's, but Kennedy's, though perhaps smaller in pageantry, was larger still than any of those, save for Bobby's, because his seemed to strike the American conscience so widely and so deeply. It was, like Bobby's, a national mourning that cut across class, race, geography, even ideology. "Esteemed by almost everyone," E. J. Dionne Jr. would write of him. "A Swelling Tide of Emotion" is how *The Boston Globe* described the public response. With full day-long television coverage, it was the big, emotional send-off of a president—bigger than that of most ex-presidents—though Edward Kennedy had never achieved that ambition, having failed spectacularly in his one attempt. But they came, many of them, not because he was a political potentate but because he was a Kennedy, and the Kennedys had been central to American life for decades. "No family has loomed as large in the course of this century, both mirroring and making the nation's manners and morals," wrote one observer, and he was certainly right. Their story, which is the story of Irish immigrants rising to wealth and influence and status and power and then to the highest office in the land, was the American Dream come true—a living myth. And to that myth they added glamour and a movie-star panache that gave the country both pride and a vicarious thrill. Yet with the soaring achievements and the glittering celebrity came a reckoning. As countless commentators said, the Kennedys had lived a Shakespearean tragedy, which became the nation's, especially the tragedies of the assassinations of John Kennedy and Robert Kennedy, who were struck down in their relative youth and at the height of their powers. In this drama, the survivor, Ted Kennedy, would become the Prince Hal, young, errant, and often irresponsible, who, with his brothers gone, was now called into service and forced to grow into King Henry to maintain the family legacy. From "kid brother" to "senior statesman" is how John Kennedy's old adviser Ted Sorensen put it, though it was hardly so smooth a transformation or one so easily embraced.

For if the Kennedys touched Shakespearean heights, they also, in Ted Kennedy's lifetime, descended to tabloid depths, in large measure because of Ted Kennedy. The Kennedys were part of the American consciousness in this sense too: major characters in the nation's soap-opera repertory company. "The Kennedys have become entertainment superstars," one analyst wrote. "This is a family identified by first names in the familiar Hollywood style—Jack, Jackie, Bobby, Ethel, Teddy—just as we knew Elvis, Marilyn, and Ringo. . . ." And that familiarity, that ongoing engagement with the Kennedys, including an engagement with their foibles and failures, was another reason they came. As pollster Mervin Field characterized it when Ted ran for president, "Kennedy's popularity is an accumulated, generational perception. He is part of American culture." That only became truer over the years. "We lived with the Kennedys all our lives," Charles Satkewich and Elise Lavidor told a reporter, as they waited in that line at the JFK Library. "We needed to say goodbye."

And they came not just because he was a Kennedy, whose life traced the ups and downs of American life, but because he was the surviving brother who evoked memories of John and Robert, and of a brief, exuberant time in America where there seemed to be unlimited hope and promise, and of men whose legend, as *New York Times* columnist Tom Wicker wrote in the wake of the tragic accident on Chappaquiddick Island that cost Ted Kennedy his own promise, "most powerfully centered on the notion that John and Robert Kennedy somehow called upon the best that is in us to deal forthrightly with the worst that is in us." This was what the Kennedys had meant politically and culturally to those who loved them: the personification of our better angels. And this was why more than forty years after the brothers' deaths, Americans still mourned them, still felt their loss as a moment when the American Dream seemed to die, and one reason why they came to honor the youngest brother. Ted was the heir, the one who said after Robert's death that he now had to pick up his brothers' fallen standard, and his own death, however tarnished his personal reputation might have been, not only stirred memories of his brothers but also signified the end of the Kennedy era in American politics and, for many, the extinguishing of a last flickering hope. In mourning him, they mourned that too. Or as one of those in the line that day, Susan Jackson from Worcester, Massachusetts, put it, "I grew up with my dad always telling me that as long as Ted Kennedy was around, everything was safe." Now it didn't seem as safe.

And they came because he was not only the last thread to his beloved brothers but also to the New Deal and to progressivism itself—the politician most identified with liberalism, the one who exerted the greatest effort to keep the liberal mission of an active and caring government alive, the one who had accomplished what his brothers had not, hadn't even cared to in their rush to achieve the presidency: Ted Kennedy had become the most consequential legislator of his lifetime, perhaps in American history. So they came.

Much of Ted Kennedy's fame was reflected glory from his brothers. But not here—not in the Senate. Here was a consensus that Ted was greater than his brothers, that he "mattered," which is how one longtime staffer put it, describing her sense of what Kennedy himself had striven for: "He wants to know he mattered." Ted Kennedy mattered. "Senator Kennedy probably has his name on more legislation that has become law than any other senator" and was without peer as a legislator (former Senate majority leader Robert Byrd). "He's one of the most effective legislators of this century" (former Senate majority leader Tom Daschle). "If I had to name one outstanding legislator during my twenty-two years on Capitol Hill, it would be Ted Kennedy" (Senator Paul Simon). "He is without a doubt the most effective legislator with whom I served during my thirty-eight years in the Senate" (Senator Ernest Hollings). And it wasn't only Democrats who thought he mattered. "Let's face it, the guy—whether you agree with him or not, whether you like him or not, whatever your feelings are toward him—he's productive and effective" (Republican Senate majority leader Robert Dole). "I don't know if they'll have a marble head down here, but they'll find a spot for him somewhere" (Senator Orrin Hatch). *New York Times* columnist David Brooks wrote that he once asked senators who was the colleague they most admired and said he got a variety of answers. Then he asked who was the "best at the craft of legislating": "Regardless of party, only one name comes up—Kennedy." Historian Doris Kearns Goodwin opined that he would rank with "the Calhouns, the Clays, and the Websters," all of whom operated at a time when the Senate was a vastly more vigorous and effective institution than when Kennedy was in office. Kennedy basked in this acclaim, realizing that it was for him, not his brothers—that it celebrated something he had that they didn't have, the patience that his mother once called a "ninth-child talent." When his father-in-law compared him to the great nineteenth-century Massachusetts senator Daniel Webster, Ted quipped, "What did Webster do?"

What Kennedy did, legislatively speaking, was Herculean. His was what one political reporter called "the most significant legislative career in American history"—one in which "the number of Americans affected easily surpasses 200 million, more than most presidents." He sponsored 2,552 pieces of legislation, just under seven hundred of which became law, and co-sponsored nearly seven thousand others. Among his achievements, Kennedy either sponsored, co-sponsored, or piloted through the Senate: the Voting Rights Act amendments that extended and secured the

Voting Rights Act of 1965 into American law; the Civil Rights Act of 1991, which restored, after an adverse Supreme Court decision, the rights of employees to sue for discrimination; the Immigration and Nationality Act of 1965, which loosened restrictions on immigration that had been in place since 1924; the State Children's Health Insurance Program, which provided health insurance to millions of children who did not qualify for Medicaid; the Americans With Disabilities Act, which prohibited discrimination against those with disabilities; the Health Insurance Portability and Accountability Act, which allowed American workers to carry their insurance from one job to the next, and the augustly named Consolidated Omnibus Budget Reconciliation Act of 1985 (because Kennedy had sneaked his bill into that larger one), which allowed workers who had lost their jobs to purchase health insurance; an amendment to the Older Americans Act, which allowed states to use federal funds to support food deliveries—Meals on Wheels—to the stay-at-home elderly; the Ryan White Comprehensive AIDS Resources Emergency (CARE) Act, which provided resources to individuals and families struck by AIDS; amendments to the Freedom of Information Act, which opened government records to the press and public; the Family and Medical Leave Act, which required businesses to allow employees leave for family emergencies or births; the Mental Health Parity Act, which gave those suffering from mental illness some of the same support and rights as those suffering from physical ailments; the National Cancer Act, which funded massive new cancer research and established a new cancer agency; the Serve America Act, which reauthorized and expanded a domestic national service corps; No Child Left Behind, which established new standards for public education; and three increases in the minimum wage over the last two decades of his life. And this list hardly scratches the surface. As *CBS Evening News* anchor Bob Schieffer commented after Kennedy's death, "Every single bit of social legislation . . . was associated in one way or another with Ted Kennedy," adding that Kennedy had accomplished more than any of the ten presidents of Schieffer's acquaintance.

But it wasn't just that Kennedy steered these bills into law. It was that he initiated most of them, and many of those he didn't initiate became law only because of his legislative skill—a skill without which they would almost certainly have languished. He made them happen. "So much flows that seems inevitable," said Nick Littlefield, who was Kennedy's staff director and chief counsel on the Labor Committee, which Kennedy chaired or of which he was the ranking member for two decades and from which he launched many of his legislative campaigns. "If you meet your wife in a train station, strike up a conversation with her, and she becomes your partner in life, it seems inevitable that that would have happened. But if you hadn't been waiting at that train station at that exact moment, you never would have met her. Everything that seems so obvious flows from the fact that Kennedy happened to be there and put in place this piece of legislation, this program, which so easily had no likelihood of being there. It wouldn't be there today if not for him."

And that, too, is why they came. Because so many had benefited from these efforts of his.

This is how he saw his legacy—the legacy that he had crafted separately from that of his brothers, the legacy that he could own because it was his own. It wasn't about personal political attainments, not even the presidency. It wasn't about the kind of soaring rhetoric and spiritual invigoration that his brothers had provided and that was so closely associated with them: the power of inspiration. It was about something much simpler but perhaps even harder to achieve. It was about results, about affecting people's daily lives as they lived them—the flesh, not the spirit. Lyndon Baines Johnson, another master legislator, used to get annoyed with colleagues who would invoke principles and ideals and high-mindedness, and he preached what his biographer Robert Caro called a "mantra of pragmatism." Ted Kennedy was a pragmatist. As David Brooks put it of Kennedy's legislative efforts: "This is not the stuff of poetry," which would have described his brothers' appeals, "but prose." The prosaic Kennedy did the plodding work, the drudgery, the negotiation, the compromising, the meticulous horse-trading, the grind that could last weeks, months, years, even decades in the case of national health care, if that is what it took. "A workhorse, not a show horse," is what some senators would say admiringly of him when he first showed legislative acumen, which is not something they expected from a Kennedy. And that made him different not only from his brothers but from nearly all his senatorial colleagues—because his ambitions were large, even if they were so incrementally achieved that one could miss the scale, and because he was, finally, so effective. "The Brother Who Mattered Most" is how *Time* magazine titled one of its posthumous tributes. The brother who would continue to matter. "I think the way he keeps score is different from the way most politicians today keep score," said one longtime staffer, Jeffrey

Blattner. "He keeps score with a hammer and chisel. It's to stand the test of time." "What is the purpose of all this?" another Senate aide once heard him asked. "To make gentler the human condition," Kennedy answered.

So they came.

And they came in tribute not only to what he accomplished but also to how he accomplished it, which, for most of his Senate career, was against the prevailing wind—in fact, in the very teeth of that wind. Ted Kennedy had entered the Senate in 1962, winning election to his brother John's old seat when he was thirty, just old enough to qualify for the Senate. He entered by catching what might have been the most powerful gust of what historians have called the post–New Deal modern liberal consensus or "the American consensus," a time when, despite yawning divisions between Democrats and Republicans—or, more accurately, between the Southern Democratic–Midwestern and Western Republican coalition on one side and the Northern Democratic–New England Republican coalition on the other—there was nevertheless a general acceptance of government activism and the social safety net. It was a time when debates were primarily over means, not ends. By Kennedy's mid-career, that had changed—changed entirely. Those old coalitions had been reassembled as the South became unshakably Republican and as moderates were largely driven from the Republican party, and that general acceptance of New Dealism had been shattered. For much of his life, as the country moved rightward, Ted Kennedy became the voice of American liberalism—a powerful voice that, as he so often said, he used to speak for the powerless to summon what was in his view the best of the American spirit, the compassion of the American heart, even as he increasingly seemed to be shouting into a void and even as he seemed to be turning into a political anachronism. "While claiming the moral high ground," novelist James Carroll fulminated as early as 1991 in a cover story for *The New Republic* titled "The End of the Dream," in what had already become a liberal lament, "the conservative establishment has been systematically destroying this country for almost two decades now—its schools, its unions, its protections of the poor and the old and the sick, its civil rights laws, its banking system, even its roads and bridges. And Ted Kennedy has almost stood alone in opposing them with any force." Kennedy's often lonely opposition was a performance that recalled Winston Churchill's comment:

"I was not the lion, but it fell to me to give the lion's roar." Kennedy gave the roar.

He had nothing to gain politically from doing so. The national mood had turned decisively against the things in which he believed. Liberal programs were under siege—discredited as expensive and counterproductive and an assault on individual initiative. He did it surely because he felt he owed it to his brothers' memories to keep their causes alive, but, more simply, he did it because he felt he owed it to those who suffered and with whom he empathized—empathized not out of a sense of noblesse oblige but out of his own pain and his own aching sense of inadequacy. So he persevered, continuing to hector the American people, though he knew that the things for which he advocated had fallen out of favor. "When people were getting tired of hearing about racism or the poor or the decay of American cities, he kept talking," wrote Richard Lacayo in *Time*, shortly after Kennedy's death. "When liberalism was flickering, there was Kennedy, holding the torch, insisting that 'we can light those beacon fires again.'" And while it is customary to think of Ted Kennedy as the beneficiary of his brothers' compassionate liberalism, it may be more accurate to say that they posthumously became the beneficiaries of his, which was far more ardent and enduring than theirs. We impute Ted Kennedy, the fighting, unflagging liberal optimist, back into John and Robert.

The optimism was real, but it didn't come easily. For the right, as the wind changed, Kennedy became not only an anachronism but also a liberal whipping boy. Conservative ideologues castigated him. Republican fundraising appeals routinely brought up the specter of a Kennedy-controlled Congress, and would-be Republican allies felt the need to apologize to him for having to keep their distance; even some moderate Democrats sheepishly refused his offers of campaign assistance for fear of angering conservative voters. That is how dramatically the Kennedy brand had diminished over the years in so much of America, how much conservatism had delegitimized liberalism—the "L-word," some called it, as if it were an epithet, which is what it had become to many.

Yet Kennedy's hectoring wasn't only rhetoric. Even as conservatives sought to disarm government assistance for those who needed it, Kennedy the pragmatist, Kennedy the expert sailor who knew how to tack against the wind, managed to get results, not by threatening or bullying, as Lyndon Johnson had done—Ted Kennedy did not wield such power as Majority Leader Johnson had—but through the power of friendship and compromise and an acute understanding of both self-interest and moral suasion. "Everybody will say, looking back, 'This was the era of the conservative ascendency,'" Kennedy aide Nick Littlefield remarked in 2008, "and that's true. Except that on domestic policy, it's really the era of the ascendency of the issues Kennedy pushed. . . . Medicare is twice as big as it was ten years ago. There's three times as much federal money being spent on education as there was fifteen years ago. The minimum wage has been raised again." Kennedy had continued to fight those battles, and he had won them.

And when those crowds came to honor him, they came, many of them, because they remembered the fight he had waged for them not just when he was catching the wind in his first decade as a senator but when he was sailing against that hard, conservative wind and when everything seemed lost—remembered and wanted to give thanks.

By Thursday evening, when the viewing began, the line at the John F. Kennedy Library, on a jut of land in Dorchester Bay across Boston Harbor, wound hundreds of yards down the walkways—an estimated 15,000 mourners. Many of them had waited hours in the hot sun, though the mood, fitting for the most extroverted of the Kennedys, was far more festive than melancholy. "I just had to be here," Leslie McMillan, who had driven from Hackensack, New Jersey, told a reporter. "The Kennedys—they were always involved with the civil rights movement, and anything that happened to them, we felt happened to our family." Told they would have at least a three-hour wait before viewing, Olga and Ned Music, Serbian immigrants, said they would stay, despite Olga's arthritis. "I will go anywhere," Ned said. "He was the champion of the poor people." Many in line held signs. One group of health workers carried a banner with Kennedy's photograph. Inside, the flag draping the casket was the one that had flown over the Capitol on the day of his death—attended now by a military honor guard and a vigil of five civilians in the Stephen Smith Hall of the library, named after Ted's brother-in-law and his 1980 presidential-campaign chief—and as people filed by, the mood turned somber. Some wept, some dabbed tears, some made the sign of the cross, one black couple embraced. The viewing was to end at eleven that evening, but the crowds kept coming, so that even the buses discharging passengers from nearby parking lots and public transit were backed up, and the viewing was held open until two in the morning.

They came again at dawn on Friday, tens of thousands more, with members of the Kennedy family—Ted Jr., Patrick, Ethel, nephew Joseph II and niece Caroline, even Kennedy's widow, Victoria—either walking the lines to thank people for coming or standing in a receiving line to greet them. Other family members hugged mourners or shook their hands. By the time the viewing ended, at three that afternoon, it was estimated that 50,000 had paid their respects. This was not just their farewell to him but the Kennedys' farewell to him too—and his to them. While Ted Jr. and Patrick were on the receiving line—their sister, Kara, had retreated to her hotel after the long day—one of their father's secretaries handed them an envelope with the three children's names on it and the instruction: "To be opened after my death." And when they finished their duties, Ted and Patrick retired to a private room on the library's seventh floor, phoned Kara, and read her the letter that Ted had written some twenty years earlier—"a beautiful letter," Patrick would say, "so moving, full of all the things you'd ever want to hear from your father." Ted, who had thought of everything, had thought of that too.

That evening, family and friends, six hundred of them, gathered for a memorial in the same light maple–paneled Smith Hall in which Kennedy's coffin had lain, its tall windows looking out across Dorchester Bay, now pelted by rain. The service, called "A Celebration of Life," was an old-fashioned Irish wake, which was just as Ted had wanted it, lively and funny and high-spirited—a remembrance of his friendship, his exuberance, and his hopefulness. They spoke not because they thought Ted was great—he wouldn't have believed that himself—but because they knew he was good. Ted's nephew Joseph Kennedy II told about how he and Ted were racing a sailboat during a gale, and how Joseph steered it into a buoy, the penalty for which was circling that buoy three times, and, having fallen back, how ashamed Joseph felt—until Ted asked him what he would have felt if he had been told the night before that they were in seventh or eighth place. And when Joseph said he would have felt pretty good, Ted answered, "Let's go win this race," which they did. His close Senate friend Chris Dodd of Connecticut, in a bright-green tie, recalled telling Ted before a 1994 campaign debate with Kennedy's Republican opponent Mitt Romney not to talk too fast, after which Ted, during the debate, paused interminably when asked why the race was so close. Why did he pause so long? Dodd asked him afterward. "I was thinking, 'That's a damn good question,' " Ted said. And, after the anecdotes and the laughter, Dodd also revealed the secret to Kennedy's legislative success: "People liked him."

Nick Littlefield, the aide who had once been a professional singer and with whom Ted often did duets, sang, "Love Changes Everything," which Kennedy had had sung at his wedding to Vicki and which he felt described his new life after meeting her. Senator John McCain, the Republican presidential candidate in 2008, recalled two freshman senators—a Republican and Democrat—in heated debate on the Senate floor and he and Ted instinctively joining in and taking sides, getting heated themselves, and then laughing "uproariously" when it was over. John Kerry remembered Kennedy's last visit to the Senate, where he kept listeners in stitches reenacting how he tried to get his broken body to throw out the ceremonial first pitch at the Red Sox game the preceding spring. And Orrin Hatch, Republican senator from Utah, who had collaborated with Kennedy on several bills, described how one night he ran into Kennedy, who was deep into his cups, and got him to agree to address a group of Mormon missionaries in Boston. "Orrin, what else did I agree to?" Kennedy asked him the next morning. And his Harvard classmate and lifelong friend, John Culver, former senator from Iowa, recounted sailing the Nantucket Regatta with Ted during a thunderstorm, even though Culver hadn't the slightest idea of how to sail, and noted Ted's complete obliviousness to Culver's incompetence. "I thought I was with Captain Ahab." And then came Vice President Joseph Biden, who recalled how, seven weeks after being elected to the Senate, he lost his wife and infant daughter in a car accident, and how Kennedy phoned him every day, day after day, and sent a "platoon of specialists" from Boston hospitals to help his two young sons who had been injured in the accident, and then encouraged him to take the Senate seat when Biden considered resigning. "He crept into my heart and, before I knew it, owned a piece of it." And he remembered this: "People didn't want to look small in front of him—even people who were small." And, finally, Caroline spoke of the way her uncle bolstered the spirits of his nieces and nephews and how fervently he expressed his belief in them so that they would believe in themselves, and she described the summer history trips on which he took his nieces and nephews—to Civil War battlefields; to Fort McHenry, where Francis Scott Key wrote the national anthem; to the Brooklyn Bridge and Mount Vernon; and to the historic sites around Boston. And she spoke of the last of these trips: the funeral cortege through Boston. And then Brian Stokes Mitchell sang

Kennedy's favorite song, "The Impossible Dream," and the service ended with everyone singing "When Irish Eyes Are Smiling," exactly as Ted wanted it.

The next morning, under heavy rains—two inches of rain—they came. At 10:04, the Cadillac hearse left the JFK Library for the trip up Tremont Street, the procession climbing Mission Hill to the Basilica of Our Lady of Perpetual Help, and again, the crowds, most of them holding umbrellas pelted so hard by the rain that one heard the muted drumbeat, cheered or saluted or held up their children. They came not just because he was a Kennedy or because he was a connection to the past or because they wanted to witness history but because many of them had a personal connection to him—kindnesses he had shown them, favors he had done for them. Michelle Nagel was living in Europe when she was diagnosed with leukemia and had no money to come home to Massachusetts. Kennedy got her the money and arranged a bone-marrow transplant in Boston. Carlos and Melida Arredondo had lost their son, Alex, in the Iraq War five years to the day before Kennedy's death; Kennedy helped Carlos gain citizenship and was working to have Alex awarded a Bronze Star posthumously. Rich Adams of Brookline, a veteran suffering from post-traumatic stress disorder and ravaged by drugs, met Kennedy on a Cambridge street, where the senator assured him he was going to be all right. "When Teddy talked to you, he talked to you man to man," Adams said. Tom McDermott of Dorchester couldn't find a job after fighting cancer. Ted Kennedy's office found him one. Franca Firicano said Kennedy sponsored a friend of hers who had emigrated from South Africa.

Just as there were thousands of pieces of legislation, there were thousands of these stories. "Throughout my life, strangers have told me how Teddy was there when a child was diagnosed with cancer, when a father lost a job or had a blow to his reputation, when a wedding was to be celebrated," recalled his niece Kerry Kennedy. His stepson, Curran Raclin, said, "I didn't even believe it until I saw it myself is that everybody has a Ted Kennedy story. . . . 'Oh, he wrote me a letter when my mother died.' What? 'Oh, yes, he sent me a card when my brother died.'. . . No one does that; that's not the norm." He wrote. He phoned. He visited with constituents who suffered or were under duress or had petitioned him because they felt that he alone would listen and understand and help. His office was called the "Lourdes of Capitol Hill."

All of this was of a piece with the old puddingstone church to which the mourners came that unseasonably chilly, wet morning and up whose narrow street the crowds spilled. It wasn't the kind of church one might have imagined for a Kennedy—not the Cathedral of St. Matthew the Apostle in Washington, where President Kennedy's service was held, or the majestic St. Patrick's Cathedral in New York, where the funeral service was held for Robert Kennedy. There was so little parking that many mourners arrived in chartered Peter Pan buses. And though it was close inside despite the chill, the church wasn't even air-conditioned. But it was the church Ted had chosen, the church he wanted, the church scaled to his proportions, as the motorcade and the memorial service had been. The Basilica of Our Lady of Perpetual Help—a name that couldn't have been more expressive of Kennedy's own mission—was perched atop a working-class neighborhood that many Bostonians considered rough, dangerous. For over a century, the poor had come to pray for intercession at the altar there, under a gold-framed painting of the Virgin Mary—first Irish and German immigrants, more recently Latino and Caribbean immigrants, many from nearby housing projects, though they came in fewer numbers now. Kennedy had come there daily to pray when his daughter, Kara, was diagnosed with cancer in 2002 and was being treated at the nearby Brigham and Women's Hospital. He returned to pray when he was diagnosed with cancer himself, slipping in quietly, unobtrusively. And now he had returned again.

This time, along with the family and friends, the dignitaries came: three former presidents and the current president, who would deliver the eulogy; fifty-eight senators by one count; Speaker of the House Nancy Pelosi; Supreme Court justice Stephen Breyer, who had been a Kennedy aide; Gerry Adams of Sinn Féin, for whom Kennedy had once argued to secure a visa from the State Department; former Boston Celtic star Bill Russell; singer Tony Bennett; actor Jack Nicholson. They squeezed into the oak pews, under which they slid their umbrellas—nearly 1,300 of them. And then the coffin was rolled up the center aisle to the altar, and the service began.

And this time, instead of celebrating Kennedy's playfulness, as at the memorial service, the mourners celebrated the strength of his conviction and his tenacity—a celebration of having endured and survived so much tragedy (and having caused tragedy too). But it was also a tribute to his faith, which had been tested throughout his life and often, by his own admission, challenged. His stepson, Curran, read from the Book of Wisdom, 3:1–9, about "the souls of the just" who "chastised a little, they shall be greatly blessed, because God tried them and found them worthy of himself." Ted Kennedy had been chastised. His daughter, Kara, read Psalm 72, with its response: "Justice shall flourish in his time, and fullness of peace forever." To his admirers, Ted Kennedy had fought for justice. His stepdaughter, Caroline Raclin, read from the Letter of St. Paul to the Romans that no tragedy can separate one from God's love. Ted Kennedy, against the odds, had suffered tragedy but had not been separated, and though one might not have thought of him as religious, given his wayward escapades, he may have been the most devout of the Kennedy children. And then Kennedy's parish priest, Father Mark Hession, read the gospel, from Matthew 25:31–32A, 34–40, in which Jesus tells the righteous, "Whatever you did for one of the least of these brothers of mine, you did for me." Ted Kennedy built his career on that premise. After Father Hession's homily, Ted's grandchildren and assorted nieces and nephews described his values during the intercessions and read a passage from one of Ted's favorite poems, Alfred Lord Tennyson's "Ulysses," which he quoted frequently, as John Kennedy and Robert Kennedy had quoted it before him:

> *Tho' much is taken, much abides; and tho'*
> *We are not now that strength which in old days*
> *Moved earth and heaven, that which we are, we are;*
> *One equal temper of heroic hearts,*
> *Made weak by time and fate, but strong in will*
> *To strive, to seek, to find, and not to yield.*

Ted Kennedy never yielded.

And after the Liturgy of the Eucharist—during which cellist Yo-Yo Ma played and then accompanied tenor Plácido Domingo on Franck's "Panis Angelicus"—came two remembrances from his sons. "He was not perfect, far from it," Ted Jr., who had the same tousled look as his father, told the mourners—something that Ted himself had asserted throughout his life. "But my father believed in redemption. And he never surrendered, never stopped trying to right wrongs, be they the results of his own failings or ours." Speaking to that resilience, Ted Jr. recalled the winter when he was twelve years old, shortly after his leg had been amputated due to a cancerous growth. There was a heavy snowfall in Washington, and Ted went to the garage to get the Flexible Flyer sled and asked Ted Jr. if he wanted to glide down the steep driveway. Ted Jr. said he struggled down that driveway, slipped on the ice, and then began to cry, insisting that he could never make it up the hill. "And he lifted me up in his strong, gentle arms and said something I will never forget," Ted Jr. remembered, now mopping away tears. "He said, 'I know you can do it. There is nothing you can't do.'" And Ted grabbed his son around the waist and hauled him up the hill, and he and Ted Jr. sledded down that driveway. Ted Jr. told the congregation, "I knew I was going to be okay."

If that story spoke to Ted Kennedy's determination, another story Ted Jr. told that morning spoke to his modesty—to his scale, to his acceptance of his own deficiencies and the way he worked to overcome them. Ted Jr. had asked him one summer night at Cape Cod why they were always the last sailors on the water. "Teddy," his father said, "you see most of the other sailors that we race against are smarter and more talented than we are. But the reason—the reason why we're going to win is that we will work harder than them, and we will be better prepared."

Ted Kennedy always worked harder because he felt he had to.

The second remembrance was Patrick's, who had struggled with illnesses and with addictions and who would later say that his proposed appearance met with some apprehension from the family, because they didn't know how he would behave or what he would say. But he spoke movingly of his asthma and how it kept his father by his bedside— "always holding a cold wet cloth against my forehead until I fell asleep again"—and of the times that his father brought him along, despite his afflictions and his lack of skill, to race with him on his sailboat and taught him that there was always room for everyone.

And then came President Barack Obama, in a dark-gray suit and silver tie—Obama, whom Ted Kennedy had endorsed during the 2008 primary campaign when the candidate needed a boost—to deliver the eulogy. Obama spoke of Ted Kennedy's travails but also of his indomitable spirit. "As he told us, individual faults and frailties are no excuse to give in and no exemption from the common obligation to give of ourselves." And Obama quoted Wordsworth to the effect that Kennedy never sought to excuse his faults or conceal them but rather learned how to use them: "As tempted more, more able to endure. As more exposed to suffering and distress, hence also more alive to tenderness." And Obama said, "Through his own suffering, Ted Kennedy became more alive to the plight and the suffering of others." And Obama praised Ted Kennedy's collegiality, his civility to the other side of the aisle, and his commitment to the nobility of politics, but also his caginess. And he told the story of how Ted won the support of a Texas committee chairman on an immigration bill by walking into the conference with a plain manila envelope, letting the chairman peek inside to see his favorite cigars. "When the negotiations were going well, he would inch the envelope closer to the chairman. When they weren't, he'd pull it back." And he read the note that Jacqueline Kennedy had written to Ted after he walked Caroline down the aisle in the stead of her late father: "On you, the carefree youngest brother, fell a burden a hero would have begged to have been spared. We're all going to make it because you're always there with your love." And Obama said, "We do not weep for him today because of the prestige attached to his name or his office. We weep because we loved this kind and tender hero who persevered through pain and tragedy, not for the sake of ambition or vanity, not for wealth or power, but only for the people and the country that he loved."

Then the coffin was rolled back up the aisle as the pipe organ boomed "America the Beautiful."

They came on the streets of Boston, four and five deep, in that rain— "We're his family," said eighty-two-year-old Theresa Antonelli, holding a plastic bag with Ted's photo inside, while she waited in the downpour—as the motorcade headed to Hanscom Air Force Base, and they came again in Washington after the coffin arrived late that Saturday afternoon at Andrews Air Force base and drove past the Capitol, where hundreds of old Kennedy staffers waited on the steps to pay tribute, alongside staffers of other legislators and several senators and congressmen, including Robert Byrd, frail, his hair snowy white, and confined to a wheelchair, wiping the tears from his eyes. As it approached, many of them broke into cheers. Here the caravan stopped, and Mrs. Kennedy emerged from her limousine to give and receive warm embraces while "America the Beautiful" was sung once again. And then the cortege moved on, down Constitution Avenue, as dusk fell, and past the Lincoln Memorial and to Arlington Cemetery, where he was to be interred beside his brothers, down the knoll from the Custis-Lee Mansion, in a grave marked simply by a white cross with a white marble headstone engraved EDWARD MOORE KENNEDY, 1932–2009, which befitted the man who had always chosen to seek not grandiosity but virtue.

For all the reasons they had come, those thousands, these past three days, there was a final one—perhaps the deepest connection to Kennedy, one so deep it was practically subconscious. It was not the connection to his brothers, or to his magnitude—to the way he had impressed himself upon history or even impressed himself upon their lives, though he had done both. It was their connection to his lack of magnitude. John and Robert Kennedy had been embalmed in history—forever sainted. Ted had gotten the gift of years that none of his three older brothers had, but it had come with a price. He had lived long enough to fail, to sin, to stumble, to fall and fall out of favor. He had been publicly abased—the accident at Chappaquiddick in which a young woman died, his womanizing and drinking, his odd behavior on an Easter weekend in Palm Beach in 1991 during which his nephew was accused of rape—and forced to ask for forgiveness. To his fiercest detractors, these missteps were unforgivable, though how much of their implacability was politics in the conservative gale and how much morality is impossible to say.

But to those who loved him, these flaws were intrinsic to that love. As President Obama said in his eulogy, if his tribulations, even those that were self-inflicted, wound up binding Ted Kennedy to his constituents with empathy because he knew what it was like not only to suffer but to fail, so did they bind those constituents to him. He was theirs more fully than John and Robert, because his scale was more human. "My father was far from perfect," Ted Jr. had said, which was something everyone acknowledged. And about the crowds at the funeral procession in South Boston—whose angry citizens had smeared Ted Kennedy's car with excrement during those anti-busing protests and where one woman had said at the time, "We mourned President Kennedy. We won't mourn this one"—Patrick would later comment, "They hated my dad, and he had everybody standing there, every sidewalk, in mourning, because as much as they may have had a problem with Ted Kennedy, as much as they liked to pillory him and castigate him for never being what they thought he should be, they also loved him. And he was one of them at the end of the day." So they came, and they mourned.

The memorial service had been about Kennedy's good humor and affability, the funeral service about his endurance. The burial service, conducted at the grave site in the fading, crepuscular light—hours later than planned because of the crowds—with only the family present, was about his frailty and his flaws. Ted Kennedy recognized those flaws. He had lived within a sense of insufficiency compared to his brothers, made all the more agonizing because he insisted on being surrounded by their memory—in the mementos and photographs in his offices and in his homes; in the frequent quotes from them and the stories he told about them; in the lonely morning visits to their grave site, where he would soon join them. Though it was virtually anathema in Joseph Kennedy's household to admit to one's own deficiencies, to ever feel less than anyone else, and though Ted had preached that same gospel to his own children and nieces and nephews, Ted Kennedy couldn't abide by it himself, because he never felt he was his brothers' equal. In the early days of his political career, he was burdened with their tragedy, from which he would never recover, in his later days with his own flaws, from which he prayed to recover. Ted Kennedy's detractors saw in him a sense of entitlement: He sinned because he knew he could get away with it. But it is probably closer to the truth that Ted Kennedy sinned, when he did, as a form of dereliction for which he could then do penance. He sinned to be redeemed.

To the end, he sought redemption. In July, when President Obama was heading to Europe and the Vatican, Kennedy had given him a letter with the request that he deliver it to Pope Benedict XVI. And so, to his past public requests for forgiveness, Kennedy added, in his waning days, this private one, asking for absolution. Read at his graveside that night, nothing may have spoken so simply of Kennedy's deepest self or of his humility:

I am seventy-seven years old and preparing for the next passage of life.

I've been blessed to be part of a wonderful family and both my parents, specifically my mother, kept our Catholic faith at the center of our lives.

That gift of faith has sustained and nurtured and provided solace to me in the darkest hours. I know that I have been an imperfect human being, but with the help of my faith I have tried to right my past.

I want you to know, your Holiness, that in my fifty years of elected office I have done my best to champion the rights of the poor and open doors of economic opportunity. I've worked to welcome the immigrant, to fight discrimination and expand access to health care and education. I've opposed the death penalty and fought to end war. Those are the issues that have motivated me and have been the focus of my work as a U.S. senator.

I also want you to know that even though I am ill, I am committed to do everything I can to achieve access to health care for everyone in my country. This has been the political cause of my life. . . .

I've always tried to be a faithful Catholic, Your Holiness. And though I have fallen short through human failings I've never failed to believe and respect the fundamental teachings of my faith.

I continue to pray for God's blessings on you and on our church and would be most thankful for your prayers for me.

And then Edward Moore Kennedy was laid to rest.

This volume, the first of two, is the story of young Edward Kennedy and his emergence as a force in American politics. In terms of his personal biography, it follows him from his birth into one of America's most famous families; to his itinerant childhood as the last-born and least of the Kennedys, a boy of whom nothing was expected but upon whom a great destiny was imposed, namely the destiny to run for his brother's vacated Senate seat; to his first years as a senator, trying to learn the chamber and earn the respect of his Senate elders; to the airplane accident that almost cost him his life; to the deaths of his two older brothers, and his commitment to complete their legacy, and the toll that the deaths and the commitment took on him; and, finally, to his confrontations with Richard Nixon in trying to pick up his brothers' fallen standard and champion their causes. It may seem a familiar story by now. Having lived with him during his fifty years of public life, many Americans assume they already know Ted Kennedy. "More is probably known about Ted Kennedy's character—for good or ill—than about the character of most other American politicians," Kenneth Auchincloss wrote of him in *Newsweek,* two years after Ted Kennedy's presidential run, with nearly thirty more years to go in his career. "His private faults have been laid bare in public, and his private generosities too. Even for a nation endlessly fascinated with the personal lives of its political chieftains, Ted Kennedy is overexposed." But that overexposure did not necessarily mean the public knew him, much less understood him.

Americans knew what they knew about him, but they didn't know everything, in no small measure because the Kennedys didn't want them to. Timothy Shriver, Ted's nephew, once told Patrick, "The family pathology, which everyone in the family does have, is secrecy." The Kennedys had an image to maintain; preserving the image demanded secrecy. So the Ted Kennedy that emerges in these pages and in those of Volume Two is not likely to be an altogether familiar one. The public saw the jovial Ted, joking and laughing and singing; they didn't see the dark Ted, lonely, sometimes monosyllabic, staring out at the ocean for hours. The public saw the optimistic Ted, telling us the dream goes on; they didn't see the fatalistic one. The public saw the self-confident Ted, luxuriating in being a Kennedy; they didn't see the self-doubting Ted, imprisoned by the expectations of being a Kennedy. The public saw a Kennedy who was open and accessible and presumably less complex than his brothers; they didn't see the inner turmoil and demons that arguably made him the most complex of the Kennedys, certainly the most roiled. Lewis Lapham, writing in *Harper's* in 1979, compared him to a minotaur—half man, half beast— representing "the worst as well as the best that can be found in man." The public saw that Ted. But in a profile in *The New York Times Magazine* shortly after Lapham's piece, Steven Roberts, perhaps thinking of the Tennyson poem, considered Ted more of a Ulysses: "alone, lost, abandoned by the gods, trying to resist temptation, searching for home and peace." The public didn't see this Ted.

But if this is a book about the shaping of Ted Kennedy, it is also a book about the shaping of American politics over the course of Ted Kennedy's nearly fifty-year career in the Senate, using Ted Kennedy, the preeminent liberal of his time, as a prism through which to tell and view that story, one in which he was both symbol and protagonist. The first part of that political story, which is told in this volume, is Ted Kennedy's legislative assault during his first and second Senate terms, his catching the liberal wind and helping to generate the liberal hour during which his brother and Lyndon Johnson fought for civil rights and immigration reform and Medicare and an anti-poverty program, among many initiatives. This volume details Ted Kennedy's general acquiescence to Lyndon Johnson, despite Johnson's antipathy to Ted's brother Bobby and despite Johnson's prosecution of the misbegotten Vietnam War, which was threatening the liberal agenda. It details, too, Bobby Kennedy's challenge to Lyndon Johnson and Bobby's presidential campaign, in which he tried to reinvigorate liberalism's flagging moral authority. It details the effect that the deaths of

John Kennedy and Robert Kennedy had on the nation and how their surviving brother, the alleged least of the Kennedys, tried to extend the liberal hour during the presidency of Richard Nixon, when the liberal wind was dying and the liberal clock was ticking down. And so this volume details the fierce antagonism between the two major political forces that emerged from John and Bobby's deaths and Lyndon Johnson's abdication—Richard Nixon and Ted Kennedy—and the personal failings, Ted's at Chappaquiddick and Nixon's at Watergate, that altered the course of American politics.

But taken together, these two volumes tell a larger story than the personal story of Ted Kennedy or the story of his political education and adventures. They tell what is perhaps the most important story of the late-twentieth and early-twenty-first centuries in American politics: the story of the shift in the nation's political tectonic plates from liberalism to conservatism. The path of liberalism through Ted Kennedy's life was a tortuous one, though its direction, despite Kennedy's best efforts, trended downward. Many books and many scholars have addressed this issue, and the reasons why liberalism declined are complex and multitudinous, a death by a thousand cuts—among them a more prosperous working class that turned on the liberal prescriptions; demographic changes; a revolt against high tax rates; a fear that traditional values were under assault; a perception among blue-collar Americans that liberals were disdainful of them, which was a perception fed by conservatives, who had constructed a massive, well-financed infrastructure of think tanks, political action committees, and especially right-wing media. One of the larger cuts, most scholars concur, was race, which reconfigured the two major parties geographically and ideologically; upon Johnson's signing of the Civil Rights Act of 1964, his aide Bill Moyers famously reported him as having said, "I think we just delivered the South to the Republican party for a long time to come." Johnson was right.

But there may be another reason for liberalism's demise, one seldom cited by scholars, and in some ways it is as much a protagonist in this book as Ted Kennedy himself, though it is often difficult to separate the fates of the two. What had helped sustain liberalism, even after the end of the traumas of the Great Depression that initiated modern liberalism and then nourished it, was moral authority—the sense that providing for the poor and helping the marginalized was the right thing to do. Liberalism had moral authority. Ted Kennedy, like his brothers, drew upon that authority. His appeals were overtly appeals to justice, compassion, and decency, and for a while his moral entreaties were also a source of his popularity, just as they had been a source of his brothers'. Over time, those entreaties ceased to stir the public spirit, in large part because liberalism lost the moral authority that undergirded it. This was not a thousand cuts but one large cut, for which Ted Kennedy must bear some responsibility.

In telling the story of the decline of liberalism, then, these two volumes must also tell the story of the delegitimization of a certain set of moral values and a certain kind of social responsibility and their replacement by another set and another kind. It is the story of political morality and how the country lost the liberals' idea of it. In writing of Lyndon Johnson, Robert Caro has said he is writing about power. In examining the life of Ted Kennedy, this book is about political morality.

This is a big story—this story of the reshaping of American politics— and this volume is only the beginning of that story. It may be too big a story to tell, a story with too many perspectives, but Ted Kennedy's life provides us with one way of telling it. Few lives were as large, as complex, and as metaphorical as Ted Kennedy's, few were at the very epicenter of American politics as his was for as long as his was, and few seemed so deeply connected to the national psyche. This book tells how he caught the liberal wind and tried to keep riding it, and in telling that story, it attempts to tell how the entire country, for a brief time, seemed to have caught the wind too, before it stopped blowing.

CATCHING

THE WIND

The Youngest

H E W A S T H E youngest, and from that nearly everything in his life would follow. And not only was he the youngest, he was also unexpected—an accident. Beginning in 1915, with the birth of Joseph Patrick Kennedy Jr., Kennedy children arrived at one- or two-year intervals for the next ten years and six more babies. Rose Kennedy said that after the birth of Robert Francis Kennedy in 1925, her friends "gently chided" her against having any more, and she seemed to agree. But three years later, Jean Kennedy arrived, which, Rose said, made her even more "skittish" about her passel of children. After Jean's birth, Joseph Sr., apparently anticipating no more offspring, named the family yacht the *Ten of Us*, and he warned his wife that if she had another child, he would give her not the customary trip to Europe that had followed each birth but a black eye. But in February 1932—February 22, 1932, Washington's birthday—almost four years to the day of Jean Kennedy's birth, Edward Moore Kennedy arrived to forty-one-year-old Rose Kennedy, not only the youngest, not only unexpected, but an afterthought.

And more than an afterthought. One Kennedy biographer surmised that he was reparation for Kennedy's torrid affair with the film star Gloria Swanson, whose career Kennedy had guided—an amends to his wife after the affair had ended. By that time, Joseph and Rose were intimate only infrequently, by most accounts, but the couple rendezvoused in the spring of 1931 at the Homestead Resort in Hot Springs, Virginia, after Joseph's four-month winter vacation at Palm Beach, Florida, and spent a few days together before Joseph left alone for New York. Edward was born nine months later. Despite her husband's threat, Rose still got her European trip shortly after the birth.

For the youngest, the circumstances surrounding the birth were an augury both of the family traditions to which he would be obligated and of the negligence with which he would often be treated. Though the family lived in Bronxville, New York, at the time, Rose insisted he be born at St. Margaret's Hospital in Dorchester, Massachusetts, so he could be delivered by Dr. Frederick Good, who had delivered each of his siblings. She recuperated in Dorchester for two weeks, near her parents, since Joseph hadn't attended the birth or provided any emotional support but instead had retreated once again to Palm Beach. "There was no need keeping Joe around in the winter, not in the middle of February for a baby," Rose later told her ghostwriter, with a certain dismissiveness toward her new child. But she said that her husband had meals sent to her from the Ritz Hotel via taxi because "he felt so sorry for me being in a hospital."

And if the baby was an afterthought, so too was his name. Edward Moore was a family retainer, a onetime secretary to Rose's father, John Fitzgerald, when Fitzgerald was mayor of Boston, which is when Joseph Kennedy met Moore back in 1912. Moore continued in the position under mayors James Michael Curley and Andrew James Peters, before accepting a job with Joseph Kennedy as his counselor, after which, according to historian and Kennedy family chronicler Doris Kearns Goodwin, "the bond between the two men proved inseparable." But "counselor" may have been both too august and too limited a word for what Moore did for Joe Kennedy. "Eddie Moore became his closest friend," Rose would say of Moore's relationship to her husband, "someone he trusted implicitly in every way and in all circumstances. His wife, Mary, became an equally great friend, confidante, and unfailing support for me." So close were the Kennedys and the Moores that Joe sold them his Brookline, Massachusetts, house on Beals Street in March 1920, which had the advantage of bringing them from Charlestown, where they had lived with Mary Moore's mother, to just around the corner from the Kennedys' new house, where they could be on call in case Joe needed them.

Still, for all the talk of friendship, the relationship was hardly one of equals. Edward Moore *served* Joseph Kennedy. He was, as *Time* magazine put it, "nurse, comforter, stooge, package-bearer, adviser, who played games with Joe and the children, bought neckties and bonds for Joe, opened doors, wrote letters, investigated investments, saw to it Joe wore his rubbers." One Kennedy biographer called him a "valet," another a "flunky." One of Joseph Kennedy's granddaughters said that the childless

Moore's duties included being an "occasional babysitter." A more important duty was to provide cover for Joe Kennedy. According to Joseph Kennedy biographer David Nasaw, Kennedy and Moore set up a real estate company, Fenway Building Trust, after World War I, in which Joe owned 98 percent of the shares but Moore was assigned the task of convincing two women to sell their real estate to the company for notes that were then used to buy more real estate. Another biographer said Kennedy used Moore's name to hide Wall Street transactions with which he didn't want to be publicly associated.

And Kennedy used Moore as a cover in other ways. He was a beard for Kennedy, so that even Rose Kennedy said Joe told her "that he kept Eddie around when he was signing contracts with some of these 'dames,' as he used to say. And then he'd [Joe], you know, get framed and get into difficulties." And if Edward Moore was a beard, he was a procurer for Kennedy and the Kennedy sons too. As a Harvard student, John Kennedy had his father's "administrator"—it could only have been Moore—find girls for him and five friends for a bacchanal at Cape Cod, after which John fretted over whether or not he had gotten the "clap."

But Joe Kennedy enjoyed Moore not just for his service, which was slavish, or his loyalty, which was total, but for his sociability. "Irish as a clay pipe," *Time* wrote of him, and Edward Kennedy himself would say that his father "cherished Eddie's convivial soul." During a 1932 train tour in support of Franklin Roosevelt's presidential candidacy, a trip on which Moore accompanied Kennedy, Roosevelt adviser Raymond Moley remarked on Moore's "infinite capacity to make friends," though vaudevillian Eddie Dowling, who was on the same tour, thought the amiability was tempered by his servility. "He never stopped telling me, and anybody else that would listen, about the greatness of Joseph P. Kennedy."

The idea that Kennedy and Moore were inseparable was less figurative than literal. Joe's "shadow," Gloria Swanson called him. Moore was with him in Boston at the beginning, in New York when Kennedy moved there for business, in Hollywood when Kennedy began assaying the movies. And when Roosevelt won the election and named Kennedy the chairman of the Securities and Exchange Commission, Moore accompanied him to Washington, where they lived together on a 125-acre estate in Rockville, Maryland. They were still living there when Kennedy became head of the Maritime Commission, and he and Moore spent two and a half months working with a former Harvard classmate of Kennedy's named John

Burns, who had become a judge, to devise the commission's subsidy structure. Moore was with Kennedy when Kennedy became the United States ambassador to England, and they sailed there together; with him when Kennedy returned to America; and with him nearly every day thereafter, until Moore was felled by a fatal illness in 1952.

Edward Kennedy would later say he found it "endearing" that his father had named him for his friend, even as he'd named his first son, Joseph, after himself and his second son, John Fitzgerald, after Rose's father, and Edward Kennedy would talk proudly about how Moore was his father's "go-to guy." But for all his intimacy with the Kennedy family, Edward Moore was still a retainer, and for Joseph Kennedy to name his youngest son after him—a man of no great distinction, a man whose chief virtue was his undying loyalty to his boss—as seemingly a small reward for Moore's service was itself a harbinger of Edward Moore Kennedy's status in the family.

If Edward Moore Kennedy was the youngest of the Kennedy children, he was also the least.

The youngest was born into Boston Irish royalty. Joseph Kennedy and Rose Fitzgerald were a charmed couple. Though Joe Kennedy didn't say much about his upbringing, possibly fearing that doing so might undermine his rags-to-riches myth, he did not grow up poor and struggling. Patrick Kennedy, a tight, taciturn man, was a prosperous saloon owner who also owned a wholesale liquor company and a share of the Columbia Trust Company. Joe's maternal uncles included a Boston mayor and a doctor. Moreover, Patrick Kennedy was a powerful political operative, a ward boss, in the Democratic Irish establishment. One Kennedy biographer said that Patrick ran a "pocket-sized welfare state" in East Boston that gave him considerable political clout, and he sat on the Board of Strategy, which selected candidates for the Democratic ticket, serving for a short time in the state House of Representatives himself. The Kennedys lived in a large colonial house set on a hill overlooking Boston Harbor, though the real sign of their status might have been sending Joseph to matriculate at the Boston Latin School, a redoubt for the Protestant elite, where John Adams and Ralph Waldo Emerson had gone, and which sent a high proportion of its graduates to Harvard, including, eventually, Joseph Kennedy.

It was while he was starring on the baseball team at Boston Latin and winning election as class president that the Irish prince began courting Boston's Irish princess, the beautiful eldest daughter of the city's mayor and a former congressman, John "Honey Fitz" Fitzgerald. Honey Fitz—the name derived from his outgoing, gregarious personality—was a born politician, at least a born Boston Irish politician: cocky, loquacious, back-slapping, fiery and unrestrained, sentimental, a man who would break out in "Sweet Adeline" at the drop of a hat. He even looked the part: short, round, and stocky, moon-faced, ruddy-complected, and blue-eyed. "Pixie-like" is how he was once described. Honey Fitz was also a student of humanity, which, with his extroversion, made for a powerful combination of charm and ambition. As a boy, he studied the Boston Brahmins while selling newspapers at Beacon and Park Streets, and his father clearly hoped he would become one of them, or as close as an Irish Catholic could come. His father had decided that Honey Fitz would be a doctor, and like Honey Fitz's future son-in-law, he attended those citadels of Protestant privilege, Boston Latin and then Harvard. But the father died suddenly two weeks before his son's final exams, and Honey Fitz was forced to leave school to care for his family. He took a job as an assistant to a ward boss named Matthew Kearney. And thus did John Fitzgerald enter politics.

His was a meteoric career. He was elected to the Boston Common Council at twenty-eight, then in short order rose to the state Senate and to the U.S. House of Representatives at thirty-one. (He was one of only three Catholics in the chamber.) After three terms, he ran for mayor of Boston in 1906 on the populist slogan "The people not the bosses must rule!" and won, then lost a reelection campaign, and, after a two-year interregnum, ran and won again in 1910, overcoming charges of corruption. When he reneged on a promise to the Democratic machine not to seek reelection, the ward bosses threatened to expose an affair Honey Fitz had had with a young cigarette girl. It would be the end of his elective political career, though not for want of trying to sustain it. He would lose a Senate race, win a House race only to see the result overturned due to vote fraud, then lose two mayoral races, two gubernatorial races, and another Senate race when he was in his seventies. Still, for all the losses, Edward Kennedy would attribute the Kennedys' political base in Boston to his grandfather and to his mother, who served as Honey Fitz's hostess during his political heyday because Honey Fitz's wife rejected the role.

When Joseph Kennedy and Rose Fitzgerald married in 1914, two scions of two powerful Irish political families, it might have seemed like a royal alliance, though the Fitzgeralds, none too happy with Rose's choice, thought of it as a morganatic one. Despite Rose's later denials, her family did everything it could to prevent the nuptials, including sending Rose on an extended trip to Europe. The Kennedys might not have been too happy either, given the vast differences of temperament between the two fathers—one reserved, the other boisterous; given the tensions between their political factions—Patrick's the Democratic establishment, Honey Fitz's their populist antagonist; and given the gap in their moral conduct. As one observer later put it, "The two grandfathers [speaking of Ted's grandfathers] expressed two sides of the Irish personality in America— P. J. its solid, closemouthed Catholic puritanism, with rigid values and strict boundaries, Honey Fitz its dervish-like energy, its drive, wit, and charm, and a grandiosity that refused to accept limits."

But if the two patriarchs were temperamentally and often politically at odds, there was one thing that united them, one thing that burned hot in them both and that would go a long way toward defining and driving their children and eventually their grandchildren: Catholic umbrage at Protestant condescension.

Above everything else, the Kennedys and the Fitzgeralds were Irish and Catholic, and defined themselves as such, and so did a large segment of Boston. The Irish had started coming in the 1830s, just before the potato famine, landing in Boston, it was said, because Samuel Cunard, the shipping magnate, had made an agreement with the Shawmut Bank to make the city the terminus of Cunard's Liverpool line. They came in droves, so that by 1855, the Irish, nearly all of them Catholic, constituted a third of the city's population. They quickly transformed the culture of the city and its politics, since two-thirds of Boston's Irish immigrants had been naturalized by 1885—a higher percentage than that of any other group. They brought with them their traditions, but they also brought with them their cultural inheritance—as historian Arthur Schlesinger, Jr., would describe it, "the pessimism, the romantic defiance, the political instinct, the irony, the sexual chauvinism, the Catholicism, the sense that the world was a mess and not likely to improve very much."

And they brought one more thing: They brought their grievances, especially their grievances against the Protestants, who were contemptuous of them. That was the great cleavage in Boston, the unbridgeable chasm: Catholics and Protestants. No Catholic could escape that Protestant contempt. No Protestant could escape that Catholic hostility.

But as much as the disdain stung the so-called "shanty Irish," the ordinary Irish men and women who couldn't begin to think of challenging the Protestant hegemony, it especially rankled the so-called "lace-curtain Irish," or "high Irish," among whom the Kennedys and Fitzgeralds numbered themselves—the Irish with money and ambition. Joseph Kennedy was ambitious. He aimed for Harvard but was held back in his senior year at Boston Latin to prepare more fully for the entrance exam and then was admitted on a probationary basis because he did poorly on that exam. That was a portent too. Throughout his four years there, Joseph Kennedy was an indifferent student.

But it wasn't the academics that daunted him; Harvard was clearly a credential for him rather than an education. It was the barrier Harvard erected against Catholics—the stigma of always being outside the social aerie of the Protestants. He would often remember what Doris Kearns Goodwin called a "negligible incident" of walking on Harvard Yard and watching three wealthy Protestant students pal around and then enter Claverly Hall, a posh private dormitory that functioned as their club—a club, like all those at Harvard, from which Kennedy would be barred. This seemingly negligible incident that had stuck in Joseph Kennedy's memory had no obvious point, save this: that Joseph Kennedy envied the boys' wealth, their easy camaraderie, their self-confidence, their sense of entitlement, and, above all, their status. And this point too: that Kennedy was angry at his exclusion. Goodwin says that is when Kennedy's resentments began to intensify, intensify and harden: "Resentment had crystallized out hard as rock," she wrote. And that may be when the Kennedy political dynasty began, that day on Harvard Yard, when Joe Kennedy, the Irish Catholic, began molding his life in the image of the young men he envied and the young men he was determined to supersede. Goodwin called it his "siege against the world."

And when Kennedy was graduated from Harvard, the siege continued. His Protestant classmates found positions with establishment banks. Kennedy, the Irish Catholic, did not. Instead, he became a bank examiner—a civil-service position. And while many of the Brahmins eventually left the business world entirely to live on trusts, Kennedy, the Irish Catholic, fiercely pursued his destiny with his own family connections. When he rescued his father's bank, Columbia Trust, from a hostile takeover, he was given the bank presidency at the age of twenty-five. With that foothold, during World War I he was appointed assistant general manager of the

Fore River plant in Quincy, where ships were made under the auspices of Bethlehem Steel, and shortly after the war he landed a position at Hayden, Stone & Co., a prestigious brokerage, gaining admission not as the Protestants did, through pedigree, but by, during a providential train ride on which Galen Stone happened to be a passenger, selling the idea of Stone buying ships from Fore River, while also selling himself. With Stone as his mentor, Kennedy became a dealmaker—he made his first killing, $650,000, when Henry Ford contracted to buy coal from a Stone-run company—and built a fortune, according to one biographer, by using insider information he gained at the brokerage. When Stone retired in 1923, Kennedy, the Irish Catholic, was sufficiently established to form his own investment firm.

He was not principally an investor. He was a juggler, taking out loans to buy real estate, then taking out loans on the real estate to buy more real estate, relying on Columbia Trust and on friends at other banks to finance him. Money was to be his equalizer, and he waded into finance with a chip on his shoulder. "Whenever you're dealing with someone important to you," he once told an adviser to his son, John, years later, "picture him sitting there in a suit of long red underwear. That's the way I've operated in business." At the same time, he was deeply conscious of elevating his status and of washing away the Irish Catholic stain. When he managed to push his way onto the board of the Morris Electric Company, even though the Irish had been blackballed, he said, "Do you have a better way to meet people like the Saltonstalls?" referring to a prominent family of the Protestant Brahmin elite.

But the Irish Catholic financial juggler was still not fully accepted by that elite, despite his success, despite his swelling wealth. It galled him that he was rejected twice for a seat on the board of trustees for the Massachusetts Electric Company before finally being admitted. And though he was driven by social acceptance, by trying to become an equal, he often found his business not in areas in which the Brahmins made their fortunes but in ones the Brahmins disdained. He was especially intrigued by motion pictures, an industry he first waded into while at Hayden, Stone and then plunged into when he raised $1.1 million to buy the British production company Film Booking Offices. Kennedy became a film mogul.

Beyond the profits of motion pictures, which were extraordinary, Kennedy found another benefit in Hollywood: The Irish Catholic was not stigmatized there. The industry was run largely by Jews, many of them

Eastern European immigrants, who had moved in, just as Kennedy would, because more-prideful Americans found the movies beneath them. One of those Jews, Jack Warner, who would later form the Warner Bros. studio, compared the status of that early film industry to pornography. Joseph Kennedy wasn't going to be considered a pornographer. He knew that as much as the Irish Catholics had been derided, the Jews were derided even more, which gave him an opportunity: He promised more wholesome movies than the ones the Jews had made. While this allowed him to raise his status by raising the status of motion pictures, it wasn't entirely as strategic as it may have seemed. Kennedy detested the Jews. He hated their values and their clannishness. He warned about letting them into Harvard or Christian country clubs. But he learned something from them too. He learned, as he would tell Rose, that the best defense against the world, that implacable Protestant world, was to "stick together."

Hollywood, according to Kennedy biographer David Nasaw, is where he made his real fortune. But he was always looking for opportunities—opportunities the Protestants might overlook, using his outsider status to his benefit. Critics said that during Prohibition he was a bootlegger, though there is no evidence for it. He did, however, after repeal, buy shares in a glass company and then got a license to distribute liquor in the United States from the English distilleries Haig & Haig and Dewar; he named his company Somerset, after the Somerset Club, from which he had been excluded. It was, wrote Nasaw, a "cash cow" for the family. But if the movies and liquor demonstrated Kennedy's willingness to find profit where he could, it was his financial conservatism that saved his wealth. He resisted the exuberance of the twenties, anticipating that there could be a crash, and wound up selling off nearly all his properties before it occurred. That is how he emerged from the depression as one of the country's richest men.

Yet the Irish Catholic still could not surmount the condescension, still seethed at it, still continued his siege against the world. "He would always be an 'Irish Catholic' first," his son Teddy would write, "and an individual second. 'I was born here. My parents were born here. What the hell do I have to do to be called an American?' he blurted after yet one more paper referred to him as an 'Irishman.'" And it wasn't just Joe Kennedy who was spurned. It was his family. "They wouldn't have asked my daughters to join their debutante clubs," he once complained, adding that they wouldn't have joined if they *had* been asked, which was highly unlikely.

Rose had to form her own charity group of Irish women—lace-curtain Irish women, whom she called the Ace of Clubs—because the Brahmins excluded them from *their* charitable organizations. (So great were Rose's airs that the ability to speak French was a prerequisite for joining her club.) "Tell me," Rose once asked a Protestant classmate of Jack's when she had her chauffeur drive them to Cape Cod for a weekend, "when are the nice people of Boston"—by which she meant the Protestants—"going to accept us?" And these indignities not only ate at Joe and infuriated him, they became a mantra in the Kennedy family. "It was always pounded into his head that they're all against us," a neighbor said of Kennedy. "It's us against the rest. And he taught this to his kids. It was us against the rest."

It was Boston he blamed—the whole Boston social structure—in which not even his success could mitigate the ostracism. "It was no place to bring up Irish Catholic children," he once told a reporter of one of the most Irish cities in America. "I didn't want them going through what I had to go through when I was growing up there. . . . I know so many Irish guys in Boston with real talent and ability that never got to first base, only because of their race and religion. In New York or Chicago, they would have been big men."

So Joe Kennedy left Boston to be a big man.

In 1925, long before the crash, he moved to New York, where he worked on the movies while Rose stayed in Brookline with the family—an arrangement that lasted for two years. Eventually Ed Moore found them a rental house in Riverdale, north of the city—a lavish estate at 5040 Independence Avenue, which had been the mansion of New York governor, Republican presidential candidate, secretary of State, and Supreme Court justice Charles Evans Hughes. Rose and the children departed Boston for New York on September 26, 1927, in a private railroad car. Two years later, Joe paid $250,000 for a six-acre estate in Bronxville in Westchester County at 294 Pondfield Road: a three-story, eleven-room red-brick mansion—Ted said it had twenty rooms—topped by a red-tile roof.

And though Kennedys would return, individually and triumphantly, that would be the end of Boston for the Joseph Kennedy family.

But it wasn't the end of Massachusetts, and it wasn't the end of discrimination. The Kennedys had continued to summer there in the twenties, and Honey Fitz had a house in Hull, in Plymouth County, off Boston Harbor. But Ted remembered that his father wouldn't be allowed in the golf club there. He tried Oyster Harbors and the Wianno Club and found them just as discriminatory. And he tried Cohasset, and the Cohasset Golf Club, and he was denied entry there too. In 1925, he wound up in Hyannis on Cape Cod, more hospitable to Irish Catholics, in a rented cottage on Marchant Avenue built in 1902. Here the Irish Catholic finally found his refuge, though locals still called it the "Irish House." The year after he moved to Riverdale, he bought the cottage, despite the fact that it was modest and unprepossessing for a man of his wealth, largely because Rose liked the way the lawn sloped to the water. In later years, when John Kennedy was president and had his own house there, it was to be called a compound. But Joseph Kennedy knew differently. It wasn't a compound; it was a fortress against the Protestant elites.

II

At the time the youngest was born, Joseph Kennedy, having presciently sold short on his stocks just before the crash wiped out the fortunes of so many others, had $4.2 million in assets. But the crash had nevertheless shattered his faith in the economic system. One biographer called his new attitude one of "almost unshakable pessimism," and that was the vision within which Edward Moore Kennedy grew up: tremendous wealth undermined by an ongoing sense of insecurity at how easily it could all be lost. Wealth had been Joseph Kennedy's weapon. Wealth had allowed him to lay siege to the Protestant establishment. Wealth was to be his family's great equalizer. And yet wealth was unreliable. Neither Joe nor the other Kennedys ever spoke of their fortune—to do so was forbidden—as if to do so was shanty Irish, not lace-curtain Irish. "Listening to them talk about money was like listening to nuns talk about sex," said a family friend. Nor did they ever speak about how Joe acquired that wealth. Ted's father-in-law would later recall Ted discussing his childhood—picking fresh tomatoes with his father or being sent to get salt water to steam lobsters or eating chicken livers with him—but said that Ted never spoke about his father's business, because Joe never had. He said that Joe Kennedy put up a "wall" between his family and his business.

But if money was not a passion among the Kennedys, only a way to gain status through the power it conferred, the Depression jolted Joe Kennedy into an epiphany about the relationship between money and status and power. He saw that the Depression had disrupted that relationship and that money didn't necessarily lead to power. With the entire economic machinery of the country wrecked, Kennedy had come to the realization that politics would control wealth, not the other way around—that the surest path to real power was through politics. As he told his friend, the entertainer Morton Downey, "In the next generation, the people who run the government will be the biggest people in America."

And that realization would change everything for the Kennedys.

Prior to the Depression, Kennedy's attitude toward politics had been largely apathetic. Despite his father's and his father-in-law's involvement in ward politics, he seemed to think of politics differently—not as a way to rise on the backs of Irish plebeians but as another way to raise his status over them. Kennedy's father, Patrick, had come to feel an antipathy to the regular Democrats after Honey Fitz had won them over, by one account even leaving Boston for Winthrop when Honey Fitz sabotaged Kennedy's primary campaign for street commissioner. Joe Kennedy's antipathy went deeper—to the lack of status attached to being a Democrat. In the early twenties he flirted with the idea of joining the Republicans, and he did become a member of the Middlesex Club, the oldest Republican organization in New England. According to Doris Kearns Goodwin, it was Rose who insisted he stick with the Democrats out of family fealty, but biographer David Nasaw said he quit the Middlesex when Massachusetts governor Calvin Coolidge replaced an Irish Catholic appointee with a Protestant one; Kennedy fumed about it, complaining that Republicans had to learn how to treat Irish Catholics respectfully. Still, Nasaw speculated that Kennedy voted for Republican Herbert Hoover in the 1928 presidential race against fellow Catholic and Democrat Al Smith because Smith's vulgar, working-class style offended him.

But in 1932, after his epiphany about politics and power, Kennedy threw his support to the Democratic presidential candidate, New York governor Franklin Roosevelt, and after spending the summer following Ted's birth with the family at Hyannis, he and Eddie Moore joined Roosevelt in September for that cross-country whistle-stop tour from Albany to Los Angeles, during which Joe ingratiated himself with the candidate by proselytizing for him with wealthy friends, including the influential newspaper magnate William Randolph Hearst. When Roosevelt coasted to victory in November, Kennedy clearly felt that these efforts would be rewarded with his own political power in the new administration—power that would serve as a foundation for his sons' political power. He was wrong. Roosevelt, thinking Kennedy overly ambitious and untrustworthy, was no more grateful to him or admiring of his talents than other Protestant Brahmins had been. Kennedy grandiosely wanted to be secretary of the Treasury or ambassador to England. Instead, Roosevelt offered him the ambassadorship to Ireland (Roosevelt must have known how much that offer would sting Kennedy) or the chairmanship of a trade commission to South America. Kennedy was insulted. Revealingly, he wrote his son Joseph, "I told him that I did not desire a position with the government unless it really meant some prestige to my family."

It was always for family: the wealth, the power, the ingratiation, the desperate need to elevate his status. His children would be the beneficiaries and, he dreamed, the victors—the ones who would finally win the siege, the ones who would at long last expunge the Irish Catholic stigma that so haunted him. It was because of deficiencies in family, he believed, that the Irish were snubbed by the Brahmins. The Boston Irish, he said in a speech to the Clover Club in 1937, "suffered under the handicap of not possessing family tradition adequate to win the respect and confidence of the Puritan neighbors. The Yankee pride of ancestry developed a boastfulness and snobbishness which, though difficult to understand, explains many of the strange idiosyncrasies of Boston"—and, he might have added, of the Kennedys. Even Rose spoke approvingly if enviously of the "advantages of inherited wealth and status and close-knit interfamily ties" that created a "self-perpetuating aristocracy" among the Brahmins. Joe was determined that the Kennedy family would emulate those ties in hopes of creating their own self-perpetuating aristocracy. He was determined that the Kennedys would triumph not only over the Protestants; they would triumph over their own Irish Catholicism.

No one believed more fervently in family than Joseph Kennedy. No one was more invested in family than Joseph Kennedy. And of all the lessons he taught his children, there was none more important than this one, which he had learned from a lifetime of affronts: Family takes precedence over everything else. In a world of uncertainty, in a world of betrayal, as he felt Roosevelt had betrayed him, in a world of humiliation, where not even wealth could finally shield you from disdain, the one redoubt, the one sanctuary, the one protection, the one repository of trust, was family. "From our earliest days," Ted would write, "I think all the Kennedy children were made to feel that our father's principal interest in life was his

family. As the youngest, it appeared to me that the family was his only interest." It was.

Joe Kennedy cultivated family. He would say of his children that
"they've always been very close to each other" and that the Kennedys had
"togetherness long before it became a slogan." But this understated the
case, making it seem as if their filial bonds were normal. They weren't. So
powerfully had Kennedy instilled in his children a belief in family that it
had an almost metaphysical effect on them. "I never expected any of us to
get married," Ted would write. "We would be brothers and sisters, unchanging forever." Columnist Stewart Alsop would later put it more succinctly: "The Kennedys were all in love with one another." Elsewhere, Ted
noted that "the overarching sense that we all had is we were enormously
happy together. Our best friends were our brothers and sisters," and to the
comment that they thought they would never get married he added,
"They all got married somewhat older than most of their colleagues."
And though, amid the devotion, Joseph was cautious not to inculcate in
them a sense of entitlement, he did not stint on inculcating in them a
sense of superiority, even over relatives who were not part of the nuclear
family. As a girl, Jean Smith would measure her wrists and ankles and
then sniff at a cousin that the cousin's ankles weren't slim enough to be
"really aristocratic"—like the Kennedys'.

That is how Joe and Rose saw themselves and how they wanted their
children to see themselves—as aristocrats. Few families were as class-
conscious, and for all the animus Joe felt toward his Protestant social su-
periors, he assiduously emulated them and forced his children into the
mold. As one political writer would put it, "Joe Kennedy was hardly a patrician, but he brought up his boys as if they were the sons of one." For
Rose, the bug bit early. She would recall a trip to Palm Beach, where
American aristocrats wintered, and gush, "Rich, very rich people like the
Astors, medium rich, and people of ordinary circumstances like me were
all accommodated in the same place. I was thrilled in those days to see the
Vincent Astors, the Vanderbilts, and especially the Wideners, all promenading up and down the foyer of the hotel after dinner." It wouldn't be
long before she would join those ranks of wealth; no matter how ordinary
she might have thought herself, according to her biographer she had a full
household staff from the moment she was married. Later, in a possible
stab at seeming more aristocratic, she would label the staff: the Secretary,
the Cook, the Chauffeur. The Kennedys were, said onetime Massachusetts

governor Paul Dever, "the first Irish Brahmins." Joe was determined to remove "Irish."

And it wasn't only that he taught his family they were superior. Joe taught them the family was sacrosanct, insulated not only from the business world but also from the political world Joe Kennedy was beginning to invade. "This house was a sacred place for all of us," Ted would later say of the Hyannis Port cottage. "I don't ever remember my father having a political meeting in this house. There was never a cocktail party in this house," until John Kennedy ran for president. "Never any other time. My brother Jack didn't have them, my brother Bobby didn't have them, I didn't have them." The house was for family—only for family. And Joe would tell his children this: "Home holds no fear for me," by which he meant that whatever happened to them in the outside world, whatever failures or indignities they may have suffered, they could always come home to safety and to love—to the Kennedys. "None of my children give a damn about business," he once said proudly. "The only thing that matters is family. I tell them that when they end this life, if they can count their friends on one hand, they will be lucky. Stick with family."

But if family was a refuge, a defense from the world, it was also, in Joe Kennedy's mind, a weapon, an instrument to beat the world. And the Kennedys had to be trained, drilled, for it. Their competitiveness was legendary. "Daddy was always very competitive," Eunice would tell a Kennedy biographer. "The thing he always kept telling us is that coming in second was just no good. The important thing was to win—don't come in second or third—that doesn't count—but win, win, win." When young Ted came in third in a sailing race, Joe was furious. "We've got the best boat; we've got the best teacher. How come you're coming in third?" When Ted lost another race, Joe sent him to his room. Competition was as ingrained as love and possibly more pervasive. "We competed in every conceivable way: at touch football, at sailing, at skipping rocks, and seeing whose seashell could float the farthest out to sea," Ted would write. "We competed at games of wit and information and debate. We competed for attention at the dinner table, which meant a good deal of boning up." During the 1960 presidential campaign, in which John Kennedy ran, Joe told his friend, *New York Times* columnist Arthur Krock, "For the Kennedys, it's either the outhouse or the castle, nothing in between." And that is why the Kennedys were always "out for blood," as one family friend put it, referring not only to athletic competitions but also to their later political competitions. And that is why, as Doris Kearns Goodwin observed, Joe seldom provided moral guidance for his children, only competitive guidance. "Not once in more than two hundred letters," she wrote, "did he put forward any ultimate moral principles for his children to contemplate. On the contrary, he stressed to his children the importance of winning at any cost and the pleasures of coming in first." But it wasn't about success and it really wasn't about pleasure, because there was very little pleasure in it—mainly agony and fear of failing. It went deeper. For Joe Kennedy to lose was to revisit every defeat he had ever experienced. For Joe Kennedy to lose was to challenge the very basis of his life.

There was one place, however, where the competition was not blood sport, and that was within the family itself. Joe encouraged healthy interfamilial competition, and Rose cited fraternal rivalries between Joe Jr. and Jack or between Bobby and Ted. And Joe wasn't above comparing one child of his to another, albeit in the interest, Ted would say, of raising the expectations of each. But it was done, Ted said, with such tact that it never engendered any resentments, which, among Kennedy siblings, would have violated Joe's family code. "I can't deal with the fact that they're differing or fighting with one another," Joe would say. So they didn't. There may never have been a family with fewer intramural squabbles, at least overt ones. And this lack of sibling enmity or jealousy was bred deep in them too and lasted into their adulthood, so that they never even *spoke* disparagingly of one another. "The Kennedys were amazingly considerate of each other," wrote a nurse who had worked for the family, "and during all the years I was with them, I never heard one gossip about another." That is how inviolate the Kennedy family bond, the bond forged by Joe Kennedy, was.

Family was fortress, family was weapon, but Joe Kennedy's family was also art—a "conscious work of art," one political observer would say, of the sort Kennedy had produced in Hollywood. Joe Kennedy had learned lessons about imagery in his California foray. He frequently paraded his family before the cameras, not only so that they would be seen but so that they would know *how* to be seen—developing a consciousness of the camera. Rose would arrange family tableaux for the camera—how often does one see the Kennedy family en masse in old photographs?—and she instructed them to turn sideways to make them look thinner. Even the much-vaunted, toothy Kennedy smile was the product of Rose's orchestration. The children were sent to the orthodontist every few weeks, and toothbrushing was a serious routine in the Kennedy household.

This heavy emphasis on aesthetic values might have seemed incongruous with Rose's even heavier emphasis on spiritual values. Rose Kennedy was devout—beyond devout. She attributed that devotion to her mother, a quiet introvert who was the antithesis of the rowdy, carousing Honey Fitz and who "drilled us in our catechism and other religious lessons." And Rose drilled her own children—stopping at St. Aidan's in Brookline with them every day when they lived in Massachusetts; saying grace at every meal and reciting the rosary each night; learning the prayers in Latin; recruiting the sons as altar boys even when they were too little to lift the prayer books onto the altar; and attending mass every Sunday, even forcing Joe, whose religious fervor was considerably less than his wife's and who chafed at the Church hierarchy as he chafed at social hierarchies, to go. Religion, Ted would say, was as "much a part of our identity as the large family was, the Irish tradition was." And Ted would tell the story of how he was eagerly planning to sail up to Edgartown for a regatta, until his mother returned from mass and ordered him to attend a religious retreat in Lawrence instead.

But the imposition of religion on the children obscured something else: It wasn't just about Christ or, perhaps, even primarily about Christ. It was about Rose. First, Rose's piety was another way of asserting her superiority over less religious Protestants by showing that Catholics, especially Irish Catholics, were more deeply committed, more deeply moral. And second, Rose's religiosity was finally as much, or even more, a matter of aesthetics as of faith. She would tell of how, when her father denied her wish to attend Wellesley, she went to Blumenthal, a Sacred Heart convent school in Holland, and how at Blumenthal she made a commitment to "try harder to dedicate myself to the standards of convent life." That meant perfection as, she said, the Virgin Mary was perfect. "I shall be the model of *perfection* for the next few months," she wrote home. But it was for more than the next few months. It was for a lifetime. Rose Kennedy spent that lifetime in pursuit of perfection, as her husband spent his in pursuit of retribution.

But it wasn't religious perfection she sought. Her interests were no more spiritual than her husband's, her guidance no more moral than her husband's. Her interests were that she and her children be the very models of social, cultural, and physical perfection, that they stand straight, dress well, be clean, well spoken, well mannered, presentable—in short, the personification of the wealthy aristocrats the Kennedys so detested and so envied. Many years later, her grandson Robert Kennedy Jr., would marvel at a typical note Rose wrote in which she glided effortlessly from fashion to religious observance, without missing a beat: "They are wearing parchment-shade gloves this year—not white—if you are thinking of wearing them with black dresses, for instance. They can be bought at Bergdorf's. Also say rosary in month of October"—a marvel because to her, the realms of the material and spiritual were not different; they were both a matter of aesthetics. And it was true of her family too. The Kennedys were an aesthetic object—a perfect aesthetic object. And in this, Rose was no less interested in power than her husband was. The family was to be her weapon as it was for Joe—her rebuff to those who had rebuffed her. "My great ambition," she would say, "was to have my children morally, physically, and mentally as perfect as possible." Religion was just a stick to get them that way.

And the Kennedy children had to live up to the image—had, in fact, to live *for* the image, because however much Joe Kennedy may have said, and may sincerely have felt, that everything he did was in service to his children, the fact was that everything his children did was in service to him. For all the tributes to the solidarity and joy of the Kennedy family, there was also great pressure on the children to be the objects they were expected to be. "There was always a good deal expected of us, and we all knew it," Ted would say when he first ran for the Senate, citing, as one example, the parental order to read a book a day during the summers. "Whatever we did, we were expected to do as well as we could." And though most of this was attributed to the diktats of Joe Kennedy, Eunice Kennedy cited the "terrific drive" and "quite a little pressure" her mother inflicted upon them as well.

There were rules, and not just the rules of conduct. Joe wanted his children to be "natural" and "able to smile no matter how tough things were." One of his pet expressions was, "I don't want any sourpusses around here." Another was, "Tears accomplish nothing." And a favorite word was "bellyaching," which was something he abhorred. But he was also quick, said Ted, to "scold a child who tried to smile too readily, or charm his way through life." He said he wanted his children to have a "good time" but never a "frivolous one." "Ride a horse, yes, but play polo, no." He tolerated mistakes but only the first time, never the second. He didn't need to. He disciplined, said a childhood friend of Ted's, through his eyes—"with that glare"—though Ted would say that both his mother and father also administered punishment more prosaically, with a coat hanger.

Again, none of these rules constituted a moral education. They were an education in survival and social advancement—two of the things that Joe and Rose most prized. To the extent that there was any moral component, it was, like Rose's piety, an aesthetics of morality: the appearance of morality without real spirituality. This was true of what was perhaps the most salient of the commandments from both Kennedy parents: that the children use the opportunities that had been given them, that their lives be purposeful, not necessarily because there was some moral imperative to do so but because not to do so would be to waste all the effort that Joe Kennedy had expended on them, that not to do so would reflect badly on the family Joe and Rose had so carefully constructed. Oft quoted in the Kennedy household was Luke 12:48, "To whom much has been given, much will be required," though it wasn't so much being required to give to others as to do something constructive—even, as Ted later interpreted it, if it was only selfishly to win praise. Achievement reflected favorably on the family and added honor to the Kennedy name. It burnished the family aesthetic.

But as much as the family aesthetic was designed for public consumption, to show the Kennedys as those models of perfection, the Kennedy children largely bought into the image or at the very least willingly promoted it for a long time. In the familiar Kennedy saga, Joe and Rose were always devoted. They were perfect complements to each other. Joe was, in Ted's words, "strong," "dominating," "motivating"; Rose had "softness," "gentleness," and a "sense of understanding and love" that tempered her husband's high expectations. And though Joe was away a good deal of the time, he was nevertheless always a presence and "never seemed far away," according to Rose. And though he could be a stern taskmaster, Joe Kennedy's "criticisms were always positive and constructive," his "guidance was for our own good and the family's," and he always gave his children his "unqualified support," in Ted's words. The Kennedy family—wise father, doting mother, loving siblings—was what every family aspired to be, not just in its physical aesthetics but, according to the Kennedys' own testimony, in its emotional support.

And they had learned their father's lesson. For them, as for him, family would be everything. "Family was the abiding metaphor of their lives," the author Richard Rhodes would say in an early profile of Ted, "their reference point, their pool of knowledge, their place of retreat, their source of strength. They said: We have all this, who can dream what we might do with it? They made it a metaphor of nationhood. They spoke of a new generation. They said we can work together. They said we should love one another." And referencing a line from the speech that Robert Kennedy made in Indianapolis the night that Martin Luther King Jr. was killed—"I had a member of my family killed"—a speech that managed to bank the crowd's angry fire, Rhodes continued, "That simple sentence stopped a riot, if only for one night."

Family would define their politics. Family would undergird their image. Family would be both their vehicle and their message.

And yet the glowing image hid a reality, several realities. For one thing, the great paterfamilias of the Kennedy clan, the man who was said to rule them all, was almost never there—either in Hollywood or New York or Washington—for long, long stretches. For another, far from having a loving marriage of two complementary partners, Joe and Rose had a marriage of convenience that functioned largely as show. According to Doris Kearns Goodwin, Rose, disillusioned and unhappy, had actually left Joe Kennedy in 1920 and retreated to Honey Fitz's house. Honey Fitz promptly commanded she return to her husband, and it was after going on a religious retreat that she decided her family was to be her life's mission. And as Goodwin put it, "From here on, Rose and Joe appear less like lovers than like partners in the common enterprise of welding their children together into a family group with its own standards, its own language and its own traditions." But Rose's threat didn't change Joe Kennedy. Despite his wife's new resolve, Kennedy continued his womanizing. Rose certainly knew about these affairs, though she pretended she didn't. She seemed to accept them the way her mother had accepted Honey Fitz's dalliances—as the price she had to pay to keep her family intact and its reputation impeccable.

This was, by many accounts, not as great a sacrifice as it might seem. Rose was a prude. Her niece, Ann Gargan, said that Rose believed sex was for procreation only—a view about which, Gargan remembered, Joe would tease her. Near the end of her life, Rose asked her twenty-year-old grandson, Robert Shriver, how he was getting on with a girl to whom he had introduced her. When he said he had kissed her, Rose was aghast, even more aghast when Shriver said he had kissed other girls before. "You know," Rose said, "your grandfather was the only man I've ever kissed." After Ted was born, the intimacy stopped altogether. A friend told Goodwin that Rose announced, "No more sex," and from that point forward they slept in separate bedrooms.

But that didn't mean that Rose now redirected all her attention and her love to her children, which was nevertheless the image she purveyed during their campaigns in later years. That image was for show too. For all the Kennedys' emphasis on family, Rose was not a nurturing mother. She would complain that when she was growing up, her family was so large—six children—that she never got sufficient attention, and she said she was frequently left alone or with caretakers while her father was in Washington or her parents vacationed without their children. But rather than spare her children the emotional deprivation she felt she had suffered, she perpetuated it. She was cold, aloof, self-interested, and often, like her husband, absent. "Gee, you're a great mother to go away and leave your children alone," six-year-old Jack complained when she left him for six weeks—one of many barbs he would fire at her. And it only got worse as time went on. After Ted's birth, she reached an accommodation with Joe for him to send her on frequent trips to Europe to give her a respite from the children. By one account, in the mid-thirties, when Ted was an infant, she took seventeen of these trips. She told her granddaughter Caroline that she and Joe never fought, and when Caroline asked how they resolved their differences, Rose answered, "I would always just say, 'Yes, dear,' and then I'd go to Paris," which was evidently the price Joe paid for his infidelities.

And it wasn't just that she was frequently absent; she was emotionally distant too. The children often talked about her influence on them, her regimentation and scheduling, her unceasing demands for punctuality and good behavior, her nitpicking corrections of their grammar, her "awakening of educational and intellectual pursuits," as Ted would put it, at the expense of more-maternal feelings. They would always try to put the best gloss on this discipline—on the aesthetics of a well-regulated family. But as Eunice Kennedy would later say, Rose's relationship to her children "wasn't a great emotional thing. . . . She was more a teacher or inspirer. She was more interested in whether you were reading or whether taking skating lessons." She had begged off breastfeeding her children because a "baby is usually fed at ten or ten-thirty [P.M.]. You're at the theater, so what do you do?" When Jean complained about being shuffled off to boarding school when she was only eight, Rose parried, "Well, what was I to do? Your father was always gone, or we were having dinners at the embassy or attending formal affairs. I had no time to spend with you children." Ted would recall a rare interlude when he left Riverdale with whooping cough and went to Cape Cod with his mother, where he had her to himself for the first time in his life, reading to him, walking with him, caring for him, and said that "it cemented a special bond between my mother and me," except that Ted, according to medical records—records kept meticulously by Rose—had whooping cough and light pneumonia in June 1942 and spent two weeks at St. Vincent's Hospital in New York, where his mother almost certainly did not tend to him, not on Cape Cod, unless his recovery was unusually long. More accurate than these loving, confected vignettes might have been Rose's own unguarded admission on discipline: "I used to have a ruler around and paddled them occasionally because when they're young that's all they understand."

And there was one more secret, one more blot on the image: the Kennedys' eldest daughter, Rosemary. Physically, Rosemary met the Kennedy standards, Rose's standards. She was lovely. But as a child, she lagged behind her two older brothers' benchmarks, was slower than they had been both physically and mentally, and when she was five and enrolled in kindergarten at the Edward Devotion School in Brookline, she was declared "deficient"—what was then called "mentally retarded." The Kennedy response was denial, at first—deep denial—then, over time, strenuous intervention in the belief that they could correct Rosemary's disability while also attempting to hide it from others. Some of this fell to Eddie Moore, who, as Rosemary's godfather, took an abiding interest in her and helped make arrangements for her. Still, as Joe and Rose hunted for solutions to a condition for which there was no solution, they were determined that she "pass" as normal, and Joe Jr. and Jack often took her to dances in that effort, Jack once commenting that his friends couldn't seem to tell she was disabled.

But it was a losing effort. In a family of competition, Rosemary wanted desperately to be her siblings' equal, and when she was sent off to a special boarding school, she wrote plaintive letters to her parents about how well she was doing, about how proud she hoped they would be of her. She could never, however, match her siblings. Both Joe and Rose were deeply sensitive to her situation and to theirs. They understood that the Kennedys' desire for perfection threatened Rosemary; they understood, too, that Rosemary threatened the Kennedys' desire for perfection. She was, Eddie Moore told Joe Kennedy's paramour, Gloria Swanson, after she'd asked about Rosemary and Kennedy had exploded, a "very sore subject with the boss." And perhaps more for Rose. "Our family was the perfect family," she would say in a speech on mental disability many years later, "boys brilliant, girls attractive and intelligent, money, prestige, a young father and mother of intelligence, devoted exemplary habits and successful in the education of their children. . . . But God or 'destiny' just does not allow a family to exist which has all these star-studded adornments." In effect, she saw Rosemary as a means for God to show them humility—a way for him to show them imperfection in the Kennedys' perfect world.

III

Rose would assert that when she learned she was pregnant with her last child, the child who was an afterthought and surprise, she resolved that this would be no disadvantage to the baby, or, she added, to her. "The baby, boy or girl, would always know it was a welcome and cherished member of our family," she later recalled, "always feel loved, and would grow up knowing the profound meaning of love in joy and confident service and happy relationships with others." And after Teddy's arrival, she would write, "I went out of my way to make sure that these resolutions—for me and for him—were kept in every way I could do so." That is the way it appeared in her memoir. But she was more candid to her ghostwriter, telling him that she got "indignant" over friends' disbelief that she was having another child after eight and that, as a kind of defiance, she was going to make sure that no one felt sorry for either her or Teddy, that neither would "suffer" and that they were going to be "independent and make it in superior fashion." And as if to verify her success, she told the ghostwriter that Teddy was "happy . . . He would never get upset with anybody or anything."

"Happy" is how young Teddy was usually described. He had, Rose said, a "cheerful and outgoing character" and "always had a 'sunny disposition.'" "Cheerful and docile" was how a friend of Rose's described him. "He never got into the scrapes at home like Joe and Jack and Bobby." Rose had to spank them, the friend said. She rarely spanked Teddy, who was "gentle and lovable," she said. "Outgoing and friendly," said his sister Eunice of the young Teddy, an extrovert that the brothers and sisters all loved to be with. "People naturally gravitated to him," said his sister Jean, calling him the leader of the family games and outings. "You never had to push Ted—you always had to hold him back." So much younger than the rest—seventeen years younger than Joe Jr., fifteen years younger than Jack, even four years younger than Jean, the next youngest Kennedy—he took from his sister Kathleen the mantle of family pet. Upon Teddy's birth, Jack wrote a note to his mother asking to be godfather—a note that Ted as senator kept framed on a wall in his office, alongside a congratulatory letter from President Herbert Hoover to Rose that arrived, Ted would later joke, with five cents' postage due. He was always spoken of with a diminutive: "Eddie" to his siblings and later "Teddy."

But the façade also hid a truth. If Rose thought that the youngest was a happy, perfectly contented child, she was mistaken, very mistaken, and for all her professions of going the extra mile for him, she even, on occasion, seemed to acknowledge her failure. "We tried to keep everything more or less equal," she told *Time* magazine, "but you wonder if the mother and father aren't quite tired when the ninth one comes along. You have to make more of an effort to tell bedtime stories and be interested in swimming matches." And she said something even more revealing: "When you have older brothers and sisters, they're the ones that seem to be more important in a family, and always get the best rooms and the first choice of boats, and all those kind of things, but Ted never seemed to resent it." Or as Jean Kennedy would later say, "My mother's great theory was to concentrate on the older children and the younger ones would come along."

So Ted never exhibited resentment when he was always being evicted from his room to accommodate guests, even spending one night sleeping on a massage table and another in the bathtub. He didn't exhibit resentment when he and Jean were exiled to the children's table at dinner while all the other siblings sat at the main table. He didn't seem to resent it when he was constantly chided by his parents and ribbed by his siblings for his chubbiness, in a house where physical attractiveness was so highly valued, and he didn't seem to resent it when his brother Joe angrily threw him off a sailboat into the water because Teddy didn't follow his instructions adequately. (So deep in denial may Ted have been that he told that story with only the barest hint of irritation.) And he didn't seem to resent his mother trying to shunt him off to kindergarten when he was only four and too young to be admitted, or her persistence, when a principal nixed that idea, in trying to find a school that might admit him to the first grade the next year, when he was scarcely five.

Whatever attention Joe and Rose had paid to the older children and whatever sacrifices they had made for them—which weren't many—they ceased making them for the younger children and especially for the youngest, the afterthought. After Rosemary, the youngest had it worst. Ted attended ten schools by the time he was eleven years old, sometimes being pulled from one school in the middle of a semester and thrust into another to accommodate Rose's schedule—and it was always Rose's schedule that took precedence over Ted's. When she traveled, she put him in boarding school, even admitting that she shouldn't have done so at his age but not stopping either. One biographer said that during the school year, from ages seven through fourteen, Ted was home only on holidays.

And the youngest had it worst when, in March 1938, Roosevelt appointed Joe Kennedy the United States ambassador to England, though, again, no one in the family seemed to recognize the boy's distress. Roosevelt's son James said his father had "almost toppled from his wheelchair" when Kennedy first requested the appointment after Roosevelt's election in 1932. But now the president told his Treasury secretary, Henry Morgenthau, that Kennedy had become increasingly critical of the administration, and Roosevelt wanted him out of Washington, saying the appointment was to be for six months only, just enough time to neutralize Kennedy. Kennedy was elated with the appointment, after having served in relatively minor roles as chairman of the new Securities and Exchange Commission to supervise Wall Street and as the chairman of the Maritime Commission responsible for regulating international ocean transportation. Neither was commensurate with his status, and both he and Roosevelt knew it.

The Court of St. James's was different. Whatever else it was, it was a high attainment for a social climber, especially an Irish Catholic social climber—a perfect vindication, since there had never been a U.S. Irish Catholic ambassador to England—and he and Rose were clearly in their element there. The ambassador's residence at 14 Princes Gate in London was an amalgamation of two houses once owned by the American financier J. P. Morgan. It was six stories tall and, depending on who did the tally, had either thirty-six or fifty-two rooms manned by twenty-three servants with three chauffeurs for the automobiles. (Of course, Ed Moore, who accompanied Rosemary and Eunice to England after they finished school in May, served as the ambassador's chief secretary.) Ted, who had often been dispossessed of his room in America, at last had a large room to himself, with a desk, a chaise longue, and a breakfast table. Better still, there was an elevator, which Bobby and Teddy loved to ride up and down, playing department store, until Rose forbade it. And in addition to the residence, Joe rented a country house at Ascot and sent the family to St. Moritz and the French Riviera for vacations. As for Rose, she bought two hundred dresses for herself and her daughters.

If Joe and Rose loved the status, they also loved the display. The Kennedys, with their brood, made for a novelty, often photographed for both British and American papers and magazines in the standard lineup like ducklings. "Nine Young U.S. Ambassadors," one article called the children, describing young Ted as a "real American boy with a trick a minute and boundless self-confidence and enthusiasm." It added that he and Bobby would take the embassy car to school each day, where Ted "adjusted quickly." And Luella Hennessey, the Kennedys' longtime nursemaid, would pick the boys up from school and take them through Hyde Park, where, she said, they would kick pebbles. As Hennessey saw it, Teddy in England was "always bubbly and happy, always wanting to talk," just as he had been in America. He seemed to love it. There was no question Joe and Rose loved it. As Joe Kennedy neared the end of his first year—Roosevelt had not recalled him after six months as he said he would—he and Rose were weekend guests of the king and queen at Windsor Castle. As Rose told it, Joe said to her, "This is a helluva long way from East Boston," which had been the point all along.

But what was social advancement for Joe and Rose was social displacement for their youngest son. Despite the outward appearances, Ted Kennedy was no happier in England than he had been in America when he was being shuttled from school to school. He was lonely and friendless, and, he would later write, "the loneliness I felt was obvious to those around me," no matter how much they might have tried to blind themselves to it. Bobby, Ted told his father's biographer decades later, tried to keep him company, but he was six years older and had found his own circle of friends. With no one else to befriend his youngest son, Joe, who was living with the family for the first time and recognized Ted's difficulties, made an effort to spend time with him—riding horseback with him in the mornings, attending his cricket games, reading to him in Ted's room at night. It was the closest they had been. Nursemaid Hennessey recalled how, early in the evening, as the ambassador dressed for the night's appointment, he would first talk with Bobby and then Ted. Joe had never fully understood Bobby, nor did he appreciate him. He wasn't big, athletic, and outgoing like his brother Joe or witty and acerbic like his brother Jack. He may have had a little too much of his mother's piety in him for Joe's taste. But Joe enjoyed Teddy—beamed when he saw him. "Teddy was like the sunshine," Hennessey would say, "lighting up everything in sight and keeping his father young." She said you could hear them laughing "as Teddy jumped up and down on his father's bed until he was exhausted." And then Rose would calm him down and get him ready for bed.

Even then, Ted must have realized that his antics and Joe's amusement at them, like so many of the interactions in the Kennedy family, even the sincerest ones, were a transaction. If Joe and Rose had taught their children to be purposeful, that extended to the Kennedy family itself. Each child had a role to play in the family structure to sustain the family's survival, as if it were an organism. Sometimes the role fit the personality: Carefree Kathleen, or "Kick," as she was aptly nicknamed, was the spirited rebel in temper and part. Sometimes the personality was made to fit the role: Bobby, the runt of the Kennedys and a boy of sensitive disposition, became the family tough guy to cancel that sensitivity. But everyone in the family was cast in the Kennedy movie: Joe and Rose's movie. And to the youngest fell the job not necessarily to be happy himself but to make others in the family happy—to tease and be teased, to joke and laugh, to serve as both jester and pet, as both comic relief and adored object. Especially because of the disparities in age between him and all but Jean, Ted couldn't help but be taken less seriously than the others, and he didn't seem to fight it. Teddy Kennedy always appeared happy, always cheerful, always of sunny disposition, always a ball of fire, a naughty but good-natured prankster, because that is what the family needed from him, what it expected from him—the youngest.

And Ted cultivated these skills, the way Bobby cultivated toughness, and he also cultivated the skill of hiding his unhappiness, because Ted Kennedy had to be the family joy, whether he was joyful or not.

But especially in England, he was not joyful. Yet again, he started at one school, the Sloane Street School for Boys in London, where the headmaster remembered nothing about him save that he passed on servings of cauliflower, only to be sent to another, the Gibbs School, where the head-master remembered him as a "very normal, cheerful little boy." Ted saw it very differently. "I struggled to learn my lesson," he would write. "I strug-gled to learn cricket. When I broke the rules, I was invited to the headmas-ter's office, where he made me hold my palms up and then whacked them with a ruler until they were bright red." And, despite his educational dis-ruptions in America, he would remember this passage at Gibbs as the be-ginning of his unhappiness in school and something worse: his confrontation with not having friends and being disliked. "I liked to be liked," he would write, "and up until my school years I'd taken my likabil-ity for granted. After all, I was the youngest, used to being doted on by everyone." But by "everyone," he meant the Kennedys. What he discov-ered in England was that "the world of strangers proved different."

And his sense of alienation couldn't have been helped by his father's increasing untenability as ambassador: When British prime minister Neville Chamberlain appeased Adolf Hitler in Munich to stave off war, Rose recalled that Joe "kissed me and twirled me around in his arms, re-peating over and over what a great day this was and what a great man Chamberlain was"—a verdict not vindicated by history. Nor was he helped by his mother's absences: As Bobby and Teddy were beginning the new school year, Rose had chosen to go to Scotland just five days after return-ing from a trip to France, then reluctantly came back to London because Joe insisted upon it. She did not return, however, to nurse Ted, who was having his tonsils out just four days after the Munich Conference. She wrote in her diary: "Did some shopping and got a report about Teddy," which expressed the level of concern she had for her six-year-old son even when he was hospitalized. Four months later, she left on a six-week shop-ping trip, missing his birthday. When the family finally did gather, it was for another publicized tableau, this one in Rome for the investiture of the new pope, Pius XII. As Eugenio Cardinal Pacelli and Vatican secretary of state, the pope had visited the Kennedys' Bronxville home in the fall of 1936 during a tour of America and after a meeting with Roosevelt. Though the visit was a favor to Joe Kennedy for having arranged the meeting between the cardinal and the president, it nevertheless attested to the status of the Kennedys in the American Catholic community. Ted crawled into the cardinal's lap while the churchman sat on a sofa. (The family kept the sofa in Hyannis thereafter.) It was another testament when the new pope gave the family a private audience on March 13—the pontiff, calling Ted a "smart boy," told him he remembered him from Bronxville—and then, two days later, officiated at Ted's first communion in a small chapel at the Vatican. "I hope you always be good and pious as you are today," the new pope told him. But the investiture attested to something else for young Teddy Kennedy. "There were eleven of us in seven seats," he would recall. "I, being the youngest, was squeezed to the far end of a very small bench. I remember one of the central thoughts I had during the whole ceremony: being squeezed in but still not being separated. That had a lot of significance to me over the course of my life." He was the youngest, the afterthought, but he was still a Kennedy.

It was to be a brief interlude of calm before a brewing storm. Chamberlain's agreement with Hitler did little to slow the march toward war, and Joe Kennedy was more vehement than ever about keeping America from becoming entangled should war break out. As Ted would later put it of his own feelings at the time: "I was seven then, and understood dimly that a big war was happening, and that it might come to London soon, and that my dad was working very hard to prevent this." This made it sound as if Joe Kennedy was working for peace. Other interpretations were that Kennedy's prevention amounted to appeasing Hitler, to sacrificing Britain because Kennedy was at base an Anglophobe, to resettling the Jews, toward whom he had never had especially warm feelings or sympathies and who he feared would incite animus against the Germans in the press (Joe Jr. had remarked during a 1934 visit to Germany that the Germans' hatred of the Jews was "well founded" and that Hitler's attack on them was "excellent psychology"), and to doing his best to sabotage any attempts at American assistance to England that, he believed, would only prolong war, should it come.

Roosevelt had long been suspicious of Kennedy, not only because he thought he had presidential ambitions but also because, as he told Secretary of the Interior Harold Ickes, he felt that if Kennedy were ever to fulfill those ambitions, he "would give us a Fascist form of government" with a "small powerful committee under himself as chairman and this committee would run the country without much reference to Congress." Roosevelt was wrong. Kennedy didn't seem to have any affection for fascism or for Hitler. What he had was fear: fear that Hitler was too strong to be defeated, fear that war would topple the entire economic system of capitalism, fear that it would bring, in addition, "the destruction of democracy and the onset of the dark ages," as columnists Joseph Alsop and

Robert Kintner reported Kennedy's remarks. "He says that only peace, at almost any price, can save the world." So Kennedy was willing, even eager, to capitulate. And there was a very personal stake that motivated him beyond the economic or political one: Joe Kennedy, as his grandson Robert Kennedy Jr. would later put it, "found the thought of losing a child unbearable." And thinking of other mothers and fathers who might lose children in combat, his grandfather "found it nearly impossible to conceive of any political dispute that would make such a sacrifice worthwhile," Robert Jr. wrote. It was family over fascism.

The British obviously disagreed that fighting Hitler wasn't worth the sacrifice, and with war bearing down in the summer of 1939, Joseph Kennedy, with his push for appeasement and his predictions of doom, had become a pariah there. His influence declining, his main concern now was no longer saving capitalism or democracy or the world but his own family. When Russia and Germany concluded a nonaggression pact in August 1939 while the Kennedys, in the midst of the crisis, were vacationing on the French Riviera, Joe rushed to London to meet with Chamberlain, as Ted later told it, and then instructed Rose to plan to take the children back to the United States. Within a week, Germany invaded Poland, and Joe moved the family to the country for safety. Two weeks later, they began their departure, in shifts, Ted leaving with sisters Pat and Jean and nurse Hennessey on the *Manhattan*. Only Rosemary remained, because Joe had found a school for her where she seemed to be progressing.

Joe stayed, along with Ed Moore, but not because the British wanted him there. Even as the nation girded for invasion in 1940, Kennedy was vilifying the Royal Air Force for not succumbing to the German Luftwaffe, again on the basis that Britain's survival would only prolong the war. Roosevelt didn't want him in England any more than the British did, but he wanted him in the United States even less, worried that he might be a rival or an antagonist of the administration in the upcoming 1940 presidential election. So Roosevelt kept him there, and Kennedy hung on, even though he realized his situation in England was impossible and his efforts empty. He was a lost man, filling out his days. He phoned the family every Sunday, and the children exchanged letters with him while he remained there. He watched as England suffered. During the air blitz on London, Joe wrote to young Ted: "I am sure you would have liked to be with me and seen the fires the German bombers started in London. It is really terrible to think about, and all these poor women and children and homeless people down in the East End of London all seeing their places destroyed. I hope when you grow up you will dedicate your life to trying to work out plans to make people happy instead of making them miserable, as war does today." Happiness was still Ted's job.

Ted was happier back in the States than he had been in England. The family returned to Bronxville, and Ted was enrolled in Lawrence Park West Country Day School and, as his sister Pat reported to her mother, "loves it there." But it didn't take long for Rose to subordinate Ted's education to her migrations and for the same educational peregrinations to follow. As one biographer commented, the family followed the weather—south in winter, north in summer—and so did Ted's education. He stayed at Lawrence for only two months—October and November—before Rose withdrew him, apparently to take him to Palm Beach for the winter. "Interruptions at this point in his progress are apt to prove difficult and will no doubt result in slowing up his advance," wrote an administrator. Still, she added, "We shall miss him very much with his happy disposition and smile in our midst." Always the smile. But it seems he had no sooner enrolled at the Palm Beach Private School that winter than Rose decided to bring him back north again to the Lawrence Park West Country Day School in the spring. He stayed in the fall. And then Rose took him back to Palm Beach for the winter.

By now Joe had gotten his wish and was finally recalled from England that October. He landed firing this last bullet in an interview with *The Boston Globe:* "Democracy is all done." So in some ways were the Kennedys, or at least the image of the Kennedys. The family didn't reassemble. Joe Jr. left Harvard Law School to enlist in the Navy Reserve in June 1941, and Jack followed him a few months later and was assigned to Washington. Kick went to Washington to work as the secretary to Frank Waldrop, the editor of the *Washington Times-Herald.* Ed Moore found a home for Rosemary. The younger children were scattered to their boarding schools. "Suddenly, this wonderful, nurturing family is kind of divided," Ted would later say. "Suddenly. We'd had a very wonderful time together, where my brother Joe taught me to sail and my brothers taught me to ride a bicycle, and I was always around with all of my brothers and sisters. Then suddenly at this time, at this very young age here, there was real separation and a sense of confusion. And wondering. You wondered whether you were ever going to see these people again." He called it a "lonely existence," though most of his existence had been lonely.

And he was not just lonely but adrift. Ted wound up in Palm Beach again that winter, where, unsurprisingly, a teacher wrote on his report card: "No foundation for fourth-grade work." But that Easter, after Ted had spent only three months at the Palm Beach Private School, Rose decided to embark on yet another lengthy trip now that the winter season was over—to South America with her daughter Eunice—and she had to find somewhere to park her youngest. The idea she came up with was to send Teddy to the school that Bobby had been attending since his return to the States: Portsmouth Priory. By this time, Ted was so confused that he had trouble determining which grade he was in—he later wrote that he attended three different schools for second grade "with three different curriculums, with three different peer groups and sets of friends to make," though he was actually in England then—or which schools he had attended. (One transcript listed him as having attended a Bronxville Country Day School, even though no such school of that name existed.) He called himself "nearly always a stranger."

But nowhere was he more a stranger than at Portsmouth Priory, a Benedictine school in Rhode Island that had been founded largely for the wealthy sons of Catholics aiming for the Ivy Leagues. The trouble with Rose's idea—one that seemed designed purely for her own convenience—was that Teddy was only nine years old at the time and not even ready for third grade, much less fourth, and the school didn't begin until the seventh grade. (Rose forced them to take Ted.) So he was thrust, in the middle of the semester, into an impossible situation where all the skills of appeasement that he had cultivated failed miserably. "I was the subject of some teasing at the time," he told his biographer Adam Clymer in 1995. That was an understatement. He was more candid in his memoir, where he called his time at Portsmouth Priory "not an education; it was a battle," and where he talked not of teasing but of torment. He was three years too young, a poor student, hopelessly out of his depth, and he was a social outcast, constantly bullied and harassed. Nor would Bobby come to his aid, insisting that he had to fight his own battles. When a boy named Plowden began pummeling Teddy and demanding that he declare, "The Plowdens are better than the Kennedys," Bobby refused to intervene, one of the rare instances Bobby's own self-interest overrode the family interest, most likely because Bobby didn't want to be a pariah too. (Ted never forgot this contravention of family solidarity and discussed it in numerous interviews.) But there was worse. Friendless, Ted had sought comfort with a pet turtle, which died. Ted buried him. His classmates then disinterred the turtle and played hockey with him and afterward dropped him on Ted's bed. (He would retell this story too, to underscore his unhappiness.)

But he didn't stay long at Portsmouth Priory, where the headmaster, Father Damian, called Ted young and immature and said he didn't get on with the other students. That fall he was sent to Riverdale Country School in the Bronx, not far from where the Kennedys lived. This proved to be yet another disaster. "If Portsmouth Priory taught me about the cruelty of children," Ted was later to write, "then Riverdale taught me about the cruelty of adults." Ted said that the dorm master there was a pederast who abused the students—conducting games of strip poker and even chasing one student down the hall, grabbing his suitcase, and tossing the clothes into the Hudson River. Ted was "terrified of him." But he wasn't in Riverdale long either. His mother removed him once again to join her in Palm Beach, which, as Ted later wryly noted, was "not exactly conducive to keeping and making friends or doing well in school." By the fall he was back at Riverdale, but this was when he came down with pneumonia and whooping cough and allegedly spent his recuperation at Cape Cod with Rose. Even then, however, with what he remembered as this precious time with his mother—his only precious time with his gallivanting mother—he was sad, realizing that the Kennedy clan had lost its rapture. "The underpinnings, I think, both of the family and support and faith weren't there," he told an interviewer of the way the war had torn them apart. "It was almost getting like you're in a tender that is getting loose. You're losing your mooring as a child."

The Kennedys themselves had no mooring *other* than themselves. They lived in resort communities: Hyannis Port in the summer and, after 1933, Palm Beach in the winter, where Joe bought a house that Addison Mizner had designed for the department-store magnate Rodman Wanamaker, with an orange-tiled roof and a living room that opened onto 176 feet of beachfront. Living this way, from vacation home to vacation home, Ted himself said that he felt homeless. The one constant—the one physical mooring, especially for Ted—was the Bronxville house to which he had been brought after his birth and where he had lived most of the time until the family departed for England. He described it lovingly—the six acres with tall trees; the balconies supported by Ionic columns; the porches that surrounded the home; the billiards table in the basement;

and the train set on the third floor that had belonged successively to Joe Jr., Jack, and Bobby. But when he returned from London, Joe Sr., who was clearly shaken by the antipathy toward him, decided to sell the house, which was another sign of how much the family had begun to disperse and how much the Kennedys were no longer the Kennedys as Joe and Rose had designed them. For Rose, with her customary obliviousness, the selling of the house meant nothing. "I feel quite relieved and very free with nothing on my mind except the shades of blue for my Palm Beach trousseau," she wrote to her children. For Ted, the selling of the home was devastating—another "loss of stability," as the nursemaid Luella Hennessey told Doris Kearns Goodwin. He had lost his last mooring.

Now having lost the anchors of his home and his family, Ted Kennedy was left to drift again from school to school. And, again, he was miserable. He was miserable in part because he was lonely, with few friends and even fewer visits from his family and less time with them, only on vacations and holidays—a "pretty lonely, bleak kind of period," he called it. A friend said that during the three years he and Ted matriculated together, neither Joe nor Rose ever visited their son, though it appears Joe did make at least one appearance. (Teddy excused them on the basis of wartime gas rationing, which seemed a rather feeble justification for Joe Kennedy.) And he was miserable because, save for his few months at Portsmouth Priory, which he detested, he was a Catholic when nearly all his classmates were Protestant. When he attended Fessenden School, in West Newton, Massachusetts, for three semesters over two years—given Rose's continuing habit of moving him about—he was one of only thirteen Catholics in a class of two hundred. And he was more miserable because the Catholics were conspicuous, in part because Rose insisted on the school making provisions—"my mother made such a deal out of it"—for the Catholic boys to have a separate time for religious instruction; Ted said he was always aware of "tension between Protestant and Catholic." On Sundays, the one Catholic teacher at the school would drive them to church. A classmate said the other boys would stare at them as they left.

He was miserable because he was fat. This was an issue both within the family and at school, where he would be teased for his weight. Kennedys were not supposed to be fat. Both Joe and Rose assiduously watched their weight and expected their children to do so as well, which was an unusual request for a boy his age. Each did—all but Teddy, the youngest. (Rose's vanity extended to wearing adhesive tape to pull away "frownies," or frown lines.) Teddy's weight became a family obsession long before Fessenden. "Ted is getting bigger, better, and fatter," Eunice wrote when he was seven. "He looks like two boys instead of one." "Teddy is as fat as ever and rising steadily in weight," Bobby had written to his father early in 1940. "Teddy is fatter than ever and looks as healthy as it is possible to look," Joe Jr. had written to the ambassador in April 1940, when he was in England. "Teddy now has to go on a diet," Jean wrote Joe a month later, adding that he had to wear "extra-large suits." And Rose wrote to Joe when he was in England and she back in America, "Teddy is such a fatty." When Ted griped about the food at school, Joe wrote back sarcastically, "I am sorry to see that you are starving to death. I can't imagine that ever happening to you if there was anything at all to eat around, but then you can spare a few pounds." He was always smuggling food from the kitchen at school, and while Joe was still in England, Rose wrote to him about a misunderstanding before mass the previous Sunday, where Ted accepted the priest's breakfast invitation after already having eaten breakfast at home. "I think he has put on the ten pounds which he lost at Riverdale," she reported. And at Windsor Castle, Joe told young Princess Margaret, who ate quickly so as not to be the last to finish, that his son Teddy ate quickly and ate too much. His sister Jean called him "Biscuits and Muffins," and the name stuck.

And if he was miserable because he was teased for not being slim like his siblings, he was also miserable because he wasn't a particularly good student like them either, though neither Joe Jr. nor Jack was an academic star, and Bobby was an indifferent student too. This was understandable given his nomadic education, but it raised concerns for Joe and Rose. After Ted's bout with whooping cough at Riverdale, Rose hired a tutor that summer to work with him. "I can understand your concern for Teddy," wrote a school official, "as he is such a delightful, able youngster." Delightful but perhaps not, his parents worried, smart. After Ted received a particularly bad report at Fessenden, Joe wrote to him disappointedly, bristling that Ted "didn't pass English or Geography and you only got 60 in Spelling and History. This is terrible—you can do better than that. You wouldn't want to have people say that Joe and Jack Kennedy's brother is such a bad student, so get on your toes." But that is exactly what they did say: The youngest was the least intelligent. And Rose complained to Fessenden's headmaster that Teddy was an awful speller (he would be an awful speller throughout his life) and that he counted on his fingers. "Will you please bring it to the attention of his arithmetic teacher in the fall?"

The Fessenden motto was *Labor Omnia Vincit*—"Work Conquers All"—though this didn't seem to describe Teddy, who seemed uninterested in his studies. He became instead a prankster, a jester at school as he had been in the family, presumably as a way to ingratiate himself with his classmates. Because Joe gave his permission for Fessenden to mete out corporal punishment to Ted—a sign that he did not trust his son's self-discipline—he was paddled thirteen times (fifteen by another account) for various infractions, from, he said, dropping water balloons on the faculty to sneaking into the faculty lounge to peek at grades. Once, he was given the punishment of sleeping in a bathtub for having searched for a teacher's stash of candy. These punishments were so frequent and yet, Ted believed, fair, given his transgressions, that he came to consider the disciplinarian who administered the paddlings a "good and trustworthy friend" and would occasionally return to Fessenden to see him. At one point, when he was expected home in Hyannis Port for the weekend, he was instead restricted to his quarters after a water fight in the lavatory, though Rose was certain that "the boys who were there provoked him to mischief." But Teddy didn't seem to need provocation. After all those years of being teased and bullied and harassed and pummeled and ostracized where his charm hadn't worked as it did in the family, he had become incorrigible. Following that one visit Joe Kennedy apparently did make to Fessenden, he wrote Rose that Teddy was "a riot, as usual." *As usual.* And Joe indicated that his son's mischievousness outside the classroom also operated within it, possibly, he realized, as a way to cover his shortcomings. He said the consensus was that Teddy had a "fine head" and was "getting along much better with boys than he did when he first started" but that he "goes off half-cocked when anybody asks any questions and he gives them an answer even though most times it is wrong. . . . So if he isn't a bright student"—a tough concession for Kennedy—"he is a good salesman." But salesmanship was not the Kennedy way.

Though his loneliness wasn't abated by his newfound puckishness, Ted did have one refuge after he returned from England, one "constant in my life during the difficult nomadic years of boarding school," as he later put it. He had his grandfather Honey Fitz. On Sundays, when Ted was at Fessenden in 1943, he would take the subway to Boston, only ten miles away, trudge up Beacon Hill to the Hotel Bellevue, where his grandfather kept a room, and wait in the lobby until his grandfather came down the stairs. Even at eighty, he was the same old Honey Fitz that he had been in his heyday: gregarious, loquacious, charming, full of blarney, amiable but ambitious. (All of these things would later be said of Ted Kennedy too.) His pockets would be stuffed with newspaper clippings—"he collected information" was how Ted put it—on which he would write notes and then send off his ideas, often asking his grandnephew to hand-deliver them to various political figures. And after he descended the stairs on those Sunday afternoons, he would begin politicking—first in the kitchen among the staff and then in the dining room, where he would circulate among the diners like a host. "Everyone knew him. He knew everyone," Ted said. And eleven-year-old Ted Kennedy watched him, watched him closely, "observed his relationship with people and the joy he had from relating to people, and how he related. He was outgoing and warm," and Ted later admitted that he had not seen those qualities in his own family, certainly not in his parents with their formality and hauteur. And he said it affected him deeply.

The political education would continue on those weekend afternoons. After lunch, Honey Fitz would take his grandson on walks around Boston—the Boston the Kennedys had escaped—where he discussed history, some of which he had lived himself as mayor, and he discussed ethnic divisions, and he discussed the Irish and the prejudice against them, which was still vivid to him. He talked about Irish persecution in Ireland and Irish persecution here. He recalled as a young man going to Cambridge to watch the rowers on the Charles River, rich boys, Brahmin boys, and he, an Irishman, walking up to the Cabots or the Lowells to introduce himself, while being bitterly aware of the distance between him and them. That bitterness sharpened in the stories he told his grandson, told often so Ted wouldn't forget, about the signs that had hung in Boston windows: NO IRISH NEED APPLY. (Ted later framed and hung one in his house.) And, of course, he discussed how this had affected politics, his métier—how, for example, Massachusetts Republicans curried favor with the French in Lowell and Lawrence by giving them jobs that had belonged to the Democratic Irish, or how, when he decided to appoint an Italian as fire commissioner, ten thousand Irishmen demonstrated outside his house, shouting, "Appoint one of your own, Honey Fitz!"

But Honey Fitz provided more than a political education or an historical one to his grandson—much more, as far as Ted Kennedy was concerned. John Fitzgerald provided a psychological education, one that had been lacking in the more aesthetically inclined Kennedy family, where people's feelings were largely disregarded or repressed. Honey Fitz not only loved people—clearly loved them and loved to be around them. Honey Fitz *understood* people, had an instinct for them. As Ted put it, thinking back on watching his grandfather walk those Boston streets and greet passersby, "He knew people's problems and motivations and needs." And this made as deep an impression on young Ted Kennedy as the glad-handing or the tales of Irish misfortune. Deeper: Honey Fitz cared.

None of this was the Kennedy way. Ebullience was not the Kennedy way. Many of them thought of old Honey Fitz as an embarrassment— a vulgar old pol—and when he visited the Kennedys in London and wrote invitations for a tea to his friends in Boston on embassy stationery, Joe and Rose were mortified. Her father was an "extrovert," Rose explained to her ghostwriter, "and Joe wasn't and that was it." But that wasn't it. Honey Fitz had no airs or pretensions, and Joe and Rose lived by pretensions. Feelings were not the Kennedy way either—not in a household where Joe Kennedy derided "sourpusses" and forbade tears and where he demanded stoicism. Empathy was not the Kennedy way. For all Rose's religious pro-nouncements and her repetition of Luke 12:48, this was not compassion but noblesse oblige—high-Irish noblesse oblige.

None of this was the Kennedy way. But it would become Ted Kennedy's way.

During this time in the early forties, Ted Kennedy would call Honey Fitz "sort of an extra parent," though in most ways he was closer to Teddy than Joe and Rose were, certainly closer in temperament. When Ted ran for office, he would admit that he inherited his political style from his grandfather, that he enjoyed the rituals of retail politics as much as Honey Fitz did—enjoyed them as much as his brothers Jack and Bobby disdained them and who performed them only by force. He could do a dead-on imi-tation of his grandfather, loved to do it, and the high trill that later in-vaded his speeches in a way that almost mocked grandiloquent political oratory was another gift from Honey Fitz. He loved his grandfather's jovi-ality too. He loved the way he enjoyed life and embraced people. But most of all, more than his grandfather's enthusiasm or his history lessons or his dissertations on discrimination, Ted was shaped by that deep, sincere feeling Honey Fitz had for people, that un-Kennedy-like feeling.

On those Sundays watching Honey Fitz, Ted Kennedy, who had been

victimized so often, saw something that he said stayed with him throughout his life and affected its course. Watching his grandfather, Ted Kennedy, who had received no moral education from his own parents, saw
what empathy meant.

IV

Ted wasn't the only Kennedy who was miserable during the war. Joe Kennedy was suffering through his own slough of unhappiness. He had returned from his ambassadorship disgraced and humiliated, continuing to
insist that the country would be better off fighting to keep the Nazis out of
our own hemisphere rather than fight them in theirs, and, when Pearl
Harbor was attacked on December 7, 1941, and America finally entered
the war, Kennedy was, in the eyes of many Americans and in the eyes of
the Roosevelt administration, on the wrong side of history. Whatever political ambitions he harbored for himself—and he had even harbored ambitions for the presidency—vanished. With America at war and Joe Jr. and
Jack in the service, Kennedy begged for some post—"I feel that my experience in these critical times might be worth something in some position"—
but he had disqualified himself from one. "My energy from now on will be
tied up in their [his children's] careers rather than my own," he wrote
Radio Corporation of America head David Sarnoff shortly after Pearl Harbor, in yet another concession that certainly must have been difficult for
him. Even his days of financial maneuvering were over. With the war, he
put his money in oil and real estate. He was morose. "Mr. Kennedy began
to withdraw more and more into himself," Luella Hennessey, the children's nursemaid, would remember. "He was not as outgoing or as happy
as he had been before, and the kids felt it."

With the sale of the Bronxville house, he retreated with the family to
Hyannis Port for the summer, and he tried to stir himself from his mood.
He made sure, according to his niece Mary Jo Gargan, that there was
"plenty going on in the house to take Aunt Rose's mind off things." But the
war overshadowed everything, especially with the two older boys waiting
for deployment, and it fell on Teddy once again to do what the youngest
had always done, what it was his job to do—in Gargan's words, to be
"there with his smile, winning sailboat races and just being himself, giving joy and saying happy things at a time when his parents needed what
he had to give."

Ted never had the best of his father. None of the Kennedy children really did. He was, Eunice said, "always" absent—always—which was literally true from the fall of 1939 through 1940, when he remained in England as ambassador after the family returned home, save for a three-month visit during the Christmas holidays. When he was present, during those summers at Hyannis Port, he was "a very strong and wonderful figure," Ted later called him, amending that to an "inspiring and authoritarian figure," which was hardly the highest commendation for a son to make of a father. And he would say that no matter how busy his father was, he "seemed to have a moment to listen and to encourage us"—again, not the tenderest of expressions, because encouragement from Joe Kennedy usually came in the form of pressure. It was Honey Fitz and Bobby, six years Ted's elder, who were his paternal figures—a "second father," Teddy called Bobby, because Bobby, despite his indifference to his younger brother at Portsmouth Priory, was now the one who would call to check up on him or visit him at Fessenden on weekends when his parents didn't, and Bobby was the one with whom he would share the empty Hyannis Port house when the boys were on leave from school, and Bobby was the one who took on the paternal duty, in their cousin Joey Gargan's words, "to get Ted to make the extra effort." "Bobby was in charge, taking care of me and always making sure I had something to do," Ted later said.

But in his despondency after his ambassadorship and in semiretirement, Joe Kennedy was finally home, and in those summers during the war, when Ted was also home and most of his siblings away, the two bonded. "It was a quantitative difference of a large order," Rose would later say of this period. "Joe spent a great deal more time with Ted than with the other boys, and that counted." He had always enjoyed Teddy's company, which is why he had welcomed those evenings in London when they would share an hour together. Everyone in the family saw the delight he took in Teddy. Mary Jo Gargan said that during the war, Teddy was his parents' "golden child." "Ted can do no wrong in the old man's eyes," Jack once told a friend. "When Teddy comes into a room, you know you are in for a good time." And the friend concluded of Joe, "He related to Teddy more than he did to Bobby."

But for all that, Jack also said that his father could be tougher on Teddy than on the other children, enforcing sterner discipline on him. During those wartime summers, Joe was always making Teddy toe the line, always trying to teach him responsibility because he had that streak of irresponsibility. In Hyannis Port, he was never allowed to ride his bike outside the driveway, and he had to be home before the streetlights went on. One time, he asked his father for five dollars for a kayak. Joe, figuring he would get bored with it, made him a deal: If Ted did get bored, he would have to pay his father back from his allowance. "For two weeks," Ted recalled, "I practically lived in the boat, and then I just forgot about it." And Joe made him pay back the money. Another time, Joe allowed Ted and Joey Gargan, who was Ted's constant summer companion, to sail to Bass River overnight. Then it rained, so instead of staying in the boat, they took a dinghy and returned and had the handyman pick them up. No sooner did they get home than Joe sent them back to pick up the sailboat. And Joe always made sure that Teddy worked in those summers, assigning him and Joey Gargan to his stables in Osterville, where Mary Jo Gargan said, they would "cut bridle paths through the woods . . . hard work, buggy and hot."

Joe Kennedy, a "stern" disciplinarian, Ted would tell his wife, doubtless meant this for Teddy's own good—to teach the youngest maturity. But it was also, as were most things for Joe Kennedy, for the family's good, for the good of its image. For Joe Kennedy had a concern about his youngest son, and it chilled him: He feared that he might be less a Kennedy than a Fitzgerald.

Among the Kennedys, including Rose Fitzgerald Kennedy, this was not a good thing. Teddy *looked* more like a Fitzgerald than a Kennedy (though, for that matter, so did Joe Jr.). He acted more like a Fitzgerald than a Kennedy. He had his grandfather Honey Fitz's extroversion—"Joe wasn't" extroverted—his grandfather's blarney, his grandfather's volubility, his grandfather's desire to entertain and please, his grandfather's flamboyance, his grandfather's lack of discipline as well as his lack of pretension, his grandfather's amiability, and, as one of the Kennedys' nurses put it, his grandfather's "tendency to cut corners." Ted was, as his father had observed at Fessenden, a "riot." He was a Fitzgerald *among* the Kennedys. The same nurse said that when Rose heard him "laughing and singing," she would say, "Teddy was our surprise baby, and he's brought more joy into our lives than we ever thought possible." It was Fitzgerald joy.

But the very things that made him so appealing in the family, the very things that Joe loved about him and that Ted had conditioned himself to do to fulfill his family service, were also the things that concerned his parents and that they felt could jeopardize his eventual success. From the earliest, Joe took pride in questioning his children during dinner on current events. Ted talked about sports. And from the earliest, Joe and Rose made sure that the other children engaged in activities. "We played games," she wrote, "we read all the available stories, we made puzzles, we bought countless gadgets from the 5 & 10, blew bubbles." Ted didn't engage. "He sits comfortably in his bed next to his radio, requests a proper program and then by a mere turn of the wrist conjures up entertainment by the minute." (Rose said he loved *The Lone Ranger*.) From the earliest, the children were ordered to read; there was that book a day during the summers. Jack read books "by the cartload." Ted read comic books. And there were his poor scholastic performances, and his impish escapades that landed him in trouble, and his laziness, and his attempts when confronted to finesse rather than address. Ted Kennedy, the youngest, made the Kennedys laugh, but he didn't uphold his other end of the Kennedy bargain. He didn't make them proud.

Even while Joe Kennedy could be tougher on Teddy than on the other children because he seemed afraid of his Fitzgeraldian tendencies, he also seemed to have lower expectations of him, in part because he was the youngest, in part because Joe seemed to think Ted couldn't rise to the older children's higher standards even if he wanted to. ("He held up standards for us," Jack once told historian Arthur Schlesinger Jr., "and he was very tough when we failed to meet his standards.") Rose seemed to concur. She told her diary, "When we have a number of children, we cannot understand why they are all not alike, especially if the older ones are brilliant scholastically or outstanding in athletics. Then when the younger ones come along, we naturally expect the same thing and we become critical and impatient if this is not the case." The youngest, who was neither academic nor athletic, was held to the lowest standards—adored but not extolled—and he knew it, knew that no one thought he was up to his brothers. He once pondered running away from home, apparently ashamed, until Jack asked him to go to the movies with him, a war movie; and, walking home afterward, Jack advised him, as Ted put it, that it "wasn't entirely about matching my brothers' accomplishments. It was about conducting myself like them"—a lesson that really implied Ted's inferiority to them. And that summer, as the war wound down, Ted had a conversation with his father, one he would frequently reference. "You can have a serious or a nonserious life, Teddy," is how Ted recalled his father's admonition, saying he would love him either way. "But if you decide to have a nonserious life, I won't have much time for you. You make up your mind. There are too many children here who are doing things that are interesting for me to do much with you." And Ted also recalled, "It didn't take me long to decide which kind of life I wanted to lead." Not long to decide, perhaps, but it would take him a long while to do.

If Joe Kennedy was morose over the end of his political ambitions and the continuation of the war, he was also morose over the family, which in that period had not only scattered but was also beginning to disintegrate. With her disability, Rosemary had always been an issue for her parents. The Kennedys had tried to mainstream her, to make it appear as if nothing were wrong with her, but as she got older, their state of denial was impossible to maintain. They had found a school for her in England during the ambassadorship, where, secure and free from any family pressures, she seemed to be progressing. When she returned to the United States, however, she regressed. School after school found her difficult to deal with, suddenly abrasive, aggressive, defiant, uncontrollable, even violent. (Some attributed it to puberty.) One sent her to a psychiatric hospital for evaluation. She was, in effect, mustered from the family and sent away because Rose and Joe decided the Kennedy competition, the Kennedy standards, were too high for her and only frustrated her, though it was equally true that she frustrated the family. Still, searching for some answer, Joe had heard of a new, experimental treatment, lobotomy, which would tame her bouts of violence and render her more docile. Rose said that he decided to have Rosemary undergo the procedure without consulting her and that she wouldn't learn what had been done to Rosemary for another twenty years. What had been done, in November 1941, was a prefrontal lobotomy. It made Rosemary more docile, but it also destroyed most of what little mental capability she had. For her own good again, but also clearly for their own, Joe had her institutionalized afterward, in a psychiatric hospital in the upper Hudson Valley called Craig House. She was gone to them now. Rose wouldn't see her for more than twenty years.

To Ted, even before the lobotomy and the hospitalization, Rosemary was a kind of ghost. "She was a presence," he told an interviewer. "I never saw her too much, but she was always sort of a presence when I went home at Christmas or so," and she was "almost gentler and tenderer and more loving even than other brothers and sisters." He said none of the Kennedys made much of her disability. "She was sort of challenged, but she seemed very natural . . . Everybody else was sort of cool about it. I was the youngest and I was cool about it too." But as much as Rose insisted that the procedure and the reasons for Rosemary's absence were secrets, the rest of the family seemed to know, and Ted's response was damning about the price of Kennedy perfection. He later told a biographer that as a boy he feared "the same thing could happen to me."

Jack was the next to leave. Having joined the Navy even before the war and been stationed in Washington doing naval intelligence, he was eager for active duty after Pearl Harbor, even though he was sickly and couldn't pass the physical. His father pulled strings and got him assigned as a PT-boat commander in the Pacific. During a mission to engage a Japanese convoy in August 1943, his boat was split in two by an oncoming Japanese destroyer, and Jack Kennedy was forced to lead his men to safety, swimming three and a half miles to land, towing one wounded sailor by a life-vest strap clenched between Jack's teeth. It was the first of several long swims to islands where they hoped they might find food and fresh water. Meanwhile, he was reported missing in action. He was rescued six days later and returned to the United States. But he was sick with malaria, in excruciating pain from his chronically sore back, suffered from intestinal distress and fatigue, and was emaciated to skin and bones.

A month after Jack's rescue, Joe Jr. arrived in England as a member of Bombing Squadron 110, flying anti-submarine missions. He flew twenty-five of those missions over 1943 and 1944, which made him eligible to return to the United States. But leaving the battlefield was not the Kennedy way. There had been a going-away dinner for him as he was about to debark to England—a dinner at which, according to some accounts, younger brother Jack was toasted for his heroism in the Pacific. Later that night, it was said, Joe Jr. sat on his cot, "clenching and unclenching his fists," presumably because he felt his younger brother had outdone him. Whether or not this is true—and Rose indicated it was, writing that Jack's heroism was "the first time Jack had won such an 'advantage' by such a clear margin. . . . It cheered Jack and must have rankled Joe Jr."—Kennedy volunteered for a dangerous mission, Operation Aphrodite, in which the Army and Navy Air Corps deployed dummy planes filled with explosives. Each plane, only barely airworthy, would be flown by a two-man crew to two thousand feet. The crew would then pull the safety pins on the detonators, signal the radio controllers in nearby planes, and parachute to safety, after which the controllers would remotely guide the now-unmanned, explosive-laden plane to its target—in this case to a U-boat installation in the North Sea. On August 12, 1944, almost a year to the day that his brother was rescued in the Pacific, Joseph Kennedy Jr. took off from the RAF base at Fersfield, southwest of Norwich, for the first of Operation Aphrodite's naval missions. His plane had just made its first pass over the target when he pulled the safety pin and radioed the controller as planned. And then, minutes later, the plane exploded in midair before he could evacuate. Joe Jr. and his co-pilot were killed instantly. A pilot in a tracking plane said it was "the biggest explosion I ever saw until the pictures of the atomic bomb."

Early that afternoon, two priests came to the house in Hyannis Port and asked to speak with Joe, and Joe came out on the sunporch afterward and said that Joe Jr. had been "lost," Ted remembered. His voice cracked and "as tears came to his eyes he said in a muffled voice: 'I want you all to be particularly good to your mother.' " Joe Jr. was the chosen one of the Kennedy family—the eldest and the one on whom the highest expectations were laid. He was tall, handsome, athletic, confident, easygoing, charismatic, and far less complicated than his younger brother Jack. Joe had anointed him to be president, the first Catholic president, and Joe Jr. knew it, went through the paces for it, including his military service. His loss was incalculable to Joe. It was the loss of both a son and a dream, and Joe Sr. never quite recovered from it.

And later that afternoon, Jack tried to shake himself and Ted from their grief by taking his brother and their cousin Joey Gargan sailing, the sea being the great Kennedy balm even then. As Ted recalled it, "This was the first of many times when taking the tiller has steered me away from nearly unendurable grief across the healing waters on the long, hard course toward renewal and hope." To allay their grief in the time that followed, as their father indulged his silently and alone, Jack spent time with Ted, teaching him about literature and the Civil War, reading *John Brown's Body* with him, and even, later that summer, taking him to a naval base in Florida and one night smuggling him onto a PT boat. And the next summer, with his brothers' example, Ted began to take command of the sea himself—learning how to read the winds, the tides, and the currents, learning how to navigate by landmarks. It was in those days when the family was in pain, he said, that "the sea transformed itself into a home for me, a charmed universe that I could enter in any season, any weather, and find comfort, transcendence."

There was to be one more loss that last war summer, this one in the form of an excommunication. Kathleen Kennedy, the most vivacious of the Kennedy sisters, the wildest of the Kennedy sisters, had been a belle in England during her father's ambassadorship, with a wide circle of friends and male admirers, and when the war began and the other Kennedys were sent home to safety, Kathleen remonstrated with her father to stay. He refused. Back in the States, she attended a finishing school and a commercial college in Florida, did volunteer work for the Red Cross, and got the job at the *Washington Times-Herald,* eventually landing a society notes column of her own, which was an irony for the status-conscious Kennedys. But she pined for England and for a beau there—William Cavendish, the Marquess of Hartington and the heir to the Duke of Devonshire—and she was determined to go back, despite her parents' objections. Her way back to England came as a Red Cross volunteer in 1943. Once in England, she promptly renewed her romance with Billy Hartington.

Rose was furious. Hartington was Anglican. If Kathleen were to marry him, she would be marrying outside the Catholic Church, which Rose was neither prepared to allow nor to accept, since in Catholic doctrine Kathleen's marriage would be a mortal sin. Joe lobbied the Church for a dispensation, and when that failed, Rose pleaded with her daughter, but to no avail. Kick and Billy Hartington were married on May 6, 1944, by a county clerk. Of the Kennedys, only Joe Jr. attended, and Rose was none too pleased about that either, refusing to answer his notes. But if Rose had been furious on hearing of the engagement, she was "horrified" and "heartbroken" when Kick informed her that they were to be married in a registry office, not a church. She called it a "blow to family prestige" and tried to think of a way to "extricate" her daughter. Ted was too young to fully understand the situation, but he said he couldn't help but feel the tension in the house—a great deal of tension. Four months later, and just a month after Joe Jr.'s death, Major William Cavendish, while on a mission to liberate a Belgian village, was killed by a German sniper. Rose was unmoved, telling her daughter that she had sinned. Now Kick was lost to the family just as surely as Rosemary was.

V

And the melancholy continued. Ted may have found his transcendence in the sea, but when the summers ended, Ted's school tribulations began anew. He attended Fessenden again that fall, but only until October, when Rose, shuttering the Hyannis Port house for the season, pulled him and enrolled him in Palm Beach Private, where he had been the previous winter. After another year there, in the fall of 1945 he was sent to the Cranwell School, run by Jesuits in Lenox, Massachusetts, in the Berkshires. "The kind of boy you like to have in school, a happy boy, a real All-American boy-type, a good student," a school administrator later told one of Ted's biographers. But the description didn't fit young Ted Kennedy, neither in scholastics—Joe upbraided him in a letter for spelling "know" for "no," "scating" for "skating," "tommorow" for "tomorrow," and "slauter" for "slaughter," saying, "You're getting rather old now, and it looks rather babyish"—nor in temperament. Ted said he was unhappy there—"too distant, too remote"—and lonely. Always lonely.

Bobby had suffered from the same educational inconstancy. He reacted, he said, by inexplicably dropping things and falling down. But Bobby said he was "quiet most of the time," and that he learned "not to mind being alone." This was very different from Teddy, who was far from quiet and minded very much being alone. Still, when he first ran for the Senate and was asked about constantly changing schools, Ted said, "I don't think I felt anything particular about it. I don't have any complexes, if that's what you mean." Bobby and Eunice pointedly said the same thing about him. He was unaffected by being uprooted every year and sometimes two or three times a year. It rolled right off him.

But his was Kennedy talk, Joe Kennedy–mandated talk, talk that denied trauma as weakness. As he grew older, Ted would admit not only his sadness in this period—essentially his entire youth—but also the deep impact it left upon him, the scars. "He would talk about kind of the emotional trauma of having been bounced around," his son Patrick said. There were stories of hazing, of being made fun of and picked on: "He would talk about how he really had to kind of struggle, in a self-deprecating way that was, 'I can't really complain because I have it good, but not for nothing, there's some pretty strong stuff here that was tough for me to have to face.'" Patrick thought he was always deflecting the "pain" of that period. One of his closest friends, his Harvard roommate John Culver,

speculated that it was this pain, the constancy of loneliness and alienation, that would connect Ted to others in pain—that it was this childhood pain that would become the basis for his politics.

And then, finally, in the fall of 1946, when he was fourteen and about
to enter high school, the rootlessness ended. It ended because Bobby, who
was on his way to Harvard after having served in the Naval Reserve for
the previous two years, had attended the Milton Academy in Milton, Massachusetts, outside Boston, and thought Ted might like it. Ted, as close as
he had become to Bobby over those summers early in the war, did not go
willingly. He said he was so sad at going that, all the weight considerations
notwithstanding, his father allowed him to take some of Katie Lynch's
Butter Crunch with him as a consolation—but Ted stuffed his pockets
with two boxes' worth and Joe rescinded the offer. Still, despite his trepidations, Ted Kennedy, for once, was not unhappy at school. He felt as if he
had finally found himself at Milton. And for once, Rose let him stay.

He had not necessarily found himself academically. He got basically B's
and C's, and his test scores rose early on only to fall again. Nor had his
work ethic on his studies improved appreciably. Milton's headmaster
called Ted a "pragmatist," which, of course, he was. He said he didn't like
"sitting in a chair and mulling over philosophy. . . . Life for him was to act."
A master at the school called him a "plugger." "The favorite customer of
the school's tutor," the head football coach and later headmaster Arthur
Hall called him. It was that tutor, Kernel Holloway, affectionately known
as "the Colonel," who got Ted through by working with him every night,
Hall said.

But Ted flourished outside the classroom with a slew of activities. He
played intramural basketball and tennis and wrestled, and he joined the
football team for two years on both offense and defense as left end, where
his play was described as "dogged" and he scored a touchdown against
Milton's rival, Noble and Greenough. Headmaster Arthur Bliss Perry
called him "absolutely fearless" and said, "He would have tackled an express train to New York if you asked." He joined the debate team, where,
unlike the student he had been at Fessenden, who had tried to charm and
double-talk his way through an answer, he "always knew what he was
talking about" and even in the classroom could "speak more intelligently,
with great concern and feeling and knowledge of public affairs," according to his debate coach. (Public speaking was the only course in which he
won honors.)

And this time something else happened that hadn't happened before: Ted Kennedy was accepted by his classmates. He was no longer an outsider—no longer too young, too Catholic, too fat. He had blossomed. Everyone could see it. Jack's old friend LeMoyne Billings recalled Ted at ten or eleven as a "kind of wiseass fresh kid, kind of fat, not terribly appealing"—though he was appealing among the Kennedys. "Then suddenly, when he was twelve or so [it had to have been later], this terrific appeal, his personality emerged and overcame the rest. His sense of humor couldn't be equaled. It was very adult for his age." And he now engaged in the family games, when he had previously retreated to his radio. "He became . . . just damn good company."

At Milton, the former outcast was social. He was well liked, loose, gregarious like his grandfather Fitzgerald, a class politician. "The Politician" was one of the nicknames the Milton yearbook, *The Orange and the Blue*, gave him. "Good company," Billings had called him, and he was good company at Milton. "Fun," his family had called him, and he was fun at Milton. "If there was some horsing around that was going on, Ted was probably in the middle of it," said a classmate. "Good-humored, fun sort of kid," said his football coach. "Cheerful, fun-loving, exuberant," said one of the masters, and "generous and considerate to his fellows as he could be charming to grown-ups." Joe had taught him that—not to show up other students with his family's wealth.

And they had another nickname for him in the Milton yearbook: not just "the Politician" but "Smilin' Ed," who, it was said, would actually practice smiling in the mirror. The shy, lachrymose boy at school, who hid his misery with a plastered smile, had not only blossomed. He had blossomed into "Smilin' Ed Kennedy." And this time, the smile, if studied, was real.

As Ted later described his transformation during his four years at Milton, he had gone from a boy to a man, and, figuratively, he had. It could have been his age that shocked him into recognizing his inadequacies and moved him to address them. It could have been the agonies the family endured during the war that matured him. It could have been, at long last, the stability of one school that allowed him to thrive. But perhaps the most important cause was something much simpler and more literal: During those four years, Ted Kennedy had *physically* gone from a boy to a man. A late bloomer, he had shot up to a strapping, broad-shouldered young man, over six feet tall and nearly two hundred muscular pounds by the time he left Milton. And the baby fat had disappeared, so that his face was no longer round, boyish, and chubby but handsome, like his brothers'. And he had athletic ability, if only because of his size, that he hadn't demonstrated before. He blossomed because he was transformed—physically transformed. LeMoyne Billings was right. Ted Kennedy was different now, but he was different in no small measure because Ted Kennedy looked different now, which made people perceive him differently. He had a presence.

And there was something else that followed inevitably—another discovery Ted made at Milton besides discovering himself. He discovered girls. Milton held dances with its sister school, the Milton Academy for Girls, and Ted, who his mother had said was a good, light-footed dancer even when he was heavier, happily attended. After one of these dances—a "big teen dance"—he wrote his parents eagerly that he had gone to a girl's house for supper, presumably the house of Nancy Burley, who would become his dance partner during three of his years at Milton and, he would say, his first girlfriend. "I am gradually getting to know more girls, which couldn't please me more." As Ted would later put it, his Milton years were a "bright dawn after the cheerlessness of my early boarding school years."

Yet there was one more pall to come over the family, even as Joe continued to grieve for Joe Jr., four years after his death—an ongoing, unshakable grief that unsettled Ted and that he couldn't fully comprehend. He was in his room at Milton that May of 1948 when he heard a knock at the door and was told that his sister Kathleen had died. He got dressed, went downstairs, and waited for a car to come to take him to Hyannis Port. He was the first of his siblings to arrive. The family gradually appeared for another mourning.

The circumstances of her death were difficult. She had stayed in England after her husband's death, where she celebrated the end of the war, then returned to the States, only to realize that she really belonged in England now. "It's rather nice not having to be a Kennedy," she told a friend after her return. She met Peter Fitzwilliam in 1946, two years after Billy Hartington's death, at a charity event in England she was chairing. He was a rugged, dashing commando, a man's man, and extremely wealthy as well. That evening they danced, and the romantic sparks were embarrassingly unmistakable to the people watching—embarrassing because Fitzwilliam was married with a young daughter. By that time Rose and

Kick had finally reconciled, but when Kathleen reluctantly announced her intention to marry Fitzwilliam, Rose was so outraged—another Protestant, and a married one—that she not only threatened to cut her daughter off from the family once again, but she also threatened to leave Joe if he didn't stop the marriage. So determined was Rose that she went to England herself to implore her daughter not to go forward with the nuptials. But Kathleen said she was infatuated and couldn't be dissuaded. That May 1948, Fitzwilliam had invited Kick to fly to Cannes with him for the weekend, and Kick, who still held out for her father's blessing, arranged for him to meet them in Paris on the return trip to England. The plane never arrived there. Flying into a storm—largely because Fitzwilliam ignored a warning and delayed his takeoff to have a long lunch with friends—the small plane crashed just north of Ardèche in the mountains of the Cévennes. None of the four passengers survived.

The Kennedys had been constructed as an organism, in which each part worked in conjunction with the others to create the Kennedy solidarity and advance the Kennedy brand—all except for Rosemary, who was exiled precisely because she had no function save as a reminder of God's will. And the Kennedys had been constructed as a movie, a beautiful image of beautiful people who were smart, ambitious, productive, fun, and happy—*perfect*. The political dynasty Joe envisioned would be based on that organism and on that movie. The movie was for public consumption, and it would remain so; no one outside the family would see the stresses. But with Joe Kennedy broken by his beloved son's death, the son on whom he had staked so much, the son who was to settle Joe's score with the Protestant establishment, and with Rose burrowing deeper into her faith with the losses of Rosemary, Joe Jr., and Kathleen, it was nearly impossible for the family to sustain that vision for itself. Even as they continued to sell it, the Kennedys knew the movie had ended. A solemnity hung over the family now.

And yet, Ted Kennedy, of all the Kennedys, tried to will the movie to keep running, even as his role of family pet and jester diminished. He tried to suspend his disbelief in the Kennedy image, almost as if he needed the image himself, needed it to survive. And for him, somehow, it did. "In some persistent region of my mind," he would write near the end of his life, "Joseph P. Kennedy remains to me, eternally and solely, *my dad*. Just as I remain the ninth and youngest child of all the Kennedys."

CHAPTER TWO

The Least

N OW TED KENNEDY was going off to college, but not just any college. If the Kennedys lived within their aesthetics as a means to raise their status, education was a form of aesthetics too, which is why Harvard University figured so prominently in Joe Kennedy's arrangements, even though he harbored his own deep resentments against it. To Joe Kennedy, Harvard was less an educational institution than a path to social advancement. Ted was graduated from Milton in May 1950, just a passable student, even with the constant tutoring—thirty-sixth of fifty-six in his class. Nevertheless, it was a foregone conclusion that he would attend Harvard, where all the Kennedy boys had gone. But Ted was not just another Kennedy boy. He was the most self-conscious of them, the one most sensitive to his failure to measure up to the others, the one most riddled with doubt, and the poorest student among them, even if the others hadn't exactly been academically outstanding. So the passage to Harvard was, for Ted Kennedy, by no means inevitable. Moreover, Ted, seeming to realize his own inadequacy, tried to resist his father's expectation. He seriously considered Stanford, which Eunice had briefly attended to regain her strength in the warmer climate following a series of health problems that left her severely underweight. Ted said he was "dissuaded" from attending Stanford, no doubt by his father, who wouldn't have regarded it as eminent enough, and it was on his weekend visits to Bobby, who had gone to Harvard after leaving the Navy, that his father's and brothers' alma mater began to exert its appeal on him, but not because of its reputation or its educational benefits or even the family tradition; it was because of its football team. Despite being undersized, Bobby had joined the team— another Joe Kennedy imperative—and he would take Teddy to football games and introduce him to his teammates like the O'Donnell brothers, Cleo and Kenny, excellent players whose father had been the longtime football coach at Holy Cross. And Bobby would also invite those teammates to Hyannis Port, where Ted mingled with them. And those encounters converted him. Ted admitted he got "stars in his eyes" for Bobby and his teammates but "also for Harvard and playing football there." But even if it hadn't been for football, he really had little choice. Ted Kennedy's life, like his brothers', had been constructed by Joe Kennedy. His education would be no different. "I suppose it would be almost a sacrilege not to have the last of the Kennedy boys attend the school where his father and brothers went," Joe Kennedy wrote the dean of freshmen at Harvard that July, "and now that he is fortunate enough to be admitted to Harvard that he will have a reasonable chance, in spite of the war"—North Korean troops had invaded South Korea, and American troops just a few days earlier had entered the conflict on the South Korean side—"to finish his course there." Ted Kennedy was not about to commit a sacrilege against his family, even if he could, and, of course, he couldn't.

But Ted Kennedy, whose admission to Harvard had been in some doubt, did not enter the university without misgivings, because he brought with him something his brothers had not: He was not only the youngest of the Kennedys; he was the least of them—the one of whom little was expected.

Even Ted seemed to realize that he might not be quite ready for Harvard, not seasoned enough, and that summer before his enrollment, almost certainly under pressure from his father, he did something uncharacteristic. He and his cousin Joey Gargan took a long trip through Europe, nearly two months long, clearly a trip intended for self-betterment. (His brothers had made similar trips.) And what was even more uncharacteristic, Ted—who as a boy was the worst of the Kennedy correspondents and whose father while in England scolded him for writing so infrequently and even then writing so little—kept an extensive travel diary documenting his trip, as if to prove to himself, and his father, that he was absorbing what he saw. What he saw included most of the traditional tourist sites and events: St. Peter's Basilica and the Colosseum and Pompeii and the Uffizi Gallery in Italy; the Oberammergau Passion Play and Hitler's Eagle's Nest and a beer garden in Germany; Lake Geneva and the United Nations offices in Switzerland; the Arc de Triomphe, Eiffel Tower, the Louvre, Versailles, and the Chartres Cathedral in France (where he also saw Elizabeth Taylor and said he embarrassed himself "bobbing and weaving" to get a photo of her). But what he saw, too, was war-ravaged Europe, which provided a different kind of education—this one in the destruction of the war. In Rome he was "impressed with extreme poverty and dirtiness of Italians"; in Cologne, Germany, he saw a city "bombed most and very little reconstruction"; in Munich, "many bombed museums and churches"; and everywhere, even in the countryside along the roads he and Gargan drove, gutted areas, no-man's-lands where bombing and battles had occurred. In Brussels, he saw the political consequences of the war: street demonstrations, one of them violent, with windows smashed and trolley wires cut. In Frankfurt, he met a defector from the Russian zone, who told Ted that everyone hated the Russians, a sentiment Ted said he heard frequently expressed and that he frequently repeated, and in Heidelberg he argued with an old Nazi and then with a young communist who insisted America had started the Korean War. And he had political sentiments of his own, one of which was that the Italians "loved" Mussolini and that he would be regarded as a "national hero" in a few years—a prediction as misguided as his father's about Britain's certain defeat at the hands of the Germans, which only demonstrated that Ted was still an eighteen-year-old who hadn't developed political sophistication yet. He lunched on the Waterloo battlefield, and he walked the Dunkirk beach, where the British had evacuated during the war, and he crawled through the pillboxes there. And he saw the Dachau concentration camp, saw it with three visitors who guided him and his cousin—one of whom had been imprisoned in a concentration camp herself. "We saw gas chambers, crematory [sic], the ovens, and the places where they hung people," he wrote in his diary. But if it left a deeper impression than that, Ted didn't say.

And if Ted was feeling the old tug of inferiority that necessitated such a trip, it was no doubt intensified by Jack's postwar success. Despite his father's ambitions for him, Jack had never had a political temperament like his older brother. He had a wry detachment about life, probably engendered by his endless series of health problems, and a much more intellectual approach than Joe Jr.'s had been. He was bookish. He thought of a journalism career or a career in academe. But with Joe Jr.'s death, that all changed. There was a succession in the Kennedy family, a succession in Joe Kennedy's siege against the Protestant establishment, and in that succession, Jack Kennedy was to take Joe Jr.'s place. "It was like being drafted,"

Jack said. "My father wanted his eldest son in politics. 'Wanted' isn't the right word. He demanded it." So in 1946, Jack, diffident and publicly ill at ease and not yet thirty years old, ran for Congress in a safe Democratic Boston district, and, as a war hero backed by his family fortune, he won. It was, as Joe had always intended it to be, a family effort, even for the youngest, fourteen-year-old Teddy. "Teddy is chafing at the bit," Rose wrote Kick—this was two years before Kick's death—during that first congressional campaign, "but I think I have prevailed on him to stay the weekend here," meaning at Hyannis Port. But Jack's victory put additional pressure on his younger brothers, pressure to succeed, as Joe Jr.'s Harvard successes had put pressure on Jack. Even Jack, however, admitted it was worst on the youngest, the last in line. "The pressure of all the others on Teddy came to bear," Jack once told *Newsweek*, "so that he had to do his best. It was a chain reaction started by Joe [Jr.], that touched me, and all my brothers and sisters." Teddy had the most to live up to but also the fewest personal resources to do so.

Ted Kennedy entered Harvard with trepidations, and he entered with sorrow. He had been there only a month when Honey Fitz died after a brief illness, at the old Hotel Bellevue where Ted used to meet his grandfather in Ted's Fessenden days. He had lived to eighty-seven, vigorous to the end, and they had remained close—Ted and the man who taught him empathy. On family vacations in Palm Beach, Ted, as a teenager, would drive Honey Fitz to the Breakers Hotel, where his grandfather would once again work his political magic as he had in Boston. "He'd go and sit in the lobby with twelve newspapers," Ted remembered. "He'd go up to the concierge and give the concierge ten dollars, for the concierge to ring the bell once if the person was from Massachusetts and twice if they were from Boston. And just as I would be ready to walk out, I'd hear, ding, ding, and Grampa would go up, 'I'm Honey Fitz from Boston, you must be from Boston too!' " Eight months before his grandfather's death, Jack had had a long conversation with Honey Fitz at the Bellevue that lasted late into the night, and he would say that his grandfather had passed the political torch to him during that conversation, and he would say that Honey Fitz affected his political career by showing him the powerful bonds forged in a political life and by showing him, according to Jack's close friend LeMoyne Billings, "the extraordinary impact a politician can have on the emotions of ordinary people"—this for a young man, Jack, who seemed to have little feeling for people. For Ted, who spent much more time with his grandfather than Jack had, Honey Fitz's impact was larger; it was on his entire life, not just his political life. The death, he said, was a "bright line marker for the end of my childhood."

Harvard may have been another. Ted wasn't going to be coddled by his parents now. His hijinks—a "riot as usual"—weren't going to be tolerated now. And Joe was more watchful over him now. One of his roommates said that when Joe called, Ted would shush them, shush them forcefully: "You guys, shut up!" Another roommate said that Joe "controlled everything Ted did." John Culver, who became friends with Ted that freshman year, said that Ted buckled down because he had "his father looking at those report cards," and Culver remembered even Congressman Jack Kennedy, clearly also worried about Ted's academic career, telling his youngest brother that he should never be without a book, that he should be reading something all the time. So great was Joe Kennedy's power over Ted that when he gave him a gray-green mustard winter coat, an awful-looking coat, Ted felt obliged to wear it, at least on weekdays. And Joe was watchful of Ted's Fitzgeraldian flamboyance too, which Joe perceived as a kind of arrogance. Ted had a car horn that sounded like a cow's moo. When Joe heard about it, he issued a reprimand: "I don't want to be complaining about the things you do"—though he often did—"but I want to point out to you that when you exercise any privilege the ordinary fellow does not avail himself of, you immediately become the target for display and for newspaper criticism," which, of course, would hurt the family's political prospects. And he added, "It's all right to struggle to get ahead of the masses by good works, by good reputation and by hard work, but it certainly isn't by doing things that people would say, 'Who the hell does he think he is?,'" which wasn't so much a moral injunction as a social and even political one.

But Ted Kennedy wasn't arrogant at Harvard, any more than his grandfather had been arrogant, any more than Ted Kennedy had ever been arrogant. Like his father before him, he felt he was the victim of arrogance. Despite the passage of time since Joe Kennedy had matriculated there, Harvard was still a bastion of Protestant elitism; only 15 percent of the class was Catholic, which was a significantly smaller percentage than even the Jews at 25 percent. And it was a bastion of Eastern elitism as well; only 8 percent of the class was from the West or South. Ted Kennedy may have come from one of the wealthiest families in America, but given his low status in it, he didn't feel entitlement at Harvard; he felt his classmates' condescension. Ted Kennedy thrived in warmth, but he said he found Harvard not a "particularly hospitable place," nor a "terrifically warm and wonderful kind of experience." And he said he felt something else with which he was all too familiar from all his years of bouncing from one school to another: unhappiness. At Harvard, Ted Kennedy found, "I wasn't all that happy."

But Ted Kennedy, like his father and brothers before him, who had suffered from the same condescension, did find camaraderie at Harvard, just not among the general student body. He found it among his fellow Catholics. And he found those Catholics where his brothers had found them—in the one purely meritocratic place at Harvard, a place where neither pedigree nor status nor even wealth like the Kennedys' mattered. He found them on the football team. When Joseph Kennedy, who was a superb athlete himself, sent Joe Jr. to Harvard, it was with an injunction for him to join the football team because it provided, he wrote, a "great chance to meet a lot of fellows, and, after all, that is the first requisite of a successful college education—learning how to meet people, and getting along with them." Joe Jr. followed that injunction, joined the team, and befriended football star Timothy Reardon, as Jack would later befriend star Torbert Macdonald, and Bobby the team captain, Kenny O'Donnell, who had so awed Teddy. But, contrary to Joe's instruction, it wasn't for establishing connections that they joined; these friends were poor boys, outsiders themselves. It was for finding refuge. And while some ascribed the Kennedys' passion for football, with the famous rollicking, rough-and-tumble touch football games on the wide lawn at Hyannis Port, to their penchant for competition—the Kennedys played for blood—at Harvard it may have been less a passion for competition than for the comfort of meritocracy. It wasn't football they loved, surely not Jack or Bobby, one of whom was frail and sickly, the other small; it was the democracy of the football team.

But unlike Jack and Bobby, Ted Kennedy, who had always followed his father's orders, didn't need orders to become a football player. He had gone to Harvard as much for football as for academics—more, in fact— and promptly joined the freshman team, as had his brothers before him. Though he hadn't been a great player at Milton, he was better than Jack or Bobby. What he had was size and, once he had shed his fat, strength. And determination. One of his signature plays there was called the "Lumbago Pass," in which Ted would get the ball, his teammates would pile on him, and he would drag them over the goal line. "Teddy was always big and strong for his years," Rose would write of him. "Who knows where this came from? There were athletes on both sides of the family. From someplace in his ancestry, no doubt on both sides, Teddy got the right genes to give him all the physical attributes a boy needs to excel at sports and the spirit to go with them." Strength he had. Spirit he had. "He never shirked from any drill," said Richard Clasby, one of the Catholics with whom Ted became friendly—a working-class boy from Natick, Massachusetts, "very poor," Ted said—whose parents worked at the local prison and who was admitted to Harvard because he was a star athlete. Clasby said that Ted was "always in the middle of it. He liked the contact, and he was just a very good guy who you wanted him [sic] on your team, that's for darned sure." Culver, a Catholic from Iowa who was himself massive, called him "tenacious and tough." Ted, he said, "didn't have the most athletic gifts, was not very fast, but was very good defensively and worked hard on his weaknesses." To improve his tackling, he enlisted a teammate after practice and kept hitting him without his pads, punishing himself. No one else on the team, said Culver, stayed like that after practice, only Ted.

These teammates, these poor Catholic football boys at the citadel of the wealthy, became Ted's Harvard compatriots. Not just his compatriots but his closest friends there. When Ted invited these boys to Hyannis Port, as Bobby had invited his teammates, they had never seen anything like it. By the same token, the Kennedys had never seen anything like them. Clasby said that Rose took his only sport jacket and gave it to the Salvation Army. But it was more than the Kennedy wealth that impressed, even dazzled, these poor Catholic boys; it was the Kennedy energy. Clasby was astonished watching the Kennedys play "mind games," answering questions as Joe Kennedy tested them. And there was "energy all over the place. Everything was done quickly. There was sailing and then, 'We're going to have dinner in twenty-two minutes.'" Culver remembered a steak fry at Hyannis in the spring of that freshman year and seeing Jack drive up and enter the house. And then he heard a shout from the window, "Culver's a bum!" Culver had never met Jack Kennedy, didn't know him, but Jack had gotten his name from a member of the house staff and decided to prank him. Then Jack came down to play touch football with them—gingerly, as quarterback for both sides, since his aching back didn't permit him to do anything else. But Clasby noticed something between the older brother and the younger one. He said that Jack was "frail. . . . Everybody watched out that they didn't bump into him too much." And in that frailty, Clasby saw Jack's admiration for Teddy's stamina, his health and strength, saw a transaction between the two of them. "I could almost see that the older brother just felt that this other guy had everything. He was bigger and stronger, and every one of them was good-looking. He would really call Ted aside and talk to him, and no one ever knew what they were talking about, but there was a lot of laughing going on. You could just see the beam in Jack's eyes about this guy." Jack Kennedy actually admired Teddy Kennedy.

And that is what had transpired in the Kennedy family about the least of them. Whatever deficiencies Ted had, however much he had been the comic relief, however low the expectations of him were, "Biscuits and Muffins" had become not only big and strong and robust, he had also become a paragon of size and strength to the Kennedys. He may not have been a great football player, not like Clasby or Culver, but he was the best player in the Kennedy family, the *only* thing he was best at, and just as Joe Jr. had envied Jack his war heroism, Jack envied Teddy his prowess. So would Bobby. Even old Joe would come to practice, standing on the sidelines in a beret, to watch his youngest son. If football had been the Kennedys' niche of meritocracy at unmeritocratic Harvard, their comfort zone, for Ted football was also something more. It was the way for him finally to earn the respect of his family, by providing that family with the vicarious thrill of his vigor.

Kennedys admired physical ability. As sickly as many of them were, a Kennedy signature was vigor—a word that would become closely identified with the Kennedy administration in a conflation of physical and political fortitude. And Ted was the most vigorous of them. At Hyannis, he and his new football friends would take out Joe Kennedy's yacht, attach a raft to it, and then play King of the Raft, trying to knock one another off, even as the yacht accelerated. In physical combat is where Ted Kennedy found himself. In physical combat, at least, Ted Kennedy was the King of the Kennedys.

But if football was Ted Kennedy's salvation at Harvard that freshman year, and not only at Harvard but within the family, it would soon prove his ruination—the engine of an embarrassment so great, so un-Kennedy-like, that it would hound him throughout his life and nearly eclipse his accomplishments. Ted had been only a fair student before Harvard, and that didn't change in college. He struggled. He especially struggled with Spanish class. He had no aptitude for languages; at Milton he had dropped his Latin class but got a tutor to help him keep up, then complained that the tutor "wants to start at the beginning of the book." He wrote one of his father's advisers, Paul Murphy, during his midterms at Harvard his first year that "I am now having exams and so far they have been going fairly well." But Ted didn't mention Spanish, which wasn't going well. As the final exams approached, he was terrified that he wouldn't get a C- in the class—terrified not because of embarrassment or even at what his father might say. There was something much larger at stake for him: He was terrified because he needed a C- to keep his football eligibility.

As he later recounted it, he had finished studying early that evening before the exam but was still feeling apprehensive. He and a few friends went out for a walk. Warren O'Donnell, Kenny's younger brother, asked Ted how he was faring, and Ted admitted that he wasn't faring very well with the Spanish test hanging over him. They were passing through Harvard Yard when O'Donnell "jokingly," as Ted put it, suggested that he should just have someone else take the exam for him. They headed toward the dorm of a friend named Bill Frate, another Catholic and another member of the football cabal, and O'Donnell, clearly warming to the idea of Ted having someone else take the exam, called Frate out and asked if he had an aptitude for Spanish. (In another version he told, Ted said *he* was the one who "jokingly" mentioned the possibility to Frate.) Ted called the conversation "spontaneous," but it escalated with O'Donnell and the others goading Ted to do it. Frate laughed too, but he nevertheless checked to see if he was available to take the exam the next morning, so it was becoming something more than a harmless suggestion. Later that night, Frate offered, saying, "Fine, hell, I'll be glad to take the test." Ted said he thought of it as a kind of prank and that he hadn't been exactly secretive about it—at least not among his own friends, who were the ones to rouse Frate the next morning for the test.

But it wasn't a harmless prank like the ones he had pulled at boarding school. It was cheating. The proctor of the exam was someone who had hung out around Warren O'Donnell's dormitory room, so he knew Ted and he knew Bill Frate. (Ted said the proctor was actually Frate's tutor.) When Frate dropped the exam on the desk at noon that day, he "looked him [the proctor] square in the eye," almost, it seemed, as if Frate were daring him. And as Frate later told it to one of Ted's biographers, "He practically had an orgasm. He saw the name on it, and he was out of the room before the test was over." Ted got the call shortly afterward from an administrator, saying that he and Frate were to be expelled.

Joe Kennedy was not accustomed to embarrassment. Gloria Swanson, Joe Kennedy's onetime paramour, recalled Kennedy's reaction when the film they had made together, *Queen Kelly*, turned out to be a critical and financial disaster. "He charged into the living room of the bungalow," she said, "slumped into a deep chair," and, holding his head in his hands, emitted "little, high-pitched sounds . . . like those of a wounded animal whimpering in a trap." And he said: "I've never had a failure in my life."

Never a failure, but now the youngest had visited a terrible failure upon the family—a disgrace upon a family whose head had nitpicked about something as small as possible hostility toward a loud car horn. Ted didn't tell his father at first; he couldn't. Instead, he called Jack and then Bobby. Their advice was that he had to call Joe and tell him. But before he made the drive to Hyannis Port—"the longest and worst drive I ever had to make," he would say—he stopped at Milton to see his old headmaster, Arthur Bliss Perry, to confess. "His first reaction," Perry said, was "horror that he got caught," which fit the amorality in which he had been raised. But then, Perry recalled, Ted reiterated, "again and again," how badly he felt for the boy who had taken the exam for him—for Bill Frate. (Perry said something else: that the incident "grew inside him as he got older.") And now, after visiting Perry, Ted had to face the shaming. He met his father in the sunroom at Hyannis Port. As he told it to his mother's ghostwriter— saying, in this version, that he called his father before arriving, to report the expulsion—he described him as "very calm." Joe Kennedy asked his son, "What exactly was the situation I'm involved in? What impact could it have on my life and relationships?" And it was only later, eighteen to twenty-four hours later, that Joe Kennedy was "absolutely wild and went up through the roof. For about five hours." And then the calm returned: "How do we help you?" And Ted said that after that his father never brought up the incident again.

But that was the authorized version—the version portraying old Joe Kennedy as a solon who was analytical before he was furious, tender before he was censorious, who was always looking out for his children's welfare, and who had told them that home held no fear for them. But home did hold fear, paralyzing terror, and Ted told a different story years later. In that version, he said, his father "alternated between disappointment and anger for quite a while." ("Outraged and upset" was how he put it in still another telling.) And Joe Kennedy said something to his youngest son, to the least of his sons, that even Ted admitted was all too true. He said, "There are people who can mess up in life and not get caught, but you're not one of them." Less nimble, less clever than his brothers, Ted Kennedy always got caught. (In this, too, he was like his grandfather Honey Fitz, whose political career was derailed by charges of corruption and moral turpitude.) And being caught cheating at Harvard only certified the position he knew he occupied in his family—his position as the least. "There was a period where I had a lot of disappointment," Ted would say, "disappointing him [his father], disappointing my brothers, disappointing my family. It was a difficult time." And a pivotal time. Jack said that Joe had gotten tough on Teddy, that he needed to, that in doing so he saved him from himself. "If it hadn't been for that, Teddy might be a playboy today," and that "cracking down on him in a crucial time of his life . . . brought out in Teddy . . . discipline and seriousness. . . ."

But it wasn't as simple as Jack made it sound. (Joe had issued that admonition about living a productive life to a teenage Teddy long before the cheating, with seemingly little effect.) Ted had been expelled with the possibility of being readmitted if he demonstrated "constructive and responsible citizenship," but only the possibility. Ted and Gargan had been planning another long European trip that summer, from June through August, but the expulsion put an end to that. Now he—and his father—had to decide the best way to proceed. Joe posed two options. He said that Ted could attempt to enroll at another college; he mentioned Notre Dame, where Joe had a close personal friendship with Father John Cavanaugh, the university's president.* Or he could join the military, obviously build character, and try to return to Harvard, though Joe warned that Harvard had given Ted no guarantee of readmission. Ted was immobilized—humiliated and confused. According to a Kennedy maid at the time, he sat "brooding . . . sometimes for hours." It was after consulting with his brothers that he made the decision not only to enlist in the armed services

---

* At that same time, ninety-six cadets at West Point were also implicated in a cheating scandal and expelled. As a result of Ted's transgression, Joe Kennedy made arrangements with Father Cavanaugh at Notre Dame to finance the education of each if they chose to go there. He remained anonymous. He made a similar offer to finance Bill Frate's education. Frate refused and later re-enrolled at Harvard.

Honey Fitz. He said that 30 to 35 percent of the unit was black, and Ted Kennedy had never been around black people. He had to find different survival skills than the ones he had always used: the smile and the appeasing congeniality. And for someone who had never won respect in his own family, he had to find ways of earning respect in the Army. But Kennedy was big now, strong now, which meant a lot more in this arena than his wealth did. (His sergeant said that when Ted took the swimming test, "I never saw anything like it, and I tested thousands of guys. He probably could have been in the Olympics.") He was able to take care of himself, and in the Army he needed to. He fought now. He had a fight with a fellow boot camper, a black man named Wharton. Ted, Wharton, and a soldier named Fessier had been "gigged"—meaning punished—for having dirty weapons, the sentence for which was cleaning the officers' mess hall. It was a Saturday, and Ted and Fessier began the cleaning early, because Ted wanted to watch a football game. Ted asked Fessier to get Wharton, and Fessier returned with this message: "Wharton says he may come, but he may not." Ted, now suddenly assertive, said, "Well, he's going to come." Ted marched off to the barracks, where a group of eight or so black soldiers were rolling dice, and he called out Wharton, whom he had never met. When Wharton answered, Ted saw a man even bigger than he was and solid. Still, Ted was adamant; Wharton had to come. They volleyed: "Maybe I'm coming and maybe I ain't coming." "You're coming." And a fight ensued. The sergeant, Joseph Maguire from Waltham, Massachusetts, arrived to break it up and suggested they go clean the mess and then rendezvous at the flagpole at six o'clock to finish their dispute. Wharton was sullen. They finished the gig duty. Ted went to the flagpole. Five minutes later he left.

This was Ted Kennedy's new life.

And he learned something in this new life of his—this tough, hard life in which the Kennedy name meant nothing to his fellow soldiers. He learned about character, and what he learned was quite the opposite of what Joe and Rose, the social climbers, had taught him—about how the better people had it, and the Kennedys needed to be among the better people. But Ted watched those soldiers in his unit, as he had watched Honey Fitz with people who were like these soldiers, ordinary people, people without conceit or self-importance. Those things didn't matter in the Army any more than Ted's ingratiation had. He watched his gig partner

Fessier, a Notre Dame graduate who, after a forced twenty-six-mile march at night, carrying forty-six pounds on his back, would set up his tent, while the others just collapsed under theirs, and wash his socks in his helmet, while humming cheerfully. And he watched Washburn, the toughest guy in the unit when you looked at him, a Brooklyn guy, a "mean son of a gun," and Washburn would collapse after eleven miles. And Ted saw this: "You began to see who were the people who stayed the course, who were the people who were reliable . . . and who were the ones who did their duty." And he learned this: "You've got to value the people for what they were and what they did . . ." Honey Fitz had taught Ted Kennedy empathy. The Army taught him what character meant and who had it.

And Ted Kennedy sought to build his own character. There were no special privileges for Kennedy in basic training, and he didn't ask for any. (He only made it up to Hyannis Port once that summer.) Maguire called him a "pleasant kid, very easy to get along with, never gave you any guff," and Ted once told him, "You know, you're the only one who ever told me what to do, except my mother." (Pointedly, Ted didn't say his father.) But if there were no special privileges or airs, there was nevertheless one thing different about him. He had a rich kid's prerogative. On Sundays, Maguire remembered, he would be driven back into camp with a blonde at the wheel, and "All the guys would be looking out the window at that."

And he had one more prerogative, an important one, whether he asked for it or not: his father. After basic training ended that November, Ted was scheduled to be stationed at Fort Chaffee in Arkansas, the home of the Fifth Armored Division, the "Victory" division, which had landed on Utah Beach on D-Day and had recently been reactivated for possible deployment in Korea. (In the event, it wasn't deployed there, but Joe couldn't have foreseen that.) But Ted's orders were revoked without any cause given. He was sent instead to Fort Holabird, outside Baltimore, to the Counter Intelligence Corps, the area in which Jack had worked before he pressured his father for PT deployment. Ted said he had applied for intelligence work, a request that the Army apparently hadn't honored, so the revocation may very well have had the hand of Joe Kennedy on it, like the reduction of the four-year commitment and the promise to keep Ted from Korea. But Ted didn't stay at Fort Holabird long, only for a few weeks into January, before he was dropped from the program. He didn't know why. Ted told his biographer Adam Clymer that he suspected someone there had found out about his cheating. In any case, he was out of the Fifth Armored Division and out of the CIC, though he had asked to be released from neither.

But if Ted Kennedy didn't seek privileges after boot camp, his father sought privileges for him. After being mustered out of the CIC, Ted was sent to Fort Gordon in Georgia for military-police training, which was a kind of sinecure, provided one got the right assignment. Joe Kennedy made sure his youngest son got that assignment. Matthew Troy, who would later become a Democratic boss in New York, was Ted's squad leader, and he said that Joe "fixed it so that we would be assigned as MPs to Supreme NATO Headquarters in Paris." Troy was ecstatic at the prospect. But when they took their physicals, Troy was an inch under six feet—six feet being the minimum to be placed on the honor guard. Ted went to Paris, Troy to Korea. But this wasn't just an accident of height. Joe had asked a "tremendous personal favor" of the Army's foreign liaison, Anthony Biddle: to get Ted an "interesting assignment," and he mentioned Paris. Joe clearly had little interest in the others or where they went. So Ted arrived with the 520th Military Police Service Company on June 4, 1952, at Camp des Loges near Versailles and the Supreme Headquarters. Such were the benefits of being the son of Joe Kennedy, even when one didn't ask for them.

If Ted—or his father—was trying to avoid being measured against his brothers' martial glory by trying to avoid danger, Ted or Joe couldn't have found a better, cushier assignment. In the States, Ted had been just another grunt. In Paris, he was ornamentation and was largely left to his own devices. He skied the Alps with his sisters. He attended a black-tie gala for the Grand Ballet du Marquis de Cuevas with his mother—it was consistent with Rose's parenting that she hadn't seen him while he was in service in the United States but saw him in Paris—then drove back to the base with her in her chauffeured limousine; she called out to him as he approached his barracks: "Teddy, dear! You forgot your dancing shoes!" which prompted his fellow soldiers to thereafter call him mockingly "Teddy Dear" and ask him about his dancing shoes. He romanced women. Rose wrote Joe after her visit, "His girl, the nurse, is to come over this week and his girl from Texas has left, so he is lucky as usual." But the best part of his Paris duty may have been that it included playing football, because Ted was assigned to the battalion football team, first in France and then, when he was transferred, in Germany. This was the easiest assignment of all. The team traveled around the two countries, playing exhibitions, with the players setting their own schedules and hours. And that is how Ted Kennedy spent the next nine months of his military service—as an ornament and as a football player. On March 5, 1953, he returned to Fort Devens, where his service had begun. He was released from active duty on March 17 and discharged, still a private first-class, on June 24, having seen his only action on the football field.

Yet, for all that, the Army had been a seminal experience for him—a "very maturing experience, very quickly," he said. Much of this was just the discipline he had never had before, other than his father's withering glare, his mother's orders on etiquette, and football practice. And some of it was the self-assertion he displayed that he had never displayed before, the physical confrontations he had—"a couple of very tough, bad fights in the military, but survived," he said. But that may have been the least of it. More of it was the new socialization he had, was forced to have, with those soldiers so very different from him. "A lot of diversity, a lot of minorities," he remembered, especially black people—that 35 percent at Fort Dix, 45 percent at Fort Holabird, a third of his football team in Paris. And he cited "the kinds of high emotions that exist on racial questions" as something he addressed for the first time. At his basic training in Fort Dix he had gotten his education in character—in watching people under stress and seeing how they performed, seeing who made it and who didn't. But throughout his two years of service, he got to know these men, these men so different from him, got to separate them from the stereotypes and prejudices, got to appreciate the best of them. Ted Kennedy had been no racist; he never uttered a racist remark. But the Army widened his experience and his vision. Before the Army, black people had been unknown to him. Now they weren't.

And there was another maturing process he had undergone in the Army. Twenty-one-year-old Ted Kennedy was more serious than nineteen-year-old Ted Kennedy had been—more sober, more determined to do right, determined to expunge the stain of his cheating, which was a dark stain. He had concentrated on his uprightness, knowing there was no latitude for the least anymore. "I didn't want to make any more mistakes" is how he would put it, though it was really that his father would no longer tolerate his son's mistakes. But when it was over, Ted Kennedy purged nearly everything from the service save for the lessons he had internalized and couldn't purge. The young man who would learn how to make friends everywhere and keep those friends, many of them for life, didn't stay close to anyone in the service. "It was sort of a time that I put behind me." It was a time of penance for the great disgrace. And then it was over and lost.

He returned to Harvard, looking for further redemption from the disgrace. Late that April of 1953, when he was seeking reinstatement, he was interviewed by the dean of students, Delmar Leighton, to demonstrate his new seriousness. Leighton was impressed. "I send you a copy of a somewhat formidable letter which I am writing to Ted," he wrote Joe Kennedy. "I was favorably impressed by Ted's appearance and attitude in my recent talk with him. It looks to me as if he has made good use of these last two years." To demonstrate his seriousness, Ted spent that summer taking two courses in government and did well. To demonstrate his seriousness, he and his old football friend John Culver, who had just graduated from Harvard and who had reconnected with Ted the summer before in Paris, drove down to Washington to visit Jack and attend the Senate Subcommittee on Investigations hearings that Joseph McCarthy was conducting on alleged communist subversion for which Bobby was serving as assistant counsel. To demonstrate his seriousness, and as a result of the new racial sensitivity he had acquired while in the service, Ted volunteered one or two afternoons a week at the South End Settlement House, taking fifteen or so poor black children around Boston, as Honey Fitz had taken him, and coaching the boys in basketball. Perhaps above all, Harvard *made* him demonstrate his seriousness, by putting him on academic probation so that Ted Kennedy couldn't play varsity football that first year back, only club football for the house in which he now resided, Winthrop, where Jack had lived too, though it was a "jock" house—the House of Mesomorphs, as some referred to it.

Friends noted the change in him—the new seriousness. Culver said that Ted didn't "gab" with the football players the way he used to. He went to the business library instead to study. "I was really interested," Ted recalled of this time, speaking of his classes, which is not something he could have said before, and he said that he "worked, worked hard." Deciding to major in government, he focused now on government courses, difficult courses—Arthur Holcombe's course on the Constitutional Convention, which all his brothers had taken, and a course on Constitutional Studies from a brilliant young professor named Robert McCloskey, who would become something of a Harvard legend. The seriousness didn't suddenly turn him into an excellent student. ("He was no aristocrat at college" was how classmate and later aide Milton Gwirtzman put it.) Holcombe, like so many who judged Ted by his demeanor, had low expectations. "I didn't think he was in the same class with his older brothers, but that was merely because I didn't have any evidence to form a high opinion of him," he later told one of Ted's biographers. He came to believe that Ted was above average, but, for all of Ted's sudden desire to apply himself, Holcombe said he couldn't tell how *much* above average he was, because he suspected Ted was still thinking more about athletics and socializing. "I think academics came third," said Holcombe, and he thought that, finally, "He did just what was necessary to remain in good standing," though he was now pulling B's where, as a freshman, his best grades were two B-'s. And, ironically, he received his highest grade, an A-, in Spanish.

But if there was no full classroom redemption, there was still a source of family redemption at Harvard. By the next year, he was back at football, his real love and his real source of status among the Kennedys. (One biographer said Ted "majored" in football.) Having missed three seasons now, his was not an easy return to the field. He had fallen on the depth chart to the eighth end, he said, and had to work his way back. Though big and strong, his football aptitude was in some ways like his academic aptitude: He had a "lack of natural ability," said the Harvard coach Lloyd Jordan. But he compensated, said Jordan, "with a fierce sense of determination," which was the difference between Kennedy on the football field and in the classroom. "He was the kind of player a coach appreciates."

"The harder you played against him, the harder he'd play against you," said the longtime ends coach Henry Lamar, who had also coached all three of Ted's brothers. And Lamar remembered a series of plays in which Ted, on the defensive line, was designated to hit the quarterback. On the first play, he "laid the quarterback out just after the handoff." On the second, the quarterback anticipated Ted's rush and gave Ted a forearm. On the third play, Ted "hit the quarterback with everything he had, carefully avoiding the forearm." Lamar agreed with Jordan: "not what I would call a natural athlete." But he was nevertheless an "outstanding player, the kind that carried out his assignments to the letter." And Lamar said something else about Teddy—that he was "the easiest to know" of the Kennedy brothers, "more open and outgoing." He didn't play a great deal in his junior year. When he finally did get on the field, against Bucknell, he said he was so ecstatic that he didn't even notice when an opponent knocked out one of his teeth.

But the ecstasy was short-lived. To earn his football letter, he needed only four more minutes of playing time in the final game of the season, the biggest game of Harvard's year, against its archrival, Yale, which was vying for the Ivy League title. Jordan inserted him near the close of the first half at right defensive end. And the player who lacked great talent but who never missed an assignment promptly missed his assignment, allowing a Yale player to sweep around him for sixty-two yards. (Ted would later claim it wasn't he but the linebacker who missed the assignment.) And just like that, four minutes short of his letter, Ted was pulled from the game, never to return. "It was like they signed your death warrant," he would lament years later. Harvard won, rallying from a 9–0 deficit with less than five minutes to go and scoring twice in the fourth quarter, 13–9, thus costing Yale the Ivy title outright (they shared it with Cornell), so Ted had to feign enthusiasm, but he felt as if he had failed yet again—this time at the one thing he was reasonably good at.

In his last year at Harvard, redemption was still coming hard. "Hope things are going well and that you will make your last year at Harvard a real big one," Joe Kennedy wrote his youngest son, adding, "if only for your future." With so much to overcome, the least of the Kennedys was, in fact, acquitting himself. In the classroom, his grades improved. "There was quite a bit of difference between his scholastic ability as a sophomore and as a senior," said a teaching fellow named Fred Holborn. Holborn observed that the sophomore Ted was "pretty disorganized," an "average student," this despite the new seriousness with which he had returned to Harvard after his expulsion. The senior Ted was focused, Holborn said, which he attributed to Ted's taking public-speaking courses—the courses in which Ted had received honors at Milton—that helped him organize his thoughts. That last year, he earned one C, four B's, a B+, and an A- and finished in the top half of his class.

But the seriousness with which he had returned to Harvard after the Army had dissipated as the stigma if not the pain of the great disgrace had dissipated. Ted's natural extroversion reemerged, which made the year unlikely to be a "real big one," as his father had hoped. He reverted to form. Once again, he exhibited what his classmate Claude Hooton called a "zest for life." Once again, he was puckish. He joined the Hasty Pudding Club, as his brothers had, which was known for its conviviality and for its all-male cross-dressing theatricals. (He was not, however, selected for any of the exclusive Harvard clubs; the Catholic prejudice remained.) He pulled pranks as before, but the pranks were harmless: he and Clasby tricking students by performing a mind-reading routine in which they had rehearsed "tells"; Ted challenging a roommate, Ted Carey, who had been annoying him, to fly to Africa if Ted paid the fare, and then, when Carey took him up on it and Jack and Joe heard about it, frantically phoning the airport, begging him not to go (Carey flew to Hartford, Connecticut, instead, without telling Ted); bringing a sheep into the barracks of the Harvard rugby team, on which he played that spring, when the team had a match in Bermuda (the sheep evacuated everywhere). Ted Kennedy caused troubles, innocent troubles, but he stayed out of trouble.

Still there was the matter of redemption, his family redemption for the great disgrace, and it came elsewhere—where it had come before: on the football field. After barely seeing the field in his junior year, he averaged fifty-six minutes a game in his senior year. The Kennedys were overjoyed. Jack and Bobby attended all his games, and, as Clasby had noticed back at Hyannis Port, Jack was particularly mesmerized. Save for the summer of 1944, the summer during which Joe Jr. was killed, Jack and Teddy hadn't been particularly close. "It was sort of an older brother looking after a younger brother and interested in the books that I read and the activities I was involved in, and the studies that I was working on," Ted recalled. But Jack was preoccupied with his own activities. It was different with football. Jack took an interest in that and in Ted. The Kennedys were proud of him, bragged about him. After talking to some of Ted's teammates, Bobby wrote Joe enthusiastically, "They said he had no qualms about lowering his head and crashing in and that he has great potentialities and is one of the best ends they have. That is certainly good when his fellow players think that." Tenacious. That was the Kennedy way.

And Joe Kennedy, who had previously taken notice of his son more for his transgressions than for his successes, now took notice. For the big Harvard–Yale game, the conclusion to an undistinguished losing season—Harvard was 2 and 6, limping into the final—Joe brought a group of his friends to New Haven to watch Ted play. And this time Ted did not disappoint. In freezing weather, on a field blanketed with snow, with Harvard trailing 14–0 in the third quarter—Yale's points had come off a Harvard fumble and an interception—tailback Walter Stahura led a seventy-nine-yard march, capped by a seven-yard touchdown pass lofted high into the corner of the end zone to a leaping "Ed Kennedy," as he was described in the front-page *New York Times* account of the contest, which also cited him as among the half dozen Harvard players who "excelled" in the game. It was to be Harvard's lone touchdown in the 21–7 loss. But, the loss and a shoulder injury he incurred in the game notwithstanding, it was a triumph for Ted. Jack and Bobby came into the locker room to celebrate with him, and then Ted went down to the New Haven railroad station to see his father and his father's friends off. Moreover, Ted finally received the football letter he coveted and had been denied a year earlier. (In the tally for the season, he would have six catches for eighty yards, including another catch in the Harvard–Yale game, this one for fifteen yards, and two touchdowns.) Later, he would say, he received an invitation from the Green Bay Packers of the National Football League to try out for the team. More important, however, was that the game, the catch, were partial redemption for the great disgrace of his having cheated, and redemption is what he sought.

Joe Kennedy's eyes were fixed on the future, and he had long worried about the future of his youngest son. Despite the Packers' invitation, Ted Kennedy would not become a professional athlete, and upon graduation he had to find a path forward, or, rather, the family had to find him a path that would bring honor to them, for that is how it was among the Kennedys. He had not spent his Harvard summers productively. After his sophomore year, he and his big, boisterous, equally fun-loving Harvard pal, Claude Hooton, borrowed money from Joe to start a water-skiing school in Newport Beach, California. (One account reported the location as Panama, another that Joe eventually scotched the idea.) After his junior year, he worked as a forest ranger in the Sequoia and Kings Canyon National Parks. The summer after his graduation, however, was to be a summer of preparation since Ted was now in the line of succession, after Jack and Bobby, whether he wanted to be or not. "I was drafted," Jack had said when he ran for Congress after Joe Jr.'s death, and so now was Teddy. He had majored in government, clearly as a prelude for government service. The next step, the step that both Joe Jr. and Bobby had taken, was law school—the step from which Jack was saved by his war heroism. (Such was Ted's reputation in the family that when Rose learned Ted was going to law school, Bobby said she asked him, "What side of the court my brother is going to appear on when he gets out of law school: attorney or defendant?") Ted was to say that he had gone to law school without ever intending to practice law. "I just enjoyed the mental gymnastics, and I think that legal training gives you perspective and judgment." But Ted Kennedy had never been particularly interested in mental gymnastics or perspective or judgment. What law really gave him was something else in which he was interested, or in which his family was interested on his behalf: a way into politics, or what he called "public service." That was the path Joe Kennedy had cleared for him.

The problem was that law school was competitive, and Ted hadn't excelled at Harvard. Even Bobby, a better student, had been rejected by Harvard Law and told by the University of Virginia that with his grades, he was "unlikely to be admitted to this Law School unless you do well on the [Law School] Aptitude Test." He did and was admitted. But Ted had an additional problem. Like Bobby, his grades would have disqualified him from admission to Harvard Law, even if he hadn't been expelled for cheating, but he had. He considered Stanford Law, as he had considered Stanford for his undergraduate career, again as a way of creating distance between himself and Kennedy expectations, but Joe Kennedy nixed the idea, and, even if he hadn't, there is no certainty Ted would have been admitted there either. (Ted had an independent streak, his family said, but if he did, he always surrendered to his father in the end.) Rather, Ted would be staying east, whether he wanted to or not. Since Bobby had attended Virginia Law, it was a natural option, Ted's default, but Ted said it was Jack who encouraged him to go there because of its proximity to Washington and its ties to Washington. (Ted was present when Jack, now a senator, cornered fellow senator Hubert Humphrey outside the Foreign Relations Committee room and convinced him to speak at Virginia Law's Student Legal Forum, where he himself had spoken recently.) Yet Virginia was no more welcoming than Harvard to one who had cheated. According to one Kennedy biographer, Max Lerner, the law faculty revolted when it learned that Ted was being considered, since the school operated on an honor principle that Ted had already violated. It was only after a special vote of the university's full faculty that Ted was admitted.

None of this seemed to be directed by Ted, who was following the family's dictates as he always had. It was his father's doing and even his brothers'—looking out for the youngest, looking out for the family. Now, the summer before law school, the summer of 1956, Jack again took his youngest brother under his wing, clearly pushing Ted's political prospects, even though they were a long way off. As part of the ongoing enterprise to educate Ted and make the least serious of the Kennedys more serious, Jack urged him to tour North Africa—a serious trip for a serious summer—because the countries in that tier were just shaking free of colonialism, or, in Algeria's case, attempting to do so, and Jack thought the trip would be highly educational and, in time, politically valuable. Ted took one of Jack's staffers, the former Harvard tutor Fred Holborn, with him, to provide context, and, with Joe's help, Ted obtained a press pass from the International News Service on the basis that he would be reporting on what he observed. That gave the young man access to most of the leaders in the area.

At his family's behest, Ted was slowly building a portfolio—slowly being transformed into a prospective political figure. From the Army, Ted had learned race. From his trip to North Africa, he learned about colonialism and independence. He and Holborn visited Morocco first, which had just won its independence from France. Mohammed V had become sultan once again, and Ted and Holborn attended a kind of two-day coronation up in the mountains among the Berber tribes, where Ted and Holborn slept on rugs under a capacious tent—holding hundreds—while the new king and his harem camped in another tent. And the next day, the Berbers swept across the plains, fifty abreast, firing their guns, delivering a "rebel yell," and pledging their allegiance to their leader. Then Ted and Holborn went to Algeria, traveling with the French forces as the insurgency by the National Liberation Front was beginning to boil. The French told him that they had the rebels under control, but Ted felt differently and conveyed that to Jack, who would later publicly call for the French to abandon the country. And then they arrived in Tunisia and observed Habib Bourguiba, whom Ted described as "one of that group of postwar revolutionaries who—in Earl Attlee's phrase—became 'tenacious prime ministers.'"

For someone who had usually taken the path of least resistance, except when it came to football, this was not a vacation. It was an opportunity to show his family his maturity. Armed with his press credentials, Ted met with ambassadors and government officials. He saw violence erupting. He kept extensive journals, as Jack had during his trips and as Ted himself had done during his travels in Europe, cramming page after page after page with observations. (He couldn't decide whether to write his press reports as he went or write them all when he returned.) And, most of all, for a twenty-four-year-old of fairly limited experience, he was surprisingly tough-minded now about what he saw, incisive, and what he saw was the collapse of colonialism and new countries aborning, although he was less than optimistic about the course those countries might take and the motives of their leaders. And he gave Jack this assessment: that he believed communism was most likely to bloom where there were unresolved tensions, which is to say when the colonialists and the indigenous populations were at loggerheads.

It was the first time he had dared make a political suggestion to one of his brothers. It was the first time anyone in his family took the advice seriously.

III

Like his grandfather Honey Fitz, Ted Kennedy had a gift for friendship. On the very first day of classes in his first year at the University of Virginia Law School in the fall of 1956, Ted was milling about outside a classroom in Clark Hall when John Varick Tunney, another law freshman, introduced himself. That past summer, Jack had made a last-minute bid for the Democratic vice-presidential nomination but had lost narrowly to Tennessee senator Estes Kefauver. Still, young John Kennedy had made a name for himself at the convention—he was a comer—which is why another student had pointed Ted out to Tunney and why Tunney wanted to meet him, though Tunney had no knowledge of Joe Kennedy or the Kennedy family beyond Jack. Tunney was no unknown himself. In the 1920s, his father, Gene Tunney, had been the light-heavyweight and heavyweight boxing champion of the world—he took the latter title from the immortal Jack Dempsey and then defended it against him in one of the most famous fights in boxing history, the night of the "long count," where Dempsey refused to go to a neutral corner after knocking Tunney down and subsequently lost the fight. John Tunney's mother, Polly Lauder, was a wealthy socialite. Despite his profession and his lack of formal education, Gene Tunney was erudite—both a thinking boxer in the ring and a thinking man's boxer outside it, who numbered among his friends Ernest Hemingway, George Bernard Shaw, Philadelphia Orchestra conductor Eugene Ormandy, and, though Tunney's son John didn't know it, Joseph Kennedy. Ted's first comment upon the introduction was that John's father had arranged to have a sauna built at the Kennedys' house in Hyannis Port like the one Tunney had in his own home. That was the icebreaker, but Tunney said he immediately realized that "this was a person I was really going to like—just the way he carried himself when he talked [and] the smile," adding, "He had a warmth to him." And Tunney said he immediately detected a "kind of chemistry between them. . . . Instant friends." They quickly became inseparable and remained that way over the next three years.

They were kindred spirits, both tall, athletic, handsome, wealthy, and Irish Catholic, which meant they bore those grievances against the Protestant establishment. (The only thing they didn't share at that time was their politics: Gene Tunney had been a Roosevelt supporter but turned Republican in 1940 when his friend, the businessman Wendell Willkie, captured the Republican presidential nomination, and John Tunney and Ted would argue heatedly, Tunney said.) And they shared anxiety—"such anxiety," as Tunney described it. "You knew that everybody in the school was pretty smart. They wouldn't be there if they weren't. And you also knew that not everybody was going to make it, and you didn't want to be one of the ones who failed." Tunney admitted that that first year they both had their doubts, as Ted had always had self-doubt, so they "worked our heads off" and "we got through."

But there was a deeper source for their anxiety, a deeper and more terrifying source, and they shared that too: "Are we going to be adequate to live up to our family's names?" as Tunney posed it. They discussed it. They discussed how they had to carry the "burden"—that is what Tunney called it—of not disappointing their families, but what Tunney really meant was disappointing their fathers. Joe Kennedy overshadowed everything Ted did, perhaps more so after the cheating scandal, when Ted had so much more to prove to him, had to try so hard to lift the disgrace. Like Ted's roommates at Harvard, Tunney called Joe Kennedy a "major figure in his life in those days. I mean a *major* figure," and he observed, as Ted's Harvard roommates had observed, the fear and obeisance Ted demonstrated when he talked to his father on the phone. Tunney knew that feeling, knew it well. They were partners in their terror—and it *was* terror—of inadequacy. That first year at Virginia Law, Ted Kennedy, "Smilin' Ed," who had been so easygoing, who had a "zest for life," developed an ulcer.

They always felt they had to prove themselves. The summer after that first year, the summer of 1957, the two friends decided to go to the Hague Academy of International Law for a series of lectures delivered by Hardy Cross Dillard, a Virginia Law graduate and professor (they managed to wangle a credit from him without having to take exams), though the motive for going seemed less to extend their legal education than once again to prove their seriousness to their fathers. "Thank you for the newsy letter," Joe wrote Ted that July, "and I'm sure that, as dull as some of it sounds, you will get some good out of it." And: "I think I notice a greater maturity in your letters." When the course was finished, they traveled around Europe, "trying to live out our Ernest Hemingway fantasies," as Tunney put it. "We'd take a brandy now and then and talk about the great thoughts of Western civilization."

But Tunney said he noticed something about Ted on that trip that he hadn't noticed before, despite all the time they had spent together. As the two of them roamed Europe, Tunney recognized that Ted had "more raw charisma than almost any man I'd ever met. . . . The man had this incredible ability to attract other people to him and to lead." And he couldn't help but notice something else: Ted had "incredible physical courage," raw courage, reckless courage, which may have been another way for him to impress the Kennedys, to show them he was up to *being* a Kennedy. The reckless courage had a long history. When he was small, his brothers had coaxed him to jump off the garage roof at the Bronxville house while holding a jerry-rigged parachute, and Rose recalled Jack and Joe Jr. exhorting young Teddy to jump off a cliff at Eden-Roc on the French Riviera during the time when Joe was the ambassador to England, then Teddy doing so and "kept doing it, egged on with great applause." (He would repeat the performance at Eden-Roc while traveling with Tunney.) But what most impressed Tunney about Ted's courage on their European excursion was Ted's decision to climb a mountain in the Alps, even though he had no mountain-climbing experience whatsoever, then slipping on the way up and dangling three thousand feet above ground until Tunney, who had preceded him, managed to pull him to a ledge, where Ted calmly took out cheese and an orange and exulted over the story he would tell about the adventure, no doubt to his brothers and his father.

Now Ted had to prove himself to them in the classroom. When he and Tunney returned to Virginia Law that fall for their second year, they rented an old house, a converted stable on Barracks Road in the Charlottesville countryside. Jacqueline Kennedy, Jack's wife, had a cook named Carmen who quarreled with the other kitchen help, so Jackie had to let her go and she recommended that Ted and Tunney hire her as their housekeeper, since there would be no one else at their house with whom she could argue. Now, without having to fend for themselves, they began a new routine, a serious routine, a "tough schedule," Tunney called it: sharing breakfast, driving separately to class, returning for lunch, and then spending the afternoon studying in their rooms, after which they would reconvene for dinner. After dinner, they would talk or argue politics for an hour or so over cups of coffee—Tunney said he had never been able to communicate with anyone the way he could communicate with Ted, in part because Carmen did all the housework, leaving them free to converse—and then they would retreat to their rooms once again for more studying.

Later, when Ted ran for office, stories would circulate that he didn't abide by the routine as strictly as Tunney had said, that he was as reckless in Charlottesville as he had been in the Alps, that he was always getting in and out of scrapes, that he and Tunney loved to carouse, and that the boy who had cheated his way out of Harvard nearly drove his way out of Virginia. "Cadillac Ed" was one of the nicknames Ted's Virginia classmates gave him. (His boat-sized car was actually a large Oldsmobile.) Tunney admitted that they both liked speed and that Barracks Road, with its curves, provided a kind of raceway for them, but Tunney also insisted that neither of them ever drank and drove. Still, Ted had several run-ins with the police that spring—once when he ran a red light and then sped away after a police officer flashed him, and again the following Saturday, when he ran another red light and then led the officer on a chase, with the officer saying that he was "driving as fast as his police cruiser could travel with safety on Barracks Road." Ted's lights were off—a mechanic later substantiated that there was a short in the wiring—and when the chase finally ended, outside Ted's house, he was crouched in the front seat. He was ticketed, though the warrants were never placed in the court's docket drawer—whether by accident or to spare Ted is impossible to say—and Ted later pleaded not guilty to reckless driving and paid a $35 fine for speeding.

Over the years the litany of charges against him would grow. He was accused by a woman of stealing two of her horses, but she claimed she didn't press charges because she was told that if she did, Ted would not graduate. He and Tunney were said to frequent the Chi Psi fraternity, of which neither was a member, and Tunney once got into a fight there. They threw parties, one at the end of their second year and another at the end of their third, huge raucous parties that, as Tunney put it, "went

down in the annals," though he said that was not because the parties he
and Ted hosted were particularly riotous but because they were the only
parties to which the entire class, all 150 of them, were invited. In short,
Ted Kennedy at Virginia Law was accused of having reverted to his old
self and of playing dangerously close to the line he had crossed as a freshman at Harvard. Again, more Fitzgerald than Kennedy, he was accused of
being irresponsible because he was irrepressible.

But there was another possible reason for Ted Kennedy's ongoing flir-
tation with disaster—a darker one. It wasn't because, as a Kennedy, he felt
entitled and thought he could get away with anything, which was a
charge that would dog him throughout his life; Ted Kennedy had never
felt entitled, not at Harvard, not now. It wasn't because he couldn't control his Fitzgeraldian impulses; Ted Kennedy had largely controlled those
impulses. It wasn't because he was fundamentally unserious; Ted Kennedy was serious now. It was because the only times that Ted Kennedy
was in control of his own life, the only times he could escape the prison of
his family, were those times when he seemed out of control—when he
transgressed against the strictures that his father had imposed on him
and on all the Kennedys. And more, it was because Ted Kennedy, the boy
who actually returned to Fessenden to visit the disciplinarian who had
meted out punishment to him and to thank that disciplinarian, and the
boy who was firmly convinced of his inadequacies, the boy who was
steeped in his mother's Catholicism and in Catholic guilt, seemed to need
to sabotage himself to validate his own negative judgment and then accept the punishment, even as he also tried, manfully if often unsuccessfully, to disprove the judgment. Ted Kennedy felt so unworthy that he had
to demonstrate his unworthiness. And Ted Kennedy could only be freed
from his sense of unworthiness, his sense of being the least, by being re-
buked. This was the process of his life. Ted Kennedy wanted redemption,
but he needed to sin and then be punished in order to get it.

Ted would later say that he had made one change at Virginia. He would
say that "for a while, at least, I stopped worrying about 'catching up' and
savored the moment," presumably meaning catching up to his brothers.
The escapades of which he was accused may have been his way of savor-
ing his time at Virginia, of giving himself a break, but he never stopped
trying to catch up, even though it always seemed to be a losing race. The
"plugger" continued to plug along. Tunney attested to how hard Ted continued to work, how he kept to their schedule after that first year, "study-

ing all the time," save for Saturday afternoons, when a group of students played touch football. Ted had to work hard, "*very*, very hard," Tunney attested, because—the comment that had trailed Ted everywhere—he "wasn't a great student, I wouldn't pretend he was. . . . He was always pretty much in the middle, sometimes lower-middle segment of the class," though it was a sacrilege among the Kennedys to finish even second. (Joe Kennedy had admonished his children, "Do the best you can. And then the hell with it." But this was not the way the family actually operated. It operated under the principle: "Do the best you can. And win.") Another close friend, Timothy Hanan, said that Ted would sit in the law library for hours, poring over his books with a jar of Maalox on the table for his ulcers. One of his professors said that Bobby was brighter but that he gave Teddy a higher grade "because he worked harder." (Shortly before he graduated, Ted sent the professor a thank-you note, one of only a half dozen students who had ever done so, the professor said.) Another professor called him "handsome, good-mannered, and a hell of a nice boy," but, he said, "he didn't have the best grades," mainly C's. A professor who flunked him in a course nevertheless praised him because he "took his medicine like a man" and made "no attempt to get around it." But these were not the sorts of comments that a Kennedy wanted to hear or that any other Kennedy had heard. They were comments for the least.

IV

While he struggled at law, there was a second thing, besides football, at which Ted Kennedy was not the least of the Kennedys: In a family of womanizers, Ted was a world-class womanizer. He had come late to this achievement, given his adolescent weight issues, though it wasn't for want of trying. But as he grew older, taller, thinner, and more handsome, his interest in women and his success with them intensified. At Harvard he had no steady girlfriend, preferring, one of his roommates said, to date girls from Pine Manor Junior College outside Boston rather than girls from Radcliffe and Wellesley, though this might just have been discretion. His friend Dick Clasby said he would rate the girls he met, A through F, and added, "He had a twinkle in his eye for pretty girls." Jack would bring girls with him to New York, and Ted and Clasby would take them to the Stork Club. The interest continued in the service when, as Rose had reported to Joe, Ted was shuffling out one girl as he was bringing in another.

But while Joe, who had his own roving eye, had often warned Teddy to be cautious with women, he did not exactly discourage Ted's womanizing; rather, he took pride in it, seeing Teddy's attractiveness to women as yet another form of winning. "I don't know whether you know it or not, but the reports of your goings on with all these beautiful women at Cape Cod," he wrote Teddy early in September 1955, "is slowly but surely driving your oldest brother insane." This though Jack was married to Jacqueline. "There was a time when I think he thought I was a little strict with you by insisting that you have something else on your mind besides girls, but after having heard from Morton Downey [a Kennedy friend] that he saw you at the airport with a more beautiful girl than Grace Kelly, Jack, I am sure, has changed his whole outlook on your future." He concluded, "If there are so many beautiful girls looking around for a Kennedy, it should be for the oldest brother and not the youngest."

Joan Bennett knew the exact day, the exact moment, the exact place, she met Ted Kennedy: on the early afternoon of Monday, October 28, 1957, in the Prom Room of the Benziger Building at Manhattanville College of the Sacred Heart in Purchase, New York, where she was a student. And she vividly remembered her first impression of him. "I'll never forget that moment," she later said about when she was told the youngest Kennedy was at the school. "I expected to see a small boy. Instead, I found myself looking up at somebody six feet two inches and close to two hundred pounds. And, I must say, darn good-looking." In another recollection, she was more succinct: "He was tall, and he was gorgeous." Tall and gorgeous Ted Kennedy was. The most inferior of the Kennedys had become the most attractive of the Kennedys.

But if Joan Bennett was smitten, she was not necessarily impressed. Joan didn't know much about the Kennedys. "I took no interest in current events," she said. She had met Jean Kennedy Smith in August 1956, at a party at the Greenwich, Connecticut, home of George Skakel Jr., the brother of Bobby's wife, Ethel. Joan arrived accompanied by two men who were friends of Jean and her husband, Steve Smith (by several accounts, including Joan's, one of the men had once been Jean's fiancé), and when Joan was introduced to Jean, they discovered that they had both grown up in Bronxville and that Jean had also attended Manhattanville. Joan said that Jean "took me under her wing" at the party, but that was more or less that. Joan had no idea that Jean was a Kennedy, nor would it have mattered if she had.

Rose Kennedy had a deep interest in Manhattanville, her alma mater, which she had forced her daughters Eunice and Jean to attend as well, and she and Joe had decided to donate a gymnasium to the school in the name of Kathleen. Jack was to speak at the dedication that October 27. By coincidence, Ted, who was then beginning his second year at Virginia Law, was in New York that weekend for the Giants–Redskins football game, staying at his father's apartment in the city. As Ted later told it, Jack stopped by the apartment that night, said he wanted to see the game himself, and asked Ted if he would fill in for him at the college. Joan had no intention of attending the dedication. She had spent the weekend at Yale, as she often did for football weekends, and had a paper to type, so she skipped the dedication itself. But her roommate, a girl named Margot Murray, warned Joan that attendance was going to be taken at the reception, which, by Joan's date, was the next day, and as a senior, she would get a demerit if she also skipped that. Joan Bennett was not the kind of girl to get a demerit. When Jean Kennedy Smith spotted Joan at the reception, she took her over to meet Ted. (Ted remembered it differently. He said that Jean introduced him to Margot Murray, who knew many of Ted's friends, and that Murray introduced him to Joan.) This Ted remembered: Joan was an "exquisitely beautiful young student." And on this they would agree: Joan said that they both felt something "instantaneous," almost a "shock of recognition," she called it, "as if each of us realized, 'This is it, this is the one.'" Ted said that he might need a ride to the train station, and Joan and Margot Murray volunteered. Joan said that as he entered the car, he asked if he could call her. He phoned her the next night. It was only after several more calls that he finally asked her out, for the Sunday after Thanksgiving. Joan already had a date for Sunday night, so Ted agreed to Sunday brunch. He drove out to Bronxville after coming in from Hyannis Port and took her to the Sherry-Netherland (another account says the St. Regis) in the city with his sister Pat and her husband, the movie actor Peter Lawford. They returned to Bronxville just as her evening date was arriving.

If Ted was fast, like all the Kennedy boys—all but diffident Bobby—Joan Bennett was slow. She had grown up in Bronxville, as Ted had (the Kennedys decamped for England when she was a toddler), but she went to public school, stuck to the community, and wound up, she said, "knowing mostly people pretty much like myself." A "cloistered background," she called it. Her grandfather, Harry Bennett Sr., had been something of a buccaneer and rapscallion, a fortune seeker who roamed the world, but her father, Harry Bennett Jr., an advertising executive, was conservative in both temperament and politics; it was an upper-middle-class family, a Republican family, though, unlike the Kennedys, politics was never a subject of conversation at their dinner table. "A nice quiet kid" is what Joan's assistant pastor at St. Joseph's Roman Catholic Church in Bronxville called her. Her younger sister, Candy, was the cannonball, the live wire. "When I'd come home from work," Harry Bennett said, "Candy would be halfway down the block to meet me and would throw herself at me. But Joan would sit in the living room." Her happiness, he said, was "bottled up inside." She was an introvert. She felt misunderstood, ignored. "When I was a kid, nobody asked me what I was going to do," she told an interviewer. As a teenager, she was tall, five foot seven, and gangly, only ninety pounds, and she wore braces on her teeth. She said she identified with Eleanor Roosevelt, homely and lonely.

But Joan Bennett was no Eleanor Roosevelt. She may have been lonely. She may have been shy and quiet. But she wasn't homely, not once she had blossomed, as Ted Kennedy had blossomed. Once she blossomed, everyone said, Joan Bennett was beautiful—not just beautiful but, as Ted Kennedy had appraised her that first day, "exquisitely beautiful." A friend observed of her: "With that absolutely perfect nose and her equally faultless backside, some divinity must have shaped her ends." And Joan Bennett was a *blond* beauty at a time when blond-haired Marilyn Monroe was the reigning movie siren, and blond was fashionable. When Joan's father recommended her to a modeling agency, the wife of the agency's head, a former model herself, said, "She was one of those rare beauties we get infrequently. I found myself comparing her to an Ingrid Bergman when she was Joan's age." While at Manhattanville, she worked steadily—print ads and national television programs like *The Colgate Comedy Hour* and *The Perry Como Show*. During a spring break trip to Bermuda, she was crowned the queen of the Bermuda Chamber of Commerce.

And more than beautiful, as far as Ted Kennedy was concerned, Joan Bennett was a *Catholic* blond beauty. Though her father was Protestant, her Catholic mother raised her in the faith and then sent her to the all-girls Manhattanville College, where Joan majored in music, having studied piano since she was a child. Candy Bennett said that Joan "loved" the school: "She loved the nuns, her studies, her friends." Years later, however, Joan sounded less enthusiastic. She said that if you wanted to sign out, you had to do so in triplicate. "I joked about wanting to climb the walls but being afraid the nuns would come after me." But Joan Bennett was not the kind of girl to climb walls. "I did as I was told," she said. "Life was so much easier. You got married or became a nun." The girls' great transgression, she recalled, was taking the train into New York City, wearing big hats and white gloves, and then changing into a second pair of gloves on their way home—an "assurance that we remained pure, immaculate, and inno-cent," presumably for their prospective hubands. A friend of Joan's called Manhattanville a "marriage mill."

Whether twenty-five-year-old Ted Kennedy had matrimony in mind, he had Joan Bennett in mind that fall. They didn't see each other much that school year, only twice. Ted was in Charlottesville, Joan in Purchase. But he phoned—phoned often. At Christmas, they took a ski trip to Stowe, Vermont, with Margot Murray and her boyfriend, who happened to be a classmate of Ted's, but since Joan was a good Catholic girl, the boys and girls roomed separately. It was on that ski trip, Joan later said, that she fell in love with Ted, because she had never skied before and Ted was "always there to pick me up and urge me on with such patient, sweet encourage-ment." They met for a weekend in Charlottesville that spring, again with others, and she told Kennedy biographer Adam Clymer that they had sev-eral dates in Bronxville. By this time she had stopped dating other boys, or, as she put it, they had stopped dating her when they discovered she was seeing a Kennedy.

Though they had scarcely seen each other—"as often as possible, which wasn't very often"—and though they had seldom spent any time alone, Joan would say that "almost before we knew it, we were on a fast track toward marriage." After Joan's graduation that June, Teddy invited her to Hyannis Port, the royal invitation, to meet Rose, who subjected her to a lengthy interrogation, beginning with questions about Manhattan-ville and ranging, Joan told her biographer Laurence Leamer, from values to religion to music, a passion they shared. Joan stayed the week, strolling along the beach with Ted and accompanying him on the golf course, and it was "very cozy," she thought, comfortable. Later that summer Ted joined her at her grandparents' summer house in Alstead, New Hamp-shire, where she had spent most of her summers, and there, she said, she got a "glimpse of how much fun he was." They attended a square dance, and Ted got up and began calling. They also spent quiet time—painting landscapes, which was an activity in which Joan's mother had led the children of her extended family.

Though they knew they had fallen in love, the decision to marry was not one to make alone. There was the Kennedy family movie to cast, and anyone marrying into the family was marrying into the Kennedy image. Joan needed to be vetted. So the couple returned to Hyannis Port two more times that summer of 1958, including the last weekend of the summer, Labor Day. Already, Rose had called Mother Elizabeth O'Byrne of Manhattanville to gather intelligence on Joan, and the reports were good. It was on that weekend, when Ted and Joan were walking down the beach from the house to Squaw Island, about a mile away, that Ted blurted, "What do you think about our getting married?" Joan said she answered, "Well, I guess it's not such a bad idea." Ted then slumped to the sand and asked, "What do we do next?" Joan said it was up to him, and then and there Ted decided they should be married as soon as they could make the arrangements.

There was, however, one last hurdle before those arrangements could be made—an important hurdle. Joe Kennedy had been away in France that summer, sheltered from the hubbub of Hyannis—he detested the flurry of activity there and preferred quiet—and he had only just returned that afternoon. Ted had already gotten Rose's approval. In fact, Rose was ecstatic. She told Joan that she had been saying her rosary that Teddy would meet a nice Catholic girl and had even told Eunice after meeting Joan, "I can't believe our luck." But Rose graded the religious test and the etiquette test. Ted needed Joe's approval for the aesthetic test—not just beauty, which Joan would easily pass, but also poise, which would be necessary for his political career. Bobby had chosen Ethel Skakel—wealthy, dynamic, vivacious. Jack had chosen Jacqueline Bouvier—regal, beautiful, cosmopolitan, the perfect consort for the presidency that Joe had in mind for his son. Joan met Joe for the first time that evening, the evening of the proposal, in the living room. As Joan recalled it, he sat in a great wing chair while she sat on an ottoman before him. "Do you love my son?" he asked, though Joan would later tell an interviewer she thought the question unnecessary. And then he proceeded to conduct what Joan called an "interview," at the end of which, satisfied, he gave his blessing. Joan returned to Bronxville with Ted at the end of the weekend. She told biographer Laurence Leamer that she wouldn't see Ted again until her engagement party. But Joan wrote her future father-in-law a thank-you note, telling him that "Ted delivered me into the arms of my father, who promised Ted he would take very good care of me over the next month," and closed with "Lots of love from a very healthy and happy little girl." Meanwhile, Rose, who had left Hyannis Port before the proposal, sent her future daughter-in-law a congratulatory telegram, expressing how "I had hoped he would win you from the moment I first met you at the Cape." But, with her customary detachment, she mistakenly called Joan "Connie."

Now the marriage train was hurtling down the track. The wedding was scheduled for November 29, Thanksgiving weekend, because Ted was still in school and couldn't take time off. (It would also be three weeks after Jack's expected reelection to the Senate—a campaign for which Ted was the nominal campaign manager.) The venue was St. Joseph's in Bronxville, Joan's lifelong church. Joan had wanted her favorite priest, Reverend John Cavanaugh, Joe's old Notre Dame friend, to officiate, but Joe Kennedy wanted Francis Cardinal Spellman, America's most well-known and powerful Catholic prelate, instead. And "that was that," Joan later recalled. As the planning continued, the couple reunited at the engagement party at Joan's home—Joan said that it was Joe who had picked out the engagement ring, which was so large she called it a "skating rink," and that Ted hadn't even seen it when he handed it to her—and then Ted was off again, shuttling between law school and helping on the final weeks of Jack's campaign, though, according to one of Jack's aides, "No matter how late he [Ted] arrived back at our house, he would always hurry to our upstairs telephone for a lengthy long-distance call to her in New York."

But as the wedding day approached, a storm was brewing. Ted had proposed impulsively. It was, it seemed, a matter of aesthetics; he felt that it was time he should be married, and Joan was the right candidate. And it was a matter of desire more than deep devotion. Joan was beautiful and dutiful and Catholic, which is what a Kennedy wife had to be, but she was also chaste. She would not be intimate with Ted before marriage; they had only shared kisses. "All our dates were well chaperoned," she told biographer Leamer. "It was sort of romantic." Romantic for Joan, but for Ted, who was a womanizer, it was also frustrating, maddening. Hence the urgency. Years later, Joan's secretary was to say that Joan had told her, "The only reason he wanted to marry me was because he couldn't get me any other way," meaning sexually. (Of course, it could also have been that in the competition between the brothers, Ted wanted to ensure that the least would land the most beautiful spouse; Jack, upon seeing Joan, dubbed her "the Dish.") In those few months, however, Ted and Joan came to realize, separately, without telling each other, that they barely knew each other and that they were rushing into the marriage, though it was Ted who had done the rushing. Ted, out sowing wild oats a few days before his wedding, confessed as much to a friend. (It may have been a sign of Ted's wavering commitment to Joan that in May, when he was dating her, Joe wrote him with another of his admonitions: "If you're going to make the political columns, let's stay out of the gossip columns.") Joan confessed her trepidation to her father, who concluded that they should postpone the wedding for a year. But when Harry Bennett made the proposal to Joe Kennedy—Joan said she had no idea her father had made such a request—Kennedy erupted, falling back again on aesthetics and shouting, by one account, that "they're not going to put in the papers that my son is being tossed over." And so the wedding proceeded, even though the two participants now had reservations about whether they should be marrying so soon—reservations that one was not allowed to have in the Kennedy family.

The wedding ceremony itself was full of portents, not only that it proceeded when the couple was so uncertain; or that Joan's choice of an officiant was denied; or that a storm blew through Bronxville the night before, sending debris through the streets; or that Jack had to exchange suits with Dick Clasby because Jack had gained weight after his spinal surgeries and his own suit didn't fit him; or that the wedding was much smaller than Bobby's wedding or Jack's wedding, only 475 guests to 3,000 at Jack's and 1,500 at Bobby's; or that during the reception, at the Siwanoy Country Club on Pondfield Road, the same road on which the Kennedys once lived, Jack, Bobby, and Ted sneaked away to watch the Army–Navy game, while Joan wondered where her groom had gone. Not only all that, but beyond all that may have been the worst portent: Harry Bennett had hired a film-and-sound crew for the wedding, and, at least as the story has been reported, while Ted, the groom, and Jack, his best man, stood at the altar waiting for Joan to come down the aisle, Jack whispered to Ted a piece of brotherly advice Joan was later to hear on her father's recording—that just because Ted was married, he didn't have to be faithful to his wife. That was the Kennedy way.

The honeymoon was a portent too. They spent their first two nights back at the Kennedy home in Palm Beach in Jack's old room, then, at Joe's insistence, flew to Nassau, to the estate of Joe's friend Lord Beaverbrook, the Canadian-born English newspaper magnate. The estate came with an unexpected amenity: Beaverbrook himself, which meant, Joan later said, that they had to have "breakfast, lunch, and dinner with this old man" and that "we had to eat what he liked to eat." One lunch was just a baked potato, and they were limited to one daiquiri because Beaverbrook only drank one daiquiri. When Beaverbrook lent them an island of his so that they could finally be alone, Joan complained that it was unbearably hot— "the most miserable day and a half of our lives." She said, "All we did was scratch ourselves. It was so awful, we just laughed. That was our honeymoon."

What Joan Kennedy didn't say is that it was their honeymoon because Joe Kennedy had dictated it to be their honeymoon. What she didn't say is that Joe Kennedy made the rules in the Kennedy family, and everyone else had to obey. Now she did too.

When Ted Kennedy had returned to Charlottesville for his final year of law school after the summer of 1958—he had spent it working on Jack's Senate reelection campaign—and just months before his marriage, he returned, as he did when he returned for his final year at Harvard, with the hope of yet another stab at redemption. Ted was a mediocre student, but there was one thing he was good at, one thing, besides football and womanizing, that he was better at than his brothers. Like Honey Fitz, Ted Kennedy could talk. Jack and Bobby were shy, uncomfortable in public; Jack had to overcome that when he began his political career, but he would still fidget, still exhibit nerves. Ted didn't fidget. Ted didn't have nerves. The youngest knew how to speak up, how to get attention, how to entertain. And Ted Kennedy couldn't only talk. From his days on the debate team at Milton and his time in public-speaking class at Harvard, he knew how to frame an argument, how to sell an argument. Ted Kennedy may not have been the most brilliant legal mind, but Ted Kennedy could present a case.

And he had been working on a case since his second year of law school. Like most law schools, Virginia had a moot court competition, a chance for two-man teams to argue a case before a panel, which would then render a decision. Every student at Virginia was required to argue two cases in class, but that was just for the experience. Those who wanted to compete needed to prepare a third case. And Ted wanted to compete. He approached Tunney with the idea; it was "something we should do," he said. Tunney hadn't given it much thought. Some of the best students in the class would compete, students much better than he and Ted. It would take tremendous preparation, hours and hours, even weeks or months of preparation; the ability to speak well wasn't enough. And the competition lasted two years—both the second and third years. And Tunney didn't think they would win. Nobody thought they would win. But Ted Kennedy could speak, and Ted Kennedy could compete. And Ted Kennedy was a plugger—not quick but slow and steady and determined, the qualities he'd had on the Harvard football team. For him, moot court was like Harvard football, and like Harvard football, it had the same goal: a chance for Kennedy to prove himself.

The plugger worked hard, "*extremely* hard," Tunney said, at "writing our briefs and preparing our arguments and practicing our arguments." He added, "Up early every morning." There were three oral arguments that first year of competition—the second year of law school—each one an elimination round. They won the first—narrowly, 2–1—with three senior students acting as judges. One of the judges told Tunney afterward that the only reason they won was Ted. Ted was "forceful," Tunney recalled, right from the outset. He was, Tunney said, "by far the outstanding one," between the two of them. "He had great energy, great ability to succinctly phrase an argument, an excellent voice and timbre, one that projected a lot of vitality and dynamism." But Tunney took the criticism to heart. He improved largely, he said, by watching Ted, seeing Ted's command—and then they won two more decisions, unanimously, which qualified them for the competition in their senior year.

Now they were a team—a good team—and they trained to get better, trained just as Ted had trained for football during his Harvard years. They would find another team—a team they would not be competing against in the next round—and practice against them, honing their skills of argumentation. And they would go out into the woods around their house and declaim, "just speak to the trees," Tunney said—he compared the routine to Demosthenes practicing his speech—to work on their projection. And the two pluggers, the two middling students, won the quarterfinals and then the semifinals. By this time, the two, previously known more for their revelry than their academics, had become a phenomenon. Underclassmen were attending their oral arguments to see, Tunney would say, "how this team of Kennedy and Tunney were able to do it."

The final argument, though, was different, very different. This time, the judges were not students but three jurists—prominent jurists: former Supreme Court justice Stanley Reed, chancellor of England Lord Kilmuir, Circuit Court of Appeals judge Clement Haynsworth, and Andrew Parker, the president of the Law School Association. And this time the competition was an event, a big event, held on Law Day. And this time there was an audience of hundreds, including Tunney's mother and Ted's sister Pat and brother Bobby, who had only advanced two rounds when he competed. And this time, with no other team to practice against, since all but one other had been eliminated, Ted and Tunney recruited some of the best students in the class to pepper them with questions, to sharpen them: the two average students using brilliant ones. And this time Ted was newly married—Joan had assumed the role of housewife in Charlottesville—and, despite his pre-marriage jitters, he was extremely happy. Ted called what Joan and he shared in those early days of marriage "euphoria," but euphoria wasn't necessarily the best state of mind for the painstaking, detailed preparation necessary for the competition. Thankfully, there was more than euphoria, and this *was* helpful. Years later, Ted told his son Patrick that he had a sense of "adventure and optimism" with Joan, that he had "started to feel that he was the master of his own destiny"—this young man whose destiny had always been determined by his father. So, despite the distractions of a new marriage, Ted Kennedy applied himself because he had started to feel that he wasn't inferior, that he could succeed. And that was critical. Because this time, everything was at stake, not only a validation of Tunney's and Ted's law school education but a validation of the two young men themselves and proof that they were not the least. "Coming in second was just no good," Joe Kennedy had always said in direct contradiction of his other advice to just do your best. "Win, win, win."

That afternoon of April 18, 1959, Law Day, Ted and Tunney argued before a packed house in the ballroom of Newcomb Hall. They argued a mock case, the *United States v. the Akkro Corporation*—a case involving a provision in the Taft-Hartley Act, an act governing business-union relationships, that prohibited corporate executives from making campaign contributions. Tunney and Ted argued for the appellee, Akkro, which had given $8,600 to defray the cost of a television ad endorsing a candidate. Tunney asserted that the law was an infringement on free speech and that in a modern society where mass communications were necessary to promote one's point of view, to prohibit contributions like Akkro's would be to prohibit Akkro from exercising its first amendment rights. Ted, who made the concluding argument, made the point that the statute was vaguely drawn, and he used the example of a contribution to a nickel cup of coffee to demonstrate that the statute contained no time frame as to what was permissible and what wasn't. Tunney and Ted argued well. And that afternoon, the two ordinary students won the Moot Appellate Court competition—won it over fifty other teams that had competed over the previous two years. When the decision was announced, Ted pounded his fist on the table triumphantly. Congratulating each other afterward, Ted and Tunney talked about how they had spent two years "dreaming of achieving this goal," and Tunney would say that "it seemed so impossible"—impossible because of their own sense of inadequacy. Tunney called it the "principal academic achievement in our lives up to that point," and said that afterward, he got two job offers from Wall Street firms based on his oral argument. Decades later, Ted would call the victory the "most exciting and rewarding moment of my life to that time and among those of all time." But it wasn't just the fifty teams they had beaten that gave Ted that thrill. It was being able to say that he had beaten a Kennedy. "Ted just loved the fact that he had been able to excel at something in law school where Bobby had not done as well," Tunney recalled. And there was another thrill, this from one last commendation—the most important commendation, the only commendation that could lift the "burden" of disappointment that Tunney had referenced, the only one that could redeem Ted Kennedy. Joe Kennedy sent Ted a congratulatory note: "Scholastically, it certainly fits with anything anybody has ever done before—including your father!"

But exhilarating as it was, as rewarding as it was, it wouldn't be victory that would leave the most lasting impression on Ted Kennedy from these years at Virginia. It would be all those defeats and disappointments along the way that had led to Virginia. Ted Kennedy, the boy who, as his father said, couldn't get away with anything, had known what it was like to fail, what it was like to disappoint, what it was like to be disrespected. The moot court triumph couldn't expunge that. Ted Kennedy knew failure, and Ted Kennedy would use that knowledge.

The Succession

JOE KENNEDY HAD plans for his sons, big plans, the biggest plans. He had had them for decades, and the sons acceded because the Kennedy boys always acceded to their father. In those plans, they would assume the political role Joe Kennedy himself had abandoned, was forced to abandon, when he preached defeatism during World War II. The Kennedys would later be identified with moral passion and with firing the nation's soul, but there was no morality in those plans, no civic mission or public good. The plans were political, and politics for Joe Kennedy was an instrument for power, for retribution, for status. The presidency that he sought for his sons after he had once hoped to attain it for himself was the highest rung on his social ladder, the rebuff to all those who had rebuffed him, and it was the beginning of what he believed would be a dynasty—the surest rebuff. As early as 1957, in a *Saturday Evening Post* article that was engineered by Joe Kennedy to promote Jack Kennedy's 1960 presidential aspirations, those plans were being disseminated. "Fervent admirers," the article said, "confidently look forward to the day when Jack will be in the White House, Bobby will serve in the Cabinet as attorney general, and Teddy will be the senator from Massachusetts."

Joe Kennedy had plans, but he had no moral purpose or ideology to purvey; his politics were incoherent, patchwork, and while he had a path that his sons were expected to follow, *had* to follow, he didn't try to indoctrinate them in his views, confused as those views were, and in fact encouraged them to think independently, sending Joe Jr. to England to study with the socialist political scientist Harold Laski. "The generation that follows me may have to stand for everything that I stood against," he once said, "and that includes my sons." To the extent that Joe Kennedy had any kind of political-belief system, it was his allegiance to Irish Catholicism and its discontents, a politics that challenged Protestant disdain, which became the basis for the Kennedy juggernaut. Recalling Jack Kennedy's first congressional race, in 1946, *Boston Globe* reporter John Aloysius Farrell, said, "They put on a tea at the Commander Hotel in Cambridge, and the Kennedy girls were there with Joe, Rose, and Jack. If you were an Irish American woman or maybe even an Italian American woman in the district, you were there that day. The line stretched out of the ballroom, out into Cambridge, down the sidewalk. Everybody was dressed up. They had their white gloves on and all they wanted to do was touch the Irish American royalty, because that's what they [the Kennedys] were." Joe Kennedy's resentment at the Brahmin establishment had fueled his life. Now it fueled his son's campaign.

That fuel, however, was the fuel of liberalism. Joe Kennedy was not a liberal as so many Irish Catholic Democrats were, especially after Franklin Roosevelt's election had seemed to give the nation's poor and marginalized new purpose. He had no particular concern for the disadvantaged or dispossessed, save for Irish Catholics. Joe Kennedy was not a New Dealer, despite serving in the Roosevelt administration, and he had no interest in government palliatives. Though he defended Franklin Roosevelt against charges of undermining capitalism—"There has scarcely been a liberal piece of legislation during the last sixty years that has not been opposed as communistic," he once told a business group—what he took away from his experience with the administration was umbrage at the way Roosevelt had treated him, which was, he felt, disrespectfully. Shortly after Roosevelt died in April 1945, Kennedy wrote his daughter Kathleen that the death had very little impact on the nation: "You rarely, if ever, hear his name mentioned, and there is no doubt that it was a great thing for the country. He had stirred up a hatred in the minds of at least half the country, and no matter whether he proposed anything good or bad, half the country would be against it and half for it." (Of course, this was patently false—an angry man's distortion.) And Joe Kennedy was not a defender of civil liberties or an opponent of red-baiting. He had supported Richard Nixon's Senate campaign against Democrat and liberal Helen Gahagan Douglas, whom Nixon had accused of communist leanings, donating $150,000 to Nixon's war chest, and he was an ardent supporter of his fellow Irish Catholic Joseph McCarthy and of Senator McCarthy's war on alleged communist subversion in America. "The strongest man in America next to Eisenhower," he told his friend Lord Beaverbrook of McCarthy. And when an aide to Jack circulated a statement attacking McCarthy during Jack's 1952 Senate race, Joe snapped, "You and your . . . sheeny friends . . . are trying to ruin my son's career." So supportive of McCarthy was Joe Kennedy that he got Bobby the position of minority counsel on McCarthy's Investigations Subcommittee.

Joe Kennedy was none of these things, but his son John Kennedy, over time, would become many of them—including a liberal—in no small measure because his father had underestimated how difficult it would be to separate stoking Irish Catholic resentments, which he had done throughout his sons' childhoods, from the liberalism that seemed an amelioration of those resentments. Like his father, Jack had come to politics with no essential belief system. Having arrived through succession, replacing his brother Joe as the anointed Kennedy, his primary interest was placating his father and getting himself elected, though with no great enthusiasm over the latter. "When the war is over and you are out there in sunny California giving them five and a half inches for a six-inch pavement," Jack wrote his Navy buddy Paul "Red" Fay, "I'll be back here with Dad trying to parlay a lost PT boat and a bad back into a political advantage. I tell you, Dad is ready right now and can't understand why Johnny boy isn't 'all engines ahead full.'" In the beginning, he did share his father's skepticism about liberals, suspecting them of elitism at the very least. "I'd be very happy to tell them [liberals] I'm not a liberal," Jack said, adding, "I'm not comfortable with those people." And in the beginning he also shared his father's anti-communist truculence, telling a Harvard seminar conducted by his old professor Arthur Holcombe that he was "happy" Nixon had beaten Douglas and that he supported Joseph McCarthy's crusade, though he was less enthusiastic about it as time went on— a concession to his presidential aspirations. By 1958, when he was asked if he considered himself a liberal, he said he did—meaning, presumably, that he backed the initiatives of the New Deal and that he supported civil rights. In the Democratic party, he really could not have said otherwise if he hoped to be the party's standard bearer.

But that was in the beginning, when Jack Kennedy was basically an old-fashioned ethnic ward politician, not a reform politician in the mold of Adlai Stevenson, the Democrats' erudite two-time presidential nominee, and that was when he was still his father's son, politically speaking. Jack Kennedy would change, and he would change out of political necessity. If he wanted the presidency—and he did want the presidency, if only as a form of personal vindication over his late brother or as a gift to his father—he had to moderate his more conservative positions. The reform Democrats, those Stevenson Democrats, were already distrustful of Kennedy for being a temporizer, for being Catholic and supporting Joe McCarthy, and for being Joe Kennedy's son—Joe Kennedy, who was anathema to liberals. Jack needed to disarm them—disarm them because a booming postwar economy that would increase personal income 80 percent between 1945 and 1960 and reduce working hours and increase educational opportunity was creating new social dynamics, liberal dynamics. And, on a more practical note, he had to disarm them because those dynamics, along with a recession and general sense of discontent over America's lagging in the Cold War against Russia, had helped generate a Democratic wave in the 1958 midterm elections, giving the party forty-eight more seats in the House and fifteen more in the Senate. (Ten Republican incumbents lost.) In the Senate, it was the largest swing from one party to another in United States history. The incoming Democratic Senate class constituted a new generation of liberals, which included Philip Hart of Michigan, Edmund Muskie of Maine, and Eugene McCarthy of Minnesota, and began to tip the Senate's center of power from the Southern conservatives. More, these liberals brought a new moral energy to the Senate, especially when it came to civil rights. Politics had been little infused with morality since Eisenhower's election, except for touting America's moral superiority over communism. Now it was. Jack Kennedy, who was reelected to his second Senate term by a record margin in Massachusetts in that same wave, 874,608 votes, the largest margin in the nation, had to woo those liberals, prove himself to them, to get their support for his presidential aspirations. In effect, he had to disown his father politically. And he did.

But pragmatism wasn't all that guided Jack Kennedy, only mostly pragmatism. Joe Kennedy was right when he said that his sons might have to stand against everything he had stood for. Even as he had carefully guided their careers, he had inculcated independence of thought in them—independence made more powerful by how domineering Joe Kennedy had always been, more powerful by how much his sons chafed at that dominance even as they benefited from it, and more powerful because of their own life experiences. Bobby Kennedy, who was in thrall to his father and listened to his anti-Semitic tirades, would, as a young man scarcely out of college, come to challenge that prejudice, saying it violated the teachings of Catholicism, and he would exhibit a sensitivity to the poor, some speculated because he himself was the runt of the Kennedy litter and because Joe made him feel that way. Jack, who was less in thrall to his father, was also less inclined to defy him, though perhaps his frequent illnesses, his infirmity, and his sense of his own mortality—he had a mordant wit about when he would die—connected him, as Franklin Roosevelt's infantile paralysis had, to those who suffered. Not much of this empathy surfaced during his Senate career. His aide and chief speechwriter, Theodore Sorensen, would say of the young Jack that he was "shaped primarily by political expedience instead of basic human principles," but out of his expedience gradually arose a certain moral sense—that, for example, one needed to support civil rights if one expected to be the Democratic nominee for president, which would eventually transform him from a trimmer to an advocate when it came to those rights; Sorensen would also write, later, that "beneath the cool exterior of the ambitious politician was a good and decent man with a conscience that told him what was right and a heart that cared about the well-being of those around him," which certainly couldn't have been said of his father.

Teddy, the most empathetic of the Kennedys, in part because he was the most disrespected of the Kennedys, had watched most of his brother's political ascension from afar. He was only fourteen when Jack first ran for Congress in 1946, and he became an errand boy for the campaign when he wasn't in school. But he did remember his brother taking him to Washington after that election and taking him to the House floor and then the Senate floor, both chambers empty with Congress out of session, and he remembered Jack's advice to him: Now that he'd seen these places, he should take an interest in what happened in them. When Jack ran for the Senate in 1952, Bobby ran the campaign, and Ted was in the Army. But during the 1958 reelection bid, Jack's big campaign to position himself for his presidential run, Jack appointed Ted his campaign manager, and even though it was more titular than actual, another way to fuse the family—Bobby's old friend Kenny O'Donnell and another political veteran, Lawrence O'Brien, ran the campaign in reality—Ted shuttled from Charlottesville, where he was still in law school, to Massachusetts every week, to do his part for his brother and the family. He would shake hands at factory gates, flag down cars to slap on Kennedy bumper stickers (when Joe Kennedy complained that he didn't see enough bumper stickers,

Teddy grabbed a stack and raced to Sumner Tunnel to pass them out), and canvass door-to-door to get pledges of support. One old Massachusetts operative named Gerard Doherty called Ted "the chief signature getter in the world" and said Ted would do whatever it took to win them, even sing or dance a jig.

This is how Jack liked it. He liked pressuring Teddy, liked to know his errant younger brother, over whose future he often fretted, was exercising discipline. And Ted Kennedy *was* disciplined. Jack had told O'Brien at the beginning of the campaign, "Teddy's starting from scratch. Push him. Make him work." But O'Brien said he soon realized he didn't have to push Teddy. Teddy was up at dawn every day he was in Massachusetts, working to get his brother elected. His brother-in-law Stephen Smith said Ted "worked like hell," worked at everything except the retail politics of dealing with people. He didn't have to work at that. Dealing with people, Smith said, came easy to him. Like Honey Fitz, he loved people.

The one who didn't work hard was Jack Kennedy, who had a well-deserved reputation for indolence. In Congress, he was frequently absent from the House and then the Senate due to his illnesses and his debilitating back condition, but he wasn't particularly industrious when he was there. The House and the Senate were stepping-stones. He had almost no interest in legislation, only in promoting his presidential ambitions— a show horse. Tip O'Neill, Jack's successor to his congressional seat, said of Jack, "In all my years in public life, I've never seen a congressman get so much press while doing so little work." Political columnist Clayton Fritchey wrote in *Harper's* of Jack in Congress: "It was quite clear to his colleagues from the first that he was not going to spend a lifetime gradually working his way up in the Senate by dutifully adhering to the Club rules of self-effacement, routine chores, routine thoughts, and cultivation of his elders. He was bent on a national constituency from the outset. . . ." It was no different in his 1958 campaign. He spent fewer than twenty days in Massachusetts that fall, which provided Ted with an opportunity to be his brother's surrogate. Early on in the campaign, Ted would attend fundraisers with Jack and listen to him, listen to the issues. Later on, in the last two to three months of the campaign, when he wasn't in Charlottesville, Ted would fill in for Jack, speak for him. And with Jack absent, Teddy would travel with O'Brien around Massachusetts, learning the state "intensively," he said. He learned the scheduling and the field operations and the TV and radio buys. He even learned the ethnic rivalries when a group of state Italian leaders objected vehemently to Ted one day about Kennedy's slogan, "Make your vote count." Ted explained that the slogan implicitly meant, "Make your vote count for Jack for president in 1960." They countered that *they* interpreted the slogan as meaning that a vote only counted if it was cast for an Irishman, and they resented it. Ted said the campaign had to tear up all its literature, bring in an advertising executive who was a friend of Joe Kennedy's, and then sit down with the executive all day long trying out new slogans. But this was, in his brother's absence, an education in the vicissitudes of electoral politics. And when Ted Kennedy learned something, something political, he wasn't likely to forget it.

And he wasn't likely to forget it because he knew his father had political ambitions for him, and he would need that knowledge if he was to fulfill those ambitions, which he intended to do.

Now began the final preparations for the culmination of the big plan—the plan of Joe Kennedy's lifetime, the plan to elect Jack Kennedy president of the United States. The first organizational meeting was held at Palm Beach on April 1, 1959. But Ted wasn't there. Ted was still finishing his final term at law school. He was present at a second, bigger organizational meeting at Hyannis Port in October, which was a sign of his older brother's respect—there were only sixteen men invited, the inner circle—as well as a sign of how deeply involved the family was expected to be. He also attended a later meeting in New York, at which Jack asked him what part of the country he would be interested in stomping to help Jack win the nomination. Ted chose the eleven states of the West because he hadn't spent much time there, but he also said later that he chose the West because none of the Kennedys had had much experience there and, always looking to carve out his own niche, "I wanted an area of my own responsibility." Shortly after that meeting—armed, he said, with memoranda written by Jack's chief aide, Ted Sorensen, listing delegates and local party leaders—he headed west for the next six weeks, primarily to make contact with those leaders, learning about them and about their states the way he had learned his own local politicians and Massachusetts in 1958. But Bobby and Jack were not going to entrust the Western states entirely to their young brother, even though that section of the country was regarded as more partial to Senate majority leader Lyndon Johnson, a potential candidate, than to John Kennedy. (Johnson, however, was too proud to declare his interest in the race, thinking Kennedy was no match for him and thinking the race would come to him, which left those Western states open to Ted's blandishments.) Teddy shared the duties with a seasoned white-haired attorney and political operative from Chicago named Hyman Raskin, who was a veteran of the Stevenson presidential campaigns, and the two—the twenty-seven-year-old freshly minted lawyer, and the dignified fifty-year-old pol—formed a team, albeit an odd one, traveling through the West. Ted said his job was to excite the contacts about Jack's candidacy, give them the emotional pitch, then Raskin would sit down with them and talk pragmatics: What did Chicago Mayor Richard J. Daley think of Kennedy? What did Pennsylvania party boss David Lawrence think? "It was a one–two punch," as Ted described it.

And that fall of 1959 and into the winter of early 1960, he traveled through Colorado, where he spent a week with the Colorado campaign chairman, Byron White, a former football All-American turned lawyer who, Ted said, ate a T-bone steak every night of that week, washed down with a Coors beer, and then got up every morning at six o'clock to do push-ups. And during that week, White introduced him to party leaders, two or three dozen of them. At week's end, White suggested they take the red-eye to Washington but also suggested they go skiing before the flight. When they arrived in Washington and Jack saw Teddy's tan, he asked suspiciously whether he had been skiing with White instead of making calls and meeting delegates, and Teddy sheepishly confessed he had skied, but "only for a day." White, meanwhile, assured Jack that Ted had been working.

And Ted *had* been working, working hard, as the plugger always did, to compensate for what he felt he lacked in ability, though it wasn't a duty for him. It was what he was expected to do for family and what he was doing for his own political education, and he professed to enjoy it. He had gone to New Mexico, not once but three times in 1959 alone, and again in January 1960. He had gotten his pilot's license while at Virginia and spent three days flying around Arizona in a tiny plane, carrying Sorensen's four-page list of contacts, to places like Globe (for breakfast), Show Low (for lunch), and Flagstaff (for dinner), meeting with delegates to the national convention, delegates who could vote for Jack. "Called all the people. They all came out to these little places. Wrote my own notes," Ted recalled. And the notes were extensive, detailing who he had met and what they might do for a Kennedy candidacy. Then the next day, Prescott (for breakfast), Yuma (for lunch), and Nogales (for dinner), and the same routine. Three days alone in that small plane. And then on to the next state and the next, eventually hitting Montana and Utah as well.

Ted Kennedy's schedule was unrelenting. The campaign was always intended to be a family affair—Joe believed family were the only ones you could really trust—and everyone was expected to be on hand, no matter what. Only the meaning of "on hand" had changed. By late winter, Ted was no longer a roving ambassador, collecting delegates one by one, but was now, as the primary season began, a surrogate on the stump for his brother. No matter what. Joan was about to give birth to their first child, and she retreated to her parents' home in Bronxville to await the delivery. She gave birth on February 27 to Kara Anne, but Ted had to race to get there before Kara arrived. He'd been in New Hampshire, working for Jack, even though the primary there was uncontested. That made no difference. Joe had taught them that Kennedy siblings always came first. No matter what.

And Jack Kennedy needed those primaries—only sixteen of them then—needed them desperately, even though the bulk of delegates were chosen not by primary but by party conventions, because Jack Kennedy's roots in those conventions were not as deep as those of his competitors. His competition for the nomination—Senator Hubert Humphrey, Senator Stuart Symington, and Senate majority leader Lyndon Baines Johnson—were all institutionalists of the Senate, and all had deeper roots in the party than he, especially Johnson, so deep that Symington and Johnson decided not to contest the primaries but to rely instead on their support among party officials. (In the wings was two-time nominee Adlai Stevenson, who was still the favorite of the intellectual liberals in the party.) Kennedy not only had to prove his liberal bona fides; he had to prove he could win, despite his youth (he was forty-three), his questionable liberal credentials, and, above all, his Catholicism. The primaries were the means of doing that. With much more limited resources, Humphrey did challenge Kennedy, choosing two states to square off against him head-to-head: Wisconsin, bordering his home state of Minnesota, on April 5, and West Virginia on May 10.

The Kennedys hit Wisconsin like an invading army. Ted spent seven weeks there, with Joan and his newborn daughter parked at the Hotel Milwaukee while Ted did what he had done in Massachusetts in 1958, the plugger plugging, getting up at 5:30 A.M., shaking hands, making speeches, handing out campaign literature—anything to secure his older

brother a victory. When Ted was campaigning at a ski-jumping tourna-
ment near Madison, someone dared him to don skis and jump himself,
and reckless Teddy said he would, if they promised to vote for Jack. Then
he did jump—a story that would become part of Ted Kennedy lore—
though he admitted he would have taken off the skis and gone down the
side of the jump if he thought his brother wouldn't have sent him "back in
Washington, licking stamps and envelopes" if he had. (Later that day,
while slapping stickers on the inside rear windows of cars instead of slapping them on the bumpers, he was bitten by a dog.) In the end, Jack Kennedy won handily, 56 percent to 44 percent, with Humphrey complaining
that he "felt like an independent merchant competing against a chain
store." He was.

But Wisconsin, Kennedy detractors felt, hadn't been a fair test. Wisconsin had a large Catholic population, 32 percent Catholic, and the Kennedys had steamrolled Humphrey there with superior organization and
much more money and that large Catholic vote. (Moreover, Republican
Catholics could cross over there, which was why Humphrey felt he lost.)
West Virginia was different. It was coal country, union country, which
would favor Humphrey with his deep ties to labor, and it was Protestant
country—95 percent Protestant. Early polls showed Humphrey well
ahead. But once again, the Kennedys invaded a state, fully realizing that
if Jack won there over Humphrey, he was likely to win the nomination, but
that if he lost, his campaign would have suffered a serious, possibly fatal
blow, demonstrating that a Catholic could not win. This time Ted was sent
down into the mines in the West Virginia backwaters; he later said that
one image of miners there, heading to a shed in which, for forty-five minutes, they slowly removed their sooty clothes, remained with him long
after the election. (Joan campaigned there too, despite having given birth
less than three months earlier; all the Kennedys were expected to be on
hand, to pitch in, no matter what.) It was while Ted was doing this duty in
Beckley, West Virginia, that he received what *Time* magazine called a "crisis message" from Jack. Delivering twenty or more speeches a day, Jack
had lost his voice and needed a replacement. Ted arrived in nearby Ravens-
wood and, with Jack standing by his side, enthusiastically read his brother's speech. As *Time* reported it, Ted was saying, "Do you want a man who
will give the country leadership? Do you want a man who has vigor and
vision?" when Jack grabbed the microphone from him and rasped, "I
would just like to tell my brother that you cannot be elected president until

you are thirty-five years of age." "So back to the boondocks I went," Teddy said.

It was a rough primary, a dirty primary. The diplomat and educator Max Kampelman recalled being at a Washington airport and seeing the Democratic national committeeman of Connecticut, John Bailey, a Kennedy supporter, holding a suitcase full of cash to give to ministers and local officials in West Virginia to get them on the Kennedy bandwagon, when Ted brushed past him. Bailey, he said, "shooed" Ted away, fearful that the suitcase might pop open and Ted would see what was going on. But Ted must have known. All the Kennedys must have known. The highest morality for Joe Kennedy was victory, and he wasn't going to let his son lose this primary. "What's a hundred million if it will help Jack?" Joe asked one of his closest confidants. The Kennedys even recruited Franklin Roosevelt Jr., his father practically a saint in West Virginia, to campaign for Jack—and Roosevelt cast false aspersions on Hubert Humphrey's activities during the war, saying he had sought draft deferments when he was actually prevented from serving, despite his best efforts, because of physical issues. And in the end, the money, the Roosevelt imprimatur and the Roosevelt slander, and the family assault succeeded. So did a speech that Jack delivered the day before the primary on his fealty to America over the Catholic Church—a speech that election chronicler Theodore White called "the finest TV broadcast I have ever heard a political candidate make." Jack beat Humphrey, 61 percent to 39 percent, or, more accurately, the Kennedys beat Humphrey, who withdrew from the race the next day. At a victory party in Hyannis Port, as *The Boston Post* reported it, Joe Kennedy's "eyes glowed when he spoke of the work his three sons had done in the primaries across the country. . . . He had special praise for his youngest son, Ted. 'When Jack's voice was gone in West Virginia, Ted really took over and kept the ball rolling.'"

But the nomination was still not Jack Kennedy's. Having vanquished Humphrey, there was still the convention in Los Angeles, still Lyndon Johnson and Adlai Stevenson to contend with. Johnson was especially fearsome, with his Southern support and his roots in the Democratic establishment, and Johnson aide Bobby Baker would later accuse Teddy of circulating stories about the condition of Johnson's heart—he had suffered a near-fatal heart attack in 1955—before the convention to weaken that support. Whether or not Ted did so, the Kennedys were enterprising. Ted said that they reviewed the delegate counts every morning and "we knew where we stood to within a vote and a half." The Johnson forces felt that if they could stall Kennedy on the first ballot and get to a second ballot, they would stop his momentum and build Johnson's. As the balloting approached, the Kennedys knew it was going to be close. They had determined from their head counts that Wyoming would cast the votes that could put Jack Kennedy over the top—Wyoming, which Ted had visited seven times that year on Jack's behalf. But only *could.* By their reckoning, Kennedy was four votes short of the nomination. Just before the balloting, Ted went down to the convention floor to talk with Tracy McCracken, the state's leading newspaper publisher, and, as a Democratic national committeeman, a man with tremendous influence within the delegation. Ted knew they already had ten of the state's fifteen delegates, but he also knew they needed those four additional delegates to win. So he asked McCracken, who was personally leaning to Lyndon Johnson: If the nomination came down to those last few votes, could he deliver the final five to John Kennedy? McCracken was incredulous. He couldn't see how it would be that close, but he promised Ted, "If it comes down to it, though, I will." Ted was standing in the middle of the delegation when Wyoming was called during the roll. At that point, Wyoming senator Gale McGee, knowing how tight the balloting was, took the microphone and pleaded, "Give me four votes! We can put him over the top! Please give me four votes!" One of Johnson's supporters attempted to take the microphone from McGee, and others were screaming at him, but McGee held firm, and with Ted hovering over McCracken and shouting, "Do it! Do it! Do it!" McCracken announced the vote: all fifteen delegates for Kennedy. McGee began jumping and slapping Ted on the back.

Ted Kennedy had wrangled those votes. And Jack Kennedy was the Democratic nominee.

There had never been a presidential candidate quite like Jack Kennedy. For one thing, there had never been a candidate as young as Jack Kennedy. (Theodore Roosevelt had assumed the presidency at a younger age, but he had ascended to the office through the assassination of William McKinley.) Kennedy had come into politics young—he was twenty-eight when he first ran for Congress; thirty-four when he first ran for the Senate—and he appealed, said Robert Kennedy, to "people who had not been involved in politics and a lot of servicemen." And because he was in a hurry, he had been the youngest candidate in all his races. Kennedy himself thought that made a difference in 1960. "I've come on the political scene when the leadership is old," he told one reporter. "The president is old, his health has been affected, his leadership is not wholly successful, and therefore I think there is a desire to turn a new page and start with newer leadership, fresher, and we hope more vigorous."

There had never been a candidate as telegenic as Jack Kennedy—"the most telegenic person in public life," *New York Times* television critic Jack Gould called him as early as 1956, when he captivated the Democratic National Convention that year. And Jack Kennedy was not only telegenic; Jack Kennedy understood television. As early as 1959, Kennedy himself had written an article for *TV Guide,* describing the influence of television on politics and how it had "altered drastically the nature of our political campaigns, conventions, constituents, candidates and costs." Kennedy had benefited, benefited greatly, from that alteration. And having lived his life within an image, the image Joe Kennedy had purveyed of his family, Jack Kennedy thought that the images the public saw on the television screen were "likely to be uncannily correct." And again, having lived within a family in which aesthetics were primary, Kennedy understood the value of aesthetics, understood how easily aesthetics could usurp policy, even usurp the entire party structure, so that Jack Kennedy didn't seem to *need* the old pols the way previous candidates and his competitors had—though he knew how to manipulate and use them. But he could appeal to the public over their heads, could sell his persona—a star's persona—directly to the public.

There had never been a candidate as self-possessed as Jack Kennedy or one who seemed as self-knowing as Jack Kennedy, not even Franklin Roosevelt. Teddy Kennedy was roiled by doubts of his own adequacy. Jack Kennedy was never ruffled by doubts of any kind, so secure was he in who he was, which was one endowment from his father, who instilled confidence in all but Teddy. When asked if the campaign would tire him, Jack answered that he wouldn't be tired but his opponent, Vice President Richard Nixon, would be. "Because I know who I am and I don't have to worry about adapting and changing," he said. "All I have to do at each stop is be myself. But Nixon doesn't know who he is, and so each time he makes a speech he has to decide which Nixon he is, and that will be very exhausting."

And perhaps above all, there had never been a candidate who understood America's untapped desires the way Jack Kennedy did, who understood politics as a kind of ongoing movie the way Jack Kennedy, who had lived within the Kennedy family movie, did. In an essay on Kennedy, "Superman Comes to the Supermarket," in *Esquire* magazine that November, Norman Mailer analyzed the psychic underpinnings that made Kennedy so very different from conventional politicians like Nixon. Mailer thought Kennedy operated underneath the nation's politics, where Jack fired what Mailer called "the subterranean river of untapped, ferocious, lonely and romantic desires . . . which is the dream life of the nation." And Kennedy, eschewing conventional politics, appealed to the voters' vision of a dream life. Whether by design or good fortune, he hit the American psyche the way movie stars did. He excited the country the way movie stars did. He stirred yearnings and passions the way movie stars did, though he had little passion himself. He created a "new life of drama," the way movie stars did. Jack Kennedy opened the country to its romantic possibilities. One could vote "for glamour or for ugliness," Mailer wrote of the choice between Kennedy and Nixon, and he questioned whether the country "would be brave enough" to choose glamour and the things that came with it.

Those were the stakes. And they would be the stakes raised not only for John Kennedy but for his brothers too, including his youngest brother, who would also summon "the dream life of the nation." That would henceforth be what Kennedys did. They would be called America's royalty. But they were really America's political movie stars and, as such, they would reshape American politics.

And so began the battle Norman Mailer had characterized as one between ordinary politics and the politics of romance. Ted again was responsible for the West, now including Alaska and Hawaii, mostly states that Kennedy had little realistic chance of winning, which made Teddy the least in the campaign as he had been in the family, even though, according to his Harvard friend Claude Hooton, who accompanied him on some of his swings, he was, as everyone had always said, "the hardest-working man I've ever known." He got up at 4 A.M. He hit the factory gates, as he always had, and, by his own reckoning, spoke at four or five college campuses each day. In Wyoming, taking another dare like the one at the ski jump in Wisconsin, he attended a rodeo and rode a bucking bronco.* In California,

---

* In Ted's memoir, he dated the bronco ride to a pre-primary visit to Montana where he was

with his law school roommate John Tunney, who took a leave from the Air Force to join him, he stumped the state for twenty days. Over the three and a half months between the convention and the election, he saw Joan and his new baby, who were living in an apartment in San Francisco, only thirteen nights. But that was the Kennedy way—Joe Kennedy's way. In the end, Jack narrowly won the election—glamour, Mailer had said, could be terrifying—but lost all but three of the thirteen states Teddy managed for him. In the end, Joe Kennedy finally had his president.

But it was still not quite over. Nixon had won California by only 35,000 votes out of 6.5 million cast, and Jack sent Ted and Bobby to California in case there was a recount. There wasn't—Kennedy didn't need the state's electoral votes to win in any case—so Bobby and Ethel, and Ted and Joan, and Bobby's close friend David Hackett and his wife went to Acapulco to recuperate for a few days. When they returned, Jack rewarded his family with engraved silver cigarette cases. Joan's inscription, prompted by reports that when she campaigned in West Virginia, listeners were too distracted by her looks to hear her message, was: "Joan Kennedy—Too Beautiful to Use"—though, of course, Jack Kennedy had used her, as he had used all of them.

But even then, for Ted Kennedy, it was not over. He returned from his brief Mexican vacation with the idea that he was going to have some position in the administration and that "I was going to be thinking big thoughts and be talking to important people." But Jack had another campaign in mind for him: Teddy's own future campaign. Always looking out for Ted's career, Jack suggested that his younger brother join a three-man delegation of the Senate Committee on Foreign Relations, senators Frank Church, Gale McGee, and Edward Moss, who had already embarked two days earlier on a tour of West Africa; Jack thought it would be helpful for Ted to familiarize himself with that part of the world, and he believed Ted could then write a speech about Africa that he could deliver around Massachusetts, should he decide to seek state office. (Given Joe Kennedy's ambitions, there was little doubt Ted would seek such an office.) Jack phoned a Foreign Relations Committee staff person himself to make the arrangement. Though Ted was just off the campaign trail after nearly two years—

---

told everyone had gone to the rodeo, and when he asked if he could be announced to the crowd was advised that he could be announced only if he rode a bronco—which he did. Edward Kennedy, *True Compass* (New York: Twelve, 2009), 128–129.

Jack brushed off his protest that Joan might not understand his leaving so soon—Ted took a flight to London that night, December 1, to catch the weekly plane to Rhodesia. He was gone a month—nearly all of December—during which time Joan rented a small fourth-floor apartment on Louisburg Square in Boston, near the capitol, and then, while it was being renovated, took a loft, which had formerly been servants' quarters. As he had been nearly absent for his daughter's birth, Ted was absent for his family's housewarming, which, again, was a matter of Kennedy priorities. Ted had no choice. Joe Kennedy's family came first.

Ted hadn't made the choice to go to Africa any more than he had made the choice to go to Harvard or law school or to work on his brother's campaign. There were no choices in the Kennedy family, at least not career choices. There were only wishes—Joe Kennedy's wishes and now Jack's too.

The interregnum between the election and the inauguration should have been time for the Kennedys to rest and reunite after their long siege on the presidency and before the presidency itself began. When Ted returned from Africa, he and Joan were finally together after all the months apart—long months devoted to his brother. Over Christmas 1959, anticipating Jack's campaign, Joan had resolved "to be ready to go anywhere and accommodate myself to my husband's schedule," and she had. Now that was over. But the election victory had only served to solidify the Kennedy tribe at the expense of Ted and Joan's own new family. "I loved the Kennedys right away," Joan would say. "They were so warm to me and interested in so many things. I never felt in any danger of being swallowed up by such a large family because I saw all the in-laws were individuals in their own right and were respected as such." And she said, "The Kennedy girls were just terrific to me, and I felt accepted as a little sister almost at once." But this wasn't true—none of it. The Kennedys weren't warm. The Kennedys weren't welcoming. The Kennedys weren't inclusive. Joan's comments were more of the old Kennedy smoke screen to protect the Kennedy image. And it became even less true the more time she spent with the Kennedys, and she was spending more time with them in that interregnum and in the early days of the administration.

Joan suffered from the same inferiority complex that had afflicted her husband, and being around the Kennedys only made it worse. Jackie Kennedy told Doris Kearns Goodwin that in the beginning, Joan and Ted were happy. "Whenever we were in Hyannis Port you could see the pride on

Ted's face when she walked into the room with her great figure and leopard-skin outfit. If only she had realized her own strengths instead of looking at herself in comparison with the Kennedys." But Joan did compare herself. And, what was worse, the Kennedys compared her. "They think we're weird," Jackie told her that summer when the rest of the family was playing touch football and Joan and Jackie weren't. And even when Ted invited Joan to join them, it wasn't easy, whatever Joan said, to enter the Kennedy circle—a circle that had been explicitly constructed by Joe Kennedy to repel invasion. Rita Dallas, who would join the family later that year to nurse Joe Kennedy, observed, "The compound could be alive with celebrities and dignitaries, but you would never see a Kennedy alone. There was always another nearby," and they were so tight a clan that they would "cut out everyone else, including in-laws." She continued, "United, they were a formidable group." Too formidable for Joan, which is why both she and Ted contemplated trying to escape the Kennedys' gravitational pull that year—a pull made even stronger by the new presidency. Even Ted now wanted to get away and begin a life of his own—a life that had not been constructed to the Kennedy specifications.

II

But Ted Kennedy was an afterthought yet again. Jack Kennedy was the cynosure of the family and of the nation. A political romantic, he had entered the presidency at a propitious moment. Though he was only a grudging liberal—a liberal not by deep conviction but by electoral necessity to win over the leftist faction of his own party—he was not ideological, and neither were the times. Kennedy preferred to think of himself as a pragmatist—a "managerial politician," an "efficiency liberal, a man, at his best, looking for the most efficient means of attaining the greatest happiness for the greatest number," as political analyst Richard Reeves would put it. Historian James MacGregor Burns put it differently: "The essence of Camelot decision-making," using a term that would later be applied to the Kennedy administration, "was not calculation in terms of a governing principle but judgment on the basis of rigorous comparison of alternatives." Kennedy was measured, cautious. He did not want to get out too far ahead on any issue, and particularly not on any issue where Congress—still controlled by a coalition of old Southern bulls and conservative Republicans, despite the liberal wave of 1958—could thwart him.

He was cool, detached, the very opposite of his belligerent father, which is what the times called for. "America's history of ideological disputation seemed to be over," political historian Rick Perlstein would say of this period. "The nation had settled into a governing equilibrium." The prevalent word was "consensus," as in a consensus had developed throughout the 1950s that Roosevelt's New Deal was a permanent fixture of America and could not be dismantled ("Should any political party try to abolish social security, unemployment insurance, and eliminate labor laws and farm programs, you would not hear of that party again in our political history," President Dwight Eisenhower had written his brother Edgar); consensus as in a consensus had developed that the government had a prominent and continuing role to play in solving problems and in energizing the economy; consensus as in a consensus had developed on a globalist foreign policy that sought to contain communism while also seeking some accommodation with the Soviet Union and that sought to bring capitalism and democracy to the rest of the world—a consensus that marginalized isolationists like Joe Kennedy. Historian Arthur Schlesinger Jr. would call these views "the vital center." Harvard sociologist Daniel Bell called them "the end of ideology." Journalist Karl Meyer called them "the smooth deal." Others would call them simply "the American consensus." But whatever one called them, it was basically a post–New Deal liberal consensus, following Franklin Roosevelt's definition of a liberal as one who "recognizes the need of new machinery" but also "works to control the processes of change, to the end that the break with the old pattern may not be too violent." Jack Kennedy understood the need for change, but Jack Kennedy wasn't going to break violently with old patterns. In America, the center now held.

And that is how John F. Kennedy governed—from the center. He supported tax cuts to stimulate the economy, as advised by economists Walter Heller and Paul Samuelson, then approved his Treasury secretary C. Douglas Dillon's suggestion that they be tax neutral, thus defeating the very purpose of them. ("You may be right," he told James Tobin, a member of the Council of Economic Advisers, about creating stimulative deficits, "but they would kick us in the balls," meaning big business and their Republican allies. "They're just waiting for the chance. We'd lose everything.") In the end, the tax cuts wound up benefiting business and the wealthy. He was skeptical of the military, which was equally skeptical of him, but he nevertheless proposed heavy increases in defense spending to stave off Republican charges of softness. He was sympathetic to advancing civil rights for African Americans, but he moved slowly, justifying his caution on the basis that while integration should be American policy, "other people have grown up with totally different backgrounds and mores," and "we can't change that overnight," though he also recognized the political cost of advocating for African Americans. On other occasions, speaking of civil rights, he would say, "Life is unfair," which became a kind of mantra.

But this wasn't the impression most people had of their young president—that he was cool, dispassionate, slow to move, always searching for compromise and devoid of conviction. Nor was it the impression he wanted to convey. Because if Jack Kennedy came to the presidency at a time of liberal consensus, he also came to the presidency at a time of pent-up energy after the relatively enervated postwar period. Jack Kennedy helped release that energy. "There was simply a new step, a new cadence, to American life from the minute Kennedy gave his inaugural address," his old adversary Hubert Humphrey would write. "The whole country seemed to have awakened from the dormancy of the Eisenhower years, and the White House and the presidency served as a foundation of inspiration and a source of national renewal." Jack Kennedy gave Americans hope, gave them the possibility, as Arthur Schlesinger Jr., a Kennedy acolyte, would write, "to feel as if all the world were young and all dreams within grasp." John Kennedy made the country feel good about itself, feel as if there was nothing it couldn't do, no challenge it couldn't face. If he wasn't a crusader or a firebrand or a moral force, he was an inspiration.

And John Kennedy had the same effect on his youngest brother. Ted had always idolized his older brothers. "It was a pure and simple case of hero worship, and he made no pretense about it," nurse Rita Dallas would say. But it intensified, intensified significantly, when Jack became president, as if the office had made him even bigger in Teddy's eyes. Dallas said Ted was "like a small boy full of the thrill and excitement of having a brother who was the president," and he would literally "jump up and down for joy" when Jack's helicopter landed at Hyannis Port, shouting, "There's the President! Everybody, look, there he is!" And she said he loved calling his brother "the President." More, Jack now became not just his idol but his model—the person who provided the course he wanted to follow. "He'd constantly say, 'Jack did this, Jack did that,'" John Tunney remembered. "And he wanted to live up to it. I think he already thought largely in terms of politics." Ted had huge blowups of Jack in his rec room. Bobby never did. And thinking back decades later on his brother's presidency, Ted would write, "Some of the happiest memories of my life are from those early, impossibly sunlit days I shared with him, when there seemed no limit to the splendid quests and triumphs that lay ahead."

And if Teddy worshipped Jack, saw in him everything that he aspired to be, Jack enjoyed Teddy. Jack and Bobby were closer, much closer. But Jack and Teddy had more fun together. Rita Dallas said that Jack would tease Teddy, tease him "unmercifully." Teddy would be discussing an idea with the president, clearly trying to impress him, and Jack would crane his neck as if he were looking behind Teddy's ears and say, "Hmmmmmm, still wet, I see," and Teddy, embarrassed, would change the subject. But for all the teasing, Jack admired Ted, still envied Ted his strength, just as years earlier, watching them play football at Hyannis Port, Dick Clasby had observed the transaction between the brothers—Jack, playing gingerly, quarterbacking, and Teddy snatching his passes out of the air. They formed a partnership. Jack's friend and aide Dave Powers said that Jack "loved to throw passes, and Ted, with those big hands of his, could catch anything." The Kennedys kept track of pass attempts and receptions, and Ted made Jack look good.

But the transaction between the brothers was predicated on more than football, more than physical activity, in which Jack, with his back injury, could not fully participate. Their sister Eunice speculated that *because* Jack couldn't fully participate, Teddy, who "wanted his admiration," became "more interested in doing all those things Jack wished he could do but couldn't." So Teddy became *more* physically active, and not only more physically active but also more extroverted, because Jack was not a natural extrovert; he was less inhibited because Jack suffered from inhibitions. And while Jack had begun to take a deeper interest in Ted when Ted was a teenager—"He could look at situations in a way that made things look not so grim as the headmaster might have reported," Ted said—and while he had worried about his youngest brother's lack of discipline, his recklessness, and advised him to keep pushing himself, stretching himself, he also took enormous pleasure in many of Ted's transgressions and foibles, transgressions that as a congressman or senator Jack could not commit, even encouraging Ted to take chances. Rose saw the transaction. She recalled Jack urging Ted to dance with a scantily clad dancer at a charity event during the 1960 campaign because, she said, he loved having Ted do "what he could and should not do himself." When Jack became president, Teddy became his comic relief, as he had with Joe Kennedy's family when they were young, and even became, in some ways, the president's id. At Bobby and Ethel's eleventh-wedding-anniversary party in 1961, Arthur Schlesinger Jr. wrote in his journal, "Teddy Kennedy emerged as the dominant figure, singing, plunging fully dressed into the swimming pool and demonstrating in general that the Kennedy vitality is far from extinct in the lower reaches of the family." And as much as Teddy lived vicariously through Jack, Jack's closest friend, LeMoyne Billings, thought "the president lives vicariously through Ted." Ted relaxed him more than anyone else, Billings said. And Billings recalled to one Ted Kennedy biographer a time during the 1960 campaign when Jack was watching Ted deliver a speech, and "the president was just sitting there, his hands open in his lap, and he was just dying with pleasure."

Behind Joe Kennedy's big plan for his son to win the presidency, there had always been his other plan: his succession plan. Joe Kennedy didn't just want a president; he wanted a dynasty to give him the retribution he desired. Now that Jack's position had been secured, he turned to Bobby and Teddy. After the election, Bobby had considered returning to Massachusetts to run for governor. Though Jack's Senate seat was now vacated, to be filled first by the governor's appointment and then by a special election during the next midterm, Bobby had no desire to be appointed to it, telling *Time* magazine's Hugh Sidey, "The only way I'll go to the Senate is to run for it." But Bobby really had no choice. Joe Kennedy had already decided that Bobby was going to be Jack's attorney general, both because he felt that Jack needed the protection of having a family member close by and because Bobby was due a reward for his service to his brother during the campaign, when he served as Jack's manager and point man. "Bobby is going to be attorney general," Joe told longtime presidential counselor Clark Clifford. "All of us have worked our tails off for Jack, and now that we have succeeded, I am going to see to it that Bobby gets the same chance that we gave to Jack." It was unclear exactly when Bobby was let in on this decision. Jack's secretary, Evelyn Lincoln, wrote in her diary on December 15, 1960, that Jack called Bobby to lobby him to take the attorney generalship, or the Senate vacancy, or undersecretary of State for Latin American affairs. Lincoln said that Bobby told his brother he was interested in none of those and that he would rather write a book, though John Kennedy biographer Robert Dallek believed that this was all just a ruse, a way to make Bobby look as if he was resisting pressure, in order to allay a growing public outcry against nepotism amid rumors of his joining the Cabinet. Bobby took the attorney generalship.

And then came Ted's turn. Ted said he had considered running for office from the time he was in high school and was on Milton's debate team, and he had run for class office at several of the schools he attended, despite the fact that he was always an outsider. Elsewhere he said he first began thinking of running for public office while a freshman at Harvard watching Jack's career. Still elsewhere he said he first thought of politics after he was discharged from the Army and his father sent him to Tulsa and then Chicago to look after some family interests, and he said he returned from that trip telling his family of the appeal of a political life. (His Harvard friend Dick Clasby claimed that his first political address may have been a speech he made on his family's behalf to the Boys and Girls Club of Boston—a speech he practiced endlessly, even jumping onto a pool table to improve his delivery.) And John Tunney, his Virginia Law roommate, said he knew Ted was going to be a politician from their nightly political arguments. Jack had clearly chosen him, at least nominally, to run his Senate reelection campaign to train him for his own political career, and on the night of Jack's overwhelming victory, Ted raised a glass in his brother's honor and toasted, "Here's to 1960, Mr. President—if you can make it." To which Jack riposted, "And here's to 1962, *Senator* Kennedy, if *you* can make it."

But that was still in abeyance. Ted knew he was going to run—had to run—was ordained by the new family business, politics, to run. It had been ordained almost from the time he was born. As he would later write, all his life he had "wanted to catch up" to his father and his brothers, who were "godlike figures to me." Politics was the way to catch up. The first question, however, was: What would he be running *for*? He was only twenty-eight, devoid of any political experience outside his brother's campaigns. Bobby admitted that if Ted had his choice, he probably would have run for Massachusetts state attorney general, a modest position, a stepping-stone to higher offices. But Joe, who was pushing Teddy to run on the basis that Jack and Bobby had their positions and now Ted, who "sacrificed himself" for Jack, as Joe put it, should get his, felt it would be demeaning for him to run for state attorney general—Joe Kennedy, Bobby said, "felt that it was a mistake to run for any position lower than" United

States senator—and that essentially, as a Kennedy, he really didn't need a stepping-stone to anything but president.

And while that issue was being debated, there was another question: *Where* would he be running? When Ted asked to take the Western states for Jack's campaign, he had another consideration besides the one he gave his brother—that he wanted to see that part of the country. At the time, he assumed that his brother was going to win the presidency, and he assumed as well that Bobby would be appointed to Jack's old Senate seat, which would foreclose the opportunity of higher office in Massachusetts for Ted unless he ran for governor. The West was open for political opportunity. And there was yet another reason for looking west: It would be a way for him to make his own mark away from the family pressures, which he had been trying to escape since he pondered attending Stanford rather than Harvard. He was at a point, his son Patrick would say, where he was the "freest in his life" and a "kind of autonomous, self-actualizing architect of his own life." Away from the Kennedys, he could "shape his own identity." He wanted to "succeed or fail on his own" was how Joan put it. During the campaign he had taken Joan to New Mexico and Wyoming with him to give her a sense of what living there might be like. He was especially intrigued by New Mexico, a Democratic state whose senators were both aging. The plan was that he would practice law there—despite his professed intentions not to practice—for five or six years, then run for office. Ted said he talked with people, local politicians, about it, and about Colorado and Arizona as well. (Joan said they had both "fallen in love" with Arizona.) "It passed through my head," Ted later said. Meanwhile, his sister Pat, living in Los Angeles with her actor-husband Peter Lawford, was urging him to move to California. He discussed that possibility with Tunney too, even mentioning buying a stake in a National Football League team there to put down roots, as Tunney put it, for his political future.

But Ted Kennedy didn't have the final say in his political future any more than Bobby Kennedy had the final say over the attorney generalship. Joe Kennedy said that California was too difficult a state to navigate politically; there was mixed party registration there, which meant independents could vote in the Democratic primary (he was wrong); it would take too long to establish himself in the state; and Ted said that he himself had concluded that California State Assembly speaker Jesse Unruh, who ruled the state's Democratic party with an iron fist, was a force too big to reckon with. Joe, Eunice said, spoke with "great conviction and assurance. He discounted all objections. He predicted unparalleled success for Teddy." But the success would be in Massachusetts. Joan would say, "We really wanted to go out west, but in those days, my late father-in-law said, 'You do this' and you did that." And, though Ted did it, did return to Massachusetts, Patrick would say that his father always spoke longingly of that point in his life—that point when he was almost the master of his own destiny.

III

Now it was the Senate, and now it was Massachusetts. Bobby had already told Ted over their Acapulco vacation after the election that he had no interest in the state's Senate seat. That sent Ted into a conversation with Jack a few days later at Palm Beach, asking for a position in the administration on arms control, a subject about which he said he felt "passionately" and one upon which he hoped he could build his résumé for a Senate challenge. Jack counseled a different plan. He told him to get back up to Massachusetts and travel the state, get to know it. "If you get involved in arms control, the world is never going to know about you or what you're doing." But he advised that Ted first go to Africa and join the Senate Foreign Relations Committee delegation of senators McGee, Church, and Moss there. And that is when Ted left for Africa for the month of December. While he was gone, Jack, vacationing in Palm Beach, told *Boston Globe* reporter Bob Healy that Ted might run for the Senate, even though Teddy hadn't fully committed yet. (Once again, Ted was not in control of his own destiny.) Healy published the piece on December 21—he actually reported that either Bobby or Ted was likely to run for the seat—and as in so many things in Ted's life, the decision seemed to have been made for him.

The Senate was a big ambition for a novice, but no more than the presidency was for an indifferent young senator only eight years in the Senate. "The gold ring doesn't come around very often," Jack had said of his run for the presidency, "and when it does, you better be ready to grab it." Honey Fitz had had the same philosophy; he was thirty-one when he first ran for Congress and won. But not everyone in the president's circle, notably Kenny O'Donnell and Larry O'Brien, was enthusiastic about the prospect of the president's youngest brother running for the Senate; they thought it could damage the president's standing. Ted knew there were dissenters, and he himself harbored some doubts, but he said that Jack kept encouraging him—that he was "always very positive." While encouraging him, however, and telling him to get back up to Massachusetts as soon as he could to begin laying groundwork, Jack also warned Ted that he would be monitoring Ted's progress, getting reports from the field—"I've got people up there"—and that he would "hear whether you are really making a mark up there." Then, after gathering this information, he would tell Teddy if a Senate race was worth seriously considering, which was a way of saying that Jack was going to protect himself from a poor showing. Even as president, however, and even as the one who might be affected by Ted's race, Jack would not be the one who decided whether Ted would run. That decision was always left to the family's chief executive, Joe Kennedy, and he was already warming to the idea.

Ted Kennedy had begun warming to the idea too, if only by convincing himself he could do it, but that was largely because the decision had already been made for him, so he had no choice. Still, Ted Kennedy couldn't just go up to Massachusetts and declare himself a candidate for the Senate. He needed a base from which to operate, and he needed some experience beyond his campaign experience. Joe began looking for a position for him. He was friendly with a municipal judge named Frank Morrissey, who was well connected politically—he knew all the pols in the state—and religiously—he was close to Boston's Richard Cardinal Cushing, who was also close to the Kennedys. Joe had recruited Morrissey fourteen years earlier to work on Jack's first congressional campaign, and he had worked in every one of Jack's campaigns thereafter. (He was also obsequious to Joe, "the guy who never let Joe Kennedy's overcoat touch the floor," as one detractor put it.) Whether at Joe's instigation or because Morrissey had been searching at Joe's behest and found the position of assistant district attorney himself, Morrissey talked to the Suffolk County district attorney, Garrett Byrne, who had won fame in the Boston area back in the early 1950s for prosecuting the gang that had robbed a Brink's depot of $2.7 million—the "Great Brink's Robbery," people called it. The Kennedys seemed to realize that for the president's brother to work in the DA's office would seem suspicious, beneath him. They needed a pretext, which was that Jack was concerned about corruption in Massachusetts state politics, and the president wanted to get his youngest brother involved. Joe first inquired about the position on January 24. Ted was appointed assistant district attorney two weeks later, on February 7, 1961, the day that Kevin White resigned the job to take the position of secretary of the commonwealth, to which he had been elected in November, and just eighteen days after John Kennedy's inauguration. (White would soon become mayor of Boston.) Ted asked to be paid only a dollar a year. Meanwhile, Joan found the red-brick townhouse on Charles River Square, within walking distance from Ted's new office, and they bought it for $70,000, moving from the fourth-floor apartment on Louisburg Square, which they had occupied not long before.

Despite the pretext, the job was obviously a stepping-stone, a brief stop to allow Ted to explore his candidacy, the way the Senate had been a stop for Jack on his way to the presidency. He certainly could have coasted in the job, as Jack had coasted in the Senate. Ted was a Kennedy, the president's brother, and he would be given a lot of latitude. But Jack could coast without guilt. Jack was self-confident, implacable. Ted couldn't. So deep was Ted Kennedy's sense of inadequacy that he took his work seriously, very seriously, as he had taken law school and campaigning seriously. His third day on the job he tried his first case, concerning a man named Hennessey, who had gone to a Red Sox double-header, then to the Brown Jug saloon, where he downed over twenty drinks, then got into his car and plowed into another car, in Kenmore Square. Though it seemed an open-and-shut DWI case—Hennessey was clearly inebriated, and he clearly drove into the other car—Ted nevertheless prepared assiduously, not only studying the evidence—"hard," he said—but poring over the final arguments of famed defense attorney Clarence Darrow and then revising them for the prosecution. When they handed Hennessey's folder to the public defender, a man named Stanziani, Ted thought Hennessey was cooked. But then the defender began his defense, telling the jury that Hennessey had been working since he was twelve—Ted wondered what that had to do with anything—and then looking up at Ted, prompting the jury to look at him too, as if to say that Ted Kennedy never had to work. And he continued that Hennessey's principal crime was that he cheered for the Red Sox, perhaps cheered for them a bit too enthusiastically, but then, "I think most of us can understand that, when the Red Sox win." And Ted kept thinking: *What does this have to do with anything?* And the defender continued that Hennessey was a carpenter, and if he was convicted he would lose his driver's license, and if he didn't have that license he couldn't get to work, and if he couldn't get to work, he would be forced onto welfare, and if he was forced onto welfare, with his seven children, it would cost Suffolk country $1,500 per month. Hennessey was acquitted in twenty-two minutes. Ted said he discovered that DWI defendants were almost always acquitted. The prosecutor's office knew that. These were just cases they gave to new attorneys to let them get their feet wet. But in these trenches where ordinary people met the legal system, Ted discovered something that neither Jack nor Bobby had experienced: the real grass roots of law, the way that ordinary people felt and thought, and the things that could move them. The DA's office was supposed to be a way station. It wound up providing a liberal education.

And Ted Kennedy, who couldn't coast, who didn't know how to coast, kept working hard. His boss, Garrett Byrne, said that he tried roughly twenty cases during his time in the Suffolk County office and that Ted annoyed his fellow attorneys by working so hard. Byrne also said that Jack and Bobby phoned him for reports on how Ted was doing and that Joe asked him when they saw each other at the Cape. And Byrne said, "I give them a regular report, and it's always the same: Teddy's the hardest worker I've got." But if he was the hardest worker in the office, he wasn't interested in scoring easy victories like so many DAs. One public defender against whom Ted argued said he didn't try to "pad" his record with easy, winnable cases but took cases that required "immense preparation." And the defender said that he wasn't just out to get convictions but rather to get justice, openly sharing information with the defense at pretrial, in the interests of fairness, even if it damaged his own case. (Prosecutors were supposed to do this, but not all did.) And as he advanced from those early cases, those unwinnable DWI cases, his liberal education expanded. Ted's supervisor said that Ted was exposed not only to those ordinary people, like Hennessey and Hennessey's jurors, but to an underside of American life that his brothers hadn't seen either: armed robberies, cases of nonsupport, a case of an elderly woman being raped, a "begetting" case, in which a woman was charged for "getting with child" and in which Ted won a conviction against the woman's boyfriend.

These were not the kinds of cases, however, that would win Ted Kennedy any kind of political advantage, and political advantage was what he would need to contend for the Senate. To seize that advantage, Ted turned to Frank Morrissey, the pol who had found him the job. Morrissey looked the part of an Irish pol—he was short and slight, with thick dark hair and bushy brows, and a round congenial face—and he acted like one: extroverted and voluble. He had helped introduce Jack to the Irish ward heelers back in 1946, and now he was doing the same for Teddy. Now that he was laying his political groundwork, Ted eased his workload in the DA's office and increased it outside. He typically worked from ten to noon, then broke for lunch. During this lunch hour, Morrissey began introducing him at clubs around Boston—all sorts of clubs—at which the president's youngest brother would speak. Ted would give a forty-five-minute talk about his recent trip to Africa, complete with slides. (Jack was keeping track, as he had promised. He called Ted to tell him that forty-five minutes was too long. If Jack could give the State of the Union address in twenty-three minutes, Ted could describe his African experience in twenty-five.) But Ted was good. One of those who heard Ted's talk said he was "perceptive, so interesting, and so sophisticated, and articulate about the people and the leaders to whom he talked and what was going on there." Then Ted would return to the office or court and work from two to four. Then Morrissey would arrange more meetings for him, more speaking engagements, for the late afternoons and evenings.

Now Teddy's plans were coalescing. He only needed his father's formal approval to embark on his candidacy, and he broached the subject of the Senate with him that spring, even though a Senate run had been Joe Kennedy's idea all along. The only remaining consideration seemed to be if Ted might prove an embarrassment to the president and his family, and some of Jack's advisers still seemed to think he would be. Morrissey had been reporting back to Joe about Ted's appearances, and his reports were glowing. "Morrissey had this wonderful gift of gab," Ted would say, "and was enormously enthusiastic and always knew that my father wanted to hear positive things. He would gild the lily on my talks and speeches and the receptions I was getting. My father thought I was just on fire up there." And so, Ted said, his father became his "co-conspirator" in the Senate effort. But though it seemed a foregone conclusion—in 1960, when Joe asked a prospective gubernatorial candidate looking for a contribution whom he might appoint to Jack's seat, and the man named a close friend of Jack's, Joe dismissed him because the right answer was Bobby or Teddy—Joe hadn't given Ted the go-ahead, not quite yet. That didn't come until early that summer at Hyannis Port, when Ted and his father went sailing and Ted discussed his aspirations for the Senate. Joe, he said, was now "enthusiastic," repeating yet again that Jack and Bobby had their positions and it was time for Ted to get his and giving Ted the "full measure" of his "focus and advice." Speaking of Jack and Bobby, Joe said, "I'll make sure they understand it." And Ted said something else about their conversations that summer: that he had "seen what a wonderful relationship he [Joe] had with my brothers when they were running," and that Ted was now enjoying that experience with his father as they had. It was the first time, he said, that the family energy was focused on *him* and on *his* future—the first time it wasn't Joe Jr. and Jack and Bobby.

But as Ted closed in on his decision to run for Jack's vacated seat that summer, there was a problem: The vacated seat wasn't vacant. In an effort to placate Jack the previous December, departing Massachusetts governor Foster Furcolo had appointed Benjamin A. Smith to the seat. Furcolo would later say that Jack had asked him to appoint Smith, who had been Jack's Harvard roommate (another athlete) and an usher at his wedding but who had little political experience, only a brief time as a councilman and the mayor of Gloucester. The rest of the time he ran his family's successful box-manufacturing company in which the local fish were packed. Furcolo said he did as the president-elect asked, but he came to realize that Jack had made the request because he wanted someone compliant, someone without enough political clout to get elected to the seat at the special election in 1962 to fill out the last two years of Jack's unexpired term. (In fact, when Furcolo made the announcement of Smith's appointment, it was made with the condition that Smith would not run in the special election in 1962.) Jack was keeping the seat for one of his brothers.

Ted liked Ben Smith. Smith was a Kennedy stalwart—"enormously devoted to my brother," Ted would say. He and Ted had spent a good deal of time together campaigning for Jack during the West Virginia primary, and he had told Ted that if he had to shovel every ton of coal out of West Virginia to elect Jack, he would. All the Kennedys liked Ben Smith. And Ben Smith was now the senator from Massachusetts, in the seat that Ted had targeted, even though many in the Massachusetts Democratic establishment felt that, as one of them put it, the appointment of Smith was a "slap in the face of every single Massachusetts Democrat." But if Ben Smith, quiet, loyal Ben Smith, was a seat warmer, Ted wasn't sure anyone had told him, despite that condition upon his appointment, and Ted said he hadn't talked to his brothers about it either. Smith apparently thought he could run if he wanted. And Smith was proud of the appointment—"delighted" about it, said one of the Kennedy aides—and neither Ted nor his brothers seemed to have the fortitude or the decency to tell Smith that Ted was going to be running for his seat. Instead, Ted would say, it was "quite apparent" by the end of 1961 "that I had every intention of running." And that was the end of Ben Smith, family friend and devoted supporter.

But even with Ben Smith dispatched, there was another obstacle to Ted's candidacy, and this one wasn't as easy to overcome. The obstacle was Edward McCormack, Massachusetts state attorney general and the thirty-nine-year-old nephew of House majority leader, soon-to-be speaker, John McCormack. Edward McCormack was another aspirant with his sights on Jack Kennedy's old Senate seat. McCormack's father was Eddie McCormack Sr., or, as he was known among the Democratic pols, "Knocko," for his days as a semiprofessional prizefighter—a short, three-hundred-pound behemoth with clout among the Boston ward heelers. The contrast between Joe Kennedy and Knocko McCormack couldn't have been more stark. Knocko said he came from "the poorest family in South Boston." His father, a bricklayer, died when his boys were children, and the McCormacks moved to a tenement that rented for $1.25 a week. Knocko joined the Teamsters, then the Ninth Massachusetts Volunteers in Mexico, and then the 101st Infantry in World War I, then became a bootlegger and a tavern owner, before entering Boston Democratic politics, largely as an enforcer for Mayor James Curley. Knocko was a familiar figure in South Boston. As "self-effacing as a bass drum," one legislator called him. His son, young Eddie, however, was hardly a chip off the old block. He was something of a wunderkind. Tall and handsome, with blond wavy hair, an aquiline nose, and a lantern jaw, he looked like anything but a Boston machine politician. His background wasn't that of a machine politician either. He had graduated from the Naval Academy at Annapolis and then graduated first in his class at Boston University Law School, where he was editor in chief of the law review. A self-made man with political connections, Eddie was ambitious. He ran for and won a seat on the Boston City Council in 1952 at twenty-nine, then became council chairman, and then was appointed attorney general by the Massachusetts legislature in 1958, when Attorney General George Fingold died and McCormack won the Democratic primary. He went on to win a full term in 1960, by 430,000 votes, despite the fact that Republican John Volpe won the governorship. As McCormack later told it on *Meet the Press*, no sooner had he won the attorney generalship in 1958 than he was looking at the Senate, figuring that Kennedy would win the presidency and the seat would be open. He called his preparations to run while attorney general a "calculated risk."

There was no love lost between the McCormacks and the Kennedys. If the Kennedys boiled with resentment at the Protestant establishment, the McCormacks boiled with resentment at the lace-curtain Irish Kennedys. In the hurly-burly of Boston Irish politics, the two clans had fought over the Democratic State Committee in 1956, when Jack attempted a takeover to reform the state party and John McCormack counterattacked. As Larry O'Brien told it, their respective candidates for state chairman—an onion farmer on the McCormack side, named William "Onions" Burke, and a small-town mayor on the Kennedys', Pat Lynch—nearly came to blows. And while the clans had forged a truce since, it was a tense one—one that could easily shatter. In taking on Ted's presumed candidacy, Eddie McCormack knew exactly what he was doing. For the family honor, as well as for his own ambition, he was taking the fight to the enemy, and the enemy was the Kennedys.

The Kennedy camp tried to defuse the situation the way they had always tried to defuse problematic situations: by trying to co-opt McCormack. John McCormack said that Joe Kennedy called him and offered to support and finance his nephew's run for governor if he left the Senate race. Meanwhile, Jack was also working to dissuade Eddie. Tip O'Neill, who represented Jack's old congressional district and had ties to both sides, recalled that Jack called him in and said that he and John McCormack had reached a "rapprochement" and he didn't want to disturb it with Teddy's candidacy, but his father was insisting. So, Jack said, Ted had proposed a solution and wanted to present it directly to O'Neill. O'Neill said he met Ted on Washington's birthday—also Ted's twenty-ninth birthday—and that Ted's solution was that he and McCormack take a poll with a pollster of McCormack's choosing; the Kennedys would even pay for it. If it showed Ted beating McCormack by more than five points, McCormack would abandon the Senate race and run for governor, with the Kennedys' blessing. (O'Neill blanched, saying that if Ted lost, there was nothing to prevent him from running against O'Neill himself, but Ted insisted he would never do that.) But when O'Neill took the proposal to McCormack, McCormack had no interest. Like so many others, he underestimated Ted, had contempt for him, and thought that Ted running for the Senate, at thirty, without any experience, was beyond audacious. He felt that he had staked a claim on the nomination long before Ted began considering a run, that it should be his, not Ted's. And he was sure that he would beat Ted. By one account, he told his uncle, "He may win in the polls, but I've got the delegates sewed up at the state convention," where the party would make its endorsement.

But Ted Kennedy, who was finally catching up to his brothers, wasn't about to leave the race. Instead, he was deep into his Senate preparation. That spring, after only a few months on the job, he took a leave from the DA's office to tour Italy, from Rome down to Naples and Sicily, with Joan, Frank Morrissey, and a travel agent named Phil Cordaro—what Italian papers puffed up as an "extraordinary delegation"—for the one hundredth anniversary of Garibaldi's unification of the country. He had the trip filmed and edited so that he could later show it at talks in Italian communities in western Massachusetts. And that summer he took another leave, for a trip to Latin America—a fact-finding tour not unlike the one he had taken to West Africa. He had secured a young Harvard professor named John Plank, who was a Latin American specialist, to accompany him, and, clearly thinking of his image, he also brought along a biographer named Bela Kornitzer, who was pondering writing a book on the Kennedys. But he also called his old friend John Tunney to invite him along, and Tunney leapt at the chance, knowing that the president's brother would get to meet, as Tunney put it, "heads of state, the top religious leaders, the top labor leaders, academics everywhere we went, students." But as Ted was meeting heads of state, religious leaders, and others in positions of power, he also made a point of meeting with the leftist opposition, as a way of learning what ordinary people might really be thinking and feeling, which is one reason he brought along Plank, who had connections in that community. (The FBI, following Ted's trip, found this suspicious.) And he said that he saw villagers powering their radios with kerosene just so they could listen to Radio Havana Cuba. At the time, when American hostility to Cuba ran high, Ted's meetings with leftists constituted a risk to his own political ambitions. He took meticulous notes, as he had on his previous trips—two hundred pages' worth—then, typical of Teddy, left the notebooks on the plane. (His observations wound up in a five-part series in *The Boston Globe*).

He returned with momentum. He wrote his parents and Bobby about the trip, which had bolstered his Senate credentials, then discussed other developments: Harold Case, the president of Boston University, had asked him to be a trustee, "which I think should be helpful as well"; he had also begun doing extensive charity work in the community. But he added, somewhat disconsolately, McCormack had told Hal Clancy, the editor of the conservative *Boston Herald Traveler,* that he was definitely going to run and said he doubted that Ted would, because Bobby had congratulated McCormack on a brief he'd filed on school desegregation. That only showed how little McCormack understood about Kennedy solidarity. When Ted complained to Bobby about the congratulations, Bobby said he didn't see what was wrong with complimenting McCormack, because he would compliment Teddy too, to which Ted groused in mock despair, "So you can see what I'm up against."

But Ed McCormack would be up against more, much more. He would be up against Ted Kennedy. Ted never forgot anything. He had learned a great deal from his brother's campaigns, and he put that knowledge to use that summer and fall. He rented a small office-cum-apartment at 122 Bowdoin Street for $115 a month from which to explore his candidacy—the same apartment from which Jack launched his first congressional campaign. (When they raised the rent to $125, Ted said, he debated whether he could afford it.) He got involved in charity work, as he had written his father, specifically the Cancer Crusade, headed by an oncologist named Sidney Farber and Lloyd Waring, the Republican state chairman, and he fundraised with them for two or three months "every single night," which was a form of campaigning without the overt politics. And Eddie McCormack would be up against not only Ted Kennedy. He would be up against Joe Kennedy too. By late that summer, Joe Kennedy was fully involved, reliving Jack's earlier campaigns through Teddy's, reestablishing contact with old friends, people like Basil Brewer, the conservative editor of the New Bedford *Standard-Times,* or Hal Clancy, or the old families he remembered from the Boston waterfront, the fishing families—he would ask Frank Morrissey, who knew everybody, whether they were still around, and Morrissey would tell him who was, "calling, touching base with people, seeing what was going on, what was happening." Ted said that "for that year, it was the central part of his life," meaning making the contacts for Teddy's Senate run.

And Ed McCormack would be up against the Kennedy network that Jack had constructed for his election campaigns. Morrissey was taking Ted around—"keeping me on the go day and night," Ted wrote Joe. On one Sunday that October, as *Time* reported it, he drove from Hyannis Port to Natick to deliver a breakfast speech at Temple Israel (usually a speech about his trip to Latin America), went to mass, then raced to Framingham for a kaffeeklatsch followed by a luncheon talk, followed by a get-acquainted tea in Medford hosted by the St. James Church Women's Guild, followed by a talk to a parents' group at the Wrentham State School for mentally disabled children. That night he attended the General Casimir Pulaski Skyway Committee banquet in Dorchester, recited part of the Polish national anthem in Polish, and danced the polka "with a score of girls." Ted reported to Joe: "I think that the reaction has been quite good, except for a few cynical old pros." And he said that he had found "some old Irish stories that Grampa used to tell which have really helped out."

And it wasn't just Morrissey who had come aboard Ted's bandwagon. Working in the DA's office, Ted met a crusty old gadabout from South Boston named Jack Crimmins, who had been Governor Paul Dever's driver back in the early 1950s, and Crimmins now drove Ted around Massachusetts, knowing all the back roads. But Crimmins was more than a driver. He was a streetwise adviser, with, Ted's cousin Robert Fitzgerald would say, "good street and political sense," and with a deep loyalty to Teddy. ("Teddy never had anyone who was more loyal than Jack Crimmins," Fitzgerald said.) And Ted's old football friend John Culver, who had gone to Harvard Law School and entered practice, had returned to Harvard earlier that year with his wife, serving as a freshmen proctor, living in a dormitory basement; and Ted looked him up and asked if he might be interested in joining the nascent campaign—nascent because Ted had yet to declare his candidacy—and Culver was. Culver would remember a conversation at Hyannis Port with Joe not long after—a conversation about loyalty. "Brains are a dime a dozen," Joe told Culver. "I can always buy those. What you can't buy is judgment and loyalty." Culver was loyal. And later that fall, Joe asked Hal Clancy for a recommendation for a possible press secretary for Ted, and Clancy mentioned a young *Herald Traveler* reporter and former Marine named Ed Martin. Ted invited Martin to the apartment at 122 Bowdoin and asked if he would be interested in heading the press operation. Martin protested that he didn't have any experience and that he didn't cover politics exclusively. Ted said a generalist was exactly what they wanted, and Martin concluded that "they figured I didn't support anybody else, and I was probably coming to them clean." So he took the job. What he didn't realize was that, by hiring him, Joe and Ted also believed they were neutralizing opposition from the conservative *Herald Traveler*. (Clancy, in fact, became an adviser.) Ed McCormack would even be up against Rose Kennedy, who was thinking of delivering lectures in French to aid Teddy in the French areas of the state.

And if Ed McCormack would be up against this ragtag network of politicians and fixers and volunteers and loyalists and old friends and family even before the real campaign had begun, he would also be up against the Kennedy *organization:* the Kennedy "secretaries," women who had supported Jack Kennedy since 1952 and held receptions for him—"teas," they called them—in their neighborhoods; the thirty women who were manning the operation; the sixteen to eighteen attorneys and insurance agents and friends who had taken leaves to assist Ted; the advertising man, Don Dowd, who took Ted's Italian movie to meetings around the state; and Ted's cousin Joey Gargan, and later Ted's brother-in-law Steve Smith, who would join the campaign at Bobby's request. Ted Kennedy had people willing to go to war for the Kennedys. And Ted Kennedy would be at war with Ed McCormack.

But if Ted Kennedy had an enthusiastic grassroots organization and a number of low-level pols on his side, the one thing he didn't have, at least not yet, were the state party leaders, the "bigwigs," as one of his supporters called them, who were close to the McCormacks and who were hedging their bets on the prospect that Jack and old John McCormack would eventually settle the war and that Ed McCormack would get one nomination, either senator or governor, and Ted get the other. But that was not how Ted Kennedy was thinking. Ted, now emboldened by his father's encouragement, was thinking that he was going to be senator. So he had Morrissey convene a lunch meeting of ten Democratic state congressional leaders that November at the Locke-Ober restaurant, one of Boston's oldest and most venerable, and then go around the table asking each of them how many delegates they could deliver for Ted at the state convention. When he got to Billy Bulger of South Boston, a tough Irish politician from McCormack's district, Bulger said he wouldn't deliver any—that he was sticking with McCormack. (Bulger had gone to the meeting at the suggestion of the McCormacks, who told him to order the most expensive item on the menu, which was lobster Savannah, while the others ordered sandwiches at $1.85.) Another legislator, Gerard Doherty, trying to mediate between the factions, suggested they just keep the dialogue going and meet again in a week, to which Ted quipped, "I don't know whether we should try to persuade him. I don't think we can afford to feed him."

But Doherty's attempted mediation turned out to be a stroke of luck and one more force that Ed McCormack would find himself up against— a big force. *Boston Globe* columnist Bill Lewis got wind of the second meeting, got wind of Doherty's mediation efforts, and wrote the following Sunday, acidly, that Doherty was at risk of destroying his political career by getting between the Kennedys and the McCormacks and speculated on his sanity. That night, when Doherty returned home from a semiprofessional football game he'd attended, his wife told him that "some damn idiot" pretending to be Ted Kennedy had called him—called him three times. Doherty recalled that, just as she finished, the phone rang again. It was Ted, apologizing profusely for getting Doherty in the middle of the dispute and then inviting Doherty to come to his townhouse on Charles River Square that night. Doherty did, and after another long apology, Ted asked him if would join the campaign. Doherty, another poor Irish Catholic Harvard grad, agreed, giving Ted a very valuable asset. A state representative from Charlestown, Doherty was hardly a political heavyweight, and he was so disheveled, he looked like an "unmade bed," according to one associate, but he had this: He knew the state inside and out, every nook and cranny of it—knew "more about the Massachusetts situation than anybody," Jack had said of him. And Doherty was very close to a collection of other state legislators, who, Ted said, became the "backbone" of his early campaign organization. With their guidance, he was attending communion breakfasts on Sundays at "every church I could" and school dinners at "any school I could."

And Ed McCormack would be up against something else too. He would be up against the president of the United States. Ted's undeclared campaign had a slogan now, a theme that fall. Jack had suggested it during a sail on the *Marlin* at Hyannis Port: "He can do more for Massachusetts." Jack had had a similar slogan when he ran in 1952 against Henry Cabot Lodge Jr., with the implied message that Lodge was so involved in Eisenhower's presidential campaign that year that he had forgotten Massachusetts. This time the slogan had another implied message, which infuriated McCormack with its nepotism and its promise—that Ted's ties to President Kennedy would give him more clout in Washington. And Jack, who never missed a detail, had another suggestion for his brother. In his own campaigns, he had handed out PT-boat tie clasps—mementos that would remind voters of his war heroism. Jack advised that Ted have tie clasps too, and he drew a map of Massachusetts on a piece of paper and told Ted to put "Kennedy in '62" on the clasp, which Ted did.

But what Ed McCormack would really be up against was a whirlwind. No one had ever outworked Ted Kennedy, and with the campaign heading into election year, Ted Kennedy was now unrelenting. By early 1962, he was going to Europe and the Middle East, traveling with another Harvard football friend, Claude Hooton, for another fact-finding mission like the ones he had conducted in Africa and Latin America, making sure to touch bases that would resonate with constituents back in Massachusetts, and making sure that the trip was covered extensively in the American press. He met with Common Market officials and trade unionists in Brussels; visited Christian holy sites and a kibbutz in Israel, met with Prime Minister David Ben-Gurion, spoke at Hebrew University of Jerusalem—where a shouting match ensued between communist hecklers and Kennedy supporters—and was yelled at by Jordanian border guards when he wandered too close to the neutral zone in Jerusalem; attended a cabinet meeting in Greece with Prime Minister Konstantinos Karamanlis and met actress and politician Melina Mercouri (he said he was struck by how little security Karamanlis had); flew to Poland, where he met with the Polish foreign minister Józef Beck, saw the Black Madonna of Częstochowa, and fended off questions about magazine reports that he was running for the Senate ("Well, it would be rather inappropriate, I guess, to announce it in Warsaw"); sped through the Polish countryside on a lavishly appointed train provided by the German government to Berlin, where Bobby, who was visiting Germany at the time, had finagled an invitation for him from West German mayor Willy Brandt (Brandt hosted a birthday dinner for Ted) and rendezvoused with his brother there; and then sneaked into East Berlin, where he argued with a young East Berliner about the necessity of the wall dividing East from West, and where he asked a woman who was waiting in line for apples whether she had to do so every day—to which she answered, "No, because they do not have apples every day." (East German officials would later claim that by showing his passport at Checkpoint Charlie, the entrance point across the wall, Ted had respected East German sovereignty, even though the United States did not recognize the division, setting off a diplomatic tempest.) He ended his trip in Ireland, at County Wexford, the ancestral home of the Kennedys, where police battled crowds to open a path for his convoy. "It's good to be home," he said.

Meanwhile, Ed McCormack suddenly hustled to Europe and to the Middle East during Ted's trip so as not to be usurped.

And it was not only Ed McCormack who was caught in the whirlwind. It was Ted Kennedy. The campaign had not been something he had originally sought; it had been sought for him by his father and to a lesser extent his brothers. He was uncertain about himself; he had always been uncertain about himself, and the prospect of running for office, much less the United States Senate, had unnerved him. Yet there was no denying his father or his brothers, even though they had trepidations of their own over Ted's readiness. Nor could he deny that, despite his self-doubt, he relished the opportunity to elevate himself in his family's estimation, and there was only one way he saw for himself to do so. And as the time neared for a declaration, as he schooled himself and honed his political instincts, he was carried along by the momentum of the campaign and began to feel ready and gain confidence that he could do this, that he could be senator. He began thinking like a Kennedy.

Now it wasn't so much self-doubt that plagued him. It was the doubts of everyone else. Even though Jack was monitoring Ted's progress carefully and giving him advice, the hesitation within his administration about Teddy's run had not abated, and Jack himself was conflicted about what effect the candidacy might have on his own standing. "The whole thing struck Jack as too gimmicky," a friend of Jack's said. "He was far more sensitive about the dynasty charge than people ever realized." When another friend and Democratic insider, state committeewoman Betty Taymor, visited the White House, Jack made a point of asking her what she thought. "Not so good," she told the president. "He's just sitting there in that Bowdoin Street office," which couldn't have been less accurate; Ted never just sat. And she said that "the liberal crowd at home simply will not buy Ted's candidacy," which was more accurate, because they thought him too raw and inexperienced. Jack's answer: "Well, get back there and help." Even after all the trips and preparation, after the speechmaking and stumping, Kenny O'Donnell and Lawrence O'Brien remained adamantly opposed and told the president so, and according to O'Brien, the president asked him to have a talk with Teddy to see if he could convince him to run for a lesser office. (O'Brien said he didn't have the talk.) And when the president was asked about his brother's plans at a press conference in January, he kept his distance, answering, "Well, I think he's the man . . . who's running, and he's the man to discuss it with," even though Ted had yet to announce officially. Ted said he never held it against his brother's advisers for wanting to protect the president. "If I'd been somebody else, I'm not sure I would have supported the idea." But the one who did hold it against them was Joe Kennedy, and Joe Kennedy made it clear to everyone, Jack and Bobby included, that Teddy was going to run for senator whether they liked it or not, and that whether they understood it or not, Ted's temperament, so different from his brothers', was actually likely to help them, not hurt them. As Jack's close adviser Ted Sorensen put it, Jack had had "enough disagreements with his father on policy not to pick any new arguments on family matters," though he continued to insist publicly that he was neutral in the race and would not actively aid Teddy.

But try as he might to seal himself off, Jack Kennedy was not neutral. He wanted to make sure that Ted didn't embarrass himself or embarrass the president. When Ted was scheduled to appear on *Meet the Press* on March 11, 1962, he went to the White House the night before to see Jack, who asked Ted if he thought he was ready. (Ted had also finally visited Ben Smith that day, the first time he'd done so, to break the news to him that he was going to run.) *Meet the Press* wasn't just another appearance. The expectation was that Ted would either announce for the Senate on the program or soon thereafter, and the show would be a kind of audition for the campaign and for a candidate who was still roundly scorned by a good deal of the national press. Ted said he didn't feel "rattled" and that he was "fairly confident," so Jack told his secretary, Evelyn Lincoln, not to bother him and arranged chairs around the desk and had Ted sit behind it, then began grilling him. "I went right back out and practiced a lot more after that," Ted said. But that wasn't exactly how Ted would later recall it happened. Later, he would say that Jack told him he had to "sharpen these up a bit." And then Jack called in Sorensen and another adviser, Myer Feldman, and for the next hour and a half they prepped Teddy, writing up answers for him.

For well over a year, the drama had been mounting, and it was about to explode that Sunday morning. Ted's confidence had been shaken by his trial in the Oval Office, and when he made his appearance, the man who had felt he was ready no longer was certain how he would perform and whether he would embarrass his brothers. He wasn't the only Kennedy with jitters. The president had left for Florida, where he turned on *Meet the Press*, but during the broadcast he kept walking in and out of the room nervously. When it was over, he asked his close friend and aide Dave Powers how Ted had done. Powers said Ted had done fine. Still unsatisfied, Jack called the host of *Meet the Press*, Lawrence Spivak, and asked how Ted had done. Spivak said he had done fine, except that he couldn't get an answer out of him about aid to Catholic schools, which was an important issue in Massachusetts. Jack laughed and said that was just where Ted ought to be. Ted had done well. He had been deft. Asked whether the Kennedys had commissioned a Harris poll in 1961 to gauge his strength, he said they hadn't. Asked if the Kennedys were gaining too much power, Ted said, "If you are talking about too many Kennedys, you should have talked to my mother and father at the time they were getting started." And he said what everyone had been waiting to hear him say: that he would put his name before the Democratic State Convention, though he cannily refused to say for what office. Three days later, on March 14, at his Beacon Hill apartment at 3 Charles River Square, he finally declared his candidacy for the Senate, calling for a "new vitality, a new image, and a new vigor," which was a tacit admission that there was little substantive difference on policy between the two contenders, both of whom were liberals, consensus liberals, just with a difference in style. For his part, Ed McCormack, who had announced nine days earlier, ridiculed Ted as "just a kid three years out of college," but added, "Competition is healthy."

But there was already a feeling from some quarters that competition from Edward Kennedy was *not* healthy, that it was arrogant and damaging. *Time* said he had "no visible qualifications" and that relatives of "prominent officials" should "present some solid evidence of talent before they make the sacrifice of starting at the top." Anticipating Ted's entry into the race just before the *Meet the Press* appearance, *New York Times* Washington bureau chief James Reston was especially lathered over Ted Kennedy's temerity to run at the age of thirty, just old enough to qualify, and with his lack of experience. "Any way you look at it, this adventure promises to be an embarrassment to the president," Reston opined. "If Teddy wins, it will inevitably be said that the president put him over, even if the president doesn't say a word in his behalf, and if he loses, it will be regarded as a rebuke to the Kennedys for overreaching themselves." But, Reston went on, "Teddy figures: why not go after what you want; everybody else in the family has." (Reston was right in assessing Ted's reasoning.) As for the president not saying a word on Ted's behalf, he didn't. Presidential press secretary Pierre Salinger had drafted a release that said Ted had made an independent decision, that he had not asked for the pres-

story?" Maguire wanted to know what Healy knew, but Healy didn't know much, only scuttlebutt he had heard from Harvard faculty members. Maguire excused himself, left the room, and then returned and told Healy, "I got a phone call for you." The president was on the line, asking what Healy knew about the cheating episode—again, not much—and if Healy could sit on the story. And Healy told him, "Yes, and Eddie McCormack will blow you out of the water in the first debate." Jack just laughed, said, "Yes, you've got it," and told Healy to visit him when he returned to Washington.

When Healy did visit the White House, he quickly realized that the president was now managing the release of the story for Teddy. Over the years, Healy recounted a number of different versions about how this proceeded. In one, he met with the president one-on-one, after which the president invited McGeorge Bundy—the national security adviser who had also been dean of the faculty of the arts and sciences at Harvard—and Kenny O'Donnell into the Oval Office. (In another version, Healy said historian and presidential adviser Arthur Schlesinger Jr. was also in the meeting.) The president was negotiating—"like a union negotiation," Healy would later say, though his editors had told him not to negotiate. The president wanted Healy to bury the scandal episode in a longer profile of Teddy rather than have it be what journalists call the "lede," or opening. Healy told Kennedy, "Christ, you've got to be kidding. I'd write that story, put it in the tenth paragraph, and the AP [Associated Press] would lead with it all over the country that Teddy got caught cheating at Harvard." By one of his accounts, Healy said that was the end of their first session, but he met with the president three more times, an hour each; at one point, the president, cognizant of how much time he was spending on the reporting of Ted's transgression, snapped, "I'm having more fucking trouble with this than I had with the Bay of Pigs," the botched CIA operation to invade Cuba. To which Bundy said, "And with about the same results." In the end, Kennedy had Bundy call Harvard to get the entire record for Healy and gave him access to the parties involved, including Bill Frate, on the condition Healy wouldn't use his name. (Bundy would later deny that he did this.) Healy also met with Ted, though Ted never spoke about their discussion, and neither did Healy. The brief story ran tucked in the lower left-hand corner of the *Globe*'s front page on March 30, with the title TED KENNEDY TELLS ABOUT HARVARD EXAMINATION INCIDENT and with Ted's statement that he wanted to set the record straight, which was considerably softer and less sensational than it could have been. Healy said he and the president had massaged the lede and admitted to having "soft-pedaled" some of the story at, he said, the behest of his publisher, William Taylor, who told Healy not to "kill this guy"—this guy being Ted—because Taylor believed in "not hurting the presidency." And Jack Kennedy did one more thing: He made sure that the article was published late enough in the week, a Friday, that the newsweeklies wouldn't be able to pick it up for their next editions.

But now that the story was finally public after more than a decade of it being buried, Ted was terrified. "I thought that was the end of the whole campaign, and I remember that being a long, long day." That night, he had a scheduled appearance at a hall in Milford, Massachusetts, with a capacity of more than three hundred. He stood in the parking lot agonizing about whether he could screw up the courage to face that crowd— every member of which, he was certain, had read that day's *Globe*—and face the public humiliation. And he thought, *What in the world is going to happen with this thing?* But he realized he had no choice, so he headed in disconsolately. When he did, the crowd was cheering—"everybody was supporting" him, he would remember, and it was a "terrific shot, a lift." And he said to himself that now, maybe, he could get through this after all, that maybe he could overcome the disgraces that seemed to dog him.

But not everyone was cheering the candidacy of Ted Kennedy. Outside that contingent of the Washington press that found his candidacy insulting, even appalling, there were also the McCormack loyalists and others among the Massachusetts pols who chose to remain neutral until they saw how the race unfolded. Nevertheless, Ted was carefully courting them. He had gone down to Washington in early February, before his European trip, to meet with the entire Massachusetts congressional delegation, coming to them via taxi through a snowstorm after, notably, first visiting his brother in the White House and his brother in the Justice Department—a clear message to the recalcitrant among those congressmen about the power behind him. But there was also a message of a different kind: On the very day of Ted's Washington visit, a testimonial dinner was being held for Ed McCormack back in Boston, at which Tip O'Neill, John Kennedy's congressional successor, would be appearing. The wooing would have to continue.

And Gerard Doherty, the state legislator who was helping Ted, told another story—a story about holding a delegate party at the Parker House in Boston. But as the hour approached, none of the delegates had arrived. They were, Doherty realized, staging a boycott as a courtesy to the McCormacks. When Ted arrived, Doherty told him that they had gotten the time wrong and sent him away. Then, he said, he got on the phone and began calling all his friends in Charlestown and told them to dress up and get down to the Parker House with their wives and girlfriends and to applaud at the right time. When he got off the phone after making all those calls, Teddy was just returning, just getting out of the cab, and Doherty sent him off again, told him to go to headquarters, because the food servers had a problem setting up. And when Ted returned a third time, the room was filled. "He got a tremendous reception, and he really felt great."

But while most of the boycotting politicians were simply being cautious, biding their time, playing both sides, there was another group that had no caution, another group that was vigorously, immovably opposed to Ted Kennedy's candidacy. Boston academics and intellectuals hated Ted Kennedy, and "hate" was not too strong a word. One close observer of the campaign said, "Nobody could possibly overestimate the hatred of the idea of Edward Kennedy's candidacy by the intellectual community." When a Harvard law professor named Mark DeWolfe Howe heard that Ben Smith would be stepping aside for Ted's ambition, he wrote a furious broadside to his fellow academics, excoriating Teddy's supporters and calling his candidacy "both preposterous and insulting" and saying that Ted himself was a "coattail candidate" whose academic career was "mediocre" and whose professional career was "virtually nonexistent." (Howe had a personal motive too: He helped write an amicus brief for Attorney General McCormack on the Gideon case, which sought to provide free defense attorneys to indigent clients.) And Howe didn't stop at the letter. He was so outraged that he would buttonhole Kennedy supporters among the faculty at Harvard and elsewhere and denounce them, which prompted one of those supporters, MIT professor Robert Wood, to tell Howe, "We're only trying to make him a U.S. senator, not a Harvard professor." Gerry Doherty said that Ted was intimidated by academics and hurt by their response to him—that "the almost total boycott by the liberal establishment" had "bothered him the most" of anything in the campaign, and that he was more than hurt, he was angry, when a supporter hosted a reception for him in liberal Brookline and there was only a small turnout.

And as the campaign wore on, the hatred didn't subside; it grew. Howe and others, including Harvard historian Arthur Schlesinger Sr., poet Archibald MacLeish, and foreign affairs expert Hans Morgenthau, formed the National Committee for an Effective Congress, which seemed primarily designed not to improve congressional effectiveness but to attack Ted Kennedy, issuing yet another broadside against him, even criticizing his trip to Europe and the Middle East—"the usual political Three I Circuit," it called it, meaning Italy, Israel, and Ireland—and disparaging his work in the DA's office, saying he "went through the motions of serving for a few months." (He had actually served fourteen months before resigning to run.) And this time they implicated the president too, for this "affront to the Senate." Theologian Reinhold Niebuhr went further. He called the candidacy an "affront to political decency," and his wife held a fundraiser at their summer home for McCormack. Even the Young Democratic Club of Harvard and Radcliffe announced its support for McCormack. When Arthur Schlesinger Jr. confronted the president with reports about his behind-the-scenes efforts on his brother's behalf despite the intellectuals' outcry against Ted as a mediocrity, Jack said, "Teddy's not running against George Washington."

The intellectuals made it seem as if Ted was coasting into the Senate on his name, but Ted Kennedy wasn't coasting here any more than he had coasted in the DA's office. He was always having to *prove* he was worthy of his last name. And the same intellectuals griped that Ted was not only privileged but also incompetent. "When he made a speech, he could barely complete a sentence," said Harvard professor Samuel Beer. Another said that during an early confrontation between Ted and McCormack—it could only have been the first debate, since there was no previous joint appearance—Ted was in a "state of shock." He was "so nervous, he could barely get sound out of his body." And when he did speak, the answers were all canned, memorized, not even the right answers to the question asked. But like so many attacks on Ted Kennedy in those days, none of this was true. Kennedy was articulate on the stump, a charmer. And Kennedy did not quiver in fear. He was always composed. What is more, Ted Kennedy was prepared for the campaign ahead. He was not winging it, despite what his polls showed. He welcomed expertise. John Culver had invited one of his old Harvard law professors, Charles Haar, who had his own doubts about Ted's competence, to accompany Ted on a campaign swing, and Haar came away impressed, especially impressed because Ted did not pander to his Catholic audiences on the issue of federal aid to parochial schools. He explained that there was a constitutional issue involved, the separation of church and state, and that this had serious implications for democracy. And he said that his brother, the president, had decided the wall between church and state should not be parted on this particular issue. And Haar remembered a woman in a basement where Ted was speaking to a small group, who said, "Ah, come on, Teddy. Eddie was here a while ago, and he told us that he was going to get money for this purpose [for the school]. Why can't you do the same?" But Haar said that Ted didn't budge.

So Haar became an adviser to Ted Kennedy. He gave him books to read. He thought aloud with him on issues. And Ted would ask questions, lots of questions. "It's kind of an intense curiosity that drives his questions," Haar would say. "He likes to get to the bottom of issues, probing further and further until it becomes a part of him." And Haar saw something that others had observed in Ted: "He doesn't get tired. I think he was virtually indefatigable." When Ted had gone down to Washington in March, just before announcing his candidacy, and visited Ben Smith's office, Smith offered him the services of his legislative assistant, Milton Gwirtzman, a Harvard man with extensive knowledge of the issues as well as a gift for speechwriting; and as the campaign wore on, Gwirtzman and Culver would go up to Boston or, when summer arrived, to Hyannis Port every weekend to discuss issues with Ted, brief him, prepare him for the week ahead, and to give Gwirtzman a feel for the way Ted spoke, so he could craft speeches expressly for him. And finally Ted was able to win over some academics who were less exercised over Kennedy's lack of credentials than they were over corruption in Massachusetts and the need for reform. (Massachusetts politics was riddled with corruption.) Bobby had held a meeting at the Justice Department with a handful of Boston regulars, among them Dan Fenn Jr., whom Jack had tapped to be a "talent scout" for the administration. When Bobby heard about the academic opposition to Ted, he asked Fenn to go up to Boston and spend some time with the academics, especially those who were angry about the sorry state of the Massachusetts Democratic party. Fenn said he spent two or three days circulating, hearing the academics' grievances, one of which was that John Kennedy had not done enough to rid the party of corruption, and then drafted a letter in Ted's name, which Ted signed off on, promising that he would help reform the party if he was elected, even encouraging the creation of an advisory committee to suggest policies to the state legislature. And with this promise in hand, the reformers, who included Samuel Beer and Bob Wood and James MacGregor Burns of Williams College and John Plank, the Latin American expert who had accompanied Ted on his trip there, were able to pry others away from McCormack, because McCormack, who had benefited from the incestuousness of Massachusetts politics, would never make such a pledge.

As the negotiations over the cheating-scandal story demonstrated, the president was involved, deeply involved. There was one group, however, that took the president's professions of neutrality seriously, took them seriously because they wanted to, because they had been intractably opposed to Ted's candidacy in the first place, because they had been as opposed as the intellectuals to the very idea of his candidacy and had not changed their minds even after he declared. And these dissenters were closer to home than the holdouts with ties to the McCormacks, the local pols, or the Harvard highbrows. Closer because these were members of the president's own inner circle, men like O'Donnell and O'Brien. And these dissenters were still so loath to aid Ted, so fearful of tying the president to Ted, that they wouldn't even answer his campaign's phone calls. And Ted needed assistance. Ted had lots of troops, good troops, men like Morrissey and Doherty and now Gwirtzman, and he had the shell of the Kennedy organization that Jack and Bobby had constructed for Jack's own campaigns—an organization with which McCormack couldn't hope to compete. But the Kennedys never left anything to chance, never, and neither Ted nor Jack nor Bobby was going to leave something as important as Ted's Senate election to chance.

So Doherty headed down to Washington the week after Easter, on April 27, 1962, to coordinate with the administration that had said it would not be coordinating. He went with a close colleague, Maurice Donahue, the president of the Massachusetts state Senate and a former gubernatorial candidate, because he felt Donahue would have more standing with the White House aides than Doherty himself, the lowly state legislator and "unmade bed." The two traveled under assumed names, lest anyone in the press discover the collaboration. And they left Boston just as Ed Toohey of ABC News reported that the president was going to "yank" Ted out of the race because he was doing poorly—a report that may have emanated from those dissenting aides. (In truth, the president might very well have yanked him had Ted been doing poorly, but a Gallup poll showed more respondents favoring his campaign than opposing it, and private polls showed Ted leading McCormack by a substantial margin.) And the president had asked other Massachusetts operatives to fly down as well—again, so that nothing would be left to chance.

But it wasn't just that the president wanted intelligence on his brother's campaign and a sense of its direction, or even that he was distrustful about how it was being conducted, though he may have been. It was clear from the start of the meeting that the president was reveling in the campaign, reliving his own early campaigns, enjoying the combat—clear that he couldn't keep away, even if he had wanted to. And when Doherty brandished a blue file on the Democratic officials in Berkshire County who were backing McCormack, the president, the coolest of the Kennedys, began railing: "Those bastards, they were against me; they're against my brother." And he named the names of the people in that county who were for him and against him, remembered them all, and said those people were likely to be for or against Teddy too. As Doherty ran through the districts and counties, the president had anecdotes about each. "He knew them all." And from his own recollections, he told Doherty that what Doherty had compiled was "pretty accurate." Then there was the thump-thump-thump of a helicopter outside on the lawn; the president said that British prime minister Harold Macmillan was arriving, and he asked if the delegation would stay over and talk with Bobby. But before he left the room, he said, "I'm excluding my guests," meaning the guests from Massachusetts, "but let me remind all of you here in this room"—and O'Brien and O'Donnell were in the room with the other advisers—"if my brother doesn't do well, it will be an awful crack in the balls to me, so we understand that he's going to do well." The next day at the Justice Department, Bobby gave Doherty the same grilling, going over names of Massachusetts politicians one by one, asking how he knew who was for or against Ted. And when Doherty was through, Bobby told him, "I want you to take control of this thing, and if anybody gives you a hard time, you call me," and he gave Doherty his phone numbers. Now the doubts and fears about Ted's chances dissipated, and now the president's advisers were on board—*had* to be on board. If the campaign had been aimless and leaderless before, those meetings gave it direction and a leader. From then on, what Doherty called a "turning point," O'Brien dispensed advice and Steve Smith money. Or, as Ted later put it, his brothers "kick-started the campaign."

And Doherty, the new leader, didn't leave anything to chance any more than the Kennedys had. When Betty Taymor, the state committeewoman who had earlier disparaged Ted's campaign to Jack, visited Ted's headquarters on Bowdoin Street, he showed her a big map stuck with hundreds of pins—red and black—indicating where Ted had been and where he was intending to go, and she thought that he had a lot to learn about running. But Doherty didn't rely on just a map and pins. He broke down the state into its forty Senate districts and then assigned ten districts each to four young women—"boiler-room girls," he called them. They were expected to learn about those districts, read the local newspapers, know the local issues and politicians, and they were expected to know everything Ted would need to know when he visited a particular district, including where a couple might be celebrating their fiftieth wedding anniversary, so Ted could send them a personal note. The boiler-room girls would meet every afternoon at four to share their information with one another. And Doherty kept files on each district—like the files he had shown to Jack Kennedy on Berkshire County—and he kept index cards on individual delegates to the state Democratic convention, and he would go to regional political meetings, "wiggle my way into the car," and introduce himself to the local representatives, because in Massachusetts, nearly all politics was personal; there were connections and alliances, but there was no overriding machine as in Boston. Then Doherty would assign individual towns, many of which were small personal fiefdoms, to Kennedy workers, and those workers would keep track of individual delegates, so that, in the end, young Ted Kennedy, with the help of Gerard Doherty, had an operation that was at least as sophisticated as his older brother's had been. Bill Evans, Ted's campaign manager before Doherty took command, had worked in the Central Intelligence Agency, but he didn't think breaking down districts and delegates this way was important. But Ted Kennedy, young as he was, inexperienced as he was, knew this: He knew that he would have to work harder than his brothers, getting right down to each of those individual delegates.

And now, with his troops in place and his strategy set, Ted Kennedy, who had almost been superfluous to his own campaign to this point, was about to engage in hand-to-hand combat against Ed McCormack.

FOUR

"If His Name Was Edward Moore..."

Now, with eddie McCormack and Ted Kennedy having declared their intentions and girding to face off, the campaign began in earnest, and so did the first test of Ted Kennedy's political mettle. Though the Kennedy sons had all been forged in the same family crucible, and though they all pursued the family business of politics, the surviving boys were very different from one another, and that difference manifested itself in the way that they campaigned and in the way that they led. Jack was always regarded as imperturbable, unflappable, elegant, the cool one. But that was a learned response as much as Teddy's jollity was a learned response. As a boy Jack was slovenly and disengaged, seeming "to lack entirely a sense of responsibility," his father said of him when Jack was at Choate. "Sloppy in almost all of his organization projects," wrote Choate's headmaster. He studied at the last minute, was habitually late (this from a boy who grew up in a household where tardiness was unforgivable), and had "little sense of material value." Through an act of will, he transformed himself—in part, one suspects, because he had to in order to assume his late brother's mantle, in part because of his war experience, and, in the largest part, no doubt, because he was constantly ill, often at death's door, and it had given him a detached, fatalistic vision that seemed to erode his youthful carelessness. Jack Kennedy was enigmatic, even to those who knew him best. (Ted would describe him that way.) He kept a good deal of himself hidden. "He lived within himself, a private man," wrote the author Richard Rhodes of him. Ted Sorensen, who had probably spent as much time with him as any man had, said he could not "remember everything about him, because I never knew everything about him. No one did. Different parts of his life, work, and thoughts were seen by many people—but no one saw it all." To his mother, who was absent so often during his childhood, he was a "child of fate," who, "if he fell in a puddle of mud in a white suit would come up ready for a Newport ball." He was not, like his youngest brother, a boy who could never get away with anything. Jack Kennedy got away with everything. But for all his luck and for all his self-confidence, he was a shy campaigner, uncomfortable with people, seemingly ill-suited for the political world of glad-handing, as ill-suited as Teddy was well-suited. "In the early years we had to shove Jack into the streets to meet people," said an aide. Perhaps it was the diffidence and the mystery that made him so compelling a figure—a movie star, as Mailer had said.

Bobby, so close to Jack, was so different from him temperamentally: "volatile and intense," Sorensen would say, where Jack was calm; deeply admiring of physical courage (almost certainly because of his stature, which forced him to compensate), where Jack, Sorensen said, admired intellectual and moral courage; overtly emotional where Jack hid his emotions; more judgmental than Jack, angrier than Jack, less likely to forgive than Jack, overall more like his father than his brother, or at least the younger Bobby was. Rose had called him "unsociable" as a boy, said he didn't seem to like any of the boys at the Bath and Tennis Club at Palm Beach. Others found him self-righteous—"Bobby lived in a heaven-and-hell world," said Lyndon Johnson's aide George Reedy; his friends William vanden Heuvel and Milton Gwirtzman said he had a "Puritan's sense of right and wrong, good and evil"—and his own mother called him "sanctimonious." There was a time he thought of becoming a priest.

But the adjective that became attached to him like a Homeric epithet was "ruthless." Bobby Kennedy lived without compunction, and not just toward his enemies, the most hated of whom were usually the enemies of his brother because he so worshipped his brother and sought to protect him. John Tunney remembered going up to Hyannis Port for the first time and playing touch football. Teddy threw him a pass, and as he jumped to catch it, Bobby submarined him, knocking him "head over heels," and Tunney was furious, yelling, "What the hell are you doing?" Bobby just flashed him a smile and said, "What's wrong, can't you take it?" And Tunney said he thought he was a "punk." A lot of people felt that way about the young Bobby Kennedy when he was running Jack's campaigns, taking the flack for doing things that Jack wanted done but didn't want to take responsibility for—Bobby was the one who took the fall when Jack wanted to disassociate his 1952 Senate campaign from Governor Dever's campaign, infuriating Dever—always making sure that Jack's hands were clean even when his were dirty. And a lot of people felt that way when he was the chief counsel of the Senate Rackets Committee, hounding the Teamsters' union for corruption. Bobby was relentless, and he was merciless.

He wasn't soft. Softness was a curse in the Kennedy family. But this, too, was a learned response—an act of will on Bobby's part—since he was generally shy, quiet, and sensitive, which were not characteristics much valued in the Kennedy family either. He had, said one reporter who covered him, a "contempt for self-indulgence, for weakness," which had been engendered in him by Joe Kennedy. And a contempt for conviviality. He hated the rituals of retail politics as much as his older brother did—more, even. "The entire hand-shaking, small-talking side of politics was repugnant to him," Larry O'Brien remembered. "He often said to me, 'Larry, I don't know how you stand it.'" He hated being touched too, though crowds would clamor to touch him, clawing at his hands, tearing at his shirt, pulling off his cuff links. But he had to endure these things when he was running for himself if he was going to fulfill Jack's legacy after Jack had died. He told writer Gail Sheehy, "People can hear everything about a candidate, and it's the touching him they never forget." He was not built for retail politics. He didn't have the joie de vivre of most retail politicians. There was a bleakness in him, a sadness. Gladys Gifford, the wife of one of Ted's earliest aides, said of him: "Looking into Bobby Kennedy's eyes, you felt like you were looking into the soul of the earth."

No one would have ever said that about the youngest of the Kennedys, the least of the Kennedys, the Kennedy who had made an art out of hiding his sadness. No one ever saw Teddy sulking or Teddy melancholy or Teddy snarling. "Teddy always sang around the house, and his favorite expression was, 'Let's make it fun time,'" said Joe Kennedy's nurse Rita Dallas. His father said of him that he had "the affability of an Irish cop." He once told one of his nephews that if he hadn't gone into politics, he would have liked to be an opera singer: "learning those songs and having pasta every day for lunch." But, he sighed, he had gone into politics instead, so "Now I can't eat and I don't sing!" (Though sing he often did on the campaign trail.) No one ever saw Teddy acting standoffish, the way his brothers could act, or condescending, the way he had so often been treated himself and was still being treated in his Senate campaign. "Nothing formal about Ted. Nothing formal about him," said a longtime Hyannis neighbor, Melissa Ludtke. No one ever saw Ted burdened by doubt, though he often was—very often. "Stalwart and optimistic from the time he was a little child," said his mother. No one ever saw Teddy cold or ruthless or calculating. People called him "fair." Betty Taymor, the Democratic official, called him "kind." And she said, "I think that comes through." No one ever saw Teddy disparaging people. His sister Jean Kennedy Smith said of him, "If there are five people in a room, I might not like two of them. He'd find something [to like] in all five." And no one would have ever said of Teddy Kennedy that he was withdrawn or enigmatic or unknowable, or lost in his own thoughts, even though he could be all of those things. When *Boston Globe* political reporter Bob Healy was asked by his wife the difference between Jack and Ted, he said, "Jack was all head. Ted's all heart."

And when it came to politics, because he was exuberant, because he was gregarious, because he had no diffidence in him, because he was kind rather than cold, because he was nonjudgmental—because of all these things, he loved retail politics as much as his two brothers abhorred it, which may be another reason he was so eager to run. He just wanted the joy of running. "The reincarnation of Honey Fitz," Ted Sorensen called him, and he was. The joy of it was so palpable that it was infectious, which was another reason why his brother Jack was so willing to get involved in his campaign despite the warnings against doing so, not only willing but excited to get involved. As he fed off Ted's physicality, which he had been denied, as he fed off Ted's incorrigibility, which he wasn't permitted, he also fed off Ted's great political elation, which he envied but which was so alien to him. Jack's mantra was fatalistic: "Life's unfair." Teddy's mantra was both hopeful and bemused: "I can't believe it!" It was an expression of his astonishment at the unpredictable vicissitudes of life, especially those of his own life. With all this, it was hard to resist him. Jack's friend LeMoyne Billings said, "I don't think the president loved anybody the way he did Ted." Loved him so deeply that he would do almost anything to assist him in his first political foray.

When Ted Kennedy began his campaign for the Senate, he had not just a joy for politics but an instinct for it, a great natural gift for it. "The most naturally gifted political person I've ever met," Frank Morrissey said, and he had met quite a few. One old Boston pol opined that he had "the best street personality of them all." Milton Gwirtzman, who had also spent a few years around politicians, said he was "impressed by his political skills. I had never seen that in somebody that young." Even his old friend John Tunney was surprised by Teddy on the stump, saying that while he had once seen the two of them as comparable, Teddy had surpassed him. His campaign manager, Gerard Doherty, saw the gift as Ted's way with people. "The thing that broke for him first," Doherty observed, "was he quickly became a people person." Doherty said Ted would go up to people in what Doherty called a "riveting way": "How are you, Charlie Brown? Jesus, that's a great-looking tie you've got. Can I buy it from you?" And if, as John Kennedy speechwriter and adviser Richard Goodwin said, Ted didn't have "exactly the quickness of John Kennedy or Robert Kennedy," he nevertheless had something else: a "shrewdness about human motivation." Even his opponent Eddie McCormack would later say of Ted that in 1958, when Ted was just a novice working on his brother John's Senate campaign, he was "better with people he didn't even know than Jack Kennedy was ever to be. Jack Kennedy didn't really like adulation, open flattery embarrassed him, but Teddy was already a . . . a freewheeler, a swinger, he liked to be with people, good with the glad hand, the big smile, the slap on the back. . . ." Columnist Stewart Alsop put it simply: "Teddy Kennedy was designed by his maker to be a politician."

And if there was a joy in him, a great love of people, off which his audiences fed, there was also a preternatural self-confidence in his political gifts that they enjoyed. Ted Kennedy *knew* he was good at this. He *knew* he had the political instinct, the gift. He doubted many things about himself—most things—but this he never doubted, and it made him unflappable. His old friend and now campaign adviser John Culver remembered a campaign appearance in one of the liberal redoubts, Brookline or Newton, where he was subjected to a "barrage of very tough, hostile questions" from an audience Culver described as self-consciously "sophisticated and enlightened" and "brutal." He and Ted got into the car and headed to the next appearance, with Culver still shaken. But not Ted. "Ted got up and I think he gave the best talk I'd heard him give up to that point. Just a half hour later." And Culver said he learned from that, as he thought Ted had learned from football. "You're knocked down, you get up, and you don't let that last play upset you. . . ." Ted was so confident that when he was being driven into South Boston, McCormack territory, his driver—probably Jack Crimmins—asked him if he heard some banging out back

behind the house they were passing and said that was Knocko McCormack, making signs for his son. So Ted got out of the car and went out
back and walked right up to Knocko, who wouldn't even acknowledge
Ted's presence. "At least you could look up at me," Ted joshed. "You're
working very hard." To which Knocko growled, "I'm not working hard
enough. Every time I bang a nail into one of these signs, I think of banging it right into your ass, so get the hell out of here!"

And Ted Kennedy didn't just have a gift for people, didn't just have a
politician's self-confidence, he understood the minutiae of politics, things
he had gleaned from his brother's campaigns. One of his campaign aides,
Charles Tretter, had to get money to Ted to drop into a collection for a
saint's festival. But Ted told Tretter he couldn't just hand him the money.
He had a very specific way he wanted it to be given to him, slipped into his
hand—probably so that it wouldn't seem as if he was collecting the money
from an aide. Tretter said if it was money, or a note, or even if you wanted
to say something to him, "You had to be discreet. . . . You had to work on
being graceful about it." Campaign aesthetics from a man who grew up
with aesthetics. And on another campaign visit, this one to a shoe factory
in Hadley, Ted glanced down at Tretter's loafers (Tretter thought Ted was
admiring them) and asked where they had been made. Tretter said Italy.
Ted made him go home and get another pair of shoes, American-made
shoes, so the factory workers wouldn't be insulted.

But even though Ted Kennedy could be brusque, Milton Gwirtzman
noticed something else about him, something as remarkable, he thought,
as his political acumen: Ted Kennedy had manners, deeply internalized
manners. Ted Kennedy always opened the door for his campaign workers.
He always made it a point of introducing his aides or informing them of
something they might not know. "He was really brought up well," Gwirtzman said. And Charles Tretter said Ted was always careful about dressing
anyone down—stern, yes, cruel, never.

It was in some ways incongruous: the millionaire's son courting and
winning factory workers against an opponent who had pulled himself up
by his bootstraps, even if that opponent couldn't discount the help of his
uncle. Steve Smith had been worried that voters might resent Ted, the rich
boy. They didn't. One labor leader told them that it was quite the opposite:
"People in industrial situations have a remarkable respect for a man who
doesn't have to work himself up from dogcatcher to senator but can start
as a United States senator. They respect the power." And there was con-

cern among his campaign team, too, that the rich boy might not be able to connect with those factory workers, might not understand them. But Ted did, had always understood them, from his days walking Boston with Honey Fitz. One JFK aide, Jim King, remembered taking Ted to his very first factory gate, the Fisk Tire Factory in Chicopee, during Jack's 1958 campaign. "[Larry] O' Brien was with Ted and we could see immediately that he could communicate with those people—pols, cops, guys going in a gate. They gave him a helluva greeting, although at least a third of them thought he was Jack." And King said what would later be said of Ted during his own campaign—that they could see "he was interested in them, interested in their lives." *Time* reported an incident in his own campaign at a textile plant in Worcester, where Ted moved through "the din and smell of hot metal" to shake hands with the foundrymen. When one of those men gestured that his hand was too greasy for Ted to shake, Ted said, "Gimme that, buddy!" and grabbed the man's hand, shook it, then "strode on, his hand black with grease below his neat white cuff." And Ted loved the story—told it again and again and again throughout his life, sometimes changing the venue to fit his audience—of campaigning at a bakery on the North Shore the day after his first debate with McCormack, at which McCormack had lambasted Ted for never having worked a day in his life. Ted was wading through the workers, their hands caked with flour and sticky with jam, and he was uncertain whether or not to shake their hands, until one of them shouted to Ted, "I heard what they said about you last night. 'You never worked a day.' You didn't miss a thing."

Ted Kennedy connected.

But there was more to Ted Kennedy on the stump than the fact that he knew how to connect with the voters. He had what his brothers had, which was something even rarer than connection. He had that overused word, charisma—the ability not only to connect to them but also to excite them. "There was something magnetic about him," recalled Harvard Law professor and onetime Ted Kennedy skeptic Charles Haar. "They called him Teddy and they felt comfortable with him." Haar watched those factory workers, fifty or a hundred of them, changing shifts, going in and out of the factory, and he said that they would gather around Ted, gather around him naturally. John Tunney called it a "magic with crowds," and said, "It's hard to know what it is in the brain and the heart of a candidate that enables him to catch whatever fire there is as background music in the community, that allows that candidate to synthesize hopes and aspirations and needs, and get it out there in a way that that person then becomes an image of what people want. . . . There is a connection between the brain and the heart. There's a fire that develops in a really successful candidate," and Teddy "just had it."

Crowds went wild for him. One McCormack aide told political scientist Murray Levin, "The women politely clapped for Eddie McCormack [during a parade]—but all the joy of seeing Ted Kennedy . . . these women just get a chemical reaction when Ted Kennedy comes along, a spontaneous reaction." *Time* reported that he "reduced the women to squeals of delight with his rugged good looks" and described how, at his appearances, he was often surrounded by "searchlights, drum majorettes, flying flags, and marching bands that whipped the crowds into football fervor." Another political worker said, "Teddy is a Hollywood star." But another commentator, this one in *The Berkshire Eagle*, found another analogy—not a star, but a prince. "There is a sort of princely effect in the Ted Kennedy campaign. In any dynasty the king is respected and obeyed, but everyone loves the prince, and Ted Kennedy seems to have that attraction wherever he goes." In a way, then, it was because he was the least that he roused the fervor—because he was both one of them and bigger than they were.

But Ted Kennedy had something else besides instinct and connection and charisma—something even more important than any of those when it came to winning elections. Ted Kennedy had energy, had always had energy. He took nothing for granted, despite his polls, which showed him far out in front of McCormack. Ted Kennedy had always worked harder than anyone. And now, in his own campaign, he worked harder than he had ever worked before. "He basically outworked McCormack," said Barbara Souliotis, who managed his Boston office. "I mean, it was nothing for him to start at five-thirty in the morning and finish at eleven at night. . . . No breaks. It was just seven days a week. Never stopped. If he had fifteen minutes, it was, 'What're we doing now? What're we doing now?' The schedules were unbelievable." He even had perfected a routine where he could shower, shave, and dress in twelve minutes, then jump into the car to be at the factory gates when the morning shift arrived. On one day, he might hit five different factories—the "pit," the pros called it—back-to-back, in the course of just an hour and a half, and not just hit them at the gates but walk the floors, talk to the workers, as many as 450 an hour, Ted would say: Marum's High-Grade Knitting, with 300 workers; the Hy-Grade Textile Mending plant; Ace Knitting; Cardinal Shoe; Barre Textile

Manufacturing, with 500 workers; the Gas Light Company. On another day, a typical day, he hit Ware High School at 9; Belchertown High School at 10; Amherst High School at 11; met with the student council and then gave an address at Warren High from 12:15 to 12:45; Warren Town Hall at 1:30; North Brookfield High at 2; coffee at Francis Lee at 2:45 [his schedule didn't describe what or who this was]; a tour of Mary Lane Hospital at 3:30; a tour of Ware Woolen Company at 4; a tour of Ware Town Hall at 4:30; the house of a supporter to run down a telephone list at 5:10; a meeting with French-speaking constituents in Ware at 5:45; the League of the Sacred Heart, Mount Carmel Parish, at 6:30; and a social gathering at the home of a supporter at 8:30.

And this schedule didn't include those outdoor rallies—the ones with the searchlights and the bands, usually the local high school band, and the majorettes—three a night once the weather permitted, right up through September, when the weather got cool again. And it didn't include the ethnic picnics on Saturdays and Sundays all along Route 128. Or the communion breakfasts on Sunday mornings. Or the weekly parades in Boston on Sunday afternoons, celebrating one nationality or another. Or the "house parties," as they called them, as many as nine a day for Ted, where women hosted get-togethers in their homes, as they had done for Jack Kennedy. Or the events at the Kennedy compound in Hyannis Port— events that broke Joe Kennedy's long-standing rule that the compound was hallowed ground and not to be used for politics—at which Teddy had to reassure his mother that he, not she, was paying the tab. Only Friday nights were off the stump, reserved for strategy sessions and issue conferences back at Hyannis Port with Milton Gwirtzman and John Culver. They would sit at the table of the house Ted and Joan had bought in March, on Squaw Island, about a mile down the beach from the big house, and the cook would prepare a dinner for them, and they would talk. According to Gwirtzman, old Joe Kennedy, who had no tolerance for downtime, couldn't understand "why we were not out on the hustings again." But they would be, the very next morning, Saturday, and the routine would begin again, until at least nine every night. "Those stories of him getting up at four or five in the morning, they're absolutely true," said his press secretary, Ed Martin. "What used to bother us was, we'd be exhausted by the end of the day, and nine at night, he'd still have an appointment. He was just strenuously strong. Amazing." Forty or fifty stops a day sometimes, Martin said. And if Ted had a spare moment, he would walk through Filene's Base-

25,000 new voters. And Ted had a far better organization than McCormack, even a better-*looking* organization. Advance man Charles Tretter said that when he entered Kennedy's headquarters, the first thing he noticed was how different it was from the good-old-boyo political operation— McCormack's kind of operation. "All the women were attractive; all the guys were well dressed and young. There was not a lot of cigar smoke. The place seemed organized, and there was a vitality, a real spirit." Organized it was, with not only a coordinator for every Senate district but a ward leader in every ward and a precinct captain in half the precincts; some apartment buildings even had their own captains. And Ted had not just his father's money and influence but also the influence of the president. When the *Boston Herald* ran a front-page picture of Ted along with a negative piece about Knocko, the McCormack camp attributed it to the paper's desire to get a television license from Washington. The Kennedys didn't just want victory; they wanted a knockout. When McCormack asked John Reilly, a Bobby Kennedy aide, why they were pulling out all the stops for Teddy when he was almost certainly going to win anyway, Reilly said, "Because we've got it," meaning all the resources.

These would have been disadvantages, tremendous disadvantages, for any opponent, but they were especially severe for Eddie McCormack because Eddie McCormack, though an honorable public servant with a distinguished liberal record, particularly on civil rights, was not a good candidate, certainly nowhere near as natural a candidate as Ted Kennedy. Where the Kennedys were well organized, McCormack was disorganized. He put a Jewish liberal reformer in charge of a campaign whose foot soldiers were nearly all Irish Catholics, and those soldiers resented him. According to Murray Levin, who wrote an account of the campaign, when the campaign manager scheduled a meeting, no one would show up. Eventually he was called up to the Army Reserve, missing two weeks of campaigning. Nor did the foot soldiers, many of them old pols, mesh with the Cambridge academics who disdained Teddy and supported McCormack and wanted to work for him. And if McCormack's campaign organization contrasted poorly with Ted's, so did McCormack's personal style. McCormack lacked warmth, the sort of warmth Ted Kennedy had in abundance. Kennedy supporters spoke of McCormack's "artificial smile" and asked, "Did you ever shake his hand?" Everyone shook Ted's hand. And Eddie McCormack lacked charisma. Even one of McCormack's own advisers admitted, "The presence isn't there." Ted Kennedy had presence.

And McCormack had what one reporter described as a "slight speech impediment that could be mistaken for a brogue," a thick South Boston accent, and he spoke out of the side of his mouth, which made him look "shifty."

And looking shifty mattered because Eddie McCormack was part of a political culture, the culture of Boston ward heelers, at a time when one of the most salient issues in Massachusetts was political corruption: graft, payoffs, kickbacks, boondoggles. Ted gave a speech in May, which was self-serving but also honestly felt: Its central theme was that for far too long people had been running for office in Massachusetts for money or power. The Kennedys hadn't done business with those grafters. Those people, he said, had had their day. Now a new day was arriving. No one could ever accuse a Kennedy of running for office for money. Ted said he was running to serve, which was, as Milton Gwirtzman said, "the code word for 'get rid of the old-line politicians.'" Everyone could read the code. Whatever else Eddie McCormack was, however honorable he may have been in most respects, he was a professional politician, and one who, some felt, had attacked corruption with something less than alacrity. Ted Kennedy posed as a citizen-politician who would deliver the state from the old pols and change the state's political culture. "Running against a Kennedy is almost like running against the Church," said one Democratic officeholder. That was Eddie McCormack's unenviable task.

But even though he faced almost certain defeat at the polls, McCormack soldiered on—soldiered on because he held out hope that he could still turn the tide if he could win the endorsement of the Massachusetts state Democratic party as its official nominee at its June convention at the Municipal Auditorium in Springfield, the convention he told his uncle he had "sewed up," and the convention whose endorsement would give him the first spot on the primary ballot and momentum against Ted in the September primary vote. McCormack had some reason for that hope. The convention wasn't a model of democracy. Kenny O'Donnell would call it a "whore's paradise," packed with old pols on the take, and several of Ted's advisers told him to skip it, believing that the long-standing bonds between many of the delegates and the McCormacks were too strong to break, not to mention that there was no love lost between many of those delegates and the Kennedys; Jack, who never genuflected to the pols, had been booed by them at the 1954 state convention. Gwirtzman was pessimistic. He wrote Ted a memo telling him that it was going to be an "uphill battle." But Ted Kennedy said that Jack had stood at the convention when he ran for the Senate, ignoring the hostility, and Ted felt that he should too.

Despite these presentiments of doom, Teddy had never conceded the convention to McCormack. He had been aiming at the convention long before his announcement. It was the convention that had prompted him to bring on Gerard Doherty, with his granular knowledge of the state; the convention that had led to his intense organization, right down to individual precincts; the convention that had triggered rumors the Kennedys were promising postmasterships to delegates who fell in line behind Ted, the convention that had moved his staff to prepare dossiers on every single delegate, right down to their personal interests, so that Ted could find a supporter in the community who shared those interests; the convention that brought Ted to small house parties to meet delegates individually and that sent Joan to meet with the wives of delegates; the convention that had taken him into some of the smallest Massachusetts backwaters, where he might pry loose a delegate. "I don't say he's been in every town," a McCormack aide said, "but I guarantee that he's been in seventy-five to eighty percent of them. He's been in places like Gill. . . . Who ever goes to Gill? This guy went to Gill to see one delegate they've got there. Most people wouldn't know where Gill is, including Edward McCormack." By one account, Ted had visited 1,300 of the 1,800 delegates. By another account, he had personally contacted every single delegate, phoning those he hadn't visited. He found one delegate, from Lynn, on a rooftop at a construction site. Others he found on their front porches or in their living rooms, making, by one report, "like a Dutch uncle with the children." One delegate told a McCormack staffer, "Nobody has been here to visit me," explaining why he was going with Kennedy. "This man came to my house and rang my bell and spent an hour with me and talked with me on every phase of politics. . . . He just made me feel good."

Still, as the convention approached, Ted didn't know whether he would win, partly because of that affinity between the pols and the McCormacks and partly because the Massachusetts Democratic party, with its deep ethnic roots, was more conservative than the national Democratic party. While neither Ted nor McCormack was a conservative, the conservatives felt more comfortable with McCormack, who was one of them by blood if not by ideology, than with young Ted. (One reporter described the delegates as a "cast of characters plagiarized from *The Last Hurrah*," a popular novel about an aging Boston mayor and his cronies.) Ted's task was to describe their self-interest to them: to convince them that it was better to be allied with the president than with the speaker of the House. But it wasn't until the bosses of two wards in Hyde Park, Wards 20 and 21, decided to cast their fate with Ted, after concluding that Ted was going to win the primary regardless of the convention, that he knew he would win the convention too. "They were old guard, and they were very important symbolically," Ted would later say. After their defection, others fell in line.

Yet Eddie McCormack acted as if he didn't know his old power structure was crumbling, acted as if he could still pull out a victory, acted as if he didn't realize his politics of individual fiefdoms was giving way to a politics of personality abetted by efficiency. He arrived in Springfield "quietly," *Time* reported, with his headquarters in a small suite at the Sheraton-Kimball Hotel. Teddy arrived loudly, behind a brass band and standing on a sound truck with a small crowd assembled, including his attractive female campaign workers, and he proceeded to give a short speech. Another *Time* report observed of Ted at the convention, "Teddy thought like a winner, talked like a winner, and acted like a winner. He urged delegates to vote for him and thereby 'do yourself a favor.'" But if he thought like a winner, and if he was fairly certain by this point that he was going to win the delegates, he still didn't take anything for granted, because he never took anything for granted. "The greatest thing in the world he likes," a campaign official told Murray Levin, "is for you to say, 'There's seven delegates all against you and they want to sit down and talk to you.' 'Beautiful,' he'd say. 'Beautiful!' He'd go into that room and take his coat off, and the thing always happens—halfway through, two of them would jump up and say, 'I'm with you!'" That was the challenge—to test his likability. And the official said that if Ted walked into a hall and only one member of the audience was booing him, that would be the person he would focus on.

As he had been throughout the campaign, Eddie McCormack, in his big stand, was outmanned, outhustled, outworked, and outorganized— a mom-and-pop store against a department store, as Hubert Humphrey had said of his own experience with the Kennedys. McCormack had a single telephone line in his suite, over which he called delegates. According to Murray Levin, Ted had a switchboard in his suite and another in a backroom on the convention floor at the Municipal Auditorium, where he also had a map of the floor with every delegation notated, 240 floor workers, and six aides with walkie-talkies. "Away from the turmoil of soundtracks and placards," reported one journalist, "one glimpsed platoons of pretty girls and purposeful young men methodically correlating the silent index cards that represented the noisy humanity on the convention floor." In the upper reaches of the auditorium, Steve Smith, Ted's brother-in-law, watched on a television monitor, "tirelessly putting his team through dry runs." McCormack, by comparison, had "two or three chairs, a table, and two telephones" in his command post off the floor. Instead of walkie-talkies, he had aides shouting above the cacophony. And Ted had something else that McCormack didn't have: He had a head count, an exact head count, borrowed from his time on the floor at the Democratic National Convention that had nominated his brother. (In the final tally, Doherty's count was off by only two votes.) When a reporter from *The Boston Globe* told Eddie Martin that he had a delegate count showing McCormack would win, Martin dared him to publish it. Martin knew the count was wrong.

McCormack watched the convention from the balcony—watched it, one reporter said, "as though it was his convention." But it wasn't, and he knew it. Now, in what could be the death throes of his campaign, McCormack had one thing that Ted Kennedy didn't have. He had charges—desperate charges that the Kennedys were buying off delegates by promising them those postmasterships that the president appointed, charges of corruption, essentially, of the sort Ted Kennedy had railed against. McCormack had been making those charges throughout the campaign. He specifically accused former assistant postmaster William Hartigan of meeting with Kennedy aides at the Parker House hotel in late April to dole out those postmasterships, though Hartigan vehemently denied it, saying he had been discussing post office business. When asked for affidavits as proof, McCormack didn't produce them, claiming that doing so would embarrass those who took the patronage and embarrass the president. He said he didn't "want to win the Senate at the cost of the 1964 presidential election." Knocko McCormack was especially aggrieved and especially angry over the alleged bribes. As he sat "sadly" in the Cheshire Cheese Room deep in the Sheraton-Kimball, he told one reporter of getting into the elevator late the night before with an old friend from Northampton, a fellow American Legionnaire. Knocko greeted him with "Hello, Commander." "And," as Knocko recalled it, "he hangs his head, and he says, 'I can't be with you, Knocko.' 'What do you mean?' says I.

'I've been offered a good federal job if I go with Kennedy,' says he." And Knocko told the reporter of another friend, over in Worcester, "like a first cousin to me for forty years," who told Knocko that the Kennedys had offered him the postmastership in Worcester, so he was going with Ted.

It was a last, desperate effort to turn the convention to him, and while McCormack's charges were desperate, they weren't entirely untrue. "Because we've got it," Bobby's aide had said of why the Kennedys expended so much on the campaign they were certain to win. And they didn't let up at the convention either. By Ted's own admission, some delegates did get those postmasterships, though he said McCormack's accusations about the number awarded were a "vast overstatement." And he later admitted that he had pressured his brother, who had had a frosty relationship with the former Massachusetts governor Foster Furcolo, an Italian, to appoint Cleveland mayor Anthony Celebrezze as secretary of Health, Education, and Welfare to help Ted capture the Italian vote, a gambit that Ted himself conceded was a bit extreme. "He was thinking about who he was going to put on arms control, and I'm talking to him about getting this thing through in time, you know, for the convention." (The president did appoint Celebrezze, though Bobby denied it had anything to do with Ted.) There were those who said that Ted didn't need to arrange for appointments, that the implied promise of patronage or the implied threat of withholding it worked to Ted's advantage when the McCormacks had little patronage to offer, especially when Eddie McCormack would be leaving his office after the election. By one story, Ted asked a local politician to join him at the convention, and when the politician hesitated, Ted said, "All right. But remember: Win or lose, I'm handling the patronage in Massachusetts." And it wasn't just patronage about which the pols worried. They worried about power, some of them even saying that the Kennedys were vindictive. Jack Kennedy had "jawboned" the steel companies into rolling back a price increase. Said one delegate, explaining why he was supporting Ted, "After all, the guy [President Kennedy] broke the steel companies. Think of what he could do to us!" And it was true. The Kennedys were not old-fashioned pols; they weren't in politics to line their pockets. But they *were* in politics to accumulate power—a more personal form of strong-arming but as morally suspect as graft. They would do just about anything to advance themselves, which they seemed to justify as politics as usual.

Reading the tea leaves, the delegates—those characters right out of

The Last Hurrah—had largely defected to Ted Kennedy. Knocko was so incensed that he threatened to shut down the convention, to cut the lights, and his son's staff had to stop him from making good on the threat. And there was another threat. In a last-ditch effort, McCormack had managed to swing two hundred of Ted's pledged delegates his way, provoking the Kennedy forces to launch a counterattack, with Kennedy supporter—the only Kennedy supporter on the Massachusetts congressional delegation—Representative Edward Boland racing around the floor, "haranguing" delegates, according to one report, while the six aides armed with walkie-talkies identified the rebels and put down the revolt. Boland then placed Teddy's name in nomination, declaring that the convention's endorsement "should not be given as a reward for service rendered. It should be given to the man who will best perform the work that must be done." While Ted sat in his hotel room rehearsing his acceptance speech, the roll call—a "turbulent" roll call by one account, in a raucous convention—was proceeding. When one McCormack delegate's district was called, he yelled, "Being too old for a post office job, I'm for McCormack." By midnight, with Ted well ahead, two to one, and McCormack carrying only three of twenty-four districts, Knocko lumbered backstage and phoned his son, telling him he should concede rather be humiliated. McCormack acceded at 12:28 that morning, to a rousing ovation. "With all this enthusiasm, how did I lose?" he quipped. And then, in what was described as the "smoky murk," Ted arrived before the packed house of three thousand and held a late-night press conference, with Joan at his side. "I can see I'm among friends," she told the crowd. "We'll be seeing you again and again." To which a supporter shouted, "In Washington."

And then it was over.

Except that it wasn't, not quite. Ted had won the party endorsement and the first line on the ballot. But there was still the primary balloting itself, and McCormack hadn't given up contesting it, despite his convention defeat. Once again, the Kennedys tried to dissuade him. The president personally called Tip O'Neill and asked him to talk to Kenny O'Donnell to see if they could work out some accommodation with McCormack, and when O'Neill objected to working through O'Donnell, the president told him that he didn't want the press to think he was involved. "The papers will say I'm a Boston pol who can't stay out of a local fight," even though that was true. O'Donnell explained to O'Neill that the Kennedys had no desire to see McCormack humiliated, which he would certainly be if he stayed in the primary. And O'Donnell offered that if McCormack withdrew, he would get an ambassadorship and have his campaign debt retired. Joe Kennedy would even send law clients his way. But when O'Neill approached Speaker McCormack with the proposed deal, the speaker said he couldn't get his nephew to retreat, though Eddie McCormack did make it known that he had no interest in an ambassadorship; as an Annapolis graduate, he wanted to be appointed undersecretary of the Navy, a post already held by Jack Kennedy's close friend and Navy shipmate, Paul "Red" Fay. Still, the Kennedys persisted. By one account, O'Neill met again with the speaker, and this time with the speaker's top aide, Charles Hamilton, and with Eddie McCormack's wife, Emilie, to try to broker some agreement. But Emilie McCormack was adamant. "I don't want my children to have a quitter for a father," she said, and she said she didn't want one for a husband either. McCormack himself conveyed that he would only withdraw if asked to do so by the president, and the president would do no such thing. So McCormack stayed because Eddie McCormack hoped he might still turn the tide after he wasn't able to do so at the convention. McCormack kept hammering away at Ted Kennedy—at his fortune, his connections, his lack of experience, his youth—and was advised to keep hammering away, even though McCormack, by temperament, was not an aggressive or belligerent man. Now he had to be. And in this belligerence, the hope to which he clung, a slender hope but his only hope, was that he could engage Ted in debates, that in doing so he could unsettle Ted, rattle him, knock him off his game, expose him as callow and uninformed. He issued his first challenge, for two debates, on July 15. Ted had moved his headquarters from the cramped apartment on Bowdoin Street to more spacious quarters on Tremont Street. McCormack moved his headquarters right next door and hung a large sign in the window saying he had challenged Ted to debate but that Ted had refused, and McCormack posted a running tally on a blackboard in that window of the days remaining until the primary. Still, Ted resisted, and McCormack issued another challenge, on July 25, this time for eight debates with ten questions for each candidate. Ted still resisted. He was far ahead; there was nothing for him to gain. But Ed Martin, Ted's press secretary, thought that passing that sign every time he entered his headquarters finally had an impact on Ted, that it wore him down, though it may have been that Ted had never dodged a challenge and to do so here would have made him less than his brothers. So one day he said, "Let's do it." Eleven days of negotiations later, the sides had reached an agreement on two debates with five-minute opening statements and questions posed by newsmen, the names drawn by lot, allowing two and a half minutes for answers and a minute and a half for rebuttals. But Ted had not only agreed to debate. As he often did when he accepted a challenge, either to demonstrate his prowess or to tempt defeat, or whether, in this case, to underscore McCormack's ties to the sordid politicos of South Boston, he said that the debate should be held there, in South Boston, on McCormack's home turf, and not only on McCormack's home turf but at South Boston High School, McCormack's alma mater. When Steve Smith told Gerard Doherty to set it up with McCormack's representatives, Doherty exploded and told Smith "[you're] out of your mind." But Smith calmly explained that if Ted lost, they would say it was because he was on hostile territory. Though Ted had hatched the idea of the location himself, whether he knew it or not, the Kennedys were always lowering expectations for him.

The Kennedys knew as well as Eddie McCormack did that the first debate, on August 27, would be the most important event in the campaign, the only event that could possibly be game-changing, and they didn't anticipate it would be polite. They expected McCormack to come out firing. Ted's debate-preparation book, assembled by *Boston Herald Traveler* editor Hal Clancy, warned him to be "prepared for a purely personal attack. Mr. McCormack knows that public interest can't be excited by argument over a few nitpicking differences between the candidates on foreign and domestic affairs. . . . Nothing less than a clean shot at our jugular can bring about the dramatic swing in voter attitudes he desperately needs." What the Kennedy camp didn't know was that, after McCormack had rejected an opening statement drafted by his staff as too negative, the staff had begun goading him, trying to raise his temperature, stoking his resentments, telling him that Steve Smith had said derogatory things about him, telling him the Kennedys had called him lazy and said of him that every man had his price. Day after day, over the course of a week, they incited him, until McCormack finally surrendered and agreed to take the offensive. Meanwhile, the president had secretly dispatched Bobby and Ted Sorensen to Cape Cod—"Have no feah, we are heah," Bobby said upon his arrival—to drill Teddy at the dining room table of Joe and Rose's big house, not unlike those sessions at which Sorensen coached Jack for his Nixon debates or for a presidential press conference. They fired questions at Ted to see how he responded. Sorensen said he found him "surprisingly relaxed and informed." Beyond the questioning, Bobby also told his brother to emphasize his commitment to public service—"Tell them you don't want to be sitting on your ass in some office in New York"—and to raise the issue of West Iran—McCormack would "talk about the Middle East, and he'll look like a fool."

But one big question remained: Just how aggressive should Ted be in response to the anticipated attacks? This had already been argued throughout the campaign as McCormack had issued his sallies, and Ted had never responded in kind. It was relitigated the afternoon of the debate among Bobby, presidential aide Kenny O'Donnell, Bobby's old friend John Seigenthaler, and Ted, and they all reached the same conclusion, but only after what Seigenthaler called a "tough discussion": Ted would take the punches and refuse to swing back. "Just take the high road," Doherty advised too, "and no matter what he says or does to you, or what the crowd does to you, just remain aloof from it all and you'll come out okay."

Ted arrived at South Boston High School at seven-thirty that night for the eight o'clock televised debate and for what seemed to be Eddie McCormack's last chance to turn the race. It was a poor, downcast neighborhood to which he came, McCormack's childhood neighborhood, a neighborhood of three-story tenements that surrounded the school. But that evening it was buzzing. Sound trucks were parked outside through which other politicians, taking advantage of the people and the attention, shouted their messages, and several hundred onlookers crowded the entrance, cheering McCormack and then Ted when they entered. It was a shanty-Irish, not lace-curtain, environment. The school auditorium was packed with an audience of 1,100, many of them young people, presumably students from the school; the paint was peeling, the seats were worn, and the air was close and muggy. ("Why couldn't they have staged it in a place with air-conditioning?" one audience member complained.) The men removed their jackets; the women fanned themselves. Though they had been warned against doing so, some of those audience members had smuggled in political signs, mainly McCormack signs, which were quickly confiscated by guards. It was an energized crowd, a crowd that came to shout and cheer, more a fight crowd than a debate crowd, and if they had come to see a fight—the fight in which Ed McCormack hoped to deck young Teddy Kennedy—they were going to get one.

And as the two contestants waited ten minutes at their respective podiums for the debate and broadcast to begin—Ted on the audience's left and McCormack on their right, both of them dressed nearly identically in navy-blue suits with blue shirts and dark ties—they were tense. Ted had forgone makeup. McCormack had had it applied, grotesquely, noted columnist Mary McGrory, who was among the observers, with dark lipstick so that it made him look, she wrote, "as though made up for an early Lon Chaney movie." While McCormack waited, some of his supporters in the audience signaled him with alarm, and he rubbed it off, seeming to realize, as the crowd had, that this wasn't going to be a TV show; it was going to be that prizefight—Eddie McCormack's last chance.

The Kennedys had assumed the debate would not be polite, assumed that it would be rough and aggressive, but they had anticipated neither the level of vituperation that McCormack would unleash nor the relentlessness of it. From his opening statement, where he laid out his qualifications and Ted's lack of them ("You graduated from law school three years ago. You never worked for a living.") then dug into Ted's campaign slogan, "He can do more for Massachusetts" ("Do more, how? Because of experience? Because of maturity of judgment? Because of qualifications? I say no!"), McCormack fired one salvo after another. He cited Ted's failure to vote in any election in which his brother was not a candidate ("You didn't care very much, Ted, when you could have voted between 1953 and 1960 on sixteen occasions and you only voted three times"); his opposition to federal aid to parochial schools; his attending the University of Virginia Law School ("While I was fighting to eliminate the 'black belts' and the ghettos, you were attending a school that is almost totally segregated"); his trip to Ireland, which McCormack called politically motivated, which, of course, it was; even Ted's arrest in Pamplona for throwing a pillow into the bull ring when he was in the service. And McCormack did something else as he lobbed these charges, something belittling. While Ted referred to him throughout as "Mr. McCormack," McCormack always referred to Ted as "Ted" or, more frequently, "Teddy."

Ted was itching to return fire, despite a lifetime of appeasement and strained happiness, but he couldn't because his political instincts, those well-tuned political instincts, wouldn't let him. Instead, he stared straight ahead, uncomfortably, sternly, seething. He would recall later that if McCormack "had just fired a shot or two, I'd have been tempted to come back. But this thing just kept on going and going and going. I thought,

There's so much in there that if I start off on this part—it's probably better to let this thing go." So he stood and took it, took it for an hour, calmly, punch after punch after punch, answering questions, even countering McCormack by asking him to discuss his investigations into state corruption, and he stayed calm, if tight, though the questioners themselves, hardened journalistic veterans—the ones chosen by lot—were "hostile" to Ted, "caustic," said Gerard Doherty. And Doherty said this was anticipated too. The Kennedy camp *wanted* hostile questioners to make Ted look victimized, so they had stacked the deck of potential questioners. "And the thing we kept saying to Teddy was, 'Just don't get mad. If they call you a son-of-a-bitch, just say, "I disagree with you respectfully." ' "

But there was one thing for which the Kennedy camp had not prepared. They had not prepared for McCormack's go-for-broke closing statement—a statement in which McCormack couldn't restrain his snideness or his bald contempt for Ted Kennedy, a statement that Gwirtzman called "vicious," a statement that was so personal, so overbearing, so contemptuous, that it stunned the Kennedys, who had been expecting viciousness. Ted had just finished his own closing statement, a temperate one, only aimed obliquely at McCormack—"We should not have any talk about personalities or families. I feel we should be talking about the people's destiny in Massachusetts"—and one in which he paid tribute to Boston itself for its historic role in promoting free speech, like the debate then being conducted—a statement for which he received an ovation from the crowd, a McCormack crowd, with Bobby and Sorensen tucked unobtrusively at the back. But Eddie McCormack was having none of it. "I'm not starting at the top," he snarled, and snarling he was. "I ask, since the question of names and families has been injected, that if his name was Edward Moore, with his qualifications—with your qualifications, Teddy—if his name was Edward Moore, your candidacy would be a joke. And nobody is laughing, because his name is not Edward Moore. It's Edward Moore Kennedy." And he concluded by asking the voters to go into the booth, "without fear, without favor," and vote for "the candidate whom you feel is the qualified candidate." Even before McCormack's haymaker, Ted seemed uneasy. Some observers thought that Ted's voice was "shaking" during his closing statement. Some said his eyes were misty. One said he turned white and bit his lip. Another cited a "quiver" in his voice, and by one account McCormack actually considered tempering the attack he had rehearsed, then decided that having come this far he had to forge ahead. But these were not signs of fear in Kennedy; Ted Kennedy did not fear Eddie McCormack. They were signs of rage that he was having to suppress. And when Mc-Cormack delivered his final statement, his attempted knockout blow, Ted could scarcely control himself. It was the reference to Eddie Moore, his family's beloved retainer, that did it. Ted told Charles Tretter that "he had everything he could do to keep himself from punching McCormack in the mouth when he brought up Eddie Moore." After the debate, Ted asked Doherty, "Where is that bastard? I'm going to punch him." And Doherty had to restrain him, calm him down, as he stormed off the stage without the traditional post-debate handshake.

For McCormack's part, nothing he did—save his brief hesitation over whether to unleash his full fury—was on impulse. After that week of his staff's goading, he had decided on going in to provide what he called "shock therapy" to the voters—voters he knew were likely to be against him, given the aura of the Kennedys. He felt he had to "shock the people into understanding," presumably that Ted Kennedy was unsuitable for the Senate. And even years later, he said that he had no regrets for his performance that night, the continuous onslaught. He said he had no choice. "There are two kinds of contests in which one engages in an election," he told Kennedy biographer Lester David. "One is a very gentle type in which you try to outdistance your opponent as in a foot race. The second is to try to have a confrontation in which you dramatically emphasize your opponent's weakness." Since he said that he wasn't running just against Ted Kennedy but against all the Kennedys, he had to bring the issue back to Ted and bring it back forcefully.

And when it was over, the consensus was that McCormack's onslaught had succeeded, that he had delivered a blow to Ted Kennedy's candidacy. "He swung from the floor," one reporter wrote of McCormack. "He jarred Kennedy with the force of his attack." Brushing off reporters' questions, Ted left the auditorium hurriedly, his blue shirt soaked with sweat. McGrory said he looked "shaken." McCormack, for his part, appeared "jubilant," with supporters slapping him on the back and congratulating him for seeming to have delivered the knockout he needed. Afterward, one supporter out on the sidewalk said that McCormack had "wiped the floor with him," meaning Ted, and that he had told McCormack before the debate that he was "fighting for him in my community, and I wanted him to fight tonight. He did." Most people in the auditorium agreed. "They were sure McCormack had won the debate," recalled Doherty. Eddie Martin, Ted's own press secretary, thought McCormack had won the debate. Another Kennedy aide said, "McCormack's attack was just so earthy and so shattering that our candidate might not be able to bounce back." McCormack himself remarked that "some of the Kennedy lieutenants felt that their candidate had been slaughtered," while his own staff thought Kennedy might very well have been eliminated from the race. *Eliminated.* And the sentiment was shared by Jack's aides in the White House, who thought that "Teddy got whacked all over the stage in front of the entire country." (This was an exaggeration, since the debate was televised locally, though the press postmortems were national.) Worst of all, Ted Kennedy agreed. He returned to his townhouse on Charles River Square with, he would later say, no sense of how the debate had gone, but that wasn't entirely accurate. His demeanor indicated that he felt he had lost—and possibly not just the debate but the election itself. After big events, Ted typically phoned his father first and then Jack. But this time, he phoned Jack and almost immediately handed the receiver to Gwirtzman to give the president an assessment. And Gwirtzman, who had never spoken directly to the president before, was candid. He said, out of earshot of Ted, that McCormack had won on points: "He made a lot of the people take things he said about Ted and think about them." But Gwirtzman went on to say that those watching on television were likely to think that Ted had won because he was "the good guy," not letting himself get rattled. The president interrupted. He said he didn't want to hear any of this on-the-one-hand, on-the-other-hand stuff, and he didn't want Ted to hear it either. "He's the candidate. He has to get up in the morning and go out and campaign. Tell him that he did great. None of this objective shit, not with somebody who's running. Not with somebody who's just gone through that." And the president said, "Make him feel good." Meanwhile, the president asked Larry O'Brien to call pollster Joe Napolitan and commission a poll on the debate. Napolitan said he would draft questions and conduct it over the weekend, but O'Brien said the poll needed to be conducted immediately, with results by five the next day. So Napolitan took out the phone book and began calling people randomly.

But Ted Kennedy did not feel he had done great. While the White House was arranging intelligence on the debate's outcome, Ted was still shaken, still not assuaged, fearful that he had failed. The next call Ted made after speaking to the president was to Mary Moore, the widow of Edward Moore, who had passed away ten years earlier. Ted realized that she might have been watching the debate on television, watching as her late husband was belittled and, in Ted's mind, ridiculed. As Gwirtzman told it, Ted felt obligated to call her and apologize for McCormack's remarks, which the Senate race had occasioned. And then he and Joan and Gwirtzman and the other aides turned on the radio to listen to call-ins discussing the debate, listening until midnight, listening tensely, listening in complete silence for the next forty-five minutes to an hour—silence because their phone wasn't even ringing, so deathly was the feeling about Ted's performance.

But as Ted listened nervously, dejectedly, to those ordinary citizens calling in to express their feelings, something strange seemed to happen, something that contradicted the conventional political wisdom that Ted had been hearing that night, the wisdom that said McCormack had decked him: The callers, many of them Irish women, were defending Ted Kennedy, saying that McCormack had bullied him, disrespected him, insulted him, saying that Ted's restraint was admirable, saying "Oh, that Ted, he was such a fine boy," and saying McCormack was a "dirty politician." The calls, Ted remembered, were running three to one, four to one, for him and against McCormack. And then the phone finally started ringing in the townhouse with the same message. And Eddie Martin, who was sure McCormack had won, went to the headquarters after the debate, where the switchboard operator asked him, "What happened over there?" because the board was jammed with calls—calls complaining about McCormack's behavior. Martin also said that a bus driver pulled up in front of the headquarters that night and hollered, "Hey, I'm with Kennedy too." And McCormack, on the drive home, was listening to those same call-in shows and heard the same anger among those Irish women, and he turned to his campaign manager, Sumner Kaplan, and told him to turn it off, told him that "the race is over." (Kaplan said his own mother wouldn't talk to him for three months because of the way McCormack had treated Ted.) The next morning, a state representative who supported Kennedy and who had assumed McCormack bested him arrived at his office to make calls for his own race and found that all anyone wanted to talk about was the debate, and all anyone had to say was that they wanted to "lacerate" McCormack. That same morning, Ted tentatively got into his car to face another campaign day, still uncertain as to what the effect of the debate might have been—"I didn't know whether I was going to come out of my house after that"—and listening to the morning radio heard what he had heard the night before and realized that he had won the debate and that he had effectively put away McCormack. And Ted Kennedy realized, as McCormack now realized, that he had effectively ended the campaign—at last.

The rest was anticlimactic. For the second debate, nine days after the first and held at the Holyoke War Memorial, the president once again sent Bobby to drill Ted as a way of blunting the inexperience issue. Ted said that Bobby was "very incisive and tough-minded. . . . He would keep hammering and hammering and hammering on answers until they became just really razor sharp and spontaneous and lively." The campaign had also sent a plane to ferry Gwirtzman from Rochester, New York, where he had business that week, to Hyannis Port, and he and Ted and Joe Kennedy and the president went out sailing to discuss debate preparation, during which the president pressed Teddy to bring up the issue of the increase in the crime rate. But Teddy demurred. The pugnacity he had felt in the aftermath of the first debate had dissipated with his victory. In the event, the debate was "gentlemanly," as Gwirtzman called it. McCormack, chastened by the outcry against his performance in the first debate, had not only abandoned his attack mode, he had also changed his presentation entirely, abandoning what *The New York Times* called "the rasp of a prosecuting attorney for the softer tones of a family lawyer."

After the months of tumult, in the end the campaign sputtered to a finish. Ted gave a five-minute television address the night before the vote, taking a soft shot at McCormack ("Our officeholders must be the kind of people our citizens can trust and respect") and making a soft reminder of his brother in the White House ("Our state needs in the Senate its most vigorous champion"). McCormack, without the resources to go on television, stood on the tailgate of a station wagon, "forlornly pleading his cause," as one reporter put it, asking voters to look at his record but nursing grievances privately that he had led all the polls before Teddy came along and grousing, "If this is politics, if they can get away with this, then I don't want any part of politics." Tom Wicker, in *The New York Times*, called Ted and McCormack "two tired and nervous young men," but said that for all his lamentations, McCormack told him, "I just feel it coming my way."

But it wasn't. At 8:32 on primary night, September 18, an aide gave Steve Smith a slip of paper with voting results on it for South Boston,

Ward 7. "Here's where Knocko lives," he said—not only lived but had been the Democratic leader for thirty years. Kennedy had beaten McCormack there, 396 to 347. He won McCormack's own precinct in Dorchester as well. He won every ward in Boston and 269 of the city's 275 precincts, and statewide Ted won 69 percent of the vote. Ted knew even before the final tally when a voting machine in Salem malfunctioned and had to be opened for a manual count. Ted was leading handily, which, he said, was a "tip-off that it was going to be a good ballot."

"Enormously exciting" was how Ted remembered it—the fulfillment of his ambitions, his first big step toward catching up to his brothers—and he remembered phoning the president, who was also "very excited and pleased." "Enormously exciting" was an understatement. Ted was now a full-fledged Kennedy. He had accomplished something himself. He had vindicated himself. Even if his father had engineered the victory, Ted had at long last put to rest all Joe Kennedy's worries about his youngest son's future. But Ted Kennedy's joy, especially that reward to his father, would be short-lived. Even as he was celebrating that night, there was an almost eerie coincidence, a sad, tragic coincidence that undercut the excitement. That very night, the night of Ted's triumph, Joe Kennedy suffered a massive stroke. Ted canceled all his appearances, didn't even appear on television to take a victory lap, and raced to the hospital to be at his father's bedside.

Joe Kennedy had been in uncertain health for several years. He had suffered from heart issues, and he had been resting frequently. "Your father's not coming down for lunch," Rose would say. "He's not feeling well." In December 1961, he had returned from a golf outing at Palm Beach complaining of fatigue, took a nap, and then awoke a short time later, gasping and unable to speak. Jack and Bobby immediately flew down on Air Force One, and Ted flew in from Boston with a vascular surgeon. Joe Kennedy had suffered a stroke, which had paralyzed him on his right side and robbed him of his speech. Ted remained with him then for three days. The stroke, he would write, "hit me very hard." He said that they had finally "been together as men, sharing a common purpose"—his preparation for his Senate run. Now his father couldn't fully share that with him. "It was almost more than I could bear." From that point, observed Joe Kennedy's nurse Rita Dallas, "Teddy always tried hard to keep his father in a light mood and usually succeeded."

But Joe Kennedy was still sentient after that first stroke; he could still make his feelings known and his sons could still interpret his sounds, which is how he impressed upon Jack that he wanted Ted in the Senate and how he was able to "confer" on Ted's campaign. The second stroke made even that difficult. "He would try to say things and he would slobber," recalled Jack's good friend Senator George Smathers, " '*tu-tu-tu-tu-eh-eh-eh*,' and his face would get all red . . . It was pitiful." Ted had waited all his life to earn his father's respect, not just his love, waited all his life to join the family enterprise as his brothers had. Now, at the very moment he had achieved his greatest success, the opportunity to share it with his father was lost. It had all been done not only by Joe Kennedy but for Joe Kennedy. Now there was no one to please, no one to bestow upon Ted the redemption he so badly desired. Now it seemed empty. It was a succession without the man for whom it was intended.

III

But even after the long primary campaign—six months on the stump and months of preparation before that—and even with the primary victory, Ted Kennedy could not erase perceptions. *The New York Times*, in a blistering editorial that echoed Eddie McCormack, opined that the victory only showed "if a man has the right connections, those are all the qualifications necessary for nomination to the United States Senate," and that the victory was "demeaning to the dignity of the Senate and the democratic process." And the president was still being harassed with questions as to whether three Kennedys in Washington might be one Kennedy too many, to which the president said, "I would think the people of Massachusetts could make a judgment as to his qualifications and as to whether there are too many Kennedys." At another appearance, on a midterm campaign swing through Pennsylvania, he joked, "I will introduce myself—I am Ted Kennedy's brother." But the perception that Ted had won on his name and his connections was not the only one in the postmortems of his primary win. There was another perception—the perception that Ted's victory marked a change in Massachusetts politics, maybe even in American politics generally; that it was the triumph of charisma and personality over political traditions and that the bonds engendered by mass media were now stronger than the nearly familial bonds between voters and ward heelers, as John Kennedy's own Senate and later presidential victories had suggested; that voters preferred an outsider, a citizen-politician like Teddy, over the old pols with their taint of corruption; that a campaign with its "sheer intensity of purpose," as *Time* had described Teddy's, was more appealing than a campaign based on experience and past history; and that the Kennedy brand of youth and excitement and glamour, the brand so assiduously cultivated by Joe Kennedy as the basis for his dynasty, had trumped everything else. "One of the hottest political properties outside 1600 Pennsylvania Avenue," *Time* said, though one seldom thought of politicians as being hot commodities.

But there was still one campaign, one election, to go: the general election. Many considered this just a formality, even though the campaign would be another joust between two formidable and very different dynasties. Ted's Republican opponent was George Cabot Lodge, a member of one of the most revered political families in Massachusetts. He had come from a long line of senators, the most famous of whom was his great-grandfather, Henry Cabot Lodge, the powerful senator who had derailed Woodrow Wilson's League of Nations, and the man who had defeated John Fitzgerald, Honey Fitz, in the 1916 senatorial race. George Lodge's father was Henry Cabot Lodge Jr., the incumbent senator whom John F. Kennedy had narrowly defeated in 1952 and who later ran as vice president on Richard Nixon's ticket in 1960. George Lodge had been a journalist, then held a series of government posts; John F. Kennedy had actually reappointed him as assistant secretary of labor for International Affairs when he took office, and Bobby threw a party for him when he left to join the faculty of the Harvard Business School. He was young, only thirty-five, tall—taller than Ted, which wasn't easy—handsome, urbane, intelligent, articulate, having overcome a stutter, and a moderate in his party; his father had been Dwight Eisenhower's campaign manager, and Lodge later said he was running for the Senate on three issues: advancement of civil rights; opposition to America's support of dictators; and reducing unemployment. He was also a close friend of Bobby's, who had begged him not to run for the Senate, and Lodge said he might not have entered the Republican race if he had known that Teddy was going to run. For the Kennedys, however, his virtues notwithstanding, his nomination made this a race between old Protestant wealth and new Irish Catholic wealth—the sort of race the Kennedys relished, the sort of race that would give them vindication if they won.

And there was yet a third dynasty in the race. In March, H. Stuart Hughes—the grandson of Charles Evans Hughes, onetime New York governor, associate Supreme Court justice, Republican presidential candidate against Woodrow Wilson in 1916, secretary of State, and then chief justice of the Supreme Court—announced his entrance into the race. He had collected enough signatures, 144,000 of them, to get on the ballot as an independent reform candidate, who eschewed the liberal consensus and called for national health insurance, a higher minimum wage, a tax cut, expanded welfare, and, most important of all to him, unilateral nuclear disarmament, which earned him the sobriquet "peace candidate." The president himself was astonished by the number of signatures Hughes collected and, rightly recognizing it as a possible harbinger of growing left-wing sentiment in the party, questioned Teddy whether this could be a factor in the campaign and whether Hughes, who was endorsed by *The Harvard Crimson*, was gaining any traction.

But no one, least of all Ted Kennedy, seemed particularly worried about the outcome. Russell Baker of *The New York Times* wrote that Ted "rises each dawn in his austerely elegant Beacon Hill townhouse to face the problem every politician dreams of. For one more day of brutal campaigning, he must keep himself convinced that he can still be beaten in his Senate campaign against George C. Lodge." For his part, Lodge only casually touched upon the dynasty issue—after all, he had a dynasty issue of his own—or even the qualification issue, because that had been a point against him in his own primary campaign against an old conservative congressman, though Lodge's supporters touched on both. Republican National Chairman William Miller managed to do so simultaneously when he said, "We're going to take a lot of votes all over the country out of this because people are going to think twice about the dynasty issue now. It was bad enough making Bobby attorney general. But even that wasn't the joke this one is. The idea that Teddy is qualified to be a U.S. senator is ridiculous." And former president Eisenhower, at a Lodge fundraiser, ridiculed Ted's qualifications, without mentioning him by name, by sneering that the primary question of Ted's campaign was a "crass, almost arrogant query: Who can get the most out of the United States Treasury for Massachusetts?" To which Ted responded that in a "Democratic Congress, in a Democratic Senate, and in a Democratic administration, we must have a Democratic voice to speak for Massachusetts."

Lodge, instead of attacking Kennedy as McCormack had, stressed his own independence. "When I came to the conclusion that I would like to hold office," he said, "I did not wait to be requested by friends, but I went out and told the men who had much to do with winning elections that I would like to run." He stressed that because the Kennedy administration was beholden to the old Southern bulls of the Senate, who controlled the most powerful committees, the South would get most of the defense largesse and that Massachusetts needed a Republican senator to fight for the state. Meanwhile, Ted emphasized his policy positions: national medical insurance through Social Security; relaxed immigration laws; an end to poll taxes; federal enforcement of racial integration; and federal aid to education. And Ted had staked his own personal claim to advancing civil rights. In May, he had formed a committee to assist black "refugees" from Arkansas who were being forced north by segregationists. The committee met in his office.

Still, in contrast to the primary, it was a lethargic campaign, even though the candidates themselves were far from lethargic. Lodge worked from morning to night, sleeping only five or six hours (he told his campaign manager that if the candidate didn't drop of exhaustion at the end of the campaign, then the manager should be fired), and Ted hit the hustings tirelessly as he had done against McCormack. He was driven around the state by Jack Crimmins, who also dispensed political advice (he knew all the pols as well as he knew all the roads) and who once even let the air out of the tires on Hughes's car. Ted didn't let up. Rose believed this had less to do with politics than with Ted's dedication to his stricken father, who, she said, had so wanted his son to run. And he ran, she said, particularly hard. "If there is anything beyond 'going all out,' that's where Teddy went, because he knew how much a victory would mean to his father."

But it wasn't only for his father. Meeting the voters continued to have its effect on him, continued to impress upon him the good he could do for them if he won. He would visit the tanneries, where, he said, the acid on the floor that was used to treat the hides would peel the soles right off your shoes, and where the factory workers were all missing fingers sheared off by the presses, and where the water wasn't potable because of the chemicals. Or he would meet the women in the mill towns, in Fall River and New Bedford, who sat at the sewing machines doing piecework, hour after hour, day after day, four or five hundred of them in a row. And he said, "It's the representation of those individuals who are working like the devil," individuals who were "getting the short end of the stick," that motivated him and that "it isn't difficult to get worked up" about representing them. This wasn't just campaign talk. This was the empathy that Ted felt—empathy that Kennedys weren't noted for feeling.

And he recruited Joan—Joan, whose parents never discussed politics and whose lowest grades in college were in current-events courses—to help him on the campaign trail. "Let's show them, Joansie," she said Ted had told her. And she said, "It was just us kids. And it was one of the happiest years of my life." And though she was reluctant, though she said she couldn't have campaigned that way even for her brother-in-law Jack, "who I love," she did it for Ted because, "after all, Teddy's my life." But if she did it to help Ted, she also did it to impress him. Don Dowd, one of Ted's campaign coordinators, said she was constantly asking him, "Do you think I did the right thing?" or "Do you think he would be happy with what I said?" And Gerard Doherty, who said that the other Kennedy women had taken to politics like ducks to water, described Joan as a "duck who had never been in water like this," where she had to prove to people that "Teddy wasn't just a smart-ass kid." But she did. Joan would be in a receiving line and women would be passing through and telling her they had heard Ted speaking and answering questions, telling her, "He's so smart." And Joan, Milton Gwirtzman said, would be "amazed and delighted" to hear people talk about Ted that way, since his own family never would.

But if Ted and Joan were campaigning hard, the tenor of the general-election campaign was nevertheless less contentious than the primary campaign, because Lodge was more gentlemanly than McCormack, because the Kennedys genuinely liked him, because there seemed to be less at stake since Ted's eventual victory was assumed, and because Ted had felt no need to engage Lodge directly, believing that voters had already formed an opinion of him from his debates with McCormack. Lodge debated anyway—debated Hughes without Kennedy present, in hopes of promoting Hughes's candidacy and peeling away liberal votes from Ted. Hughes, a Harvard professor, later admitted that he regarded Ted "as a kid" and had a "somewhat supercilious" attitude toward him, though Ted wasn't there to take the criticism or the hauteur.

As the campaign wound down, Ted came to realize that there could be no harm in debating Lodge, who he knew would not go on the offensive as McCormack had, and so they staged a series of low-key debates and joint appearances, some of which were broadcast on radio. The most consequential, on foreign policy, was set for October 22—consequential not because it was antagonistic (it wasn't) but because, at the time, the Kennedy administration was in the midst of its greatest crisis. On October 14, American reconnaissance planes had spotted Soviet nuclear missiles in Cuba. No one outside the inner sanctum of the White House knew about them. Ted Kennedy didn't know. What he did know is that he had phoned the president earlier that day, the day of the debate, and the president had told him, "This is going to be an easy night for you tonight." But he couldn't tell Ted why. He just said cryptically that Ted would find out later, presumably after a presidential address scheduled for that evening at 7:30 Eastern Time.

Both Ted Kennedy and John Kennedy had wanted to detach Ted's campaign from the presidency, but the debate that night, staged in Worcester by the Brotherhood of Temple Emanuel before six hundred people, demonstrated just how impossible that was. Two television sets had been stationed at the front of the hall, where a pre-debate dinner was postponed so the audience could hear the president's speech. Then dinner was served, and Lodge said that he and Ted debated over fruit cups. But there wasn't much to debate after the president had informed the nation that the reconnaissance planes had photographed Soviet nuclear missiles in Cuba, that the president was ordering a blockade of the island to stop Soviet ships from bringing more missiles, and that America might be on the brink of war with Russia. When an audience member questioned Ted about the crisis, he said that he agreed with everything his brother just said, which, he recalled, drew a laugh—apparently a nervous laugh. At least, that was one recollection, and it was Lodge's as well. But Ted had several different recollections of the evening and of the day after. In one, he said he first heard about the crisis on the radio while out campaigning and had pulled over to call the president. In another he said he didn't reach the president that next morning but did reach a member of the National Security Council, who explained to him the gravity of the crisis, and that he finally reached his brother, who couldn't give him any further details but who did send Bobby and Ted Sorensen to Massachusetts once again because Ted had a scheduled appearance on *Meet the Press;* and they didn't want him to say anything about Cuba that might be construed as coming from the president, since the situation was so delicate. In another, he said this had all occurred on the day the Soviets had agreed to remove the missiles, though the president made no address to that effect.

And there was another recollection: that in the middle of the most serious international crisis in decades, Carroll Rosenbloom, the owner of the Baltimore Colts football team, had informed Ted, Bobby, and the president that the Philadelphia Eagles were for sale if they could come up with $6 million. So the three brothers began dickering, as the president asked for a study before they made their bid of how his attending games might affect ordinary fans.

In the end, the Kennedys didn't buy the team, and in the end, the missile crisis was successfully resolved, which gave the president a victory and cemented what had already been a foregone conclusion: Ted's election to the Senate. And in those waning days, despite the relief of having averted war, whatever campaign energy remained seemed to deflate. "Campaign fatigue," Russell Baker called it when, he said, crowds were sparse. And this time Ted spent election eve not on television but on the tailgate of a truck in Dorchester, as McCormack had on the last day of the primary. Lodge had fought gamely and gallantly, but his main handicap was that he wasn't Ted Kennedy. "He's a very nice boy," a woman in East Dedham said of Lodge. "Very friendly. You'd never know he's running for anything." And political columnist Stewart Alsop said of him, "At thirty-five, George Lodge is a good-looking man, but his are not the sort of looks to make a bobby-soxer squeal." And that was contrasted with Ted Kennedy—Ted Kennedy, who had both the name and the charisma and who never let anyone doubt that he was running for something. At *The Harvard Crimson*, where he was viewed with contempt, two or three Radcliffe girls had disparaged him throughout the campaign, until one night one of the paper's photographers, Donal Holway, who was doubling as Ted's campaign photographer, entered the office with Ted Kennedy himself trailing behind, carrying Holway's bag of lenses and equipment. Ted made eye contact and small talk before departing. "He was impossibly handsome," wrote Hendrik Hertzberg, who was on the *Crimson* staff then. "We were junior sophisticates, scornful of 'mediocrity' and the rest, but we were dazzled. The 'girls,' for their part, literally swooned. The tingle of excitement was something they—we—never forgot." And that is what George Lodge and Eddie McCormack before him were competing against. That is what they lacked.

So it ended, all the months of campaigning, the years of planning. The president flew into Boston at six on election eve to cast his vote the next day at the Joy Street Police Station in Beacon Hill, and that night he visited his ninety-seven-year-old grandmother, Honey Fitz's widow. Later that same night, following a long Boston tradition, Ted closed his campaign by appearing at the G & G Delicatessen on Blue Hill Avenue in Dorchester, addressing the crowd from a platform outside, and then Lodge appeared too, endorsing a health-insurance plan for senior citizens.

And then they waited. In some respects, it had been more like a long siege than a campaign. By his own estimate, Ted had sent 1.5 million mailings and his staff had made 300,000 phone calls. By one unofficial tabulation, he had only spent $226,009 on the campaign, with another $275,112 in contributions, slightly less than Lodge spent, if one were to believe the figures, but that didn't seem accurate. By another account, advisers admitted the number was closer to $1 million. "It wasn't so much a victory as a purchase," one reporter would later write, as others had written of John Kennedy's election triumphs. But, of course, that wasn't true either. It wasn't even true, as George Lodge would generously later say, that Ted won because "Ted ran a perfect campaign." Truer would be that Ted Kennedy was a perfect candidate, that he had been bred to be a perfect candidate, that the skills he had acquired as the youngest and the least of the Kennedys and that the drive with which he had fired himself to catch up to his brothers had delivered his victory. No one had been able to resist Ted Kennedy. The voters hadn't been able to resist him either. "Teddy is the best politician in the family," Jack would say. His father went further. Two years earlier, at the convention that would nominate Jack for the presidency, Joe told a family friend, "Teddy is very young, but he might be the brightest of all," referring clearly not to his intelligence, but to his acute political instincts.

He won the election 1,162,611 votes to Lodge's 877,669: 55 percent of the vote. Hughes received just 2 percent, though his influence as a "peace candidate" would subsequently have greater influence than the vote suggested. Now the election was behind Ted, but there were still simmering resentments. A few months later, after Ted entered the Senate, he received a congratulatory card from Eddie McCormack, at whom he was still fuming for the rude treatment. He showed it to the president with some disdain, but Jack told him, "I'll tell you what to do. For the rest of the time you're in the Senate, just at election time, have a successful fundraiser, and then call Eddie McCormack and ask him if he'll do a fundraiser for you and leak how much you expect from him. Then, when he has that fundraiser, raises that money for you, when you pick up the checks and

The Lowest Expectations

N OW TED KENNEDY was a senator-elect, but when he arrived at the Senate chamber, just thirty years old, he arrived with very little sense of the institution or of the enormity of what lay before him. He had gone down to Washington the day after his election victory because Ben Smith, ever accommodating, had agreed to resign so that Ted could get seniority over those other newly elected senators, who would be sworn in on the customary day in January. (Ted would be sworn in on that day too, as a formality.) Vice President Lyndon Johnson administered the oath of office in the gallery with Joan, Pat, Jean, Eunice, and Joe and Rose Kennedy looking on.

But if Ted Kennedy arrived with little sense of the Senate, he nevertheless arrived with a sense of exhilaration. The 1962 midterm election had been a good one for the Democrats, which meant it had been a good one for his brother. The Democrats had lost only four seats in the House, when the party in the White House typically lost many more in a midterm, and they had actually picked up four Senate seats, giving the Democrats a 258 to 176 House majority and a 68 to 32 Senate majority. There were some portents of cracks in the old Roosevelt Democratic coalition of minorities, cities, blue-collar workers, and the solid South—Republicans' proportion of the Southern vote had risen from 16 percent in the 1958 midterm to 31 percent, while the Democrats' proportion of the Catholic vote had decreased—but the national enthusiasm with which John Kennedy had entered office had scarcely waned; if anything, the successful resolution of the Cuban Missile Crisis in October had boosted that enthusiasm at election time. Historian Arthur Schlesinger Jr., who had taken a leave from Harvard to serve as a special assistant in the Kennedy administration and who would become one of its chief proselytizers, had already, before John Kennedy's election, forecast a "new mood in politics," the "threshold of a new epoch in our national life," and he wrote, "We have awakened as from a trance; and we have awakened so quickly and sharply that we can hardly remember what it was like when we slumbered." This was what John Kennedy's adherents felt about him. Ted Kennedy shared that attitude, that faith in his brother, whom he not only loved but for whom he also had a kind of hero worship. "There was a great optimism in the country," he would remember, and he especially remembered the confidence that people had in their government—the confidence *he* had. "The basic concept when I went as a young, very impressionable person," he would say, "is that the institutions were all functioning and working. You had belief in the presidency and what they were going to do."

And if Ted Kennedy arrived in Washington with a sense of exhilaration over his brother's presidency, he also arrived with a sense of his own mission and of his own place in the historic constellation. It was very hard for a new senator not to feel that sense; the Senate chamber practically demanded it. The chamber, which had been built in 1859, was grand to match the ambitions within it or to elevate those ambitions: Roman Corinthian in style, subdued in color, a ceiling "encrusted with floral and other embellishments in high relief," 1,700 yards of tapestry carpeting with flowers on a purple background, even a retiring room fashioned entirely of marble. It was a place "where calm dignity sits enthroned, and where business really seems to be done," as *Harper's Monthly* described it at the time of its opening. And when it was renovated in 1895, after complaints by senators that it had deteriorated over the years, become "tawdry," when its mahogany desks were stripped of their layers of varnish, when the purple carpeting was replaced by dark green, when the walls were reappointed in gold silk damask, and the floors in cream and dark-red marble, the effect was even more august. "It takes a new man considerable time to overcome the feeling of awe which takes possession of him when he subscribes to the oath and becomes privileged to breathe the air of the upper legislative chamber," observed *The New York Times* when the renovation was completed. And Ted Kennedy had that feeling—a feeling of "reverence," as he called it, and he said that "something profound and fundamental happens to you when you arrive there, and it stays with you all the time that you are privileged to serve." The Capitol had that effect on him. The Senate chamber had that effect.

And then the initiation began. The night before his formal swearing-in that January, he spoke publicly for the first time as a senator, at the Women's National Press Club, which fetes new senators, and joked that when he visited the White House to give his brother some suggestions for the upcoming State of the Union address, the president only asked, "Are you still using that greasy kid stuff on your hair?" referencing a Vitalis hair tonic commercial. And Ted joked that he should not be regarded as exploiting his brother's position "just because I had a rocker installed in my Senate seat this afternoon," referencing the president's penchant for rocking chairs in the Oval Office to ease his backache. At noon the next day, January 9, Ted took his formal oath, on the arm of Massachusetts senior senator Republican Leverett Saltonstall, as was customary, and alongside a freshman class that included Milward Simpson of Wyoming, Thomas McIntyre of New Hampshire, George McGovern of South Dakota, Daniel Inouye of Hawaii, Birch Bayh of Indiana, Gaylord Nelson of Wisconsin, and Abraham Ribicoff of Connecticut. This time Joan, Kara, and Ted Jr., who had been born the fall of 1961 during Ted's Senate deliberations, were in the front row of the diplomatic gallery, along with his sisters Eunice, Pat, and Jean, and Jean's husband, Steve Smith, Bobby's wife, Ethel, and Rose. (He said he had managed to secure extra tickets.)

And then his Senate term began.

He needed a desk. Desks in the Senate were meaningful. The position of a desk was meaningful; the closer one got to the front of the chamber, the higher the status—senators generally moved up as they gained seniority—though unless a freshman class was unusually large, most of them got back benches. The history of a desk was meaningful, who had sat behind it in the past was meaningful. The assignments were made by the majority leader, Mike Mansfield of Montana, who had succeeded Lyndon Johnson when Johnson became vice president. This could be a long process, weeks sometimes, according to the Senate majority secretary at the time, J. Stanley Kimmitt. And Ted had a special request. He wanted John Kennedy's first Senate desk, in the back row on the left side. By one account, he lost a coin toss to Senator McIntyre, who got a mid-chamber back row desk next to where John Kennedy had sat. By other accounts, Ted got Jack's desk, between McGovern and Lee Metcalf of Montana, who had two years' seniority, with senators Phil Hart of Michigan, Edmund Muskie of Maine, and Eugene McCarthy of Minnesota in the same back row. But it wasn't just the distinction of his brother's desk that Ted desired. The desk was nearest the entrance to the Democratic cloakroom, where Ted could greet senators as they arrived on the floor, because Ted Kennedy's political instincts, his political gift, was still active, even though he was now in the Senate. Ted Kennedy still liked people, still wanted to be in the midst of them.

Ted had a desk, but he needed committee assignments, which were the very lifeblood of the Senate, the source of power and influence and action, but about which Ted had almost no knowledge. Traditionally, assignments were dispensed by the party's Steering Committee, which was composed of the Democratic leadership and senior Senate members, and nervous freshman senators would lobby them to get the committees those fledglings wanted. Birch Bayh, who entered with Ted's freshman class, said he "knocked on doors" of the Steering Committee members when he first arrived in Washington, even called on Vice President Johnson, who had retained his influence among the members of that committee, to introduce himself and gain an advantage. But Ted Kennedy was no ordinary freshman senator, and Ted Kennedy didn't petition the Steering Committee, either because he didn't fully understand the mechanisms of the Senate (Bayh had been the speaker of the Indiana House, and did) or because he feared those members might misconstrue his requests as arrogance, as pulling rank because he was the president's brother, not really asking for assignments from the committee members but telling them. He had consulted Jack, who told him that rather than ask for committees he should take whatever committees they offered him; and Jack told Ted that he didn't want to get personally involved, because if Ted failed to get the committees he wanted, it would reflect poorly on the president. But in this, as in Ted's campaign, John Kennedy was not about to leave his youngest brother, the brother he loved, adrift. So, rather than have Ted make inquiries, Jack made some inquiries himself and told Ted that the Senate leadership was considering the Labor and Judiciary Committees for him. Ted had also approached Majority Leader Mansfield, a strong supporter of President Kennedy, and Mansfield said that Jack had always been on the Labor Committee because of the large union contingent in Massachusetts, and Ted, not knowing the jurisdiction of committees, said, "I thought that was fine." Ted said he met with the chairman of the Senate Labor and Public Welfare Committee, Lister Hill of Alabama, shortly after his November swearing-in, and Hill assigned him subcommittees, though not the ones Ted wanted. (He asked and was granted the courtesy to attend meetings of the subcommittees to which he was denied membership.) But Ted Kennedy, who could not petition, did not complain.

Nor did he complain when he met with Senator James Eastland of Mississippi, who was the chairman of the Judiciary Committee. Jack had thought that Ted might like Judiciary because he was a lawyer, but, then, most of the senators were lawyers. In one story, Ted only got the assignment because the Southern bulls who ran the Senate—including Eastland—had decided to punish Senator Quentin Burdick of North Dakota, who was actually in line for the appointment; Burdick had voted to limit the filibuster, the Senate rule that required a two-thirds vote to end debate and a rule that the Southern conservatives had found necessary to thwart civil rights legislation. So Ted got Judiciary, but that March he had to discuss subcommittee assignments with Eastland. Eastland was tall, balding, paunchy, jowly, bespectacled, often with a cigar clamped in his mouth—almost grandfatherly looking. But Eastland was no mild-mannered grandpa. A "very foxy, shrewd individual," Ted would call him, and foxy James Eastland was about to school Ted Kennedy in Senate power. Eastland had told Ted to mull over assignments on the weekend, and Ted used that time to confer again with Jack. Together they made a short list. The following Tuesday morning, Ted's office received a call from Eastland's, saying the chairman wanted to see him—immediately. When Ted arrived in Eastland's office, Eastland's aide, Courtney Pace, brought in a tray with bourbon and scotch on a coarse white napkin. "Now, Ted, I've been thinking about what subcommittees you might want," Ted recalled Eastland telling him. "I bet you want the Immigration Subcommittee," and when Ted asked how he knew that, Eastland said, "Well, you have a lot of Italians up there, a lot of Italians, a lot of immigrants." Then, when Eastland asked him if he preferred scotch or bourbon and Ted said scotch, Eastland had Pace put five cubes of ice in a glass and poured Chivas Regal over them—poured until, Ted said, "all the ice was covered and it was still absolutely amber." Eastland said he preferred bourbon himself, and Pace poured him a glass. "Now," said Eastland, nodding to Ted's glass, "if you drink that drink down, you're going to find yourself on that immigration committee." So Ted did. (In some tellings, he said he surreptitiously poured half of it in a nearby planter.) Then Eastland poured him another glass of Chivas and said that Ted had to decide on a second subcommittee. "You Kennedys care about nigras," he said, pronouncing it with the emphasis on the first syllable and hard "g" that was customary among white Southerners. "Always hear about your caring about those. You finish that off, and you're on the civil rights committee." And Ted tossed down the second glass. And then Eastland poured him a third glass. "I suppose we're going to try to fix you up with a third committee. Not a lot of people want a third committee, but I think you're always caring about the Constitution. Kennedys always talk about the Constitution. You finish that, and I'll put you on the Constitution committee." And so Ted had his three scotches and his three subcommittees. He had been in Eastland's office for roughly an hour—elsewhere he said two hours—and returned to his own at noon to find about forty constituents waiting to see him. "I'm bouncing from wall to wall down that corridor," he would recall. "Yes, the new boy in town was just getting his committee assignment." Eastland's recollection was simpler: "We had a long talk. I was very impressed with him. He told me he wanted to be on the Judiciary Committee, which I did." But Eastland was indulging in understatement. Eastland had, of course, been testing him, seeing what he was made of, and of how he well he would operate in a system based on seniority and power and collegiality. And Ted Kennedy passed that test.

But the reason that Eastland was testing him was that Ted Kennedy, who arrived in Washington with ignorance of the Senate but also with exhilaration and reverence and humility, had arrived with something else—something with which he had become all-too-well acquainted. He had arrived with the lowest expectations about him. Those who had seen him campaign in Massachusetts knew that Ted Kennedy had been underestimated. But none of these senators had seen him campaign. They only knew him by reputation, and Ted Kennedy did not have a good reputation outside Massachusetts. One reporter said he was dismissed as an "aristocratic waster" when he arrived. A fellow Democratic senator complained, "Frankly, the Democratic party wasn't too thrilled to be getting Teddy down here. We knew the Republicans would make hay over the idea of a 'dynasty,'" but he also told a reporter that "three Kennedys in Washington seemed just a bit tasteless. And you would have thought so too, if you had heard some of the cloakroom jokes." One Kennedy staffer said that another Democrat, Robert Byrd of West Virginia, would say of Ted, "When I first met him, I hated him." And if you asked Byrd why, he would say, "Because I'm supposed to. I'm in that club that doesn't like him, and, goddamn it, there it is." Republicans called him "Little Brother," and one senior Republican dubbed him "Bonus Baby." Of course, everybody called him "Teddy," never Edward or even Ted. (Bobby hated being called "Bobby," and those close to him didn't.) Columnist and longtime Washington insider Stewart Alsop wrote that unless Ted could show a "talent for surmounting the insurmountable," he would always be the butt of jokes "about King Kennedy III, and a politician no one takes seriously." Another columnist and close friend of Jack Kennedy's, Charles Bartlett, confessed to one of Ted's friends that, while he loved Jack and Bobby, "I think Ted's just a playboy," and he said that Joe Kennedy himself had told him, "Listen, Ted would be just as happy being on a beach in Cannes playing with the babes." Yet another reporter wrote that "the Senate does its best to ignore him." Even a member of his own staff told his biographer Burton Hersh, "A lot of the time that first couple of years, socially at least, I thought Ted wasn't much more than a really happy-go-lucky arrogant brash kid, always out for a good time." And Ted himself admitted that when he came to the Senate, he was out of his depth. "I knew I was very lucky to be there, and I knew I had a lot to learn," he said, and he realized he had to work hard—four times as hard as other senators, he told a reporter, because his name was Kennedy.

The work began almost immediately. A little over a month after his swearing-in, he had, much to the chagrin of New York Republican senator Kenneth Keating, visited the Grumman plant on Long Island in an effort to lure it to Massachusetts—a "virtual campaign of pirating," Keating called it, though Ted was just serving his constituents. But he could also be un-senatorial. Just two months later, while skiing at Stowe, Vermont, with Joan, he grabbed a camera from an intrusive photographer and exposed the film, prompting Jack to call him to the White House for a stern dressing-down by Clark Clifford, the veteran Washington counselor to presidents, during which the president, according to one witness, wagged a finger at Ted as if to say, "Na-na-na. Shame on you." That was the Ted Kennedy that most senators recognized, not the hardworking one, though it was also the Ted Kennedy that charmed his brother.

Ted obviously knew about his reputation. He knew he needed to burnish his image among the senators, that he needed to be respectful, even deferential. Just weeks after entering the Senate, he told *Newsweek*, "I appreciate the wisdom of saying that a freshman should be seen and not heard." He told his staff the same thing: "You can't use your influence. You can't show off." And his behavior underscored his words. He turned down an invitation to speak at the Gridiron Dinner, a Washington tradition, and only accepted the Women's National Press Club appearance because other freshmen were scheduled to appear. He refused other invitations to speak as well, limiting his engagements to Massachusetts until mid-November, when he made what was basically a campaign speech supporting Jack's reelection. He remained inconspicuous on the Senate floor too, speaking only a half dozen times, and then only in response to a roll call. He held only a single press conference, for Massachusetts reporters, and didn't give an interview until April. Even his first appearance as the Senate's presiding officer was so impromptu—the Senate secretary asked him while he was walking down the hall—that Joan couldn't come, because she was occupied with the children. And his legislative agenda was low-key, Massachusetts-oriented, virtually guaranteed not to grab national attention. His first bills, according to biographer Burton Hersh, were focused on fishing—promoting fish research, subsidizing fishing boats, keeping foreign fishermen out of American waters, including fish in the Food for Peace program—and the first bills he co-sponsored were the Urban Mass Transportation Act, the Youth Employment Act (both of which passed), the Senior Citizens Hospital Insurance Act, and the National Service Corps, each of which either had direct application to Massachusetts or were part of his brother's legislative program. Nor was he interested in empty crusades that wouldn't result in legislation. "I'm not going to support something that is going to fall on its face," he said. He wanted results to prove that he was a workhorse. He wanted results to disprove the image.

And Ted Kennedy, who didn't fool himself about how little he understood, needed staff. He needed people who knew the ropes of Washington and the Senate, as Gerard Doherty had shown him the ropes of Massachusetts politics, and people who could provide him with the substantive knowledge of issues that he lacked. Senate offices were allocated by the population of the senator's state, with those representing the most populous states, fifteen million and over, getting eight rooms; seven to nine million, six rooms; and fewer than seven million, five rooms. (Massachusetts had a population of a little over five million.) Ted got Ben Smith's office, 432 Senate Office Building, which had also been John Kennedy's office. He decorated it after his own fashion, unpretentiously: an 1802 Simon Willard banjo clock, an M14 rifle made in Worcester, a model of a sailing schooner that had been a wedding gift from Bobby. Near the entrance was the framed letter from Jack to Rose, scrawled on Choate stationery, asking if he could be the new baby's godfather. And above the fireplace hung a portrait of old Honey Fitz. Ted sat at an English antique desk, which was the one his father had sat at while ambassador and the one that Jack had sat at in his House and Senate offices and later in the Fish Room of the White House.

And if he had taken the office from his predecessor, he took much of his predecessor's staff as well. In Senate offices, staff was generally divided between the administrative side, which ran the office and set the senator's schedule, and the legislative side, which concentrated on Senate business, though that made the delegation of authority much neater than it really was. Smith's administrative assistant, an elderly Senate veteran named Joe McIntyre, whose experience ran all the way back to the 1940s, when he was on the staff of former Massachusetts governor and then senator David Walsh, became Ted's first administrative assistant. A "wise old fox," Barbara Lahage, another Smith staffer who moved to Kennedy, called McIntyre. "He knew everything. He knew how to get things done," said Barbara Souliotis, who moved from the campaign into Ted's office. She said that because of McIntyre, they were able to "hit the ground running." Ted retained the services of Milton Gwirtzman, Bobby's old Harvard friend, who was working in Smith's office when Smith lent him to Teddy's campaign; Gwirtzman, shuttling back and forth between the administrative and legislative sides, continued to write speeches and brief Ted on issues, even though Gwirtzman had formed his own law firm immediately after the election. And on the legislative side, Ted retained the services of a young—just twenty-five years old—Ben Smith staffer named Terri Haddad Robinson, who, despite her age, had been through Massachusetts political wars and became what she called a "den mother" to the other women in the office. Ted retained two or three of Smith's caseworkers as well, the staff people who served constituents' needs, one of whom, Margaret Stalcup, had been working in the Senate almost as long as McIntyre.

But Ted needed his own people too, his loyalists. So he asked John Culver if he would become his legislative assistant, even though Culver later admitted he knew nothing about legislation. And Culver also functioned as press secretary, though he admitted he knew nothing about press relations either. Because they were both so protective of Ted, so invested in his success, Culver and Gwirtzman promptly got into a turf war, and at a party one evening, Culver—a little drunk, according to Gwirtzman— even charged him, forcing Gwirtzman to seek asylum in a closet. (Both Ted and Culver called Gwirtzman the next day to apologize.)

And Ted asked Bill Evans, the former CIA agent who had been his first campaign manager, to work alongside McIntyre as executive assistant, due to McIntyre's age, and recruited a Chicago attorney named Jerry Marsh, who had been a football teammate of Ted's at Harvard, to serve as legislative assistant while Culver was upped to legislative administrator. And Ted hired a young Mount Holyoke graduate named Anne Strauss as a "clerk"—nearly everyone but the administrative and legislative executives were called clerks—which meant she typed and handled mail, but she later became secretary to Jerry Marsh, which gave a sense of how catch-as-catch-can the office operation was. "Jobs simply evolved based on what you were able to do," Strauss would recall.

And Ted brought down a couple of staffers from Massachusetts to serve as what one observer called "factotums," dealing with the new complications in his Senate life: Ed Moss, who took a leave from the New England Telephone Company and who was part companion, part bodyguard, and Charles Tretter, who had been the Boston advance man in Ted's campaign. Tretter compared his job to that of a maître d', since Ted's schedule was, as Tretter put it, "always so fouled up that he'd keep people waiting in the reception room." Tretter would have to stall them and banter with them until Ted could see them. And Tretter also became chauffeur, driving Ted from his three-level brownstone on 28th Street in Georgetown, which Ted leased for $600 a month, to the office in an old blue Chrysler, one of a series of oversized Chryslers that Ted leased from a friend in Lawrence, Massachusetts. Frequently, Tretter would arrive at the house, and Ted's cook, Andres, would offer him breakfast, even though Tretter had already eaten. But he wouldn't refuse, and as he was digging into his second plate of pancakes, Ted might come in, ask him if that was his second plate, and then begin teasing him. And then in the car, Ted would begin a "nonstop kind of exhortation," because "you can't start the car that he doesn't tell you *how* to start the car." Then, later that morning, Ted might phone him, ask what Bill Evans had assigned him to do that day, and then tell him he wanted him to "take Joan to the doctor" or "take the kids to the doctor" or "take the governess, Teresa Fitzpatrick, she needs to go there," wherever she needed to go, or "pick up a friend of mine." Tretter said that in retrospect friends of his called him a "manservant," but Tretter said he never saw himself that way. He was helping Ted Kennedy.

Ted Kennedy needed help because he had so much to prove. Though he had benefited from the smooth operation of his campaign, he was terribly disorganized himself, more disorganized now with his Senate responsibilities. Tretter said, "It was a joke around the office that if the senator was in charge of anything, you could be assured it was going to be screwed up. His sense of being able to organize anything and get it executed—forget it." And when Ted would say, "I'm going to straighten them out," Tretter said, "he was *not* going to straighten them out. It was going to be worse by the time he got through." So it was up to his staff to organize, up to his staff to straighten out. And when he started, the office correspondence was careless. "People didn't proofread," said Anne Strauss. "Nobody checked anything." Strauss had a friend who received a letter from Kennedy's office that had so many typos in it, he thought the senator had typed it himself. What made it worse was that Kennedy received letters from around the country, hundreds a day—"close to overwhelming," Strauss recalled—so many that the clerks began stuffing them into file cabinets, as if the letters didn't exist. "Everyone turned to Ted," Terri Haddad Robinson said, and the office had to hire volunteers to file those letters properly, but the volunteers had to work on the floor, because there wasn't enough room for desks. And the volunteers could only file, not type, because there were not enough typewriters for them. And there were no Xerox machines, only mimeograph machines. "But we did it," Robinson said. "We did it." And they didn't just do it. Because so much was on the line for Ted, his whole reputation, and because everything that left the office reflected on him, the president's brother, he was determined that they do it well, that they correct mistakes, that they proofread carefully now, that they vet everything that left the office. And if that meant longer hours, as it often did, that was all right too. "Everyone loved working there," Robinson said. They loved working for the president's brother.

II

But however much Ted Kennedy tried to get his political house in order, order would not be enough to improve his image among the senators who mattered. The United States Senate was a club, the world's most exclusive club, it had been called. But there was a club within the club, and even though he was the president's brother, even though thousands of people were already turning to him for assistance, even though he was striving for approval and would do almost anything to get it, Ted Kennedy was not a member of that club, and that club ruled the Senate. "Minnows and whales" was how Lyndon Johnson divided the Senate, and the whales, the chairmen of the major committees, who had come to those chairmanships through seniority, were the ones who ran the club. It was a club whose members were old. The average age of a senator when Ted entered the body was fifty-seven-and-a-half years old, but the ones who ran the club were older. It was a conservative club. The Senate, John Kennedy's Senate, had those large Democratic majorities and a growing cohort of liberals, but the ones who ran the Senate were not those liberals. "We should realize that some of the Democrats have voted with the Republicans for twenty-five years," John Kennedy said, explaining the difficulties he was having pushing through bills, "really since 1938, and that makes it very difficult to secure the enactment of any controversial legislation." The New England states, the Northern states, and the Midwestern states together outnumbered the Southern states, but the senators from those states were not the ones who ran the Senate, despite their numbers. "Southerners colonized the Congress," wrote one political scientist of this period, "shaped its rules to their needs, and made it a bastion for protecting Jim Crow at home and keeping Washington at a distance." Or, as *The New York Times*'s Tom Wicker put it more colorfully, "Those old chairmen would put their rumps together like mules. There they stood in an unbreakable circle, one for all and all for one." They stood in a circle, those Southerners who ran the club, primarily to stop civil rights legislation from advancing, and they had largely succeeded. (Only the timid Civil Rights Acts of 1957 and 1960 had passed.) But if race was their primary focus, maintaining the status quo was another. "Congress is like a waterlogged scow," said Senate Minority Leader Everett Dirksen. "It doesn't go fast, but it doesn't sink."

When Ted Kennedy entered Congress, the engine of that scow was at long last being revved. Speaker of the House Sam Rayburn and John Kennedy had conspired during Kennedy's first year in office to expand the House Rules Committee, where the chairman, Howard Smith, a crusty Virginia segregationist, had managed to block any progressive legislation; the Senate, too, was in transition, as those liberals from the class of 1958 were beginning to gain seniority and chairmanships. But if the scow moved more rapidly than before, it still moved slowly. One senator had so little staff—Ted had roughly twenty-five staffers, but two-thirds of them answered mail—that he said the Senate almost worked as a parliamentary system: The president or the Cabinet secretaries approached the committee chairmen with proposals, and the chairmen from that point on did everything, made all the decisions, advanced legislation or bottled it up, since legislation had to be reported to the Senate floor from the appropriate committee. The committee members themselves were basically powerless, though one was unlikely to get on a committee unless he either supported the chairman or was assured of being thwarted by his fellow committee members, as Ted would be thwarted on civil rights issues on James Eastland's Judiciary Committee. In order to get on the powerful Senate Finance Committee, for example, which reported out legislation to the full Senate on oil matters, Ted said that one had to take a "pledge" to support the oil depletion allowance and the oil import tax, which aided the oil industry by giving it tax breaks.

But Ted Kennedy had an advantage with the Southern bulls who ran the club—an advantage that most of his fellow freshmen did not have—and it wasn't that he was the president's brother, which actually made some of those bulls suspicious that his loyalties lay not with the Senate but elsewhere. Ted Kennedy's advantage was that he had grown up in a family where he was the youngest, the least, the one who was forced to entertain and appease his siblings and parents, which he did—"a ninth-child talent"—and that talent would be instrumental in entertaining and appeasing the elders in his new family, his Senate family. So if Ted Kennedy was made to be a politician, he was also made to be a senator in an institution run by old bulls, an institution in which the sort of deference he had always displayed and the sort of comity he had always exuded could go a very long way. As Milton Gwirtzman put it, "He knew how a young person should deal with the old people."

Ted may not have understood the operations of the Senate, but he understood the operations of its members. He had read William White's classic study of the Senate, *Citadel,* but that was a book. Now he was invading the citadel. He needed to get inside it—"There's no school for senators," Jack had told him. "You learn the job by listening to other senators, observing and studying the great institution and how to make a contribution to it"—and he said he entered the Senate with the intention that he would "learn the institution and learn how it worked, and learn how my colleagues, you know, functioned with the institution and how they got things done." He knew that in order to learn those things, he had to visit a "lot of old bulls here." When Jack had first arrived in Congress, one old Boston pol advised him to "marry" John McCormack, the House majority leader, to "hang around with him in the House, eat dinner with him a couple of nights a week, listen to everything he had to say and ask for advice," which is how young congressman Lyndon Johnson had cozied up to Speaker Sam Rayburn, a fellow Texan, and became his protégé. But Jack Kennedy was different. The pol said, "He backed away from me in horror as if I had pointed a gun at him." But now that Jack was dispensing advice to his youngest brother, he suggested that he first go around and pay his respects to the congressional leadership—to Majority Leader Mike Mansfield and Speaker McCormack and the Senate committee chairmen, those bulls. He should tell them that he was there "to learn and listen and ask what kind of advice they have for you." And he should go see Georgia senator Richard Russell, widely regarded to be the biggest of the Senate bulls, the smartest and canniest of them, the real leader of the chamber. "When you see Russell," the president said, "you should just tell him, Teddy, that although the president told you that he rarely voted with Senator Russell"—who was an ardent segregationist—"that there were very few men that he had greater respect for as a senator." Jack also told him to attend the Wednesday prayer breakfasts, where a dozen or so of the bulls held forth, which was an opportunity to, as Ted put it, "get some sense and feel for people and how they were related to the Senate." And Jack told him to eat in the senators' dining room, not the one where senators could invite guests but the inner dining room, the private dining room, where it was admission by Senate membership only. "Have lunch there every day," and mingle with the senators and talk with them. And Jack told him to go to the Senate steam room, in the bowels of the Senate gym, at about 6 P.M., where he would be likely to meet a different group of senators from the ones at the prayer breakfast or at lunch. And Jack told him to roam the halls of the Old Senate Office Building, just drop in on senators to show his respect for his colleagues, since senators seldom went to one another's offices. Whether Jack had done any of these things himself was another matter.

Ted Kennedy followed his brother's advice. He introduced himself to the leaders and the bulls, dropped by to pay his respects, went to Richard

Russell's office on a courtesy call, told Russell that he was "honored to be sitting in the same body with you," to which Russell replied that "it's good to have you here." But when Teddy, making chitchat, said that he and Russell had something in common—they had both arrived in the Senate at thirty—Russell parried that he had had a "little seasoning first." He said, "I was the county attorney of Barrow County, a member and speaker of the [Georgia] House of Representatives for ten years, and governor of Georgia." (Culver, who had accompanied Ted, said that, far from chastened, Ted went down the hall laughing over Russell's expert putdown.) And he attended those prayer breakfasts, attended them regularly for three or four years, and got to meet the bulls, men like Sam Ervin of North Carolina, and John McClellan of Arkansas, and Willis Robertson of Virginia, as well as the Republican conservatives—and Jack, who had his own motives in his advice to his youngest brother, would often call him afterward to find out what they were saying. And he did have lunch daily in the inner dining room, passing the Republicans, who sat in one room while the Democrats sat in another, and even the Republicans, when Ted passed, would engage him, telling him that they had been back home and there were some polls taken, and they'd share that intelligence with Ted. And he went to the steam room and sat with the four or five regulars there, who would discuss the day's events and other things that were happening. And he not only met with those Senate bulls but he listened to them, listened closely and courteously, even when, said Charles Tretter, they would "just go on and on." But Tretter remembered that Ted would be "very gracious, and he'd be listening to them, and he'd say, 'Well, Charlie will come back and get that, Senator.'" And he did begin roaming the SOB halls, dropping in on senators, and not just the SOB halls but the halls of the executive departments, going to the Labor Department, for example, and asking people to brief him, so that he gained contacts and information.

He did all of those things. And he did more. He sent Joan out to socialize with the other Senate wives, even though she was the youngest of them by far, save for Birch Bayh's wife, Marvella, who was only three years older and who could sympathize with the pressure Joan faced attempting to balance her personal life with her political one. "Like jugglers trying to hold four or five plates in the air at the same time," said Marvella Bayh. Joan joined the Senate Ladies who met to sew bandages for the Bethesda Naval Hospital, and she headed the Hope Ball for charity, and she ingratiated herself with the other wives with her modesty as Ted was ingratiating himself with their husbands with *his* modesty. And Ted invited his legislative colleagues to parties at his Georgetown home, and when, at the first of these, the guests began to leave at eight o'clock— thinking that Ted would be as parsimonious with alcohol as Jack had been when he was a senator—and were milling around outside deciding where to go next, Ted ran out to urge them to come back in, protesting that he was not Jack and that he had drinks and food inside. Tip O'Neill, who was one of the invitees, said they stayed until three in the morning.

And beyond the ingratiation and the socializing, Ted Kennedy did something that he had always done: Ted Kennedy worked hard—worked hard because he knew his Senate colleagues had "an impression about me, just on the basis of stories, and the rest," and he was determined to prove them wrong. Every six weeks or so, Bobby had been holding meetings—seminars, really—at his house, Hickory Hill, in McLean, Virginia, inviting government officials, academics, think-tank staffers, and other experts to discuss issues, sometimes having everyone read a book prior to the meeting to discuss that. And Ted said he adopted this idea, holding similar sessions at his own house in Georgetown to analyze particular issues, to familiarize himself with them, to gain expertise in them, to show that he was a workhorse. And when John Kennedy submitted his civil rights bill in June 1963, Ted was especially dedicated. He said it was at one of those meetings where he became educated on the issue of the poll tax, a "voting tax" that Southerners had enacted to prevent African Americans from exercising their franchise—an issue that would become important to him.

He had done all these things to learn the Senate, to learn the issues, and he had done them to change his reputation among the senators. One advised him to keep his mouth shut, and the senator said, "He kept his mouth shut." Russell told him, "You go further if you go slow." So Ted went slow. He didn't even introduce legislation, those fishing bills, until he had been in office nearly a year, and he had been reluctant to co-sponsor any legislation that didn't affect Massachusetts directly or that didn't emanate from his two committees, Justice and Labor. Everyone watched to see how much of a show horse he would be, how much attention he devised to attract. So Ted didn't devise to attract attention and didn't court the media; he did the opposite. "He was very sensitive to anything that would take the attention away from them," away from the old bulls, said

Milton Gwirtzman. And because of all that—because he had kept quiet and gone slow and remained as inconspicuous as the president's brother could remain, and because he seemed studious, and because he diverted attention to his seniors in the Senate, and because he was courteous and deferential and affable and charmingly self-deprecating, and because he so clearly, legitimately, enjoyed being with them, as he had enjoyed campaigning ("He enjoyed understanding these other members," John Culver said)—those old bulls, and even younger senators who had also harbored doubts about Ted Kennedy, began to think differently about him, began to be disabused of those low expectations. Missouri senator Stuart Symington called him a "terrific fellow" and said he had never seen anyone learn the job as quickly as Ted had. Senator Joseph Tydings of Maryland, who arrived two years after Ted, found him "one of the most attractive young men I've ever seen." Republican senator Jacob Javits of New York took a liking to him and invited him to a breakfast with the Federal Reserve chairman, Arthur Burns. Senator George McGovern, one of his seatmates in that back row, would admit, "I suppose that in early 1963, I shared the common reaction that the president's kid brother had come to the Senate," and that he "didn't expect much of Ted." But "I quickly got over that misimpression," seeing that "Ted was determined to be a good senator." Some of those bulls were even asking Ted to speak in their states—the senator who had refrained from speaking outside Massachusetts because he feared being seen by those bulls as self-serving—so thoroughly had he won them over. And Ted passed the sternest test of all. One Democratic observer said, "Why, even Senator Russell now respects him. In fact, I haven't heard an unkind word about him."

But of all the Senate bulls, the one who mattered most to Ted Kennedy was James Eastland, the chair of the Judiciary Committee on which Ted sat, the committee from which Ted would be making his own legislative forays. Judiciary was powerful. One-fifth of all measures referred to Senate committees passed through it, and more important for Ted, and for the president, it was the committee that would either be reporting out or bottling up, as it had for years, civil rights legislation and immigration legislation, and it was the committee that considered constitutional issues, like the poll tax, in which Ted had taken that interest. And if Judiciary was powerful, James Eastland was the power behind Judiciary. Eastland, Ted said, had "complete control over every aspect of the committee," despite the other Senate luminaries who served on it. "They had just stars on that Judiciary Committee," Ted would say: Minority Leader Dirksen; Hugh Scott of Pennsylvania; Sam Ervin; Republican veteran from Nebraska Roman Hruska; John McClellan; Hiram Fong of Hawaii; Phil Hart. "They'd come in and have a drink in the afternoon, and they'd decide. They'd decide what judges they were going to confirm, or if they weren't going to do judges." And they would decide which bills would be reported out. And they would decide how much funding each subcommittee would receive, though in all these decisions, Eastland's was always the decisive vote, the only vote that really mattered. So, over and above his interest in being accepted by the Senate bulls, which was a very large interest, Ted Kennedy had a reason to court James Eastland, as Lyndon Johnson had courted Richard Russell when Johnson first entered the Senate—young men lavishing praise, attention, and respect on old men in exchange for their support and mentorship.

And Ted Kennedy would visit Eastland, because Eastland had told him at the outset, "You want something, you come over and speak to me. I don't ever want to get a letter from you." And Ted thought that this personalization was as much a test of him as the scotch, that Eastland wanted to be Ted's mentor and pass on to him the importance of interpersonal relations in the Senate and wanted to see that "you picked up on [it], just the way you were dealing with people. That was very important to him." But even though Eastland was a power in all matters Judicial, Ted thought his real interests laid elsewhere—in money. When Ted visited Eastland's office, he said he invariably found Eastland poring over oil maps alongside oil men from Mississippi and Alabama, and they would be looking at oil wells, talking about deals, and they would be doing that for days on end. Occasionally, Ted said, Eastland would "drift by the floor," the Senate floor, and read a short statement. And then, at the end of the day, Eastland's "little drinking club" of those old, conservative Judiciary members would convene in his office. But, Ted said, Eastland "no more cared what was happening in the United States Senate . . . than the man in the moon. It was all about the oil." He even had a private oil-company plane fly him back to Mississippi on Thursdays and return him to Washington on Mondays.

But as Ted Kennedy knew all too well, it was not *all* about oil. There was something else that moved James Eastland as much as oil, perhaps more, an animus deep in him, in his very bones. James Eastland was also moved by race—moved to keep the races separate, moved to prevent any civil rights legislation from being reported from his committee, through which all civil rights legislation had to pass. Eastland would joke that he had his tailor put especially deep pockets in his suits: pockets where civil rights legislation went to die. And his wasn't ordinary Southern racism, the racism that was second nature to many white Southerners. It went deeper. The Eastlands hailed from Doddsville in Sunflower County, Mississippi, in the Delta, one of the poorest counties in America, where Eastland's grandfather, Oliver, had bought a 2,400-acre cotton plantation. But the Eastlands had no interest in their poor neighbors of Sunflower County, none whatsoever. They had no interest because most of those neighbors, 80 percent of the population, were black, many of them former slaves who had become sharecroppers. And the only interest the Eastlands *did* have was in maintaining white supremacy over those poor African Americans. When one of the Eastlands' laborers, a longtime servant named Luther Holbert, took up with a fellow laborer's wife or girlfriend, Oliver's son, James, and the alleged cuckold went to Holbert's cabin and confronted him. A gunfight ensued in which the cuckold and James Eastland were both killed. Now the slain James's older brother, twenty-five-year-old Woods Eastland, set out after Holbert with an army of vigilantes. Leaving a trail of black bodies in their wake, they brought him and his girl back to Doddsville, tortured them, driving a corkscrew into their bodies and pulling out chunks of their flesh, cut off their ears and fingers (these were passed out as souvenirs), cracked their skulls, dragged them to a black church, and then set them afire in front of a crowd of one thousand people. Woods Eastland was Senator James Eastland's father, and Eastland's mother was pregnant with James at the time Woods was acquitted of the murders.

The apple didn't fall far from the tree. As James Eastland would say, "My father completely controlled me," which meant, among other things, that Eastland became a white supremacist. A portrait of General Nathan Bedford Forrest, who had massacred black Union troops at the Battle of Fort Pillow and after the war became the first grand wizard of the Ku Klux Klan, hung in Eastland's Senate office. Lyndon Johnson would later say of Eastland, "Jim Eastland could be standing right in the middle of the worst Mississippi flood ever known, and he'd say the niggers caused it, helped out by the communists—but he'd say, we gotta have help from Washington," which neatly summarized Eastland's racism, his red-baiting, his hy-

pocrisy, and his belief in government largesse, from which he had greatly
benefited when cotton prices were depressed during the Depression and
Franklin Roosevelt provided cotton farmers with relief.

That was the barrier Ted Kennedy had to surmount. That was the barrier all liberal senators had to surmount if they wished to pass civil rights
legislation. But Ted Kennedy courted James Eastland, courted him to gain
acceptance, courted him to give himself some legislative footing, courted
him to gain funding for his subcommittees, since parceling out that funding was one of the ways Eastland kept liberals in line. And Ted Kennedy
knew how to court, had the youngest's talent for courting. The enormous
political differences between Eastland and him notwithstanding, he knew
that, in the words of one Senate colleague, "you have to be extremely careful that you handle the situation in which you ask for something in a delicate way." The colleague added, "Ted's a master of that." He would flatter
Eastland, charm him, share a convivial bourbon with him in his office.
But this wasn't just a pretense, a strategy to disarm Eastland, though it
did succeed in doing that. Ted Kennedy, who seemed to like everyone and
was practically incapable of hatred, developed an affection for Eastland, a
chemistry with him, which was an important ingredient in the Senate and
an important capability of Ted's. "There was a lot of chemistry then," Ted
would say of the Senate at that time. A Kennedy staffer called Ted's relationship with Eastland "genuine" and said they "giggle together like children. It is beyond explanation, except chemistry." And because he liked
Ted Kennedy too, Eastland bestowed favors upon him. When Ted was trying to get something out of the committee, Eastland told him that even
though he was personally opposed to it, he would get it out of committee.
But when Ted heard that another senator had "flipped," deciding to vote
against Ted's bill after saying he would vote for it, Eastland said he would
flip his own vote and told Ted to go ahead and offer the bill, saying afterward, "I told you [that] you were going to get the thing out. I didn't think it
was going to be this way, but if I give my word on it, you're going to get it
out." Ted did. And that was part of his Senate education: that even racists
occasionally would come to one's aid, but only if they liked you, only if the
chemistry was right, and only if the issue wasn't race.

But if Ted Kennedy had to court the bulls, had to show them deference,
had to win their trust and approval, he had arrived in the Senate at a time
when the power of those bulls, power that had lasted for decades, was fi-

nally beginning to decline and the institution itself was finally changing—a time when he had the possibility of gaining not only acceptance but also some small degree of power with which he could counter those lowest expectations. Much of this had to do with the decrepitude of the bulls themselves. Senator Eugene McCarthy said that after John Kennedy submitted the Civil Rights Act in 1963, Vice President Johnson—who had once been majority leader of the Senate, the most powerful and tenacious majority leader in the Senate's history—corralled several senators and told them that this was their moment to act, because the bulls, the bulls whom Johnson himself had so assiduously courted in his Senate days, were physically incapable of holding on to their power. "He started down the list of Southern senators," McCarthy said, "and he began to tick off their various disabilities. . . . He said that 'there [are] only two of them who will fight on civil rights and are able-bodied. Mostly, they're old and sick. You can break them down in two weeks. You can kill them." This about the men with whom Johnson had worked hand-in-glove, the men who had taken him under their wings and advanced his ambitions. And McCarthy said that it was "inconceivable that Mansfield would have uttered those words."

Mike Mansfield, who had succeeded Lyndon Johnson as Senate majority leader, could not have been more dissimilar from him. Johnson was a Texan, a hardscrabble Texan, whose family had descended from country nobility into poverty, and who used his considerable wiles and energy to scale the heights of power while carrying a huge chip on his shoulder. Mansfield was born in Greenwich Village in Manhattan, in 1903, but was sent to live with his aunt and uncle in Montana after his mother died when Mike was three. If Johnson was as tough as Texas and as garrulous as the stereotypical Texan, Mansfield was as dry and laconic as Montana—literally professorial since, after dropping out of school to work in the mines, then enlisting in the Navy at the age of fourteen and serving in all three branches of the service during World War I, then returning to Montana to get a college degree (his sweetheart wouldn't marry him if he didn't) and then his master's degree, he became a history professor at Montana State University. He went from the classroom to the U.S. House, and from the House to the Senate in 1950. And he went from the Senate to the Senate leadership when Johnson named him whip as a compromise candidate over Hubert Humphrey and Florida senator George Smathers, who were both vying for the position.

And if Johnson and Mansfield, though friends (Mansfield wouldn't have gotten the whip without Johnson's approval), couldn't have been more different as men, they also couldn't have been more different as leaders. Johnson had run the Senate the way the bulls ran their committees, and in fact with the full support of the bulls and in conjunction with them—with an iron fist. Mansfield, who even looked professorial—thin, hollow-cheeked, his hairline receding, his temples graying, and always smoking a pipe—ran it with an open hand. "Working for Mike Mansfield compared to working for Lyndon Johnson was like lolling on the beach as opposed to picking cotton," said Bobby Baker, whom Johnson had appointed Senate secretary to the majority leader and who then served Mansfield when Johnson became vice president. Another Johnson aide, Harry McPherson, said that under Mansfield, senators were "like boys in a prep school when an old tyrannical headmaster who believed in the redeeming power of work was replaced by a permissive young don." Mansfield had little use for the bulls and less use for the club through which they ran the Senate. To undercut them, he used his power as leader to appoint allies, liberal allies, young allies, to investigative committees and committees formed under his jurisdiction, select committees, which chipped away the bulls' power. Lyndon Johnson had twisted arms, yelled, harassed, intimidated, tyrannized. He would use the meetings with committee chairmen to pressure them. Mansfield didn't twist arms; Mansfield patted backs. The "anti-Johnson," Senate parliamentarian Robert Dove would call him. John Stewart, the special assistant to Hubert Humphrey, who was Mansfield's whip, said he based his leadership "on an appeal to the senatorial interests of institutional pride and personal participation, interests seemingly far removed from Johnson's harsh world of political reality. Mansfield seemed to believe that belovedness would become the guiding force in the Senate." And Johnson would dole out Democratic Senatorial Campaign Committee contributions as rewards for support and withhold them as punishments for dissent. Mansfield did not reward. Mansfield did not punish. Mansfield was so imperturbable, so composed, that one of the members of his own Democratic caucus, Senator Thomas Dodd, attacked him on the Senate floor for being too docile. Mansfield coolly rebutted by admitting that descriptions of him "ranged from a benign Mr. Chips, to glamourless, to a tragic mistake," and he said he could own up to all of them, "although I cannot claim either the tenderness or the perception of Mr. Chips for his charges," and he admitted that he was neither a "circus ringmaster" nor the "master of ceremonies of a Senate night club" nor a "tamer of Senate lions" (though he had helped tame them) nor a "wheeler and dealer." What he was, he declaimed, was what he was, "and no title, political face lifter, or image maker can alter it."

But Mike Mansfield, in all his casualness, even because of his casualness, *was* altering the Senate. By reducing the bulls' power, by nudging the caucus to appoint more liberal committee chairmen, and then by giving those chairmen more authority and independence rather than cajoling them, as Johnson had done, by encouraging even freshman senators like Ted to speak, when they had been forbidden by custom from speaking, he was slowly disrupting the old power structure and letting loose the members of the post–New Deal liberal consensus. And he had done all this not just because of his serene temperament and not just because he wasn't Lyndon Johnson and had no desire to be. He had done it because pieces of legislation were piling up—Medicare, immigration reform, especially a civil rights bill on desegregating public accommodations—legislation that the president had been pushing, legislation that the bulls had not let out of committee or had mustered the votes to kill on the floor by filibuster or by an alliance with the conservative Republicans, and the time had come to pass this legislation. Lyndon Johnson wanted to pass it over the bodies of the bulls. Mike Mansfield wanted to pass it by changing the institution itself and changing the apportionment of power therein. For all his temperance, Mike Mansfield was bringing moral suasion to the Senate leadership.

This was how the Senate was being transformed when Ted Kennedy arrived, at the transition point between an old Senate run by bulls and this new, more liberal and moral one. A "bipartisan liberal institution" was how Senate historian Donald Ritchie described what it was evolving into. And Ted Kennedy, who had spent his first months in Washington learning how to navigate the old Senate, hoping to raise expectations for himself there, was hoping to raise them even higher in this evolving one. And not only higher expectations but new expectations—expectations that would alter completely his career path. Jack had hated the Senate, even though he sometimes felt nostalgic twinges for it. "We were just worms there," he told historian James MacGregor Burns, which was true for most of the members of the old Senate, the Senate of minnows and whales, and in any case Jack was just killing time there, preparing for his presidential run. But Ted Kennedy loved the Senate, loved it almost from the moment he entered it. Milton Gwirtzman said that even at the beginning, "He really talked about being a senator all his life. He thought maybe he could break the record [for longevity] that was set by that guy from Arizona, Carl Hayden." He loved the old mahogany desks in the Senate, those desks from 1819 that were purchased after the British had torched the Capitol in the War of 1812; loved the traditions of the Senate, like the picnics on the Capitol grounds, when the senators kept their windows in the Old Senate Office Building open so they could hear the bells calling them for a vote; loved even the strange folkways of the Senate that he was beginning to pick up. As an example of those folkways, he would tell the story of watching Senator Willis Robertson, an old Virginian, speak "very passionately" in favor of a bill, and Ted, swayed by that passion, voted for the bill during the roll call—only to hear Robertson himself vote against it. And when Ted approached him afterward, seeking an explanation, Robertson said, "Well, Senator, in my state the people are evenly divided, and to those who favor the issue, I send my speech, and to those who are opposed, I send my vote." (Ted joked to himself, "I think I might be able to make it here after all.") Most of all, he loved his fellow senators and the bond that formed among many of them because they realized that they were members of the world's most exclusive club, a small club, and because they shared such deep respect for the institution, which included respect for one another. "The impressive thing is to discover the relationships between the senators," he told a reporter in his first months, "to see the mutual respect they have for each other and for each other's ideas and philosophies."

He had come to love the Senate so much that, even though he loved his brother, he saw himself increasingly as a Senate man, politically speaking, and hoped his fellow senators would see him the same way. A staffer said they seldom contacted the White House, for fear the senator's loyalty would be suspect: "We always felt that we were being screened as to our every move, so we were very guarded." And to prove his independence, to prove, as Gwirtzman put it, that he wasn't just a "lackey for his brothers," Ted would occasionally diverge from the White House positions. He called for diplomatic relations with Red China and broke with his brother on a Cold War GI bill, on a tariff amendment, and on farm aid that would help his constituents. He lobbied his brother personally about the closing of a rifle plant in Springfield that would cost six hundred of those constituents their jobs—lobbied him during a dinner at Treasury secretary Douglas Dillon's house. But the president was unmoved. "Tough shit," he said, smiling. Ted wasn't breaking with the White House just to prove his bona fides. He was doing it because he identified with the Senate, wanted to be a Senate man, saw himself in the continuity of the Senate, saw it as another family, saw it as a place where he might be able to make his own mark. He kept a framed letter of Daniel Webster's, the great Massachusetts senator who fought secession before the Civil War, in the vestibule of his Charles River Square townhouse, and he treasured a silver humidor that John Culver had given him that first year on which were engraved the names of all the senators who had held his seat before him. On a four-day weekend with his friend John Tunney later that first year, Ted enthused over the Senate. "He told me that he had decided his career was really going to be there," Tunney recalled to Kennedy biographer Theo Lippman. "He urged me to seek a Senate career. He told me how he had established a really good relationship with members of the hierarchy, particularly the Southern members, which was perhaps not to be expected, considering their political views." And Tunney got the sense not only that Ted loved the Senate, was finding his way within it, but also that Ted had determined "a person could get an awful lot done in the Senate."

III

That summer of 1963 was good. During the week, when neither of them was up at Hyannis Port, Jack would often phone Ted at his Senate office and invite him to the White House for an evening swim and dinner, usually creamed chicken and rice, and peas, just the two of them, and Jack would ask for stories; he loved those Senate stories, loved hearing how Senator Jennings Randolph, a huge bear of a man, was in the Senate steam room, discussing postmasterships, when he almost passed out from the heat right in the middle of his discourse. Or they would sit on the porch, smoking cigars and making small talk, until nine-thirty or ten, when the president might excuse himself to read. (Sometimes, Jack would just ask Ted over to smoke those cigars and talk.) Or, more rarely, they might go out on the presidential yacht, the *Sequoia*, typically with Cabinet members. Or they might fly up to Hyannis together. He tendered these invitations because Jack Kennedy, like Joe Kennedy, just loved Ted's company. He *sought* Ted's company. Bobby and Jack didn't have those kinds of moments.* "Red" Fay, Jack's old Navy friend, told Arthur Schlesinger Jr. that he thought "JFK was much easier and more relaxed with Ted than with Bobby. RFK was too intense, too much involved with issues, too demanding for the president at the end of a long day." And Schlesinger himself said, "Teddy made the president laugh. Bobby was his conscience, reminding him of perplexities he wished for a moment to put aside."

There was reason for laughter among the brothers that summer and fall. The Kennedys seemed especially blessed. Jack was riding high, preparing for his reelection and pushing those signature pieces of legislation on health care and civil rights. Ted was looking forward to his own reelection campaign, this time to win a full Senate term, since the 1962 election had only been for the end of Jack's term, and Ted was making nearly weekly visits back to Massachusetts. It was the best of times.

Ted was in the Senate at 2:20 that afternoon of November 22—not only in the Senate but in the chair on the rostrum presiding over the chamber, as freshman senators often did, because more-senior senators didn't want the assignment—when, 1,300 miles away, it happened: a cataclysmic event that was to change his life, his family's life, and the life of the nation, change each so dramatically that none of them would ever be the same. Rein J. Vander Zee, the assistant to Senate Democratic whip Hubert Humphrey and the assistant secretary of the majority, was sitting at a corner desk in the chamber at a duty station there, when a page approached him and told him that something had just come across on the news ticker, something the page had been told to tear off and post: President Kennedy had been shot while appearing in Dallas, Texas. Vander Zee knew that Ted was in the chair, so he told the page to find another junior senator to relieve him. Then Vander Zee went to Mansfield and told him about the news on the ticker. Mansfield left the floor immediately. At the time, Ted was reading correspondence on the rostrum while eight senators on the floor were debating or listening to a debate on an amendment to the Library Services Act. A research assistant to Senator Wayne Morse had heard the news and told an assistant Senate press liaison officer

---

* It is notable that Jackie drafted a will in 1960 and entrusted Caroline and John Jr. to Ted should she and the president die. Bob Holher, "Bottom Line on JFK Auction," *The Boston Globe*, March 20, 1998.

named Tom Pellikaan, and Pellikaan told Richard Langham Riedel, the Senate press liaison officer, who rushed out to the Associated Press ticker to verify the news. Ted said he had heard a shout in the Senate lobby and saw Riedel head out to discover what was going on. Once Riedel had done so, he ran back into the chamber—he later said that in all the years he had worked in the Senate, and he had been a young page there, he had never run on the Senate floor—and told Senator Spessard Holland and Minority Leader Everett Dirksen and anyone else who was within hearing distance. And then Riedel, a big, lumbering man, headed to the rostrum, the rostrum where Ted sat. Riedel said he told Ted, "The most horrible thing has happened! It's terrible, terrible!"

But Ted recalled it differently. He said that Riedel, wearing a "strange expression," told him to follow him out to the teletype machine. All Ted knew was that something had happened—something serious. George McGovern said he had just arrived at the rostrum when he saw Riedel whispering to Ted, and Ted motioned to him and asked him to relieve him. "Something has happened," Ted said gravely, then touched McGovern's arm and said, "Thank you." (McGovern's recollection was wrong. Actually, Spessard Holland relieved Ted.) And then Ted followed Riedel out to that teletype, which, by now, was surrounded. And it was on the teletype, Ted Kennedy said, that he learned his brother, the president of the United States, John F. Kennedy, had been shot.[*]

Ted was numb with disbelief. He would say that the only thing he could hear was the clatter of the AP machine. And then, he recalled, he heard someone say, cutting through the clatter, that the president was dead. There was confusion then, and there would be confusion thereafter when the story was told. Depending on the version, Ted went to Lyndon Johnson's office off the Senate floor and tried to dial Bobby at the Justice Department but couldn't get a dial tone, so he bolted out to the street, where a legislative aide offered him a ride to the Senate Office Building. Or Ted raced out of the Capitol and down the steps and ran directly to his own office and then phoned Bobby, who he thought was at home in Hickory Hill. When Ted himself told the story, he recalled that he either spoke with

---

[*] Riedel told it differently to Kennedy biographer Lester David. There he said that he did tell Ted. "He asked me how I knew, and I told him." It is Ted himself who said he learned the news from the teletype. William Manchester in *The Death of a President* tells it differently still, with Riedel telling Ted the president had been shot but nothing else. Boston: Little, Brown, 1967, 197–198.

Bobby and learned that the situation was very serious (he hadn't yet confirmed that Jack had died in one version; in another Bobby told him he had learned from FBI head J. Edgar Hoover that Jack was dead) and that he should go home, or he said that he didn't speak with Bobby then because the phone lines had gone dead. Milton Gwirtzman recalled that he was in Ted's office when Ted arrived. Since so much was still unknown—"bedlam" Ted called it—Ted didn't dismiss the possibility that there was a conspiracy and that—thinking of the night of Lincoln's assassination, when the conspirators attacked members of Lincoln's Cabinet—he and, more important, his family might be in danger. His impulse was to race home, but his Chrysler was in the repair shop, so Gwirtzman offered to drive him in his Mercedes. Ted's old Harvard football friend Claude Hooton, who had come to Washington for Ted and Joan's fifth anniversary party that night, slid into the back seat of the car while Ted took the passenger seat, holding a transistor radio one of his secretaries had given him. Then Gwirtzman sped from the Old Senate Office Building—from Pennsylvania Avenue around the White House to E Street to Virginia Avenue, down the Rock Creek Parkway—to Ted's Georgetown house, ignoring the red lights along the route. Ted motioned to the oncoming traffic to get out of the way but didn't say a word during the trip. It took twelve minutes to get there. But when they arrived, Joan wasn't home; she had gone to the Elizabeth Arden salon on Connecticut Street to get her hair done for the party. Gwirtzman volunteered to go get her—the manager of the salon had already heard about the shooting and told the stylist not to tell Joan but to rush—and he hustled her into the car and told her that the president had been shot, hurt, and that Ted wanted her to come home now. When Gwirtzman dropped off Joan at the Georgetown house—Joan's sister, Candy, and her husband had just arrived for the party—Ted was distraught, frantic, because all the phones there were dead as well and, by this version, he still didn't know the president's condition. (The phone lines were overtaxed because the news of the president's shooting was breaking.) Gwirtzman said that he and Ted walked up and down the 1600 block of 28th Street, desperately knocking on doors, hoping to find someone whose phone was working. Hooton told biographer Peter Canellos that he was the one who accompanied Ted up the street and that they found a maid at one of the homes, but she refused to let them in until she recognized Ted and relented so that he could phone his brother, the attorney general. It was then, by the version William Manchester told in *The*

Death of a President, that Bobby simply told Ted, "He's dead," and asked him to call Rose and Joe. But the line suddenly cut off. *He's dead.* Whenever exactly Ted received that news, during his first call to Bobby or during this one, he said, "In that moment, the world lurched apart from me." He said he felt "unmoored," but he knew that he had "to keep moving" and that he had to inform his parents. At Gwirtzman's suggestion, they went to Gwirtzman's house, but they had no better luck with the phones there, and Ted said, "between his teeth," as Manchester wrote, "Let's go to the White House." Gwirtzman told this differently too. He said Ted despaired of finding a phone, so they hopped back into the car and headed back to the White House, not stopping at Gwirtzman's house, and, Gwirtzman remembered, "As we go in, you could just—And I knew right away. We did not turn the radio on. I did not want to be there when he was hearing on the radio that his brother . . . I didn't know, but you could see as you drove into the White House, the secretaries were crying. You could see. You could know that he was dead."*

Ted said he felt "unmoored." But Ted Kennedy couldn't afford to be unmoored. He had responsibilities—family responsibilities. From the White House, he called his mother at Hyannis Port. When he reached her, she had already heard the terrible news, but Rose said that Joe Kennedy had not, and Ted offered to fly up to break it to him. Eunice had come to the White House too with her husband, Sargent Shriver, and Ted and Eunice made arrangements to fly to Hyannis Port. They flew together on a military plane from Andrews Air Force base, but it was Ted who arrived to find his father napping, and Ted who ripped out the wires from the TV set so that Joe Kennedy wouldn't see the news when he awoke. And it was Ted who, after what he called a "hellish" night, told his father at breakfast the next morning—Ted whom, Rose said, the family had chosen to tell him, Ted whose job it had always been to leaven the family mood. And Rose, an aesthete even here, described it as a quiet tableau, with Joe, heavily sedated, hearing the news and then going to sleep.

But Joe Kennedy's nurse Rita Dallas told a different story—a story not of control but of uncontrollable grief. She said that Eunice "exploded" into the house when she and Ted arrived the afternoon of the assassination and that Eunice bolted up the stairs, while Ted, "his face white, his

---

*In *True Compass,* his memoir, Ted writes that he learned of the president's death from Bobby during their phone call.

eyes glossy with tears," hung at the bottom of the stairs before slowly making his way up to the nurses' station; he spoke to them and then gave a "long, trembling sigh" as Eunice asked the nurses whether Joe had been told yet, and when they said he hadn't, Eunice flashed Ted a "firm look," and the two entered Joe's room. And while Eunice caressed her father's hand and kissed him, Ted cried, "Dad, Jack was shot." And, Dallas said, Eunice lowered herself onto a footstool and laid her head on her father's hand, and Ted leaned across her and kissed his forehead, and then Ted got up to the head of the bed and touched his father's shoulder. But it was too much for Ted. He dropped to his knees, Dallas said, buried his face in his hands, weeping. And Eunice told her father. Eunice said, "He's dead, Daddy. He's dead."

And now the Kennedys once again suffered a ritual of loss, as they had with Joe Jr. and Kathleen. They stayed in Hyannis Port, Ted and Eunice, to comfort their parents, stayed in the big house, where there were hourly prayer sessions. And then Ted flew to Washington, to visit the Capitol, where the late president was lying in state under the rotunda. First, however, Ted went to the White House, where Milton Gwirtzman, who had been working on the 1964 presidential campaign, was waiting. "He looked terrible," Gwirtzman said of Ted. "He hadn't slept, obviously." But Ted said, "Let's go up," meaning up to the Capitol to see Jack's coffin, and the long lines of people waiting to pay their respects parted when he arrived. And Ted went to the bier, got on his knees and prayed, and then returned to the White House.

He had come to Washington to send off Jack. And he had come to Washington to help plan for Jack's funeral. Ted's office was inundated with requests from Massachusetts friends for tickets to the service—"begging to get into St. Matthew's Cathedral," Terri Haddad Robinson said—and the office was handling those requests in concert with the White House and Jacqueline Kennedy's staff. It was chaos. The office kept an open line to Western Union to send out invitations, while on another line they were fielding requests: "Send this one. Send that one." And when Ted thought they couldn't get enough tickets, he asked them to arrange to have televisions set up in his house and invite guests there to have breakfast and watch the funeral, which the staff did. And throughout all this, Ted had to maintain his composure, had to be strong for the family, for the nation. He suppressed his own grief, he would say, because Bobby was so deep in his and couldn't perform that function of strength, but he would also admit that this might have been an excuse he gave himself, a way to avoid having his grief "swallow" him up as Bobby's grief had swallowed him up, a way to keep it at bay by prioritizing Bobby's.

John Culver, who was in Iowa at the time of the assassination, flew back to be with Ted. "He outwardly was holding up in a very manly fashion," Culver recalled, saying that Ted kept himself busy so as not to indulge his sadness. John Tunney, who had flown east from California with polls he had taken for his own possible congressional race, and who was dining with his parents in New York when the maître d' gave them the news about the president's death, hopped a plane down to Washington to spend the weekend with Ted, who had flown back to Washington himself from Hyannis Port to be with Joan. "Oh, what a weekend that was. Whew!" was all Tunney would ever say about what was clearly a time of inexpressible sorrow and unremitting pain.

And then, that Sunday, Ted and Eunice accompanied Rose to the Capitol, to pray beside Jack's coffin. The following bright, crisp morning, November 25—with the entire nation watching on television, united in mourning—there was the funeral itself. Ted walked alongside Bobby, both hatless, both in morning coats (Ted's attire had come with articles missing, so he wound up wearing the striped trousers that Jack had worn to the inauguration), and Jacqueline, sheathed in black and wearing a veil, was solemn, stoic, because, publicly at least, Kennedys lived by Joe's injunction never to cry. As the funeral procession moved down the Washington streets, Ted and Bobby whispered to Jacqueline, "Faster" or "Slower," to keep their march to the cadence of the drums. And after the funeral, Tunney said, he and Ted spent an hour and a half or two hours with Jacqueline. And then Ted and Tunney returned to Ted's house to continue their own mourning.

But Ted Kennedy would not wallow in grief because he was afraid he might be paralyzed by it as Bobby was. So even before the national grief had begun to lift, while the country was still in shock, and Ted's office was handling mail, thousands of letters of condolence—Ted asked to see the most touching letters from average Americans—after all that, Terri Haddad Robinson was in the office leafing through magazines and newspapers full of accounts of John Kennedy's death when, to her astonishment, Ted appeared and asked to see those newspapers, wanted to read them all, wanted to steep himself in them, wanted, she thought, to get some handle on the great tragedy that had befallen him and the country. "Get me *Paris Match*," he said. "They have the best pictures." Bobby remained at home. Bobby couldn't face anyone. Bobby couldn't shake his grief. But Ted had to, trying to inure himself to it, in order to save himself and his family.

A fog settled on them all now, a dense cloud of unbearable suffering. They gathered the next week, the week after John Kennedy's funeral, for Thanksgiving at Hyannis Port, all but Bobby, whose grief was so deep, so all-consuming, that he couldn't bear to be there; he went instead with his immediate family to Hobe Sound in Florida. "Insupportable emotional shock," Rose called his reaction. With Bobby lost in his grief, with Bobby now unable to do so, Ted had to shoulder the family despondency, had to temper the despondency. The night before Thanksgiving, he hosted an Irish wake for his dead brother, surrounded by a group of their friends. It lasted the night, a night of drinking and laughing—"Teddy laughed louder than usual," remembered Rita Dallas—and telling stories about Jack, not sad stories but humorous ones. "They actually made a game of seeing who could come up with the most outlandish stories about the president and his family," said Dallas. Kara and Ted Jr.'s governess quit the next day, thinking Ted "heartless," not recognizing the pain under the carousing.

There would be no participating in Irish wakes for Bobby Kennedy. Jack Kennedy had been Bobby's life. As a boy of limited natural abilities, he looked for charismatic figures to whom to attach himself—one of his closest friends was David Hackett, the best athlete and the most popular boy at Milton—but the charismatic figure to whom he attached himself for life, the one who compensated for his deficiencies among the Kennedys, was Jack. Bobby knew powerlessness as a boy. He also knew how to cheat it. Jack was his means. Jack was his alter ego. Jack was everything he felt he was not. And Bobby was more than a brother to Jack, John Kennedy biographer Richard Reeves would write. There might have been no political career without him. "He had no hidden agenda, no other loyalty than to John Kennedy. Among his many services, he played the political wife, intuitive judge of who could be trusted and who could not, a role rejected by Mrs. Kennedy." As Jack himself put it, "With Bobby, I don't have to think about organization. I just show up." Their mutual friend John Seigenthaler, who served in Bobby's Justice Department, said that Bobby would "have taken a bolt of lightning for Jack." In many ways, as Jack's political point man, he had.

And Bobby took Jack's death hard. Richard Goodwin, a John Kennedy adviser, compared the post-assassination Bobby to "a landscape riven by an earthquake, familiar landmarks shattered, displaced by novel contours." Political columnist Murray Kempton said he seemed to have shrunk, "not as though he had wasted, but as though he had withdrawn." Withdraw he had. Seigenthaler said, "If you were around, you knew he was not—sometimes not really with it. He was really hurting, bruised spiritually and emotionally." Jacqueline Kennedy gave him Edith Hamilton's *The Greek Way*, which he devoured, underlining passage after passage, internalizing them, which was Bobby's way, trying to understand, trying to rationalize the tragedy, trying to accept that suffering was man's lot. Norman Mailer wrote of him that he had "come into that world where people live with the recognition of tragedy, and so are often afraid of happiness." There was no happiness for Bobby Kennedy now. He had lost his lodestar. He had lost his meaning.

Ted was just as brittle, just as ravaged. If Bobby had lost his other half, Ted had lost his personal hero and his father figure now that Joe was disabled. "Almost a second father," he would say of Jack. "He was my mentor, protector, wise counsel, and constant friend." Always searching for a present, emotionally generous surrogate father to replace his absent, emotionally ungenerous one, he had said practically the same thing of Bobby and of Honey Fitz. Luella Hennessey, Ted's childhood nurse who was now helping with his children, told biographer Lester David that after Jack's death, Ted was "so overwhelmed, so shocked, he could barely speak. . . . His face was so white and drawn. I got the feeling that if he said any more he would break down and cry." But Ted Kennedy, whose job had always been to pick up the family's spirit, couldn't permit himself to cry. He said he had to keep his grief from "disabling" him, letting go only when he walked the beach at Hyannis and faced the sea—only then because he knew he couldn't reveal those feelings to his parents. (He would refer to his brother's assassination only obliquely, as "the events of November.") And, instead of searching the Greeks, he prayed, as his mother had always prayed, though he admitted that his faith was shaken and that he thought perhaps the tragedies were some divine retribution against his parents for some undefined transgression though others might very well have defined it as Joe Kennedy's politics.

But there was another feeling welling up in Ted Kennedy. One of his last times with Jack was on October 19, at a speech at the Commonwealth

Armory in Boston, when Jack joked, "My last campaign, I suppose, may be coming up very shortly—but Teddy is around, and therefore these dinners can go on indefinitely," and he thanked his youngest brother for "offering me his coattail." They would meet again a few weeks later in Florida when Ted asked Jack for advice on a speech he was to give in Michigan, a speech in which he would chide Barry Goldwater, one of Jack's prospective Republican opponents, and they talked again in mid-November on the phone. But the remark about Ted's coattail, however humorously intended, now had a different resonance with Jack's death. Bill Evans, Ted's administrative assistant, told Lester David that after Jack's death, "there was a void left in what his brother [Jack] had launched." And he said Ted felt, "Now I have more of a part." Now he felt he had to help fulfill his brother's unfinished legacy. Now he had to rise above the expectations.

Ted Kennedy wasn't the only one whose faith was shaken by the president's assassination. Much of the country was shaken by the tragedy, by the loss of its handsome, glamorous, seemingly vigorous young president—shaken as it hadn't been in a long, long time. It had been a short presidency, only a thousand days, and there would be arguments about how consequential it was. "Camelot" was the designation Kennedy's presidency got after Jacqueline told journalist Theodore H. White that Jack liked to listen to the Broadway cast album of that musical play about King Arthur, his wife, Guinevere, and his knight Sir Lancelot. "Camelot was the opium of the intellectuals," another journalist, Garry Wills, would gripe of the Kennedy aura. Wills said that Kennedy was the intellectuals' "surrogate," their "dream-self," and he especially complained about the perception that the Eisenhower years were somnambulant and the Kennedy years a sudden awakening. But Wills was wrong about the intellectuals. Not all of them were taken with John Kennedy. Many felt he was an example of style over substance. Henry Kissinger, foreign policy expert and later secretary of State in the Nixon administration, said, "He could get people excited, but what exactly did he accomplish?" English political observer Henry Fairlie said that Kennedy aroused expectations, expectations that "poverty and discrimination, ignorance and disease, could all be conquered as easily as the technology could be mastered to take a man to the moon"—expectations that wouldn't be realized, thus leading to frustration and disillusion.

But if Wills was mistaken about the intellectuals' affection for John Kennedy, the intellectuals who derided John Kennedy were also mistaken about his effect on the nation. The optimism his election and presidency engendered were real. Critics concentrated on legislative accomplishments, of which there were few. But John Kennedy's presidency wasn't about policy, though he championed those bills on national health insurance, immigration, and civil rights—crusades he lost to the Senate bulls and their Republican allies, crusades he knew he was going to lose. Kennedy's presidency was about setting the stage for battles to come, not about arousing expectations, as Fairlie had complained, but about energizing hope, about building America's confidence, about lifting the country's aesthetic and even its moral values, especially after John Kennedy had embraced civil rights, about transitioning, as he so often said, the country from one generation to another. "The Kennedys, with their cosmopolitan style, their devotion to art and the intellect"—they had invited artists to the White House and embraced intellectuals—"enabled us to break not only with the Rotarianism of Ike and Nixon, but also with the earnest dull liberalism of Stevenson and Humphrey," novelist James Carroll opined some years later in a *New Republic* essay titled "The End of the Dream." "JFK gave us the world." Kennedy adviser Richard Goodwin wrote of Kennedy's influence that "he seemed to embody the idea of America. Not the nation itself. That would be presumption. But the idea by which we have defined America, and, by extension, ourselves as Americans." And that idea, Goodwin said, was a "belief in America's possibilities; that we were a nation with a large purpose, a mission, perhaps dangerous, certainly difficult but within our powers." And though he was a reluctant liberal, Kennedy advanced liberalism not just through the legislation he promoted, however cautiously, but through that general sense of mission Goodwin identified. John Kennedy may have given us the world. He also helped give America a revitalized political soul. During the campaign, Norman Mailer was right when he cited John Kennedy in "Superman Comes to the Supermarket" as a cinematic figure even more than a political one and elaborated on the ways that he tapped into the country's romantic psyche. And his tragic death from an assassin's bullet was more like the hero's death at the end of a film than like a politician's death. His death seemed to diminish our capacity to dream. He had cast a spell on the nation. Now the spell was broken.

Ted Kennedy was one of those who was charged with reinvigorating it and casting the spell once again. And that task would be both a thrilling obligation to honor his brother and an agonizing burden he would never be able to lift.

IV

Part of the diminution of the capacity to dream, Bobby Kennedy felt, was the new president, Lyndon Baines Johnson. Ted Kennedy was not a hater, but Bobby Kennedy was, and Bobby Kennedy hated Lyndon Johnson. He hated his cornpone style, hated his ham-handed legislative techniques when Johnson was Senate majority leader, hated his cohabitation with the Southern bulls, who impeded every progressive piece of legislation and would later block John Kennedy's agenda, hated what he saw as Johnson's reduction of everything to politics, even hated his intelligence, which he thought negligible. He saw Johnson's success, said Bobby's deputy attorney general, Nicholas Katzenbach, as "the product of sleaze and manipulation, maybe even corruption," and he didn't, Katzenbach felt, "want to share the Kennedy dream with this man." He had tried, without success, to dissuade Johnson from accepting Jack's offer of the vice presidency—basically begged him not to accept—but Johnson's big role in winning John Kennedy the election and his place in the administration did not dissipate the hate. And now, after Bobby's brother's death, the hate, if anything, burned harder, brighter, not only because Bobby knew he was dispossessed but also because he saw in Johnson an impediment to all the things John Kennedy had hoped to achieve, the entire liberal program, and while Bobby was no raging liberal himself, not yet, he was committed body and soul to his late brother's program and to his late brother's legacy. "People just don't realize how conservative Lyndon really is," Bobby told his aide Ed Guthman, shortly after the assassination. "There are going to be a lot of changes." The month after Jack's death, Bobby told Schlesinger and Goodwin at the Justice Department that they had eleven months—the time until the 1964 presidential election—*just* eleven months, to do something, on the assumption that once Johnson was elected, John Kennedy's grand ambitions would be over. "My brother barely had a chance to get started—and there is so much now to be done—for the Negroes and the unemployed and school kids and everyone else who is not getting a decent break in our society. This is what counts.

The new fellow [meaning Johnson] doesn't get this. He knows all about politics and nothing about human beings," which was, of course, a terrible misjudgment of Johnson, who knew a lot about human beings. And now Bobby was fired by his hatred, roused from his grief by it, the only thing that could rouse him, and he became more fervent about his brother's causes than his brother himself had been, became determined to salvage his brother's legacy from the threat of Lyndon Johnson.

Johnson knew. And Johnson, who was a world-class hater as well, returned Bobby Kennedy's enmity—a book about their relationship was titled *Mutual Contempt*—and wanted to pay him back for the humiliations he had suffered from the Kennedys, and he had suffered many.

Lyndon Johnson was not a man whose enmity one wanted to incite, because everything about him, including his enmity, was oversized, like the man himself. Johnson was tall and beefy—gargantuan. "He is not only big physically," wrote columnist Joseph Kraft. "He hates more, loves more, worries more, boasts more, talks more, cries more, laughs more, eats more, conceals more, exposes more, works more, plays more than normal men. He is a giant in all things, something larger than life and out of size. . . ." This had been his strength as majority leader. He was too large a force, too overwhelming, to be domesticated, even by the bulls. But this was his torture as vice president, where he was simply too big for a small office. When Mike Mansfield was elected as Johnson's replacement by the Democratic caucus, he proposed that Johnson be invited to preside over the caucus, to which those senators who had felt the lash of Lyndon Johnson when he ruled the Senate immediately objected. Johnson was wounded by the hostility, but he also realized how much the calculus of power had changed now that he was powerless, and though Mansfield's motion carried, Johnson boiled. "I now know the difference between a caucus and a cactus," he said. "In a cactus, all the pricks are on the outside."

But now the calculus had suddenly shifted again. Now, in a moment, Lyndon Johnson was the most powerful man in Washington, holding an office for which he had striven all his life, the only office that was large enough for the man, as he saw himself. He made gestures toward the Kennedys and their men, gestures of goodwill, but gestures they were. The Democratic party was his now, not the Kennedys', and not too many months into the new presidency, he told Bobby that it wasn't really even the Democratic party anymore, at least not the liberal party into which

John Kennedy had been fashioning it; it was the "All-American party." Bobby groused to John Bartlow Martin, a friend and John Kennedy's ambassador to the Dominican Republic, that "the businessmen like it. All the people who were opposed to the president like it. I don't like it much." Which is probably exactly what Johnson intended.

But Bobby Kennedy had both overestimated his brother's liberal bona fides and underestimated Lyndon Johnson's. John Kennedy, who had been elected as a liberal pragmatist, governed as one. Speaking at Yale of the economy—though the speech could have applied to any number of other issues as well—he explicitly waved off ideological divisions and called economic decision-making "basically an administrative or executive problem." As one analyst later put it, "The liberalism of Kennedy's later days responded to utilitarian concerns and never appeared impassioned," though one could also have said that John Kennedy, who liked being the cool one, didn't appear impassioned about much of anything, despite having an uncanny aptitude for stirring passion in others. Still, Kennedy knew something about legacies. As his presidency advanced, he was moved to work on immigration reform by the country's draconian policies, which had shaped his own family history, and he understood that strict limits on immigration had hurt his Massachusetts constituents, many of whom had come from other countries and had relatives there seeking to come to America. He submitted a Medicare bill, long a Democratic promise, providing health insurance to seniors, only to see Southern Democrats in the Senate, twenty-one of them, vote with Republicans to narrowly defeat it, 52 to 48. And during his 1960 campaign, he had made a stirring plea to end poverty, and he instructed his staff to draft an anti-poverty plan—one that he didn't live to see presented. In effect, if the election had made Kennedy more of a liberal than he had been in the Senate, his presidency had made him more liberal than he had been as a candidate.

But there was one issue, one overriding issue, one incendiary issue, one dividing issue, one defining issue, about which John Kennedy had been especially slow to heed liberal calls for action: civil rights. As a senator, he had never been a civil rights firebrand; when Kennedy was in Jackson, Mississippi, to speak before the Young Democrats, the state Republican chairman issued a public challenge on where he stood on segregation. Kennedy answered evasively that he accepted the Supreme Court's decision on *Brown v. Board of Education.* "We didn't lay awake nights thinking about it" was Bobby Kennedy's attitude toward civil rights before Jack took the presidency. Even after he won the presidency, Jack Kennedy didn't act with urgency. He appointed racist judges in the South, one of whom, William Harold Cox of Mississippi, had in open court called black plaintiffs a "bunch of niggers . . . acting like a bunch of chimpanzees." After Freedom Riders seeking to integrate bus stations in the South were savagely beaten, and his civil rights adviser, Harris Wofford, asked him to make a statement affirming the right to travel, Kennedy demurred, doubtless because a Gallup poll showed 63 percent of Americans opposed the Riders. It wasn't until the night of June 11, 1963—two and half years into his presidency, after protesters in Birmingham, Alabama, were beaten by police during a march, knocked down by water cannons and attacked by dogs, and on the same day that Alabama governor George Wallace had stood in the doorway of the University of Alabama, physically barring black students from entering—that Kennedy, in response to these events, made a national speech supporting a civil rights bill, the most important plank of which would end segregation in public accommodations. His biographer Robert Dallek said he did so as much because of the national embarrassment in the eyes of the world as for moral reasons, especially since by this point he knew he was likely to lose the South in the 1964 election anyway. Still, Kennedy demonstrated moral courage and called for it: "I hope that every American, regardless of where he lives, will stop and examine his conscience," the president asked that night. There was no great yearning for the bill in the nation, beyond the black community and its liberal allies, and nothing much to be gained from it politically; in fact, there was much to lose. A Gallup poll in 1963 showed that 78 percent of white Americans would move out of their neighborhoods if black people moved in. And there was no great yearning for the bill in the Senate, outside those liberal senators, like Hubert Humphrey, who had championed civil rights all their lives and had consistently been denied; the Senate had its liberals, but it was not yet a liberal institution. Kennedy had been told that the bill had no chance of passage—Johnson, the master legislator, had told him that—but Bobby had finally concluded that the president needed to introduce it, whether it passed or not, to gain "the confidence of the Negro population," and Jack Kennedy himself, uncharacteristically bold, told his secretary of Commerce, Luther Hodges, "There comes a time when a man has to take a stand and history will record that he has to meet these tough situations and ultimately make a decision." He had finally taken that stand.

But it was an ambivalent stand. When, in August 1963, longtime civil rights leaders Bayard Rustin and A. Philip Randolph, the president of the International Brotherhood of Sleeping Car Porters, a largely black union, organized the March on Washington to advocate for civil rights and economic opportunity for African Americans—the march at which Martin Luther King Jr. delivered his "I Have a Dream" speech—Kennedy rebuffed attempts by the leadership to arrange a meeting with Dr. King. And when Ted, who had been urged to attend the march by his supporters and who wanted to be a "fly on the wall" there—he seemed to have more interest in and empathy for African Americans than his brothers did—asked the White House for advice, both Jack and Bobby dissuaded him from going. In part, Ted would write, this was for fear of possible violence, but also, he would admit more candidly in a later interview, it was for fear that his brothers, who had been severely criticized by civil rights leaders for slow-walking legislation and then for supporting a bill that was weaker than the leaders would have liked, would be ridiculed, and Teddy could not tolerate ridicule of his brothers. Instead, Jack and Bobby advised that he meet with marchers in his office, which Ted did. Ted said he didn't fully understand the issue or the passions then, that he was just being introduced to them, though during his campaign he had already fought for civil rights in Massachusetts—when an Arkansas segregationist group that paid for black people to leave for Boston sent a black short order cook to Hyannis Port just to spite the Kennedys, Ted made sure he was there to greet him. But he also said that, his brothers' cautions notwithstanding, he wanted to be among the marchers, and he slipped out of his office, "unnoticed and alone," and walked to the Reflecting Pool, and he said it was then, watching the hundreds of thousands gathered there to fight for their rights—an "awesome sight," he called it—and later listening to the speeches back in his office that he was "fully baptized" into the civil rights movement.

And civil rights was one of the issues—the primary issue—on which Bobby Kennedy distrusted the commitment of the new president, who had never shown any zealousness for civil rights laws until the Civil Rights Act of 1957, and then only to curry favor with Northern liberals for his anticipated presidential bid. Jack Kennedy had appointed his vice president to head up the Committee on Equal Employment Opportunity, and when Labor Secretary Willard Wirtz gave Bobby statistics about how few companies doing business with the government had employed black people, Bobby gave them to Jack, who held Johnson responsible for the lack of progress. "This man can't run this committee," he told Bobby. "Can you think of anything more deplorable than him trying to run the United States? This is why he can't ever be president."

But Jack Kennedy and Bobby Kennedy had no understanding of Lyndon Johnson, had no understanding of the humiliations he had suffered and the sympathies he had felt consequently toward the dispossessed. They knew that Lyndon Johnson gravitated toward power, that power was his aphrodisiac, and congressional power, the power of the bulls, was set firmly against civil rights. But while Johnson hadn't been especially zealous in Congress on civil rights legislation, making league with the bulls to thwart it, he had nevertheless engineered, with guile, intimidation, toadying, horse-trading, and tactical brilliance, the Civil Rights Act of 1957 through the Senate, the first civil rights law since Reconstruction, and in the Kennedy administration he had been a more forceful voice for civil rights than John Kennedy himself, a more forceful voice for moral leadership, until Kennedy decided at last to introduce his Civil Rights Act. "The Negroes are tired of this patient stuff and tired of this piecemeal stuff," Johnson counseled the president when protesters were marching in Jackson, Mississippi, "and what they want more than anything else is not an executive order or legislation, they want a moral commitment that he's behind them." And he said, "I want to pull out the cannon. The president is the cannon. You let him be at all the TV networks just speaking from his conscience."

And now that he was president, now that he had a legacy of his own to create, Lyndon Johnson pushed the Civil Rights Act that John Kennedy had introduced the previous June and that had been voted out of the House Judiciary Committee on the day that John Kennedy left for Dallas, the bill that had then stalled as the Congress recessed and absorbed the loss of the president. But Lyndon Johnson wouldn't let it stall. He was maneuvering to advance it. By February, the bill had passed the full House, where party loyalty typically triumphed. The Senate, however, Johnson's Senate, posed a huge obstacle, with those twenty-one Southern Democrats uniformly opposed, and, as Ted would put it, a "very important part of the Republicans opposed to it as well," those who thought it a government intrusion on individual and states' rights. Johnson was maneuvering around them, through them, over them, cutting a deal—which would reduce the budget and break the logjam so the civil rights bill could move—with Senate Finance chairman Harry Byrd, who was holding off passing the tax cut bill as a way of preventing the Senate from considering the civil rights bill, manning the phones to lobby senators, twisting arms, counting votes for cloture that would end an almost certain filibuster.

But among those twenty-one Southern Democrats, many of them bulls, was one who was extremely important in these deliberations and one who had dedicated his life to segregation. That man was Ted Kennedy's Judiciary chairman, James Eastland, who had called the bill a "complete blueprint for the totalitarian state," and whose committee had jurisdiction over the bill and had to report it to the full Senate. This time, though, there was no custom. Johnson didn't try to cut a deal with Eastland; he probably knew he couldn't, and, by one account, the man who was expert in reading the tides of the Senate was beginning to fear that, even deploying all his considerable powers of suasion, he might not be able to get the bill through, and he didn't want to be pinned as the one who failed. So, with the new president backing off, it was his successor, Mike Mansfield, who steered the bill away from Eastland and away from what one historian of the Civil Rights Act called the "Judiciary Committee purgatory," where civil rights bills went to die. First, Mansfield violated the Senate tradition of letting the relevant committee chairman manage a bill: He bypassed Eastland as the bill's floor manager and gave the assignment instead to Hubert Humphrey, the majority whip and a fervent civil rights advocate, who had gained a national reputation for his stirring speech at the 1948 Democratic National Convention, endorsing civil rights. And then Mansfield contravened another tradition, something that Lyndon Johnson had been forced to do to the then newly appointed Judiciary chairman Eastland, when Johnson was majority leader and trying to gain passage of the Civil Rights Act of 1957: Immediately after the House bill was read in the Senate the first time, before it could be read a second time—which, by custom, would have automatically referred the bill to the relevant committee, in this case Judiciary—Mansfield moved to have the bill considered by the entire Senate, not by Judiciary. And thus began one of the longest filibusters in Senate history—seventy-five days of debate.*

And Ted Kennedy, though still a very junior senator, was determined to be part of that debate—in some measure because he felt an obligation to his brother to do so, and in some measure because he was now "baptized in civil rights" and was caught up in the swirl of the movement and felt he owed it to the black community to do so. More than his brothers, Ted Kennedy had empathized with the poor and marginalized. Now he turned his empathy into action. He had become, he said, involved in "the substance of the discussion" behind the scenes and in the debate on the floor. And he weighed in because he knew the bill was under assault both from the Southerners and from conservative Republicans and that it needed protection—protection he could help provide as the late president's brother. A month into that debate, on April 9, 1964, shortly after a heated session of the Republican caucus in which Minority Leader Everett Dirksen had offered forty amendments, including one to gut the newly added equal employment provision—Johnson had argued privately that the bill could not be tampered with in any way, because doing so would give its opponents a pretext to sink it—and with Joan and Ethel Kennedy sitting in the gallery, Ted made his first major Senate address, what he called his "maiden" speech. He had, in fact, delivered short remarks on the floor previously. But he had never delivered remarks like these, never a full address, never an address so obviously crafted for the occasion (probably by Milton Gwirtzman), never one so eloquent, never one so clearly intended not just to put Ted on the record but to influence the debate, never one so nakedly emotional, never one that invoked his late brother's moral authority as this address would, and, perhaps above all, never one that seemed to recognize the salience of moral authority in liberal politics as this address did. Ted Kennedy had not been a moral leader; he had been too junior to be one. Now he assumed that role.

Ted rose in the Senate at his desk in the back row—the freshman row. He was nervous, his voice thin and "faltering," as one report put it, though that was largely because he was so filled with emotion at speaking on behalf of his late brother's legacy. He began apologetically, acknowledging

---

*Ted himself said it was fifty-seven days, the Official Senate History said sixty working days, and civil rights historian Clay Risen said seventy-five, each depending on when one started the clock and whether one counted all days, including weekends, or just working days. I have chosen the last as most accurate.

the Senate custom by which he had, for his first sixteen months in office, so closely abided, that a "freshman senator should be seen, not heard; should learn, and not teach," and he praised the dignity of the debate so far. And he said that while he had planned to deliver his maiden address at this time, he had, in keeping with his local focus, intended to discuss industry and employment in Massachusetts. "But I could not follow this debate for the last four weeks—I could not see this issue envelop the emotions and the conscience of the nation—without changing my mind." And he said that to focus on local issues while ignoring this great issue would be to "demean" his Senate seat. He said that the "basic problem," as he saw it, was one of "adjustment," of white Americans (though he didn't use the word "white"; he spoke of Americans generally) having to adjust to black people entering America as fully enfranchised citizens. And with what seemed to be a nod to his grandfather Honey Fitz, he told the story of how Massachusetts had had to adjust to immigrants—"fully 40 percent of the people of my state . . . are either immigrants or children of immigrants"—and how the state made that adjustment, and how the state benefited from making that adjustment. He told his fellow senators that afternoon that while prejudice existed in the minds and hearts of men, prejudice that laws could not eradicate, "fairness and goodwill also exist in the minds and hearts of men" and that law "expressing the moral conscience of the community" could elevate the latter over the former. And as he spoke, several senators took chairs and pulled them up near Ted and turned them around and sat, sat listening intently—a sign of respect, Ted later said. He read letters he had received from religious leaders, from Cardinal Cushing of Boston and the Episcopal bishop of Massachusetts, Anson Stokes, endorsing the bill—the rights it protected were "sacred rights," wrote Cardinal Cushing, and those rights could not be left to "chance," wrote Bishop Stokes. And Ted called for a "reign of justice" in the country. In invoking these religious leaders and others, he said he was not mixing politics and religion but rather politics and morality—the morality of doing what was right. But he said that morality "must be backed up by law to be effective."

And then he spoke of the provisions of the law—of one that would allow black people deprived of their voting rights in federal elections to seek legal redress in the courts, and of the public-accommodations provision that would ban discrimination in public facilities, ban the separate restrooms of the South, and the separate drinking fountains, and the seg- regated sections of restaurants. And he spoke of segregated schools in his own city of Boston, which opponents of the bill had cited, but he said that there was no law in Massachusetts forbidding integration and that no state official stood in a school doorway to stop it. And he spoke of the pro- vision that would prevent federal funds from being used to support segre- gation. And he spoke of the provision that prevented discrimination in employment, calling the deprivation to make a decent living a "family tragedy." And then he ticked down, one by one, how moderate these pro- visions actually were, how fair they were; "mild," he called them, so that they shouldn't arouse animosity. And finally he discussed "some personal reasons why I am so interested in passage of this bill," and, his voice now breaking with emotion, he quoted Lyndon Johnson: "No memorial ora- tion or eulogy could more eloquently honor President Kennedy's memory than the earliest possible passage of the civil rights bill for which he fought so long." And he said this: that his brother was the first American presi- dent to "state publicly that segregation was morally wrong." And he said, "His heart and his soul are in this bill." And he said, "If his life and death had a meaning, it was that we should not hate but love one another. We should use our powers not to create conditions of oppression that lead to violence, but conditions of freedom that lead to peace." When it was over, Joan wept and dabbed at her eyes.

It was unlikely that the speech changed votes. Speeches seldom did, and in any case the Republicans were not there to hear it; they were cau- cusing over several provisions introduced by their leader, Everett Dirksen. But if Ted Kennedy didn't change any votes that day, he did change perceptions—the perception of Ted Kennedy. When it was over, liberal Il- linois senator Paul Douglas—a former economics professor, World War II hero (he had enlisted in the Marines at the age of fifty), and one of the most respected men in the Senate, if not one of the bulls—congratulated Ted on the floor, calling the speech "magnificent" and "noble and ele- vated." Hubert Humphrey, who was floor-managing the civil rights bill, said the speech provided "new inspiration." Others came too—Ted kept a pencil sketch he had been given of the senators sitting, listening to him—to congratulate him. *The Boston Globe* called it "the most moving moment of the current civil rights debate."

One who was not impressed was Bobby. When Senator Phil Hart visited Bobby's office later that day and reported on how well Ted had done, Bobby—perhaps resenting Ted's so prominently taking up Jack's cause, or because he was now angry at the world—snorted, "I suppose it's possible. Who do you imagine wrote it for him?" Still, Bobby's comment notwithstanding, Ted Kennedy had raised the expectations of him.

And Ted didn't just *speak* about civil rights, however eloquently, however impassioned. He *acted.* Humphrey had appointed him one of six senators charged with rounding up a quorum every time the Southern senators, in yet another gambit to stall the civil rights bill, would call for a vote, and they would call for a vote often. As a member of the Judiciary Committee, he was invited to a session in Minority Leader Dirksen's office opposite the Old Senate Chamber in the Capitol to hammer out the bill, which, despite Lyndon Johnson's counsel not to alter it, was being amended behind the scenes, mostly with minor amendments—the Southerners would submit more significant ones to try to eviscerate the bill's effectiveness. This was primarily a way for Dirksen to demonstrate to his Republican caucus that he was fighting to mitigate the worst aspects of the bill, which helped pacify conservatives, even as he was now helping guide it to passage, which pacified Republican moderates. (There were rumors that Johnson had persuaded Dirksen to drop his opposition by promising him federal largesse for Illinois, but Dirksen seemed to be acting out of conviction that the party of Lincoln couldn't just turn its back on civil rights.) It is unclear precisely when it occurred, probably in early May— there were daily meetings called by the leadership among senators, Justice Department officials, and even lobbyists during the filibuster—but Ted recalled that the Judiciary senators, who were permitted one staff person each; Deputy Attorney General Nicholas Katzenbach; the head of the Justice Department's Civil Rights Division, Burke Marshall; Dirksen; and others stayed in Dirksen's Capitol office, didn't leave it save for brief breaks, for eight hours negotiating and negotiating, until an agreement was reached. "We got everybody to sign off on it, and everybody stuck with it," Ted said. "It was an extraordinary phenomenon" to get the senators themselves to negotiate for that many hours and to have that kind of cohesion. And Ted felt that the meeting finally resolved Dirksen's onagain, off-again commitment to the bill—a commitment that was absolutely critical to any prospect of its passage, since the Democrats needed Republican votes to end the filibuster and since no filibuster of a civil rights bill had ever gotten cloture. What Ted Kennedy, the freshman senator, provided in those meetings was clearly a reminder of his brother. And what he provided was that dead brother's moral authority.

Ted Kennedy had given his "noble and elevated" speech and had worked on the bill for his brother's legacy. And then, in the middle of the debate, he left for Europe with his friend William vanden Heuvel for another legacy to his brother: to raise money for the John F. Kennedy Presidential Library to be built in Cambridge and to discuss European memorials to the late president. They met with English prime minister Harold Macmillan, "tears streaming down his cheeks as he talked about his relationship with President Kennedy." (The English were erecting a memorial at Runnymede.) French prime minister Georges Pompidou told them that when French president Charles de Gaulle got news of the assassination, he buried his face in his hands and said that Lyndon Johnson wouldn't politically survive the assassination that had occurred in his home state. "It is Banquo's ghost," he had said, citing *Macbeth*. "You cannot have the king killed when he is a guest in your house." And they met with the pope at the Vatican and with Italian prime minister Aldo Moro. And they went to Germany, where former chancellor Konrad Adenauer, in his late eighties, raced down the hall so as not to be late in greeting Ted. But the most dramatic was the visit to Ireland, where they arrived on May 29, what would have been John Kennedy's forty-seventh birthday. (There were observances throughout the world, including in Washington, where Jacqueline attended mass with the Irish president Éamon de Valera and visited her husband's grave site with him.) Thousands of people lined the streets of Dublin as Ted was driven to St. Mary's Pro-Cathedral, where a memorial mass was celebrated, and crowds mobbed him both when he arrived and left the cathedral, breaking through the police lines, reaching for him, grabbing at him, calling to him. "A Beatles reception," one person in the crowd called it, referencing the British rock group. Another observed that one could "see in that crowd the hope that, although John Kennedy was dead, perhaps in this young Kennedy their tribe of Irishmen might again rise." Vanden Heuvel said of the cathedral visit, "You could feel the weight literally shift as the audience stood to greet him." And he said, "There wasn't a dry eye," including that of President de Valera's wife, Sinéad, who sat near Ted and wiped away tears. Afterward, addressing the huge crowd gathered outside, Ted called it a day of joy and sadness—joy because he was in Ireland, sadness because it was the late president's birthday, and his voice broke as he said it, and he paused to collect himself as the crowd suddenly went silent, and when he recovered he said, "My brother will not be able to come back and enjoy any more spring days here." As late as midnight, crowds were still lining the Dublin streets, hoping to catch a glimpse of him. And with the sadness came still more sadness. While Ted was in Ireland, at the very end of his trip, Joan suffered a miscarriage, almost a year to the day after suffering one in 1963—yet another loss in a year of tragic losses.

Now, having worked on brick-and-mortar memorials, there was still his brother's legislative memorial to resolve. Ted returned to the Senate early in June and to the long-sought but difficult cloture vote that would end the filibuster and allow the Senate to pass the civil rights bill. It had taken months, years really, to reach this point—years of delay by the Southern bulls. It had taken Lyndon Johnson's intervention, though the only vote he seemed to sway was Arizona senator Carl Hayden's, and that only by promising him a water project. And it had taken the steady strategizing of Bobby Kennedy's Justice Department; and it had taken the canny but ultimately courageous efforts of Everett Dirksen, whom Johnson had advised Humphrey to flatter as courageous because Dirksen always wanted to be considered courageous (he would wrangle twenty-two Republican votes); and it had taken the unceasing lobbying efforts of the civil rights groups; and it had taken Martin Luther King Jr.'s moral courage and rhetorical eloquence; and it had taken all the foot soldiers of the civil rights movement, those protesters and Freedom Riders and sit-down strikers; and it had taken the deaths of many African Americans, including four little girls killed in a bombing of a Birmingham, Alabama, black church by white supremacists in September 1963. It had taken all these things. But in the end, at 11:15 A.M. on June 10, 1964, the United States Senate voted 71 to 29 to close debate. Among those voting for cloture was California Democratic senator Clair Engle, who was wheeled into the chamber despite a debilitating brain tumor that had robbed him of speech, and who, when his name was called, could only gesture to his eye with his right index finger to signify "Aye." And now all that remained were more stalling tactics by the Southerners, more amendments, and more debate. But stall as they might, and stall as they did, the passage of the Civil Rights Act of 1964, John Kennedy's primary memorial, was inevitable. And it was appropriate, perhaps symbolic, that as the biggest of the bulls, the one who had probably been most responsible, given his status, for stopping civil rights legislation from passing, Senator Richard Russell was on the Senate floor yet again, on June 19, the last day of the debate, declaiming against the bill, denouncing it, though, knowing his efforts were now futile, declaiming without his customary fervor, and that while he was delivering his message—"We did not deceive anyone as to our purposes"—Ted Kennedy, who was sitting on the dais and presiding over the Senate at that moment, cut Russell off in mid-sentence. "The time of the senator from Georgia has expired," he said. And Russell glowered at him, said that he hoped the same rule that the chair had applied to him had been applied to others, and asked whether Humphrey, who spoke a day earlier and yielded himself a minute, had taken longer than that, and when Ted said he took nine minutes, Russell snapped sarcastically that he was "glad to hear it." Then Russell took his seat—sagged in his seat, by one account—reportedly with tears in his eyes, tears of recognition that everything to which he had dedicated his life was about to change, both in the South and in the Senate. The next day, Humphrey delivered his final address, a conciliatory one—"Let us be exalted but not exultant. Let us mark the occasion with sober rejoicing, and not with shouts of victory"—and so did Dirksen, movingly, answering the rhetorical question "How have you become a crusader in this cause?" with "I am involved in mankind, and whatever the skin, we are all involved in mankind." And then, finally, Mansfield spoke, invoking the late president, and said, "This is indeed his moment." Then came the vote, at 7:40 P.M., one year to the day after the legislation had been introduced by John Kennedy. It passed 73 to 27.

Throughout the debate, Dirksen had frequently quoted a line he ascribed to Victor Hugo: "No army can withstand the strength of an idea whose time has come." Now, at long last, the time had come. But it was more than the time having arrived. It was the moral purpose with which it had arrived—the moral purpose that Ted Kennedy had cited in his address during the debate. He said then that his brother had been the first president to declare that racial segregation was morally wrong, which made the bill's passage not only a victory for John Kennedy and for Lyndon Johnson, for African Americans and for America itself. It made the passage, above all, a victory for morality.

CHAPTER SIX

"Do a Little Suffering"

A FTER THE VOTE on the Civil Rights Act, Hubert Humphrey exited the Capitol to find a crowd on the steps, cheering him. He stayed there with them for three hours, late into the night, exulting with them, even though he had promised he wouldn't exult. But Ted Kennedy didn't have time to celebrate. Despite the lateness of the hour when he left the Capitol, Ted Kennedy had another appointment that night. He was scheduled to speak at the Massachusetts State Democratic Convention in Springfield, which was going to award its endorsement to Ted that very evening for the 1964 Senate nomination. And Ted had recruited a fellow freshman, Birch Bayh of Indiana, to accompany him to Springfield and deliver the convention's keynote address. By this point, unlike in his contest two years earlier against Eddie McCormack, the party's endorsement was a formality—a coronation. But Ted Kennedy's trip to Springfield was not about accepting the convention's nomination. It was about making good on his promise to the reformers that he would be active in the state party, which had been riddled with corruption. Jack had had no interest in such matters. When, back in 1956, Jack Kennedy's advisers Kenny O'Donnell and Larry O'Brien schemed to get William "Onions" Burke, the state Democratic chairman and a McCormack ally, ousted, Joe Kennedy complained, "Leave it alone and don't get in the gutter with those bums up there in Boston." The only reason Jack finally battled John McCormack at the state convention and sought to depose Burke, one of "those bums," was that Burke, disdaining his party's leading presidential contenders, Adlai Stevenson and Estes Kefauver, had arranged for the party to stage a write-in vote for John McCormack as a favorite son; so that Burke, who had no fondness for the Kennedys, could control the state delegation to the Democratic National Convention. That would have been an embarrassment to Jack, who had vice-presidential aspirations and needed the votes of his own state delegation. Still, other than for his own career advancement, Jack followed his father's advice and steered clear of state intraparty skulduggery and the bums and the gutters.

But Ted Kennedy, a people person, that chip off Honey Fitz, loved state politics, loved to get his hands dirty with the local pols, one of whom said, "Ted is always ready to jump in, no matter how small the fight." And when *The New York Times*'s Tom Wicker complained during Ted's Senate campaign that the Massachusetts Democratic party was weak, disorganized, and corrupt, a "wild collection of personalities, families, and petty satrapies that passes for the party," and asked if Ted Kennedy could clean it up, Ted replied evenly, as his brother never would, "I am not going down to Washington after the election and retire. I'm going to be active in the party." And active he was. With Jack and Bobby basically abandoning the state party, and with Teddy having toppled Eddie McCormack and the satraps who had supported him, there was now a power vacuum, and young Ted charged right in and filled it. He installed his campaign manager, Gerard Doherty, as the state chairman and then had the wisdom to introduce him to Speaker McCormack, after which McCormack told Ted, "Senator, you've been down here two years, and you've always come and sought my advice and treated me like the speaker. You are the leader of my party in Massachusetts, and if this man is your leader, he is my leader." And, according to political columnists Robert Novak and Rowland Evans, Ted made allies of the president of the Senate, the state treasurer, and the chairman of the Turnpike Commission. He even began handpicking legislative candidates. And after Jack's death, his power play intensified. The "unchallenged leader of the Democratic party [in Massachusetts]," wrote Robert Donovan in the *Los Angeles Times*, which was an accomplishment for a thirty-two-year-old political novice, who only two years earlier was being berated for his inexperience. A Boston reporter told Donovan that Ted "used to walk on tiptoes up here. Now he moves in and gets involved. He's become a stand-up guy. He's all muscle now. He can speak out. The difference between Ted Kennedy now and a year ago is the difference between night and day." But there hadn't been any sudden transformation in Ted, at least not in his personality. He was doing what retail politicians always did, what Honey Fitz did: wade into the fray. The only difference was that Ted now had the confidence to assert himself while being wise enough to demonstrate his magnanimity, which made party members feel that he wasn't asserting himself. This was why he invited Eddie McCormack, Governor Endicott Peabody, Lieutenant Governor Francis Bellotti, and Boston mayor John Collins to his Boston townhouse for a series of get-togethers. "Passing the peace pipe," a reporter called it. And Ted Kennedy knew how to do that, knew how to make people feel comfortable around him, knew not to vaunt, even when he was in control. And he was in control now.

So when Ted Kennedy headed to the state convention the night of the great civil rights victory, he was heading into a group of his own, a group that loved him as they hadn't loved Jack, who always seemed to them a bit too imperious, a bit too lace-curtain Irish for them. Ted Kennedy didn't act lace-curtain Irish. He had the instincts and the bonhomie of a shanty-Irish pol. And despite the long legislative day and despite the difficulties of getting there now, Ted Kennedy headed there because he wanted to, wanted to accept their coronation, and didn't want to disappoint them. Because he was running so late, he addressed them by phone, as a kind of teaser while they waited, asking them jokingly "not to nominate Joan until I get there." Ted's personal assistant—his "body man," as he was called—Ed Moss, who had worked in Ted's campaign, was to make the arrangements for the flight. Moss asked Ed Martin, the press secretary from Ted's campaign and now a staffer in Massachusetts, if he would fly down to Washington, get Ted to the plane at National Airport, and fly up with him, but Martin couldn't get a flight down, so he offered to pick up Joan and drive her to the convention, which left Moss flying down to Washington himself to get Ted and Bayh and Bayh's wife, Marvella, who would be flying up to Springfield with them. With time of the essence, Moss, Ted, and the Bayhs headed to the airport with a police escort. Because of the upcoming campaign, Ted had been flying up from Washington regularly—at one point, he spent twenty-seven straight weekends in Massachusetts. A man named Daniel Hogan, who was an industrialist and the owner of the company that made Lestoil household cleaner, and who owned the Aero Commander on which Ted had been flying, had been his recent pilot. Hogan was going to fly Ted up this time too, but he changed his mind at the last moment to attend a Yale class reunion and assigned his own pilot, Ed Zimny, to sub for him.

It was not a hospitable night for flying. The skies were dense with fog, the moon, Bayh said, alternately shining brightly and then hiding behind clouds, and when Ted asked the pilot why it was taking so long—they had been flying for ninety minutes, when the flight typically took an hour and fifteen minutes—Zimny said that he'd had to skirt storms on the way up. But Ted was unconcerned. He was a pilot himself; he got his license during law school and flew those small planes around Arizona and New Mexico for Jack's campaign. He appreciated the vicissitudes of flying. John Tunney would recall an incident when Ted was flying them into National Airport and was instructed by the air traffic controllers to follow a plane, and Ted followed the wrong one, so that there was a commercial airline right on their tail. The controllers yelled for Ted to take a left—"Hard left!"—and he did. "One of the more terrifying experiences of my life," Tunney called it. But he said that Ted was "full of enthusiasm and didn't appear afraid at all."

But, then, Ted Kennedy, who had that reckless streak in him, was seldom afraid. He was sitting behind the pilot, facing the rear of the plane, while Bayh sat across the aisle from him, the two of them working on their speeches, when Ed Moss got up to sit in the co-pilot's seat to give them more room. And Moss told them they would be landing shortly at Barnes Municipal Airport in Westfield, just outside Springfield. "Flying through a black void" is how Bayh described the descent—so black that Zimny had to make an instrument landing. Ted turned off the cabin lights and a short time later heard a radio transmission that visibility was 800 feet obscured. At that point, he loosened his seatbelt so he could turn and watch the approach and check the altitude on the instrument panel. He heard the wheels being lowered. "I remember looking down at what I thought was going to be the approach," Ted would later recall, saying he then buckled and tightened his seatbelt. But it wasn't the approach he expected. Instead of the runway, he said, he was "seeing rocks and a field almost directly in front of us, and trees sort of beyond that. It looked like we were coming right on down in sort of a rocky bluff." He also described it as "like a toboggan ride." Zimny pulled the throttle to raise the plane's nose, but not quickly enough. The plane rode along the treetops, tall thick pine trees. Bayh said the engine stalled, and said he heard a *crack* and assumed it was lightning. A "tremendous impact," Ted called it. But it wasn't lightning. Actually, the plane's left wing had hit one of the pines, which spun the plane off to the left. It slid 166 feet into an apple orchard, which slowed it down, but then the cockpit split—"opened up the front," Ted said, "right at the face." As the plane lurched to a halt, Bayh was momen-

tarily shell-shocked, unconscious. But he recovered and called to Marvella, who responded that she was all right, and he shouted to Ted. But
Ted was unable to respond. "I remember being hit in the head, hanging
between what was the pilot and Moss," Ted said in one account. And he
remembered mosquitoes coming in through the broken window. And he
remembered "absolute silence, nothing going on, absolute silence."

Bayh had managed to squeeze through the window, which had popped
out on impact, and then to pull out Marvella. But now there was another
danger. Smelling gasoline and fearing an explosion, the two of them
began to run from the site. Then Bayh stopped. He couldn't leave Ted behind, so he headed back to the wreckage, where Ted still dangled. "We
gotta go back and help Ted," he told Marvella. Hearing the mention of
gas, presumably from the Bayhs, Ted had managed to summon enough
strength to crawl to the rear of the cabin—"I was conscious that something was seriously wrong with me"—and drag himself to a window. He
could hear Marvella Bayh outside, repeating over and over, "We've got to
get help. We've got to get help. We've got to get help." But Ted couldn't
speak. Bayh said he saw an emergency light glancing off Ted's cuff link—
his coat sleeves had been torn off by the impact—and finally Ted grunted,
"I'm alive, Birch."

Bayh tried to drag him out of the wreckage, though Bayh had hurt his
back and couldn't bend, and Ted told him he couldn't move from the waist
down himself. In fact, Ted thought he was paralyzed. So Bayh told Ted to
grab his neck, and Bayh, in an act of Herculean strength, pulled Ted out
through the window and dragged him through the orchard "like a sack of
potatoes," for, Ted said, "what seemed an extraordinarily long time." Bayh
told Ted he would let him go when they were at a distance to be safe from
a possible gas explosion. Finally Ted heard, "We're far enough away," and
Bayh dropped him onto the grass, where he lay motionless, fighting for
breath and "fighting to remain conscious," as he later put it. Meanwhile,
Bayh headed back to the plane to see if he could rescue Zimny or Moss. He
couldn't. So Bayh left Ted, and he and Marvella headed out of the orchard
and up the road to seek help. By one account, they tried flagging down
cars, and nine passed in the course of twenty minutes before a farmer
named Robert Schauer stopped, picked them up, and drove them to his
house, where they called an ambulance. By another account, the Bashista
family, who owned the orchard, heard a sound like a motorboat and then
heard their collie barking, so Walter Bashista and his daughter Joanne

went out to see what was causing the noise and why their dog was agitated. In this version, they found Marvella Bayh, dazed, and hurried back to their house to call the ambulance. By this time, people were gathering at the site, and rescuers with power saws were cutting Moss and Zimny out of the plane, which was crumpled like "tinfoil," by one report. When they were removed, Zimny was clearly dead, but Moss was still clinging to life, though with a serious head wound. According to this version, by biographer Burton Hersh, Joanne Bashista ministered to Ted, whose eyes kept closing, and brought him a glass of water, blankets, and a flashlight. He asked about the condition of the Bayhs and of Moss. Ted doubted his own survival. He thought he was going to die. It *felt* like death. "It was sort of pain, but it was more numb, but you could just feel, sort of feel everything going out of you. . . . I felt the tide was going out." It was at least ninety minutes after the crash that the ambulances arrived, and another thirty minutes before Ted was taken to the hospital. He had insisted that Zimny and Moss be taken first. Then the medics came for him. He asked them for a shot of sodium pentothal, which he had taken once to relieve the pain for a shoulder dislocation, but they said they couldn't administer that because he had massive bleeding. (This was likely from a large wound on his hand.) And then they cut off his clothes. And then he passed out. Through it all, the red taillight of the plane kept rotating.

With the tragedy of John Kennedy's assassination still fresh, a sense of terror hit Ted's associates. Ed Martin said he had no sooner arrived at the convention with Joan than he and she got word about the crash. He called the White House and asked to speak to Sargent Shriver, who had been working with Johnson, to inform them. Then he went to Cooley Dickinson Hospital in Northampton, to which Ted was being brought—the ambulance wouldn't arrive until after midnight—and instructed the staff to set up fifty phone lines. By that time, telegrams were already arriving.

But by another account, Joan had heard the news from Ted's old driver, Jack Crimmins, who had been assigned to drive her to the convention. Crimmins had heard it on the radio and relayed it to Joan, who, in order to avoid curious onlookers, was staying at a house of friends of friends, Don Dowd and his wife, Phoebe. Presumably Crimmins did so when he arrived to pick her up. By Dowd's own account, he was waiting at the airport with a Democratic pol, Ed King, for Ted's plane to land when he got word of the accident and then drove immediately to his friend's house to tell Joan. Joan, almost catatonic, as Lester David told it, crawled into the back seat and kept saying over and over that the news might be wrong and that, in any case, Ted would be all right, while, by still a third account, Crimmins was the one who drove her and the Dowds to the hospital, where Joan wandered about in a dream state trying to find her husband. But there was one thing on which all the accounts agreed: Joan Kennedy was lost in her own thoughts, benumbed by her terror, trying desperately to keep reality at bay—to keep at bay the idea that her husband might be gone: another Kennedy casualty.

And the terror spread. At Hyannis, where Bobby had gone to spend the weekend, Jean Kennedy Smith rushed in to tell him that she had been watching the convention proceedings on television and heard the news. Meanwhile, Birch Bayh—whose muscles were torn all down his side and who needed medical attention—phoned Bobby as soon as he arrived at the hospital, which was long before Ted arrived, to tell him of the accident. So accustomed to grief was Bobby that Bayh said his first words were reflexively, "Is he dead?" That was the thought that permeated the Kennedys: *Is he dead?* Then: *Would he die?* Bobby ordered the late president's plane, the *Caroline,* to fly him and Jean from Boston, but the weather was still too treacherous, so they took a car the 150 miles to the hospital, telling the driver to "Gun it," and arrived at four that morning. At the same time, Pat Kennedy Lawford was arranging to fly in from Pittsburgh. As soon as he got word of the crash, Lyndon Johnson, who was on a fundraising trip in California, ordered four specialists from Walter Reed Army Medical Center to fly up to Northampton to see if Ted's life could be saved, and his wife, Lady Bird, phoned Joan to offer her support. Kenny O'Donnell, who was traveling with Johnson, immediately arranged to fly east. William vanden Heuvel, who had accompanied Ted to Europe, and Nicholas Katzenbach, the former deputy attorney general, were in upstate New York working for Bobby when they heard; they jumped into a car to get to the hospital and arrived to find Ted in an oxygen tent. They could have been arriving for a death watch.

Would he die? "White as anyone," Ed Martin said when Ted was wheeled into the hospital on the gurney. "I thought he was dying." He was given three blood transfusions and intravenous bags of glucose and salt. He was in "deep shock," had two broken ribs and three fractured vertebrae, a bruised kidney and a punctured lung, was bleeding internally, and his blood pressure was so low that it was "almost negligible," his doctor, Thomas Corriden, said. And his pain was unbearable, though his doctors, fearing injuries to his spleen or kidney, refused to give him painkillers. He was still immobile. Neither he nor his doctors knew yet whether he was paralyzed. The doctors had doubts whether he would survive.

And as Ted teetered near death, there was still Ed Moss, Ted's tall, genial administrative assistant, his "body man," who had been in the copilot's seat when the plane tore through the orchard and the pines tore through the plane. Moss arrived at Cooley Dickinson just before midnight, unconscious, but his eyes were open, staring blankly, and he was bleeding profusely from cuts on his tongue, and he was rushed into surgery. Four doctors worked on him, assisted by ten nurses and technicians. They worked through the night. They worked for over six hours. They intubated, transfused him, stemmed the flow of blood, sutured the cuts on his tongue, and called in a neurosurgeon to remove pressure on his brain. Meanwhile, after visiting with Teddy for twenty minutes, Bobby sought out Moss's wife, walked around the hospital perimeter with her, tried to console her. But Moss's case was hopeless. He expired at 6:15 A.M.

Would he die? But Ted Kennedy, somehow, broken as he was, wounded as he was, immobile as he was, did not die. He rallied, almost as if the young man whose job had always been to boost his family's morale in times of despair had to now boost that morale when his own survival was the source of the despair. When Joan arrived at his hospital bed, Ted, in his agony, moaned, "Hi, Joansie. Don't worry." When vanden Heuvel arrived, Ted had the presence of mind to ask him if he would fill in for Teddy on a speech he was set to deliver in New York. And when Bobby arrived at his bedside, Ted cracked, "Is it true you are ruthless?" Milt Gwirtzman, who was supposed to rendezvous with Ted the day after the convention for a getaway up in the Adirondack wilderness, arrived about ten to twelve hours after the crash and told Ted this would be the time to write a book—whether humorously or not, from the humorless Gwirtzman, it was difficult to say. "You could see that he was a little spacey," Gwirtzman said. "But he wasn't at all mopey. He was looking forward." This from a man who was near death and whose survival remained in question.

And dead Ted Kennedy would have been—"deader than a mackerel," said a member of the Massachusetts Aeronautics Commission, who was the first agent to reach the crash site—had it not been for one thing he did just before the descent: He refastened his seatbelt. Had he not done so, he would have been thrown fifty feet from the plane. And paralyzed he would have been had his most severe spinal injury—a fracture of the third lumbar vertebra—been an inch higher, which would have severed his spinal cord, though it would be some time before the doctors knew and Ted knew whether he would walk again. There was so much to do that night of the accident, and for several days thereafter, that it wasn't until much later that anyone bothered to stitch a six-inch gash on his right hand—the gash that had bled. And it would be a full week before his doctors were finally sure he was going to survive.

The morning following the crash, after he had taken his walk outside the hospital with Ed Moss's wife, Bobby Kennedy took another walk, this one with Walter Sheridan, a former FBI agent and an old friend of his from the rackets investigation days. At one point Bobby stopped, lay out on the grass, and mused, "Somebody up there doesn't like me." And so it seemed of all the Kennedys.

II

Ted Kennedy had lived, but it would be a long road ahead—a long and torturous road. The damage done to his body—damage that he survived largely because of his superb physical condition—would not heal easily, especially his fractured vertebrae, which required he be immobilized. He had been strapped into—and "strapped into" was the appropriate term— a Foster frame, which was a metal bed that sandwiched a patient with cervical issues like Ted's between two long mattresses that would restrain the patient and allow him to be rotated, like a rotisserie, facedown then faceup. The Foster frame was cumbersome, and it was uncomfortable— a kind of straitjacket. But the alternative was worse. The alternative was surgery in six to eight weeks to fuse his vertebrae, when he had sufficiently healed to undergo an operation, and the alternative was what the doctors Lyndon Johnson had sent from Walter Reed advised Ted to do. But the Kennedys had had experience with back operations—tragic experience.

Jack, who had chronic back issues, likely worsened by a Harvard football injury and by his PT-boat heroism when he towed an injured shipmate on open waters for five hours, decided to have an operation in 1944, when he was suffering excruciating pain. But it did not relieve his suffering. So in 1954 Jack Kennedy decided to have another operation, fusing his vertebrae with a metal plate attached to the spine. This time the surgery not only didn't relieve his pain; a staph infection developed at the site, nearly killing him and necessitating yet another surgery, in February

1955, to remove the plate. "He was at the bottom," said Kenny O'Donnell. "It seemed over." He didn't return to the Senate until late May. And he was forced to wear a brace for the rest of his life. Ted Kennedy remembered that period, remembered it well, because he was at Harvard at the time, and Jack invited him down to Palm Beach, where he was recuperating, to entertain him. (It was when Ted first began painting, because Jack had picked up painting to pass the time.)

As Ted deliberated whether to undergo the surgery, he invited his father to the hospital on July 2 to discuss the option with the doctors. But there was no discussion. Joe Kennedy, who couldn't talk but who could make his feelings known, brayed at the physicians, "Naaaa, naaaa, naaaa!" and just "stormed at the doctors," as one observer said, clearly remembering Jack's near-fatal experience. And Ted concurred. There would be no operation.

Not yet. On July 10, he was transferred to New England Baptist Hospital in Boston. (A friend wrote him a few days later: "We were delighted when you shifted from liquids to cereals, and there was a cheer which went up when we read you stopped the ambulance to get a hot dog on the way to your current residence.") But there was no celebrating for Ted. He said that he had no sooner arrived than the doctors told him that he was never going to walk again. It is unclear when they revised their diagnosis, but in Boston, Ted was tended by three surgeons: Dr. Herbert D. Adams, the director of the renowned Lahey Clinic, who covered thoracic surgery; Dr. James Poppen, a neurosurgeon; and Dr. George Hammond, an orthopedic surgeon. And Ted told Lyndon Johnson, in a phone call on August 13, that they "just announced this morning they're not going to operate, so they're giving me a few more months on my back up here." (The next day *The New York Times* reported the decision to forgo an operation, adding that the doctors expected him to be able to leave the hospital six months after the accident.) And Ted said that he was intending to "beat their estimate and be home by Thanksgiving." To which Johnson said, "They can't keep a good man down."

"On his back" meant on his back in a bed frame, this time a Stryker frame, which was an improved version of the Foster frame—improved because it didn't sandwich the patient between two mattresses but trussed him into foam pillows on a metal frame that still had to be rotated every three hours. (One of the problems was lifting Ted, who was six foot two and 230 pounds now, onto the frame.) Improved it was, but it was still uncomfortable. He could only lift his chin and move his arms and legs, and he had to read through "prism" glasses that reflected the pages of books he balanced on his chest, which prompted his mother, ever the self-improvement martinet and ever the critic of her children, to write him suggesting that when he was lying in his bed, he could read a paragraph from a book and then try to resay it, so he could "notice the difference between the succinct dramatic expressions of the author + your own discursive dull recital of the same events."

Discomfort was the least of it. He was still in excruciating pain. He was immobile. He was a "human rotisserie," as he put it. He couldn't sleep, and when he managed to do so, he would awaken only to find that scarcely a half hour had passed, but then he couldn't fall asleep again. Still, no one saw him succumb to depression, which was not the Ted Kennedy way. Ted Kennedy had always been irrepressible, and he was irrepressible in recovery. "I've never heard him complain once about the ordeal that he had to go through," William vanden Heuvel, who visited him often during this period, said. "I never heard him make reference to the pain and suffering and anguish that he had to endure during those months, which had to be significant." And vanden Heuvel saw in this stoicism the Kennedy family trait: "this determination to absorb all the fateful lashing of history and life and go forward and go forward and go forward." And Ted Kennedy did go forward. He was already doing exercises three days after the accident, his physical therapist said, and at New England Baptist he was always pushing himself, always trying to go beyond the prescribed exercises, always working to beat the six-month timetable when the doctors had predicted he would be able to leave. He had a television in his room, but his therapist said he never watched it, never even turned it on. His brother-in-law Peter Lawford sent him a Scopitone, a jukebox that played little musical shorts. But this didn't get much use either; it was kept in the corner of the room. His primary recreation in the hospital, his only real recreation, was dinner, ordering nightly meals from Locke-Ober, from which a retainer named Andy Vitale would fetch the meals—served on silver trays.

The one thing he had in the period he spent on his back was time—hours of time, days of time, weeks of time, months of time. And Ted Kennedy, the most restless of the Kennedys, was not a man to waste time, though waste some of it he did, greeting visitors—a parade of visitors who would come to pay their respects to the incapacitated young senator trussed in his bed, a sign of how in less than two years in the Senate he had been overcoming the lowest expectations. Of course, his friends visited regularly. Ted Sorensen was one of those visitors and found him "amazingly brave, determined, and cheery." Evangelist Billy Graham visited. And President Johnson, who was in nearby New Hampshire campaigning, called to say he was going to visit, though as the day grew later and later Ted tried his best to discourage him, having Ed Martin call the president and tell him that a visit at this late hour would disrupt the other patients. "You tell him I'm coming," Johnson said. "The patients can sleep a little longer in the morning." He arrived at the hospital at 12:40 A.M., "created quite a racket there," Martin said. But he also said that Johnson came because he liked Ted, liked him "very much"—as opposed to how he felt about Bobby—and wanted to demonstrate it, although with Johnson, it was impossible to tell whether he wanted to ingratiate himself with the Kennedy coterie or to show up Bobby by honoring Ted. They talked—or mainly Johnson talked, "a rambling conversation," as Ted would describe it—about how the FBI should have followed up on warnings about Lee Harvey Oswald, John Kennedy's accused assassin; about a prospective autoworkers' strike; about the violent situation in Vietnam; even about Rhode Island politics. After a half hour, Johnson kissed Teddy goodbye, held a brief press conference, at which he called Ted "cheerful and optimistic," and departed—a human tornado roaring through the hospital, leaving "confusion" in his wake, said Ed Martin.

And there was another visitor who needed to see Ted Kennedy, needed to see him more than the others. Preliminary investigations pointed to pilot error as the cause of the crash. ("Lots of pilot error," Birch Bayh would later say.) Ed Zimny had miscalculated. He had taken the plane down a mile short of the runway into that grove of pines. And now Zimny's widow came to see Ted, came to see him to tell him how terrible she felt about the accident for which her late husband had been responsible. But Ted, as he so often did, felt responsible to her too. The Federal Aviation Administration was going to conduct a thorough investigation, and Ted was trying to quash it because he didn't want Zimny to be implicated; he didn't want Zimny's memory to be tarnished.

The visitors came, but Ted Kennedy didn't want to spend his time in the hospital greeting well-wishers. Ted Kennedy needed to *do,* even if he could barely move. When John Kennedy was bedridden with his back injury, he wrote—or guided Ted Sorensen to write, depending upon whom one believed—*Profiles in Courage,* a book of mini-biographies of political figures who, when tested by political crises, had demonstrated spine. It won Kennedy the Pulitzer Prize. Ted was less ambitious—he usually was—but he had taken up Gwirtzman's suggestion to write a book too. He actually wound up editing one, soliciting contributions to a self-published volume dedicated to his father, called *The Fruitful Bough*, its title from Genesis 49:22, "Joseph is a fruitful bough." And, even while imprisoned in the Stryker frame, he took up painting again, still lifes only—a winter landscape with a covered bridge; a sleigh ride; a red cottage with a sailboat in the background; a rocky Maine coastline; a flower in a vase—because, he said, he had no knack for figures. He finished seven canvases during his recuperation, all from memory, while flat on his back, holding the canvas with his left hand, the brush with his right, and he distributed the paintings to his family members. And Ted, who loved opera, who had in a secret life aspired to be an opera singer, listened incessantly to opera, especially to *Madama Butterfly*.

But Ted Kennedy, who had the time now, had a deficiency to repair, especially with his brother gone, and especially since he would be expected to help fill the emptiness. Ted Kennedy knew politics, knew how to play them better than his brothers, but he wanted to know policy. Before the accident, he had already begun conducting those informational sessions at his Georgetown house. But now, while he was strapped into that Stryker frame, he asked Samuel Beer, the Harvard political scientist who had helped his Senate campaign, to set up tutorials for him with Beer himself and other Harvard and MIT luminaries, to teach him the things he hadn't learned but the things he felt he had to know to be a good senator, a respected senator. So Beer enlisted Robert Wood, a professor at MIT, to teach Ted about cities; John Kenneth Galbraith, Carl Kaysen, and Alain Enthoven to teach him about economics; Jerrold Zacharias and Jerome Wiesner of MIT, who had been John Kennedy's science adviser, to teach him science; and Harvard Law professors Charles Haar, whom Ted had impressed during his campaign and who assisted him then, and Mark DeWolfe Howe, who had been the Harvard professor most intractably opposed to Ted Kennedy's candidacy, the one who considered it insulting and an affront, but who now gave him a crash course in civil rights. They met in Ted's hospital room, different tutors, twice a week from 7:30 to 9:30 P.M., delivering what amounted to lectures at first, since he was incapacitated and could only read a "bit," Galbraith said, but conducting seminars later on as his condition improved. And they provided reading lists and even recruited other scholars to come in for discussions. And Ted, who had often been considered a lackadaisical student, the least intelligent of the Kennedys, worked hard—hard because he knew he was improving his standing. His physical therapist said that he now would read and jot notes even while doing exercises. "He'd somehow take notes, and he'd listen to us," Beer said. He brought Teddy a book, *Intergovernmental Relations in the United States* by W. B. Graves, a huge book—"I'd rather eat it than read it," Beer said—but he also said it was a great reference book, and Ted, strapped into his bed, read it, read the whole thing. Beer said that made him so different from Jack, this ferocity to study now, to consume, because Jack was so self-confident, he didn't think he had to study. But Ted Kennedy needed to study. Late at night, when Ted finally got out of the Stryker, aides would find him on the balcony outside his hospital window, a blanket wrapped around him, lit by a desk lamp on one of two small wooden tables on that balcony, reading and jotting those notes. There were books everywhere. Once, George Lodge, his Republican Senate opponent, visited him and saw the books piled beside him, and Joan said, "Teddy's reading all the books he should have read in college." He was. And he processed what he read. Years later, one of his staffers, Jeffrey Blattner, was working with him and a few others on some issue when Ted quoted an appropriate line from the Constitutional Convention. Blattner, surprised, asked where he had come up with that. And Ted told him: When he was flat on his back and recuperating, he had read the entire proceedings of the Constitutional Convention—and then he had remembered the important points of them.

Those long months were for recuperating, and they were for educating. But they were also for fulfilling two other obligations. First, Ted Kennedy was still a United States senator, and he needed to perform as one for his constituents. So his staff set up an office on the fifth floor of New England Baptist Hospital—not really set up but commandeered the wing. "Something surreal," Charles Tretter called it. Another called it "sheer bedlam." Ted had his hospital room with its balcony, but across the hall, in another room, he had installed his secretary, Angelique Voutselas, and Ed Martin, who was now working not only as his press secretary but also as liaison between Washington and Boston. Martin said that someone from the Washington office would phone every day to tell him about pending legislation and a feeling about how Ted should vote, and Martin would then pass on the information to Ted, who would tell Martin how he *was* going to vote. And down the hall from the "office," they built, right in the hospital, a double-doored entryway to yet another room, this one manned by two Navy corpsman whom Lyndon Johnson had dispatched from Walter Reed Hospital to look after Ted. "There were some days when you went up there," Tretter said, "and but for the fact that he was in there in this thing [the Stryker frame], he could have been in there behind a desk. The place was going like crazy. Soon there were two desks, then more phone lines. I think we even took more rooms."

But Ted Kennedy, during those long months in New England Baptist Hospital, wasn't only running *an* office; he was also running *for* office, for his own term in the Senate. It wasn't a campaign like the one for the remaining two years of John Kennedy's term in 1962. There would be no primary, no contentious convention. And there would be no serious Republican challenger either. Howard Whitmore Jr., the Republican nominee, was a Harvard-educated, fifty-nine-year-old former state representative, who had later served as mayor of Newton but had lost a bid to run for governor when the Republican state convention tapped John Volpe instead. He was also a sacrificial lamb, which didn't mean that Ted didn't take the race seriously. Ted clearly couldn't campaign. But one Kennedy could: Joan Kennedy. And Joan did. It was Joan who collected signatures to get him on the ballot, Joan who attended the meetings and conventions, Joan who even danced the polka at a Pulaski Day dinner in Dorchester. "He wants you to return him to the Senate," she would tell crowds. "He can't do it by himself, so he wants me to tell you he needs your help." She would give those audiences reports of his convalescence. She would show them home movies of Kara and Ted Jr. picking up shells on the beach to give their father and movies of them visiting him in the hospital. She "grinned and bounced," a reporter told her biographer, Lester David. "She sparkled all over the place." Her "delight was genuine," he said. And she would campaign like this six days a week, even though she was shy and private, even though crowds made her uncomfortable, even though she doubted herself. But she did it, did it for her husband. "If I weren't married to Ted, I'd be home with my children, leading a much more private life," she told Lester David. "I don't do this kind of thing for fun. I do it for Ted." So every day an aide would pick her up at Squaw Island on the Cape, and every day she would visit Ted in the hospital, and then every day she would go stumping—every day but Sunday. For Ted. And every day, after campaigning, she would return to Ted in the hospital. She wasn't entirely alone on the road. Rose took to the stump too. "I've come to tell you my version of my son Teddy," she would tell those crowds, "and why I think you should return him to the Senate." (And Joan didn't only campaign for Ted. She made an appearance for Birch Bayh, who was running for reelection in Indiana, as gratitude for Bayh's having saved Ted's life.) But as the campaign wore on, it began to wear on Joan. The delight diminished. The reporter who had observed that delight said that at the end of the day she would collapse in a chair and sigh, "I'm glad this one's over," or "I'm glad it was a short one tonight." Yet Joan persevered—persevered and carried the campaign. And when Ted won overwhelmingly—just under 76 percent of the vote—his Boston campaign manager Jim King told him, "You didn't win in 1964. Joan won in 1964."

Ted wasn't the only Kennedy running in 1964. Bobby had emerged from the melancholy into which he had fallen after Jack's death—emerged determined to protect what he saw as his brother's legacy, emerged to put himself on a course to the presidency, not for his own ambitions but for his brother's. He had changed since the assassination—that was the phrase one heard again and again from those who knew him—the same man but transfigured: The riven landscape Richard Goodwin had described of the Bobby shortly after Jack's death was "composed of the same elements of stone and soil that abided there before the earth shook," yet different. Once cautious, so cautious that he advised Jack not to meet with the leaders of the March on Washington, he was cautious no longer. Once hard in order to conceal his vulnerability, the vulnerability that his father so despised, he was now more openly vulnerable. Once ruthless on his brother's behalf, he was increasingly soft on his own behalf. Once a pragmatist like his older brother, he was now less a pragmatist; he was becoming an idealist. Once largely indifferent to the suffering of the disempowered and dispossessed, he now made relieving their suffering his primary mission. In many ways, he became the new, more ardent face of American liberalism.

But to continue Jack Kennedy's legacy, he needed a way into elective office. Just weeks after the assassination, on a flight up to Boston with Arthur Schlesinger Jr. to incorporate the JFK Library, Schlesinger said that Bobby was already contemplating whether he should angle for the vice-presidential nomination with Johnson, whether he should begin to deploy the pressure that was out in the country for him to extend the Kennedy administration. (A Gallup poll in April had showed that 47 percent of Democrats favored Bobby for vice president.) But Bobby vacillated. He wasn't sure he could work with Johnson, or if, short of pressure, Johnson would work with him. In any case, Johnson foreclosed the option late that July when he announced that he would not put anyone from the Cabinet on his ticket, a decision clearly aimed at only one Cabinet member, which prompted Bobby to express his regret at taking "so many of you nice fellows over the side with me." Still, Bobby remained in the Cabinet as a way, he hoped, of pressuring Johnson to select the liberal Hubert Humphrey as his vice-presidential nominee, which Johnson eventually did. But now Bobby's sights turned to the Senate and to New York, since the Massachusetts seat was occupied and since he had lived in New York while growing up, though that didn't deflect charges that he was a "carpetbagger"—charges that his opponent, the moderate Republican Kenneth Keating, was eager to exploit. So while Ted was in the hospital, Bobby was storming New York, hoping to lay the foundation for a future presidential bid.

And Bobby was not the only intimate of Ted's running for office. John Tunney, Ted's close friend, was running for Congress in California. He said he had caught the political bug when he worked with Ted on Jack's 1958 Senate campaign, and as he began pondering, early in 1963, the possibility of running for Congress in California, Ted invited him and Tunney's Dutch-born wife, Mieke, to a luncheon in Washington with Crown Princess Beatrix of the Netherlands, then spent the rest of the week discussing a political career with him, encouraging him to run. And Ted not only encouraged Tunney, he sent Ed Martin, Ed Moss, and Jim King to tutor Tunney's inexperienced staff on how to run a campaign, then went out to California the day Tunney announced his candidacy, in January, to tour the district with his friend. It was a conservative district east of Los Angeles, and Ted didn't return, lest he hurt his friend's chances—and then he had the accident and couldn't return. But Tunney was smart and attractive and sufficiently moderate, and he won, beating the Republican incumbent.

There was one other candidate for office in 1964 who was critically important to Ted Kennedy—this one not an intimate of Ted's but the man who would be shaping the nation's future and, of utmost concern to the Kennedys, John Kennedy's legacy. Lyndon Johnson was running for his own full term, drafting behind the national sorrow over John Kennedy's death and behind the legislation that Johnson had enacted that year—first the Civil Rights Act and then, in August, the Economic Opportunity Act, which fired the first shot in Johnson's declared war against poverty, another of John Kennedy's initiatives. And Republicans had made it easy for him to run on Kennedy's unfinished business and on his own efforts to finish it—made it easy because their candidate had stood in opposition to everything Kennedy and Johnson did. The Republican nominee was Arizona senator Barry Goldwater. Grim he looked, with a broad forehead, a firmly set jutting jaw, deep-set eyes, and black horn-rimmed glasses, and grim he was. Barry Goldwater was not a traditional Republican. The traditional Republican party—the party of agrarians and small-town America, the party of big business and economic elites, the party of self-sufficiency—was increasingly anachronistic in an industrialized and urbanized America, in an America where big business had been rendered suspect by the Great Depression, and where self-sufficiency wasn't adequate to meet many of the challenges Americans faced, like unemployment or old age or poverty or health care.

The party had adjusted. The liberal consensus had been the Republican accommodation to the post–New Deal world—a kind of truce with it. But there was another kind of reaction among a faction of angry Republicans to their party's possible obsolescence, and it wasn't accommodation. It was political war against the consensus. And Barry Goldwater was their candidate. Looking forward to the 1964 election, Jack Kennedy had already been concerned about the reactionary veins within the Republican party, and he asked White House counsel Myer Feldman to examine the ascension of the right wing. Feldman reported back that the right wing was indeed empowered, that it controlled foundations and corporations and utilities and that it had poured money into congressional campaigns, and done so successfully. Meanwhile, Kennedy commissioned Walter Reuther, the president of the United Auto Workers, to draft a plan to thwart that influence. Even Ted, during his convalescence, wrote a paper on the dangers of extremism and on "the compelling necessity of consensus in a pluralistic society." But Barry Goldwater did not want consensus. Barry Goldwater did not want pluralism. Barry Goldwater was the personification of the threat Kennedy saw to his programs and to his America, and *The Washington Post* described Goldwater's assault on the traditional Republican party as an "attempted gigantic political kidnapping" by "fanatics." His acceptance speech, at the Republican National Convention in San Francisco, was a full-throated attack on New Deal government and the post–New Deal liberal consensus, including on the Republican moderates who subscribed to that consensus, couched in the rhetoric of American individualism. Democrats, he said, were "those who seek to live your lives for you, to take your liberty in return for relieving you of yours, those who elevate the state and downgrade the citizen," even suggesting they believed that "earthly power can be substituted for divine will." The stakes couldn't be higher, he said. This election was, he said, an election to turn the tide, Kennedy's tide, Johnson's tide—"false prophets," he called them by implication—which had been running against freedom, which was the very bedrock of America, but which was endangered, in Goldwater's view, by government. He compared the slavery of African Americans in the antebellum South to the threatened slavery of Americans under liberal government. And he said in a ringing peroration: "Extremism in the defense of liberty is no vice. And moderation in the pursuit of justice is no virtue." It was an odd speech for a major-party candidate, a unique speech, the humorless speech of a scold, a speech without uplift, a speech without tolerance, without compassion, without a ringing declaration of the American community, without any role for diplomacy in foreign affairs or any role for government in domestic affairs, save to protect the "sanctity" of property. It was a radical speech for its time—not only fiercely anti-government but anti-politics itself. As historian Richard Hofstadter put it, Goldwater "wanted, in short, to drive the politics out of politics" and turn it into a belief system. It was a speech not of a political party seeking to win voters but of a movement seeking to convert adherents.

But for all the vehemence of the speech, for all its deep appeal to the individualistic strains in the American psyche, it was a testament to the enduring power of the post–New Deal liberal consensus, to the effect of John Kennedy's death on the nation, and to the vigorous defense of government by that old New Dealer, Lyndon Johnson, that Goldwater's speech won few voters, even if it did convert some adherents. The election turned out to be a rejection of Goldwater's pusillanimous view of what government should be, which was very little government at all, and an endorsement of Johnson's, as Kennedy's legatee. And despite John Kennedy's own moderation, it demonstrated that nothing so liberalized him or, possibly, his country as his death. The election was, in many ways, a plebiscite on America's moral authority in the wake of John Kennedy's presidency, and the plebiscite affirmed that authority. Johnson won 61 percent of the vote—the largest landslide in American presidential history. As for the Kennedys, Ted and Johnson got almost exactly the same percentage of the vote in Massachusetts, but Johnson outperformed Bobby in New York, where the president received 68 percent of the vote, and Bobby, hurt by his diffidence, by his seeming arrogance in running in the state in the first place though he didn't reside there, and by entering the race less than three months before the election, got 53.5 percent.

Pundits would write eulogies for the Republican party, which was now, they said, seized by those fanatics outside the American mainstream, but the vote didn't come without warnings that belied Johnson's victory. Johnson lost only six states: Goldwater's home state of Arizona and five states of the Deep South, where, as Johnson had predicted, the Civil Rights Act drove them to the Republican party and to Goldwater, who had opposed the law. Prior to 1964, race had been a divisive issue but not necessarily one that divided Democrats and Republicans, since most of the segregationists were Democrats, who could and did make common cause with some conservative Republicans—until John Kennedy and then Lyndon Johnson began promoting civil rights, marginalizing those segregationists. But the law created a new political cleavage. Before the civil rights movement, Southern Democratic legislators could vote for segregation *and* support New Deal–style initiatives that would help their poor white constituents. After the civil rights movement, they couldn't, denouncing instead those initiatives as government overreach, which meant any reach that helped African Americans too and might possibly embolden them. Speaker of the House Sam Rayburn once told Lyndon Johnson the story of an aging Southern senator who lamented the good old days, the days when the South could hate blacks but vote for Roosevelt. "Poor old state," the senator said. "They haven't heard a real Democratic speech in thirty years. All they ever hear at election time is 'nigger, nigger, nigger!'" At the same time, conservative Republicans quickly recognized that even if they weren't racists themselves, their antigovernment, individualistic philosophy gave cover to subliminal racial appeals, and sometimes not-so-subliminal ones. This was one of Barry Goldwater's bequests to his party. From 1964 on, race would redraw

America's political lines—would be, as economist and liberal columnist Paul Krugman would later write, "at the heart of what happened to the country I grew up in."

The eulogies were premature.

III

It was finally drawing to an end. Ted Kennedy had been in convalescence for nearly six months, six excruciating months, especially excruciating for someone as active as Ted, and though he had worked hard to get out before those six months, swore he would get out before, he couldn't. As time went on, as the wounds and bones began to heal, he was released from the Stryker frame and allowed to sit up in bed. And, no longer trussed, he could sit out on the balcony too. With his congressional race over, John Tunney came to visit often. But Tunney said they never talked politics; they talked about Ted's recovery. Come December, as Rita Dallas told it, Ted phoned and asked that his father be brought to the hospital. On December 3, with his father looking on, Ted walked for the first time since the accident: twenty feet, tentatively, ten feet out and ten feet back, with a cane, and the doctors close behind, lest he fall. And Dallas said that Joe Kennedy took a "deep and startled breath, then grinned from ear to ear. Bursting with pride, he struggled to his feet and stood beside his son."

The fractures were all healed now. Ted's muscle function, they said, was normal, though he had lost thirty pounds in the ordeal. He was now sitting or standing most of the day and would start to take short evening walks. And soon he was climbing the back stairs, however painful it was, to tone up his legs. "Very few people could recover the way he did," Dr. Adams, the Lahey Clinic director, said. One day shy of two weeks after taking those first steps, on December 16, he left New England Baptist Hospital. But Ed Martin told biographer Burton Hersh that at 5 A.M., before the formal discharge, he, a friend of Teddy's named Ray LaRosa, and Ted quietly slipped down the back stairs, and LaRosa drove Ted to a cemetery in Andover, where, up a knoll, Ed Moss, his "body man" who had perished in the crash, had been laid to rest, though the site was still without a headstone. It would have been Moss's forty-first birthday. And then Ted asked to be driven to Moss's home, to see his widow, Katie, and their three children. They had gotten a German shepherd and named him Teddy, and the dog jumped into Ted's lap.

And then he returned to the hospital for his release. Afterward he flew to Washington and in Washington took the *Caroline* to Miami, then was driven to Palm Beach, where his father awaited him. Father and son exercised together over that holiday, stepping slowly together into the rehab pool, holding on to the parallel bars together. But Ted was different with his father now, Rita Dallas noted—less carefree, less the family jester, more serious. The two, she said, would sit for hours together, watching a ball game on television, but Teddy wouldn't root the way he used to. He would analyze the game. And when Joe would fall asleep during the game, Ted would shut off the television and wait in the chair until his father awoke again. And she said he would read the newspaper to Joe or sit by his bedside and adjust his covers while he slept. He was tender with his father, sensitive to his suffering now that he had suffered himself.

Others noted changes in him too, profound changes. Ted was resilient. Kennedys were trained to be stoic in tragedy and resilient in recovering from it, but the boy who would always get caught, the boy who could never escape, not even tragedy, had never emerged from his afflictions unaffected. He had come back from the cheating episode more mature, more determined. Now he emerged from the accident more contemplative, more introspective—this from someone who had never been terribly introspective. He lived with pain now. He would always live with pain. The best athlete in the Kennedy family would have to wear a four-pound plastic back brace for the rest of his life, so restrictive that he couldn't bend over to tie his shoes, and he would never be able to stand fully erect again. He had to soak his back every day, as Jack had, sometimes having to stop in the middle of a campaign day to do so. He couldn't walk stairs without agony. The pain informed him. Samuel Beer, one of his Harvard tutors, compared his personal transformation to the one Franklin Roosevelt had undergone when he was diagnosed with polio. A "spiritual rebirth," Beer called it. (Ted Sorensen thought John Kennedy had undergone the same kind of transformation in his brush with death after his back surgery, as did Bobby in the aftermath of Jack's death.) Ted thought more deeply now, challenged himself more intellectually after his hospital seminars. When Ted got out of the hospital, John Kenneth Galbraith, who had been one of those tutors, hosted a dinner for him, to which he invited experts in various fields. It was a kind of Pygmalion moment—the experts firing questions at Ted. And Ted answered adroitly. Beer said, "He did very well." And when Beer was leaving, he and Galbraith embraced "because we'd pulled it off. We'd really sold Ted Kennedy to the academic elite." But it wasn't a matter of his mentors selling him. Ted had sold himself by having challenged himself.

He was deeper now, less callow, more focused on his future. "I had a lot of time to think about what was important and what was not, and about what I wanted to do with my life," he told reporter William Shannon, who had been Jack's ambassador to Ireland. He thought long and hard about the Senate—a subject that had preoccupied him for years—and his accident and recuperation only strengthened his conviction about how he would use his office. Robert Wood, another of his tutors, said that he and Ted would discuss what kind of senator he wanted to be and whether he should rest on his notoriety, as Jack had, or seek something else, and Ted said that he "wanted something with more substance." He told a reporter about a note he received from Senator George McGovern, a note that he said affected him deeply, in which McGovern wrote that he believed there was a "call to greatness stirring within you" and felt the accident and the recovery may "set you on an even finer course than would otherwise have been the case." Arthur Schlesinger Jr. felt similarly, writing in his journal that "in retrospect this interlude will turn out to be one of the luckiest things that ever happened to him" and that "I have no doubt he will be an effective and hardworking senator." Ted himself had tentatively concurred, even before his recovery was under way. Talking to Lyndon Johnson on the phone a little more than a week after the crash, he said that he was receiving a lot of mail, and "They say: . . . 'After all that, you get on your back a little, and think, and do a little suffering, you'll be a better man.' So I guess I'll take my chances with that."

And suffer now he had.

SEVEN

"A Heightened Sense of Purpose"

W HEN TED KENNEDY returned to Washington from Palm Beach, on January 3, 1965, to take his Senate seat, he arrived a different senator than when he had left the previous June—a man transformed. He was physically different. He was still in convalescence, walking slowly and with a silver-headed cane given to him by Barry Goldwater, who had somehow acquired it from Joe Kennedy. He was temperamentally differ-ent. A "grimace and a smile," reported *The Washington Post* of his expres-sion as he arrived at the Capitol, which captured a sense of the agony that tempered his usual ebullience without erasing it. His reception from his fellow senators was different. Though still the youngest senator, now, hav-ing survived his brother's assassination and then a plane crash, he was no longer a kid, no longer a punch line, no longer the senator of whom his colleagues had the lowest expectations. He had pulled up to the Justice Department in his old blue Chrysler early on January 5, the day of the swearing-in, to pick up Bobby, who slid into the driver's seat and asked half-jokingly, "Which way do I drive, Eddie? You know this routine now." And when the two of them arrived at the Capitol, their fellow senators swarmed Ted. As *Life* magazine reported it, John Stennis of Mississippi bellowed, "Mighty glad to have you back." Stuart Symington shook his hand. Clinton Anderson of New Mexico told him that "the best news of the session is having you back." And Richard Russell, the biggest of the old bulls, walked across the room to greet him and told him to take care of his back. Then Ted and Bobby entered the chamber and, at 12:23 P.M., flouted Senate convention by being sworn in together—the first brothers who would serve together in the Senate since Theodore and Dwight Foster in 1803.

Democrats couldn't help but feel giddy. It was not the hopefulness they felt with John Kennedy's election. It was less aspirational than that, more pragmatic. This was an enthusiasm that after all the years of having legislation, progressive legislation, bottled up by the bulls and the conservative Republicans, many of those bills would now see passage into law, as had the Civil Rights Act. Lyndon Johnson's landslide had resulted in 295 Democratic representatives in the House to 140 Republicans, and 68 Democratic senators to only 32 Republicans—enough to invoke cloture were the conservatives to filibuster and the liberals to gain a few Republican moderates. "We've been a long time in the wilderness," said a veteran liberal senator. "It's awfully nice to look forward to better times." They felt emboldened. The previous May, at the University of Michigan commencement, Johnson had announced an ambitious new agenda—a Franklin Roosevelt New Deal agenda—that he called the "Great Society." And he asked the graduates that day: "Will you join in the battle to give every citizen the full equality which God enjoins and the law requires, whatever his belief, or race, or the color of his skin? Will you join in the battle to give every citizen an escape from the crushing weight of poverty? Will you join in the battle to make it possible for all nations to live in enduring peace—as neighbors and not as mortal enemies? Will you join in the battle to build the Great Society, to prove that our material progress is only the foundation on which we will build a richer life of mind and spirit?" In his State of the Union address, he elaborated upon these challenges, delivering a long list of objectives, an ambitious list of objectives, the most ambitious since Franklin Roosevelt: on improving education and health, renewing faltering cities, protecting the environment, relieving economic distress, reducing crime, establishing voting rights for African Americans, even promoting art. And on this list he elaborated still further, leaving no part of America untouched and no liberal dream undreamed. Lyndon Johnson had a mandate. Even 74 percent of Republicans approved of the new president, whose program was every conservative's worst nightmare— the very governmental "tyranny" that Barry Goldwater had deplored and warned against. But Lyndon Johnson intended to fulfill his mandate with the 89th Congress, which is what Ted Kennedy, as he had pondered his future in his hospital room, hoped.

Lyndon Johnson couldn't have fulfilled that mandate with the old Congress, the old Senate, where the bulls and their Republican allies would have resisted him at every juncture. But the changing Senate had changed further with the election. The club was no longer as restrictive, no longer as powerful as it had been. "A greatly depleted coalition," Meg Greenfield wrote in *The Reporter* of the Southern Democrats and conservative Republicans who had blocked liberal legislation for years, and she cited one Northern liberal who spoke now of "the astonishing silence of the South." "The Establishment—that mysterious conservative cabal which for years dominated the world's most exclusive club—is crumbling," opined *The Wall Street Journal*, in yet another obituary for the men who had prevented liberal initiatives from becoming law, and it talked of an ascending power center, "a group of brainy young liberal Democratic newcomers"—Ted was certainly one of them—"unimpressed by the old rules about the sanctity of seniority." One longtime political observer, Clayton Fritchey, writing in *Harper's*, said the club still existed, but when he enumerated its members, it included "half to three-quarters" of the Senate. Majority Leader Mike Mansfield delivered the same verdict, telling a reporter, "All senators are equal in my opinion," which would have been heresy just a year earlier, when senators were hardly equal, and he added bluntly for good measure, "There is no club in the Senate anymore." Even before the election, this is what the Civil Rights Act had wrought; in one momentous vote, it brought down the old power structure, the old rules, the old disciplines, the old Senate itself (Richard Russell pleading with Ted for more time), and in its place arose what *The New York Times*'s Tom Wicker called a "mildly progressive legislative body in which the Old South has lost its grip, in which junior members are playing increasingly important roles, in which the fabled power of the committee chairmen has been scattered, and in which the dominant influences are those of urban industrialized America and the president of the United States."

And the president of the United States was prepared, was eager, to take advantage of this new Senate—not only prepared and eager but in a hurry to do so. Lyndon Johnson had known the Senate well, known it probably better than any other man had ever known it, knew how it could put the brakes on legislation, how it could stall and divert and block, things he had done himself. But knowing that, Lyndon Johnson also knew how to propel legislation through the system, how to speed it up. Before Johnson's presidency, the Senate was a rather relaxed institution, according to Ted. He said his "central impression" upon arriving was "how little people really worked." In the mornings, many members, and nearly all the members of the club, would go to the congressional golf course. Then they would return at noon and repair to the Senate dining room, where Ted himself, at Jack's instruction, had spent his lunches. After lunch, they would go to their offices to sign their mail—"I'd see fifteen piles of papers on their desks," he said, though apparently little headway was made through those piles—and then possibly go to the floor. Then they would retreat to one of the senators' offices for their bourbon and branch water. And then they would socialize again at night. And added to this relaxed schedule were long recesses when the senators departed for home.

But lassitude was not President Lyndon Johnson's pace. He had his agenda to fulfill. So senators now worked five days a week, often long days. Ted said he would fly up to Massachusetts on Friday—the crash had not deterred him from flying—but was rarely home in time for dinner. And then he would fly back to Washington on Sunday and was up early on Monday, at nine-thirty or ten, when the Senate started up again, and the hearings, he said, were going "full blast," and they "rarely got out until late Friday afternoon." He said that senators stayed often now in the evenings to work, usually Monday through Thursday nights. And Ted said senators worked through the summer now too, with only the Fourth of July and Labor Day off, and then worked until Thanksgiving. And even in summer, the routine was so rigorous that Ted would offer his amendments and then have Joan bring the children for a picnic outside on the lawn, alongside other senators with young children, while military bands played between the Senate Office Building and the Capitol. (These were the picnics he was referring to when he talked about Senate comity.) Even then, however, there might be a roll call, and staff would shout from open windows, and the senators would race to the floor.

And it wasn't only the workload that changed. The pace changed. Lyndon Johnson wanted action, and the Civil Rights Act demonstrated that things could move if one worked at it and that things could move quickly now that Lyndon Johnson had his Senate. "Lyndon came in like a tiger," said Stewart McClure, the chief clerk of the Senate Committee on Labor and Public Welfare, "and everything that had been dormant and stuck in conference or committee went *whoosh*, like a great reverse whirlpool spinning it out. We passed everything in the next year or two." Ted recalled a railroad strike and Johnson calling the House and Senate Labor Committees—Ted was a member of the latter—in to the White House for a sit-down with Labor Secretary Willard Wirtz and Defense Secretary Robert McNamara; the strike, Johnson felt, was endangering the Vietnam

War effort. Johnson handed them a bill, already drafted in the White House, and he told them all to meet over in the Roosevelt Room and get the bill passed *that afternoon,* and he would sign it in three days. He said he would call the majority leader and speaker and get it put on the agenda. And the House passed it almost immediately. "No notice, no nothing, *nada,*" Ted said. Then it came to the Senate Labor Committee, and the chairman, Wayne Morse, asked if there was any objection. And Bobby, who had that simmering hatred of Johnson, leaned over to Ted and, just to make trouble, said, "Ask for one day of hearings," which any member of the committee, under senatorial privilege, was entitled to do. So Ted did. (He immediately suffered remorse for listening to his brother.) Morse was aghast and warned Ted he would have to tell the president that he had asked for a hearing. The hearing was held, and it was discovered that the strike was not actually slowing war materiel headed to the troops. But in relating the story, Ted's point wasn't that Bobby would do anything to impede Johnson, though, in this case, Bobby was probably invoking the fact that the bill was anti-labor. Ted's point was this: Lyndon Johnson could commandeer the entire legislative process. Lyndon Johnson could snap his fingers and get what he wanted, unless some wiseacre like Bobby had the temerity to slow him down, and few, very few, did.

Whatever hostility Lyndon Johnson felt toward Bobby Kennedy, he seemed to have nothing but genuine affection for Ted. "I like Teddy. He's good," Johnson would tell Ted's chief of staff. Even privately, he would tell advisers, "Ted Kennedy has the potential to be the 'best politician in the whole family,'" though he probably also intended that as a dig at Bobby and even at Jack, the two Kennedys who had disdained him. Johnson was fulsome in his praise of Ted and frequent in his praise of Ted. After watching him on *Meet the Press* in March 1964, he had phoned Ted to tell him that "the president [meaning Jack] would have been so proud of you, and I was, and I just thought that you hit a home run every time they asked you a question," and said, "You can take my job anytime you're ready." But Johnson had also used the call to try to smooth the turbulent waters between the Kennedys and him. "The last thing he [Jack] would want us to do is to wind up disagreeing with each other, and we're just not going to do that." He told Ted that "anytime something happens that you or the attorney general or your mother or your father or your sisters feel ought to go differently, you put on your hat and walk in that office and sit down and say your speech. . . . I'm just a trustee that's trying to carry on the best he can." And in May 1964, Johnson had called Steve Smith, telling him, "Teddy is burning up the league down here. . . . He's the hero of the Senate." And he added, "He certainly does know how to handle himself, and he's also doing us a lot of good throughout the country." Later that same day, Johnson phoned Ann Gargan, Ted's cousin, who was caring for the stricken Joe Kennedy, and told her, "Every place he goes—he was down in Georgia, and he was over in Maryland, and he was up in New York—and every place they're just crazy about him. And every member of the Senate, both sides, Democrats and Republicans, just thinks he's more popular than Jack or Lyndon or anybody that was ever in the Senate."

For Johnson, "doing us a lot of good" meant that Ted was out working for Lyndon Johnson's reelection and for other Democrats, before the plane accident felled Ted. And his support was not tepid. In a January 1964 speech at the Biltmore Bowl in California, Ted said that people may have wondered whether the Kennedys, after the assassination, would remain in public life, and he answered, "As long as there is a job to do, we intend to do it." But then he did what Bobby would not. He tied that job to Lyndon Johnson, asked the crowd to support Johnson and give him a mandate for an unabashed liberal agenda, which he described as "Whether our government has a responsibility to those who live in poverty. Whether our citizens of one color have a responsibility to those of another. Whether those of us who are young and working have a responsibility to those who are old and retired. Whether in sum we are all one people or whether we are separate societies of the rich and the poor, the white and the non-white, the haves and the have-nots—with no mission except that of increasing our own comforts and maintaining our own prejudices." Bobby doubted Johnson's liberalism, thought him insufficiently liberal. Ted Kennedy did not; in fact, Johnson's new liberal fervor seemed to have stoked Ted's and made him more liberal than he had been during his own brother's administration. He was catching the gust of liberal wind. And Johnson appreciated the support, even as he curried it. On election night, he phoned Ted at the hospital at 3 A.M. to congratulate him for his victory. To which Ted responded almost sycophantically that the national victory was a "great tribute to you and what you've done" and that Johnson had "certainly won the support and the hearts, the loyalty and the affection, of all people."

But Lyndon Johnson's affection for Ted Kennedy was not only the product of self-interest. Ted thought that Johnson was "somewhat affected by how I came into the Senate," by which he meant how he came into the Senate with great respect for, even love for, the institution—an institution that Johnson himself loved—how hard he worked in that institution, how serious he was about it, how he had made himself a Senate man as Johnson had been a Senate man, perhaps even how well he worked the Senate, as Johnson himself had worked it as a young senator. And Ted was not averse to working Lyndon Johnson too—supporting him and praising him to get something in return, which Lyndon Johnson could certainly understand, even appreciate, from his own Senate experience. Ted was going to be making a speech before the Massachusetts legislature, and he phoned Johnson to ask if he could discuss a New England Regional Commission, along the lines of the regional development program that Johnson was pushing through Congress for Appalachia. The commission would formulate an economic-stimulus plan for the region—something with which, Ted plainly said, he could "become identified," rather than have it identified with his colleagues in the region. And Johnson told him that he didn't know the "technicalities," but he did know this: "There's not a member of the Senate that I'll go as far to meet as I will you, because I just think that you've been fair and decent and fine as anybody." Then Johnson added another gripe about the supposed rift between him and the Kennedys: "This business about my being at crossways with the Kennedys is just a pure lot of crap." And he closed: "You just go on and make your speech, and write your ticket, and I'll do my damnedest to make good on it." That was how Lyndon Johnson and Ted Kennedy cooperated—as political partners.

But the business of Lyndon Johnson being at crossways with the Kennedys was not "a lot of crap," because however much Lyndon Johnson and Ted Kennedy seemed to understand each other, however much they might have even felt some degree of affection for each other, Bobby Kennedy and Lyndon Johnson did not understand each other, and Lyndon Johnson and Bobby Kennedy did not have any affection for each other. They viewed each other as usurpers: Bobby trying to usurp Johnson, and Johnson usurping Jack. And that enmity figured into Johnson's wooing of Ted. However genuine the affection he might have felt for Ted Kennedy, Lyndon Johnson did few things without an ulterior motive, and one of his motives here was clearly to divide the Kennedy brothers, pit them against each other, as he had tried to split their brother-in-law Sargent Shriver from the rest of the family by bringing him into the White House and attempting to make him a Johnson man. (Bobby was incensed at *any* of the Kennedy men who stuck with Johnson, feeling it was a betrayal.)

Ted was fully aware of the effort, fully aware that Johnson's blandishments toward him had a design. "There were times that Johnson tried to play Bobby off against me," Ted would later write, "which was totally bizarre, since there was no way that a Kennedy would side with an outsider against another Kennedy." And as shrewd as Lyndon Johnson was, Ted called this a rare failure in his political acumen. The senators Kennedy—they called each other "Robbie" and "Eddie"—were a formidable pair. They were the stars of the new Senate. "Each Kennedy draws bigger crowds, attracts more mail, gets more speaking invitations, packs more people into the galleries, runs a longer gantlet of autograph hunters and Brownie snappers, and captures more and bigger headlines than any man in public life except LBJ himself," *Newsweek* reported in a cover story on them. "Their favors are courted, their will—when they choose to express it—attended." Robert Dove, who worked for the Senate parliamentarian and who would later become parliamentarian himself, said that when the two of them were on the floor, "You could feel the electricity." Since Jack's death, the two had become closer, filling the hole for each other that Jack's absence created, and once Bobby arrived in the Senate, they shared what John Culver called a "much more intimate professional life." They had private office phone numbers to reach each other directly, and they spoke in what two friends described as "shorthand." For Ted, who was so sociable, it was joyous having "my teammate from college [Culver], and my roommate from law school [Tunney], and my brother to work with." It made the Senate a "wonderful place," he said. But there was an even deeper bond than the deep bond of being Kennedys. They had the bond of being Kennedy survivors—two men who knew the pain of loss, knew the emptiness, knew the capriciousness of fate. Lyndon Johnson would never be able to loosen that bond.

And yet, for all their closeness and for all the similarity in their politics, the brothers were very different kinds of senators, which reflected their very different personalities. "Bobby was intense," said Dun Gifford, who joined Ted's staff that year. "He was severe on the issues. It was his nature. It was his way. Teddy was much more of, 'Let's talk it over, and let's laugh together a little bit, and see what we can work out.' Bobby was, 'Let's get the job done.'" But getting the job done wasn't the way the Senate typically did things. Like Jack, Bobby didn't have a senatorial temperament. (Arthur Schlesinger said that Jack and Bobby had "executive" temperaments, while Ted's was "parliamentary." He was impatient with the Senate's slowly grinding wheels, even as Lyndon Johnson got those wheels turning faster. Ted took sixteen months to deliver his maiden speech. Bobby took a month. And during a long hearing of the Labor Committee, the only committee on which both brothers sat, Bobby was wiggling in his seat impatiently wanting to ask questions and then catch a plane to New York, but the more-senior senators kept droning on. "Is this the way I become a good senator—sitting here and waiting my turn?" he whispered to Ted sarcastically. And when Ted told him it was, Bobby asked how *many* hours he had to sit there. And Ted said, "As long as necessary, Robbie." By contrast, when one of Ted's staffers once asked him if he didn't get frustrated with the Senate's snail-like pace, he said, "I look at it like a river, and you can change the course of that river to the left or the right." He joked that he chose the left.

But Bobby Kennedy didn't want to change the course of a river in geologic time. He wanted action now, which should have made him an ally of the other man who was impatient for action, Lyndon Johnson, but the breach between the two was too great for accommodation. Ted attributed Bobby's impatience and his disaffection with the Senate to his "fast-blossoming idealism" after Jack's death, which didn't comport particularly well with Senate politics. He was intensely conscious of how little time there might be and how much there was to be done, and he was more accustomed as attorney general, in his brother's administration no less, to making things happen with a phone call. Senator Ralph Yarborough said that "the delays were so abrasive to Bob, his mind always seemed out beyond the narrow confines of the committee room, the floor—he wanted to solve the problem, jump ahead to the solution."

But no single senator, not even Richard Russell or Lyndon Johnson in his time, could *make* things happen. That was not the way the Senate operated. The Senate was not only a slow-moving body—that scow Everett Dirksen had described—it was a body that depended upon collegiality, chemistry, to get things done, and if Bobby Kennedy was not patient, he was also not collegial. He thought of professional politicians as hacks, not recognizing that Jack had been a professional politician, and Tip O'Neill complained that Bobby held him in such contempt, he called him "that big fat Irish bastard." And of the Senate bulls, one of Teddy's aides told a reporter, "Teddy listens to old Senate windbags more patiently than Bobby, which is not a bad attribute in this chamber." Bobby not only didn't listen to colleagues, he insulted them—"would pull a quip that would get a laugh at the expense of another senator," said Ralph Yarborough. Thruston Morton, a Republican senator from Kentucky, said that Jack and Bobby both "had a way of talking down to the rest of us," which Ted would never do. At one hearing, where consumer advocate Ralph Nader was testifying, Senator Carl Curtis from Nebraska complained that Nader "loses me," at which point Bobby interrupted acerbically, "With big words?" And if Bobby bristled at the forced decorum of the Senate, he also bristled at the horse-trading. At one point he asked a colleague to support a bill, and the colleague said he would if Bobby would agree to speak in his state. "Is this what you have to do to get votes?" he sneered to Ted. To which Ted replied, "You're learning, Robbie." But Bobby didn't want to learn. He didn't want to be a Senate lifer. Like Jack, he wanted the White House. He told Russell Long of Louisiana and Robert Byrd, after they had reneged on a promise to let him speak against a welfare bill he opposed, that their broken promise was a "reflection on all those who participated, not just as United States senators, but as individuals and as men," which was both harsh and a violation of Senate etiquette. Bobby was the obverse of Ted. As *Newsweek* put it, "He is respected but not loved by his Senate colleagues." That was an understatement.

II

In his two years there, Ted Kennedy had come to know the Senate and understand it. And for a while Bobby deferred to him. Not fully grasping a piece of legislation yet, he once slipped a note to Ted on the Senate floor: "All I want to know—when I shake my head from side to side and you nod your head up and down, does this mean I will vote no and you agree? Obviously not. In other words, when I wanted to vote no, I should have nodded my head up and down—you would have shaken your head from side to side—then I would have known how to vote." But the deference didn't last long. In the Kennedy family there was always primogeniture, always the younger yielding to the older, and Ted's Senate experience didn't finally matter. "Clearly, Bobby was the lead dog," even John Tunney observed. "He was the alpha dog in the relationship." Milton Gwirtzman concurred: "For everything that was said at that time about . . . Teddy sort of indoctrinating Bobby in the ways of the Senate and taking him around, the fact is that whenever push came to shove and something tough had to be done or decided, Bobby was the one who did it. And Ted deferred to him." Gerard Doherty told biographer Burton Hersh that an expert had given Ted information on drugs, only to see Bobby use that information in a television interview, and concluded, "I think Ted had a real fear of center stage." It is also possible, though, that Ted was yielding center stage to his brother, who had presidential ambitions, which it was Ted's job to further.

But despite their closeness, despite Ted's deference, despite the fact that Ted claimed Lyndon Johnson could never come between them, there was an undercurrent of competitiveness between the brothers and on Ted's part even an unacknowledged resentment. Some of this expressed itself in mildly barbed humor. Ted's new legislative assistant, David Burke, said that Ted told Bobby he was going to introduce an amendment and asked him to "stay off the floor, because I need some votes." On another occasion, Senator Gaylord Nelson remembered, Bobby introduced a bill, then embarrassed himself by not being fully versed in its particulars. "Well, that's par for the course," Ted gibed. Sometimes it was not so jocular. Ted attended a dinner in honor of Governor Robert Docking of Kansas, while Bobby sent his apologies in a telegram, saying he had dispatched his little brother in his stead and they should send him "right home" when it was over. "I thought it was a nasty telegram," Ted said later, a demeaning telegram. And Ted added in reference to the carpetbagging charges against his brother, "But at least when I go home, I know what state it's in." Some of the competition was more bare-knuckled. Ted and Bobby had decided to climb Mount Kennedy in the Yukon, which Canada had named in Jack's honor, but Ted was recuperating at the time from his plane crash and asked Bobby to wait. Bobby climbed the mountain anyway. And there was a time when Defense Secretary Robert McNamara, a close friend of the Kennedys, called both brothers to the Pentagon and told them that he was going to have to close either the New York Naval Shipyard in Brooklyn or the Boston Naval Shipyard. Bobby said that since he had known McNamara longer, they should close Boston. "And I was in absolute disbelief," Ted later said. So Bobby relented and told McNamara to close the one that would have the least impact on working people. McNamara closed Brooklyn.

And beneath the competitiveness was something else, something much deeper: Bobby triggered Ted's inferiority complex. Ted had already been a senator for two years when Bobby entered the Senate. Ted was already gaining recognition when Bobby entered the Senate. Early in 1964, Robert Donovan of the *Los Angeles Times* was already reporting a "political development fraught with possibilities: the gradual transformation of Senator Edward M. (Ted) Kennedy into a national political figure." Donovan listed the speaking engagements across the country that Ted now had. And Ted Kennedy, who had always lacked for confidence because he was always being compared to his brothers, had been gaining confidence when Bobby entered the Senate. When Bobby arrived, it had seemed like a godsend to Ted; they were now equals. A "wonderful place," he had called it with Bobby's entrance. But they weren't equals, at least not in Bobby's eyes, and it didn't take long for Ted's confidence to erode under Bobby's criticisms and under comparisons to Bobby. "I was okay in the Senate until Bobby came in and upset everything," he would say.

Bobby loved Ted, but not the way Jack loved Ted. Jack would tease him, playfully needle him. Bobby was not playful with Ted. Bobby was caustic. ("Who do you think wrote the speech for him?") And now that Bobby was in the Senate, Ted Kennedy, who, during his convalescence had dedicated himself to being a good senator, a serious senator, who had studied to be a good senator, felt inadequate again. "He was under pressure," David Burke said. "He was under pressure from Bobby because Bobby was 'smarter' than him," by which Burke meant not necessarily more intelligent but "well tested." When administration officials would come to Capitol Hill to testify at hearings, Bobby was never awed. These had been his colleagues. But, Burke said, when those same officials came to testify, Ted *was* awed by how articulate these men were, how self-confident. "You could see his desire to be like that at some time, and he wanted to make sure he didn't falter when questioning someone like that, so that person would think less of him. It was very important to him. He wanted to be highly regarded by people whose high regard is a mark of some kind on our society." Ted, who was so great and natural a stump speaker, even took elocution lessons, so he would be more articulate on the Senate floor. Bobby would have never thought of taking elocution lessons, though he stammered more than Ted.

And if Ted thought Bobby was smarter than he was, better than he was, he knew Bobby's staff was smarter and better than his staff too. Bobby had told him so. Ted's office had been staffed by the old-timer Joe McIntyre, who had worked in the Senate forever, and by the former CIA operative Bill Evans, and by his Harvard pals Jerry Marsh and John Culver, and by old campaign associates like Charlie Tretter. (Tretter had attended law school but failed the bar exam, so Ted told him to leave Washington, go back to Boston, and start thinking about himself, which Tretter called a "gracious gesture.") Bobby's office was staffed by the Harvard elite. When David Burke told friends he was going to work on the Hill for Kennedy, he said the initial response was, "Oh, you'll love Bobby. He's great." And when Burke said he was going to work for *Ted* Kennedy, they would say, "Why are you going to work for Ted?" Burke said, "It was like I settled for less when I worked with Ted."

And he *had* settled for less, given the brothers' respective statures. But during Ted's convalescence, when Ted had undergone that rededication, some of his brothers' friends and advisers told him he would need a better staff if he was going to make any kind of headway in legislating, not just in being liked. McIntyre had died of a heart attack in December 1964. Evans had left for a job at Pan American Airlines. Jerry Marsh was back in Illinois. And Culver had quit to run for Congress from his native Iowa and would be entering the House. With Ted's staff depleted, Milton Gwirtzman was given the assignment of finding a new legislative assistant for Ted, essentially a chief of staff. Gwirtzman had found Burke, a young Irish Catholic, the son of a cop, from Boston, who had attended parochial schools up through high school, then gone to Tufts University outside Boston, and then to business school at the University of Chicago, from which he received his MBA, "all of which meant," Burke would say, "that I could read without moving my lips." After graduation, at the recommendation of one of his professors, he got a job in the Kennedy administration working on labor-management issues. That is how Gwirtzman got wind of him. Burke said that Ted interviewed him early in 1965 at the senator's office, and that Ted was "white as a ghost" and "frail," clearly in pain and easily fatigued, after returning from the plane accident. But Burke said he obviously "passed muster," because Gwirtzman called him later and asked when he could start.

At some point shortly thereafter, Ted designated Burke to find him other staffers, first-rate staffers, staffers who could compete with Bobby's staff, which was now Ted's standard, and Burke's idea was that Ted shouldn't be bringing in his pals and hangers-on. Rather, he should hire "nothing but the best." Burke wanted "people who are smarter than you and me." Ted, whose own sense of inadequacy had made him worshipful of those smarter than he, knew he needed those kinds of people now too—people who could build his reputation as a serious legislator. "And that was when the sun came out," Burke said. So he began looking for recent Harvard Law grads, people who had made law review, and people with expertise and experience. Dun Gifford, who had gone to Harvard—he met the Kennedys when he was interning for Rhode Island senator Claiborne Pell, and he and Pell would hop a ride on the *Caroline*—and who went to work for the Department of Housing and Urban Development and then for Bobby, now joined Ted's staff. And Ted hired George Abrams, another Harvard Law grad, to become general counsel of Ted's Refugees and Escapees Subcommittee. The pay wasn't much. Gifford made $26,000 as his legislative assistant, which was the second-highest position in the office. But this wasn't about remuneration. They signed on because of the opportunity to do something special, something important, now that Ted had decided *he* wanted to do something important.

But if Ted Kennedy had ambition, he didn't yet have a direction in which to aim that ambition. His philosophy was evolving. One thing was plain: He was an increasingly ardent liberal in increasingly liberal times. His legislative agenda, however, was vaguer. Burke said Ted didn't always apprise him of what he was doing or what he wanted—"He didn't see himself as having a responsibility to tell me what was happening"—even though other staff people would badger Burke for guidance. And Burke could never be certain whether this was just dereliction on Ted's part, because he didn't know what he wanted done, or deliberation. Burke sometimes saw a "glint in his eye," as if Ted wanted to "catch me off base because I didn't know if something was happening, which had the strange effect, whether he meant it or not, to sharpen my skills and make me defensively more reliant so that I knew what was happening in life around us all the time." But it could be nerve-racking not to be on top of things, and Burke said he often retired to the Catholic church down the street, where he would sit in the last pew and ask God, *Why did you do this to me? How did I get into this situation?* and think huffily about who Ted thought he was, leaving Burke with so much to answer for. Meanwhile, the new, improved staff, all of them liberals, were mapping out programs of their own that they wanted Ted to pursue and that they funneled to him through Burke. And Ted was more demanding now of his staff than before, less easygoing with them. He wanted a memo on every piece of legislation moving through the Senate. He would complain about not having a speech ready on time when his brothers' staffs had always drafted their speeches when they needed them. He dismissed one committee staff member when he felt that Bobby was better prepared than he during a Labor Committee hearing. And Burke said that one of his own duties now was spending time walking the marble corridors of the Old Senate Office Building, stroking those staff members and soothing their egos—"people who had been first in their class, first in this, first in that, and they had just been destroyed by some criticism" of Ted's. But Ted had to be tougher because he was in a new competition now, a competition with his brother, and his staff was in that competition too. ("Toppers" is what the staff called those little things that gave them an advantage over Bobby's staff.) Ted Kennedy had entered the Senate having to prove himself. Now he was having to prove himself in competition with his own brother.

As one of his advisers told a reporter, Ted Kennedy "had to do after an election what other people had done to get elected." He had had no record on which to run, which was one of Eddie McCormack's criticisms of him. He had run on his pedigree as a Kennedy son, on his personality and on his possibilities. And he had come into the Senate to be a student of the institution, learning its mechanisms and its members, but he was not yet, despite his Civil Rights Act speech, a full participant. Freshmen never were. But then, Ted was to say, senators underwent some sort of spiritual alteration. "Something profound and fundamental happens to you when you arrive there, and it stays with you all the time that you are privileged to serve. . . . It may take a year, or two years, or three years, but it always happens; it fills you with a heightened sense of purpose." It had taken Ted Kennedy two years, but after surviving the plane accident and after subsequently feeling the need to raise himself to Bobby's level, he was now filled with that heightened sense of purpose himself.

Yet he was still groping his way toward what that purpose would be. Bobby, after Jack's death and the transformation he had undergone, had dedicated himself to alleviating the suffering of the disadvantaged, especially minorities, Native Americans, and the Southern black population mired in poverty and disease. A liberal through the trauma of his brother's death, Bobby took helping these people as his new life's mission. "The man who saw life rigidly in moral terms discovered a social conscience" is how writer Richard Rhodes described it. "He convinced the weak and the disenfranchised, by pouring out his feelings to them, that whatever needed to be done to relieve them of their deprivation and at the same time to hold the country together, he would do. And of the lesson of his brother's death, he would say, 'Tragedy is a tool for the living to gain wisdom, not a guide by which to live.'" Bobby had gained that wisdom.

Ted Kennedy was not a liberal by trauma, like Bobby, but by instinct, those instincts implanted by his own childhood ordeals and then honed by his grandfather Honey Fitz. And though he and Bobby had the same passions for justice, the brothers were not, Ted would say, especially close Senate allies. This was a time when the Senate was considering a plethora of issues, from Medicare to the Voting Rights Act to expanded poverty programs—"major legislation every month," an historian would say. Find your niche, Ted had been told by senior senators. Find your niche if you want to be an effective senator. Ted knew his mission now—to help those who needed help—but he hadn't found his niche. While Bobby early in his term focused on those minorities in America, Ted, sitting on both the Immigration and Refugee Subcommittees, had begun focusing on groups trying to come to America. They were difficult groups for which to advocate. Immigration, which Judiciary chairman James Eastland chaired himself as a way to prevent reform legislation from passing, was not a particularly coveted one on which to sit. A "rather sleepy subcommittee," Ted called it. Its budget was tiny by subcommittee standards, only $100,000, and there was only one assigned staff member. And there was a reason for the small budget and the single staff member: No one in the Senate much cared about immigration, or, rather, those who did were always obstructed by the Southerners and conservative Republicans. Americans had generally been antagonistic to immigration—Honey Fitz had argued against an immigration-exclusion bill while in the House—and since 1924, when Congress, in a bout of hysterical nativism, set strict quotas on Southern and Eastern Europeans (essentially Catholics and Jews) and on nonwhite immigrants, there had not been much of a hue and cry for reforming immigration law. On the contrary, when an immigration law was passed in 1952, over President Harry Truman's veto, it simply reinforced the Northern European bias, while adding political discrimination—restricting immigration of communists and leftists—to ethnic discrimination.

But among those in Congress who did raise the issue was John F. Kennedy. With his family's great sensitivity to Irish immigration, and with an eye to the political appeal of immigration reform among urban ethnics, Kennedy had denounced ethnic prejudice that reduced immigration and had written a book, *A Nation of Immigrants,* which made the case for a new immigration policy that would take discrimination out of the law and put a premium on family reunification, special skills, and the admission of refugees. (Ted often carried a worn paperback copy.) Jack even had one of the rare successes in immigration legislation when the Capelinhos volcano erupted on the island of Faial in the Azores, a Portuguese territory (Massachusetts had a large Portuguese population), and he sponsored the Azorean Refugee Act of 1958 to lift quotas for Azoreans hoping to enter the United States. Ted Kennedy remembered his brother's advocacy—remembered that his brother, even as a congressman, had worked to reform immigration. "This was something alive and evident in the early years of my life," he said.

And yet, despite his interest and despite the political benefits he foresaw, when he became president, John Kennedy could not move on immigration reform, and he could not move because there was an impediment. That impediment was Representative Francis Walter of Pennsylvania, the chairman of the House Judiciary Committee and a vehement foe of immigration reform. For years, liberals had sought to change the national-origins quota system, which had led to nativist and racist consequences. And for years, Francis Walter had thwarted their attempts, as the Southern bulls had thwarted the Senate liberals' attempts to pass civil rights legislation. Instead of relaxing the quotas, Walter sponsored the McCarran–Walter Act, the 1952 law that continued the quotas, and, mixing his obsessive anti-communism with his nativism, he later warned that "communists, their fellow travelers, congressional 'liberals,' and spokesmen for the so-called ethnic minority blocs" were leading "the assault on America's immigration system." Kennedy couldn't circumvent Walter. The president needed him to help steer legislation through the House, but he had Bobby's Justice Department draft an immigration reform bill anyway, so he had one at the ready. When Walter died of leukemia in May 1963, Kennedy, who had shown reluctance to move forward on so many other issues that might ruffle conservatives in Congress, moved quickly on immigration. In July, he proposed a massive overhaul of the immigration law, essentially overturning McCarran–Walter by phasing out the national-origins quota system, which he called "without basis in either logic or reason," and suggested a seven-member immigration board to advise the president on immigration policy henceforth. When John Kennedy died five months later, the bill died too. But Lyndon Johnson, who was determined to show his fealty to the Kennedy agenda, announced his support for immigration reform in his State of the Union Address on January 8. Five days later, in a demonstration of his seriousness, he invited a group of immigration lobbyists to the White House to sit with congressmen and senators, including Ted, who was no doubt invited because of Jack's passion for the issue, and discuss the bill's passage. Feeling pressured, and apparently wanting to pacify his old friend Lyndon Johnson—though no doubt also realizing that a reform bill was likely to pass—Eastland removed himself as an immediate obstacle and deputized Ted as the acting chairman of the Immigration and Naturalization Subcommittee while the bill was being considered. Eastland had almost certainly done so, again, in part because of the late president's interest in immigration. Later that month, Ted held hearings, the first on immigration reform since 1952, with Phil Hart, who had introduced John Kennedy's bill in the Senate, as the opening witness. And then the issue languished. As Ted would say, 1964 was for civil rights, not for immigration reform.

It languished for a year, but it did not expire. During that time, immigration reform was one of the issues that Ted studied, and studied hard, during his hospital tutorials, presumably to determine how he could realize his brother's hopes—one place where he might find his niche. Then, on January 13, 1965, a year to the day after he had first introduced the bill, Lyndon Johnson declared in his State of the Union address that he would again ask Congress to pass a new immigration law "based on the work a man could do and not where he was born or how he spells his name." Ted Kennedy wasn't on the floor the day Phil Hart formally submitted it for Senate consideration later that month—he was still feeling the effects of the plane accident—though Hart commended him for his work on the bill the preceding year. For Ted, however, this was not just another legislative errand. He had a deep personal connection to the bill, both because of his long-standing concern with Irish immigration through his grandfather and because of his brother's crusade to end quotas: a "great scorching issue," he told Burton Hersh. And he also had an understanding, like Jack's, of the political capital to be won in Massachusetts, a state shaped by immigration, by supporting reform. Ted wanted to take an active role in passing the legislation, and he asked both Eastland and Johnson if he might floor-manage the bill. Given John Kennedy's advocacy for reform and, in Johnson's case, no doubt recognizing the power of having Ted push his brother's legacy, they agreed. And now Ted Kennedy had found a niche, an issue— one to give him his "heightened sense of purpose."

Ted Kennedy hadn't drafted the Immigration and Nationality Act of 1965. (Actually, Adam Walinsky of Bobby's staff was one of the authors.) Nor had he been involved in the origins of the bill. Nor was he the primary sponsor of the bill; Phil Hart was the sponsor in the Senate and longtime New York representative Emanuel Celler was in the House. It was called the Hart–Celler Act. But Ted Kennedy was the one who now had the responsibility—who had *asked* for the responsibility—for steering the bill to passage. It was the first major bill he had floor-managed, and he took that responsibility seriously.

The bill was the most significant change to immigration law since 1924, when Congress, by pegging the issuance of visas by country to percentages that their nationals represented in the 1920 census, had effectively guaranteed that 70 percent of immigration to the United States would come from Northern Europe—actually, from just three countries: Ireland, England, and Germany. Over a five-year period, Hart–Celler would eliminate the national-origin quotas—the provision that had severely limited immigration from Southern and Eastern Europe, and the provision that liberals found so pernicious. It eliminated, too, what was called the "Pacific Triangle" limit, which imposed even stricter quotas on Asia as a whole. Moreover, in the new bill, spouses, minor children, and parents of a citizen or legal resident would not be subject to quotas. Hart–Celler also allowed the president to reserve up to 20 percent of the visas for refugees in danger of sudden relocation and up to 50 percent in the first five years for people from countries that might have been disproportionately affected by the new formula—namely, Western Europe—as a concession to opponents. It left unchanged the lack of any quotas in the Western Hemisphere on the basis that such immigration was small and that restrictions might be used as propaganda by the communist Castro government in Cuba. Above all, while it maintained the total number of visas at roughly 170,000, it would now apportion them not by country but by seven categories by which immigrants would be given priority. The highest priority would be given to those with special skills or education regarded as "especially advantageous" to the country; lower priority would be given to relatives of American citizens or permanent residents who did not qualify for nonquota status, such as unmarried adult children or brothers and sisters, or to those with hardships and whose occupations were in short supply here.* It represented a trade-off—higher skills for broader immigration—but it was the only way that immigration reformers could blunt opposition.

With the momentum of Johnson's post-election legislative juggernaut, passage might have seemed a formality at this point, regardless of past history. The bill had thirty-two co-sponsors in the Senate, a sign that the antipathy toward immigration reform had abated. Ted conducted new hearings beginning in February and running through August with fifty-six witnesses, and the bill seemed well on its way to becoming law. But if antipathy to immigration reform had abated, it had not disappeared. Many Southern Democrats and conservative Republicans were still intent on America remaining overwhelmingly white and Northern European. And, since Eastland had stepped aside, the most important among them now was Representative Michael Feighan of Ohio, the chairman of the House Subcommittee on Immigration and Citizenship.

Like Francis Walter, Feighan was a conservative Democrat, obsessed with anti-communism, as Walter had been, and devoutly nativist, as Walter had been. Feighan had derailed John Kennedy's efforts in 1963 by demanding funding for an investigation into immigration policy as a quid pro quo for considering the bill—an investigation that Celler saw as a ruse to stop reform by finding communist involvement. Now, two years later, in 1965, despite President Johnson's call for passage, Feighan had resisted even holding hearings on the Hart–Celler Act. When he finally begrudgingly did so, after a narrow primary win in which his opponent emphasized Feighan's foot-dragging on immigration and after arm-twisting by Johnson, Feighan still didn't ask his committee to report the bill out. Instead, on June 1, he introduced a bill of his own. On its face, it looked innocent enough, perhaps even more progressive than Hart–Celler. As in Hart–Celler, Feighan wanted to repeal the quotas, only he wanted them repealed immediately, and as in Hart–Celler, Feighan wanted the seven preference categories. He even wanted to raise the ceiling on the number

---

*The bill added a complex provision to admit individuals with mental-health issues, who had previously been barred, so long as the attorney general ruled they would not be charges of the state. One immigration historian believes Ted was instrumental in this because of Rosemary. Roger Daniels, *Guarding the Golden Door* (New York: Hill & Wang, 2004), 132.

of immigrants permitted to 225,000. But Feighan also wanted two additional provisions: He wanted no more than 20,000 immigrants to be admitted from each country, and he wanted the top priority to be given to uniting families—what would later be called "chain migration"—rather than to employment and skills, which Johnson and the bill's sponsors had touted to give the bill an economic basis. Innocent Feighan's bill may have seemed, but innocent it was not. Feighan's reasoning, which he shared with his fellow conservatives, who were adamantly opposed to removing national-origin quotas, was that by emphasizing family unification and letting family members, including brothers and sisters, into the country—the long "chain" in chain migration—his law would maintain the present ethnic and racial proportions, those proportions highly favorable to the desirable Northern Europeans. In short, Feighan saw his bill as a white Protestant bill—national-origin quotas by another name.

But that was on the House side, where Celler and Feighan quarreled, where the president and the House leadership decided to expand the House Immigration Committee to add liberals who would defy Feighan, and where, notwithstanding the expansion, the bill was held up in a tenday impasse followed by eighteen executive sessions, until Feighan and Celler, under prodding from Johnson, who wanted a law, finally reached a resolution that included Feighan's chain-migration priority. ("Just shove it any way you can," Johnson ordered House majority leader Carl Albert when Albert complained about Feighan's obstruction.)

On the Senate side, Ted was conferring with the very groups that had supported Feighan—among them, a nativist group called the American Coalition of Patriotic Societies, the American Legion, the Daughters of the American Revolution, and the National Association of Evangelicals—trying to convince them there had been so many exceptions to the national-origins quotas (congressmen could propose what were called "private bills," which sought visas for individual constituents) that a new, more regulated system would be preferable. And there was yet another group in opposition, this one closer to Ted's heart. Among the nationalities that were likely to lose visas in the new process were the Irish, who had been favored by the old system. Ted's legislative assistant, David Burke, warned him not to take on the issue. "Remember, we're talking families and reunification and so on. Why do we have to get into this?" But just as Charles Haar was surprised to see Ted refuse to pander to Catholics seeking federal aid to parochial education during his 1962 campaign, Burke was surprised to see Ted refuse to buckle to his own Irishmen. To him, this was larger than the Irish. This was a matter of the injustice done to other immigrants. "He took it on," Burke said. "It just was not right." And Burke said that he discovered "there were certain things that he is deaf on, and one is political advice like, 'I'd stay away from that issue, it's a killer.' That's not a good way to open a conversation with him. He just looks at you with sort of wonderment, like . . . 'It's just not fair.' "

And while Ted was trying to disarm those outside opponents to the bill, he had stumbling blocks of his own in the Senate. Both Judiciary Chairman Eastland and Senate bull Sam Ervin, another Judiciary member, supported national-origins quotas, supported them strongly, Ervin saying that they gave recognition to "groups who historically had the greatest influence in building the nation." Eastland, perhaps realizing that it was futile to challenge the bill now that the Great Society was under way, basically recused himself from the fray, but not without wresting a concession from Johnson to confirm a Mississippi judge Eastland wanted appointed. Ervin, a wily old legislator who looked like and affected the folksy pose of a simple country lawyer but who was greatly admired in the Senate for his expertise in constitutional law, his segregationist sympathies notwithstanding, was another matter. Ted used his best ninth-child talent to win over Ervin, especially after Ervin and Bobby had a testy exchange when Bobby testified before the subcommittee in favor of the bill—an exchange in which Ervin tried to school Bobby by reading him the dictionary definition of "function," because the new law would give a preference to those who could perform a "specific function" for which there were not a sufficient number of Americans, and Bobby curtly told him he didn't need to hear the definition. But Ted understood, as Bobby did not, that you didn't make enemies in the Senate, that it was run on chemistry, even chemistry with men whose views you might find abhorrent, and that you needed that chemistry, even if it was only a way to make your opponents less vehement in their opposition. So, shortly after the hearing, on St. Patrick's Day, Ted sought to soothe any hurt feelings by pinning a shamrock on Ervin's lapel in a gesture of affection.

But shamrock or not, Ervin wasn't through just yet. The House passed the bill, 318 to 95, on August 24, with Johnson having caved to Feighan's demand for chain migration to get it out of committee, and the Senate Immigration Subcommittee, now Ted's subcommittee, deciding to accept the House bill in order to speed passage. But that acceptance came with one addition. Ervin, who Ted said had changed his mind on the bill and become an "able advocate" for it, insisted now that the bill place a 120,000-person quota on immigration from the Western Hemisphere, where immigrants had not been subject to quotas previously, even in the most draconian bills. Both John Kennedy and Lyndon Johnson were insistent that quotas not be imposed in any reform because they would seem an affront to our Latin American neighbors, whose goodwill America desired. Moreover, the House had already rejected the quota. On this issue, however, Ervin, who saw it as another way of restricting immigration, would not budge. More important, he had also gotten Minority Leader Everett Dirksen to support it. Angry at the limit and angry at Ervin, Bobby, who was distrustful of compromise and may have seen it as a betrayal of Jack, advised Ted to dump the bill, let it fail, and then reintroduce it the following year without Ervin's provision. But however much they personally disliked the new limit, Ted and Johnson were too close to victory to ditch immigration reform now. (As one immigration history put it, Johnson was more interested in the "moral principle" of the bill than in its specifics.) Thus, the bill was approved on September 8 by the full committee, 14 to 2, with the Ervin exception.

And now passage *was* pro forma. On September 17, Ted began the floor debate to a largely empty Senate chamber, a tower of lawbooks and briefs beside him, and holding a stack of fifty blue notecards with debating points. (Ted would develop the strategy of having Burke take a number of books randomly from the office bookshelf and haul them to the Senate floor, then pile them on Ted's desk, where he would often lean on them as he spoke—lean because of his aching back. "Anyone who was frivolous enough to oppose what he was proposing," Burke said, "they'd say, 'Oh, Jesus! He did his homework. He has all these books there and he's going to kill me.'") As Ted spoke, he invoked Honey Fitz, who he said had inspired John Kennedy's original bill, and John Kennedy himself, and the late senator Herbert Lehman, who had introduced the first bill to repeal national-origin quotas in 1953, and Vice President Hubert Humphrey, who submitted a repeal bill every year he was in the Senate. And he declared, as Johnson had in proposing the bill, "We will no longer ask a man where he was born. Instead, we will ask him if he seeks to join his family or he can help meet economic and social needs of the nation." He argued that the bill is "not concerned with increasing immigration to this country"— a major concern of opponents—"nor will it lower any of the high standards we apply in the selection of immigrants." He estimated that immigration would only rise by 62,000, with another 18,000 "no-quota" admissions coming largely from Asia and from Jamaica and Trinidad and Tobago, which were given nonquota status. He held the floor for five days, but the chamber remained largely empty because the debate was no longer contentious. Eastland spoke in opposition, but not heatedly so, and so did South Carolina senator Strom Thurmond, who called for an overall reduction in immigration to 50,000. Senator Spessard Holland asked Ted "exactly how many nigras" the law would admit, but that sort of question seemed passé now in the blizzard of equal rights legislation. The only amendment offered in those five days, by Jack Miller of Iowa, backing Thurmond's idea to impose a ceiling on immigration, was defeated by a voice vote. The bill passed on September 22, 76 to 18, went to a House–Senate conference, where Ervin's Western Hemisphere provision was added to the final bill, and was signed by President Johnson on October 3, in a ceremony beneath the Statue of Liberty. At the signing, Johnson singled out Ted, who stood just behind him to his left, for his stewardship. But there was another encomium, this one from Sam Ervin, who said the legislation would not have emerged as it did had "it not been for the tact and the understanding and the devotion which the senator from Massachusetts gave to the bill," though Ervin also meant to the opponents of the bill. Ted hadn't succeeded by intimidation. He had succeeded by tenacity, pushing the bill even when his brother and others told him to withdraw, and he had succeeded by charm—succeeded in shepherding through the Senate a piece of legislation that would be, as one historian called it, "perhaps the single most nation-changing measure of the era," though what those changes would be were still to come.

But he had succeeded as well by the invocation of one other force. He had asked to manage the bill because he wanted to fulfill his late brother's moral mission, and he had *been* asked to take a central role in its passage by Lyndon Johnson because he summoned his late brother's moral authority. With the Civil Rights Act and now the Immigration and Nationality Act, Ted Kennedy had come to appreciate the power of that authority—the way it could propel legislation long stalled. Ted Kennedy was finding his niche, helping the helpless, but he was also finding his lever. Even senators could be moved by morality. Even senators could feel the rightness of undoing injustice.

III

All that year, the legislative juggernaut, Lyndon Johnson's juggernaut, the Great Society, was rolling. Johnson submitted eighty-seven pieces of legislation in 1965; eighty-four eventually became law. These included the Social Security Act Amendments of 1965, which established a national health-care program for senior citizens (Medicare); the Model Cities Program; the Federal Cigarette Labeling and Advertising Act; the Elementary and Secondary Education Act; the Higher Education Act, which established the Teacher Corps; the National Foundation on the Arts and Humanities Act, which established the National Endowment for the Arts and the National Endowment for the Humanities; and a series of environmental protections, including the Water Quality Act and the Motor Vehicle Air Pollution Control Act. There was virtually not an area of American life that was untouched. It was the largest governmental program of social engineering since the New Deal.

But despite the similarities to Roosevelt's initiative, there was one significant difference. Roosevelt had launched his programs in the midst of a Great Depression to lift the nation from its economic and spiritual doldrums. And though his programs had very real moral implications, they were designed primarily to ease the suffering from that catastrophe and to aid those in future catastrophes and to help prevent others from occurring. Johnson's Great Society programs had their economic implications—many of them were designed expressly to help the poor—but they were surrounded by a moral nimbus at a rare moment, perhaps a singular moment, of national conscience, inspired in no small measure by John Kennedy's death. For if nothing so liberalized John Kennedy as his death, nothing may have so liberalized the *country* as the shock of his death. "My brother was the first president of the United States to state publicly that segregation was morally wrong," Ted Kennedy had said of Jack during his speech supporting the Civil Rights Act. Lyndon Johnson had picked up that baton, and when he introduced the Great Society, he framed nearly all his programs as morally driven, only adducing economic arguments, as he did with the Immigration and Nationality Act, to neutralize critics who disdained political morality. And many Americans responded, seeming to see themselves in the image of John Kennedy. The death of the young president who had appealed to the nation's better angels inspired those angels to pay tribute through moral purpose. Though Bobby Ken-

nedy doubted Lyndon Johnson's sincerity, though he thought him a cra-
ven, self-interested politician, Johnson understood power as well as any
man, and, no less than Kennedy, he understood the power of moral authority and the way it could move mountains. The legislative agenda of
1965 was a victory for many things, but it was, perhaps above all, a moral
victory for the great unfinished business of American justice, equality,
and decency. "Martyrs have to die for causes," he would tell Doris Kearns
Goodwin, speaking of John Kennedy. "But his 'cause' was not really clear.
That was my job. I had to take the dead man's program and turn it into a
martyr's cause." The cause was moral. At least that is what Lyndon Johnson claimed, and that was how Lyndon Johnson sold it to Congress and to
the American people. He had found a moral crease in the nation.

And this may have been nowhere more true than with the Voting
Rights Act of 1965, which Johnson introduced on March 15 before a joint
session of Congress, declaring, "Our mission is at once the oldest and the
most basic of this country—to right wrong, to do justice, to serve man."
As the brutality in Birmingham, Alabama, had stirred the national conscience and given impetus to the Civil Rights Act the previous year, so did
the brutality in Selma, Alabama, the vicious beatings of marchers protesting for their voting rights, the *deaths* of some of those protesters, including one from Massachusetts, tweak the national conscience and give
impetus to the Voting Rights Act. ("There is no cause for pride in what has
happened in Selma," Johnson said in his speech.) The Civil Rights Act had
sought to give black Americans the same rights as white Americans—
rights they had been denied for a century—the right to eat at the same
restaurants, to sleep in the same hotels, to drink at the same drinking
fountains, to swim in the same swimming pools. Now Johnson sought to
let those black Americans exercise one more right to which they were entitled as citizens, the essential democratic right: the right to determine
their futures through the franchise, which was arguably the most important right for black Americans and the most perilous right for Southern
whites who feared black empowerment. Since the end of Reconstruction,
that right had been wrested from black Americans through a variety of
means, "ingenious" efforts, Johnson called them, like invalidated applica-
tions or literacy tests. ("He may be asked to recite the entire Constitution
or explain the most complex provisions of state law," Johnson had told
that joint session.) The Voting Rights Act was designed to guarantee the
right to vote by putting the full force of the federal government behind the

Fourteenth and Fifteenth Amendments—that no state shall make a law to abridge rights or deny citizens due process, and that no state shall deny them the right to vote, respectively. It was a complicated piece of legislation, including tests to determine which jurisdictions had prohibited African Americans from voting, and including a series of remedies, from federal registrars who would do what state and local officials would not do—register blacks—to federal monitoring to make sure that the law was being enforced and not circumvented. It was complicated and it was critical, arguably the single most important piece of legislation in the Johnson agenda.

Senator Phil Hart, whom Ted Kennedy had taken as a role model, had told Ted that in the Senate you measured accomplishments not by climbing mountains but by climbing molehills. Ted Kennedy had been climbing those molehills in his first two years—with legislation like the fishing bills and a bill to reverse a Civilian Aeronautics Board ruling to deny Northeast Airlines, which served Boston, a Boston-to-Miami route. But climbing molehills was not the Kennedy way. Earlier that year, he had begun working on the Immigration and Nationality Act to stake his claim on a peak. The Voting Rights Act was an even taller mountain, and Ted Kennedy wanted to climb it. His problem was that he didn't quite know how yet. David Burke recalled Ted telling him one day that a voting rights bill was coming up, and "we have to amend it." When Burke asked *what* amendment he had in mind, Ted answered that he didn't know, but he did know that "Bobby's going to do something"—in fact, Bobby's former deputy, now the attorney general, Nicholas Katzenbach, had drafted the bill in conjunction with Everett Dirksen—and that "We just got to—so let's try to figure this out." It may have seemed flip, Ted using a critical piece of legislation to win the competition with his brother, and it was; but it was also Ted Kennedy's way of saying that he needed to be as much part of the process of securing voting rights as he was part of the process of reforming immigration. At that point, Burke said, he called Joseph Rauh Jr.

In the liberal community, the fifty-four-year-old Rauh was a titan—first in his class at Harvard Law, a clerk for Supreme Court justices Benjamin Cardozo and then Felix Frankfurter, an aide to General Douglas MacArthur during World War II, and after the war a leading antagonist of Senator Joe McCarthy. Rauh was also deeply involved in civil rights. He had helped draft the minority civil rights plank at the 1948 Democratic convention, the adoption of which became a signal moment in the history of the movement; he was the chief lobbyist for the Civil Rights Act of 1957 that Majority Leader Lyndon Johnson maneuvered through the Senate that year, and in 1963 he was one of the organizers of the March on Washington. The next year he led the battle—a pitched battle—to have a black delegation representing Mississippi seated at the Democratic National Convention instead of the all-white one selected by the state's segregationist Democratic machinery.

At the time Burke called him, Rauh, who was the longtime attorney for the Leadership Conference on Civil Rights as well, was fresh off lobbying for the Civil Rights Act of 1964 and was lobbying for the Voting Rights Act. Burke said that Rauh, with a sweet affability for a man who had spent his life battling intractable forces, was "the kind of guy I liked, because if you said to him, 'We want to do something on civil rights, come down to my office right now,' he'd say, 'Come on. I'll feed you. I'll do anything you want.'" When Burke and Rauh met, Burke was somewhat ashamed that he didn't know the hot issues on the Voting Rights Act, but Rauh promptly tutored him. The hot issue, he said, was the poll tax—the tax that several Southern states levied on voters, which was yet another way in the South to discourage African Americans from voting. The Twenty-fourth Amendment, ratified the previous year, had banned poll taxes in federal elections, but four Southern states insisted that the taxes were still permissible in local and state elections. That, Rauh said, was a problem.

By this time, the Voting Rights Act was wending its way through the Judiciary Committee, and the liberals on that committee were becoming fearful that Majority Leader Mike Mansfield, Minority Leader Everett Dirksen, and Attorney General Nicholas Katzenbach, acting at the instruction of the president, were gutting some of its stronger provisions in order to get it by the Southern Democratic–conservative Republican coalition and allow the Senate leadership to invoke cloture and thus avoid a filibuster. The House bill had included a poll-tax ban. The Senate bill had not, and Ted, who had obviously been briefed by Dave Burke, couldn't understand why the law would ban literacy tests but not the equally heinous poll tax. (One ostensible reason was that courts had found that the poll tax was not racially discriminatory; it hurt poor whites as much as it hurt poor blacks. Another was that under the Constitution the states were the stewards of their own elections, and opponents of the poll-tax ban argued that could not be undone by federal statute.) Ted's distress over why the poll-tax ban was left out of the bill was fueled by meetings he was now holding with civil rights leaders, who kept raising the issue with him, pressing him on it, while Rauh, with whom he was also meeting, was, Ted said, "particularly worked up about this issue" and was obviously goading him. And if Ted needed any more incentive, the Judiciary's senior liberal and the Voting Rights Act's floor manager, Phil Hart, frustrated at the compromises in the bill, encouraged Birch Bayh, Joseph Tydings, and Ted, three young Judiciary liberals, to fight back by asking each to select a provision of the bill to strengthen and then push it. But James Eastland, who had allowed the Immigration and Nationality Act to pass because he knew his opposition would be futile, was not so agreeable when it came to voting rights. He managed to stave off most liberal amendments by having Sam Ervin stage a committee "filibuster," reading the Constitution slowly—*very* slowly—for three hours while the other senators sat idly and angrily. As part of his general education while hospitalized, Ted had already spent a good deal of time examining the poll tax, not connecting it explicitly to the Voting Rights Act. Now, caught up in the excitement of the Voting Rights Act, he spent a good deal more time discussing it with Rauh, who tutored him as he had tutored Burke. And he conferred with other experts: Thurgood Marshall of the Second Circuit Court, who recommended he speak with Clarence Ferguson, the dean of the Howard University School of Law, and with Howard professors Jeanus Parks and Herbert O. Reid; Charles Haar, his old supporter, and Mark DeWolfe Howe, and, finally, Paul Freund, who was widely regarded as the great expert in constitutional law, all of them from Harvard Law. Many of these advisers, Ted said, came to his house frequently in 1965, often on weekends, to go over the arguments. And all of them concurred that there was not only something that could be done legislatively to attack the poll tax but also that it was important that something *should* be done to attack it, that doing so would be constitutional, and one wouldn't have to wait for a Supreme Court decision. Still, it was a sign of how unaccustomed Ted was to making that ascent up the legislative mountain that when it came time to present the poll-tax ban in committee, he called out to Burke, right in the committee room, and asked, "Where is my amendment?" Caught by surprise, Burke, who had no amendment because Ted had never asked him to draft one—Burke wasn't an attorney, in any case—raced back to the office, had a lawyer on the staff write a few lines, and then raced back to the hearing room with it. (Rauh would eventually write the amendment when it was added to the bill.) And then Ted made a powerful and cogent argument for the repeal of the tax. The amendment passed in committee—the committee where civil rights bills had always gone to die—with nine votes, which demonstrated how dramatically things had changed in the Senate in a short time.* As Burke would later put it to biographer Burton Hersh, "That's how the poll-tax fight began."

And it *was* a fight, even though Lyndon Johnson, Attorney General Nicholas Katzenbach, now Lyndon Johnson's point man on the Voting Rights Act, and Majority Leader Mike Mansfield were all just as desirous of eliminating the poll tax as Ted Kennedy was. But one reason that the bill had not included a poll-tax ban, besides those previous court rulings that the tax was not discriminatory against African American voters and that states controlled their own election process, was that a case on whether a state poll tax violated the Twenty-fourth Amendment—the amendment that banned the tax in federal elections—was likely to be argued before the Supreme Court shortly, and the court would more than likely find it unconstitutional. "And that would finish it," Katzenbach said with finality. Ted, morally impatient, wanted to end it earlier. There was, however, an issue of the constitutionality of a poll-tax ban in the Voting Rights Act, that is, a congressional ban, which was why Congress had felt it necessary to introduce a constitutional amendment to end the federal poll tax. If Congress passed a poll-tax ban, Katzenbach argued, the current case would probably be remanded while another case, on the new law, would be heard in the lower courts and then make *its* way to the Supreme Court, which, Katzenbach felt, could take another two or three years. (Ted rebutted that Katzenbach could add the Voting Rights Act to the brief in his case rather than be forced to bring a new action.) Politically speaking, and politics were important in trying to pass this difficult piece of legislation that would radically change race relations in the South, the ban would also raise a red flag—Dirksen was opposed in part because Vermont, with two Republican senators, had a poll tax for town meetings—that would rouse the old Southern Democrat–conservative Republican alliance and threaten the cloture vote to end debate, for which the bill needed sixty-seven votes. And that was another reason the admin-

*To avoid having Eastland kill the bill in committee, Mansfield had gotten the Senate to pass a resolution ordering Judiciary to report it out by April 9, which is why Ervin's "filibuster" was so aggravating.

istration opposed a poll-tax ban: It might upset Everett Dirksen. "If you can tell the states, 'You can't impose a poll tax,' why can't you tell them, 'You can't impose a cigarette tax, or any other tax'?" Dirksen would say.

In short, the administration feared that the poll-tax ban would wind up jeopardizing the entire bill. Already, Ted's fight had delayed floor consideration of the larger bill—the bill without his amendment—for a month. Katzenbach had made these arguments to Ted personally, made them several times, without moving Ted. (Burke Marshall, a close friend of the Kennedys and the head of the civil rights division in Bobby's Justice Department, had made them to Ted too, over a long lunch, also without effect.) And Katzenbach admitted to feeling that Ted was grandstanding, finding his mountain, but that he was, in Katzenbach's view, finding it at the expense of passing a voting rights bill. David Burke, though, felt that Katzenbach, like so many of Jack and Bobby Kennedy's courtiers, was being condescending to Ted, dismissive, as if he didn't know what he was doing.

Katzenbach was wrong. Ted Kennedy may have been finding his mountain, but he was not grandstanding, and he did know what he was doing and why he was doing it. There were legal reasons for waging his fight. The law professors who advised him felt that there was no reason to wait for the Supreme Court and that Ted could hasten the end of the poll tax because the Fifteenth Amendment, as it might now be interpreted in the era of civil rights, outlawed such a tax, in their view. And those same scholars wanted Congress to be on record in finding a poll tax unlawful, which would, they felt, help the case currently before the Supreme Court when the court rendered its decision, whether they needed that decision or not. And there were political reasons for waging his fight. Liberals, especially those young liberals in the Senate, had felt snubbed by Johnson and Mansfield, who, they thought, were too eager to appease Dirksen by stripping out of the bill some of its more strenuous provisions; this was one reason why those liberals, among them Ted, had, at Hart's instigation, revolted in the first place with their own set of amendments. By fighting for the poll tax, especially against the Democratic establishment, Ted earned chits with those liberals, which he would use in advancing future legislation and in advancing his political career.

Finally, there were personal reasons for waging his fight, and these may have been the most compelling reasons of all. Ted Kennedy had been disdained and even disparaged by the Boston intellectuals when he ran for the Senate—intellectuals who had embraced Jack and Bobby. And Ted, who so admired intellectuals because he wasn't one of them, desperately wanted their approval and, more, their respect. Ted understood that by taking on a big issue, an important issue, an issue with ramifications, and by working with those intellectuals, he might win them over. That was very important to Ted Kennedy, the young man of whom everyone, especially those intellectuals, had had the lowest expectations. And there was another personal reason—an even bigger one. Ted Kennedy had been deferential to his Senate elders. He had minded his manners and bided his time, as freshman senators were trained to do. "I've never seen any new senator ingratiate himself so quickly with the older members of the leadership," one of those older members told William Shannon of *The New York Times*. But Ted Kennedy, particularly in the wake of his brother's death and after the plane crash, when he had devoted himself to becoming an important senator, a senator who could make a difference, and particularly with Bobby in the Senate providing competition, and particularly in a time of liberal fervor, when the liberal wind was blowing and great legislation was being passed—for all those reasons, Ted Kennedy wanted to be deferential no longer. He wanted to find his niche and make his legislative mark. He had spoken for the Civil Rights Act. He had floor-managed the Immigration Act. But he had yet to introduce a major piece of legislation—one that would not only let him make his mark but also win him the respect of those Senate elders, not just their friendship. Now he would. The poll tax was fully his—his amendment—an amendment with lasting consequences and an amendment dealing with constitutional law, which was one of the areas in which senators won respect from the elders. A "fundamental problem" is how one of those elders approvingly described the poll tax and immigration reform on which Ted had worked. "Nothing cheap or flashy." And there was yet one more element, this one to win not only his colleagues' respect but his own self-respect: the moral element. Ted Kennedy's fight to end the poll tax was a righteous fight, a good fight, a fight against searing injustice.

In effect, then, Ted Kennedy chose to fight because he *needed* a fight to establish his stature in the institution he loved and among the intellectuals whose respect he yearned for. And he needed it to establish his moral bona fides to that institution and to himself. His amendment was his chance to achieve a heightened sense of purpose.

• • •

And Ted Kennedy, who had already been working on the immigration reform bill when the Voting Rights Act suddenly seized center stage, had
learned a few things in his first two years in the Senate about how to move
legislation. Having passed Judiciary, where the liberals now had a majority, the bill—with the poll-tax ban—headed to the floor. Though he appreciated that he faced opposition from the president, the majority leader,
and the minority leader—a powerful array of opposition, especially for a
young man who believed so devoutly in deference and comity—Ted was
personally lobbying senators, working the phones, visiting twenty of
them in their offices, palavering with them in the Senate Office Building
hallways in what one reporter called his "gentlemanly ways" with "quiet
chats," and keeping a careful head count on a large white poster in his office. It sat on a tripod on which he had divided senators into four lists, the
way Lyndon Johnson might have done when he ran the Senate: those
senators who were with him; those new liberal senators who were likely to
be with him; those senators who were vacillating whether to be with him
and were persuadable; and those conservatives who were likely to oppose
him but who, Ted felt, needed to be engaged as a way of showing respect.
"At all hours of the day and even into the night, as the showdown vote
neared," *Newsweek* reported, "the tall, slim figure could be seen walking
the corridors of the two Senate office buildings, his back held stiffly in a
brace, his right hand clutching a silver-headed cane." And he didn't lobby
just senators. He called interest groups and the press and civil liberties attorneys and labor leaders—basically waging a campaign. And because
Ted was calling senators, visiting senators, lining up senators who also
wanted to see the poll tax abolished, Mansfield, who said he had no idea
Ted was lobbying this way and felt ambushed, was now forced into calling
senators too, asking them to vote against the ban, fearing that if the
Southerners didn't think he had the votes for cloture, they would begin a
filibuster, while Dirksen was working his side of the aisle. (By one report,
Mansfield offered Ted a seat on the Foreign Relations Committee if he
would desist.) And the president too, for whom this battle was also personal—a battle to put the Kennedy boys, but especially Bobby, in their
place—had his Senate liaison, Mike Manatos, contact every senator and
ask them to vote against Ted's amendment. And that wasn't the only activity. Dirksen and Mansfield, hoping to mollify the liberals and disarm

Ted, were quietly collaborating on sending a new voting rights bill of their own to the floor instead of the Judiciary bill—a new bill that stripped out the poll-tax ban but directed the attorney general to bring suit immediately to test the constitutionality of the tax, based not on the Twenty-fourth Amendment, on which the Supreme Court was already deliberating, but on the Voting Rights Act itself, meaning to test if Congress had the right to overturn the poll tax regardless of the constitutional amendment. Meanwhile, Vice President Humphrey had asked Mansfield to postpone a vote on the Judiciary bill, so that he could line up senators against it. But Mansfield was apparently so worried about the outcome that he would not wait and decided to rush his own and Dirksen's bill to a vote after an abbreviated debate. When Ted heard that Mansfield and Dirksen had put their own bill up instead of Judiciary's, he was furious.

Furious or not, Ted knew the odds against him were high. But he was not yet defeated. On May 1, the day after Mansfield had introduced his bill, Ted flew back to Boston to confer with his Harvard experts: Freund, Haar, and DeWolfe Howe. So intent was he on getting his argument right in order to fend off opponents on the Senate floor that he and Haar met outside Langdell Hall at the Harvard Law School, and Haar laid out for him the entire history of the poll tax—"many hours we spent," Haar said— explaining the basis of a property requirement to vote, going back to *The Federalist Papers*, reading him early cases on the poll tax, and examining different viewpoints, trying to make them clear to Ted. Those professors also had sixteen of their students draft a brief for Ted that laid out the reasons for an outright ban on the poll tax. And, having heard that Thurgood Marshall had prepared for his argument on *Brown v. Board of Education* before the Supreme Court by practicing in a moot court, Ted invited those professors to his Georgetown house when he returned to Washington; he would conduct a moot court of his own, like the one he had won at the University of Virginia, having the professors pepper him with questions as he knew his opponents would do on the Senate floor. "Ted gives the impression of being brought along carefully with much coaching and preparation," William Shannon had written in a profile of Ted for *The New York Times Magazine*, "while Bobby appears decidedly more self-reliant and confident." And Shannon was right. Ted was a natural politician, not a natural intellectual. But Ted Kennedy had been coached. And Ted Kennedy had been prepared. And Ted Kennedy was ready.

Now the fight between the freshman senator and the Senate leader-

The Kennedy family in 1938. Seated from left to right: Eunice, Jean, Teddy (on his father's lap), Joseph Kennedy, Patricia, and Kathleen. Standing from left to right: Rosemary, Robert, John, Rose Kennedy, and Joseph, Jr. Rose and Joseph had created the family as an aesthetic object, beautiful and well-mannered, to appeal to the world, but they had also created it as a fortress against the world—one in which devotion to one another was paramount. *ullstein bild via Getty Images*

Joseph Kennedy's aide-de-camp, Edward Moore, with his namesake, Edward Moore Kennedy (front center), at the family retreat in Palm Beach, Florida. Bobby and Mrs. Moore are behind them. It was a reflection of the youngest's status that he was named for a man whose chief attribute was his unflagging loyalty to the boy's father. *Copyright John F. Kennedy Library Foundation/ Kennedy Family Collection/John F. Kennedy Presidential Library and Museum, Boston*

Teddy and Joseph Kennedy in London during the latter's tenure as the United States ambassador to Great Britain—a position that brought him disrepute for his promotion of appeasement to Adolf Hitler. Though Joseph Kennedy was an absent father, he spent more time with his youngest child than with his other children and was highly entertained by him. *Hulton-Deutsch/Hulton-Deutsch Collection/Corbis via Getty Images*

Teddy at the Kennedy home in Hyannis Port on Cape Cod. He was the family jester, the Kennedy whose role it was to amuse the rest and keep up their spirits. In a family where great emphasis was placed on appearances, he was also nicknamed "Biscuits and Muffins" for his appetites and his struggles with weight. *Copyright John F. Kennedy Library Foundation/ Kennedy Family Collection/John F. Kennedy Presidential Library and Museum, Boston*

Ted at Harvard, where his dedication to football overshadowed his dedication to academics. His fear of failing Spanish led him to ask a classmate to take an exam for him, which led to the dismissal of both. *AP Images*

Ted Kennedy and Joan Bennett on their wedding day, November 29, 1958. Ted would say that it seemed "everything was coming up roses." As it turned out, it wasn't, and the marriage was a troubled one. *Bettmann/Getty Images*

From the *University of Virginia Law Weekly:* Ted and his roommate John Tunney win the Moot Appellate Court competition, which Ted calls one of the highlights of his life. For a young man of whom the expectations were always low, the victory is a signal triumph.
CCBY image courtesy of Virginia Law Weekly and University of Virginia Law Library

Three brothers in 1959. From left to right: Robert Kennedy, the majority counsel of the Senate Select Committee on Improper Activities in Labor and Management (though it was labor that took the brunt of the investigation); Ted Kennedy, recently graduated from Virginia Law School; and Senator John Kennedy, a member of the committee and an aspirant for the 1960 Democratic presidential nomination. *Bettmann/Getty Images*

Ted at the 1960 Democratic National Convention in Los Angeles that would nominate his brother John. As the western state coordinator of his brother's campaign, Ted is in the center of the Wyoming delegation at the moment the delegation's votes would put John Kennedy over the top for the victory. *Ralph Crane/The LIFE Picture Collection via Getty Images*

Campaign 1960: In the Kennedy family tradition, Ted would do anything to elect his brother president. When a local official in Miles City, Montana, told him he would be allowed to address a local rodeo to tout his brother's candidacy only if he rode a bronco, Ted mounted the bronco. *AP Images*

Ted in February 1961, being sworn in as an assistant district attorney of Suffolk County, Massachusetts, by the secretary of the commonwealth, later Boston mayor, Kevin White. Ted was laying the groundwork for elective office. *Bettmann/Getty Images*

Ted campaigning for the Democratic Senate nomination, to fill his brother John's Senate term, outside the G & G Delicatessen in Dorchester in September 1962. It was a contentious primary pitting Ted, who had never held elective office, against Ed McCormack, the state attorney general and the nephew of House speaker John McCormack—a scion of one Massachusetts political dynasty against a scion of another. *Carl Mydans/The LIFE Picture Collection via Getty Images*

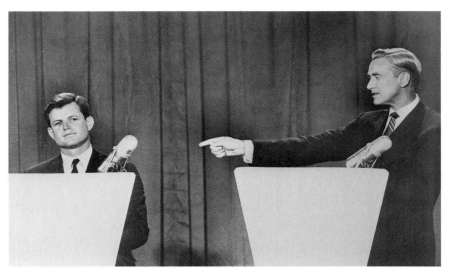

"If his name was Edward Moore . . . your candidacy would be a joke," Ed McCormack assailed Ted during their first debate, held that August at McCormack's old high school in South Boston, over Ted's lack of qualifications for the senate. Ted was certain he had lost the debate and possibly the nomination. Instead, voters turned on McCormack for bullying his young opponent. *Bettmann/Getty Images*

Senator-elect Edward Kennedy and his family in November 1962: Ted; daughter, Kara; wife, Joan; and son, Edward, Jr. *Jack O'Connell/The Boston Globe via Getty Images*

Senator Edward Kennedy and his brother, President John F. Kennedy, in Boston at a fund-raising dinner in October 1963, their last joint public appearance. The two traded gibes, Ted saying that the president would be "running on my coattails" in the 1964 election, "and he's going to have to treat me better," and the president saying that Teddy was "tired of being called the younger brother" of the president and a "Kennedy" and was thinking of changing his name . . . to "Teddy Roosevelt." *Edmund Kelley/The Boston Globe via Getty Images*

The funeral march for the assassinated president, John F. Kennedy, on November 25, 1963. From left to right: Bobby, Jacqueline Kennedy, and Ted, wearing his late brother's pants because his didn't arrive. *Wally McNamee/CORBIS/Corbis via Getty Images*

Ted in Dublin, Ireland, outside St. Mary's Pro-Cathedral on May 29, 1964. He received a Beatles reception, according to one observer, and Dubliners even lined the streets at midnight to catch a glimpse of his motorcade. *Independent News and Media/Getty Images*

The plane crash on June 19, 1964, at Southampton, Massachusetts, that almost cost Ted Kennedy his life—and took the lives of the pilot and of Ted's administrative assistant, Ed Moss—and that kept Ted hospitalized for six months while Joan campaigned for his senate reelection. *Charles Dixon/The Boston Globe via Getty Images*

The long recuperation: Ted, his back broken, was placed in a Stryker frame so that he could be rotated like a "human rotisserie," he said. He spent much of his time with a series of Harvard "tutors" who schooled him in issues so that he could return to the Senate a more informed and better legislator. *Leonard McCombe/The LIFE Picture Collection via Getty*

Back in the Senate: Ted and the chairman of the Judiciary Committee on which Ted sat, Senator James Eastland of Mississippi, one of the Senate "bulls." Eastland was a racist, but he accommodated Ted, and Ted learned how to defer to him to get what he wanted. *Bettmann/Getty Images*

Ted and President Lyndon Johnson shortly after Ted's return to the Senate following his recovery from the plane accident, hence the cane. Johnson was in a bitter rivalry with Bobby Kennedy, but he felt a kindred spirit in Ted, which didn't prevent him from occasionally tormenting him to redress his grievances against the Kennedys. *Alamy*

Ted at work in his Senate office early in 1966. He is surrounded by photos of his family—ever-present reminders of the expectations placed upon him. *Joe Runci/The Boston Globe via Getty Images*

Celebrating the passage of the Voting Rights Act of 1965. From left to right: Thomas Kuchel, the Senate minority whip; Phil Hart, one of Ted's mentors; Ted; Mike Mansfield, the Senate majority leader; Everett Dirksen, the Senate minority leader; and Jacob Javits, a Republican moderate with whom Ted often collaborated. *Universal History Archive/Universal Images Group via Getty Images*

Francis X. Morrissey before the microphones during his Senate confirmation hearing for an appointment to the federal District bench. While his brothers had demurred in promoting Morrissey, Ted pushed the nomination at his father's behest, and wound up spending political capital because Morrissey was manifestly unqualified for the position. *UPI*

Ted at the provincial hospital at Hoi An in South Vietnam during his second trip there—early in 1968. He had been a supporter of the war, but that support had gradually eroded as he watched the toll the war had taken on the civilian population of Vietnam, to whom he felt a special responsibility as the chairman of the Senate Refugee Subcommittee. *Bettmann/Getty Images*

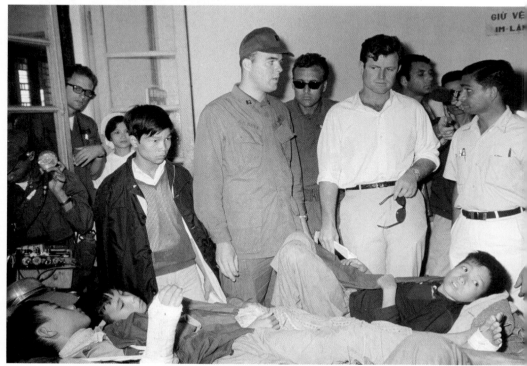

Ted and Bobby in the Senate at a Labor Committee hearing in 1967. With Bobby's election to the Senate in 1964, they became both partners as they supported liberal legislation and rivals as Bobby chided Ted for his deficiencies and forced Ted to compensate for them. *AP Images*

The engine behind the senator: Edward Kennedy awaits delivering a Democratic fund-raising speech in 1967 while his administrative assistant, David Burke, makes last-minute changes to the address. Burke was largely responsible for assembling Kennedy's staff early in his first full term, setting the stage for what would be considered the best staff in the Senate. *© Robert Nandell/USA Today Network*

Ted at St. Patrick's Cathedral in New York, delivering the eulogy for his brother Bobby in June 1968, after Bobby's assassination during his presidential campaign. "My brother need not be idealized," Ted said, and asked that Bobby be remembered as a "good and decent man, who saw wrong and tried to right it, saw suffering and tried to heal it, saw war and tried to stop it." *Bettmann/ Getty Images*

Ted on a jetty in the bay at the family compound at Hyannis Port, 1969: an image of the long, sad emotional devastation after Bobby's death, from which Ted would never really recover. *John Loengard/The LIFE Picture Collection via Getty Images*

ship and the president of the United States was finally coming to a head on the Senate floor, which had been debating the Judiciary Committee's bill since April but had not yet addressed the poll-tax amendment. The speech Ted gave was different from the one he would give a few months later on immigration reform. On that issue, there would be little blowback—none from the administration or the Senate leaders. But here he was challenging those leaders, doing something that as a conscientious Senate man he had never done before. He continued to go over the arguments repeatedly. And he rehearsed the speech itself, though it was brief, only eleven minutes, going over it "again and again" at his home, Burke said. He was nervous—"very nervous," Burke recalled. This was climbing the mountain, his Senate rite of passage, and he had never taken anything in the Senate more seriously.

The morning of the floor debate, May 11, there was chaos. It still wasn't clear as the vote approached if Ted would win or lose against the president. No one, however, was a better head counter than Lyndon Johnson, and Katzenbach had met with Bobby, who had only reluctantly joined his brother's cause, to tell him that Johnson had the votes to defeat the amendment, but he said, "If it does Teddy any good," presumably meaning helping his reputation with the civil rights groups and with his Senate colleagues, "go ahead and work on it." And he added, "If you can beat me, beat me, but I don't think you can." Ted's head count was less certain. He had thirty-seven co-sponsors. Of those liberals who hadn't joined him, he wasn't sure about Eugene McCarthy, who had voted against the poll tax in the past, and Vance Hartke of Indiana, who had yet to declare himself on the issue. What Ted didn't know was that Hartke had phoned Johnson just four days before the floor debate was to begin, to complain that he was being heavily lobbied by Joe Rauh and Clarence Mitchell of the National Association for the Advancement of Colored People; that he had been meeting with McCarthy and Mansfield to solidify opposition to the amendment; and that he was irritated by Ted telling McCarthy that Humphrey was in favor of the bill, when he obviously wasn't. (As Johnson's vice president, he couldn't be, whatever his personal inclination.) Humphrey then told Hartke that Rauh, who was one of Humphrey's closest friends, was just trying to round up votes by telling Teddy that Humphrey was with them. But if Joe Rauh had been trying to round up votes, he was also sowing mischief by pitting liberal against liberal. Bobby confronted McCarthy angrily on the Senate floor with the charge, which he said he heard from

Rauh, that the only reason McCarthy was opposing Ted's amendment was that he hated Bobby. And Bobby told Hartke that Rauh had said the same thing about him—that he hated Bobby. Johnson told Hartke, "I will get right on it," apparently meaning that he would do some more arm-twisting, necessary because he knew Democrats were reluctant to vote against a poll tax on the seemingly arcane basis that passage would upset some legal strategy.

At the same time, Teddy, the best politician in the Kennedy family, was beginning to hedge his bets in anticipation that he might lose. That morning, before the floor debate, he had called Humphrey—who was sitting with the president at the time; Johnson remained silent throughout the conversation. Ted was joined in his office by Rauh, Senator Hart, who was the floor manager of the entire Voting Rights Act, and representatives from both the American Federation of Labor and the National Council of Churches, and he began haggling with Humphrey over a possible compromise. What Ted proposed was that he would agree to remove the ban in return for a "declaration and finding" in the bill by Attorney General Katzenbach that the poll tax had resulted in an abridgement of voting rights, that he would bring suit against the states still using a poll tax (the same provision as in Mansfield's bill but with the declaration to strengthen it), and that he would reestablish federal poll watchers without court procedures and federal registrars without first going through state registrars, both of which had been added to the bill in committee by the liberals and then stripped out in the Mansfield–Dirksen substitute. Humphrey said he would head off to discuss this with Mansfield and Dirksen. But as Humphrey was ending the call, Hart warned him, "We're running out of time."

By that point, they *had* run out of time. Johnson tried to calm his restive troops by telling congressional leaders at a breakfast that morning that he was against a poll tax and had actually asked for a ban in the original bill but that Katzenbach had told him it was probably unconstitutional. Later that morning, Humphrey phoned Ted back and told him to speak directly to Mansfield, but, as Hart had warned, it was too late. The Mansfield–Dirksen substitute bill was already headed to the floor, amid a flurry of activity—"noise and confusion on the floor," one report called it—with Humphrey racing around trying to cajole a few undecided senators, and Mansfield and Dirksen buttonholing members of their caucuses, and the floor buzzing with so much noise that when Humphrey finally gaveled them to order, he had to tell them to quiet down or go to the cloak-room.

In the midst of this, Ted—wearing one of the PT-109 tie clips that Jack used to pass out to intimates—set down his silver-headed cane and rose stiffly, flanked by Milton Gwirtzman, who had written his speech, and Mike Mansfield. Looking pale and uncertain and standing at the front of the chamber rather than at his seat in the back, he began to make his case. It was a "rare moment of high drama," as *The Washington Post* reported it. (By sheer coincidence, Bobby was in the presiding chair.) Ted spoke eloquently—the poll tax was "not only conceived in discrimination, not only has it operated in discrimination, but its effect is obviously discriminatory"—and carefully—"Why are we asking the Supreme Court to make this declaration if we are unwilling to make it ourselves?" he asked, which went to the heart of his amendment—and he answered questions expertly, clearly well prepared for the moment. Even then, for all the head counting by both sides, the result was in doubt, and when the roll was called, many Democrats retreated to the cloakroom to see if the president would need their votes or whether they might vote their conscience with Ted. And when the votes were tallied, Ted Kennedy's amendment had lost, barely lost, 49 to 45. And Ted "cheerfully," it was reported, accepted congratulations for a fight well fought, picked up his cane, and hobbled to the back of the Senate chamber, where Bobby was waiting for him and where the two brothers huddled in conversation, most likely Bobby praising his younger brother for his tenacity.

But even though he had lost the vote, even though he hadn't scaled the mountain to its peak, there was a kind of victory in his losing. One senior senator remarked, "I never thought Ted would have the guts to buck Lyndon. We felt he was too soft to try anything like this." But Ted Kennedy had demonstrated guts in taking on the entire political establishment. Columnist Mary McGrory called it his "bar mitzvah," and labeled the loss "the best kind of defeat," and said he had "earned the right not to be called 'the kid' anymore." And Ted Kennedy had demonstrated maturity in the way he conducted the debate, the assiduousness with which he conducted it, and the graciousness with which he lost it. And Ted Kennedy had demonstrated moral passion. A longtime Kennedy detractor, journalist Robert Sherrill, cited Jack's unwillingness to appoint a single black justice to the federal bench in the Southern circuit and his willingness to appoint white racists, but he wrote, "Ted's willingness in 1965 to put himself out, to risk retaliation from the White House, for the sake of stiffening a pro-black piece of legislation, would have to be seen as a radically new direction for the family." Ted Kennedy, the most empathetic of the brothers, had pointed the Kennedys in that new direction—not following the moral vanguard, as Jack so often did, but leading it. (In fact, he was arguing for something more liberal than Lyndon Johnson had.) Ted always was likable to his Senate colleagues. But now he had impressed them with his diligence and with his knowledge and with his obvious hard work, when, as *The Washington Post* reported, "his late brother had often failed to immerse himself in issues," and also with his moral commitment. Even Mike Mansfield in victory was congratulatory to Ted, calling Ted's leadership "brilliant," and his mastery of the subject "complete," and his argument "lucid and compelling," quipping, "He almost—but not quite—persuaded me." And Mansfield said that the fight left "no scars," because "No one dislikes Ted." A "moral victory," *The New York Times* called it. A "personal triumph," said the *Los Angeles Times*. And in the black community, Ted won not only plaudits but gratitude. An "insult and blasphemy," said Dr. Martin Luther King Jr., who had gotten out of a sick bed in Selma to denounce the poll-tax defeat.* Ted Kennedy had lost the vote, but he had won the respect of both those in the Senate and many outside it. And he had won self-respect.

And he had won not only respect, theirs and his own. He had shown remarkable political skill, the power of soft persuasion, beating the president in the Democratic caucus, with thirty-nine Democrats voting for Ted's amendment while twenty-four voted with Johnson. Still, despite the defeat, the deliberations continued, and a compromise was finally reached. Mansfield and Dirksen agreed to a "congressional declaration," the one for which Ted had asked Humphrey, that in "certain states"—not including Vermont, the four states that still exacted a poll tax: Alabama, Mississippi, Texas, and Virginia—the right to vote was being denied due to the poll tax, thus putting the sense of the Congress behind the attorney general's effort to challenge the poll tax in court, which even Katzenbach thought would strengthen his hand. Hart supported the addition, and it

---

*King may have been disingenuous. In his memoir, Ted said he later discovered that King had written liberal senators and urged them to vote against the amendment because he, like Johnson, thought it might threaten the passage of the entire bill. *True Compass*, 232.

passed 69 to 20. Now Mansfield called for unanimous consent to end debate on the Voting Rights Act, but Louisiana senator Allen Ellender objected, though he admitted he had been "unable to awaken the South from its slumber to the obnoxious provisions of this law." The Southern bloc awakened long enough to submit sixty amendments in an attempt to emasculate the bill—Dirksen let them proceed, and Johnson, not wanting to fight Dirksen, concurred—but they didn't have the votes. Mansfield finally got cloture, 70 to 30, on May 25, and the bill passed the next day, 77 to 19, with only Southern senators in opposition. A House–Senate conference reconciled their differing bills, with the House deleting the poll-tax ban, and Johnson signed the bill into law on August 6.

The next year, the Supreme Court ruled the poll tax unconstitutional, which meant that just as he had lost the vote on the poll tax but won both respect and his point, so, in the end, had Ted Kennedy won the war itself after having lost the battle. He was now, one reporter said, a "heavyweight senator"—a heavyweight because he waged the fight and waged it well, a heavyweight because the fight he waged mattered. At last, African American voters would no longer be burdened by the poll tax.

IV

After the great Voting Rights Act battle, Francis Xavier Morrissey hardly seemed the kind of figure who would cause a political contretemps, much less for one of the most well-liked men in the Senate coming off his great legislative and moral victory a few months earlier and his legislative victory with the Immigration and Nationality Act scarcely a few weeks before that. Ted Kennedy had spent the year involved in two great causes, two mountains: civil rights and immigration. Frank Morrissey was not a great cause. Frank Morrissey was less than a molehill. Morrissey, a municipal judge, was a guileless Boston pol, pleasantly nondescript, a born bit player, whom Joseph Kennedy had recruited to help introduce Jack to some of the local ward heelers when Jack first ran for Congress in 1946. As a secretary to Governor Maurice Tobin in the mid-1940s, Morrissey had entrée to the denizens of low-rent Boston politics, and as a fundraiser for Catholic charities, he had entrée to Richard Cardinal Cushing—two worlds that the politically ambitious Kennedy sons had to navigate. A "personal factotum" is how Kennedy adviser Richard Goodwin described him, a man who had been assigned "to keep watch on young John's activities so the father could be alerted to any hazards—personal or public—that might obstruct the career of his swiftly rising son." When Jack ran, Morrissey was the one who escorted him around the state, and after Jack won, he worked in his Boston office. And when Jack ran for the Senate, it was Morrissey once again who tended to the pols for him.

Frank Morrissey was in service to the Kennedys, a lackey, but he was not without ambition. In 1958, Massachusetts governor Foster Furcolo appointed Morrissey to the Boston Municipal Court, dealing primarily with minor infractions—hardly the highest bench, and apparently not high enough for Morrissey. For two years he quietly lobbied Joe Kennedy for an appointment to a higher bench, and when Jack Kennedy became president—Jack Kennedy, whose career he had helped launch—he came to believe that he been "marked," as he put it, for a federal judicial appointment. Joe told Morrissey that he was "mistaken," that Joe had made no such promise, that he would work "very hard to get the job for you," but that Morrissey was "way off base" to think of it as any kind of guarantee. Nevertheless, Joe Kennedy forwarded Morrissey's name to Jack with the request that he be appointed to the federal District Court. Jack said he felt obligated to his father to help Morrissey, but he did not do so happily. For all the service Morrissey had provided him, Jack Kennedy did not like Frank Morrissey. In fact, he had always felt that his father planted Morrissey in his campaigns as a spy, and he felt no compunction about humiliating him. *Boston Globe* reporter Robert Healy recalled how once, during a campaign trip from Worcester to Boston, Jack stopped the car in the "boonies" and ordered Morrissey to get out. "And Morrissey is standing there in the street, saying, 'What do I do now, Coach?'" And Jack told him to stick out his thumb. Another time, down in Palm Beach, Jack was with Morrissey and queried why he had never run for office himself. "Well, a lot of people have asked me to run for the State House," he answered with a certain puffery, and, as Healy told it, "Jack looked at him very coldly and said, 'Frank, you're a fucking liar. You ran in 1932. You finished seventh in a field of eleven, and you had, you know, 640 votes.'"* So while Jack tried to pacify his father by considering Morrissey's appointment, he did what he could to sabotage it, asking Bobby to have a prominent Bos-

---

*In fact, Morrissey had run for the state legislature in 1934, finished twelfth in a field of sixteen, and received 420 votes. Robert Healy, "Candidacy Raises New Morrissey Issue," *The Boston Globe*, October 15, 1965.

ton attorney and American Bar Association officer named Robert Meserve informally investigate Morrissey's qualifications. When Meserve found him unqualified, Bobby took the step of submitting Morrissey's name to the ABA, which rated nominees, and to the Massachusetts Bar Association, both of which deemed Frank Morrissey unqualified to serve on the federal bench. At the same time, Robert Healy, who was about to become executive editor of *The Boston Globe*, had told the president that the paper would not support Morrissey's appointment, which led to a confrontation between Bobby and Healy at a party for the president's departing congressional liaison at Duke Zeibert's restaurant. This was almost certainly less because of Morrissey, for whom Bobby had no particular affection, than because of Healy's perceived disloyalty to the administration. Jack intervened, pulled Healy aside, and said, "It ain't gonna happen," meaning Morrissey's nomination. Jack had fulfilled his obligation to his father. The nomination rested without being submitted to the Senate for confirmation. The possibility of his nomination arose again, briefly, in late 1963, but Jack was killed. And the seat remained open.

But that wasn't quite the end of Frank Morrissey and the Kennedys. When Teddy ran for the Senate in 1962, the call went out once again to Francis X. Morrissey, and Morrissey pulled the same duty for the youngest brother that he had for Jack. When Ted took his lunch hours while working in the Suffolk DA's office, Morrissey was the one who went to the East Boston Chamber with him, or the East Boston Lions Club, or the North End Seniors, or the Charlestown Civic Association. And after work, once Ted had stopped home to see Joan and the children, Morrissey would be the one who would go to the bean suppers with him. "Teddy's eyes and ears," Gerard Doherty, Teddy's 1962 campaign manager, called him. Teddy saw it differently—in fact the way Jack had seen it. He said that Morrissey would report back to Joe on his progress. "Frank raised my approval rating with the only 'constituency' who then counted."

And though the Kennedy boys had little use for him once they had established those relationships and once they were safely ensconced in office, Joe Kennedy did, especially after he suffered his stroke. Morrissey would visit the ailing patriarch every week when Joe was no longer relevant and largely ignored. "Morrissey and only Morrissey," Milt Gwirtzman said. And before he made those weekly visits, Morrissey would first visit Cardinal Cushing, so he could tell Joe that "the cardinal said this, and the cardinal said that," and that the cardinal had said, "God love you."

Frank Morrissey became the liaison between them. So obsequious was Morrissey that Gwirtzman and Ted's aide Bill Evans used to do skits about him, mocking him, saying, "God love ya, Teddy. I just saw the cardinal, and he said to tell the ambassador . . ." No one took him very seriously. "He was a sketch, and the people in the White House knew it," Gwirtzman said.

But if Frank Morrissey was a joke among the Kennedy associates, his life was anything but. Born in the Charlestown section of Boston to a stevedore, he was one of twelve children in a poverty-stricken family. He worked his way through Charlestown High School by selling newspapers at 3 A.M. on the docks. His higher education was piecemeal: He worked as a bank teller for five years, while at night attending Suffolk University Law School, which was unaccredited at the time, failed to get his degree and then failed the bar exam three times before returning to school, getting the degree, and finally passing the bar twelve years later; attended night school at Boston College; attended the Staley College of the Spoken Word in Brookline, from which he got a social-work degree that, Gerard Doherty said, was "always ridiculed." His career was just as piecemeal, from an insurance broker to a salesman to a social worker to Governor Tobin's secretary to the deputy commissioner of the State Department of Corrections to a gofer in Jack Kennedy's campaign and, after the campaign, to secretary in Jack's Boston office. So if he was a factotum, it was because so little in life had come easily to him and so much in life had kept him down.

But while Morrissey was helping Joe Kennedy, visiting him, gossiping with him, extending compliments to him, and worshipping him, a worship that seemed wholly sincere, he had not surrendered his dream to sit on the federal bench, and apparently he kept prompting Joe to fulfill it. Bobby knew that his father had wanted this favor for his retainer. But Bobby, who had presidential ambitions, was not going to risk embarrassment for the benefit of Francis X. Morrissey. Ted knew it too and asked his father if he still wanted it. Though Joe couldn't speak then, Ted said he "made clear to me that he cared very much." And Ted said then what Jack had said when the request had first come to him: that "this was the only request my father had ever made of me." Ted called it "a matter of loyalty." And not just loyalty to his father but to his late brother. Morrissey, Ted said, kept telling him that Jack had promised him he was going to get the seat: "He certainly led me to believe he had a commitment." Morrissey had even said this publicly. (Of course, Jack had also said that Morrissey was a liar.) And Ted felt he had to honor that commitment, regardless of the fact that the nomination had previously been derailed. Moreover, Ted had his own commitment to Morrissey for the services he had rendered during Ted's campaign, and loyalty meant more to Ted Kennedy than to his brothers. "Teddy is one of the most loyal people you'll ever meet," his nursemaid Luella Hennessey said of him. Jack made sure that Morrissey would never sit on the bench. Ted was determined that he would, for his father's sake, his brother's sake, for Morrissey's sake, even though he had the same misgivings about him that Jack and Bobby had.

But it was unclear if Ted had disinterred the dead nomination himself or if he had been prodded into it by Lyndon Johnson. Ted's Refugee Subcommittee staffer, George Abrams, recalled that Ted was holding a hearing when he was beckoned into an anteroom and told that Johnson was on the line and that he was going to appoint the fifty-five-year-old Morrissey to a district judgeship. Abrams said Ted seemed surprised by the news and that "he came back and told me, and he wasn't very happy." By another account, it was Ted who, as Massachusetts senator, was given the courtesy of submitting names to the president for the federal bench in his state and had approached Lyndon Johnson with the request. (Senators generally submitted several names; Ted submitted only one: Morrissey's.) Johnson acceded but not before asking Ted privately, "Do you really want this?" Ted said he did. Several days later, with Ted present in the Oval Office, Johnson phoned Joe Kennedy to tell him about the nomination and asked Ann Gargan, who was handling the phone for Joe, if he had heard. "He was quite emotional about it," she said, and Ted piped in, "Dad, it looks as if you're the man with all the influence," and joked that he was trying to "get a few lessons on how you get these things done." And, always trying to puff up his invalid father, he added, "The president said he is doing it for all of you and Jack and Bob and myself . . . but I think he is giving it a little extra push because of your interest in it."

Just how committed Lyndon Johnson, the Lyndon Johnson of ulterior motives, really was to Francis X. Morrissey would be a matter of some dispute. There were rumblings that he was upset by Ted making a nomination that would reflect badly on the president (Katzenbach himself was "pissed," Gwirtzman said); others said that Johnson was taking a small measure of revenge for the poll-tax fight by appointing a man clearly unqualified for the bench but who was closely associated with the Kennedys, so that the stigma would be theirs, not his; still others thought it was another bit of retribution against the Kennedys generally, because Johnson thought people would realize the Kennedys were the ones behind the appointment and Johnson knew the appointment would embarrass them. Whatever the motive, according to William Sullivan, the third-ranking member of the Federal Bureau of Investigation, no sooner had Ted left the Oval Office that morning than Johnson phoned Cartha DeLoach, the deputy director of the bureau, and asked him to conduct an investigation of Morrissey: "one of the most exhaustive investigations of its kind we ever conducted," wrote Sullivan, making it seem as if it was more than the routine investigation that nominees underwent. He said it turned up very little, but whatever negative information they found, Johnson leaked to the press, as a way, Sullivan felt, of tarnishing Ted and, no doubt, Bobby. There was also something odd about how the president chose to announce the nomination. He did so while at his Texas ranch, the day after the phone call to Joe Kennedy, and then held a press conference at which the only subject was Francis X. Morrissey and the Kennedys' involvement in his appointment. According to Dave Burke, the press reaction was, "Is that it?" To which Johnson said, "That's it," which got the press thinking about who Francis X. Morrissey was and why Johnson made such a show of his appointment. And that, given Morrissey's history, was not a good thing for Ted Kennedy.

But just a few days after announcing the nomination, and after hearing from press secretary Bill Moyers that Bobby's and Ted's people were accusing Johnson of "taking advantage" of them by naming Morrissey, Johnson laughed and told Katzenbach, "They're trying to stir trouble between the Kennedys and the president again about this judge in Boston." And he said that when Bobby left the Cabinet, one of the things he had asked for was Morrissey's nomination, and Johnson said that he had called Bobby just last week to confirm it, even after Johnson told him that there was negative information in Morrissey's file, which is when, Johnson said, Bobby suggested he talk to Ted about the nomination. (Either Bobby was clearly being disingenuous about wanting Morrissey's nomination and was eager to shuffle it off to Ted, or Johnson was lying to Katzenbach about the whole thing.) "I'd withdraw it tomorrow, if they wanted to withdraw it," Johnson told Katzenbach.

But Ted Kennedy, who was convinced that Johnson was not trying to undermine him, was not about to torpedo Frank Morrissey's opportunity to get a federal judgeship after making a promise to his father. On the contrary, he sent George Abrams up to Boston for three or four weeks to drum up support for Morrissey in the legal community, especially the Boston Bar Association and the Massachusetts Bar Association, both of which had rated Morrissey unqualified when Jack first floated his name, and Ted pressured prominent Boston lawyers with Kennedy connections to get the bar associations to reverse themselves. (The Massachusetts Bar Association eventually did.) "They tried to reach as many members of the bar associations as they could," one attorney said. "They tried to reach various houses of delegates and those in leadership positions. They tell what a great guy Morrissey is and how he worked his way through school." But, the lawyer said, "They usually don't say much about his qualifications." Still, Abrams managed to line up fifty judges who attested to Morrissey's fitness and especially to his likability. "To them a federal judgeship was not that big a deal," Gwirtzman, who worked on Morrissey's judicial campaign, said. And Massachusetts senior senator Leverett Saltonstall had submitted his "blue card"—both senators from a state had to approve a nomination by handing in a blue card with the nominee's name on it— and said he would support Morrissey's candidacy, not because he necessarily thought him qualified but because he didn't know much about him. Thus did Ted Kennedy's loyalty to Joe Kennedy outweigh his loyalty to the law.

And yet, opposition was already mounting. Albert Jenner Jr., the chairman of the ABA's judicial committee, which had rated Morrissey unqualified in Morrissey's first attempt at the seat, reiterated that assessment the day after the nomination, with brutal clarity. Looking at Morrissey's scholarship and his experience, Jenner said that he "does not measure up." But at least the ABA had been on record in its opposition. What was shocking, even unprecedented, was the step the chief judge of the Federal Court in Boston, Charles Wyzanski Jr., took in sending a letter to the Judiciary Committee excoriating the nomination, saying it "corroborates the cynical view that judicial place goes not to those who will honor it, but to those who by service have bought it," citing Morrissey's service to the Kennedy family as "the only discernible ground for the nomination." That same day, the *New York Herald Tribune* called the nomination "nauseous," and a *Washington Post* editorial reprimanded Ted personally for tendering it. All of this prompted Ted to take the Senate floor briefly, scold the press for prejudging Morrissey, and ask that he be given the chance to defend himself before the Judiciary Committee.

But even as he was lining up support, Ted was being warned by his own associates about Morrissey's negatives. Back in Washington in the Refugee Subcommittee room, after his trip to Boston, George Abrams had been prepping Morrissey for his confirmation hearings before the Judiciary Committee and realized that there were going to be problems with his record, which was, indeed, less than exceptional, and that Morrissey himself was not an especially good advocate, since he seemed to have no idea of what he was getting himself into. He was a "naïf," Gwirtzman said, who believed that a federal judgeship worked the same way local Boston politics did: "If the guy on top likes you, you get the job." But that was not the way the Senate worked. Abrams even brought Morrissey up to Ted's office so Morrissey could tell him face-to-face about his difficulties with getting his law degree and passing the bar. But there was nothing to be done. Ted was already committed both to his father and to Morrissey, and the embarrassment of forcing him to withdraw, after all Ted had gone through, seemed worse than the embarrassment of having him face confirmation hearings. So Ted told them that they had to go forward. "We've got the witnesses. We'll do the best we can."

But Ted Kennedy was not just going forward on an endangered nomination, a nomination that could not possibly help him. He was working even harder for it now that it was endangered. With the hearings about to begin, he approached Minority Leader Dirksen. Dirksen had not been well disposed toward Morrissey when John Kennedy had first raised his name, and Dirksen was likely to be one of Morrissey's fiercest antagonists, especially now, because having worked with Johnson on both the Civil Rights Act and the Voting Rights Act, he had to mend fences with the more conservative elements of his party and show that he was not a Johnson patsy. Taking on Ted Kennedy was a way of proving his conservative credentials. But others, including George Abrams, thought there was a more personal animus: Everett Dirksen, as a Senate elder, a sage, still resented the way Kennedy had just marched into the Senate and then had the gall in the current session to take an active role in legislation, even taking on the Senate leadership in the poll-tax dispute. Now Dirksen, some felt, was going to give the upstart a lesson. But when he came to the minority leader, Ted wasn't thinking of Dirksen's revenge. He was thinking of Senate collegiality. He admitted to Dirksen that Morrissey had had "difficulties," that he had failed the bar three times. Dirksen, with a great basso voice that sounded like a church organ, told Ted not to worry. He had failed the exam twice himself. "So your words don't fall on unsympathetic ears," Dirksen said. And Ted asked a favor. He asked that "consideration be given" to allowing Morrissey to make his case and allow Ted to help make his case for him. And Dirksen replied that he would. "We'll do that. We'll do it in a fine way. A fine way." And Ted returned to his office with Dave Burke, feeling that he had possibly charmed Dirksen into being less antagonistic, fairer.

But Ted had been outfoxed by Dirksen. Morrissey was now a *cause célèbre* in the press, an object lesson in political favoritism and back-scratching, a moral affront, and neither Dirksen nor the liberal elites, who were not typically Dirksen's allies, were going to let Morrissey off easy. On the first day of the hearings, October 12, Morrissey received a string of endorsements, two and a half hours' worth, beginning with Ted Kennedy's, which commended Morrissey for his civic-mindedness, and including that of Speaker John McCormack, making a rare appearance in the Senate to say that he had known Morrissey for twenty-five years and could attest to his character and decency ("honorable and trustworthy in every respect"), and by the president of the Massachusetts bar, and by several judges and attorneys, and by a college president. But then came the afternoon session, and the tone changed, sharpened, especially under the questioning of Dirksen. The ABA's Albert Jenner reiterated his condemnation of the nomination, and then he leveled a new charge, something that Morrissey hadn't previously revealed: When Morrissey failed the bar in Massachusetts, he went to Georgia, enrolled in the Southern Law School in Athens (a fly-by-night operation—a "diploma mill," Dirksen called it), and, almost immediately after arriving, was admitted to the Georgia bar, for which no examination was necessary, and then left again for Massachusetts. Jenner suggested that Morrissey intended to circumvent his failure to pass the Massachusetts bar by using a reciprocity agreement between Georgia and Massachusetts that would grant him admission to the latter. Jenner was followed by two more critics: Robert Meserve, another ABA official and the Boston attorney whom Bobby had originally asked to investigate Morrissey (Meserve added that Erwin Griswold, the dean of the Harvard Law School, also opposed the nomination), and Bernard Segal, who had been the chairman of the ABA's standing committee on the federal judiciary and who called Morrissey the worst candidate he had ever reviewed. Then, at just before 6 P.M., after six hours of waiting, Morrissey himself finally took the witness stand. He was penitent. He was submissive. He admitted his "weaknesses," but Morrissey insisted that he had never tried to practice in Massachusetts using his admission to the Georgia bar; that he had gone to Georgia in June 1933, at the age of twenty-two, when a classmate at Boston College evening school told him that with his class work at Suffolk Law School and an intensive class at Southern Law, he could gain admission to the Georgia bar; that he actually spent three months studying at Southern with the intention of staying in Georgia, which he did for at least six months longer to see if he could set up a practice there but was unsuccessful, and finally returned to Boston late in 1933—much of which was at variance with Jenner's testimony. And, as he testified, with Ted having left the committee room to attend to other business, Dirksen and Joseph Tydings "tore into him," as George Abrams recollected. And then Jenner was re-called and stated yet again that he had no evidence Morrissey had stayed in Georgia to practice.

But the legal establishment and Everett Dirksen, who asked Morrissey what *The Washington Post* called "embarrassing questions," weren't the only ones determined to sink Morrissey's nomination. Morrissey's testimony that he had been a Georgia resident during and shortly after his law training there triggered a memory from someone else who wanted Morrissey's nomination to fail: Jack Kennedy's old appointments secretary and current Johnson staffer, Kenny O'Donnell. Robert Healy, *The Boston Globe* executive editor, who had gotten into that dustup with Bobby Kennedy over the nomination four years earlier, got a call from O'Donnell that night. "I'm going to just tell you this once, and then I'm going to hang up," O'Donnell said. And O'Donnell recalled that time when Jack Kennedy baited Morrissey on why he had never run for office, and then Jack sprang on him the fact that Jack knew he *had* run for office in 1934. Healy said he didn't see the relevance of what O'Donnell was talking about. And then it dawned on him. If Morrissey had run for office in 1934, he had to have signed an affidavit that he was a Massachusetts resident for a year prior to the election, even though he had signed an affidavit that he was a Georgia resident through most of 1933 in order to get admitted to the bar there. Healy, who was in Washington, said he went up to Boston and found Morrissey's affidavit at the State House. And then he told Bobby and Ted and Dirksen that he was going to write a story saying that Morrissey had lied. It ran on the front page of the *Globe*—CANDIDACY RAISES NEW MORRISSEY ISSUE—two days later, on October 15.

Ted was clearly both desperate and perplexed, having gotten himself into a situation that threatened to tarnish his new-won respect. Meanwhile, Dirksen smelled blood. However much senators might have disregarded Morrissey's qualifications as a nod of senatorial courtesy to Kennedy, it was harder to overlook the discrepancy between his being in two places at one time, which prompted Senator Hugh Scott to cite *Alice's Adventures in Wonderland*, saying that the case had become "curiouser and curiouser." To discuss the new revelation, the Judiciary Committee met in executive session and questioned Morrissey again for another hour (after which the affable nominee emerged saying that he had "no hard feelings toward anyone"), and though only three copies of the transcript of that hearing existed, the *Globe* called them "the best-read documents in recent Senate history." Meanwhile, the FBI opened a new investigation into the residency issue; Attorney General Katzenbach met with Ted over lunch, presumably to convince him to withdraw the nomination; Tydings, who had once been appointed a U.S. attorney by John Kennedy and who was usually a reliable liberal ally of the Kennedys, delivered a scathing speech on the Senate floor—a speech he said he had been preparing to give long before the Morrissey nomination—in which he declared that "the easiest way to remove an unqualified judge is not to appoint him in the first place"; and Saltonstall, Massachusetts's senior senator, was even expressing second thoughts about his blue card, which soon turned into a withdrawal of his support, practically unheard of for one senator to do to another senator from his own state. Ted was scrambling, begging for his colleagues' support when he clearly was embarrassed by Morrissey himself. "Phil, do you think this guy is competent? Can you vote for him?" Ted said he asked Phil Hart, a senator he deeply respected, before the committee vote, revealing his own doubts. And Hart said he could vote for him in "all good conscience." Still, all the senators' reservations notwithstanding, the power of senatorial courtesy and the desire to help Ted Kennedy, whom most senators genuinely liked, were enough for the committee to recommend the nomination to the full Senate, 6 to 3, though it was an ominous sign that seven members declined to vote.

And still, despite all the opposition, the furious editorials and the *Boston Globe* investigation, the near-unanimous angry chorus of the legal establishment, and the pressure by Johnson's own Justice Department for Ted to withdraw the nomination—despite all that, Ted Kennedy persisted to try to get the votes to have the nomination confirmed on the Senate floor. Once again, as he had on the poll-tax amendment, he manned the phones, calling senators, trying to line up their votes, though for a less admirable cause. "One of the hardest sells recently seen in the Senate," *The Washington Post* said of Bobby and Ted's full-court press—Bobby trying to salvage his brother from defeat and even disgrace—and it quoted one Senate staffer who said that within forty-eight hours his office had been contacted by Bobby and Ted and two of Ted's staff members, arguing that a defeat could possibly jeopardize Ted's reelection chances and promising to help fundraise if their senator voted for Morrissey. Another Senate source told *The Boston Globe* that Ted was "collecting all his coupons [political debts] on this one, and he's writing quite a few new ones. Don't ask me why, but he is." He had even sent a letter to his fellow senators charging the ABA, wrongly, with having opposed Louis Brandeis's elevation to the Supreme Court, presumably on the grounds that he was a Jew. Meanwhile, Johnson also was instructing his aides to round up aye votes. " 'Work hard on this one,' " Johnson assistant Joseph Califano Jr. said the president told his staff. "And, with a cat-who-ate-the-canary smile on his lips, he added, 'Teddy's gonna get his ass beat on this one, and I don't want him to accuse me of not helping him, 'cause he ain't going to blame himself when he loses.' " Even Vice President Humphrey was out coaxing senators to vote. And Ted thought he had the votes. He thought that Dirksen had turned the nomination into a partisan squabble to help the Republicans in the midterm election the next year and that Democrats were rallying to him.

And there was some indication that Dirksen and the ABA *had* overplayed their hand, if only slightly. On October 18, six days after Morrissey first testified, Katzenbach wrote a letter to Judiciary chairman James Eastland with the results of the FBI probe into Morrissey's residencies and found that he had not, as Jenner had indicated, gone to Georgia for a few days, got his bar admission, and then returned to Massachusetts. In fact, Katzenbach reported, "There is no basis whatsoever to question either Judge Morrissey's credibility or his recollection of the events surrounding his studies in Georgia." And Morrissey's contention that he had studied law for several months, that the "diploma mill" actually had three faculty members, and that he had stayed in Georgia with the hope of practicing law were all verified, and that the FBI had several witnesses who testified as much. (Katzenbach, who had been pressing Ted against the nomination, had apparently done this to save face for Ted.) Ted said a "large number" of senators told him the report "cleared up any questions they had" and that they were now prepared to vote for him, and he challenged Jenner's attack on Morrissey—rightly, it turned out. But Dirksen pushed back, saying the report hadn't cleared up anything at all and that he had the votes to recommit the nomination to committee. And Dirksen wasn't prepared to leave the matter there. That same day, Dirksen talked with Johnson and told him he had more information—he didn't say what—but said he wasn't going to use it and instead would just make a "frontal assault." "This guy doesn't have what it takes," he told the president. And Johnson answered noncommittally that the decision was up to the Senate, not to Johnson, which was Johnson's way of letting Ted Kennedy dangle.

Nevertheless, the stakes of the fight, and the lengths to which Dirksen was prepared to go to win it, were suggested by the information he had hinted to Johnson—a "bombshell," Dirksen had told several reporters. When asked if he was withholding the bombshell, Dirksen replied cryptically, "I'm just a country lawyer, but when I prepare a case, I try to get everything." That bombshell was a 1961 clipping from an Italian newspaper, showing Ted and Morrissey during their trip to Italy when Ted was gunning for the Senate nomination. They were at lunch in Capri when a man approached Morrissey to ask a favor of Kennedy. Morrissey listened, then returned to the table and asked if Ted would meet the petitioner. The man told Ted that he had lost a son in Vietnam, and he wanted to go back to the United States, but he was having visa trouble. Could Ted help? Ted offered to be of assistance and took down his information, and the man then asked if he could have a picture with Ted, to which Ted assented. The day of his return to Washington, Ted was having dinner with Jack, who wanted to debrief Ted about the trip, when Bobby phoned and told Jack, "I just want you to know that your brother Teddy just had his picture taken with the biggest Mafioso figure in all of Italy in Capri." The man who allegedly had lost his son was Michael Spinella, a Mafia don, who had been deported. Once again Jack tut-tutted: "Can't we keep you out of trouble, Teddy?" But while the photo did emerge, Dirksen apparently was not the one who released it. Bobby, hearing about Dirksen's scheme, challenged him to make the charges on the Senate floor. (In any case, it was more a dud than a bombshell.) Dirksen then called Bobby that Wednesday to his office and told him, "I'm not interested in you or Teddy. I'm out to get Morrissey," and he pointed to a bronze statue of John Kennedy. "You see that bust on the mantel? That was one of the best friends I ever had."

And now it was down to the vote and down to who was the better head counter, Everett Dirksen or Ted Kennedy, though one surprise still remained. By this time, in a week of frantic activity since the hearing, even sympathetic senators were wondering why Ted was so invested in Frank Morrissey, why he had been risking so much of his political capital on him—and as the fight dragged on, the amount of that capital had kept rising. But it wasn't just the political capital that was rising. As the animus toward Morrissey rose, so did Ted's determination to defeat it. Ted was no political naïf, like Morrissey. Not anymore. He knew that he would lose even if he won. But his crusade for Morrissey went beyond paternal or fraternal loyalty to something very deep in Ted Kennedy—something that neither of his brothers felt, something that pitted his sharp political instincts against his even more acute human ones, something that the attacks on Morrissey aroused. Ted Kennedy could sympathize with Frank Morrissey—with the ridicule and humiliation and the jokes and the deprecations, the insults to his intelligence and to his education by the Harvard elites who had never had to struggle the way Frank Morrissey had, and though Ted admired those elites, even tried to emulate them, he was not blind to the condescension in them, because they had once trained that condescension on him. Frank Morrissey may have been negligible, may have been unqualified for the federal district bench, may have been nothing more than an agreeable fellow, but Ted Kennedy, who was called unqualified for the Senate when he ran, could sympathize. In fighting for Frank Morrissey, he was fighting for all those who had suffered the same indignities, including himself. He said as much. Frank Morrissey was a victim of class hauteur. So was Ted Kennedy. And as he headed to the Senate on that morning of October 21, accompanied by Gerard Doherty, Ted wasn't concerned with himself but with Morrissey. "Here's a guy who could out–Abraham Lincoln Abraham Lincoln," he told Doherty. "If someone could just sit at a typewriter and write the story. It's all there," meaning the story of a man who had come from nowhere and had nothing and only wanted to succeed against the odds. But "because he didn't go to Harvard, he got bombed," even though Ted seemed myopic to the fact that he was also getting bombed for not being of judicial caliber. Kennedy called it a "tragedy for the man." And Kennedy said as much when he rose to deliver his speech defending Morrissey on the Senate floor shortly after 11 A.M., in his blue suit, his desk once again piled high with books, and with Joan, Eunice, and Ethel watching in the gallery and Bobby grabbing a seat to be close to him. Gwirtzman had written the speech, but Gwirtzman had shown it to Adam Walinsky, a brilliant member of Bobby's staff, and Walinsky made a few additions, which Gwirtzman called "Adam as only Adam can do."

There was near silence when Ted rose, near stillness. He looked drained, observers said, fatigued. He attacked the ABA's inquisition that had questioned Morrissey's veracity. He said, "No one who knew Frank Morrissey could doubt that he was telling the truth." He said, "It is one thing to pass on a man's qualifications. This is entirely proper, and we welcome it in the Senate. It is another to attack by innuendo and accusation and insufficient evidence a man's character. We do not welcome that in the Senate." He said of the ABA's assault on Morrissey's legal education that perhaps they had not been satisfied "because he attended a local law school at night and not a national law school by day." And now, addressing the issue of Morrissey's Georgia juncture that had come to define the nomination, came Walinsky's additions: "Senators may nevertheless ask why did Francis Morrissey leave Massachusetts for Georgia in 1932? Simply stated, the answer is that he was young and he was poor—one of twelve children, his father a dockworker, the family living in a home without gas or electricity or heat in the bedrooms; their shoes held together with wooden pegs their father made . . ." And at this point, Ted, moved by Morrissey's plight, as he was often moved by the plight of outsiders, choked back tears, reached for a glass of water on the desk, and took a long drink. And as he tried to continue, his voice "quavered," in one report's description, and quavered again, until he was able to compose himself. When he recovered, he said, "And so we are asked to vote. After a careful assessment, I have determined that a majority of the members of the Senate are prepared to support Judge Morrissey's confirmation. If we took up the nomination this morning, the debate would be prolonged, but the nomination would be confirmed." But he said that some senators still had reservations given the controversy swirling around Morrissey. "I have been asked why, in view of the unfavorable publicity given this nomination, I would not, in my own interest, ask that it be withdrawn. Let me say simply that when a man has been unfairly attacked and unjustly accused, I cannot in good conscience desert him. And I should not." He said that a full and fair examination of the record would support his view.

And then, to the surprise of nearly everyone, he closed: "I therefore ask unanimous consent that the nomination of Francis Morrissey be re-committed to the Committee on the Judiciary" for further consideration. But there was no doubt there would be no further consideration. Morrissey's nomination was finally dead.

Virtually no one knew because Ted had had a last-minute change of heart—a reluctant change of heart. A few days earlier, Bobby, who had been working the phones, asked Charles Ferris, the general counsel of the Democratic Policy Committee, the party's Senate policy engine, and a close adviser to Mike Mansfield, how Ferris thought the Morrissey vote would go. Ferris told Ted he thought Morrissey might win by a vote or two, "but you're going to have to make an awful lot of good guys walk the plank, on a personal basis." Already reports were circulating that a dozen Democrats, not wanting to embarrass Ted but not wanting to embarrass themselves either, were going to be absent during the vote. Ferris also thought it was too late to withdraw. Bobby disagreed. "If it's the right thing to do, we can get him to withdraw his name in minutes."

But it wasn't really Morrissey's decision to make. It was Ted Kennedy's. Bobby was already growing angrier, primarily at Dirksen and his tactics, and more exasperated. He had spoken with his Senate and New York colleague, Jacob Javits, who was adamantly opposed to Morrissey, about re-committing the nomination to Judiciary rather than withdrawing it outright, as a face-saving gesture for both Morrissey and Ted, but Bobby had to sell the idea to his brother. (Bobby would "be the one to be the tough guy," Gwirtzman said, "and to take the heat.") So Bobby went to Ted's office with Gwirtzman and proposed Javits's solution. When Gwirtzman asked about their commitment to Morrissey, Bobby "looked at me with as icy a stare as I'd ever received from anybody, saying, 'I think we've fulfilled our commitment to Frank Morrissey.' " But it was not the commitment to Morrissey that Bobby cared about honoring. It was his own commitment to protect his little brother. Bobby convinced Ted that this was the best re-sult for everyone. Gwirtzman didn't think Ted would have ever done that to Morrissey on his own. He would have fought to the death. But when Ted walked into the Senate that morning, still lamenting to Doherty how Morrissey had been treated, he had made the decision. The previous night, he'd phoned Johnson at Bethesda Naval Hospital, where Johnson was recuperating from a gallbladder operation, and told him the news. Then he told Dirksen. Ted had counted the votes. He knew that Dirksen would hold the entire Republican caucus (he had ordered three senators back from home visits), and he knew that there would be those Democratic absentees (fourteen of them, as it turned out), and he thought he might be five or six votes short. "Faced finally with a choice between inglorious victory and unpalatable defeat," *Time* reported, "Ted Kennedy went all the way to the brink—and chose defeat."

To the brink. He had dragged the Senate into a fight that few of its members wanted. He had assailed both the legal and the political establishments and had especially run afoul of Dirksen. He had threatened to embarrass the institution into confirming a man who no one much thought was suitable for the federal bench. And he had humiliated himself in the bargain after working at gaining and succeeding at gaining such goodwill from his colleagues on the poll-tax and immigration bills. Pundits who only weeks ago were praising him predicted that he would lose standing. "Only by dropping the fight in the showdown Senate session Thursday did he cut his losses in strained relationships and political IOUs," opined *The Washington Post,* and "only the senator's reputation for political loyalty was enhanced." Meg Greenfield wrote in *The Reporter* that he seemed to have lost some of his confidence after the imbroglio.

And yet that morning, after his speech and after what *The New York Times* called his "surprise retreat," Ted Kennedy was far from a pariah among those Senate colleagues. Dirksen ambled up to him and shook his hand and said loudly in his basso that a "disconsolate spirit and anxiety had beset me" over the nomination, but "I want to salute the junior senator from Massachusetts. I think he has risen to every expectation of what the country desires in a senator fulfilling his oath, his duty, and his sense of responsibility." Mansfield said he had listened to Ted's speech with "a deep sense of regret" and that he agreed with Ted that the nomination would have been confirmed had it gone to a vote but that Ted had exercised "superior judgment" and that "had the vote been carried to its conclusion in the atmosphere which exists at the moment, the results might have been anything but beneficial." David Burke said that the defeat, "strange to say, left a good taste in the mouth of everyone in the United States Senate. He just got whacked. He took it right. He did the right thing for the things he had to do." The secretary of the Senate, Francis Valeo, recalling that Ted had entered the Senate to his colleagues' "mixed feelings, in part, that he was profiteering on his brother," thought the Morrissey affair may actually have increased his standing. "I was impressed greatly by the speech," Valeo said, "because it seemed it was not politically expedient. It showed an indication of character which I felt was not to be denigrated." *Time*'s postmortem was that Ted's campaign for Morrissey would be forgotten, "while his retreat from the brink of embarrassment will be warmly remembered as an act of high courage."

But if it had demonstrated a kind of courage—the courage of admitting one's failure—the Morrissey fiasco also demonstrated how Ted Kennedy's personal strengths—his sympathy for the underdog and his empathy for the weak, his loyalty, his doggedness, and his commitment to keep his word—could also become political weaknesses. The poll-tax fight, in which Ted deployed all those strengths, had shown Ted's new heightened sense of purpose; the Morrissey affair, a lowered one. That was a difference between Ted and Bobby. Bobby could be passionate for his causes and personally invested in them, but he would never have been caught between his sense of personal obligation and his political duties, his lower and higher senses of purpose, which is precisely why he jettisoned Morrissey, despite his father's entreaties. Ted often would be caught because he had a difficult time distinguishing between the two. For Ted, the personal often was the political, as it had been in both the poll-tax and the Morrissey battles. Bobby would never have fought for Morrissey. Ted would never not have.

EIGHT

A Dying Wind

TED KENNEDY HAD been catching the liberal wind in the two years since John Kennedy's death, catching it and riding it, but that fall of 1965 there were already harbingers that the wind was beginning to die, exhausted by another of Lyndon Johnson's missions. Later on the afternoon of the Francis Morrissey defeat, Ted Kennedy was off to Vietnam. It was a far-from-pleasant flight. The trip, a fact-finding mission, had been planned long before the Morrissey affair, with Ted scheduled to join now-representatives John Culver and John Tunney, two of his closest friends, and Senator Joseph Tydings in Saigon, after those three had first flown to the Philippines. But Tydings had not gone to the Philippines. Tydings, a former United States attorney in Maryland, who claimed to have fostered judicial reform in that state and who then took over the Improvements in Judicial Machinery Subcommittee of the Judiciary Committee, had first considered leaving on the trip to avoid having to vote against the Morrissey confirmation but then decided to stay in Washington to oppose it and delivered that blistering speech on the Senate floor. Ted Kennedy did not typically hold grudges—Bobby was the hater in the Kennedy family—but he held a grudge against Joe Tydings. Though Tydings later said that Bobby Kennedy was the more furious of the two Kennedys over his opposition to Morrissey, Ted was angry himself at what he considered Tydings's betrayal of their friendship. The two were, as Ted put it, "stuck together" on the plane to Asia, a near-thirty-hour flight, and then, once in Saigon, were assigned to be roommates for four days. "It was about as hard a jaw-biting as I've had," Ted would later say, and years afterward he would do something else he seldom did: He gloated over Tydings's defeat in the 1970 election.

Though he was now engaged in his first overseas mission on Senate business, Ted Kennedy was far less interested in foreign affairs than he was in domestic issues. Stuart Hughes's "peace campaign" during the 1962 Senate run notwithstanding, Vietnam hadn't really been on Ted's radar until a luncheon during a conference of the Inter-Parliamentary Union in Belgrade, Yugoslavia, on September 13, 1963, where he was seated next to Tran Le Xuan, known as Madame Nhu, the sister-in-law of South Vietnam's president, Ngo Dinh Diem, and a formidable power behind the scenes in the country. During that lunch, Madame Nhu lobbied Ted for ninety minutes on the rightness of a campaign by the Catholic Diem government against Buddhists. Eleven days later, Ted, in a speech to the Advertising Club of Boston, delivered what one of his biographers, Adam Clymer, said were his first remarks on Vietnam, emphasizing its strategic importance to the United States but also chastising the Diem government for its persecution of Buddhists. And then Vietnam fell off his radar again.

But Vietnam, though nearly nine thousand miles from Washington, had been on John Kennedy's radar almost from the moment he entered the White House, when his predecessor, Dwight Eisenhower, warned him about how Laos was being destabilized by a communist insurgency, which could threaten all of Indochina with a communist takeover—that, one after another, nations could topple like dominoes, including Laos's neighbor, Vietnam, which had been divided between a communist north and a non-communist south at a 1954 conference in Geneva after the French colonialists had left the country. This put intense pressure on Kennedy, not just because of the tenuous Cold War global situation but even more because of the tenuous political one domestically. Kennedy felt compelled to disprove a right-wing perception that Democrats were soft on communism and were unwilling to use American power to fight it. And that pressure only intensified after a summit in Vienna with Soviet premier Nikita Khrushchev, in which Kennedy himself admitted he was bested, and after the disastrous Bay of Pigs invasion of Cuba, in which a CIA-backed invasion force of Cuban exile commandos was easily defeated by the government forces of leader Fidel Castro. Kennedy told *The New York Times*'s James Reston that he would now be forced to increase the defense budget, which he did: by $6 billion in the first months of his presidency. But, as Kennedy biographer Richard Reeves wrote, this increase was not a "direct response to a real Soviet threat." It was instead "the result of runaway

American politics, exaggerated threats of communism, misunderstood intelligence, inflated campaign rhetoric, a few lies here and there, and his own determination never to be vulnerable to 'soft on communism' charges that Republicans regularly used to discredit Democrats." *Soft on communism.* That was the abiding terror of Democrats ever since the right-wing debate after World War II on "Who Lost China?"—a debate that helped propel red-baiting and communist witch-hunting. And that was the terror that still drove American foreign policy more than fifteen years later. "Too liberal to fight," the poet Robert Frost had said upon returning from a visit to Russia about how Russians were viewing the United States. The remark reportedly incensed Kennedy, but it also was the sort of thing, the terror, that motivated him.

And it was not just the fear of being regarded as insufficiently anticommunist that motivated John Kennedy. It was the fear of being regarded as insufficiently masculine, a particular sensitivity among the Kennedys as well as a driving force on the right, which had taunted Democratic presidential candidate Adlai Stevenson in the 1952 campaign as a homosexual. (He wasn't.) Kennedy adviser Arthur Schlesinger Jr. would say that John Kennedy had already proved his manhood in the Solomon Islands during the PT-109 incident, and Kennedy complained to editor James Wechsler of the *New York Post* during conservative saber-rattling over Berlin about "many of his countrymen who believe our national manhood can be affirmed only by some act of bloody bluster." But manhood was always at issue, the demonstration of toughness always a political imperative. This was the lesson that the National Security Council had drawn from the Cuban Missile Crisis: Toughness won. And this was the posture that was urged upon Jack Kennedy by the Cold War hawks among his own foreign policy advisers. Toughness wins. And this is how John Kennedy came to view Vietnam in those first two years of his presidency. In that same conversation with James Reston about pumping up the defense budget, he said, "Now we have a problem in making our power credible." And he said, "Vietnam is the place."

But as with so many things in John Kennedy's reckoning, this had less to do with conviction than with political calculation. Kennedy was no admirer of the military. During one of those summer conversations he had with Ted, he told him that someday he might be in the White House, and that if he was, he should never trust the military brass, who were all too eager to apply military solutions to political problems. And yet Kennedy often succumbed to the hawks as a way of protecting himself from the soft-on-communism charges. When it came to Vietnam, those hawks, the old staunchly anti-communist wing of the Democratic party that followed the lead of Harry Truman's secretary of State, Dean Acheson, were advising him to be aggressive, to face down the communists, to use military force in Vietnam. But there were others, also among his advisers, who believed in diplomatic and political solutions to Vietnam—namely, replacing the Diems—and who thought that the greatest threat Vietnam posed to America was not of encroaching communism but of encroaching American adventurism, which would commit the country to a long and ultimately futile slog. This wasn't only a tactical difference. It was a moral one. "Maybe we have two different liberalisms," Carl Oglesby, a founder of the Students for a Democratic Society and a onetime technical writer at a defense think tank, wrote, "one authentically humanist; the other not so human after all." Such was the intramural war within the Democratic foreign-policy establishment, and such were the sides between which John Kennedy was trapped—between so-called "hawks" and "doves." Neither position fully satisfied him. On the one hand, he complained of timorous liberals "who cannot bear the burden of a long twilight struggle." On the other, he criticized hard-liners who thought that anything short of war was appeasement.

So he vacillated. At the suggestion of his favorite general, the urbane Maxwell Taylor, whom he had dispatched to South Vietnam to assess the situation and then report back to him, he sent military "advisers" to Vietnam, ostensibly to assist the Diem government's own army in resisting communist forces, even though this was in direct violation of the Geneva Accords that had established North and South Vietnam. Defense Secretary Robert McNamara and the Joint Chiefs of Staff were proposing six combat divisions, or 600,000 troops, to "show that we mean business." But Kennedy resisted sending American combat forces. Despite that resistance, as time passed, the number of advisers continued to grow, ultimately reaching 16,000. All of this concerned critics of escalation. Senate majority leader Mike Mansfield, who had had extensive experience in Indochina as an envoy to China—Senator Joseph McCarthy labeled him "China Mike" when he first ran for the Senate—had warned as early as 1954 that any war in Vietnam would be a "nibbling war," nibbling away at mechanized forces, and that a nation's independence could be preserved only "if they have it in the first place and are willing to fight to keep it." Undersecretary of State George Ball predicted late in 1961 that Vietnam would be a losing proposition and that involvement there would eventually lead to 300,000 American troops. To which Kennedy said, "Well, George, you're supposed to be one of the smartest guys in town, but you're crazier than hell. That will never happen." By 1962, Mansfield was advising withdrawal of the American advisers and came to the White House to plead his case in person. But Kennedy responded, "If I tried to pull out completely now from Vietnam, we would have another Joe McCarthy red scare on our hands, but I can do it after I'm reelected. So we had better make damned sure that I am reelected." He told his friend, columnist Charles Bartlett, the same thing: "We don't have a prayer of staying in Vietnam . . . But I can't give up a piece of territory like that to the communists and then get the American people to reelect me." Political considerations won out.

Nevertheless, Ted would later say that at the time of John Kennedy's death, his brother was engineering a withdrawal from Vietnam and that he had sent Maxwell Taylor to do another review "obviously based upon his judgment that he needed a new direction and a different direction." And Ted said he had "the clearest feeling and sense that there wouldn't have been this dramatic escalation of the conflict" and that Jack was "beginning to understand that this was a conflict that ultimately wasn't going to be resolved militarily." Whether or not that was true, Lyndon Johnson entered the presidency bound by the same Cold War mentality and, more, by the same political restraints. "The terrible beast we have to fear is the right wing," he told George Ball. "If they ever get the idea that I am selling out Vietnam, they'll do horrible things to the country, and we'll be forced to escalate the war beyond anything you've ever thought about." And, barely six months into his presidency, he cited to his friend Senator Richard Russell, a stern Vietnam hawk, notwithstanding doubts about Indochina as a theater of war, the old liberal fear of seeming unmanned. "They'll forgive you for anything except being weak," he told Russell, quoting a maxim his friend A. W. Moursund had said the night before in a conversation with Johnson. Johnson wasn't going to seem weak, no matter how many troops it took.

At the time Ted visited Vietnam, in October 1965, the escalation had already begun, and Vietnam was becoming a national issue, a controversial issue, but Ted was not caught up in that controversy. He still subscribed to the so-called "domino theory" and still supported Johnson's efforts there. "I do not think the effect would be so quick or immediate," he told the Associated Press of the domino theory shortly before he left, "but I do believe that if we abandon our commitment to South Vietnam, it would lessen the ability of nations like Thailand, Malaysia, and the Philippines to stand up to the pressure of communist China." On the ABC News program *Issues and Answers*, he suggested it was a matter of loyalty: "If we are not going to fulfill our commitment there, our words will not be good in the other countries throughout the world."

But this wasn't just about commitments. Ted Kennedy was empathetic, and his interest in Vietnam had less to do with the political or military consequences of America's engagement there than with the human ones. During his convalescence from the plane accident, Ted had received his first subcommittee chairmanship: of the Subcommittee to Investigate Problems Connected with Refugees and Escapees. It was a minor committee, even more insignificant than the Immigration Subcommittee that James Eastland would hand to Ted during Johnson's immigration reform, and while Phil Hart had chaired it, the subcommittee had been basically moribund. But when Hart decided to take the chairmanship of the Antitrust Subcommittee and handed the Refugee Subcommittee to Ted, Ted was determined to reinvigorate it in the interests of further pursuing the "heightened sense of purpose" that had overtaken him in the hospital. He still didn't know exactly what he wanted to do with the subcommittee; he was soliciting experts to give him advice on possible initiatives. And from his hospital room, he had recruited George Abrams, a Harvard classmate and Harvard Law grad, telling him that he was "very anxious" to get back to the Senate and that he was eager to make his first foray into foreign affairs. The pay was derisory, $18,000, and Abrams was in private practice at the time of the offer, but he said he would take the job on two conditions: that it look into immigration, which was not technically within its purview, and that it investigate the treatment of Vietnam refugees, which is how Ted found himself suddenly involved in Vietnam.

And he was actively involved. He had always been a quick Senate study and had already become legislatively adept enough to realize how he could leverage his small, seemingly unimportant subcommittee into something with clout. As Abrams put it, "We used it as our foreign-policy vehicle," specifically on Vietnam. If Vietnam hadn't been of overriding interest to Ted Kennedy, neither was it a particular concern of Congress at the time, less from disinterest than from fear of the consequences of

criticizing American policy. "It was considered a very politically dangerous subject," Abrams said, and when the hearings were launched in July
1965—the summer of the Immigration Act—a young staff holdover
named Dale DeHaan was chiefly concerned about communist infiltration
into the refugee community. That focus quickly changed to the disruption
the war had created among the civilian population. Ted conducted the
hearings, thirteen of them, and among the witnesses he called into executive session were the ambassador to South Vietnam, Henry Cabot Lodge
Jr.; the secretary of State, Dean Rusk; and the assistant secretary of State,
and one of the architects of Johnson's Vietnam policy, William Bundy.
Ted didn't go into the hearings with any antagonism to Johnson's policy.
And he didn't conclude the hearings antagonistically either. But the hearings did open the first crack between Ted and the administration on Vietnam. Lodge was, Abrams said, "patronizing" (which is an attitude that
Ted always found degrading), and when Abrams directly challenged Rusk
and Bundy on their tallies of the number of refugees displaced in Vietnam, he found "absolute proof that they had two sets of numbers"—one
real and one for public consumption. As the number of displaced Vietnamese rose over the course of the year to one million, Ted was forced to
say, however reluctantly, that the Johnson administration had given little
or no thought to the refugees and had no refugee policy in place. It was,
Abrams said, a lesson for Ted. "He was learning how to move an administration, and how sometimes it's impossible to move an administration,"
because Johnson wasn't about to expend much money or time on those
refugees. And Ted was learning how to draw attention to an issue—
through hearings. Abrams said that after the hearings, Phil Hart stopped
by Ted's office to tell him how proud he was, and when Abrams had dinner
with Massachusetts representatives Tip O'Neill and Ed Boland, they both
pressed him for information about the refugees. Because of the hearings
and Ted's lobbying, the U.S. Agency for International Development
(USAID) created a new section to deal with refugees. Before the hearings,
no one had cared. Now they had started to.

And yet, regardless of the refugee situation, when Ted Kennedy went
to Vietnam in October 1965, with Culver, Tunney, and Tydings, he still
supported Johnson's general policy objectives in Vietnam as well as his
prosecution of the war, in part because the group had been briefed extensively by Bundy; by the recently departed ambassador to Vietnam, Maxwell Taylor; by longtime diplomat and undersecretary of State for political

affairs Averell Harriman; and by CIA officials, all of whom assured them that the war was going well. Ted's primary concern was still the refugee situation, and even on that issue, he held to the administration position that it was the North Vietnamese who were responsible for the displacement. "Robert [Kennedy] was politically more involved," Abrams said. "Ted was pragmatically involved. . . . [He was looking at] the immorality of what was happening to the Vietnamese people but not the bigger picture that Robert was looking at." And once he landed in Vietnam, everything was done to dissuade him from looking at either the larger political picture or the moral one. Immediately upon arrival, the group was outfitted in full military gear and then briefed by the military command, including General William Westmoreland himself, the top United States commander. "Congressmen and senators were immediately put into a cocoon by the military and not allowed to have contact with any dissident voices," Tunney recalled—a "movable cocoon"—and "we moved with helicopters and military transports." They met with generals Nguyen Cao Ky ("the General Patton of Vietnam," Taylor had called him), and Nguyen Van Thieu, who became head of the South Vietnamese government after the Diems were assassinated in a coup. They went to Laos and Cambodia to observe the situation there. And Ted said he later went to Singapore, where he conferred with Lee Kuan Yew, the prime minister, who believed devoutly in the domino theory and who invited him to visit captured communist insurgents. Yew said those insurgents would tell him that they wanted to stay in jail so that when the communist liberators came, after beating back the United States in Vietnam, those liberators would view the prisoners as allies and not as traitors. That is how tough the communist opposition was, and that is why they had to be beaten, Yew said.

But for all the rosy prophecies of American success in Vietnam, and for all the endorsements of the righteousness of the cause, and for all his professed belief in both, Ted was uneasy. In part, he was uneasy over Westmoreland's assessment that, despite the American B-52s pounding the North Vietnamese troops infiltrating South Vietnam—a pounding Westmoreland called a success—"this will last a long time." But what he found even more discouraging was what those military operations were doing to the people of Vietnam. It became "immediately apparent" to him, he later said, that there was an "incredible gulf between what was happening over there from governmental action and military action, and what was happening to the . . . civilian population." Tran Ngoc Linh, the Vietnamese minister of social welfare, said in a meeting with the delegation that for the cost of one B-52, he could finance a work relief program desperately needed by the refugees, but he also said that there was little interest in doing so. Both in Vietnam and in the United States, the primary focus of the mission was military, not humanitarian. As *New York Times* reporter Neil Sheehan would later write, Ted Kennedy, whose priority had always been people, was "the only political figure in Washington to take a consistent interest in the plight of the Vietnamese civilians."

And *still,* despite the human toll, Ted Kennedy returned to the United States voicing full support of the war, even visiting Massachusetts high schools to rally the students. "If we do not support freedom in the world, who will?" he asked a group of them. "All of us came back hawks," Tunney would say. And, like Ted in Massachusetts, Tunney was going around his congressional district giving glowing reports on Vietnam and cheering the war effort. But then something happened. Within weeks of their return, Tunney said, "Fissures began to show up in the edifice of propaganda that they had surrounded us with." For Tunney, the fissures first appeared after a phone call from Tydings, who asked if he had ever heard of Bernard Fall. Tunney hadn't, and Tydings explained that Fall was an Austrian-born French journalist—his parents had escaped to France after Hitler's annexation of Austria—who had covered Indochina since the days of the French colonization and who had a deep expertise in the area, not from the colonialists' point of view but from the indigenous population's. Tydings told him that he had talked with Fall upon their return, that Fall had a "very different take on this war than what we heard" in Vietnam, and that he thought Tunney should hear it. Tunney took Fall's number and called him as soon as he got back to Washington. He spent two or three sessions with Fall, long sessions, at which Fall asked what the officials had told Tunney and then described in great detail, painstaking detail, how wrong not only the American assessments of the war were but also how wrong the figures on which they based those assessments were. The Americans and their Vietnamese allies had cooked the figures. And Fall, who understood the Vietnamese from his years of intimate contact with them, told Tunney that this was not a civil war between communists and democrats, as the administration would have it. This was a revolutionary war against Western colonialism, only the Americans now had replaced the French oppressors. What the delegation had heard was spin. What the delegation had seen in the pristine new refugee camps were Potemkin villages, arranged expressly for them. And what Fall told Tunney was that this war would be long, it would be bloody, and it would be unwinnable.

Tunney thought Ted needed to hear this information. It is unclear—Ted gave different versions—whether he was briefed by Culver and Tunney on Fall's analysis, or whether Ted actually met with Fall himself, or both. But as he recounted it in one interview, he and Fall met over dinner at Fall's house, and Fall asked him his impressions of Vietnam. Ted told him, "I think it's going reasonably well. Inflation is getting under control." And immediately Fall stopped him. "Oh, inflation is getting under control?" Fall asked skeptically. "Well, where did you go?" And Ted said Hue. And Fall asked where in Hue. And Ted fished through his notes and told him. Then Fall went to his bookshelf and pulled out a volume, the U.S. Agency for International Development book on Vietnam, and he opened it to Hue and found the listing of the price of rice, which showed that the price had risen six hundred percent in the last seven months. "So you think they're pacifying that road?" Fall asked Ted. "Do you think they're getting through? Why do you think it's gone up six hundred percent?" And point by point, in the same way, Fall refuted nearly everything Ted had been told in Vietnam. And Ted said that "was the first sort of *whing* that went off in my mind about it." He began rethinking everything he had been told.

But Bernard Fall did more than refute the fabrications of Ted's American handlers in Vietnam. As he did with Tunney, he tried to get him to rethink the very nature of the war itself. The United States was dropping tons upon tons of bombs on people who were "running around in their diapers," Fall said affectionately. "And they're going to beat you," he warned. "They're going to beat you silly because you don't think they have a brain in their head." And in looking at the war this way, as a battle of massive mechanized forces against those individuals in "diapers," Ted was forced to begin to square his support of the war with his advocacy of those refugees. "When you watched the [air] strikes from twenty-five thousand feet," David Burke would say of the beginning of Ted's reeducation on the war, "you can bomb anything, and it doesn't bother you because you're just pushing buttons." But Ted wasn't oblivious to the effects of those bombings. Ted knew "what was going on below," knew that civilians were being killed, the very people whom he was dedicated to helping.* That had an emotional impact on Ted that all the briefings he had heard could not possibly have. *The Vietnamese people were dying.* Ted Kennedy had a visceral attachment to those people.

And there were other voices encouraging Ted to be skeptical of what he had been told. William vanden Heuvel, who had accompanied Ted to Europe the year before to raise money for the John F. Kennedy Library, stayed at Palm Beach with Ted over the New Year's weekend, and Ted told him how impressed he had been with the briefings he received there. But vanden Heuvel had been to Vietnam himself in the mid-fifties, had seen the French departure there, knew Diem, and still had friends in Vietnam, and he cautioned Ted not to believe the positive forecasts he heard. And all of these cautions, Ted said, "fit into the internal anxiety that I had," triggering memories of his experiences in North Africa, where he saw not the East–West Cold War dichotomies but the dichotomy that Fall had identified between a native population and colonialist occupiers. "I think that was the beginning of my transition," he would say, from a Vietnam hawk to a Vietnam dove.

But only the beginning—the very beginning. Ted was physically reckless but usually politically cautious, moving carefully to protect his political flanks and to make sure he wasn't making enemies. (Even his anti-poll-tax effort was popular within the Democratic caucus.) Before leaving for Vietnam, Ted, who was hoping to use the trip to draw attention to his entrance into the foreign-policy arena, had contracted with *Look* magazine to write a piece on his experience. After his session with Fall and the warnings of vanden Heuvel and his own internal anxiety, he was still loath to break with Johnson, and he was intending to have Abrams and Burke write a piece defending Johnson's Vietnam policy under his byline. But Abrams and Burke were both appalled and begged Tunney, who was swiftly moving away from his pro-war position, to come to the house and talk Ted out of it. "It was a very dramatic thing," Abrams recalled. The article was due the next day, and Tunney had arrived late at night. Tunney agreed with them that Ted could not write in defense of the war. "It would be a disaster," he told Abrams, presumably both for Vietnam and for Ted. And Tunney convinced Ted to back away. Now the issue

---

*Fall himself would be one of those casualties, when he stepped on a land mine near Hue while accompanying a Marine patrol in 1967.

was what the article *could* address. Abrams and Burke said it could be about the Vietnamese refugee problem, which was Ted's real concern anyway. So that night, Abrams and Burke debriefed Tunney and Ted on the refugee situation, and then the two aides wrote a story about it, knowing full well that *Look* would be less than happy about their new approach.

Ted—or, rather, Abrams and Burke—wrote of two wars in Vietnam: one against the Vietcong, and a second, which was a "struggle for the hearts and minds of the Vietnamese people themselves. . . . It is a war for the hopes and aspirations of the people that must be escalated in Vietnam." They wrote of the 600,000 refugees in June 1965, 500,000 more than the government had estimated, and they wrote of the lack of a program to help them. And they wrote of how, in just six months—the article was published in February 1966—the number had soared to one million. "While in Vietnam," they wrote for Ted, "I saw for myself the indifference of the Saigon government to the plight of their own." And they wrote of the "sham" the government had staged for his arrival—the promised construction of camps, the distribution of blankets, the cheers led by government officials, the newly painted buildings, and the freshly cleared roads. And Ted called for a new American humanitarian program to aid refugees; for a democratic process to be established in the refugee camps; for the recruitment of experts in refugee affairs from other countries; for the appointment of a refugee official who would report directly to the ambassador and the president; and for a volunteer, nonmilitary international force to provide assistance to those in distress. The article did not indict American policy in Vietnam. Ted was not ready to do that, even though, by one account, he was telling friends privately that he worried the Vietnam hawks might escalate the war into a nuclear confrontation with China. And when Ted did consider whether to speak out on the war after he returned from Vietnam, National Security Adviser McGeorge Bundy wrote Johnson reassuringly, after speaking with Ted, that he got the "impression that he was not likely to say anything very tough," and that he had been talked out of making a speech calling for prolonging the bombing pause. But, for all his caution, Ted's article did indict the government for its lack of concern about those most deeply affected by the war.

And that was a beginning too.

II

Bobby Kennedy was not cautious like his younger brother, at least not when it came to Lyndon Johnson. Though Bobby was hamstrung in his opposition to the war by one of the same emotions as Ted—to disavow the war and its underpinnings would be to disavow John Kennedy, who had promoted American involvement—he had less compunction now that the war was Lyndon Johnson's. After two skirmishes between several North Vietnamese gunboats and the American destroyers *Maddox* and *Turner Joy*, which were patrolling the Gulf of Tonkin just off the North Vietnamese coast—skirmishes that the Americans seemed to invite— Johnson asked Congress for a resolution authorizing him to "take all necessary measures" to repel further attacks and "prevent further aggression." It passed the Senate with only two dissenting votes. (Ted was convalescing at the time, but he would certainly have voted with Johnson, and during a telephone call he congratulated the president for his success in getting it passed.) Six months later, acting under the resolution, Johnson introduced combat troops into Vietnam. By the end of 1965, when Ted went to Vietnam, the number of American forces had escalated far beyond 16,000 advisers to 189,000 ground troops. Now Bobby could pounce.

But even then, the pounce was less than an attack. On February 19, 1966, when bombing was resumed after a brief Christmas lull, Bobby called for negotiations with the communist Vietcong and for a coalition government of the sort that John Kennedy had agreed to in Laos. Vice President Humphrey immediately labeled the proposal "putting a fox in a chicken coop." (The *Chicago Tribune* called Bobby "Ho Chi Kennedy," after the North Vietnamese leader, Ho Chi Minh.) But between the choice of a Kennedy supporting a Kennedy or a Kennedy supporting Johnson, Ted, however cautious, naturally chose a Kennedy, and on *Meet the Press* three weeks later he echoed Bobby's sentiment that there must be talks between the South Vietnamese government and the Vietcong. And to Humphrey's charge, Ted said that giving communists control of the post office would not create the same opportunity for subversion as handing them the interior department.

But Ted was not as ready to wade into the Vietnam fray as Bobby was. Few were, fearing both the wrath of Lyndon Johnson and the brickbats of the Republicans, most of whom were even more aggressive on Vietnam than the president and who were already unsheathing, yet again, the soft-on-communism sword. So Ted continued to lobby for refugees with what one reporter called "quiet consultations" with Secretary of State Rusk, UN ambassador Arthur Goldberg, and others in the administration. He didn't make waves. Instead, he spent most of 1966 charting his own domestic legislative territory, building his reputation among his fellow senators, and gaining respect. Ted was not yet a grand strategist. He didn't think in terms of radical departures and bold new programs. He was a people person, a pragmatist with an idealistic streak, looking for what would be effective to help individuals in need, and he framed his politics that way too. After his anti-poll-tax measure, which made him a player in the civil rights movement, he waded more deeply into civil rights and accepted an invitation from the Reverend Martin Luther King Jr. to attend the Southern Christian Leadership Conference convention in Jackson, Mississippi. What happened at the convention illustrated that the Civil Rights Act and the Voting Rights Act, whatever good they did, had very little effect on racial attitudes. Demonstrators outside the hall threw nails under the tires of Ted's car, and he had to be hustled out through the back door. But it wasn't just the South where racial animosity was boiling. Over dinner, King told Ted that he had been working on a housing program in Illinois and had marched through the Chicago suburb of Cicero. King said that he had felt hatred in the South, deep hatred, but that he had never before felt the intensity of hatred he experienced walking the streets of Cicero. And he said that while it was easy to castigate the racism of the South, it was going to be far more difficult to address the racism of the North. Ted was on notice.

And in his ongoing search for a heightened sense of purpose to build himself up in the Senate, Ted had caught the wind of another liberal crusade, a big crusade: the crusade for improved health care. Part of this was the result of his own convalescence and the gratitude he felt to the medical profession after doctors saved his life. And, having survived his own near-death experience, Ted became curious about how others survived their medical calamities. While in the hospital, he had a conversation with Gerard Doherty, who, years earlier as a college student, had to leave Harvard and spend two years in a tuberculosis sanitarium. How did his family survive? Ted wanted to know. Doherty told him that his father was a "string saver, and he saved a lot of string." And Ted asked him about a neighbor of Doherty's who had had health problems. Doherty felt that these conversations had sparked Ted's curiosity about the health-care difficulties the poor faced.

Ted wasn't thinking at the time of how to translate his sympathies into policy. But in January 1965, just as he was returning to the Senate from his accident, two physicians from Tufts University, Jack Geiger and Count Gibson Jr., submitted a proposal to the new Office of Economic Opportunity, one of Lyndon Johnson's Great Society anti-poverty agencies, to establish community health centers geared toward the poor. In December 1965, they opened a pilot project funded by the OEO in a renovated two-floor office of a housing project at Columbia Point in Boston. The following August, on a sweltering day, Ted, with his growing interest in health care, visited the Columbia Point Health Center, as it was named, and he was intrigued. He spent three to four hours there, observing, questioning the patients and staff, even going over Geiger's grant proposal. And Geiger could see that Ted was "very taken." As Ted later recalled, "I saw mothers in rocking chairs, tending their children in a warm and welcoming setting. They told me this was the first time they could get basic care without spending hours on public transportation and in hospital waiting rooms."

And that was another beginning. Geiger said that Ted called him soon after the visit, possibly even that night, and the two of them, while on the phone and then over a dinner with Gibson as well, worked through a proposal for legislation setting up a pilot program for community health centers, beginning with the one in Columbia Point, and another in Mount Bayou, Mississippi, which Ted had read about and then visited. And now Ted Kennedy was hooked, seeing another way to help people in distress. Yet, despite the momentum of the Great Society, it wasn't an easy sell. At the markup session for the bill in the Senate Labor and Welfare Committee, there was resistance from the Southern Democrats and from the Republicans, recalled Dun Gifford, Ted's legislative assistant. Both groups were opposed to the project, so that the committee was split nearly fifty–fifty. "The Republicans were scared of the poverty program because they knew it had a political side to it, not overtly, but poor people were coming together and feeling their power," Gifford said, and Republicans questioned whether these health centers might become political centers. And because Bobby also sat on the committee, and because Bobby was increasingly engaged in and identified with efforts to empower the disempowered, this led to an "intense" debate over farmworkers and their unionization and the poor in the Mississippi Delta and other issues far afield from community health, but Bobby held his ground, Gifford said. He fired back at the Southerners and their conservative Republican allies that the poor needed all kinds of help, including health centers, and that he would fight to help them. "Hard and pushy" was how Gifford described him, daring the committee to oppose a bill with such an obvious moral justification. But, as if they had been working in tandem, Ted took a softer tack, as he usually did, the good cop to Bobby's bad cop, "negotiating and teasing and saying, 'Let's do it this way. Let's do it that way,'" defusing the tension. And Gifford said it was both of them—Bobby flaring with moral outrage and Ted pacifying with his collegiality, though he was no less morally motivated than his brother—that got the bill out of the committee. "They were sure the stars of that long, tense morning."

Ted now was fully engaged, committed to providing health care for the poor. But there was yet one more hurdle. The bill, which Ted had attached as an amendment to another health bill, had to go to conference to reconcile the Senate and House versions. The chairman of the House Committee on Education and Labor, and the chairman of the conference, was Representative Adam Clayton Powell Jr., a bon vivant who had represented Harlem since 1945. As evening approached and Powell was eager to end the meeting, he asked Ted what his amendment entailed, and Ted explained it was to provide funding for community health centers. "Well, how much money is in there now?" Powell wanted to know. Ted answered that he was asking for $35 million, enough to fund three centers. "Write in the legislation to put one in my district, and you can put the other two wherever you want," Powell said, and then he ended the conference. "That was it. That was the start. That's how it got done," Ted would say. And now he was a player in the health-care arena.

Ted Kennedy had been moving—on immigration, on civil rights, and now on health care—to build his reputation and his importance. Since his hospitalization, he had become a liberal stalwart, carried along by the wind of the Great Society. But Johnson's foreign adventure in Vietnam had by 1966 already begun to lessen the wind. When it came to Vietnam, Ted continued to hew closely to refugee issues rather than making any frontal assault on the Johnson policy, as Bobby was increasingly doing, though this didn't indicate any split between the brothers. Bobby "knew very well what I was doing," Ted would say, "and he supported me." Yet Ted was growing impatient himself, defending Johnson by, as he would later say, "lessening degrees" that spring and into the summer of 1966. At four-thirty on June 29, the president convened a meeting at the White House of thirty-five congressmen and five senators, including Ted, at which Secretary of Defense McNamara gave another glowing assessment of American progress in the war. But the object of the meeting wasn't information. The object was to quash growing congressional criticism of the war, and Johnson went around the table asking for comments while he sat sipping a Coke. Most of the participants told Johnson exactly what he wanted to hear: either that the bombing was working or that it should be intensified. But when Johnson got to Ted, he encountered "the first note of discord of the evening": Ted called for a halt in the bombing and greater diplomatic efforts for peace. Johnson immediately dismissed Ted's suggestion, insisting that bombing was the only way to bring the North Vietnamese to the bargaining table. And the meeting ended with Johnson discoursing on why he couldn't find a better, incorruptible prime minister for Vietnam. He told the story of how the good people of Polk, Texas, had asked him to find an upstanding mayor to replace their drunken, gambling one, and Johnson said he had recruited a seemingly incorruptible young man, only to have him go down the same wayward path as his predecessor. "If I can't keep a good mayor in Polk, Texas," he told the congressmen, "how the hell do you think I'm going to keep a prime minister in Saigon?"

Ted called that White House meeting his "break" with Johnson, but it was not a break, not even close to a break. Privately, he had all but broken with Johnson by late 1966, and George Abrams recalled a conversation with him—an "extraordinary conversation," he called it—when the two of them were driving back to Ted's house after he had delivered a speech on the Senate floor. Abrams mentioned an anti-war statement by Bobby and then remarked how "the bulk of the political people" kept making the case for staying in Vietnam. And Ted parried, "You know, George, I've listened to that, I've listened to it, and, and, I've listened to it. I am convinced now that the Vietnam [war] is a disaster, that we can't win there, and we've got to get out. We've got to do everything we can to end our involvement." And Abrams said he was "shocked" because, after all the hearings and the briefings and the meetings, that was the first time he had heard Ted talk that "definitively and precisely."

But Ted was still not talking that way publicly. At an appearance at the University of Wisconsin in October in support of the Democratic candidate for governor, Patrick Lucey, he was heckled by anti-war protesters for opposing a unilateral withdrawal, then won a standing ovation when he invited one of those hecklers to the stage and let him air his grievances for seven and a half minutes. At least that is what the *Los Angeles Times* reported. Ted viewed it differently. What he saw in that arena were sheets with skeletons drawn on them to signify the people lost in Vietnam—those Vietnamese civilians for whom Ted was fighting—and he recalled that after yielding the stage to the heckler, he retook it and tried to make a case for doing whatever was necessary to get to the bargaining table, but the crowd grew restless and he had to be escorted out. And on the same Midwestern swing, campaigning for one of the great Senate liberals, Paul Douglas of Illinois, who was also still supporting the war, Ted saw the anger in those protesting against Douglas and against the war, and it moved him. But *still* Ted Kennedy would not denounce the war or Lyndon Johnson publicly. Dun Gifford said Ted told him that while he opposed the war "totally," he was reluctant to say so, because public support was still running high and he didn't want to undermine Bobby's future presidential chances, even though Bobby himself was bolder in his statements on Vietnam than Ted was.

But it may not have been only Bobby's presidential fortunes that concerned Ted; it may have been his own. Almost from the moment Bobby entered the Senate, with his obvious presidential ambitions, Ted was being favorably compared to him by his Senate colleagues. Asked how Bobby was doing in the Senate, a longtime member of the chamber told John Herbers of *The New York Times*, "I'll tell you who I like. I like Teddy." Ted, Herbers wrote of the affection colleagues felt for him over Bobby, "spends more time in the Senate, works harder on legislation, wears his hair shorter, and shows more respect for the elders in the institution." But it wasn't just that his fellow senators saw him as a better Senate man than Bobby, which he clearly was. It was that they saw him as a better potential president. Robert Dove, who began working in the Senate parliamentarian's office in 1966, said that when he arrived, Ted was "seen as the future, even more so than Robert." And that attitude was beginning to seep beyond the Senate as well. "The Next President Kennedy?" columnist Drew Pearson asked as early as the week after the 1964 election, noting, "It is becoming increasingly obvious that Ted, more than Bob, has inherited the late President Kennedy's political style. Ted has the same charm and wit. Bob has a tendency to be grimmer and less gregarious." And at the annual Democratic steer roast in Euclid Beach Park, outside Cleveland, where Ted, as the featured speaker, drew a crowd of 75,000, Senator Stephen Young introduced him as a "future president of the United States."

But while Ted may have been protecting his own future presidential ambitions by deemphasizing Vietnam and currying favor with Johnson, the 1966 midterm elections proved disastrous for the president and the Democrats. They lost forty-seven House seats, more than they had gained in the 1964 landslide, and three seats in the Senate, including Paul Douglas's. Republicans also gained eight governorships, including that of California, where the former actor Ronald Reagan took the State House. Though the Democrats retained control of both houses of Congress, the great juggernaut of the 89th Congress, the most productive Congress in history, the Congress of the Immigration and Nationality Act, the Civil Rights Act, the Voting Rights Act, Medicare, and a dozen other pieces of landmark legislation, the Congress that had redefined America and that had promoted an unprecedented political morality, was gone, and with it much of the energy of the Great Society. How much Vietnam figured into the midterm loss is impossible to say, though it certainly didn't help the Democrats. Some called the election a referendum on Lyndon Johnson's moral crusade—a referendum that seemed to amount to a repudiation of government expansion and intrusion. But a Gallup poll found that 36 percent of Americans believed the government was exercising the right degree of power, and another 31 percent thought it should exercise even more. Other pundits said that it wasn't government expansion that prompted the Republican victory so much as it was government assistance to black Americans, and those pundits pointed to what they called a "white backlash" against civil rights and anti-poverty legislation. (In fact, Republicans had made gains among black voters.) Johnson dismissed that interpretation. He did worry, however, that the Republican victories might imperil his Great Society, as they almost certainly would. It wasn't Republicans, though, that posed the greatest threat to the Great Society; it was the Vietnam War. However much Johnson may have tried to hide the war's cost—and that cost ran to $5 billion in 1966—the gradual collapse of his social agenda told the story. The public still supported the war. In May 1966, 48 percent opposed withdrawal, while only 35 percent favored it. In January 1967, only 32 percent thought entering the war was a mistake. But the war was already diverting the funds needed for the Great Society and was already eroding the confidence and sense of purpose that both John Kennedy and Lyndon Johnson had engendered. A sense of disequilibrium seemed to be affecting the country. It was as if the moral crusades for the poor and the marginalized to which Johnson had summoned Americans and on which he had acted, and the more dubious moral crusade to save Vietnam from communism, had exhausted the nation.

The liberal hour, America's great moral moment, was ticking down.

Ted Kennedy had not surrendered to that exhaustion. Given the continuing public support for the war, even as it was sapping domestic programs, most politicians were reluctant to oppose it openly, instead griping about it privately as Ted did, which was a form of cowardice from a man who seldom displayed it. Ted's tack after the midterms was avoidance. He would not take on Vietnam. Rather, as he had done with civil rights and the community health centers, he focused his attention on domestic matters, continuing to build his portfolio on big issues in his quest to become an important senator. Among the issues Paul Douglas had championed was one man, one vote, which addressed the matter of disparities in the sizes of congressional districts. The way congressional districts were drawn—by state legislatures, which meant by the politicians in those legislatures—the voters in more populous districts effectively had their votes diluted, those in less populous ones strengthened. In 1946, in *Colegrove v. Green,* the Supreme Court had ruled that state legislatures had the authority to devise whatever districts they liked, inequality of district population notwithstanding, because this was a political matter to be resolved through the political process, not the judicial one. But in 1962, in *Baker v. Carr,* the court overturned *Colegrove* and ruled that claims against disproportionately sized districts were, indeed, subject to judicial review, under the equal-protection clause of the Fourteenth Amendment, rather than left to the political process, as the two dissenters in the case argued. (Chief Justice Earl Warren would call it the most important decision rendered by his Warren Court.) Two years later, in *Wesberry v. Sanders,* the court applied its review to congressional districts, ruling that those districts must have roughly equal numbers of constituents.

The ruling was straightforward. The implementation was not. Because the court had not determined just how great a variance in districts would be constitutionally permissible or when the redistricting had to take place, Congress was forced to take up those issues. And when it did, the constitutional decision took on a political cast. The House, whose members now fretted that they might have to run in newly drawn districts or even at-

large while the mechanics of the decision were worked out, voted to remove the judicial review on apportionment from the federal courts.
Liberals argued that there should be no more than a 10 percent variance.
Southerners and conservative Republicans argued for a 35 percent variance, and among the most vehement of those was Minority Leader Dirksen, who feared that in his own state of Illinois, Chicago would overwhelm
less-populated rural areas in representation—Dirksen himself had come
from one of those areas. Dirksen was so lathered by the issue that he had
even submitted a constitutional amendment to blunt *Baker v. Carr.* Ted
had opposed Dirksen then, when the minority leader had sought to undermine the decision. (Some believed it was Ted's opposition, not his poll-
tax fight, that fired Dirksen's ferocity on the Morrissey nomination.) "Like
an aging wolf standing off a challenge to his leadership of the pack" was
how *The Wall Street Journal* described Dirksen on the floor at that time,
"the survivor of a thousand Senate battles faced his tormentors—
evidently relishing the exchange, but sadly aware he was absorbing more
punishment than he inflicted."

But that was in 1965, when the matter first reached the floor and before courts had begun ordering redistricting in compliance with *Wesberry.*
Now, two years later, House Judiciary Committee chairman Emanuel Celler, one of the sponsors of the Immigration Act, struck a compromise,
permitting a 30 percent disparity between districts—a disparity that
would gradually scale down to 10 percent by 1972—and steered it to passage in the House. But this didn't satisfy those who wanted prompter and
more equitable action. Paul Douglas had led that effort, with the support
of a group from Judiciary that included Ted. But Douglas's election defeat
had left the one-man, one-vote side without a leader in the Senate. It
wasn't hard to see why Ted got involved, beyond the fact that he was looking to expand his portfolio and keep Vietnam at bay. He had fought vigorously for black voting rights in the previous session, and one man, one
vote was also a civil rights issue. Disproportionately populated electoral
districts and "gerrymandering"—the creation of districts, often oddly
shaped, to favor one party or another—had typically reduced the power
of black voters, either by concentrating them all in one district to reduce
their representation or by scattering them over districts so that they could
not gain a majority in any one of them. This was unfair. And that may
have been the bigger motivation. Ted Kennedy, the man who felt he had
often been treated unfairly himself, was committed to fighting unfairness,

as both a personal matter and a political one. (He had even refused to succumb to Irish pressure on the Immigration and Nationality Act, because
what his Irish constituents wanted was, he felt, unfair.) The Voting Rights
Act had allowed black Americans to vote. Equalized, compact districts
would allow their votes to matter.

But if there were reasons why Ted Kennedy involved himself in an
issue that pitted him against some of the most powerful men in Congress,
it isn't clear exactly how Ted became the point man in the Senate now. By
one account, Representative John Conyers, a young black congressman
from Detroit, presumably thinking of Ted's anti-poll-tax amendment,
asked Ted to carry the fight in the Senate against the Celler bill. (Conyers
had been a beneficiary of redistricting when Michigan added a second
black-majority congressional district in Detroit.) Ted himself said it was
Bobby who encouraged him to take the issue on, since Ted sat on Judiciary, and it was Bobby who brought him together with boyish Republican
Tennessee senator Howard Baker Jr., who also wanted to fight the unfairness of unequally drawn districts. *Baker v. Carr,* the case that established
judicial review over apportionment, was brought by disgruntled Tennes-
seans (Howard Baker was not the Baker in the case), who complained that
the state had not had its districts redrawn since 1901, despite a law requiring them to be redrawn every ten years after the census. In Tennessee, this
had led to significant disparities in the population of districts, and Howard Baker had campaigned on the issue of one man, one vote, though
Baker now had his own ulterior motive, and it had nothing to do with increasing black representation. He felt that with demographic shifts to the
Southwest and with the Republicans' new political muscle there and in
the South, one man, one vote would eventually increase Republican representation in the House. (On the other side, Southerners felt it would increase black representation too, especially in the North.) Baker had
known Bobby since serving as a volunteer counsel on the McCarthy Senate Subcommittee on Investigations, where Bobby had been minority
counsel. Baker, too, said that Bobby had arranged for him and Ted to work
together, but Baker also said that Conyers had been pressuring Ted's Judiciary aide, a Harvard Law grad named Jim Flug, to take action, and that
Flug had called Baker's aide, Lamar Alexander, and in this roundabout
way, the partnership was struck. But there was one additional fillip to the
collaboration: Howard Baker was Everett Dirksen's son-in-law.

And so, once again, young Ted Kennedy found himself in a pitched battle against the Senate bulls and the minority leader. Celler had expected the Senate Judiciary Committee to accept his bill, which had passed the House 289 to 63, as a courtesy, which it usually did with House bills on which disagreements with the Senate seemed to be slight. But he was wrong. The committee had retained the provision postponing implementation until 1972, but it had not included Celler's scaling down to 10 percent. And it retained another controversial provision, which permitted the states themselves to determine whether their districts were sufficiently "compact"—compactness being a way to avoid gerrymandering. This would have stripped that power from the federal courts and left the states to their own devices. The committee also made one significant addition: Instead of keeping Celler's 30 percent variance, Eastland convened an ad hoc subcommittee headed by Sam Ervin, which upped the variance to 35 percent and then, the very next day, sent the amended bill on to the full committee. On May 23, Ted, upset with the new, larger variance, the postponement of full implementation, and the state determination of compactness, offered his 10 percent variance plan in committee, effective immediately. Eastland wouldn't even hold hearings on it, and it failed, 10 to 5.

But Ted Kennedy had gained confidence in nearly five years in the Senate and in his crusades for immigration reform and an anti-poll-tax amendment, and now he did what he had done with that poll-tax amendment when Mansfield, Dirksen, and Johnson had all been in opposition. On May 25, he offered his one-man, one-vote amendment on the Senate floor, bypassing the Judiciary Committee on which he himself sat, which was an unusual tactic. (The committee reported out bills, but those bills could be amended by anyone.) He knew passage would be difficult. He was tampering with the very basis of electoral politics: the size and the determination of the election district. And while he knew that district size would have no effect on elections to the Senate, those Senate bulls were intent on carrying water for their House brethren, who *would* be affected. Ted's own tally sheet had question marks beside the names of thirty senators whose votes he could not predict. A "doomed crusade," *Time* called it. Knowing how fierce Southern opposition would be, he prepared for the debate just as assiduously as he had prepared for the anti-poll-tax debate two years earlier. Flug told biographer Burton Hersh that he spent several nights at Ted's house rehearsing questions and answers. "He was tremendously well prepared," Flug said. "Probably more than we [meaning the staff] were. Probably more than anybody else in the Senate." But Ted couldn't choose the timing of his presentation. To make it more difficult for the opponents, the committee—over Ted's objections—sent the bill to the floor in the middle of the Arab–Israeli War, when the chamber's attention was clearly diverted.

And now, on the Senate floor, Ted Kennedy took on the opposition, especially the foxy Sam Ervin, who had inserted the 35 percent variance in committee and then defended it. But this time, Ted was not alone. He was joined by Howard Baker and by Bobby, to help establish a legislative history for the bill that could later be used to defend it in court, and both warned that the House bill—the one that Judiciary had amended—would likely be ruled unconstitutional by the Supreme Court because the variances would be too large and because it gave states the right to construct the districts without review. But Ted didn't only rely on the floor debate to press his point. As he had with the anti-poll-tax amendment, he organized a lobbying effort with interest groups, or, as he later put it, he worked the phones, while Baker worked the press. And this time, there was a difference from the anti-poll-tax battle—a big difference. The aging wolf, Dirksen, didn't win. Ted's amendment carried, 44 to 39, and the entire bill passed, 57 to 22. (The low vote totals may have been a testament to how many senators didn't want to go on record either way, for fear of alienating their House party colleagues or alienating their constituents.) And now it was sent to conference, where the House and Senate bills were to be reconciled.

But Ted was only one of those six conferees. After three months of wrangling—wrangling that indicated just how resistant Southerners were to redistricting—the other five conferees, including Ervin and Dirksen, voted against Ted's amended version, the Senate's version, of the bill and opted for the House version instead, but without any guidelines on variance and without any anti-gerrymandering provision. All it retained was the five-year moratorium on implementation, which made the bill an obvious attempt to obstruct the courts from proceeding. Ted was enraged. If it was uncustomary for senators to vote against their chamber's own bill, what Ted did next was also uncustomary—a rare violation, for him, of Senate tradition. He declared war on the conference-committee report. When the conference report came back to the Senate that November, Ted argued on the floor that it would be better to reject the bill and leave the issue for the courts to resolve than to pass a bill that was, he stormed, "unconstitutional, unconscionable, unclear, unworkable, and unresponsive." And just as it was unlikely for senators to opt for a House bill over their own, and as it was unlikely for a senator to challenge the conference report, it was unlikely for the Senate to reject that report—their own report. Ted was taking another big risk. But when the bill came to a vote, Ted Kennedy scored another victory, a remarkable victory, a "notable personal triumph," as *Time* called it. The Senate voted against the conference report overwhelmingly, 55 to 22, which meant that the Senate had endorsed Ted's view that disproportionate districts and gerrymandering must stop because they were unfair. Ted Kennedy had taken on the bulls, had taken on Everett Dirksen (Dirksen was not on the floor that day), and Ted Kennedy had beaten them. (So had Howard Baker, who had beaten his own father-in-law.) "By blocking H.R. 2508," Jim Flug later said, "he kept the legislation off the court's back, let them [the justices] continue modernizing the political units, got them into the gerrymandering field. We think it worked out nicely." And yet, somehow, Ted Kennedy in victory did not make enemies but, rather, as he did during the anti-poll-tax fight or the fight for Francis X. Morrissey, managed to gain respect. "He isn't sneaky," one of those who opposed him said afterward. "He isn't a wise guy." And David Broder of *The Washington Post* paid him a high compliment that suggested the lowest expectations were continuing to be expunged and Ted's rebuilding process was successful: "While it is impossible for any Kennedy to be overlooked, this one has surely been underestimated."

He wouldn't be underestimated again.

III

Whatever Ted Kennedy was accomplishing domestically, Vietnam had come to overshadow everything—a dark, foreboding national cloud. "The center of our concerns," Johnson had called it in his 1966 State of the Union address, just a year after introducing the Great Society, when social justice was the center of the nation's concerns. Vietnam not only overshadowed everything, it permeated everything. It had become both the text and the subtext of American politics, and, though it had been launched as a moral defense against communism, to many it signified a political immorality that canceled the Great Society's short-lived political morality. Throughout 1966, Americans had continued to support the war effort and to support Johnson, and even the political opposition was tepid. But in 1967, the national mood began to change. By the end of that year, there were nearly 500,000 American troops in Vietnam—George Ball hadn't been crazy—and 11,000 military casualties, nearly double the number of the preceding year, and there were continuing scenes of death and destruction on the nightly news broadcasts. Within Vietnam, there was political instability, protests, and violent government crackdowns against the Buddhists, some of whom had begun immolating themselves. In America, there were protests too—tens of thousands marching against the war in April and a hundred thousand again in October. That same month, Gallup polls found that only 42 percent of Americans thought that the country's involvement in Vietnam was not a mistake; by year's end only 39 percent approved of Johnson's prosecution of the war. That same month, 44 percent of Americans favored withdrawal, 26 percent a negotiated peace, and only 21 percent military victory. But polls also suggested the confusion Americans felt. While opposition to the war grew, so did support for more aggressive approaches like invading North Vietnam (49 percent) or occupying the demilitarized zone between North and South Vietnam (42 percent). And while protests against the war grew, so did opposition to even the *right* to protest. And opinion was not only confused; it was volatile, swinging wildly from one month to the next.

Among those who publicly vacillated was Ted Kennedy. He didn't shy from legislative combat when he felt a moral issue was at stake, but he didn't like making enemies—"I like Ted" was the Senate refrain—and he especially didn't want to invite the enmity of Lyndon Johnson, whose enmity was legendary. And though Ted had come to think of the war as a tragic mistake, he continued to tread lightly in expressing his opposition to it, citing the deleterious effects of the war rather than attacking Lyndon Johnson's leadership and strategy and taking the politically expedient course of siding with neither the peace movement nor with the hawks. While Bobby had called for a cessation of bombing against North Vietnam in March 1967—it was a sign of the Democrats' trepidations that this was considered a bold move—Ted preferred to lament Vietnam's effects on the Great Society. Speaking before the Americans for Democratic Action that same month, he said, "The simple and brutal fact is that the liberal program, the concern for the unfinished agenda among our people, has been a casualty of the war in Vietnam." So was the Democrats' moral authority. And throughout the year, he continued to emphasize the refugee situation and the woefully inadequate medical facilities for civilians there. Since stressing the human cost of the war had a powerful appeal, peace groups began pressuring Ted to deploy his Refugee Subcommittee to underscore the larger catastrophe of the war, and the Johnson administration was concerned he might do so. John Roche, a special consultant to the president, warned Johnson that "Dr. Spock's outfit," referring to the renowned pediatrician who had become one of the most vehement critics of the war, had been agitating to get publicity from the subcommittee.

But despite being pressured by peace groups and being inundated with reports from government agencies, NGOs, and private citizens on the dire situation of civilians in Vietnam, Ted still did not move forcefully—in large part, it seemed, because he still did not want to rouse that legendary enmity of Lyndon Johnson. He worked behind the scenes, meeting with Averell Harriman that March to discuss the medical program for the civilian population and noting to Harriman that civilian casualties were higher than enemy military casualties; that only a small fraction of civilians got treatment; that treatment was usually delayed; and that treatment was usually inadequate. He was deeply disturbed by the situation. As much as he feared the president's wrath, his conscience was inflamed—an instance of his own moral sense being stoked by what he had seen and heard—and he was conflicted over whether he could continue to hold his fire. And this time, to underscore the point of the civilian tragedy in Vietnam, he issued his own warning: If the administration didn't act, he would hold public hearings on the issue, which would likely embarrass Johnson. Johnson reacted. Three weeks later he promised to build three field hospitals in Vietnam, at a cost of $15 to $20 million, with between six hundred and one thousand beds, that would treat the most severe civilian casualties, with the implied trade-off that Ted would desist from publicizing the civilian situation. The first hospital was to open later that year. And so Ted had seemed to wrest some moral good from what he now regarded as an immoral situation.

But then Johnson did something he rarely did when it came to politics. He misplayed his hand. He reneged. He didn't open a hospital by year's end in 1967; in fact, he never opened any of the hospitals. And Ted was displeased. During that summer of 1967, he had sent Tip O'Neill, an increasingly ambivalent supporter of the war, a copy of a speech that former Kennedy and Johnson aide Richard Goodwin had delivered, in which he called the war a "triumph of the politics of inadvertence," and Ted talked to O'Neill about endorsing a bombing halt, though O'Neill wasn't ready to take that step. By this time, Bobby, who had endorsed the bombing halt, was pressing Ted for information on the civilian casualties, which would buttress his growing resistance to the war, and Ted's refugee aide, George Abrams, briefed him for two hours. "Ted and Robert were talking more," Abrams said. "Ted was giving Robert facts"—clearly facts about civilians and refugees—"and Robert was giving Ted kind of . . . his view of the big picture." In short, Bobby was stoking Ted's conscience, just as the refugees were. Ted was funneling information on the refugee situation to other opponents of the war too, among them Tunney, Roger Hilsman, a former State Department official under both Kennedy and Johnson, who had concluded the war was unwinnable, and I. F. Stone, a prominent left-wing journalist. "We were feeding everybody we could," Abrams said. And Abrams described Ted as a "sponge trying to get information, assuming he didn't know anything, wanting everyone else to tell him what they thought." And as information flowed into Ted, he and his staff set up meetings to share that information, creating a kind of clearinghouse for the moral case against the war.

All this time, Ted Kennedy continued to prod the administration to provide civilian relief, but while others, including Bobby, were addressing the military futility of the American effort and the harm to America's reputation of a superpower pounding away at a small country, Ted, still not wanting an open break with Johnson even though Johnson had betrayed him on the hospitals, was determined to address Vietnam on his own terms, which was ignoring the military component of the war and concentrating exclusively on the human cost. To shift the discussion from refugees alone to civilian casualties, Abrams had recommended that Ted arrange for a group of prominent physicians, under the auspices of USAID, to visit Vietnam and report back on what they found. When the team returned and filed a hundred-page report citing the medical disaster in Vietnam (30 percent of citizens with tuberculosis, 80 percent with worms, 30,000 to 50,000 amputees) and calling for a vast expansion of health services there, USAID quickly spun it into a much sunnier press release. But Ted wasn't sunny. After meeting with the group of doctors and hearing their stories, he was boiling. By that point, he had already decided to hold public hearings of his own, the hearings that Johnson so dreaded, on the civilian and refugee problems in Vietnam.

Ted had finally broken with the administration publicly on moral grounds. But he could not find it within himself to break with it politically. As for the moral break, at the five days of hearings that were conducted that October, doctors and aid officials testified to a litany of suffering among the Vietnamese civilian population: terrible casualties, the lack of facilities, unsanitary conditions, housing units unbuilt and food allowances unfilled, the decrease in funding to help refugees at the very time that Ted was calling for increased funding, the sheer number of refugees (more than two million displaced, with over 100,000 casualties), and, perhaps above all, the "scandal" of what Ted would call "the cavalier and almost disdainful attitude" toward those civilians, as reflected in General Accounting Office reports that plainly stated the civilian side of the war was not seen as "critical to our success in the political-psychological side of the war effort," a direct contradiction of Ted's feelings. As one witness said, the refugees used to be fleeing the Vietcong; now they were fleeing American bombing. *The New York Times* editorialized that "the hearings created a graphic picture of what it means to be a Vietnamese peasant caught in the crossfire of the war in South Vietnam." What it meant was death and destruction. The administration tried to parry. When Ted argued during one session that the administration had to take civilians into account if it was to be successful in Vietnam, William Bundy, the assistant secretary of State for East Asian and Pacific Affairs, said that Vietcong recruiting had declined, showing, he said, growing support for the South Vietnamese government. But Ted immediately brandished a new Department of Defense report, dated October 4, that indicated just the opposite, to which Bundy responded feebly that he was relying on figures from one office in the Defense Department and Ted on another.

The hearings were a stern indictment of the administration—one of the sternest. But if Ted Kennedy had prosecuted the case, he was *still* not yet ready to call for a guilty verdict against the war itself or the administration. Instead, at the very time when a peace movement was building within the Democratic party to find a candidate to challenge Johnson in the upcoming 1968 primaries, and as pressure was mounting on Bobby to be that candidate, Ted continued to act as if the civilian casualties and Johnson's war policy were somehow unrelated, as if the casualties were unfortunate collateral damage rather than an integral part of a strategy to uproot the population. Even Bobby was confounded by Ted's reluctance and confounded as well that Ted didn't take more criticism for his unwillingness to break with Johnson. Why wouldn't he join those peace forces when he so clearly seemed sympathetic to them?

One could have attributed his reticence to his ongoing political calculation not to get too far out in front on a divisive issue, especially one that was rending his own party, though he could no longer use the excuse that he was protecting his brother's future presidential ambitions, since Bobby himself was critical of Johnson and the war. And while it wasn't beyond Ted, as had been suggested, to think of his own presidential future, that was a very long way off. And though it was undeniable that Ted thought his human approach was the most politically salable one to those who thought the peace movement was undermining American troops in Vietnam, his approach had shown very few results. In fact, the administration had not only backed away from its promise of hospitals; it was backing away from funding almost any civilian relief, though that relief paled in comparison to the military expense—$80 million for refugees that year against $25 billion for the war.

But there was another explanation for Ted's reticence to take on Lyndon Johnson—one that Bobby should have understood: In politics, as in the Kennedy family, Ted Kennedy had a youngest child's ingrained deference to authority. And while Ted Kennedy was astute enough not to trust Lyndon Johnson and to realize that he was a conniver, he liked Lyndon Johnson, appreciated Lyndon Johnson's favors (early one rainy morning in March, when John Kennedy's body was disinterred and reburied in a permanent plot in Arlington Cemetery, Johnson had accompanied Ted and Bobby to the ceremony), bathed in Lyndon Johnson's praise, and saw in Lyndon Johnson a kind of kindred spirit, personally (both men had been humiliated and underestimated in their youths) and politically (Teddy was a Senate man, as Johnson had been, which was also a source of Johnson's attachment to Ted). And, as the youngest, Ted Kennedy simply could not bring himself to attack Lyndon Johnson, however much he had come to disagree with him on Vietnam. Dave Burke said as much in describing why he thought Ted kept deferring to Johnson, especially when it came to foreign policy, with which Ted had little experience. "You can argue all you want about crime and health care, schools, public education," Burke analyzed, "because laymen are supposed to have some expertise on that. But not on foreign policy. That's really rather different." Ted had gained confidence in domestic policy, had made a mark on domestic policy. He had no confidence, had made little mark, on foreign policy.

And so, even at the conclusion of his hearings, Ted Kennedy didn't argue for withdrawal from Vietnam but rather that the war was unwinnable if we didn't take the civilian situation into account: to win "the hearts of the people." And right before his hearings would provide point after point of American negligence toward those people, Ted Kennedy still delivered a speech at a Democratic fundraiser in Des Moines, Iowa, saying that had it not been for John Kennedy and Lyndon Johnson, American troops would be fighting in Red China and that voters would give Johnson a "vote of confidence and gratitude" for Vietnam in the next election. And Ted Kennedy, speaking at the Harvard Medical School, shortly after the hearings, insisted that America "rethink her approach" to the war and "ask ourselves whether the losses we have suffered and the resources we have expended have resulted in any real gains in affecting the political inclinations of the South Vietnamese," and he asked that, if not, "Must we continue to pour young Americans into that abyss?" But at the conclusion of his speech, rather than call for withdrawal explicitly or criticize Johnson's policy outright, he said, as he had said so many times, "the bullet will never defeat the Vietcong or the soldiers of the North." And in another speech, to the International Rescue Committee, not long after, he again cited "the almost total disruption and, in many cases, destruction of the fabric of life and society in that nation" and said the misery "staggers the imagination," but, again, said that it was not too late "to use our men and resources in a different kind of struggle"—from military battle to social assistance. Ted Kennedy wasn't ready to get out of Vietnam yet or to attack Lyndon Johnson yet. He still believed in redeploying our forces there for a moral mission, but only because he was afraid to admit to himself that Lyndon Johnson had no interest and would never have any interest in providing relief to the civilians and refugees of Vietnam.

And it wasn't only the Vietnamese about whom Ted Kennedy worried, though he was worrying about them a great deal now. "He has a natural inclination to the humanitarian side," David Burke said. " 'People getting hurt! Oh, my God! Have you seen them? Isn't it terrible?' " Ted was concerned about the other casualties of the war: the American soldiers. He would admit that it was because he was in favor of the war in 1966 and

1967 that he began looking at modifications to the draft, though he also said that Bobby had pushed him to work on a draft lottery because "the soldiers who were dying [in Vietnam] were poor and urban." Again, as with the Voting Rights Act and one man, one vote, he considered draft reform a matter of fairness, as someone who had tasted unfairness himself. He testified before the House Armed Services Committee in 1966, which was examining the draft, that deferments worked to the disadvantage of the poor, who seldom received them, and that there should be national guidelines for deferments rather than leaving them to local draft boards. He also called for drafting nineteen-year-olds first, rather than older men, because they weren't likely to have families or careers yet. When Senator Joseph Clark of the Labor Committee began raising questions at the same time about the equity of the draft, Ted introduced three amendments to create, as Bobby had suggested, a draft lottery—all of which failed when the director of the Selective Service System, General Lewis Hershey, opposed them. But Ted was not through. He revived the proposal the next year, as the war escalated. In February 1967, with the draft law due to expire in June, he submitted a resolution asking that Johnson reform the draft by executive order and again called for a lottery, the drafting of the youngest first, deferments for trade apprentices and not just for college students, and national induction standards. The draft was the province of the Armed Services Committee, headed by Richard Russell. (The Labor Committee had addressed the issue on the pretext that the draft was also a manpower issue.) But it was yet another sign of Ted's acceptance by the bulls and their affection for him that Russell now permitted him to conduct hearings under the auspices of the Senate Subcommittee on Employment, Manpower, and Poverty, which Clark let Ted chair temporarily. Johnson responded rapidly on March 6, saying that he endorsed recommendations of a National Advisory Commission on Selective Service and would institute the "youngest first" proposal and a draft lottery by January 1, 1969. General Hershey, testifying before Ted's committee two weeks later, said that he now supported the "youngest first" and lottery reforms too, because, as he bluntly put it, "when the quarterback [meaning Johnson] calls the signals, that is the way I play them."

The Labor Committee sent Ted's bill to the floor, and the Armed Services Committee sent a bill with Johnson's recommendations, which were essentially the same as Ted's, even though Russell said he wasn't sure a lottery would result in greater fairness, and the full Senate passed the bill, 70 to 2, on May 11. But once again, Lyndon Johnson made a rare miscalculation. Johnson's Senate may have been compliant. The House was not. Mendel Rivers, the chairman of the House Armed Services Committee, was so opposed to a lottery—he apparently thought it unworkable—that he proposed legislation to strip the president's authority to institute one. In May, with the members eager to leave for the Memorial Day weekend, Rivers rushed through approval—those proposing amendments were allowed only one minute to explain them—of a four-year reauthorization of the current draft bill, 369 to 2, with an important stipulation: Congressional approval would be required for any changes Johnson made. Now the two bills went to conference. But when they emerged, Ted Kennedy was once again unhappy. Russell had conceded on keeping the congressional-approval requirement of the lottery in the bill as well as a provision that would retain student deferments, which Ted felt were unfair to those who could not or did not attend college and were not provided with vocational deferments. "Both groups are learning to become productive citizens," he would say on the Senate floor, "but one group—the less privileged—has no protection from exposure to the draft." And now Ted confronted Richard Russell on that floor, asking for more time for the bill to be considered, hinting at a filibuster, and the exchange became snippy. As Adam Clymer described it, when Ted said he had some questions for Russell, Russell snapped, "I do not like to answer questions under threat of a filibuster." At which point Majority Leader Mansfield called for a two-day postponement to ease the tension. When the bill came back to the floor after the postponement, Ted announced that he wanted to have new conferees appointed—conferees who he felt would support the Senate bill with Ted's provisions. And he waved letters from administration officials who also opposed the conference bill. And then, finally, Ted urged his colleagues to reject the bill, Richard Russell's bill, the bill Russell had personally floor-managed, and called instead for a one-year extension. But as popular as Ted Kennedy had become, he was still no match for Richard Russell. The bill passed, 72 to 23, though twenty-three votes was an unusually large number to oppose a reauthorization bill or, for that matter, a non–civil rights bill with Richard Russell's imprimatur.

But despite the confrontation, as Ted's aide Dun Gifford told it to Clymer, there was no animosity between Ted and Russell afterward. "Ted, that's a hell of a fight you put up," Russell told him in the cloakroom. "You did a great job." And the two went off to have a drink. "I know you got problems in Massachusetts with the young people up there and all those liberals," Gifford said Russell told Ted. "I don't like you to go away empty-handed." And Gifford said that Russell agreed to allow some changes in the draft law the next year. Then Russell said he needed some help on getting a naval base built in Savannah—help that he obviously didn't need. But he asked for Ted's support, and Ted gave it. "We're a Navy state and a Navy family, and I'll be glad to help you with that," Ted said. Ted would get some draft reforms. Russell would get another ally.

And that was the way the Senate worked between those who were Senate men—even between those who disagreed vehemently about the Vietnam War, which was beginning to tear the country apart. But it wouldn't be that way for much longer.

IV

A "noxious atmosphere." That was how *Time* described the mood of the capital as 1967 wound down and the war continued to flare. Vietnam had not only ended the Great Society, it had divided the nation, expended most of its moral capital, drained its energy, created a sense of disorientation, even seriously injured the American economy. "We are in danger of losing our sense of confidence in each other," Ted warned. That summer, as attention was focused on Vietnam and as the social fabric was fraying, one hundred American cities, notably Newark and Detroit, erupted in race riots in response to police brutality—riots that added to the growing sense of national division and disruption. America seemed ablaze from without and within. And Bobby Kennedy was angry—angry about Vietnam and how it had wracked the American soul, angry about how it had diverted attention from his own personal mission: to help the poor and disempowered. Bobby had gone to Paris in January 1967 to take the pulse of the French about the possibilities of a settlement with North Vietnam. Among those with whom he spoke was François Mitterand, who had led the left-wing opposition against President Charles de Gaulle. Mitterand told him that Vietnam was "the single most important reason why there has been a loss of U.S. 'moral authority' in France and elsewhere in Western Europe," and Étienne Manac'h, the head of the Asian Affairs of the French Foreign Ministry, told Bobby that a bombing cessation would lead directly to peace talks with the North Vietnamese, which administration officials strenuously denied. Bobby returned to Washington and met with Johnson, offering to help broker a peace agreement. But Johnson was immovable, and Bobby then gave his speech on the Senate floor on March 2, calling for a bombing halt. From that point, the rupture between Robert Kennedy and Lyndon Johnson on Vietnam was irreparable. Bobby was now in opposition.

And Ted Kennedy was finally beginning to sharpen his tone too, as it became increasingly clear that the administration was unlikely to de-escalate the war, much less end it. Ted had endorsed Bobby's call for a bombing halt three days later in a speech before the Massachusetts chapter of Americans for Democratic Action (ADA) and even warned that if the war wasn't over in 1968, the American people might "pass a protest vote" to sweep Johnson from power, which was, for him, a remarkably bold prediction, especially after having been so supportive of Johnson. But Bobby was now the main event, and Ted's remarks received little notice. Two months later, speaking at the University of North Carolina, Ted said that guerrilla movements like the Vietcong "offer discontented people a purpose, a faith, an organization, and a way of life. But it is not our mission to suppress them. It is not our mission to make Asia safe for the mandarins and landlords." Then came the doctors' mission and the reports of neglect and the refugee hearings—and the continued inaction by the administration.

But for the tens of thousands now organizing in 1967 to end the war, words were hardly sufficient. There was only one way to end the war: *Dump Lyndon Johnson.* So long as Johnson was in office, the war would proceed and, with it, all the damage that war had inflicted on both the Vietnamese and the Americans. To those in the peace movement, Lyndon Johnson was too invested in the war to stop it, too fearful of showing weakness, too entangled in his lies and distortions and estimates of victory. He had had moral authority, only to squander it on a misbegotten adventure overseas, and he could never regain it now. *Dump Lyndon Johnson.* And Bobby Kennedy had heard those murmurs turn to shouts, heard them and listened.

After John Kennedy's death, Bobby had turned himself into a living memorial to his brother, a powerful memorial, which necessitated reinventing both himself and his brother as far more ardent liberals than they really were. The death had "humbled him, softened him," said John Kennedy's longtime adviser Ted Sorensen. "He became a gentler, warmer person." And Sorensen said that while Bobby started out like Joseph Kennedy, "he ended up far more liberal than both his father and JFK." More liberal and more driven. The memorial dedicated himself to completing Jack's mission to help the poor and the marginalized. He became, virtually overnight, their tribune and their protector. "He was preoccupied with suffering and despair," the journalist Jack Newfield wrote—at first his own over his brother's death, but then his own suffering transmuted into the suffering of others, as Ted's humiliations had transmuted into his sensitivity to the humiliations of others. And Bobby felt that Lyndon Johnson could never be dedicated the way Bobby was. Lyndon Johnson could never understand suffering as Bobby did. Lyndon Johnson might use moral authority to boost his own prospects, but he was too much the politician to believe in moral authority. And though Bobby had felt this way even before Johnson became president, even before Johnson plunged the nation into Vietnam, Vietnam had provided proof of Johnson's insincerity, as Bobby saw it. Bobby would tell Ted that he opposed Johnson not because of Vietnam but because of Johnson's growing indifference to the poor and neglected and that Vietnam had only served to reorient Johnson's priorities and expose him. Bobby had gone to the Mississippi Delta, had seen the distress of the black Americans there, had known how much help the people there needed. Melody Miller, who worked for him then, remembered him coming back to the office from his trip. "He'd seen people living in tar-paper shacks and little black children with swollen bellies, and nobody having correct nutrition, and the threadbare existences inside those houses." And as she stood in the office doorway, she watched Bobby "pulling pieces of paper out of his pockets and laying them out on his desk, and he picked up the phone and started calling all his rich friends in New York. He said, 'Could you send a box of blankets to this address? Can you send a box of soup to this address? Can you send canned goods and blankets to this address?' " And she said he told them that he would submit legislation to help but that it would never happen fast enough. The crisis was *now*. (Of course, the crisis had been going on for a very long time before Bobby discovered it.)

But after piloting the Great Society to help the people Bobby wanted to help, Johnson in his 1966 State of the Union had placed Vietnam, not poverty, at the center of his political considerations. And his 1967 State of the Union, as urban expert Daniel Patrick Moynihan would write, nearly eliminated mentions of civil rights and poverty altogether, "to be replaced by disquisitions on Safe Streets and Crime Control Acts and other euphemisms for the forcible repression of blacks," as if the political winds had shifted and Johnson was now following them. This was what had always concerned Bobby—how tenuous Johnson's commitment to the poor was. And now, as Bobby was devoting himself to their fight, his suspicion had come true. *Dump Lyndon Johnson.*

And Bobby felt this too: Liberalism, which had fed the great accomplishments of the 89th Congress, was withering. In his address to the Massachusetts ADA, Ted had also made the argument that liberalism had become "tired and weak," that Vietnam had broken liberalism's promises and exhausted it. But Ted was not in despair. "Once Vietnam is behind us," he said, "we can turn again to the causes that have traditionally tested us—the expansion of opportunity, the extension of human dignity, the improvement of the quality of American life." First, however, one had to put Vietnam behind. First one had to defeat Lyndon Johnson. And the most promising candidate for doing so was Robert Kennedy. Bobby had long been spoiling for a fight with Johnson. Vietnam offered him an occasion, and all that year, 1967, he had been putting distance between himself and Johnson. But as impulsive as Bobby could be—"existential," he was often called by friends—he was still a politician with a promising presidential future, and he was not about to challenge a sitting president unless there was an organized effort for his doing so. Bobby had disdained liberal intellectuals for their ineffectuality. (He thought this was one reason that they had been so attracted to Adlai Stevenson: Stevenson was too rarefied to win.) "They like it much better to have a cause than to have a course of action that's been successful," he told *New York Times* reporter Anthony Lewis. Bobby Kennedy didn't just want a cause. He wanted the presidency.

And there were those who were encouraging Bobby to take Johnson on. Liberal activist Allard Lowenstein, who was organizing a campaign to dump Johnson, approached Bobby. Bobby admitted to Lowenstein that he thought Johnson a coward, that if Johnson was beaten in the early primaries, he might actually withdraw. But Bobby was tentative. He feared that if he ran against Johnson, he would be seen as personalizing the race, that people wouldn't see him as trying to change policy and rescue the country from Johnson's mistakes and reinvigorate liberalism but, given his reputation, as someone who was so ambitious, so opportunistic, that he would do anything to be president. Whether this was an excuse, a way to protect himself for future runs without alienating the Johnson forces in the party, is impossible to say, but Bobby said the same things to Ted. "It was going to be blind personal ambition for power," Ted recalled of how Bobby's campaign was likely to be characterized, "and using the war as a lever to steal away the nomination because the Kennedys felt that they were entitled to it." And Ted agreed that Bobby was especially sensitive to fueling the charges that he was ruthless and, in a practical sense, worried that the characterization would harm his chances of beating Johnson.

All his life, Bobby had run vicariously through Jack, until he was forced to run on his own to be Jack's memorial. Political tentativeness was built into him. Harvard psychologist Robert Coles, a friend of Bobby's, said he had the mien of "a man who has a lot to say, but isn't quite sure how to say it; who has a lot stirring in him but doesn't know how to put it into words; who has a lot of emotional things happening to him." So he waffled. Ted said that he and Bobby had discussed the prospect of his running against Johnson "many, many times." Should he do it? Should he take the risk? And Bobby would say at the end of those conversations, "I'm going to give it some more thought." But Ted thought that the fact that Bobby kept returning to the idea gave it a kind of "inevitability." Inevitable, perhaps, but he was taking a very long time to get there.

Part of that, beyond his personal qualms, was his own sense of political reality. Johnson was not particularly popular at the end of 1967, but he controlled the Democratic party, and, Johnson's alleged cowardice notwithstanding, Bobby didn't underestimate the difficulty of beating him. If anyone understood the strength of the party stalwarts, it was Bobby Kennedy. And Johnson was not only powerful; he was also shrewd. In fact, even as Bobby dithered, reports circulated that Johnson was thinking of asking Ted to run as a favorite son in the Massachusetts Democratic primary, on the pretext that Johnson then wouldn't have to run against an anti-war Democrat who might decide to take him on in that liberal state, though the reports might also have been a way for Johnson to smoke out Bobby's intentions.

Lyndon Johnson wasn't the only one wanting to smoke out those intentions. As Bobby pondered whether to run, the peace movement was getting impatient, and it was beginning to sound out other possible candidates. Even Bobby's own brain trust was getting impatient—so impatient that on October 8, Jack's former press secretary, Pierre Salinger, rented a suite, Room 212, at the Regency Hotel in New York for a meeting of a dozen Kennedy insiders, among them Ted, Sorensen, Goodwin, vanden Heuvel, Kenny O'Donnell, and Steve Smith, to discuss Bobby's plans and chart a course for him. (At Ted's suggestion, Bobby did not attend.) Ted led the discussion, which settled upon three options: that Bobby oppose Johnson in the primaries, that he position himself as an alternative should Johnson decide not to run, or that he angle for the vice presidency should Johnson decide he needed Bobby to win the fall election. The group immediately ruled out the last option, but it was a sign of their own timidity that they ruled out the first as well. Instead, they resolved to have Bobby not endorse Johnson, while they worked to canvass Democratic politicians and see how viable a challenge might be. There were, Ted said, "varying degrees of intensity about him running"—Arthur Schlesinger Jr. would send Bobby a note urging him to run—but most were unenthusiastic, and Ted was the least enthusiastic. Ted, though, was not thinking morally but politically, believing that the run would not only jeopardize any future candidacy, were Bobby to lose, but that if Bobby ran and Johnson lost to a Republican, Bobby would be blamed. (At the time, Jack's old nemesis Richard Nixon was among the leading Republican aspirants.) Nine days later the brain trust met again, this time in Ted's office, joined by John Culver, Dave Burke, and Massachusetts congressman Ed Boland, who had nominated Ted at the 1962 Massachusetts Democratic convention. The consensus again was to move slowly, conduct some polling—basically on the issues of Vietnam and Bobby's personality, which showed what the group considered the two major issues—continue to sound people out, and make a covert outreach to the peace groups, which had been urging him to run.

But Bobby Kennedy wasn't the only one thinking of taking on Lyndon Johnson. Senator George McGovern of South Dakota, a Vietnam dove, had been approached by peace groups during the summer of 1967 about considering a run. McGovern demurred because he was up for reelection in 1968, but he suggested two like-minded senators who were not: Lee Metcalf of Montana and Eugene McCarthy of Minnesota. Later, when he saw McCarthy in the Senate, McGovern apologized to him for sending the activists his way, but McCarthy told McGovern that he was actually considering a run—a sentiment that McGovern passed on to Schlesinger and to Joe Rauh, who had been talking to McGovern about getting a peace plank into the Democratic platform. McGovern said that within an hour, Bobby phoned him to discuss McCarthy's comment—an alacrity that showed how much Bobby really wanted to run himself. "He was highly agitated and pressed me on how certain I was about the information I had given Schlesinger," McGovern would later write. "It was clear that he was deeply distressed about the possibility of a McCarthy candidacy."

No doubt Bobby was concerned about being co-opted, though if that was his fear, he hadn't been in any hurry to make a decision, and he—and Ted—seemed more interested in Bobby's political fortunes than in ending the war that was tearing the country apart, which was to the credit of neither. But there was another consideration about Eugene McCarthy, a more personal consideration: Neither Bobby nor Ted liked him very much. McCarthy was aloof, arrogant, self-regarding, unpredictable in the worst sense. Tip O'Neill remembered McCarthy delivering the nomination speech for Adlai Stevenson at the 1960 Democratic National Convention, the convention that would nominate John Kennedy, and telling O'Neill and Ed Boland afterward, "Actually, I'm the one who should be nominated. Any way you measure it, I'm a better man than John Kennedy." This to two Kennedy supporters. "I'm smarter. I'm a better orator, and if they're looking for a Catholic, I'm a better Catholic." O'Neill said he was smiling when he said this but "there was meanness in his heart."

Meanness in his heart. That is how Bobby and Ted thought of McCarthy too. Ted couldn't help but remember approaching McCarthy in the Senate dining room the day of the anti-poll-tax amendment vote and McCarthy brushing him off, saying that he was eating his lunch, and then casting his vote against the amendment for, Ted believed, no better reason than that he didn't like Bobby. Still, if the Kennedys resented McCarthy, thought him arrogant and mean, Bobby understood that if he himself wasn't ready to run, McCarthy at least had the gumption to do so—of course, Bobby almost certainly thought that McCarthy had nothing to lose, whereas Bobby had his future presidential aspirations to lose. Both Kennedys discussed McCarthy's potential race with him. Ted said that McCarthy had come to his office on November 28 and told him that he was going to run and that he intended to enter four primaries, presumably cherry-picked to help him beat Johnson, but not necessarily Massachusetts. Ted advised him that the Democratic State Committee would be meeting on December 2 and a vote would be taken on a peace resolution then, which might, in any case, obviate McCarthy's need to run in the state. And Ted said that he put McCarthy on notice that he himself would likely run as a favorite son. McCarthy didn't seem terribly interested in what Ted said but agreed that he would discuss the matter with Ted before he made any decision about Massachusetts. Two days later, on November 30, McCarthy declared his candidacy. When the state convention wound up endorsing Johnson's policy overwhelmingly rather than the peace plank, McCarthy paid a second visit to Ted's office, on December 6, to inform him that he would now be running in Massachusetts after all. (That announcement was apparently the consultation McCarthy had promised.) Ted wanted to control his state's delegation himself and wasn't pleased with McCarthy's decision, though McCarthy understood that at the time Ted would be holding the delegation for Johnson, not for any peace candidate. "He was just buffaloed, blinking," a Kennedy supporter told biographer Burton Hersh.

Ted had no reason to blame McCarthy. While the Kennedys couldn't seem to make up their minds on what to do about Lyndon Johnson, McCarthy was running to change Vietnam policy, and the Massachusetts Democrats—with, Ted would later admit, "a bit of behind-the-scenes work from our people"—had endorsed Johnson's policy.* McCarthy told Ted he had no choice but to run. Moreover, after McCarthy's announcement of his candidacy, Ted had declared, "I expect President Johnson to be nominated in Chicago, and I will do everything I can to help his reelection." At the time, that no doubt was an accurate expression of his sentiments, though not one that would endear him to the man who was trying to end the war: Eugene McCarthy. Nor was it a terribly courageous expression from a man who himself professed to hate the war. But Ted was still loath to break with Johnson on his reelection, no longer out of affection for him or kinship with him but largely, it seemed—though he would never say so—to keep himself in good standing with his party after having devoted so much energy to building his Senate credentials; and also, more understandably, because he no doubt also feared a Republican victory. It seemed a case where expediency won out over Ted's better instincts.

Bobby was different. As much as he disliked McCarthy, he wasn't going to help Lyndon Johnson. Instead, through an intermediary, the columnist Mary McGrory, he offered to set aside an hour and discuss political strategy with McCarthy. Bobby even came with lists of "key people" who could

---

*Publicly, Ted said that he opposed the pro-war resolution, though, puzzlingly, he commended the committee for taking a stand. "Parlay in Boston Backs President," and "Edward Kennedy Opposed," *The New York Times*, December 3, 1967.

aid McCarthy's candidacy. But much to McGrory's amazement and cha-grin, McCarthy showed little interest in Bobby's help either, and the meet-ing lasted only seven minutes.

With McCarthy in the race, still Bobby wavered. On December 10, 1967, the Kennedy brain trust held yet another meeting, this one at Wil-liam vanden Heuvel's New York apartment, and this time with Bobby in attendance. Once again, there were presentations for why he should run, by Schlesinger and Goodwin, who had devised a plan for him to enter the primaries and to dog Johnson all the way to the convention once McCar-thy, as anticipated, withdrew, and another by Bobby himself, who argued for the necessity of running on moral grounds at a time when the na-tion's morality was clearly in danger. Vietnam had ripped the country's soul, and the country, he said, couldn't survive five more years of Lyndon Johnson. But once again when it came to his brother, Ted played the prag-matist, not the moralist, and Ted Sorensen agreed. Johnson was going to be renominated and likely reelected, though if Bobby tore the party apart, it was quite possible a Republican would be elected; given the fact that Republicans, and Richard Nixon in particular, had demonstrated no in-terest in ending the war (most of them thought Johnson not aggressive enough) and even less interest in helping the poor and black, this was not an acceptable alternative. And more practically speaking, however un-popular Johnson was, as president he still had the ability to control events. He had already regained some popularity by meeting the preceding June with Soviet premier Alexei Kosygin at Glassboro, New Jersey. He could have other surprises in store. For Bobby to oppose him would be political suicide. All he had to do was wait four years. And yet Bobby was champing at the bit. As Schlesinger told it, "Bobby was torn, rueful, enormously at-tracted by the idea of moving, but at the same time impressed by the lack of belief on the part of serious politicians that he should."

V

Now Ted Kennedy had an idea. That same December, he had received let-ters from the director of a Quaker assistance group telling him that the "Forgotten Ward," as the director of the Quang Ngai hospital called it, was "overrun daily" with victims of South Vietnamese and American ar-tillery, shrapnel, and napalm. This made a deep impression on Ted. So he invited Dave Burke to dinner at his Georgetown house—a small dinner.

After the other guests had left, he asked Burke to take a walk with him through the neighborhood. And he mused to Burke that maybe it was time to take another trip to Vietnam—not a trip like the first one in 1965, when Ted was an innocent, gulled by everything the officials told him and ultimately embarrassed, but a "really good trip," as he put it, a well-prepared trip, a trip with an agenda and a purpose, a trip that would eschew reporters and publicity for on-site experience. He sent Burke and a four-man team of attorneys, one of whom spoke Vietnamese, to lay the groundwork in Vietnam, and Burke assigned each of them to one of the four Civil Operations and Revolutionary Development Support areas (CORDS)—areas that had been set up in May to separate the South Vietnamese from the Vietcong and pacify them. (That was the word the American officials used: "pacify.") The attorneys were to collect information in thick briefing books on what was really going on there, not on what American officials said was going on, and they were then to report to Burke in Saigon, so that when Ted arrived, he would know exactly what he wanted to see, without interference from the Army. In short, this was less a fact-finding mission than a fact-confirming mission.

Ted intended the trip to be his introduction, his real introduction, to Vietnam after all these years. He and Burke rendezvoused in Manila on New Year's Day 1968, and Ted pored over the briefing books as he always did. They arrived in Saigon the next day and were met by the military. But this time there were no Potemkin villages, no newly painted huts that would go unoccupied, no recently fed refugees who wouldn't be fed again anytime soon. This time Ted and Burke, accompanied by Dr. John Levinson, an obstetrician–gynecologist who had made four previous trips to Vietnam to assist in provincial hospitals there, went into the countryside, visiting over twenty-five refugee camps, and saw children burned by napalm, their arms melted to the sides of their bodies. "Just horrible things," Burke recalled, "that you don't want to see." They spoke with a sobbing plane spotter, who admitted he couldn't tell the difference between civilians and Vietcong. They searched for a notorious mental hospital where the patients were said to be fed garbage—searched fruitlessly. They visited prisons and saw the holes filled with lime and oil into which captives were thrown. They visited a base near Dong Tam, which had been bombed nightly; and when Ted asked if the area had been cleared of civilians, the officer showed him a map that had been drawn by the French during their occupation more than twenty years earlier, and then the officer described how, before raids, he notified the province chiefs who in turn notified the village chiefs, though when Ted met with a province chief, the man admitted he was not notifying villagers. And they visited a hill above a free-fire zone—zones in which Americans were allowed to fire at will, on the grounds that these were occupied by Vietcong. One young soldier had carved Ted's name into a shell—the five-thousandth shell on that hill—and they fired it into the zone. And when Ted asked where it had gone, the soldiers said it was a free-fire zone and there were obviously Vietcong there. But Ted told them that he had come in by helicopter and had seen farmers in fields and rice paddies, and he asked the soldiers if they would have shot the shell in Iowa or Illinois. Burke said that Ted didn't want to reprimand these kids who were risking their lives and who thought they were honoring him by firing a shell with his name on it, but the "disgust just got stronger and stronger." He had intended to stay ten days. He stayed twelve.

And he saw something else. He saw the photographs of his brother John pasted to the walls of Vietnamese huts—John Kennedy, whom they had seen as their protector. And that moved Ted, because America was the Vietnamese protector no longer.

The Army complained that Ted had come in with an agenda, and they were right. General William Knowlton was assigned by Westmoreland to debrief Ted before Ted left. But Ted was in no mood for the Army spin. Knowlton said that Ted asked him a question and then began reading the newspaper. Knowlton stopped speaking and said Ted didn't even realize it for four minutes. Knowlton called it "arrogance" and groused that Ted "really didn't give a damn what we were going to say." And Knowlton was right about that too. Ted Kennedy was not normally discourteous—far from it—but he had heard all the excuses and the lies. And now he had seen the damage with his own eyes, and felt the indifference. Burke said that after the military briefing, Ted just "tore it apart. . . . They would say something, and he would say, 'How can you tell me that? I was just there. It's not true!'" He was no more respectful to President Thieu, Ambassador Ellsworth Bunker, or Robert Komer, the head of CORDS, the so-called pacification program in Vietnam. Each of them delivered the rosiest of prognoses, and none of them was happy about Ted trying to contradict them. When Ted called the program a "sham," Komer actually shouted at him for "sticking your nose into something that is much larger than refugees." And Burke said, "There was no way home after that. No way back." After seeing the devastation to the civilians and hearing even more lies, Ted knew the war had to end; it had to end now. Ted was so distraught he admitted, "I drank a great deal of liquor on the flight home." Burke said, "That trip had an enormous impact on him. An enormous impact. It just made a whole difference in his life." From that point, his opposition to the war was solidified; he argued with anyone who challenged him: "I've been there, and you haven't."

And Lyndon Johnson was watching carefully, wanting to know what difference it had made. When Ted's advance team first arrived, Bunker and Komer had fired off a telegram to Secretary of State Dean Rusk, saying that Ted's team was "extremely active visiting the countryside" and was "querying refugees on motivation for leaving their homes" and that the team clearly thought the money spent on the war was wasted. They then called a press conference on background—not for attribution—in which they issued a preemptive counter that the refugee program had taken a turn for the better. That was before the trip. By the time Ted returned from the trip, Johnson himself had begun to worry about the report that Ted would issue—so much that he had his appointments secretary, Marvin Watson, call Larry O'Brien, a Kennedy intimate and at the time postmaster general, to see how Johnson might head Ted off. This wasn't Bobby Kennedy, whose criticisms could be discredited as politically motivated. This was Ted Kennedy, who had supported Johnson and was less interested in the prosecution of the war than in the treatment of Vietnamese civilians. O'Brien advised that they should tell Ted his report would be "looked at very carefully." Forty-five minutes after Johnson's conversation with O'Brien, by one account, Ted and David Burke were invited to the White House for an alleged debriefing.

But it was not a debriefing. Quite the opposite. The meeting on January 24, 1968, was a way for Johnson both to charm and intimidate Ted. As David Burke described it years later, Ted was "concerned . . . nervous" about the visit. He had been so loath to break with Johnson that he had carefully crafted his criticisms so that he couldn't be mistaken as criticizing Johnson, but now at last he had turned, and he knew that Johnson would not be happy about it. Johnson, who knew how to wield power even if it was only the power of controlling a room, greeted them both effusively, asked them to sit on couches, introduced them to a State Department official who would relay Ted's observations to the department, and just as Ted was about to speak, condemning the rampant corruption he found in Vietnam, Johnson offered him a Fresca—"We're not in any rush here"—which Ted declined. And then Johnson introduced them to his dog Yuki, and the dog put his head in Burke's lap. Now Johnson encouraged Burke to have a Fresca—"Dave, your president is going to have a Fresca, and you mean you won't have one with me?"—so Burke did. And then, finally, Ted began to deliver his report, which basically came down to what he had long been saying: that we could not win the war through military means but only by winning the hearts and minds of the Vietnamese people and that it was imperative to de-escalate, to stop the policy of search-and-destroy, and to move resources to protecting the population in a clear-and-hold policy, though Ted had become deeply suspicious of the metrics used to determine whether an enclave had been pacified or not. Johnson listened intently—listened with his head resting in his hand—listened looking at him as if to say, "I am bored to tears, but I am going to let this fellow continue," as Burke saw it. And both Ted and Burke could see that the president wasn't pleased with Ted's message. Johnson advised that he would speak with Defense Secretary Robert McNamara, a friend of the Kennedys, though McNamara had announced on November 29 that he would be leaving the administration in February to become the president of the World Bank, and there would be little McNamara could do, which may have been Johnson's way of sidelining Ted. (Ted had said on the Senate floor that McNamara authorized him to say that he had been fired by Johnson.) And Johnson, per O'Brien's instructions, said that the administration would work with Ted. Burke said the ninety-minute meeting ended inconclusively and tensely. Ted would later describe the ending just a bit differently. He said Johnson asked him if he had seen any progress in Vietnam since his 1965 trip, and Ted tactfully answered that there may have been, but it depended on how you measured progress. Then, Ted said, Johnson waxed philosophical, saying it was difficult to evaluate progress. And in Ted's remembrance, the meeting ended with Johnson leaning into him and saying, "If we flop on this one, then Nixon will be in there, and we don't want that, do we, Ted?"

But Ted, who had capitulated to Johnson on Vietnam for years, would capitulate no longer. To him, Johnson had already failed. Though the final subcommittee report wouldn't be issued until May, the very day after his visit to the White House he delivered a scathing denunciation of Johnson's Vietnam policy, in a luncheon speech before the World Affairs Council in Boston. He lashed out at corruption—"brazenly practiced"—that deposited half of the money dedicated to refugees into the pockets of South Vietnamese officials. "I would urge a confrontation between our government and South Vietnam on the question of corruption, inefficiency, waste of American resources, and the future of the 'other war,'" meaning the war for hearts and minds. And he stated unequivocally that if the South Vietnam government couldn't attract its citizens to it, Americans should rethink their commitment, since the goals of this war, unlike those of past American wars, in which the country was defending itself, were more "nebulous," and he cautioned about "applying the traditional canons of patriotism, or the clichés of the past, in judging this war." He detailed resentments that the Vietnamese felt toward Americans and said he found that 80 percent of those he talked with said that the Americans had either herded them into camps or that fear of American artillery—not of the Vietcong—had driven them into camps. "I believe the people we are fighting for do not fully have their hearts in the struggle, and I believe as well that the government that rules them does not have its heart in the cause of the people."

The Johnson forces were enraged. By one account, Ambassador Bunker, General Westmoreland, and pacification director Komer worked "into the night" to prepare a rebuttal to Ted's charges and concluded, after conferring with senior diplomatic officers, that the report was a "most unfortunate statement, apparently based in large part on incomplete, biased, or false information." Bunker derided Ted's report as appealing "heavily to the emotions," and he was especially exercised over Ted's demand that the Vietnamese government curb its corruption, saying that the Vietnamese were "an Asian people with a sense of fatalism that has little to do with Occidental rationality" and that if the United States pressured them, they would possibly distance themselves from us. And as for Ted's complaint that Americans had caused the casualties, he said that the civilians were "victims of a war deliberately undertaken by a cruel and murderous communist enemy."

But Johnson was so clearly incensed by Ted's seeming betrayal that he wasn't content with Bunker's response. The day after the Bunker memo, he lunched with former South Vietnamese ambassador Henry Cabot Lodge Jr. and asked *him* to weigh in, which he did, with a thirteen-page memo also excoriating Ted. He argued once again in favor of the domino theory, said that the United States had to support President Thieu, that, as Bunker had said, corruption was endemic to Asians because, according to

Confucianism, a man's first obligation was to take care of his family. And to all this he added a bizarre theory that because Vietnam was hot and damp, and people didn't have to venture far to sustain themselves, it was much more difficult to establish a centralized government than in temperate zones, "where a man has to span a much larger area in order to satisfy his needs." Meanwhile, former general Maxwell Taylor, John Kennedy's original envoy to Vietnam, attacked Ted and said his recommendations would put America on the road to withdrawal.

But Ted would not desist. His trip had lifted the scales from his eyes and sent him on a mission to rescue the country from Vietnam and Vietnam from the country. He had suppressed his frustrations—suppressed them out of his fear of and deference for Lyndon Johnson and his desire to protect his career. Now, driven by the agony he had seen among the Vietnamese, driven by his moral instincts, he feared no longer and finally released those frustrations. Three days after his World Affairs Council speech, he went on the CBS public-affairs program *Face the Nation* and repeated his charges, then called for a troop reduction and a strategy emphasizing protecting population centers. A week later, before the American Advertising Federation convention, he reiterated that if the South Vietnamese didn't have sufficient interest in the survival of their own country to mobilize for war, to draft their own eighteen- and nineteen-year-olds, to stop the sale of deferments, to put themselves on a seven-day week, and to eliminate corruption, they couldn't expect us to maintain our interest. And a week after that, back in Massachusetts, he barnstormed, delivering speeches at two high schools, two colleges, three city halls, four editors' offices, and a movie theater in Beverly, where he asked for a show of hands on which Vietnam policy they preferred. Ted's on de-escalating and clearing-and-holding won. Everywhere he went, he received an enthusiastic reception.

And now, after the trip and the meeting and the report and the barnstorming and the displaced Vietnamese (four million by one count) and the casualties to both Vietnamese and American soldiers and the "noxious atmosphere" settling across America—after all that, Ted Kennedy was at long last finally off the reservation.

precedented. The North Vietnamese invaded one hundred cities simultaneously: down the coastline from Quang Tri to Hue to Da Nang to Hoi An
to Quang Ngai to Qui Nhon to Nha Trang; through the middle of the
country from Khe Sanh to Lang Vei to A Shau to Kham Duc to Dak To to
Kon Tum to Pleiku to Ban Me Thuot; in the south at Bien Hoa, Vin Long,
Can Tho, Ca Mau. The North Vietnamese seemed to be everywhere, as, in
the words of Vietnam historian Stanley Karnow, they had "exploded
around the country like a series of firecrackers." The most startling attack, however, the attack that seemed to blow away the years of encouraging reports—months earlier, Westmoreland had told the press that a
"sense of despair" pervaded the enemy ranks—was an attack right in the
heart of Saigon, and not just in the heart of Saigon but an attack on the
seemingly impregnable, solid concrete fortress in Saigon that was the very
symbol of indestructibility in the heart of the heart of Saigon: the American embassy. That night, and for days thereafter, Americans watching
television saw the invaders, the corpses, the damage, the sheer volume of
battle, spread across that faraway nation. And if the invasion of the
American embassy became the symbol of the nation's own vulnerability
in a small country of guerrilla soldiers in pajamas, where we were thought
to be invulnerable, there was another symbol, this one of the ugly brutality of the war, of the way this war had become unmoored from morality.
It was an image—an image shot by photographer Eddie Adams in Saigon,
when he came upon General Nguyen Ngoc Loan, the chief of the national
police, to whom an apparent Vietcong sympathizer had been dragged.
And Loan coolly took his revolver, pointed it at the man's head, and, in a
terrifying instant, pulled the trigger, turning the man's face into a rictus
of pain. The photograph would be plastered on front pages throughout
America, and it would become one of the defining images of the war.

American officials would later declare the Tet Offensive a victory, since
the cities were retaken, the North Vietnamese beaten back, and serious
casualties inflicted upon them. This all was true. But the North Vietnamese had not designed the campaign for territorial conquest, nor had they
cared about their costs in manpower. It had been designed for
demoralization—particularly demoralization of the South Vietnamese. It
had that effect, but it had demoralized Americans as well. Within a month,
Gallup polls showed that the percentage of Americans identifying themselves as hawks plummeted from 61 percent to 40 percent, and those identifying themselves as doves soared from 25 percent to 40 percent. And for

the first time since the beginning of the war, a majority of Americans said they opposed it.

And now, with confidence in the legitimacy of the war and in the truthfulness of the administration at low ebb, the time was right for a serious challenge to Lyndon Johnson. Eugene McCarthy in November had already sworn to make that challenge, but few outside the peace movement thought he had any chance of actually beating Johnson. The point was to make a point. Asked on his *Face the Nation* appearance why, if he opposed the war, he wasn't supporting McCarthy, Ted made the same argument: "Senator McCarthy himself, I believe, stated at an early part when he announced for the presidency that he didn't feel that he was going to win the nomination," though Ted went on to say that McCarthy had taken protest from the streets to the ballot box. The implication, however, was that while the campaign was noble, it wasn't going to be effective. Robert Kennedy could be effective. But after spending Christmas with Bobby at Sun Valley and having discussed the presidential bid with him there, Ted was reasonably certain that his brother had decided against a run. Then Ted went to Vietnam. He was resting in Hawaii after the chaos and misery he had seen in Vietnam, "intending to clear my mind in the sun there for two or three days," and getting ready for bed when he got a call from Fred Dutton, another of Jack's old hands, asking him to fly back for a summit on Bobby's candidacy at Hickory Hill. Ted got dressed immediately and arranged to catch a flight to Washington. But for all the urgency, yet again no decision was made. It now seemed that Bobby was holding meetings just to get some affirmation for his desire to run.

But the Tet Offensive gave the deliberations a new urgency and gave Bobby a new bravado. On February 8, at a book luncheon at the Ambassador East Hotel in Chicago, he leveled his most searing denunciation of the calamity in Vietnam yet. The Tet Offensive, he began, had "finally shattered the mask of official illusion with which we have concealed our true circumstances, even from ourselves." It was imperative now, he said, that we "face the facts . . . freed from wishful thinking, false hopes, and sentimental dreams," foremost of which was that we were winning the war and protecting the population. And, he said, we had misconstrued the nature of the struggle, thinking we could win with military force when the real issue was the "will and conviction of the South Vietnamese people." He compared it to "sending a lion to halt an epidemic of jungle rot." And he attacked the corrupt South Vietnamese government, which had failed to win the allegiance of its people. "We have an ally in name only. We support a government without supporters." He attacked the illusion that our efforts had helped the Vietnamese people, and he condemned fighting the war "as if moral standards could be subordinated to immediate necessities"—using the argument that Ted had used in railing against American disinterest in the Vietnamese civilians. He said we had to surrender the illusion that we could win the war on our terms. And he called for a peaceful resolution, including putting the Vietcong in the South Vietnamese government, which, he said, was the "only" path to peace. Stressing again the need to face reality, he closed by citing "the bravery to discard the comfort of illusion" and to see the war for what it was and what it had done to us. And what it had done was destroy the nation's moral standing.

But if Bobby was ready to run—and readying himself to run—he had yet to convince Ted, who, Bobby told Arthur Schlesinger Jr., was "the strongest opponent of his moving" to a candidacy. Ted's main objection had been that Bobby couldn't win when Johnson had the backing of the Democratic establishment—an objection that still seemed likely, although the Tet Offensive had opened a small crack for a possible victory—and that his candidacy would only divide the party and help elect a Republican. But Ted had been holding back another reason—a reason he could never share with Bobby, because it might foreclose Bobby's own decision-making, an emotional reason that went deep in Ted. Ted knew Bobby was a volatile figure, even an incendiary figure, and Ted had an awful presentiment that some crazed person would be looking, as Dave Burke put it, for a "twofer"—John Kennedy and Bobby Kennedy. "He really believed it," said Burke. Ted was so worried about Bobby's safety that he approached George McGovern in the Senate gym and asked him if he would speak to Bobby and discourage him from running. (Dun Gifford believed that if Ted had shared his concern with Bobby, "if he'd given him the real reasons he was worried, I don't think Bobby would have done it.") At the same time, Bobby was imploring friends to speak with Ted and convince him why a run was advisable. Among those he urged was Richard Goodwin. On February 13, five days after Bobby's Chicago speech, Ted had dinner with Goodwin at a restaurant in Beacon Hill, where Goodwin argued that another term of Johnson would kill liberalism altogether and, with it, any chance that Bobby would ever have of being president. Afterward, they walked to Goodwin's apartment on Chestnut Street and talked idly over brandies. And as Ted got up to leave, he stopped and said, "Just the same, maybe he should do it. All his instincts tell him to go. And he's got good instincts." Goodwin asked Ted what he thought Jack would have done. Goodwin said Teddy thought for a moment and then grinned. "He would have advised against it. But he would have done it himself."[*]

But Ted knew now that Bobby's heart was in running and there was no convincing him otherwise. That had, in fact, been a fear of his: Bobby was too impulsive. Despite the months of deliberation, he lived in the moment and acted in the moment, acted on his instincts, so that rational arguments wouldn't matter. And Bobby had a fear of his own, a lament, really, that may have also accounted for his hesitation. As he told his aide Peter Edelman, "My problem is that I don't have anyone to be for me what I was for my brother." Not even Ted, he felt, could be for Bobby what Bobby was to Jack—his chief counselor and his hatchet man. Now, however, the brain trust met again, over the weekend of March 2, and this time it was clear the die had been cast, even though Ted was not on board and still fretted about his brother's political future and, more, his brother's safety. On March 4, Monday, Bobby sent Fred Dutton to see Ted for one last plea. Dutton was nervous, knowing how set against a run Ted was. He cleared his throat to begin, but Ted beat him to it. "I think Bob is going to run, and it's up to us to make some sense out of it," he told Dutton with, Dutton said, "a kind of resignation." Then, at noon the next day, he and Dutton strolled to Bobby's office and met with Bobby and Kenny O'Donnell for three hours to plot the campaign that Ted had so insistently opposed.

And yet, after all those months of dithering, a speed bump still arose. By one account, after those March deliberations, Ted Sorensen had, at Bobby's behest, gone to New Hampshire to discourage Bobby's backers there from putting his name on the ballot—a task for which Johnson was so grateful that he invited Sorensen to the White House. It was during a discussion on Vietnam with Johnson that Sorensen proposed a national commission to recommend a new course—and also to dissuade Bobby from running, since Sorensen had the same concerns as Ted. Johnson professed interest. Meanwhile, Bobby had phoned Chicago mayor Richard J. Daley, a longtime Kennedy supporter and a major power broker in

---

[*]Elsewhere, Goodwin told it differently. He said Ted cracked, "I'm not so sure about that, but I know what Dad would have said. . . . Don't do it." Richard Goodwin to Robert Kennedy, "Conversation with TK on Feb. 13," RFK Papers.

the party, to tell him of his decision. But Daley, who well understood the fallout of a Kennedy running against the sitting president, told him he had hatched a plan to save his party without having Bobby run. Daley said he had recommended to Johnson a commission, a presidential commission, to chart a new course in Vietnam that would obviate Bobby's running. Now both Sorensen and Daley had made the same proposal to Johnson, and Bobby offered to discuss it with the president. At least that was Sorensen's version, and he said he called Bobby to have him suggest members for the commission.

Clark Clifford told a different story, and a more plausible one. Clifford, the professional presidential wise man who had recently succeeded McNamara as Defense secretary, said that he received a call late one night in March from Ted, asking if Clifford would agree to speak with Bobby and Ted Sorensen. When the two came to his office at the Pentagon on March 11, the day before the New Hampshire primary, in which McCarthy would be facing Johnson (Sorensen said they met on March 14, two days *after* the primary), Bobby explained that he was under tremendous pressure to run, and the only way he felt he could resist this pressure was for something to be done to resolve Vietnam. As Clifford told it, *Bobby* suggested a "peace commission," with members selected by him, possibly even including him, to investigate the war and draft a report for the president—a report that would be made public. Clearly, the idea was to pressure Johnson into making some sort of concession toward peace. And Clifford saw it for what it was. An "ultimatum," he called it. But Clifford met with the president afterward anyway, and Johnson, who had supposedly encouraged Sorensen, now rejected the proposal outright, calling it an abdication of his responsibilities. And though Ted reluctantly went along with the idea as a last-ditch attempt to discourage his brother from running, Fred Dutton told biographer Burton Hersh, "I think Teddy thought the peace commission idea was absurd." He knew that there was no way Johnson would accept it.

Two days before the meeting or two days after, depending on whose dates one believed, the political world was rocked by an earthquake. Eugene McCarthy—the afterthought candidate who was nevertheless the only candidate with the courage to confront Lyndon Johnson in New Hampshire (so confident of victory was Johnson that he hadn't filed to put his name on the ballot, lest he seem to be lowering himself, but asked supporters to write it in); the candidate with virtually no support among the apparatchiks of the Democratic party, who relied instead on an army of college students that invaded the state, knocking on doors, after cutting their hair and shaving their beards to "Get Clean for Gene"; the candidate who some saw as a possible stalking horse for a real candidate like Robert Kennedy; the candidate who seemed aloof and whose speeches sounded less like campaign volleys than like academic disquisitions; the candidate who was dry and had the attitude of a patrician (he even looked like a Roman noble in a Hollywood movie); the candidate who had never really declared for the presidency but only said he would run in four primaries; the candidate who had only $400 in his campaign war chest—Eugene McCarthy won 42 percent of the vote. And even though he lost the election—Johnson's write-in campaign won him 49 percent—McCarthy won a moral victory by shattering Lyndon Johnson's aura of invincibility.

To those who saw McCarthy as a stalking horse, the moral victory might have seemed like an opportunity, opening the race for Bobby, who had already committed himself to run but was waiting to announce his candidacy until after the primary. Bobby still had no affection for McCarthy, who had never shown any passion for the liberal causes Bobby espoused, only for opposition to the war, and Bobby told Ted somewhat ruefully, "If Gene McCarthy talked about the cities"—by which Bobby meant black Americans and poverty—"I wouldn't have run." But McCarthy's showing in New Hampshire complicated matters rather than clarifying them and sent everyone back to a reassessment of what Bobby should do. He already had the enmity of the Johnson partisans. If he were to enter the race, as he had intended, after McCarthy's shocking success, he would seem to be an opportunist and earn the "passionate hostility," as William vanden Heuvel put it, of McCarthy's partisans—the very people he would need to beat Johnson. Moreover, Bobby admired those young idealists, longed to have won them himself, hated the idea of alienating them, and he told a Justice Department associate, "I'm going to lose them, and I'm going to lose them forever."

Ted was distressed, not by McCarthy's near victory but by the likelihood that it might give further encouragement to Bobby to enter the race. The next afternoon, the brain trust, which now had expanded to include Milton Gwirtzman, former assistant attorney general Burke Marshall, and old John Kennedy advance man Jerry Bruno, among others, met at Steve Smith's apartment at 1030 Fifth Avenue in New York City. Schlesinger said that Ted, "who looked flushed and a bit unhappy," laid out the options, which spanned total inaction to full-on participation, and the meeting soon devolved into chaos. At seven that evening, they stopped and turned on the *CBS Evening News*. Bobby was being interviewed by the anchor, Walter Cronkite, and was telling him that he had all but decided to run, telling him that he would no longer be dividing a party that was already divided, and that "if I decided to run, it would be on the basis that I could win." Ted griped, "I don't know what we are meeting about. He has made all the decisions already, and we're learning about them on television." But when Bobby entered the Smiths' apartment later that evening, the group broke into applause. They had no choice. Ted was right. The decision had been made.

In a season of political fits and starts, there was one more fit: how to appease Eugene McCarthy. On March 7, five days before McCarthy's victory, Bobby asked Ted to give notice to McCarthy, as a courtesy, that he was probably going to enter the race. Ted decided to ignore the request, feeling that McCarthy might use it against the Kennedys, but Bobby didn't discover that until March 10, when he impulsively decided to fly to California to join Cesar Chavez, the head of the United Farm Workers, in ending Chavez's twenty-five-day hunger strike. Chavez had used the strike to pressure the big growers to reach a contract. Now Bobby phoned Ethel to have one of their friends—either Schlesinger or economist John Kenneth Galbraith or Goodwin—place the call that Ted hadn't placed. Ethel demurred, and Ted finally contacted Goodwin, who had grown so weary of Bobby's foot-dragging that he'd joined McCarthy's campaign. Goodwin grudgingly delivered the message to McCarthy, though, as Goodwin told it to Burton Hersh, Ted hadn't told him Bobby was running, only that he "hadn't foreclosed involvement, definitely," which meant that McCarthy was being treated with the same vacillation. But at that point, before New Hampshire, McCarthy himself hadn't been too certain of his prospects. After New Hampshire, that changed. His arrogance had ballooned, and he certainly didn't feel he owed the Kennedys anything, especially under the circumstance that Bobby seemed to be using McCarthy's near victory to nudge McCarthy aside.

So Ted was delegated to see McCarthy, who was campaigning at the time in Green Bay, Wisconsin. Ted himself said in one interview that he was going simply to tell McCarthy that Bobby was *definitely* running and was going to explain why. But somewhere along the way, the mission to notify McCarthy and tell him Bobby's reasons turned into a peace mission. Vanden Heuvel claimed it was his idea. Schlesinger said the idea actually emanated from the McCarthy camp, when Goodwin, who was bent on defeating Johnson by any available means, and McCarthy's campaign manager, Blair Clark, met at the Georgetown Inn to discuss whether the two candidates could form an alliance. By another account, McCarthy's New Hampshire campaign manager, Curtis Gans, realizing how difficult it would be for McCarthy alone to take down Johnson, talked with Clark about having the two peace candidates divide the remaining primaries so that they wouldn't be running against each other, and Clark took the idea to Goodwin.

Whoever hatched it, by the time Ted flew out to Wisconsin, very late on the night of March 15, the day before Bobby was scheduled to announce, he was no longer delivering news; he was looking to broker a truce, and McCarthy had agreed to listen. (It was a sign of how intensely Goodwin, Gans, and Clark wanted to find some modus vivendi between the candidates that, when they flew into Chicago and bad weather grounded commercial flights, they chartered a flight for $2,000, putting the expense on Clark's personal American Express card, with his not knowing whether or not he would get reimbursed.) In Green Bay, Gans and Clark went immediately to McCarthy's suite in a ratty old hotel named the Northland— "modernized now with a veneer of commercial-grade carpeting, of plastic, and Grand Rapids versions of Danish furniture and lamps" is how Abigail McCarthy, Eugene's wife, described it—while Ted waited in a room reserved for him at the Holiday Inn. But McCarthy apparently had had a change of heart. When Abigail and their daughter Mary went in to see him, he was "adamant," Abigail said, that he wasn't going to meet with Ted, even though Ted had, after all, flown halfway across the country to see him. Instead, McCarthy went to bed, and when the delegation arrived, Abigail refused to wake him up, until Clark insisted on it. It was Mary who roused him at two that morning, but neither of the elder McCarthys, Abigail nor Eugene, was particularly happy about it, and Ted, who had sneaked in the back way so that the meeting would remain secret, said later, "I knew right away it was a mistake. I should have known it when I went out there that it was a mistake." Still, Ted, "radiating good grooming, charm, and bonhomie," as Abigail put it, charged on. He said that he brought two messages from Bobby, whom he referred to as "Bob." First, if McCarthy agreed to talk about the cities and urban policy as much as he was talking about the war, Bobby would not enter the race. (No one but

Ted seemed to remember this offer.) Second, Bobby was willing to divide the primaries, as Goodwin and Clark had discussed, in a joint effort to defeat Johnson. But Ted said that McCarthy was dismissive: "tired, uninterested, rather disdainful. . . . He was on a big high. It had all moved for him. He was pretty much in the catbird seat, wondering why in the world he was being disturbed." Clark called the meeting a "disaster." He said it lasted barely twenty minutes, with Abigail "glowering and Gene hardly awake."*

There would be no accommodation. Ted flew back later that night, arriving at 5:30 A.M.—the morning of what was to be Bobby's announcement—at Hickory Hill where Schlesinger, Sorensen, and vanden Heuvel had bunked, awaiting Ted's return and his report. "Abigail said no," he told them. Breaking the news to Bobby, he told him that McCarthy was "really angry at Bobby even thinking that there was some reason why he should make any accommodation." Later, Bobby wandered in absently on Schlesinger, looking morose, not knowing whether he should announce or not, since he realized that the two peace candidates were likely to split the vote and get Johnson nominated and that his entry would revive the charges of ruthlessness and opportunism. Schlesinger advised that he just endorse McCarthy, but Bobby looked at him "stonily" and said, "I can't do that. It would be too humiliating. Kennedys don't act that way." But Ted had come to the conclusion that no matter how much Bobby disliked McCarthy, Kennedys *should* act that way, that running against McCarthy *and* Johnson would be a calamity for the party and the nation and, most important, for Bobby. And, later, over breakfast with Schlesinger, Sorensen, and vanden Heuvel, Ted groused, "I just can't believe we are sitting around the table discussing anything as incredible as this," meaning having Bobby run.

But Bobby was running, saw no other choice but to run, felt it would dishonor the Kennedys not to run, especially since he knew, no doubt, that Eugene McCarthy had no realistic chance of unseating Lyndon Johnson. And Ted had finally conceded. He told the assembled brain trust that any further discussion was out of order, that it would shake Bobby's confidence at a time—the announcement—when he needed to be confident.

---

*Ted was incensed that McCarthy hadn't been too tired to alert CBS News reporter David Schumacher about the meeting, so that CBS had its cameras filming Ted's departure, apparently to show that the Kennedys had come to McCarthy and he had rejected them.

And when a barber arrived to trim Bobby's hair, which he had worn long and tousled after Jack's death, almost as a sign of grieving, Ted ordered the barber to "cut it as close as you can. Don't pay attention to anything he says." He had to look presidential.

It was not a day of elation. Dave Burke said that as Ethel was picking out Bobby's tie and, much to Bobby's consternation, making a "big fuss about everything," Ted invited Burke to go out and get some air, and the two of them walked the large yard that surrounded Bobby's big white house. "We have to do the best we can on this," Ted told Burke resignedly. "This is going to be very difficult." And then, as if to mollify himself, he said, "Well, we're going to be all right." Then they all drove to the Senate Caucus Room, the room where Jack had announced his presidential bid, to watch Bobby announce. It was an unusual speech, a muted speech, not a speech with grand promises but with grave commitment, not with ebullience but with solemnity. He talked about the "perilous course" he felt the country was on, the new policies he sought: "policies to end the bloodshed in Vietnam and in our cities, policies to close the gaps that now exist between black and white, between rich and poor, between young and old, in this country and around the rest of the world." And he was running, he said, because he wanted the Democratic party and the nation to "stand for hope instead of despair." He commended McCarthy for proving "how deep are the present divisions within our party and within our country" and insisted that his decision did not signal a personal battle with Lyndon Johnson—though it obviously did—but a political one. And he closed oddly too, not with some buoyant send-off or with patriotic boilerplate but with a different kind of injunction, a different kind of cause: "At stake is not simply the leadership of our party and even our country. It is our right to moral leadership of this planet."

"Morality" was not a word often associated with politics, at least not overtly. Dun Gifford said that Ted had invoked morality sparingly in those early years in the Senate, even though so much of what he was doing was morally driven, because "he didn't believe you should use up what capital you had on a moral issue," since morality, he thought, didn't ordinarily move people. He was wrong, and he would come to see he was wrong. In fact, he would come to see just how powerful a force morality could be, and he would use it repeatedly: in advancing civil rights legislation, in his campaign for Vietnamese civilians and refugees, in health legislation, and in one piece of legislation after another that bettered the lives of the poor.

Morality would not be incidental to him; it would be the foundation of nearly everything he did. But Ted wore his morality lightly, as he wore nearly everything lightly. Bobby did not. He had been accused of seeing the world in black and white, and though after Jack's death he was softer, more tolerant, more likely to see grays, he was no less passionate about them. Ted saw morality in tangible terms, in terms of people, and he spoke of injustice with indignation. Bobby felt deeply for people too, but he saw morality in larger, more abstract terms, and he spoke of it with a plaintiveness rather than an anger, his voice filled with ache. Now Bobby Kennedy, who had been his older brother's political henchman and who had seemed anything but a moral figure before Jack's death, had decided to wage a moral campaign, had decided that was exactly how he wanted to expend his political capital. In Bobby's reading of America, the country had gained its soul—no doubt, he felt, in some large measure because of his brother John, who had called upon America's better angels—and then lost it in Vietnam, when America's overweening sense of power blunted it or corrupted it, which is what Mitterand had told him: America had lost its "moral authority." Now Bobby wanted to restore that authority, wanted to help return the country to its better angels. When he talked about the weakening of liberalism, he was talking about policy but also about this: Liberalism had subsisted on moral authority, on helping the poor and weak and voiceless and marginalized. He felt it could not survive otherwise. Neither, he thought, could America.

And so Bobby Kennedy wasn't running for president to topple Lyndon Johnson or to change policy or even to help the people he so desperately wanted to help. He wasn't running to bring rationality to governance, as dispassionate Eugene McCarthy seemed to be doing, or to depersonalize government after Johnson, and John Kennedy for that matter, had personalized it. Bobby Kennedy, whose own mother had called him sanctimonious, felt he was running to save the nation's soul.

II

It would not be easy, since so many of those who agreed with his views nevertheless doubted his own soul when he jumped into the race after McCarthy had led the way. When Ted invited the liberal columnist Murray Kempton to a book party after Bobby's announcement, Kempton declined with a note: "Sorry I can't join you. Your brother's announcement makes it clear that St. Patrick did not drive all the snakes from Ireland." Bobby understood the animosity against what seemed like blatant opportunism; it was one of the reasons he had kept waffling. And he understood what a lonely journey this would be—a grim journey, like his speech, without the highs of his brother Jack's presidential campaign. Though McCarthy was regarded as the aloof intellectual, it was Bobby who, having made the decision against nearly all advice, campaigned as if he was alone in this venture, as if he *had* to campaign alone. At the St. Patrick's Day parade in Boston, the day after the announcement, he and Ted were marching when Bobby raced ahead to a loud ovation; Ted raced to his side, but Bobby nudged him away as if to say, Ted would recall, that he didn't need him, though perhaps the truth was he didn't want him. "My brother thinks I'm crazy," Bobby told reporter Sylvia Wright on the way to a campaign event. "He doesn't like this. He doesn't go along. But, then, we're two different people. We don't hear the same music. Everyone's got to march to his own music." He even distanced himself from Jack, telling interviewer David Frost that the New Frontier, Jack's name for his political program, was over and that we are "living in a different time." And he said, "Until November 1963, my whole life was built around President Kennedy." But after the assassination, he said, "I had to play a different role, because what had existed for me then didn't exist." And he might have added that no one but Bobby himself could fully appreciate that new role, which was to reshape America in Bobby's image of his brother, which is why he felt so alone. He was aloof from the party leaders, who wouldn't break from Johnson. He was aloof from his late brother's old hands, many of whom had joined the Johnson administration—those men who had long assumed that one day they would be helping Bobby to the presidency and manning his administration. The night after the announcement, Ted had dinner with Larry O'Brien, Jack's close associate from the Massachusetts days and now Johnson's postmaster general, to ask—"it was implied," O'Brien said—if he might head up Bobby's campaign. But "we didn't pursue the subject," O'Brien added, and O'Brien didn't offer. As Bobby had said, "We're living in a different time." He was even aloof from his younger brother.

Now Bobby was preparing for the primaries. The first in which he could run was to be held in Indiana on May 7. Indiana was not a promising contest for Bobby Kennedy. It had been a hotbed of Ku Klux Klan activity in the 1920s, and the state, in many respects as much Southern as it was Midwestern, was still rent by racial divisions. Moreover, Johnson had a well-oiled organization in place, thanks to the governor, Roger Branigin, who would be running as a favorite son so that Johnson wouldn't have to run there. And the main newspapers in Indianapolis were staunchly conservative. At a meeting in New York, Bobby's brain trust discouraged him from contesting there, certain he would lose. But Gerard Doherty, the "unmade bed" who had guided Ted's first campaign, phoned to offer his services, and Ted called back to ask if he had a crew he could send to Indiana to get enough signatures to land Bobby on the ballot. Doherty got enough Catholic high school and college students in the state to gather the signatures, then returned to New York to tell the campaign cognoscenti, as he called them, that Bobby had a fighting chance to win there. On that feeling, Bobby committed. And Ted became the state campaign chairman, trying to perform the service for Bobby that Bobby had so often served for Jack.

But while Ted, Doherty, and others hunkered down in Indiana—their headquarters was above an old movie theater, which was showing *Gone with the Wind*—the campaign was shaken by another earthquake. On March 31, a Sunday, Lyndon Johnson was to address the nation after his New Hampshire humiliation. The expectation was that he would modify his Vietnam policy in some way, perhaps make some sort of concession to the North Vietnamese that, like previous concessions, he knew they would never accept but that might blunt the peace candidates' efforts. Johnson, a steely man, a man who never gave an inch, a man who knew how to read men and get from them what he wanted, a proud man, an intimidator, was teetering. His approval rating had fallen to 36 percent, and Eugene McCarthy was poised to beat him in Wisconsin—a punishing defeat, a debilitating defeat. Though he still controlled the Democratic party, Johnson felt former allies beginning to distance themselves from him. California Assembly speaker Jesse Unruh met with Johnson that March and promised his support but said he wouldn't join the state delegation. (At the same time, Unruh was coaxing Bobby to run.) United Auto Workers president Walter Reuther pledged his support as well but couldn't say what his board would do. Governor Robert Docking of Kansas also said he would support Johnson, but Johnson felt his support was lukewarm and was sure he would defect to Bobby. And just as Ted was pressuring O'Brien, so, too, was Johnson, trying to get O'Brien to stay in the administration, but Johnson felt him inching away, prompting Johnson to remind him who had given him a Cabinet position. (O'Brien would leave shortly thereafter to aid Bobby.) Even his own majority leader, Mike Mansfield, was against him, he complained, and after a two-hour White House meeting—a meeting that Johnson called "just awful"—he said Mansfield gave his support, but not on Vietnam, and then went out and attacked Johnson's Vietnam policy.

And it wasn't just his former allies whose abandonment he feared. It was the press. On February 27, Walter Cronkite, the CBS News anchorman, who was often called "the most trusted man in America," stepped out of his role as news reader after a visit to Vietnam and delivered an editorial in which he said "it was now more certain than ever" that Vietnam would end in a "stalemate" and that "the only rational way out" was to negotiate, "not as victors but as an honorable people who lived up to their pledge to defend democracy." The effect of Cronkite's analysis rippled through the media and the country. Moreover, despite Johnson's insistent message that America was winning the war in Vietnam, Americans no longer believed it; 49 percent that March called it a mistake. But what was worse, Johnson's own advisers, the men who had told him he had to prosecute the war in Vietnam, the men who prodded him to keep pouring in more troops, the men who had provided those glowing assessments ("There is a light at the end of the tunnel," General William Westmoreland had said scarcely six months earlier, and "The enemy's hopes are bankrupt," a month after that)—those men, by March 26, had finally concluded, as the former national security adviser McGeorge Bundy told Johnson, that "we can no longer do the job we set out to do in the time we have left and we must begin to take steps to disengage."

But with all these blows raining down upon him and with other primary defeats ahead of him, the biggest humiliation in this series of humiliations was the entrance of Robert Kennedy into the race. Johnson said so himself. After telling biographer Doris Kearns that "I was being chased on all sides by a giant stampede coming at me from all directions"—the hawks and doves on the war, those concerned about an inflationary economy, rioters in the cities, "hysterical reporters"—he faced "the final straw. The thing I feared from the first day of my presidency was actually coming true." Bobby Kennedy was going to run against him. "And the American people," he told Kearns, "swayed by the magic of the name, were dancing in the streets. The whole situation was unbearable for me."

And now, on that Sunday night, Johnson faced the nation, a speech he had been planning for weeks, to tell about the situation in Vietnam, though the speech he had been preparing was a truculent one, a speech with no olive branch, a speech that would announce a major escalation. That was not the speech he gave. Of Vietnam, he now said, "No other question so preoccupies our people." He praised his previous peace proposal, announced in August, to stop the bombing if North Vietnam would agree to negotiate. He claimed a victory in the Tet Offensive and said that the North Vietnamese could not win. Still, he mourned the continued loss of life. To reduce it, he announced a unilateral end to bombing over 90 percent of North Vietnam—all but a strip just above the demilitarized zone, which had been used by the North Vietnamese as a staging area— and he said he hoped for a response from North Vietnamese leader Ho Chi Minh. He praised the South Vietnamese army and the South Vietnamese government, though he laid out further efforts they needed to undertake. He said he would be sending an additional 13,500 troops—this despite heavy lobbying by supporters not to escalate the war—and he would be spending another $5 billion in the coming two years. He urged Congress to pass his budget and a tax surcharge to tackle the deficit. He called for a political settlement in Vietnam, not a military one. And while he acknowledged the pain and sacrifice, he also reaffirmed that the war was necessary for American security. And then he spoke of division: "There is division in the American house now. There is divisiveness among us all tonight." And then came the earthquake, though it rumbled with such a quiet tremor that one might have barely noticed it until it was over: "I do not believe that I should devote an hour or a day of my time to any personal partisan causes or to any duties other than the awesome duties of this office, the presidency of your country. Accordingly, I shall not seek, and I will not accept, the nomination of my party for another term as your president." *Dump Lyndon Johnson,* the peace movement had shouted for nearly a year. Now Lyndon Johnson had dumped himself.

And the whole political world rumbled, rattled, and cracked.

Among the Kennedy partisans, there was celebration. Bobby was watching the speech in his New York apartment with twenty family members and members of the brain trust, and they erupted in euphoria. Ted was at the Marott Hotel in Indianapolis, and when Johnson uttered those words of withdrawal, he whooped so loudly that the chicken sandwich he was eating flew out of his mouth. As Thurston Clarke reported it in his account of Bobby's campaign, Ted raced into the room of a local campaign staffer, Louis Mahern, and the two tried to reach Bobby, without success, so they went to the law firm of a supporter named Mike Riley, who was president of the Indiana chapter of the Young Democrats of America, and used his office's phone bank to reach Democratic notables. They stayed for three hours. But they could not get commitments, in part because Hubert Humphrey had Johnson aide Marvin Watson also calling those same notables—a hundred calls, Humphrey said Watson made, lasting until well past midnight and asking them to hold their pledges until Humphrey returned from a dinner that night. And as Ted and Mahern returned to their hotel, Ted kept repeating, "What startling developments! What startling developments!"

But there was one man that Sunday night who was not euphoric: Bobby Kennedy. Kennedy had been running not against Johnson personally but against the moral rot that he felt Johnson represented—the rot of Vietnam and the rot of abandoning the poor and powerless. (Apparently, other Americans looked at Johnson the same way. A greater number of McCarthy voters in New Hampshire favored a more aggressive policy in Vietnam than a less aggressive one; it was Lyndon Johnson they disliked, presumably for throwing the country into chaos and division.) And now, as vanden Heuvel, who was with Bobby Kennedy that night, put it, "He understood immediately that this made it a much more difficult race for him in many ways, because his reason for running was that Johnson represented one course and one direction for the Democratic party and for the nation, and he represented a stark contrast. Now, suddenly, that was different." And vanden Heuvel said that when he reached Ted that night after the flush of excitement had worn off, Ted felt the same way. Johnson's departure would not help the cause.

And if Johnson's withdrawal did not lift Bobby Kennedy's spirits, neither did it dispel the curse that seemed to haunt the nation now—a curse in which, quite possibly because of Jack's death, Bobby, always a fatalist, deeply believed. "I am dissatisfied with our society," Bobby had said on *Meet the Press* the previous August, talking not just about political leadership but about the society generally. "I suppose I am dissatisfied with my country"—which was something no candidate for the presidency had ever said, for fear of being labeled an apostate against the civic religion of optimism. Bobby Kennedy was no optimist. "What do you think is going to happen to this country?" the poet Allen Ginsberg had once asked him. "It'll get worse," Bobby answered.

And it did get worse. Five days after Lyndon Johnson's withdrawal, the civil rights leader Martin Luther King Jr. was assassinated on the balcony of a Memphis motel, while visiting the city to march with striking sanitation workers. The effect on the nation and on Bobby Kennedy was to engulf both in an even deeper despair. Bobby got the news while he was campaigning at a rally in Indianapolis—his first full day of campaigning in Indiana. In the cold, misty evening, he climbed on a flatbed truck and broke the news to those who hadn't already heard it and then spoke extemporaneously, quoting Aeschylus—"Even in our sleep, pain which cannot forget falls drop by drop upon the heart until, in our own despair, against our will comes wisdom through the awful grace of God"—and calling for "love and wisdom and compassion" and a "feeling of justice toward those who still suffer within our country." And he asked that those in the crowd dedicate themselves to "what the Greeks wrote so many years ago: to tame the savageness of man and make gentle the life of this world." But Bobby understood the near impossibility of this. The next day, America erupted in violence—riots in Washington, Chicago, Kansas City, Baltimore, Pittsburgh, and nearly one hundred other cities—violence that Richard Nixon would use to exploit his implicit racist appeal to "law and order." Dr. King's death—"perhaps the darkest moment of the entire decade," as one observer would write—only underscored the existentialism of this already existential man, only underscored the fatalism of this already fatalistic man. "I don't think this will mean anything," Bobby told journalist Jimmy Breslin while the two walked in Dr. King's funeral cortege, and he turned to Charles Evers, the black civil rights leader whose brother, Medgar, had also been assassinated, and asked him what effect *he* thought it would have. "Nothing. Didn't mean nothing when my brother was killed." And Bobby quoted Jacqueline Kennedy when she returned from Medgar Evers's funeral: "Of course people feel guilty for a moment. But they hate feeling guilty. They can't stand it for very long. Then they turn." And if the assassination made him feel as if he were, in the words of reporter and confidant Jack Newfield, "the last friend left" among the dispossessed, which gave his campaign new urgency, it also made him even more alert to his own vulnerability. "I'm afraid there are guns between me and the White House," he told the Reverend Walter Fauntroy, while touring Washington, D.C., with him after Dr. King's assassination. And to Associated Press reporter Joe Mohbat, who asked about the possibility of his own assassination, he said simply, "This really isn't such a happy existence, is it?"

The first test of Bobby's candidacy would be Indiana, where Governor Branigin was now suddenly thrust into a different role: not as Johnson's stand-in but as Hubert Humphrey's, since Humphrey, as vice president, was Johnson's heir apparent. And in many respects, it wasn't Bobby's state to win. It was Ted's to win for him. In Indiana, Ted was the organizer—the one who, along with Dave Burke and Doherty and his staffers, Dick Drayne and Dun Gifford, was setting up state organizations around the country—and Ted was the one reaching out to Democrats in the state. This had been Bobby's job in Jack's campaigns: the organizer, the pol handler, the delegate wrangler. Now it had devolved to Ted. And in Indiana, it was Ted's strategy based on Ted's political instincts, which were more acute than Bobby's, that prevailed. Ted read Indiana. He realized that while Bobby would not want to trim his sails, the best approach—the only approach—in Indiana was to be moderate. Rather than emphasize his concerns for the poor, Bobby should emphasize his role as attorney general, the nation's chief law-enforcement officer, a law-and-order candidate, and focus on his support for welfare reform, increasing federalization of government, and private initiatives rather than public programs that put the entire burden on the federal government—downplaying the very reasons Bobby had said he was running. And rather than seeming to identify with black Americans at the expense of white Americans, he had to appeal to those white voters. When liberal professor Richard Wade, the Chicago commissioner of housing and a Kennedy supporter, stressed the importance of black voters in industrial Gary, Indiana, Ted told him that this was not a productive strategy and steered Bobby away from Gary's black mayor, Richard Hatcher. It was the kind of advice Bobby would have given Jack, though it was not the advice of a moral force. The object was to win, because Kennedys *had* to win. Ted even advised Bobby to cut his hair, as Bobby had before his announcement, to pacify the conservative Indiana voters, and so the hair got progressively shorter.

And the relationships were Ted's. Given how high the stakes were—

Bobby had to win Indiana to get his campaign off on the right foot—Ted was the one who spent nearly two months living in Indianapolis along with those staffers of his, and Ted was the one who traveled the state, reaching out to the local pols, the civil rights leaders, and union officials, who had little affection for Bobby because of his Rackets Committee investigations but who had great affection for Ted, who was approachable and likable. (The pols appreciated that dedication.) The "filter" for Bobby, Gerard Doherty called him, because he would soften Bobby's hard edges, and Bobby needed softening because, even as a candidate seeking support, he could be tough and uncompromising. During the Indiana campaign, a teamster from Charlestown, Massachusetts, a "devout Catholic," Ted said, and a "thoroughly decent man" who cared for a handicapped wife, approached Ted with a proposition: If Bobby would agree to listen to the recommendations of the parole board on former Teamsters' president Jimmy Hoffa, who had been jailed because of Bobby's efforts, and then accept those recommendations, the Teamsters would give him $1 million for the campaign. And when Ted passed the proposal on to Bobby—while Bobby was taking a bath, which is when the two of them often spoke—Bobby kept washing his arms and his neck and said offhandedly, "Well, you tell so-and-so that if I get to be president, Jimmy Hoffa will never get out of jail, and there will be a lot more of them in jail." To which Ted, the filter, said, "Well, thanks, Bobby. I don't think I'll pass that on."

And the attitude of the campaign organization was Ted's. Bobby was insular, diffident, abrasive—better at ginning up crowds than placating delegates. Ted was outgoing, gregarious, congenial—the old Honey Fitz backslapper. As Doherty told Burton Hersh, "Teddy provided the atmosphere to keep people going, keep them happy." And it was Ted who tended to Bobby, who would sit next to him for "one-on-one time," while Bobby soaked in that tub at the end of the day when he was campaigning in the state, and Ted who kept him abreast of everything that was going on. Bobby was always "interested in hearing about the campaign and talking about it," Ted said. Bobby had lamented before the campaign that he didn't have anyone to be to him what he was to Jack. But he did. He had Ted, who was a very different kind of alter ego to Bobby than Bobby had been to Jack, but who was every bit as dedicated to him as Bobby had been to Jack—this, even though he still didn't believe in the campaign. Bobby couldn't help but see that dedication. And, according to one staffer, "The Indiana primary changed the balance completely between Bobby and

Ted." Ted rose in Bobby's estimation. The least was now the skilled political operative.

Like the speech that launched it, the Indiana campaign was an odd one—a harbinger of the strange campaign to come. The Kennedys made an assault on the state, as Jack had done in his primaries and Ted had done in his first Massachusetts campaign. There were the cadres of old Kennedy hands, and the lists of local supporters, some 14,000, that Doherty had parlayed from the get-on-the-ballot petitions, and the meticulous breakdown of the state into districts, and the money (nearly $1 million by some accounts), and the Kennedy family—even Bobby's dog, Freckles—parachuting into the state. But that was business as usual: the Kennedy political machine purring. What was unusual was the response the candidate elicited, the spirit of the crowds he drew, the electricity of his appearances. Bobby Kennedy, the shyest and most tentative of candidates, the candidate who wore a bashful smile and almost looked as if he were ashamed to be campaigning, and who was always nervously brushing his hair from his forehead, was greeted from the outset like a rock star. In this relatively small, conservative state, the crowds that greeted him were large ("rolling mobs of teeny-boppers," *Newsweek* called them), and they were frenzied, sometimes hysterical, as his convertible slowly rolled past and he stood up in the back seat, his shirtsleeves rolled up, the girls screaming in an uncontrollable, shuddering ecstasy that Americans hadn't seen since the Beatles toured the country, running alongside his car, reaching for him, almost plaintively, grabbing at his arms, pushing him up against the car so forcefully when he debarked in Mishawaka that he chipped a tooth. "Children were sometimes trampled in the crush, women fainted, men lost their tempers," *Newsweek* observed. "Kennedy often seemed a prayer away from being dismembered." The journalist Theodore H. White called it "the response of passion to passion." But it was not the passion of campaign rhetoric that drove them to these flights of ecstasy. Kennedy's message was the moderated one Ted had advised, delivered haltingly—though, Bobby being Bobby, he couldn't help but sermonize about the destitute and the desperate, those people, especially children, for whom he now advocated and for whom he was running. And he frequently closed his stump speech not with a rousing call to arms but with a sober call to heed those better angels, quoting Albert Camus: "Perhaps we cannot prevent this world from being a world in which children suffer. But we can reduce the number of suffering children. And if you don't help us, who else in the world can help us do this?" What seemed to incite the crowds was a pent-up hopefulness—pent up at least since Vietnam began draining America's will and confidence—a sense that Bobby Kennedy could revitalize the country as his brother had, that he could rescue Americans from their malaise, that he could make Americans feel good about themselves again. When the results came in, Bobby had won 42 percent of the vote, Branigin 31 percent, and McCarthy, who entered late and ran a lackluster campaign there, 27 percent, which he nevertheless claimed as a kind of victory since it exceeded predictions. (Bobby quipped dryly, "I always thought that it was much better to win. I learned that when I was about two.") But reporters—and Kennedy supporters—seized on another result. Bobby had won the black vote overwhelmingly, as expected (85 percent), but he also won the seven white working-class counties that the segregationist Alabama governor George Wallace had won in the primary four years earlier. And this created a new narrative for the campaign and for the pundits covering it, especially in the wake of Martin Luther King's death: Bobby Kennedy was hanging on to the old New Deal coalition, which had threatened to break apart when the passage of the civil rights laws exposed the fissures in it. A week later, in the Nebraska primary, where he won just over 50 percent of the vote, he achieved a similar feat. Though Nebraska had a small minority population, Kennedy won 60 percent of the rural vote and 60 percent of the blue-collar vote.

And there was a feeling now that Bobby Kennedy was not only reinvigorating the country; he was also reuniting it.

Primaries were about voters, about giving candidates a head of steam by demonstrating they could win those voters, but nominations weren't necessarily won in primaries, in part because there weren't enough primaries to provide a majority of delegates. Nominations were won among the party bosses, the pols in the trenches, who actually controlled the nomination process. As the campaign hit the road, Ted Kennedy was working to find delegates and line up support among those Democratic officeholders and the heads of the party's constituencies. Hubert Humphrey would not contest the primaries; he wouldn't formally announce until April 27, when the deadlines were past. But Humphrey had inherited most of Johnson's party support, and Humphrey, who had come on the national scene as a maverick, the man who, at the 1948 Democratic National Convention, had dared the party to pass a civil rights plank even though the Southern delegations would walk out if the convention did so (it did and they did), was now the party establishment—the man who defended Lyndon Johnson against all comers and who even continued to support the Vietnam War. Bobby was no insider—not anymore, not after his brother's death. Most of those insiders gravitated toward power, and Johnson and Humphrey had it now. It was no easy task for Ted to win them over, even if Bobby demonstrated his popularity by winning the primaries. So Ted kept working the phones, kept calling those Democrats who had voiced displeasure with Johnson, men like UAW president Walter Reuther and other labor leaders who distrusted Bobby but whom Ted hoped to woo anyway, and Harvard professor Daniel Patrick Moynihan, and the civil rights leaders. He visited George Meany, the president of the American Federation of Labor and the Congress of Industrial Organizations (AFL–CIO), the big labor confederation, but Meany was a robust supporter of the war and doubted Bobby on labor, and, as Ted put it, he was "very unresponsive and quite antagonistic." And Ted attended the Democratic state conventions, where most of the delegates to the national convention were chosen. But he was no more successful there. "We went to their convention and spoke up there," Ted said of the Pennsylvania session, "and we thought we made some inroads. They weren't very significant, as things turned out. At a subsequent meeting of the state central committee, Humphrey was strongly endorsed." That became a familiar scenario in other state conventions. "It was quite clear Bobby was not close to them," Dave Burke, who accompanied Ted on many of these convention forays, recalled. Humphrey was close to them, had been close to them for years after he shed his outsider status, was one of them. And Burke said that even though Ted never discussed it with him, Burke had the sense that, besides his dread that someone might try to kill Bobby, Ted also had a sense that, despite the crowds and the hysteria and the hopefulness and his brother's ability to inspire voters, Bobby might not only lose but might lose "badly," because this was the pols' nomination and not a people's nomination.

Bobby Kennedy was not the pols' candidate, and his campaign was not the pols' campaign; a Gallup poll in early June would show he had the support of only 16 percent of Democratic county chairmen, to 70 percent for Humphrey and 6 percent for McCarthy. He was not the pols' candidate because he did not rely on them and their organizations—he actually harbored contempt for them. Instead, he relied on his personal charisma—those screaming girls—just as John Kennedy had used his charisma in the beginning to circumvent the party regulars and establish an organization of his own, and just as he would use his movie-star charisma as president against the regular politicians when he had to. "Bob seemed to be in color and everyone else in black and white" was how *New York Times* reporter Steven Roberts would describe Bobby entering a room. And Bobby Kennedy was not the pols' candidate because, despite the dream he roused in Indiana of resurrecting the crumbling New Deal coalition, Bobby Kennedy had his own dreams of a new coalition, which would disrupt the Democratic party of the pols. "We have to write off the unions and the South now," he told Jack Newfield during the campaign, "and replace them with Negroes, blue-collar whites, and the kids," obviously disassociating those blue-collar workers from the big labor he so detested. He was opting for the party to write off the very basis of *their* party. And Bobby Kennedy was not the pols' candidate because he was calling for a revised liberalism, not the New Deal liberalism of Franklin Roosevelt and Lyndon Johnson, which was based on federal paternalism and provided spoils and patronage on which the pols had come to depend, but a liberalism that was decentralized right down to the community and that called upon the private sector—like the Bedford Stuyvesant Restoration Corporation, in a nearly all-black Brooklyn neighborhood, a massive, community-based, multifaceted redevelopment plan he had devised, and one with little pork barrel in it.

Perhaps, above all, Bobby Kennedy was not the pols' candidate because, unlike a Lyndon Johnson, he had very little interest in or tolerance for realpolitik or even political power, after his post–John Kennedy assassination transformation. True to his presidential announcement, he cared primarily about moral power, which made him less a politician than a priest, which is what he sometimes sounded like on the stump, and which made his campaign less an electoral mechanism to gain power than a crusade to redeem the national soul—and those pols were comfortable with neither. He called this an election "not for the rule of America but for the heart of America," and he said it would determine "what kind of men we are." And because it was a moral crusade rather than a conventional election, he didn't see his role as winning votes by making promises, which is what traditional aspirants did, so much as by challenging voters, even making them uncomfortable, which violated every political tenet. "From the moment I met him," his high school classmate Dave Hackett recalled, "I knew that he would embarrass his friends." Now he was embarrassing voters, shaming them, calling them out, working their guilt. Where would he get the money to finance his grandiose health programs for the poor? medical students in Indiana sneered at him. "From you," Bobby would answer. *From you.* "What other reason do we really have for existence as human beings," he asked in a speech at Notre Dame university at the outset of the campaign, "unless we've made some other contribution to somebody else to improve their own lives?" That was the essence of his campaign, but it was foreign to the pols, and it was disturbing to many Americans too, even frightening. "Why Do They Hate Him So?" columnist Stewart Alsop asked in his column in *The Saturday Evening Post*—it was a question Ted Kennedy had often asked too, of why Bobby Kennedy seemed to elicit not only such extreme devotion but also such extreme antipathy. Alsop concluded that white middle-class Americans feared his moralism and his stridency and his scolding and his insistent idealism—feared that they could lead to economic redistribution, said Alsop—but it might have been more accurate to say that they feared the redistribution of power from whites to minorities and resented the shame that Bobby called down upon them for not doing more to help their fellow Americans.

All of which made Bobby Kennedy an anomaly and, worse, a threat to the very people who would decide whether or not he would get the Democratic nomination.

But Ted didn't let up, even though he harbored those serious doubts that Bobby could win, even though the defeat would hurt the Kennedy brand, a winner's brand, and his own future presidential prospects. Dave Burke said Bobby's campaign revealed to him Ted's own presidential desires: "That was the first sense I had that underneath a ton of baggage, and underneath the horrors of the sixties, was a yearning on his part to someday have a shot for the presidency of the United States of America." Since Ted was a Kennedy, it was probably true. Ted persisted for his brother, fought for delegates, stayed on the road as he had for Jack's campaign even when Joan was pregnant, spent all but five nights of those two and a half months traveling for Bobby, because that is what Kennedys did and because that is what Bobby needed. And Bobby had to keep winning the primaries—those primaries in which Humphrey would not be on the ballot—to prove to those party bosses that he was the only one who could lead them to victory, to prove to them that he had the voters.

Oregon was the next battlefield, but it was the kind of state that raised doubts in the Kennedys—albeit different doubts from those in Indiana. "One giant suburb," Bobby had once called it, with few segments of the coalition he was hoping to assemble. "Bobby, I think, said that there wasn't a black or a poor kid or a city out there in Oregon—you know, his natural constituency," Ted would say. (Ted never set foot there; he was busy in California, which held its primary a week after Oregon's, and where the stakes were much higher.) Oregon was a perfect McCarthy target, white and fairly affluent, and Bobby Kennedy couldn't generate the frenzy there that he had generated in Indiana and was generating in California. When he lost to McCarthy, 44.7 percent to 38.8 percent, he became the first Kennedy to finish second in an election. But if it didn't come as a complete shock, it nevertheless shook Bobby's confidence: Kennedys never lost. It was akin to a sin. "I sometimes wonder if I have correctly sensed the mood of America," he admitted afterward. "I think I have. But maybe I'm all wrong. Maybe the people don't want things changed."

California was different. California was Kennedy country. In California, the crowds were large and enthusiastic, even ecstatic—all those images of his motorcade chased by people clamoring for him—and Bobby spent the last day of his campaign there racing around the state, a sprint from San Francisco to Los Angeles to San Diego to Long Beach, in what he realized would be his final chance, really his only chance, to prove himself to the bosses by overwhelming them with the strength of his support. "If we lose here, we can all go home," an aide remarked, though a Gallup poll that week among the national Democratic rank and file had shown Humphrey out in front of Kennedy by 48 percent to 36 percent.

But that was not the rank and file in California. As the votes rolled in, Bobby took a big lead over McCarthy, and the networks began calling the state for him. Ted was working San Francisco on election day, June 4, and late that evening he spoke before a victory rally at the Masonic Temple. But there was a portent in it. Dave Burke, who was with Ted, said the rally felt less celebratory than unsettled, with a current of tension. Something seemed amiss. He told Lester David that there were a lot of unfamiliar faces, a "lot of people who were pushing and it was difficult to reach the stage and get off." He said a group in the balcony was chanting, "Free Huey!" meaning Huey Newton, the Black Panther leader who had been incarcerated. "There was an awful lot of physical shoving of the senator," Burke said, and "no sense of control." And he said that people were shouting things that "had nothing to do with Robert Kennedy's victory." Burke and Ted, feeling uneasy, left the rally as quickly as they could and returned to the Fairmont, the hotel where they were staying.

At that same time, the mood was different for Bobby. Feeling celebratory and smoking a cigar, he was holed up in the bathroom at the Ambassador Hotel in Los Angeles, with Ted Sorensen and Richard Goodwin, working on his victory speech, while guests milled about his suite. Just before midnight, as the returns kept rolling in, he asked California Assembly speaker Jesse Unruh, now a supporter, if they knew enough for him to declare victory. "Oh, yeah," Unruh said, "there's no doubt about a victory," and Unruh headed to the Embassy Ballroom, while Bobby and Ethel prepared to follow. John Lewis, the civil rights leader and a Kennedy supporter, who was in the suite, said that Bobby looked so happy "he would have floated out of the room." In the ballroom, Bobby gave a speech, a humorous speech—he thanked his dog, Freckles, who he said was so sure of victory that he had already gone to bed, and supporter Roosevelt Grier, a massive defensive lineman for the Los Angeles Rams, who he said would "take care of anybody who didn't vote for" Bobby. He mentioned winning in both rural and urban areas and taking the South Dakota primary earlier that day, and then he discussed the ruptures within the country and said, "We are a great country, a selfless country, and a compassionate country, and I intend to make that my basis for running." Then he spoke beyond the crowd to the delegates, saying that the primaries had indicated people wanted a change in the country and, more than implying that those delegates should deliver one. He congratulated McCarthy and said he hoped to engage Humphrey in a debate on the direction of the country. And he closed, "On to Chicago," which is where the convention was to be held that August, "and let's win there." Then he headed off the dais and to the kitchen and toward a back entrance to reach the service elevators to his room.

The timing was practically choreographed. At that point, Ted and Burke had just arrived at Ted's room in the Fairmont and switched on the television to watch the returns. They saw chaos instead, and they assumed that there had been some outbreak of violence at the festering rally they had just left. And then Steve Smith, Ted's and Bobby's brother-in-law, was on the television screen, asking the crowd to stay calm and to leave the ballroom, and Ted and Burke realized that this was obviously Los Angeles, not San Francisco, that there had been a shooting, and, in what

Burke described as a "sudden, horrible dawning realization," that Bobby Kennedy had been shot. Ted watched impassively, then said, "We have to get down there." But they stood silent, in the middle of the hotel living room, transfixed by the screen—"frozen," Burke said, though for how many minutes he couldn't say. And then Burke raced down the eleven flights of stairs—he was so pumped with adrenaline he forgot the elevator—to the reception desk to book a flight. (In a later recollection, he said Ted had raced down the stairs, but this seems unlikely.) One of the receptionists reached American Airlines, and Burke took the call in the assistant manager's office, but the airline said they would have to call him back. As he waited, he phoned other airlines, taking breaks to head back up to the room to check on Ted, who remained motionless, expressionless, silent, standing in front of the television, his mind gone "black," he would say. Unable to secure a plane, Burke spotted Congressman Phillip Burton in the hotel lobby, and Burton offered to arrange through the National Guard for an Air Force jet to fly them from Hamilton Field in nearby Marin County, but he had a condition: that he accompany them to Los Angeles. (This infuriated Burke, who thought Burton wanted a photo-op off Bobby Kennedy's shooting.) By this time, John Seigenthaler, the newspaper editor who had been an aide of Bobby's at Justice, and Robert Fitzgerald, a cousin of Ted's and Bobby's, had arrived at the hotel. A state trooper herded all of them into a car—all but Burton, since Burke had ordered the police to "shoot" anyone else who tried to get in the car—and drove them to the base, about twenty-five miles away, accompanied by four motorcycle policemen. Burke told Lester David that he noted the time of their departure as 1:16 A.M., which was exactly one hour after Bobby had been shot.

It was a silent trip—"he set his jaw and he said nothing," Burke recalled of Ted, which was also Ted's demeanor when he rode back home after hearing of Jack's shooting—the silence broken only when Ted took a call from Pierre Salinger, Jack's old press secretary, who had been working on the campaign and who was at the Central Receiving Hospital in Los Angeles, where Bobby was awaiting surgery to remove the bullet and fragments from his brain. They spoke for a minute. When Burke asked what Salinger had said, Ted answered evenly, "It's going to be all right," which, of course, Salinger had not said. Ted did not utter another word throughout the flight, though he did get up and get coffee for the three other passengers. "Solicitous" is what Seigenthaler called him, though Ted was the one who could have used solicitousness. When they arrived at the airport, a helicopter was waiting to fly them to Good Samaritan Hospital, several blocks away, where Bobby had been transferred for surgery.

It was a grim arrival, but Ted's impassivity concealed fury. Dun Gifford was there when Ted walked in. "He was like a frozen man, he was so angry," Gifford remembered. "He was just barely controlling himself." A specialist had already said that Bobby would survive only eight to eighteen more hours before his systems would shut down. Ted Sorensen, Pierre Salinger, Milton Gwirtzman, Bobby's close friend and old classmate David Hackett, the singer Andy Williams, Bobby's aide Ed Guthman, even Martin Luther King Jr.'s widow, Coretta, who insisted on coming, and, of course, Pat and Jean had all preceded Ted there. (Joan was in Paris with the Shrivers, attending a reception at the Élysée Palace, when she got the news, and she and Eunice flew to New York—six hours during which, Joan said, she meditated on Ted and the new "family burdens" he would have to assume.)

Ted went to his brother's bedside, while Burke watched the screen showing Bobby's vital signs on the monitor outside his room. Ted had no illusions. He knew there was no hope. Even if Bobby were to miraculously survive, Ted was told, he would have severe brain damage. Nevertheless, Bobby underwent three hours of surgery, and Ted phoned Dr. James Poppen of the Lahey Clinic in Boston and asked if he would come, which he did, on a plane that was provided by Vice President Humphrey. (Poppen's prognosis was no more encouraging.) And then Ted phoned Hyannis Port to inform Rose, but Ann Gargan told him that Rose had already heard the news. In the morning, Ted and Steve Smith made funeral arrangements. Burke picked out an African mahogany casket. And then they kept vigil as Bobby lay there. "I can't let go," Ted told Gifford, meaning he couldn't let his emotions go. "We have a job to do. If I let go, Ethel will let go, and my mother will let go, and my sisters." At one point, he left to walk the parking lot and to be alone. But strong as Ted may have appeared in controlling his grief, Frank Mankiewicz, Bobby's campaign press secretary, said he saw Ted later in the bathroom of Bobby's hospital room, bending over the sink, clutching the sides of the basin. "I never expect, for the rest of my life, to see more agony on anyone's face. It was beyond grief and agony." When Richard Goodwin arrived and entered the room, he saw Ted at the foot of the bed, on his knees, praying. Ethel was beside Bobby, sitting on the bed. The rest of the family stood there, without breaking the silence. And Tunney, who had heard the news while in Boston with his father, delivering a speech at a Police Athletic League dinner, immediately jumped on a plane to Los Angeles and joined Ted at the hospital. And he, too, said, "Never had I seen such anguish."

So much anguish. And the anguish continued through the day as Bobby Kennedy languished. At 5 P.M., Mankiewicz, who had been providing updates to the press throughout, appeared before microphones set up across the street, to announce that there was a "continuing failure to show improvement during the postoperative period," and that there would be no further bulletins until the morning. By now, others had come to the hospital—the Kennedy entourage, but also Eugene McCarthy to pay his respects. Burke, who was manning telephones in a nearby suite on Bobby's floor, said that Humphrey called every half hour, asking if Ethel or Ted or Rose needed anything. President Johnson, who had been awakened by his national security assistant, Walt Rostow, at 3:30 A.M., Eastern time, on the night of the shooting, issued a statement—"All America prays for his recovery. We also pray that divisiveness and violence be driven from the hearts of men everywhere"—and then sent personal messages to Ethel and Rose and Joe and called Ted at the hospital. Crowds had gathered around the hospital, and in many parts of the country there was a kind of national keening over the impending loss—a sense that this was the loss of more than a man. It was the loss of an opportunity. "I can feel history slipping through my fingers," Jack Newfield told John Lewis.

At 2 A.M., Mankiewicz, his eyes watery, approached the microphones. Choking back his emotion, barely able to speak, he said tersely: "I have a short announcement to read, which I will read at this time. Senator Robert Francis Kennedy died at 1:44 A.M. today, June 6, 1968. With Senator Kennedy at the time of his death were his wife, Ethel; his sisters, Mrs. Stephen Smith and Patricia Lawford; his brother-in-law Stephen Smith; and Mrs. John F. Kennedy. He was forty-two years old.'"* (Eunice and Joan, flying in from Paris, would arrive in time to meet the plane carrying Bobby's

---

*The last line was an addition by Pierre Salinger, who anticipated its effect. Milton Gwirtzman interview, August 5, 2009, Miller Center, University of Virginia.

Ted personally helped lift the casket onto Air Force 707, stooping to recover a wreath that had fallen. The coffin was placed in the front of the plane, near the pilot. Ethel slept beside it, and Ted stayed next to it throughout, motioning newsmen to speak with him about the future, and later falling asleep briefly just before the plane landed. It was a different kind of flight than the one that had taken him from San Francisco to Los Angeles. Ted comforted the passengers as he had done then—a list that now included widows Jacqueline Kennedy and Coretta Scott King—but he was less restrained. NBC newsman Sander Vanocur, on the plane as a friend of the family's, said at the time, "He's mad. I might as well say it, he's mad. He's mad at what happens in this country. He does not know whether it is the act of a single person or whether this is the act of a conspiracy." Ted told the newsmen on the plane, "I'm going to show them what they've done," echoing what Jacqueline Kennedy had said on *her* death flight back from Dallas, "what Bobby meant to the country, what they lost."

But the country knew. While the casket lay at St. Patrick's Cathedral, where Ted kept another vigil all that night, he had to prepare a eulogy for his fallen brother. Dave Burke was adamant that Ted should not deliver a eulogy, that he had gone through too much, that it would be yet another ordeal, and Burke was so opposed that he said he wanted nothing to do with it. But Ted was equally adamant. He needed to send his brother off. Still, he didn't think he could write the eulogy himself. He didn't feel he had the skill. So he recruited Milton Gwirtzman once again, and Gwirtzman, Bobby's aide and friend Adam Walinsky, and Tunney met in Ted's room at the Waldorf Astoria to bat around ideas. Walinsky had provided some of Bobby's sayings, because Ted wanted to incorporate those into the eulogy. But Ted and Tunney also wanted to express Ted's own words and feelings. As Gwirtzman later told it, "Ted and Tunney felt very deeply that they wanted the eulogy to be about love, and the love that Ted had for his brother, and the love that his brother had for people." So Gwirtzman repaired to his hotel room. He said that the eulogy he wrote was not necessarily suffused with love, as Ted had requested. He thought it necessary to acknowledge something else, something that he had read in a Tom Wicker column in *The New York Times*, that John Kennedy's assassination had made him more beloved a figure than he would otherwise have been, which prompted Gwirtzman to write a passage about not making more of Bobby in death than he was in life. He sent the draft to Pierre Salinger to review. But Gwirtzman said no one touched a word of it. And he said he wrote it out of his feelings for Ted. And while Gwirtzman wrote, Ted and John Culver cruised the streets of New York, just the two of them and a driver, all night, a sleepless night of sad, quiet reverie.

The eulogy Ted Kennedy delivered that morning at St. Patrick's Cathedral was one of eloquence, poetry, emotion, and inspiration, both a call for reconciliation and a challenge to change the world. It was a summary not only of what Ted felt about his beloved brother but also of how Ted himself was coming to see the world. "Love is not an easy feeling to put into words," he said, his voice soft and wavering, his eyes fixed on the cards from which he read, seldom looking up. "Nor is loyalty or trust or joy. But he was all of these. He loved life completely and lived it intensely." He quoted Bobby's words about their father, about his father's love—"the kind of love that is affection and respect, order and encouragement, and support"—and about the social conscience Joe Kennedy had inculcated in his children: "There were wrongs which needed attention. There were people who were poor and needed help. And we have a responsibility to them and to this country." And then Ted quoted at length, great length, from a speech, a remarkable speech, that his brother had given in South Africa during a visit in 1966 in which he addressed "slavery and slaughter and starvation," government repression, the inequality of wealth, and "the imperfection of human justice and the inadequacy of human compassion," but said, "We can perhaps remember—even if only for a time— that those who live with us are our brothers; that they share with us the same short moment of life; that they seek—as we do—nothing but the chance to live out their lives in purpose and happiness, winning what satisfaction and fulfillment they can. . . . The cruelties and obstacles of this swiftly changing planet," Bobby had said, and Ted now quoted, "will not yield to the obsolete dogmas and outworn slogans," and he cited how change is often inspired by a single man. "Each time a man stands up for an ideal, or acts to improve the lot of others, or strikes out against injustice, he sends forth a tiny ripple of hope, and crossing each other from a million different centers of energy and daring, those ripples build a current that can sweep down the mightiest walls of oppression and resistance." He said, "Moral courage is a rarer commodity than bravery in battle or great intelligence." He said, "All of us will ultimately be judged, and as the years pass, we will surely judge ourselves on the effort we have contributed to building a new world society and the extent to which our ideals and goals have shaped that event." He said, "It is the shaping impulse of America that neither fate nor nature nor the irresistible tides of history, but the work of our own hands, matched to reason and principle, that will determine our destiny." And then Ted turned to those words Gwirtzman had written, influenced by Wicker's observation: "My brother need not be idealized or enlarged in death beyond what he was in life; to be remembered simply as a good and decent man, who saw wrong and tried to right it, saw suffering and tried to heal it, saw war and tried to stop it." And here Ted's voice quivered, almost broke, but not quite, though one could feel the strength, the struggle, it took for him to finish. "As he said many times, in many parts of this nation, to those he touched and who sought to touch him: 'Some men see things as they are and say why. I dream things that never were and say why not.' "

When the service ended, Ted accompanied the casket to a hearse outside, which carried it to Pennsylvania Station, where it was loaded onto a train bound for Washington and sent on a trip during which it passed thousands upon thousands of mourners standing alongside the track, all of whom had come to say goodbye. And then to Arlington National Cemetery. And then, late at night as the fog rolled in, to burial, not far from his beloved brother John.

Bobby Kennedy was gone now. And so much else too. From the first, his campaign had been singular: not, as McCarthy's was, a one-issue movement to end the war, or, as Humphrey's was, a vindication for administration policies that he announced as the "politics of joy"—a characterization Bobby ridiculed—but a deep reevaluation of America that would empower the powerless. Richard Goodwin said Bobby had discovered this theme while stumping through California, but he had actually discovered it much earlier. "He would be the 'tribune of the underclass,' not just the blacks or the impoverished but all those who sensed that their needs, their desires, were disdained or denied by the ruling forces of American life. For behind the varied problems of the day," Goodwin wrote, "was a single issue—impotence; the sensed helplessness of citizens to shape the conditions of their own life and that of the country." In impotence, Bobby brought together black Americans and working-class white Americans, that coalition much discussed in the Indiana primary. "I think we can end the divisions in the United States," he said in his California victory speech minutes before being shot. "The only white politician left who could speak to both races," said NBC News anchor David Brinkley. "The last liberal

politician who could communicate with white working-class America,"
said Paul Cowan in *The Village Voice*. And though some disputed that he
had actually bridged the racial divide in Indiana or elsewhere—vanden
Heuvel and Gwirtzman noted that he had lost fifty-nine of seventy white
precincts in Gary, Indiana—and though his success was surely overstated,
Bobby himself never doubted it, even though he was often exasperated
during the campaign when he failed to spark white audiences with calls to
justice for black Americans. McCarthy had had no interest in black people
and not much in working-class white people either. Humphrey had built a
career on civil rights, but the war had diverted his attention elsewhere.
Only Bobby Kennedy had staked his chances on reconciliation. Ruthless
he had been called. Ruthless he had become for the dispossessed.

And Bobby Kennedy, alone among the candidates, found an essential
truth about liberalism at the very moment when it was under siege and
losing its strength. Liberalism had become "pragmatic" and "realistic,"
Jack Newfield complained. It was "less visionary, less politically combative, less intellectually flexible." It had become "suburbanized," devoting
itself less to righting wrongs than to maintaining the status quo against
new assaults. There was a backlash against the old liberalism, with its
stridency—or, at least, what many whites regarded as its stridency—in
advancing the rights of black people and the poor. In 1961, 59 percent of
Americans believed the government had a responsibility to see that everyone had a job and an adequate income. By 1969, after the Great Society,
only 31 percent thought that. But Bobby Kennedy knew this truth: that
liberalism was predicated on moral authority, that the only reason it had
lasted as long as it did, long after the exigencies that had brought it into
being during the Great Depression had passed with postwar prosperity
among most of the citizenry, was because it still maintained vestiges of its
moral authority—the powerful summons to do good, to help those who
needed it, to provide aid and justice and equality and power to the least
among us. Civil rights had made many white Americans uncomfortable
with that summons, and Vietnam had begun to strip away that authority.
In mounting his moral crusade for the presidency, Bobby Kennedy understood that if liberalism lost its moral authority, if Americans no longer
thought of their nation as a moral enterprise, all was lost. He was a moralist not because he was a scold but because he thought it was the only way
to save his country.

And now his death had ended that promise, because no other politician could or would make it, and certainly no other could ever make good on it as he might have, even though his prospects for wresting the nomination from Humphrey had been slim. When people grieved for Bobby Kennedy, especially those people for whom he had so vigorously advocated, they grieved for that, for the end of the promise, for the end of the hope for national moral redemption. Even the normally unflappable Hubert Humphrey, the promoter of the "politics of joy," called Larry O'Brien to his room at the Waldorf Astoria that night, after the funeral service, depressed, shaken, hopeless. "Men struggle for worthy goals, and yet they have no control over their own destinies. It all seems futile and pointless," he told O'Brien. "I'm afraid they will all opt out now," United Auto Workers president Walter Reuther told Arthur Schlesinger Jr. of those who had championed change, as the two waited to board Bobby's funeral train, adding, "They will be like the college kids before New Hampshire— completely skeptical about any possibility of change within the system." Barbara Mikulski, who later became Senator Mikulski, recalled of Bobby's death, "Really, it was a generational broken heart, that's what we had," a broken heart she tried to salve with political action. "The music died for me," John Bartlow Martin, a speechwriter for both John and Bobby, and a diplomat, wrote in his diary. "It's over, the brief bright dream." He felt nothing but "bleak despair," Martin said. "He was a conscience in our midst," newsman Sander Vanocur said, "and now we have come to understand how little some people wish to understand conscience." Jack Newfield made this benediction at the close of his memoir on Bobby: "We are the first generation that learned from experience, in our innocent twenties, that things were really not getting better, that we shall *not* overcome . . . And from this time forward, things would get worse: our best political leaders were part of memory now, not hope." Civil rights leader Roger Wilkins would declare, "And it was over. The whole thing was over. The whole period of lift and hope and struggle was all over. It was just over."

IV

American soldiers in Vietnam would describe especially fierce firefights as "all hell fell." Now all hell had fallen politically for the country and personally for Ted Kennedy. Playing off Franklin Roosevelt's optimistic incantation that Americans had a "rendezvous with destiny," Ted would say of the sixties that it was the decade in which Americans had a "rendezvous with reality." In a message videotaped on the front lawn of the big Hyannis Port house on June 15, Ted and Rose, with Joe sitting in a wheelchair beside them, expressed their thanks to President Johnson, Vice President Humphrey, UN Secretary General U Thant, and "the people themselves with outstretched hands of sympathy and strength that have most touched the hearts and members of my family. . . . It is the ones who could give the least who have given the most," Ted said, in a sentiment reflective of Bobby Kennedy, and he said that the family would continue to express their thanks "in our deeds in our public and private lives."

But that wasn't true. Ted Kennedy wasn't ready yet for deeds in either his public or private life. Ted Kennedy was incapacitated by grief. It was different than the grief he had suffered over Jack's death. Given the disparity in their ages, the relationship between Jack and Ted was like that between an indulgent father and a winsome son, and as traumatized as Ted was when Jack had died—and he was terribly traumatized—he recovered, if only because he still had Bobby. Ted's relationship to Bobby was more complicated. When Ted was in high school, Bobby was a kind of mentor to him—"When we were boys he spent so much time with him," Joe Gargan would say of Bobby. And though, while Jack was alive, Ted and Bobby didn't share the same intimacy as Jack and Bobby did, and though Bobby would snipe at Ted and assert his intellectual superiority when Bobby entered the Senate, he came to admire Ted's senatorial prowess and, in Bobby's presidential campaign, Ted's political skill. The two grew close, very close, if only as replacements in each other's lives for Jack and as ongoing solace for each other. There had been a physical proximity too. When Joan was pregnant with their third child, Patrick, in the spring of 1967, Ted bought six acres in McLean, Virginia, a mile down the road from Bobby's house, on which to build a home of his own. "They're like crossed fingers," one Kennedy would say of them. In Bobby's first public appearance after Jack's funeral, he attended a Christmas party at an orphanage, and a young black boy, not more than seven or eight, raced up to him and shouted, "Your brother's dead! Your brother's dead!" The adults in the room gasped, and the boy, sensing he had committed some transgression, began to cry. And Bobby scooped him up and held him close and whispered to him, "That's all right. I have another brother." But Ted Kennedy didn't have another brother now. Ted Kennedy was alone. "He had no one to talk to," Jean Smith said, though the loss went deeper than that, much, much deeper.

Yet Kennedys had been taught never to display grief or acknowledge unhappiness. They had been taught to be stoic, even as the tragedies piled up, even as they had been shaken to their core. "I don't want sourpusses around here," Joe Kennedy would say, as if sadness were weakness. "There'll be no crying in this house," he would also say, and "pronounced it with the force of moral law," Ted recalled. And Ted added this, revealingly: "To understand the profound authority of this charge to us is to understand much about my family." It was to understand the devotion to the aesthetics of fortitude, the emotional repression under which the Kennedys were forced to function, which led to the denial of their deepest feelings and ultimately of themselves, and it was to understand the ways in which that denial tortured them and warped them and even brutalized them, forcing them into themselves rather than allowing them to give expression to the agony they were enduring. *Kennedys don't cry.* But Kennedys often felt like crying, and they paid an enormous price for not doing so. Ted's youngest son, Patrick, said the entire family suffered from post-traumatic stress disorder, the condition from which soldiers often suffered when they had been in combat and all hell had fallen. The Kennedys were shell-shocked. Always.

Ted tried to maintain the pretense of imperturbability that summer of Bobby's death. One journalist visiting the Kennedy compound at Hyannis called it a "pretty hilarious time," adding, "Fiercely competitive tennis games. Merciless teasing." And he cited Teddy leading a procession singing "Southie Is My Hometown" up the stairs and dumping Jean and Steve Smith out of their bed. "They never talked about death or assassination," the journalist said. "They never talked about the pain or how we all felt." Ted seemed to think that action would inure him to grief. One time that summer, Ted and Joe Gargan and a group of Green Berets rappelled up the big house on the compound, then went to Squaw Island, where Ted had his house, then to a neighbor's house, and then to a bar, where they ate steaks that Gargan had ordered earlier in the evening and had forgotten until night. Ted buried himself in trying to find jobs for his brother's staff, putting together a master list of all the people, firms, NGOs, and other Senate offices that he had coaxed to volunteer—a book an inch thick—and he kept at it into the fall, until he had placed them, because he felt he owed that to Bobby and because he had promised it to them. He gathered the brain trust once again, only this time to discuss a memorial to Bobby—a foundation to support his work to help the disempowered. In July, he accompanied Bobby's eldest son, Joe II, to a finca in Spain, to study Spanish and history. In August, he decamped to Greece and joined Jacqueline, who was affianced to the Greek shipping magnate Aristotle Onassis, and vacationed on the island of Skorpios, which Onassis owned. He took the Kennedy children on a white-water rafting trip on the Green River in Utah—though, under the circumstances, it was not the festive trip that white-water-rafting ventures had been with Bobby. "The adults floated along with their daiquiris and Pouilly-Fuissé and didn't want to be bothered," said one of the cousins. "They were angry."

But try as he might to distract himself, Ted couldn't. Try as he might to carry on as normal, he couldn't. He was going through the motions of normalcy because he felt he had to. "A lot of it is duty. Some of the gaiety is forced," recalled his former aide Charles Tretter, who visited the family then. Ted Kennedy understood that duty. He had been regarded as the blithest of the Kennedy brothers, "the least intellectual and introspective," as *Time* put it. "He never seemed to have a care in the world. Life to him was 'fun time,'" said Joe Kennedy's nurse Rita Dallas. "The most open of the Kennedys," observed one reporter. But this had always been something of a misconception; it had always been the way that Ted portrayed himself, felt he had to portray himself. In truth, the boy who harbored such deep doubts about himself, the boy who was bounced from school to school to school, the boy who was never good enough, harbored a darkness too. Bobby knew. The bonhomie couldn't hide it. Bobby had inscribed a copy of his account of the labor-rackets investigation, *The Enemy Within*, to Ted this way: "To Teddy, who has his own enemy within. Love, Bobby." Ted's apparent openness notwithstanding, the same reporter who had cited it also noted a "deep reserve" in Ted, a wariness. Rita Dallas, who had called him seemingly carefree, also said that his "ever-present smile didn't quite reach his eyes. To me, they were often clouded," and she said, "There was still a sadness in them at off moments." Majority Leader Mike Mansfield called him "the sad one . . . the one who's had a black shadow over his life."

At first, with Bobby's death, there had been that rage—a "rage so deep and black that," *Newsweek* observed, "aboard the funeral train, the word went down the line, 'Don't close headquarters yet—Teddy's fighting mad,'" as if he would pick up Bobby's fallen sword and challenge McCarthy and Humphrey himself. (Rage was how Ethel coped too—storming around the tennis court even though she was pregnant with their eleventh child, screaming, blasting music in the garage.) But Ted's rage passed, and then a darkness adumbrated everything. And that darkness he couldn't hide, at least not from anyone who knew him. *Time* described him in "kind of hibernation." A friend said, "He almost looked like he had a death wish, almost like he didn't care." A "fatalism," the friend called it. "Teddy went into a downward spiral," said another friend. "There's no other way to talk about it. You just ached to see him. He was always able to be up and cheerful, keep everybody up, but this was one time he couldn't do it. He just couldn't." And she said there was "just a sadness toward everything." John Tunney recalled, "It was horrible. . . . He was not able to function effectively for a while. Part of his brain was not working, and it was because of this extraordinary grief that he felt, and almost to the degree that was fatalistic, that he was going to be gone, he was dead, he was going to kill himself, he wouldn't be around much longer, and what the hell, what's going on? This world is crazy. It's chaotic. What am I doing here? All this stuff." Tunney said the death destroyed Ted's sense of identity and forced him to ponder whether he should even be in politics anymore. "It was just [as if] a nuclear bomb had been tossed on the family's psyche," Ted's son Patrick would say, assessing his father's debilitation from the distance of decades. "It obliterated any sense of hope, happiness, security, possibility. Boom. Gone. But there they all were, standing as shells of their former selves." One Boston pol said, "There are two Ted Kennedys. The pre-1968 Kennedy with a terminal case of adolescence, and the post–June 5, 1968, Kennedy. For all practical purposes, he had a nervous breakdown that summer of '68 after Bobby was killed." Still another friend said that Ted had lost his sense of self. "I don't know if he's real. I think he's a composite of what he's seen as the good qualities of the others . . . as if he's taken a little from each one." But the brothers were gone now, and the father was incapacitated, and Ted had become a composite of the lost.

All that summer—a summer darkened by the shadow—there were constant scenes of pain and sorrow, unremitting scenes. He would go silent—this most voluble of men—and take long walks along the beach with Ethel or Jackie. More often, he would walk the beach alone, his arms linked behind him, or walk the compound, a "lost soul," as Rita Dallas described him. Sometimes he would lie on the long gray-stone jetty that formed a breakwater in the bay off the compound. Other times, he would ask his chauffeur to drive anywhere but home, because he wasn't up to facing anyone—including his family. And still other times, he would weep with others or weep alone—usually alone. He wept for the loss and he wept for the burden he now had to assume. "I remember seeing him sitting on the steps of the porch," Dallas would write, "watching the children at play: Bobby's, the president's, his own. From the pain in his eyes, I could tell he knew there was no way for him to replace their losses. He tried valiantly, but it was too much."

Though Joan would say that she and Ted grew closer in this period, that she could commiserate with him and that he would confide in her, friends said he sought refuge in women, which had been Joe's and Jack's recreation, "one after the other," as one profiler wrote of this period. And he sought refuge in drink. "It's inaccurate to say he was drunk most of the time," an associate told biographer Burton Hersh. "It's also inaccurate to say he wasn't drunk at all." Ted had always drunk more than Jack and Bobby, ignoring his father's injunctions against it. But that was social drinking, drinking for conviviality. Now the drink inured him to the pain. "The freneticism of booze and sex," a friend told a reporter. "Afterward there were times of great guilt. He was so raw." But it wasn't just the pain to which he had to inure himself. There were the expectations now—this of the boy for whom the expectations had always been the lowest. "He would go through the necessary performances," the friend recalled, "and then, a lot of times, it would be, goddamn it, it's me now, it's me for the bullet; it's me for the brass ring."

He called this period a "blur in my memory," though it was also a time when he sought to obliterate his memory. His real escape, his balm, was the water. It was the water, as much as anything, that connected him to Joe Jr. and Jack and Bobby—all of whom had taught him to sail, and he could recall Jack telling him when Ted was just a boy how the proportion of salt in our bodies is equal to the proportion of salt in the sea, which, in Ted's mind, created a mystical communion between man and the sea from which he sprang. He had perfect recall of the details of those sailing expeditions with his brothers—where they went and what they saw. And as he grew older, he saw the sea as a personal metaphor—its roughness, its ungovernability, and its danger all analogues for life, but also, for all that, its peacefulness and implacability, which were analogues too. "There are eternal aspects to the sea and the ocean," he had told a friend. "It anchors you." Bobby liked to quote Albert Camus: "I was born halfway between poverty and the sun. Poverty taught me that all was not well under the sun and in history. The sun taught me that all was not history." The sea was Ted Kennedy's sun, his cosmological perspective.

And as he recovered, Ted needed to be on the water. That terrible summer, he had gone back to the Senate, answering mail and organizing Bobby's campaign papers, and he suddenly asked Dun Gifford if he would go charter him a boat, a big sailboat. There were no further instructions, not even where Gifford should get it—"We'll go wherever the boat is"—so Gifford, an expert sailor himself, rented a sixty-foot yawl named the *Mira* in Oyster Bay on Long Island, and Ted spent the better part of that summer living on the water. On that first voyage, he picked up Joan and the children in New London and later that summer picked up Jackie and Ethel and all their children in Hyannis, sailing up and down Long Island Sound, the Vineyard Sound, and Nantucket Sound. There was no set destination. The object was to sail wherever the wind took him. "It was hard at first," Gifford said. "He had a hard time." But he would ask Gifford to rotate his friends for various legs, and that is how he coped. "He coped by having friends with him, family with him," Gifford said. "A lot of times he would be morose, and I could recognize it. He had a vast support structure of family and friends, coming and going, but sometimes you just knew he was down. So I'd say, 'Why don't we go anchor off this island?' And he'd either swim in or take the dinghy in and just walk off by himself for a while and then come back. That happened a lot at the beginning. There were other times when he needed to have a whole lot of his friends around, raising hell, making jokes, telling stories, whooping it up." Sometimes he would stop at a cove just long enough to lead a run down the beach. Sometimes he would be gone for a day, sometimes for four or five days at a time, and he once returned home unshaven, rumpled, annoying his father with his unkempt appearance; Rose threatened to shave his beard, but Ted shaved it off first. Sometimes he would sail alone, just him and the captain, and maybe Joan or Joey Gargan or a friend, eschewing other company—even Rose went occasionally, to calm him, though she detested the sea—and he would lie on the deck, as he had lain on the breakwater, staring silently at the sky. And sometimes, the best times, he would sail the night, all night, usually with the smaller boat, the *Victura*—the best times not just because he felt "the momentous joy I have always felt at the way a sailboat moves through the water" but because he also felt his "grieving was subsumed into a sense of oneness with the sky and the sea" and because "the darkness helped me feel the movement of the boat, and the movement of the sea, and it helped displace the emptiness inside me with the awareness of direction. An awareness that there was a beginning to the voyage and an end to the voyage, and that this beginning and ending is part of the natural order of things." And that was both the most powerful metaphor and the most comforting metaphor—that there was a shape to tragedy, a vector to it.

But that summer there was little sense of direction, only drift. He thought seriously about leaving politics, getting as far away from politics as possible until, as he put it, his wounds could heal. On those trips, he and Gifford would talk about setting up a boat charter company, with an office in Marbella, Spain, and one in Palm Beach and one in Newport. But Gifford said he figured that while Ted was drumming up business, Gifford would be stuck with actually running the operation. William vanden Heuvel joined him on the boat then too, and they would also discuss career options, maybe buying a newspaper or becoming a university president—talking politics, vanden Heuvel said, was too painful for Ted— but vanden Heuvel concluded that Ted was only musing about these things because "he was so wounded by Bobby's death" and that ultimately any life outside politics, however safe, however liberating, would have bored him.

But with the sorrow and pain and grief and drift, there was that overriding despair. He spent a good deal of his time sailing up the coast to Maine, docking at Gene Tunney's summer house there or at the home of Douglas Dillon, who had been Treasury secretary in Jack's administration, or Tom Watson, the head of IBM and a Kennedy family intimate. Ted was "determinedly buoyant," *Newsweek* observed. But there was no real buoyancy here, as there was no real buoyancy elsewhere. "I think I probably kind of checked out," he would tell an interviewer years later. He just wanted to escape. He hated to return to Hyannis but said he "felt I owed it to them," meaning Joe and Rose, "to come back and see them," and so he would sail home and then sail back to Maine again. "I love to sail into one of those Maine harbors where nobody knows you . . . couldn't care less," he said. He was hopeless and faithless, and he was not alone in that. Rose Kennedy, who had always been sustained by her religious faith, even had what Ted called a "moment of despair" and cried out, "But how could they [meaning God] have taken the father of ten children?" She was able to accept Jack's death, Ted confided to James Wechsler, the editor of the *New York Post,* "but after Bobby . . ." He later told an interviewer about his own crisis of faith: "That was the big one that made you wonder about how that could happen. Children, all the children, they were going to grow up without a father." And now those children were his responsibility. He said that while sailing in Maine, "I felt that whatever justice there was, whatever the meaning of life in terms of spirituality and reliance and source of strength that would come from my faith—I found it was pretty empty. I mean . . . the losses, his loss." And in Maine, "just breathtakingly lovely, beautiful, and you could . . ." but even all those years later he trailed off, unable to say what he wanted to say: that he'd hoped he could lose himself there.

But there was no escaping what he faced now, which was being the paterfamilias of the Kennedy family, the leader of them all, though he was only thirty-six. At summer's end, Gifford later said, Ted would sail over from Hyannis with the Kennedy cousins, and Gifford would sail from Nantucket with his family and friends, and they would meet at a "sand spit of an island" called Muskeget. And these gatherings were the opposite of the solitary and melancholy voyages they had shared earlier. These were large and boisterous—picnics with swimming and games and grilling over big fires—until the day ended, and Ted and Gifford went their separate ways. Gifford speculated that these outings were Ted's way of telling the family and himself that he was up to the task of leading them all now. "Grieving is one thing, and you get over it," Gifford said, though Ted never really did. "But then you think, 'Oh, my God! Now what? Now they're all going to be looking at me.' And they *were,* everybody. 'Now what, Teddy? Now what are you going to do?'"

Which was the same question he was asking himself.

TEN

A Fallen Standard

BOBBY KENNEDY'S DEATH had left an emotional void in the Kennedy family, but, as the Democratic National Convention approached in late August, it had also left a political void in the Democratic party. "It had always been assumed that if anything should happen to Robert Kennedy, his brother Edward would take on the quest for the presidency, just as Robert had done after John F. Kennedy was assassinated in Dallas, and just as John Kennedy had entered politics to fill the intended role of Joseph Kennedy Jr., who was killed in World War II," John Herbers wrote in *The New York Times* of the Kennedy succession, just ten days after Robert Kennedy had died. Herbers concluded, "Those who know Edward Kennedy expect him to be less persistent than Robert would have been in upholding the family tradition. But he still is a Kennedy and his friends do not expect him to remain in politics without aspiring to a higher goal."

At the time Herbers wrote, Ted Kennedy *was* considering leaving politics, abandoning the violence and the madness and what he increasingly saw as the futility of politics. But as he gradually emerged from his mourning, he realized that this was an impossibility for a Kennedy, regardless of his own desires. Though he didn't know about Allard Lowenstein stopping Ted in the hospital elevator to beg Ted to run, Milton Gwirtzman said that the pressure on Ted to join the Democratic ticket began "immediately" after Bobby's death, even on the plane carrying Bobby's body back to New York, when an associate of Bobby's, a man named Paul Corbin, who had helped Bobby in Wisconsin, collared Ted and pleaded, "You gotta run. You gotta run for president." And pressure was mounting from the party too. Within days, Humphrey let it be known to Ted that he would be "welcome," in the words of a *New York Times* report, to be Humphrey's running mate, and a few days after that, Humphrey indicated again that he wanted Ted on the ticket, rebuffing reports that Ted was not interested with "I have no reason to believe that. I hope it's not true." Six days after Bobby's assassination, Gwirtzman wrote Ted a six-page memo laying out considerations for accepting or rejecting a vice-presidential nomination and for dealing with Ted's reintroduction into public life. Gwirtzman knew that the party bosses, who had never warmed to Bobby's candidacy but who liked Teddy, were receptive to the possibility of him on the Democratic ticket, and not necessarily just for vice president, though, as *Newsweek* put it, "his party was fairly begging him to run for vice president." A Harris poll late in June showed Ted beating Richard Nixon and third-party candidate, former Alabama governor George Wallace, 42 percent to 38 percent for Nixon to 13 percent for Wallace, and beating another Republican contender, New York governor Nelson Rockefeller, 40 percent to 36 percent. The same poll showed that a Humphrey–Kennedy ticket would beat a ticket of Nixon and Illinois senator Charles Percy by ten points and one of Rockefeller and California governor Ronald Reagan by twelve. A poll a month later found that Ted especially provided a boost for Humphrey among African Americans (by 18 percent), Catholics (by 13 percent), women (by 11 percent), union members (by 10 percent), and young people (by 7 percent). Yet another Harris poll later that summer found that Ted would add five million votes to Humphrey's ticket. At the Governors Conference in Cincinnati, Sam Shapiro of Illinois and Richard Hughes of New Jersey publicly endorsed Ted for vice president, and seven other governors joined forces to phone Humphrey and demand that he put Ted on the ticket. At the same time, Mayor Richard Daley of Chicago, at sixty-six one of the most powerful of the Democratic bosses, with a smooth-running political machine and who had used that machine to aid John Kennedy's candidacy, said, "I hope the convention will draft him," though for president or vice president he didn't say. And former Ohio governor Mike DiSalle announced that he would be putting Ted's name in nomination at the convention—a "one-man" draft, he called it.

But eager as the bosses were to have him, Ted was deep in depression and in no condition to entertain a presidential or vice-presidential run. "Anyone who had seen him with his family at that time"—meaning that summer—"would have known that seeking higher office was simply not possible for Teddy. He realized that he was being sought only as a sentimental talisman," wrote Joe Kennedy's nurse Rita Dallas. Nevertheless, with all the calls for Ted to make a move, the brain trust that had advised Bobby on his presidential deliberation assembled at Hyannis Port on July 2, to discuss ways to advance both Bobby Kennedy's agenda and Ted's political options. No one thought much of Humphrey, whom they considered a "symbol of failure," or of Eugene McCarthy, whom they felt petty for not congratulating Bobby on his primary victories or acknowledging Bobby's telegram after McCarthy's Oregon victory. But, as Richard Harwood of *The Washington Post* reported, Ted, still frozen in grief, listened to the deliberations and said little. The only conclusion among some of the staff—a minority—was that Humphrey would offer the vice presidency to Ted, who could then demand concessions on Vietnam. (In his memo, Gwirtzman had promoted an idea from columnist Charles Bartlett that Ted introduce an anti-Vietnam resolution in the Senate, which Humphrey could use as an excuse for changing his position. But Ted didn't return to the Senate, was in too much pain to return, and Humphrey was wary of antagonizing Johnson, his patron.) Indeed, Humphrey had spoken with Steve Smith and Ted Sorensen about whether Ted would accept the vice presidency, but Smith was adamantly opposed to his doing so—so much so that he said he would sit out the campaign if Ted ran.

But Ted seemed to have already made a decision through his inaction. On July 26, while he was sailing, he issued a statement that it would be "impossible" for him to run for the vice presidency, citing "purely personal reasons," and that this decision was "final, firm, and not subject to further consideration." (The day before, however, Mayor Daley said he had spoken to Ted and that Ted said he was open to being drafted at the convention, though this might have been a ruse by Daley to pressure the convention into drafting him.) This was not, Ted asserted, a political abdication. He said that he would be speaking out on "certain vital foreign and domestic policies our party must pursue if it is to be successful in the coming election," and, though little was made of it at the time, he said nothing about the presidency, only the vice presidency.

Ordinarily, Ted's unequivocal statement would have ended the speculation, except that Ted announced he would be making his first public address since Bobby's death on August 21, in front of the Worcester, Massachusetts, Chamber of Commerce, five days before the opening of the convention—an announcement that some took as a change of heart. But Ted Kennedy had had no change of heart. His speech was not designed to further a political bid. It was a speech on behalf of Bobby's crusade, and, while it was seen as Ted's reintroduction to the political scene after the tragedy, Ted had clearly calculated to have it affect the Democratic platform on Vietnam, to move its position closer to Bobby's position on the war, and it was intended to keep Bobby's flame alive.

It was a big speech, a highly anticipated speech, a speech in which Ted Kennedy would return to public life after ten weeks during which he spent time with the sea, he said, "clearing my mind and spirit of the events of last June." The live audience for the televised speech was so large that the address had to relocate to the campus of the College of the Holy Cross. Ted Sorensen, Jack Kennedy's own wordsmith, drafted most of it. It clearly bore Sorensen's flourish, as Ted began citing calls for him to withdraw from public life for his own safety. But this had never been the Kennedy way. "There is no safety in hiding," he told the crowd, as he stood on a dais adorned with red, white, and blue carnations and battled his emotions, fighting back tears, "not for me, not for any of us here today, and not for our children, who will inherit the world we make for them. . . . For all of us," he went on, "the path is to work in whatever way we can to end the violence, the hatred, and the division that threaten us all.

"So today I reassume my public responsibilities to the people of Massachusetts. Like my three brothers before me, I pick up a fallen standard. Sustained by the memory of our priceless years together, I shall try to carry forward that special commitment to justice, to excellence, and to courage that distinguished their lives." And just like that, simply, directly, solemnly, he assumed his role in the succession from Bobby as Bobby had assumed his from John, the succession Joe Kennedy had set in motion years earlier, and he dedicated himself to fulfilling Bobby's mission as Bobby had dedicated himself to fulfilling John's. Ted had been cautious; Ted had been wary of spending moral capital; Ted had been more of a pragmatic idealist than a romantic idealist like Bobby. But Bobby's death had not only emptied Ted; it had refilled him, changed him, just as John's had emptied and refilled and changed Bobby's, and not only because Bobby was gone but because Bobby had died waging his moral campaign. From Bobby, Ted's impulse for moral justice was converted into a passion for moral justice. Ted was less cautious now after the months of despair, less morally inhibited, less the pragmatist and more like Bobby, even though they had such different temperaments. And having reentered the political arena, he decried the social chasms separating Americans and the hopelessness felt by so many who had worked to change the system through political means, and, in an allusion to the prospective Republican candidate, Richard Nixon, who had been emphasizing law and order over more-humane solutions to problems, he said, "We cannot let the new leadership of this country be swept into office on a tide of fear." Then Ted launched an attack on Lyndon Johnson's Vietnam policy: "the tragedy of our generation," he called the war, and a "bottomless pit." And he proposed an unconditional cessation of bombing, a negotiation of withdrawal of foreign forces from South Vietnam, assistance to the South Vietnamese government, and, prior to withdrawal, an immediate reduction in American troop levels as a demonstration of our good intentions. And he emphasized that there would be no military victory. Finally, he asked, as Bobby had asked, for each American to reaffirm "a profound personal and moral commitment" to "passion and action in the service of our fellow man and the nation we love." *A moral commitment.* He closed with Bobby's quote about "the end he so tenderly sought for all of us," to "tame the savageness of man and make gentle the life of this world." Then he left. He had arranged his arrival and departure to avoid reporters.

He had to. By this time, Richard Nixon, who was anathema to most Democrats as a onetime red-baiter and a political sharpie, had won the Republican nomination, and the pressure on Ted began anew. Despite his renunciation of any immediate political ambition, many, including many in the party, assumed the speech had reopened the door to a possible candidacy. Even Herbers wrote that Ted had "left the impression" that he had "recovered from the shock of his brother's death," which was not true. On the drive back to Hyannis Port with columnist Jimmy Breslin and Dave Burke, Ted was "drained," Burke said, and he believed that "the ice got thicker and thicker" as Ted began to come to terms with the fact that he was now the hope his brother had been, that he was the person on whom the fate of the nation rested. It was almost insurmountable pressure—the pressure to be the liberal savior. The next day, August 22, Ted met with Hubert Humphrey, the presumptive Democratic nominee, at Ted's new McLean home, for a half hour or forty-five minutes—a "warm and touching conversation," Ted called it—during which Humphrey tried to convince him yet again to accept the vice-presidential nomination, even while expressing his understanding that Ted was under enormous strain and that Ted was fully committed to a different policy on Vietnam, which Humphrey, beholden as he was to Johnson, couldn't endorse, though Humphrey said he was going to "try and work that issue through" once he was on his own. Ted knew there could be no accommodation on Vietnam unless Humphrey renounced Johnson's policy, that his brother's supporters would be aghast if he were to run with Humphrey given Bobby's feelings about the war, that he couldn't even think of putting his family through a campaign without an assurance of some resolution of the war, and that, in any case, he had little interest in being vice president when he was becoming so active in drafting legislation in the Senate. "I liked him," Ted said of Humphrey, "but I wasn't prepared to sign on."

In the meantime, as Humphrey hoped that Ted would change his mind on the vice presidency, and others hoped he would change it on the presidency, the political sands had begun to shift. Bobby's supporters and those on his staff feared that with Bobby's death the entire mission of moral regeneration would simply sputter. They considered throwing their support to McCarthy but decided against it—"inappropriate," they called it, because it wasn't likely to stop Humphrey's nomination—and despite some affection for Humphrey, supporting him was unconscionable to most of them, including Ted. On Bobby's funeral train, Bill Dougherty, who had headed Bobby's winning South Dakota primary effort, had already approached Senator George McGovern to declare his candidacy as a way of holding Bobby's delegates at the convention. McGovern said he was reluctant because Ted should be the one to make that decision, and he called Steve Smith to see if Ted might enter the race. Smith said he saw no chance of that, so McGovern announced his own candidacy on August 10, still hoping that Ted might run. When McGovern phoned Ted after the Worcester speech to congratulate him, he said that Ted "expressed clear sympathy with what I am doing," namely, trying to hold Bobby's delegates as a bloc in order to move the convention leftward, but McGovern didn't expect any kind of endorsement and he didn't get one.

As the Democratic convention opened in Chicago that last week of August, the party was in a state of panic and depression: panic because thousands of young anti-war protesters had invaded Chicago to march against Humphrey's nomination and his position on the Vietnam War; depression because the party was deeply divided between its hawk and dove wings and because Humphrey, still carrying water for Lyndon Johnson on the war, was an almost certain loser in the general election, dooming the Democrats—*unless* either the convention turned to another candidate or nominated a vice-presidential candidate who could unite those warring factions. The only candidate who could do so was Ted Kennedy, not necessarily because Ted was personally popular, though he was, but because he was a Kennedy carrying the Kennedy brand and carrying it more lightly than Bobby had. And Ted was not unmindful of that. Mike DiSalle had still not surrendered his plan to nominate Ted, despite Ted's disavowal, and Congressman Tip O'Neill told DiSalle that he would support Ted himself once he discharged his obligation to vote for McCarthy on the first ballot. "Able, talented, confident, a worker, and a great man," O'Neill said of Ted. But when he and Representative Ed Boland got Ted on the phone and pleaded with him to reconsider his decision not to run, O'Neill said that Ted just laughed. "No way was he going to get involved."

On the eve of the convention, however, Ted Kennedy's decision was not quite as ironclad as it may have seemed. Ted was clearly still suffering the effects of Bobby's death. His emotional wounds were still grave. "He was still in a state of shock," said Lester Hyman, a longtime Kennedy family associate whom Ted had tapped as the Massachusetts Democratic state chairman. "He would be doing fine; then he would stop, stare out the window. Ted [the old Ted] didn't do that." William vanden Heuvel remembered of seeing him at Hyannis Port, "Ted was quiet. He kept very much to himself whenever I saw him. He kept asking—mostly to himself, but aloud at times—'What was it all about?'" That was the human side of Ted, the doubting side of Ted, now the tortured side of Ted. But there was also the political, Joe Kennedy–inspired side—the side that had been inculcated in Ted, that the Kennedy children should never forgo an opportunity. "The ring only comes around so often," Joe Kennedy would say. "You better get ahold of it when it comes around." And Ted, thinking of the pressure to take the vice-presidential nomination, which was his for the asking, began thinking of his father's instructions, began thinking that perhaps this was his chance, perhaps his last chance, given the vagaries of life. And Ted wasn't the only one in his camp with these notions. Steve Smith didn't want Ted to accept the vice-presidential nomination, but he wasn't averse to his accepting the presidential nomination—Bobby's rightful nomination. "Steve Smith was churning" is how Ted would put it decades later. "He'd been very emotionally tied into Bobby's campaign, and he was personally frustrated by all of this," meaning the indecision among the Democrats. "I think he was constantly trying to think of what's out there and what can be done." Presumably, what was out there was the possibility of Ted being drafted for president, since he had said repeatedly that he had no interest whatsoever in the vice presidency. And presumably what could be done was continuing Bobby's lost campaign, boosting liberalism and restoring that moral order Bobby had so badly wanted to restore. Ted didn't actively pursue that chance. He was too emotionally disabled to run for the presidency, but he would say of Steve Smith that "I might have talked to him about my concerns about whether this [presidential draft] was real. I may very well have. . . . And he might have thought, 'Let me just explore this further.' " So the brother-in-law of the man who said emphatically that he would not be on the Democratic ticket went to Chicago and holed up at the Standard Club, a distinguished Jewish club, where Smith was not likely to be discovered, and there Smith began his exploration, working the phones, talking secretly to those bosses who had rejected Bobby but who feared an impending Humphrey defeat and were encouraging Ted.

But in implying that he might have given the impression to Smith that he was mildly interested in seeing what might develop at the convention, Ted was being disingenuous. He had also called John Tunney, who was then on vacation in Maine, and asked him to go to Chicago as well, Tunney would recall, to "keep my eyes and ears open and try to find out what was happening politically as it related to him." And Tunney raced to Chicago and conferred with delegates and bosses, including California Assembly speaker Unruh, who had become a Ted advocate. "He knew that people were pushing very hard for him to be a candidate," Tunney said of Ted, "and he took it seriously, but he didn't want to make a decision that was not based on the best information that was available." And Tunney added, "I didn't go there for my health." Nor were Smith and Tunney the only listening posts for Ted. Fred Dutton, Gerard Doherty, Charlie Tretter, Dun Gifford, Lester Hyman, John Seigenthaler, even Ted Sorensen, who had stopped at McLean to discuss the presidency with Ted before heading to Chicago, were all at the convention on Ted's behalf, seeing if it might break for him, working to see if they could get it to break for him, even though they weren't certain he wanted it. At the same time, during that weekend before the convention, Ted asked Gwirtzman and Burke to fly up to Hyannis Port to strategize, while Ted coyly kept his distance, alternately teasing them with a commitment to run and then withdrawing it. "He'd call, clowning around," recalled Burke, "say—you know—'Why not?' Or—'Okay. I'll write my acceptance speech myself.' " And Burke said they were also getting calls from delegates on the convention floor pledging their support and begging Ted to announce his availability. "They were in despair," Burke said. But not Ted. Ted finally seemed to be enjoying it— enjoying the cat-and-mouse game—the first real diversion he had had since Bobby's death and, more, something that seemed to put him on the same footing as his late brothers: the prospect, however improbable, that he could be president.

The pressing question among the courtiers was whether Ted should come to the convention. As the anti-war protesters gathered and the Chicago police attempted to corral them, Gwirtzman said that word was sent to Ted that he might come to quiet the disturbance, that "his presence there would be a healing thing," and that only Ted Kennedy among the Democrats could have that effect. But Burke Marshall, Bobby's old deputy at Justice and one of the coolest heads in the Kennedy camp, warned Ted not to come, that it would only worsen the situation. Others phoned Ted to tell him that Chicago was "about to erupt." Sorensen told him the same thing, warning that if he came, he could become a pawn for Daley and for the students, each side trying to use him to their advantage. "Things are just so bad here, just stay away from it," Sorensen advised. Nevertheless, Mayor Daley, whose police force it was that was clubbing the protesters, pleaded with Smith to have Ted come, not to pacify them but to change the political dynamics of the convention: If Ted came, Daley told Smith, he would sweep the convention and win the nomination by acclamation.

Ted was conflicted. Once the convention began, on August 26, Ted was, Burke said, "under an onslaught of phone calls from politicians around the country" with the same message as Daley's: Come to Chicago and be anointed. And Daley promised Ted via Smith that if he came, he would be perfectly safe: "Don't you worry. We'll take care of everything. We'll have cops in everyone's bedroom. Nothing bad can happen here." Burke said that Ted was "buoyed" by the phone calls and that he now thought of going, especially when Daley told him point-blank: "If you want to have the nomination for president of the United States, you could have it tomorrow morning if you want. You come into town, and Chicago will be stood on its ear, and you will, by acclamation to the whole nation" be the nominee. "The momentum was there, and the madness was in the air," was how Burke put it. Richard Daley, who had been Chicago's mayor since 1955, had that kind of clout in the party. He didn't make idle promises. He could make good. And with Daley behind Ted, Steve Smith was more direct than Burke. "We had it," he would later declare. "There was no question but that the senator could have had the nomination. All he had to say was yes."

And the momentum kept building. Mike DiSalle, with no encouragement from the Kennedy camp and even with a call from Ted asking him to desist, set up draft headquarters at the Sherman House Hotel, hoping to line up delegates to vote for Ted and *make* him the nominee despite his resistance. Ted's disclaimer meant nothing. Jesse Unruh publicly disregarded it, saying it wasn't dispositive, and telling the press that a Kennedy draft would provide an "incalculable lift to what looks to be almost a disastrous year for the Democrats." And he said that he didn't think Ted, 1,500 miles away, could fully appreciate the tide running in his favor. He even said he might nominate Ted himself or second the nomination if DiSalle placed Ted's name in nomination. Some California delegates, all of them pledged to Bobby, began wearing DRAFT TED buttons, and Students for Kennedy, a group that had formed to support Bobby, spread out in the lobby of the La Salle Hotel, the California delegation's headquarters, and painted signs for Ted. But California was Bobby Kennedy country already. William vanden Heuvel, who was a McGovern delegate, said he ran into Senator Russell Long. Long told him that Louisiana was sticking with Johnson, meaning Humphrey, but then he said that if Ted made himself available, Louisiana would go for him "in a minute." And Long added, "This is his convention, if he wants it." Vanden Heuvel phoned Ted at Hyannis Port with the news. "You know, this is a long hill, the presidency," he told Ted. "It's a hard hill to climb, and all I'm saying to you—and I'm not trying to persuade you—that the mountain in my judgment is yours, if you're willing to be available to it." Vanden Heuvel said Ted laughed, and said, "No. I'm not going to do it."

But as the momentum kept building, that comment wasn't dispositive either. Rumors were sweeping through the Democratic ranks that Daley was threatening to withhold Illinois's 118 votes from Humphrey to promote a Kennedy draft, and former Texas governor John Connally was purportedly so upset with Humphrey for repudiating the unit rule, which awarded a primary winner all the votes of the state's delegation, that he was considering submitting his name as a favorite son. And there was more momentum still, this time from one of the contenders himself. On Monday morning, the first day of the convention, after a staff meeting in Eugene McCarthy's suite at the Conrad Hilton Hotel overlooking Grant

Park, where the protesters were massing, McCarthy, speaking of the "Draft Kennedy" movement, asked Richard Goodwin, who had returned to the McCarthy fold after Bobby's death, "What about this Ted thing?" Goodwin said he didn't believe that Ted would allow a draft, which prompted McCarthy to ruminate on how "we might do this together" and beat back Humphrey. This was not the usual McCarthy approach. He had always chosen to go it alone. But Harvard economist John Kenneth Galbraith, who knew McCarthy, said that Bobby Kennedy's assassination had taken the steam out of McCarthy as well, that McCarthy had been "deeply depressed" by it and felt, as Ted did, that it "showed the hopelessness of the game." And though McCarthy's mood lightened later, Galbraith didn't feel that "his heart was ever again wholly in the battle." Now McCarthy, who had been so haughty toward the Kennedys, even boastful, was considering how he might help Ted overcome concerns about his youth and inexperience, ending the conversation with, "Let's see how things develop." But things didn't develop in McCarthy's favor. Even as the antiwar protesters were being beaten, creating a violent, bloody tableau on television screens across the country—"The whole world is watching," chanted the protesters—the convention was marching toward Humphrey, unless Ted could stop him. The next day, August 27, McCarthy asked Goodwin again about "Teddy," and Goodwin advised that McCarthy contact Steve Smith directly. The two, McCarthy and Smith, met in McCarthy's twenty-third-floor suite at four-thirty, but Smith, as Goodwin later recounted it, said that Ted was not making himself available for the nomination, to which McCarthy replied that since he couldn't win himself, he was willing to ask his delegates to vote for Ted. As they walked to the elevators, Smith said, "Let's keep in touch."

And the momentum wasn't only building in Chicago. It was building at Hyannis Port, where Ted was still waffling. Burke said there was one night, presumably Monday, the first day of the convention, when "the phone calls were red-hot." Smith kept calling, telling Ted he was the favorite, and as he did so, Burke said, you could feel the energy shift, the enthusiasm build, among the group gathered there, a dozen to twenty supporters. Smith said that Daley had told him, "The roof is going to come off the convention hall. It will physically come off the convention hall when Ted hits the floor." And Smith would get some party boss on the phone to talk to Ted, and Ted would listen and banter with the caller but remain noncommittal. And as Ted listened and spoke, Burke said, "the temperature in the room rose and fell" among the supporters, because everyone there realized, "This is the last moment." As Burke put it, "We either grab it now, or you'll never" get a chance. And Ted, Burke said, was almost jovial, as if he were riding the energy of the prospect. Seigenthaler told Smith after walking the convention floor, presumably that Monday, "If Teddy wants to be president of the United States, this is right now, this year. He's the nominee." And Smith told Seigenthaler to call Ted and tell him. Ted even told a friend, "Daley says we can just have it." And Smith, who was no political novice, agreed. They had done the delegate math, and Ted had the votes to win.

The nomination was Ted's for the taking.

But Ted Kennedy, young as he was and as much as he was pondering the presidency as a way to fulfill Bobby's aborted mission and as stirred as he was by the Kennedy succession, had become a shrewd politician, and, his ambivalence aside, he didn't fully trust Richard Daley. Daley was a crafty politician, a tough infighter, and a hard pragmatist, neither a liberal nor a true believer (his affinity for the Kennedys had been the affinity of one Irish Catholic for another), a strong supporter of the Vietnam War, and a leading figure of the Democratic establishment headed by Lyndon Johnson. Ted knew that if he came to Chicago and made himself available for the presidential nomination, the Humphrey forces, of which Daley might be a double agent, could easily perform a bait and switch and draft Ted for vice president, and then he would be trapped. He called it a "dicey situation." (Ted might have misjudged Daley. Years later, Daley's son, Bill, would tell Robert Shrum, a Kennedy speechwriter and staff person, that just before the convention he saw TED KENNEDY signs in his father's basement and asked him what they were doing there, since his father had publicly committed to Humphrey. To which Richard Daley said, "Not if Kennedy will take it.") And Ted didn't trust Eugene McCarthy's offer to step aside either. By one account, that of Peter Maas in *New York* magazine, McCarthy had told Smith that he still wanted his name placed in nomination and that, while he refused to nominate Ted himself, he would make it known beforehand that he would be stepping aside and then afterward would come to the floor and ask his delegates to support Ted, which seemed to Smith like a hedge. A "typically mystical performance by McCarthy," griped one Kennedy aide.

But it wasn't mysticism that destroyed the opportunity. It was more of

McCarthy's pettiness. What infuriated Ted, as McCarthy told Robert Healy of *The Boston Globe*, is that while he was discussing the situation with Smith, McCarthy had mentioned to him that he couldn't have supported Bobby, whom he described as a "mean shit." Maas reported it more decorously: "While I'm doing this for Teddy, I never would have done it for Bobby." In Maas's version, the meeting broke after ten minutes with McCarthy asking Smith, "Would you think with my support Teddy has a chance?" and Smith saying, "It would be a real ball game," but that he would have to talk to Ted. McCarthy probably knew Smith would relay his comments on Bobby to Ted and knew what effect those comments would have on Ted, which is probably why he made them. McCarthy told Healy that he heard Ted was "really upset" about it. But still, according to Maas, the possibility of a deal remained open as Smith and Ted deliberated. What Maas said torpedoed the proposed alliance was a report, clearly leaked by someone in McCarthy's camp, from David Schumacher of CBS—the same reporter whom the McCarthy camp had alerted to the Wisconsin meeting with Ted—that Smith had come to McCarthy and spent two hours begging for his support. Smith was enraged. (Kennedys didn't beg.) And so, whether because of the insult to Bobby or the deception to Smith, the proposed McCarthy alliance fizzled.*

But there were stalwarts who kept the faith that Hubert Humphrey could still be defeated, and for them there was one last, desperate gambit: the Vietnam plank of the Democratic platform. The Platform Committee, packed with party regulars and Humphrey supporters, had passed a plank that, according to reports, was written in the White House to Lyndon Johnson's specifications, precluding a cessation in bombing without a quid pro quo from the North Vietnamese, withdrawing American forces only after negotiating an end to hostilities, establishing a South Vietnamese government through free elections without provision for a Vietcong component, and praising the president for bringing the North Vietnamese to the peace table. (In May, the North Vietnamese had agreed to talk with the Americans in Paris.) All of this was anathema to the peace forces—McCarthy, McGovern, and the "Draft Ted" activists. They had proposed another plank, a dovish plank, calling for immediate unconditional cessa-

*By one account, McCarthy told an associate, "I wanted Teddy to take it and then be beaten. It would have broken the chain." Lewis Chester, Godfrey Hodgson, and Bruce Page, *An American Melodrama: The Presidential Campaign of 1968* (New York: Viking Press, 1969), 576.

tion of bombing, a reduction of hostilities, and encouragement of the South Vietnamese government to negotiate a political reconciliation with the North Vietnamese. Of course, the differences between the planks were the very divisions that had torn the party asunder. But these weren't just policy disputes. They had political consequences—big political consequences. If the "peace plank" somehow passed, it would be virtually impossible for Humphrey to run on it—indeed, Johnson would surely disavow it—which would open the door for Ted's nomination, without Ted having to raise a finger. Some delegates felt this was exactly the point: The peace plank would serve as a test for Ted Kennedy's candidacy.

But if this was the scheme of Ted Kennedy's supporters, this was not Ted Kennedy's scheme. By this point, after the McCarthy breakdown, Ted had signaled to his main advocates that he would not accept a draft—he had phoned McGovern on Wednesday morning to notify him and added that if Daley and others publicly supported him, he might have come to Chicago—but he withheld a public announcement because he had another agenda, which was to use the possibility of his candidacy to promote Bobby's ideas. When Lester Hyman told reporter Mike Wallace of CBS "with certainty" that Ted would not allow his name to be placed in nomination and Wallace ran with the story, Ted phoned Hyman on the convention floor and said, "Lester, take it a little easier next time," meaning, Hyman said, "He didn't want people to know that he wasn't going to run, because he wanted to preserve his power." Bobby's interests were so important to Ted that he had even toyed briefly with the idea of attending the convention, not to whip up a frenzy for his own candidacy—though he must have realized any appearance would have had that effect—but to speak in favor of the anti-war plank that he knew Bobby would have endorsed. He felt he owed it to Bobby and to Bobby's supporters. "Sheep without a shepherd," he called them. This was also one of the reasons McGovern had declared his candidacy: to rally Bobby's anti-war supporters and possibly hold them should Ted run. Vanden Heuvel, who had gone to the convention expressly to fight for an anti-war plank, had planned to submit one to the floor once it had been voted down by the Platform Committee, and if it failed on the floor, as he assumed it would, he would then place Lyndon Johnson's name in nomination on the basis that if the convention were to support a pro-war Johnson plank, Johnson should be made to walk it. When he met with a Johnson representative under the podium to reveal his plan, the representative threatened to place *Ted's* name in nomination—though why that would have been a real threat, given that Ted might very well have stampeded the delegates and turned the convention away from Johnson's handpicked candidate, is hard to figure.

In any case, the floor fight over the Vietnam plank only introduced more pandemonium into a convention already in full-blown chaos. The fight lasted seven hours—seven hours of speeches, procedural votes, shouting, hooting—and only ended past midnight when the Platform Committee chairman, Congressman Hale Boggs of Louisiana, took to the dais to read the platform. When he got to the Vietnam plank, the delegates from Wisconsin—a McCarthy delegation—began to clap and shout, preventing Boggs from continuing and forcing the convention chairman, Representative Carl Albert, the House majority leader, to recognize Wisconsin chair Donald Peterson, who called for an adjournment to the chants of "Let's go home! Let's go home!" But Albert, now incensed by the disruption, called the motion out of order, touching off still more booing, which intensified when Mayor Daley, his jowls shaking and his face red and wild, shouted that the convention was for "the delegates and not for anyone in the balconies trying to take over this meeting." And as the shouting and mayhem continued, Albert, fuming and red-faced himself at the peace advocates, finally recognized Daley, who, realizing that the situation had escalated out of hand, asked for an adjournment until 4 P.M. the following afternoon.

It was a last-ditch effort, an all-but-certain-to-fail effort to defeat the Johnson plank and put the party on record to oppose the war its president had been prosecuting for four years, and its failure seemed to doom Ted's presidential chances too, since he could never run on the Johnson plank any more than Humphrey could run on the McCarthy–McGovern–Kennedy plank. But Richard Daley would not relent in his pursuit of Ted Kennedy, not because he was in sympathy with Ted's views—he was a vociferous, nearly apoplectic opponent of the protesters, who were turning his city into bedlam before the entire nation—but because everyone was now expecting an electoral debacle if Humphrey was nominated. Even amid the commotion of the Vietnam-plank debate, Daley told Steve Smith that he was eager to hand the nomination to Ted but that there were two provisos: Ted had to say he would accept it, and Ted had to appear in Chicago to get it. (By another account, Daley wanted Ted to ask Daley for the nomination—an "overture," one of Daley's allies called it—

which is something Ted would never have done.) Smith's answer, relayed from Ted, was that Ted would only submit to a legitimate draft arising spontaneously from the sentiments of the delegates, not to one that Ted had helped engineer. And when Daley kept pressing his case, Smith finally told Ted that he had to speak to the mayor, who'd told Smith he had planned to support Bobby and that Ted had to clarify his position to Daley.

By that point, Ted seemed to have finally let go of his presidential aspirations. He had left Hyannis Port and was sailing on the *Mira* up the Maine coast to escape the clamor. But Smith had gotten word to Ted aboard the boat, which was anchored off Stonington at the time, that Daley needed to speak with him. So Ted, who now sported a short beard, rowed ashore through a thick morning fog and talked to Daley from a phone booth in the middle of a general store. But once again Ted told Daley, recalled vanden Heuvel, who was with him on the sail,* that while he wouldn't categorically rule out being a candidate, he was not going to come to Chicago and he was not going to declare his availability. And for all practical purposes, that was the end of the Ted Kennedy for President boomlet.

The boomlet had been serious, and it had been imminent. But Ted had had doubts not only about McCarthy's and Daley's motives; he had doubts about his own. "He wasn't ready, and he knew it, and the people close to him knew he wasn't ready" was David Burke's assessment. And it was more than his not being politically equipped. It was his not being emotionally equipped. As he sat at his home on Squaw Island, down the beach from the Kennedy compound in Cape Cod, with his sisters Jean and Pat fielding Smith's calls, Ted said he felt the pressure steadily building to run but didn't feel the passion that he needed to subject himself to the physical dangers of a campaign or to the emotional ones, since he was certain Nixon would attack him for being young and inexperienced and trading on his brothers' names. "I simply could not summon the will" is how he later put it. It was to be Bobby's nomination, not his. "I have a gut feeling that this is not the year, that it is too early for me," he told Arthur Schlesinger Jr. when Schlesinger phoned him during the convention to sound him out. "I would rather try and do it as an individual in my own

---

* Vanden Heuvel claimed to have been at the convention and sailing with Ted, which seems impossible unless he left Chicago immediately after the platform vote. It is more likely that at some later time he and Ted sailed to Stonington and Ted *told* him about the phone call. Ted had told a similar story on a similar sail to at least one friend, Lee Fentress.

right, to carve out something of my own, establish myself to some degree in control of events." In effect, he was admitting to the larger truth of his life: He had never really been in control of his own destiny. And he said he feared he would be seeming to "take advantage of people's sympathy." But he also said that he wanted to do everything he could to advance Bobby's agenda, which was why he had been so conflicted and indecisive. And he admitted frankly that there was the issue of losing the opportunity to be president, which he fully realized might never come again. Reflecting back on his father, he quoted another slogan of Joe Kennedy's: "Things just don't happen; they are made to happen." And Ted told Schlesinger, "All I can say is that we are not making this one happen."

Now there was one last issue to resolve: the vice presidency. And Ted was to have a say in it. As expected, when the convention reconvened on Thursday, the Johnson–Humphrey forces won the platform fight on the Vietnam plank, which meant the convention endorsed Johnson's war policy—the policy that had driven Johnson from the race—and that Humphrey had secured the nomination. No sooner had he done so than he contacted Ted once again with the same plea to accept the vice-presidential nomination. And Ted once again refused. (There had been fear among the Kennedy claque that Humphrey would try to draft him anyway.) Still, Humphrey seemed fixated on some Humphrey–Kennedy alliance, even it if couldn't be an alliance with Ted. As Sargent Shriver's biographer Scott Stossel later told it, two months earlier Bill Moyers, the former Johnson aide and now the publisher of Long Island's *Newsday*, acting presumably at Humphrey's behest, had been sounding out the Kennedy camp's attitude toward Shriver as a possible alternative to Ted, thus uniting the Humphrey and Kennedy factions. At the time, Moyers had asked Fred Dutton if the Kennedys would accept Shriver on the ticket, to which Dutton said he thought they would. He was wrong. A friend of the Kennedys, Don Petrie, wrote Humphrey on July 17, saying that he had spoken with Steve Smith, who had spoken with Ted, and that Ted denied he had any intention of running for anything. But when Shriver's name arose, Smith told Petrie that "the family resents it," apparently referring to the fact that Shriver had accepted Johnson's appointment as ambassador to France the very week that Bobby was to announce for the presidency and that Shriver had remained in the position even after Johnson renounced reelection, which showed that ambition among the Kennedys was a matter of blood, not relationships. As the idea of a Shriver vice-presidential nomination brewed, Ted called his brother-in-law in Paris shortly before the convention—a conversation that Shriver described acidly to a friend the next day: "Many K[ennedy] boosters really are sore at me—even bitter—because I didn't help more [on Bobby's campaign]," and he complained that "the palace guard (now without a palace) (or a pretender) find it hard to accept the prospect of a prodigal son-in-law (let alone son) sitting down to their feast." Ted, though, did promise to "slow him down or shut him up," meaning Steve Smith, if he continued to undermine Shriver. Kenny O'Donnell was nevertheless blunt. He told Humphrey that the family would consider Humphrey's selecting Shriver an "unfriendly act." If there was to be a Kennedy on the ticket, it was to be Ted or no one. Now it was no one.

Ted nevertheless had a stake in the selection, even if it wasn't to be a Kennedy. Though he didn't want it himself, he was looking out for himself, and he didn't want Humphrey to choose someone who might eventually challenge him for primacy in the party. That Wednesday of the convention, Humphrey had narrowed the field of candidates—he even discussed McCarthy but dismissed him because he had a "cynicism about life" that Humphrey said he could not tolerate. It seemed he had settled on two—Oklahoma senator Fred Harris, young, vigorous, well spoken; and Maine senator Edmund Muskie, a political veteran with a Lincolnesque look and mien—and he asked Ted which of them he would recommend. Ted said he didn't know Harris very well but that he knew Muskie, that he had, as Gwirtzman remembered the conversation, "worked with him," and that he had a "great deal of respect for him." At conversation's end, Humphrey made one last entreaty—"please do it for me, please run with me"—but Ted was firm, and Humphrey ultimately chose Muskie—a choice, Ted told his advisers, that he had endorsed not so much because he knew Muskie but because he felt Muskie was of a "another generation" than he and "wouldn't be competition even if Humphrey and Muskie were elected." Then, Gwirtzman said, Ted went off sailing again.

II

It was an ugly campaign in a season of ugliness. Humphrey had to carry the albatross of a discredited Vietnam policy because Lyndon Johnson demanded it of him. The Republican presidential candidate, Richard Nixon, promised that he had a "secret plan" to end the war, but his was essentially a campaign of division, a campaign that set old against young, whites against blacks, rural Americans against urbanites, conservatives against liberals, Republicans against Democrats. It was a campaign dedicated to shattering the post–New Deal liberal consensus that had predominated for the past twenty years, and in many ways, though Nixon was no Barry Goldwater, no hardened ideologue, his campaign was the fulfillment of Goldwater's crusade and the crusade of the extreme conservative faction of the Republican party to reshape the party to accomplish that very end. And to that end, it was a campaign that actively challenged the moral authority that Bobby Kennedy and then Ted had worked so hard to restore and that had been a basis of the post–New Deal consensus. In describing conservatives' reaction to the first year of Johnson's presidency, political historian Rick Perlstein would write, "For them, the idea that calamitous liberal nonsense—ready acceptance of federal interference in the economy; Negro 'civil disobedience'; the doctrine of 'containing' the mortal enemy, communism, when conservatives insisted it must be beaten—could be described as a 'consensus' at all was symbol and substance of America's moral rot," which was precisely the obverse of the moral rot Bobby Kennedy had identified. For Bobby, the idea of a national moral redemption in the service of the poor and the dispossessed was the whole reason for running. For Nixon, whose principles were nowhere near as fixed as Bobby's and whose moral engine nowhere near as active, moral redemption was a convenient political device—one designed to appeal to the general disaffection many Americans were feeling over Vietnam and race, especially after the race riots the preceding year and again that spring, by poising Americans against one another and against their government.

"What Has Happened to America?" That was the title of a *Reader's Digest* article Nixon had written in October 1967, in what would be a blueprint for his campaign. The country had been making racial progress, Nixon wrote. Now it was aflame in race riots, making it "among the most lawless and violent in the history of the free peoples." Nixon's diagnosis for what had caused the black ghettos to erupt was not deep social problems. Rather, they had erupted, in a somewhat tautological formulation, because of a "graver national disorder—the decline in respect for public authority and the rule of law in America." And to what did Nixon attribute this decline? To "permissiveness toward violation of the law" and to "indulgence of crime because of sympathy for the past grievances of those who have become criminals," presumably the grievances, though they were far more than that, of slavery and then Jim Crow. And Nixon then went on to blame "judges" who had gone "too far in weakening the peace forces as against the criminal forces"; "opinion-makers [who] have gone too far in promoting the doctrine that when a law is broken, society, not the criminal, is to blame"; and "teachers, preachers, and politicians [who] have gone too far in advocating the idea that each individual should determine what laws are good and what laws are bad, and that he then should obey the law he likes and disobey the law he dislikes." He decried Vietnam War protesters and those who practiced civil disobedience, and he called for a crackdown using more and better-financed police. Thus were the great moral causes and actions of the early 1960s reinterpreted as lawlessness and anarchy.

Ted Kennedy had no affection whatsoever for Richard Nixon, whom he saw as the antithesis of his brothers and whose defeat he felt essential to preserving his brothers' values, which was the very reason he was so loath to disavow Johnson even as he was prosecuting the Vietnam War. But he also had little appetite for politics that fall, little appetite even for legislation—this from a man who had loved legislative combat. Earlier in the year, before Bobby's assassination, the Senate was considering a Civil Rights Act of 1968, which outlawed discrimination in housing. But a group of Southern senators decided to use the bill as a bludgeon against black rioters, so Russell Long proposed several amendments, one of which would have made it a federal crime to manufacture or transport explosives if there was any reason to believe that they might be used unlawfully in a riot. Long said openly that he was targeting Molotov cocktails for black rioters, but Ted, to the shock of the Southerners, embraced the amendment because he said it would prohibit *any* firearm from being transported or manufactured under the same circumstances. Even though they realized that Ted had smuggled gun control into their anti-black bill, something that was anathema to them, the Southerners felt they had no choice but to vote for it. Then Bobby joined the scrap. He supported another Long amendment—this one making it a federal crime to commit or threaten to commit any unlawful act of violence in furtherance of a riot. Bobby told them it would give the federal government unprecedented force—which was also anathema to the Southerners. Working in tandem, Ted and Bobby had hoisted the opposition on their own petard. But that was when Bobby was alive and Ted was spirited. In September, right after Ted returned to the Senate for the first time since Bobby's death, Johnson asked Ted to lead the battle for gun-control legislation restricting the mail-order sale of guns and imposing a waiting period. But, as important as the issue was to him, and it was very important, this time Ted demurred, sitting in his seat in the last row of the Senate, chin in hand, watching others debate. Senator Joseph Tydings, who had introduced another bill to license and register handguns and who had encouraged Ted to join him, said Ted didn't even come to meetings on the bill. He just didn't have the heart for it.

He didn't have the heart for much of anything. A reporter found him devoid of his old energy: "visibly older, somewhat slow of step, the gray flecks at his temples more apparent. His waist has begun to thicken." Tydings recalled, "Teddy's role in the Senate and his leadership and activism during that period diminished substantially. He went into a period of deep, dramatic depression. I couldn't talk to him on things where I needed his advice." He continued, "His friends were worried. He was decimated." And Tydings had another observation of Ted that fall. He said that he had never noticed Ted's drinking until then. "But looking back on it now, I have to think that he started drinking far more heavily and that had to have an effect on his total conduct." He could scarcely come to the Senate. He would drive to the Capitol and then turn back, unable to enter. His voting record in the year after Bobby's death was only 39 percent.

But if Ted Kennedy was swirling in a vortex of grief that fall, and if he seemed to need to take a pass on the 1968 election—"The Kennedy people do not expect him to do any campaigning this year," John Herbers wrote in *The New York Times*—there were nevertheless calls, *pleas*, for him to emerge from his isolation and rescue the party. And, despite his courtiers' belief that he would resist those pleas and refrain from action, Ted Kennedy knew that he would have to heed them if he was to be true to his brothers and true to himself. One of those calls came from Hubert Humphrey. Ted was still dubious about supporting Humphrey, because of the war. As late as July, Humphrey had told *The New York Times* that he would not repudiate Lyndon Johnson, because, "We don't need an Aaron Burr in this republic." But as he wooed Ted for the vice presidency during the convention, he asked him for understanding on the difficulty of his situation with Johnson and assured him, "I can work out the problem of my Vietnam position. I'll be right on those issues." Ted waited for that change in position, but as he recalled, "It got delayed and delayed and delayed, by weeks." In his Worcester speech, Ted had vowed to reenter the political arena, and as grief-stricken as he was, as dedicated as he was now to ending the Vietnam War, he had come to believe Humphrey's promise and believed, as he put it, that it was "important to be involved and engaged and explain the reasons why I wanted to get back into the fray," especially given the alternative, which was Richard Nixon. Ted finally agreed to campaign with Humphrey on September 19 in Boston—a nervous agreement, since Humphrey had yet to soften his support of the war and since Ted realized there were going to be anti-war protesters screaming at them, even though he opposed the war. As Ted recalled, he and Humphrey had driven down Tremont Street to dine at the Parker House, and he saw the demonstrators practicing getting up on one another's shoulders to unfurl an anti-war banner. Later that night, in introducing Humphrey at a rally of some five thousand Bostonians at Summer and Washington Streets, Ted praised him as an "outstanding and progressive leader," who had been "in the forefront of every vital domestic problem before the United States in the last twenty years," pointedly saying nothing about Vietnam. Humphrey said that Ted was still so fraught by Bobby's death that he "shook" when he got up to speak. But when Humphrey took the microphone, the protesters began heckling him, provoking Humphrey to yell back that they were going to "disgust the American people and injure the cause of peace." As they persisted, drowning him out, Humphrey finally discarded his speech to take on the hecklers, while Ted, by one report, "frequently looked at the sky or at his feet" and "applauded mechanically." Afterward, Ted said cautiously in his defense, "I think our force, myself, McGovern, and the moderate Republicans, can work more effectively in a Humphrey administration."

Humphrey hadn't misled Ted. He wanted to disengage himself from Lyndon Johnson, but he worried that doing so might be perceived as betrayal not only by Johnson but also by the public and that it would do more harm than good. But he also knew he had virtually no chance of winning the presidency unless he did so. A Gallup poll in late September showed him with only 28 percent of the vote, fifteen points behind Nixon but, even more worrisome, only seven points ahead of the segregationist independent candidate George Wallace. It wasn't just defeat he faced; it was humiliation. Moreover, the campaign was in shambles. Liberal fundraisers had deserted him over Vietnam, but since he seemed like a sure loser, contributors who normally gave to both sides to protect themselves didn't step up, so he had little money. His message was indistinct, still in support of Johnson's Vietnam policy but feinting to step away. The mainstream press, who didn't care much for Nixon and had been fond of Humphrey, had lost that fondness over Vietnam. And everywhere he went, as in Boston, he was hounded by anti-war protesters so that he could barely speak, turning his rallies into shouting matches and making him look besieged, which he was. Often, he had to slink into cities and keep crowds at bay. One account would say that he "carried a stench of disaster with him." All of this had been building slowly, week after week—building into inevitable defeat unless Humphrey could do something to jolt his campaign. After a particularly raucous event in Seattle, where a protester shouted through a bullhorn that Humphrey should be tried for "crimes against humanity," he had finally had enough. He told his staff that he realized he was probably going to lose, but "win or lose, I'm going to speak my mind, and I'm going to fight."

And the fight now was not against Richard Nixon. It was against Lyndon Johnson's intransigence on Vietnam—the war that had cost the nation so many lives, and cost the Vietnamese so many more, and cost America its claim to moral authority. The speech Humphrey had decided to give on Monday, September 30, in Salt Lake City, at the end of a Western campaign swing—a speech on which his campaign had spent its last $100,000 for national television time—was much debated by the staff, torn between those who felt Humphrey had to make a clear departure from Johnson and those who felt he shouldn't, couldn't, without risking the wrath of Johnson. In the end, Humphrey exploded that there was too much skittishness, and he wrote the draft himself. The speech he delivered that night was hardly a bombshell. Humphrey merely said that as president, "I would be willing to stop the bombing of North Vietnam as an acceptable risk for peace, because I believe that it could lead to success in the negotiations and a shorter war," something that Bobby had said much earlier; that he would gradually de-escalate and de-Americanize the conflict; and that he would propose an immediate ceasefire supervised by an international force. But tepid as it may have seemed, it nevertheless constituted a break with Johnson, and it gave the doves an opening to support Humphrey against a candidate whose pronouncements were significantly more hawkish. Ted wired him immediately and perhaps too extravagantly: "To all who look for peace in Vietnam, you've given great encouragement and hope. . . . I believe you deserve the support of all who have worked and prayed for peace." Larry O'Brien, who was running Humphrey's campaign, said Humphrey was "beaming" as he showed Ted's telegram—which Humphrey said was the first one he'd received afterward—to his staff. Two days later, back on the stump, he phoned Ted to tell him that Ted's "support has made a difference in the campaign," given the size of his crowds now, and that Humphrey would never forget it. By that time, Ted had already arranged with O'Brien to cut television commercials for Humphrey—"You've done enough for me," Humphrey told Ted, "but obviously this will be very helpful"—and had shot a short film on the beach at the Cape in conversation with O'Brien, discussing how helpful Humphrey had been to John Kennedy and how much respect Humphrey and Bobby had shared—a film that was shown on election eve on national television. Hubert Humphrey had been liberated.

But salient as it was, there was more than Vietnam to the campaign, more to it than Humphrey and Nixon. Former Alabama governor George Wallace, the segregationist who had barred the doors for black students to prevent them from entering the University of Alabama—the action that had stirred John Kennedy's conscience—was also running, as a third-party candidate, and while Nixon thumped for "law and order," which many liberals read as a euphemistic racial signal to whites riled by the riots in the ghettos, Wallace unleashed a louder version, a less euphemistic version, a vicious and blatant attack on black Americans and their liberal sympathizers—"They're building a bridge over the Potomac for all the white liberals fleeing to Virginia," he said, beaming—and added an even uglier hostility to an already ugly campaign. "The ablest demagogue of our time," Richard Strout of *The New Republic* called him. Wallace, a snarling little man with a lip permanently curled into a sneer, had turned the Great Society on its head. He had taken government efforts to help the powerless—in this case black people, especially those in the South, who had been suppressed by Jim Crow—and portrayed those efforts as a mortal threat to working-class whites; he inflamed those white supporters so that his rallies frequently rang with cries of "Sieg heil!" and "Kill the niggers!" But his was not just a Southern appeal. "There are a lot of rednecks in this country," Wallace liked to say, "and they don't all live in the South."

And so Ted Kennedy, who now trembled when he was at the lectern, made one more speech for Hubert Humphrey that fall. This one was on an afternoon in New Bedford, Massachusetts, on October 24, the evening of which some 16,000 people would jam Madison Square Garden in New York City to hear Wallace speak, and this one aimed squarely at those backing George Wallace, many of them, presumably, onetime Bobby Kennedy backers, to whom Ted alluded when he said, "I know the kinds of citizens who are considering voting for the third party." Ted called Wallace's voters "decent people who believe in America . . . citizens who feel that their needs and their problems have been passed over by the tide of recent events" and who "feel the established system has not been sympathetic to them in their problems in everyday life, and in a large measure, they are right." But Ted also felt they had been misled by thinking that a vote for Wallace would simply be a protest vote, a way to express their grievance. Instead, a vote for Wallace, he said, "would lift the haters and wreckers to positions of formidable influence in the country. It would be a signal for the forces of suspicion and repression . . . to restrict our liberty." He cited the fact that a "large number of the party [Wallace's American Independent party] are members of the Ku Klux Klan, the armed Minutemen, and the White Citizens Council." He spoke, he said, out of fear that Wallace could gain enough electoral votes to throw the election into the House of Representatives but also out of fear that Wallace's party could become a permanent political institution of "division and hate," electing officials throughout the country. Only with "the greatest effort and the greatest pain" had America been able to rid itself of the "poison" of similar movements in the past. "Let us not in this election set that dark process in motion again." And after delineating the differences between his brothers and George Wallace, he concluded that it wasn't enough for the Wallace movement to be defeated. "It must be repudiated."

And thus did Ted Kennedy end the Kennedy portion of the 1968 campaign as his brother Bobby had opened it: with an appeal to moral decency.

After Salt Lake City, Hubert Humphrey closed, and he closed fast. The speech had been a tonic to the candidate and to his prospects. His numbers rose. Nixon's and Wallace's dropped. But Humphrey couldn't close quite fast enough. Nixon won 43.4 percent of the vote, Humphrey 42.7 percent, and Wallace 13.5 percent. Humphrey lost by only 500,000 votes, though the percentages indicated just how little any of the candidates was able to stir the voters. It was as if, with all the turbulence of the campaign—the daily reports from Vietnam, McCarthy's near-win in New

Hampshire, Johnson's withdrawal, Martin Luther King Jr.'s assassination and the riots that followed, and then Robert Kennedy's assassination, the violence at the Democratic National Convention, and the ongoing heckling that served as accompaniment to Humphrey's appearances, the Wallace racial instigation—Americans just wanted it to be over and some semblance of normalcy restored. Even Humphrey himself accepted his defeat, for the office he had sought for a lifetime and had come so close to grabbing at the last moment, with surprising equanimity. "I take some solace in feeling that 1968 was simply not the year when the American people wanted liberal leadership," he would later write in his memoir, "so much as they wanted a respite from anxiety and frustration." It had all changed so quickly. Four years earlier, Lyndon Johnson had won in a landslide championing liberalism. In 1968, three-fifths of the voters seemed to have repudiated both it and George Wallace.

Nixon's was a narrow victory, but it was a victory, and there would be years of analysis trying to account for it. The most obvious factor was Vietnam, without which Humphrey would most likely have won, but without which Johnson certainly would have run. Vietnam had created disruptions, sapped resources, cost lives, eroded confidence, forced national self-examination, and opened divisions within the Democratic party and within the nation that were not easily healed. Vietnam was a blot—a moral embarrassment. Nixon promised to solve it, while Humphrey was part of the team that had created it. Then, too, there was the domestic side of the Johnson agenda. The South had already begun peeling away from Democratic hegemony with the passage of the civil rights bills, though Democrats might have withstood that—Johnson did in 1964—if measures like open housing and school busing for integration hadn't also peeled away some white voters outside the South, and if the Republicans, spotting a chance, hadn't been so aggressive in exploiting it as part of what they saw as a new conservative coalition. "From Day One, Nixon and I talked about creating a new majority," Nixon speechwriter and aide Pat Buchanan told the *New Yorker*'s George Packer years later. "What we talked about, basically, was shearing off huge segments of FDR's New Deal coalition, which LBJ had held together: Northern Catholic ethnics and Southern Protestant conservatives—what we called the Daley–Rizzo Democrats in the North [after Chicago mayor Richard Daley and Philadelphia mayor Frank Rizzo, a former police commissioner] and, frankly, the Wallace Democrats in the South." And Buchanan said that when he attended a meeting of angry Republicans in Columbia, South Carolina, with Nixon in 1966, Nixon told him, "This is the future of this party, right here in the South." The future hadn't arrived in 1968—yet. Wallace took the heart of the South, and the Democrats lost it. Meanwhile, without the South, the Democrats were looking to forge a new coalition of their own—slight variations on the coalition that Bobby Kennedy was trying to build—of minorities and young people and affluent whites and disgruntled blue-collar workers. But the coalition was unstable, and without the blue-collar workers, who were growing increasingly resentful over black gains—or, at least, the appearance of them—it wasn't a majority.

Others would point to contradictions and grandiosities within the liberal consensus that undermined it: that the nation was strong enough and united enough to solve its own problems and those of the world at the same time; that it could successfully separate racial issues from economic ones; that it could promote both equality and liberty; that it could use military force to bring freedom and morality to the rest of the world; that it could be simultaneously pragmatic and moral. Each of these raised problems and each caused political backlash. And within the new so-called post-ideological consensus of the sixties may have been the most grandiose idea of all—an idea to which John Kennedy subscribed—that the solutions to many of America's problems were simply a matter of expertise. This led to "the best and brightest," as writer David Halberstam dubbed them—Johnson himself called them "the Harvards"—the brilliant, well-educated, self-confident, and hubristic cadre of staffers and bureaucrats who deigned to tell ordinary Americans what to do, even though their rational approaches didn't always prove workable, as Vietnam had illustrated. Out of a similar impulse, Johnson, in his overweening political optimism, had overpromised. He had called upon Americans to end poverty, end racism, end communist adventurism, end struggles for health care, end the insufficiency of housing, end gun violence. But he proved *too* optimistic. When he and they couldn't, he fomented disappointment and frustration instead. As one observer put it, the liberals "lost the confidence of the majority," though one might also have said that the majority lost confidence in itself. Among the casualties was the moral sense to which Americans had clung.

Nixon's victory—Humphrey's loss—was a product, no doubt, of all these things, and many others. (And one could also read too much into it.

A study by University of Michigan political scientists concluded that Robert Kennedy, had he lived, might have beaten Nixon "and perhaps with greater ease than he would have won his own party's nomination.") But the 1968 election was not just an election about liberal failures and miscalculations; in that fractious, tumultuous, raw, and angry year, it was an election, above all else, about resentment and about fear, and this is where Hubert Humphrey, the avatar of the politics of joy, could not compete. Wallace, a bundle of vitriol, thrived on fear, provoked resentment, loved to raise the temperature of his audience, and even encouraged violence against protesters in the crowd. He professed to speak for all those who had been afflicted by Lyndon Johnson's Great Society, all those who felt its disruptions as the disruption of the certainties of their lives, all those who were now feeling left behind in the liberal draft Johnson had generated, most of all the blue-collar whites who resented the civil rights movement, resented black violence, resented intellectuals ("Any cab driver in Montgomery knows more about why we're in Vietnam than a Yale professor sitting up there in his ivory tower," Wallace would say), resented government bureaucrats, "who can't even park their bikes straight," and resented even government itself. But it wasn't only blue-collar whites to whom he appealed. As Wallace had said, there were rednecks in suburbia too. Wallace had tapped into a great pool—an ocean—of resentment in white America that rose with the passage of the Civil Rights Act and the Voting Rights Act. Wallace understood the value of resentment and understood how to incite it.

But he didn't understand it as well as Richard Nixon did, because he didn't feel it as powerfully or as personally as Richard Nixon. Wallace played upon the resentments of the aggrieved without fully sharing them. For him, it was a means of advancement in the racial politics of Alabama, where a white candidate was obligated to denigrate black citizens, and which he then expanded to the rest of America with its discontents. Richard Nixon was no Snopes. He was a virtuoso of resentment. A poor boy from Whittier, California, a smart boy but from the wrong side of the tracks, a boy who was disdained by the popular kids, he had lived within his resentments and actively nursed them—nursed them until they became his governing passion. Nixon's boyhood resentments as an outsider led him to an insight that Rick Perlstein phrased as: "When the people who felt like losers united around their shared psychological sense of grievance, their enemies felt somehow more overwhelming, not less."

That was the fear part. And this would lead directly to the resentment part, which was the source of Nixon's political genius: "Do the people's hating for them. Emerge as the people's champion. Except to the people who hate you more than ever." Ted Kennedy had understood what it was like to be an outsider and then used it to build compassion for the disempowered. Richard Nixon understood what it was like and used it to channel the jealousy and antagonism of his fellow Americans. In effect, he took his own anger at the hurts to which he had been subjected and nationalized it. "We thought he did not know, thus could not reach, the country he aspired to govern," Richard Goodwin would write of Nixon. "We were wrong. He knew a lot about America. He could reach, with uncanny intuition, the buried doubts, the secret dreads, the nightmare panic of the threatened soul." And in this, he was a better, smoother, softer, and more politically attuned and acceptable figure than Wallace, who made many of the same appeals to law and order and against restive minorities, the allegedly undeserving poor, the spoiled young, the seemingly condescending intellectuals, and the federal government in a country of increasingly threatened souls, but who was never taken as seriously as Nixon was. Nixon normalized Wallace's hate-mongering.

And he disguised it. He pretended to be a healer. In his victory speech the morning after the election, Nixon recalled a young girl in Deshler, Ohio, holding a sign: BRING US TOGETHER, it read. And he said that after a contentious campaign, unifying the country would be "the great objective" of his administration. Not even Nixon's own staff took this too seriously; one of his speechwriters, William Safire, doubted there even was a sign. If the 1968 election had proved anything, it was how great, and how unbridgeable, the divide in the country now was. He could not bring America together, even if he had really wanted to, and he didn't. In milking the resentments of people he extolled as honest, ordinary, hardworking, taxpaying, "good," and "decent"—a "silent majority," he would label them almost exactly a year after his election—as opposed, it was understood without his having to say it explicitly, to black Americans and the poor and the war protesters and the young student radicals who had occupied university presidents' offices that spring, Nixon had helped widen a divide between these groups as surely as Lyndon Johnson had with the Vietnam War. It was a divide widened over resentments of perceived entitlement. And in milking the resentments of those good and decent people against those allegedly smug, superior elitists—those "Harvards" and "pointy-headed" intellectuals he and Wallace so detested—he had opened another divide, this one more personal for him, between those ordinary folks and their snotty social betters. This was a divide widened over resentments of perceived condescension—Nixon's revenge for his boyhood mistreatment. (This populist anti-intellectualism had been a thread in postwar conservatism; Joseph McCarthy had used it to brilliant effect. Now Nixon used it to even more brilliant effect.) Decades after the election, a cunning Republican operative named Roger Stone, whose career stretched back to Nixon, would tell *The New Yorker*, "Remember. Politics is not about uniting people. It's about dividing people. And getting your fifty-one percent." Nixon divided and got his 43 percent.

But perhaps the greatest resentment Nixon and Wallace tapped, the greatest division they exploited, was nervousness and conflict over how rapidly the country was changing and the *way* in which the country was changing, tumultuously, and over the guilt those ordinary Americans were expected to feel in trying to slow or even prevent that change. "Raw, dislocating change has been moving in America at such speed and with such force," the presidential election chronicler Theodore H. White wrote a year later, "that in 1968 it reached the point of overpowering American understanding." And American values. Nixon and Wallace understood the vestigial power of the moral authority that liberalism had borne, and they knew that they had to delegitimize it. They seemed to understand that in many ways, the Great Society had been compensation for John Kennedy's death—a way to ease the national pain by giving the death meaning through action. The great achievements of the Great Society had been moral achievements—to bring equality and justice and succor to those who had long been denied them. But that could only work if the majority of Americans, white Americans, felt the beneficiaries themselves were deserving. Johnson and the Kennedys insisted they were. Nixon and Wallace insisted they weren't, insisted that their gains came at the expense of the majority, insisted that those beneficiaries did not share the values of work and thrift and honesty with the majority, and tens of millions of white Americans had come to agree with them. This was Nixon's message and perhaps his most enduring contribution to American politics: He legitimized resentments by removing the moral opprobrium against those resentments. But there was another way of putting it: The majority of Americans had grown tired of the effort and sacrifice required to be good. And Richard Nixon absolved them of that duty.

III

If Kennedys didn't cry, neither did they wallow in grief. Now Ted Kennedy, the last brother, was determined to shake off the stupor into which he had fallen in the months since Bobby's death. When he returned to the Senate after the election, he drove himself, drove himself hard, as an anesthetic against the pain that enveloped him and as a way of maintaining his sanity. "I feared that despair and darkness might overtake and smother me if I slackened my drive," he said. A lover of speed, he drove himself literally, jumping into his car and driving fast, driving to outrace the grief. And he drove himself figuratively. "I drove myself in the Senate," he would write of this period. "I drove my staff; I sometimes drove my capacity for liquor to the limit. I might well have driven Joan deeper into her anguish, but the sad truth is that she needed no help from me. Bobby's assassination had devastated her." Bobby's death obsessed him, overwhelmed him. When James Wechsler, the *New York Post* editor, brought up Bobby's name, Ted unleashed what Wechsler called a "wave of reverential nostalgia and lament," calling his brother a "very real patriot," saying he was "misjudged" as ruthless, and insisting that the only reason he had been so reluctant to run for the presidency was that he was afraid "people would just regard his campaign as a personal bid for power."

But it wasn't only Bobby's memory that drove Ted Kennedy, nor was the drive intended only to lessen Ted's pain. There was also Bobby's legacy, and the drive was now to fulfill it—to pick up, as Ted had said in Worcester, his brothers' fallen standard and fill the national void Bobby's death had left. That is what it meant to be the last brother. It was, he felt, his responsibility "to work toward the goals that had been most important to them," Rose Kennedy would write of Ted's dedication to Jack and Bobby. "There was this crushing drive and desire to fulfill their agendas, and be worthy of his brothers' initiatives, and at the same time continue his own," his close friend John Culver would say. "He matured rapidly," is how Theodore Sorensen assessed Ted's response to Bobby's death as he emerged from mourning. "He knew he bore responsibility for the family name, assumed the mantle of family leadership from his brothers, and took on the job of nurturing and guiding their children, comforting their widows, and supporting their causes." He spent a good deal of time late that summer and fall commuting between Washington and Boston to tend to Bobby's children—a "surrogate father," his cousin Robert Fitzgerald called it. That was for the family. In the Senate, it was about those causes. In a book of remembrance about Bobby, Ted said that his most vivid memories of his brother were walks they took together from the Senate Office Building through the park to the Capitol (they eschewed the Senate subway that connected the buildings) and Bobby's repeated entreaties to him during those walks: that he speak at an assembly at a local high school to encourage students to continue their studies; that he support a fundraiser for Cesar Chavez; that he remember the poor, malnourished black people in the Mississippi Delta whom Bobby had visited and the Native Americans whose causes Bobby championed. Ted said those conversations, "as much as any speech he made, revealed his deep feeling and passionate concern for the forgotten American." Now that Bobby was gone, Ted returned to Washington to make Bobby's concerns his concerns too. Now that Bobby was gone, he returned to finish Bobby's unfinished business.

Barely able to stir himself that fall during the election, he willed himself into becoming a whirlwind after. "I felt that coming back to the Senate," he told one reporter, "I had to be involved and active and busy. It was important for me to do that . . . in very personal terms." Said a new staffer of the reinvigorated Ted: "There was all this rising, boiling feeling about this meteor getting ready to take off." He began to travel. In December, he visited Morgantown, West Virginia, to dedicate a federal rehabilitation center named for Bobby and told the crowd, "husky-voiced," *Time* magazine reported, "These hills, these people, this state, have had a very special meaning for my family," recalling the 1960 West Virginia primary. "We tried to make your problems and misfortunes ours and the nation's. You made our misfortunes yours." He met with leaders, including an hour-long tête-à-tête with Lyndon Johnson, which he used to thank Johnson for his kindnesses after Bobby's death. He even tried to touch the nation's conscience as Bobby had. Where he had earlier ignored gun-control efforts because he lacked the emotional capacity, he now took on an issue that had occupied Bobby: the humanitarian tragedy in Biafra, a small secessionist state of Nigeria that had triggered a civil war leading to the starvation deaths of millions of Biafrans, many of them children. "We hold ourselves out as something different on this globe," he said, "a nation that has responded to suffering, has helped the helpless, has looked beyond our narrow interest. . . . Perhaps the starvation of people in Nigeria-Biafra is not in our vital interest. But it is in our conscience." Through his efforts, he managed to pressure the State Department to arrange relief flights to the area, then called on United Nations secretary general U Thant to convene a conference to reach a ceasefire in the war.

But these were random gestures. He needed more to restore himself, to save himself—a larger mission. "I knew at the end of the summer when we all had to go back to work on Labor Day in Washington," said Dun Gifford, his legislative assistant, "that he had to do something. I had no idea what it would be." At the time, Ted didn't either. He loved the Senate. "The greatest forum for change in our country and in the system," he told William Honan of *The New York Times.* "It's the forum that I very much want to be part of and have some influence with." He loved it even though he and John Tunney would confide to each other their frustrations with it, the frustrations Bobby had felt: "not to be able to get things done, and see changes made, and the fact that there's an inertia in the system which is so difficult to break through." Ted may have been much more of a Senate man than his brothers, but most observers thought that, like his brothers, he would nevertheless use the Senate as a stepping-stone to run for the presidency. He had never talked of being part of the Senate leadership. He had never seen himself as a Lyndon Johnson, working the levers of power there in order to get to the presidency.

But there were rumblings in that leadership, which had become more important with the election of Richard Nixon. Majority Leader Mike Mansfield was unassailable. But the assistant majority leader, known as the whip—because one of his chief assignments was "whipping" senators to come to the floor to vote—was very assailable. That position was occupied by Louisiana senator Russell Long, son of the bumptious populist Huey Long and a member of the Senate bulls. Long was "fun-loving," "humorous," "bombastic," as Secretary for the Majority J. Stanley Kimmitt described him—a real Senate character. But he was also an alcoholic, an obstreperous, disheveled alcoholic, which did not always endear him to his fellow senators. Long would arrive on the floor inebriated, and Mansfield would order Democratic staffers to "get him out of here." Senate parliamentarian Robert Dove recalled, "Senator Mansfield was very unhappy" with Long. And that wasn't the only thing that annoyed his colleagues. He had tied up the Senate for five weeks in the spring of 1967 to oppose a rider to the Presidential Election Campaign Fund Act of 1966 and threatened to ask President Johnson to veto the tax bill, which Long's Finance Committee had passed, if the rider wasn't withdrawn; he had called for a vote on a welfare bill, inserting a work requirement early in the morning when liberals weren't on the floor to oppose it (Mansfield got the vote rescinded); and he vehemently attacked the Senate Select Committee on Standards and Conduct when it recommended Senator Thomas Dodd, a fellow alcoholic, be censured for using campaign funds for his own personal benefit. The committee's chairman, John Stennis, was said to be "black with rage" at Long. (Ted, while not supporting Dodd and eventually voting for his censure, was the only senator to visit his office and express his sympathies on the day the Senate Select Committee on Standards and Conduct issued its report against him—a human gesture devoid of political motives.) Moreover, Long had been a frequent opponent of Lyndon Johnson's Great Society agenda and a critic of Mansfield for not acting boldly enough, neither of which endeared him to the leader. Rather than rely on the unreliable Long, of whom he had tired, Mansfield appointed four junior senators to a Legislative Review Committee to serve as his floor leaders.

The whip's job was a largely thankless one, basically a legislative errand boy, and the fact that nine first-term senators had been elected whip testified to just how negligible its power was. The position had apparently arisen in 1913, when the then-majority leader, Senator John Worth Kern of Indiana, complaining about the poor attendance of his charges, appointed an assistant to rectify it. (Later, the caucus would elect its whip.) And it remained a subordinate office until 1946, when the Legislative Reorganization Act recommended a policy committee for each party to plan and execute a legislative program. Whips were made *ex officio* members of those policy committees, and they received several perks, including additional staff, office space, and invitations to events. But whatever power the position conferred was ultimately less a function of anything that inhered to the office itself than of the tenacity of one of its occupiers, Lyndon Johnson, who, when he became whip, ignored the Democratic Policy Committee and made decisions unilaterally, then used the position as no other occupant had: to ascend to majority leader.

But unless one had a lust for power, as Lyndon Johnson did, and the ability to convert the office to one's own ends, as Johnson did, there weren't a whole lot of reasons to seek becoming whip. Ted Kennedy didn't have that lust, nor did he have Johnson's single-minded ingenuity to scheme his way into the ranks of the mighty. And yet Ted Kennedy admitted that as he headed west over the Christmas vacation in yet another attempt to forget Bobby's death, he began pondering the possibility of challenging Long, who he knew was vulnerable. "Flabbergasted" is what Ted's aide David Burke thought when Ted first broached the idea. "It hadn't occurred to me," Burke would recall, "because it was such a strange role for him to want." Ted certainly didn't need the recognition. He was already perceived, especially after the convention, as being a future presidential candidate, which, as journalist Garry Wills observed, "won him special treatment from his Senate peers, special attention from the press, the brightest and best speechwriters and legislative assistants." And as a Kennedy, he already had "star power." When he arrived at a hearing, *U.S. News & World Report* noted, "Television cameras rolled. Photographers ignored the witness who was still talking and blocked to snap the senator sitting quietly in a chair reviewing his presentation."

Ted himself admitted that the idea of running wasn't the product of any great deliberation. It just suddenly sprang up. "He [Long] was having a bad spell of it and wasn't really interested in it, and I don't know who talked to me." It might have been Mansfield, who "pushed Edward Kennedy as much as he could," said parliamentarian Robert Dove. "I just arrived there," is how Ted put it. Another time he said, "I think I saw an opening for advancement." Yet another time, he said he ran because he wanted to be in a position to help set the Democratic agenda and advance issues, "which I thought were going to be threatened with the new administration"—in effect, resuscitating liberalism. And he said that was particularly important because Mansfield, whom Ted greatly liked and admired, had that rather casual leadership style of his. Senators would agree on a time for debate, and Mansfield would then retire to his office to eat a hamburger and read a book. And the quorum would continue, and Mansfield wouldn't announce any more votes, which would send senators knocking on Mansfield's door to tell him that they had worked out the issue and to ask for consent and the bill would pass. But as laissez faire as that method was, if Mansfield wasn't around, "turmoil" ensued. Ted said that was not *his* style. "I am much more of an advocate for causes. And this [Mansfield] was an accommodator and a compromiser," which he said he found "frustrating and unsatisfying." He felt that as whip he would have more of a "constructive impact" on the Senate, as he put it. For all that, he gave a more nonchalant reason when he told a reporter that he had decided to challenge Long in part because he didn't have a committee chairmanship to occupy his time, as Long did.

But his seemingly casual interest in the position might have just been a way for him to protect himself should he lose, and if the decision to run was casual, the real reasons may not have been. Indeed, there were other reasons that even Dave Burke failed to discern—"My strong sense is the getting of it was what it was all about," Burke would say—more-personal reasons, reasons beyond his desire to drive himself and keep the agony at bay, which was no small thing in itself. The senator who had had to overcome the lowest expectations realized, as one reporter who interviewed Ted at the time put it, that "by becoming a member of the Senate leadership, he would be perceived as having a 'legitimate' interest in issues for their own sake, and thus not always arouse speculation that his every action was devoted by designs on the White House." In other words, after dedicating himself to being a senator with a heightened sense of purpose when he returned from his accident, he was hoping to further entrench himself as a Senate man. And in the same vein, he told one of his biographers, the whip job afforded him an "opportunity to learn more about the range of issues that was coming up, to be more of a generalist rather than a specialist," which was a way of raising his status among his colleagues. And there was this: While his brothers were not Senate men, as he was, and had no interest in the institution, his becoming part of the leadership was a way for him to distinguish himself from them, to succeed in an arena where they had neither the desire nor the ability to succeed, and to show, as one reporter put it, that he was not "coasting on his family reputation but has earned his stripes the hard way." He had to do things in his own right. "All of a sudden, he was not Bobby's little brother anymore" was how Dun Gifford saw it. "Didn't want to be . . . He had to be the chief. He was, but he had to be it. More than the title. And he knew that." In this respect, Ted Kennedy *was* more like Lyndon Johnson than like his brothers. He was laying down his marker on the Senate as Johnson had. He was demonstrating that he could make the institution work. It was as if he was seeking to escape the politics of charisma that his brothers had personified and that had, arguably, cost them their lives; as if he was seeking to reposition himself as a pol, not a messiah, burying himself in Senate drudgery, retreating into the institution, following Johnson's lead and Humphrey's, both of whom had been whips, protecting himself physically but also spiritually. It was totally uncharacteristic for a Kennedy to do so. No Kennedy had ever been an institutionalist, much less an errand boy. But Ted Kennedy was: "More modest, more retiring, less ambitious" than his brothers, Mike Mansfield had said of him, and "the only one who was and is a Senate man." The Senate was his fortress; the Senate was his retreat. And the Senate was his way of establishing his own path rather than following the path that had been laid out for him.

But whatever thoughts were churning in his head to pursue the whip position—and Ted said that "Christmas was the first time I had to think about other things" beyond Bobby's death—the decision to run was nevertheless impulsive, a last-minute decision, a decision not entirely rational. He had no animus against Long. Ted said that he actually had a friendly relationship with him, that the two often sat together in the caucus. But Ted had also concluded that Long was "running out of gas" and that he seemed to care more about appeasing oil interests than he did about the Senate; Ted also noted, though, how Long used his influence with his oil and insurance friends to direct campaign contributions to senators Long favored, and Ted recognized the power in that.

Then came Christmas. Over the holiday, Ted had gone on a ski vacation to Sun Valley with his family and John Tunney's family. One story had the airline misplacing his ski boots and Ted calling the baggage department trying to track them down, then, given the idleness as he waited for his boots to arrive plus his natural sociability, he began calling a few of his Senate colleagues to pass time, which is when he heard that Edmund Muskie, the defeated Democratic vice-presidential candidate who had been considering challenging Long himself, had decided to back off. And that is when he began to think about the whip possibility more seriously. (One staffer said that Ted's losing his boots was entirely consistent with his carelessness.) Ted phoned Ed Muskie, coaxing him to reconsider his whip run, but Muskie, by one account, said that he didn't think he could get more than twenty-three votes—he would have needed twenty-nine to win—and encouraged Ted to think about running himself; by another, Ted told Muskie, "If you're absolutely sure you won't run, maybe I will," to which Muskie said, "Do. I urge you to." Now Ted, who had been driving himself all that fall and into the winter, took the initiative. The day after Christmas he began working the phones, as he often had in the past, working them so hard that, Joan said, he hardly did any skiing. He called Humphrey to notify him that he was considering making a run. And then he spent the next five days phoning aides and allies: Joe Tydings, Birch Bayh, Henry Jackson of Washington, George McGovern. "Why?" some of them, perplexed, asked him, according to *Time* magazine. "Are you sure this is something you want?" Kennedy's "standard" comeback was, "Why not?" though by this time his effort wasn't casual. Ted Kennedy wanted to be the whip, wanted to be a Senate leader, wanted to demonstrate that he wasn't an adjunct to his family but now was the leader of it. And then, because there was no time, because he couldn't send them notes or, even better, meet them in person as he preferred to do—"The telephone is not very satisfactory," he complained, "but it is the only way"—he began calling the Southerners, the bulls, Long's natural constituency, and this is where his deference to them, his likability, came into play. "Wha'chew wanna run against Russell Long fo'?" asked one of them. Eastland said, "Ain't no vacancy." But John Stennis said that while he wouldn't support Ted, couldn't really support him, he wouldn't actively oppose him either. And the biggest of the bulls, Richard Russell, who was embarrassed by Long's drunkenness, told him, "I will put no stone in your path." Now that he was finally running, Ted phoned Muskie again to ask for his support, which Muskie pledged. And then, at last, he called Long. It was another testament to Ted's standing among the bulls that they had kept his confidence and that Long was surprised by Ted's news. But it was a sign of Long's own confidence in retaining the job that he flew to the Sugar Bowl football game in New Orleans rather than spend his vacation time lobbying for his job.

Ted Kennedy, however, never rested on overconfidence. He called every one of the fifty-five other Senate Democrats and spoke to nearly all of them, making his pitch: "It was that I felt the job of majority whip was important, that it could be effective, that although the job was not clearly defined, I would try, if I won it, to make it important to the nation, the Senate, and the party." And in a clear dig at Long, he reminded his fellow senators of Humphrey's tenure as whip, of his dignity and stature, of the way he had promoted legislation. And to his fellow liberals, he said that it was "important that someone in the leadership should be sensitive to the things they felt strongly about," even though Mansfield clearly did. What Ted was really saying is that it was important to have someone in the leadership to *fight* for those things. And he was saying that he would. He made so many calls and was so preoccupied with his new campaign that he left Sun Valley without even saying goodbye to Tunney.

It was, he realized, a risk—a big risk. *Kennedys don't lose.* But Long had his oil people calling senators and applying pressure, and they had influence. Ted said he was his own one-man campaign, that he didn't ask others to pressure senators for him, that when he made the commitment to run—and he didn't tell Long until December 29—he had no idea whether or not he could get the votes to win, which was a bit like his poll-tax and Morrissey efforts. "I suppose some other calls were made," he conceded, "but the people who made them did so on their own." But this wasn't entirely true. Though Dave Burke was steadfastly opposed to Ted's running on practical grounds—the job was "meaningless," in his mind—he was thrilled that the fight for it had seemed to energize Ted. "After Bob's death, he had been a different person," Burke told biographer Theo Lippman. "There was a lot of the wind out of him. He was very slow in coming back. It ended when he ran for whip. . . . He was spunky and wanted to do something—even if it wasn't a good thing to do." So Burke and Charles Ferris, Mansfield's chief of staff and a good friend of Burke's—the two played poker every week at the house of columnist Mark Shields—started making calls of their own, and, as Ferris put it, the effort "took on a life of its own." When Ted returned from Sun Valley and met with Ferris and Burke, the three realized that they might actually have the votes after all, in part because Long was, as Burke put it, "walking around thinking everything is coming up roses."

But there was one more call to make—one important call when it came to the inner workings of the Senate and the machinations among Democratic senators. Late on the night of December 30, Ted phoned Lyndon Johnson to apprise him of the whip campaign. Ted had already spoken with Humphrey three times about the race, including once that morning, and Humphrey had given the heads-up to Johnson. Humphrey told the president that Long had called him too and thought he had thirty-six votes, but Long asked Humphrey if he might pressure his young Minnesota protégé, Walter Mondale, a request that Humphrey deflected. (Mondale had already told Humphrey he was likely to vote for Kennedy.) Then Humphrey and Johnson got into head counting—a Johnson specialty. Humphrey thought Long might "try to twist the arms of the committee chairmen," but Long had come to the floor "with a few snorts under his belt," which disgusted them. Johnson concluded that "Kennedy would have the votes."

When Ted called Johnson that night, he was not entirely honest with him. He told him that he had "given some thought" over the last "two to three days"—he had been pursing it since the day after Christmas—and that "some of my colleagues" had spoken to him about running—he had initiated it—and that he had told them he was holding back in deference to Ed Muskie until Muskie told him he wouldn't be running. And only then, Ted said, did he begin making calls. "I wasn't interested in getting in it if, you know, the horses were out of the barn," which was certainly something Johnson could appreciate. But Ted said he discovered that he could make a "creditable showing," though he realized all in all that it would be an "uphill fight." Long was a "very able fellow"—Johnson knew he wasn't—but as chairman of the Finance Committee and with "all his other responsibilities," Ted said, Long was "stretched pretty thin there," and with the new administration coming in, "it might be of some value in being in that position." Of course, while Ted was being coy with Johnson, Johnson was being coy right back. He cited the time that Franklin Roosevelt weighed in on the side of Senator Alben Barkley in 1937, when Barkley was running for majority leader against Mississippi senator Pat Harrison after the death of Joseph Robinson, and Johnson said Roosevelt wound up dividing the party by doing so. And Johnson claimed—not credibly—that he hadn't talked to a single senator about the race. In fact, Johnson, who loved intrigue, had spoken to Long himself and had run down the list of senators with him just as he had done with Humphrey. When they got to Mansfield, Johnson asked Long what he had told him. "I asked him, and he said I didn't have to worry about his vote," Long answered. To which Johnson, that reader of men, immediately cracked, "He's against you. That is not a commitment." And Johnson told Long that Mansfield would never vote against a Kennedy. Now that it was Ted's turn to speak with the president, Ted, still coy, said he had already talked with senators Russell, Eastland, Stennis, and Alabama's John Sparkman—all bulls—and had then phoned Long. "I'm afraid he's been busy on the phone ever since," Ted told Johnson, and both of them laughed.

Long must have thought that his seniority and his association with the bulls would protect him. They didn't. On January 3, with Muskie placing Ted's name in nomination, Ted beat Long 31 to 26. Now he was officially a Senate leader. He had won, in part, some felt, *because* he was not part of the old guard but rather part of a new, ascendant group of young senators. (By contrast, Representative Mo Udall ran against Speaker John McCormack and suffered ignominious defeat. Such was the difference between the House and Senate, now that the Senate bulls were aging out of power.) Long said he took some consolation in the fact that he couldn't have been defeated by "anyone else in the U.S. Senate" and that he would have taken "any other opponent by a two-to-one margin." And he said, less graciously, "This happens to have been a race where it was a nation-wide proposition, and while I had Senator Kennedy outgunned in the United States Senate, he had me outgunned in the United States," mean-ing that Kennedy had succeeded in nationalizing the contest. If he had—and Long's alcoholism certainly had as much to do with his defeat as Ted's national standing—it was yet another indication of Ted's growing sup-port among rank-and-file Democrats as well as a sign of the declining support of the bulls in the chamber. Liberals, who were now increasingly in charge of the party, were jubilant. "The best thing that has happened to the Senate in years," Joe Rauh wrote Ted shortly after the victory, and he added, "Ever since your superb performance when we worked together against the poll tax, I have hoped you would do just this." Ted himself was hopeful that he could energize the Senate, and he said he viewed his vic-tory not as a personal triumph or a way station to the presidency (though he was certainly hoping to use it as that if he chose to pursue the presi-dency) but as "expressing the sense of the Democratic senators in favor of an aggressive and creative program in the upcoming Congress," the kind of program Bobby would have promoted. Even Long himself agreed, warning the incoming president on *The Huntley–Brinkley Report* NBC News broadcast that night that Nixon had better look out because, "in all probability, he had a very able opponent ready for him." When Ted, watch-ing in his office, saw that clip, he laughed. And then later that night, a bitterly cold night, after celebrating his victory at his McLean home, he drove himself to Arlington Cemetery to visit the grave sites of his lost brothers. As Nixon was about to enter the Oval Office, Ted Kennedy, the new Democratic whip, flush with victory, had picked up his brothers' fallen standard as he had promised he would, and he had become the par-ty's new leader-in-waiting.

And he was looking forward to the battle ahead.

ELEVEN

A Shadow President

WITH THE ELECTION of Richard Nixon to the presidency, Democrats braced themselves for the worst. Nixon was a man whom nearly everyone in the party abhorred, seeing him as a vicious political slasher, a zealous partisan lacking all scruples. Ted Kennedy had no affection for Richard Nixon either, but neither did he feel any personal antipathy toward him. They had first met back in 1953, shortly after Jack Kennedy was elected to the Senate, when Ted, then not quite twenty-one, took the night train down from Boston to Washington to visit with his brother and arrived at Jack's office early in the morning, before Jack did. Ted was sitting on his suitcase in the hallway of the Senate Office Building outside Jack's door when Nixon, then the vice president–elect, strolled by on the way to *his* office, which happened to be next to Jack's. He invited Ted to wait there with him, and, over the next forty-five minutes, as Ted remembered it, "We had a pleasant talk, sparring about who got in first in the morning and that sort of thing." And Ted would later say that there were several occasions when he was visiting Jack and wound up chatting with Nixon. But these friendly encounters did little to break the ice between the two of them. For a politician, Nixon was, as Jack Kennedy had observed during their presidential campaign, uncomfortable in his own skin and unable to relax. He was studied, mechanical, uneasy, incapable of charm, a brooding man with a smile that seemed the result of great effort, an insincere smile, but, then, he exuded a general sense of insincerity, which was one of his political liabilities. And if Nixon was generally uncomfortable, he was especially uncomfortable in the presence of the Kennedys, who seemed to press all the buttons of Nixon's deep insecurities. In the first month of his presidency, Nixon visited the Senate, where he had served for two years before becoming vice president, and Ted noted to Arthur Schlesinger Jr. that Nixon seemed to have "some sort of odd feeling about me." Ted continued, "Every time we are together in the same room, I feel he has this particular awareness of me, and this means we keep getting thrown together and then have nothing to say," though they had once made plenty of small talk. Standing in Minority Leader Everett Dirksen's office that afternoon, Ted said that Nixon was "very nervous" and broke the tension by remarking, "Well, this is a strange room, isn't it?" even though Ted thought there was nothing especially strange about it.

But if Ted had no personal animosity toward Nixon—he had shown little personal animosity toward anyone—he did have political animosity toward him. Most liberals did, for Nixon, a dark man with furrowed brow, jowly, heavy of spirit, seemed to draw on the darkness of the electorate. He had a gift for it, as Ted had a gift for lightheartednesss, and since he had won the presidency by teasing out the fears and resentments of Americans worried about race and youth and Vietnam and a country seemingly spinning out of control, he was threatening to govern by fear and resentment too. It was as instinctual to Nixon as conviviality was to Ted Kennedy. ("*I* think I've got a lousy personality, and I'm not a personality kid," Nixon himself told pollster Louis Harris.) He had risen to prominence in the House and was catapulted into the Senate by sowing fear of communist infiltration of the government and branding his opponents as communists or communist dupes. He had won the presidency with the same playbook, by sowing fear of black Americans and young protesters and liberals. In this, Nixon had the advantage of a teetering economy—basically stagnant wages—which could easily be sold to those disaffected Americans as a zero-sum game: Whatever gains Johnson's (and Kennedy's) poor got were subtracted from those "forgotten Americans," the same term Franklin Roosevelt had used during the Great Depression, until Nixon discovered the term "silent majority," a perfect formulation that bundled the resentments of white Americans against what Nixon implied was a noisy minority. "In a time when the national focus is on the unemployed, the impoverished, and the dispossessed," he had said in his acceptance speech, citing three categories of prominence for Democrats generally and the Kennedys specifically, "the working Americans have become the forgotten Americans."

Democrats were defeated, chastened, demoralized. Many felt their moment had passed and that the Great Society was endangered. "I figured when my legislative program passed the Congress," Lyndon Johnson would lament several years after Nixon's election, "that the Great Society had a real chance to grow into a beautiful woman. . . . And when she grew up, I figured she'd be so big and beautiful that the American people couldn't help but fall in love with her . . . they'd want to keep her around forever, making her a permanent part of American life, more permanent even than the New Deal." But then came Nixon, "and everything I've worked for is ruined. . . . She's getting thinner and thinner. . . . Soon she'll be so ugly that the American people will refuse to look at her; they'll stick her in a closet . . . and there she'll die." Just before he left office, Johnson convened a congressional-leadership breakfast at which he asked whether his last budget should continue the 10 percent surtax he had enacted to help pay for the Vietnam War or whether he should leave the decision to Nixon. Every one of the leaders, in what was an acknowledgment of their distress, told Johnson to leave it to Nixon. All but Ted, who, after telling Johnson that he wanted to give the question more thought and would get back to him, phoned Johnson aide Joseph Califano later that day to say he would urge Johnson to continue the tax rather than reduce the budget with what he called "fake cuts." Johnson later agreed. He wasn't going to let Nixon starve his programs.

But despite their deep distrust of Nixon, a distrust born of two decades of red-baiting, vehement partisanship, and political deviousness that had earned him the sobriquet "Tricky Dick" among his detractors, Senate Democrats still hoped they might find some modus vivendi with him. Just a week after Nixon's inauguration, Mike Mansfield met in the conference room of the Senate secretary with the Democratic Policy Committee, on which Ted, as whip, now sat, to discuss their prospective working relationship with the new president. "One must avoid getting in a position of opposing for its sake alone," Richard Russell argued, "but should be selective in taking our stand." Mansfield agreed, even saying he trusted Nixon's sincerity in wishing to end the war in Vietnam. The majority leader's position was that the interests of the country should always supersede the interests of the party, though as much of a principled stand as it was— and Mansfield was a deeply principled man—it, too, was an acknowledgment of how far the Democrats had fallen. Nixon held the upper hand.

As whip, Ted Kennedy now moved, as one reporter put it that first month, "at Mansfield's elbow." But that did not mean that Ted shared

Mansfield's more charitable view of Nixon or that he was willing to conciliate, as Mansfield was. Like Mansfield, Ted was not by temperament intransigent. He didn't, as Russell had warned his fellow Democrats, oppose for the sake of opposing. Still, the Ted Kennedy of 1969 was different from the Ted Kennedy of even a year earlier—different from the one before Robert Kennedy's death. Bobby's death had broken him personally, driven him into despair, but it had also annealed him politically, toughened him, forced him not only to pick up the fallen standard but also to fight hard for Bobby's constituencies and for the America Bobby had envisioned. As columnist Max Lerner would later describe Ted's new resolve in this period, he treated Bobby's death as an affront, and "the we-against-the-world motif operated to firm up Ted's allegiance to revealed liberal doctrine." Lerner noted, too, that the "we" didn't mean only Ted as the "last survivor" but a growing entourage who viewed him, as many of those convention delegates had, as their best and perhaps their only hope to beat back the conservative tide. Though he said he had run for whip in part to discourage presidential speculation—"I want to give my full attention to the Senate," he told the press upon beating Long for whip. "I'm not planning for four years or eight years or twelve years into the future"—he had become the presumptive Democratic nominee for 1972, both among his party confreres and, according to polls, among rank-and-file Democrats. *Time* observed, "Whatever he accomplishes for the party and the Senate, his already lustrous presidential prospects are clearly enhanced." In the view of many Democrats, with the party in ashes, leaderless and aimless, Ted was the only one with the authority to assume its leadership and take the battle to Nixon, as he had had to assume the leadership of his family. Ted had come to see himself in the same way. Part of it was that Ted Kennedy was one of the few Democrats who was unbowed by the election defeat, one of the few who didn't want to make accommodation or need to make accommodation to Nixon. He saw Nixon as Johnson saw Nixon, a mortal threat to liberalism, a man who sought to both attack liberalism's moral underpinnings and unravel the liberal programs for which Ted's brothers had fought. Ted had already dissuaded Senator Henry Jackson, a Democratic hawk, from considering becoming Nixon's secretary of Defense. By one account he told Jackson, who still harbored presidential aspirations, in no uncertain terms that his career as a Democrat would be over if he accepted. And Nixon had scarcely settled into office when Ted, sitting on the Select Committee on Nutrition and Human

Needs, fought a proposed cut of $100,000 from the food-stamp budget and even pressured the new secretary of Agriculture, Clifford Hardin, to offer new stamps to affected counties in South Carolina.

But these were mere skirmishes. Ted Kennedy was girding for more. In those early months of the Nixon presidency, Ted Kennedy was already girding for war: a war to save liberalism from what he saw as the depredations of the new president and a war to save the constituencies he served and that Bobby had served—the poor and the powerless—from the new president's neglect. He had sought the whip position with, he acknowledged, more than a subliminal understanding that Mansfield had no appetite for tangling with Nixon. Ted did. But he had also sought the position with almost no deliberation about what he would do with it; as David Burke had said, not entirely accurately, it was just the winning of it that mattered. But now, during the interregnum, that changed. Ted began to think of the office both in terms of what it could contribute to his presidential ambitions, though he was loath to say so, and in terms of the ways in which he could use it to challenge Nixon and preserve liberalism and thus help those who needed help. The position had been so marginalized that when he had solicited one senior senator's vote, the man said he didn't even know who the present whip was. Ted would make sure that every senator would know now. He had no sooner won the whip job than he sought to redefine it, reinvigorate it, turn it into a position of real power, liberal power; he would not just be a servant of his fellow senators. As Ted saw it, the whip office would become a battle station—a Lyndon Johnson strategy to gain greater power by proving oneself within the Senate, rather than his brothers' strategy of proving themselves outside it. It was telling that no liberal, save Mansfield and Humphrey, had held a Democratic leadership position in the Senate since 1947. (Johnson was no liberal during his Senate time.) Russell Long himself, who had opposed John Kennedy's Nuclear Test-Ban Treaty and Lyndon Johnson's civil rights and Medicare bills, all keystone pieces of legislation, and who was clearly a puppet of big-oil interests, had won the job over John Pastore of Rhode Island, a traditional liberal.

But now a liberal *had* won, and he was aiming to change the dynamics in the chamber. One of those dynamics was the hegemony of the bulls, whose power was already in slow decline. Ted knew better than to challenge them directly; there was no benefit in doing so, especially since he had profited from working with them, and especially since, as he pointed out to one reporter and as Johnson had pointed out as vice president, he realized that they would soon be aging out of power. But without infuriating them, he actively set up a liberal counterweight. Though he told reporter William Honan that he realized the whip had to serve all senators, he also told Honan that he was "aware of the fact that a senator such as Richard Russell consults with, works with, and identifies with a certain group of senators," those conservative bulls, and that Ted now would "identify myself with a certain group of the Senate: that is, the group dedicated to change and progress and to meeting the needs of the country as I see them."

But it was about more than identification. The bulls and their conservative allies were legislative artists who knew how to work the levers of the Senate. Now Ted, who had spent so much of his time observing the chamber's operations, watching those bulls, was learning how to work those levers to advance his issues—liberal issues. At the behest of Harold Hughes, a freshman from Iowa, Ted gathered a group of twelve liberals, including Ed Muskie, George McGovern, Walter Mondale, Frank Church, and Alan Cranston of California to discuss how they might accrue power—the sort of power the bulls had had. The conservatives had always made sure that one Southerner was on the Senate floor at all times to monitor debate. The liberals resolved that they, too, would have their members on the floor to hear speeches and ask questions and monitor debates. When liberals had threatened to dominate a committee, the bulls had always moved quickly to get a conservative on that committee, as they had done when they reassigned Robert Byrd from Armed Services, where the conservatives already held sway, to Judiciary, where the liberals were gathering force. And the conservatives did more, conspiring to deny Birch Bayh a spot on the Appropriations Committee, even though, by seniority, he was entitled to it. "Whether or not they moved into these committees by plan or design," Ted told William Honan, though he very well knew it was by design, "I can't be sure." But Ted said that now that he was whip, liberals would be using the same techniques. "Maybe we could get liberals to give up certain committee assignments even when they have a great interest in a particular committee, when shifting them somewhere else would tip the balance in our favor." He recommended that the Steering Committee, which made those assignments, be reconfigured for better "geographical and philosophical" balance—in essence, reconfigured to reduce the power of the Southern conservatives.

And it wasn't just a matter of maneuvering to circumvent the bulls. It was a matter of empowering the whip, *him*, to help dictate policy, which had never previously been a function of the whip but which Ted saw as a way of increasing his own leverage and that of the liberals. Soon after assuming the position, Ted met with David Burke and Wayne Owens, his new whip assistant, to discuss the purpose of the whip and concluded that he needed not just to corral votes or nose count or even strategize about increasing liberal influence within the caucus but to be much more proactive in the setting of a legislative agenda and in the formation of legislation itself in order to create a Democratic opposition to Nixon. "Whip up the majority in terms of issues, not telephone calls," is how Burke would later put it. And Ted thought the Democratic Policy Committee, which had been formed expressly to devise a coherent Democratic program but had abandoned that role, needed, in the absence of a Democratic president, to fulfill that function: "that is, to formulate ways and means of enacting the party platform into the law," as he told *The New York Times*. And since Mansfield didn't seem particularly interested in doing so and was willing to grant Ted, his new protégé, a fair degree of independence, Ted decided that he would take the initiative himself. Ted Kennedy would become the self-appointed Democratic policymaker. And Ted Kennedy would become more.

II

The whip's rooms in the Capitol—S148, S149, and S150—located just thirty steps from the Senate chamber, now became the command center of the Senate. They had once been, in the early nineteenth century, the home of the Foreign Relations Committee and the Naval Affairs Committee—a hallway between them had been converted to S149 to make one large suite—and then the Court of Claims and then the Committee on Revolutionary War Claims and then the Census Committee and then the Commerce Committee, when the great senator Hiram Johnson chaired that committee and had his offices there, and then, after it housed a succession of senators, it became the office of the secretary to the majority, and only when Ted took over did it become the whip's office. It was a grand office, an ornate office, an office with an expansive view of northwest Washington—high-ceilinged, with crystal chandeliers and marble fireplaces and gilded mirrors—an office that radiated power and even majesty, befitting the large role Ted Kennedy wanted the whip to play. Ted had told Owens that he believed the whip could serve as a force to "educate and communicate" with fellow senators, and he began setting up seminars for the staffs of the freshmen and launched a whip newsletter. And, as he did with the meetings of experts at his McLean home to educate himself on issues, he invited experts to his office to advise other senators and to speak to the Policy Committee as a way of forging some unity on a legislative program—*his* unity. "So what is his role?" Harvard law professor Samuel Beer, who had advised Ted in his first Senate campaign, asked rhetorically of the new whip. "He gives the Democratic party a sort of coherence and purpose that develops what the issues are. This is a kind of party government. What you can do depends on the legislature." But since America didn't have a parliamentary system, it only worked if, Beer said, a congressional leader was skillful enough to attract some votes from the other side. "If he's like Teddy," Beer added, he "can make that work." And Beer, noting Ted's new assertiveness, recognized that the presumptive Democratic presidential nominee was using the whip's office for a larger purpose than devising policy, larger even than laying a political foundation. In that physically majestic office, Ted Kennedy was making himself into what Beer called a "shadow president"—he said he got the term from Kennedy biographer Burton Hersh—positioning himself to be Nixon's opposite number and to parry him. Ted clearly had that in mind: a shadow presidency. Beer wasn't the only one who saw Ted as Nixon's nemesis on his way to being Nixon's successor. "He carried about him the aura of a shadow government," a reporter observed, "a thriving and palpable government-in-exile, just waiting to take over." Of course, Congress had taken on presidents before, preventing them from enacting their programs, putting up stop signs. The Senate bulls had stymied much of John Kennedy's agenda. But while Ted was erecting his own stop signs, this wasn't just stymieing presidential initiatives. This was working on an entirely new agenda—a liberal alternative to Nixon's. Not even Lyndon Johnson as majority leader had dared something so audacious as to use the Democratic caucus in the Senate as an alternative government. Thirty-seven-year-old Ted Kennedy would try.

What made the attempt even more audacious was that Richard Nixon was no easy mark. If this shadow presidency required Ted to redefine the whip's office and enlarge its scope, it also required him to redefine his own staff, strengthen it. He had done this once before, in 1965, under the challenge of his own brother when he realized that his staff was deficient compared to Bobby's. Now under the challenge of taking on the entire executive branch, he began enlarging and upgrading his staff once again, and once again the task fell to David Burke. "To actually go out into the marketplace and look for people who had recently graduated from Harvard Law School and were on the law review and were smarter than I could ever be, or anyone else I knew—that's the person you wanted to work for you," Burke recalled, which is what he did when he had first arrived. But it wasn't as difficult this time to recruit staff, because Ted's stature had grown so appreciably and his future burned so bright— a presidential future. "High excitement and enthusiasm" was how Robert Bates, Ted's first African American staff member, who had come to him from the Office of Economic Opportunity, described the mood. "I called him the Great White Hope, because at that point, in January of '69, there began this surge toward his being the new Democratic nominee for president." (One of the first things Bates did was try to organize striking black Senate dining room employees, with Ted's full support, he said, even though the employees were protesting the low wages paid by the Senate administration—an administration of which Ted was technically a part.) Another new recruit was a former Harvard varsity football player and Harvard Law grad who had worked in Bobby's presidential campaign, Paul Kirk Jr.; the Massachusetts native arrived at Ted's Senate office so overcrowded with fellow staffers that he was shuffled off to Ted's whip's offices in the Capitol. A third recruit that month—the one who would be the most important recruit—was Carey Parker, a slight, balding, quiet, studious, almost recessive young attorney who had clerked for Supreme Court justice Potter Stewart and then gone to work as a special assistant in the criminal division of the Justice Department, where he'd helped draft Lyndon Johnson's crime legislation and met Jim Flug, Ted's staff person on judiciary issues. With Nixon cleaning out the Justice Department of Johnson's people, Flug tendered the offer to join Ted's staff, which Parker accepted on the same basis that Bates had: "It was Kennedy for president, no question. That was part of the appeal. . . . I probably wouldn't have come to work for any other senator." Parker became the office buddha— a figure of preternatural serenity. As Burke put it, "The butterflies would be flitting around, having all sorts of ideas," while Parker "sat in the corner and didn't say much," though it didn't take long for his gravity to speak for him and for Ted to come to rely on his judgment.

There was a lot of flitting because there was a lot to be done. Ted had wanted a legislative package of his own to contrast with Nixon's, to *challenge* Nixon's, and within a month he had introduced tax incentives to industry for job creation and housing; a "minimum tax" bill to prevent the wealthy from avoiding taxes altogether; an expansion of the community health centers he had first promoted in 1966; and a draft-reform bill. It wasn't a big package or a radical package, no Great Society. *The New York Times Magazine,* in William Honan's story on Ted's budding senatorial leadership, was unimpressed. "Headlines notwithstanding," it opined, "Kennedy continues to plod at a respectable hiker's pace; he is no flashing rabbit." But this assessment may have had more to do with Ted's reputation as a cautious Senate insider than with the reality that Ted, after scarcely six years in the chamber, was forcefully pushing his own agenda and taking the fight to Nixon on these and on a series of other issues. Whether the press yet recognized it or not, Ted was becoming a rabbit.

And while his presidential prospects played a role in his aggressiveness—even if he wasn't quite sure whether he wanted to be president or to become a Senate eminence instead—there was that other motive, a far more powerful motive, that explained why he suddenly transformed into a firebrand and that explained his newly energized liberal proclivities, a motive that engulfed him, a motive that was bred into him as a Kennedy in the Kennedy succession and as a brother whose devotion was boundless: It was for Bobby. It was all for Bobby and the people for whom Bobby had worked. It was to do the things that Bobby would have done had he lived. It was to honor Bobby's memory, not just to fulfill his legacy but to carry the fallen standard as Bobby had done after Jack's death: passionately and with moral fervor. That is what Kennedys did. Passion hadn't come naturally to Ted Kennedy. He didn't have Bobby's fire or belligerence or moral fever. He had been the plodder, as the *Times* described him, the legislative conciliator who always seemed to know his place and who picked his spots—the poll tax (despite the administration's opposition); immigration; one man, one vote—carefully. But in some ways, with Bobby's death, he had subsumed his brother. He felt it was his duty to do so. There was so much unfinished business. Ted felt he had to finish it. There was such a grievous threat to the things in which Bobby believed. Ted felt he had to defeat it. "In 1969, it seemed to me that there were a number of things that Bobby was interested in and I thought I ought to try and sort of pick up on," Ted would recall years later, much more dispassionately than he really felt at the time—dispassionately, no doubt, because he was still coming to grips with Bobby's death and its meaning and, in fact, would always be coming to grips with it.

And this was how he tried to come to grips with it. Ted Kennedy, who had toyed with the idea of accepting the Democratic presidential nomination for Bobby, now embraced the burden in the Senate of saving the country's soul for his late brother, who had given his life, Ted believed, in that same effort.

That spring of 1969 was Bobby's spring. Bobby's issues were the important issues, the ones that needed tending, and Bobby's constituencies were the important ones, the ones that needed a voice. The staff knew it—they were "extraordinarily sensitive to the kinds of things that Robert was promoting," said Robert Bates, who was brought on staff to deal with black issues—knew that this was what Ted wanted. But not everyone was on board with Ted's new advocacy. David Burke tried to dissuade Ted from speaking in Memphis on the first anniversary of Martin Luther King Jr.'s death—a surprise appearance, it was called—though Bobby would have done it, or from joining president Cesar Chavez and United Farm Workers members in a one-hundred-mile march from Indio, California, to the Mexican border to publicize Mexican farmworkers who were being shuttled across the border as cheap "scab" labor. Burke said he was worried about security. In the past, Burke said, Ted might have listened and weighed the benefits against the dangers. But Burke told Kennedy biographer Burton Hersh that Ted was much more decisive now, much more willing to take risks. For Bobby. Others called it a rebelliousness, an impulsiveness, a "kind of what-the-hell attitude" that had come to grip him after Bobby's death, because his own life seemed cheaper to him now. So he went to Memphis and spoke to an enthusiastic crowd at an outdoor observance—even though Bates, who had been sent there in advance, had heard gunshots at the venue shortly before Ted arrived. And, after first bowing to advisers who told him that going to California to march with Chavez would seem to be trading on Bobby's death, he abruptly changed his mind during a touch football game that Sunday at Hickory Hill and directed Dun Gifford to book a plane for him immediately, realizing that it was the right thing to do—again, the thing Bobby would have done. And at Calexico, near the Mexican border, he jumped on the back of a truck, in shirtsleeves in blazing 106-degree heat, and told the crowd that "the voice of Cesar Chavez was being heard in Congress" and that "injustices to farmworkers can no longer be tolerated," which were the words Bobby would have uttered. As *Time* put it of these appearances, he would "help remind the nation of those beyond affluence's pale," which is what Bobby had done on his visits to Appalachia and the Mississippi Delta. And while *Time* also noted that there was political "mileage" in his "rapport with America's downtrodden"—though it was difficult to see exactly what that mileage was—he also made a plea for Bobby's assassin, Sirhan Sirhan, to be spared the death penalty, because he knew Bobby would have done so, even though there was no political mileage in it whatsoever for Ted. "My brother was a man of love and sentiment and compassion," Ted wrote the district attorney before the sentencing hearing. "He would not have wanted his death to be the cause for the taking of another life."

He fought for Native Americans for Bobby—because Bobby had championed their cause. "It wasn't just a matter of voting on legislation when it came along," said a staffer. "He allocated two of his most precious resources to the subject of Indian affairs, Indian rights, and Indian education. One was his own time: floor time for debates, committee markups, chairing hearings, travel, speeches, and that sort of thing. The other was staff time, because during those years [after Bobby's death] I [the staffer] spent a lot of time on Indian matters." When the Special Subcommittee on Indian Education, which Bobby had chaired, was set to expire in March 1969, Ralph Yarborough, the new chairman of its parent committee, Labor and Public Welfare, encouraged Ted to take the chairmanship himself and get the Senate to extend it through November, which Ted did. For Bobby. Over the next five years, he held hearings on Indian education, traveling throughout the West to conduct them. And these weren't perfunctory appearances either. Once, he held a hearing on a Navajo reservation in Window Rock, Arizona, where a medicine man, heavily bejeweled in turquoise, was testifying through a translator. Ted had another hearing scheduled for later in the day, to which he would be flying in a propeller-driven Indian Health Service plane, and the forecast was for a storm. Still, Ted listened to the medicine man through the end of his testimony, even though the storm had now precluded his flying out. In the end, remembered staffer Thomas Susman, the tribe formed a caravan and drove him three hours to the destination. "Kennedy has done more for

Indians than almost any other member of Congress," an aide to another senator told Kennedy biographer Theo Lippman, "certainly more than any other Easterner." He did it because Bobby no longer could.

He fought the military draft for Bobby—because Bobby had told him that his opposition to Vietnam had as much if not more to do with the fact that the soldiers who were dying there were poor and urban than with the immorality of the war itself, though the loss of those soldiers was another form of immorality. And while he was alive, Bobby had pressed Ted to work for a random selection of draftees through a lottery, a system without student deferments, which Ted did in 1967. Ted won agreement from Senator John Stennis, the chairman of the Armed Services Committee, to fund a commission to study random selection, even though the House–Senate conference made a concerted effort to remove the funding. Stennis said he included it "out of a personal respect I've developed for Senator Kennedy." And Ted would say that his inspiration for offering the amendments on the draft and working for their passage were conversations he had had with Bobby, who had nettled college students by questioning, "Can you really defend draft deferments for students on a moral basis?" By year's end, Ted had convinced Stennis to send the lottery legislation to the Senate floor, on the condition that Ted withhold other reform measures, especially ending deferments, until Stennis could hold hearings on them the following year, and on December 1, a draft lottery was held.*

The biggest of his legislative battles that year, the most consequential, and the one that pitted him directly against the new president was another that Bobby had instigated: a fight against an anti-ballistic missile system. The ABM had actually surfaced first in the Johnson administration, when the Defense Department, under Secretary Robert McNamara, began a research-and-development project into the feasibility of such a system to defend American cities against incoming Chinese missiles by knocking them out of the air with land-based missiles, and it intensified when Congressional hawks authorized $168 million to build hardware for it, even though Johnson himself harbored some concerns. But Nixon had no such trepidations, and shortly after entering office, he decided to de-

---

*Ted believed that the end of deferments did as much to wind down the Vietnam War as the Tet Offensive had, because it put middle-class and upper-middle-class young men at the same risk as poor young men.

ploy a modified three-site pilot system, this time not only against Chinese missiles but also against a possible first strike of Soviet missiles. Bobby had been no fan of the project: He was skeptical of any new massive military outlays, but he also felt that there had been too little congressional consultation in its development, which he thought had been a problem with Vietnam as well. Though Ted's senatorial friend Phil Hart and Hart's Republican ally Senator John Sherman Cooper carried the fight against the ABM system throughout the Johnson administration and into Nixon's, Ted had come to share Bobby's views, especially about the White House's disregard for congressional input, and decided to take a leading role in opposing the system. In this, he seemed to be moved as much by Bobby's example in leading legislative battles as by Bobby's position on the issue. After Bobby's death, Ted had begun reaching out to experts in numerous fields as Bobby had done, not only as a way of building his Senate portfolio and his stature but also as a way of fulfilling his obligation to Bobby to be involved in critical issues like the ones in which Bobby would have been involved. Among those to whom he had reached out were John Kennedy's former science adviser, Jerome Wiesner of MIT, and a Harvard professor named Abram Chayes, who specialized in international law. Chayes had been a campaign adviser to Jack, and was now working on arms control. Both men had been among Ted's hospital tutors when he was recovering from his plane crash. Chayes and Wiesner had serious reservations about the ABM system on the basis that it would be prohibitively expensive, it would threaten to escalate the arms race, and, last but not least, it would not work. The Nixon administration dismissed those concerns. It was fixated on an ABM system.

And that set up a confrontation between the president and the would-be shadow president—a first test of Ted's burgeoning senatorial power. Because one of the sites was to be built in Massachusetts, Ted assigned Dun Gifford to explore the situation, and when Gifford, after consulting with the scientists and selected military officials, concluded that it should not be built, Ted sent a letter to the new secretary of Defense, Melvin Laird, on January 31, asking that construction be halted. Laird promptly and somewhat surprisingly agreed to do so while the department conducted a review, then, just as promptly, decided to proceed once the review unsurprisingly wound up endorsing the system. Still, Nixon knew he was jousting with Kennedy, so to circumvent him, the new president, a cunning political operative himself, revised the ABM from the one Johnson had proposed, protecting cities and called Sentinel, to one protecting American missile silos and now redubbed Safeguard, his reasoning being that a smaller, less ambitious, and less expensive modified system would be more likely to blunt opposition.

Now the two political goliaths and would-be presidential adversaries stood toe-to-toe. A "very big fight," Dun Gifford called it. "The biggest challenge at the moment," Nixon's chief of staff, H. R. Haldeman, called it in April, seeing it as "the first battle of '72 vs. Teddy Kennedy," already looking forward to the next presidential election, and adding, "We must win," though Nixon, more sanguine than Haldeman, felt he could lose a vote in the Senate and still get his ABM in a House–Senate conference. But despite the fact that it was a wrestling match between two savvy opponents, and despite the fact that Nixon saw it as a chance to take down Ted early, both realized that what was at stake was more than politics. There was policy. For congressional liberals, ABM threatened to undermine the basic predicate of nuclear deterrence, which was "mutually assured destruction," or MAD, the idea that no nation would launch a first nuclear strike because it would be subject to retaliation; ABM reinforced the idea that the Pentagon could move forward as it pleased with only minimal involvement from either Congress or the scientific community; and ABM constituted yet another large investment in defense, which would inevitably come at the expense of domestic social programs. Defeating the ABM would, in a single blow, reassert MAD, balance the presidency and the Congress, put new brakes on the military-industrial complex, as President Dwight Eisenhower had called the alliance between the armed services and big business, and, perhaps above all, reapportion government spending from defense to social programs. This became the shadow president's primary mission that spring.

But in attacking Nixon's ABM, Ted now was not only challenging the president, he was challenging something even more sacrosanct in the Senate: the defense establishment, which had its own defenders, among them Senator Henry Jackson. And this, Ted understood, meant that he had to be both aggressive and careful. With Dun Gifford leading the operation, Ted mobilized. On February 19, he announced that he had commissioned Chayes and Wiesner to prepare an extensive report on the ABM system. They, in turn, mobilized their own colleagues in academe. "He knew the arms-control community was very interested in having access to experts around the country who would look at the issue, who would contact their own people who had sources of information, and who would then formulate the case either for or against these anti-ballistic missile systems," Carey Parker recalled. That is exactly what Chayes and Wiesner did. And while the two arms-control advocates were gathering information and rousing the grassroots of their own community—working at breakneck speed because Nixon was racing to construct his system before Ted could build opposition to it—Gifford was also working the Senate itself, meeting with the staff of other senators to forge a coalition. "We had almost daily meetings of like-minded Senate staff," Gifford remembered, and meetings with those who advocated for the ABM too. "We had a staff-designate from all senators who were opposed to it and kept on trying to talk quietly with the same group on the other side," Gifford said, telling them that they didn't want to get into "some kind of disaster crazy mode, way out there on a limb." And Ted was shepherding yet another group, a bipartisan group, called the National Citizens Committee Concerned About Deployment of the ABM, this one of notables that included former Supreme Court justice Arthur Goldberg, former New York governor Averell Harriman, former Federal Reserve chairman Marriner Eccles, Urban League president Whitney Young, and Arjay Miller, the president of the Ford Motor Company.

The forces began to converge that spring. In May, Gifford rushed out the Chayes–Wiesner report in a commercially published version, nearly four hundred pages long, with each of its fifteen chapters written by a prominent scientist, all of whom concluded that the ABM was unreliable, would trigger a new arms race, and should be, at the very least, deferred. That rush, however, was preceded by an internal struggle within Ted, a moment of reflection, as to whether or not he might be moving *too* rapidly, whether or not he might risk offending the Senate bulls with his aggressiveness. He agonized, wrote William Honan, who was following Ted for a book at the time, for three weeks, "changing his mind almost every day" over whether or not to write an introduction to the published Chayes–Wiesner report himself, over whether the size of the type of his name on the cover was too large, over whether the title was too sensational (in the end the title made it sound like an academic treatise), whether the jacket was dignified enough—which only demonstrated how difficult and unnatural it was, even then, even as shadow president, for Ted to break free from his customary senatorial deference. But when he did make the decisions and when the report was released, rather than call a press conference and risk charges that he was politicizing the science, Ted delivered a copy to each senator's office, and later that month, Wiesner, now the provost at MIT, testified against the ABM before the Senate Armed Services Committee, where even Chairman Stennis had some reservations. The senators "began to see and hear questions that should have been asked before in Congress" but hadn't been, said Carey Parker: questions about cost, questions about how it might destabilize the U.S.–Soviet nuclear stalemate. "Awakening the country to the nuclear issue" is how Carey Parker put it of Ted's achievement. The debate would drag on through the summer, by which time Nixon had already scaled back his plans, but short of a shutdown, the scale-back wouldn't be Ted Kennedy's triumph. Ted Kennedy's real triumph was that there was a debate at all over the ABM (*The New York Times Book Review* in an essay on the Wiesner–Chayes report said as much) and even skepticism about it. Few senators ever took on defense appropriations. Few senators wanted to invite the wrath of the powerful defense establishment. Few senators wanted to be accused of opposing America's military and undermining the nation's soldiers. Those appropriations normally sailed through Congress with little debate. (This had even been true of the Vietnam War.) So in opposing the ABM system, Ted Kennedy had not only taken on Richard Nixon; he had also taken on the whole Senate tradition of bowing to the armed services and, in doing so, changed it. Even Majority Leader Mansfield thought that defense procurement would henceforth be more rigorously scrutinized as a result of Ted's effort. "They [the scientists Ted had recruited] changed the tone of the defense debate in the country," Carey Parker would later say, though he might have said that they didn't change it so much as let Ted create it. It was no small achievement, though it was his first achievement as the shadow president.

III

Still hanging over everything, casting its dark shadow over the nation as it had for several years, was the Vietnam War. Richard Nixon, despite his professions to do so, despite his alleged secret plan to end the war, did not de-escalate the conflict. And now Ted Kennedy, the shadow president, fought against the war for all the Vietnamese refugees and civilians and for the American soldiers there. And for his late brother Bobby. Meeting with *New York Post* editor James Wechsler, Ted, Wechsler would recall, talked repeatedly about "how, after Bobby's death, he felt his major obligation was to carry on Bobby's fight against the war—you know, that was the thing he really cared about at the end. It dominated everything else." Still, Ted held his fire in those first months of the Nixon administration. When, in March, McGovern fumed on the Senate floor that "there must be no further continuation of the present war policy" and called for an "immediate end to the killing," Ted thought it "precipitate" and counseled patience, in part, no doubt, because a good many Democratic senators, including those bulls, still supported the war. Instead, he took the tack he had taken against the ABM. He railed against a bloated defense budget and called for redirecting funds from the space program to helping cities and the poor. But that approach was to change in May—changed because of a grievous action. On May 10, American troops, assisted by South Vietnamese forces, launched an attack on a hill covered in dense jungle—Hill 937 it had been designated, for its height in meters—in the A Shau Valley near the Laotian border, which was held by North Vietnamese regulars. The assault was part of a mission called Operation Apache Snow to clear the area of the enemy and disrupt his supply lines, but there was no particular strategic importance to the hill itself. It was seemingly yet another example of American forces demonstrating strength and attempting to demoralize the enemy, but the American officers had greatly underestimated the enemy's strength, and the assault continued for ten days— ten grueling, agonizing, bloody, and deadly days. Again and again, the troops were ordered up the treacherous mountainside of 937, ordered in the face of a massive enemy barrage, only to be forced back down to wait for another assault into another massive barrage. By day six, Jay Sharbutt, a twenty-eight-year-old Associated Press reporter who had heard about the Sisyphean battle, went to A Shau, observed the fight, and wrote a scathing account of the American paratroopers repeatedly being sent up the hill and then retreating, "their green shirts darkened with sweat, their weapons gone, their bandages stained brown and red—with mud and blood." He called the battle a "meatgrinder." One of the soldiers, writing a sign on the torn-off bottom of a C-rations box and then nailing it to a tree, dubbed the battlefield "Hamburger Hill." Another soldier wrote underneath: "Was it worth it?" Americans lost seventy soldiers, with nearly another four hundred wounded. Major General Melvin Zais, who headed the operation, called it a "gallant victory."

As with the Tet Offensive, which was also called a "victory," that verdict was in dispute. David Burke was in his Volkswagen, driving from his home in northern Virginia to the Senate Office Building, when he heard "for maybe the fourth time that morning" about the continuing futile assaults up Hamburger Hill, and, for what he said was the first time in his tenure with Ted, he became "personally infuriated"—so infuriated that when he got to Ted's office, he grabbed a yellow pad and began dashing out a statement on the "meaningless killing of people on both sides" for "no advantage, no tactical [purpose], no nothing." And, as he later told it, he took the statement to Ted, who was in a hearing at the time. Burke said that up to this point Ted hadn't been focusing on Hamburger Hill, and when Burke showed him the statement, Ted questioned what it was about "because he could see that I was agitated." As soon as Burke explained the situation, Ted took the statement, stormed off to the Senate floor, and read it. "It caused an uproar," as Burke recalled, because Ted was not known for acting rashly. In fact, his staff had been preparing a speech cautiously criticizing Nixon's Vietnam policy, to be delivered at the Fordham University commencement. But this was the new Ted Kennedy, the post-Robert-Kennedy-assassination Ted Kennedy, the incautious, rebellious, rabbit Ted Kennedy. And this Ted Kennedy wasn't holding back.

At least, this is how Burke recollected it. Dun Gifford had another recollection. He said Ted came into the office that day, May 20, 1969, the tenth day of the Hamburger Hill assaults, "with a huge head of steam" and said that he was going to the floor at noon. "I'm taking the lid off this thing. I'm going to do it," he told his staff. The staff was more restrained and more concerned about Ted going off half-cocked. "We all went, 'Ohhhhh, Jesus!'" And then Ted told them what he wanted to say, and Burke wrote the statement. ("Kept him from being crazy" is how Gifford put it.) "But we loved that day," Gifford said. "It was one of the best days we ever had in that office. Ted took the gloves off, said the right things. We were thrilled. It helped change the debate. It just did."

It wasn't a long statement. He began by recounting how, after Johnson had ordered the cessation of bombing in North Vietnam, the level of actions against the enemy actually rose and, with them, the number of casualties, and he cited Nixon's press conference of April 18, in which the president said that he was keeping the military pressure on the North Vietnamese in order to improve the American bargaining position at the Paris peace talks. Ted said that it defied logic to think that intensified force would help the peace process. But he said more. He said that the deaths were pointless: "I feel it is both senseless and irresponsible to continue to send our young men to their deaths to capture hills and positions that have no relation to ending this conflict." If, as President Nixon asserted, Americans sought only peace, he asked, "How then can we justify sending our boys against a hill a dozen times or more, until soldiers themselves question the madness of the action?" And he said, "The assault on 'Hamburger Hill' is only symptomatic of a mentality and a policy that requires immediate attention. American boys are too valuable to be sacrificed for a false sense of military pride." Four days later, he spoke with George McGovern at the New Democratic Coalition, a reform group, and called Hamburger Hill an example of "cruelty and savagery," and a week later, in a speech at the University of Massachusetts at Amherst, he repeated the charges.

Now Ted was making a frontal assault on the issue for which Bobby had been fighting when he died: to end the war as quickly as possible. Hamburger Hill had jolted Americans, whose support for the war had already been declining to the point where a large majority considered the war a mistake. But Nixon and the Republicans had no intention of ending the war on any basis that would leave them open to the sort of criticism *they* had leveled at President Truman when China fell to the communists. Seizing an opportunity to accuse Ted of damaging the peace process and undermining the military, they fired back at him, just as Johnson had when Ted had criticized Vietnam policy at the time of the Tet Offensive. While Ted was in Arizona delivering a speech at a graduation in a Native American school, Minority Leader Everett Dirksen, with whom Ted had tangled on the poll-tax ban, the Morrissey nomination, and one man, one vote, took to a nearly empty Senate floor to ask, "When senators twelve thousand miles removed from Hamburger Hill call the ten-day action 'senseless and irresponsible,' can it be interpreted in any other way than a direct reflection on the judgment and competence of our field commanders in Vietnam?" And he said that while he had "affection" for Ted, Ted's statement "did jolt my estimate of his wisdom and judgment." It was left to Mansfield to rebut Dirksen, saying that Ted had every right to criticize the prosecution of the war and that the blame for the problems in Vietnam should not be laid upon Ted or the generals but on the leaders in Washington. And he called the war a "tragedy," citing the 179 Montanans, servicemen from his state, who had died in the conflict. "And for what? For what?"

Ted's vehement condemnation of Nixon's policy and his accusation that American lives were being wasted in a lost cause, along with the equally vehement pushback by Republicans, had the effect of Ted crossing the Rubicon. As the media saw it, it boldly refuted William Honan's earlier characterization of him as a plodder. The very next day after Ted's floor speech, *The New York Times*'s James Reston, in a column titled, "Edward Kennedy's Challenge to President Nixon," wrote that "the old pugnacious Kennedy spirit," by which he meant *Bobby's* spirit, "is beginning to be heard again in the Senate," and that Ted, who had previously been deferential and quiet, was now "clearly cracking the whip" and "aiming to be head of the party." As evidence, Reston cited Ted's criticism of Vietnam and his rebuke of South Vietnamese corruption, his call for funds to be diverted from the space program to help the poor, his demand that oil exports be increased to lower oil prices, his promotion of wage and price restraints, his recommendation for greater leniency toward Red China— a "fairly strenuous week's work," Reston called it, though he added that it was only when you looked at his speeches since Nixon's inauguration that you realized "his challenge to the administration has been building up week by week." And Reston finally acknowledged how Ted had changed since Bobby's death. "The paralysis of last year is over. He is moving." A week later in the *Times*, Warren Weaver Jr. made a similar observation: "It has become increasingly clear Senator Kennedy is not going to hang back deferentially. . . . He is about to speak out as loud and as often as he sees fit. . . ." And Weaver acknowledged what was also becoming increasingly clear: Ted's "position of political preeminence" as Nixon's primary antagonist. Ted Kennedy's shadow presidency was on the march because Ted Kennedy, a man who was seldom angry, was angry now.

The media weren't the only ones taking notice. Richard Nixon couldn't help but take notice. In a Gallup poll in May asking which Democrat respondents would want to see "take over the direction of the plans and policies of the Democratic party," Ted was named by more people than Humphrey and Muskie combined, and a poll of college students in *Fortune* magazine tabbed Ted as the most admired. By the spring of 1969, with Nixon having served only a few months as president, Ted's aide Paul Kirk was already drawing up a list of states in which Ted might organize, and "Draft Kennedy" groups were forming. Meanwhile, early polling showing Ted competitive with Nixon prompted Milton Gwirtzman to write a five-page memo outlining Ted's presidential prospects, and Gwirtzman said he wasn't the only Kennedy acolyte doing so. Gwirtzman thought Ted's age, only thirty-seven, was a handicap, and he believed as well that Ted couldn't counter the issue through legislative leadership alone but had to do things outside the Senate to burnish himself. But even as counsel had begun to stream in, Gwirtzman said that Ted didn't especially encourage the speculation. "It would be a hint here, a hint there, that he was talking about it," and, like Bobby before him, "he'd blow hot and cold." William vanden Heuvel, the longtime Kennedy adviser, also met with Ted late that spring over lunch and told him that Muskie was gaining strength and that if he wanted to run for the presidency, he had to give some signs of interest. But vanden Heuvel said that Ted told him, "Well, you know, when they killed Jack, I thought that was an accident of history. But when they killed Bobby, I didn't feel that way anymore. And I have no doubt that if I were to get out there, they would kill me too." Vanden Heuvel said, "He just felt that there were forces in motion that were so dark and determined to destroy what the Kennedys represented that he would be the immediate target for those same forces—not in a conspiratorial sense, but just the way life and fate came together."

And yet, despite those fears, deeply held fears, Ted was clearly preparing for war against Nixon, be it legislative or presidential, and he was manning the battlements. As he quickly discovered, the whip job, which Ted had calculated would be his engine to lead Democratic opposition to Nixon, wasn't up to the task, in part because it wasn't designed to generate legislation or to thwart it—that was Mansfield's job, and he didn't seize it—and in part because Ted's intended redesign of the office hadn't been entirely successful. The position had given Ted standing in the party and in the press; what it hadn't done was reinvigorate the party. To do that, Ted had to redesign another institution, one that would allow him to extend himself legislatively into nearly every corner, one that would enable him to continue to pursue Bobby's broad agenda, and one that would let him confront Nixon.

Ted Kennedy had such a vehicle. It was an odd institution, a virtually toothless institution, practically a moribund institution, a kind of senatorial afterthought. Ted himself called it "obscure." Even the name of the institution—the Senate Subcommittee on Administrative Practice and Procedure—was mundane, dull, uninspiring. James Eastland, the chair of the Judiciary Committee of which AdPrac, as it was known, was a subcommittee, would, according to one AdPrac counsel, assign junior liberal members to negligible subcommittees, powerless committees, and then fund them lavishly as a kind of bribe to maintain his own power. Eastland also let his subcommittees operate more or less autonomously, which was not always the case among committee chairmen, some of whom controlled their subcommittees' staffing; AdPrac had its own staff appointed by its own chairman. No doubt that is why Ted took the otherwise thankless AdPrac chair with the seating of the new Senate in 1969. It at least gave him something.

But clever, ambitious junior members like Ted Kennedy—members who could not yet chair a standing committee due to lack of seniority—could nevertheless use their subcommittees to advance their own aims. In fact, after a Senate reorganization in 1946, the number of standing committees shrank from thirty-three to fifteen, but the number of subcommittees mushroomed from thirty-four to forty-four and then to sixty-six in 1950 (twenty years later, when Ted was whip, there would be 140), and so did the staffs, giving subcommittee chairmen much greater latitude and power if they chose to use it. Many did not. John Kennedy did not attend a single session of the Afro-Asian Subcommittee, which he chaired. One who did was Lyndon Johnson, who, as a first-term senator, was handed the Preparedness Subcommittee of the Armed Services Committee to chair; Johnson used it to generate what his biographer Robert Caro called a "publicity bonanza," adding it was "less preparedness than publicity that was the subcommittee chairman's primary concern."

AdPrac hardly seemed the kind of subcommittee to generate publicity. Its jurisdiction seemed limited to investigating bureaucratic practices. But Ted Kennedy had larger plans for his "obscure" committee—or, at least, he was going to try to devise larger plans. Ted's staff was nothing if not "entrepreneurial," as one staffer put it—"opportunistic" was another word he used—and Ted had assigned his staff to, as one of them, Thomas Susman, put it, "develop portfolios for the committee." What Ted discovered is that even though it had previously restricted itself to rather arcane matters, it actually enjoyed, in Ted's words, a "surprisingly broad mandate—essentially the entire federal bureaucracy—for administrative oversight." In the right hands, a chairman could stretch its authority to cover nearly anything. And Ted Kennedy's were those hands. The moribund committee to which no one had paid any attention suddenly was energized. AdPrac in short order took on oversight of the Federal Trade

Commission ("No FTC position for you guys," Ted joked to his staff when he grilled the commission's chairman, Paul Rand Dixon), investigated equal opportunity in federal contracting and the marketing practices of the pharmaceutical industry, looked into deregulation of natural gas and the airlines, reported on Selective Service reforms, even assumed jurisdiction on Native American affairs when Bobby Kennedy's Subcommittee on Indian Education expired later that year. These were just a few issues on a long list that kept getting longer as Ted, prodded by chief counsel Jim Flug and Susman and fellow staffer Joe Onek, searched for new areas to investigate. "People who joined his staff were amazed at how the Senator was able to add yet another issue, no matter how full his plate was already," Carey Parker would say. And that was largely because of the expansiveness of AdPrac. At the beginning, the eager staffers would sit in the subcommittee's cramped room in the Dirksen Senate Office Building and brainstorm over what they might do next. "A number of hare-brained ideas," Susman said of some of his suggestions to Ted. But Ted, who signed off on many of those ideas, would eventually gather so many staffers that they had to be crammed into several offices—seven in Ted's own office, and another ten in the subcommittee office. Ted called the AdPrac office, not the whip's office with its ornate suite, his "base of operations" in taking on Nixon. Jim Flug was more direct. He called the committee the "fire brigade for liberal causes." And consumer advocate Ralph Nader's Congress Project described it perhaps even more accurately as "racing feverishly from one conflagration to another." Ted Kennedy was now putting out those conflagrations.

But it wasn't just that the subcommittee had the capability to pry into whatever cranny Ted desired to investigate. The key to AdPrac's efficacy as a weapon against the Nixon administration was its hearings, because, as Ted had learned from the Refugee Subcommittee, well-constructed hearings attracted the press, and the press, inevitably, featured Ted, which allowed him to promote issues by putting his name, face, and voice on them. So AdPrac, the committee that seemed unlikely to generate publicity, wound up generating a good deal of it, just as Johnson's Preparedness Subcommittee and Ted's Refugee Subcommittee had. "When he recruited me," recalled one staff member, "he said, 'What you have to do around here is you've got to help me. You've got to get us to show our leadership. We've got to get press, because that's the way we get these other good things done.' He asked me what I'd be interested in working on, I told him, and he liked all that stuff, and he said, 'We can get that done, but if we don't maintain my leadership role, we don't get to do anything.' " It was Ted's way of saying that he was willing to use the press's interest in him and his Kennedy brand to shine a light on his issues. And Ted, like Johnson before him, understood exactly how hearings worked, how one could use them to grab media attention, which in turn could create public pressure, which in turn could produce policy. "First, you set up what you want the hearing to produce," said one staffer, describing Ted's modus operandi, "either in the way of an outcome that forces the administration to take executive action to enforce the law that it's failing to enforce—setting school-bus safety standards—or to demonstrate why there needs to be a law—migrant health. You go around and hold hearings around the country and show that the farmworkers are getting screwed and that there are no health facilities. . . . Then you pass a law that says you have to have these conditions, these standards." That's how Ted did it—repeatedly. Through AdPrac, he became his own public-relations machine.

And this barrage of hearings and press attention and bills, over the next few years, pitting AdPrac against the administration, had exactly the effect Ted intended: It put the president on the defensive. Much of the time, Nixon responded in typical political fashion: by assailing Kennedy, having Dirksen accuse him of "harassment" of business in his hearings on discriminatory hiring, or vilifying him for using his position on the Select Committee on Nutrition and Human Needs to get those food-stamp cuts restored. But rather than counterattack constantly, Nixon, again the consummate politician, also devised another tactic. As he had done when he scaled back the ABM system after Ted's opposition, he tried to preempt Ted—to find more temperate ways of doing what Ted was demanding so that he could both disarm Ted's criticism and get credit for taking action. In this, Nixon was encouraged by his domestic-affairs adviser, Harvard social scientist Daniel Patrick Moynihan, a former Labor Department official in the Johnson administration. Moynihan had sparked controversy with a report on the "Negro family" that cited government welfare policy as helping destroy black families by denying benefits to households with men. Though a liberal himself, Moynihan understood Nixon's predilection for beating liberals at their own game and cleverly introduced him to the idea that he could be an American Disraeli—a conservative who could co-opt his liberal opponents as the British prime minister Benjamin Disraeli had co-opted his liberal adversary, William Gladstone. Playing to

Nixon's pride as well as to his political gamesmanship, Moynihan convinced him that this was the road to greatness. And it was also along this road that Nixon, a conservative, became something of a mild reformer on issues like welfare and the environment and workplace safety and, eventually, on health care, so that the man whom Lyndon Johnson feared would destroy the Great Society had done no such thing. Instead, Nixon would try dealing a blow to Ted's more-progressive agenda, and to Ted's presidential prospects, by proposing a less-progressive agenda rather than by undoing progressive programs altogether.

Ted was certainly conscious of Nixon's strategy. He instructed his staff to start keeping a file on how Nixon and his advisers reacted to Ted's "words and deeds," and the key word was "reacted." When, a few years into the Nixon administration, Ted announced that AdPrac would hold hearings on Native Americans, Nixon issued a statement on Native Americans three days later, and Interior Secretary Rogers Morton held a news conference on Native Americans a week after that. When Ted left for a trip to Pakistan, Secretary of State William Rogers spoke of Pakistan at the United Nations, and the day before Ted's Refugee Subcommittee was to hold hearings on Pakistan, Nixon created a special committee on refugees. ("It was a hurry-up thing," Ted said. "Some of the people on it tell me they were called at midnight.") When Ted introduced a bill providing low-cost life insurance for policemen, Nixon proposed a $50,000 life benefit. When Ted proposed his draft lottery, Nixon endorsed his own lottery. And when Ted, after his fierce criticism of Hamburger Hill, sat down with Nixon's national security adviser, Henry Kissinger, to express his frustration over Vietnam, Nixon, whether in response or not, announced a force reduction a short time later. As one of Ted's staffers told Warren Weaver Jr. in *Esquire*, "You know how the State Department has an Israel desk and a Laos desk? Well, somewhere down in the White House, there's a Kennedy desk, keeping track of everything we do. At first, we thought we were imagining it, but there's no doubt anymore."

But there was more to Nixon's fight with Ted Kennedy than preemption, something worse. There was also skulduggery. The youngest child, the pacifier, Ted never personalized politics, never turned politics into a direct competition between himself and an antagonist; he hadn't even done that with Nixon. His arguments with Nixon were arguments about policy or power, not personality. In fact, that was the very reason he said he had discouraged Bobby from running for president—because, as he told a reporter, "I felt the issues . . . despite his deep feeling for them . . . the issues were going to get lost . . . that it would turn into a personal kind of conflict." This attitude couldn't have been further from Nixon's. Nixon always personalized politics—always saw politics as a contest not of ideas but of personalities, always wanted to pit himself against his foes, and the Kennedys were among his biggest foes. Nixon had envied Jack and Bobby Kennedy and hated them, hated them *because* he envied them, and he had envied them because they represented all the people who had disdained him, ignored him, excoriated him. With Jack and Bobby gone, Nixon visited that envy and hate on Ted. Ted believed that Nixon was so paranoid about him and his presidential prospects that he would even undermine legislation just because Ted had helped pass it, and Ted cited the National Institute of Law Enforcement and Criminal Justice, for which Nixon cut funds because Ted had promoted it; the administration also curbed a summer internship program Ted had sponsored placing college students with law-enforcement agencies.

And Ted wasn't wrong about Nixon's Kennedy paranoia. Richard Nixon lived in terror of a Kennedy restoration—terror that Ted Kennedy would do to him what Jack Kennedy had done to him before and what Robert Kennedy was threatening to do in 1968, had not an assassin's bullet prevented him from capturing the Democratic presidential nomination. When Nixon was at his retreat in San Clemente, California, he would routinely invite editors—mostly those of right-wing newspapers—to dinners there, but he usually made it a point to have *Boston Globe* political editor Robert Healy helicoptered in from Los Angeles International Airport before the others arrived. "He had a fixation, Nixon did, on the Kennedys," Healy said. "Of course, what the hell? He was looking down the barrel of a gun at Bobby and Jack, and the guy was paranoid anyway, and the Kennedys just wiped him out," meaning politically. And Healy said that the first thing Nixon would ask him when they were sitting on the deck sipping martinis was "everything about Teddy Kennedy. What was he doing? What were people saying in Massachusetts? What were people saying elsewhere? What did I pick up from Democrats?" But Nixon was not just fixated on Ted Kennedy or paranoid about him. He actively sought opportunities to ruin him politically. "Whenever we were face-to-face, he was always gracious," Ted would later say, "but he was very tough behind my back, encouraging dirty tricks and other kinds of activities." As early as March 1969, when Ted first began criticizing Nixon on Vietnam, Nixon presidential assistant John Ehrlichman suggested that the president put a tail on Ted, presumably in the hope that they might catch Ted in some compromising position with a woman, because Ted's womanizing was by now fairly well known in Washington circles. Nixon authorized it— authorized it because he, too, was at war, and there was no weapon he wouldn't use to win against so formidable an opponent, nothing he wouldn't do to stop the restoration.

In battle, taking up Bobby's causes, winning the whip, and attacking Nixon with AdPrac, Ted Kennedy might have seemed healed from the deep wounds of the previous summer—a man back to his old self, affable, spirited, hardworking, if newly combative, which is how the press now portrayed him. He was racing around the country, holding hearings, strategizing, speaking out forcefully, acting presidential, leading the opposition. But these actions disguised one awful fact: Ted Kennedy had not healed. He was still broken. The hectic activity was, in some measure, an attempt to conceal this and a way to keep the pain at bay. How broken was revealed during a bipartisan congressional trip that April to Eskimo villages in Alaska—a trip that Bobby had scheduled for himself before his death and that Ted had taken up when he assumed the chairmanship of Bobby's Subcommittee on Indian Education. The ostensible object was to investigate how to improve educational and anti-poverty programs for Eskimos, but Ted understood that the best way to achieve that end wasn't just touring and listening to stories. He needed press attention. The subcommittee chief of staff, Adrian Parmeter, who had visited Alaska and found a direct link between poverty and a lack of education, prepared a forty-three-page brief for Ted in which he advised that "the major focus of the trip, particularly in terms of the photographers and TV cameras . . . should be on native property contrasted with the affluence of the government installations which can be found in practically every village," and Parmeter invoked the word "colonialism" to describe the Eskimos' situation in relationship to the federal government. Once the Republican senators on the trip got wind of the memo—Ted said it had been distributed to the Republicans before they left, which they denied—they exploded in indignation. Senator Henry Bellmon of Oklahoma complained that the trip was "arranged to confirm preconceived conclusions." Senator George Murphy of California, who had once been a Hollywood song-and-dance man—and who had told the press on the first day of the tour that what the Eskimos really needed was to learn how to tap dance, since there were plenty of jobs for tap dancers in the movies—called the trip a "stage-managed scenario" to boost Kennedy's presidential prospects; a Republican committee aide explained Murphy's pique by saying Murphy was "just tired of a one-man show." ("This isn't Air Force One yet," griped a Republican representative, referring to the president's plane.) Those two and Senator William Saxbe of Ohio quickly abandoned Ted's tour—Alaskan Senator Ted Stevens remained—for what the Democrats on the trip called a "prosperity tour." Senator Walter Mondale, one of those Democrats, described it as "instead of looking at people in trouble, look at people who have money." (When, after Murphy's departure, a reporter cracked to Ted, "I told you to see that Murphy got his box lunch on time," Ted took a pen and wrote "Murphy" on several of the boxes.) What the Republicans had done was something that Ted always dreaded: They had personalized the politics, made it about him rather than about the issue. "Ted can take care of himself," Mondale lamented after the Republican defection, "but I worry that the walkout will distract public attention from . . . the natives of Alaska."

But as it turned out, the defection wasn't the real distraction. On a C-130 transport plane that was ferrying the group around Alaska, Ted sat with *Life* reporter Brock Brower and began ruminating disjointedly on the politics of the trip and on his future and on his public reception, then began removing gingerly from his bag a silver flask that had belonged to Bobby. "First time I used it," he said defensively, though another reporter on the trip remarked what all those who knew Ted already acknowledged: He had begun drinking more heavily since Bobby's death. It was a warning sign that all was not quite right with Ted. There were other signs on the trip—an almost manic energy, dips and rises. "Look, look, look," he shouted to *Time*'s Sylvia Wright one night, pointing to the sky, as Wright would tell it to biographer Burton Hersh. "Stars! Stars! First one to find the northern lights gets a beer." He drank again with the reporters on the flight from Fairbanks to Seattle and then again on the flight from Seattle to Washington, D.C., drank a lot, by now weaving up the aisle, throwing dinner rolls and pillows, trying to awaken sleeping reporters, saying, "They're going to shoot my ass off the way they shot Bobby's," and yelling, "Eskimo Power!" and even standing, swaying with a cup of hot coffee to sober him, above a hapless family with whom his entourage shared the plane, until his press secretary, Dick Drayne, steered him back to his seat, lest he spill the coffee on a sleeping baby.

Most of the reporters were embarrassed for him, embarrassed that he had lost control, that he wasn't conducting himself like a potential president, even though most of them had joined in his chant of "Eskimo Power." (He was behaving the very way that Russell Long had behaved.) But most of them also saw the pain and saw that his behavior was a tacit admission that he had not, even then, recovered from Bobby's death. He had assumed Bobby's causes, Bobby's leadership, even Bobby's passion, without also having Bobby's equanimity and balance. He had been, in his sister Jean's word, the "enjoyer." But he was now often uncomfortable with people, where he had always been extremely comfortable in the past. "He seemed in private more fatigued by the demands of his public image," as *Time* put it. "T.M.B.S.," he would whisper to his aides: "Too Many Blue Suits," meaning that he was feeling suffocated by officialdom, though it might have been telling that *he* was the one who typically wore a blue suit. And he told one reporter as he ran his fingers through his hair, "I am so tired of trying to figure things out."

He was lost again. Right after the Alaska trip, *Newsweek* reporter John Lindsay phoned Lester Hyman, Ted's old Massachusetts Democratic party chair; Ted was in "deep psychological trouble," he told him. "Everybody else is just saying, 'Ah, he just had a few drinks,'" Lindsay told Hyman out of concern for Ted. "This is a guy who is suffering, and if you guys don't do something soon, something terrible will happen." Ted's good friend William vanden Heuvel had read about the Alaska trip too, and said he thought, "This is a person who's in trouble. I think the trouble was he didn't have any real help in handling these enormous burdens of grief and responsibility that were put upon him. Those of us who loved him and who were his friends would have done anything for him to help him, but it was such a personal burden in so many ways." John Tunney, perhaps his closest friend, concurred. "I could tell that there was a wildness in his brain, and although he was still performing very well as a senator, getting legislation introduced and legislation heard and legislation passed . . . there was a kind of wildness there that was almost a flaunting [*sic*] of the rules of the game, so to speak, because he was so angry. There was an anger that he felt about the unfairness of the way his brothers had been gunned down." And Tunney would tell an interviewer some years later,

"He hadn't healed. He hadn't healed at all. The healing hadn't even begun, if you want to know the truth."

Ted Kennedy was a man in agony, trying hard to outrace it, which is another explanation of why he waged his fight against Richard Nixon. It was for Bobby not only in the sense of completing Bobby's mission but in the sense of inuring himself to the ongoing pain of Bobby's death by plunging into battle. But no matter how hard he tried, he couldn't deaden the pain.

Ted was certainly self-aware enough to realize his predicament, even as he piled more political responsibilities upon himself as both another manifestation of his mania and another form of self-medication. Speaking years later of Alaska, he said, "I'm back, but sort of wasn't back. I never really thought I was back. I never quite thought that it was . . ." And he trailed off. But a few months after the Alaska trip, just two days after the first anniversary of Bobby's death, on a plane back to Hyannis after giving a speech in Kentucky, he was more reflective, more candid, with Associated Press reporter Joseph Mohbat, saying that he was "unresolved" about his political future and asking, as he had asked shortly after Bobby's death, "What's it all for? I used to love it. But the fun began to go out of it after 1963, and then after the thing with Bobby, well . . ." And he concluded, when Mohbat asked him about whether the Kennedy name would still resonate in 1972 or 1976, with his new fatalism: "I really think all these things are just predetermined."

changed into dry clothes, and then they drove back to Edgartown, where Ted and his nephew Joe raced the regatta in the *Victura* that afternoon, finishing ninth out of thirty-one entries. Then Ted retired to the Shiretown Inn to "freshen up," he said, for the evening at Chappaquiddick, to which Crimmins drove him at seven-thirty.

The regatta was Ted's release—a chance to get away and be on the water. Chappaquiddick was no release. Chappaquiddick was an obligation. Joey Gargan had arranged a small get-together for what were known as the "boiler-room girls" of Bobby's presidential campaign, so named because they worked in a windowless basement of the campaign headquarters—a boiler room. These young women, six of whom had accepted the invitation—Esther Newberg, Rosemary Keough, sisters Nance and Mary Ellen Lyons, Susan Tannenbaum, and Mary Jo Kopechne—had manned the campaign in the bowels of the Washington headquarters, where, each of them working on an assigned section of the country, they did a lot of the grunt work: contacting local leaders and press, making arrangements for rallies and meetings, scheduling appearances, collecting information, answering phones, and, above all, tracking delegates. As Gladys Gifford, the wife of Dun Gifford, who took a leave from Ted's staff to run Bobby's boiler-room operation, said, "Everyone in the Kennedy orbit knew the boiler-room girls." And not only knew them but felt protective of them. After Bobby's death, the women had regrouped at Hyannis Port at a party Ted and Joan hosted at their Squaw Island home. They met again the following January in Washington, at a "bachelor's ball" dinner that Gifford and Bobby's close friend David Hackett hosted for them, ostensibly to marry off the boiler-room girls—Gifford and Hackett had invited two bachelors for each girl—but also to express their appreciation to them and to provide some small levity to distract them from their own indescribable grief. It didn't work. Ted made an appearance—"There was a special relationship between the boiler-room girls and Teddy," Nance Lyons, who had joined his staff, recalled—and the dinner was, Lyons said, the first time that Ted cried in public. "He broke down, and I thought afterward that maybe that was good." They regrouped again in the spring and then again that July at Chappaquiddick. These weren't parties where the mood was celebratory. "They were wakes, a form of grief," is how Gladys Gifford described them. "It was as if they were in an army platoon," said another of Ted's assistants, Melody Miller, of the group of young women and the staff who gathered, "that had all gone off to war together. They weren't people who had been dating each other. Some were married, some were not, some were aged. It was just a whole mishmash of folks getting together to have a reunion, even a mourning of Robert Kennedy, and to tell war stories."

The party, to which the bone-tired Ted dragged himself for Bobby's sake and the sake of Bobby's young campaign women—Nance Lyons had told him it would mean a lot to those women if he made an appearance— was another of those wakes. This one was perhaps Joey Gargan's way of taking initiative he was often denied by the Kennedys but also, clearly, he organized it because he felt a paternal affection for the girls. As the son of Rose's sister, Mary Agnes, who had died suddenly when Joey was six, Gargan was of the family but not really in it, because no one who was not a Kennedy would ever be embraced as a Kennedy in that insular clan. "He felt in some ways a charity case," said Melody Miller, which he was. Because of the large disparity in ages between Ted and his brothers, Joe Kennedy had tapped Gargan, almost two years to the day older than Ted, to be Ted's constant companion in the summer of 1940 and for many summers thereafter, and the two traveled together, sailed together, caroused together, until Ted left for Harvard. But for all the camaraderie, there was no mistaking Gargan for a Kennedy. He didn't look like a Kennedy, wasn't handsome like a Kennedy. He was tall and broad like Ted, and a good athlete like him, but his face was long and plain, his lips thin, his hair brushed straight back and receding, and he wore glasses. He wasn't bred like a Kennedy either. While Ted went off to Harvard, Gargan went to Notre Dame, where his father had been a star athlete—"You were kind of a fairy if you went to Harvard," Gargan said—and then to Notre Dame Law. As the Kennedys pursued their political careers, Gargan got relatively menial jobs in their campaigns, despite august-sounding titles, eventually joining a Massachusetts law firm rather than receiving a staff job from his cousins. "He was a gofer," said Gladys Gifford, and Gargan didn't dispute that, even though he chafed at it—chafed hard. Rose's onetime secretary, Barbara Gibson, wrote that Gargan "laughed about all the work the family caused him through their unthinking attitudes and arrogance. Yet they never seemed to appreciate him." This was the way Kennedys often treated people who weren't part of their nuclear family. Gargan wasn't singled out. He was just regarded as an outsider, despite his relationship to them. Even Ted had basically cast him aside once they were grown-ups. "Joey was not one of the people you put in charge of a lot of stuff," Melody

Miller said. "He was a good guy to have if you had a party and you needed somebody to organize the barbecue, and somebody who was a warm hail-fellow-well-met, that type of guy. He wasn't somebody who was in the circles of the Kennedy brothers, who was consulted like Steve Smith." Rita Dallas observed of Gargan, "An extremely likable man, but he had always been a shadow in the background. He was the one who carried Teddy's sails and cooked special breakfasts for him and his guests every Sunday."

And so it was Joey Gargan who arranged the party, Gargan who rented the cottage on Chappaquiddick, a gray-shingled saltbox with yellow shutters, for eight days beginning on July 12 from a Scarsdale, New York, attorney named Sidney Lawrence, with the idea of Joey using it for a family vacation before the get-together (a plan that was scotched when his mother-in-law was felled by illness), Gargan who reserved Ted a room at the Shiretown Inn, Gargan who got the steaks to grill, and Gargan who served as host. It was Gargan's party. Ted arrived at eight o'clock, reluctantly. "He didn't want to be there," Charles Tretter, another guest, said. "I think he wanted to go sailing, but I don't think he wanted this whole burden . . . of putting on a party." The girls arrived about a half hour later from Edgartown, brought from the ferry in a rented white Valiant by Raymond LaRosa, a good friend of Ted's late administrative assistant, Ed Moss, who had died in the plane crash that had injured Ted. LaRosa himself had been a campaign worker for the senator. It was a small gathering, just the six young women, Ted, Gargan, Crimmins, Tretter, LaRosa, and Paul Markham, a friend of Gargan's, who had been United States attorney for Massachusetts, and it was a quiet gathering. "There was talking, some laughing and singing, but no raucous noise," a neighbor told a reporter for *The Washington Post*. "I wouldn't even call it a party. I would call it people in for the evening." Gargan admitted, "Some people were bored to death with it." Crimmins had driven up the liquor from Boston—three half gallons of vodka, four fifths of scotch, two bottles of rum, and a couple of cases of beer—though he later said his intention was to take back the remnants to Hyannis Port "if anybody dropped in to say hello." In any case, the guests consumed three-quarters of a half gallon of vodka, one and a half bottles of rum, and "very little scotch," by Crimmins's account. As for Ted, he would later testify that he had drunk a third of a beer after the race at the Shiretown Inn and had two rum and Coca-Colas at the cottage, one poured by Crimmins upon Ted's arrival at eight o'clock, and another that he poured himself at nine. They listened to music and danced—Tretter and Rosemary Keough had gone back to Edgartown to get a radio—but mainly they reminisced about the campaign. Ted was somber. "I worked for the senator for a long time," Tretter recalled to biographer Burton Hersh of the evening, "and I think I know him pretty well, well enough to realize that he was—he was not exuberant. He was not having a helluva good time." At about ten, Gargan grilled the steaks, and by ten-thirty, dinner was over. It was a hot night and buggy with mosquitoes. The air was listless. It was getting late. The day had been long for all of them. Ted would write in his memoir that in the lull after dinner, he spoke with Mary Jo Kopechne about Bobby and that they both "became emotional." And Ted said: "I needed to get out of that party. I needed to get outside, to breathe some fresh air." And he said that Mary Jo gave him the excuse to do so when she said she wanted to leave and return to Edgartown. (Elsewhere, Ted would say that she had told him she had had too much sun that day and wasn't feeling well.) As he recalled it to Burton Hersh, Ted glanced at his watch. It was eleven-fifteen or eleven-thirty. He asked Crimmins for the keys to the Oldsmobile rather than have Crimmins drive them, because Crimmins was "enjoying the fellowship," though there had been some discussion about the ferry stopping its run at midnight and about whether they would make it and about having to pay the ferryman to take them after that if they didn't. And Gargan would say that Crimmins, far from enjoying the fellowship, later got "agitated" that the guests were not leaving to catch the ferry, meaning that they would be stuck at the cottage for the night.

But that was later. Before then, Ted and Mary Jo headed to the Oldsmobile, she climbed into the passenger seat, and they left the party.

Only two people would ever know what happened next or why. In the aftermath, there would be rumors, salacious rumors, about what led Ted to drive the Oldsmobile down the road he took, but these discounted the kind of woman Mary Jo Kopechne was. A "real straight arrow" is how Gladys Gifford described her. The only child of Joe Kopechne, an insurance salesman, and Gwen Kopechne, a housewife, twenty-eight-year-old Mary Jo had been born in Plymouth, Pennsylvania, outside Wilkes-Barre, and moved to New Jersey with her parents when she was an infant. She had attended parochial schools and then the Caldwell College for Women, a Catholic school near Newark, New Jersey, and later, in a bout of religious

devotion, she taught black children at the Mission of St. Jude in Montgomery, Alabama. By one account, she felt she was too emotionally attached to the children to continue teaching, so she left for Washington
and landed a job working for Senator George Smathers of Florida, who
had been a close friend of John Kennedy's. But it wasn't Smathers for
whom she wanted to work. She loved the Kennedys, and when Bobby was
elected to the Senate, Bobby borrowed her as a secretarial temp until he
recruited his own staff. She returned to Smathers's office, but not for long.
One day he came in with Bobby and told him, "Well, you might as well
take her. There are no pictures of me around. Just you and the president."
Back with Bobby, she worked as a secretary to his speechwriters, as a legal
secretary to an adviser named Joe Dolan, and then, when Bobby declared
for the presidency, she entered the boiler room. After Bobby's death, she
helped Ethel answer sympathy cards. Later, she helped register black voters and then joined a consulting firm in Washington that advised Democratic candidates.

She was a quiet young woman. She worked hard—she once stayed up
all night to type one of Bobby's speeches on Vietnam—and she went to
bed early. A "sleeper," her mother called her. She seldom socialized, and
she vacationed with her parents. She had a boyfriend who worked in the
Foreign Service and whom, it was said, she hoped to marry, but her friends
were concerned that he was more interested in one of Mary Jo's few in-
dulgences, a little green sports car, than he was in her. Another man she
had met stole her checkbook and defrauded her. "Not somebody men hit
on at all," Melody Miller said, who also said her nickname among her co-
workers in Bobby's office was "the virgin." Though the photograph that
would circulate afterward—her college graduation photo—showed a
reasonably attractive young woman, Mary Jo would not have qualified as
glamorous. She was by all accounts a nice girl, a bright girl, a bighearted
girl, an ambitious girl, but she was no siren. Ted said, implausibly but to
this point, that he hadn't remembered meeting her before that day at
Chappaquiddick. On that muggy July night, she simply seemed like a tired
young woman who wanted to go back to her hotel.

All these things are just predetermined, Ted had said. He drove up Schoolhouse Road for about a half mile, then came to a fork. Chappaquiddick
Road, a paved road of black asphalt, ran off to the left and to the ferry slip;
Dike Road, unpaved and plain dirt, went to the right toward Poucha Pond,
which was actually a fairly large body of water, its name notwithstand-

ing. In the postmortems, it was said that Ted couldn't have failed to recognize the difference between the paved road and the unpaved one, though Ted hadn't driven it before (Crimmins had driven him both times, in the afternoon and earlier that evening), and it was said that Ted couldn't have mistaken the one for the other, though Ted was notorious for getting lost. "His sense of direction was always so bad," wrote Rita Dallas, "there was a family joke about his never knowing what turn to take." (She said he frequently got lost driving his father around Hyannis, which was an area he had known since boyhood.) Ted took the right turn, the turn onto Dike Road, and bumped along three-quarters of a mile, thinking, he said, that he was heading for the slip. At that point, at the point where the road crossed the pond, there was a low bridge called "Dike Bridge"—hardly a bridge, just a few planks of wood supported by thin, rough-hewn wooden pilings. It had been built in 1949 to replace a dirt dike. It measured ten and a half feet wide and eighty-one feet long. It was pitched at a twenty-seven-degree angle to the road. It had no guardrail and no lighting. It was treacherous. If a "driver goes onto the bridge at exactly the same angle he has been traveling, he will automatically wind up in the water," by one report. "Perilous even in broad daylight," *New York Times* columnist James Reston, a Vineyard summer resident, told Arthur Schlesinger Jr. "That bridge . . ." Charles Tretter, who had been driven over it with Ted that afternoon, recalled, "how somebody didn't do what happened before, and how somebody wasn't sued before—I mean, that bridge was ridiculous." Brock Brower would write in *Life:* "That Dike Bridge out there on the end of Chappaquiddick, every islander knows, is a danger to man. Too narrow, angled all wrong to the dirt road, humped up too high in the middle, no railings, no warning, just all of a sudden, planks under your tires. Something was bound to happen there one day."

And that night it did.

Ted would later say that he hit the brakes a fraction of a second before his car sailed off the bridge to the right—sailed off at about eighteen feet along the planks—and fell into the black water. He said he remembered the vehicle "just beginning to go off the Dike Bridge." He said the next thing he recalled was "the movement of Mary Jo next to me, the struggling perhaps hitting or kicking me" and that he then opened his eyes and "realized that I was upside down, that water was crashing in on me, that it was pitch black." He said he took a gulp of air and knew he and Mary Jo had to get out of the car. He said he could remember "reaching down to try and get the doorknob of the car and lifting the door handle and pressing against the door and it not moving." He said he reached down but it was really up—since the car had overturned and landed on its roof—and remembered feeling along the window, which was closed, and he said, "I can remember the last sensation of being completely out of air and inhaling what must have been half a lung full of water and assuming that I was going to drown," assuming that his life was over, and "then somehow I can remember coming up to the last energy of just pushing, pressing, and coming up to the surface." He said he had no idea how he managed to escape, though it had to have been through the driver's broken window.* He said he was conscious of "the rushing of the water, the blackness, the fact that it was impossible to even hold it back."

He said he was "swept away by the tide," about thirty or forty feet—the water was shallow, about seven feet deep, but the tide ran swiftly there— and called out Mary Jo's name and made his way to the east side of the cut, then waded up to his waist and started back toward the car, "gasping and belching and coughing." He said he could distinguish the front of the car from the rear because the headlights were still on, so he waded to the front and dove—dove to try to rescue Mary Jo, dove, until the tide would sweep him out, and dove again, until the tide swept him away again, and dove again. "I would come back again and again to this point [near the front of the car] or try perhaps the third or fourth time to gain entrance to some area" where he could find some steadiness. He dove, he said, seven or eight times. But "at the very end when I couldn't hold my breath any longer, I was breathing so heavily it was down to just a matter of seconds," so that he could barely stay underneath the water, clinging to the metal undercarriage. He said he couldn't dive any longer. His "head was throbbing, and my neck was aching, and I was breathless, and at that time, the last time, hopelessly exhausted." And then, after fifteen or twenty minutes of attempting to rescue her, he let himself float until he reached the shore, and he crawled and staggered and fell onto the grass on the west bank, and lay there, coughing up water, for another fifteen or twenty minutes.

And then he started down Dike Road, "walking, trotting, jogging, stumbling, as fast as I possibly could," with only the silhouettes of the

---

*He would tell a doctor who examined him that he had escaped through the window. "Chappaquiddick Revisited," *The Washington Post*, February 22, 1976.

trees on either side of the dirt path in the blackness to guide him, until he eventually reached the cottage and the white Valiant outside and saw Ray LaRosa and asked him to get Gargan. (LaRosa recalled that Ted asked him to get *both* Gargan and Markham.) And while LaRosa fetched Gargan, Ted crawled into the back seat of the Valiant, without entering the cottage and without telling the guests what had occurred, which he later admitted was a mistake. When Gargan arrived at the car, Ted told him to get Paul Markham too (Gargan, then, by his recollection, actually instructed LaRosa to get Markham), and when Markham came out of the cottage, he got into the car, and Ted explained that there had been an accident— a "terrible" accident—and the three of them—Ted, Gargan, and Markham— drove out to Poucha Pond, drove fast. Once there, Gargan pulled the Valiant to the far end of the bridge and turned it around so its headlights shone on the water. "Holy God!" Markham exclaimed when he saw the overturned car peeking above the water. While Ted, sapped of energy, stood mute in front of the Valiant, Gargan and Markham proceeded to strip off their clothes, and with Markham stationed at the rear of the car, Gargan felt along the submerged auto with his feet, trying to find the windows, and then dove to see if he could rescue Mary Jo. "You could not open your eyes underwater," he later said. "The current just forced your eyes closed." At this point, Ted recalled, he believed it was roughly 12:20 A.M., because he had looked at the Valiant's clock. (The Valiant didn't have a clock, but later he said he could have glanced at Markham's watch.) Gargan managed to get partly into the car through the broken driver's window, scraping his arm as he did so, Ted said, up to the elbow, but he was unable to extract Mary Jo. He got stuck and was losing his breath, then squeezed back out and was carried by the current until Markham grabbed him some twenty-five yards downriver. He dove several more times, pulling at the door handles, but was unable to open the car. After forty-five minutes, Gargan and Markham were exhausted and returned to the Valiant, and they told Ted that he must report the accident. And Ted would say that during that ride to the ferry, a "lot of different thoughts came into my mind . . . about how I was going to really be able to call Mrs. Kopechne at some time in the middle of the night to tell her that her daughter was drowned, to be able to call my own mother and my own father, relate to them, my wife," what had happened. But Ted also said that "even though I knew that Mary Jo Kopechne was dead and believed firmly that she was in the back of the car, I willed that she remain alive." And he said that as they drove down that road after the rescue attempt, "I was almost looking out the front window and windows trying to see her walking." He would write in his memoir: "Perhaps I could wish it all away." Markham said that Ted was "sobbing" in the car. Gargan described him as "very emotional, extremely upset, very disturbed," and said he kept repeating one of his familiar expressions: "Can you believe it, Joe? Can you believe it? I don't believe it. I don't believe this could happen. I just don't believe it." Gargan asked Ted to explain what had happened, and Ted told him of the Oldsmobile flying off the bridge, but Gargan also said he told him something that "still sticks in my mind." As Ted recalled the water rising over him, he told Gargan, "Then I gave up. I thought that was it and I gave up." And after giving up, he said, he found himself inexplicably on the surface of the water. And then, after Ted's recitation, they arrived at the ferry slip, where they spoke for another ten minutes, with Gargan and Markham reiterating that Ted had to report the accident and Gargan advising him to call Dave Burke in Washington, to inform Ted's family, and Burke Marshall, Bobby's old Justice deputy, now an IBM executive and the family wise man, to advise Ted on what to do legally—though Gargan and Markham made no attempt to report the accident themselves. "The Rosencrantz and Guildenstern of this dark evening," writer John Gregory Dunne would call them. And Ted told them, "You take care of the girls. I will take care of the accident."

And then he took three steps and suddenly dove into the water, fully clothed in a polo shirt and slacks, and began swimming across the channel toward Edgartown. But the tide there was strong too, and it began to pull him down, and the water became colder, and the tide drew him out, drew him "well out into the darkness," and he thought, for the second time that evening, that he would drown. And the strength left his body, possibly, though he didn't say so, because he wanted to surrender himself to the fates after the accident. But when he reached the middle of the channel, the tide lessened, and he summoned what little strength he had and was able to swim to the Edgartown side, where he pulled himself onto the shore and then walked to the Shiretown Inn at around 2 A.M., resting in the parking lot by leaning against a tree, gathering himself, trying to get his mind around what had happened—"all the nightmares and all the tragedy and all the loss of Mary Jo's death . . . right before me again." When he got to his room, he removed his wet clothes and collapsed on the bed. But he was kept awake by noise—"around me, on top of me, almost in the room"—and rose, put on dry clothes, opened the door, and saw a man standing in a pool of light under the balcony, a tourist he assumed, and descended the stairs and asked him the time. The man, glancing back through the window at the clock in the hotel office, said, "Two-thirty," and Ted returned to his room.*

The next hours would turn out to be the most problematic to Ted Kennedy's account, because Ted didn't report the accident that evening or even the first thing that next morning. And there is no indication of when or even if he intended to report the accident in that time. He said that even after the disruption, he couldn't sleep that night. At roughly 8 A.M., Ted, now wearing white loafers, white trousers, and a navy polo shirt, came down the stairs, saw the receptionist and two of his fellow sailors, with whom he spoke briefly on the porch, and then Gargan and Markham arrived—"unkempt," Ted said; "ruffled and looking damp," said one of the sailors—and Gargan, Markham, and Ted retreated to Ted's room, where Gargan and Markham asked if Ted had notified the authorities. But Ted said that he hadn't, *couldn't*, that he still "willed" that Mary Jo had survived. "I told them how I somehow believed that when the sun came up and it was a new morning that what had happened the night before would not have happened and did not happen, and how I just couldn't gain the strength within me, the moral strength, to call Mrs. Kopechne. . . ." Markham, who said he was aghast at Ted's dereliction, recalled Ted saying that he had failed to report the accident because it was "just a nightmare" and that he wasn't sure it had even happened. By one account, Ted then emerged from his room, got copies of *The Boston Globe* and *The New York Times* at the desk, and borrowed a dime to make a call—to his brother-in-law Steve Smith, to get Burke Marshall's number, except that Smith was vacationing with his family in Spain. Instead, he called Helga Wagner, a vivacious blond jewelry designer in Key Biscayne, Florida, who had known Ted for years and who was rumored to be a long-time girlfriend. Wagner would later dismiss any indiscretion about the phone call, saying that Ted was merely seeking Smith's phone number

---

*Ted told a somewhat different version elsewhere—that he left his room and spoke to a hotel clerk (actually Russell Peachey, a co-owner of the Shiretown Inn) to complain of noise from an adjacent building and inquired the time. "The Mysteries of Chappaquiddick," *Time*, August 1, 1969.

because Smith had asked Helga, who had also been a friend of Jack's, to join his family in Spain, so she was likely to know his whereabouts. After the call, now roughly 9 A.M., he, Gargan, and Markham—still not having reported the accident—walked to the ferry slip and took the ferry to Chappaquiddick. There Ted placed a call to David Burke, asking him to get in touch with Burke Marshall. He used a phone on the Chappaquiddick side of the ferry because, Gargan would later say, it was difficult to find a phone with any privacy on the Edgartown side; Ted would say it was because he wanted to talk to Marshall before he reported the accident and knew he "would be involved in a myriad of details" after he had done so. (It is unclear whether Ted tried to reach Marshall himself and was unsuccessful.) Burke's wife, Beatrice, remembered it differently. She said her husband had returned in the middle of the night from watching the launch of the moon shot in Florida and was sleeping when Ted rang. They spoke for roughly fifteen minutes, with Burke being the one to tell Ted to call Burke Marshall. And Beatrice Burke said her husband told her he gave another bit of advice to Ted: "Get your ass to a police station."

Meanwhile, about an hour earlier, at 8 A.M., a mile or so away, two young fishermen visiting from upstate New York had spotted a car wheel sticking up from Poucha Pond and had gone to the nearest house to report it. Mrs. Pierre Malm, who lived one hundred yards from the bridge, then phoned the police to alert them. The thirty-eight-year-old Edgartown police chief, Dominick Arena—a former football star, at six foot four and 225 pounds—came over to Chappaquiddick, put on swim trunks, and tried to investigate the wreckage, but the current pulled him away from the car, as it had Ted and Gargan. While Arena made his attempt, the chief of the Edgartown Fire Department Scuba and Rescue Division, John Farrar, heard from someone in his Turf 'n Tackle Shop about the accident and headed to the site. He also struggled against the current and had to tie a rope around Mary Jo Kopechne's neck to secure her body. It took him about twenty-five minutes to remove her corpse from the automobile. At virtually the same time as her body was being removed: A tow truck from Jon Ahlbum's gas station was driving off the ferry and heading to the pond to pull out the wreckage; Ted was at the slip, calling David Burke; and the ferryman, Dick Hewitt, was told by a friend from the medical examiner's office about an accident involving a car belonging to Senator Edward Kennedy. (Arena had traced the license plate to Ted.) Hewitt advised his friend that Kennedy was right there on the dock just a few feet away, and the friend approached him, Gargan, and Markham to inform them of what had happened. But Ted hung back, shielded by some cars, while either Gargan or Markham told the man they had already heard. By another account, it was Hewitt himself who asked them if they had heard, and one of them, not Ted, responded, "Oh, yeah. We just heard about it." And it was only then, at 10 A.M., the very time at which the car was being pulled from the pond and the time at which Chief Arena, having traced the license, was phoning his office to get contact information to apprise Ted, that Ted returned to Edgartown and, accompanied by Markham, went to the police station to report what had happened the evening before. And it was at the station that Ted, with Markham's help, dictated his account of the accident, written out in longhand by Markham—though Ted didn't know how to spell "Kopechne," calling her "Miss Mary," with Markham drawing a _____ instead of her name. By that time, Chief Arena had arrived and later typed the statement. Ted stayed at the station for several hours, being debriefed by Arena, who was still in his swim trunks, and then tried to reach Burke Marshall. And it was then that everyone would know.

But it wasn't reporting the accident to the police that was difficult—though Ted knew both the personal and political ramifications of the report, knew that the report would serve as a kind of sentence on him. Much more difficult was telling the Kopechnes, which was one reason, the primary reason, why he said he hadn't reported the accident earlier. "I just can't do it. I just can't do it. I just can't do it," he recalled to *The Boston Globe* five years later of his state of mind that morning. But now, facing the inevitable, he did. Mrs. Kopechne said she was alone that morning when Ted called, the tone of his voice conveying "sorrow" or "sadness," and told her there had been an accident. She asked if it had been a car accident, and when Ted said it was, she said she knew instantly that Mary Jo had been killed, though Ted hesitated saying so and only reluctantly said yes when Mrs. Kopechne asked. "I do remember screaming," Mrs. Kopechne said, prompting a neighbor who had been hanging clothes outside and had heard her screams to look in on her. Mr. Kopechne said that when Ted first called him (it is unclear if he came on the phone with his wife or if this was a later call), Ted was sobbing so loudly that Mr. Kopechne barely understood what he was saying and that he and his wife didn't get the full details of the accident until a *Boston Globe* reporter phoned them later. He compared hearing the news to "watching a TV program and waiting for the end of the program and turning it off and it's all over."

And then came the gathering of the clan—all the Kennedy acolytes who in time of tragedy and disaster, out of both love and duty, would come to Hyannis Port to ameliorate whatever had befallen the family. Ted had left Martha's Vineyard later that Saturday afternoon, July 19, on the private plane of the chairman of the Edgartown selectmen, a man named Bob Carroll, who also piloted the plane. Ted arrived, a maintenance man at the Hyannis airport observed, "sweating" and looking in a "state of semi-shock." Rose Kennedy would recall, "He was so unlike himself, it was hard to believe he was my son. His usual positive attitude, which he displayed so clearly at times of difficulty, had vanished. He was disturbed, confused, and deeply distracted, and sick with grief over the death of the young woman." Nurse Rita Dallas said that Ted appeared at his father's bedroom door "drawn, downcast, intimidated." He told his mute father he had been involved in an accident, that there would be "all sorts of things" said about him—"terrible things"—but that the truth was that the incident was an accident. And Dallas said that Joe Kennedy reached for his son's hand and brought it to his chest and nodded and patted the hand and then closed his eyes. A visitor told biographer Lester David that Ted was clearly in shock. "His eyes would mist over, and you could almost feel his pain." By this time, David Burke had finally reached Burke Marshall, who arrived at Hyannis Port that afternoon to counsel Ted. Marshall found him "disoriented" and so deeply in denial about Mary Jo's death that he feared he had a brain "blockage" of some sort and advised he get medical attention. A doctor, Robert Watt, then was called to examine Ted that day and found "concussion, contusions and abrasions of the scalp, acute cervical strain," and advised bed rest and a muscle relaxant. When his condition didn't improve two days later, Dr. Watt had him X-rayed and suggested a cervical collar (Ted resisted it at first, saying he didn't want people to think he was eliciting their sympathy) and then Watt recommended a neurosurgical consultation, which confirmed the concussion and "acute cervical strain." But the general mood on the compound was not concern either for Ted or for Mary Jo and the Kopechnes. The general mood, as Rita Dallas described it, was "rage and horror and anger"—she said at the fates, but it was not only at the fates. Rose was incensed that there had been no one to protect Ted at Chappaquiddick, no one to guide him, no Eddie Moore (she specifically cited Moore) to take the hit for him, as Moore was always willing to take a hit for Joe Kennedy. She especially focused her wrath on her hapless nephew, Joey Gargan, even later disinheriting him for not displaying better judgment when Ted was clearly not in his right mind.

Americans had been directing their attention elsewhere that weekend. While Ted was on Chappaquiddick, astronauts Neil Armstrong, Buzz Aldrin, and Michael Collins were hurtling toward the moon, and Armstrong was about to be the first man to set foot on its surface—a mission that had been initiated by President John Kennedy. Still, despite the epochal nature of Apollo 11, the Chappaquiddick accident shared front pages that weekend with the moon landing. The initial press response treated it as another tragedy visited upon a family all too familiar with tragedy. The Associated Press wire service opened its story by citing Ted's "narrow brush with death" and then proceeded to recount the litany of family disasters. *The New York Times* called it another "in a series of violent events that have hounded the Kennedy family ever since it came to prominence in American political life." *The Washington Post*, speaking of other dynasties, said that "none has been so tragedy-ridden as the Kennedy clan." But while not entirely unsympathetic, and while putting the accident in the context of previous Kennedy tragedies, the press soon transitioned from focusing on Ted's brush with death to Mary Jo's actual death, from what had happened *to* Ted Kennedy to what had been done *by* Ted Kennedy, and it demanded answers: "Why Teddy told no one about the accident and did not seek help for the girl, why no one called a doctor or even asked Kennedy what had happened—and indeed how he got back to the hotel—are questions that must now puzzle not only the police but also Ted Kennedy and his nationwide constituency," as *Time* put it that first week. Left unsaid, though it clearly hovered over the incident, was what Ted was doing alone with a young lady. (The *New York Daily News* headline the day after the accident foreshadowed what was to come: TEDDY ESCAPES, BLONDE DROWNS.) The conservative *Chicago Tribune* was more blunt than *Time* in an editorial calling out Kennedy: "It may be that there is some defect in the senator's character," and cited the Harvard cheating scandal. This converted the accident from tragedy to mystery and even to soap opera, which now filled pages and airwaves. In its issue one week after Chappaquiddick, with its cover bannered THE KENNEDY DEBACLE, *Time* said that "the Kennedy debacle became a topic of more interest in much of Washington and elsewhere in the country than man's landing on the moon. Americans in Saigon discussed the case more than they did the war." And everywhere there was another question—not why Ted had acted inexplicably but whether his inexplicable actions would doom any presidential prospects, this for the man who had assumed the role of shadow president.

Now Ted had to answer those questions. Up to this point, he had said virtually nothing publicly, having been forewarned by Burke Marshall that any statement could affect his legal status. The only comment was a short summary that the police had released quoting from his written account, ending erroneously with: "When I fully realized what had happened this morning, I immediately contacted police." The clan had not necessarily gathered to draft a more comprehensive statement or even to save Ted's now-endangered career, though that would become the public assumption. "Certainly, in terms of what the perception was to the media," said William vanden Heuvel, one of the arrivals, "who saw this avalanche of the Kennedy army approaching, how do we save our leader? Instead of being what I think Teddy felt much more genuinely, [which] was the grief and the sadness of the event that had happened. He wasn't thinking, in my recollection of those days in talking to him and being with him, he wasn't thinking about how he could come out of this looking differently," which is to say better. Lester Hyman, the former Massachusetts Democratic chairman, said he was at his summer home in the Berkshires when he heard the news and immediately phoned Hyannis Port and got Milton Gwirtzman* and told him that from the account Hyman had heard, Ted was in shock and needed hospitalization. To which Gwirtzman said, "Oh, don't worry. It's a one-day story." Hyman wanted to go up there himself, but he was dissuaded from doing so and later regretted it. "Most of them were John Kennedy people. I believe they were there to preserve John Kennedy's reputation, not Teddy's, and I think they disserved him."

Whether they had come to comfort Teddy, as vanden Heuvel had, or to preserve John Kennedy's reputation, or to save Teddy's presidential prospects, they came, more than a dozen of them, and congregated in the big

---

*Gwirtzman was not yet there, so it might have been Richard Goodwin with whom he spoke, or he might have spoken to Gwirtzman later than he remembered.

house, Joe's old house on the compound, while Ted was largely sequestered at his home on Squaw Island, a half mile down the beach. "A caravan of stars," Dave Burke called them, "coming and going and coming
and going. There was not one time when everyone was there at once."
Stars many of them were, some within the Kennedy constellation, some
outside it: Gwirtzman; Burke Marshall; former Defense secretary Robert
McNamara; John Kennedy and Lyndon Johnson speechwriter Richard
Goodwin; John Kennedy's aide and speechwriter Ted Sorensen, and his
special assistant, Kenny O'Donnell, and his boyhood chum, LeMoyne Billings; historian Arthur Schlesinger Jr., who flew in from Rumania; Ted's
friends John Tunney, John Culver, and Claude Hooton; Ted's local counsel,
Richard McCarron, an Edgartown lawyer, and Robert Clark and Robert
Clark III, experts in motor-vehicle law; economist John Kenneth Galbraith, who was too ill to be there in person but who remained in contact
by phone from his Vermont summer home; and then the family, Steve
Smith, and the sisters, Pat, Jean, and Eunice—who, upon her arrival,
shouted, "Where's Teddy? Where's my brother?" and raced about looking
for him—and even Jacqueline Kennedy Onassis. "They weren't dragooned," Dave Burke would say. Most came as if they were beckoned by
fate. Sorensen came because Steve Smith had asked him. Tunney came
because he got a call from Pat Kennedy Lawford while he was campaigning for a Senate seat in California, and she told him, "Your best friend is in
terrible trouble," and Tunney caught the next plane out and then sat with
Ted at Squaw Island for the next three or four days, consoling him, talking to him, listening to him try to parse what had happened. Gwirtzman
came because he had gone to Ted's office on the Saturday morning Mary
Jo's body was discovered, and Burke had shown him Ted's full statement,
and they both realized that this was going to be difficult for Ted, personally
and politically, especially because James Reston of *The New York Times* was
on the island visiting his son, who edited the local paper on Martha's Vineyard, the *Vineyard Gazette,* and Reston would be making inquiries. But it
wasn't until Wednesday that Gwirtzman realized the full magnitude of
the accident and decided that he had to go up to Hyannis to help out, writing notes on the plane for a statement, since Ted's secretary, Angelique
Voutselas, had told him that Ted only intended to issue an apology and
condolence to Mary Jo's family, not an explanation of what happened and
why. "I couldn't believe someone who was this fine a person and that was
concerned about everybody would let this girl drown," Gwirtzman

thought. "There must be some reason for it, and he should tell what his reasons were."

The mood was tense. "The Cuban Missile Crisis all over again," a critic would call the conclave. The exception was Joey Gargan, who, Rita Dallas observed, walked right into the room, fixed himself a drink, and then plopped into a chair, which, she said, he would have never done before. "This was the same man," she wrote, "who once stood outside a room until he was invited in and then waited until someone said, 'Sit down, Joe.'" Chappaquiddick seemed to have changed him, seemed to have re-dressed the imbalance between him and his cousin. "Joe became his own man after Chappaquiddick," Dallas would write, "and he was the only one who did not seem to be going around in a state of shock—who did not seem horror-stricken over what had happened. If I had to describe his manner, I would say he was suddenly self-assured." And Dallas assumed it was because Ted needed him now—needed him to substantiate Ted's story about the rescue. This was Joey Gargan's moment. It was the moment when Rosencrantz or Guildenstern became Hamlet. It was the moment he had lived for.

But there was no such calm among most of the assembled group, only nerves. Now they settled in, though they didn't know exactly what they were settling in for. "A great headless talented monster" is how Richard Goodwin described the team to biographer Burton Hersh. "Nobody could decide what to do." There were telephones, typewriters, and black coffee. What there was not was a strategy. (Lyndon Johnson, observing from afar at his Texas ranch the bungling attempts to rescue Ted, said, "Never would have happened if Bobby was there.") Burke Marshall and the local attor-neys argued that Ted should remain silent while they fought charges—primarily leaving the scene of an accident—in court. Others contended he should plead guilty and then issue a statement. Though the assump-tion in the press was that the team members were plotting Ted's survival, even working on a cover-up, they were basically waiting, killing time. As the week dragged on and as the attorneys met with the special prosecutor, Walter Steele, no plan of action was undertaken until late Thursday, when Steele told them that Ted was likely to get a light sentence, and Ted's attorneys withdrew their pretrial hearing request for a full trial and agreed to plead guilty. And it was only then that the team had a direction because, as Goodwin would assess it, they had turned a personal and moral problem into a manageable political one. The issue was finally not how to save Ted's soul but what they could do to salvage his political prospects. Now they went to work on a plan.

It was not Ted's plan. He was in no condition that week to plan. He described that week after Chappaquiddick to Burton Hersh as one of "great and searching speculation over the incidents surrounding the whole tragedy" and said that he was loath to discuss it with Mary Jo's funeral approaching. He was confused, his mind jumbled, which was evident even when, years later, he discussed his mood in that period. "Many cross streams," he told Hersh. "People coming up and saying you ought to go to press conferences, my own feeling about the circumstances." And he said that "what seemed important one hour seemed unimportant a second hour, enormously difficult and complex." Rita Dallas said that he walked around in a "stupor, more alone than I had ever seen him," sometimes meeting with his mother at the flagpole, while the army of acolytes spent "long hours of loud, argumentative discussions over what to do about Teddy." He wore—"ostentatiously," Sorensen said—a huge bandage around his head, though Sorensen questioned whether he needed it or whether he wore it to gain sympathy. He was aware that the accident might very well end his career, probably would, and that his silence in the face of calls for an explanation for his actions worsened an already difficult situation. "It is nearly certain," editorialized *The Washington Post*, "that saying nothing will do him grave damage politically. . . ." One Democratic leader told the *Chicago Tribune* that he doubted Ted could "ever recover from the fact that he left that girl's body in the water for nine hours. That's too much." A Republican senator told *The New York Times* of Ted's not having issued a statement: *"Res ipsa loquitu"*—the thing speaks for itself. Even Dun Gifford, Ted's own legislative assistant, said that as he flew over Chappaquiddick that week on the way to Martha's Vineyard to assist in the transport of Mary Jo Kopechne's body back to her parents, he told the pilot, "There goes the presidency."

But politics was not Ted's primary consideration as he retreated to Squaw Island that week, a gray, drizzly week, lost in himself. Certain that the presidency was now out of his reach and that his Senate career was hopelessly compromised, he discussed with Dave Burke resigning his seat. But Burke, who was less than sympathetic to Ted at this point, snapped, "What can you do? Are you going to be the duke of Windsor?" When Schlesinger, who had left Hyannis before Ted delivered a statement, phoned Ethel Kennedy later that week and remarked that he was worried Ted was going to resign, Ethel told him, "You will never know how close it was." Ted's main concern now was morality—moral, not political, absolution. Talking with Tunney, he insisted that he had "a point of view of the morality of her [Mary Jo's] death." He told Tunney that he didn't feel guilty about it, that while it was a "terrible thing," and while he "shouldn't have been there," and while he should never have driven after having a few drinks, he had nevertheless tried to save her, had "tried to dive down and I couldn't," had "almost drowned myself," and once again repeated that when he didn't see her in the car, "I thought she had gotten out," which was clearly wishful thinking and denial. But he refuted the idea that he had killed Mary Jo, that it was anything but a tragic accident. "He really strongly felt that," Tunney recalled. "And I know he would have told me the absolute truth at that time. I just know he would have. Who else was he going to tell it to if he wasn't going to tell it to me?" Ted had said the same thing to Gwirtzman: "I willed her alive." Gwirtzman recalled, "He thought she had gotten away." And Gwirtzman said that after that, he left Ted and worked with Sorensen.

While Ted was sequestered, often restricted to bed, whether by physical illness or mental strain, the work began on a statement that Ted could deliver to address the growing consternation about his behavior. Ted Sorensen, who'd been charged by Steve Smith with precisely this kind of work, met with Ted in "long, emotional sessions," during which Ted related the facts of the accident. Sorensen, however, called himself a "very reluctant participant," especially because he was considering running for office himself and knew he would be tainted by writing an apologia, and he said he only came because he "obviously felt very sorry for Ted." But having come, Sorensen and Milton Gwirtzman drafted a statement, which others on hand, like Schlesinger and Goodwin, touched up, making the final product something of a patchwork. Still, it was primarily a Sorensen speech, a florid speech rather than a plainspoken one, a speech that was designed to give Ted political cover, which he had been forswearing, rather than a moral defense, which he wanted, a speech that was both plaintive and groveling—not the speech that the occasion called for, as even Sorensen would admit in retrospect, though it is hard to imagine any speech that would have fit the circumstances. ("It was not the high point of either my career or his," Sorensen would say.) And if it was the wrong speech, the wrongness of it was compounded by the fact that it wasn't Ted's own speech. Once again, as he had so often done in the past, Ted, who was shattered and confused and numb and self-flagellating, had surrendered himself to others—reading their words, expressing their sentiments rather than his own, serving their needs instead of his. Ted wanted and needed penance. Goodwin, who left Hyannis Port before the speech was finished, said that Sorensen and Gwirtzman were "trying to say something and still avoid the connotation of immorality—the old Irish Catholic fear of ever suggesting that you were screwing somebody outside of marriage." Gwirtzman's major contribution was to have Ted ask the voters of Massachusetts to render the final decision as to whether Ted should resign or not, which seemed both abject and too clever by half, since they were unlikely to turn on the Kennedys. But he also included having Ted say that in light of the accident, he would never seek the presidency. (Biographer Adam Clymer claims Ted desired to say this.) It was Eunice who, unwilling to forfeit her younger brother's future, insisted that the passage be struck, and it was. Sorensen said that the final draft wasn't shown widely and was hardly vetted, though younger staff members who did see it thought it should have been simpler, more sincere. And there is no record of the debate over having Ted deliver the speech on television rather than have it submitted in writing. All three broadcast networks provided him free time. And that was that.

And there were other duties that week, moral duties—not to service Ted, but to service the grieving Kopechnes. And Ted took these duties seriously. Mary Jo's body was still in Edgartown. Dun Gifford was in Nantucket at his summer house the morning after the accident, a Saturday, when Dave Burke and then Ted called him and asked if he would go to Martha's Vineyard to identify the body and make arrangements to have it transported to Pennsylvania, where the Kopechnes wanted her interred. Gifford flew in a small chartered plane that afternoon, piloted by a friend, and identified Mary Jo's body—he also examined her to see if there were any wounds, which there weren't—and then arranged for the funeral home to contact the Kopechnes. Ted was in anguish that afternoon and disoriented, but Gifford said that he called "regularly during the day" and "volunteered" Gifford, as Gifford put it, to accompany the body to Pennsylvania. The next day Gifford flew to Nantucket to get a change of clothes, then back to Martha's Vineyard, where the body bag was loaded onto a small twin-engine plane—laid into the aisle—and took off on what Gifford described as a "miserable day," flying through thunderstorms, with

Gifford thinking that God was "smiting me down for being involved in this." They landed in a downpour in Wilkes-Barre, transferred the body bag to a hearse, and Gifford rode beside it to the Kielty Funeral Home in Plymouth, just outside Wilkes-Barre. The directors there found a dress for Mary Jo and made her up with lipstick and styled her hair, while Gifford protested that she seldom wore lipstick and always wore her hair straight and that the dress was too frilly, and he forced them to redo the preparation—take off the lipstick, fix the hair, put on a different dress. And then the Kopechnes arrived to see her. "The worst part of it for me," Gifford would say. "Decent, trusting people," he would tell his wife—people who "loved the Kennedys" and "didn't want to be negative about Ted."

Ted was thinking of them too and had Dave Burke make another call, this one to William vanden Heuvel, who was in New York, to ask if he would go to Berkeley Heights, New Jersey, where the Kopechnes lived, to console them. (Ted would call him later that day as well.) Vanden Heuvel drove to Berkeley Heights and met the Kopechnes at their home, and he said the first thing they asked him was: " 'Is the senator all right?' They had such concern that he might have been injured, and they absolutely understood that this was a terrible accident, nothing more. It was a terrible accident." And vanden Heuvel sat with them into the night, talking with them, trying to protect them from the rush of press that was descending upon them—sat with them because Ted had asked him to.

But there was another obligation—this one Ted's alone. On Tuesday, July 22, he flew with Joan to Wilkes-Barre for Mary Jo's funeral, Ted still wearing his neck collar and walking stiffly. "Like a man in a catatonic trance," William vanden Heuvel, who accompanied them, said. They met the Kopechnes at the St. Vincent's rectory before the service, but Ted was still in anguish. Mr. Kopechne said, "He was talking, and I still couldn't understand a word he said, he was so emotional." Mrs. Kopechne had dealt with her grief by taking Valium and scarcely remembered the day. "I was working automatically to greet people," she would later say. Ted had offered to cover the funeral expenses, but the Kopechnes refused, paying with a bank loan and savings they had put away for their daughter's wedding. Instead, the Kennedys provided a vase of yellow flowers that sat beside the coffin. It was not a sedate ceremony. One reporter described the atmosphere as "festive." By one estimate, seven hundred spectators had collected outside the church, basically to get a glimpse of the Kennedys, which, Mrs. Kopechne later said, she fully understood. "Nothing that big had happened around there since thirty-four settlers were killed by the Indians, and that was before the Revolutionary War." Girls in the crowd screamed, "Isn't he beautiful?" "I saw him! I saw him!" Inside the church, Ted and Joan sat in the fourth pew, across from the Kopechnes. Mrs. Kopechne wept into her black gloves throughout the service, except for those moments when her husband helped her to her feet for the responses and held her close to him. The boiler-room girls were in attendance, and they wept too. And when the mass ended and the mourners left the church, they made their way through a crush of spectators to their cars for a slow procession to the grave site, which sat on a hillside "above the slag heaps of this mined-out anthracite town," as one report described it. Afterward, Ted, Joan, Ethel Kennedy, and the Kopechnes went to the Kingston House Inn, and "We had a great time," said Mr. Kopechne, referring primarily to Ethel, who made him feel as if he were "talking to my sister." And then the Kennedys left, boarded their plane, and returned to Hyannis and the clan there.

But for the Kopechnes, there would be no relief. "Every once in a while, we get angry, and we get mad, and this mad anger we wake up with sustains us through the day," Mrs. Kopechne would tell *Time* magazine a month after the funeral. "We've reached a breaking point many times, but I'm controlling myself for my husband, and he's controlling himself for me. It's holding us together." She said the worst time was the night, when their friends had left them to themselves and there was no one and nothing to comfort them, and they'd fight going to bed, because lying there awake—always awake—only focused them on their loss. "When we finally go to bed, and the lights are out, we can't help thinking."

After Ted returned to Hyannis Port, the army of Kennedy courtiers finally constructed his apologia, and now, on July 25, three days after the funeral and six days after the accident, came the televised statement from the big house. Dun Gifford told Burton Hersh that when he visited Ted after returning from Pennsylvania, Ted was in a "state of mind I'd never quite seen in him before—down but determined," eager to make a statement, to resolve the legal issues, and to get the accident behind him. But Rita Dallas said that when she saw Ted being prompted on the speech, he was "dull and listless, hardly able to respond or function." The day of the speech, Eunice had cleared the house of everyone but family, though there was one family member, Joe Kennedy, who would not be allowed to watch the broadcast. Ted sat at a desk in front of a white bookcase filled with what seemed to be sets of books. His hair was short and neatly combed. He wore a navy suit and matching tie. He held his script in his hands, seldom glancing up at the camera. He spoke evenly, quietly, grimly, as he had when he delivered Bobby's eulogy. He said that he had pleaded guilty to leaving the scene of an accident that morning and that he was now "free to tell you what happened and say what it means to me." He described Mary Jo as a "gentle, kind, and idealistic person" and said that the Kennedys had tried after Bobby's death to show her that "she still had a home with the Kennedy family." He denied any "immoral conduct" or any private relationship between them, and he decried "ugly speculation" to that effect. He described the accident briefly and his efforts to rescue Mary Jo from "the strong and murky current." He admitted, "My conduct and conversations during the next several hours, to the extent that I can remember them, make no sense to me at all." And while citing his "cerebral concussion" and state of shock, he insisted, "I do not seek to escape responsibility for my actions." He called his delinquency in reporting the accident "indefensible." And he described his mental state at the time: "All kinds of scrambled thoughts—all of them confused, some of them irrational, many of them which I cannot recall, and some of which I would not have seriously entertained under normal circumstances—went through my mind," including, he said, the possibility that the Kennedy family was cursed. He was "overcome . . . by a jumble of emotions." And he said, "No words on my part can possibly express the terrible pain and suffering I feel over this tragic incident."

And then, laying down the script, clasping his hands in front of him, and looking directly into the camera, he began Gwirtzman's peroration—the appeal to the people of Massachusetts for them to determine whether he should continue to represent them, in the process ticking off a list of the state's most distinguished senators, his voice cracking on the last name: John Kennedy. He closed with Sorensenian sententiousness: "A man does what he must," which is "the basis of all human morality," and he must follow his conscience, whatever sacrifices that entails. "Each man must look into his own soul." He said he hoped "I shall be able to put this most recent tragedy behind me and make some further contribution to our state and mankind, whether it be in public or private life." It took just under twelve minutes, which must have been the worst twelve minutes of his public life. Afterward, he entered his father's room and told him, "Dad, I've done the best that I can. I'm sorry."

Ted had said nothing in his statement that he hadn't said privately to his closest confidants. His very brief description of the accident was consistent with his written account to the police, save for the mention of the Gargan–Markham rescue attempt, which he had excluded from his police report in order not to embroil them. His description of his state of mind was doubtless accurate, given accounts of his words and behavior at the time, and short of a confession that he delayed reporting the accident to give himself time to come up with a cover story to preserve his presidential prospects, or of extreme self-flagellation, it is unlikely anything he said would have satisfied critics in the press who assumed that his only calculations after the accident were political ones. He called his actions "indefensible," which they were. He expressed contrition, if not sympathy to the Kopechnes, though he had already expressed that privately three times—when he first informed them, when he called them again that Monday, and when he met them before the funeral. The end of the speech—the appeal to the voters and the high-blown clichés about conscience and sacrifice—seemed insincere and, worse, self-serving, the swerve from tragedy to politics that had disgusted Goodwin, but it was hardly egregious.

And yet the speech received scathing reviews. Journalist William Honan would call it "one of the most devastating confessions an American public figure ever made. And it was not believed." Many of those reviews compared it to Richard Nixon's mawkish "Checkers speech," during the 1952 presidential campaign, when he was accused of having benefited from a slush fund provided by rich donors; Nixon defended himself by pleading poverty and declaring that his wife, Pat, wore a "good Republican cloth coat" and that the only political gift he had ever received was his dog Checkers. (Cartoonist Bill Mauldin drew Ted looking into a mirror and seeing Nixon holding Checkers.) "A Checkers speech with class," one politician called it. James Reston called it a "kind of tragic 'profile in courage,'" drawing on the title of Jack Kennedy's book. "What he has really asked the people of Massachusetts is whether they want to kick a man when he is down, and clearly they are not going to do that to this doom-ridden and battered family," even as, he wrote, Ted was ducking questions, evading the press, and avoiding cross-examination in court by pleading guilty. But there was more to Reston's critique. Reston wondered whether the accident had "startled him out of his rather casual ways and made him choose between his impulses and his responsibilities and family ambitions," which incorporated an awful assumption: that Ted Kennedy, who had been working so diligently to be a great senator, *had* casual ways and that he succumbed to his impulses—in short, an assumption that Ted must have been up to something that night other than taking a young lady back to the mainland. (Even after the Alaskan trip, Ted's drinking was regarded as a form of anesthetization; he was no lush. Nor, when it came to his womanizing, while widely rumored, was he a sybarite.) It wasn't what Ted said, even with its closing mawkishness, or how he said it that offended Reston. It wasn't his plea for sympathy when something else was called for. What seemed to disturb Reston was his doubt that Ted's innocent description of the accident could possibly have been true, given the rumors about Ted Kennedy's drunkenness and womanizing, and his doubt that Ted's failure to report the accident immediately wasn't actually some sort of cover-up to hide his reckless, wanton behavior.

It was an assumption widely shared, leading to the "ugly speculation" that Ted had referenced in his speech and that was the subtext of so many editorials condemning it. "He will have to face the sneers and the doubts of millions who did not agree with him politically and who feel he has added immorality to his drawbacks," read an *Atlanta Constitution* editorial. "Nothing that Senator Kennedy said last night explains that conduct convincingly," *The Baltimore Sun* said of his behavior. "He remains a man who failed badly in long hours, not just in a moment of crisis." In the *Hartford Courant:* "It seems to us the senator failed to level on exactly what happened that night." The *Kansas City Star* called the speech "deeply moving" but said it did not "excuse Kennedy's strange reactions after the fatal plunge of his car into a pond, nor did it answer all the still-unanswered questions in connection with that event." And *The New York Times* said his account may be "entirely true" but nevertheless found it "unsatisfactory" and wanted to know why he waited to report the accident, why he remained silent for a week, and why he did not subject himself to reporters' questions. And there was one more conclusion shared by most of the commentators—a conclusion expressed in *The Christian Science Monitor:* "It is doubtful if what is often spoken of as the Kennedy aura can ever be won back."

That was the press. Among his congressional brethren, there were some who were just as dubious, just as unkind. Senator George Murphy, one of the Republicans who had decamped from the Alaska trip, would later tell the *Los Angeles Times* that he now thought a Republican would win Ted's Senate seat. One Democratic congressman said that he felt "nothing but compassion" for Ted but that he still didn't think "the full story was told. . . . I wanted to hear a full explanation in his favor—and I don't think I got it." Other colleagues were more forgiving. Vermont Republican senator George Aiken said, "By God, he told the truth." Edmund Muskie called it a "straightforward story. I believe it." Thomas McIntyre wired him: "I trust you. Stay with us." Wisconsin senator William Proxmire said, "It would be a tragic setback for peace and liberalism if he should resign." Hubert Humphrey urged him to stay. So did Speaker John McCormack. The secretary of the Senate, Francis Valeo, remembered Majority Leader Mansfield speaking to Ted or someone close to him—he couldn't tell—and then hanging up and sighing, "My God, what an ill-starred family." And Chicago mayor Richard Daley promised to support him if he ran for president in 1972. Perhaps the most important individual verdict came not from a senator or congressman but from Gwen Kopechne, who had watched the speech at a friend's house and emerged afterward saying, "I am satisfied with the senator's statement and do hope he decides to stay on as senator."

But there was still another verdict to be delivered, the deciding one— the verdict of the public, to whom Ted had appealed. Even Milton Gwirtzman, who had hatched the plan to have Ted put his fate in the hands of his constituents, wasn't entirely sure how those constituents would react. But Ted, who knew those constituents well, must have anticipated their response. *The New York Times* reported that after his speech, the switchboards of Boston newspapers and television stations were "bombarded" with calls, running two to one in Ted's favor, and it quoted a *Boston Globe* editor, "All hell's breaking loose here. I've never seen anything like it." A *Globe* poll showed that 84 percent of Massachusetts voters approved of Ted, only 5 percent opposed him, and 78 percent wanted him to remain in the Senate. Two-thirds wanted him to run for president. Boston radio stations said the calls ran three to two and four to one for Ted; Western Union said it delivered 100,000 telegrams to Hyannis in just a single batch, and one aide said they ran 100 to 1 in Ted's favor. When he attended mass at St. Francis Xavier Church in Hyannis Port with his family and his friend Claude Hooton, he was cheered, and bystanders shouted, "Don't give up, Senator," and "We're with you," though Ted only responded with a slight nod. And the support extended beyond Massachusetts. A national Harris poll showed that, as *Time* put it, "The American public takes a generous and forgiving view of Ted Kennedy and his Chappaquiddick troubles." According to the poll, 68 percent felt it was unfair to be critical of him; by 58 percent to 30 percent they thought he had suffered and been sufficiently punished; and 63 percent to 28 percent said the incident had no effect on their regard for him. (Still, 44 percent believed he hadn't told the truth.) But Ted was not assuaged. He sailed with his family on the Sunday after the speech with Joan, Ethel, his own children, and several of Bobby's, but when they stopped for a picnic, Ted didn't leave the boat. And a visitor to Hyannis Port a few days after the speech found him transformed yet again. "Overnight, Teddy had turned from a young to a middle-aged man," the visitor told a reporter. "He had lost a good deal of weight, and somehow, for the first time, he looked like Bobby. I thought to myself: 'Now he is becoming Bobby, just as Bobby became Jack.'" And he said, "He had been lifted by shock into the final recognition that he is the one, the inheritor, the boy-come-of-age." Except that after Chappaquiddick, Ted Kennedy was fairly certain he had cost himself the inheritance his brothers had left him.

II

As one conclave met at Hyannis Port to save Ted Kennedy's political career the week after the Chappaquiddick accident, another conclave was meeting in Washington that week to destroy that career—this one headed by the president, with whom Ted had been jousting that year. Nixon had been at the presidential retreat of Camp David with his chief of staff, H. R. Haldeman, when he got the news and immediately began grousing about the press "as they try to cover up real implications of what happened." And Haldeman noted that the president "wants to be sure he"—meaning Ted—"doesn't get away with it, but of course no reaction from us." Like the editorialists, Nixon told Haldeman that he assumed Ted was drunk, escaped from the car, let Mary Jo drown, and only talked when the police got to him. In his memoir, Nixon would write, clearly thinking of himself, that if "anyone other than a Kennedy had been involved and had given such a patently unacceptable explanation, the media and the public would not have permitted him to survive in public life," the implication being that the media and the American people favored the Kennedys, as if this was the result of some sort of duplicity on the Kennedys' part and not, at least as far as the public was concerned, the result of genuine affection and gratitude for their efforts.* But Nixon then went on to express his sympathy for Ted, saying that when he saw him not long after the accident at a meeting in the Cabinet Room, "I was shocked by how pale and shaken he looked," and made a point of taking him aside in the Oval Office to encourage him to "overcome this tragedy and get on with his life." (Ted, laughing "derisively," according to biographer Theo Lippman, said that he "appreciated the gesture" but remarked that "it was in the papers that afternoon!") And in the memoir, after expressing sympathy and pontificating on how it was "possible to feel genuine personal concern for an opponent and still be coldly objective about his position as a competitor," and how he thought the accident would "be one of his greatest liabilities if he [Ted] decided to run for president in 1972," Richard Nixon, this most vindictive and grudging of men, this self-pitying man who had no sympathy for others, then lamented that he doubted the press would "try very hard to uncover" what had really happened and instructed his assistant for domestic affairs, John Ehrlichman, to assign someone to investigate, with the stern admonition, "Don't let up on this for a minute." (When his speechwriter William Safire told him that the moonwalk would overshadow Chappaquiddick, Nixon, after having condemned the press, gloated that wasn't necessarily true because "too many reporters want to win a Pulitzer Prize" for them to keep the story quiet.) In ordering an investigation, he was motivated, he told Ehrlichman, by what he thought Kennedy would do to him if the roles were reversed, though this was obviously a case of projection. Ted Kennedy bore no malice. Richard Nixon bore little but malice—a malice born of resentment.

But Richard Nixon, in his malice, did not settle for an investigation. The man who envied and loathed the Kennedys, who was obsessed by them, was obsessed now by Ted Kennedy's accident. Within two hours of the discovery of the car in Poucha Pond, Ehrlichman had had Jack Caulfield, a White House aide and former New York City policeman, send another retired New York detective, Tony Ulasewicz—part of what Caulfield described as the White House private intelligence operation—to Martha's

---

*Lyndon Johnson had exactly the same reaction. Kennedys would always be acquitted, he groused, while he, a Southerner, would always be convicted. "If I had been with a girl and she had been stung by a bumblebee, then they would put me in Sing Sing." David Halberstam, *The Best and the Brightest* (New York: Random House, 1972), 435.

Vineyard to provide information on the accident to the president, though already, according to Ulasewicz, there was a "hotline from Chappaquiddick and Edgartown to the White House." Ulasewicz spent a week there hunting for evidence of Ted's transgressions and posing as a reporter at news conferences, asking embarrassing questions about him. "The only way I could counteract White House doubts about the accuracy of my reporting," Ulasewicz would later write, "was to get others to start verifying the accuracy or inaccuracy of Kennedy's story on their own." In short, the White House was manipulating the news coverage. Apparently, Caulfield himself also went to Edgartown in the days after the accident—columnist Jack Anderson would later say he had—and reported to Ehrlichman having observed Bobby's son, Robert Kennedy Jr., examining Ted's wrecked Oldsmobile. ("A little aside—he apparently has all the Kennedy instincts, including an eye for pretty girls!") And when Caulfield, watching TV, saw Jim King, a onetime Bobby Kennedy bodyguard and yet another former New York City detective, driving Ted, he reported to Ehrlichman that "we may be able to develop some useful information in time," indicating that they might use King as an informant.

But even as Ulasewicz was collecting information, the president's obsession would not abate. On the day he was to give a televised national address about the moon landing, he called in Haldeman to discuss Chappaquiddick. "He is very interested in the whole thing," Haldeman wrote in his diary, "and feels it marks the end of Teddy." Later that day Haldeman wrote: "He's going to push hard on the Ted Kennedy thing, mainly because he feels it greatly reduces Teddy's influence in the Senate and may help us on ABM and surtax, as it takes the wind out of opposition's sails." The next day Nixon was still obsessing over Ted at a meeting with Haldeman, Ehrlichman, and his national security adviser, Henry Kissinger. "Lots of talk about Ted Kennedy episode," wrote Haldeman. And again the next day: "P still fascinated with Kennedy case." And several days later, as they flew to Guam after greeting the Apollo 11 astronauts, Nixon had Haldeman listen to Ted's speech via phone—an aide held the receiver to the television back in the States—and take notes, then had Haldeman check with Ehrlichman for an evaluation. "P still very interested," Haldeman wrote in his diary. "Discussed it with him on the plane (to Manila) and he still has a lot of theories." And when Nixon heard a report that Haldeman was talking to the press about it, he was concerned that the White House switchboard might be tapped. And *still* Nixon's obsession continued. Within a week, Ehrlichman authorized wiretaps—illegal wiretaps, since Nixon was now willing to break the law to disable Ted Kennedy—on the phone of Mary Jo Kopechne's Georgetown house, where she had lived with three roommates. Two weeks later, Nixon instructed Ehrlichman to talk with Kissinger, who had spoken with Kennedy friend John Kenneth Galbraith, as to "what really happened in the EMK matter," and then "you, of course, will know how to check it out to get it properly exploited," clearly meaning exploited in the press. A few months later, Nixon had yet to relent. This time, his deputy attorney general, John Dean, asked the FBI to "discreetly" determine whether Mary Jo Kopechne had traveled to Greece in 1968—the clear intent of the request being to find something that would link Ted and Mary Jo romantically, that would compromise both of them, something in which Mary Jo Kopechne's reputation would be collateral damage in the president's war to render Ted Kennedy harmless to him. (In the end, there was nothing to find.) According to Ulasewicz, the White House compiled a scrapbook of every negative mention in the press of Ted's behavior during Chappaquiddick and labeled it "At an Appropriate Time." Haldeman, who was ruthless in his advancement of Nixon, justified these activities on the basis that they were necessary to stop a Kennedy restoration. "This was at least a chance to get something while it was still hot with some guys that ought to be able to find it out," Haldeman said, lamenting that they had failed to get something on the Bay of Pigs invasion or Vietnam, which would have besmirched John Kennedy and undermined Ted. Such was Richard Nixon's sympathy, and such was his antipathy.

There was another casualty in the accident at Chappaquiddick—one who had been given little consideration that week. Joan Kennedy hadn't accompanied her husband to Martha's Vineyard because she was four months' pregnant with the couple's fourth child. To get pregnant with Patrick, after having already suffered two miscarriages, she had taken hormone shots, massive doses, she said, and then was committed to bed rest throughout the entire pregnancy. But she had told herself, "I'm gonna do this one more time, so I can give Patrick a little brother or sister." And she did. It was a difficult pregnancy and a difficult time. Not long before Chappaquiddick, Joan's father had asked her mother for a divorce, and the woman, broken, left for Europe with a friend. And then came the accident and the gathering of the clan and the insinuations over Ted's conduct. According to her secretary at the time, Joan remained upstairs during the Kennedy army's deliberations, but at one point on that first weekend, she picked up the phone and heard Ted talking to Helga Wagner, a presumed paramour. Joan was devastated. "Nothing ever seemed the same after that," her secretary would say. Still, Joan was devoted to Ted—a good soldier for him. So she accompanied him to Mary Jo's funeral, knowing that her appearance would help Ted resume his career, despite the fact that she was pregnant and that the charter plane was small and the ride rough. She admitted that deciding to go was like "choosing politics over our baby." A month later, on the night of August 28, she suffered a miscarriage and fell into an unshakable depression. There would be no more pregnancies, no more children. "After that I just thought we tried hard enough."

Now it was Joan who retreated to her room at Squaw Island. Luella Hennessey, the nurse who had tended to Ted as a boy and who now tended to Kara, Ted Jr., and Patrick, said that Joan operated in denial too, as her husband had, never mentioning the accident, ignoring mentions of it when she heard them on television or radio, focusing her attention on the children or on Joe Kennedy, who was growing weaker that summer, holding up as Ted had felt it necessary to hold up when tragedy struck. She bristled when friends offered sympathy—"Oh, poor Joan," or "You poor thing"—and bristled more when they hinted at her husband's infidelity. "I told them where to go," she confided to biographer Lester David. "It was kind of like I got up on my high horse for the first time in my life." She claimed that "if anything good can be said to have come from that tragedy, it is that Ted and I were brought closer together."

Ted saw it differently. He called it a "difficult time with her." As much as she tried to maintain a stoic front, she was no more able to do so than Ted had been, and like Ted, she was emotionally crippled. Alcoholism ran in her family. Both her parents were alcoholics. (Her mother, upon hearing about Chappaquiddick while on her European excursion, collapsed; when she returned home, she was committed to a sanitarium in White Plains, New York, to deal with her illness.) Now Joan, who had already had a difficult time coping with the deaths of her brothers-in-law, crumbled, drinking heavily, anesthetizing herself to the tragedies and to the rumors. "She tried, and tried hard, to get help during this time," Ted would recall, "and she went to different places," meaning rehabilitation centers.

"It looked like it was okay for a while, and then she had a tough period." And so the long descent began.

Though Ted Kennedy had pleaded guilty to leaving the scene of an accident ("looking like a ruined man," *Time* had said of his appearance at the hearing), though he had been sentenced to a two-month incarceration, which was then suspended (the judge said that he "already has been and will continue to be punished beyond anything this court can impose"), and though he had made a remorseful public statement that he hoped would provide closure, the case would not yet be laid to rest. Critics, who included most of the press corps, believed that the authorities had been less than zealous in their investigation. Chief of Police Arena, who was under pressure to charge Kennedy, said he did not do so because he saw no skid marks on the bridge, which indicated to him that Kennedy had simply driven off it thinking he was still on the road, and that he failed to test Ted's breath for alcohol because he said that when Ted appeared at the police station the next morning, he showed no signs of inebriation. "A Roman holiday" is how *Washington Post* reporter Richard Harwood described the proceedings, in which the town counsel, a man named Richard McCarron, represented Ted and in which the local district attorney, who was allegedly investigating the accident to see if any further action was necessary, failed to interview Arena. That district attorney, Edmund Dinis—forty-four, square-jawed, with thick, wavy black-and-gray hair, and handsome enough to have once attracted the attention of an MGM talent scout—agreed with Harwood's characterization. He himself described it as a "Roman circus"—"the press kept giving the whole thing a more and more macabre turn"—but later admitted to Burton Hersh that he was feeling bullied by the press commotion, especially demands by his local paper, the New Bedford *Standard-Times*, to open an investigation. So two weeks after the accident, Dinis requested an inquest, a fact-finding hearing into Mary Jo Kopechne's death, to answer the media's unanswered questions.

At least that was Dinis's stated motive. (Steve Smith later griped that inquests had been designed under an 1877 statute for investigations of railroad accidents and that an inquest hadn't been held in Massachusetts in "I don't know—Never.") But in reopening the case after it had seemingly been closed, Dinis may have also been harboring a long-standing grudge against Ted. He had a reputation for resenting wealth and power and felt that the Kennedys had ignored him in his various bids for public office. When he remained neutral in Ted's primary battle against Ed McCormack after Ted had asked him to head an organization of Portuguese Democrats, it led to an angry exchange in which Ted warned, "The Kennedys never forget," and Dinis snapped, "I don't need you, and I don't need your brother." Meanwhile, adding the morbid to the circus atmosphere, Dinis, on the basis that there had been bloodstains on Mary Jo's blouse, petitioned a Pennsylvania court to have Mary Jo's body exhumed for an examination to determine if she had actually died by drowning— a request that was vehemently opposed by the Kopechnes, who said there was no doubt she had drowned, and that was ultimately rejected by the court as well, which ruled, "To consider any other cause of death at this time would give loose rein to speculation unsupported by any medical facts of record."

In deciding to hold an inquest that September, Dinis and Judge William Boyle, who acceded to Dinis's request, were essentially casting doubt on Ted's story and giving legal credence to assumptions about his motives and behavior that evening, which lent the proceedings a slight political cast. Ted—reluctantly, he said, and only under the advice of his counsel— requested a postponement at the last minute, on the grounds that Ted's rights would be violated since the inquest did not allow him to have counsel present or to allow cross-examination of witnesses and since the proceedings would be open to the press. The Massachusetts Supreme Court eventually allowed the hearing to be held but ordered any transcript embargoed until the hearing had been completed and barred the press and public, as Ted's attorneys had requested.

The inquest began on a snowy January 5, 1970, in the red-brick Dukes County Courthouse of the Edgartown District Court of Judge Boyle. Crowds had gathered outside, but Ted had rejected the town's offer of police protection and waded through the spectators, almost as if he was, once again, tempting fate. The hearing lasted four days, with twenty-seven witnesses testifying, including Ted, who took the stand for six hours, and it produced 763 pages of transcript. Ted's story hadn't changed significantly. And there was little testimony in contradiction to it, save for that of a part-time deputy sheriff named Christopher Look. Look claimed he had been patrolling Chappaquiddick on the night of the accident and saw a large dark automobile passing by, with what seemed to be a male driver and female passenger, at the junction of Dike and Schoolhouse Roads at roughly 12:45 A.M. The auto then stopped, causing Look himself to stop and get out of his car in case the passengers needed directions or assistance. Then, he said, the car backed up and drove down Dike Road— the significance being that if this was indeed Ted Kennedy's car, the time of the sighting would have challenged Ted's chronology. Otherwise, the inquest was anticlimactic. "It is a nonstory," James Reston wrote in *The New York Times*, "held behind closed doors, to repeat old tales, which few people quite believe anyway, yet it is a ghoulish mystery, and even Chet Huntley and David Brinkley [NBC News anchormen] thought it more important than any other story in the world on the day the senator merely went in and came out of a courthouse door."

The inquest was over quickly, but then came the long wait, a nearly four-month wait, for the release of the transcript and the judge's report. Those months were not to be entirely placid ones either for Ted Kennedy. Given the boiling hostility in Edgartown toward the Kennedys—a Republican stronghold so hostile to Kennedys that once, when Joan was having difficulty negotiating a disembarkation from a boat on the wharf, the local citizenry nearby watched without offering assistance—and given the growing certainty among the citizenry that Ted Kennedy must be guilty of something other than leaving the scene of an accident, a grand jury was impaneled in April. The jury foreman, a young pharmacist named Leslie Leland, said that he had been encouraged to seek the hearing by District Attorney Dinis, though it didn't take much encouragement, since he had already concluded that Kennedy had escaped justice. The grand jury was a homegrown event, and a useless one. The presiding judge, most likely in an attempt to protect Ted from further scrutiny in what seemed an instance of favoritism, did not give the jurors access to the inquest transcript (Leland later said that when he asked for it, the judge looked at him with "what seemed like daggers in his eyes"), and they were told they were not permitted to call witnesses who had testified at the inquest—which hardly made the session worth impaneling. The grand jury lasted two days, heard four new witnesses for a total of twenty minutes, and then adjourned without issuing an indictment, though Leland later complained that the jurors were "manipulated" and "blocked from doing our job" and that "if you want to use the word 'cover-up,' then, okay, that's what it was." He also blamed Dinis for reversing himself and telling them, "You are just looking for Mickey Mouse charges," though

Dinis, who had no love for Ted, might have come to that conclusion. In the end, one juror said that most of them felt Ted was "morally responsible," and another said, "I don't believe this will ever be resolved as far as some people are concerned."

But there was still one more step before Chappaquiddick could be put to legal rest: the judge's report from the inquest. Judge William Boyle, sixty-three years old, a lifelong Massachusetts resident and conservative Republican who had been appointed to the court only after twenty-seven years as a clerk—which probably contributed to a simmering resentment—looked curmudgeonly, with a deeply furrowed brow and long wattles and a white brush mustache. The only effect that lightened his appearance and irascible demeanor was the red bow ties and soft fedoras he favored. And those bow ties notwithstanding, Boyle *was* curmudgeonly—a martinet whose temper attorneys feared. Boyle, who had also presided at Ted's sentencing, had remained more or less quiet during the inquest and had performed judicially if, according to critics, incuriously. But he clearly had his opinions, and after listing the findings of fact, he expressed them in his report, for which, he said, he used a standard not of "proof beyond a reasonable doubt," as in a criminal trial, but of "probable guilt" based on an "inference" that a reasonable man would draw from certain facts. And Boyle's inference was not kind to Ted Kennedy. He inferred that Ted and Mary Jo did not intend to return to Edgartown that night, as Ted had testified; that Ted had intentionally turned onto Dike Road; that Ted, driving at a speed of twenty miles per hour, as he had testified, "would at least be negligent and possibly reckless"; and that Ted knew of the hazard of the bridge but failed "to exercise due care." In short, Boyle called Ted a liar—a charge that so disturbed and even infuriated Ted that he told reporter Willian Honan, when the two were walking through Boston Public Gardens shortly after the report's release, that he was once again contemplating leaving public life. He told another visitor to his home that weekend the same thing—that he was considering writing, teaching, or traveling. And as Ted pondered his future, there was more at stake than the charge of lying. There was legal jeopardy. Though Ted had avoided a charge of manslaughter, *New York Times* legal reporter Fred Graham argued that Boyle's finding of negligence required him by statute to have Ted arrested for trial. But Boyle, though curmudgeonly, seemingly did not have the stomach for doing so, statute or not. The transcripts, which detailed Ted's state of denial and his inexcusable tardiness in reporting the accident, would stand as his real sentence. He had not behaved admirably. He would have to live with that.

But that would not be sentence enough for many, especially for Ted Kennedy's detractors. Doubts abounded, and doubts would persist—intractable doubts. There were doubts that he was sober, though no one at the party and no one afterward—Shiretown Inn owner Russell Peachey had spoken to him just hours after the accident—suggested any signs of inebriation or any indications of a hangover the next morning, and his alcoholic intake, even if one included several drinks he later remembered having right after the race, would not have exceeded the Massachusetts limit for intoxication. (If he had been impaired by anything, it would have been fatigue.) And in any case, while Ted had been drinking more heavily since Bobby's death, there were no reports of public drunkenness, save for the Alaska trip, and a *Time* correspondent who had followed Ted for months said he had seen him drunk in that period only once—on that Alaska flight.

There were doubts about Ted's insistence that he and Mary Jo were not having and had never had any kind of romantic relationship, though Mary Jo was a devout Catholic, the office virgin, and not the kind of woman to allure Ted Kennedy—"not his cup of tea," as his aide Melody Miller put it. "When people made the suggestion that the senator and she were going off to the beach," said Miller, "and that's why he turned right, for a tryst, the Robert Kennedy staff women all looked at each other and laughed. We laughed because we knew that was absurd." Moreover, Ted's mood that night was somber, even sour, not amorous. And, above all, for him to have had a romantic dalliance with a young woman devoted to his late brother would have been a breach of faith with Bobby and an insult to Bobby's memory, which he would never have done.

There were grave doubts, perhaps the gravest, that he was driving to the ferry, the doubts that Judge Boyle had voiced in his report, on the basis that Ted had known the road and should have recognized the difference between the asphalt Chappaquiddick Road and the rutted, washboard-like dirt Dike Road, though Ted did *not* know those roads, had *not* driven those roads himself, and had a notoriously bad sense of direction. And even if one were to draw the most lurid conclusions about their drive, even if he *had* been heading toward the beach, that "doesn't seem to me the most sinister thing in the world," as one Kennedy associate told Burton Hersh. It certainly wouldn't have led to the conclusion that he was responsible for Mary Jo's death.

There were doubts about the time frame, especially prompted by Deputy Look's inquest testimony of when he spotted that dark car and by his claim to have seen a license plate with an "L" and a "7" at the beginning and another "7" at the end, which Kennedy's plate had, though Look had not reported seeing the car that night or recorded its plate number or told Arena about it. According to *The New York Times,* his story was later said to have "materially expanded" as time went on, and according to a *Washington Post* investigation nearly seven years after the accident, he had changed his story three times, making it more damaging to Ted each time.

There were doubts about the speed at which Ted estimated he was traveling (twenty miles per hour)*—reckless speed, Judge Boyle had said, though Ted, even by the least charitable estimates, had hardly been racing toward the bridge. A *Reader's Digest* analysis by an expert in auto accidents determined he had been driving at least thirty miles per hour, which would not have been inappropriate if he did not anticipate a little hump of a bridge ahead. One Chappaquiddick investigator said that the bridge could be seen in headlights three hundred to four hundred feet from the approach and that running off it would require a "driving error so grandiose as to defy the imagination," but *The New York Times* reported that a "nighttime examination [apparently the night after the accident] showed that the bridge could easily be mistaken for something else when looked at with automobile headlights."

There were doubts about his description of his rescue attempt, though the current at Poucha Pond was strong by Gargan's admission, Chief Arena's admission, and John Farrar's admission, and there is no reason whatsoever to believe he didn't attempt to rescue Mary Jo if only because he knew the consequences of not doing so. There were doubts about why, immediately after the accident, he didn't head to the Malms' house nearby or to the fire station, where a red light was shining, to report it or seek help, though Ted insisted he never saw those lights or any lights on his way back to the cottage, not necessarily because those lights weren't shin-

---

* At the inquest, George Kennedy, the supervisor of the Registry of Motor Vehicles in Oak Bluffs and no relation to Ted, estimated from skid marks on the bridge that Ted had been driving between 20 and 22 mph, though Chief Arena said he had seen no skid marks.

ing but because he was dazed. "I'm sure anybody who was making that walk would have seen them," he once told William vanden Heuvel. "I didn't see them. I didn't see anything," and vanden Heuvel attributed it to a "profound state of shock."

There were doubts about the swim across the channel that he claimed to have taken, doubts about the strength of the current, though Ted was a strong swimmer, even with his aching back—a nearly Olympic-caliber swimmer, his Army trainer had said—and though both the ferryman, Jared Grant, who told *The New York Times* that he had checked the tides that night, and the scuba diver who recovered Mary Jo's body, John Farrar, said the channel was entirely swimmable. Moreover, the ferryman who was on duty the next morning, Dick Hewitt, after telling *The Washington Post* that he was dubious about Ted's swimming story, said that he had seen people swim the channel that summer, but "each time they were so exhausted, they took the ferry back." Ted didn't have to take the ferry back; he was in Edgartown. And he was exhausted.

There were doubts especially about Ted's reason for the delay in reporting the accident, which he attributed to his confused state of mind, adamant denial, and irrational hope of Mary Jo's survival, though these were evident to Gargan and Markham immediately—Ted talked repeatedly about Mary Jo having lived—and *Time* consulted three experts in trauma who said of his behavior that it was "not unusual for a person who had suffered such an experience." This did not absolve Ted Kennedy of the responsibility to report the accident, and it did not dispel concerns over whether he postponed the report because he had alcohol in his system or because he was searching for some way to spin the accident in his favor, though to inculpate him based on these speculations was no different than exculpating him. There was no evidence.

And from these doubts arose theories of conspiracy, complicated Rube Goldbergian conspiracies, like the theories that arose after John Kennedy's assassination, including one saying Ted had been framed by Nixon's CIA, another that Ted had already murdered Mary Jo because she was pregnant and then drove her off the bridge, and a third that Ted and Mary Jo had had an earlier accident in which she was killed and Ted then recruited Gargan and Markham to help him push the damaged car over the bridge to give the appearance that she had driven into the water herself. Nixon's deputy attorney general, Richard Kleindienst, reported to FBI chief J. Edgar Hoover that a personal friend of his who knew the Kenne-

dys' doctor told him that the doctor was on Martha's Vineyard the weekend of the accident and said that Ted had changed clothes to go swimming
with Rosemary Keough, another of the boiler-room girls, but that unbe-
knownst to them, Mary Jo, feeling ill, had curled up on the back seat of the
car; when Ted then drove off the bridge, he rescued Rosemary Keough but
had no idea about Mary Jo, and Ted and Keough returned to the party
and joked about losing their car—a story substantiated by absolutely no
one, though the Kopechnes themselves would come to believe it, perhaps
as a way, understandably, to exonerate their daughter from having know-
ingly gone off in the car with Ted. (Keough said that at five foot two inches
and ninety-five pounds, her chances of making it out of the car would
have been "nil.") Another theory, flogged by scuba diver John Farrar, was
that Mary Jo had survived the accident and found a pocket of air that
could have sustained her until Ted sought help—a damning charge. According to reporter Jack Olsen, though, Farrar, "a strong conservative,"
had earlier told him his assessment of the accident was that a "car gyrat-
ing into the water in such a fashion would be likely to smash its occupants
into unconsciousness, or at least disorient them thoroughly." This hardly
makes it sound as if Mary Jo would have survived. (Like many accounts,
Farrar's became progressively more negative toward Ted Kennedy; twenty
years later he said that Mary Jo could have survived for at least two hours
in the wreckage.)* And had Farrar been correct, had Mary Jo been conscious, she almost certainly would have struggled to free herself by clawing her way through one of the broken windows—in this case, the window
on the passenger side—as Ted had apparently done on the driver's side,
but Dun Gifford, who identified her body at the funeral home, said that her
hands and fingernails were "pristine." Olsen himself had his own theory.
He surmised that Ted had abandoned the car when Deputy Look approached, not wanting to be caught, even if innocently, with a young
woman, and that Mary Jo drove herself off the bridge without Ted knowing about it.

And there was yet another account by someone who, as right-wing
journalist Leo Damore put it, would "suffer in silence wounds inflicted on

* A study conducted for Ted by the Arthur Little consulting firm determined that Miss Kopechne could not have remained conscious for more than four minutes or lived more than
fourteen, while an Indiana University study found that an automobile upside down in water
with an open window would not have a significant air pocket and that she could have survived only a minute. "Chappaquiddick Revisited," *The Washington Post*, February 22, 1976.

him by the accident that killed Mary Jo Kopechne." Except that this witness didn't suffer in silence. Joey Gargan, the so-called flunky, the Rosencrantz or Guildenstern of that July evening, had seethed with resentment
at his cousin, or at least that was how he unburdened himself to Damore
years after the accident, saying that in 1976, during Ted's Senate campaign, Gargan had "exploded" at him: "I've given you thirty years of my
life and what do I have to show for it? I'm a fool in the eyes of my own
children because of Chappaquiddick." After having righted his life with
the help of Alcoholics Anonymous, Gargan told Damore his version of
what really happened that night: how Ted had suggested to him and
Markham that Gargan could "discover" the car in the pond and say they
found Mary Jo alone in it (Gargan said he vehemently opposed that proposal); how, despite Ted's obvious distress and confusion, Gargan assumed
he would report the accident, and how Gargan himself returned to the
cottage without thinking to report it; how Ted insisted the next morning
at the Shiretown Inn that he was going to say Mary Jo was driving the car;
how Nance Lyons, on the drive from the cottage to the ferry, told Gargan
that he could take the blame for driving the car (a charge Lyons forcefully
denied and one no one else corroborated, though there were others in the
car who could have done so); how Gargan told Ted at the Shiretown Inn,
in no uncertain terms, "You've got to do what I've been saying right
along"—report the accident; and, finally, how Gargan tried to dissuade
Ted from delivering his televised statement. By his revised account, Gargan, the self-described hero of an evening in which there were no heroes,
gave credence to the idea that Ted delayed reporting the accident in order
to cook up some alibi or cover story. But Markham never corroborated
Gargan's new version, and there never was an alibi or cover-up of any
kind—if there had been, it certainly would have been a better story than
the one Ted told. Ted had explicitly left Gargan and Markham out of his
first statement in order, he had told them, to spare them rather than implicate them. And when Ted did report the accident, the first thing he told
Chief Arena, by Arena's own statement, was, "We've got to do what's
right, because if we don't, we'll both be criticized for it."

And so, for all the doubts and theories, the answers to the questions
about the accident at Chappaquiddick may be a matter of Occam's razor:
that the simplest explanation is the likeliest explanation. Ted's behavior,
as he said in his televised statement, may have been "indefensible," "irrational," inexplicable," "inconsistent," and "inconclusive," not to mention

inexcusable, far from heroic, the conduct of a man already in ruins and now in shock, and there may be small discrepancies in his testimony that were magnified by Kennedy haters and conspiracy theorists into seemingly large ones, but there is no credible evidence that Ted Kennedy wasn't telling the truth. There is nothing implausible about his account, nothing in all but the most outlandish conspiracy theories to suggest that the incident was anything but a tragic accident, nothing to provide the slightest hint of a romantic liaison, nothing to suggest a cover-up, nothing even to indicate that the courtesies that had been extended to Ted—courtesies normally extended to notables—resulted in any miscarriage of justice, since a suspended sentence for leaving the scene of an accident was standard for first-time offenders. Nothing points to any crime on Ted's part, save leaving the scene, and Judge Boyle's inference of Ted's recklessness or negligence was not only unlikely given the facts but also would have been impossible to prove given the condition of the bridge. There was, in sum, nothing whatsoever to undermine Ted Kennedy's credibility, except for those who had a stake in undermining it (the word "murder" kept cropping up on the right), or those who were convinced of Ted's reputation as the least of the Kennedys and for whom his conduct confirmed it, or those who felt the Kennedys were driven by opportunism and political calculation and saw Ted's behavior as a way to save his career, or those who now searched for doubt of any sort wherever they could find it. This last included the press, besotted with Kennedy hysteria and a soap-opera fever so virulent that even reputable journalists would write that "the only theory that still plausibly" explained Ted's behavior was that he was "trying to fabricate an alibi while the girl was lying at the bottom of the pond," when there were many other more plausible theories, or that what made Chappaquiddick "indefensible" was not the accident but "the attempt to cosmeticize its aftermath into something 'irrational' and 'inexplicable,' a moment of panic or trauma," when anyone who knew Ted Kennedy after Bobby's assassination knew that is most likely what it was. ("I see Chappaquiddick as the last looming incident in Ted's life," Gladys Gifford, Dun's wife, would say, "as a result of Bobby's death.") In the end, the mysteries were not so mysterious, the discrepancies not so significant, the "science" that purported to prove or disprove Ted Kennedy's story not conclusive. In the end, he was a flawed man, often in trouble, overwhelmed by another tragic situation, paralyzed by shock, and tortured by torment, all of which led to a kind of irony. As Garry Wills, no Kennedy admirer, would write, "It may seem Kennedy has such a genius for getting caught that he is caught even when there is nothing to catch him out in." Chief Arena would say years later, "I will always be convinced that what happened was an accident." Kennedy's friends would say that his public account was also his private account. "I don't think he ever lied to me about anything I asked him," Dun Gifford said. "I am convinced that when we'd talk about it that he was telling me the truth," his closest friend, John Tunney, averred. And Ted himself never wavered, insisting that the skepticism about his account was "unwarranted and unjustified." Still, he knew that the cloud would never lift: "No matter what I said, it would not satisfy those who had already made up their minds."

And he was right.

III

All these things are just predetermined. He had been on "the wrong side of destiny." That is how John Tunney thought his friend Ted Kennedy had come to think of himself after the accident at Chappaquiddick, a position that may have been yet another Kennedy inheritance. As Doris Kearns Goodwin had written of the family, theirs had been a "tale, repeated in three generations, of great achievement followed by decline and failure— self-inflicted or at the hands of a merciless fate." Ted's was both self-inflicted *and* the result of merciless fate—a fate so merciless that even after the legal proceedings had concluded, even after Ted had told his story, even after the press had taken its whacks at him, the accident at Chappaquiddick would continue to reverberate through political and cultural history for decades, generating ripples, waves even, out of all proportion to the event itself. Almost immediately, Chappaquiddick seemed to have written a political epitaph for Ted Kennedy, the presumptive Democratic presidential nominee. "The end of the Kennedy era," Tom Braden and Frank Mankiewicz, Bobby's campaign press secretary, declared in their inaugural political column. Ted said as much himself. Chappaquiddick had "effectively ended all of the activities in terms of a national campaign." While Massachusetts had rallied to him, and the general public had been sympathetic, the latter's mood soon changed, as the press coverage grew more hostile. A national Harris poll in August after the accident showed Ted running worse than Muskie or Humphrey against Nixon. (In May, before Chappaquiddick, Ted had run ten points better against Nixon than both of them.) By November, only 28 percent had a "highly favor-able" opinion of him, down from 49 percent before Chappaquiddick, and Nixon held a fourteen-point lead over him. "Ted's Crumbling Position," *Time* titled its polling story. "Would you let this man sell you a used car?" ran a new joke referring to the old characterization of Nixon as a used-car salesman. "Yes," went the punch line, "but I wouldn't let that Teddy drive it." But the jokes couldn't disguise the sense of disappointment, even de-spair, in many pockets of the nation or the realization that Chappaquid-dick had rewritten not only Ted Kennedy's fate but America's fate too. As political columnist David Broder analyzed the consequences of the acci-dent, "Our shock at what happened is based not just on our sympathy for the victim and her family and for Kennedy, but on our hurt that the future we had arranged for him—in our own minds—is now altered." Even the movie gossip magazine *Photoplay* weighed in, with Ted and Joan on the cover and the headline THE PARTY'S OVER.

Because Chappaquiddick clung to the collective memory, there would be no resurrecting Camelot after it, no Ted Kennedy regency. "You just knew it would never be the same again," Dun Gifford recalled. "You knew that right away. It didn't mean he couldn't have a life in public service, but it wouldn't be a charmed life. It was going to be different." And as *The New Yorker* observed on the accident's twenty-fifth anniversary, Chappaquid-dick not only trimmed Ted's political prospects, which very likely altered the nation's trajectory; by opening an "aperture into the underhistory of the Kennedys," it also affected his brothers' place in the national pan-theon. "Lurid insinuations about what might have happened at Chappa-quiddick fed curiosity about the secret history of the martyred president and his administration." Thus, "the Kennedys began their descent from mythic figures to human beings," though Ted Kennedy had always been the most human, most fallible of Kennedys. Now he had simply visited that fallibility on his brothers.

And if Chappaquiddick halted another Kennedy presidency, and if it recalibrated how Americans thought of the Kennedys, it also wound up transforming American political discourse itself. "What happened to Ted was in part a matter of chance, while Ted's response was a matter of char-acter," Max Lerner would later write of him in the aptly titled *Ted and the Kennedy Legend: A Study in Character and Destiny*. "It was his character, engraved in him by the circumstance of his biography, that shaped his ac-tion." He must have some defect in character, Nixon had mused about Ted after Chappaquiddick, voicing what many had come to think of the youngest Kennedy. But that focus, triggered by Ted's behavior, now injected the character issue into the larger political conversation as well, and not the issue of *political* character—qualities like courage, compassion, probity, and honesty—but of *personal* character—qualities like abstinence, faithfulness, thrift, and religiosity. "After Chappaquiddick, amateur psychoanalysis of politicians became commonplace," *The New Yorker* commented in that twenty-fifth-anniversary piece. "The psychological dynamics of John Kennedy—and of Robert Kennedy—had seldom been publicly discussed during their lifetimes; through the 1970s, Edward Kennedy's were probed ceaselessly." But it wasn't just the 1970s, and it wasn't just Edward Kennedy. Character became yet another standard against which to measure all political aspirants, another way for pundits, and opponents, to examine a candidate's fitness for office, so that personal character came to overshadow political character, personal behavior to overshadow political ideas.

And character led to morality. The Kennedys had traded on their moral authority. They had profited from it politically. So had liberalism. Moral authority had, indeed, helped sustain liberalism when the benefices of the New Deal had been so assimilated into American politics that they were no longer identified as liberal. But just as Chappaquiddick fixed a lens on personal character, so, too, did it fix a lens on moral authority—in the first instance, Ted's. Of Mary Jo Kopechne and Ted Kennedy, Charles Pierce would write in *The Boston Globe*, "She denies to him forever the moral credibility that lay behind not merely all those rhetorical thunderclaps that came so easily to the New Frontier, but also Robert Kennedy's anguished appeal to the country's better angels. He [Ted] was forced from the rhetoric of moral outrage into the incremental nitty-gritty of social justice. He learned to plod because soaring made him look ridiculous." And the loss was not only Ted Kennedy's. To the extent that Ted Kennedy had become the face and the voice of modern liberalism, the liberals' shadow president and the only figure in the party with the Kennedy inheritance, it was liberalism's loss as well—a devastating loss—the loss of its moral authority, an especially powerful tool in contrast to Richard Nixon, whose moral authority was suspect. "He took us with him over that bridge," Senator Walter Mondale would lament of Ted, "because he was sort of our star. I think if that hadn't happened, he might have been in the White House himself. There was a huge transition period there that we had to go through because the parameters of his leadership had been damaged." A "party left groping for a center," wrote one columnist of the Democrats after Chappaquiddick. A "serious blow to our party and country," Democrat Joseph Califano Jr., Lyndon Johnson's aide and later Jimmy Carter's secretary of Health, Education, and Welfare, would say. It was a blow from which liberalism and the Democratic party never fully recovered.

And once on the wrong side of destiny, Ted Kennedy could not find his way back to the right side. Chappaquiddick was indelible—a stain he bore that no amount of penance could erase. He tried. Racked by guilt over not having been able to save Mary Jo, he felt that the $50,000 benefit from his auto insurance to the Kopechnes was inadequate, so he asked them to choose an actuary, who recommended an additional $90,904, which he paid himself. And he would meet again, twice, with the Kopechnes—once in May 1970 at the New York City Central Park South apartment maintained by Rose, where he said yet again in explanation that he had headed down the wrong road, and then at his Virginia home. Dun Gifford, who drove the Kopechnes back to their home after the New York meeting, said they told him they were satisfied with Ted's explanation, but twenty years later they were howling at fate themselves, and Mrs. Kopechne was asking a journalist, "Can't he relieve us of this? Isn't there something he could tell me that would lift this heavy, heavy burden from my heart?" He couldn't. There wasn't.

Nor would there be relief for him. Shortly after Chappaquiddick, before the press had turned against Teddy, before it had reconstituted Chappaquiddick as an example of Ted Kennedy's irresponsibility rather than as another Kennedy tragedy, *Boston Globe* reporter Martin Nolan wrote an article in tribute to Mary Jo and said that when she was vindicated of the malicious gossip against her, there would be no bands playing and no lawyers with leather briefcases, as there would be for Ted. And after Ted returned to Washington, Nolan said he got a call from Ted's press secretary, Dick Drayne, who told him Ted wanted to see him. Nolan went to Ted's office in the Capitol tentatively, expecting Ted to reproach him. But when Nolan entered and tried to welcome Ted back with a cheerful salutation, Ted, still using his silver-headed cane, said nothing, but hobbled over to him, put his head on Nolan's shoulder, and sobbed.

Indelible was the stain. Chicago columnist Mike Royko said he once mentioned that Ted Kennedy's phone number was similar to that of a pizzeria and that Kennedy kept getting calls to order a pie. "Bam!" said Royko. If you wrote *anything* about the Kennedys, the next day's mail was "all about Chappaquiddick." Republican senator Alan Simpson remembered getting off the Capitol subway with Ted early one morning and a woman coming up to Ted—"nasty, very aggressive." She snapped, "What you did, leaving that woman in that car, was shameful." And Ted, with no one around but Simpson and the woman, said softly to her, penitently, "It is with me every day of my life." *Every day.* "I will never escape the realization and the belief and feeling that I bear a very heavy responsibility for it," he would tell *The Boston Globe* five years later, "and it is one which I do today bear responsibility for, and I did then and I will for the rest of my life." It "haunts me every day of my life," he would write in his memoir. He seldom spoke of it. Rose said that she never discussed it with him. His son Patrick said he only spoke of it once to him, when Patrick was a boy and another Chappaquiddick anniversary was approaching and the two took a walk on the beach. "His face was pure anguish," Patrick would write. "And all he said was, 'You're going to hear a lot of people talking about what happened at Chappaquiddick, and I just want you to know how bad I feel about everything, and I'm really sorry you have to hear about it.'" And then he fell into silence.

Indelible was the stain. Joyce Carol Oates would write a novella titled *Black Water,* a very thinly veiled *roman à clef* about a powerful, sexually predatory senator who romances a young woman during a Fourth of July celebration, convinces her to drive off with him to his hotel, and then crashes through a guardrail into a marsh on the way to the ferry, leaving the girl to expire in the car. (She narrates the novella as her lungs are filling with "black water.") And there would be a 2018 film titled *Chappaquiddick,* in which Ted is depicted as infantile, self-interested, cowardly, sniveling, unconcerned with Mary Jo while he ponders how to save his political career by shifting blame. These were two iterations of Ted Kennedy—one heartless, even monstrous, the other weak and hollow. Though different, both would play on the idea of the impunity of power and the arrogance of privilege—the idea that Ted failed to act because he had always expected his father to clean up his messes and had escaped punishment because, as a Kennedy, he was too powerful to be punished. But in real life, stroke-crippled Joe Kennedy was in no position to clean up a mess—*Chappaquiddick* has him drooling the word "alibi" to his son, when he had been mute for years. (That the film received generally favorable reviews as an allegedly honest retelling of the story spoke to the endurance of the hostility to Ted Kennedy and resentment of the Kennedys generally as well as to the magical hold of conspiracy.) In real life, instead of shaking off the tragedy, Ted Kennedy, who had been afflicted so often, would now be afflicted forever. "He set out to achieve such wonderful things, bold, courageous things in public life," John Tunney would say of the effects of Chappaquiddick on Ted, "and all of a sudden, he is looked upon as being something quite different from that." On the tenth anniversary of the accident, Ted told *The New York Times* that Chappaquiddick had changed not only the perception of him but had changed him, had forced him into a "greater reexamination of my own life, my own values, the importance of family, faith, the question of continuation of involvement in public life." And he would tell CBS newsman Roger Mudd that he was a "different person than prior to that tragedy. I know just from my inner views or inner attitudes about life and people and faith in God. I am a different person."

"What agonies of remorse has he reserved for himself?" one commentator asked rhetorically in *The New York Times* shortly after the accident. For Ted Kennedy after Chappaquiddick, those agonies, while in no way comparable to those of the Kopechnes, would be deep, they would be daily, and they would be lasting.

THIRTEEN

Starting from Scratch

TED KENNEDY RETURNED to the Senate on July 31, less than two weeks after the incident on Chappaquiddick, but it was not the triumphant return he had experienced after his plane crash or after Bobby's death the year before. He was driven up to the Capitol in a blue convertible by his old Harvard football friend Claude Hooten—Ted's license had been suspended for a year after leaving the scene of the accident—where police escorted him through a crush of reporters and spectators on the Capitol steps, a horde that followed him into the building, shouting questions at him, until he stopped briefly outside the Senate chamber to look at a news ticker, then entered the chamber and headed to Majority Leader Mike Mansfield's desk. "I'm glad you're back," Mansfield told him. "This is where you belong." Ted had already released a statement the day before in which he said that he would run for reelection in 1970, having determined that the informal Massachusetts plebiscite had gone in his favor, and, if victorious, that he intended to serve his entire Senate term and would not run for president in 1972. Though he was received warmly on his arrival by his colleagues—Muskie spent several minutes at Ted's desk and squeezed his arm; other senators approached him to say hello—he was "terse and solemn," wrote one reporter, "slouching . . . distracted, almost as if not wanting to be seen," wrote another, "thinner and perceptibly grimmer," wrote a third, and "dejected, bedraggled-looking," wrote a fourth when Ted joined a contingent of other senators to greet Nixon on the president's return from a world trip a few days later. He had lost so much weight that his blue suit seemed to hang on him. He had come back to argue against the anti-ballistic missile system for which President Nixon had fought so forcefully in the spring and against which Ted had fought just as forcefully. If his mood was tense, defeated, it was also ruminative and penitent. The day of his return, he lunched with former Massachusetts Democratic chairman Lester Hyman, at Ted's desk. Hyman said that as soon as he began to speak, before he had even gotten a word out, Ted raised his hand, "just like a little kid," and said, "Lester, I swear to God, I had nothing to do with Mary Jo Kopechne, and I was not drunk." Hyman expressed his belief in Ted's oath but said the real problem had not been the accident but Ted's conduct afterward. "Well, let me explain that to you," Ted said, but just at that moment the Senate buzzer sounded, calling the senators to the chamber for a vote, and Ted got up to leave. "By the time he came back," Hyman said, "he wasn't ready to talk anymore, and I always wondered what he would have said," though it is highly doubtful he would have said anything he had not already said. Ted had another long talk shortly after his return, this one with Senator Phil Hart, one of Ted's Senate mentors and a man often called "the conscience of the Senate," though the content of that conversation was never divulged.

Ted had been welcomed with "genuine warmth and affection," columnist Drew Pearson reported, but Pearson also cited "old Senate hands" who questioned, as the press had, "whether he can continue to be effective following the tragedy of Chappaquiddick." That first week back, when he delivered his speech on the Senate floor supporting a bill by Phil Hart and Republican senator John Sherman Cooper to stop the ABM program, few senators were there to listen, and though some who were commended Ted for the speech, and though Hart called it a "hallmark of his entire distinguished career in the Senate," the bill failed when Vice President Spiro Agnew cast a tie-breaking vote for the Safeguard system to proceed. Ted suffered a similar result with a package of amendments to Nixon's tax-reform bill, including a minimum tax for the wealthy and an increase in the capital-gains tax. His arguments were delivered haltingly, by one account, and without "his usual well-founded sense of political assurance," and the amendments failed by large margins. They were likely to have failed anyway—but the margins of the loss suggested that Ted's shadow presidency was over.

His confidence was shaken too. "Kennedy looked and acted like a man in ruins," Sylvia Wright reported that October in *Life* of Ted's return. "He seemed devastated. The massive body had grown thin"—yet another observation on his weight—"the jowls which had always made him seem like a caricature of himself were barely noticeable. The ashen face was melted down, leaving a bone structure so visible that one could only think that there, under all that cheek and baby fat, had been the face of his brother Bobby all the time." (It was the same remark a visitor to Hyannis had made to a reporter after Chappaquiddick.) "The tortured eyes looked out tentatively, seeking signs of loyalty or defection, then were cast down again. He walked and moved more softly, more slowly." Ted himself would later describe this period as "sort of living in a nightmare." He said, "You would wake up and this would not have happened. It was really too much for me to take in and absorb and try and think through. I kept thinking, 'This isn't [real]—I'm going to wake up and we're going to be headed down the dock for the next day's race.'" And he said the sense of unreality stayed with him for a "considerable period of time"—one staffer told journalist William Honan that Ted often mused over whether his travails would ever end or "if they will just go on and on and on"—but he admitted that he "should have had a different frame of mind . . . from the time of the accident on, instead of a state of almost disbelief. . . ." Arthur Schlesinger Jr. visited him at Hyannis Port later that summer after Chappaquiddick, just after he had returned to the Senate, and wrote in his journal of how sad it was to see him, sadder even "in a more painful way" than in 1964 after Jack's death and in 1968 after Bobby's, because Ted's wounds were self-inflicted. "When I first saw Ted," Schlesinger wrote, "we were playing tennis. He came in from sailing and sat down to watch us. He looked terrible and, for a moment, his glance was averted, as if he was not sure whether I would wish to greet him." They would speak at length that Sunday morning, with Ted yet again expressing how inexcusable and indefensible his behavior had been after the accident. "He talked calmly and sorrowfully but seemed to exude a sense of defeat." And Schlesinger said that his spirits revived only when he talked about the Senate. Yet another account, in *Time*, described his "sallow" complexion and noted that his "bright blue and usually merry eyes had become dull and distracted." He greeted old acquaintances with a "hesitant, questioning glance," as he had greeted Schlesinger, and with the doubts about their loyalties that Schlesinger had detected. He avoided looking people in the eye. "There are moments when shadows fall across his face," Mike Mansfield told Honan. It was not when he spoke of his brothers, Mansfield said, because he had learned to deal with those losses. "But at certain times, for no palpable reason, he will withdraw into himself. Not for long—just for a few moments. Then someone will make a remark, and he'll snap out of it." And a Massachusetts congressman told Honan the same thing: "Whenever I am with him, I get the feeling that he is constantly thinking of other things—that his mind is elsewhere." An aide told biographer Lester David that he would "listen to you and begin an answer." But "pretty soon you would see his eyes move from you to a corner of the room or a faraway point, if we were outside, and his words would just fade away. You knew what he was thinking, and it was hurting like hell, and there wasn't a damn thing either he or you could do about it." He went sailing for three days that summer, but he couldn't escape. "This was a summer I was anxious to have end," he told friends.

And though Schlesinger said that Ted's spirits had revived when he talked of his Senate work to come, he could not shake his malaise when he returned to the chamber. Walter Mondale said he admired his "courage to walk on the Senate floor the first time after he got back from Chappaquiddick," admired that "he got right up and tried to function, for Senate purposes, as if nothing had happened, and that he tried to hold on to his leadership position in the Senate caucus and tried to reassert his leadership role in the Senate on progressive issues," admired all of these things but also said, "It was painful"—painful because, while he tried to act as if nothing had happened, he didn't succeed. But it wasn't so much how Ted looked now or how he acted, which was defeated and deflated, that testified to his downfall; it was how he was regarded by his colleagues. "He was still liked and admired, to be sure," Robert Sherrill would write, "but he was also subject now to the one leprous and untenable quality in politics: pity." One of Ted's aides told Burton Hersh, "These guys are all traders of power, legal prestige, moxie, and when it becomes obvious that you are no longer a presidential candidate, you lose a lot. I don't think they liked him any less. They just needed him less." A senator told Hersh, "Whenever he was around here, he was like . . . like a god. Now he's . . . just another man." A former aide to Lyndon Johnson, who had obvious contempt for Ted, said, "He can't even make those lighthearted speeches and tell the Irish tales he was so good at. That won't sit well. He can't lead a crusade either. He can never moralize again. He is finished." And still another senator told William Honan that if Ted was going to reestablish his clout after Chappaquiddick had destroyed it, he would have to "start all over again from scratch."

Even some members of Ted's staff had their doubts about him after Chappaquiddick. For some there was what Sylvia Wright described as an almost "manic gaiety," meant to buoy his sagging spirits as they reviewed the hate mail that had poured in and checked on old speaking invitations to see if they were still valid. But there were tensions. Nance Lyons, the only one of the boiler-room girls who was on Ted's staff, said she stayed because "one didn't want to jump off a sinking boat, or look like that," and Ted's boat was certainly sinking. Still, she said, she was made to feel uncomfortable in the office—by the staff, some of whom seemed to blame her for Chappaquiddick, and by Ted himself, for whom she was undoubtedly a constant reminder of the tragedy, especially since she was the one who had talked him into going. Though she worked within ten feet of his office, she said, he "never, never asked how I was doing or said how sorry he was that I and the other women were subjected to such scrutiny." Nor did he ever thank her for supporting him or mention Mary Jo to her—"no call during each year's anniversary scrutiny." She felt that was "unbelievable," and she would never forgive him for what she called his "insensitivity." Even though Ted already knew she wanted to leave the staff and even though she stayed long after Chappaquiddick, she assumed that he had engineered her departure, having one of his associates in New York offer her a job.

But there was a bigger departure: Dave Burke, Ted's administrative assistant, his right-hand man, the person who had built the staff, guided Ted, and even, in some ways, shaped him. Burke was a straight-arrow—a Catholic moralist—someone who had kept Ted in check because Ted was afraid to disappoint him. On the staff, he was called "Monsignor" for his rectitude. But Chappaquiddick had had the same effect on his regard for Ted as it had had on so many others. He had lost faith in him. "Chappaquiddick was a bad event for me," Burke would say years later, "and it tore a lot of foundations away that had been holding me up. His behavior had been on and off, errant on many occasions, and I heard, 'That's all right. We'll always see our way through. it.'" But this time, Burke couldn't see through it. This time, Burke couldn't excuse Ted. Burke's wife said it was like creating a "sculpture and all of a sudden it melts." Burke had threatened for years to leave for a better-paying job—his wife, Beatrice, said he was seldom home during the years he worked for Ted—only to have Ted coax him back with the lure of important legislation and the ongoing tease of the presidency. Now the legislation would be more difficult. Now the presidency was lost. Beatrice Burke said she didn't remember the day her husband told Ted he was leaving, nor does she remember her husband telling her Ted's reaction. His leaving just seemed inevitable. The Monsignor moved on. Others couldn't excuse Ted's behavior either. They left too, their faith betrayed.

Even Ted wasn't sure he could start over in the Senate, wasn't sure he would be *accepted* doing that. "I thought there was still the possibility to regain confidence and regain trust and regain support," he said years later of that period. "I believed that, but I wasn't absolutely sure. I knew that the only way you're going to do it is a lot of—lot of hard work, a lot of slogging away, and a lot of working with colleagues and deference to them, you know, re-earning your stripes, so to speak. So that's what I did."

He started from scratch. He applied himself as he had applied himself when he had entered the Senate—no longer a shadow president but a fledgling again. And yet, as a fledgling, he faced setbacks—the rejection of his anti-ABM position, of his tax amendments, of an amendment to include ammunition in the Gun Control Act of 1968. The consensus was that he had lost not only his status but his effectiveness when he lost his presidential prospects. And he had lost more than his presidential prospects. The Chappaquiddick accident had cost him his moral authority, which may have been even more important than his presidential potential in his accrual of power. But a few years later Warren Weaver wrote in *Esquire* that the press had underestimated Ted Kennedy's resilience in this period, underestimated his ability to get things done; Weaver thought that when they depreciated his efforts, "it simply means that he is not impressing a group of people [the press] who no longer watch him as closely or with the same mixture of fascination, envy, and fear." And Weaver added that he detected a "lurking feeling" in the press that Chappaquiddick was a betrayal of *them* and that, by destroying his presidential candidacy, Ted had ended a "great unfolding story," that to the media now "everything that has happened since is of modest consequence, a flawed record at best." As early as October, *Time* made the same determination that Weaver would. Ted had returned as that man in ruins, it reported, but he had quickly restored himself, regained, at least superficially, some of the confidence he seemed to have lost just a few months earlier.

In some ways, he had no choice. Despite all his ruminations on other possible professional avenues, there really were no other avenues. Ted Kennedy was a politician, and he realized as well as anyone that a spent politician was a worthless politician. There was no reason for him to be in the Senate if he wasn't going to advance his causes, and he knew this too:

If he wasn't going to advance his causes, if he wasn't going to challenge Nixon, who would? Carey Parker thought he arrived back in the Senate with "much of the same spirit, at least outwardly." (Parker said he couldn't speak to what Ted was feeling inwardly.) Sylvia Wright thought that after his brief slough through July, August, and much of September, he had become increasingly combative, even cocky. When the Federal Trade commissioner Paul Dixon, testifying before Ted's AdPrac Subcommittee, said he felt the subcommittee members were laughing at him, Ted asked him to whom he was referring. "I don't see anyone here laughing. I don't think anyone here would do that. Is it all right if they smile? Can we smile? Would that just be okay?" The *Los Angeles Times* called him "aggressive." The twenty-pound post-Chappaquiddick weight loss, which had made him seem haggard that first month, now made him seem in fighting trim, prompting a joke about him: "There must be an easier way to lose weight." And *Time* observed that he was "clear-eyed, the puffy jowls are gone, his hair is razor-cut in the back with the sideburns shorter. His handshake is firm once again." And it cited an incident of Ted rushing to a Senate–House conference when a father was about to snap a picture of him. Ted stopped, asked the man's wife and teenage daughter to stand with him, and invited the man to snap away. "A few weeks ago," *Time* wrote, "Kennedy would have walked by with his eyes on the floor."

There were those who believed that the accident at Chappaquiddick had made him a better senator, and that, as Arthur Schlesinger Jr. said, "the iron went into Edward Kennedy's soul." Always diligent, he became even more so, some felt, once he collected himself after Chappaquiddick, versing himself in Senate procedural rules so that he could be a more effective whip. His aide Robert Bates thought that once Chappaquiddick wrecked his presidential chances, he refocused himself on Senate business. "There was a redirecting of ambitions," Bates said. "He had to figure out which way to go. And I think he felt the weight of that and threw himself into his work, and it allowed him to become a more serious legislator." Robert Sherrill, a Kennedy critic, believed that Chappaquiddick liberated him, "giving him the recklessness of despair" that "turned him into a superior senator"—a senator who would later stand up to hostile audiences rather than pander to them, because he felt he had nothing to lose. And there was certainly the possibility that for Ted Kennedy, for whom sin and repentance were such central features of his belief system, Chappaquiddick represented the biggest sin and being a truly great senator the only commensurate penance. Everything he did as a legislator would have to be better now, not just to regain his effectiveness but to try to erase the stain—the stain of Chappaquiddick.

He resumed his battle late that September by renewing his protest against the war in Vietnam, taking what *Time* called a "routine dinner speech" before an American Cancer Society fundraiser in Boston and turning it into an attack on Nixon's war policy with, *Time* said, "even more sting than before." He called Vietnam "difficult to justify, impossible to win, a war not worthy of our lives and efforts, a conflict that has made us ill as a people as surely as any disease that attacks the body." He scolded the administration for having made "only token troop withdrawals on the battlefield" and accused it of an "exercise in politics and improvisation." And he said there would be no peace so long as Nixon insisted on propping up the current South Vietnamese government, which itself was refusing any postwar power-sharing coalition. "Why should General Thieu control the destiny of America or dictate the future of young American lives?" he questioned. But what made this appearance more notable than the brio of his attack was that he felt he could make a moral argument again—this from a man who had been morally castigated for his behavior at Chappaquiddick just two months earlier. (It was a kind of hubris that he did, since Chappaquiddick had hardly been expunged.) And what made it more notable still was that, beyond the politics of it, Ted seemed finally at ease, finally able to come out of hiding, finally not ashamed of himself. Reporting on how he circulated through the audience before the speech, Sylvia Wright reported, "He nodded, leaned over again and again to whisper and grin, laughed as he listened to smiling faces, pointed and gestured almost playfully when he spotted familiar ones." When he met with the Democratic National Committee that same week and was warmly received, an aide said, "It made him realize that he's still a voice to be listened to." And he realized that somehow the accident hadn't destroyed him as completely as he had feared, which may have spoken to how much his party really needed him to battle Richard Nixon.

The proof was that Richard Nixon's aides were listening. The day after Ted's speech, Lyn Nofziger, Nixon's deputy assistant for Congressional Relations, wrote a memo to Bryce Harlow, the head of Nixon's Congressional Relations office, suggesting how to counterattack: "I think that first we should get general agreement from the leadership that Teddy Kennedy is not sacrosanct *for any reason* and that they should attack him wherever he is vulnerable." And as to those vulnerabilities, Nofziger wrote: "For instance, I see no reason someone should not refer to those who desert their friends in their hour of deepest need, who make a habit of running at the moment of crisis, and who put their own political interests before their obligations to their fellow man," though Nofziger added this should be done "subtly," as if his references to Mary Jo Kopechne's death were subtle. Above all, he said, "We should make it clear that Teddy Kennedy is not to discuss the great issues of war and peace and honor and decency—with impunity." And he said he didn't think the Democratic leadership would have the "gall" to defend Ted. Nixon himself called Ted's speech "irresponsible" but thought it "clever" of Ted to deliver it as a way of deflecting attention from Chappaquiddick. And Nixon told his underlings to circulate the fact that the North Vietnamese had used Ted's remarks to try to undermine the administration. "It is absolutely essential," said a Nixon memo to H. R. Haldeman, "that we react insurmountably and powerfully to blunt this attack."

But Ted, perhaps because he had been so bloodied, suddenly seemed unbowed. In that same speech at the Cancer Society fundraiser, he had taken on another cause. Nixon had nominated Fourth Circuit Court of Appeals judge Clement Haynsworth to replace Abe Fortas on the Supreme Court, when Fortas, a close associate and friend of Lyndon Johnson's and a Johnson appointee, was forced to resign for financial improprieties. The right had long sought to curb the liberal Warren Court, the court of chief justice and Eisenhower appointee Earl Warren, the court that had outlawed school desegregation in *Brown v. Board of Education,* that had overruled anti-miscegenation laws in *Loving v. Virginia,* that had equalized voting rights with one man, one vote in *Baker v. Carr, Reynolds v. Sims,* and *Wesberry v. Sanders,* that had given impoverished criminal defendants representation in *Gideon v. Wainwright* and ordered police to read them their rights in *Miranda v. Arizona,* that had enlarged the right to privacy and access to contraception in *Griswold v. Connecticut,* that had forbidden school prayer in *Engel v. Vitale,* and hundreds of other cases that changed the face of America and that enraged conservatives who detested the changes. One conservative, Yale law professor Alexander Bickel, lambasted the court for imposing "moral imperatives" and establishing a "dictatorship of the self-righteous." The Warren Court was as much an engine of the liberal transformation of America in the 1960s as John Ken-

nedy or Lyndon Johnson had been, probably more. IMPEACH EARL WAR-
REN read billboards that dotted the countryside where conservatives felt
their America under siege. And now Richard Nixon had his chance to arrest and even roll back those changes. Warren had resigned in 1968,
awaiting a successor, who was to be Associate Justice Abe Fortas, before
Fortas's resignation under duress. Nixon appointed a Warren critic, District of Columbia Court of Appeals judge Warren Burger, to replace him.
A moderate judge, a traditional legal intellect, he was confirmed with little
debate.

But Haynsworth was another matter. Nixon had clearly made the
nomination with the intent of turning the court to the right—first Burger
for Warren, and now Haynsworth for Fortas. Despite a distinguished legal
reputation, Haynsworth, a South Carolinian, was suspected by liberal
Democrats of being less than fully committed to civil rights, which was
Phil Hart's line of attack against him. Ted, still in his post-Chappaquiddick
retreat, did not take the lead in the fight. Birch Bayh did. And Ted had no
particular grievance against Haynsworth. (After the battle, Ted would
say that Haynsworth, who was one of the judges of Ted's great mock-trial
victory at the University of Virginia, told Ted that he had voted for him.)
His opposition to it, he said, built slowly, "cumulatively," beginning with
accusations that Judge Haynsworth had a conflict of interest when he
heard a case involving an unfair labor practice against a company that
had contracts with a vending-machine business in which he owned a
small stake. In failing to reveal that conflict, Haynsworth was not "completely frank with the [Judiciary] committee," said Ted, though what
seemed to rankle Ted was when Haynsworth declared that Bobby had
cleared him of any conflict of interest, to which Ted snapped that Bobby
had done no such thing; he had only cleared Haynsworth of any criminal
conduct. Ted also thought that Haynsworth was being "canny" in dodg-
ing Ted's questioning during the confirmation hearing. Then came information about Haynsworth slowing the pace of desegregation, which
prompted Ted to say he was not a "contemporary man of the times." Still,
Haynsworth was approved by the Judiciary Committee, 10 to 7. And then,
as Ted put it, "the bottom really fell out for him fast," not because of any
one thing, or even because of an accumulation of small infractions, but
because of what liberals thought he represented. In the end, he was defeated on the Senate floor, 55 to 45, with seventeen Republicans voting

against him—the first Supreme Court nominee not to be confirmed since 1930.

Now Nixon was furious, and, as Ted put it, he ordered Harry Dent, another South Carolinian and Nixon's liaison to the state Republican parties, to find him a nominee further to the right than Haynsworth. Dent found him: G. Harrold Carswell. Haynsworth had been a Harvard Law graduate and a respected judge. Carswell was something else—a graduate of Mercer Law School, where he had not made law review, and someone who had written not a single article for a law journal since. Moreover, 58 percent of his decisions had been reversed. (Upon the nomination, *The New York Times* ran an article titled "Carswell May Make Some People Long for Haynsworth.") "Vengeance" is how one moderate Republican senator described the nomination, after learning that the Justice Department had rated Carswell well down the list of prospective candidates. Vengeance "to make us sorry we hadn't accepted Haynsworth, and at the same time," said the senator, "it was an attempt to downgrade the Supreme Court and implement the Southern strategy," which was Nixon's attempt to placate the South and thus woo it away from its Democratic tradition. Jim Flug, Ted's Judiciary aide, was incensed by the nomination. According to Richard Harris, who chronicled the fight for *The New Yorker*, Flug and Ted met on January 23 in Birch Bayh's office with a group dedicated to defeating Carswell—a group that included Joseph Tydings, who had been one of the leaders in the Haynsworth defeat; Phil Hart; Joe Rauh, the civil-liberties attorney who had helped Ted on the poll-tax amendment; Clarence Mitchell, the director of the Washington bureau of the NAACP; Marian Wright Edelman, a black activist; Andrew Biemiller and Thomas Harris of the AFL, and Brad Brasfield of the UAW; and Verlin Nelson of Americans for Democratic Action. The consensus was that it would be nearly impossible to stop Carswell, especially after Haynsworth's defeat, since there was little appetite for another battle. And because it was nearly impossible, there was little enthusiasm to take it on. "No one was jumping up to lead it" was how Jim Flug put it. As Harris reported it, Hart had been a defender of Abe Fortas and had been sullied for it. Bayh had already led the Haynsworth fight and was girding for another against Carswell, but his staff warned him that doing so might cost him Republican votes on an issue to which he was deeply devoted: a constitutional amendment to end the Electoral College. Tydings grudgingly agreed to lead the fight and accepted the responsibility at a meeting of the Leadership Conference on Civil Rights, but then Bayh followed him with a speech—a "stemwinder," Harris called it—that so energized both the conference and Bayh himself that he offered to lead the battle again, as he had against Haynsworth.

Bayh was now the face of the opposition, but working behind the scenes was Jim Flug, who believed that Carswell could be beaten and convinced Ted to join the fight. "Huge, huge amounts of work—not all of it, but huge amounts of it—were done by them," *Boston Globe* reporter Thomas Oliphant recalled, meaning Flug and Ted, though he also said that because of the stigma of Chappaquiddick, Ted "left no fingerprints," even as he was engineering the defeat. Flug wrote a memo, a tough memo, pointing out Carswell's deficiencies, not least of which was that he was a racist, and he suggested that Ted ask James Eastland, the Judiciary chairman, to postpone the hearings while the opposition could muster its forces. Eastland, a racist himself, refused. And Flug, whose broad smile and bright eyes belied his tenacity, convened a meeting of Senate staffers at which he invited Joe Rauh to lay out the case against Carswell as a way of bucking up the staffers' spirits and convincing them the nomination could be beaten. (He would hold meetings with these staffers throughout the hearings and the debate. "Monday Morning Meetings," they were called.) Meanwhile, Flug, in a flurry of subsequent memos, compiled evidence of Carswell's racial prejudice, including his refusal to desegregate a municipal golf course in Florida while he was United States attorney there.

Carswell had Nixon, but he didn't have much else. Only eleven of the nineteen active and retired justices of the Fifth Circuit Court of Appeals, on which Carswell sat, endorsed him. And then there were the witnesses. Testifying before the Judiciary Committee, several attorneys claimed Carswell had been "insulting and hostile" to black and civil rights lawyers and had even advised one city prosecutor on how to avoid a civil rights law. Yale Law School dean Louis Pollak said Carswell had "the most slender credentials of any man put forward in this century for the Supreme Court." (During the floor debate, Roman Hruska, a Nebraska Republican, would defend Carswell on the basis that "mediocre judges and people and lawyers" are "entitled to a little bit of representation, aren't they?") Edward Brooke, Ted's junior colleague from Massachusetts and the only black senator, read a speech on the floor that Carswell had delivered in

1948 to the American Legion, in which the prospective Supreme Court justice declared, "I believe that segregation of the races is proper and the only practical and correct way of life in our states. I have always so believed, and I shall always so act," and in the speech Carswell firmly committed himself to "the principles of white supremacy." (Carswell repudiated the statement.) Still, as the case against Carswell mounted, only three senators—not including Ted—had publicly announced their opposition to him before the hearings concluded. And when the hearings did conclude, and Judiciary took its vote on February 16, Carswell's nomination was reported to the floor, 17-4, with Ted, Bayh, Hart, and Tydings the nay votes. (Ted, bedridden with pneumonia in Palm Beach, telephoned in his vote.) But even then, even though the odds against defeating the nomination seemed long, Flug shot Ted another memo, this one titled, "How to Beat Carswell." In it, he wrote: "I smell blood."

The blood Flug smelled was the accumulation of many drops—from Carswell's seeming racism to his legal mediocrity to his ethical lapses for hearing cases involving clients he had once represented. (When Ted asked for a list, Minority Leader Robert Griffin, implicitly invoking Chappaquiddick, questioned Ted's integrity, which, Richard Harris observed, made Ted even more hostile to the nominee.) The long consideration—the committee delays, a decision by Mike Mansfield to postpone a vote until after voting on an extension of the Voting Rights Act, an unsuccessful attempt to get the nomination recommitted to Judiciary, a prolonged three-and-a-half-week floor debate—had taken its toll on Carswell's support and on the idea that the Senate, having rejected Haynsworth, now had to bow to Nixon's wishes on Carswell. "Can we accept the proposition that the appointment of a Supreme Court justice is the president's own to make, unfettered by Senate review?" Ted asked sarcastically during the debate, in a comment that would reverberate for years to come in later debates over Supreme Court nominees. It was a contentious debate, a vicious debate. At one point during that debate, two Republican senators, Edward Gurney of Florida and Robert Dole of Kansas, raised the issue of Frank Morrissey, which sent Ted bolting from the cloakroom to the Senate floor and arguing vehemently that when Morrissey's nomination had faced opposition, he withdrew it. And then, his anger dissipating, he smiled and suggested that the Republicans do the same with Carswell.

And it wasn't just the debate that drew blood. *Boston Globe* reporter Thomas Oliphant remembered getting a call the weekend before the vote from Flug, who passed a tip to Oliphant on the condition that Flug not be on the record. The tip was that the vacancy on the Supreme Court had also opened a vacancy for a justice to oversee the First Circuit, which covered New England, and that Carswell would be appointed that justice. And Flug knew the effect of that news—knew that there was a Republican senator in New England who was wavering over her vote: Margaret Chase Smith of Maine. Oliphant printed the story, presumably Smith read it, and she decided to vote against Carswell. "Not a fingerprint," Oliphant said.

And so, despite the traditional deference to a president's nominees, the Senate, after four months of deliberation, rejected Carswell as it had rejected Haynsworth, 51 to 45, with thirteen Republicans voting this time with the liberal Democrats against him, and seventeen Southern Democrats voting with the Republicans for him. "By the end of it, I thought Carswell was a kind of buffoon," Ted would recall. "I didn't have any respect for him at all, but you couldn't help having some respect for Haynsworth. He had been an important jurist." And Ted said, "I never relished the thought of defeating these people." But Flug, who had goaded Ted into action and had goaded him to forget Chappaquiddick for this fight, did relish the thought. When the vote was taken, he was at the back of the chamber, "laughing and weeping at the same time," as Harris reported it. "I just can't believe it," Flug kept repeating to himself. "It's too good to believe." Carswell declared for the Senate shortly thereafter—he lost—and Nixon would appoint Harry Blackmun, a comparative moderate, to the seat. But Nixon was so enraged by the defeat that, as Haldeman wrote in his diary, he "wants to step up political attack. Investigators on Kennedy and Muskie plus Bayh and Proxmire," meaning that Jack Caulfield and Tony Ulasewicz, the two former detectives who had been put on Ted's tail after Chappaquiddick, would be ordered back into action to find dirt. As Nixon put it to Haldeman: "Have to declare war."

II

Ted Kennedy, who had expected Chappaquiddick to destroy his career, had actually been liberated by it, convincing himself that he had been so degraded that he had nothing left to lose. But he did. There had always been a pair of eyes watching him, judging him, measuring him against his brothers. For years—ever since his stroke in 1961—Joseph Kennedy had been a shadow of his former self: incapacitated, unable to speak and communicating by grunts, unable to give advice, sequestered from the tragedies that had befallen the family. His grandson Christopher Lawford said that Joe would be brought down in his elevator by Ann Gargan and set before the window so that he could look out across the broad Hyannis lawn at the ocean. He would be surrounded by pillows on which his favorite sayings had been embroidered: "Applesauce!" "You're dipping into your capital!" "You have just made a political contribution," which meant, Lawford said, that Joe had tithed his children's bank accounts to contribute to Jack's or Bobby's or Ted's campaigns. Ted had said that he became closer to his father just before the stroke in 1961, that he had spent a lot of time with him that summer as Ted was pondering whether to run for the Senate, that he and Joe would go out sailing and that Joe Kennedy had become "focused," as Ted put it, on him and not on his brothers. And then the stroke hit, and Joe had a "terribly difficult time," Ted recalled, and had a "very difficult time from then on." But even mute and disabled, he remained a presence—a powerful presence. Robert Shriver, Eunice's son, said that even after the stroke, his parents were in "fear" of Joe. "Oh, boy, Dad is . . . We have to report to Dad" was the tenor. And as years went on, Ted would frequently quote his father's sayings, aphorisms, words of wisdom: "Well, as my dad always says . . ." It was always to Hyannis that Ted would return when something befell him or when he felt he was on the wrong side of destiny, always to his father, whose approval he sought, though Joe could no longer grant it. Teddy hadn't received the most attention from his father or been held in the highest esteem by him, but he and Joe had that special bond. "The fair-haired boy," Richard Clasby, Jack's old Harvard classmate and frequent visitor to Hyannis, called him. "He could do no wrong in his father's eyes," though, of course, he could do a great deal of wrong. It was just that Joe always forgave him, was far more forgiving with him than with Jack and Bobby. Rita Dallas said that Ted received "no stern looks or reprimands, no impatient frowns" from his father. When Ted would "burst" into his father's room, Joe's face would "light up," she said.

But it became harder to cheer Joe Kennedy as time passed and harder still with the series of tragedies, including Chappaquiddick. Rita Dallas said that Rose and Joe fretted over Ted that summer, "for he seemed to be lonelier and more lost than anyone at the compound," spending long hours with his father, then pulling himself away, often to Joey Gargan, from whom he sought the fraternal companionship that Gargan couldn't possibly provide. And Dallas felt that Joe Kennedy deteriorated after Chappaquiddick, that the accident was one blow too many. (Whether Joe Kennedy really appreciated enough of what had happened to fret or whether this was Dallas's projection is impossible to determine.) That November, Joe Kennedy suffered another stroke, which blinded him and cost him his ability to make any sounds and robbed him of what Dallas said was his "one pleasure": to be with Teddy. Ted implored, "Dad, it's me, Teddy. It's me, Teddy. Can you hear me? Please talk to me. Please answer me." But Joe Kennedy couldn't. As Dallas described the scene, Jackie, Jack's widow, spent the night of November 17 with her father-in-law. In the morning, the nurses were discharged, and Dallas found Ted in the living room with Steve Smith. He was "slumped in a chair, staring moodily out the window, and when he told her she could leave too, he buried his face in his hands. The next morning, she arrived at Joe's room to find Ted there, cocooned in a blanket in a chair next to his father's bed. He left to get breakfast, until Dallas, tending to Joe, alerted the family to come: Jean and Steve Smith, Eunice and Sargent Shriver, Pat, the widows Jackie and Ethel, Ann Gargan. Ted went to get his mother, who then knelt at her husband's bedside and laid her head on his hand and wept. Eunice prayed aloud, and Jackie got a rosary, which Rose brought to Joe's lips and then slid into his hand. And on that November 18, Joe Kennedy, the patriarch, passed away.

It was not easy for Ted. After the funeral—he had spent the night before in a sleeping bag underneath the casket—he walked down the beach with Ann Gargan and his son Patrick and then alone, "letting the tears come, and struggling with thoughts more wrenching than those following any of my previous bereavements"—more wrenching because he wondered "whether I had shortened my father's life from the shock I had visited on him with my news of the tragic accident on Chappaquiddick Island." And he said, "The pain of that burden was almost unbearable." Joe Kennedy had been not only the patriarch of the Kennedys but also the architect of the Kennedys. He had created them all, even as many of them rejected his values and his politics, but perhaps none was as much his creation as Ted, who was forced to conform to the role Joe had designated for him and the course Joe had charted for him; as the youngest, he had the least power to resist. "You'll see a tremendous change in Teddy when his father dies," Joey Gargan had predicted. Gargan was right. Now Ted was more truly alone than he had ever been. But now he was more truly liberated than he had ever been. There was no pair of eyes directing him, watching him, judging him, measuring him against the past. Now it was all up to him—starting from scratch.

He was recovering. *The New York Times*'s James Reston reported that, by January, "the visible edginess of last summer is gone. He now seems a little more solid, a little more composed, and a little more patient with the crowds that still point and mutter as he goes by." That March, *The Boston Globe*'s Martin Nolan brought Washington pundit David Broder to the St. Patrick's Day parade, where Ted was marching. Ted was walking through Dorchester Heights, as his bodyguard, Jim King, "peeled off the older and middle-aged ladies of Wards 6 and 7 from his boss's topcoat," when Ted approached Broder and Nolan and smiled. "In Southie, they love you when you're down," he told them. But that was Southie—Irish Boston. They weren't going to love him everywhere. Reston thought that because of Chappaquiddick, the "routine of living" was going to be a "very complicated business" for Ted Kennedy henceforth, that he "could not go anywhere and not feel on display," and that he now would lead a "calculated life" in which he would be "like an actor going onstage," always on, always wary. And though Ted was easing back into his old gregarious style, another political columnist, Joe Klein, recalled seeing him in a back brace at a Memorial Day Greek picnic later that year, where he seemed to "writhe in the public eye," and also seeing him at a campaign appearance at a supermarket, where he was uncomfortable and stilted. "So, uh, your family, ah, likes . . . meat?" he asked one woman.

On display, calculating his every move, writhing in the public eye—and yet Ted Kennedy continued to subject himself to the exposure in order to do his work and in order to atone for Chappaquiddick. California Assembly speaker Jesse Unruh, who had been one of the forces behind Ted's presidential draft in 1968, thought that Chappaquiddick had made a "hell of a better man out of Ted," that "everything had been so easy for him" until then—which certainly wasn't true—that he was almost "insufferable" after winning the whip, but that he had been humbled by Chappaquiddick. One of Jack Kennedy's former aides, who played tennis with Ted, thought he had changed too. "Teddy bends over backward to be fair, is scrupulous about the calls, always giving advantage to his opponent, and I haven't seen that in any other Kennedy." Arthur Schlesinger Jr. thought that Chappaquiddick infiltrated Ted's politics in a positive way.

"Ever since Chappaquiddick, he has been spending his life trying to redeem himself," Schlesinger told John Gregory Dunne. "I think the cease-
less effort at self-redemption may be for Teddy Kennedy what polio was for
FDR," which had also been said of him about his plane crash.

He had readily accepted the responsibility of being his brothers' heir,
of promoting their causes, of speaking for those whom Bobby especially
had championed. That was his duty as a Kennedy. But after Chappaquiddick, he had rededicated himself, taken it upon himself to be more than his
brothers' legatee. It may have been his only way to expiate the sin of
Chappaquiddick. He wanted to be the voice of the powerless, and if he was
no longer the shadow president that he had been in the early days of the
Nixon administration, he nevertheless rapidly became the single most
powerful proponent of liberalism, the very symbol of liberalism to both
Democrats and Republicans. There were other liberal voices. Ted Kennedy's was the loudest, the most distinctive. Chappaquiddick did it. Stripped
of his moral authority, even ridiculed for the temerity of having used that
authority, he compensated with the intensity of his beliefs and the magnitude of his initiatives. Part of his penance was to be a great senator. But if
he was to be redeemed, truly redeemed, he needed to be more. He needed
to be what Bobby was aspiring to be when he was killed: the senator of all
those in need, all those who had been marginalized, all those who had
been dispossessed, all those who had been beaten down, all those who
were suffering. Ted Kennedy, sent to purgatory by Chappaquiddick, would
be the man to whom those in purgatory could turn.

And this time it wasn't just for Bobby. It was for Ted himself.

None of this was a radical departure for him. In this, he wasn't starting
from scratch. He had been inclined toward social justice from the moment
he entered the Senate, and he saw, as he would recall, that "the wealthiest
individuals and the most powerful corporations had powerful spokesmen
and women speaking for them, in the Finance Committee and the Ways
and Means Committee." But "it's the working American, it's the senior
citizen, it's the young child, it's the small businessman, it's the person
who's concerned about the fragile areas in our environment, the people
who are concerned about a more sensible nuclear arms policy—they
need that spokesman, and that's who I want to speak for, and that's who I
will speak for as long as I have a voice in the Senate." And this would become a mantra, invoking the "voiceless and powerless" and saying, "I'd

like to be their voice, their senator." Or telling an interviewer, "My greatest passion is with regards to the human condition." Or telling a new staffer named Stephen Breyer, later Supreme Court justice Stephen Breyer, "We're going to live up to this thing." Remembering the conversation, Breyer would ask rhetorically, "What is this thing?" The reply: "I can't describe it. But it's not just being a senator." But Breyer knew what exactly it was; it was being the moral force for those who needed it. And even a Republican senator would tell political reporter Richard Reeves, "Whatever you think of Teddy's personal morality, he is a publicly moral man." And in the wake of Chappaquiddick, with, as Ted saw it, his soul at stake, his public morality, that *thing*, would have to salvage the loss of his personal morality. *It was not just being a senator.*

That *thing* had been deep in the Kennedy family. John and Bobby Kennedy had been associated with social progress, albeit, for John, somewhat reluctantly. And yet the question seldom asked was: Why? Why were the Kennedys liberals? The Kennedys were enormously wealthy, and Joe Kennedy was, if anything, a conservative despite his streak of resentment toward his alleged social betters, not unlike Richard Nixon's. Neither his instincts nor his politics spoke of liberalism; they spoke of self-interest. He had given his sons their political independence, encouraged them to blaze their own trails, even as he stage-managed their electoral victories, but Joe Jr., despite his tutelage under the British socialist Harold Laski, had conservative instincts like his father's, and so, too, did John and Robert. Robert served as a counsel on Joe McCarthy's red-baiting Subcommittee on Investigations and later served as chief counsel for the Senate Rackets Committee, as the Select Committee on Improper Activities in Labor and Management was called, in which he conducted hearings that seemed far more interested in union improprieties than in business ones—hearings that many in the labor movement considered anti-labor. There was certainly nothing to distinguish either brother as particularly liberal, and to the extent that John Kennedy moved leftward, it was largely as a concession to Democratic party politics; it was virtually impossible for a conservative to win the party's presidential nomination, and it was the nomination toward which John Kennedy (and his father) had aimed his entire political career. But he changed only in part due to political pressure. As president, he had undergone a kind of Oval Office conversion, introducing the Civil Rights Act and Medicare. Bobby's conversion came later, with Jack's death and Bobby's disappointment with Lyndon Johnson, which forced Bobby into the role of moral avenger. But he changed too—far more radically than Jack had.

Ted Kennedy had inherited that legacy, but it didn't explain fully why he would become the self-appointed liberal gladiator. It didn't explain fully why he would dedicate his life to that *thing*—being the champion of the underprivileged, when there was little to gain politically from doing so, especially as the country was turning rightward under Richard Nixon, turning away from the bigheartedness of the Johnson years and the sense of moral mission that Bobby had stoked, turning against the poor and against black Americans, who had rioted and were portrayed as lawless and undeserving of assistance. In embracing liberalism so tightly, in giving liberalism full voice, in identifying himself so closely with it that liberalism and Ted Kennedy would become inextricably bound up with each other and would remain so, even as Nixon was discrediting liberalism and identifying it with loose morals, sneering elitism, and national dysfunction, Ted Kennedy was delivering a lesson in public morality—in helping the very people that Middle America was now disavowing. His brothers' inheritance did not explain that fully, though it would be Ted Kennedy's life-defining question.

The answer, Ted's widow would say, was "complicated." There was an answer in religion—in the Catholicism that Rose Kennedy, whose life spun around the poles of materialism and piety, took so seriously and that she enforced upon her children, even as the aesthetics of religion seemed to her as important, if not more important, as the spiritualism. Her favorite biblical quotation, one she drilled into her children, was Luke 12:48: "And to whomsoever much is given, of him shall much be required." This was an expectation upon all the Kennedys. John Tunney would cite a "Jesuitical philosophy running through the Kennedy family," which encouraged the "desire to serve," and said that Ted thought of public service as a "higher calling" more than "just being politically successful at what you do." Ted was not generally thought of as religious; he was regarded among the public as the most debauched of the Kennedys, a perception that Chappaquiddick only reinforced. But it was precisely because Ted Kennedy seemed so self-indulgent, at least when it came to drink and women, that his religion came to matter so much to him as a counterweight and a guide to redemption. And Ted would say that the Gospel of Matthew, "in which he calls us to care for the least of these among us, and feed the hungry, clothe the naked, give drink to the thirsty, welcome the stranger, visit the imprisoned," was at the center of his own belief system. "It's enormously significant to me that the only description in the Bible about salvation is tied to one's willingness to act on behalf of one's fellow human beings." He would tell an interviewer, "Choosing a life that helps others" would lead to "our ultimate and eternal reward" in heaven. It would lead to salvation—his own too.

And there was an answer in the Kennedys' sense of grievance, an ongoing sense of grievance, still raw, their wealth and power notwithstanding—grievance over being Irish and Catholic and debarred from so many of the benefits that came naturally to the Protestant Brahmins, a grievance nursed by Joe Kennedy and explained by Honey Fitz, both of whom saw their success as a form of revenge. "The two-dimensional backdrop," Doris Kearns Goodwin called the social scene of Boston: "the Irish versus the Yankees." When asked once why he fought for minorities, Speaker of the House John McCormack, an Irish Bostonian, answered simply: "No Irish need apply." This was burned in Ted Kennedy's consciousness too, by his grandfather Honey Fitz, burned deep, as surely as Luke and Matthew had been burned into his consciousness by his mother. It wasn't only the NO IRISH NEED APPLY sign that Ted kept posted on his wall throughout his life, it was the photograph that hung on a wall at his Washington home—a photograph of the water main being laid on Meridian Street in Boston, the street on which Joe Kennedy had been born, and of the Irish immigrants digging the trenches while the supervisors stood over them, issuing orders. And Ted would recall with bitterness the political structure of Boston in the postwar period, how it was run by a group called VAULT, which, as Ted said, "by its name you can imagine who were the members of it." And those members of VAULT, those Brahmins, made the decisions for the city: who would run for municipal office, where the money would go, what the agenda would be. But they had nothing to do with the ordinary people of the city—the people with whom Ted Kennedy identified. They were like the supervisors on Meridian Street. And Ted Kennedy remembered. "He had access to everything power wise, financially and politically and socially," his son Patrick would say, "and yet he acted as if he was an Irish [kid] who had just gotten off the boat. . . . He was emotional about these things."

And there was an answer for the least of the Kennedys in what he learned from the least fortunate of the Kennedys. If, on his Sunday visits with his grandson, Honey Fitz introduced Ted to the working people of Boston, Ted's sister Rosemary introduced him to the afflicted and challenged. The Kennedys did not coddle Rosemary. Anything but. They tried to disguise her disability, pass her off as perfectly normal. But even as she tried so hard to conform—indeed, *because* she tried so hard to conform— she informed the lives of her brothers and sisters. Ted often cited her as one of the most important influences in his life both personally ("Rosemary enriched the humanity of all of us," he would write in his memoir) and politically, listing her alongside Honey Fitz and his father and his brothers.

But Jack and Bobby had grown up with Rosemary, had known her better than Ted did, and she seemed to have little influence on them. Jack, benumbed by his abundant blessings, was oblivious to the struggles of ordinary people, as oblivious as were the members of VAULT. "Careless days growing up in England, the effortless C's of a young gentleman at Harvard, serving in a Navy without Negroes and then going to Congress before he was thirty years old," Richard Reeves would write of him, "had left him with no particular feelings and great voids of knowledge about the day-to-day lives and cares and prejudices of his fellow Americans." Bobby, whose frailties were far greater than his older brother's, had more feeling. When he worked for his father's Columbia Trust and collected rents at the tenements, he would return to tell his mother about the families huddled in their apartments. But Bobby subordinated whatever feelings he might have had to his brother's political ambitions. He desensitized himself to anything that didn't serve Jack's interests. It was only much later, with Jack's death, that, in the words of the civil rights activist Roger Wilkins, he "became a man who was connected to the world's pain," because he had now experienced such a deep pain himself.

Ted had been directly connected to pain, physically excruciating back pain after the plane crash (Senator Richard Durbin called him "disabled" and said that "at any given moment you can look and see the pain") and equally excruciating emotional pain with the family tragedies he endured, especially the deaths of Jack and Bobby. Those deaths made him bereft and forced him to find a new solidarity to replace the solidarity he had lost with his brothers' passing. He found it with the powerless and dispossessed—those who had suffering forced upon them. "There's so much wrong in the world, so many people suffering needlessly," he told a reporter after Bobby's death as to why he felt the need to dedicate himself to them, "and if I think I can help, it seems to me I just try." But long before those deaths, he knew pain—pain of a more quotidian sort—and there was an answer in that. It was the pain of being the least of the Kennedys. "His awful vicissitudes," as Harvard Law professor Samuel Beer called them, "have given him a sympathy with human frailty." He lived within the pain of his insufficiency. "He was constantly disappointing, constantly letting people down. He had a huge dose of humble pie throughout his life," Patrick Kennedy would say, and he would say it connected his father to the pain of insufficiency in others. "In his soul he felt the vulnerability that the migrant workers felt who had a grower tell them that they could just sit out there in the baking sun and just tough it out, or the laborer who was just turned away and not given an opportunity to provide for their family, or the family who had a loved one who was denied health care." It was, Patrick said, his father's "sensitivity to the concept of feeling [disregarded]." And Patrick said that when he was a boy, his father prayed with him every night, and Ted's favorite prayer was: "Angel of God, my guardian dear, to whom God's love commits me here, ever this day be at my side, to light and guard, to rule and guide." And Patrick thought his father loved the prayer because it indicated that Jesus didn't have the "bandwidth" to focus on him, that "he's just not worthy" for Jesus's focus, so Jesus sent him a guardian angel in his stead. This is how Ted always thought of himself: as unworthy. He had a "losing-side consciousness," as columnist Murray Kempton put it.

The Kennedy siblings, despite the image they cultivated, could be rude and arrogant. But not Ted, not the boy with the "losing-side conscious-ness." He had little sense of entitlement. He even insisted on flying coach rather than first class. "Humble" is what one Republican Cabinet secre-tary who worked with him would call him. "He's not going through the Boston airport like 'I'm the big man on campus' kind of thing. It's more familial." His longtime aide Eddie Martin said that Ted would distinguish between "the givers and the takers" and that the givers "suppressed" their egos, which is what Martin said Ted would do. "Focusing on other people always," Stephen Breyer said of him. A dance instructor at an Arthur Murray school remembered how Ted, "the smallest boy in the class," would go up to "one of the oldest and fattest ladies," who might be watch-ing her grandchild or great-niece or nephew, and he would bow and ask her to dance. He understood. Jack Kennedy had once spoken disdainfully to his father about a former aide, who was making $5,000, working nights to put himself through law school, saying that the $5,000 he earned from Jack was enough money to do so. To which Joe Kennedy replied, "Do you realize *you've* been spending $50,000 a year on incidentals?" But Ted was never disdainful. While prepping Ted for a debate in which the Republicans were seeking to repeal the Davis–Bacon Act of 1931, which required the federal government to pay prevailing local wages to workers on its projects, an aide of his made a similar sort of complaint—that the General Accounting Office found some workers getting $22,000 rather than $20,000 as mandated; Ted looked at the aide, leaned over, and said, "God forbid that a working man should make another two thousand dollars a year." And the aide, realizing that Ted had caught him on his "white-boy reflexes," said that was "the day that the scales fell from my eyes." On another occasion, after a fierce blizzard had paralyzed Boston, an aide rhapsodized over the beauty of the "pristine and white" snow, and Ted erupted, "You say it was nice? I flew over the homes that had been destroyed . . . so don't tell me it was nice." And the aide said, "I was struck then that here's a guy who seems to use as a template for all kinds of things, things as simple as a blizzard: What is its impact on distributional equity?"

But Ted Kennedy would have never put it that way, would never have thought in terms of "distributional equity," and there was an answer in that. Other politicians might have theorized that way. Others might have thought of people as groups to be flattered and won; a "silent majority," Nixon had characterized his supporters, lumpen and undifferentiated. Not Ted Kennedy. Ted Kennedy, for all his sincere and moving invocations of the powerless and the suffering, always thought in terms of individuals. His basic political outlook was not ideological; it was the particular because his own experiences were so particularized. His basic political unit was not the group, it was the person. And other politicians might project themselves onto their constituents, see their constituents as extensions of themselves, as Nixon did, perceive the slights he had suffered as theirs. Ted Kennedy, who understood so much about suffering, also understood how personal suffering was. "The more I discover about people's personal lives," he told biographer Burton Hersh, "the more I see that every household has . . . problems, in one form or another." As his son Patrick said of him, "It was always about the particular," about "individual stories." Even those who applied to work for him were advised to have a story to tell for each item on their résumé—a personal story. He wanted to know them at ground level. He was a great talker, a great storyteller, but one of his later Senate colleagues, Barbara Mikulski, would say that he was just as skilled in getting other people to talk about themselves and tell him their stories. A "schmaltzy, softhearted guy," she called him, who was "touched" by the lives of people. Political journalist Al Hunt would write of him that "more than almost any figure of this or any age, he reveled in the human element of politics and genuinely liked and cared about people."

And if all this helped explain why Ted Kennedy sought to become the face and the voice of modern liberalism, it also explained why he was accepted as such. The people for whom he purported to speak knew he understood human frailty better than most politicians because he was so frail himself. They knew he understood suffering because he had suffered so much himself, and those who had suffered sought consolation from him, which he was always eager to give. "Somehow, families, when he would write, or he'd call when they were going through some horror, drew strength from him," his staffer Melody Miller would say. "They immediately knew that he really did empathize, and when he would tell them, 'You will get through this,' that made them believe that they could." They knew he would try to help, because he never condescended to people but rather always respected them. They knew. Chappaquiddick had destroyed a good deal of his moral authority, and his opponents drew on that to undermine his political effectiveness. Ted understood that too. But Chappaquiddick could not erase his experiences, nor could it erode his empathy. The epigraph of his brother Bobby's commonplace book was: "None can usurp the height but those to whom the miseries of the world are a misery and will not let them rest."

Ted Kennedy, who had lived many of them, understood those miseries. And, understanding them, Ted Kennedy could not rest.

III

However much Chappaquiddick damaged Ted Kennedy's moral authority, it also largely deconstructed something that the Kennedys had worked tirelessly to construct: the image of perfection. The Kennedys were the great American family. Ted and Joan were a beautiful couple. They lived in a glorious home at 636 Chain Bridge Road in McLean, Virginia. The U-shaped, gray-shingled building of 12,500 square feet had been designed by the firm of architect John Carl Warnecke, who also designed John Kennedy's grave site; it sat on six acres and, by one description, was "perched on the edge of a bluff" that fell down steeply to the Potomac River. It had six bedrooms, ten bathrooms by one count—ten bedrooms, thirteen bathrooms, by another—a sauna, office, library, rec room, servants' quarters for four, and a wine cellar; outside were a tennis court, a forty-four-foot-long swimming pool, and a children's playground. "Cape Cod on the Potomac," Ted liked to call it, and it had antiques and raw beams salvaged from old barns and oak floors to give that effect—a cozy effect. But that effect was offset by the two-story drawing room, and by Joan's baby-grand piano, and by a white marble fireplace topped by an eighteenth-century mantel from Bradbury Kent, England, and by the large pink-and-white master bedroom. A magnificent house. A picture-perfect house. And, inside, a picture-perfect family: Joan and Ted and Kara and Ted Jr. and Patrick, a year after whose birth in July 1967 they moved into the McLean house. A family suffused with love. ("I have talked with him about how his three children were conceived in love," said Melody Miller, a longtime staff person who became a friend of Ted's). And they lived what seemed to be a picture-perfect life, which was reported that way in magazines and newspapers—Ted having breakfast with the children almost every morning, then driving his Pontiac GTO to the Capitol ("rapidly"), except for the time when his license was suspended, and coming home for dinner with them "as often as possible," by one account; picnicking with Joan and the children on the Capitol lawn on Fridays when the Senate was in late sessions; hosting the Tunneys to swim and play tennis and maybe football on weekends when he didn't fly up to Boston; taking the children to guitar mass on Sundays at Holy Trinity Church in Georgetown; and visiting Bobby's children twice a week at Hickory Hill close by. The man who was often neglected as a boy was a devoted parent, a parent who lavished love on his children. A Hyannis neighbor and friend averred that "his children were his life." *Beyond* his life, she said. All perfect—so perfect that Ted engaged a photographer to film the family on their vacation trips, as his father had filmed his children, just to show the world how perfect they were. Meanwhile, Joan was portrayed as a perfect homemaker. As *Time* reported it, she paid all the family bills, oversaw the homes at McLean and Hyannis, wrote letters, and "does such thoughtful chores as sending snapshots to parents of children who attend the three Kennedy youngsters' birthday parties." Joan told biographer Laurence Leamer, "Everyone thinks this is a marriage made in heaven. Both my mother- and father-in-law, and my parents and me"—she included herself—"and all my girlfriends and Ted's friends. Everyone thinks this is a marriage that will just be perfect."

Perfect. That's what everyone thought, what everyone was supposed to think. But there were cracks in the façade—terrible cracks—not least of which was that Ted and Joan were largely incompatible. Even after more than ten years of marriage, Ted admitted that he and Joan didn't really know each other, because they hadn't spent sufficient time together either during their courtship or early in their marriage. (Joan would say they married for desire, Ted because he wanted to be a "married man," a "family man," given that " 'family' virtually defined my entire consciousness.") "And so we never benefited from that critical but fleeting interval in which a young husband and wife get to know themselves and each other as a married couple," he would say. They were uneasy with each other. Joan called Ted "the last of the Irishmen who revere their mothers and put their wives on a pedestal but don't talk to them." A "real mismatch," said a friend of the couple. "Fundamentally different temperaments," Ted would write years later. "Joan was private, contemplative, and artistic, while I was public, political, and on the go." Joan told biographer Lester David that even during their time together when Ted was finishing law school in Charlottesville, the time that Ted had told Patrick was wonderful, she felt something was missing—felt that she didn't measure up to the Kennedy sisters and sisters-in-law, which was exactly what Ted felt about himself toward his brothers. She even said that Ted should have married her sister, Candy, who was much more athletic than she and extroverted and would have fit more neatly into the competitive Kennedy family. To remediate, the self-described "most unathletic girl imaginable" took tennis lessons and asked Ted to teach her to ski. But she felt she lost herself doing so. "I tried to be like the Kennedys," she told a reporter years later of this period, "bouncy and running all over the place. But I could never be like that. That's not me. I'd rather take long walks, sit by the fire, or play the piano." She felt inadequate, too, in childbearing, suffering three miscarriages—one of them seven months into the pregnancy—while Bobby's wife, Ethel, had baby after baby. And the sense of disjunction only got worse when Ted won his Senate seat and they moved to Washington. She often spent her evenings alone, playing her piano, while Ted worked. Then she began taking courses at American University and Georgetown University to fill her days, but Ted would ask her if she wanted to join him on a congressional jaunt overseas, and she usually acceded.

"I'd miss half a semester, a final exam one time, a midterm paper another, and then I'd just drop it." Betty Friedan could have been writing about Joan when she described the woman who "made the beds, shopped for groceries, matched slipcover material, ate peanut butter sandwiches with the children, chauffeured Cub Scouts and Brownies, lay beside her husband at night" and dared ask, "Is this all?" Joan Kennedy asked herself that.

Even McLean was a disappointment. The grand new house was supposed to mark a new beginning—starting from scratch after Patrick's birth. But there was no starting over. Joan's sense of inadequacy only grew. The one attribute that gave her confidence, she said, was her beauty. "You know, I was Miss Bermuda," she once boasted to Melody Miller with slight exaggeration. "And that was before I was a Kennedy." (The Kennedy women didn't take it lightly. When Joan emerged at Hyannis in a leopard-skin-print bathing suit before a sailing trip, Ethel snipped, "Really, Joan, did you expect the photographer?") Younger than nearly all the Senate wives, more attractive than the other Senate wives, Joan flaunted it, though it was clearly her way of compensating for her perceived deficiencies. She showed up at a White House reception for Congress hosted by First Lady Pat Nixon in March 1969 in a silver miniskirt and at a White House reception for Philippine First Lady Imelda Marcos wearing knee-high black leather boots, a mid-length skirt, and a see-through blouse with a blue brassiere underneath. Both appearances drew snark from the press and created embarrassment for Ted. "I wish I'd never done that," she told Lester David a few years later, admitting it was a bid for attention. "And I wouldn't do it today or tomorrow. At the time, though, I didn't even think about what I was doing. Now I feel a little ridiculous not to have anticipated the stir it would cause." But she did know what she was doing. She was using her beauty because she felt she had little else. "The only thing I knew, that I was sure of," she told David, "was that I was a very attractive young woman and that I had a pretty good figure."

That wasn't enough, however, to overcome her feelings of inadequacy and insecurity. Asked by a reporter how she would describe herself, she said, "Vulnerable." She felt she had to temper herself, censor herself. "I was supposed to be the 'sweet good girl' all the time," she said. "Not allowed to cry or be grumpy. Do you realize the terrible strain that is? You were told, 'Don't let your emotions out. Ladies don't do that.'" She tried to stand on her own. She made an appearance on *The Andy Williams Show,* playing the piano, Debussy's First Arabesque and the theme from *Love Story*, which Williams sang, and she later told a reporter, "Maybe I can have a musical career of my own. Maybe I can be more than Ted Kennedy's wife. It's sort of like coming out of the shadows." But she couldn't come out of those shadows. She had been broken down by the Kennedy pressures. Her fingernails were chewed to the nub.

And what made it worse, what destroyed the few remnants of confidence she still held, was that despite her great beauty, Ted Kennedy was neither affectionate to her—"I don't think Kennedy men know how to show their affection except to their children," she would say—nor faithful, any more than Joe Kennedy had been faithful to Rose or Jack to Jacqueline. Save for Bobby, infidelity had been a family inheritance. Even Ted's beloved grandfather Honey Fitz had had a roving eye, which was what forced him from the 1914 mayoral race: He was caught "canoodling" with a young woman named Elizabeth Ryan, whose nickname was "Toodles." Joe Kennedy was flagrant. As Garry Wills put it, "Far from covering up his affairs, Joseph Kennedy tried to claim more of them than there were—even when it might hurt his business ventures. . . . He obviously thought this was part of his charm." Wills added, "Passing women around, and boasting of it to other men and other women, was a Kennedy achievement." There was a consensus that Joe Kennedy's philandering was not a matter of biology, though Rose seemed to care little for sex and though the two of them were separated for three hundred days out of each year in the 1930s. It was about power. Political reporter Frank Kent Jr. observed that for Kennedy, women were "another thing that a rich man had—like caviar. It wasn't sex. It was part of the image . . . his idea of manliness." A "predator," fashion designer Oleg Cassini, who knew him, called him. He "wanted a symbolic success in life and thought that women were one of the ways of showing power." And Joe Kennedy didn't hide his wandering eye from his wife. When Ted, then in high school, brought home his girlfriend Nancy, who, Rose wrote her daughters, "looked fifteen," Joe "made the startling announcement to her that when she was about eighteen he would be waiting for her. As she is already eighteen, she was really dumbfounded." Nor did he hide his infidelities from his sons, and Doris Kearns Goodwin speculated that the "risks" and "sexual daring" Joe Kennedy took with the actress Gloria Swanson, a daring that threatened the family's well-being, would be duplicated by those sons. "It would seem almost as if, in repeating their father's behavior," she wrote, "they were unconsciously trying to gain some sort of mastery over this early trauma that had nearly destroyed everything they had."

Jack certainly followed his father's lead. "Interested, very interested in girls," Jack's close friend and Harvard classmate LeMoyne Billings said of him, adding that, as with Joe Kennedy, it was a "form of being successful at something"—more successful than his older brother. As far back as World War II, the FBI was keeping a file on John Kennedy's relationships with women—a file that the director, J. Edgar Hoover, would later send to President Richard Nixon to use against Ted should he decide to run against Nixon in 1972. When Jack was still a senator and one of his researchers asked him why he would threaten his presidential aspirations by having affairs, he answered, "I can't help it." Neither could Ted. When the actress Gene Tierney was dating Jack in the 1940s, and he brought her to Hyannis Port, Teddy, then only thirteen, kept insisting on dancing with her. Years later, she encountered Jean Kennedy Smith and mentioned how Ted was interested in girls even then. To which Jean "winked" and said, "Yes, and he still is." Interested, and yet women were largely dispensable for the Kennedy men—again, all except Bobby, who, by most accounts if not by most rumors, was faithful to Ethel. Jack was lounging on a yacht off the Riviera in the Mediterranean with fellow senator George Smathers and with Ted in 1956 when Jackie suffered her first miscarriage. He didn't return immediately. It was Bobby who came to comfort her.

Kennedy detractors believed that this philandering could all be laid on old Joe Kennedy, that he was reckless in his womanizing, that he encouraged his sons to womanize too—hence his note to Ted in 1955 encouraging him to share his "beautiful women at Cape Cod" with his "oldest brother," who also happened to be married—that he saw womanizing not only as a demonstration of his own power or as a perquisite of his wealth but also as an expectation his sons felt duty-bound to fulfill. The apples, he hinted to them, shouldn't fall far from the tree, as if their womanizing would reflect back on his masculinity. But there may have been another explanation. It was just as likely that it wasn't so much Joe Kennedy's indiscretions that influenced his sons as Rose Kennedy's attitude toward those indiscretions that gave them license to treat women as they did. For if the boys saw their father's infidelities, his flaunting of those infidelities, they also saw Rose's forbearance of them, her feeling that they were part of her marital bargain. Joe Kennedy got his women; Rose Kennedy got her trips to Europe and other extravagances. And this may have led to the idea that the boys, at least Jack and Ted, didn't have to be especially discreet about their dalliances either. Rather, their women had to be tolerant of them.

So the Kennedy women, blindsided, made their marital bargains—made them with Rose Kennedy's encouragement. Rose admitted as much. She told her daughters-in-law that she had grown up watching her father's dalliances (she pointedly left out her husband) and said she felt duty-bound to apprise them of what they were up against; and what they were up against was, though she put it more delicately, philandering. "So each time, in turn, Ethel, then Jackie, then Joan," she would write in her memoir, "I made sure to warn them in advance of what they were in for: that they might be hearing and reading all sorts of scandalous gossip and accusations about members of our family, about their husbands, and for that matter about themselves," and she said that "they should understand this and be prepared from the beginning, otherwise they might be very unhappy," which was her euphemistic way of saying that they should understand and be prepared not just for the gossip about their husbands' infidelity but for the infidelity itself. And Rose wrote sanguinely, "They took the burden with the blessing, and all three have managed well." Other times, Rose recommended denial. As Joan herself remembered it, while she and Rose were vacationing at Palm Beach, *Women's Wear Daily* was writing about an affair Ted was reportedly having with a beautiful socialite, and Rose dismissed it. "My dear," she said, "you can't believe any of these things you are reading. Women chase after politicians." Jackie, speaking from personal experience, was more honest when Joan asked her for advice on Ted's affairs. "He adores you," she said. "He thinks you're a wonderful wife and you're smart and you're talented and you're a wonderful mother. His mother and father adore you, and the whole family loves you. You're just the perfect wife. But he just has this addiction."

But even though Rose thought her daughters-in-law had all managed well, as she herself had managed well—meaning managing their husbands' infidelities—Joan Kennedy, in truth, did not manage well. Joan managed badly. Her self-esteem, already at low ebb, disappeared entirely during this period—in drink. Already fragile, she broke. "When one grows up feeling that maybe one is sort of special and hoping that one's husband thinks so," she told a reporter candidly several years later, "and then suddenly thinking maybe he doesn't . . . I began thinking, well, maybe I'm just not attractive enough or attractive anymore, or whatever, and it was awfully easy to then say, 'Well, after all, you know, if that's the way it is, I might as well have a drink.' " She drank. She drank heavily. And she told biographer Laurence Leamer that "after Chappaquiddick . . . it became worse. For a few months everyone had to put on this show, and then I just didn't care anymore. I just saw no future. That's when I truly became an alcoholic."

And whether or not her drinking drove Ted even further away, Joan deeply resented the narrative that it had. "When he was in trouble with his womanizing," she told Leamer, "he fed certain trusted journalist confidants. He would feed them through his press secretary, Richard Drayne, and the whole idea was that people would say, 'Poor Ted,' because she drinks. The irony is that maybe I drank because there was another mistress." There were many mistresses. Ted had been discreet early on, even diffident with women. "I don't think Jack was so careful. I thought Ted was very careful not to embrace women," recalled a close Kennedy friend, Betty Taymor. "He wouldn't even kiss women supporters." Senator Strom Thurmond would bring beauty queens from his state, South Carolina, to Ted's office because the girls wanted to meet him, and Ted would roll his eyes and have his aide tell Thurmond that he was busy, or, if he felt he couldn't snub Thurmond, prayed there were no cameras, because he knew the conclusions to which people would jump if they saw him with a pretty girl, given his family's reputation.

Milton Gwirtzman thought that David Burke kept Ted in line too. "He wouldn't do any shenanigans if David was around," Gwirtzman said. "David had a strong moral sense." But Ted seemed to have very little sense for women, morally or politically. He had opposed a constitutional amendment, the so-called Equal Rights Amendment, which would have explicitly extended to women Fourteenth Amendment protections—opposed it on the basis, variously, that he didn't want to tamper with the Constitution, or that court decisions had been sufficient to protect women without an amendment, or that women constituents, having listened to opponents, had told him they didn't want an amendment, or that an amendment would, as his aide Nance Lyons, who had argued the point with him, said, put women on the battlefield and even in unisex bathrooms. And Ted wasn't alone in this. David Burke and Jim Flug were also urging him not to co-sponsor the amendment. Lyons said that Ted told her, "Convince me," and eventually, in March 1971, after nearly two years of trying, she did, so that from that point on Ted began co-sponsoring the amendment every year it was introduced.

But his diffidence toward women had been political, not sexual. With Joan's drinking, and with the fallout of Chappaquiddick that dashed his presidential hopes, and with the departure of Burke, and with the death of his father, the last restraints were lifted. He was now uninhibited. "Trying to keep him reined in was often like trying to keep a bull from charging a red flag," an aide would say. "The least discreet guy on the Hill," one source told historian James MacGregor Burns, who was writing a biography of Ted. "I have told him ten times, 'Ted, you're acting like a fool. Everybody knows wherever you go.'" And Ted looked down sheepishly and said with "a faint smile, 'Yeah, I guess you're right.'" But the source said he still didn't reform. Joan herself said, "There was always an aide who got the women up one staircase and down the other." Another source, a veteran reporter, told Burns that the womanizing showed "how reckless Kennedy is with his career," and said, "He just doesn't care," which was another consequence of Chappaquiddick, though his behavior also showed how confused Ted was, how torn he was, how willing he was to rebuild himself by battling for the dispossessed and trying to expunge the stain of Chappaquiddick, only to recklessly endanger that very mission by reinforcing the image of himself as a hedonist. It was the cycle of sin and expiation that had come to define his life, though now it was expiation and sin, as if the sin itself were the punishment and as if he didn't really want to release himself from his guilt.

Reckless he was. By one account, he wound up in the library romancing the Greek dancer who entertained at his secretary's engagement party, which he had hosted at his house. On the eve of the late French president Charles de Gaulle's memorial service in Paris, a tabloid photographed Ted with Princess Maria Pia, the daughter of the deposed Italian king, Umberto, dancing at a club until 5 A.M., and by one report, he had a weekend tryst with Margaret Trudeau, the wife of the Canadian prime minister, Pierre Trudeau. He was linked to Amanda Burden, the daughter of fashion doyenne Babe Paley and stepdaughter of CBS founder William Paley and a stunning New York socialite—the socialite about whom *Women's Wear Daily* had written when Joan was complaining to Rose. He adamantly denied it, saying he had only met her three times and always with other people present and claiming, "People write this sort of thing about me all the time," but gossip columnist Joyce Haber reported that they had actually flown separately to Los Angeles and then holed up out of the public eye in the Holmby Hills residence of a famous singer.

These were not all brief romances. Helga Wagner, the woman whom he had called the morning after the Chappaquiddick accident, was a serious relationship, a long-term relationship. Austrian-born, Wagner was the daughter of a wealthy Viennese father and an "adventurous" Florentine mother who pushed her out into the world, and she studied painting in Paris while still a teenager. Helga and her sister were vacationing in Nassau when a professional golfer named Chris Dunphy invited them to Palm Beach for Easter. She said it was her first time in America. No sooner had the two sisters landed than Dunphy told them they were all going to be having dinner with the president at the Kennedys' Palm Beach winter home—Joe Kennedy's winter residence. (Helga said she was so stunned to be introduced to the president that she kept asking, "How do you do, Mr. President?" to which Jack replied kindly, "I heard you. It's okay.") That night she met Ted Kennedy too. Wagner, blond, beautiful, lively, stayed in the United States and married shipping magnate Robert Wagner, with whom, after six years, she said, "I felt trapped in a golden cage." She said the marriage was annulled without her "taking a penny." At loose ends, she became a Scientologist, settled in Florida, and began a jewelry business there, using seashells as the primary component. Throughout it all, the relationship with Ted endured, though when it became romantic is difficult to pinpoint. Wagner became a confidante—the confidante that Ted clearly felt Joan could not be. It was when he phoned to confide in Wagner from Hyannis during the Chappaquiddick deliberations and Joan eavesdropped on the call that Joan felt devastated yet again.

And humiliated. Joan Kennedy was now a woman in despair, as Ted had been a man in despair. Whenever Joan's descent began, and it had begun before Chappaquiddick, it was steep, and it was fast. Ted said he initially noticed her drinking when he first ran for the Senate. "We were supposed to go to the State [Democratic] Committee meeting, and I asked her if she was ready," he recalled, "and I walked into the room and saw that she was unsteady. I thought, 'That's strange,' because it was sort of the first time that she hadn't been able to make it to an event." He said it "picked up during the period of '62," that it was a "difficult thing to cope with," and admitted he was "not sure I dealt with it very well in terms of how you get through it . . . until the election." And he said it was "increasingly a problem that was gnawing at me." Since both of Joan's parents had been alcoholics—her mother had an "ugly, ugly alcoholism that none of us talked about," said her son Patrick—she was aware of the danger, but she couldn't confide in the Kennedys, for whom all so-called defects had to be hidden to protect the image. Rose was especially exasperated with her, seeing Joan's problem as a sign of weakness. On one occasion, when Joan, after visiting her mother in Cocoa Beach, showed up inebriated at the Kennedy home in Palm Beach, Rose sighed, "Oh, baby!" and ordered Ted to get her home. (Joan was clearly ashamed. When a friend of Rose's went to see Joan recite *Peter and the Wolf* with a high school orchestra and complimented her afterward, Joan asked, "Would you write a letter to my mother-in-law and say I was good?") Only Eunice, among the Kennedys, was sympathetic; Joan suspected it was because Eunice knew Ted was cheating and knew how much it hurt Joan. She did confide in Jackie, whom she considered a kindred spirit, both in terms of being cheated on and in temperament—"They must think we're some kind of kooks not to want to be with everybody all the time," Jackie told her—but Joan never said if Jackie dispensed any advice to deal with the illness. In the early seventies, Joan started seeing a psychiatrist, but she called the therapy a "disaster," saying that her problem wasn't taken seriously. "No one paid attention to me," meaning presumably the Kennedy family, especially Ted. And she said the drinking got worse. "At times I drank to feel less inhibited, to relax at parties," she would say. "Other times, I drank to block out unhappiness, to drown my sorrows." She was a well-intentioned but indifferent mother. "She spent much of my childhood in her room, doing little but drinking and surviving," Patrick would write. "Occasionally, she would come out and try her best to be attentive, like driving us somewhere," but he said that as the car slowly weaved down the street, all that the nonplussed children could do was "giggle." And then at other times, especially in the early and mid-1970s, she would vanish into rehab centers—a series of them. She became a family ghost.

She no longer tried to hide her affliction and couldn't even if she had wanted to. Lester Hyman remembered going to the McLean house for a party, and Joan coming over to him and asking if he could do her a favor: "Take this water glass and just fill it with vodka, please . . . and don't tell Ted." John Seigenthaler, had attended a party in New York at Steve Smith's apartment and saw Joan get off the elevator, clearly drunk, and "just immediately crumple into a chair." The gardener at Hyannis once found her at Squaw Island on an eating binge, presumably after a drink-

ing binge, with mayonnaise in her hair. A reporter friend of Ted's told
Burton Hersh of visiting Hyannis for drinks and of Ted escorting him out
back to have him say goodbye to Joan, who was passed out on the back
seat of the car. "She was a rag mop," the reporter said. "I've seen drunks
often enough, but what I was looking at there was the result of a two- or
three-day bender. I think Kennedy just wanted me to see what he was up
against." Saying, "She looked like she had crawled through a rathole,"
after always having been so exquisitely dressed and perfectly coiffed, one
reporter concluded, "She just doesn't seem to give a damn," which, of
course, was what was also being said of her husband about his womanizing. Arthur Schlesinger Jr., at yet another party, was more succinct: "Joan
was there; she had drunk too much, alas, and was forlorn."

And forlorn in her marriage. Of all the Kennedys, the harshest to her
was the man who was never harsh to anyone else, the man whose empathy seemed boundless, the man who understood pain and suffering firsthand. But Ted Kennedy had no empathy for his wife, no feeling for her
suffering or appreciation for what she was going through or any recognition of what he had done to worsen it. He was cold to her, indifferent, resentful of her weakness, as his mother had been, seeing the alcoholism
not as an illness, which is what it was, but as a character flaw. He was
angry that she couldn't show the Kennedy fortitude, even though the
pressure of maintaining that fortitude had often crippled him, as it was
crippling her, which may have been one explanation for his coldness—
that she reminded him too much of his own weakness and his own
illness—and there is no question that her drinking doomed whatever love
he had had for her. Ted Kennedy always drank, had drunk more after Bobby's death and then after the Chappaquiddick accident to drown his sorrows. He drank prodigiously at times. "I was always amazed at how much
he could drink," his Hyannis neighbor, Melissa Ludtke, would say. He
would go out on the boat with white wine and "large pots" instead of
wineglasses. "He had a bit of a hollow leg," Dun Gifford's wife, Gladys,
would say. But Ted Kennedy could always handle his liquor. Ludtke said
some nights they would be showing a film at the big house, and he would
drink throughout it and at night's end say, "See you at eight," and there
he would be the next morning, at eight sharp, ready for tennis. Gladys Gifford said she never saw him "stumbling bumbling . . . He just got funnier
and funnier." Another friend who had partied with Ted said, "Never acted
what you would call wild [obviously not having seen him on the Alaskan

flight]. Never said anything that wasn't right or forgot what he said the next morning. He was always crystal clear." Other senators might show up on the floor, red-faced, bleary-eyed, swaying, barely coherent, as Russell Long had done. Never, never Ted Kennedy. And Ted Kennedy could stop drinking for days or even weeks at a time if he needed to. A year or so after Chappaquiddick, by one report, he had reduced his alcohol consumption to a Dubonnet before lunch or a Cutty Sark or two before dinner and limited himself to a few scotches at parties. Away from home, he preferred a Heineken beer.

So Ted Kennedy couldn't understand why his wife lost control—couldn't understand it and couldn't tolerate it, though he could understand it and tolerate it in others less close to him. But, then, those people didn't jeopardize Ted's career or threaten the image of the perfect family. He was judgmental of her. "I can still hear him," Patrick said. " 'Here she goes again . . . oh, my God . . . I can't believe it!' " There was "a palpable level of frustration and also rage," Patrick would also say of a man who was seldom enraged. And the worst fear among the children, a fear inculcated by Ted, was "to be likened to my mother." Rose's secretary said that Ted and Rose both watched Joan as "though watching an animal that might be expected to turn at any moment." And yet as impatient as he was with her drinking, he was equally impatient with her attempts to treat it, lest the secret get out and the façade crumble. He discouraged her from going to the psychiatrist. He grew upset when she left for treatment at facilities. "Let's get Sister Hargrove on the phone," he would tell her, referring to the president of Joan's alma mater, Manhattanville College, thinking Sister Katherine Hargrove would help and apparently believing she would be more discreet than a trained therapist. But it was discretion that was one of Joan's prisons—the Kennedy prison of never revealing anything behind the façade. "The family pathology was secrecy," Ted's nephew Tim Shriver would say. "I was in public life and I just had to keep everything to myself," Joan told one interviewer. "Things I knew, I couldn't even tell my girlfriends." And she said she didn't realize "how dangerous it is not to be able to speak to anybody about your troubles in the family that bothered you," adding, "How the h-e-l-l did I make it through?" But the truth was that she hadn't.

Silence was one of the great afflictions of the Kennedys—the unbearable pain they experienced that they dared not express, "the compounding sense," as Patrick put it, "of horror and shame and tragedy and trauma." They were all scarred, all damaged. But the damage had to be hidden, internalized, which is precisely what Joan Kennedy could not do. Ted did and paid a price for doing so. "A person is basically hopeful," he said of this period. But the most hopeful of the Kennedys was hopeful no longer. "I just saw things getting worse."

IV

Though Ted Kennedy tried to regain his voice after the Chappaquiddick accident, though he began to take on the administration again, the next years—1970 and 1971—would be fallow ones for him. Nixon was emboldened by the backlash against liberalism—a backlash he had helped facilitate. Lyndon Johnson, in the wake of the 1967 race riots that tore apart so many American cities, had impaneled a commission, headed by Illinois governor Otto Kerner, to determine the cause of the riots. The commission found a racially divided country and pointed to a number of social factors that had contributed to fanning discontent into violence and prescribed a massive program to deal with them. Johnson, preoccupied with Vietnam, largely discounted the report. Nixon actively challenged it. It "blames everybody for the riots except the perpetrators of the riots," he said when the report was issued. Now that he was president, Nixon saw little advantage in helping black Americans. At a bipartisan breakfast, he declared that he was in favor of school desegregation but not in favor of federal enforcement of it. When the Voting Rights Act was up for extension in 1970, Nixon again said he supported voting rights but would prefer a bill that forbade literacy tests nationwide and not just in the South, in an obvious attempt to sink it. He was no more forthcoming on aid to the poor, which pushed Ted into taking the initiative. In front of a group representing the elderly, Nixon had proposed a program to provide nutrition for seniors but had put no timetable on it. Johnson had already initiated a similar program on a pilot basis. Late in 1971, Ted sought to spread it nationwide by calling Nixon's bluff. So that same morning of Nixon's address, as Ted would tell it, he approached Republican senator Charles Percy, a moderate and a fellow member of the Senate Special Committee on Aging, and asked, "Why don't we put in a hundred million dollars in appropriations and start this program to feed the elderly?" (Actually, they were expanding it.) The two of them made their proposal, which was an amendment to Johnson's Older Americans Act of 1965, got it on the agenda, presumably to the Special Committee on Aging, debated it for forty-five minutes, and the result was an expansion of what became known as "Meals on Wheels," bringing hot lunches into the homes of senior citizens. "Starting a program in one day," Ted would exult years later. Nixon vetoed the project—the project he had proposed—because the bill included a provision calling for an end to the bombing of Cambodia that Nixon had begun to interdict North Vietnamese troops flowing into South Vietnam, but Congress overrode the veto.

Still, Ted, despite the moments of boldness he showed and the press accounts noting it, was generally more timorous than he had been before Chappaquiddick and before his brief term as shadow president. He retreated. He continued to speak out against the Vietnam War, especially after Nixon initiated the bombing of Cambodia, calling for Congress to stop funding the bombing and at long last demanding that America withdraw all troops unilaterally by the end of 1971. But he did not lead the process to do so. He rebuffed an appeal from conservative columnist Stewart Alsop to disassociate himself from the more vehement elements of the peace movement just days after National Guardsmen killed four students during an anti-war protest at Kent State University in Ohio in May 1970. He seemed to hedge, though, saying that in denouncing the war it might seem that he had "allied myself with the naïve, the idealistic, and the young," but that he allied himself with no one. "I simply protest the war and its consequences as one person who has obligations of office, some sense of the responsibilities memory has placed upon me, and as a man who has not escaped the 'harshness of the historic process.'" And he was critical of student radicalism and violence and had delivered a speech that March, two months before Kent State, at Trinity College in Dublin, in which he promoted tolerance and reason. "The objective of the discontented should not be revenge but change," he said, though he was equally critical of "the words 'law and order,' the trials, the jailings, the public statements, and name-calling by men in high office," by which, of course, he meant President Nixon and those in his administration and in his party who excoriated anti-war protesters. A month later, speaking at an Earth Day rally in New Haven, Ted was jostled off the stage by six protesters. When he regained the floor, he condemned violence and even traditional protest. "We can protest anything now," he declared, clearly concerned that those protesters might wind up empowering Nixon, "using the same old procedure, writing on the same old cardboards with detachable handles. If you want to bring an end to the war, then work to elect men who agree with you and mount that political campaign this fall. . . . If you are still insistent on racial equality, then go where you are needed to register blacks, to assist with their arguments in court, to offer your services to their cause. If you care about poverty, go live it. . . . In short, act in a way meaningful to someone other than yourself."

But timorous as he may have been, worried no doubt about becoming a foil for Nixon after Chappaquiddick and about the implications of social disruption on the liberal agenda, he did fight for one cause during the winter of 1970 as the Vietnam protests were mounting. While he was summoning youth to work for change rather than simply march for change, a call that reflected his own deeply held belief that action was more powerful than rhetoric, he was working to allow eighteen-year-olds to vote. Congress had debated the issue for years, and senators Jennings Randolph and Warren Magnuson had introduced a constitutional amendment to that effect. But most Republicans were opposed, assuming that young voters would be Democratic voters, so the amendment could never get the two-thirds vote required to send it to the states for ratification, and the issue vanished. Now, however, it arose again, as a result of the Vietnam War and the proposition that anyone who was old enough to fight for America and perhaps give his life for America was old enough to vote in America. Morally, that may have been inarguable. But there was a legal question as well as the moral one. Did Congress have the authority to lower the voting age by statute, or was a constitutional amendment required—the constitutional amendment that Democrats could not pass? Ted, who had long been exercised by the iniquities of the draft and who had helped introduce a random-selection system, now was exercised by voting rights, in part because the Voting Rights Act of 1965 was coming up for an extension. (This was the extension that Nixon had tried to torpedo.) It was Carey Parker, the calmest, quietest, and most studious of Ted's aides, who, while gathering information for the Voting Rights Act debate, found an article by Harvard law professor and former solicitor general for President Kennedy, Archibald Cox, in the November 1966 issue of the *Harvard Law Review*. In it, Cox cited a Supreme Court decision upholding a provision of the original Voting Rights Act that voided a New York state law requiring voters to speak English. Cox argued that the decision would allow Congress to make other adjustments to voting law, including reducing the voting age. Parker jumped on this, writing several memoranda for Ted, which were then circulated around the Judiciary Committee. Now Ted was excited. The only sticking point was that the civil rights community and some of their allies in Congress thought attaching this to the Voting Rights Act might wind up threatening the extension, since many Republicans opposed it; that opposition might cost supporters their chance of getting a two-thirds cloture vote if, as expected, the bill were to be filibustered. And since some Democrats in the House of Representatives opposed it as well, on the basis that the addition of eighteen-year-olds to the voting rolls in their districts might threaten their reelections, and since another opponent, House Judiciary Committee chairman Emanuel Celler, lobbied Speaker McCormack by saying that eighteen-year-olds lacked the maturity to vote, its passage was no certainty. Nixon, for his part, said he favored an eighteen-year-old vote but wanted a constitutional amendment, which he knew was unpassable.

Now Ted was determined to get the bill passed. Ted, Parker, Dave Burke (this was shortly before he left), and Ted's Judiciary aide, Jim Flug, met in Ted's office to strategize and decided that the amendment would not hurt the prospects for passing the Voting Rights extension but that, given the House's trepidations, the Senate should pass the bill first; that way the House could pass the Senate bill and thus avoid a conference in which the provision might be excluded. Ted spoke to representatives Thomas Railsback, an Illinois Republican, and Allard Lowenstein, the New York Democrat, and came away convinced that the House would wind up passing a bill if the Senate sent it one. Such was the strategy, except that John Finney of *The New York Times* got ahold of one of the memos Carey Parker had prepared for Ted and revealed what Ted and Birch Bayh, the chair of the Judiciary Subcommittee on the Constitution, were planning and the basis for their move, which allowed the opponents to prepare to counter it.

And then Ted left for Ireland that March to deliver his speech on tolerance and violence.

But despite overcoming his reticence and pushing the legislation, he was subverted by something that happened in the brief time he was away. While they were, by one account, driving home together, Majority Leader Mike Mansfield and his close friend Senator Warren Magnuson, who had long labored for a constitutional amendment to lower the voting age, talked about Ted's proposal to amend the Voting Rights Act with the eighteen-year-old vote rather than go the constitutional route, and Magnuson suggested that it was a good idea and that they introduce the amendment themselves. Mansfield said he would sleep on the idea that night, apparently realizing that he would be breaking Senate protocol by co-opting his whip, whom he genuinely liked. But notwithstanding that break, the next morning Mansfield told Magnuson that he was in, which also meant that Ted was out. It was left to Mansfield's aide, Charles Ferris, to break the news about the move to Carey Parker while Ted was still in Ireland, and not only break the news to him but also notify him that Mansfield's and Magnuson's names would be first on the bill, ahead of Ted's, though Ted had done all the spade work for it. (In fact, Parker had to ask Ferris to put Ted's name on the bill at all.) Parker sought to postpone the introduction until Ted's return, but there would be no stalling. "It's as though Ferris came to you and said, 'Stick 'em up, kid. Gimme your amendment,'" Dave Burke would tell Parker. Ted didn't find out until he came back from Ireland, when it was already a *fait accompli,* and he wasn't pleased. When Ferris phoned him to discuss it, he slammed down the receiver.[*]

But this wasn't just a matter of Mansfield wanting his name on legislation. Mansfield was no egotist. There was another issue, an issue that wasn't publicly broached, because it spoke to the diminution of Ted's power and would have embarrassed him: Mansfield felt that after the Chappaquiddick accident, Ted didn't have the suasion to get the bill passed. Mansfield could. Still, Ted was so committed that, despite his personal hurt, he worked to get the bill passed, worked to get McCormack, his fellow Massachusetts legislator, to lobby for it over the objections of Celler and of those members who didn't want to disrupt the voting demographics in their districts, worked in the Senate to convince his colleagues by testifying at length in favor of the bill before Bayh's subcommittee and carefully laying out the legal groundwork for the bill. It passed the Senate easily and then, as Ted had predicted, it passed the House, with a provision that if its constitutionality was challenged in court, it would go directly to a three-judge panel in the District of Columbia and on appeal

---

[*] In another interview, Ferris told a different story. He said that Parker had written an op-ed supporting the vote for eighteen-year-olds, to be published under Ted's name, but that Mansfield, hoping to put pressure on the House by broadening the coalition of supporters, had Ferris contact Barry Goldwater and Magnuson to add their names to the op-ed. Ferris said that was what made Ted so furious—that his initiative had been co-opted by these others. Charles Ferris interview, June 29, 2006, Miller Center, UVA.

directly to the Supreme Court before the 1972 election. Nixon signed it into law because, Carey Parker said, "He could not have vetoed the voting rights legislation," but Nixon also thought it was likely to be found unconstitutional.

It was Ted himself who argued the case before the District Court—the first time he had made an argument in federal court, and the first time he had appeared in court as an attorney since his days as Suffolk County assistant district attorney, and he spent a lot of time in preparation. "There were a lot of people who wanted to help," he would say, "and I used them all." Representing a coalition of liberal groups, Ted spoke, *The New York Times* reported, as if he were delivering a speech on the Senate floor, and the three justices did not interrupt him. (The *Times* also noted the rare instance of a legislator appearing before a court to defend his very own law.) His central argument was that the law remedied "invidious discrimination" against eighteen-, nineteen-, and twenty-year-olds, who could fight, marry, and be taxed but who could not vote. The District Court ruled in Ted's favor, then sent the case to the Supreme Court, where it met a somewhat odder fate. The court divided 4 to 4 to 1, splitting on the law's constitutionality but with Justice Hugo Black finding that Congress had the right to set the rules for federal elections but not for state elections, which effectively created two sets of rules. That led to a new push for a constitutional amendment, which Jennings Randolph submitted and which was passed quickly the next year, in March 1971, and ratified by three-quarters of the states just four months later—the "fastest ratification of a constitutional amendment ever," Carey Parker said. (No doubt Vietnam played a role, with eighteen-year-olds giving their lives, as Ted had said when he proposed the amendment.) Though the constitutional amendment was the very thing Ted had wanted to avoid in submitting his legislation, he later called the amendment one of the "three most important decisions made by Congress and the courts in terms of the sanctity to vote," along with the end of the poll tax and the enforcement of one man, one vote. Ted Kennedy didn't have to mention that he had taken a leading role in promoting all three. But Chappaquiddick had prevented him from finishing the last of them without Mike Mansfield's assistance and usurpation. Chappaquiddick still hung over him.

And now, after a year of torment and timorousness, came the referendum from his own constituents. He formally announced his candidacy for reelection to the Senate on June 11, 1970, at his Beacon Hill apartment. His popularity had tumbled. Murray Chotiner, a longtime Nixon associate, wrote Nixon's special counsel, Charles Colson, that "John Lindsay of *Newsweek* did a spot check and finds that it is the opinion of a number of people in Massachusetts that Senator Kennedy is in trouble and that the man who can defeat him is Henry Cabot Lodge," whom Jack had beaten in the 1952 Senate race and whom he had beaten again when Lodge ran as Nixon's vice-presidential candidate. But Lodge would not run. In the Republican primary, a former state chairman and moderate named Josiah Spaulding, who questioned Nixon's policy in Cambodia and his Southern strategy, and whose wife had been a bridesmaid at Jack Kennedy's wedding, ran against a conservative named John McCarthy, whom Nixon was implicitly backing. Spaulding won and attacked Kennedy on the basis that he "is not a leader, because it just isn't in him," which seemed a rather odd criticism but one that played upon the differences between Ted and his more aggressive brothers rather than on the negligible differences between Ted and Spaulding. But Spaulding wasn't Ted's real opponent. Ted was running against himself, against the 72 percent of the vote he had run up in 1964 and against the wounds that the Chappaquiddick accident had inflicted upon him. "Poll Finds Kennedy Is Losing Esteem," *The New York Times* reported of a Harris survey after the release of the inquest report in which Judge Boyle had determined Ted had not told the whole truth about the accident; the percentage of respondents who "respect Ted less" had risen from 28 percent shortly after the accident to 43 percent in May, which was not exactly an endorsement. Nevertheless, a *Boston Globe* survey taken at the same time found that three-quarters of Massachusetts residents approved of Ted's performance. "I've always been for the Kennedys, so why should I change now?" one voter told Johnny Apple of the *Times*.

It was not a happy campaign; it was a challenging campaign—a campaign in which Ted had to convince the voters that Chappaquiddick had not destroyed him, and a campaign in which he had to convince himself as well. By one account, when early that summer yet another magazine repeated Judge Boyle's charge of Ted's untruthfulness, he exploded in the Georgetown living room of a friend. "The hell with it," he was reported to have said. "Two of my brothers murdered and now they're rubbing my nose in this stuff every day. A man has a right to live his own life." And he declared, "I'm through," meaning through with politics. The next day he delivered his decision to Joan and then to Joey Gargan and then flew to Hyannis to tell his mother. At the end of long talks, according to this version, Rose made a request of her son: that he run again as a birthday present for her. He did so—he couldn't deny her—but reluctantly, and he admitted to William Honan, "It's a lot more difficult to work up the same enthusiasm as before, given recent events," which he had said after Jack's death and then Bobby's death and now after Chappaquiddick. And he said what he had said on those occasions as well: that "the excitement is gone for me. I expect it to be gone forever."

It was not a campaign of issues. It was a campaign of trust—trust of Ted Kennedy. "The voters need reassurance," Ted told Johnny Apple. "They need to see that I'm reliable and mature. You can't counter the Chappaquiddick thing directly. The answer has to be implicit in what you are, what you stand for, and how they see you." He would call this effort to restore the voters' confidence in him "cruel and difficult and painful." And Dave Burke, who had left Ted's staff to work at the Dreyfus Fund but continued to assist him when Ted requested his help, said of the campaign, "It was to be survived." Almost as another form of penance from the man who seemed always to be doing penance, Ted exposed himself to the voters, let them have at him, though Ted would say that he had "yet to find a single person, except newsmen—and few of those—to raise the issue" of Chappaquiddick. Paul Kirk Jr., one of the more recent additions to his staff, who accompanied Ted on the campaign trail, said it "became a special kind of campaign in the sense that he wanted to be in front of as many people as possible, who could ask us whatever questions they wanted—all because after the Chappaquiddick incident, and the court ordeal and the rest of it, there was a feeling that maybe he hadn't been forthcoming." It was a series of "one-on-one, face-to-face town meetings." And "it was exhausting," Kirk said.

And so he was back to doing what he had done when he first ran in 1962: campaigning all day, hitting the plant gates at six-thirty in the morning and then making twenty more appearances, at Kiwanis clubs and churches and high schools and those town meetings, his back aching, aching so badly that he would have to schedule a "tub stop" every evening at the home of a supporter to soak before the dinner engagement. A "brutal" schedule, Paul Kirk said. And all the while, Ted's driver, Jack Crimmins, the curmudgeon from the first campaign and then Chappaquiddick, was loving to "rag" Ted, telling him that a candidate like Ronald Reagan, who was running for reelection to governor in California, got up at ten in the morning, did a press conference, went home, had three Bloody Marys, ate lunch, took a nap, got up for another press conference, and was finished for the day. But Ted Kennedy pushed himself, needed to push himself, needed to show people that he was not the man the accounts of Chappaquiddick made him out to be, needed to do so even though the excitement was gone. Sometimes, a friend told William Honan, the "twinkle" was there. "But at other times, I can see by the way he tightens his jaw and grits his teeth that he's thinking of those things he's been through." He debated Josiah Spaulding twice, both times without reporters present, and both times without much heat, given the candidates' agreement on most issues. Spaulding, who received no support or money from the national Republican party, even admitted he didn't care who won. And as the campaign wound down, such was Ted's growing confidence that he left Massachusetts to campaign for threatened Democratic candidates in other states.

Ted won, won easily, but scored eleven fewer percentage points than he had in 1964. Even so, the victory was a vindication—one he badly needed. In his victory speech, he hit the themes that he had been sounding before Chappaquiddick: an end to the war in Vietnam and bringing home our troops, an implicit attack on President Nixon for sowing discord and pitting American against American, a theme he had sounded at a May commencement address at Mount Holyoke, and his familiar promise to "give voice to the powerless groups that exist within our society," pointedly singling out not just minorities and the poor but the "thousands of unemployed I met on the Massachusetts streets" and the "thousands of consumers that do not have a voice in the highest councils of government," which made it appear not as if he was concluding a campaign but as if he was gearing up for a new one, even though he had explicitly rejected the idea that he would make any bid for the 1972 presidential nomination. One reporter, speaking to biographer Burton Hersh, remembered watching the returns on election night with Ted at the Parker House hotel and telling Ted that he could now start thinking about the 1972 presidential race, to which Ted snarled, "Always trying to shove me out in front where I can get shot." The reporter apologized and said he would seek out another presidential possibility. "Well—check with me before you do that," Ted parried. A Gallup poll three weeks later showed Ted just two points behind Edmund Muskie as the favorite for the nomination among the Democratic rank and file. Having won and overcome the doubts, Ted may have thought he no longer was starting from scratch. Having won, he may have thought he could challenge Richard Nixon once again.

V

Ted Kennedy wasn't the only one who believed he might have rehabilitated himself politically. So, it seemed, did the North Vietnamese. Earlier in the year, while the peace talks dragged on in Paris, the North Vietnamese had issued invitations to various figures—religious, artistic, and political—to visit Hanoi and, as Dave Burke put it, "to see what kind of people they really were and to bring back good news about them so that the United States in its bargaining position would be more at a disadvantage." Obviously realizing the propaganda value of having Ted Kennedy come, the North Vietnamese opened a channel to him and had engaged in several discussions with him about coming to Hanoi. Ted was no naïf when it came to these sorts of political maneuvers, but he was caught in a conundrum. He insisted that there be some quid pro quo, namely a list of prisoners of war held by the North Vietnamese, and he felt that, as Burke said, "If there was anything you could do that would alleviate the condition of a prisoner and didn't do it, how are you going to live with that fact?" On the other hand, "You don't want to look as though you were a sap and you were taken in because of your naïveté." As a favor to Ted, Burke had agreed to talk to Averell Harriman, the Democratic elder statesman and former diplomat, now retired in Westchester County, New York, to get his assessment. Burke said Harriman was blunt. "Teddy Kennedy is no Unitarian minister or no lady-do-gooder," like many of the others whom the North Vietnamese had enticed. If Ted was to go to Hanoi, Harriman said, he could only do it "if he comes home with no less than fifty or more" names of POWs. Burke passed this on to Ted, who promptly dispatched Burke to Paris to meet with the North Vietnamese. It was a clandestine visit. Burke spent a weekend there holed up at a hotel, but the North Vietnamese reneged, and Burke flew back empty-handed. Burke went back to the Dreyfus Fund, and that seemed to be the end of it.

But not quite the end. The North Vietnamese seemed to be wooing Ted. On December 14, five weeks after the November elections, he heard from the North Vietnamese president, Ton Duc Thang, with the news that Thang was now willing to provide a list of POWs to him. This time Ted called Harriman himself, and Harriman advised that Ted send someone over immediately. Ted contacted John Nolan, a longtime Kennedy adviser who had graduated from the Naval Academy, attended Georgetown Law School at night, worked with Bobby at the Justice Department to help negotiate the release of prisoners captured during the Bay of Pigs invasion (Nolan knew the CIA's James Donovan, whom Bobby despised), and later joined Bobby at Justice full-time as an administrative assistant. Nolan had also been one of the advance men for Ted himself before the 1968 trip to Vietnam. Nolan flew to Paris, got the twenty-two-page list—the "first complete and official list of American prisoners of war held in North Vietnam," which Ambassador Mai Van Bo said he was only providing as a courtesy to Senator Kennedy—and then went directly to the American embassy to deliver it. Bo, looking to circumvent Nixon, also invited Ted to come to Paris to discuss an end to the war, which Ted declined. The invitation, however, seemed to indicate one thing: Ted Kennedy was a player again on the world stage or the North Vietnamese wouldn't have tendered that invitation.

But despite the North Vietnamese overtures, there was one more indignity to come—one more backlash from Chappaquiddick. With the seating of the new Congress, there would be a vote for majority whip. Ted had become disillusioned with the job, and that disillusion was intensified by his retreat after Chappaquiddick. Kennedy critic Robert Sherrill thought he had been "Chappaquiddickized," meaning that his colleagues stopped listening to him, which is what had concerned Mansfield on the eighteen-year-old-vote initiative. It didn't help his cause that in early 1970 he had suffered a serious bout of pneumonia—the bout that prevented him from coming to the Senate floor to vote against Carswell—or that he was running again for the Senate in a desperate race to acquit himself, and both prevented him from conducting Senate business, even though it was the business itself that he had come to loathe. The "worst thing in the world" is how Burke described the whip job. "People liken it to a shoe shiner. . . . It's sort of like a legislative concierge." And while Ted had grown up learning to serve others, especially those in his family, he saw little advantage in being servile to his fellow senators. "He wasn't built for that job, hustling around and taking care of everybody's little problems, or sitting on the floor endlessly, minding the store," Dave Burke would say. Ted was a doer. He aspired to be a leader, not a servant. He wanted to use the job—

and had used the job before Chappaquiddick—to set policy for the Democratic caucus. But it was not a policy-setting job, and Ted came to realize that early on. It was "holding hands with all these members and their staffs," as Paul Kirk described it. Even worse, Ted's whip assistant, Wayne Owens, said it had actually prevented Ted from being his own man and "getting out in front on the gut issues," and Owens admitted that "he's been going at it maybe two-thirds of the way." Mike Mansfield was more blunt, saying that Ted seldom showed up, though Mansfield added that the same could have been said of Ted's predecessors in the position, Hubert Humphrey and Russell Long. Yet even when he did run legislation, he was not his own master. Once, Ted called up an amendment that Mansfield had promised would not be voted upon, and it passed, which forced Mansfield to come back to the floor, call it up, and withdraw it.

Dirty work. Servile work. But there was one senator who did not mind the dirty work, did not mind the servility, did not mind being the shoe-shiner or concierge or hand-holder for his colleagues, did not mind staying on the floor hour after hour after hour while Mansfield and Ted abandoned it, someone who understood the job and was built for it in a way Ted Kennedy was not, someone who did not complain—though he did bristle when Mansfield and Ted would show up on the floor in the morning before the session opened and conduct what was called "dugout chatter" for the press and then leave the floor to him from 10 A.M. to after 5 P.M., and he'd bristle again when Ted would return at day's end and ask for a quorum call so that Ted could make a statement and adjourn the Senate. He was someone who was called "the Uriah Heep of the Senate," after Charles Dickens's obsequious, oleaginous character, but who nevertheless resented the implication, as J. Stanley Kimmitt put it, of "the lord and the serf," as he had come to think of Ted's relationship to him. That man was the secretary of the Democratic Conference, the third in line of the Democratic Senate leadership, Robert Byrd of West Virginia, who, as Mansfield said, was "there almost every day and undertook any chore." And Robert Byrd had essentially been doing Ted's job for him.

Now, as the whip vote approached, Robert Byrd wanted not only the duties of majority whip but also the title. Byrd's hardscrabble upbringing couldn't have been more different from Ted Kennedy's. Born in North Carolina in November 1917, Byrd was adopted by his mother's sister and her husband, who lived in West Virginia, after his mother died of influenza in the great 1918 epidemic. He was educated in a two-room schoolhouse in a mining camp, married his high school sweetheart, and after a series of negligible jobs ran for the West Virginia House of Delegates and won, largely on the basis of campaigning by playing his fiddle; he then moved on to the House of Representatives and the Senate, earning his law degree from American University at night. When fellow senator George Smathers kept inviting Byrd down to Florida and Smathers pressed Byrd on why he declined those invitations, Byrd told him, "I have never in my life played a game of cards. I have never in my life had a golf club in my hand. I have never in my life hit a tennis ball. I have—believe it or not—never thrown a line over to catch a fish. I don't do any of those things. I have only had to work all my life." And work he did—worked and waited. But Ted had leapfrogged him when he ran for whip against Russell Long—leapfrogged because the secretary of the conference was generally next in line for whip. And for two years—the two years during which Byrd had done all those thankless duties that Ted should have done while Ted was trying to use the whip's office for his shadow presidency—Robert Byrd seethed. And Robert Byrd, the Uriah Heep of the Senate, schemed to topple him.

Ted wasn't blind to the resentment. The two men didn't much care for each other. After his reelection, Ted phoned Byrd, who was at the Greenbrier resort in West Virginia, and asked Byrd point-blank if he intended to challenge Ted for whip, because Ted was planning to leave the country for a junket and wouldn't do so if Byrd was running. When Byrd professed not to know yet whether he would run, Ted snapped, "Well, of course you know." To which Byrd riposted, "Well, if I did know, I wouldn't tell you." But within ten days of the November elections, Byrd was talking to Senate colleagues about whether he should take Ted on. He was stealthy. He didn't want Ted to think that Ted didn't still have the upper hand, even as Byrd had asked Lyndon Johnson to phone some of his colleagues on Byrd's behalf, which Johnson happily did. And Ted *was* confident, as Russell Long had been when Ted challenged him, making calls of his own and collecting promises, and having his staff make calls, and doing a nose count and tallying twenty-eight votes in his favor—so confident that he and Joan left for four days in Montego Bay while Byrd continued campaigning.

But Ted was oblivious to the growing opposition—oblivious to the fact that senators resented his seeming uninterest in the job and his absences while Byrd did the work; resented his leaving the floor as soon as he finished a speech; resented his grandiosity in moving the whip's office to a suite that was larger than Mansfield's; resented his redefinition of the job as one to generate legislation rather than to perform services. Ted Kennedy was not generally given to a sense of entitlement, but when it came to the whip job, he had felt entitled. Not even Mansfield pushed for Ted, remaining neutral while, according to the secretary of the Senate, Francis Valeo, giving "no sense that the Senate would fall apart if Kennedy weren't reelected." (Mansfield also detested Ted's staff people—"furiously ambitious," Valeo said—especially Wayne Owens, who was often on the floor.) And Ted had sown ill will with a number of colleagues, including some who had never forgiven him for ambushing Russell Long two years earlier. He had angered senators Henry Jackson and Warren Magnuson of Washington, the home state of Boeing aircraft, when he opposed funding for a supersonic transport, the prototype for which was to be built by Boeing; a filibuster against the appropriation prolonged the Senate session until January 2, 1971. He had angered Senator William Fulbright, the chairman of the Foreign Relations Committee, when, as a courtesy, he informed him about the North Vietnamese offer to provide the names of POWs; Fulbright told him that he would be sending someone to Paris the next week to pick up the list, and Ted said that he had already sent Nolan—in fact, had sent Nolan the very afternoon of the day he received the offer. Fulbright fumed that Ted had no right doing that, that it was the province of Fulbright's committee to arrange to get the list, even though the North Vietnamese had specifically contacted Ted. "He had an edge from that point on," Ted recalled. And Ted had threatened the potential presidential candidacies of a number of senators by the prospect of his own candidacy, despite his repeated disavowals that he would be running. And then there was Chappaquiddick. "The whole mood around the Senate was: Why would you kick out a sitting leader?" Walter Mondale said. "Something must have happened. And that's what happened. . . . Chappaquiddick got him."[*]

But for all that, Ted still believed on the morning of the vote that he had those twenty-eight commitments, twenty-eight out of fifty-five, counting Richard Russell, and still believed he was going to win. Russell's vote was uncertain because he was in Walter Reed Hospital at the time, on his

---

[*] Byrd, however, had a black mark of his own. He had once been a member of the Ku Klux Klan.

deathbed, though he had pledged his proxy to Byrd because he deemed Ted's support for Russell's beloved military insufficient. It was a close vote. Senate parliamentarian Robert Dove felt that if Russell had died before the vote—he died four hours later—Byrd might have withdrawn his name, since, as Ted recollected, Byrd had parlayed Russell's vote into convincing four freshman senators to support him. (Ted knew he had lost at least two freshmen because two voters, obviously newcomers, had spelled his name "Bird.") But Russell survived just long enough, and Byrd won, 31 to 24.

The bonhomie that had sustained Ted hadn't worked. Four senators had lied to Ted. Melody Miller said that afterward she was standing by the door of his private office, and the "phone was ringing off the hook." The callers were senators swearing they had voted for him, and Ted patiently fielded the calls and told each caller, "I believe you. I know you voted for me." (Of those who had betrayed him, he said he could forgive Warren Magnuson but not Henry Jackson, because he felt Jackson had benefited substantially from his brothers' support.) In the end, it was not only a failing of Ted's job as whip that led to defeat. It was a failing of his political instincts. One staff member admitted that "we should have known we were going to lose." William Hildenbrand, who would become secretary of the Senate, said that Ted had too often let staffers call his fellow senators for commitments. "It's easy to lie to a staff person. It's hard to lie to another member." Another political analyst said, "In the old days, the Kennedys didn't mark you down unless they had you." Ted didn't have them. He had been outhustled, outpoliticked, outdone, by the Senate's Uriah Heep—because, in the final analysis, while Ted wanted to win just to have a victory, he didn't really want the job itself.

Ted took the loss with equanimity. When William Honan asked if it had hurt to lose, Ted said, "There's something about me I had hoped you would understand. I can't be bruised. I can't be hurt anymore. After what's happened to me, things like that just don't touch me, they don't get to me." When Martin Nolan of *The Boston Globe* remarked to him immediately after the loss that it was the first time Ted had ever lost anything, Ted said simply, "The Kennedys have known personal tragedy before." Carey Parker recalled, "He didn't sulk. Amazingly, he was laughing about it, telling people, 'That's probably the best thing Bob Byrd has done for me, freeing me from the whip job so that I can spend my time on health care, education, the Vietnam War, and many other issues.'" And Parker said it "appealed to Byrd that Kennedy could take defeat and get back up and want to be a senator even more." In his memoir, Byrd would write of Ted's reaction: "I learned a long time ago that as long as you don't know how to lose, you don't deserve to win." To Dave Burke, Ted said, "I'm not that concerned with who said they were for me and weren't. It's over. Let's go on."

One of the few who realized that the defeat wouldn't hurt Ted's political prospects and might actually free him was Richard Nixon, who responded to the news of the defeat, H. R. Haldeman said, "quite indifferently." Nixon told Haldeman that "you don't kill a man who's been built up the way Teddy has, by a defeat, any more than you killed Nixon by his defeat [for governor in 1962] in California." And Haldeman said, "He thinks it will provide a momentary setback but that Teddy will move ahead in spite of it, with considerable strength." Nixon was right. The defeat did free Ted—freed him from the chores, freed him from the obligations, even freed him from the Republicans. Ted said that when he was the whip, the Republicans had "an opportunity to make life more difficult for me" by delaying the Senate recess if they knew Ted had a speech to give or a place to go. "Games," Ted called them. Freed from the games and the tedium of the job too, Ted used the defeat as a springboard to come back. "I burrowed in," he would write in his memoir, almost as if he was starting from scratch yet again. "I gave myself over to contemplation and study. I absorbed the Senate's history, the careers of its greatest members, the principles that lent it constancy over the years, and the many social movements and powerful figures that at times altered its influence and character." He said he reread the Constitution and then sought out mentors, as he had earlier in his career, like John Kenneth Galbraith and Carl Kaysen, the director of the Institute for Advanced Study at Princeton, and business executives and union leaders, and Mike Mansfield. Always a student of the Senate, he would learn even more in order to be an even better senator, and after Chappaquiddick he had more incentive to be a better senator—this man who had always worked to be a great senator. And Byrd would say that one day on the Senate floor Ted thanked him for having defeated him—"one of the best things that ever happened to me," Ted told him—and the two old adversaries would eventually become close. The defeat had not only liberated Ted Kennedy from the thankless labors of Senate minutiae; it had liberated him from the strictures of the party he had longed to liberalize. He regained his voice. "You are the most important force for liberalism in the Democratic party today," Joseph Rauh, the veteran liberal firebrand, wrote Ted shortly after the whip defeat, "and I hope you will never get too discouraged or downhearted to carry out that role."

Despite everything that had happened to him and everything that had happened by him, despite the deaths and defeats and the accident at Chappaquiddick, he hadn't. He was readying himself to wage war once more against Richard Nixon. Despite everything, he was readying himself.

Ted wins the Democratic majority whip in 1969, joining the Senate leadership. From left to right: Ted, majority leader Mike Mansfield, and the secretary of the Democratic conference, Robert Byrd. Ted tried to use the whip post to build a seat of power, but the position was designed for subservience, not command. *Alamy*

Joan Kennedy being greeted by President and Mrs. Nixon at a White House reception for legislators in March 1969, where she scandalized the first couple by wearing a miniskirt rather than a formal gown. Joan later admitted that at the time she was living in a void and trying to attract attention. *Bettmann/Getty Images*

Dike Bridge at night on Chappaquiddick Island off Martha's Vineyard, where Ted drove over the side and into Poucha Pond, resulting in the death of a young woman. *Bettmann/Getty Images*

Ted's black Oldsmobile being pulled out of Poucha Pond the morning after the accident on July 18, 1969, that cost Mary Jo Kopechne her life and Ted Kennedy any chance to be president. *Bettmann/Getty Images*

Mary Jo Kopechne—a bright, ambitious, compassionate young woman who had worked in Robert Kennedy's presidential campaign and had attended the party for Bobby's "boiler room girls" on Chappaquiddick. *Bettmann/Getty Images*

Ted and Joan at Mary Jo Kopechne's funeral outside Wilkes-Barre, Pennsylvania. Ethel Kennedy, Bobby's widow, is at the center. Ted wears a neck brace after suffering an injury in the accident. Joan was pregnant at the time but suffered a miscarriage. *Alamy*

After Chappaquiddick: Ted on television on July 25, 1969, speaking to his constituents and asking them whether they wanted him to continue to represent them. The speech, written by John Kennedy's courtiers, was considered bathetic and misguided and inadequate. *AP Images*

Ted returns to the Senate in late July 1969, where hundreds await him outside the Capitol, after the Chappaquiddick accident. *Bettmann/Getty Images*

The president and the shadow president: Richard Nixon and Ted Kennedy at the signing of an amendment to the Older Americans Act, which Ted co-sponsored, in September 1969, along with other sponsors of the bill. Left to right: Rep. John Brademus, Rep. Ogden Reid, Rep. William Ayres, and Sen. Harrison Williams. Ted kept pushing the administration leftward; Nixon kept trying to co-opt Ted to foil any presidential hopes of Ted's. *Bettmann/Getty Images*

Ted, as chairman of the Senate Refugee Subcommittee, visits starving East Pakistani refugees in a West Bengal camp in August 1971. Ted had become the champion of refugees around the world, while he accused the Nixon administration of dithering. *Bettmann/Getty Images*

Ted with United Auto Workers president Walter Reuther. It was Reuther who recruited Ted to be the legislative force behind a campaign for national health care that would become the cause of Ted Kennedy's life. *Alamy*

Ted with House Ways and Means chairman Wilbur Mills as both testified at Democratic Platform Committee hearings on health care in 1972. The two—Ted, who was dedicated to expansive national health insurance, and Mills, who was dedicated to budgetary restraints— made unlikely allies, though their joint effort came closer to full national health care than anything up to that time. A scandal involving Mills and an Argentine stripper dashed Ted's hopes. *Alamy*

Ted and Ted Jr. on a sled after Ted Jr.'s leg was amputated due to bone cancer. Ted had told his son he could accomplish anything, and he helped him up the sledding hill to demonstrate. Ted Jr. would say that it was after that climb that he knew he would be fine. *AP Images*

Ted and Alabama governor George Wallace at a picnic in Decatur, Alabama, on July 4, 1973, honoring Wallace. Ted defended the appearance saying it was a way of reaching voters he could not otherwise reach. But the Southern Christian Leadership Conference, seeing it as Ted currying favor for a presidential bid, condemned it as the "height of political opportunism." *UPI/Newscom*

The portent of things to come: Ted being harassed by anti-busing protesters at a rally on the City Hall Plaza in Boston in September 1974. These had been his people, but they had turned on him when he defended busing to end racial segregation. *Bettmann/Getty Images*

FOURTEEN

"People Do Not Want to Be Improved"

FOR ALL HIS disavowals, for all his promises not to run for president, still Ted Kennedy thought of the presidency, not because he lusted for it—if he had, he very well might have gotten it in 1968—or because he felt entitled to it—he was not like his brother Jack in that respect, who *did* feel entitled, or even like Bobby, who thought of it as a kind of inheritance to extend and then burnish Jack's legacy—but because he so feared and detested what he felt Richard Nixon would do to the country and thought himself perhaps the only man to save it from him. Ted was Nixon's putative rival, his most feared rival, when in June 1969, with Nixon not even six months in office, Milton Gwirtzman wrote his memo advising Ted he needed to do something outside the Senate to promote his candidacy. "It was just a constant hum," Gwirtzman said of the presidential consideration. But even aside from Chappaquiddick—and nothing now was aside from Chappaquiddick—events were conspiring to halt a Ted Kennedy candidacy. The climate was wrong, columnist Joseph Alsop had written that April. Alsop said that Ted, "mainly as a rub-off from his brother Robert," was being branded as an ally of the new left and black militants, among the very people Richard Nixon had demonized. "One may guess that he [Ted] groans aloud each morning when he sees that day's front page with its now-customary news of this or that university's campus in a state of unpardonable disruption because of SDS [Students for a Democratic Society] and black militant uproars." And then in July, Chappaquiddick seemed to put an end to any hope Ted might have had of a presidential ascension. But the Democratic field for 1972 was thin, seeming lightweights, at least as Nixon perceived them, and after Ted's 1970 Senate victory, his Judiciary aide, Jim Flug—always proactive, always aggressive—was reported as having told labor leaders to keep their options open. Ted might still run. It is unlikely that this advisory came from Ted himself. "I feel in my gut that it's the wrong time, that it's too early," he told Warren Rogers Jr., for a *Look* magazine profile titled "Kennedy's Comeback: Will He or Won't He?" And he talked about how "sometimes you can't help thinking about how it could be different," not meaning the country but his own life. He said, "There are books I haven't read. Places I haven't seen. Maybe I'd like to take my family and go sailing in the Caribbean, just going around from island to island." But in the same interview Ted, a notorious vacillator, vacillated. Just after discussing how much he might like to expand his life beyond politics, he said, "But then you look around you and see the suffering and the unfairness, and you say to yourself that you must do everything within your power to help set things straight." Rogers said that in discussing these deliberations, Ted wore his "Gethsemane face."

He was agonizing over his direction. Over lunch with Bobby's longtime aide and friend Fred Dutton, he asked Dutton what would happen if he decided not to run again—his old uncertainty arising. When Dutton asked what he had in mind, Ted said, "Maybe return to law practice in Boston. Maybe see if I can buy the *Boston Herald*. Maybe sit in the South of France." But even as Ted was yet again pondering leaving politics, "I could tell instantly that Ted was looking for just the opposite," Dutton said. *New York Post* editor James Wechsler spent two hours in private conversation with Ted and found him "obviously a very troubled, even tormented guy, and there were moments when I wondered whether he isn't masking almost unbelievable tensions, perhaps partly related to private problems as well as the shattering blows he has taken." But Wechsler's "overwhelming impression" was "of a man who finds it hard to sit back for another four years, even while recognizing that he has to maintain that posture until Muskie et al. have had a chance to prove something"—presumably something that could land them the 1972 Democratic nomination. Ted told Wechsler that the outcome of the nomination would depend on whether "the country just wants to go along quietly—or whether it really wants to turn around," and he indicated that Edmund Muskie, the Democratic front-runner at the time, was the quiet candidate, while adding that he thought the next president would be the "guy who's saying let's get out of the war now—or at least in ninety days. Not next year or in six months." He told Wechsler that he had continued to review his decision to remain in public life after Bobby's death, thinking of the risks involved, especially now that he was the sole surviving son, but that the "corollary seemed to be that if you decided to expose yourself, you might as well think of going all the way to the top." And he admitted that there was ongoing tension between the old Kennedy loyalists, especially Jack's people, and himself about whether to run, because those loyalists clearly were hoping for the same restoration that so terrified Richard Nixon. And then Ted mused that Jack had a much more formidable group of candidates in the 1960 primaries than Ted would have were he to run, but he said that George McGovern, whom he clearly admired and who had become a fierce critic of the Vietnam War, would take "all the courageous positions—maybe more than I." Wechsler felt this "strange counterpoint" within Ted between "personal fatalism and what seemed to be his clear feeling that he could be the most formidable candidate against Nixon." Ted told Wechsler that he foresaw a "very brutal campaign," especially, one could only assume, after Chappaquiddick. But his personal freight aside, he thought the current aspirants were a "lot of guys scurrying around" without inspiring people as Bobby had. And the great Senate temporizer now called for "much more radical domestic programs." When Wechsler mentioned that he could wait until 1976, Ted countered that Bobby had hedged in 1968 for precisely that reason—he had time— and that "time had a different dimension for the Kennedys." And no doubt Ted knew, as Larry O'Brien put it to old Johnson hand Joe Califano: 1972 was his only real opportunity to be president. "The longer he waits," O'Brien told Califano, "the slimmer his chances. This story"—meaning Chappaquiddick—"will fester and grow."

And yet still he vacillated, not because he feared Nixon or even because he thought he couldn't win, despite the political epitaphs that had been written for him. He vacillated largely because of his personal safety: Ted was almost certain that he would be killed were he to run and that the fear of such an eventuality obviously haunted his family. He told Wechsler that the Kennedy family was "numb" and "brutalized" after Bobby's death and said—"grimly," Wechsler observed—"I suppose our kids can see themselves standing in Arlington Cemetery again three years from now." He saw a kind of inevitability in it. "For the Kennedys, the die is cast." After Ted's Senate victory, Joan told Lester David, "I feel very strongly that I don't want my husband to be president. I've been very close to the presidency, so I don't see it as glamorous and exciting. I think of it as a lot of work. It's tough. It's risk-taking. It's everything I find unattractive." But what she really feared was the vulnerability of it. "Whenever Ted is away, say on a speaking engagement, and the phone rings, I have to force myself to pick it up," she had told a friend.

Fatalistic—Ted Kennedy had always been that. His son Patrick thought it was one of the sources for his recklessness and transgression—because he seemed to know that there was always a "shitstorm coming," and he might as well cut loose. And that might very well have been true: Ted Kennedy felt he had nothing to lose, not because he was rich and privileged, as Kennedy haters would have it, but because he was sure he was going to be cut down or, short of that, because some form of tragedy always lurked. He had been so intimate with death—all three brothers killed violently, and then Mary Jo Kopechne's drowning—that he also seemed to sense that he would never be able to outrun it. It was impossible to be a Kennedy and not feel that way. "We took a trip together," John Tunney recalled of this period, "and I could tell that this grief that he felt, which he hid pretty well from the public, was just extraordinary and very, in a way, emotionally self-destructive. I think he really thought that he was going to get his too, and this was . . . It wasn't fear. It was a sense of the futility of what was going on in his life. What had happened to Bobby and Jack, after having contributed so much, suddenly they were gone because of a crazed act of a madman or person who was psychotic." Ted talked frequently of his being the final target—of someone wanting to add him to the list of dead Kennedys. Even his staff operated in expectation of assassination. "We plan the best funerals," one aide told Lester David mordantly after Bobby's death. Almost as if to steel himself to fate, Ted kept a small blue-covered copy on his desk of Shakespeare's *Julius Caesar*, with one passage underlined in red:

> *Cowards die many times before their deaths;*
> *The valiant never taste of death but once.*
> *Of all the wonders that I yet have heard,*
> *It seems to me most strange that men should fear;*
> *Seeing that death, a necessary end,*
> *Will come when it will come.*

There was another candidate vacillating that year, this one deliberating not about whether to run or not but about which of his prospective opponents to target. That candidate was President Richard Nixon. Though Nixon gloated that Chappaquiddick seemed to have destroyed Ted Kennedy's presidential prospects and left the Democrats with that group of lightweights, any of whom Nixon was certain he could vanquish, still he obsessed over Ted Kennedy, obsessed over the idea that Kennedy might somehow rise from the political dead and bedevil him as his brothers had done—the glorious, charismatic Kennedys once again overshadowing poor, downtrodden, self-pitying Richard Nixon. "One of them gets killed, another pops up to take his place," wrote one journalist, comparing Nixon's Kennedy obsession to that of Captain Ahab with Moby Dick. "This one is slain, and a third brother emerges, stronger than ever. . . . There seemingly was no end to the Kennedys, no escaping them." Nixon was surprisingly candid about his paranoia. He would write in his memoirs that the 1968 election had been "too close for comfort"; that had it not been for the "debacle of the Chicago convention and the burden of Johnson's unpopularity," and Humphrey's delay in separating himself from Johnson, Humphrey might have beaten him (a huge admission about his own unpopularity); and that "there was no reason to expect that Democrats would be so obliging as to provide me with similar advantages in 1972." He said that if the Democrats were to unite around a candidate—he cited Ted, Muskie, or "even Humphrey again"—they might be difficult to defeat. And then Nixon delivered his seemingly innocuous strategy for his victory, framing it not as a way of attacking those opponents but of protecting himself from them: "We must begin immediately keeping track of everything the leading Democrats did. Information would be our first line of defense."

But this was not innocuous; it required stealth, skulduggery, and illegality. And it was not directed equally at his prospective opponents, though he did engage in underhanded activities against them all. His primary target was the man he most feared, the man he most loathed, the man he felt he needed to destroy: Edward Kennedy. Nixon's sensitivities to Ted Kennedy had not abated in his two years in the presidency. They had not abated after Chappaquiddick. If anything, they had intensified as the election approached. While preparing for his 1970 State of the Union Address, he advised Haldeman to give him a report on what was being done to "sanitize" the White House staff, meaning sanitize it of possible Kennedy admirers, since he had seen "big pictures of Kennedy" in an office where form letters were drafted. A short time later, in March, when Kennedy loyalist Lawrence O'Brien was reappointed chairman of the Democratic National Committee, Nixon saw it as a sign that "Teddy is back in control" (Ted wasn't) and ordered a surreptitious campaign to undermine O'Brien, about whose "effectiveness" he worried. He called it "Operation O'Brien" and put a longtime friend, Murray Chotiner, his 1950 Senate campaign manager, to whom he had given a job on the Republican National Committee, in charge of the effort—obviously as a way to hurt Ted, whom he now perceived as a growing threat, regardless of Chappaquiddick. And it wasn't only the Democratic party about which Nixon fretted. Though Chappaquiddick had derailed Ted's shadow presidency, Nixon felt that Ted had begun to reestablish it at the Brookings Institution, a liberal think tank, even though Ted had little connection with Brookings. A Kennedy "government-in-exile," he called it at a meeting with John Swearingen, the chief executive of Standard Oil of Indiana, and asked Swearingen to raise funds for the American Enterprise Institute, a conservative think tank, which could serve as an "ammunition factory" against the left.

But nothing Richard Nixon did seemed to lessen his paranoia about Ted Kennedy, however politically damaged Ted Kennedy was. Alexander Butterfield, Nixon's deputy assistant, later said, "If Ted wanted to run, you know, Nixon imagined everyone in America running to vote for Teddy." As he ginned up for the 1972 election, Nixon would say that he attempted to separate the White House from politics but realized that he couldn't do so—although it was more likely that he had no real interest in doing so, because given once again how he invariably projected his own dark devilry on his opponents, he could justify any tactic as tit for tat, payback for what he felt had been done to him in undermining his presidential aspirations. So, instead of erecting a wall between governance and politics, he would write, "I ended up keeping the pressure on the people around me to get organized, to get tough, to get information about what the other side was doing." He admitted that he might occasionally have "ordered a tail on the front-running Democrat" or that he might have urged that "department and agency files be checked for any indications of suspicious or illegal activities involving prominent Democrats." And why? "I told my staff that we should come up with the kind of imaginative dirty tricks that our Democratic opponents used against us and others so effectively in previous campaigns."

"Dirty tricks" sounded harmless, almost playful. And the ostensible driving force behind those tricks, old-fashioned political hardball, might have seemed business as usual—the sort of thing every political operative did. Except that the tricks weren't harmless; they were a dangerous abuse of power. They weren't business as usual; Ted, for one, had never deployed these sorts of "tricks," and neither had most politicians. And the motive wasn't hardball or even self-protection; it was Richard Nixon's hateful vengeance against the Kennedys, his willingness to undermine democracy to further his ambition to triumph over them. His was a personal vengeance—a vengeance meant to harass Kennedy, to embarrass him, humiliate him, destroy his political viability. "Goddamn it," Nixon griped to Haldeman that April, "there ought to be a way to get him [Kennedy] covered. I wouldn't bother with McGovern. I think with Teddy, the reason I would cover him is, from a personal standpoint—you're likely to find something on that," meaning womanizing. "You watch. I predict something more is going to happen." This led to a rumination among Nixon, his press secretary Ron Ziegler, and Haldeman on how "weird" the Kennedys were, on Joan's miniskirted appearance at the White House ("What the hell's the matter with them? What's she trying to prove?" Nixon commented, with as little understanding of Joan as Ted had), and on how the Kennedys' jetsetting lifestyle wouldn't win votes in Middle America, despite Nixon's mortal fear that it would. Two months later, Haldeman wrote Nixon about a plan to harass his opponents, again referencing "TK" and noting, "Get him—compromising situation . . . Get evidence—use another Dem as front."

To "get" Ted Kennedy. That became Richard Nixon's political mission—the *White House's* mission. In April, as Nixon was pondering how to get Ted, Jeb Magruder, a young special assistant to the president, had suggested that they assign an investigative reporter to do "in-depth background research" on Kennedy, with the caution that they route it through the Republican National Committee so that it couldn't be traced back to the administration. But Nixon didn't find that sufficient or efficient. On May 28, after stewing over a press report on his daughter Julie's new job as a teacher, Nixon told Haldeman to "go after" the Democratic presidential aspirants: "That's why I want a lot more use of wiretapping" and "tailing and so forth. . . . That's better than hiring eighteen more researchers." But even as he ordered them to go after all the Democratic contenders, there was one special target: "I mean particularly on Teddy." When Haldeman remonstrated that Kennedy wasn't a candidate, Nixon answered, "We've got spot coverage of Teddy just because, you know, wanting to know what he's doing." And he added one more admonition: "Keep after him, see?" A month later, Nixon still wasn't assuaged. Crowing over his presidential accomplishments to Ehrlichman and Haldeman, he pivoted once again to his nemesis, saying, "We've got to do some long-range planning regarding him, on the basis that it may very well go his way, and if so, there will be great pressure to forget Chappaquiddick, which is, of course, his most vulnerable point, that we can't let be forgotten." A few weeks later, Haldeman noted, "Need tail on EMK," in what he called preparation for the Democratic National Convention, which was a full year off. "Get caught w/ compromising evidence," he wrote, and then listed women with whom Ted had been rumored to have relationships, including the actress Candice Bergen: "Hit Candice Bergen." Such were the preoccupations of the president of the United States and his chief of staff.

Get Ted Kennedy. And for this mission, a year and a half out from the election, Richard Nixon, in his obsession and paranoia, had found a willing accomplice, a fellow hater: Former Marine, local Republican operative-turned-corporate-attorney, Boston-born and Boston-bred Charles Colson was, journalist Gary Paul Gates wrote, the most "impassioned" of "all the Kennedy haters at the White House," which was some achievement given how much Ted Kennedy was hated there. A "hit man," Haldeman—a hit man himself—would call him. He would run over his own grandmother to reelect Richard Nixon, it was said. "Ruthless," he called himself, though his round bespectacled face and calm demeanor belied the ruthlessness. And when Colson the hit man entered the White House late in 1969 as Nixon's special counsel, even though Nixon had averred that he couldn't have Colson carry out his nefarious schemes lest they be traced back to him, he nevertheless was assigned a role that came naturally to him: the role of Kennedy destroyer. After Ted criticized Nixon during his 1970 Senate campaign, Colson said, "I might have attacked him physically" had he encountered him. Instead, he attacked him clandestinely. It was Colson who had sent a private detective to Paris to get photographs of Ted dancing with Princess Maria Pia the night before Charles de Gaulle's funeral and Colson who, at Nixon's directive, made sure the photographs "leaked" to the press. (Two weeks later, he was still reporting to Nixon on the "Teddy Kennedy question.") It was Colson who sent a former CIA spy named E. Howard Hunt to Hyannis that July after Hunt told Colson he had a source with new, confidential information on Chappaquiddick—information that proved fruitless. (Hunt wore a red wig as a disguise.)

Get Ted Kennedy. At Nixon's instruction, Ted was being tailed everywhere: "when he goes on holidays, when he stopped in Hawaii on his way back from Pakistan," Ehrlichman told the president. "Does he do anything?" Nixon seemed eager to know. And when Ehrlichman said he was "clean . . . very clean," and that while in Hawaii he was "just as nice as he could be the whole time," Nixon warned, "Be careful now," adding, "The thing to do is to watch him, because what happens to fellows like that, who have that kind of problem"—meaning philandering—"is that they go for quite a while—" But Ehrlichman cut him off. "Yup. That's what I'm hoping for." (But Ted, though occasionally reckless, was no wildly promiscuous philanderer, and after Chappaquiddick he was not as incautious as his staff had worried.) Meanwhile, Nixon suggested that the Internal Revenue Service investigate him, just as he was considering instructing the IRS to investigate Muskie and Humphrey. "I can only hope that we are, frankly, doing a little persecuting," Nixon said. "We ought to persecute them." That same day, Richard Allen, a foreign-policy aide, had passed on to Haldeman a rumor that Ted had a stake in a Toyota auto dealership, which, Haldeman crowed, might compromise Ted with American labor since Toyota was a Japanese company. (He had no such stake.) And it wasn't only Ted Kennedy who was in the White House crosshairs but also those with whom he associated and who became collateral damage. By year's end, another Nixon aide, Gordon Strachan, had sent a memo to Haldeman saying that he was "trying to get boiler rm girls," referring to the Bobby Kennedy workers who had been at Chappaquiddick, and noting he had "stud visiting & home phone" but also observing they were "not terribly attractive." In fact, Ehrlichman had approved a scheme to recruit Lotharios to seduce the girls at a New York apartment he had rented and, as White House counsel John Dean told it, to get them to "volunteer some details of Kennedy's conduct in a moment of tenderness, or under fear of extortion."

Nixon was so fearful of Ted that he told Haldeman he was considering not delivering the State of the Union address in person, because he felt the television cameras would focus on Ted's reaction to him. And so, driven by fear, Nixon insisted the campaign to destroy Ted Kennedy—the wiretaps, the tailing, the personal investigations, the IRS audits, the Colson dispatches—would continue. "It was the sordid beginning to all Nixon's later dirty tricks," Garry Wills would write, "the break-ins, the name-blackenings, all that scurrying in back alleys to bring down the shining

Kennedy name." All of it so that Ted Kennedy could not take the presidency from Richard Nixon. All of it so that Ted Kennedy would be stripped of the very last vestiges of his moral authority.

II

While Richard Nixon and his henchmen were waging this clandestine war against Ted Kennedy and the other Democratic presidential contenders throughout 1971, Nixon was also waging a more public war: a war against liberalism. This, too, may have been a consequence of Chappaquiddick and the erosion of Ted Kennedy's moral authority. A "decisive event for the Nixon presidency," journalist Gary Paul Gates would call the accident, because "after Chappaquiddick, the restraint provided by the daily thought that Nixon might have to face Kennedy for reelection was gone. . . . And with it went the early Nixon administration goal of trying to be more centrist than conservative in domestic policy." Gates's analysis wasn't entirely correct. Nixon had continued to fear Ted Kennedy, continued to try to drive a stake into the heart of his presidential possibilities because of those fears. But the legislative preemption with which Nixon had countered Ted before Chappaquiddick was, if not gone entirely, significantly diminished. He had been emboldened not only by Ted's demise but also by the advice he was receiving—prophecies about the souring mood of the country of which he could take advantage. He admitted that he was highly influenced by a book called *The Real Majority*, co-written by two moderate Democrats, the demographer Ben Wattenberg and the former head of the census bureau, Richard Scammon. It was a primer in moderation, which argued that the average American was a forty-seven-year-old housewife from Dayton, Ohio, married to a machinist. And, Wattenberg and Scammon argued, that average American was not content. She lived in the grip of fear—fear of black people, of drugs in the college her son attended, of the decline of her neighborhood. "To know all this," they wrote, "is the beginning of political wisdom," which is to say that to understand the rupture within America, the divisions between white middle-class America and the rest of America, those very divisions that Nixon loved to nurse, was to understand how to win elections. Nixon hadn't won his presidency that way, though he had done his best. The Democratic shambles, as he had admitted, abetted him. He worked the divisions better in the 1970 midterm elections in which the Republicans had lost only nine seats in the House—a party in power typically lost many more—and gained two Senate seats. Nixon knew he was onto something. Scammon and Wattenberg's theories were reinforced by another prognosticator, Kevin Phillips, who had written a memo called "Middle America and the Emerging Republican Majority," which attracted the interest of several Nixon aides. Phillips argued that "elections were won by focusing people's resentments"—something that Nixon certainly knew and of which he was living proof—and that the new target of resentment was what Phillips called the "toryhood of change," those condescending liberal elites who sneered at Middle America. Thus did Nixon find his enemies: minorities, the young, the educated elite, and, of course, liberals. And thus did he reconfigure the political landscape around those enmities. His natural instincts for self-righteous self-pity turned into political advantage by inciting other self-righteous, self-pitying Americans. Reject the "politics of fear," Edmund Muskie had importuned in a Democratic election-eve broadcast. But Americans embraced them instead.

This was why Ted Kennedy was even countenancing a run for president, despite trepidations about his personal safety. And this was why Ted Kennedy sought to reinvigorate himself as the election approached: because he believed Richard Nixon promoted the politics of fear. Previously cautious, he once again surrendered his caution in 1971, as he had after Bobby's death. The man who had warned young people to abjure radicalism and violence, and who had delivered a cautious speech in Dublin about the risks of alienating the mainstream through civil disobedience, told students at Iona College on May 4, the first anniversary of the killings at Kent State University and just a month after a massive anti-war march in Washington, that those protesters in the capital "felt they had to do something desperate to dramatize the involvement of all Americans, and especially of all government workers, in the war, and that blocking traffic and entrances to federal buildings was all they had left." He said that most Americans could understand why the protesters "feel they should take to the streets," could understand their frustration. And he blamed Richard Nixon for that frustration—blamed him in scorching tones for failing to act. He told another crowd of students, this one at Harvard Law School, that "Richard Nixon lives in a Skinner box," referring to the boxes of the psychologist B. F. Skinner in which animals were conditioned to respond to stimuli. "He responds only to rewards and punishments that his senses can appreciate. Your silence is not neutral in his environment; it counts distinctly as pleasure. And this reinforces the rewards he gets from his own narrow constituency whenever he appeals to their basest instincts and panders to their prejudices." Ted Kennedy developed a stump speech as he traveled across the country that fall, in what many in the press were beginning to suspect was a pre-presidential candidacy tour. They called it the "forgotten promises" speech because he cited the "depressed" spirit of the country and a "sense of pessimism and defeat" that now stalked the land—the worst pessimism since the Great Depression—and he attributed it to one central fact: "Republicans had broken their promises." Nixon had promised to end the war. He hadn't. He had promised to end inflation. He hadn't. He had promised to get people off welfare. He hadn't. He had promised to reverse the rising crime rate. He hadn't. Most of all, he had promised, on the very morning after his election and citing the sign that thirteen-year-old Vicki Lynne Cole had held aloft in Deshler, Ohio, that he would "bring us together." And here Ted would grow angry, red-faced, nearly uncontrollable, shouting, "That promise lies broken now, broken like all the others, shattered by an administration that has set black against white, rich against poor, old against young, business against labor, North against South." And he would close with an appeal to support the "leadership and vision of the Democratic party."

This was Ted Kennedy as 1971 inched closer to 1972, shaking off the fatigue of Chappaquiddick because he believed he had to. After two years of doubt, he felt energized again, speeding to his Senate office in his power-blue Pontiac GTO now that his driver's license had been restored. And once again, he broadened his portfolio—the portfolio that had shrunk after Chappaquiddick and during his subsequent political retreat. "There is only one way for a Kennedy to operate," one staffer told *Newsweek,* of Ted's political reemergence, "and that is at top speed." Now he was. Carey Parker compared him to Isaiah Berlin's fox who knows many things: "He likes to keep three or four balls in the air at all times." He had a full agenda: setting up a UN relief force, funding programs for the elderly, supporting Native American education, promoting aid to refugees, reforming the draft, holding hearings on Cuban immigrants, and promoting the recognition of Cuba. If he was no longer a shadow president, he operated as if he were a shadow secretary of State. That summer, working under the auspices of his Refugee Subcommittee, he visited refugee camps in India, where eight million East Pakistanis—35,000 a day—had fled the West Pakistan government, and for whom the Nixon government had done lit-

tle or nothing. And seeing Ted walking through the camp, seeing him acknowledge them, the refugees shouted, "Zindabad Kin-a-*dee!*" "Long live
Kennedy," as *Life* magazine reported it. He saw fields awash in human
excrement, because there were no latrines in a camp of 150,000. He saw
women who kept the corpses of their babies in pipes in which they lived,
because they didn't know what to do with them. He saw children sleeping
next to dead children. He saw a tent of elderly people dying. At a refugee
hospital he lingered over a baby, who stared back at him blankly as it
awaited death because parents only brought their children there when
the children were about to die. Ted Kennedy had been intimate with death,
and he saw death. "Burned into my soul" is how Ted described the experience. Twenty carloads of reporters trailed him on these visits, drenched in
monsoon rains. But despite the rains, Ted walked a mile through one of
the camps, rejecting offers of an umbrella, to see the new arrivals, who
cried, grabbed at him, and told him how the West Pakistanis had burned
down their houses "because we are Hindus." But when Ted asked to go
into West Pakistan, where he could discuss the situation with officials, the
government rescinded its earlier invitation. So Ted stood on the banks of
the Kapathaki River, watching boat after boat filled with refugees in flight.
And Richard Nixon watched too, from afar—watched Ted Kennedy getting publicity for the suffering Pakistanis—and this is when he employed
his preemption again: He sent Secretary of State William Rogers to New
York to deliver a check to the secretary general of the United Nations,
U Thant, for $1 million for refugee relief—"blood money," Ted called the
administration's payments to West Pakistan—on the very day Ted arrived
in India, and he announced a special committee on refugees the very day
Ted returned. All this time, East Pakistan, the separatist state of Bangladesh, was awaiting independence and recognition. There was no encouragement from the Nixon administration. But Ted Kennedy would not
forget Bangladesh. In February 1972 he would make another visit, during
which he was taken to a mass grave of Bangladeshi casualties, where, by
one account, the bones lay bleached in the sun. Yet this time he had also
come to attend the inauguration of Sheik Mujibur Rahman. Sheik Rahman had finally been released by the West Pakistanis and allowed to assume leadership, and Ted spoke at his inauguration, where he was mobbed
and cheered and had garlands thrown around his neck and petals tossed
in his hair, because the people knew he had focused attention on their
plight. And he bristled at the hypocrisy of an administration that spent

money and lives on the undemocratic government of South Vietnam while showing no interest in the new, freely elected government of Bangladesh, though a State Department official admitted to biographer Theo Lippman that Ted had forced the administration's hand in providing financial support for refugees.

Meanwhile, Vietnam, the war that Nixon had promised to end during his 1968 campaign, still raged on, still preoccupied Ted, still incensed him, and he had continued to move deeper and deeper into the dove camp after having spent so much of his time protesting the war on the basis of its harm to civilians and refugees, rather than, as some of its more severe critics, on the war's overall immorality. One State Department official complained to Theo Lippman that Ted had become a captive of his staff and of the peaceniks—a "lightweight," he called Ted, and called his staff "irresponsible," while defending Nixon's prosecution of the war. But Ted, who had exhibited patience over the years as the war continued, had lost his patience. In May 1971 he visited a tent encampment in Washington erected by protesting Vietnam veterans—John Kerry, later a senator, was one of those veterans—and stayed until 2 A.M. talking with them. And in a speech on June 7, 1971, before the National Convocation of Lawyers to End the War, he issued his most blistering denunciation of Nixon's war policy yet and made his most damning and incendiary charge: "The only possible excuse for continuing the discredited policy of Vietnamizing the war, now and in the months ahead," he declared, "seems to be the president's intention to play his last great card for peace at a time closer to November 1972, when the chances will be greater that the action will benefit the coming presidential election campaign." And he asked: "How many more American soldiers must die, how many innocent Vietnamese civilians must be killed, so that the final end to the war may be announced in 1972 instead of 1971?"

Now Republicans felt Ted had crossed the line of civil political disagreement. Senator Robert Dole, the chairman of the Republican National Committee, was outraged, saying that some Democrats—he didn't mention Ted by name and didn't have to—were willing to "exceed the bounds of partisanship, reason, and common decency in their efforts to downgrade the president and advance their own personal interests." California governor Ronald Reagan, in a visit to Massachusetts the next week, drew applause by remarking, "The senator has charged that the president is playing politics with the war. This is an irresponsibility." And even Hubert

Humphrey, who had been subjected to the same charges when he was vice president, rose to Nixon's defense, saying, "I think President Nixon wants peace as badly as any senator or anybody else" and that "it is beyond the bounds of fairness to charge that any president would extend the war and cause death and injury to young Americans to get closer to an election date." Nixon phoned Humphrey to thank him.

But Ted was unchastened by the criticism. He believed from his own experience that Nixon would change policy to gain political advantage, believed that Nixon's deepest interest was his self-interest.* The next month, Ted supported an amendment co-sponsored by senators Frank Church, an Idaho Democrat, and John Sherman Cooper, a Kentucky Republican, that would stop all funding to United States forces in Southeast Asia except for those funds necessary to withdraw the forces safely. (Even Mansfield submitted a nonbinding resolution calling for total withdrawal of American troops in Southeast Asia within nine months after the return of POWs.) But Kennedy and the other doves had come to the inescapable conclusion that Nixon could not be budged and that the war would grind on until Nixon found it politically expedient to end it. And so Ted fought Nixon's war where he felt it could be most efficacious. When the draft law was up for renewal that year, he continued to press for reform, steering a bill into law that limited quotas on draft boards, enlarged the president's power over deferments, and instituted an appeals process for those denied deferments. He also opposed a proposed all-volunteer army, because he felt it might "insulate middle- and upper-class Americans from the horrors of war" and, testifying before the Armed Services Committee, said that he doubted there would have been pressure to de-escalate the war had it not been for "young men from every social background" being "threatened with service in the war"—the result of the draft lottery that Ted had encouraged. And he continued his Refugee Subcommittee hearings on Vietnam and Cambodia and Laos—hearings that infuriated the administration by directing attention at the civilian casualties. Finally, he had his all-purpose AdPrac Subcommittee hold hearings on amnesty for Vietnam draft resisters—the first such hearings on the matter—taking fire from both the administration, which was vehemently

---

*In point of fact, during the 1968 election, Nixon appears to have passed word to the South Vietnamese government not to engage in peace talks, which might have aided Humphrey's candidacy, but rather to wait instead for a Nixon administration. "Nixon Tried to Spoil Johnson's Vietnam Peace Talks in '68, Notes Show," *The New York Times*, January 2, 2017.

opposed to any amnesty, and from South Carolina senator Strom Thurmond when Ted compared amnesty for Vietnam resisters to amnesty for Southern soldiers after the Civil War.

He was aggressive, sometimes strident, delivering broadsides that fall session of 1971 almost every day—from criticisms of Nixon's planned trip to Red China, for which Ted again cited a political motive (even as he planned the trip, Nixon and his national security adviser, Henry Kissinger, were concerned that Ted might get there first and prevented him from getting a visa); to criticisms of the United Nations vote ousting Taiwan and admitting China, for which Ted said Nixon had done nothing to prepare the American people, suggesting that the lack of preparation was a way for Republicans to discredit the institution they so disliked; to criticisms of the administration's Cuban policy; to criticisms of Nixon's latest Supreme Court nominee, William Rehnquist; to a major criticism of the administration's assault on the Constitution. "They see the Constitution as a burden, an obstruction to be overcome," he told a B'nai B'rith Anti-Defamation League dinner at the Waldorf Astoria hotel in New York, "as a technical barrier to be avoided when convenient, evaded where possible, and ignored if necessary," and he cited new press restraints; overzealous wiretapping and bugging; the eagerness to prosecute the man who had leaked the Pentagon Papers on Vietnam, Daniel Ellsberg, while Justice dragged its feet in investigating the slaughter at Kent State University; the ousting of the Vietnam veterans who had encamped in Washington in May; and the "mediocrities" being considered for the Supreme Court. He received a standing ovation. "You might enjoy reading the attached," Nixon's self-described hatchet man, Charles Colson, wrote Nixon press aide Pat Buchanan of one of Ted's speeches that October, "that is, if you can get all the way through it without throwing up. It's really disgusting. It is a subtle attempt to incite riot and revolution while appearing to say just the opposite."

Bobby had been considered the Kennedy instigator, its firebrand. Now Ted was. Still, when journalist William Honan asked Ted in November whether he had moved further leftward, he hedged. "Well, it's difficult in terms of my own critical judgment to feel any change," he answered. "I feel at any given time I'm doing what needs to be done, what's right." But he revealed to another interviewer his brewing anger at the president and at the unwillingness of so many to confront him, comparing Nixon and Attorney General John Mitchell to the people who posted those IMPEACH

EARL WARREN billboards, upbraiding too many college students as being like the "silent generation of the fifties," accusing Nixon yet again of appealing to the "basest instincts" of "his own narrow constituency," and reviling him for supporting Lieutenant William Calley, who had been accused of a civilian massacre in Vietnam, and New York governor Nelson Rockefeller, who oversaw a bloody uprising at Attica prison in upstate New York where forty-three people, including thirty-three inmates, were killed. Brewing anger over the fate of the country is what Ted Kennedy was feeling that fall.

And now the question once again was: Is Ted Kennedy running? Chappaquiddick still hung heavy on him, and the weight had only seemed to increase rather than lift. In May 1971, he led all prospective Democratic candidates. By November, a Gallup poll showed Muskie leading him 50 percent to 39 percent. And a Harris poll that July indicated that while 68 percent of Americans thought Kennedy still a good senator, only 34 percent felt he had the "personality and leadership qualities a president should have," and 33 percent felt Chappaquiddick disqualified him from presidential contention, though *Time* accurately noted "seesaw polls," in which Ted would rise and fall from month to month. Nor was it likely only Chappaquiddick that had harmed him politically. As Nixon nursed those resentments, Ted's leftward swing had almost certainly hurt him. But none of this dissuaded Richard Nixon and his associates from believing that Ted Kennedy was anything but a dangerous adversary. Adverting to the dirty tricks being played on Muskie, Pat Buchanan asked Nixon that September if they should continue focusing upon Muskie, "and do all we can to damage him; or should we turn to Edward M. Kennedy—whom some consider (Nofziger among them) the most difficult candidate the president could face?" It was a fair question. With his unrelenting attacks on the president, Ted certainly sounded like a candidate, and he certainly acted like one. He just wasn't sure that he was one. That May, a confidant of Ted's had told *U.S. News & World Report* that Ted was "keeping his options open" and that it was "almost impossible to believe that at the subconscious level, he is not really thinking of the presidency," though the friend added, "Consciously, he does not want to run."

But consciously Ted Kennedy had embarked on a barnstorming tour that November of 1971—first, for two days through three Midwestern states, where he was "besieged by swarms of autograph seekers and hand shakers," by one report, and then through the West. He delivered the "broken promises" speech wherever he went—Salt Lake City, Bismarck, Denver, St. Paul. He had even taken along Joan, who gave him a back rub on the plane as it readied for takeoff and then held hands with him as it ascended, behavior that was almost unheard of between them and a sign either of Ted's high spirits or of his trying to repair his family image for a possible presidential run. Republican senator Robert Packwood, who had accompanied him on a trip to visit hospitals and community health centers in Cleveland and Chicago for the Senate Health Subcommittee on Children and Families, which Ted headed, said the reception Ted got wasn't "political. . . . It was regal. . . . People wanted to touch him, not just twenty-one-year-old student nurses but forty-five-year-old orthopedic specialists. It was astounding and a little frightening."

But was he running? William Honan, who accompanied him on the swing, said Ted kept teasing his audiences, hinting at taking on Nixon but then pulling back, telling one group of students at the University of Utah College of Law that "I intend to fulfill my responsibilities by speaking out in the Senate." Even so, Honan was certain that he had "witnessed the commencement of the third Kennedy quest for the presidency of the United States," and a former North Dakota national committeeman remarked to Honan, "If he isn't a candidate, why did he bring his wife way the hell up here?" Was he running? Ted kept saying that he wasn't, describing at a private reception hosted by Nevada governor Calvin Rampton how difficult it would be to defeat Nixon and how Nixon's only weakness was having "so many balls in the air" that "he might not be able to keep them all up" and thus might very well drop one. One afternoon after a sherry and a light lunch in his office, he told *Los Angeles Times* reporter Nick Thimmesch that he wanted to "let someone else do it this time," and that while he thought Nixon could be beaten, he didn't want to put his family through a campaign, and that "I also think I would like to do it on my own someday" and not be pressured into running. No doubt all this was true. Ted may have been champing at the bit to run. Yet he knew Nixon was formidable, the coalition of resentment Nixon had built would be difficult to defeat—especially with the sort of leftish campaign that Ted would wage and would not want to compromise—the issue of safety was a very real one, and, for a man whose destiny had always been determined by someone else, he really did want to do it in his own time and in his own way. But the crowds were large, and the crowds were enthusiastic. And the seesaw polls had begun to seesaw back in his favor, just as *Time* had predicted; by December, he led Muskie again, 32 percent to 25 percent, with Humphrey at 19 percent. When a friend asked him why, if he kept disavowing a run, he just didn't make a statement that he wouldn't accept the nomination, he said, "Why should I? I'd lose all my influence. I'd just be a senator from Massachusetts," which is what he had become after Chappaquiddick and before he had decided to reassume his role as the voice of liberalism. Arthur Schlesinger Jr. saw him that December and found him in a "jolly mood," which was certainly a change from a year earlier. "I think he is still rather fatalistic about it all, probably prepared to accept the nomination if he is asked," Schlesinger assessed, "but also prepared to see many advantages if he is not asked."

III

Among those advantages was not having to rein himself in. After having been lacerated for his June speech that accused Nixon of postponing peace in Vietnam to bolster his reelection chances, Ted Kennedy doubled down in January with a speech before the National Press Club. He said Nixon had sacrificed the lives of "tens of thousands" of Vietnamese to secure his reelection and that the failure of his Vietnam policy was "matched only by the shame of our policy toward India and Pakistan." He reminded his listeners of Nixon's election promise to end the war and of the twenty thousand Americans who had given their lives since and of the South Vietnamese government that would "immediately wash away in the stench of its own incompetence and corruption" as soon as the Americans left. And he said of Nixon's civil rights policy, which was largely talking about law and order, that "you have to go back to the era of Reconstruction to find a comparable abdication by the federal government of its responsibility." In April, after Nixon launched a new wave of B-52 strikes on North Vietnam, Ted once again excoriated him, calling the so-called policy of "Vietnamization"—letting the South Vietnamese gradually take over their own defense from the Americans—a "wholly immoral and unjustifiable test" that is being "carried out with the lives of men, women, and children." The next month, Nixon announced his mining of Hai Phong harbor in North Vietnam, prompting Ted to call it a "futile military gesture taken in desperation," though by this time even General Creighton Abrams, the commander of American forces there, had delivered a report admitting that it was "quite possible that South Vietnam has lost the will to fight or to hang together, and the whole thing may well be lost." When Armed Services Committee chairman John Stennis submitted a resolution capping the number of draftees at 150,000 unless the president deemed he needed more, Ted spoke on the Senate floor against the clause, and Stennis later approached him in the cloakroom to lower the number to 130,000 and to eliminate the president's discretion. The exclusion carried, 78 to 4.

But in his opposition to the war and to Nixon, Ted did more, much more, something that surely, had it been exposed and had he been a presidential candidate, would have roused Republican wrath and subjected him to scathing criticism. It is unclear whether Ted initiated the contact—which is likely, since he had been regularly writing North Vietnamese leader Ho Chi Minh, asking him to observe the Geneva Conventions and let the Red Cross visit POWs—or whether the North Vietnamese contacted him first. When an international law attorney named Walter Sohier, who had worked in the Kennedy administration and was now based in Paris, met with Prime Minister Pham Vanh Dong during a visit to Hanoi, Sohier brought up the prospect of Ted visiting North Vietnam, which Dong heartily endorsed, obviously realizing the public-relations value of such a visit. Ted, picking up on the offer, once again sent David Burke to see Averell Harriman to discuss the propriety of a visit. Harriman urged Burke to go to Paris in the cause of peace, on Ted's behalf. So late that July, Burke did, along with Sohier, and the two of them met with Le Duc Tho, the principal North Vietnamese negotiator at the talks there. Burke told Tho that Ted was a "voice of power and impact in the United States" and that he wanted to see the damage done by American bombing on North Vietnam firsthand. But Burke admitted that some of Ted's advisers would oppose a trip and that he would be criticized for interfering with the peace process, so the North Vietnamese would have to make some gesture, some quid pro quo, to demonstrate that Ted was right in wanting to visit North Vietnam. What Burke proposed was releasing a "substantial number" of POWs. Tho said the offer was "interesting" and that he would pass it on to Hanoi. And then Burke concluded the meeting by telling Tho something that easily could be construed as interfering with the peace talks—a tack perilously close to what Nixon had done before the 1968 election. He said he thought Ted would be president someday and that Ted would do nothing to "hamper that goal," apparently by making any deal with the North Vietnamese that did not include a release of POWs—in short, using his possible presidency as a bargaining chip. But in discussing Ted's presidential future, a future that could conceivably arrive as soon as that November, Burke was basically undercutting the administration. Tho told Burke that he assumed that if casualties continued to rise, Nixon would lose the election anyway, but Burke disagreed. It would take more to defeat Richard Nixon than that. But in any case, Ted never heard from the North Vietnamese, and he did not make a trip there—a trip he would undoubtedly have used to attack Nixon. Nevertheless, three days after the meeting in Paris, the Senate narrowly passed an amendment introduced by Massachusetts junior senator Edward Brooke, calling for the withdrawal of all American troops from Vietnam within four months, conditioned on release of all POWs and an account of missing soldiers. In supporting it, Ted said, "I believe that our whole involvement in Vietnam was wrong, wrong from the beginning, and that our sacrifice should have ended a long time ago." And he chided Nixon for continuing to believe that "our sacrifice must continue until we win our goal, even if that means that our prisoners must remain in Hanoi."

But all this did was raise yet again the issue of whether he would run against Nixon. Political scientist and historian James MacGregor Burns, who had written a campaign biography of John Kennedy in 1960 and would write one on Ted, cited Ted's schedule early that year, 1972, as a candidate's schedule, zipping around the country in April from South Carolina to San Francisco to Alabama to Louisiana to West Virginia, and then in May to Cleveland, Chicago, Des Moines, San Francisco (again), Los Angeles, and South Dakota for subcommittee hearings (which themselves lent steam to the idea that he was running), and then in June to Atlantic City and Portland. If he wasn't considering a run, why the campaign swing? Journalist William Honan, who was also writing a campaign biography of Ted on the prospect that he might run and who was following him around the country, concluded that the "special Kennedy amalgam of liberalism and sophistication, steadiness and attack" were "both bred and drummed into his sinews," and it was "much to contend with"—so much so that Honan thought he was a candidate. Still, Ted continued to dismiss the possibility. *The New York Times*'s Anthony Lewis, who had been close to Bobby and had access to Ted, reported that Ted was "determined not to be the nominee himself this year" and was ready to endorse the outspoken anti-war candidate George McGovern, "if and when his support would really make a difference." But the suspicion continued to lurk, Lewis wrote, that Ted "hopes to be a compromise candidate this July"—a suspicion that so bothered Ted, according to friends, that he felt he might have to endorse McGovern early if a stalemate developed with Humphrey. At the same time, McGovern himself knew most people thought that the nomination was Ted's "for the asking," which it probably was.

That was Richard Nixon's belief as well. Though Muskie had been the front-runner throughout the fall of 1971, Nixon dismissed him as the "George Romney of the Democratic party," referring to the Michigan governor and 1968 Republican front-runner, who faded quickly in the media glare. (In Muskie's case, Nixon's dirty tricks contributed to the fade: Nixon's minions had posted a letter in New Hampshire's biggest newspaper, the *Manchester Union Leader*, accusing Muskie of using the slur "Canucks" about people of French Canadian origin, a sizable group in New Hampshire, and then the same paper published an article attacking Muskie's wife, Jane, for drinking, prompting Muskie to deliver an emotional defense of her in a snowstorm outside the newspaper's offices; the snowflakes melting on his cheeks gave the impression of Muskie crying and created a media story about Muskie's weakness.) According to columnist Joseph Alsop, as late as March 1972, Nixon still expected Ted to emerge as his opponent. "Of course it's going to be Kennedy," Alsop quoted a top Nixon aide. "What else do you expect? The Democratic party is up to its *blank* in pygmies, so the party is bound to turn to Kennedy in the end. And if the party turns to him, Kennedy is bound to go." So convinced was Nixon about Ted's chances that he ordered an anti-Kennedy mailing in New Hampshire before the primary there, paid for by cash payments from Colson. But it wasn't only Nixon who assumed Ted would run. Despite Ted's repeated insistence that he was not running, Mike Mansfield introduced and got passed legislation providing Ted with Secret Service protection, after an attempt on George Wallace's life while Wallace was campaigning for the nomination, because, Mansfield said, the "public thinks he is a candidate."

It was not that simple, however, even if Ted had wanted to run. And no one knew that better than George McGovern. After the 1968 debacle, in which Hubert Humphrey won the nomination despite contesting none of the primaries, supporters of Eugene McCarthy pressed the convention to adopt reforms that would give "all Democratic voters" access to the nominating process by instituting procedures to open the process to public participation. And those procedures were to be instituted within a year of the convention. The Democratic party chairman, Senator Fred Harris, appointed two committees to fulfill the commitment—one to reform delegate selection and one to reform party rules. McGovern knew because he was appointed to chair the committee on delegate selection. It was not an easy task. The reformers, who had been rebuffed by the forces of Lyndon Johnson and Hubert Humphrey in 1968, were determined to lessen the power of party bosses and elected officials, the very people who had stood in Bobby Kennedy's way, by broadening the primaries—as it turned out, from seventeen states in 1968 to twenty-three in 1972, which would have provided a winner of the primaries enough delegates to get the nomination. Those bosses and party officials, however, were just as determined to retain their power—so determined that one of them, I. W. Abel, the president of the Steelworkers Union, who was a member of McGovern's committee, didn't deign to attend a single session. "Idealists versus pragmatists" is how the battle was framed (Joe Kennedy had complained of a similar division back in the early 1950s between the "fundamental principles" of the party, meaning the old-timers, and what he called the "pseudo-influence of the ADA [Americans for Democratic Action]," a group of liberal intellectuals), or "new politics" versus "old politics," though it might better have been framed as grassroots activists, who had been weaned on the civil rights movement and anti-war protests, versus the insiders. And it threatened to tear apart the party yet again.

McGovern knew. McGovern had helped devise the rules. He understood that the victor wouldn't be chosen this time as Humphrey had been in 1968, by the party brass ignoring ordinary Democratic voters. He understood that the eventual nominee would have to contest the primaries, and that while Ted Kennedy might easily win them, he could not win the nomination without entering them. Moreover, he knew the scars that Chappaquiddick had inflicted. That weekend in 1969 he had been vacationing at a wealthy friend's home in the Virgin Islands when he heard the news. He said he tried to call Ted but couldn't reach him. He then spent the evening sitting in the moonlight around his friend's pool, "thinking alternately about Ted, about my own future, and about the American spacemen—Neil Armstrong, Edwin Aldrin, and Michael Collins—who were about to reach the moon." He recalled, "The next morning when I awakened late with the sun streaming in my face, I experienced a vague feeling that I might well be the Democratic presidential nominee in 1972"—might be because Ted Kennedy now couldn't be.

None of this was a foregone conclusion. There were a half dozen candidates. Edmund Muskie, Humphrey's 1968 running mate and the early favorite, had won the New Hampshire primary, but Muskie's campaign combusted over a series of gaffes, including those fueled by Nixon's dirty tricks, like the speech in the snowstorm, and after losing Wisconsin, Massachusetts, and Pennsylvania that April, he withdrew. Humphrey was contending again, but the party had lurched leftward over Vietnam, and while he retained the support of the party machine and the old party stalwarts and most of labor (AFL–CIO president George Meany remained a staunch supporter of the war), and while he won a band of states in the Midwest, there were large factions that opposed the war vehemently and wanted the election to be a referendum on it. These were McGovern's voters, many of them anti-war activists, and they were energized against those old party bosses who continued to support the war—the new against the old. And there was Alabama governor George Wallace, who had taken 13 percent of the vote in the 1968 general election as an independent and who was now running as a Democrat, using the same inflammatory racial appeal he had used then. Wallace won Florida and narrowly lost Indiana to Humphrey before rebounding with victories in Tennessee and North Carolina, which threw a scare into the liberals. But McGovern, the outsider, the peacenik, was racking up victories too. On April 4, he won the most hotly contested of the primaries, Wisconsin, beating Humphrey in his neighboring state. Three weeks later, he trounced Muskie in Massachusetts, then lost narrowly to Humphrey in Ohio, then picked up a series of smaller states—Nebraska, Oregon, Rhode Island—before taking the big prize, a winner-take-all state, meaning the winner won all the state's delegates: California. Meanwhile, Wallace, while campaigning at a shopping mall in Laurel, Maryland, on May 15, was gravely wounded and paralyzed by a young would-be assassin named Arthur Bremer, who was looking for celebrity. (He had stalked Nixon first and opined that killing Wallace would not make anywhere near the splash that killing Nixon would have.) Wallace, the racist, won Maryland the next day and Michigan too. Ted, who always tried not to let politics vitiate human decency, visited him in the hospital and then again that fall back in Montgomery. (It was not Ted Kennedy's finest hour; there were those who assumed that he was trying to get Wallace's support, and there was little reason to think otherwise.) But with his wounding, Wallace's candidacy was over. It seemed down to McGovern, whom the party regulars despised as a renegade and who they thought was a sure loser, and Humphrey, whom they liked much better but who was freighted with the baggage of the war and who didn't seem a likely victor either.

And then there was Ted Kennedy—*still.* The old pols liked Ted, thought he could win, felt that while McGovern was a left-wing ideologue and Humphrey just a beneficiary of the party infrastructure, *their* infrastructure, Ted had bona fides with the left, the potential support of the infrastructure, and charisma as well. As the primary season rolled on, Ted couldn't discourage speculation. Moreover, Ted appealed to the activists as much as he did to the pols. The "most liberal member of the Senate— including McGovern," reporter Jack Newfield called him. Only Ted, many felt, could unite the party's warring factions and have a chance of beating Nixon, which is exactly what was said in 1968 after Bobby's death. After Wallace's victory in Florida, Senator Ernest Hollings of South Carolina, anticipating that the liberals would do anything to stop Wallace, told columnist David Broder, "Shoot, if this keeps up, there is no way he can avoid it." And Senator Alan Cranston of California told Broder that there was more talk about Kennedy's candidacy in the Senate than at any time since the New Hampshire primary. To which Ted told Broder that he wouldn't run even if Wallace—this was before Wallace's injury—threatened to win the nomination. After McGovern dispatched Humphrey in Wisconsin, Nixon told Haldeman "to be sure that we get people to follow up on the line that Kennedy is now the obvious Democratic candidate," which is why Nixon also readily agreed to Secret Service protection for Kennedy— because "there's general agreement that he's going to be the candidate," even if there was no such general agreement, and, more, because Nixon was no doubt hoping to smoke him out rather than let the convention anoint him, and he wanted to have spies on Ted. Humorist Art Buchwald found the speculation so absurd in light of the fact that Ted hadn't entered a primary or declared any interest in the nomination that he wrote a column asking "Ted" about his intentions of taking over as conductor of the National Symphony Orchestra. "Could you possibly conceive of any conditions where you would accept a draft as conductor or run for first violinist with the orchestra?" To which Buchwald had Ted answer, "I would not exclude the possibilities. If I believed my accepting the position as conductor or first violinist could have a dramatic effect on the orchestra, I would have to reconsider my position."

It was an old game, a tired game. Ted would later tell biographer Adam Clymer that he never thought of running in 1972, presumably meaning once the primaries began, because of his admiration for McGovern: "I liked him and I thought he was courageous." (This was likely untrue. Ted had thought about running, but there were too many obstacles, including the very real possibility of losing to Nixon.) As if to prove the point that he was a McGovern man, on May 23, during a campaign hiatus called in respect of Wallace's injury, Ted met privately with McGovern in Washington to offer his endorsement should McGovern need it, though not wanting to squander his future political capital, he also said that if McGovern didn't need it, it might not come. Yet even the leak of that meeting didn't dissuade the pragmatists from yearning for Ted. By one report, that month George Meany met with Ted to beg him to run and stop McGovern, and the report said Ted was noncommittal. Years later, Ted said he didn't remember any such meeting and in any case it was highly unlikely that he would have stepped in to stop someone he respected, someone he thought courageous.

Thus George McGovern arrived at the Democratic National Convention in Miami that July as the odds-on favorite. Humphrey's last gasp was challenging the "unit rule," which required California to give all its delegates to the primary victor, who was McGovern. (In this case, McGovern benefited from a vestige of the old party rules.) Once Humphrey lost that bid, McGovern's nomination was inevitable. And so the stalwarts swallowed hard, even as Norman Mailer reported that the chairman of the House Ways and Means Committee, and a former candidate himself, Wilbur Mills, was cruising convention parties and touting a plan to stop McGovern. Ted Kennedy was the plan. But Ted Kennedy was off in Hyannis sailing at the time and told reporters he would not be following the convention. Now the speculation about Ted gaining the nomination was finally over—only to spark new speculation, this time about whether he might be the vice-presidential nominee. Earlier that year, Ted had asked Milton Gwirtzman to write a memo laying out the advantages of accepting the nomination for vice president against the advantages of staying in the Senate, though Gwirtzman was blunt about the real purpose of the memo: "Which would position you better to be president?" McGovern had thought of Ted as his running mate all along. He was certainly cognizant of Ted's apprehensions, some of which they shared. McGovern's senior advisor, Frank Mankiewicz, who had been Bobby's press secretary, admitted, "We were all afraid of [Chappaquiddick]," and he said he had the "feeling he [Ted] didn't want to raise those issues," which would probably preclude him from accepting. Nevertheless, McGovern felt he might be able to convince him—because Ted could begin to deal with the Chappaquiddick fallout as a vice-presidential candidate; because McGovern would promise him high security and carefully manage his public appearances to protect him from assassination; and because he knew Ted felt a duty to the party. McGovern had also been encouraged by an interview Ted had given to Martin Nolan of *The Boston Globe,* in which Ted said he might accept the nomination if he thought it would be the difference between success and failure, but he hedged later by saying that he was only answering a hypothetical question and that he didn't think his being on the ticket would mean that much. (To help convince him, Ted Sorensen had drafted a memo telling Ted that he could serve simultaneously as vice president *and* in the Cabinet, lest he fear being no more than a figurehead.) To McGovern directly, on the Senate floor, Ted said that family obligations would prevent him from running. John Tunney said that Ted was "having some family problems at the time . . . serious family problems," no doubt referring to Joan, "and I think he felt that he just couldn't handle it," presumably meaning the rigors of a campaign. But McGovern kept pressing—pressing because he obviously appreciated the benefit of having Ted on his ticket. As soon as he had won the nomination, he repaired to his hotel room in the Doral and made the case to two old Kennedy hands, Fred Dutton and Bill Dougherty, and then phoned Ted at Hyannis and pleaded that the country needed him if it was to change direction. "He seemed both tempted and troubled," McGovern would recall. After fifteen minutes, Ted agreed to sleep on it and call McGovern in the morning if he had changed his mind. No call came. Instead, Ted told reporters he had declined the nomination. As much as he feared what Nixon was doing to the country, he would not challenge him in an election.

But there was this: McGovern had been so fixated on Ted Kennedy as his running mate that he hadn't seemed to give much consideration to others, and in any case, few were eager to accept a nomination that seemed worthless since McGovern's campaign seemed doom to fail. After being rejected by Ted, McGovern had run down a list: senators Gaylord

Nelson of Wisconsin, Abraham Ribicoff of Connecticut, and Walter Mondale of Minnesota, all of whom declined. According to Ted, the next names on the list included United Auto Workers president Leonard Woodcock, CBS News anchor Walter Cronkite, Notre Dame president Theodore Hesburgh, Texas state representative Frances "Sissy" Farenthold, and Wisconsin governor Patrick Lucey, a Kennedy ally, who was apparently disqualified when his wife, in a huff, locked him out of his hotel room. Then McGovern, as Ted told it, seemed to have settled on Ted's brother-in-law, Sargent Shriver. But Shriver was in Moscow at the time and was unreachable. (McGovern also said that Ted was "reservedly resistant" to the idea when he broached it.) Finally, there was Mayor Kevin White of Boston, who, McGovern thought, could appeal to Catholics and blue-collar voters. Since White and Ted were both from Massachusetts, McGovern realized he would have to sound Ted out about White, and he had an aide call him to see if he had any objection. Ted told the aide he hadn't, but McGovern, exercising caution, decided to phone Ted personally, which is when Ted raised what McGovern called "some serious questions" about White—the animosity went all the way back to 1962, when White endorsed Eddie McCormack, and kept building from there. Ted told McGovern that he couldn't campaign with any enthusiasm if White was on the ticket and suggested Ribicoff (again), Wilbur Mills, or Missouri senator Thomas Eagleton. Time was running out. McGovern, who had labored hard for the nomination for months, now left the most important decision of the campaign to the last ninety minutes before filing on the last day of the convention. Desperate, he asked Ted if he might reconsider. Ted said he would, then called back a short time later—at two-thirty on the day of the nomination—to say he hadn't changed his mind and that if McGovern wanted White, he would fly him down to the convention in Miami on the Kennedy family plane.* But McGovern didn't want White now. Instead, bereft of choices, McGovern settled on Thomas Eagleton, which led to a chaotic nominating process that evening, with eight names placed in

---

*John Kenneth Galbraith later said he was the one who torpedoed White, because White had headed Muskie's delegate slate in Massachusetts, and the delegation, a McGovern delegation, would not have approved of White on the ticket. He phoned McGovern to say the delegates might walk out if he selected White. John Kenneth Galbraith, *A Life in Our Times* (Boston: Houghton Mifflin Co., 1981), 524; McGovern, 198. Ted told Adam Clymer that he thought the "folklore" about his opposition to White arose because he believed McGovern would carry Massachusetts and that White wouldn't bring anything to the ticket. EMK interview, 1996–1999, Clymer Papers, Series 2, Box 5, JFK Library, October 9, 1995.

nomination and votes going as well to Archie Bunker, a character on the popular television program *All in the Family*, and Mao Zedong, and which delayed McGovern's acceptance speech, an effective speech with the refrain "Come home, America"—come home from Vietnam—until just before 3 A.M., when no one was watching. It was a catastrophe. It was also a harbinger of what was to come.

And it didn't take long. Eighteen days after the convention ended, it was revealed that Eagleton had undergone electroshock therapy to deal with severe depression and had failed to divulge it to McGovern. (In truth, there hadn't been time.) McGovern was put in the untenable situation of either supporting Eagleton, which is what McGovern did initially, despite doubts about Eagleton's mental fitness for office, or jettisoning him to save the campaign. He wound up doing the latter, which now forced him to find a replacement, essentially ending whatever slim chance he ever had of defeating Nixon, since he now seemed both disloyal and incompetent. (Ted, always the conciliator, made a point of phoning Eagleton to express his sympathy for his plight. "Your phone call to me was a magnificent act of genuine compassion," Eagleton wrote him back. "I started out my political career as a Kennedy man, and I am still 10,000 percent in the Kennedy corner.") As McGovern later described his frantic search for a replacement, he first approached Mike Mansfield—secretly, at 10 P.M. at Mansfield's house, with Mansfield in his pajamas—who said no. Then McGovern returned to Ted. This was a prospect that terrified Nixon, who thought he had finally put Ted to rest. "Bad for us" is how Nixon described that prospect. As it arose, Nixon began "agonizing," as Haldeman put it, thinking of ways to sabotage Kennedy and sitting and talking with press secretary Ron Ziegler "on the whole Kennedy story about his involvement with the socialite Amanda Burden up in New York." He remarked to his national security adviser, Henry Kissinger, "What the hell is the matter with Teddy?" still fixating on Ted's womanizing, and decided it was the "booze" that made Ted so indiscreet. This triggered Kissinger to relate a conversation he'd had with Cristina Ford, the beautiful Italian-born wife of Henry Ford II, who told him about Ted "grabbing her by the legs" during a dinner at his home to celebrate the opening of the Kennedy Center in Washington and then about how he followed her to New York and practically "beat her door down" at her suite at the Carlyle Hotel. "She said she'd been pursued by many men in her life, but Teddy just is impossible." And when Mrs. Ford asked Ted what would happen if the papers got ahold of his pursuit, she said that he told her, "No newspapers are going to print anything about me. I've got that covered." (If true, it would have been very uncharacteristic of Ted, who never bragged of his clout.) To which Nixon said, "Jesus Christ! That's pretty arrogant." And now, fearing that Ted might wind up on the ticket after all, he told Ehrlichman to reinstate the Secret Service protection that Ted had asked to be dropped in June. "You understand what the problem is," he said to Ehrlichman. "If the son of a bitch gets shot, they'll say we didn't furnish it. So you just buy the insurance. Then, after the election, he doesn't get a goddamn thing. If he gets shot, it's too damn bad." But this time, Nixon added another wrinkle: He, not the "son of a bitch" Secret Service chief, James Rowley, would pick the agents himself. "Plant one, plant two guys on him," the president said. "This would be very useful." (In the event, it appears that Nixon had a former Secret Service agent from his old vice-presidential detail, a man named Robert Newbrand, arrange the spying operation.) And when Haldeman added, "They are never, at any hour of the day or night, to let him out of their sight," Nixon gushed, "Like a goddamn blanket. . . . Let the son of a bitch squeal." And then he rhapsodized: "He doesn't know what he's really getting into. We're going to cover him, and we're not going to take no for an answer. He can't say no to the Secret Service."

And while Richard Nixon was plotting how to kneecap Ted Kennedy, George McGovern was still plotting how to lure him onto the ticket. (Art Buchwald joked in his column that whenever the vice-presidential nomination was at stake, Ted headed to sea. This time, he "ordered a sailboat ready and provisioned it for a month.") But this time Ted, for all his protestations, was listening. McGovern said that he, Ted, and Tunney discussed the matter "for over an hour" in the office of Francis Valeo, the secretary of the Senate. "Kennedy seemed about to accept," McGovern recalled, perhaps projecting his desire onto Ted. "His face was flushed; he looked and sounded as if he was grappling with the possibility. It was not one of those times when he simply said, 'No, I'm not going to do it.' Instead, this time he said, 'I don't know.'" Ted admitted that his place on the ticket might be the only escape from the Eagleton situation, and, "pacing the floor," he mentioned Sorensen's memo about his serving as both vice president and as a Cabinet officer, to which McGovern replied that they could work that out. McGovern kept pressing, and then Tunney weighed in. "Ted, I think you ought to do it," he said. "You and George could put this thing together." Ted told McGovern, "You're awfully persuasive. You make it hard," and he sat down to deliberate. Then he leapt up, walked over to McGovern's chair, and shook his hand, giving McGovern the impression that they were shaking on the deal. They weren't. "I just can't do it," he said. And now it was finally over.*

But it wasn't over for McGovern. He still needed a running mate. He considered Humphrey, and Ted agreed to speak to him on McGovern's behalf, and he did, but Humphrey declined, telling Ted that he didn't want to be perceived as an old "warhorse" who gets dragged out at every election. By this point, on August 3, McGovern told Ted at the back of the Senate that he was interested in Ted's brother-in-law Sargent Shriver, currently in private legal practice, but that he wanted to offer the position to Muskie first. Ted said he relayed this information to Shriver, who was now at the Cape, beginning a reprise of 1968, when Humphrey considered Shriver for vice president and the Kennedys rejected the idea on the basis that Shriver had remained in his post as ambassador to France rather than resign and aid Bobby's campaign. This time, Ted raised no objection. And this time, Sargent Shriver became the Democratic vice-presidential nominee. And now the race was on—such as it was.

IV

"We have the candidate we want as our opponent," Nixon had told Haldeman after George McGovern's nomination, "but if they take Teddy as the VP, then we'll have to change our tactics a little." Now that Ted was not the vice-presidential nominee, Nixon set his strategy. He had felt circumscribed during his first term of the presidency—circumscribed in part because of the looming presence of Ted Kennedy and the near-religious devotion he engendered. Though the liberals had feared Nixon, he had had to use preemption, beating Ted Kennedy and the liberals at their own game. He had created the Environmental Protection Agency by executive order, instituted wage and price controls to curb inflation, ordered affirmative action in federal contracts, introduced and got enacted the Occupational Safety and Health Act to protect workers, approved initiatives to fight hunger, and initiated Supplemental Security Income to assist the disabled and elderly who were either ineligible for Social Security or whose benefits were not sufficient. Overall, Nixon's spending on social programs

---

* Neither Ted nor Tunney ever discussed this meeting in subsequent interviews.

would eventually exceed that of Lyndon Johnson. Some of this was a function of one of the incongruities of conservatism itself: the willingness to expand government so long as the expansion further empowered the executive. Most of it was a function of Nixon trying to position himself to fend off liberal attacks. As one of his advisers, Daniel Patrick Moynihan, who was also one of those responsible for pushing Nixon in a more leftward direction, would put it, "Richard Nixon mostly opted for liberal policies, merely clothing them . . . in conservative rhetoric."

But this was not the way Richard Nixon wanted to govern or would have chosen to govern had he been left to his devices—preempting, making concessions, acting as if morality mattered. It was politics that forced him to govern this way, and he had been laying the groundwork throughout his term to recalibrate the party coalitions and vanquish the liberal establishment. Playing on Nixon's inferiority complex, Kissinger had expatiated on that liberal establishment, telling Haldeman that no matter what Nixon did, "they'll still be against us, not because of the Hiss case* and that kind of thing but because Nixon's not one of them and won't pay attention to them." As Kissinger assessed it, it had been a mistake "talking to all the liberals and so forth when there's no hope of winning or changing them." They would be better off fighting the liberals, he said, than trying to appease them, better off using Colson "in a brutal, vicious attack on the opposition." In this, Kissinger was only expressing what Nixon himself was feeling: no more appeasement of the liberals. His goal now was what the liberals had assumed he had sought all along: to destroy liberalism. "Feels that we've got to recognize what our mandate is," Haldeman said of the president in his diary, and Nixon laid out his post-election strategy, assuming that he would easily beat McGovern. "It's not toward a more liberal domestic policy. That we've had enough social programs: forced integration, education, housing, and so on."

Nixon said the liberal establishment thought people wanted these things—wanted betterment. Nixon knew they didn't, knew that they felt betterment meant betterment for others and that it came at their expense, knew that betterment was a liberal fallacy. "People do not want to be im-

---

* As a congressman, Nixon had become a national figure as chairman of a subcommittee investigating whether a former government official, Alger Hiss, was telling the truth when he denied he had been a Soviet agent. Those who believed Hiss reviled Nixon. Those who believed Hiss's accuser, Whittaker Chambers, lionized Nixon. Decoded Soviet files released by the CIA in 1995 and 1996 proved that Hiss had indeed been a Soviet agent.

proved. . . . They don't want to help the working poor, and our mood has to be harder on this, not softer." In short, he understood the moral underpinnings of the Great Society and understood he needed to work actively against them if he was to undermine the so-called liberal establishment and shore up his power. He had to appeal to people's own narrow self-interest, not the larger human or national interest. *People don't want to help other people*. That was the basis of the end of liberalism as Richard Nixon viewed it.

Nixon didn't have to work too hard to achieve his goal. It was clear that the Democratic party was divided, factionalized, and ripe for the taking. And Nixon, the great divider, continued to pry those divides and widen them in the hope of luring those disaffected Democrats to him. The Vietnam War had opened huge cleavages, as McGovern himself fully recognized. "So long as the war continued," he would write in his memoir, "it would shatter the Democratic party. The debate between 'hawks and doves' was largely a conflict between Democrats. A 'hawkish' Democratic presidential candidate risked alienating the 'dovish' faction; likewise, a 'dovish' candidate would alienate many of the 'hawks.'" McGovern, a dove, had certainly divided the party that way and had driven off rank-and-file Democrats who saw any opposition to the war as unpatriotic, notwithstanding the fact that McGovern himself had been a World War II aviator and hero with a Distinguished Flying Cross. As columnist E. J. Dionne Jr. would later observe, "The more the New Left's critique of American 'imperialism' came to be seen as the central ideology of the anti-war movement, the easier it became for supporters of intervention in Vietnam to cast their foes as anti-American." (Indeed, a study showed that Americans felt more negatively toward "Vietnam War Protesters" than toward any other political group.)

The civil rights movement had opened another huge cleavage. Nixon aide Pat Buchanan had written a seven-page memo in 1971 that suggested ways of widening that cleavage too, including promoting a black vice-presidential candidate for the Democrats by sending out bumper stickers to black neighborhoods. "We should do what is within our power to have a black nominated for Number Two," Buchanan wrote. He believed a black nominee would "cut the Democratic party and the country in half; my view is that we would have far the larger half." Nixon loved these racial antagonisms. When, in September, Nixon discussed with Haldeman the composition of his new Cabinet once he had achieved his expected victory, Haldeman wrote in his diary, "He's not concerned about Jews on either the Cabinet or the Court, or any of the courts, but will keep [Herbert] Stein [who was chairman of the Council of Economic Advisers] and K[issinger]. As a guideline, we should work for Catholics, Labor, Ethnic, Democrats. Not blacks, not Jews."

Not blacks. Not Jews. Following the Wattenberg–Scammon playbook, he would aim his campaign—aim his presidency—at the "unyoung, unpoor, and unblack" in a backlash against the liberal agenda. And political historian Rick Perlstein said that in targeting the white urban working class that had been the foundation of the old New Deal coalition, Nixon would not dangle economic carrots, as politicians traditionally did. He would demonize the Democrats and turn the working man against his party, not because the party had failed to help him, though in some cases it had, but because the party had also worked to help others whom the white working class distrusted. "The Democratic party: enemy of the working man," Perlstein observed, though, more accurately, Nixon was working "the enemy of my enemy is my friend" idea. "It was the political version of that *New York Times* photograph of the stockbroker and the pipefitter joined in solidarity in the act of clobbering a hippie—their common weapon the American flag." And Perlstein noted a Haldeman observation: "Patriotic themes to counter an economic depression will get response from the unemployed." He was right.

If anyone on the left understood this as well as Nixon, it was Ted Kennedy, who had always been sensitive to the sense of grievance in America. Even as the media had been speculating about whether or not Ted would run, he told *Time* ruefully late in 1971 that the mood of the country was fear—"fear of the worker losing his job, fear of businessmen for the collapse of their company, fear of the wealthy losing their resources, fear of the blue-collar worker that he may lose his job to a black, the fear of whites by blacks, the fear of older persons that they won't have sufficient resources to live." The fears of 1968 had not dissipated. They had increased. The country was riven by fears that Richard Nixon had done everything in his power to stoke. And Ted was fully cognizant that Nixon could use the white working class's fears to separate them from the Democratic party. He was also cognizant that the white working class's sense of grievance could be provoked and then parlayed by demagogues. "We have to recognize how often the working man has been failed by his government, failed by the Democratic party, failed by the Americans for Democratic Action," Ted told the ADA as the campaign was heating up, "failed by his employer, failed by his labor union. And then, when a clever speaker comes to him and says, 'They've abandoned you, but at least I am for you'—then we can understand why this man casts his vote for a George C. Wallace." He said Wallace, but he also meant Richard Nixon.

McGovern couldn't combat that appeal. He was the very personification of the lefty that Nixon loathed and whom Nixon could brand as out of touch with his Silent Majority. A conservative slogan—actually hatched by one of McGovern's Democratic detractors—was "acid, abortion, and amnesty," putting McGovern on the side of the outsiders who were subverting American values. (In truth, McGovern had moderated his positions, opposing the legalization of marijuana, leaving abortion out of the Democratic platform, and calling for postponement of any consideration of amnesty until after the war ended.) Another slogan, "limousine liberal"—a label that an ethnic, blue-collar candidate for New York mayor, Democrat Mario Procaccino, had flung at the handsome, elegant, liberal, Kennedy-like mayor, John Lindsay, a Republican, during Lindsay's 1969 mayoral reelection campaign, and that congealed all the sneering vengeance the working class held toward what they felt was the contempt of the educated classes—had subsequently stuck to all liberals, putting McGovern, son of a Methodist pastor in rural South Dakota and a man arguably more comfortable on a tractor than in a limousine, on the side of the elitists. Ted fought for McGovern, fought to correct the image. After a summer of sailing, he lent himself to the campaign, joining McGovern on the stump that September over four days and through nine cities and drawing huge crowds. But Ted's appearances only seemed to underscore McGovern's deficiencies—his stilted speaking style, which McGovern attributed to the discomfort he felt listening to hyper-dramatic evangelists when he was a boy in South Dakota; his inability to connect with the working class; his seeming hectoring of his audiences; his humorlessness; his lack of charisma. When the two appeared in Minneapolis before ten thousand enthusiastic Minnesotans, Governor Wendell Anderson made a gaffe by introducing Ted as the "man who will be back in 1976 as the Democratic nominee and the next president of the United States," at which point the crowd screamed. And Ted then rescued Anderson from his gaffe and McGovern from his embarrassment by saying that the governor was right. "I will be back in Minneapolis in 1976, campaigning for the reelection of a great Democratic president—George McGovern." They drew equally large crowds in Philadelphia—"popular frenzy in the streets," reported *The Washington Post*—where Ted said that the "only thing that worries me about electing George McGovern is that I'm afraid Richard Nixon is going to be so mad at us, he never will tell us about his secret plan to end the war," and in Pittsburgh, where the ovation Ted drew when he introduced McGovern—"elongating his name like a wrestling announcer," wrote one reporter—prompted the candidate to say, "I'm never sure when I get up to speak whether that applause is for his introduction or for me. We'll take it either way." Jules Witcover, covering the campaign for the *Los Angeles Times,* cited "young girls jumping and squealing, and older ones grabbing Kennedy's outstretched hands"—reminiscent of Bobby's campaign—and yelling, "Teddy!" McGovern said he was walking down the street in Pittsburgh when a woman nearly ran him over to get to Ted. "Oh, Senator Kennedy, we just can't wait until 1976," she told him, and then, seeing McGovern, apologized to him. "I'm sorry, Senator McGovern. But that's just the way we feel here in Pittsburgh." David Broder wrote, "Where he goes, there are shouts and there are tears, there is full-throated laughter and there is the crush of eager crowds." Julie Baumgold, writing in *New York* magazine, detected a "quiet forgiveness" and a "real liking" and a "wistfulness that went beyond the tumult"—almost as if the sin of Chappaquiddick had finally been forgiven.

Wistful the election would be.

It was the biggest landslide in electoral votes in presidential history, bigger even than Lyndon Johnson's. Nixon carried forty-nine of the fifty states; McGovern carried only Massachusetts and the District of Columbia. Nixon won 60.7 percent of the vote; McGovern 37.5 percent. Nixon's margin of victory was eighteen million votes—another record. "It remains the mystery of my life that this unscrupulous man could deceive so many Americans for so long," McGovern would write in his memoir. Nixon was no beloved figure, not even a great deceiver. Voters seemed to know him for what he was, but what he was, what he had always been, was that demagogue, seething with resentments, who knew how to pick at Americans' scabs. McGovern had wanted the election to be his referendum on the war and on the immorality that he believed fed it. He exhorted Americans to be better. But Nixon had bet that Americans didn't want to be told that their war was immoral and that the old liberal habit, worked so effectively by the Kennedys—the habit of making Americans feel better about themselves by first making them feel worse about themselves with reminders of the iniquities to which society had subjected their less-fortunate fellow citizens—had played out. Instead, he had made the election into a referendum not on the war or even on himself but on themselves, on their own fears and prejudices, which translated into an overwhelming repudiation of McGovern for having repudiated the old centrist liberal consensus. "They labeled the Democrats as the party of high taxes and anti-Americanism, and the label stuck," Senator Thomas Daschle, later the Democratic Senate leader, would write of this time. " 'Never again,' these conservatives said, drawing a line in the sand to separate themselves from the forces that had, in their view, nearly brought down our society. This was a historical moment. Because from that point forward, 'liberal' became a dirty word, one even Democrats came to avoid."

The 1972 presidential election isn't customarily thought of as historic—one in which the political coalitions were reconfigured. There was no transfer of power, no seeming change. Ronald Reagan's election in 1980 is the one usually seen as a realignment, with blue-collar Democrats abandoning their party for the blandishments of conservatism. But for all that, Daschle was correct: The coalitions had begun to change in 1972, which is precisely what Nixon had calculated. By one poll, 36 percent of Democrats voted for Nixon—*Nixon* Democrats—and 54 percent of blue-collar workers did, figures that testified to how successfully he had radicalized McGovern in the public mind and turned McGovern's natural constituency against him. But the significance of the election was more than Nixon having attracted disaffected Democrats to the Republican party. It was the *way* in which he had managed to polarize the country while he attracted them. As McGovern was seeming to crack the liberal consensus from the left, Nixon, far more successfully, had cracked it from the right, pitting one cohort of Americans against another, so that there were now, as Rick Perlstein would put it, "two separate and irreconcilable sets of apocalyptic fears" coexisting "in the minds of two separate and irreconcilable groups of Americans." *Irreconcilable.* That was Nixon's plan, as he expressed it to Haldeman, Nixon's dream, born of his own deep belief—clearly another of his projections—that "the new leftists"—the anti-war protesters, the civil rights advocates, the feminists, the environmentalists, the supporters of gay rights—who had commandeered the Democratic party for McGovern were not idealists but rather implacable power mongers, basically heirs of the communists against whom he had built his career, bent on destroying the establishment, while his own adherents on the right only wanted to "conserve good things." Speaking to Haldeman of the drive of the left, he said, in one of his great feats of projection, "The goal is power by any means." To stop them, Nixon would tear America apart and take the larger portion, just as Pat Buchanan had suggested in 1968.

But it didn't end there. As he pondered his certain victory, Nixon, in conjunction with former Texas governor John Connally—a conservative Democrat-soon-to-turn-Republican, a man nearly as unscrupulous as Nixon himself, a man whom Nixon had appointed secretary of the Treasury in 1971 and who then stepped down a year later to head Democrats for Nixon during the campaign, a man whom Nixon considered his successor—pondered something else, something much larger than a single electoral win, a political holy grail: *a permanent majority*. To achieve it, Nixon had thought not just of dismantling the Great Society but of shattering the liberal consensus itself once and for all by forming a new party, an Independent Conservative party, or "something of that sort," Haldeman would note in his diary. This party "would bring in a coalition of Southern Democrats and other conservative Democrats, along with middle-road to conservative Republicans"; an anti-black, anti-liberal party, as the British journalist Godfrey Hodgson would later describe it, though it would also be an anti–Wall Street party, since Nixon distrusted the elitists of Wall Street too; a party built on the "traditional values of the middle class: hard work, individual enterprise, orderly behavior, love of country, moral piety, material progress," or at least that would be its rhetoric, as it had been Nixon's rhetoric. A "new majority party," Haldeman enthused. "Under a new name. Get control of Congress without an election, simply by the realignment, and make a truly historic change in the entire American political structure." This would not be an economic party. Nixon had long believed that culture counted for more than economics, and he had campaigned that way. It would be a party with a patina of values but with the pulse of hatred underneath the patina, sworn to protect the nation from "hippies and black-power militants, from drug addicts and welfare mothers," as Hodgson put it. And while this power dream of Richard Nixon's, this dream of triumph atop hate, didn't evolve into a brand-new party, as he had hoped, it would infuse the Republican party and change it for decades to come while, as Daschle had said, marginalizing liberalism to the point where it practically became taboo. In taking on the consensus, Richard Nixon was trying to kill both old-fashioned Main Street Republicanism and old-fashioned New Deal liberalism.

Such was the political disaster George McGovern's defeat had wrought. There were some glimmers of hope. Even as McGovern was going down to his historic loss, Democrats actually gained two Senate seats and lost only twelve House seats, which spoke to the way Nixon had demonized McGovern but not also, as he had hoped, the entire congressional Democratic party. A Gallup poll came to a similar conclusion: It was McGovern's loss, or at least a loss of what Nixon had convinced voters McGovern represented. An October poll indicated that had Ted run, he would have fared better, still losing but by 52 percent to 43 percent; he would have taken the youth vote, 55 percent to 41 percent, a vote that Nixon won against McGovern; the Catholic vote, 53 percent to 43 percent (McGovern lost 59 percent to 37 in the polling); and, most important, the blue-collar vote, 53 percent to 41 percent. In short, Ted Kennedy might have upset Nixon's master plan by stemming Democratic defections. But Ted did not blame McGovern. "He spoke warmly about McGovern," Arthur Schlesinger Jr. wrote in his journal after a post-election conversation with Ted, "and felt that he had aroused a genuine intensity of support in the country, but, of course, in far too small a group." Ted told Schlesinger that "race was the hidden issue in the campaign and felt rather pessimistic about the possibility of stopping the drift of low-income whites, who feel threatened by racial change, into the Republican party." Schlesinger thought that if Ted's analysis was right, it would "make the years ahead very difficult for Democrats, especially if Republican candidates continue to be sufficiently unscrupulous to follow the Nixon example and manipulate the race issue for party advantage," which is precisely what Nixon wanted to do.

And in all of this, Nixon was exploiting not just hatred but demographic shifts that undermined the basis of liberalism and made lower- and middle-class whites feel more self-protective. Among those shifts were growing suburbanization and, with it, growing homeownership; migration westward out of the Eastern cities to the Sun Belt; and, perhaps above all, the decline of unionized blue-collar jobs. One political scientist, Everett Carll Ladd Jr., called this the "embourgeoisement of the working class" and saw it as the primary reason that blue-collar workers had turned on the Democratic party—the party that had tossed them the lifesaver of the New Deal when they were drowning in the Great Depression. "What we now call liberalism," he wrote, "frequently makes the old New Deal majority contributors rather than beneficiaries."

Ted Kennedy was typically a political optimist, even as he was a personal fatalist, but the election had shaken his belief in the electoral prospects of liberalism and, more, in the appeal of liberalism itself to large swaths of the public—Nixon's swaths. And it confirmed to him not only the role that fear had played in Nixon's reelection, as he had predicted, but also the role that anger had played—an anger to which so many liberals had been oblivious. He, too, worried that in catering, as he would put it to James MacGregor Burns, to "people who have been left behind by the economic movement in this country" and "have suffered severe deprivation," the Great Society had created a "serious sense of injustice and resentment" among those who felt they had been forgotten by the government—not, ironically, the poor, but those lower- and middle-class whites—despite numerous programs that had helped them. He had met with Ben Wattenberg after the election, and Wattenberg told *Los Angeles Times* reporter Lou Cannon that Ted had "read the results of 1972 clearly and he is resisting being painted into an ideological corner from which he cannot escape," namely the far-left corner. And Ted told Lester David of the Democratic party after 1972 that "there are no easy answers, no panacea. No one candidate will come soaring out of the sky and, after one campaign, suddenly make all things right."

But that is exactly what the most hopeful Democrats were thinking—that Ted Kennedy would ride to the party's rescue in 1976. "While living with impending defeat this fall, Democrats dreamed of victory next time with Ted," *Time* said in its election postmortem titled "Edward Kennedy Now the Hope," and continued, "No wonder that before the final votes were counted, Kennedy was being touted for 1976." But there were four years for Democrats to endure before then, not only four more years of Richard Nixon and his various misdeeds, as Democrats saw them, but four more years of Ted Kennedy. As *Time* examined the Democrats' future in its article touting Ted as the new hope, it recognized the danger of doing so. "Even casual gossip, which they would dismiss if it concerned another man, makes them edgy when it involves Kennedy." Ted was "trouble-prone," said one Democrat. Said another to *Time*, "He's got a fine future if he can keep his snoot clean." But Richard Nixon had long been determined to catch him if he didn't. And Nixon's paranoid obsession with trying to catch him would help lead to Nixon's undoing.

FIFTEEN

"Awesome Power with No Discipline"

TED KENNEDY, DESPITE his disappointment in the outcome of the election and despite his deep distrust of Richard Nixon, nevertheless extended an olive branch to him, because that is how Ted Kennedy operated politically, trying to find accommodation even with those with whom he vehemently disagreed, and that is the kind of man he was personally, reaching out. A month after McGovern's trouncing, Ted, speaking at a dinner in Los Angeles honoring Democratic contributor Eugene Wyman, said that "without abandoning any of the basic principles we have fought for," he was "confident that we can close ranks" with the Republicans— a remarkable statement given how much time he had spent hammering away at them. But Richard Nixon, newly elected and newly emboldened, was not so confident. For him, the presidency had always been a way to even the score. During the campaign he had told H. R. Haldeman that "after the election we will have awesome power with no discipline, that is, there won't be another election coming up to discipline us, and we've got to do our planning on that basis." Now Nixon was liberated. Two months after Ted's olive branch, he told Haldeman that he would seem to be conciliatory, that he would position himself as seeming to care for the underprivileged—"We have to do like Bobby Kennedy, say you care about the poor folk, say we want to do those things," as if Bobby had been making those declarations for political gain—but then in the next sentence Nixon couldn't help himself from attacking those liberals who professed to want to aid the poor. He snarled about "the poison in the upper classes, the loss of faith in the country," snarled that "they hated the country, the country is corrupt and prejudiced," or, as Haldeman put it, "the whole McGovern argument thing." There would be no closing of ranks for Richard Nixon. There would only be the same embitterment, the same anger, the same pitched battle to defeat the liberals. And Haldeman said that Nixon, always the divider, had become especially enamored of Clinton Rossiter's book, *The American Presidency,* published in 1956, and of its analysis of Dwight Eisenhower: "which is that in terms of great leadership, it is better perhaps to have half the people like what we do and the other half hate him than it is to have the great center who likes him and only a small fringe on either side who worship him and hate him." Nixon had been preempting the Democrats' agenda so as to appease that great center. Now he was thinking it no longer mattered.

Ted Kennedy was not so naïve as to think that the Democrats and Republicans would bridge their ideological divide. But he did believe that the Republicans and Democrats in Congress might bridge their political divide in opposing Nixon's executive encroachments on congressional power. An "imperial presidency" was what historian Arthur Schlesinger Jr. had called the new executive in a book that year—a presidency in which power had accrued beyond the limits that had been set in the Constitution; a presidency that was nearly unbounded, with satraps doing the president's bidding and without most of those satraps being subject to the advice and consent of the Senate; a presidency that had agglomerated a bureaucracy of its own, beholden to the president and only to the president; a presidency that had overridden the other branches of government and was now unrestrained and without accountability.

Awesome power with no discipline. It was a concept that had long been gestating in Richard Nixon's mind—something that may have driven him to the presidency to redress all those grievances of his. He needed awesome power to do so—power without check or balance. Nixon, though once a senator himself, had little interest in the Senate and even less respect for its power. "You can vote any way you want," he once told Minority Leader Hugh Scott. "No one gives a shit what the Senate does or how the Senate does." (How different a view that was from that of Ted Kennedy, who had such great respect for the Senate.) And Richard Nixon took some pleasure in proving to the Senate that it didn't matter—that he could disregard it with impunity.

It was in that spirit of disregard that two years earlier, over the five-day Christmas break in 1970, Nixon killed a bill sponsored by Ted to provide a $225 million grant to medical schools to encourage them to promote family practice, an underserved area of medicine. The Family Practice Medicine Act had passed both houses of Congress overwhelmingly, and constitutionally Nixon had ten days to sign the bill, veto it and return it to Congress for an override, or do nothing, in which case it would become law. Ten days. But Nixon had a fourth option, an obscure option, a technicality: If Congress was out of session for an extended period of time, typically over a long adjournment, and the president didn't return the bill within ten days, it would not become law; rather, it would die from a "pocket veto" on the basis that there was no Congress to which to return it. Traditionally, even if the tenth day fell during a brief recess, the president would return the bill, and traditionally, the pocket veto was not used during an intrasession recess—that is, a recess in a single session of Congress—and in this case, the lame-duck Congress had actually come back from the Christmas holiday to finish uncompleted business before the installation of the newly elected Congress, which made Nixon's move not to return Ted's bill even more egregious. (Of course, the fact that the bill was Ted Kennedy's was likely a reason why Nixon didn't return it— another way to flaunt his power against Ted's.) Nixon dug in. He fiercely opposed the bill on the grounds that it was too expensive—"piecemeal" and "unnecessary," he said—and decided to breach tradition. Despite the short adjournment, he failed to return the bill, and when the five-day Christmas break was over, he declared the bill dead since Congress hadn't been in session. No president had ever "pocket-vetoed" a bill for a five-day adjournment. Now one had.

Ted was incensed. A Senate man, he took congressional prerogatives seriously, but, as Ted's aide Carey Parker recalled, the constitutional lawyers Ted consulted said there seemed to be only one recourse: Someone would have to sue the president—someone with the standing to sue the president, which is to say, someone who was negatively affected by the president's action. Nixon had taken nearly all of Ted's assaults on his policies personally, as if the primary reason Ted opposed them was because he held a grudge against Nixon, which is precisely how Nixon would have reacted had the roles been reversed. Now Ted took the pocket veto personally—personally because he took any affront to his beloved Senate personally. He decided that *he* would file suit as an aggrieved party—the legislator who had introduced the legislation. And so Ted Kennedy filed suit in the District Court for the District of Columbia asking the court to invalidate the veto as unconstitutional and post the bill as public law. (Technically, Ted sued not the president but a man named Arthur Sampson, administrator of the General Services Administration and the senior federal official responsible for enrolling legislation on the statute books, and another named Thomas Jones, the chief of White House records.) And not only did Ted Kennedy file the suit; he also decided that he would argue the case himself before the court, which, as Carey Parker put it, was "relatively unheard of for a senator," though Ted had also argued for the eighteen-year-old vote in court.

Now, after two years and shortly after Nixon's second inauguration, at a time when Nixon was being buffeted by investigations into his campaign activities, the case was finally being heard, and it pitted Ted Kennedy against Richard Nixon. As he had done so many times before, Ted convened a group of constitutional experts, who prepped him assiduously and then drafted a brief that Ted internalized, and on February 28, 1973, in a courtroom packed with reporters, family—including his wife, Joan, Ethel Kennedy, and his sisters Jean and Eunice—and curiosity seekers who had come to see a Kennedy, Ted Kennedy nervously grabbed the lectern—nervous because of how little experience he had arguing before a court since his Suffolk DA days—and appeared before District Court judge Joseph Waddy to beat back what he felt was Richard Nixon's abuse of executive authority. Nixon's Justice Department attorney argued that Ted lacked standing. Judge Waddy ruled that he did have standing. Nixon's attorney argued that the president was within his constitutional rights to veto the bill. Ted countered that "the president's action prevented a member of the U.S. Senate from voting [either to override the veto or uphold it] as surely as if he had physically stopped this member of the U.S. Senate from voting," and that the founding fathers had never intended to give the president an absolute veto, which is what the pocket veto would amount to for any legislation he didn't like "if it came to him at spring, Christmas, or Thanksgiving recess." And he said that no president had ever used a pocket veto for a piece of legislation as significant as this one. Judge Waddy ruled for Ted here too. Ted would later admit to reporters to being tense in the courtroom at first, "but when I got to the ad-libbing"— that is, answering the judge's questions—"I eased up, don't you think? It was sort of like 'rapping,' and I feel better about doing that than the other," meaning his formal presentation. Nixon appealed, and Ted once again argued the case in circuit court, and Nixon lost yet again. But Carey Parker felt the president chose not to appeal it to the Supreme Court so as to deprive Ted of another possible victory and to spare his administration another likely humiliating defeat at the hands of the man he loathed, though as Ted saw it, the victory was not his; it was the Senate's. Richard Nixon, however, almost certainly saw it differently.

Awesome power with no discipline. That is what Ted Kennedy had so feared of Nixon's reelection and what he hoped to curb once Nixon was reelected. And now it became the president versus Ted Kennedy. They jousted—the president and his fiercest antagonist—jousted for advantage, jousted to exert their will on policy, jousted, in Ted's case, to reveal the moral hollowness of the Nixon administration. Ted still operated his own shadow State Department, so they jousted over foreign policy where Nixon seemed to have no compunction about being on the side of authoritarians. Ted sent his old Refugee Subcommittee aide, George Abrams, and another longtime aide, Dale DeHaan, to the Middle East to file reports on how peace might be achieved there, and Ted followed up with a trip of his own— a senatorial secretary of State doing what he believed the executive secretary of State had failed to do. He jousted with Nixon on Latin America, working with Senator Frank Church to end torture in Brazil, and when a military coup headed by General Augusto Pinochet toppled the government in Chile, he held hearings on the consequences and introduced Senate resolutions to, as his aide Mark Schneider described it, "release political prisoners, stop human rights violations, restore democracy, and later to bar military aid to the new government." Schneider said, "That got the attention of the Pinochet government," and added, "This was all opposed by the Nixon administration." And Ted took a delegation to Chile at the invitation of the government, which wanted him to see how they had snatched the country from the jaws of communism, but Ted insisted that his group be given full access to anyone, including political prisoners. "We did, in fact, see people who had been tortured," Schneider recalled. "We met with the widows of people who had been killed," including the mother of Michelle Bachelet, who would later become president of Chile. "We met the cardinal." And then Ted returned to Washington and held hearings to report what he had seen and heard in an effort to extend the cutoff of aid to the Pinochet government. Ted submitted a bill to that effect, an amendment to the War Powers Act, which was a way of practically forcing Nixon to veto it and show the president's willingness to support dictatorship. He did. In the interim, before Ted could resubmit it as a stand-alone bill, Henry Kissinger, the former national security adviser and now the recently appointed secretary of State, signed new contracts with Pinochet, rendering the provisions moot. They jousted over the Soviet Union and the pace of the release of Soviet Jews. The administration had promised to work to gain their release, but Ted felt it had been less than zealous in doing so, and he applied pressure of his own on the administration—chastising Attorney General Richard Kleindienst for breaking his promises, releasing summations of correspondence with Secretary of State William Rogers, Kissinger's predecessor, about Ted's desire to expedite Jewish emigration, even calling on the Intergovernmental Committee for European Migration in Geneva to step up *its* efforts. Nor was it only the émigrés on whose behalf Ted worked. He wanted to improve relations with the Soviets and avoid a military confrontation. He told *New York Post* editor James Wechsler that Kissinger had advised him in "utmost privacy": "If your brother had one-tenth the chances Nixon has had for agreement with the Russians, the world would be really different now."

Most of all, they jousted on Vietnam, the war that Nixon had promised to end—the war about which Kissinger had declared in October, during the campaign, that "peace was at hand." But two months later, just before Christmas, on December 18, Nixon ordered a resumption of the bombing—massive bombing, 20,000 tons of bombs—in retaliation for the breakdown of the Paris peace talks five days earlier (peace was not at hand), bombing that only ended after eleven days when the North Vietnamese returned to the peace table. By that point, at long last, the Democrats had had enough. On January 2, 1973, the House Democratic Caucus passed a resolution calling for the termination of all funds for the war as soon as the POWs had been returned and our troops withdrawn, the latter of which it demanded immediately. Ted introduced the resolution in the Senate Democratic Caucus, where it passed two days later, 36 to 12, which showed how Ted's position had now become his party's position. But even as the North Vietnamese and the Americans reached a tentative agreement on a truce, the Indochina War had not ended. Cambodia and Laos were still being bombarded, and while the Senate voted 63 to 26 for an amendment submitted by Republican Clifford Case and Democrat Frank Church to cut off all war funding on June 29, it permitted Nixon to postpone the implementation for forty-five days—an extension Nixon extracted on the threat of a veto. Ted was furious and harangued Church's aide, Tom Dine, at the rear of the Senate, for making the concession. The compromise, he said in a speech on the floor, would "go down in infamy in

American history," and he declared, "The Cambodian blood that is shed between now and August 15 will be on the hands of the Senate of the United States, and none of us should have to bear that stain. . . ." It was a tough indictment, a scathing indictment—the kind of indictment one seldom heard in the Senate.

Despite the Senate's capitulation, Ted would not relent, keeping the pressure on the administration, monitoring it to make sure it was really advancing peace and, more, to make sure that it was acting humanely, since Ted was skeptical that Nixon had any interest in the people of Vietnam, only in Nixon's own political advantage. He had sent Dale DeHaan to North Vietnam that April as part of an Indochina Study Mission, which primarily visited medical facilities in the country, though the group had also met with North Vietnamese foreign minister Nguyen Duy Trinh and with the leadership of the Pathet Lao (the communist group in Laos), the Cambodian People's National Liberation Front, and the Provisional Revolutionary Government of South Vietnam, a shadow government formed by the North Vietnamese communist forces—meetings that seemed to prepare for the inevitable communist takeover. Of the two weeks of saturation bombing ordered by Richard Nixon, DeHaan concluded in a report to Ted, "In contrast to the official U.S. government assessment on bomb damage, the Study Mission confirms massive destruction—to civilian installations including medical facilities, schools, housing." And Ted wrote more letters, dozens of letters: letters to John Hannah, the head of the Agency for International Development, on the treatment of orphans and on the use of defoliants by American forces and their effect on the crops of the South Vietnamese (Hannah, following the administration line, insisted that the failure of the crops was due to mold and weather, not chemicals); to Secretary of State William Rogers on the treatment of political prisoners; to Daniel Parker, the USAID administrator, on the lack of humanitarian progress in Indochina; and to Secretary of Defense Elliot Richardson on military practices. Ted had basically made himself the ombudsman for the South Vietnamese civilians and for many of the North Vietnamese as well, and a mid-level official at the State Department told biographer Theo Lippman that his guardianship had its impact, if only because Nixon was determined to blunt Ted's criticism. "A lot of times I was able to win an argument for a better system of helping refugees and civilians, and even for a higher level of expenditures," the official said, "not by saying that I wanted to do this or that, not by saying that it was the smart thing to do or the right thing to do, but by saying that if we did it, Kennedy wouldn't be able to criticize us." That was all the administration needed to hear to get it to act: that it would silence Ted Kennedy.

II

But there was one criticism that first year of Richard Nixon's second term that was far more difficult for Nixon to co-opt or dodge, because the man of great deceptions born of great paranoia had finally been caught red-handed. Having cooked up numerous dirty tricks against his possible Democratic opponents; having sicced the government on anyone who crossed him—"full list . . . full field audit," Haldeman ordered, meaning an IRS audit of the tax returns of prominent figures who spoke out against Nixon's Vietnam policy, having encouraged the planting of false stories, like the one about Ed Muskie's wife or his "Canuck" slur; having directed his associates to distribute false polls showing McGovern gaining (in order to enhance McGovern's chances of winning the nomination, since he was considered the easiest opponent); having ordered his associates to wiretap and tail his opponents and put moles in their campaigns and dig out private information on them with Charles Colson's operatives posing as reporters and spreading gossip to friendly press outlets about them; having his operatives fabricate cables to "prove" that John Kennedy had ordered the assassination of former South Vietnamese president Ngo Dinh Diem; having (as Colson later told it) his henchmen try to plant left-wing literature in the apartment of George Wallace's would-be assassin, Arthur Bremer, to link him to the Democrats—after having done all those things and many, many more, some of which were not done at Nixon's explicit instruction but all of which were done with his general blessing, the president's operatives and those working on his behalf finally slipped up.

The morning of June 17, 1972, a ragtag crew of burglars, who had been dispatched by Nixon's hand-selected representatives at the Committee for the Reelection of the President (CREEP) to plant wiretaps in the Democratic National Committee headquarters, were arrested after an alert security guard noticed the tape they had placed across the strike plate on the door lock to hold the bolt open. Those headquarters overlooking the Potomac River were housed in an office–apartment complex called Watergate, which would soon become a metonym for all of Richard Nixon's depredations.

What exactly Nixon's operatives had hoped to find in the headquarters was a mystery, even to those conducting the break-in. Presumably, the operatives, headed by a former FBI agent and self-styled swashbuckler named G. Gordon Liddy—a "cowboy," he was called by detractors, or a "wild man"—sought to get some intelligence from the taps on the phones of Lawrence O'Brien, the DNC chairman and a close associate of the Kennedys, or perhaps some dirt on the Democrats. Liddy would later say, though, that when he and his colleagues returned to the Watergate for a second break-in, the first having yielded no significant information and the taps having failed, their purpose was "to find out what O'Brien had of a derogatory nature about us, not for us to get something on him." The first break-in, on May 28, may very well have been prompted, or at least advanced, by seeking information on Ted, which made Ted Kennedy an unwitting instigator of the Watergate affair. One of the burglars, Bernard Barker, claimed that the break-in was launched because CREEP sought information about an alleged relationship between Ted, McGovern, and Cuban leader Fidel Castro. The investigative columnist Jack Anderson also cited Ted. He wrote that it was Ted's relationship to O'Brien that prompted the break-in, since Nixon was certain that McGovern was just a stalking horse for Ted, and Nixon, according to Anderson, had opened an internal investigation to determine if O'Brien would attempt to deadlock the convention and then urge McGovern to step aside for Ted—Nixon's deep, overriding fear. The break-in may have been a way to corroborate the theory. (The man who developed photos of documents that the burglars had shot during the first break-in remembered that one of those documents mentioned either Robert or Ted Kennedy—"real cloak-and-dagger stuff," he said.)

It was incontestable that a disproportionate amount of Nixon's underhandedness and abuse of power had been directed at Ted Kennedy, and it was even arguable that Nixon's so-called dirty tricks were hatched by his attempts to destroy Ted after Chappaquiddick, leading to Nixon's later subversions of democracy. By one account, two enterprising reporters for *The Washington Post*, Carl Bernstein and Bob Woodward, who had begun investigating the break-in, had made the discovery that Colson had sent E. Howard Hunt, a former CIA agent working as an administration security official, to Hyannis to dig up dirt on Ted. They also discovered that Hunt had checked out a copy of Jack Olsen's book on Ted's accident, *The Bridge at Chappaquiddick*, from the Library of Congress on the White House account, which suggested to the reporters that Hunt was not just a security official but was actively engaged in dirty tricks for the White House. "It's going to be fun," Nixon had trilled about planting a Secret Service spy in Ted's detail, so that he could catch the "son of a bitch" and "ruin him for '76." But these missions didn't turn out to be fun, because the break-in of Watergate had threatened to expose all of Nixon's operations, including one dubbed "the Plumbers," which, in the interest of sealing leaks, had conducted several illegal break-ins. So, twelve days after the Watergate burglary, John Ehrlichman, the assistant to the president for Domestic Affairs, and John Dean, Nixon's White House counsel, instructed the new FBI director, L. Patrick Gray, whom Nixon had appointed after J. Edgar Hoover's death, to destroy all the documents collected by Hunt, including the two folders that contained the falsified cables on John Kennedy, purporting to show he had ordered the murder of Diem, and the dossier on Ted. Gray tore them up and burned them on July 3—he would later say because of national security implications but more likely because, as a source would tell Woodward and Bernstein, they were "political dynamite" and capable of "doing more damage than the Watergate bugging itself." And that was all about the Kennedys.

But Larry O'Brien believed the wiretapping of his phone at the DNC may have had yet another spur that connected Ted Kennedy to him and both of them to yet another of the administration's abuses. Ted came to the same conclusion: that Watergate and all the revelations that followed from it had begun with a deal between the administration and the International Telephone and Telegraph conglomerate. When Attorney General John Mitchell had left the Justice Department on February 15, 1972, to head CREEP, Nixon appointed Mitchell's deputy, Richard Kleindienst, to succeed him. But after the confirmation hearings had concluded and before Kleindienst could be confirmed by the Judiciary Committee, on which Ted sat, Jack Anderson published a story on February 29 with an explosive accusation.* Anderson wrote that three suits brought by the new head of the Antitrust Division of the Justice Department, a Chicago attorney named Richard McLaren, against ITT—two of which had yet to

---

* Anderson was such a "thorn in Nixon's foot," as plumber E. Howard Hunt put it, that Colson told him to "stop Anderson at all costs," which Hunt assumed meant assassinating him. He was stopped only because he could find no adequate means for doing so. E. Howard Hunt with Greg Aunapu, *American Spy: My Secret History in the CIA, Watergate and Beyond* (New York: Wiley, 2007), 199.

be decided and one of which had been decided for ITT—had been dropped, Anderson said, because of a quid pro quo between the White House and ITT, effectively a payoff: a $400,000 contribution from ITT to bankroll the Republican National Convention to be held in San Diego in exchange for Nixon terminating the actions. Anderson had obtained a memo from a longtime ITT lobbyist named Dita Beard outlining the scheme, even boasting about it. Meanwhile, McLaren was shuffled out of the Justice Department and given a federal judgeship. The next day, March 1, Anderson dropped another bombshell: Kleindienst had brokered the payoff scheme and had lied about it before the Judiciary Committee. Kleindienst, feeling aggrieved, insisted that he be allowed to return before the committee and defend himself. To which Chuck Colson told his colleagues, "Kleindienst is a damn fool."

Kleindienst felt he was defending his honor, but there was a problem, as there was with so many of the president's men: There may have been no honor to defend. Ted had already been working full steam on the Kleindienst hearings when Anderson's perjury story broke and when an attorney named Reuben Robertson, working for consumer advocate Ralph Nader, visited the office and told Ted that he and Nader were fairly certain Kleindienst was involved in the payoff, as Anderson had reported. Robertson then handed Ted a legal brief from the Justice Department on the antitrust case with a "sticky" placed over the original date of the filing and a new date written in—a date that postponed the filing until after Justice had decided not to appeal the case. In effect, the postponement obviated the need for the brief. It seemed fishy, Robertson thought. Ted was unsure. One of Ted's staffers, Thomas Susman, said that when Ted asked for more evidence of a payoff and the staff told him that all they had was the sticky with a new date and Ralph Nader's instinct, Ted rolled his eyes. But when the hearings reconvened on March 2, Ted questioned Kleindienst, questioned him hard, about ITT and Dita Beard and the alleged payoff, and he did so with Jim Flug and Susman sitting behind him, handing him slips of paper with questions, and prodding him as Kleindienst insisted he knew nothing about the settlement. (Kleindienst even met with Ted privately in Ted's office and declared face-to-face that he was innocent. "He was lying," Ted later wrote.) It was, yet again, Ted versus Nixon, and Ted didn't let up. The hearings lasted twenty-two days, during which Ted was part of a five-man delegation sent to interview Dita Beard in Denver, where she was convalescing at a hospital for a heart ailment—an ailment sparked, she said, by the Anderson revelation—and insisting that the memo was fraudulent, that she supported the administration and former attorney general Mitchell and would never do anything to harm him. (It was highly unlikely the memo was fraudulent—who would have done so, or wanted to do so, except for Nixon's enemies on Judiciary—and Beard's pleas of innocence were almost certainly untrue.) But the senators had gotten there too late. Howard Hunt, wearing his red wig, had gotten to Beard first, and when the senators arrived and Senator Edward Gurney, a Republican, began questioning her—while she "alternately sucked on cigarettes and gulped from her oxygen mask," as Ted recalled—"her blood pressure went up, the arrows of all the machines went to high gear, and she gasped and grasped and every other thing she could do, and the doctor stopped the interview." Phil Hart, who chaired the delegation, said they would not interview her again. "He was scared to death that she would collapse or die or whatever," Ted later said. (Her condition, however, had not prevented her from leaving the hospital surreptitiously to be interviewed on the *60 Minutes* television program.) In the end, Kleindienst was confirmed, with Ted and his fellow liberal Democrats filing a minority report against him—Eastland himself had made a deal with Mitchell to go easy on Kleindienst in return for not having to face a Republican opponent in his reelection campaign—and that was seemingly the end of the matter.

But the liberal Democrats, suspecting that there was more here than met the eye, did not want to let it rest, and one of the most vociferous of them was the chair of the DNC, Larry O'Brien, which put O'Brien once again in Nixon's crosshairs. Ted had been blasé in the face of Nixon's chicanery against him; when Nixon was scheming to release the documents that purportedly showed John Kennedy's involvement in the Vietnam coup, Ted told them to go ahead and release them. "It won't bother me. Let history come out. Let the chips fall," was how Colson related his reaction to the president. And Ted could even be affable if sarcastically so in the face of Nixon's deviousness, telling Nixon how "thoughtful" he felt it was for him to assign a Secret Service detail to him, even though he must have realized that Nixon was not seeking to protect him but to spy on him. But Richard Nixon was not blasé, and Richard Nixon was not affable. The ITT brouhaha had disturbed him, angered him, and he fumed over Larry O'Brien, telling Ehrlichman to get to work to "worry O'Brien," and insisting that O'Brien had a secret retainer agreement with billionaire Howard

Hughes and had obtained a loan from Hughes, which especially riled Nixon since the Kennedy Justice Department had investigated *him* for a loan Hughes had made to Nixon's brother, Donald. "Hot ammunition to discredit O'Brien," is how Haldeman later described Nixon's obsession with the O'Brien–Hughes connection. O'Brien was a sore point to Nixon—a burr under his saddle. And a threat, since Nixon believed O'Brien to be the best of the Democratic operatives, and he was sure O'Brien was operating in the interests of Ted Kennedy. Ted's investigation of ITT, and then O'Brien's full-throated defense of it, not only bound the two together in furtherance of their undermining of Richard Nixon; it prompted Liddy, with or without Nixon's explicit blessing but certainly with knowledge of Nixon's hatred of O'Brien, to suggest a covert operation to find any information connecting Hughes and O'Brien and then, on the second break-in, as Liddy described it, to find out any information O'Brien had on the ITT payoff or other Republican financial shenanigans.* At least, that is what O'Brien and Ted came to think.

Whether or not Ted, or at least Nixon's hatred for Ted, had been a trigger for the Watergate break-in, Ted Kennedy's distrust of Nixon would be a primary trigger for the subsequent investigation of the break-in. Ted had spent twenty-two days in those hearings on the Kleindienst confirmation—twenty-two days of digging at the ITT–Kleindienst relationship; twenty-two days of focusing on how the Nixon administration did business with business; twenty-two days of questioning in the hearing room and then repairing to McLean in the evening to prepare for the next day's questioning, poring over huge loose-leaf binders, while his staff worked with Jack Anderson's investigator, Brit Hume, to track down issues and then worked "round the clock," according to one of them, to lay out the case against Kleindienst and the administration; twenty-two days of sowing doubt about the administration's clean hands. And all that time, as Ted's fellow committee member John Tunney put it, there were "ferocious arguments" behind closed doors with Eastland, who strongly defended Nixon. Meanwhile, the presidential campaign continued, and the Plumbers burgled Watergate, and McGovern was nominated, and

---

*There are many theories of what instigated Watergate. The most comprehensive catalog may be in Stanley Kutler, *The Wars of Watergate* (New York: Alfred A. Knopf, 1990), 198–209. We may never know the motive, but, as Kutler concludes, the burglary "ultimately must be seen as part of a behavior pattern characterizing the president and his aides that stretched back to the beginnings of the Nixon Administration."

Nixon was headed toward an easy reelection. But the ITT issue continued to simmer. (Jack Anderson had testified before the committee and under oath that Mitchell and Kleindienst had *both* perjured themselves.) Flug told Theo Lippman that after the Kleindienst confirmation hearings, "We were ready to believe anything." And he said that after the Watergate break-in, "We knew immediately that was high-level stuff," meaning ordered from a high level. Flug wanted AdPrac, Ted's all-purpose committee, to conduct hearings, but Ted was concerned that any hearings in the middle of a presidential election campaign would seem political. So Flug and Thomas Susman instead conducted an impromptu investigation under AdPrac's auspices, "looking at the dirty tricks during the election," as Susman put it, and "finding connections and weaving patterns that were just sort of mind-boggling," Ted said, speaking of the way in which ITT and Nixon's other abuses tied in to the Watergate break-in. Aside from a few intrepid reporters, they were largely working solo late that summer and fall. "Nobody else was kind of involved in it," Ted said. "A staff's frolic," Susman called it. Still, Ted's fear of seeming to politicize any investigation, especially before the election, gave him pause, however much it pained him, and gave pause to the Democratic leadership as well. On October 3, 1972, he wrote Senator Sam Ervin, the crusty, seventy-six-year-old North Carolinian who headed the Subcommittee on Constitutional Rights, asking Ervin if he would take over the investigation that Flug and AdPrac had started informally, while secretly hoping that Ervin might decline and let Ted and his staff continue their pursuit. Ervin did exactly that, telling Ted to keep going. In the meantime, Wright Patman, the chairman of the House Banking Committee, wanted to issue subpoenas and conduct his own investigation of the whole ITT uproar, and that would have been preferable to Ted's involvement, but Ted said that House minority leader Gerald Ford managed to convince several Democrats on the committee to deny Patman subpoena power. So at last, on October 12, the day Patman was blocked from his own investigation, and with the backing of the Democratic majority of the Judiciary Committee, AdPrac's parent committee, Ted Kennedy began what he called a "preliminary inquiry" into Nixon's espionage activities, including the Watergate break-in—an inquiry that Chairman Eastland allowed only after conferring secretly with the administration, which agreed because Nixon preferred having the hearings conducted by a small, nearly invisible subcommittee than by the whole Judiciary, which was bound to attract more attention. Republicans objected that AdPrac did not have subpoena power. Eastland ruled it did.

But even as he hoped to sidetrack the investigation, especially after the Watergate burglars were indicted and questions were being raised about their relationship to CREEP, Nixon had miscalculated. AdPrac in the hands of Ted Kennedy was not nearly invisible. The whole point of Ad-Prac was to gain visibility—though, in truth, nothing in the hands of Ted Kennedy was invisible. That October, Ted told reporter Carl Bernstein of *The Washington Post,* who was covering the Watergate break-in and had written a long story about the dirty-tricks campaign, that he had decided to undertake his investigation with subpoena power, because otherwise the entire affair was likely to "go down the chute and into the shredder." Bernstein said Kennedy "professed to know little if anything more than what he had read in the papers." But he did know this: "I know the people around Nixon, and that's enough. They're thugs."

The administration tried to head Ted off, as he had feared, by claiming that he was politically motivated and was just interested in advancing a presidential bid in 1976. And Ted remained cautious about not seeming to give credence to that idea. A "holding action," he called his investigation when interviewed by Bernstein. He knew, too, that the "White House would go with everything it had to smear him," said Bernstein. "Chappaquiddick would be brought up endlessly," and there would be other gossip and innuendo about him, "nickel-and-dime stuff." But Ted was not dissuaded. He knew the "thugs," and he was determined to snare them, because he knew Richard Nixon and knew Nixon would subvert democracy if it was in his own interests. He had already collected information on the ITT matter that implicated the administration, and "many of the issues that we exposed at the ITT hearings ended up being part of the file in the Watergate [investigation]," John Tunney was to say.

Now Ted was issuing subpoenas to acquire records from numerous agencies and to compel testimony from figures involved in possible crimes—"handing out subpoenas like traffic summonses," one investigator remarked. Flug and Susman went to California and Florida to track down witnesses, focusing especially on a young political saboteur and dirty trickster named Donald Segretti and on Nixon's own personal attorney, Herbert Kalmbach, who had financed many of Segretti's activities—poring over phone records and following money trails, "a week to ten days ahead of the press," Ted said, meaning primarily the

Washington Post reporters Carl Bernstein and Bob Woodward. And with the subpoenas issued and the aides investigating, the first congressional investigation of the Watergate break-in and the other dirty tricks of the Nixon administration began.

Richard Nixon and his men were on notice. And they were scared. "Kennedy is out for blood, and I'm the one treading water and bleeding," Segretti fretted to Bernstein just days after the election, when he invited the reporter to talk to him—an invitation that was itself a sign of his fear. "Kennedy will tear me to shreds." Nixon himself was no more sanguine than Segretti. "They're going to haul the thing up publicly," Nixon complained to Haldeman about Ted's initial digging. And he was especially concerned about Congress's subpoena power. "It shows you how important it is to win the Congress," he said. "You win the Congress, you take control of the committees." This from a man who had denigrated Congress, dismissed it as irrelevant: "No one gives a shit what the Senate does or how the Senate does." And now he was in a test of presidential power against congressional power but also another test, a more personal test, a test that went to the very core of Richard Nixon's being.

He was in a test of will, strategy, and power against Ted Kennedy.

While Nixon had won the election, he had not won the Congress, and now Ted Kennedy had begun calling witnesses and holding hearings and issuing those subpoenas Nixon so dreaded. Still, Ted Kennedy would not be allowed to finish the job he had started—the job to uncover the abuses of Richard Nixon, which by this time were already being widely reported—in fact, Ted did not, as he told it, *want* to be allowed to finish it, for fear once again of compromising the investigation by letting Richard Nixon label them as political. And so, reluctantly, he said, he approached Majority Leader Mike Mansfield about turning the hearings over to someone else. Mansfield remembered it differently. He said he was the one concerned that Ted's investigation would inevitably be perceived as political, given Ted's standing as a potential presidential candidate. ("If you give it to Ted Kennedy," he told Francis Valeo, the secretary of the Senate, "it will make it into a political issue, and that will be devastating to him, to the Senate, and to everyone else.") "I'm going to do all I can to create a committee to look into these matters," Mansfield said he assured Ted that December. "And I would appreciate it very much if you would go along with me in the creation of this special committee and not push your committee investigation." As Mansfield told it, Ted said he would be happy to comply and only asked that he be kept apprised. Mansfield next approached Eastland, whose Judiciary Committee would most likely have jurisdiction, but Mansfield asked Eastland if *he* would yield to a select committee headed by Sam Ervin, who was a trained constitutional lawyer and a former judge. And Eastland agreed. A special committee, devised for this purpose alone— a select committee, Mansfield wanted, on which no prospective presidential contenders would sit, at least on the Democratic side, which ruled out Ted.

But Ted, who was deeply invested in revealing Nixon's many abuses of power, was not entirely sidelined. He and his staff worked with Ervin on the resolution establishing the committee—worked to make it a serious committee, a nonpolitical committee. The Republicans, hoping to protect Nixon, had desired what Ted called a "soft" committee, a "weak" committee, equally divided between Democrats and Republicans, and "if that had been the case," Ted later said, "I think we would have had a different outcome." (They also wanted the committee to investigate past presidential election escapades, hoping to distract the committee—escapades, Ervin complained, since "George Washington was chosen for that office in 1789.") But Ted and Ervin worked together in what was clearly an orchestrated back-and-forth on the Senate floor, early that February, a well-rehearsed colloquy in support of a strong committee. Lauding the resolution his staff had helped draft, Ted said it came from the "genius of a very special talent," meaning Ervin, and Ted introduced a letter he had written to Chairman Eastland a few weeks earlier on AdPrac's findings on Watergate and said he would give them now to Ervin's committee. And then Ted asked Ervin questions, just to clarify the committee's jurisdiction, but really to show the committee's muscles. Would the resolution apply to persons who may have "ratified and endorsed the employment [of individuals involved in illegal activities] by acquiescing in it or receiving its benefits or failing to terminate it?" Ted asked, clearly referring to Nixon. It did, answered Ervin. Was the committee's jurisdiction limited to 1972? Ted asked. It applied to every relevant action pertaining to the 1972 election, even those before 1972, answered Ervin. Would the committee's purview include any acts that limited federal investigations? Ted asked, again obviously thinking of Nixon's attempts to obstruct the Watergate inquiries. It would, answered Ervin. And with Ted and Ervin having defined the committee's strength—and, not incidentally, its danger to the president—they won unanimous passage of the resolution. Then Ted, as promised, turned over to Ervin all the files his staff had compiled, big files, including, he said, an elaborate chart, like the ones on police television shows, that showed the interconnections among the various players, so that he felt his staff had "jump-started" the hearings. And he convinced Ervin to hire Bobby's dogged old investigator Carmine Bellino, who had worked with AdPrac on the preliminary investigation. Then, even after divesting himself of his research and surrendering the reins of the investigation, Ted and his staff, according to one biographer, continued to work on Watergate every day well into 1973, not because, one of his aides said, he detested Richard Nixon, though he obviously did, but because he was "deeply concerned with the state of the presidency, and would have been so regardless of which party was in the White House." And that was true. Ted Kennedy wasn't just fighting Richard Nixon. He was fighting Nixon's ability to reconfigure power in the United States government: awesome power with no discipline.

And now Richard Nixon, who had bullied and harassed and wiretapped and tailed and sullied his opponents and then gloated about it, was finally on the defensive. He was certain that Ted Kennedy was still the motive force behind the investigation. "I am convinced that [Ervin] has shown that he is merely a puppet for Kennedy in the whole thing," White House counsel John Dean told the president that February. "The fine hand of the Kennedys is behind the whole hearing. There is no doubt about it. . . . It's keeping Kennedy's push, quietly, his constant investigation." As proof, Dean cited the fact that Jim Flug got special permission to be on the Senate floor during the February debate on the resolution setting up the committee. Dean added that Kennedy had hand-selected attorney Sam Dash to be the majority counsel for the committee—he hadn't—and thought it was "something we will be able to quietly and slowly document. Leak this to the press, and the parts and cast become more apparent." Nixon responded, "Yes, I guess the Kennedy crowd is just laying in the bushes waiting to make their move," and he began a disquisition on Bobby Kennedy's ruthlessness, as if to acquit himself of his own ruthlessness. And Nixon complained, too, that Sam Ervin had seduced Senator Howard Baker, the ranking Republican on the new Select Committee, into trusting him, but that the Southern senators were "just more clever than the minority," meaning the Republicans. "Just more clever."

But Nixon had made yet another miscalculation. Clever Sam Ervin was anything but a puppet of Ted Kennedy. Ervin's folksy style and his bumbling manner, with his bushy eyebrows seeming to dance as he spoke, belied his keen mind and penetrating interrogation. If Ted Kennedy had seemed a political assassin, whose investigation Nixon might have successfully delegitimized, Ervin was no assassin. He was pure cornpone, a country lawyer, notwithstanding that the cornpone country lawyer was a Harvard Law School graduate. But Nixon, still certain that Ted was pulling the strings, decided to direct his fire at him, using the same tactics that had gotten him into trouble in the first place. As a counteroffensive against the committee, he advised Haldeman to have "our people" put out that "foreign or communist money came in support of the demonstrations in the campaign," meaning the peace demonstrations, and "tie all the '72 demonstrations to McGovern and thus the Democrats as part of the peace movement. Broaden the investigation to include the peace movement and its leaders, McGovern and Ted Kennedy. To what extent were they responsible for the demonstrations that led to the violence." Nixon suggested they use the conservative columnists Robert Novak and Rowland Evans to write this up, and when asked about it, the White House would lie: "We knew that the P ordered that it not be used under any circumstances." And Haldeman concluded, "He thinks we should play a hard game on this whole thing regarding the Ervin investigation." None of these diversionary efforts got any traction, even as the Watergate committee investigation was dominating headlines. A "traumatic national tragedy," Ted called it in a speech that May before the American Society of News Editors and said that "we must salvage the country's honor from the wreckage of leadership." And, seeing Watergate not as an aberration in the administration but as yet another example of its modus operandi, he said, "The same arrogance, the same imperialism, the same blind judgment that led to Watergate is also the attitude that led to other controversies in foreign and domestic policy."

But there was worse to come for Richard Nixon. The Democrats had no confidence that the Justice Department would aggressively pursue those who had committed Nixon's transgressions, including, almost certainly, they felt, the president himself. Joseph Califano, the onetime Lyndon Johnson aide who had become a prominent Washington attorney and who represented *The Washington Post,* one of Nixon's targets, had met with Ted, Birch Bayh, and Phil Hart, all members of the Judiciary Committee, and asked them to call for a special prosecutor—someone not directly connected to Nixon's Justice Department. To promote the idea, Ted suggested that Califano write an op-ed in *The New York Times*, which was published that April. Califano had no sooner written his op-ed than Kleindienst resigned, on April 30, saying that he had relationships with some of the individuals under investigation, and Defense Secretary Elliot Richardson was appointed the new attorney general. Ted said that he had spoken with Richardson privately during his confirmation and had been "very clear that he wasn't going to get confirmed unless he appointed a special prosecutor." Nixon was obviously opposed and so was Richardson, but Richardson knew, after subsequent private conversations with Ted, that it was a nonnegotiable condition. Meanwhile, Ted began recruiting possible candidates for special prosecutor and approached Warren Christopher, a distinguished attorney who had been a deputy attorney general under Bobby Kennedy; Judge Harold Tyler Jr., who had been appointed by John Kennedy to the District Court of the Southern District of New York; and Archibald Cox, a Harvard Law professor who had been solicitor general during John Kennedy's presidency and who had remained close to the Kennedys. (Ted had often consulted him on legal issues that arose before the Senate.) Christopher and Judge Tyler waffled over whether the special prosecutor's mandate to pursue those in the administration was secure enough to withstand the Justice Department. Cox was reluctant as well, equally worried that he would not be sufficiently insulated from political pressures and thus have his independence compromised. To satisfy him, Ted had Flug draft a charter for the special prosecutor—Ted said he drafted it in "less than a day"—which stated that the special prosecutor could only be terminated for "extraordinary impropriety," lest Nixon order Richardson to fire him. Richardson balked but hired Cox anyway, possibly to disarm Kennedy, possibly to disarm Richardson's compatriots at Harvard. More charitable to Richardson, who had been a student of Cox's and had sought his advice in the past, the attorney general said that he thought Cox "to be a man of unshakable integrity." Nixon couldn't have disagreed more. He called Cox the man "whom I would have least trusted to conduct so politically sensitive an investigation in an unbiased way" and felt, yet again, that he had been hoodwinked. When Cox was sworn in on May 25, he invited Ted Kennedy and Ethel Kennedy as guests, prompting Pat Buchanan, one of Nixon's speechwriters, to quip, "I guess we were disenchanted with Archie Cox within eighteen minutes of his swearing in."

The pressure was mounting on the president. Woodward and Bernstein's stories were appearing regularly throughout the spring in the *Post* with new revelations, the hearings were proceeding, the Watergate burglars were admitting guilt and implicating Nixon's henchmen (even as Nixon believed that Kennedy was somehow manipulating the burglars to implicate the president himself), Haldeman and Ehrlichman had both left the White House under duress, and John Dean, the White House counsel, had turned on Nixon and testified before the Ervin committee that Nixon had been involved in a cover-up about the break-in. Even worse for Nixon, the mood of the country was slowly turning against him. And now there was a new element—a potentially dispositive element. Nixon's former deputy assistant, Alexander Butterfield, who had left the White House that March to become the chairman of the Federal Aviation Administration, confirmed to the Select Committee staff in July, and later in public testimony before the committee, that the president had installed a tape-recording system in the Oval Office and that most of the conversations there had been recorded. He testified for only thirty minutes, but they were, as one Watergate historian noted, "thirty minutes that ensnared Nixon," even as Butterfield insisted they would provide the president's defense. The same day as Butterfield's testimony, July 16, both the Ervin committee and Special Prosecutor Cox asked for selected tapes, which would provide incontrovertible evidence of what the president and his aides had said—evidence that could either corroborate the testimony of John Dean, who admitted Nixon had tried to cover up the Watergate break-in in conversations with him, or refute it; evidence that could either exonerate the president or convict him. Nixon, however, had refused Cox's request and was threatening not to release the tapes, even if the Supreme Court ordered him to do so, because, as his new constitutional attorney, Charles Alan Wright, put it, he had "inherent" power as president to withhold any materials.

Awesome power with no discipline. That threat, which also threatened a constitutional crisis, troubled Ted and made Nixon's Republican supporters nervous too. Senator Barry Goldwater, in Nixon's defense, wrote an op-ed in *The New York Times* criticizing what he called a "fad" of investigations and prosecutions of politicians, and he warned that the damage would not be limited to President Nixon. He singled out Ted as having been "badly damaged by Watergate, which renewed discussion again of the senator's ill-fated accident on Chappaquiddick Island. Thus the Democrats who want to make the most of their opportunities to capitalize on a 'Mr. Clean' image will find Teddy Kennedy a hard product to sell." If this was Goldwater's and the Republicans' way of attempting to silence Ted, they had misplayed their hand. Ted Kennedy felt so strongly about Watergate that he was not about to be silenced, even if it meant subjecting himself to ridicule. The very day of Goldwater's *Times* essay, Ted rose on the Senate floor and uttered to a nearly empty chamber the word that heretofore had scarcely been mentioned: impeachment. "If President Nixon defied a Supreme Court order to turn over the tapes, a responsible Congress would be left with no recourse but to exercise its power of impeachment," Ted said. He declared that Nixon's assertion—supported by John Connally—that he was not obligated to obey a Supreme Court order derived "only from the law of the jungle, the law of raw and naked power, which the country will never tolerate." Tom Wicker in the *Times* called it "about as strong a statement on the substantive question of impeachment as any leading Democrat has been willing to make." And Wicker said that Ted's statement "seems to be a step toward the kind of leadership position he had not previously assumed on the Watergate issue"—which wasn't entirely true given his initiation of the investigation—and that it served as a refutation of Goldwater's idea that Watergate, summoning memories of Chappaquiddick, would hurt Ted's presidential aspirations, should he have them—which may have been true. (A Harris poll the next month showed that 43 percent of Americans still doubted Ted's "integrity.") As Ted saw it, his loss of moral authority after Chappaquiddick had not removed him from the debate about Watergate, though Republicans clearly wished it had. But as Wicker asked at the end of his column: Were Nixon to defy the court, how would the country react to "the man of Chappaquiddick leading an impeachment battle against the man of Watergate?" How would it react to one morally compromised individual prosecuting another?

The answer to Wicker's question came not long after Ted's speech, but not before Nixon settled yet another scandal in which he had become embroiled. His vice president and designated attack dog, former Maryland governor Spiro Agnew, had been charged by federal prosecutors in Baltimore with having taken bribes while he was a Baltimore County executive and then the state's chief executive. Though Agnew, even more unpopular among Senate Democrats than Nixon, if possible, was viewed by some Nixon supporters as "impeachment insurance," the president might have defended him more vigorously had he not been entangled in his own dire situation and worried that Agnew would only be an additional drag on him. Agnew did what he could to save himself, even lobbying House speaker Carl Albert to hold hearings that would have delayed any resolution of his situation. But Nixon finally decided to cut his losses. Agnew pleaded *nolo contendere*—no contest—to income-tax evasion and resigned early that October with a suspended sentence. Nixon, looking to protect himself, wanted to appoint Connally, a turncoat Democrat and an ardent defender, to the post, but the Democrats advised him that Connally wouldn't be confirmed, so he defaulted to the House minority leader Gerald Ford, an anodyne figure, reliably conservative but untainted by scandal, and a man who had made few enemies across the aisle. Anodyne or not, Ford as vice president did not please Ted, and he later said that after long discussions with Mansfield, Phil Hart, Robert Byrd, Howard Cannon—head of the Senate Rules Committee, which was entrusted with taking up the nomination—and other Democratic leaders, he asked the Senate parliamentarian to move Ford's confirmation hearings from the Rules Committee to the Judiciary Committee, where he could interrogate him. (Ted wanted to wrest a pledge from Ford that he would call for Nixon to obey court orders and release the tapes, and Ted said he should not be confirmed otherwise.) But the parliamentarian refused, claiming that succession was a matter of rules. And so Ford, once he passed the Rules Committee, would become the new vice president without being subjected to Ted's withering cross-examination.

But even as he had been working to resolve the issue of Spiro Agnew, Nixon had also been working on a way to resolve his own situation and defend himself from the incipient calls for impeachment. And the best defense, he felt, was disarming Ted Kennedy's close ally Archibald Cox— a "parasite," Nixon called him, the "partisan viper we had planted in our bosom." But if Nixon cast the fight as political, it was more. In reality, it must have felt cultural to him, unleashing all of his insecurities provoked by the men Lyndon Johnson had scornfully called the "Harvards" (as Theodore H. White observed, Nixon was now encircled by those Harvards— Ted and Ervin and Ervin's chief counsel, Sam Dash, and Dash's assistant counsel, Terry Lenzner, and even his own attorney general, Elliot Richardson, as well as eighteen Harvard-trained attorneys on Cox's staff of thirty-seven, only one of whom was a non–Ivy Leaguer), and the rich pretty boys, like the Kennedys, who had always had everything handed to them while he had to pull himself up by his bootstraps—an honest sentiment—and the intellectuals, of whom Alger Hiss, the Harvard-educated spy he had taken down, was one, who had always condescended to him, who felt he was beneath them, and who had been at war with him since the days of Hiss and were at war with him once again, this time for his presidency, their vengeance against his vengeance. But Nixon had the power now, and Nixon would use it. Certain that Cox was conducting a personal vendetta against him, Nixon had been crossing swords with him for weeks and privately discussing firing him, largely on the basis that Cox was exceeding his charter by venturing into matters of national security. But Cox had power too. To enforce his subpoena for the tapes, Cox, with the backing of Judge John Sirica, who had presided over the Watergate burglars' case, brought the Watergate grand jury into a public session, a virtually unprecedented step, where each juror attested to wanting to issue a "show cause" order to obtain the tapes. Nixon continued to insist that the president could ignore the subpoena and that the courts had no further recourse—which, even if it were true legally, and that was certainly debatable, was politically poisonous: a president ignoring a court order. Still, when the Appeals Court suggested a compromise—having Cox and either Nixon himself or his representatives listen to the tapes—and when Cox and the White House failed to reach agreement on it, with Cox instead suggesting a third-party transcript—Nixon remained adamant that he would not relinquish the tapes. With Nixon and Cox at a deadlock, the next stop would be the Supreme Court, which would umpire the standoff. Then Nixon made a discovery that imperiled his position. After bringing the subpoenaed tapes with him to the presidential retreat, Camp David, on the weekend of September 29, he discovered that several of the tapes were missing, other conversations might, in his opinion, be misconstrued, and, worst of all, his secretary, Rose Mary Woods, who had been transcribing the tapes, had, she believed, or so she said, inadvertently erased one of the most important conversations on those tapes. As the president and Cox continued to squabble over the next few weeks and as Agnew departed in mid-October, Nixon, realizing the jeopardy he faced, reached a decision that would prove fateful: After having talked about it for weeks, Richard Nixon decided that he would fire Archibald

Cox. As Richardson recalled, Nixon told him in the Oval Office, not long after Agnew had been dispatched, "Now that we have disposed of that matter, we can go ahead and get rid of Cox." Or, more accurately, Richard Nixon decided that he would order Attorney General Richardson to get rid of Archibald Cox.

But there was a sticking point, and it was not incidental. It was moral in an administration that had little use for morality. Richardson had given his word to Ted Kennedy that he could not fire Cox save for "extraordinary impropriety" and then had agreed to the special prosecutor's charter with that same language, something upon which Ted had insisted precisely to avoid this situation and something without which Richardson would not have been confirmed. When Alexander Haig, Nixon's new chief of staff, advised Richardson that the attorney general was being instructed to fire Cox, Richardson told him he would have to resign rather than follow the president's orders. To head off the resignation, which Nixon knew would have as disastrous political consequences for him as his ignoring the court order, he proposed another alternative: to have Senator John Stennis, a strong Nixon supporter—not to mention notoriously hard of hearing— listen to the tapes and verify summaries of the conversations. Cox did not reject the compromise outright; regardless of what Nixon thought, he was looking for some accommodation with the president. But Cox made additional demands, including that if there were trials involving the tapes, the actual tapes would have to be produced because summaries would not be acceptable as evidence.

Now Nixon was nearly apoplectic. Cox would get nothing, he insisted. And Richardson passed this instruction on to Cox via phone. (Richardson, by some accounts, was not as much of a hero as he would later be made out to be; he was ready to place restrictions on Cox to placate the president.) So Nixon unilaterally announced that Stennis—whom he now routinely called "Judge Stennis"—would verify summaries of the tapes, while Cox, countering him, announced that Nixon was defying the court order. That Friday, as the crisis was reaching a boiling point, Ted discussed the matter with Phil Hart, the conscience of the Senate and Ted's ethical lodestone, and other senators on what course of action to take if Nixon were to fire Cox, and he was already mentioning, at what he called a "pretty low level," the possibility of impeachment. The next morning, Saturday, October 20, Cox held a press conference expressing his humility at taking on the president—"I am even worried . . . that I am getting

too big for my britches"—but insisting that the president was not comply-
ing with the court order for the tapes and that Cox could not fulfill his
charter if he didn't have access to further materials, which Nixon had
now precluded. To Nixon, this was insubordination, though he was more
likely concerned about what he knew the tapes would reveal if they were
released and what action they might prompt. Whether true or not, and it
is likely he was overstating his influence, Ted later speculated that his conversations on Friday about impeachment may have precipitated what
happened next.

What happened next was that that afternoon, Nixon, no longer willing
to delay—he was in the midst of dealing with a surprise attack on Israel
by Soviet-supported Arab forces and was especially concerned about
looking weak in front of Soviet leader Leonid Brezhnev, who was threatening intervention—ordered Richardson to the White House and personally gave him the instruction to fire Cox. Instead, Richardson resigned, as
he had said he would. Then Haig called Richardson's deputy, William
Ruckelshaus, with the same order. Ruckelshaus resigned too. (There is
some dispute as to whether Nixon, furious at Ruckelshaus, fired him first,
though Nixon in his memoirs said he didn't.) And then the task fell to the
solicitor general, Robert Bork, the next in line, who thought it injudicious
to fire Cox but entirely constitutional. That night, Bork signed the president's letter firing Cox and moving the special prosecutor's investigation
into the Justice Department—the avoidance of which was the very reason
Ted and his fellow Democrats had called for a special prosecutor in the
first place. The press dubbed it "the Saturday Night Massacre." Jim Flug
would say, reasonably, that "the Saturday Night Massacre was born in
Kennedy's office," since Ted had insisted in the charter that only the attorney general could fire the special prosecutor. And now the solicitor
general acting as attorney general had. Now the deed seemed to be done.

But the deed was not done, not if Richard Nixon had hoped to halt the
inquiry into his administration's wrongdoing and prevent his tapes from
being introduced into evidence, either at trial or at an impeachment proceeding. And Ted Kennedy, Archibald Cox's patron, was among those
who was determined to see that those tapes were released. He moved
quickly. That night Ted convened a meeting—it is unclear whether it was
in his office or in Phil Hart's—with Hart; Milton Gwirtzman; Jim Flug;
John Nolan, the attorney who had gone to Paris to get the POW lists; and
other members of the Judiciary staff. By this point, the FBI, under Clar-

ence Kelley, had sealed off access to Cox's records. "Here we are, sitting in that Senate office," Gwirtzman recalled, "and we're helpless. What can we do? We've got the FBI moving against the special prosecutor. What can senators do?" Ted, however, took command. What Ted did—Gwirtzman said that Ted was the one giving orders—was say that the Justice Department officials should be alerted that they did not have to give up their files. Then Ted denounced the firing—a "reckless act of desperation by a president who is afraid of the Supreme Court, who has no respect for law and no regard for a man of conscience"—and called another meeting for the next morning, Sunday, at his McLean home, with Hart, Senator Charles Mathias, a Republican, and Ted's staff. They batted around the idea of a resolution censuring Nixon and had Burke Marshall, the Kennedys' legal wise man, draft one, and they spoke with another political wise man, Clark Clifford, who recommended that they have the Judiciary Committee convene hearings on Cox's firing rather than promote the censure resolution. Clifford felt that the House was already moving on impeachment and might not only resent the Senate's encroachment on its constitutional territory but might also feel that a censure of the president would obviate the need for impeachment. So Ted phoned Eastland, who was traveling in Turkey at the time, and pressed him to open the hearings as soon as possible. ("We *need* to have a hearing," he said.) Eastland, who had unsuccessfully tried to stave off any hearings on Nixon earlier in the year, now had no choice. He suggested that they hold a preliminary hearing on Wednesday, leaving the logistics to Ted. On Tuesday night, before the preliminary hearing, Ted held another meeting at his home with senators and staff, this time to discuss how to reestablish the office of special prosecutor, now that Nixon had terminated it, and how to make it "fireproof," which meant having the special prosecutor be appointed by and responsible to a court. The meeting the next day was raucous. "Tumultuous," Ted called it. The majority of Republicans still supported Nixon, court orders or not, and Strom Thurmond asked that the meeting be postponed for a week, presumably to build even more support for the president, which was eroding. (Still, 55 percent of Americans did not want Nixon to be impeached, according to a Gallup poll.) Ted said he spoke for "prompt action." (He was leaving for Europe the next day.) When it ended, the committee had decided to invite Cox to testify in open session on October 29, five days later.

But now the Republicans and Democrats both dug in, and the Octo-

SIXTEEN

S.3

Richard Nixon was wounded now, badly wounded, wounded and reeling from his wounds, preoccupied with fending off impeachment, which created a power vacuum. And Ted Kennedy, as the presumptive Democratic presidential nominee once again, and still reeling from his own wounds from Chappaquiddick, looked to recover by filling that vacuum. Joe Biden said that when he first came to the Senate, Hubert Humphrey took him aside and advised him, "You have to pick an issue that becomes yours. That's how you attract your colleagues to follow you, Joe. That's how you demonstrate your bona fides. Don't be a gadfly." Ted had always had many balls in the air, only one of which, and certainly not the most important of which, was health care. His interest, he would say, came early, from his mother's emphasis on good health—she kept meticulous records of every illness of every one of her children—and from his sister Rosemary's condition, and later from John's frequent illnesses (Ted said he could remember visiting him at Chelsea Naval Hospital and the "extraordinary discomfort" from which John suffered), from his father's stroke, and later still from his son Patrick's bouts with severe, debilitating asthma. He even recalled debating whether America should have national health insurance against the Harvard freshman team while he was a student at Milton. When he was preparing for his Senate run in 1962, he had joined Dr. Sidney Farber in a Cancer Crusade to raise money to fight the disease, speaking to two or three groups a night for two or three months—an experience he would later call a "cornerstone of my interest in health matters throughout my Senate career." That interest became more personal after his plane accident in 1964 and his long rehabilitation, during which he had the conversation with Gerard Doherty about

Doherty's fight against tuberculosis while at Harvard and how his family struggled to pay for his treatment, and Doherty said that Ted got involved in the case of a young campaign worker, a neighbor of Doherty's, who suffered from kidney disease. And Ted's physician at the time of the plane accident, Dr. Herbert Adams, said he and Ted spoke daily about medicine and "especially about how to provide good quality care and make it available to everyone." Adams invited Ted to become a trustee of the Lahey Clinic, and Ted did. All of these led to his visit to the community health center at Columbia Point in 1966 and to the bill he drafted after that trip, scaling the program across the country, which was his first foray into health-care legislation. "I realized that access to health care was a moral issue," he would later write of why his interest intensified—moral obviously because he saw people who could not otherwise afford health care were it not for those community centers, and he knew the terrible cost of their not receiving that care.

Some were skeptical about Ted Kennedy's choice of health care as an issue and of national health care in particular. Walter Pincus, writing in *The New Republic*, thought it was a political decision, not a moral one. "A long-term issue was wanted that he could press and to which he could attach his name," Pincus said. "He wanted something broad and classless that would help all the people, not the least those Nixon had identified in 1968 as the silent majority. Aid the working stiffs and then you can do more for the blacks and the poor, went Kennedy's argument." This was the opposite of Nixon's argument that you pretend to do something for the poor so that you can do more for the powerful. But Ted Kennedy had not exactly *chosen* health care as his issue, though he would often talk as if he had. More accurately, it had been thrust upon him, and he accepted the challenge. At the American Public Health Association meeting in November 1968, shortly after Nixon's victory, United Auto Workers president Walter Reuther announced a new organization, the Committee for National Health Insurance, dubbed the Committee of 100 because Reuther had recruited one hundred notables from labor, politics, religious groups, the arts, business, and academe with the primary purpose of working for passage of a law to provide health insurance to all Americans, at a time when eighty million of them had inadequate care and thirty-five to forty million no insurance whatsoever and health costs were rocketing. For over fifty years, national health insurance had been a dream of progressives, and it had always been a dream deferred and defeated. But Reuther was both ambitious and tenacious—more than tenacious. A veteran of Detroit's bloody labor wars—literally—when the auto companies were fighting unionization, Reuther had survived two assassination attempts, almost certainly by underworld goons dispatched by Ford Motors; the second cost him the full use of his right arm. Now, thinking as a labor leader, he had come to believe that health costs would outstrip the ability of collective bargaining to meet them and that they were already eating up an increasingly large percentage of total benefits. But Walter Reuther was more than a labor leader. He was also a social visionary, who looked beyond the next UAW contract to the larger good of the country. "Good for America" were his watchwords. To head the Committee of 100, Reuther had chosen Max Fine, a onetime journalist, insurance lobbyist, member of John Kennedy's Medicare task force—the night before Kennedy was killed in Dallas, he had visited the task force and asked how Medicare was coming along—and then one of Lyndon Johnson's administrators of Medicare once it passed. (Fine and Reuther had met on a picket line.) To head up the task force drafting the legislation, which was a single-payer, government-financed and government-run system like Medicare, he hired Yale professor Isidore "Ig" Falk, a legendary scholar in the public-health community, who had been one of the first employees of the Social Security Administration. "Medicare for All," they called their prospective plan.

Reuther had no illusions about how easy the task would be. He asked Fine to commit himself to eight years, because Reuther felt that was how long it would take for a law to win passage, though national health care had already been a progressive project for more than fifty years. Its history was long and checkered—an arduous and largely unsuccessful history that began when the American Association for Labor Legislation, a progressive organization heavily influenced by European social initiatives, first introduced a state-based program in 1915, in which the government was to contribute one-fifth of the cost. Eight states considered the plan; California even held a referendum on it. The referendum failed. Not even Franklin Roosevelt at the height of his popularity in the New Deal, when he had won passage of Social Security, could advance the idea, though he did appoint the Interdepartmental Committee to Coordinate Health and Welfare Activities, which convened a conference in 1938 to discuss the issue. This led to New York senator Robert Wagner introducing a bill providing federal funds to states to set up health-insurance programs, and when that failed, Wagner and Representative John Dingell Sr. proposed a new bill, a stronger bill, amending the Social Security Act to provide compulsory insurance funded by a payroll tax. But when the Republicans won Congress in 1946, the Wagner–Dingell effort expired and with it any hope for national health insurance. President Harry Truman made it a legislative priority in 1948, only to be rebuffed, this time by a combination of Southern Democrats and the American Medical Association. Twenty-five years later it still had not passed, despite the moral imperative of such a law in a country where only 50 percent of Americans had health insurance in 1950.

A long and arduous history it had, with enormous, even insuperable obstacles. Why didn't America institute a national health-insurance system as every other industrialized country did after World War II? Because the wartime freeze on wages pushed unions to compete for workers by offering benefits, including health insurance. Because those unions in the postwar period, terrified by the Republican congressional victory in 1946, came to realize that collective bargaining, which could include health benefits, was far more advantageous to them than government-funded insurance was. Because Southerners feared that national health insurance might wind up forcing hospitals to integrate. Because doctors were frightened that national health insurance might drive down their income and impose new regulations, so they waged a powerful propaganda campaign through the American Medical Association linking national health insurance to socialism. "Socialized medicine is the keystone to the arch of the Socialist State," the AMA's public-relations flacks had fabricated as a quote from Lenin. Because the Republican party was fiercely opposed to any government expansion and joined with the AMA to prevent it. And finally because, as two health scholars put it, "American political institutions are structurally biased against this kind of comprehensive reform," even when the vast majority of Americans desired it. Instead, Americans settled for incremental progress, piecemeal progress—Medicare for senior citizens and Medicaid for the poor—while private health insurance, usually employer-provided, kept out government health insurance. In short, the moral issue had attracted insufficient moral energy from those in Congress.

But now, in the draft of Lyndon Johnson's Great Society, Walter Reuther felt the time had finally come for this piece of social legislation, even as he realized that national health care would still require an enormous effort—a coordinated effort. One thing he knew he needed for that effort was a congressional partner—a powerful partner, a partner with a high public profile, a partner who could sell the plan both to his colleagues and to the general public. Fine said that Reuther approached several candidates, but Fine himself suggested Ted Kennedy, whom Reuther had already recruited for the Committee of 100, to be that partner, because he was at the height of his political powers, the "number one Democrat," despite his lack of seniority, and because he was the brother of the beloved late president who had pioneered Medicare. In some ways, though, it was simpler than that: Reuther and Fine in 1968 *needed* Ted Kennedy. Ted said that he had spoken with Reuther about health care in the mid-1960s in Boston and that Reuther was one of those who had sparked his interest in the subject. And as Ted remembered it, he was giving an address that January to the Public Health Association at the Sheraton Plaza Hotel in Boston, and afterward he and Reuther, who had flown to Boston with Fine expressly to see Ted, met in the corridor, before retreating to a vacant room to discuss health care at greater length. The conversation, Ted said, lasted ninety minutes. "He was enormously persuasive," Ted would later say. As Fine remembered it, they met at Hynes Auditorium in Boston, where Ted was speaking before a benefit for the New England Hospital Assembly. In Fine's version, Ted expressed initial reluctance about leading a health-care campaign, saying that he was far more interested in education than in health care, but Fine also said that he seemed receptive to their overture, quite possibly, though Fine couldn't have known it, because education had been Bobby's issue, and health care was an issue he could make his own, and because in the ongoing competition with the memories of his fallen brothers, passing national health insurance would be a way of pulling even. (In fact, Ted was already mulling whether, despite his lack of seniority, there was some way for him to take the Health and Scientific Research Subcommittee chair.) He asked a lot of questions in the interest, Fine thought, of making sure that "there was going to be a massive commitment behind this" before he put himself on the line. Ted wasn't given to quixotic campaigns. He would be willing to take a lead in something that might not have an immediate payoff but only if he felt it would have an ultimate payoff. Already, Reuther told him, they had recruited James Corman in the House to sponsor a bill, and while the Congress of Industrial Organizations, from which the UAW had recently split in a bitter struggle, was working on a bill of its own, Reuther reassured Ted that the CIO didn't have "any activity like ours." More, he promised

Ted that he would find him a Republican co-sponsor for the bill, even though national health insurance was anathema to the Republicans. But Ted had one more reservation, as Fine remembered it: that Health Sub-committee chairmanship. Though he sat on the Labor Committee, which oversaw most health issues, he was not the chair of its Health Subcom-mittee. He was fourth in line, behind Senator Ralph Yarborough, who also headed the parent Labor Committee itself, Rhode Island senator Clai-borne Pell, and New Jersey senator Harrison Williams. So Reuther prom-ised him this: When the time came, he would talk to Claiborne Pell and convince him not to take the chairmanship, obviously because he and Fine thought Ted's backing would be more instrumental than Pell's. (Ap-parently Reuther felt Yarborough, who, after all, chaired the parent com-mittee, would step aside, and Williams wouldn't be interested in the chairmanship; as it turned out, he wasn't.) "Well, if you can get it done," Ted told Reuther noncommittally, meaning if Reuther could convince Pell not to take it, then Ted probably would. Reuther and Fine left believing they had accomplished their mission, which was to convince Ted Ken-nedy to be the face and the voice for government-financed health care. And that is how the meeting ended.* Not long after, Reuther flew to Wash-ington to meet with Ted again and map strategy, while Fine met with Carey Parker. And then the final drafting of the bill began.

No less than Reuther, Ted Kennedy certainly appreciated the obstacles to getting a bill passed, and those obstacles had only become more intrac-table with time. Ted had spoken with scholars of health care, set up meet-ings with them, and most of them felt that liberals had missed the opportunities in the 1930s during the New Deal and then in the 1960s during the height of the Great Society, to enact a national health-care plan. He asked the historians why Franklin Roosevelt hadn't worked harder for health care. The answer, they said, was that he was worried about capsizing Social Security if he attached a health-care plan to it. "Let's not miss it in the 1970s," they told Ted, according to Carey Parker. And, despite his mindfulness of the obstacles, Ted was guardedly optimis-tic. As Parker recalled, "The atmosphere in the Senate in 1969 was very much that we were going to pick up where we had left off under LBJ," that

---

*It is likely that in his interview, Fine conflated two different meetings. At the first, early in 1969, likely the meeting at the Sheraton, Fine and Reuther convinced Ted to join the Com-mittee of 100. At the second, early in 1970, the meeting at Hynes Auditorium, Reuther pressured Ted to assume the Health Subcommittee chairmanship.

no matter how much Democrats might loathe Nixon and see him as a devious red-baiter, he "did not come in with a reputation" as a "hard-line conservative" when it came to health care. (Parker was wrong about Nixon, however. Leaving his doctor's office in San Diego after a physical that December, Nixon dismissed a national plan as a "government take-over.") Meanwhile, throughout 1969, Reuther's committee was laying the groundwork for its plan and promoting it, even recruiting television stars E. G. Marshall and Carroll O'Connor to make speeches. "We had a lot of things going," Fine said.

And legislatively, Ted Kennedy was now the shepherd for that plan to institute national health insurance: a major responsibility, a difficult responsibility, a moral responsibility. He had never taken any role lightly, and he didn't take this one lightly either. He spent a lot of time that year—1969—boning up on health care, inviting those experts back to his home, working through the issue, absorbing what he learned so that he could speak authoritatively about health care himself. One of those experts he consulted, Rashi Fein, a Harvard economist specializing in health care, had met Ted a year earlier, in the summer of 1968, at a conference on medical care in poor and black communities, which was Ted's primary health interest at the time. Fein said he made an opening remark and then others began discussing it, but Ted sat there impassively, silently, seemingly uninterested—so silent that Fein assumed he was "basically sleeping with his eyes open." And Fein, who would soon become an adviser to the Committee of 100, assumed that it had "all been a waste of time." That night, however, as the conference was winding down and several of the participants were sitting around talking, Ted suddenly said, "Well, we're going to have to break up in a half hour, so let me pursue some things that were said." And Fein recalled that the first question Ted asked one of the participants—presumably economist Alain Enthoven—was, "Early on, Al, Rashi said such-and-such, and you disagreed with him, but that issue was never pursued. I'd like to find out a little more about why you disagree with him, and I'd like to hear from Rashi." And Fein said that he realized then that Ted had not only been listening, he had also been listening carefully: "He had absorbed, he had processed information, and he had put it together." That is how Ted Kennedy came to know health care inside and out, which is how Ted Kennedy came to know most things. By asking questions. By listening closely. By processing. "He learned with his ears," as one of his legal mentors, Sam Beer, would say of him.

But then, just as Ted and Reuther and their allies were building momentum for a plan, came the setback, Chappaquiddick, and Fine said that the man who had been chosen to speak for health insurance because he was one of the moral forces of the country was now a liability because of doubts about his character. Just four days after the accident, Fine said he was outside Cleveland, at Oberlin College, to deliver a speech to the Lorain County Medical Society. (He had been traveling the country speaking in support of national health care.) When the president of the society introduced him, someone immediately shouted from the back of the room, "How much is the hero of Chappaquiddick paying you, buddy?" Several others joined the man in heckling Fine, and finally Fine said, "I gather you're not interested in what I have to say," and they hooted that they were not. Whether they were opposed to national health care as "socialized medicine" and were using Ted as a pretext—doctors were among the fiercest opponents of health-care-for-all—Fine didn't say, but he did say that the heckling was repeated almost everywhere he went. E. G. Marshall told Fine he faced the same ridicule. "Boy, this Chappaquiddick thing is really hurting us," he said. The renowned heart surgeon Michael DeBakey even resigned from the Committee of 100 after Chappaquiddick. "We just came to this dead stop," Fine recalled. "It picked up later, but it wasn't the same." Chappaquiddick killed the momentum.

But once he returned from his self-imposed exile after Chappaquiddick, Ted Kennedy persisted—persisted even more, believed his aide Robert Bates, because of Chappaquiddick, since passing national health insurance could be another form of penance for the accident and even possibly a way to help obliterate the stain. *It was a moral issue.* So he pressed on. And knowing health care now, in a December 16, 1969, speech at the Boston University Medical Center, Ted publicly entered the national health insurance fray for the first time, calling for a government-financed plan and promising to introduce a bill himself—Ig Falk's Medicare for All bill. As Carey Parker put it, "He wanted to begin the debate" with the "thought that he would begin to push the issue as a member of the Senate Labor Committee." Now Ted Kennedy had become the senator most determined to bring national health insurance to America.

Then, for an issue that had constantly met with setbacks, came two more setbacks—terrible setbacks. On May 2, 1970, Senator Ralph Yarborough, a liberal, a staunch advocate for national health insurance, and the chairman of both the Senate Labor Committee and its Health Subcommittee, was defeated in the Democratic primary in Texas by a conservative businessman, Lloyd Bentsen, who ran on the contention that Yarborough was out of touch with his constituents. Bentsen's victory marked the end of liberalism in Texas politics for years to come and derailed any effort Yarborough could have mounted to advance national health care, since he was now a lame duck. And exactly a week later came an even greater setback, a tragic setback, not only for health care but for social progress generally: Walter Reuther, who had birthed the new health-care initiative and then had sustained it, was killed in a plane crash outside Pellston, Michigan. Speaking in Reuther's place at the Albert Lasker Medical Journalism Awards luncheon in New York a week after his death, Ted said, "In years to come, when Congress finally responds to the demand of the American people for better health, the legislation we enact for national health insurance will be a living memorial to Walter Reuther." Ted was right. Were national health care to be enacted, Reuther, who had risked his life for his workers and then devoted his life to them, would have been the one responsible for almost single-handedly reviving the issue after it had been left for dead. And as the 91st Congress drew to a close, Ted was determined to see that memorial arrive sooner rather than later, not because health care had the slightest chance of passage then—it didn't—but because he believed he would be launching a serious debate on it that would, finally and eventually, lead to its passage, so that his efforts wouldn't be quixotic. That August, he introduced Reuther's bill—essentially the bill Ig Falk had drafted—with fourteen of his colleagues co-sponsoring it, including two Republicans, William Saxbe and John Sherman Cooper. (True to his word, Reuther had convinced Cooper to support the plan and had gotten Ted his Republican co-sponsor.) And just as Reuther and Fine had predicted when they first recruited Ted to lead the campaign, the media reacted, despite Chappaquiddick. There was a "spate of media attention," health historian Frank Campion would write: a full issue of *Fortune* devoted to national health care; a two-hour, two-part documentary on CBS, and another on NBC, titled *What Price Health?* Meanwhile, the AMA, which had successfully demonized the idea of government-funded health care for decades, but which was now clearly concerned about the momentum such a plan might gain, came out with its own plan, providing tax credits to the uninsured to purchase private insurance. A month later, Reuther's rival, George Meany, testified before the Labor Committee at a hearing on health care at which Ted had assumed a leading role. The big, tough, irascible, cigar-chomping president of the AFL–CIO, who had been opposed to national health care, preferring health benefits be left to collective bargaining, had come to the same realization as Reuther—that collective bargaining could never keep pace with health-care spending—and came out in support of Ted's bill, after declaring a truce with the UAW and calling the AMA's rival plan "legislative quackery."

But there was another illustration of how Ted Kennedy had already changed the health-care debate: the activity of the president. Richard Nixon, who at the time thought he might be facing Ted Kennedy in the 1972 election, had once again attempted preemption, recommending what he called the National Health Insurance Partnership, which was an employer-mandated insurance system—that is, a system in which employers were mandated by law to provide health care for their workers. (It had little to offer individuals who were self-employed or unemployed.) There were those who believed that Nixon was sincere in proposing a health insurance plan; he had seen two of his brothers die from tuberculosis and another fall ill, the Nixon house plagued with illness, and they believed that those experiences had affected him deeply. But in his new effort, Nixon, forever Machiavellian, was being Machiavellian again, and as early as 1969, on the day after Ted had made his public declaration in favor of national health insurance, John Ehrlichman wrote a White House attorney named Edward Morgan that Nixon was only interested in health care as a way of thwarting Kennedy and that his goal was "in seizing and holding the political initiative in an area where the administration is perceived by some to be hostile or disinterested," while making certain to "hold back the Kennedy Plan" and "get the credit for what he proposed and what gets passed." In short, there was no moral issue in health care for Richard Nixon. In any case, Ted dismissed the new plan as "poorhouse medicine" and said it would provide a "windfall of billions of dollars" for the insurance industry—not surprisingly, he complained, because the insurance industry seemed to have designed the plan.

And yet there was a certain presumptuousness to Ted Kennedy becoming the spokesman for the issue when he had little experience in the area, despite his yearlong tutorial, and no standing in the Senate to do so, which is exactly how James Corman, the California congressman whom Reuther had recruited to push his plan in the House, felt. Corman was frustrated by the delays caused by Chappaquiddick and, according to Fine, didn't understand why he couldn't carry the ball himself. (The reason he couldn't is that he was not Ted Kennedy—not the legatee of a president Americans continued to mourn.) And Corman was more than frustrated—he was angry—when Ted proposed his plan after having made an accommodation with Michigan congresswoman Martha Griffiths. She had been backing a plan authored by the AFL–CIO that was less than full single-payer; instead, it would set up ten regional agencies through which the government would contract with medical providers. "He got really mad when Kennedy jumps in," Fine recalled about Corman feeling co-opted, and he was madder still when he felt that Ted had given up on single-payer too soon, though Ted, as always, was looking for legislation to pass and not just a cause about which to speechify. Corman was not alone in that feeling. Leonard Woodcock, who had succeeded Reuther as the president of the UAW, felt the same way, and so did other members of the Committee of 100. They felt Ted was compromising before he needed to compromise, which was a charge increasingly leveled at Ted because he had always sought the good rather than the perfect. But Ted believed, according to Fine, that he understood the politics of health insurance, and he understood too, as Fine put it, "if there's going to be any kind of health-care legislation, that he had to have his name on it." This was not necessarily because Ted's ego had swelled—he did have an ego—but because *if it was going to pass,* it had to have his name on it, as a practical consideration. Ted Kennedy was the only one who could push it through—the only one whose name was big enough, the only one with a national constituency large enough, the only one with bona fides among the Democrats reliable enough, the only one with presidential prospects promising enough, and the only one with enough trust among moderate Republicans. National health care needed a big push, the kind of push that Lyndon Johnson had provided to Medicare. Ted Kennedy, even wounded by Chappaquiddick, was the only senator who could possibly hope to provide that push.

And even then, Ted knew it might not be enough. He certainly recognized that he had lost much of his luster after Chappaquiddick. Just as Reuther knew he needed a legislative point man to further health insurance, Ted knew that if he was to brand the issue as his and advance it, he needed a base of operations—a more solid base than the Labor Committee. The putative base, of course, was Labor's Health Subcommittee, save for one oddity: While the Health Subcommittee of the Labor Committee had jurisdiction over most health legislation, it did not have jurisdiction over national health insurance. Because health insurance was principally about public funding—that is, financing—it fell under the domain of the Finance Committee, chaired by Russell Long, and *its* Health Subcommittee, chaired by Herman Talmadge, a deeply conservative Georgian who was unalterably opposed to national health insurance and certainly wasn't about to hold hearings on it. As Long boasted with not a little belligerence, "Kennedy gets all the press, but the Finance Committee gets all the jurisdiction." (This is why Ehrlichman had also written White House attorney Edward Morgan that Nixon, in preempting Ted, hoped to "bring Long and Kennedy [to] each other's throats.") Still, Ted, who had told Reuther he preferred to work on education, now coveted the Health Subcommittee of the Labor Committee—coveted it because he knew what he could do with it, knew what he *had* to do with it. So after Ralph Yarborough's defeat, and after Claiborne Pell, under Reuther's earlier prodding, chose to take the Education Subcommittee, Ted became the chair of the Health Subcommittee in the 92nd Congress, the Congress in which he also lost his whip position to Robert Byrd. "A lot of his future course was shaped by that primary election in Texas," Carey Parker was to say of Yarborough's loss and Ted's ascension to the chairmanship of the Health Subcommittee. "*My* committee," Parker said Ted began calling it, perhaps as compensation for his whip loss, and one of his colleagues on the committee, Senator J. Glenn Beall Jr., agreed: "Kennedy *is* the Health Subcommittee. He controls the entire majority staff," meaning that Ted didn't let any of the other Democrats on the committee have any staff. And Parker said something else: that the chairmanship was a "big boost in terms of his morale," at a time when Chappaquiddick had deflated that morale, because he knew now that he was going to be "Mr. Health Care in the Senate." And he had become Mr. Health Care primarily to push national health insurance—a "major push," he told LeRoy Goldman, who would become his Health Subcommittee staff director—no matter how long it took, and he knew it would take long, four or five years, he told *New York Post* editor James Wechsler, though that was more optimistic than Reuther's timetable. A "steep mountain," he called the path ahead. But however steep the mountain, as Parker put it, "Senator Kennedy felt that he ought to lay down a marker and say, 'This is our goal. We have to make sure that what we do brings us closer to that goal.'" All this, even though he knew his committee would only promote health care, hold hearings for it, focus attention on it, but not finally send it to the Senate floor.

And Ted Kennedy knew from his decade of legislative maneuvering how to lay down that marker, even though he technically wasn't in charge of national health insurance, and even though doing so would pit him against Long and Talmadge, two Senate bulls. First of all, he needed staff, not just to push health care but to take care of the numerous but seemingly prosaic pieces of legislation over which Health *did* have jurisdiction—many of which had three-year sunset provisions, meaning that they had to be reauthorized every three years, and meaning that they could be time-consuming—but in which Ted had little interest. One day that December of 1970, LeRoy Goldman said, his secretary told him that Ted Kennedy was on the phone. Goldman thought someone was pulling a prank, but Ted *was* on the phone and he *did* want to sound Goldman out about taking a position with the subcommittee. Goldman wasn't a typical Ted Kennedy staffer. He was no Harvard boy. He was an Indiana boy from the steel town of Gary—his father had worked for U.S. Steel for forty-seven years—educated at Drake University and with a master's degree in political science from Northwestern University. No Harvard boy, but a boy who loved politics: When he was ten years old, he played hooky from school to see Harry Truman speak at War Memorial Coliseum during the 1948 presidential campaign. "Hooked on politics," he said he was. Out of Northwestern, he won a competitive fellowship that landed him in the National Institutes of Health. He had no previous interest in health, but he happened to be at a urinal next to one of his examiners for the fellowship; the man worked at the NIH and advised Goldman apply there if he won. Goldman spent five years at NIH, getting five promotions in that time. But having worked with Congress while at NIH, he had his sights on moving from the bureaucracy to the legislature and landed another fellowship, this one a congressional internship, which brought him to Ralph Yarborough's Health Subcommittee. When his internship ended, he took a position as director of federal liaison for the Association of American Medical Colleges. He had been on the job for only three months when Ted made his call, and after two face-to-face meetings, Ted, to Goldman's astonishment, asked him to be the subcommittee's staff director—Goldman's lack of pedigree notwithstanding. (When Goldman warned Ted about the committee's largely pedestrian mandate, Ted told Goldman that Goldman could take care of the pedestrian issues; he was focused on national health care.) Goldman recruited another health staffer, Stan Jones, a former Yale Divinity student who had wound up at NIH, where Goldman knew him. Jones had vacillated over whether to join Ted Kennedy's staff, but when he visited the senator's office, Kennedy staffer Mark Schneider happened to rush in, and Ted, pointing at Schneider, said, "Now, see that guy? He's going to be critical in getting a voluntary draft passed in this country. And I'm working with him. You could do something like that if you were here." So Jones, wanting to be critical in getting national health insurance passed, joined the staff. And two weeks later he was organizing field hearings about national health insurance—the very subject over which Ted had no jurisdiction but only, as Long had sneered, the press.

But Ted Kennedy wanted both power and publicity, not because, like Lyndon Johnson, they could inflate him and make him unassailable, or because, like Richard Nixon, they could level the playing field Nixon had found so unfair, though Ted did have an ego and he did have his sense of insufficiency to address, but because he understood that they were the means to achieving his legislative goals, which were themselves a means to expiating his sins while making him worthy of his brothers. And Ted Kennedy knew how to get both power and publicity. "People who were less secure than Kennedy would probably shy away from stepping on somebody else's turf," said Dr. Philip Caper, a Harvard-trained physician who joined Ted's staff on Rashi Fein's recommendation shortly after Stan Jones, overestimating the degree of Ted's security. Yet Ted Kennedy did not shy away. He had done this before. When he had taken over AdPrac, the inconsequential little committee that nobody wanted, he creatively extended its jurisdiction into areas it had never previously entered—and some felt it should not have entered—simply by finding "administrative practices" wherever he looked, including, as it would turn out, the Watergate burglary. Now he was going to do the same thing with his Health Subcommittee—"*my* committee"—by finding the nonfinancial aspects of health insurance that would give him jurisdiction. "We could hold hearings around the edges" is how Caper put it, saying that health insurance would impact public-health service programs and the National Institutes of Health, which *were* issues that fell under the jurisdiction of the Labor Committee and its Health Subcommittee. LeRoy Goldman called it a "contrivance that we created." So, early in 1971, Ted Kennedy held hearings on national health insurance, many hearings, twenty-three of them; hearings in the state of nearly every senator on the committee; hearings in hospitals and clinics; hearings many of those senators declined to attend because, as Goldman put it, "they didn't want to be in Ted's shadow," and hearings, Stan Jones noted, in states where Ted had supporters and alliances from Bobby's presidential bid—in case, Jones hinted, Ted wanted to make a presidential run of his own; hearings designed, Ted had told Wechsler, to "arouse the kind of human-interest coverage that people could identify with," in which witnesses told "horror stories" about having no health insurance and being driven into bankruptcy; hearings technically not on health insurance—though they *were* on health insurance—but on the "health crisis in America," as Goldman described the mandate. And at "almost every hearing we held having to do with national health insurance," Caper recalled, citing "quite a few in Washington in addition to field hearings," Republican senator Peter Dominick would rise and say, "This committee has no jurisdiction over national health insurance." And Ted would respond evenly, "Thank you, Senator Dominick. First witness please." But while the "contrivance" allowed him to hold his hearings, it did not allow him to consider the bill itself, which was still referred to Finance, where it was certain to die under executioners Long and Talmadge. So Ted proposed an amendment to the Public Health Service Act, over which his subcommittee did have jurisdiction, to improve the infrastructure of the health-care system, "in *preparation* for national health insurance," as Goldman described it. It gave Ted a back door into considering the larger bill, Reuther's bill, Ig Falk's bill, now his bill, the bill he had introduced in the last session of Congress and that he would introduce again in the new session: Senate bill 3. *S.3.* The Health Security Act.

Ted Kennedy felt that America needed that bill—needed it to repair the broken health-care system and make it affordable for millions of Americans for whom it was now unaffordable. And for those who doubted his sincerity, he said in private to his own staff what he said in public. As LeRoy Goldman put it, "The bedrock of it, the foundational aspect of it was, 'We have got a health-care crisis in this country. It's wrong. And we need to fix it, and, by God, that's what I'm going to do.'" Health-care costs had skyrocketed—overall medical costs doubling in just five years from 1965 to 1970, the cost of an average hospital stay doubling in just four years, while medical costs rose to 7.3 percent of the Gross National Product, or $70 billion. Eighty percent of Americans were insured. But that meant 20 percent, roughly forty million Americans, were not, and since Medicare covered those over sixty-five, these uninsured were likely to be the poorest Americans, the sickest Americans, the most desperate Americans, the most forgotten Americans. And the statistics, frightening as they were, did not provide the whole picture—the picture of human suffering and destitution. "Horror stories," Phil Caper had called the testimony that so many gave at those field hearings, where Ted listened intently to presentations on the failings of the health-care system—the waste, the waits, the misdiagnoses, the filth, the poor quality of services, the inconsistency between state and federal regulations, the overuse of surgery, the rapidly rising costs and the emphasis on money, always money. But above all, those horror stories described the vast disparity of care between the rich and poor and how the less fortunate were either deprived of services altogether or forced into financial ruin after receiving them. Some of those stories were told by people brought to the hearings by medical professionals who were testifying themselves; some of them were told by members of the audience whom Ted Kennedy invited to speak. And they spoke of their despair. A widow named Betty Roche, a hotel maid who earned $75 a week, told Ted how she needed an operation and wound up with a hospital bill of $1,832 even after her insurance—an amount she could not pay. Lillian Bloom told Ted about a "catastrophic illness" that befell her husband and left him permanently disabled and how his bill came to $7,001, which was exactly what the Blooms were worth—"I sometimes feel that our medical system has private eyes who go and figure out exactly how much you are worth," she said—and how it forced them into bankruptcy and how they emerged only because they borrowed money that they then invested in health stocks because they knew how rapacious the industry was. "It is beautiful," Mrs. Bloom said. "We played the game of the establishment." John Kaiser, a sixty-three-year-old brewer, told Ted how he had worked for forty years, until his kidneys began to fail and he needed dialysis three times a week, four hours each time, at $6,000 a year, and how he was told that his group policy would no longer pay for the treatments and how he was going to lose the services and how the hospital did a credit check to see how much he could afford to pay. And when Ted asked what happened to those who couldn't afford the dialysis, Kaiser said simply, "They die." Bertha Dixon told Ted how she was admitted to the emergency room, was tested, then was discharged, and, still ill, returned to the clinic, where she was twice turned away—once because they had failed to get her chart, and again because the doctor had failed to appear—and how she was charged $599.95 for this lack of services and how the hospital garnished her wages when she couldn't pay. "It seems they don't treat you, but they can sure drag you into court," Ted said.

And then there was Isabel Rodriguez. Rodriguez was a thirty-two-year-old widow, a mother of two, a Puerto Rican immigrant, now living in the Bronx, who had been a teacher in Puerto Rico but couldn't find a job teaching in America because she had an accent. She told Ted about her epileptic son, who fell and severely bruised his eye—a "big blow in his eye"—and how she had to borrow money to take him to the hospital and how, when she did, she couldn't find a doctor there to treat him and how one of the "assistants" got a doctor "upstairs" to give her eight pills and told her to give one to her son every four hours. And she told how, with her son still screaming in pain, she walked eight blocks to another hospital to find someone to examine him. But there was no eye specialist on duty because "poor people cannot get sick after five-thirty or Saturdays or Sundays." So her son suffered. She told Ted how she lived in Acey Alley, roach- and rat-infested "day and night," and how, while working as a community organizer, she had fallen through the stairway of a tenement—a "dump," she called it—where fifty-eight children lived, and how she was unable to walk and how she waited well over an hour for an ambulance and how she was hospitalized for three months, but her bedclothes and her sheets, her towels and pillowcases, were only changed once a month. She told him how she saw people in that hospital—Metropolitan Hospital, she finally said when Ted pressed her, because she was clearly afraid of repercussions—with wounds and people crying out for bedpans, and how she heard that a hospital administrator would appear every so often, and she asked one of the workers to tell her when he came so she could get in a wheelchair and confront him. And she told how she did so, but it was useless. She said she would never go to a hospital again for herself, only for her children. She told Ted how she would walk down the roach-infested hallways of her apartment building and look into the faces of her neighbors who were old and ill and how she would ask them why they didn't see a doctor and how they answered her: "They say it is no use. It is not long now. We are waiting for death." And Mrs. Rodriguez, frustrated and angry and certain that "to be poor is to be doomed," told Ted this: "I had faith in this country. This was America, the promising land. It has promised me nothing. I don't owe America a thing. They haven't given me a thing that I didn't fight for. Everything has been wrong. We need people like you, Mr. Senator. We need people like you, more of them, thousands of them, because if not, this is a real crisis. We are already frustrated and hopeless. We have no hope anymore. We have no faith. The only faith is God. And that is what I want, is faith to the people. Let's continue fighting, because we cannot give up. We must find people that really realize what is going on." Then she thanked Ted Kennedy for listening to her and for waging that fight. And that is *why* Ted Kennedy fought—because it was a moral issue to him, a moral issue to help the Isabel Rodriguezes.

II

To "hold back the Kennedy plan" and "get the credit for what he proposed and what gets passed": This was what Ehrlichman had said of Richard Nixon's intentions in co-opting Ted Kennedy on health care. And on February 18, 1971, four days before Ted's first hearing, Nixon, attempting to do just that, submitted his own health-care plan, his employer-mandated plan for full-time employees, with subsidies for children and for the working poor, based on a sliding scale, and insurance pools for the self-employed, allowing them to buy private insurance, and all of it to be regulated not by the federal government but by the states. Unlike S.3, there were deductibles and co-pays and a limit on costs, and unlike S.3, which would cover 70 percent of health costs, Nixon's would only cover half. And Nixon's plan had one other fillip that would have had enormous consequences: Its subsidies would replace Medicaid. (In effect, as the administration privately admitted, its plan was only "stretching present Medicaid money over twice as many people.") Ted immediately denounced it, as he had a few months earlier when Nixon first announced its principles. But that might have been unnecessary. LeRoy Goldman believed that Nixon had no intention of getting his plan through Congress anyway. "It was a way of having a placeholder so they could say, 'Oh, yes, here's what I'm for,'" Goldman said, speculating that Nixon was less interested in health care than in foiling Ted Kennedy's presidential aspirations. "There is a very important difference between having a placeholder that you could point to for political reasons, as contrasted to being motivated to actually enact a program." (It was basically the same thing Ehrlichman had conceded privately.) Meanwhile, the administration protested that Ted's plan, S.3, was, in Ehrlichman's words, a "demagogic ploy" that would be far too expensive—Ted estimated its cost at $40 billion; Nixon at $77 billion—and that would be detrimental to our health-care system. Even some Democrats blanched at the price tag, and Senator Alan Cranston, who was a liberal and co-sponsor of Ted's bill, said he had only done so to "add momentum to a national dialogue." Wilbur Mills, the chairman of the House Ways and Means Committee, through which national health care would have to pass in that chamber, wasn't about to move the bill either. In short, S.3 wasn't going anywhere, not in the 92nd Congress, despite Ted Kennedy's best efforts.

But there was one more effort that year. After the field hearings ended, Ted called Goldman to his office and told him that the hearings were good—"which from him means he really liked them" because "he's not given to flowery language"—but that he now had another idea: He wanted to take his subcommittee to Europe and the Middle East to study health-care systems there. So Goldman hastily arranged a tour—Ted had given him just over three months and didn't pick up on Goldman's sarcasm when he said, "Oh, well, that will give us plenty of time this summer to catch up on the legislation"—and Ted and Joan and Phil Caper went to Britain and Israel and Denmark and Norway and Sweden, visiting hospitals and meeting with health officials. (Ted also made a point of spending an evening with the Swedish economist and sociologist Gunnar Myrdal, who had written the pathbreaking report *An American Dilemma: The Negro Problem and Modern Democracy*, which the Supreme Court cited in deciding *Brown v. Board of Education*, and Myrdal's wife, Alva, a formidable figure in her own right.) Speaking on health care in the United States, Ted would always say ruefully that South Africa and the United States were the "only two industrialized nations on the face of the earth that did not have a national insurance plan on the books." When they returned from Europe that fall, Caper said Ted asked him, "Well, why can't we do that? If they can do this, why can't we?" But there were many more obstacles ahead and that steep mountain to climb, and there was a presidential election year upcoming, 1972, during which nothing of substance would advance. And so national health care was stalled—stalled yet again.

But in the year in which he introduced S.3, the year of speeches and hearings and parrying with the administration, Ted Kennedy had become the health senator, Mr. Health Care, and he wasn't about to leave the first session of that 92nd Congress without an accomplishment, in this case an accomplishment that his predecessor, Ralph Yarborough, had left him— Yarborough's unfinished business. Philanthropist Mary Lasker, the widow of the advertising millionaire Albert Lasker, had worked closely with Yarborough over the years on health issues and had lobbied him in 1970, when he headed the Health Subcommittee, to impanel a group of consultants to work on what might be the most intractable health problem: cancer. (The year before, Nixon had cut funds to the National Cancer Institute—a cut that had appalled those fighting the disease.) When the panel, which had been led by Ted's old colleague on the Cancer Crusade, Dr. Sidney Farber, issued its report later that year—a report written largely by Mary Lasker and her associate, Luke Quinn, who was a cancer survivor himself—it unanimously called for empowering the National Cancer Institute: first by removing it from under the aegis of the National Institutes for Health and making it into an independent agency, the National Cancer Authority, with an administrator appointed by the president and a budget separate from that of NIH (Ted would compare it to NASA), and second by funding it heavily, a billion dollars by 1976. Yarborough then submitted a bill to that effect on December 4, 1970, though by that time Lloyd Bentsen had won Yarborough's seat and Yarborough was about to leave the Senate, and he knew that his gesture was a symbolic one. Nevertheless, Republican senator Jacob Javits, a moderate, promised Yarborough that he would take up the cause, and Ted, the new chair of the Health Subcommittee, told Yarborough that he would consider it an "honor" to reintroduce the bill in the new legislative session. On January 26, 1971, before he launched his hearings on the health-care crisis, he and Javits did just that: the National Cancer Act, S.34. The media, though, called it not by its title but by its mission, the "War on Cancer." (Ted himself, looking to the public-relations benefits, called the new agency the "Conquest of Cancer Agency.") The bill attracted twenty-five co-sponsors, all of them Democrats save for Javits.

All Democrats. Fighting cancer was not, seemingly, a political matter. Fighting disease shouldn't have been. As LeRoy Goldman described the typical process of formulating and then passing health legislation, the protagonists were what he called a "permanent alliance" among "agency people in the executive branch" (not, Goldman specified, people at the Cabinet level, but agency heads like the director of the NIH or the Cancer

Institute); subcommittee chairmen like Ted (not, he specified, the committee chairmen or the Senate leadership) and their staffs; and "key players
in the private sector," like Mary Lasker, influential because of her philan-
thropy, or the dean of the Harvard Medical School. "It is," Goldman said,
"the discussions and agreements reached informally and *in camera* by
these three focal points that shape and determine the legislative process."
And Goldman added that when Ted took the chairmanship of the Health
Subcommittee, he looked for a Republican partner on nearly every bill. So
Goldman would go to Javits's chief of staff, Jay Cutler, hammer out a mutually satisfactory resolution, and with the majority and at least one
member of the minority on board—this was the bipartisanship Ted
sought—the bill would proceed. "The Goldman–Cutler Show," Goldman
called it. But the National Cancer Act was not the Goldman–Cutler Show.
When it came to cancer, the members of the alliance Goldman had described could not agree, understandably, because while Javits and Ted and
Lasker and her allies all wanted an independent agency, the health bureaucrats at the NIH were adamantly opposed to one—opposed to any
agency that wasn't under their command, though the argument they
used, not an implausible one, was that a new agency would separate cancer from and thus prioritize it over other illnesses, prompting advocates
for other illnesses to call for separate agencies of *their* own, and that it
would lead to fragmentation, disrupting the coordination that had developed among various researchers and organizations committed to wiping
out cancer.

There were few enough things on which Ted Kennedy and Richard
Nixon agreed. A cancer agency happened to be one of them. Cancer was
the great terror in America—a rampant disease hitting one of every four
Americans, an incurable disease, a death sentence. Nixon had already declared his own war on cancer in his State of the Union address, clearly trying to preempt Ted yet again and regain some of the initiative on health,
and in a memo to Ehrlichman that April, he lodged the same kind of complaints at the health bureaucrats as Ted had—"they simply want to fund
the bureaucracy to go along its merry way to do as it damn pleases"—
though he also saw a new agency primarily "as a matter of appearances."
Banging away at his favorite punching bag, he wrote to Ehrlichman, "Ted
Kennedy is on a surefire public-relations and political wicket when he
comes out for a special approach with a special agency. If we are going to
spend the money, the least we can do is to get some credit for having a new

approach. We will not get it if we simply put another hundred million dollars in the bowels of the NIH and have the program lost forever as far as public view is concerned." The public had to *see* Nixon's effort because Nixon wanted the credit.

But Nixon had not submitted a bill on a war against cancer. He had only announced his declaration of war, along with a sudden infusion of $28 million more in funding on research, and then left it to the Department of Health, Education, and Welfare to draft a bill, which meant that over the early months of 1971 he had left the field to Ted. So Ted proceeded to hold two days of hearings on his and Javits's bill in March, starting with the opponents, the AMA, the NIH, and the Association of American Medical Colleges, Goldman's old employer—to whose representatives, Ted, in a churlish mood, snapped that they only opposed the bill because they were fearful of losing their own control or their own funding, though, in fact, there were those legitimate concerns about how a new agency would affect research. But the supporters were not leaving anything to chance. Mary Lasker enlisted a friend of hers, the popular advice columnist Ann Landers, to write a column supporting Ted's bill—"How many of us have asked . . . if this great country of ours can put a man on the moon, why can't we find a cure for cancer?"—and urging her readers to write their senators encouraging them to vote for its passage. Bags of mail poured into Senate offices, by one estimate between 250,000 and 300,000 letters. Landers's column appeared on April 20, by which time Ted had left for his field hearings on national health care. Now Nixon, pushed not only by the Landers column but by the lobbying of a friend and supporter, pharmaceutical magnate Elmer Bobst, knew he had to act and act quickly, lest Ted steal the issue from him. By the time Ted returned from his field hearings, Nixon had sprung. At a press conference on May 11, he announced a plan of his own out of what he said was a "very deep personal concern about this problem" and because, in what could only be perceived as a jab at Ted, "direct presidential interest and presidential guidance may hasten the day that we will find the cure for cancer." And he had Republican senator Peter Dominick submit the bill, S.1828, the HEW-drafted bill, the primary purpose of which seemed to be to draw distinctions between it and Ted's bill to give Nixon a political marker—a pledge now of $100 million in Nixon's bill, as opposed to Ted and Javits's $500 million. Nixon's bill would also keep the Cancer Institute within the NIH—though with an administrator who would be appointed by and report to the president—rather than establish it as a stand-alone agency, as in Ted and Javits's, this de-spite Nixon's own fulminations just days earlier against letting the NIH maintain control. The bill had arrived with only two days of consultation because Nixon had been racing Ted to the finish line. His press conference was held the very day that Ted was set to have the Health Subcommittee mark up his own bill. It was at that markup session that Ted agreed to hold a hearing on the new Nixon bill.

Ted Kennedy was not naïve when it came to political machinations; he had, as Nixon had complained to Ehrlichman, been playing politics too, latching on to a very popular and high-profile initiative and getting pub-licity for it. And he certainly knew that Nixon was trying to co-opt him, trying to line up Republicans against Ted's bill, trying to get credit for a war on cancer while denying Ted credit. Even so, Ted didn't want to lose the cancer initiative over Nixon's pettiness or, for that matter, his own. And in his jousting with Nixon, Ted had a powerful ally that Nixon could hardly disregard: Benno Schmidt, a Texas-born investor who had been the chairman of Yarborough's panel of consultants and who had remained as a consultant to Kennedy, and who had been so furious when *The New York Times* editorialized against Ted's bill—on the same old grounds that it would fragment the health field—that he had flown to Washington, gone straight to Ted's office with a blistering letter, and read it to Ted, barely able to contain his rage. But Benno Schmidt was not just a cancer warrior. He also happened to be a hidebound Republican and a major contributor to the party. (In fact, because Schmidt was a Republican, Yarborough had opposed his chairing the advisory panel when Mary Lasker suggested it, until it was revealed to him that Schmidt had been one of his students at the University of Texas Law School.) So Ted sent Schmidt to see if he could get Nixon to relent in his opposition, perhaps reach a truce, since the two bills were not significantly different, except for the funding. Nixon was blunt, and Nixon was candid. He told Schmidt that he had another quar-rel with Ted's bill besides the money and the authority: His quarrel was that the bill had Ted Kennedy's name on it, *Kennedy*–Javits. And he told Schmidt he would not endorse any bill for which Ted Kennedy would get the credit. When Schmidt conveyed this to Ted, Ted was conciliatory. He said it was all right with him to have his name removed, because he just wanted to get the bill passed, but Javits's name would also have to be re-moved, because they were co-sponsors. And when Schmidt told Javits, as Schmidt relayed it to Ted, Javits absolutely refused on the basis that he would not do that to Ted Kennedy, not strip Ted of credit he deserved. Schmidt remonstrated with him that Ted was okay with it—"Jack, you don't understand. Ted has taken his name off"—and Schmidt said he wouldn't leave the room until Javits agreed.

Public relations, Nixon had called Ted's effort. And now Nixon was engaging in a public-relations campaign of his own. But there was one Nixon supporter besides Benno Schmidt who wasn't happy with Nixon's tactics: Nixon's old friend Elmer Bobst. As medical historian Richard Rettig reported it, Bobst felt the press conference Nixon had given and the bill Dominick had introduced were at odds—apparently, he felt that the NIH still controlled the Cancer Institute in the bill—and he complained about it to Ken Cole of the White House staff, which moved Cole to go to New York to consult with Benno Schmidt, which moved Schmidt to meet with Ted and Javits to see if some compromise could be reached between Nixon's bill and Ted's, which were essentially the same bill. All this time HEW and the NIH were excluded from the negotiations, even though they had drafted Nixon's plan. Ted held his hearing on the bill on June 10, by which time the sides had apparently reached agreement, and Ted joked, "Maybe we ought to just recess the hearing and pass the bill as long as we have everything on track." Caught in the middle was former HEW secretary Elliot Richardson, who had testified against Ted's bill at the first hearing and now testified for Nixon's nearly identical bill, prompting Senator Gaylord Nelson to quip, "Mr. Secretary, if you are not smart enough to see that they put jacks under the Kennedy Bill, jacked it up, changed its name, and let the jacks down, then you are not as smart as I have been led to believe."

But LeRoy Goldman told it differently—much differently. He said the apparent comity notwithstanding, Ted had lost patience with Nixon's maneuvering and with the Republicans' intransigence and had called for a markup session before the full Labor Committee on June 16, six days after the hearing, at which time the bill would be finalized and sent to the floor. But since there were two bills now, his and Nixon's, Ted had no choice but to move both of them to markup, pitting the parties against each other, with the Republicans—all but Javits—unyielding in their backing of Nixon's bill, the Democrats equally unyielding in their backing of Ted and Javits's—once again, despite the fact that the bills varied only insignificantly and that the battle was less substantive than political: Who would get credit? But credit for Richard Nixon was important. "Intense," Goldman was to say of the mood in the crowded hearing room on the fourth floor of the Dirksen Senate Office Building as the sides squared off. A standoff. But then, Goldman said, Ted Kennedy did something extraordinary—something that underscored how important it was for Ted to move legislation, whether or not it was his, whether or not he got credit for it. Ted Kennedy, the man who had said of national health insurance that any bill had to have his name on it, turned to Senator Peter Dominick, the Colorado Republican, and suggested that the committee just report S.1828, *Nixon's* bill, to the Senate, and "maybe," he said, "that would take some of the controversy out of this issue." He stressed that a bill needed to move forward—*some* bill—and that more research was needed to combat cancer, better research, and that they needed to get that research to people suffering in a timely way. "If we report the administration's bill," Ted said, "maybe that will help to make that clear." And, as Goldman remembered it, "You could hear a pin drop in that packed hearing room . . . because it was unheard of. *Forget my bill.*" No senator ever did that. And then, as Goldman also remembered it, before Dominick, sitting "stunned, in silence," could say a word, Ted said, "And, Peter, why don't *you* report the bill?," which was to say, "Why don't you put your name on the bill as the primary sponsor," even though Ted said years later of Dominick that he "hadn't been interested in it, hadn't shown up for any of the hearings on it, had been rather cool to the whole idea." And Goldman said Dominick's committee staffer rose at that point, walked around the table, bent down to Goldman, and whispered, "Lee, I don't know how to write a report." To which Goldman said he responded that he and Jay Cutler, Javits's staffer, would write the report for him. But Ted wasn't finished. He did something else that was extraordinary. He said, " 'I have an amendment to offer, and the amendment is'—this is now an amendment to S.1828, the president's bill—'strike all [the language] after the enacting clause and substitute in lieu thereof the text of S.34.' " And so, with that swift move, while the committee was basking in congeniality, Ted Kennedy both gave the credit to Richard Nixon and got the subcommittee to approve the substance of his own bill by substituting it for Nixon's and changing the number.* It passed the Senate, 79 to 1, the next

---

*There may be something apocryphal about Goldman's version, since one report has two of Ted's staffers—probably including Goldman—cutting and pasting parts of the two bills. "House Subcommittee Questions Wisdom of Establishing Independent Cancer Agency," *National Journal,* July 31, 1971.

month, with only Democrat Gaylord Nelson objecting, again on the grounds that it might affect the collaboration among researchers.

But that didn't quite settle the National Cancer Act. The Senate bill, now once again Ted and Javits's bill, if not in name, had to go to the House. Ted described the conference—at which the House version of the bill, which was basically Nixon's bill, and the Senate version had to be reconciled—as "difficult." The House Health Subcommittee chair, Paul Rogers of Florida, a Democrat, was close to the medical industry, which remained suspicious of giving the new Cancer Institute any prerogatives that other health agencies did not have, and he was "very cautious," Ted said, on most health issues. In another interview, Ted called him a "brick wall." The ranking Republican on the subcommittee, Tim Lee Carter of Kentucky, was a physician whose son suffered from cancer and who took the lead on the issue as, Goldman said, he took the lead on many health issues. (He and Ted wound up becoming close collaborators on this and other health legislation.) Four times Ted walked out of the conference meetings in frustration—each time the conference had to be rescheduled—until, as Goldman recalled, Carter was able to broker a hybrid agreement in which the new agency remained within the NIH, where Nixon's bill had placed it, but with its autonomy assured by a direct line to the Office of Management and Budget and a direct line to the president, who would be appointing the new administrator as well as an advisory panel. Thus amended, it passed both houses easily, and Nixon signed it on December 23, after which he conducted a tour of the White House for Ted and staffer Stan Jones. But on that very same day, a day of mutual recognition and pleasantries, Nixon had another meeting. He met with Charles Colson, his hatchet man, to devise dirty tricks against Ted Kennedy, the man he so feared would run against him. And as LeRoy Goldman was to say of the juxtaposition between Nixon's bonhomie and his devilry, "If you want a chilling insight into American politics, there it is."

III

That was how 1971 ended. Heading into 1972, an election year, a year in which Nixon still fretted that he might have to face Ted Kennedy, Nixon's attentions and energies were focused on other than health issues. The only new wrinkle in the ongoing debate was a fascination with health maintenance organizations, or HMOs, the brainchild of a Minnesota physician named Paul Ellwood. Ellwood had worked with Senator Walter Mondale on setting up medical groups in which payment was not for services rendered, as doctors typically charged, but for patients on a per capita basis—that is, a fixed fee for each patient who belonged to the HMO, regardless of the services they received, similar to a membership. The idea was that this would hold down health costs and incentivize doctors to practice preventive medicine, since there was no advantage to treating sick patients. The idea intrigued Ted, and he introduced a bill setting up an HMO pilot project, though it never made it to a vote in the House. Nixon had toyed with the idea himself for several years—Ellwood had gotten Nixon's first HEW secretary, Robert Finch, to commit to a national program early in 1970—and he had included it in his 1971 health-care plan, but it had moved in fits and starts since, until, like so many of Nixon's initiatives, Ted showed his interest, only for Nixon's interest then to flag as the election approached and as Ted's presidential possibilities ended. (Of Nixon's motives for pursuing health care, deputy assistant secretary of HEW Stuart Altman was to say, "My best sense is that he was very much afraid of Ted Kennedy.")

But Ted Kennedy's interest in national health insurance had not flagged; if anything, it had intensified as Nixon abandoned the issue, which seemed to undermine the idea that Ted had done it all for political advantage. The problem was that there was no obvious way forward, with Russell Long's Finance Committee unwilling to cooperate. Ted was stymied. LeRoy Goldman said that he and Stan Jones were having breakfast one morning before work and hashing over their respective agendas, including national health insurance. "There are only two ways to get legislation like this before the Congress," Goldman told Jones. "One's through [Wilbur] Mills's committee and the other is through Long's committee. Long's not going to do it." And that got Goldman ruminating about Wilbur Mills, the head of the powerful House Ways and Means Committee, the committee through which all tax bills had to pass and through which any health bill that relied on tax revenues had to pass, which would include national health insurance since it relied on tax revenues. And Goldman began thinking out loud. "Mills wants something," Goldman told Jones. "He wants to be president. [He had announced his candidacy.] I'll bet he'd settle for vice president, and I'll bet if Kennedy started courting him on this, he wouldn't shut the door, because who knows?" And Goldman placed a note in Ted's briefcase, the briefcase Ted took home every

night for his bedtime reading, raising the idea of coaxing Mills into joining Ted on national health care with the hint of a vice-presidential nomination as the bait, and Ted was agreeable. (In another version, Goldman
said he broached the idea personally to Ted, who was "incredulous" but
flashed a smile and told Goldman to see what he could do.)

The idea of sixty-three-year-old Wilbur Mills, an Arkansas congressman, becoming president or even vice president might have seemed like
Mills's delusion of political grandeur, but he was a House potentate who
had exulted in his power for years. He had grown up in a flyspeck town,
Kensett, in northeastern Arkansas, where he was a grandee. His father
owned the local store and bank and had deep political connections—the
family was close to Senate majority leader Joseph Robinson—so deep
that, as a boy, Wilbur played at being speaker of the House. With political
ambitions, he attended a small college nearby, Hendrix, then Harvard
Law School, dropping out to return to work at his father's bank and to
plan his political future. In 1934, at twenty-five, and against his father's
advice, he took on a longtime county judge and beat him, running for
judge because it was where the power resided in White County. (As judge,
he had initiated a program to help defray health costs to the indigent.) In
1938, when his local congressman was elected to the Senate after Robinson's death, he ran for the vacated seat—his father financed his
campaign—and won that too. He was the second-youngest member of
the House when he arrived in Washington. Astute, Wilbur Mills was. Ambitious, Wilbur Mills was. He became a protégé of Speaker Sam Rayburn—
Mills looked so young that Rayburn assigned two older members to
chaperone him, lest he be mistaken for a page—learning where the power
resided in the House as he had in White County. And power in the House
resided in the Ways and Means Committee—the committee where all tax
bills originated, the committee through which all tax bills had to pass, a
committee so powerful that it was almost never mentioned without the
adjective "powerful" preceding it: the "powerful Ways and Means Committee." Four years after his arrival, Wilbur Mills got a seat on the committee through Rayburn's intercession—it had been Mills's childhood
dream to sit on that committee—and from the very beginning, in part
because of Chairman Robert Doughton's cool relationship with Rayburn,
and in part because Doughton took a liking to Mills, Mills essentially ran
it. Sixteen years later, he ran it in name as well, becoming its chairman.
The "third house of Congress," his Ways and Means was called. He would

sit behind his green felt table in Room H208, the entrance of which was flanked by two guards, looking like Franklin Roosevelt with his mouth clamped on a long cigarette holder—Mills was a chain smoker—and take audiences with visitors. Unassailable, Mills was. "The chief reason the country does not now have a Medicare program," *The New York Times* complained when John Kennedy and then Lyndon Johnson were working on Medicare, "is a one-man blockade exercised for four years by Chairman Wilbur Mills." That is the kind of power that Wilbur Mills, the short, jug-eared congressman from rural Arkansas, wielded.

But as the years passed, Mills's lust for power had grown beyond Congress, and now he was thinking of the presidency or vice presidency. And LeRoy Goldman knew that while Wilbur Mills had no overwhelming desire for national health care—other than to worry about how to pay for it—Goldman could exploit that lust for power to push health care. So Goldman arranged for former HEW secretary Wilbur Cohen, who was conducting hearings that June for the Democratic Platform Committee in St. Louis, to ask Mills to testify about health insurance, given the jurisdiction of Ways and Means. At the hearing, Cohen lobbed Mills what Ted's health staffer Stan Jones called "soft pitches," and Mills was, as Jones recalled, "feeling so good about being able to hit them out of the park and say all the right things and make political points." And then Cohen asked Mills about Kennedy's health insurance plan, and Mills, riding high, floating on his inflated confidence, said he would do that, that he would gladly work with Ted Kennedy, that he and Kennedy could certainly work something out. Afterward, Cohen approached Ted, who was also testifying at that session, and brought the two, Mills and Kennedy, together and asked them to draft principles. Mills batted away the idea. They didn't need to draft principles. They would draft a *bill* instead, he said. Cohen called their agreement "historic." Jones recalled, "Kennedy came back and couldn't believe it," and Goldman phoned Mills's top aide, Bill Fullerton, who joked, "What have you guys been up to?" Now began a series of meetings between Ted Kennedy, Goldman, Jones, and Wilbur Mills—not Fullerton, because Mills didn't want anyone to think he was reliant on his staff—the first forty-five minutes of which, Jones would say, would be devoted to the politics of health insurance and the last fifteen minutes to the bill itself. ("Mostly he was interested in talking about politics," Ted said of Mills, "but he knew enough about it and would identify some areas that we had to make some sort of agreements on, and then the staffs would sort of work those up.") And Ted, showing his deference as well as his political savvy, made it a point of walking through the Capitol to Mills's office, just off the House floor, for these meetings, while Goldman and Jones briefed him along the way and Ted kept rehearsing the points. And all of this largely because Wilbur Mills, self-important, desperately wanted to land a spot on the Democratic ticket.

But the glimmer of hope—and it wasn't much more than a faint glimmer—soon faded, along with Mills's dream. Ted and Mills had announced that they hoped to have a bill drafted before the Democratic convention. They didn't. Then, in September, after George McGovern's nomination, the two announced the formation of a health-policy panel to advise McGovern and agreed to submit a joint bill in 1973—presumably after McGovern's election—but by then Mills had already retreated. Mills said he wanted a role for private insurers in any plan; Ted didn't. And Mills said that after the election, Ways and Means would take up tax reform first and that, in any case, he fully expected Long to revise Ted's bill and that a House–Senate conference would have to arrive at a compromise bill. Meanwhile, Richard Nixon was hosting the president of the AMA in his office that month and crowing over the impossibility of Ted's bill ever becoming law. "We have a lot of reasons why we would hope to whip it," he said, "just talking politically, which you can't do. And one of the reasons is that this kind of philosophy [big government] must be put down. Put down really good right now. You know the program costs sixty billion dollars, sixty billion dollars!" Still, Nixon chided the Democrats during the campaign for not passing a health-care bill, though he had made no real effort to pass one of his own. And so as every year before it, save 1965 when Lyndon Johnson signed Medicare, 1972 ended without any progress on national health insurance.

By the time 1973 arrived, Nixon was enmeshed in Watergate and fighting for his own survival and had little enough time to push health care or much of anything else. But while Nixon dallied, Ted Kennedy had a new reason to focus on national health insurance late that year—a powerful reason, a painful reason, a personal reason, a reason that had nothing whatsoever to do with politics or with his feud with Nixon. At the time, on November 6, his twelve-year-old son, Ted Jr., was suffering from a cold and had stayed home from school, St. Albans. As Ted later described it, he was in his library at McLean, having just ended a briefing session with his staff, when he noticed an "ugly reddish lump" under Ted Jr.'s kneecap, and Ted Jr. admitted that it hurt. Ted thought it might be a football injury, since Junior was on the school football team. But he asked the children's nurse, Teresa Fitzpatrick, to phone Phil Caper, his staffer and a physician, to come have a look. Caper arrived a half hour later—in formal wear; he had been headed to an event—examined Junior, and told them to check back with him in a few days. On November 8, Ted flew to Boston and was about to fly down to Palm Beach to visit his mother when Fitzpatrick phoned and told him that Junior's lump hadn't improved. Ted told her to phone Caper again, while he canceled his Florida trip and returned to Washington. As he would write in his memoir, Ted said that during the flight, "I began to have an almost overwhelming sense of dread, but I willed myself not to think of the possibilities." Caper had recommended that Junior see Dr. George Hyatt, the chairman of orthopedic surgery at Georgetown University Hospital. When Ted arrived at the airport, on November 9, Caper met him there with grim news: Hyatt believed the red lump was a bone tumor. Ted and Caper drove directly to Georgetown Hospital, where Hyatt now delivered his provisional diagnosis personally. And there was worse news: If he was correct, the only option was to amputate Ted Jr.'s leg. Junior returned to Georgetown later that same day for further testing. (Joan was in Europe at the time and Ted waited to inform her, perhaps to spare her the worry but also possibly to avoid having to deal with her.) Ted Jr. was released for the weekend, then returned to the hospital for a biopsy, which confirmed the diagnosis of cancer, and then, because he was still suffering from the cold that had kept him from school that day when Ted detected the bruise, the surgery was delayed until the following Saturday.

It was an agonizing wait, first the weekend before the biopsy and then the five days until the surgery, and Ted had not informed his son yet—couldn't bear to inform him. Instead, he said, "We wanted his life to be as normal as possible for as long as possible." Ted's friend Lee Fentress remembered getting a call that weekend asking if he and his son, Andrew, might be available for a touch football game at Hickory Hill, where Bobby's family still lived. It was a "tough, competitive" game, Fentress said, and at one point Ted Jr. and Andrew collided—collided hard. Teddy crumpled to the ground and grabbed his leg, in obvious pain. And Fentress noticed how attentive Ted was to his son, when previously, if Ted Jr. had fallen, Ted Sr., in typical Kennedy fashion, would have told him to get up and get going. A "tender moment," Fentress called it. And then, Fentress said, he read in the paper that Ted Jr. had had his leg amputated, and he recalled that moment when it was "just the two of them together there, the thoughtfulness." And he realized, "Teddy wanted to have him out and have a full day there," the last day when Ted Jr. could run on his two legs.*

But the week after the game, when Ted Jr. had his biopsy, Ted, at the suggestion of psychologists, had still not told his son of the diagnosis, and he had ordered a moratorium on television and newspapers, lest Ted Jr. learn about the diagnosis before Ted himself could tell him. (After the football game, Ted said, he had finally phoned Joan.) It wasn't until late that Friday in the hospital, the night before the operation, that he broke the news to him. "The hardest thing I ever had to do," he called it, though Ted Jr. would say that his father never subsequently discussed the difficulty with him. Ted had taken Dr. Caper and Dr. Robert Coles, the Harvard psychologist, with him to the hospital, and Coles later told Arthur Schlesinger Jr. that young Teddy was "deeply upset and lay in bed for a long time in silence, throwing a towel over his face so he wouldn't have to look at anyone." Ted held him tight and assured him—assured him repeatedly—that it would be all right. And then, about an hour later, in a rare act of grace and compassion, President Nixon phoned the hospital room, and Ted passed the receiver to his son. "I don't believe he is calling me up," Ted Jr. said incredulously. Whatever the president was asking him, Ted Jr. answered monosyllabically. When the call was over, he refused to say what the president had said to him, prompting his visitors to guess. Ted speculated, "I bet he told you where the missing tapes were," referring to the deletions Nixon's secretary Rose Mary Woods had caused when she transcribed an important Watergate tape—a comment that finally elicited a laugh from Ted Jr. The next morning, at eight-thirty, Dr. Hyatt performed the surgery.

But Ted Kennedy had another assignment that day of his son's surgery—a long-standing assignment that now conflicted with the surgery because of the postponement of the operation due to Ted Jr.'s cold. Since his brothers' death, Ted had become the paterfamilias—the last man of that Kennedy generation and the one responsible for all his brothers' children as well as his own. He took this obligation seriously, attempting to be

---

*In his interview, Fentress said it was while he was driving home the next day, which would have been Saturday, November 17. It is almost certain that the game was the preceding weekend.

as much of a surrogate father as he could be and not just an uncle. Bobby's eldest daughter, Kathleen, was to be married that day at Holy Trinity Church in Georgetown, and Ted was to give her away in her late father's place. She had offered to cancel the ceremony. Ted refused. He didn't want to disrupt her wedding. As soon as the surgery ended, Ted raced to the church, wearing a business suit rather than a cutaway, and performed his duty. "He walked me down the aisle," Kathleen would recall. "Talked about his own wedding. How special it would be. Talked about my father. And how proud he would be of me," trying hard not to let his tragedy overshadow his niece's joy. A reporter said the only sign of his grief was the way he and his mother knelt in prayer after taking communion, "their fingers pressed to their closed eyes." But Schlesinger said he looked "haggard and concerned," and when the congregation began singing "When Irish Eyes Are Smiling," the last song of the ceremony, a song that Schlesinger called a "melancholy song," "one's mind went back through the sad years and wondered at the future." And then he returned to his son's bedside.

Ted Kennedy's immediate future was dedicated to his son. "He focused on that almost one hundred percent of the time," Philip Caper recalled, "through surgery and the following decision as to what kind of treatment he'd get. . . . There was never any question about competing priorities. During that period, his devotion to his son was the only thing he was thinking about." As John Tunney put it, "He organized his life to handle this. It was the most important thing in his life." Still, Ted agonized about his commitment. *Washington Post* reporter Stuart Auerbach, who happened to be Ted's seatmate on a flight from Miami to Washington at this time, said that Ted told him he wondered if he had done enough for his son. The cancer was a chondrosarcoma, which attacked the cartilage and was less virulent than an osteosarcoma, bone cancer, which had a fatality rate of 80 percent, but it was nevertheless a ruthless cancer, a pitiless cancer, and when postoperative tests found traces of cancer cells in the bone, Ted, as he often did with his legislation, convened a panel of experts at his house, where they held a four-hour discussion of treatment options. They decided upon an experimental chemotherapy pioneered by Dr. Emil Frei III in Boston, using a powerful drug called methotrexate, which killed cancer cells, combined with injections every six hours of another drug, citrovorum, which palliated the effects of the methotrexate. Ted was well aware that if he was an ordinary parent rather than a famous one, his son would not have had access to the treatment—an awareness that stuck with him.

In a life of tragedies—to whom much is given, much is also taken—now began arguably the most emotionally wrenching of them for Ted Kennedy. The chemotherapy regimen started on February 1, 1974, and it was a brutal one, requiring Ted Jr. to be hospitalized for three days every three weeks at Boston Children's Hospital. Ted dedicated himself to the treatment, meeting Ted Jr. at National Airport and flying up from Washington every third Friday for each of his son's hospital stays. He would sit with Ted Jr. in the room all day and sleep beside him all night. "I would hold his head against my chest when nausea overcame him. In time, I learned the technique of injecting him myself, so that we could cut the visit short by a day and get him into his classroom on Monday mornings." And when he had learned the injection technique and when they returned home, Ted would have to inject him with the citrovorum "intensively" for the next couple of days and even during the night and then, periodically, for another four or five days. But not even the citrovorum could mitigate the effects of the chemotherapy. Ted Jr. suffered—not only the nausea, but fever, chills, and terrible pain. Sick to his stomach all Friday night, Ted would say, then "weak . . . absolutely wiped out" on Saturday, and a "little bit better" by Saturday night, and then home on Sunday. Ted had told a friend, speaking of the treatment, that it was "all very much like picking up coffee grounds with a sponge. You can scrape and scrape. But unless you get every last cell, there's no point." In time, the treatment was given at Georgetown University Hospital, where Ted made sure Ted Jr. had someone beside him all day, until Ted himself could take the night shift. There was, however, a "silver streak," Ted would tell biographer Burton Hersh, "in that grim and terrible time." He said that it had "formed a bond between him and me that has just been extraordinary. I can't tell whether it would have been so or not otherwise."

And yet, for all the apparent tightening of the bond, Joan felt that Ted often imposed the old Kennedy stoicism on his stricken son and that his doing so drew *her* and Ted Jr. closer. The postoperative week, Ted had invited guests into Ted Jr.'s hospital room—among them, the entire offensive line of the Washington Redskins football team and former heavyweight boxing champion Muhammad Ali—hoping to buck up the boy's spirits. "He should be kept entertained," Joan said of Ted's approach, which was Ted's way of trying to take his son's mind off the loss of his leg.

But Joan told biographer Laurence Leamer that after five or six days of this stream of visitors, Ted Jr. confessed to her, "I'm so tired, but I can't tell Dad." So Joan said *she* had to tell Ted and that he was angry with her when she did, accusing her of not wanting their son to have fun. But Joan said that from that point on, she guarded the door "like a traffic cop." And when her son was undergoing the chemotherapy treatments, she said, she would stay with him at those times when Ted didn't and "he could feel sick, he could cry and fall apart and be a baby, and I would hold him in my arms. But he wouldn't let anyone else know that. He was a Kennedy." "Intimidated" by his father, Joan would say of her son. He had to be strong for his father, she would say, to be a man for his father, "to be a Kennedy" for his father, which meant not feeling sorry for himself. (Of course, this was exactly how Joan said she was made to feel about her alcoholism.)

But Ted Jr. would remember it differently. He would speak of how his father's drive also got him through his trial, and he would, years later at his father's funeral, recall the huge snowstorm in Washington shortly after the amputation and how his father pulled out their Flexible Flyer sled to slide down the driveway and how, unable to gain traction going up the slippery incline, he collapsed and cried and Ted gathered him in his arms and told him that he could do it and climbed up the hill with him and went down with him, which is when Teddy said he knew that he would be fine.

But Kennedy tragedies never took just one casualty. Ted admitted that during his son's two-year convalescence, he was under tremendous strain, worried not just about Ted Jr. but also about all his brothers' children—Jack's two and Bobby's eleven—for whom he now bore responsibility, and he admitted that his Senate work suffered, which was a very difficult admission for him. Within his own family, Kara was so unnerved by her brother's cancer that she began acting out—even running away at one point. But the tragedy took its biggest toll on Joan, and as she had been a casualty of the assassinations and Chappaquiddick, so was she a casualty of this latest blow. Joan told *McCall's* magazine that she didn't take a drink while Ted Jr. was in the hospital. "But as soon as he was well and back in school, I just collapsed," she said. "I needed some relief from having to be so damn brave all the time." And she said that she was confused by the inability of the doctors to give her any prognosis for Ted Jr., to give her any sense of what the future held for him. "They just didn't know." By May, after accompanying Ted on a trip to the Soviet Union, where he was trying to win the right of refuseniks to emigrate, she suffered a relapse and at her doctor's recommendation returned to the Silver Hill sanitarium, a sylvan retreat in New Canaan, Connecticut, the same place her mother had gone when she was composing herself from her divorce. Always secretive, Ted's office said Joan was suffering from "emotional problems." She stayed for three weeks, only to be released to attend a graveside service observing Robert Kennedy's death six years earlier. "She just needed a rest," her mother said. Friends of hers told *Time* magazine that she was "testing herself" to see if she was well enough to remain home, but one cautioned that this was a "furlough" and that she would probably return to Silver Hill shortly. The friend was right.

While friends protected her, saying that she had a very low tolerance for alcohol and would get tipsy on a single glass of wine, or that one mild muscle relaxant and a single daiquiri could slur her speech, or that she only drank because she was unhappy and wasn't an alcoholic, she was clearly in crisis after Ted Jr.'s cancer and sinking. Ted's administrative assistant, Richard Burke (no relation to David Burke), said he arrived one morning at McLean and found Joan disheveled and disoriented and unable to remember how to turn on the stove. That October, after a fender bender, she was cited for driving under the influence, forcing Ted to cancel a meeting with the Polish communist party leader, Edward Gierek, so he could be at her side. Though he had chafed at therapy, feeling that Kennedys didn't open their private lives to anyone outside the family and, in any case, that one coped alone, he did agree to weekly marriage counseling that year, at an office on K Street. It spoke to the issue, however, that he and Joan always arrived separately. Ted Jr. said he knew he would be fine in spite of his cancer and the loss of his leg. Joan Kennedy, however, would not.

IV

Enduring those months with his son and the chemotherapy treatments in Boston, Ted Kennedy, the empath, was not so consumed by his own pain that he was oblivious to the pain of others. He was alert to the distress of the parents of Ted Jr.'s fellow bone-cancer patients in the protocol. Since the therapy was experimental, it was not covered by health insurance, save for Ted Jr.'s, which was paid by Ted's generous Senate insurance plan. Each treatment cost $2,700. And Ted recalled vividly, painfully, those parents in the waiting room and what they had to do to attempt to save their children's lives. "They had sold their house for $20,000 or $30,000, or mortgaged it completely, eating up all their savings, and they could only fund their treatment for six months, or eight months, or a year, and they were asking the doctor what chance their child had if they could only do half the treatment." It was, he said, a "very powerful presentation, in terms of starkness, about health and health insurance and coverage and basically the moral issue presented here. We were all in the same circumstance. This is a very rare disease that could have happened to anybody. It happened to a United States senator; it happened to the children of working families. There was nothing they could do about it, and they were being put through this kind of system." Though his son was improving and though Ted was now Mr. Health Care, Ted said he had always been reluctant to use his personal tragedies to promote bills. (He had even been reluctant on gun control.) But he returned from those experiences—his visits once every three weeks in the Boston Children's Hospital waiting room—with a sense of anger and a renewed sense of purpose to pass national health insurance.

Ted said that his preoccupation with Ted Jr. late in 1973 and into 1974 had been a "personal overlay going through a lot of these cataclysmic moments that were taking place in government." Those moments were the ongoing hearings by the Select Subcommittee, Ervin's committee, investigating Watergate, and all the consequences that followed from those hearings—namely, Richard Nixon's frantic attempts to save himself from impeachment. In his post-election reshuffling, Nixon had moved Caspar Weinberger, the director of the Office of Management and Budget, to HEW. Weinberger was an advocate for health reform, and he wasn't above using Nixon's predicament to advance the cause. As Weinberger's deputy, Stuart Altman, remembered it, sometime early in 1973 Nixon had asked Weinberger to design a new comprehensive health plan and Weinberger, in turn, had asked Altman to do the spade work for it. Now, with Watergate, Nixon had two motives: not only preempting Ted Kennedy, lest Ted preempt him, but also demonstrating that he was still in charge, Watergate or not. Melvin Laird, Nixon's first secretary of Defense, who had succeeded John Ehrlichman as the White House domestic affairs adviser when Ehrlichman was forced to resign, had suggested to Nixon that health care could be so powerful and popular an issue that, as Ted put it after discussions with Laird, with whom he had a good relationship, "it might even save Nixon from impeachment." On December 7, 1973, less than a month after Ted Jr.'s surgery, Weinberger sent a memo to Nixon saying that his plan was ready. It was called the Comprehensive Health Insurance Plan (CHIP), and it was similar to Nixon's 1971 proposal: an employer mandate to provide insurance, limited employee co-pays so that the government wouldn't have to bear the full cost, and subsidies for those who did not have insurance. The total cost, Weinberger calculated, would be five billion dollars. When, a week later, members of Nixon's Domestic Council on Health argued against a new government program, Nixon rebutted them with his old fear that Ted might best him. "First, there is the threat of a Kennedy-type plan," he told them. "There is no question that at some point in time there will be a serious move to push legislation through Congress"—obviously thinking of the Kennedy–Griffiths bill, S.3, or Kennedy–Mills—"and we must have a proposal to counter it. You simply can't fight something with nothing."

Nixon had no real interest in health care other than as a political blandishment, but he did have an interest in stopping others from passing a health-care bill without his imprimatur, especially now. Operating under both the pressures of Watergate and the pressures of his certainty that some health-insurance plan might pass, Nixon once again needed to block Ted Kennedy and show his legislative superiority. After announcing his intentions for a "sweeping new program" in his State of the Union message on January 30, he introduced CHIP on February 6, 1974, with moderate Republican senator Robert Packwood of Oregon as its sponsor in that chamber. His House sponsor, however, was something of a surprise: ambitious, self-aggrandizing Wilbur Mills, Ted's old partner in their 1972 health-care initiative. In proposing CHIP and declaring its advantages over Kennedy–Griffiths, Nixon had emphasized the exorbitant cost of Ted's plan, which, in his State of the Union address, he had pegged at between $80 billion and $100 billion. What was worse, Nixon said, pulling out the socialist card again, "they would put our whole health-care system under the heavy hand of our federal government." But David Gergen, one of Nixon's speechwriters, wrote Chief of Staff Alexander Haig on the day of Nixon's CHIP announcement with a candid admission: "Tonight it became apparent that the total cost of the president's plan was not really very different from Kennedy's ('perhaps somewhat less'). The real difference is that RN's plan would be paid for differently—about $40 billion in total government spending and another $40 billion or less in private-sector spending." And Gergen, thinking, as he knew Nixon would, of how to best Kennedy, suggested an option: disclose only *new* federal spending, which would amount to roughly $5.9 billion. Citing Weinberger, he wrote, "He thinks we can maximize our political advantages over Kennedy by holding back total cost figures until at least the hearings," meaning the congressional hearings on Nixon's plan. But Gergen also was afraid that if Nixon, who already was regarded as devious, hid the true costs of the plan, it might "eventually do him far more harm than good." Instead, he recommended coming clean. "We can beat Kennedy anyway on the question of private vs. federal control." But throughout all their deliberations, one thing was clear: Nixon's interest in health care was driven largely by his wariness of Ted Kennedy.

And Richard Nixon was not the only one with an eye on his rivals. Ted Kennedy was now looking at Richard Nixon's plan and was concerned—concerned that his own original single-payer plan, essentially Medicare for All, had no chance of passage, concerned that Nixon's plan, with all its half measures, might doom what Ted considered real health insurance for a long time to come. (As Ted put it, Nixon was proposing insurance reform; Ted was proposing health-care reform.) Even the Committee for National Health Insurance—the Committee of 100—had, by the end of 1973, conceded what Ted himself had reluctantly concluded: "Health Security [Act] as a standard had reached the end of the road," as Fine put it in a note to Ted. Now, to parry Nixon and to get something passed, Ted returned to his old ally, Wilbur Mills. Already, after only two months, Mills had decided that CHIP, the bill he had intended to sponsor, had roused no enthusiasm in the House and was unlikely to pass, and Mills even questioned now why Weinberger was pushing it. A political savant, Mills didn't want to be identified with a losing proposition. Moreover, with Nixon on the ropes, Democratic pressure was building on Mills to get health insurance moved through his committee—pressure so intense that Representative Richard Bolling, the chairman of the Democratic Select Committee on Committees, threatened to propose a new committee exclusively dedicated to health care if Mills didn't act. For his part, Ted obviously didn't want to compromise on single-payer, which he had been championing, but he had always been a legislative realist, and he felt he had no choice given the unlikelihood of its passage. In the end, as he had the year before when he first teamed with Mills, he was willing to trade single-payer for universal coverage, which is what he did. Under Ted's plan, every single American would be entitled to health insurance.

And then, suddenly, Robert Ball entered the picture. Ball, a lifetime bureaucrat who had been administrator of the Social Security Administration, a position from which he was pushed when Nixon became president, believed fervently in national health insurance but also appreciated the political obstacles to achieving it. One of the biggest obstacles was still Russell Long of the Finance Committee. But Long and Abraham Ribicoff had proposed another compromise bill—a health-care bill that would pay for only catastrophic health emergencies, and even then only after large deductibles. It was Ball's idea to write an amendment to the Long–Ribicoff bill setting up a separate fund to pay for health insurance and to be administered by the federal government—a scaled-down version of single-payer. Ball convinced Ted of this approach, and Stan Jones and Mills's aide Bill Fullerton drafted the amendment, after which Ted took Ball and Jones to meet Long in the Senate dining room, where they got him to agree to look at their plan. Long looked at it and turned it down. Still, Ball stayed on. Ted and Mills decided to revive the old Kennedy–Mills plan— the plan that had mandated employer coverage while retaining private insurance—but with much lower deductibles than Nixon's CHIP and with the program to be paid for by a combination of payroll taxes, as was done for Medicare and Social Security, and general tax revenues. And now, with Ball's involvement, their staffs drafted the bill, and Ted and Mills announced it on April 2: Kennedy–Mills II.

It was a high moment for health insurance, perhaps the highest since the issue had first been broached, because no one wanted anyone else's bill to pass but nearly everyone needed *a* bill to pass: Nixon for his own political survival, Ted to vindicate his role as Mr. Health Care, the Congress to prove that it could pass a bill, even the health community to show that it was not obstructionist. And it was historic, above all, because the moral issue of helping those who desperately needed help seemed about to be addressed at long last. The Long–Ribicoff bill barely did anything; Long had intended it largely to head off a national insurance plan. (Long had reportedly said of Ted's plan, "It's bullshit, basically.") Nixon's CHIP was better but still too feeble and put too much of the financial onus on the insured. The Health Security Act, Ted's original bill, had been too much for Republicans to swallow. But Ted now had a bill—a hybrid bill that melded elements of S.3 and elements of CHIP in the hope that he might finally find a middle way to satisfy all the various contenders, giving each of them a bit of what they wanted, while giving no single group everything it wanted. This was Ted Kennedy's typical approach to legislation: Lay out what you want, in this case single-payer, and then compromise from that as incrementally as necessary. Now it seemed as if the clouds had parted. House minority leader John Rhodes called it a "breakthrough." *The Washington Post* editorialized that the "prospects for national health insurance have brightened suddenly and unexpectedly." Even President Nixon was "very pleased," said Senator John Tower. "General consensus was that with the introduction of the Kennedy–Mills bill, we have reached the stage where negotiations, compromise, and final package can be worked out," Vernon Loen, a special assistant to the president, wrote Bill Timmons, Nixon's assistant for legislative affairs, after Weinberger testified before the Ways and Means committee later that April. And Ted, the legislative realist, agreed. "A new spirit of compromise is in the air," he told reporters. He realized that "it was going to be a long time before we were going to get something out there, and it was going to be altered and changed in terms of the floor and the committee," referring to Ways and Means. "And it was eventually going to get set up in conference," between the House and Senate versions. But he believed that after going through that process it could pass—finally. "I saw this as a way sort of expanding our base," meaning a base of congressional supporters. Hopes ran high that the sides had finally come together, that the time had finally arrived, and that Ted Kennedy would finally get national health insurance.

But the optimists were wrong, all of them, terribly wrong. Instead of the sides coming together on common ground and the base expanding, exactly the opposite happened. Ted discovered that despite the initial optimism, all the stakeholders soon found something in the bill to criticize. The AMA, hoping to head off Ted, had reintroduced a bill of its own left over from 1971, Medicredit, the one relying on tax credits and private insurance, and it now called Kennedy–Mills II "socialist"—its reflexive label for any real national health insurance. And the insurers themselves were fiercely opposed to anything that would curb their power, which is what Kennedy–Mills II did by making them essentially administrators of the plan, as they were in Medicare, rather than the masters of the plan. Russell Long had no interest in furthering health insurance, compromise or not. It was "bullshit." And most Republicans were skeptical of any further government expansion into health.

But of all the stakeholders, the most vehemently opposed to Ted's bill was the group that had lured Ted into leading the national health-care campaign to begin with: organized labor. Walter Reuther had promoted national health insurance on the basis that it was the right thing to do and, more self-serving, that it was the right thing to do for labor. George Meany had come to agree when Ted introduced the Health Security Act, S.3. But labor had had a change of heart since Ted first pushed S.3. It had come to view its negotiated employment-based health plans as an advantage, after all, as well as a central bargaining chip in union building. "They want to be able to go and say, 'Join my union, because we're going to give you health insurance,'" as Ted derisively described the union leaders' motives. The only plan labor said it was willing to accept was S.3, the payroll-tax-financed, Medicare for All plan that Ted Kennedy, its sponsor, had concluded could never get through Congress, where Republicans would block it. And those union leaders would not compromise. LeRoy Goldman thought you could make one of two arguments when it came to labor's attitude toward national health care in 1974: "You can either say that labor was never serious about the enactment of S.3 because they already had it made, or you could say that there were some seers among them who said, 'We'd better get a program like S.3 on the books, because if we don't, it's going to wreck the goose that lays the golden egg for us.' . . . I tend to think there were a lot more of the former and precious few of the latter." But Ted Kennedy wasn't promoting S.3 anymore, as much as he would have liked to. He was promoting the Kennedy–Mills II bill, the bill with employer-mandated insurance and a 4 percent payroll tax and deductibles and co-pays and private insurers to perform the administrative tasks for that insurance. And "that was a very big deal," as Rashi Fein, the Harvard medical economist, put it—a very big difference from S.3.

But Ted Kennedy had worked too hard, was too emotionally invested, to give up on this chance for national health insurance. He had met with a group of labor leaders from the AFL–CIO and the UAW in his office just before the announcement of the new Kennedy–Mills plan that April. And, as Goldman described it, "They were berserk . . . absolutely adamant that this shouldn't have been done, wrong thing to do, huge strategic and political mistake." It was an angry meeting, a meeting of shouting and aspersions and recriminations. Andrew Biemiller, the AFL–CIO's top lobbyist, called Ted a "traitor to labor" and said that "they would call him a traitor to labor all over the country." They meant it as a threat, and Ted took it as such. Bristling, Ted grabbed a copy of the Congressional Directory and ran down the names of the senators, to show them how many would oppose single-payer. "What are you going to do about him?" Ted would ask, pointing to the name of an opponent. But labor didn't intend to do anything about him, because labor had another reason to resist Kennedy–Mills II besides the fact that it wasn't S.3. With Nixon besieged by Watergate, the labor leaders were certain of a Democratic landslide in the upcoming midterm elections, certain of a veto-proof Congress that could override Nixon, and, if they waited another two years, certain of a Democratic president in 1976. Why should they compromise now when in a short time they would be able to get everything they wanted? Why would Ted compromise? Hadn't they held out for a more-liberal Congress in 1964 and gotten the Civil Rights Act and Medicare and the Voting Rights Act? But when Ted pulled out that Congressional Directory, he showed them that "the election is not going to change anything," because not a single senator on the Finance Committee was likely to lose. It seemed now as if health care was hanging in the balance, and Ted Kennedy knew it, knew the congressional politics of it. And when the labor leaders remained obdurate, refusing to support Ted, a man who had been one of labor's champions, he finally lost patience. "This is ridiculous," he told them. "This is going to be the same people that you have now pulling the strings," referring to the Finance Committee. "And here we've got the Ways and Means Committee with Mills, [who] may be ready to support something, send it to the House. And the president is in such a weakened condition, we may just make him sign this." But the leaders sat in stony, boiling silence. As *Boston Globe* columnist Thomas Oliphant was to say of Ted Kennedy, he "functioned as the liberal leader whom his peers trusted to tell them when to settle and for how much," because Ted Kennedy never settled for less than he knew he could get. But not this time, not with these labor leaders, and not with health care. Ted finally rose and said, "Well, you're just going to have to call me a traitor." And he opened the door and motioned them out. And with them, it seemed, went the last best chance for a national health-care law.

But Ted Kennedy, the alleged traitor to labor, still would not give up his hope of passing national health care, even with labor's fierce opposition and even with his own personal commitment to his son's recovery taking a good deal of his attention. That spring and summer, he decided to go over the heads of the labor leaders to the rank and file, making his pitch for his plan at labor conventions. At the convention for the International

Ladies' Garment Workers Union at the Fontainebleau Hotel ballroom in Miami Beach, a broad, low-ceilinged room, he made his entrance from the rear and headed up the center aisle trailed by photographers, their popping flashbulbs accompanying his walk to the podium, past the leaders, who glowered at him, and past the delegates, who cheered him, some of whom waved placards saying TED FOR PRESIDENT, and onto the stage. There, taking on those angry union leaders, Ted teased his presidential ambitions by telling the crowd that he had dreamed of "standing in a vast hall here in Miami addressing a great national convention," then paused, "even though this is the wrong year and the wrong convention." And as he spoke—with an IMPEACH NIXON banner hanging on the wall—some of the elderly women in the crowd began to weep, and, as Stan Jones remembered it, the delegates were "screaming and cheering and chanting . . . yelling and cheering" the whole time, as if it were a political rally. And while Ted spoke, David Dubinsky, the union's eighty-two-year-old former president and now its éminence grise—and one of the leaders who was not opposed to Ted Kennedy—sneaked up on stage and gazed at Ted, smiling, waiting to shake his hand when he finished. The scene was repeated later at the Retail, Wholesale, and Department Stores Union convention, also in Miami, a smaller convention, but its delegates still mobbed Ted, and then again in Los Angeles at the International Union of Painters and Allied Trades convention—because these delegates loved Ted Kennedy and they trusted Ted Kennedy, and, in doing so, they showed the labor leaders that those leaders might not really have spoken for their members in rejecting Kennedy–Mills. And, in hoping to apply pressure to pass his bill, now Ted Kennedy went beyond the labor leaders and beyond the delegates to the American people. Ted spoke at the National Governors Association conference to promote his health-care plan and delivered a national radio address, a rebuttal to an earlier radio address by Nixon, in which Ted defended his plan from Nixon's attacks and the insurance industry's attacks on its use of a payroll tax to pay for it, saying that Nixon's employer-mandate plan had a tax too, but it was a "hidden tax"—hidden as rising insurance premiums.

Still, the labor leaders would not relent.

But there was one last gambit by Ted Kennedy—this one so unpredictable and so certain to inflame his labor opposition that he had to keep it secret. It originated with LeRoy Goldman. After the labor leaders had fled

Ted, Goldman slipped another note into Ted's already bulging briefcase. Goldman wrote that Ted had succeeded in reaching a compromise with Nixon on the National Cancer Act, albeit by some legislative sleight of hand, because Nixon needed to seem proactive on cancer. Now the Saturday Night Massacre the previous October, coupled with Nixon's refusal to release the tapes of his conversations, had lit a fuse. When the House reconvened the week after the massacre, it voted to refer motions of impeachment to the House Judiciary Committee, and during the first forty-five minutes of the debate over that referral, not a single Republican dared rise to defend their embattled president, until Gerald Ford, the vice president–designate—designate because Nixon's woes had postponed his installation—did. Nixon had resisted delivering those tapes and had resisted with defiance, still proposing that deaf John Stennis listen to the tapes and provide a summary. His advisers still urged him to hold out, to keep the tapes, to use his power to blunt Judge Sirica's. But Nixon, an astute politician, knew that this would only make the fuse burn more quickly and almost certainly lead to his impeachment. So that Tuesday, his constitutional attorney, Charles Alan Wright, who had previously insisted on the president's right to refuse the court, went before Judge Sirica and conceded to turn the tapes over to him. Nixon knew what those tapes contained—secrets and contradictions and revelations. And he knew now that the fuse was eventually going to detonate a political bomb unless he could somehow get it to fizzle.

And for months, well into 1974, as the fuse burned, Nixon's fate became clearer. A new special prosecutor, Leon Jaworski, had been appointed, and Ervin's Select Committee subpoenaed more tapes and investigated and debated, and new damning evidence trickled out, and the grand jury, secretly, determined that the president of the United States was an unindicted co-conspirator in an effort to obstruct justice, and, perhaps worst of all, even Republicans began to peel off, realizing that they could no longer in good conscience or, more likely, in good politics support the president. Nixon tried once again to save himself, saying that he would provide an edited version of transcripts of the tapes the committee and Jaworski had demanded. But the edited versions did not save Richard Nixon. On the contrary, once released, these private conversations, in which Nixon was anything but presidential, in which he used lewd language and insulted minorities and schemed against opponents, were a bellows on the fuse. And yet again, Nixon refused to release the full tapes, and this time the Supreme Court itself, on July 24, ordered the tapes released. And now the fuse had hit the bomb.

But all this time and through all these events, Ted Kennedy had been working on health care, and Richard Nixon had been searching for ways to stave off impeachment—two wounded politicians, one by Chappaquiddick and another by Watergate. And when Goldman suggested that Ted make common cause with Nixon, who needed a major health-care victory or *some* victory in his desperate attempt to save himself, Ted, who understood political desperation, was more than willing. At least, that was Goldman's version. But Stuart Altman, the deputy assistant secretary for planning and evaluation/health at HEW, said that it was Nixon who ordered HEW secretary Weinberger to approach Ted and Mills to see if he could make a deal with them—a step that, if true, only testified to just how desperate Nixon was. He had lived in fear of Ted Kennedy snatching away his presidency. Now, by Altman's account, he was trying to partner with Kennedy because he lived in even greater fear of impeachment. Already, Ted had met with Nixon's domestic-affairs counselor, Melvin Laird, and the two discussed possible options. Laird had suggested a pay-or-play system: An employer either provided health insurance or paid into a fund that the government could use to provide it. But the talks didn't advance, and the hopes for a health-care bill seemed dashed once again.

However, Stan Jones and Altman happened to be attending a conference in Albuquerque, New Mexico, that June, and while riding a ski lift up Sandia Peak, they began chatting about health care, their mutual passion. They continued the discussion on the plane back to Washington, taking out their notepads as they brainstormed. Back in Washington, Altman said he conferred with Weinberger—though this seems to contradict Altman's story that Weinberger was the one who had initiated the process at Nixon's behest—about whether they might come to some compromise with Ted. Weinberger's main instruction to Altman was that it not exceed a certain cost. And now began meetings—highly secret meetings, lest labor find out—among Jones, Mills's staffer Bill Fullerton, and several members from HEW, including Dr. Ted Cooper, the assistant secretary of Health, to see if they might, even then, find a mutually satisfactory accommodation. They met that June three or four times in the basement of St. Mark's Episcopal Church, at 3rd and A Street behind the Library of

Congress, but Jones said that "I could tell, just from the chemistry in the room, that they couldn't stretch and we couldn't stretch enough to make it." The Nixon side insisted on private insurance, and Ted insisted on a payroll tax and a very limited role for private insurance. Eventually, Jones left on vacation, and Ted conceded that the sides would never reach agreement. "My God," he told Jones, "I've already done this"—meaning the compromises he had made on S.3—"and they're ready to crucify me out there," meaning labor. Fullerton and the HEW members kept at it, now without Jones, and they hammered out a bill among them, but they couldn't get Mills or the administration to agree to it.

But *even then,* as Nixon was hoping for some reprieve, Ted made one last attempt to rescue health insurance. On July 8, he phoned Caspar Weinberger to see if there was any deal they might reach before Nixon might be forced from office. They met the next day and then again with Mills on July 11. Though Ted had voted against Weinberger's confirmation, Weinberger said that their relations improved after he wrote Ted a note following Ted Jr.'s surgery. (Ted appreciated those sorts of gestures, having made so many of them himself.) Moreover, Weinberger was completely committed to national health insurance, and he would say that rather than operating from instructions from Nixon to help the foundering executive do something to save his presidency, "I had no instructions, so to speak. This was all on my own." And Weinberger was confident that Nixon would sign whatever bill upon which he and Ted agreed and that they could get through Congress. "The few meetings I had with President Nixon," Weinberger said, "were designed to divert attention from Watergate stuff and show that he had his hand on the levers of government." But it was too late at this point. Nixon's impeachment was imminent, and the talks got nowhere. Within three weeks, Nixon had resigned—Ted watched his departure from the Senate cloakroom, where his only colleague was Eugene McCarthy—and Gerald Ford was president.

It had seemed the last best chance for national health care. Now it was gone.

But not quite yet. The new president had signaled his support for Nixon's health-care bill and his willingness to sign a health-insurance bill if he got one. Three weeks after Gerald Ford took office, Mills did hold hearings—when he asked George Meany what he would do with all those health-and-welfare trust-fund dollars if single-payer health insurance did pass, Meany told him not to worry, that they would find a way to make good use of that money—and Bill Fullerton continued to work on the issue, preparing a thick notebook of possible compromises and fallbacks on Kennedy–Mills for those hearings, should they need them. Meanwhile, Mills proposed yet another bill—this one a hybrid of Ted's plan and Nix- on's employer-mandate plan and Long's catastrophic insurance bill, to be paid for with a payroll tax—and Weinberger met with Ford to discuss the details, while Ted and Mills met to draft a bill. "I had all this stuff ready," Fullerton told Stan Jones. But when Fullerton went into the men's room before the markup session on August 20 and saw Mills at the urinal and told him about his notebook, Mills reluctantly said he had decided not to bring any of the bills up for a vote. Fullerton was astonished and remon- strated with him. "I've done everything I could do, Bill," Mills said resign- edly. "I have talked to everybody, and I can't get the votes, and there's no point in bringing it up." In truth, after forty-five minutes of deliberation, the committee had divided 13 to 12 for Kennedy–Mills–Weinberger, as the AMA referred to the new bill, but Mills had lost five votes to the AMA's own Medicredit plan during the debate—too close to bring the bill to the floor, too close because he knew he would lose. Martha Griffiths and James Corman, the representatives who had sponsored single-payer in the House, begged Mills to keep negotiating, saying that they were willing to compromise—which was a major concession, especially from Corman— and Mills met with President Ford that very afternoon of the committee vote, leaving the meeting saying, "We're going to try to get support for a bill that will get through the House."

But there was no such bill. UAW president Leonard Woodcock sug- gested that they wait until next year. And so it might have been. But Wil- bur Mills wouldn't be there the following year to push a bill through Ways and Means. That October 7, 1974, at 2:30 A.M., Mills was pulled over by U.S. Park Police when they saw his car weaving through West Potomac Park near the Jefferson Monument. When the car stopped, a thirty-eight- year-old woman scrambled out the passenger-side door and down the Tidal Basin before the police corralled her. She was a stripper whose stage name was Fanne Foxe, though she was billed as "the Argentine Fire- cracker." Police said the most powerful man in the House of Representa- tives, Wilbur Mills, was inebriated. And now, caught with a woman nearly half his age, he was also disgraced.

Ted had been in the committee room when the Ways and Means mem- bers were debating his bill, and he returned to his office and told Caper,

"You have no idea how powerful these insurance guys are. They've just begun to flex their muscles. And they're the ones, of course, who defeated the bill, because they were opposed to any kind of national health insurance." But there was a lot of blame to go around: labor, of course, which in its overweening hubris had refused to make any concessions whatsoever, prompting Ted to think that it had all become just a way for union leaders to give themselves a leg up in union elections and that they never had any intention of passing a law; Ig Falk, the man who had drafted the single-payer bill, Kennedy's bill, who had pressed those labor leaders not to compromise; the AMA, yet again, which had attracted 180 sponsors for its Medicredit plan and rejected any other, and its lobbyist Howard Cook, who once arrived at Ted's office and showed Stan Jones a printout on every member of the Health Subcommittee and how many contributions each had received from doctors and medical societies and who said he had reminded each of them of those contributions and told Jones, "You didn't have a prayer" to pass legislation the AMA opposed; and even President Ford, who, for all his professions that health care was one of his principal issues, was not, as Mel Laird told Weinberger, really serious about it, and even if he had been, his fellow Republicans were not. John Rhodes, the new Republican House minority leader, had informed Weinberger that he would support no health-insurance plan but the catastrophic one. "We talk to all of these guys," Bill Fullerton told Stan Jones ruefully, meaning the stakeholders, "and their priorities are, 'We don't want anything. We don't want any legislation. If you have to have some legislation, the only one we'll take is ours, and we won't compromise.' " Ted sadly agreed. "You just didn't have anybody that was really pressing and pushing for it," except, of course, Ted Kennedy himself. And he would mourn the lost opportunity, mourn it for a long time, really for the rest of his life, saying later that the Nixon plan actually looked good in retrospect and that "one of my regrets as a senator is that I didn't support the Nixon plan and make it happen." His *greatest* regret, he would often say. And having lost that last best chance, the chance that would have united the two old foes, Ted Kennedy and Richard Nixon, to help the poorest and most marginalized Americans receive the health care they needed and deserved, there would be no recovering it. It was over.

SEVENTEEN

"Our Long National Nightmare Is Over"

PERHAPS THE MOST important thing about the new president, Gerald Ford, was that he was well liked by almost everyone who knew him. His predecessor, Richard Nixon, had compiled an "enemies list" of individuals he harassed and even tormented as payback for the abuses he felt had been visited upon him. Gerald Ford could have compiled no such list, because he had few enemies. He had a look of benevolence, the pleasant look of a Midwestern small-town banker, which is what his paternal grandfather had been; he was solid and square-jawed, with a broad forehead and receding hairline of thinning blondish hair and a face that wore a smile comfortably, unlike his predecessor, whose smile was always forced. Ordinary was how Gerald Ford looked. Handsome in a plain, nondescript way. A man without frills. Unthreatening. That was how he looked, and that was who he was. Though his parents separated when he was only sixteen days old—his father had been abusive to his mother and had threatened to kill her and her child with a butcher knife—Gerald (whose birth name was Leslie King) didn't know anything about the marriage or a biological father until many years later, long after his mother had remarried, this time to a kind paint-and-varnish salesman in Grand Rapids, Michigan, named Gerald Ford, the only father Gerald would know—the "very model of a father," wrote Ford's biographer—who gave his name to his new son. Gerald Ford Jr. grew up in a modest middle-class family, and he had none of the bitterness of Richard Nixon, none of Nixon's class resentments, in large measure because Ford had something Nixon never had: athletic accomplishment. He was a star football player on two national championship teams at the University of Michigan, in 1932 and 1933, and was recruited by the Detroit Lions and Green Bay

Packers in the National Football League. He opted instead to attend Yale Law School and then joined the Navy after the attack on Pearl Harbor, where he served on the aircraft carrier USS *Monterey* throughout the Pacific campaign. His subsequent political career, as the Republican congressman from Michigan's fifth district, around Grand Rapids, was ordinary too, with none of the drama or the festering tensions of his predecessor's. A quiet congressman, a modest congressman, a nondescript congressman, a congressman who didn't introduce a single significant piece of legislation, he was recruited to run for minority leader after Lyndon Johnson's landslide in 1964, which toppled thirty-six of Ford's fellow Republicans—recruited largely because, as one of those recruiters put it, "There were fewer people mad at Ford" than at the other prospective candidate, Melvin Laird. Ford served quietly. A "team player," he called himself. And when Richard Nixon needed a new vice president after Spiro Agnew's resignation, those same qualities of Ford's, his affability and the lack of enmity toward him, prompted Nixon to select him, even though Ford had no real relationship to the president, certainly no intimacy with him, and even though Nixon had really wanted John Connally. (Nixon exacted a promise from Ford that he would not run for president in 1976 but instead step aside for Connally.) But Nixon needed someone the Democrats could tolerate. Ford was more than tolerable. Indeed, Democratic speaker of the House Carl Albert had been the one to recommend him to Nixon. Gerald Ford rose—had always risen—because he was well liked.

And Gerald Ford needed that quality, because he was the first president not to have been elected to office—not the presidency, obviously, nor the vice presidency, the first president to have been "awarded" the office through a constitutional mechanism, the Twenty-fifth Amendment, which provided for succession when the vice presidency was vacant, as it was after Spiro Agnew's resignation. Ford hadn't been accorded authority by the people. He had to win that authority—in his case, win it with his best quality: being well liked. Ted Kennedy liked him, even though he had only met him two or three times and scarcely knew him personally. "It's been excellent," he told *Time* of Ford's first days in office. "I don't think he's missed a beat."

"A Ford, not a Lincoln," he said of himself modestly when he was sworn in as vice president, and now he was a humble healing president after a time of great division. "Our long national nightmare is over," he declared in his inaugural address on August 9 in the East Room of the

White House, a day after Nixon told him that he would resign rather than face impeachment and just hours after Nixon had vacated that White House and departed Washington. Ford said that "our Constitution works," that "our great republic is a government of laws, not men," which might have seemed like a dig at Nixon, whom he had defended as Nixon dangled, but it wasn't, because Gerald Ford had no malice, no digs, and he ended his speech asking for prayers for Nixon.

Richard Nixon was gone, but even as Gerald Ford was trying to heal a nation badly wounded by Watergate, Nixon had not left government without also leaving wreckage, without damaging its institutions and processes, damaging them badly. Now Congress attempted to rectify that damage, and not least among those legislators was Ted Kennedy. For years, Ted had worked on campaign-finance reform, introducing a bill in 1969 allowing a twenty-five-dollar tax credit for political contributions, but those efforts had languished. Once the Watergate story broke—and with it, its connection to dirty money to finance Nixon's stealth operations and pay off the Watergate burglars to remain silent—the efforts languished no longer. That year, Ted called for public financing of federal elections, which had long been a crusade of one of Ted's legislative heroes and friends, Phil Hart. Hart had tried to recruit Ted to co-sponsor a bill with him to that end, but, as biographer Theo Lippman would tell it, Ted begged off because, as a prospective presidential candidate in 1976, he was afraid he would be perceived as politicizing the issue and hurting its passage. As Watergate came to dominate American politics throughout 1973, Ted changed his mind. He joined with Senate Minority Leader Hugh Scott to propose a comprehensive reform bill that called for, among other things, a limit on campaign contributions, a Federal Election Commission to patrol campaign spending, and, most important of all, public financing of campaigns for federal offices. This time Hart was the one who opposed the bill, because he feared it could not pass and would set back the cause. But Ted was convinced that Watergate had finally given campaign-finance reform momentum. He was right. The Scott–Kennedy bill sailed through the Senate on July 30, 1973—just fourteen days after Alexander Butterfield made his public disclosure to the Watergate committee on Nixon's taping system and after daily revelations about huge contributions to Nixon's 1972 campaign—by a vote of 82 to 8. Fred Wertheimer, of Common Cause, a lobbying group that had devoted itself to campaign reform, told Lippman that Ted was "on the floor every day and for long hours" and that he "knew his stuff," though Wertheimer felt that Ted's greatest contribution was less his promotion of the bill than his convincing Scott to co-sponsor it with him, which gave it bipartisan cover. And yet bipartisan cover wasn't enough. Republican senator James Allen of Alabama, after submitting amendment after amendment trying to strip the bill of its major provisions and losing each vote, then filibustered it in the Senate, where Majority Leader Mike Mansfield couldn't get cloture, despite the overwhelming approval of the bill (by this time both labor and big business had weighed in against any limitations). In the House, the Administration Committee chair, Wayne Hays, who derided reformers, was as determined as Allen to strip the bill of its effectiveness, fearing that public financing would rob incumbents of their advantages—and every member of Congress was an incumbent. Nixon, meanwhile, scorned the bill as "taxation without representation."

But Ted Kennedy was determined. He brought up the bill in the next session that January—the bill that publicly financed presidential, senatorial, and congressional races—where it met with the same fate: a filibuster by Allen and a bill denuded by Hays of all its prominent provisions so that the only thing left was a limitation on campaign spending, which abetted incumbents. By this time, March 1974, the Watergate committee was still going, Nixon was on the ropes, and Mansfield was able to get cloture. Hays, however, still insisted on his toothless bill, without public financing, and after four months of his wrangling and intentional foot-dragging, it passed that August 8—perhaps symbolically, on the day of Nixon's resignation. Now the two bills—Kennedy's strong bill and Hays's weak one—went to conference, where Ted feared that the conferees from the Senate Rules Committee might side with Hays. But Carey Parker, as Theo Lippman told it, had found a loophole in the conference committee assignments—a seldom-used loophole that allowed Mansfield to appoint himself and any others he chose to the conference, which is what he did. Still, Hays remained intransigent. So now Ted, after seven futile conference sessions late that September, met with Hays and made him a compromise offer that retained the contribution limits but provided no public subsidies for House or Senate candidates (Hays had rejected letting the Senate be publicly financed but not the House), permitting them only for presidential candidates. Thus were the incumbents spared having to face adequately funded opponents. With that protection, the bill passed the Senate on October 8 and the House two days later—the "most important bill of the year," *The New York Times* editorialized—and Ford, stating his reluctance but citing the abuses of Watergate, signed it into law. (As a House stalwart, he almost certainly would have vetoed a bill with Ted's provisions for public financing of House campaigns.) And now Ted Kennedy finally had his campaign-finance reform law—a watered-down version but still "the most extensive reform of federal campaign-financing practices in American history," as the *Times* put it. And one more of Richard Nixon's loopholes had been closed.

But there was more Nixon wreckage, wreckage from Watergate, that needed to be cleaned up: the lack of transparency in government. And, again, Ted Kennedy wanted to be part of that cleanup detail. The Freedom of Information Act (FOIA) was designed to create transparency by giving the press and the public access to government documents. It had been passed in 1966, after energetic lobbying by the press and over Lyndon Johnson's strong objections, which almost led to a pocket veto; when he did surrender to both the press and to Congress—it had passed the House 307 to 0—he expressed his displeasure by holding the ceremony quietly on his Texas ranch rather than at the White House, by handing out no pens, and by including a signing statement that incorporated a number of House rollbacks on the access to documents, all of which were a harbinger of how seriously the executive branch intended to enforce the law, which was not seriously at all. Access was severely limited by a number of bureaucratic obstacles, from exorbitant search fees and copying fees, to long delays, to the mixture of nonconfidential materials with confidential ones that "contaminated" the documents and denied them to those who requested them, to long and costly legal remedies to obtain documents after denial.

But Watergate had created new pressures for greater transparency. Richard Nixon had been secretive. He had gotten away with his dirty tricks because he operated in the shadows. FOIA was viewed as a spotlight. So a bipartisan bill was introduced in the House early in 1973, when the Watergate revelations first arose, to fix the deficiencies of FOIA, especially one deficiency: The executive branch could deny access to documents on the basis of national security without any judicial review of that classification. Ed Muskie introduced the FOIA amendments in the Senate in a companion bill to the House bill. Ted hadn't demonstrated the same passion toward FOIA that he had demonstrated on issues like health care or civil rights. But his AdPrac counsel, Tom Susman, had long been interested in FOIA—he had worked on information issues at the Justice Department before joining Ted's staff—and he *was* passionate about it. Moreover, AdPrac had jurisdiction on the procedural aspects of the bill. Despite Ted's lack of interest, Susman convinced him to take it up, partly on the basis that Watergate had created an opportunity, and partly on the basis that FOIA had strong media support, and Ted, who was not averse to pushing legislation that would attract media attention, could get some here. So Ted held hearings in AdPrac on FOIA—hearings that, as it turned out, received scant press attention but that did, according to Susman, create a legislative record that could be used to challenge the restrictions in court when courts looked at congressional intentions. And then Ted drafted additional amendments, amendments on which both Susman and Ted spent a "fair amount of time," according to Susman, amendments to give requesters easier legal redress, to permit courts to impose sanctions on those who withheld documents "without a reasonable basis in law to do so," to allow greater latitude to those requesting records, and to release the nonexempt portions of otherwise exempt documents.

Ted Kennedy drafted those amendments because he wanted to bring government out of the darkness, where it was thwarting democracy. And, with Susman's encouragement, he was willing to fight for it.

It was not an easy battle Ted was waging, because Nixon, though reeling at the time, was still in office, and Nixon did not want a bill that brought the government out of darkness. Nor did most of the executive department, whose agencies had their own secrets to hide. Susman believed the FBI intentionally broke off negotiations with legislators in order to undermine the bill and Senator John McClellan, one of the Senate conferees in reconciling the House and Senate bills, was doing everything he could to assist the bureau in its efforts. (It was Nixon's Office of Legislative Affairs that told the FBI they wanted the bill to be "as bad as possible" so as to make the case stronger for Nixon's certain veto.) The CIA objected to the provision to let judges decide *in camera* whether security classifications were warranted. But Judiciary chairman James Eastland, who opposed the bill himself, thought that Ted had conned them all by promising the administration he would heed their objections, which is how it got out of committee, where Eastland would have been more than willing to bottle it up. Eastland was wrong, though. Ted hadn't really conned them. It was the administration that "stonewalled," in Susman's word, by refusing to negotiate with Ted and thereby outsmarting themselves. Rather than reach some accommodation with the bill's supporters—and Ted Kennedy was usually willing to make accommodations—their stonewalling led to two new amendments on the floor, one by Phil Hart, the other by Ed Muskie. Hart's tightened a widely used "investigatory exemption"—that is, an exemption for records from investigations; Muskie's allowed courts to review the classification of documents *in camera*. Both amendments passed, and the bill was then sent to conference.

But would Nixon sign it? As it approached a vote, it was thought that he might actually feel pressured to do so, because to veto it at a time when he was suspected of a cover-up would have been politically disadvantageous. It never came to that. By the time the bill reached a vote, Nixon was gone, and now the decision was Gerald Ford's. As a congressman, Ford had voted for the original FOIA bill, and his new chief of staff, Donald Rumsfeld, had actually been a co-sponsor of that bill. But Ford worried that the amendments might obstruct investigations and compromise national security, and he expressed uncertainty over whether it was even constitutional. His advisers lobbied heavily against the bill, though Ford understood the political consequences were he to veto it after promising an administration dedicated to "openness and candor," in the words of one aide. Moreover, as he dithered, the clock was ticking. Ford received the bill on October 8. Congress was scheduled to recess on October 18. If he didn't act by then, he would be pocket-vetoing the bill, which would make it seem as if Ford's "openness and candor" were mere words, without his having any intention of action—a damning indictment, especially right before a midterm election and after Watergate had forced Nixon from office. Even as his advisers were nearly unanimous in calling for a veto, Ford was torn. Finally, on October 17, with just a day to spare, he returned the bill to Congress—with his veto, knowing that it would almost certainly be overridden. (By one account, it was his fear of leaks—a near-obsessive fear of leaks, not unlike that of his predecessor—that had decided the issue for him.) Eight days later he sent Ted, who had headed the conference committee, a list of his objections and of suggested amendments to meet them. But by this time Congress had recessed, and in any case, neither Ted nor the supporters of the bill were inclined to make changes to weaken it. On November 20, the veto was overridden by the House and the next day, in a close vote—so close that Ted didn't know the outcome as the roll was taken—it was overridden by the Senate. (When Susman, worried that they might not have the votes to win, suggested that Ted talk to one senator whom Susman thought might be persuadable, Ted refused, saying that the senator had always demanded some sort of trade-off, and Ted wasn't about to make one.) In the end, Ted Kennedy had won another major victory to vanquish the abuses of Watergate. He had no great "emotional attachment" to the bill, as his AdPrac counsel Thomas Susman had said. But Ted Kennedy had chaired the hearings on the bill, had floor-managed the bill, had chaired the conference committee on the bill, and had floor-managed the override of Ford's veto on the bill—not, in the final analysis, because there was media interest, but because it was the right thing to do. As Susman was to say, Ted wasn't usually identified as one of the fathers of FOIA, "but the 1974 amendments are what gave the legislation the strength it has, its staying power, and Kennedy did that." Ted Kennedy had turned the spotlight on government. Ted Kennedy had helped light the darkness: the darkness in which Richard Nixon and his confederates had hidden.

II

The reason Gerald Ford had even engaged in a last-ditch effort for health care when it was nearly foreordained not to succeed, or why despite his misgivings he signed the campaign-finance reform bill to which Republicans had previously objected, or why he was tormented over FOIA, when his advisers told him to veto it, was that Ford was caught in a political trap—namely, that Republicans fully realized the midterm election, coming just months after Nixon's resignation, was likely to be disastrous for them unless Ford took action to remove Nixon's stigma and cleanse the Republican brand. Despite the fact that he was wielding his veto pen wildly—three in one week—as the Democratic Congress tried to take advantage of Watergate, he was eager to separate himself from Nixon. But Ford, hoping to put Watergate behind him and heal the nation's great breach, had chosen to take another tack—a shocking tack, a tack that was to define his presidency. On the morning of September 8, a Sunday, sitting in the Oval Office with a view of the South Lawn behind him, the freshly minted president gave a brief national television address, just ten minutes long, in which he announced that he had decided to pardon Richard Nixon because, he said, were Nixon to face criminal prosecution, the "tranquility to which this nation has been restored by the events in recent weeks could be irreparably lost."

Continued tranquility he had sought. Instead, Ford served in those ten minutes to shatter whatever tranquility he had achieved in his first month in office. Many Democrats, including Ted Kennedy, were furious that Nixon would now escape justice, would be *above* justice, and so were many Americans who had just been dragged through two sordid years of Watergate. (Just before the pardon, a Gallup poll showed that 53 percent of Americans opposed it.) "The pardon is premature and, I think, a serious mistake," Ted said. "It raises very real questions about our system of law and whether we have a double standard of justice in this country." The well-liked man was suddenly less well liked. Ford's detractors sniffed a deal with Nixon—a deal to let Nixon off the hook, presumably the vice presidency for the promise of clemency. (And not just Ford's detractors; 71 percent of Americans suspected some quid pro quo.) Within a week, Ford's favorability rating plummeted from 71 percent to 49 percent. His own press secretary resigned in protest. Republicans were aghast, having pleaded with Ford to hold any decision on a pardon until after the midterm elections. Democrats, no less aghast, reacted differently. Hearing the news on the radio that Sunday morning, James Blanchard, a Democratic candidate for the House in Michigan, said to himself, "Yes! Yes! Yes! Yes! We're going to win!"

Blanchard's prophecy proved correct. The Democrats, boosted by Watergate, by a flagging economy, and by the backlash against the pardon that many Americans clearly felt denied them closure, steamrolled the Republicans, taking forty-three seats from them. Not since Truman had a sitting president suffered such an electoral disaster. Nixon had schemed for a new coalition, even a new party, that would provide a permanent conservative majority and end liberal rule for the foreseeable future. Now his paranoia had led to events that destroyed that vision. And the 1974 election was worse than defeat; there was the nature of the individuals who had inflicted that defeat. Not only had Democrats added enough seats to their congressional majority that they could override any Ford veto, but the new freshman class was younger and more liberal and more iconoclastic than any in recent memory. Since 1968, the Democrats had been dispirited, seeing their moral authority decline precipitously, seeing their electoral fortunes appear doomed by the divisive but powerful appeals of Richard Nixon. Now, after a single election, those spirits had risen, that authority, set against Nixon's dark deeds, had been renewed, those fortunes had been reversed.

Ted Kennedy, who had been among the doom-laden after battling Nixon for six years, was now exhilarated. Shortly, after the election, he announced that he would be reintroducing S.3, his national health bill, in the new Senate, this time with its prospects considerably brighter. Back on top, *Newsweek* said of him six months later, in what seemed an astonishingly rapid reversal but may have only been a gush of excitement now that Nixon and his Republicans were vanquished. Renewed. Revitalized. "He has shed some of the fat that stretches his jowls and thickens his middle in the bad times," it reported. "His body is lean, his mane modishly shaggy, his smile a runaway Ultra Brite commercial," citing a toothpaste. "He has largely repaired his Senate reputation, which had ebbed low after Chappaquiddick; he has used the Kennedy edge to advance a whole range of favored causes, from national health insurance to the lot of the world's refugees, and his name is no longer considered a detriment to a bill." He had even made peace with the supermarket tabloid coverage that had trailed him after Chappaquiddick. *Newsweek* said that on a recent trip to the Middle East, traveling tourist class with Joan, Kara, two of his sisters, and "miscellaneous other kinfolk and bondsmen . . . they amused themselves en route with a tabloid scandal sheet announcing: JACKIE'S NEW LOVE—IT'S TEDDY KENNEDY."

Richard Nixon had not only left wreckage. He had left a great deal undone over the two years he was preoccupied with Watergate. Now the new president and new Congress had to do those deeds. As Nixon had wrestled with Congress, the economy began to sputter. Unemployment rose, the gross national product per capita fell 2 percent in his last year in office, and so, for the first time in twenty-five years, did average hourly wages. Meanwhile, inflation began to rise. America had been in a moral crisis. Now it was in an economic one. But Gerald Ford had no solutions. In February 1975, a single month, unemployment leapt a whole percentage point, to 8.2 percent, the highest figure since the Great Depression. (By June, it would reach 9.2 percent.) Nixon had implemented wage and price controls to curb inflation, to no effect. Moreover, inflation rose to just over 12 percent by the fall. Ford, on October 8, in an address to a joint session of Congress, violated Republican orthodoxy by calling for a 5 percent tax surcharge on high incomes along with spending cuts, and he created a

voluntary organization called Whip Inflation Now, or WIN, to fight inflation through various means of persuasion like encouraging personal saving. (Alan Greenspan, Ford's own chairman of the Council of Economic
Advisers, called the WIN campaign "unbelievable stupidity" and a "low
point of economic policymaking.") But Gerald Ford was proposing unbe-
lievably stupid solutions because he really had no others. Eventually, returning to orthodoxy, he lifted the surcharge and replaced it with a $16
billion tax cut, which prompted the Democrats to outdo him by proposing
a $22 billion cut targeted to the middle class. Ford was basically pressured
into signing it, though the goodwill engendered by his first months in office was, by this time, dissipating. But Gerald Ford signed it because he had
no solutions. "I don't know how they think," Ted told columnist Jimmy
Breslin of the administration. "I can't get into their minds. Their mentality seems to be that the first concern is inflation. That is not alien to a
party more concerned with the problems of business than the problems
of the people." And when Ford blamed Congress for its unwillingness to
solve the problems that beset the country, Ted riposted that the Congress
was active; it was the president who wasn't. But Gerald Ford had no other
solutions.

And Gerald Ford had no solutions after he signed a nuclear-arms limitation agreement with Soviet leader Leonid Brezhnev in November 1974,
which Senator Henry Jackson, the leading Democrat in foreign affairs,
insisted be revised to lower the limits set, even though the actual numbers
had not yet been decided upon. Ted joined with senators Mondale and
Mathias in a "sense of the Senate" resolution—a resolution without the
force of law—calling for further negotiations to lower the limits, but it
failed to pass, and now secretary of State and national security adviser
Henry Kissinger was forced to consider a new resolution, which not only
called for further negotiations but also extracted from Kissinger a concession that America would only deploy its missiles on the basis of its security and not on the basis of how many missiles it was allowed to deploy by
the agreement. It was as if the balance of power had shifted to Congress.
All of this backing and filling made Ford look as if he didn't know what he
was doing and gave Democrats an opportunity to influence policy far
more heavily than they had done during the Nixon administration.

And still there was Vietnam, the war that never seemed to end, even
though North Vietnam and the United States had signed peace accords in
Paris in 1973 and American combat forces had been withdrawn. Despite

the truce, the wounds remained—wounds to the soldiers, wounds to the nation. In September 1974, a month into office, Ford, attempting to heal those wounds, announced a program for clemency through alternative service for Vietnam draft resisters. Ted had proposed amendments to the Selective Service Act of 1971 to make the draft more equitable and to assist those who claimed conscientious-objector status, and Nixon had signed the bill including those amendments. And the next year, Ted had held hearings on amnesty, the first such hearings, at the opening of which he lauded those "young men who saw things we now see but saw them sooner and who did the only thing they could" when faced with the dilemma of violating the Selective Service law or following their own "moral imperatives. . . . They chose prison or exile." Now he conducted new hearings on Ford's proposal and won an extension of the deadline Ford had set for the enactment. But as with so many of Ford's healing measures— halfway measures—there was dissatisfaction. Conservatives howled in protest, and Ted, speaking before the Veterans of Foreign Wars, was hooted with "No, No, No," when he chastised the organization for rejecting Ford's plan, which he said has "mercy, healing, and leniency built into it." On the other side, many draft resisters complained that they were forced to do service while Nixon got his pardon without any qualifications on it. Others wanted full vindication. And in any case, few took advantage of the clemency offer. A month after Ford's announcement, of 213,000 deemed eligible by a clemency board that Ford had created, only 560 had applied.

That was here. In Vietnam, despite the truce and the withdrawal, the war had yet to be resolved between the North and South Vietnamese. By early 1975, the South Vietnamese government, for which 58,000 American lives and countless Vietnamese lives had been expended, was crumbling. That February, Ford and Kissinger called for an infusion of $522 million to prop up the Thieu regime and that of Lon Nol in neighboring Cambodia. Ted responded: "Once again, we are hearing the same old arguments and the same old controversies—over the same old war." The next month, with the collapse of the South Vietnamese government imminent, Ted called for $100 million in international aid for the refugees, to be administered not by the United States government but by the United Nations and other nongovernmental agencies. By the time the bill reached the floor, the amount had been raised to $150 million, with the intercession of Hubert Humphrey, who had returned to the Senate in the class of

1974, but when the House–Senate conference cut out the international agencies, Ted wound up voting against it, distrusting the American government's ability to dispense those funds or the South Vietnamese government's ability to use them wisely. In demanding refugee and civilian relief, Ted knew what was coming once the Thieu government fell. He had spent years working for the civilians and refugees there—years pleading their case. And now he was pleading with the administration to save them. Speaking at Berkeley that April before 12,000 cheering students, he upbraided Ford for his Vietnam policies and America for its "long and tragic pursuit of the phantom of military victory in Vietnam." He called again for humanitarian aid channeled through the UN or the Red Cross, and he called upon Ford to negotiate an orderly peaceful withdrawal rather than a military evacuation. And finally he called for a new foreign policy, a morally based foreign policy, a policy that promoted the end of nuclear war, multilateralism, and a moratorium on arms sales to small nations, one that addressed poverty and reaffirmed our belief in human rights.

But in Vietnam, the end was not to be peaceful. Within a month of Ted's speech, the South Vietnamese government fell. Civilians swarmed the American embassy, seeking to be airlifted to safety by jamming themselves into helicopters or clinging to the struts, and there was chaos, utter chaos, everywhere—no deliberate, ordered withdrawal, as Ted had called for, but instead the frenzied evacuation he had feared. Such was the conclusion of the long, cruel, and bloody war that tore America apart and ripped her soul and undermined her moral authority and destroyed a nation three thousand miles away. And such were Ted Kennedy's regrets that he would say of his dereliction in not being "more aggressive and more active in ending the war sooner," presumably in not speaking out against Lyndon Johnson, that it was his least proud moment in public life.

Haunted by those regrets, Ted Kennedy seized on the end of the war to begin what he hoped would be a reevaluation of American foreign policy in the wake of Vietnam. At Berkeley he had called for a moral policy, and having called for it, he now worked for it. He burrowed into nuclear issues and joined the North Atlantic Assembly, an interparliamentary group bringing together legislators from America and Europe to discuss common issues, and he co-chaired its defense committee. At the suggestion of his aide Mark Schneider, he began to focus on defense spending and hosted a dinner of experts at his McLean home to learn more about it; he

also joined with Senator Alan Cranston to organize liberal senators to oppose the defense-procurement bill and called for a "Great Debate" with
their conservative colleagues to set future defense policy—a "substantive
debate," Schneider called it. He traveled extensively. He sent two of his
aides, Schneider and Robert Hunter, to Cuba to meet with President Fidel
Castro and discuss future relations with the United States, and he won the
release of some political prisoners in the bargain. Conservatives had been
exasperated with some of Nixon's foreign-policy endeavors—his opening
of Red China, his détente with the Soviet Union—but these could be
chalked up to political expediency in co-opting the Democrats and, not
incidentally, co-opting Ted Kennedy, who had championed both causes.
Gerald Ford had seemed susceptible to a genuinely new strategic vision—
a new pathway to peace. But if Watergate and Ford's ascension had
seemed to halt a rightward drift, it was largely an illusion. Ford was not
ideological, nor was he rabidly partisan like Nixon, but he was conservative by temperament and instinct, a small-town Republican with a parochial mindset. More, even if he was not ideological, he had surrounded
himself with ideologues—many of them Nixon holdovers. Ford's foreign
policy did not turn in a new direction from the lessons of Vietnam, as Ted
had hoped; it had turned back in the old direction.

Nor did Gerald Ford, the modest, well-liked man, with his pledges to
heal the country (his autobiography would be titled *A Time to Heal*), his
professions of openness and candor, and his boast to have restored tranquility, eschew political expediency or dissembling or chaos, hallmarks of
the Nixon presidency, if it served his needs, and his needs now were tilting
far more conservatively in a party that, under Nixon, had lurched rightward in its efforts to pry those disaffected white working-class Americans
from the Democratic party. On the night of November 3, 1975, at a televised press conference, Ford executed what became known as the "Halloween Massacre"—a less-than-flattering comparison to Nixon's
Saturday Night Massacre—by terminating key members of his staff and
Cabinet and reshuffling others. Already, privately, Ford had nudged the
vice president whom he had appointed under the terms of the Twenty-
fifth Amendment, former New York governor Nelson Rockefeller, to re-
nounce any plans of running for the office in 1976 and then lied that the
decision was Rockefeller's alone. He fired his Defense secretary, James
Schlesinger, some said at the insistence of joint secretary of State and national security adviser Henry Kissinger, with whom Schlesinger had

clashed, and replaced him with his chief of staff, Donald Rumsfeld, while slotting Rumsfeld's deputy, Dick Cheney, into Rumsfeld's vacated position; he fired his CIA director, William Colby; and he stripped the position of national security adviser from Kissinger, though left him as secretary of State. A "large step to the right," one historian would call it. Exactly why he made these moves Ford never fully explained. Some thought he was victim to the machinations of Rumsfeld, who wanted to position himself for a presidential run by eliminating competitors. (By other accounts, Rumsfeld argued strenuously against the move, saying, among other things, that it would remove him from Ford's campaign, in which he wanted to be involved.) Others thought that axing Rockefeller was a gesture to appease conservatives who might defect to California governor Ronald Reagan, a right-wing favorite then considering taking on Ford in the Republican primaries. Still others believed that Ford, the nice man, felt he needed to portray a more muscular image by asserting control over his staff. And there were those who took Ford's word at face value: that he wanted a new team, his own team, in the White House for defense and national security. Whatever the reasons, the suddenness of the moves and the coldness with which they were executed did not go down well with the press, which was shocked at how Ford undermined his nice-guy image. As John Osborne put it in *The New Republic*, the massacre showed "Gerald Ford to be intensely egotistic behind that humble façade of his, capable of an inhuman cruelty stupidly evinced, and desperately anxious to establish and prove himself as a national leader in his own right." Gerald Ford, who had not sought the presidency, now was accused of being willing to sacrifice his most notable attribute—that he was well liked—in order to pacify the right-wingers who distrusted his moderation—pacify them to win the nomination.

III

On the horizon of that nomination was Ted Kennedy. As early as Nixon's reelection, Ted Kennedy had been giving the presidency a great deal of thought. On December 5, 1972, Ted had met over lunch with Milton Gwirtzman, his longtime counselor, to discuss his presidential prospects. Gwirtzman was to say that he was "surprised at how eager he [Ted] was to consider the presidency and how much thinking he had been doing about it," almost certainly, in no small measure, because he saw himself as the antidote to what Nixon had done to the nation. The first thing Ted had to do, Gwirtzman told him, was resolve the problem of his 1976 Senate re-election. It would be difficult for him to run for both the presidency and the Senate, though the Massachusetts Senate primary was late, and Gwirtzman said that Ted could keep out other senatorial aspirants by telling voters that he would seek the presidency but that if he didn't win it, he would run again for his seat. Gwirtzman said he and Ted would have two or three conversations on a typical day during this period, which was the period when Nixon was getting embroiled in the Watergate revelations. At roughly the same time, Ted asked his aide Paul Kirk and his former aide David Burke to take soundings among Democratic pols about his candidacy. And Ted had Kirk and Burke draw up a list of candidates whom he had helped in 1972 with fundraising and for whom he had made campaign appearances—a list, he would say, that covered thirty-nine states. Frank Mankiewicz, George McGovern's campaign coordinator, sent Ted a private memo with the lessons Mankiewicz had learned from that ill-fated campaign, but he also included a list of fundraisers and the most effective operatives. Ted began polling in 1973, and in November of that year, on a flight from Boston to Washington with Gwirtzman, he asked Gwirtzman when he thought he had to make a decision. Gwirtzman answered that Ted probably had until August 1975, provided he had done all the necessary preliminaries, and that he could go out and deliberate on his boat if he chose. And Ted yet again expressed concern for his safety—to which Gwirtzman said that he could campaign in such a way that his life would not be jeopardized. Still waffling, as he had always done in the past when the possibility of the presidency arose, Ted admitted that the "Nixon people probably did have some stuff," meaning some gossip about him, probably pertaining to women, and, as Gwirtzman recalled it, Ted asked him whether he should take the Judiciary Committee chairmanship [Gwirtzman clearly misremembered; the chairmanship belonged to Eastland and wasn't open, so Ted must have been referring to something else]. Gwirtzman told him that it was a good job, "but not as good as the presidency."

Not as good as the presidency. Nothing was as good as the presidency. And so Ted Kennedy continued to lay the groundwork for a run, laying it years in advance, as he could not do in 1972 given Chappaquiddick. At Ted's request, Ted Sorensen submitted a memo too—a seventeen-page memo—outlining the 1976 political landscape in preparation for a meeting at Steve Smith's apartment on March 9, 1973, of what Sorensen called

Ted's "informal advisory group": David Burke, Paul Kirk, Burke Marshall, Ed Martin, John Seigenthaler, and Smith. Sorensen's first question was "whether you want the presidential nomination and election of 1976 badly enough to undertake the personal sacrifices, risks, and commitments necessary," which seemed always to be a question with Ted. Did he want the presidency badly enough? If he did, Sorensen wrote, it meant that Ted had to devote all of 1973 to "strengthening your national image and stature" and building a campaign apparatus. Sorensen said that Ted would have to moderate his liberal image, even criticize liberals when necessary, court the establishment, and co-sponsor bills with folks like Wilbur Mills, which Kennedy wound up doing with the Kennedy–Mills health plan, and Georgia conservative Herman Talmadge, and Republican moderate George Aiken of Vermont. He even advised Ted to vacation with his family at modest locations so as not to draw undue attention to his wealth. And last, he advised that Ted collect polling data to build a "comprehensive picture of the American electorate in 1976," because that electorate was changing, though no one seemed to be sure exactly how it was changing.

But perhaps nothing demonstrated how badly Ted Kennedy wanted to run for the presidency and what he was willing to do to make that run as much as a decision that summer of 1973—a decision that seemed to undercut all Ted's professions of morality. He accepted an invitation from George Wallace to speak at a Fourth of July celebration in Decatur, Alabama, which Wallace, now wheelchair-bound from the wound suffered in a 1972 assassination attempt, would be hosting and at which Wallace would be honored with the Audie Murphy Patriotism Award, named for the World War II hero. Ted polled his staff as to whether he should attend. The verdict was unanimous: no. And Ted, sitting in his office, picked up the phone, called Wallace, and *accepted* the invitation. When he put the receiver back in its cradle, his staffers were appalled. But Ted had only pretended to call Wallace. Then he lectured the aides on their response. "You are all against this," he told them, "but you have to realize that you and some other people want me to run for president of the United States. A president has to be able to go to every part of the country, and I need to go to the South. I have an opportunity here to talk to people that I do not normally get to talk to, and I will be able to bring to them a message that they normally don't get to hear." As one staffer recalled, Ted grinned and said, "And besides, how often do you have a chance to speak to four thousand blue-collar guys swilling beer?" As another staffer later told reporter Lou Cannon, "The knee-jerk reaction was that liberals don't do this sort of thing. His knee-jerk reaction was that maybe liberals should." Still, by one account, lest he endanger his standing in the African American community, Ted consulted with black leaders, including the Reverend Jesse Jackson, Congressman Andrew Young, and National Urban League president Vernon Jordan—all of whom advised him to accept, presumably on the same grounds that Ted himself had wanted to accept: It was a chance to address a crowd that was hostile to civil rights.

And so Ted Kennedy went to Alabama that July in an attempt, he claimed, to heal the country during Nixon's Watergate drama but also, and chiefly, to advance his bid to be president. And while the band played "Hey, Look Me Over," George Wallace, in a white suit, pulled himself up from his wheelchair and stood against the podium to welcome Ted, who was wearing a dark suit in the hot blazing sun after a morning rain had left the parade grounds a "mudhole," as one reporter put it. "No other family in the U.S. and across the world has suffered so much or lost more in public service," Wallace told the crowd. And then Ted, with several black Alabama mayors standing behind him, spoke to the thousands of people gathered there—spoke first of how he and George Wallace were united in their condemnation of Nixon and Watergate. "We have one thing in common," Ted said of himself and Wallace. "We didn't corrupt. We didn't malign. We didn't abuse the trust which the people had given us. We don't compile lists of enemies whose careers and lives are to be shattered because of their disagreement." And as Wallace sat in his wheelchair and turned up his hearing aids, Ted saluted the segregationist who had stood on the steps of the University of Alabama to prevent black students from matriculating there. "For if there is one thing that George Wallace stands for, it is the right of every American to speak his mind and be heard, fearlessly and in every part of the country." And Ted spoke of racial divisions, though not to reprimand the South for its injustices but to implicate the North in those same injustices: "Let no one think I come to lecture you on that racial injustice which has proven to be as deeply embedded and resistant in the cities of the North as in the counties of the South," he said, adding for good measure, "We are no more entitled to oppress a man for his color than to shoot a man for his beliefs," as if the two were comparable. The crowd of white Southern Wallace supporters cheered Ted Kennedy throughout.

But men had been shot for their color—were still being shot. And Ted Kennedy's endorsement of George Wallace for his "spirit" and his willingness to speak his mind—though he most often spoke it in furtherance of racism—did not go over well and should not have gone over well with the black leaders Ted hadn't consulted before accepting the invitation. The Southern Christian Leadership Conference censured Ted at its convention later that summer, calling the speech the "height of political opportunism," which, of course, it was. "We all make mistakes, errors, blunders," remarked the conference's leader, the Reverend Ralph Abernathy, Martin Luther King's close associate, but Abernathy was still willing to give Ted Kennedy the benefit of the doubt, and he said he hoped that Ted would "repent," because "I have great love and admiration for the man." *The Washington Post* editorialized that Ted had normalized Wallace as a populist rather than a racist. "It was only a few years ago that he was publicly entertaining thoughts of running his car over Vietnam war protesters," the *Post* opined of Wallace. "Let's not confuse him with Oliver Wendell Holmes." Former Nixon speechwriter and *New York Times* columnist William Safire was more sympathetic, accepting Ted's own reasoning for giving the speech. Safire felt that in reaching out to the South, Ted was healing a breach, providing calm at a time when the nation was in turbulence. "He may grasp, as very few of the closest aides of his brothers or of Richard Nixon ever grasped," Safire wrote, "the notion that a credo that says, 'If you're not for us, you're against us,' is incredibly stupid. To understand that, as Senator Kennedy shows signs of doing, is to begin to figure out how to acquire and wield power in a democracy," which was, indeed, Ted Kennedy's aim, though not necessarily a selfless one. (Bobby, of course, would have never done so.) And Safire closed: "Just as it took a Nixon to end the cold war"—Safire was referring to Nixon's détente with Russia and his trip to Red China—"it took a Kennedy to open up the competition for the Wallace voter—and our political system is healthier for it." Tom Wicker, a liberal *Times* columnist and a Southerner, agreed with Safire. Lecturing Southerners on their immorality was no way to win their votes, he wrote—votes that Democrats and Ted Kennedy would need to recapture the presidency. Moral authority had once been a source of Democratic strength and the South a guaranteed source of Democratic support, but it was an unstable combination, a combination that Nixon and other Republicans had seen as such and of which they knew they could take advantage through race-baiting, which meant that those days where Democrats were able to draw on their liberalism in the North while tolerating racism in the South were gone. The country had changed; the political alignments were realigning. Ted, though still an advocate of moral force, was acknowledging that in going to Alabama.

Ted Kennedy had to acknowledge it because he wanted to run for president, less out of personal ambition, it seemed—though he was, after all, a Kennedy, and the ambition was great—than to shift the national tide, which had turned against liberalism, even as it had also turned from Richard Nixon, though not for his policies but for his behavior. The question was: Could he redeem the country from what Nixon had done to it? Gwirtzman said that Ted's staff had already prepared a black book that laid out his strategy early in January 1974, by which time Ted had been pondering a run for more than a year, and Gwirtzman suggested that Ted have two staffers stage a debate with the arguments for and against running. Meanwhile, Ted was buttressing himself against potential rivals, especially Senator Henry Jackson, who had staked his career on his foreign-policy and defense expertise. So while the nation's attention was focused on Watergate, Ted took a swing through Europe that spring, meeting German chancellor Willy Brandt and speaking in Bonn, where crowds, huge crowds, treated him as a president and where German leaders eagerly sought an audience with him. He returned to the United States only to fly back to Europe a short time later for meetings in Yugoslavia, Poland, and Russia—the trip on which he took Joan and on which he pressured the Russians to allow the refuseniks to emigrate. When several of his aides argued that Jackson would only criticize him for being soft on Russia, Ted told them, "I'm going because I want to make an impact." Jackson was a hawk—a believer in the power of might. Ted was promoting a different approach—a belief in soft power, the power of moral strength. "I want to broaden the options for the Democratic party and the American people," he told a reporter, clearly thinking of Jackson.

And the party, eager for victory, smelling a victory, waited. Richard Reeves wrote in *New York* magazine that the party was "paralyzed" by whether or not Ted would run, and one Democrat complained to him, "It drives me crazy sometimes. No matter what I do, people—media people and politicians—are watching Teddy to see what he'll do. Hell, I spend half my time figuring out what he'll do." So did Ted himself. On his return from the Russian trip, he allegedly told a reporter, "I will not be running in '76. Absolutely not," then his press secretary, Dick Drayne, countered that Ted was not going to make his decision "on the basis of a question that somebody asked him when he was getting into a car in New York City."

Ted wanted to run, but he wasn't sure he should run, not just for the reasons that had blocked him in the past: his sense of his unreadiness (he felt ready now), his fear of politicizing the issues he advanced and thus hurting their chances to become law (even though he realized his presidential ambitions also propelled those issues), his safety, his concerns about Joan. This time there was another obstacle to a Kennedy victory, a major obstacle, and it happened to be the very reason he thought he *needed* to run: the nation's perceived rightward turn. He knew that by promoting a liberal agenda he could be dooming his chances for election. "I have a particular view of the country and its needs," he told *The Boston Globe*'s Martin Nolan in October 1973, "the direction that it can and should go into. It may very well be that that view may not be shared by the country or the party." But he told Nolan, "I'm not going to change my views or alter my position." To historian James MacGregor Burns, he said that he was going to continue wading into controversies, because "I can't stay out of this kind of bully pulpit." But Ted also understood why the country seemed to be moving rightward and what liberals had contributed to precipitating that move and giving conservatives an advantage, even in the wake of Watergate. Liberals, he was to say of this period, had suffered a "loss of confidence," that they had themselves changed from "challenging individuals to better themselves, to telling people what they were going to do"—the same charge of elitist social engineering and moral disdain that Nixon and others had leveled at liberals, though a lot of this anger was backlash against the liberal promotion of civil rights, which many white working-class Americans resented. This sense of liberal scolding created a "very different climate and atmosphere," he believed, than the one of the Kennedy years or the early Johnson years, before Vietnam, and he said the Republicans "played on it." Liberals nevertheless held out the hope that Ted could usher in a restoration of Camelot—the very thing Nixon had so feared. Ted himself believed otherwise. He would later write, "My actual vision of the presidency, to the extent that I turned it over in my mind, was a good deal more complex and less romantic." He said he realized that the eras that had shaped Jack and Bobby had passed. The new era was "quite different in mood, in collective experience, and in the challenges the nation faced." And he wondered, as he told Milton Gwirtzman, whether he would have to "trim" or "cut back on" some of his more liberal positions in order to run, as he had so often been advised to do, and he told Arthur Schlesinger Jr. the same thing—"whether the views for which he had stood, especially on racial questions, would have any prospect of success."

Especially on racial questions. Nixon was gone in August 1974, and Gerald Ford, who had voted for the Civil Rights Act of 1964 and the Voting Rights Act of 1965 and shared none of Nixon's racial prejudices, was president now. But despite Ford's efforts to heal the nation, the wounds Richard Nixon had opened were still deep and raw—perhaps none more raw than race. Though he was no racist, at least publicly, when he entered politics, no racist when he ran against John Kennedy in 1960,* Nixon had understood the racial antipathies in America, had understood them well, and he was more than willing to exploit them if they would bring him the presidency, especially when he was contending, as he did in 1968, with Alabama governor George Wallace. Nixon's message was subtler than Wallace's but no less divisive. When he decried the lack of law and order, white Americans knew to whom he was referring, even as he insisted it was not a "code word for racism" but a call for "justice." When he attacked the social programs of the Great Society for creating what he called an "ugly harvest of frustrations, violence, and failure," white Americans knew who he thought the beneficiaries of those programs were. When he pursued a "Southern strategy" to win the presidency, white Americans knew to whom that strategy was targeted and who would be left behind. When he nominated G. Harrold Carswell, who was racially insensitive at best, racist at worst, for a seat on the Supreme Court, white Americans knew what message the president was sending. And whatever he said or did publicly, Richard Nixon was worse, much worse, in private. If he hadn't been a racist before he ran in 1968, he had embraced the tactics of racism in 1968, and when they worked, he continued to exploit them. If

---

* It was Nixon's reluctance to contact Martin Luther King Jr. when King was jailed during the campaign for civil disobedience and John Kennedy's willingness to do so that cost Nixon black support.

he hadn't been a racist before he ran in 1968, he used the vocabulary of racism out of public view. "Just down from trees," he told his domestic counselor, John Ehrlichman, of blacks.

Ted Kennedy hadn't been a leader in the advancement of black rights when he entered the Senate in 1962, though in many respects he was more sensitive to the movement than were his brothers, who kept their distance from black activists for fear of alienating the South. (It was Ted, after all, who surreptitiously attended the March on Washington in 1963, while his brothers advised him to stay away.) But as violence against African Americans increased, John Kennedy's racial consciousness was raised, and he would become a hero to the black community for proposing the Civil Rights Act, a courageous stand, and even more of a hero after his death, when the Civil Rights Act was enacted. Bobby Kennedy had inherited that lionization and fought even more tenaciously than his late brother for civil rights to justify the African Americans' faith in him. And Ted Kennedy had inherited both John and Bobby's status among black Americans and after their deaths assumed a prominent role in the battle for civil rights—a role that became even more important when Nixon won the presidency and the fight for racial justice became more difficult. "I remember walking through National Airport in the old North Terminal," Philip Caper, Ted's health aide, said, "when a black cabbie came up to him and tapped him on the shoulder and said, 'Are you Senator Kennedy?' Ted replied, 'Yes, I'm Senator Kennedy.' The cabbie said, 'You're my favorite senator.' Kennedy looks at this black guy and says, 'Right now, I think I'm your *only* senator.'" And that is the way it must have seemed in the 1970s when Nixon and then Ford was president.

While Republicans, looking South for white votes, were increasingly neglecting the black community, Ted Kennedy worked hard for it, even on issues that were not widely publicized. When Robert Bates got a call from a woman with sickle cell anemia, a disease that primarily affected black people, Bates, who knew little about the disease, studied it, wrote up what he learned, and gave it to Ted, who ordered that legislation be drafted to provide money for research and to set up a center for the disease at Howard University, which also launched a treatment center. When Bates received another letter, this one about the effects of lead-based paint poisoning—especially pernicious in black neighborhoods, where old peeling paint could be ingested by children—Ted introduced a bill providing money to treat the poisoning and to prevent it from occurring. He even invoked his own nephews, who he said would chew the paint on the banisters at the Hyannis compound, though Bates knew very well that those nephews never chewed lead paint and that Ted was only saying so to give a dramatic example that might move his colleagues. (What Bates didn't say is that Ted needed to move colleagues who might not be moved by the danger to black children.) And there had been the big political issues like Ted's support of the Fair Housing Act and his efforts in support of the Voting Rights Act extension.

Ted understood the political perils of embracing racial justice after the moral moment inspired by John Kennedy's death had passed, especially if he had any hopes of capturing the 1976 Democratic nomination and then the presidency. He knew working-class whites would not approve. And yet he had called out his fellow liberals for not being adequately aggressive for black causes. And Ted didn't only call out his fellow liberals. He called out African Americans too. He told Robert Bates that Bates had to "get some of the brothers to do fundraisers" for him for his Senate campaign in 1976, "because you know I'm going to do the right thing." Ted said he needed those fundraisers to show suspicious white voters *why* he was working for black causes, presumably to show those white voters that there was a practical political reason for him to help African Americans, that he wasn't just doing it out of pro-black sentiments—even though he was. He hoped this would soothe the fears of anxious white voters and make his efforts more palatable to them: politics instead of morals.

And whites weren't the only ones he had to soothe in this period of racial tension. There were militant blacks who didn't trust him either. His aide Paul Kirk remembered one talk that Ted gave to the Yale Political Union in 1970, when the Black Panther Bobby Seale was on trial in New Haven for murdering an informant against the Panthers, and Kirk and Ted were the only whites in the room. It was a hostile crowd, a threatening crowd, a crowd that didn't want to let Ted speak. Kirk thought, *Is this what we're going to do?*—meaning have confrontations with radicals. But Ted finally did get a chance to speak, and when he did, Kirk said, he managed to "open a dialogue" with the audience, and by the time Ted left, he had, in Kirk's thinking, "clearly made a difference, just in terms of lowering the temperature." Kirk also thought that what Ted did that evening, before that angry crowd, was even more courageous than Bobby's speech in Indianapolis on the night of Martin Luther King Jr.'s assassination, the speech in which Bobby urged tolerance, but Kirk believed that in Ted's mind it wasn't about courage. "It was one of those things that he felt he had to do." Ted had told Gwirtzman that the one policy he would not trim in his pursuit of the presidency was his commitment to racial justice, and yet he also told Gwirtzman that he felt black leadership "have it in for me" and that he "did not have to do cartwheels to the requirements of black leadership" who couldn't even "control their own people"—remarks that Gwirtzman didn't understand and that seemed to come out of the blue. But perhaps Gwirtzman didn't fully understand because he didn't comprehend the tension Ted felt, the tension between wanting to be president and to do good for the disempowered and his feeling that some of the more radical black leaders didn't appreciate how difficult the politics of doing so were—the tension, really, between the dictates of morality and the dictates of politics. And Ted was clearly conflicted, and angry, about feeling the need to bend the former to accommodate the latter. But he did.

The question had become not whether Ted Kennedy should run for the presidency but whether he could win, even against a less-than-popular incumbent like Gerald Ford, given the illiberal tendencies of the country, especially on race. Ted felt he could get the nomination. A Gallup poll that September showed him as the favorite of 46 percent of Democratic voters, with Wallace second at 16 percent and no other candidate with more than 9 percent. And Ted had told Gwirtzman that, unlike Bobby, who had to scrape for money and dip into his own wealth and whose campaign went heavily into debt—debt that Ted later held dinners to pay off—he had promises of financial support. But the general election was another matter. James MacGregor Burns, who was already writing a campaign biography of Ted for 1976, speculated that Ted might have been loath to run for the presidency because he "shrank from putting himself in a position where he might have to give up a part of himself that he did not wish to yield"—namely, his fervent liberalism. Ted himself said as much. But there were other things that gave him pause. Chappaquiddick still haunted him; he told Gwirtzman that he wanted to commission a poll on its continuing effect on his candidacy, and Gwirtzman said that he was "unwilling to take the personal risk that Chappaquiddick will defeat him." It was one thing to lose an election for a moral cause, another to lose it for seemingly dishonorable behavior.

Chappaquiddick loomed large over Ted Kennedy. The fifth anniversary of the accident that summer of 1974, especially with the expectation that

Ted would be running in 1976, reopened the case. "The Memory That Would Not Fade," *Time* titled its anniversary story, in which it enumerated what it said were contradictions in Ted's account—everything from his saying that he hadn't visited Chappaquiddick before (a ferryman said he had taken him there "many times," though that seemed highly dubious), to the time frame for Ted's rescue attempts, which had already been thoroughly litigated in the media five years earlier. *The Boston Globe* also published an anniversary reevaluation—this one a five-part series that included an interview with Ted. The *Globe* cited one hundred discrepancies in the testimony of key witnesses at the inquest. The *Los Angeles Times* and *Philadelphia Inquirer* also conducted investigations. And independent left-wing journalist Robert Sherrill wrote another long excavation for *The New York Times Magazine,* also scathing, but, again, there was little new in any of these, only the fact that Chappaquiddick would not disappear, however much Ted Kennedy hoped it might. (Mrs. Kopechne, along with her husband the most interested parties, was interviewed just before the anniversary and told a reporter that if Ted were to run for president, "I'm for him, and I would vote for him.") Ted said he could feel that Watergate had changed the national mood—that it had heightened the stakes of personal morality, which hurt him on Chappaquiddick, but that Watergate had also turned the electorate against their public officials and against government itself. Conservative Republicans had tried hard for years to discredit government. Richard Nixon had finally succeeded, not by the power of his philosophy but by the opprobrium at his nefarious actions: Government was not to be trusted, because those who governed could not be trusted. "It was a time when the outsider had a real opportunity," Ted would say years later, knowing he was no outsider but also knowing that he was morally compromised. "It was just the wrong time." Betty Taymor, the Massachusetts Democratic activist and Ted's friend, was hearing even from former Ted supporters that they didn't want him to run for the presidency because of Chappaquiddick, and she said that some of their comments were quite "ugly." She decided to report her soundings to Ted, whom she met at his Boston office. He took her into a utility closet for privacy, where she told him, "They're not going to let you make believe it's over." She said Ted looked at her unshaken and said, "Well, I'll tell you, Betty, I've got worse problems than that." Taymor didn't ask what they were, but she assumed that "he must be having domestic problems of great magnitude."

And Ted Kennedy *was* having domestic problems of great magnitude. While he certainly harbored political considerations against running, fearing his liberalism would foreclose his winning, his personal considerations were larger, more central. There was Joan. Since Ted Jr.'s diagnosis and surgery, Joan had broken down, receiving treatments for her alcoholism, then returning home only to relapse. Ted seemed to have become immune to her breakdowns, but he hadn't. After it was announced in June 1974 that Joan had returned to a sanitarium for treatment, Ted had to fly to Boston to deliver the commencement address at Bridgewater State Teachers College, and he was accompanied by a reporter. As they were being driven to campus, Ted talked about "life, death, and accidents," then Ted made an "excellent, sometimes moving graduation speech, and carried on an interview on health care all the way back to the airport. Never once did the strain show," meaning the strain about Joan's situation. Which led the reporter to conclude: "He has become cold, even callous, about his personal past interfering with the present."

Not showing the strain, perhaps, yet always present. Cold and callous, perhaps, yet still unsettled. But by this point, Ted and Joan were seldom together, and when they did go out, "They are almost never alone," a friend told a reporter for a *McCall's* article entitled "The Troubled Marriage of Joan and Ted Kennedy." Another friend of Joan's told *McCall's* that Joan had been absent from Ted's political activities for so long that "she's not even expected." (When he was mulling the run and seemed eager to take the plunge, he told Gwirtzman hopefully that there was a new trend toward "independently living by wives" and cited his friend John Tunney's wife, Mieke, who lived separately from her husband, obviously as a way to convince himself that his relationship with Joan would be publicly acceptable.) There were those who said that Joan's condition wasn't just a result of Ted Jr.'s illness but of Ted's possible presidential run and her anxiety about his safety. In any case, she was unlikely to be a help to him were he to run and may have been too fragile for him to run.

And Teddy Jr.'s illness weighed heavily not just on Joan but on Ted too. He was to say that his deliberations about running were based largely on Ted Jr. and the ongoing treatments he needed and the ongoing support that Ted felt he alone could provide his son. "After I got into it with Teddy," he said, meaning the experimental treatment regimen in Boston, "and saw what he went through, and saw the importance of it and my presence, and the dramatic effect it was having and the uncertainty as to whether the outcome [would be successful]"—the survival rate without the treatment, Ted said, was only 20 percent—"it was pretty inevitable to me what was going to happen. And I thought rather than sort of wait and drag that out on it, it didn't make any sense." After two years of pondering the race—a race, Carey Parker said, that might be his "best opportunity" to be president and one he had been eager to make—Ted kept coming back to his son. For the Kennedys, family always came first, even before ambition. In the end, he said, "I don't think that was a very complicated kind of decision."

He had been thinking seriously about abandoning the race throughout July of 1974 and arrived at his decision over Labor Day weekend at Hyannis Port, "in solitude," *Time* would report. He broke the news to his family, who seemed relieved at his decision, appreciating both the dangers of a run and how irreplaceable Ted was to the entire Kennedy clan as its paterfamilias. Arthur Schlesinger Jr. said he had raised the issue about a 1976 run at the Smiths' New York apartment while Rose Kennedy was visiting them and that Rose had immediately shrunk and that Jean Smith remained "somber and silent." Schlesinger concluded that the "Kennedy family is deeply and genuinely opposed to Ted's running," while Steve Smith thought Ted's candidacy "may become inevitable" but that Ted himself was "fatalistic about the risks" and "shifts according to the time of day from one of these positions to the other." But Ted was shifting no longer. He had come to his decision now, and at a cookout at the family compound on August 31, he told Dave Burke, his former administrative assistant, of his decision not to run. Burke, by one account, played devil's advocate—Burke's wife said that her husband and Ted sat on a wall at the compound drinking and talking well into the evening, long after everyone else had left, and she and her children sat there forlornly—but one friend told *Time* that Ted "wasn't asking for advice. He was saying, 'This is my decision. Now let's hear the arguments against it.'" Burke made them. Ted rejected them. Once again, the time just wasn't right.

There was a sense now that the time might never be right, that, as his advisers had felt in 1972, this would be his last chance. He had decided to withhold any public announcement, for fear of diluting his influence during the upcoming midterm elections; he had a number of speaking engagements scheduled, a fundraising swing for his fellow Democrats in Ohio and California, and a trip to Detroit for the AFL–CIO convention, where his friend and mentor, Senator Phil Hart, told the delegates, "To the tips of my fingers, I believe with my deepest conviction that if Ted Kennedy were to be president of the United States, there would be a belief abroad in this land that we would be a better people and this land a better place." It was only when Ted came to realize that he was not as instrumental to the midterm campaigns as he might have thought that he changed his mind on the timing. Tom Wicker wrote that Ted was "taken aback" when he learned that the big Democratic contributor Walter Shorenstein was backing Henry Jackson and when Edmund Brown Jr., who was running for governor in California, declined Ted's invitation to campaign for him, either fearing that Chappaquiddick was still a blight or that Ted's liberalism was. Several friends tried to get Ted to reconsider his decision later that September in Hyannis Port. But Ted was firm. He gathered Paul Kirk, Carey Parker, Ed Martin, Dick Drayne, Dave Burke, and Steve Smith at his Squaw Island house on Sunday, September 22, to draft a statement, and his secretary, Angelique Voutselas Lee, came up from Washington to type it. As the draft was being polished, Smith and Ted went sailing, but there was no wind—an ominous omen had there been a campaign.

With Joan at his side—she had flown in from the sanitarium in California—he broke the news on September 23. The press conference was held at the Parker House hotel dining room in Boston—the Kennedys had made announcements to run in the Senate Caucus Room—and he said unequivocally: "I will not accept the nomination. I will not accept a draft." He told the reporters that he had renounced running "to ease the apprehensions within my family about the possibility of my candidacy." And he said: "My primary responsibilities are at home."

And that was it—the "last of Joseph Kennedy's boys telling his guys that he would not be president . . . ever," wrote Robert Healy in *The Boston Globe.* And Healy wrote of Ted's old hands who had gathered at the Parker House that morning—among them Gerard Doherty, Dun Gifford, Ed Martin, Ted's friend Don Dowd, even his old driver, Jack Crimmins—they knew "the last hope was gone."

The "right decision," the *Los Angeles Times* editorialized, which would "spare his family further apprehension." He would likely have won the nomination, *Time* reported, and "was perhaps better suited than anybody else to unify the Democrats' left and right wings." But *Time* also reported that with the indelible stain of Chappaquiddick, the moral stain he bore, he would have a hard time beating Ford, unless the president made an economic gaffe, and that, in any case, "some of the Kennedy allure had been lost." It just wasn't the right time.

IV

There was something else that happened that September that may have convinced Ted Kennedy this wasn't the right time for him to run for the presidency, something that underscored how much the country had changed since Lyndon Johnson's presidency: mounting racial tension in his own backyard of Boston. Ted had been waging his battles for the black community for years, but getting funding for sickle-cell-anemia research or inserting provisions to encourage minority hiring were relatively easy battles—battles that had no direct, visible effect on white Americans. There were more difficult battles. One of those was the battle over integration, and of those integration battles, perhaps none was more difficult, none more incendiary, than the battle over school integration—a battle that would affect both black and white children. Since 1954, when the Supreme Court ruled in *Brown v. Board of Education* that schools segregated by state law were unconstitutional, the issue of how to integrate those schools had been contentious and often more than contentious—often violent. In the rural South, where black and white Americans generally lived in close proximity and school segregation was legally enforced through state action—*de jure*—there were ways of integrating the schools through redistricting and merging black school districts and white ones, notwithstanding the strenuous resistance to such efforts by white citizens. (Rather than integrate, some Southern counties, most notoriously Prince Edward County in Virginia, shut the public school system down entirely; in Prince Edward, they remained closed for five years.) But it was different in the cities of the North, most of which were segregated geographically rather than by law. In *Brown,* the court hadn't ruled that there was a constitutional right to integrated schools, only that schools could not be segregated by "state action," which is to say, by law. Later cases attacked urban *de facto* segregation—segregation in fact, not law—by allowing courts to use measures to integrate schools that were segregated by neighborhood, explicitly including busing (*Swann v. Charlotte-Mecklenburg*). These cases also broadened the definition of "state action" by including under that rubric various devices like gerryman-dered school districts, or "freedom of choice" (which had been widely used in the South to keep schools segregated after *Brown*), or discrimina-tory feeder schools, so long as there was "segregative intent" in those de-vices (*Keyes v. School District No. 1, Denver*). This was aimed squarely at segregation in the urban North.

But even as this opened those districts to court action, a problem re-mained: the remedy. Redistricting alone couldn't solve the problem in the urban North as it generally did in the rural South. In the North, one often had to *move* students from their neighborhood schools, which often meant busing students either from black neighborhoods to white schools or from white neighborhoods to black schools, or both. Since neighborhood schools were largely sacrosanct, and understandably so—parents didn't want their children traveling across the city for their education—busing was a provocative solution, even if race hadn't been involved, and, of course, it was. Ted had sponsored a bill in 1964 to provide federal funds to school boards to help them integrate their systems. It failed to pass. But no doubt thinking of the segregated schools in Boston and how busing might inflame racial tensions there—a reform group a year earlier had found that thirteen schools in the city were 90 percent black—he insisted on *Meet the Press* that March that he was opposed to busing. Racial segrega-tion remained. It remained even after Massachusetts became the first state to pass a "Racial Imbalance Act," in 1965, to withhold state funds from any school district that was racially imbalanced, with "imbalance" defined as a school being 50 percent or more black. It remained as law-suits were filed to declare the act unconstitutional. It remained as the Bos-ton School Committee—an institution dating back to the eighteenth century, to which members were elected—resisted the law as strenuously as school board members in the South had resisted integration there, all the while denying any racial intent in their opposition. It remained as black Bostonians continued to protest the inadequacies of their schools. It remained as an army of whites stormed the State House and stampeded the legislature to repeal the Racial Imbalance Act, just as the State Board of Education was about to implement a plan to integrate Boston schools. It remained as Governor Francis Sargent, attempting to find some accom-modation, vetoed the repeal early in 1974, then introduced a new plan with one-way busing for African Americans only and on a voluntary basis, basically gutting any integration attempt. It remained.

And, as it remained, lawsuits were filed by black citizens too, among them a class action by black parents in Dorchester and another by the NAACP, which were eventually joined into one case to be heard in federal District Court—a case to integrate those Boston schools. *Morgan v. Hennigan,* it was called, Morgan being Tallulah Morgan, a young black mother, and Hennigan being James Hennigan, the chairman of the Boston School Committee. To hear the case, Judge Wendell Arthur Garrity Jr. had drawn what most jurists thought was the short straw—short because everyone seemed to realize just how thankless this case would be, pitting, as it did, the increasingly enraged white Irish of South Boston, whose animosity had been stirred by the nearly all-Irish Boston School Committee, against the increasingly frustrated black Bostonians. The Irish–black tensions were long-standing and long-simmering; school integration simply brought them to a boil. Garrity certainly understood those tensions. He was deeply Irish himself, but he was lace-curtain Irish, educated at Holy Cross and Harvard Law School, and a far cry from the enraged Irishmen who had forced the repeal of the Racial Imbalance Act and now swore to stop anyone being bused into or out of their neighborhood. And Garrity was more. He was a Kennedy Democrat, a liberal Democrat, the organizer of Jack Kennedy's Wisconsin primary campaign against Hubert Humphrey and later a coordinator of a national registration effort on Jack's behalf in the general election. As a reward for his service, Jack had appointed him to the highly coveted position of United States attorney for Massachusetts. Four years later, Lyndon Johnson appointed him to the federal District Court bench—the new seat to which Francis X. Morrissey had been nominated before Ted withdrew the nomination under duress. And if Garrity had the pedigree of an egghead, he even looked like a supercilious egghead—balding with a high forehead and wearing thick, dark-framed glasses. And now, in the spring of 1972, Wendell Arthur Garrity Jr.—named for his father, who was named for the nineteenth-century Boston-born reformer and abolitionist, Wendell Phillips, though the junior Garrity went by his middle name—was to hear the case that had Boston on pins and needles, the case that would determine whether the School Committee had discriminated on the basis of race, and the case that would decide whether, if it had discriminated, students would be bused across the city—a city that was rigidly divided into proud ethnic enclaves.

The timing of the case couldn't have been less propitious. In 1971, the

U.S. House had already passed a provision to the education bill that banned busing, and Ted was among the conferees the next year when the Senate passed a less draconian bill. It was a fierce conference between the House and Senate—Nixon had rallied the opponents of busing—which ended with an agreement to postpone all federal orders for forced busing until 1974, unless the appeals process had been exhausted before then. Ted opposed the bill, one of only fifteen senators who did so, which was an indication of how politically radioactive busing had become. That same year, Nixon, up for reelection and playing the race card, sought to place an anti-busing referendum on the Florida primary ballot, which roused Ted to call Nixon's actions a "cruel hypocrisy" that belied Nixon's pledge to bring us together. (To be fair, Nixon had advocated for desegregation and had actually encouraged it, just not for forced busing.) Republicans understood the efficacy of the anti-busing appeal, and there were numerous debates on the Senate floor, ferocious debates, over the issue. And Republicans were not at all reluctant to use the anti-busing card to punish Democrats. "We had this conference," Ted would recall, "that I always remember very clearly, between the House and the Senate, as we were trying to get money to help on [racial] reconciliation—I think it was a community-services program at that time, to help communities that were going through various court decisions [to integrate]." And Ted said that Representative John Ashbrook, a conservative Ohio Republican, told him that there would be no conference report if the bill contained any money for reconciliation. Ted "didn't understand" the vehemence behind the Republican position, so Ashbrook told him: "The Republicans . . . the president wanted to see Boston burn. They wanted to teach us a lesson. If that's the only way they're [the Democrats] going to learn, it was going to burn, but it was going to be over his dead body that any money at all was going to go for reconciliation." And Ted said, "I remember that being one of the cruelest and nastiest comments."

Let Boston burn to teach liberals a lesson.

But Boston didn't burn then. Garrity was slow, deliberate, cautious, to make sure that his decision would not be overturned on appeal. He heard the case in the spring of 1972. He didn't issue his decision until two years later, on June 21, 1974. When he did, he determined that the School Committee had indeed operated with "segregative intent" in devising ways to keep black and white students divided into schools of their own and even in discriminating on the basis of race in assigning teachers. In the mean-

time, the State Education Department's Bureau of Equal Educational Opportunity, charged under the original Racial Imbalance Act with drawing
up a desegregation plan for the 1974–1975 school year, delivered its plan.
Six days after his decision, Garrity announced the remedy, which was the
plan the Bureau of Equal Educational Opportunity had devised. And
therein lay the problem. The plan not only required busing—sending
45,000 of Boston's 94,000 pupils to schools they would not have otherwise attended, and busing 18,000 of them, which the School Committee
opposed so vigorously that when Garrity offered the opportunity to submit a plan of its own, it rejected the offer because it could not counte-
nance a plan with any busing whatsoever—but it also merged diverse
districts into new districts to which students would be bused. (The decision was unpopular; 80 percent of white parents of school-age children in
Boston disagreed with Garrity's solution.) Two of those merged districts
were the Irish stronghold of South Boston, or Southie, and the impoverished black neighborhood of Roxbury: 1,271 white students to be bused to
Roxbury; 1,746 black students to be bused to Southie. This was an invitation to disaster. A "punitive" decision, one scholar would call it. A decision in which the liberal activists of the bureau, seemingly hostile to the
Irish after years of their attempts to stop integration, were looking for retribution. Garrity tried to wash his hands of the solution, saying he wasn't
the one who devised it; he was only implementing the best available plan,
as he was required to do by law. If violence ensued, he seemed to be saying, it wasn't on him. That did not pacify those Irish parents. They blamed
Arthur Garrity—blamed him for destroying their city. And they hated Arthur Garrity—hated him for destroying their city.

Ted Kennedy was hardly blind to the festering anger of those Irish parents. These had, after all, been Kennedy supporters. After voting against a
Republican bill in March 1974, one endorsed by President Nixon that
would have prohibited busing altogether—Ted said on the Senate floor
that the bill was the result of Nixon's "appeal to the fears and emotions of
the nation"—he had reluctantly voted later that year for an extension of
the 1965 Elementary and Secondary Education Act, which limited busing
to the closest or next-closest school. The House bill had a similar limitation but also provided a provision that would reopen the *Brown* decision to
make certain that previous desegregation plans abided by the new rule.
The extension would effectively stop desegregation in most urban areas,

even reverse it, and also contained a provision allowing parents to challenge court orders that violated this rule. On the floor, Ted argued, ruefully, that the only time there was an objection to busing was when it was used to desegregate schools. In fact, he said, there was less busing now than there was before the *Brown* decision, when busing was used to segregate schools. (In any case, Nixon threatened to veto the bill if it permitted any busing.) "A sad day for the country," *The New York Times* editorialized, "when the conferees must choose between a palpably unconstitutional provision [the provision to prevent desegregation] and another which seeks to impose some limits on the freedom of the courts [the provision that allowed parental lawsuits]." In the end, the conferees agreed to the limitations but said that the courts could overrule them if it was necessary to do so to ensure a student's constitutional rights. Senator Ed Gurney's amendment in March to prohibit busing—the amendment Nixon supported—had failed by a single vote. Such were the politics of busing. And such were the politics of busing, too, that when Richard Nixon resigned that August and Gerald Ford became president, he subscribed to Nixon's anti-busing position, despite his long support of civil rights—a position that only encouraged the more racially antediluvian elements of his own party to remain steadfast.

But all of this was before the Boston busing plan commenced late that summer of 1974, as the school year was about to begin. Ted was trapped in a conundrum. Boston was Ted's city. He could look out from his office on the twenty-fourth floor of the John F. Kennedy Federal Building and see the streets where his mother, his father, and his grandfather were born—Garden Court Street, Meridian Street in East Boston, and Ferry Street. He could see the old North Church, and St. Stephen's Church, where his mother had been baptized, and the Bunker Hill Monument, and the USS *Constitution* in Boston Harbor. If he leaned to the right, he could see Faneuil Hall. And if Boston was his city, Bostonians, especially those Irish Bostonians, were Ted's people. He liked them. He understood them. He had prided himself on being one of them. He had prided himself on serving them. He provided among the best constituent services of any senator, which was part of his problem. "Everyone thinks if Ted Kennedy wants it, it can be done," James King, who ran Ted's Boston office from 1968 to 1975, told James MacGregor Burns. "They think he can press a button and get things done. . . . They think he can wave a magic wand and the water would be calm." *His city. His people. His magic.* And now, with the busing decision upon his people in his city, Ted Kennedy was being looked at to wave his magic wand and make busing disappear. He spent time that summer trying to soothe the grievances. He met with the School Committee, with teachers, with white parents and black parents, with the attorney for the black plaintiffs—"a series of meetings," Ted said. And he met, too, with a new organization, an organization formed that June after Garrity's decree, an organization headed by Louise Day Hicks, a tough racial demagogue who also headed the School Committee—an organization the name of which expressed its aim and its temperament: Restore Our Alienated Rights (ROAR). "I think the real issue for me was what my role was going to be in this period of time," Ted was to say. "We tried, through a variety of different undertakings, to play a positive and constructive role in this whole process, I think with probably marginal kinds of effect."

But Ted Kennedy was being kind to himself. His effect wasn't marginal. His effect was feckless—even worse than feckless. There was no magic wand, and had there been, Ted had already broken it, as far as those working-class Irish were concerned, when he voted against Ed Gurney's amendment to end busing. That vote instantly made him an enemy of his people, as the vote of the state's Republican junior senator, Ed Brooke, the only African American in the Senate, had made him an enemy, even if he hadn't been black. That vote told them that Ted Kennedy was no longer on their side; he was on the side of the city's black citizens. At least that was how they felt—and they felt it now strongly. But even had Ted voted for the Gurney amendment, no magic wand could have changed Judge Arthur Garrity's decision—Arthur Garrity, over whose desk hung photographs of John and Robert Kennedy; Arthur Garrity, whom the Irish parents now saw as a Ted Kennedy stooge; Arthur Garrity, whose impeachment was cheered at anti-busing rallies, alongside calls for Ted's impeachment, because it was Ted Kennedy's liberalism that had brought the city to this. And Ted Kennedy, though he had never heartily embraced Garrity's decision and though he had filmed public-service spots calling for moderation, didn't necessarily want to change the import of Garrity's decision, which was his conundrum. He was trapped between the people he had loved and served and the people he also loved and for whom he sought justice. Ted Kennedy, the brother and the legatee of John and Robert, could hardly argue against school integration, though to prohibit busing would be doing just that; it would violate his every moral principle.

And while he sympathized with the wrathful Irish of Southie, sympathized with them having their children bused, he did not, could not, sympathize with the racism with which they greeted Garrity's decision, however wrongheaded or insensitive that decision may have been.

Yet *Boston Globe* columnist Mike Barnicle, a friend of Ted's and a self-styled voice of the city's blue-collar Irish, still believed in the wand. On September 8, the day before a ROAR rally to be held in the City Hall Plaza in front of the John F. Kennedy Federal Building—a rally to protest Garrity's decision and a rally three days before the beginning of the new school year—Barnicle wrote an "open letter" to the senator, in which he called upon him to intervene in the brewing warfare. "You are the one man who can heal the divisions that have arisen over the issue of busing," Barnicle wrote. "You have the voice that can help keep this city calm, leaving the clear ring of justice and common sense." He called on Ted to invoke his brothers, to tell his restive community that "law knows no neighborhood, that justice is not confined to any one block, that fear must be put aside and the fact of law adhered to." And Barnicle wrote, "And, to you, Senator Kennedy, they would listen."

Whether or not the white parents would listen to Kennedy, given their anger at him as a turncoat, Kennedy listened to Barnicle, who had phoned him that weekend at Hyannis Port to make a personal appeal to him to attend the ROAR rally—a rally at which Ted must have known he would be vilified but one at which Barnicle thought he could be a tempering force. Ted seemed uncertain about what to do, even on the very morning of September 9. ("Don't go," his Senate idol, Phil Hart, had warned.) He was scheduled to visit four high schools that day—four of the high schools to be integrated. By late morning a group of six disgruntled white mothers, representatives from ROAR, were already occupying Ted's office, waiting to meet him and present a list of demands, among which were that he arrange a moratorium on busing—impossible for him to do—and that he bus his own children to schools in black neighborhoods. But there was to be no meeting. Instead, Ted did something impulsive, something dangerous, something nearly inexplicable, but something he no doubt felt Bobby would have done. "I remember we were driving down Cambridge Street in Boston, coming up to the Kennedy Building," Joseph Kennedy II, Bobby's eldest son, would recall, "and you could start to hear this fantastic throng of people demonstrating." Joe said that the car stopped, and several of Ted's staffers—Paul Kirk, Ed Martin, Robert Bates—pushed themselves inside. "Everybody was just, like, dumbfounded by the sheer size of the number of people," which was estimated at between eight thousand and ten thousand. The staffers, concerned for Ted's safety, advised him to have the car drive around the back of the building so he could sneak into his office. But these protesters were Ted Kennedy's people—people who had turned on him, but his people nonetheless—and Ted did not want to slink away into the back entrance, nor did he want to wade into the angry crowd surrounded by a phalanx of advisers as if he were terrified of them. "I thought I ought to go by myself," he would say. "I didn't want it to look like I was coming over there with a group."

Ted and his advisers waited in the car—waited to see what to do next.

There was a "moment" then, as Joe Kennedy described it, when all of them, Ted and the advisers, were sitting nervously in the car, the crowd swelling around them, a furious crowd, and Ted looked at Joe and Joe looked back at Ted and Ted looked at a policeman outside the car and Ted finally said, "Let's go," and "off he went . . . right into the middle of that crowd and went up to the front of it." He would later tell J. Anthony Lukas, who wrote a book about the Boston busing crisis, "They had thrown out a challenge, implied that I didn't have the guts. So I felt it was important not to back down from that, to go ahead and confront them."

Heading to the makeshift stage, he waded into the crowd—*through* the crowd, since it parted—waded through insults and angry shouts, waded through the thousands of protesters, mainly women, mainly young, many of them wearing sunglasses and short-sleeve blouses on the warm day, many of them holding signs: IMPEACH KENNEDY; BOSTON IS UNDER THE HEEL OF THE KGB—KENNEDY, GARRITY, BROOKE; HELL NO, WE WON'T GO. And they shouted: "There he is! There he is! There he is!" And one shouted: "You're a disgrace to the Irish." He arrived at the platform the group had erected in front of the building to a chorus of boos, just after Mrs. Rita Graul, an officer of ROAR, had introduced two people wearing chicken masks—one white, one brown—the first identified as Edward Kennedy, the second as Edward Brooke. "What do you want to do, speak?" a protest leader named John Kerrigan snarled at Ted, no chicken now. "You're not going to speak. You've taken away our rights. We're going to take away your rights. How do you like that?" But another leader, Tom O'Connell, a father of seven, grabbed the microphone and asked the crowd to let Ted speak. They wouldn't. O'Connell said that Ted asked him why they wouldn't, and McConnell said that they would listen "when he had the guts to put his child on the same bus to Roxbury as mine." And then the crowd spontaneously began to sing "God Bless America," and as they sang, they turned their backs and faced the building in a sign of disrespect to the senator who had once been the pride of the Irish. And when the song ended, they did an about-face, and Kerrigan gave a brief speech and then several other ROAR leaders spoke. But when Ted, still standing on that platform, reached for the microphone, he was thwarted—the ROAR officers actually covered the mic with their hands to silence him. "I've listened to you," Ted shouted. "Now let me say what I need to say." But that only further incensed the crowd. Defeated, unable to speak, Ted began to descend the stairs from the platform and wade back through the crowd some fifty yards to the Kennedy Building entrance. But this time, the snarling crowd hurled invective—"One-legged son. Send him to Roxbury!" "Let your daughter get bused there so she can get raped!" "Why don't you let them shoot you like they shot your two brothers?"—and racial epithets, horrible epithets. And invective wasn't the only thing the crowd hurled. Some threw raw eggs, some rotten tomatoes. One woman hit Ted on the shoulder with her fist. One man tried to kick him. "A sense of palpable fear" was how Robert Bates, whom Ted had ordered to end his Cape Cod vacation to be there, described the atmosphere. "Scary," said Joe II. "I was afraid they were going to hurt him," Ed Martin would recall. Others attacked his car. Lukas said that Ted stepped quickly, his head down. But Ted insisted he didn't slink away. On the contrary, he kept stopping, kept turning to face the crowd because, he said, he understood that "crowds like these are always cowards. . . . If you're facing them, they're always reluctant." And as he stopped, the crowd stopped advancing on him. But when he started walking again toward the building entrance, the crowd would begin moving too, surging, closing in on him, threatening him. By this point, Paul Kirk and several of the other staffers were plunging through the crowd to get to Ted, to protect him, but it was too late. When Ted got to within thirty yards of those doors, he bolted, which ignited the crowd to new delirium, throwing rocks now and rushing forward, pounding a plate-glass panel in rhythm to their chants and smashing it and cheering lustily, while Ted raced to safety inside. And Kirk said he thought: *How will it be if the United States senator who's taken a position on an issue can't get into his own office?* An aide of Louise Day Hicks, the instigator of the rally, saw the ruckus differently. "It was great," she enthused. "It's about time the politicians felt the anger of the people. We've been good for too long. They'd pat us on the backs, and we'd go home. No more." Ted boiled afterward at his staff over his being blindsided—"Why didn't I know about this? Who did the advance?"—even though no one on his staff knew he was going to attend the rally and even though anyone could have anticipated the reaction. And afterward, his face puffy, his eyes bloodshot, his hands shaking as he held a Styrofoam cup of coffee, "visibly shaken," by one report, he had his own verdict. He said that he understood the protesters' anger but that there couldn't be two rules, one for Birmingham and another for Boston.

But there was another takeaway from the riotous events that morning on the City Hall Plaza of Boston when Ted Kennedy tried to placate the crowd. He was no longer one of them. He was just another condescending liberal who favored minority rights over their rights. "Teddy in that one defining moment became the focus of the anti-busing movement in the city of Boston and, to some degree, nationally," Joe Kennedy II would say. And with that focus, Ted Kennedy could no longer realistically harbor dreams of running for the presidency in 1976, not with the tide against busing running so high. With that focus, Ted Kennedy had lost his constituency. And they had lost him.

Two weeks later, he announced his decision not to run.

Washing his hands of the violence that might ensue: That had been Judge Arthur Garrity's wish when he implemented the plan—not, he made it plain, his own plan—that merged the two disparate districts of South Boston and Roxbury. And violence did ensue. The schools opened on September 12, 1974, three days after the ROAR rally, and when the buses carrying the black students pulled up to South Boston High School, as J. Anthony Lukas would report it, there were crowds of angry Irish parents waiting for it, shouting at it: "Niggers, go home!" When the buses pulled up again at the end of the school day to take those black students back to Roxbury, those angry Irish parents returned, this time throwing, as Lukas would report, eggs, beer bottles, soda cans, and rocks at the buses, shattering windows and hurting the black students inside those buses. On one of those buses, at Ted's insistence, was his aide Robert Bates. "Bring your ass over here!" Ted had ordered, and so Bates rode that bus from Roxbury to South Boston, rode it as the irate whites rocked it, trying to overturn it while the black students froze inside, "scared to death," as Bates put it. The whole city was taut, edgy. Three hundred police officers from the Tactical Patrol Force were assigned to Dorchester Avenue, the main thoroughfare of Southie, to keep peace, but a brick was thrown through a patrol-car window. A Haitian immigrant picking up his wife from her job in Southie was stopped at a red light when a gang of angry whites surrounded his car, pulled him out, chased him down the street, and beat him mercilessly while yelling, "Get the nigger!" He was saved, by one account, only because a white police officer fired warning shots. When a black student at South Boston High stabbed a white student that October, whites flocked to the school and blocked black students from leaving. "Niggers eat shit!" they screamed, as their leader, Louise Day Hicks, wielding a bullhorn, tried to get them to let the blacks exit the school. But they rebuffed her. Not even Hicks, who had ridden racism to her position on the School Committee and then to one term in the House of Representatives, could wrangle them now.

A city taut, edgy, and in chaos. That was Boston as its white citizens fought busing to integrate their schools. And worse was yet to come. While Garrity worked that fall on what was called "Phase II," a plan designed to integrate the entire school system—all two hundred schools, and not just eighty as he had that September, a broader plan, a supposedly new and improved plan, a plan that might actually mitigate some of the failings of the first integration plan—the anxiety and the anger among those Irish parents continued to mushroom. And they directed a good deal of that anger at Ted Kennedy, the new symbol of the busing movement, the man who seemed to personify the elitist bureaucratic indifference of the court, even though Ted had almost nothing to do with busing and nothing whatsoever to do with Garrity's plans, other than to call for respect for the law—the law that ordered students to be bused. And Ted had hardly been strident in that call. (Asked repeatedly after the City Hall Plaza rally whether he believed in busing, he answered that he believed in "quality education," which was really no answer at all but not an endorsement of busing either.) He reached out to the aggrieved parents. He met in his Boston office with seventy protesters—met with them for seven hours—while Rita Graul, the woman who had introduced the men in the chicken masks at the City Plaza rally, introduced each of the people in that room to Ted, introduced them slowly, and gave him a detailed family history of each: "Oh, golly. Now we'll hear from Mary over here. Mary O'Sullivan. You know the O'Sullivans . . . She's got two nice children, Megan and Sean. Sean was on the baseball [team]. He can't play baseball anymore, Senator," presumably because of busing. "Do your kids play baseball?" And then, unfailingly from Rita Graul, "Why are you torturing her kids?" Or, "Why are you doing this to us, and why are you doing this to me?" Ted would remark, "Seven hours of it," with a sense of both awe and exhaustion. And of Graul, he said, "The toughest cookie I've ever seen."

But it was seldom so civil as that. Protesters followed Ted now, dogged him, showed up at his appearances en masse, disrupted his hearings when he held them in Boston, and he had made a point throughout his career of being in Boston as often as he could manage it. "We never took a plane in our lives, and we can't afford it," shouted Elvira "Pixie" Palladino, a ROAR leader, when Ted conducted a hearing on airline deregulation, and then Palladino asked, "What about forced busing?" Of Louise Day Hicks, ROAR's doughty leader, Ted said, "You could spot her a half a mile away." But Pixie Palladino would just suddenly appear as if out of nowhere— "you walked into some hotel lobby and, boom, she was there with all her people, and standing in front of you, not letting you move, wanting you to push her or do something"—and wherever Ted was, Pixie was, shouting at him at the "top of her lungs." One scholar of the anti-busing protest wrote, "Hounding him like a banshee."

The nastiest, most violent of these confrontations occurred on April 6, 1975, after a Knights of Columbus breakfast at Atlantic Junior High School in Quincy, outside Boston. Once the ROAR contingent got wind of Ted's speech, several hundred packed into trucks in South Boston and Charlestown and headed to the venue. "It was pretty obvious that they had been drinking," Barbara Souliotis, the manager of Ted's Boston office, said. "We could see the beer on the trucks." And not just drinking. The group was clearly spoiling for a fight. "A very hostile crowd," Souliotis called them. She told Bill Connors, the chairman of the breakfast and an old friend of the Kennedys, to keep Ted and his aides inside after Ted had finished, while she phoned the state police. Ted didn't listen. He headed out into the crowd anyway, with Souliotis, his crusty old driver, Jack Crimmins, and his aide Jimmy King, a big man, hoping to escape, but when they got to King's car, they saw that the tires had been slashed, the windshield had been egged, the car had been plastered with stickers—STOP FORCED BUSING—and the door handles had been smeared with dog excrement. Some in the crowd had climbed onto the roof of the car, and some of the women protesters put their toddlers in front of the tires. It was useless. And now the mob, some three hundred of them, seething, raging, seeing that Ted had no way out, encircled him and began to close in, spitting on him, shouting at him, shoving him, snatching at his sleeves. One woman repeatedly jabbed him with the point of an American flag. "A dangerous situation," Souliotis said. Ted was trapped. So he began walking—purposefully, even though he had no idea where he was going. "Do we have a friend around here?" he asked an aide nervously—this, a man who had thousands of friends in Massachusetts. "Do they have a house? There must be somebody around here who's got a house." But his aides were just as lost as he was, and no one knew of a supporter nearby with a house. So they kept walking, still purposefully, but in truth they were walking aimlessly. And the crowd now followed, taunting him, yelling at him. When he passed a bus, the crowd shouted sarcastically, "Why don't you take the bus, Ted?" With a cordon of police and aides trying to protect him, Ted spotted an MTA station—the entrance to the North Quincy subway train—and he turned to Jimmy King and said, "Jimmy, we've got to get in there." And though it seemed the only path of escape, Ted was also aware that he could be trapped on the platform, waiting for the train to arrive, while the crowd surged, maybe even blocking the entrance. So Ted had to feint, as if he was going somewhere else, while Jimmy King headed to the station entrance, a gate, and when Ted got about fifty yards away, he made a mad dash. Now members of the crowd were shouting, "He's headed to the subway station!" And they were chasing him, carrying pickets they had torn from fences. One protester grabbed his leg, but the police pulled the man off. Ted and Souliotis squeezed through the gate, the only access to the station, and King pushed it closed and braced himself against it while the mob tried to push it open. Meanwhile, Ted and Souliotis raced down the stairs to the subway, which, thankfully for him, arrived soon after—sheer providence. Ted boarded the car—leapt on the train, he would say—headed for Boston, and it rumbled off. And as it did, the angry mob threw rocks at its windows. Some of them jumped in their cars, apparently hoping to follow the train and harass Ted when he got off, but they lost it.

And now, at last, he was safe but, as *The New York Times* described him afterward, "irritated" and "bedraggled." Ted and Souliotis disembarked in, of all places, South Boston, the very source of the anger (though Ted's press secretary, Dick Drayne, would say that he believed most of the protesters had actually come from the Italian enclave of East Boston, which had not been affected by Garrity's ruling). They headed to Crimmins's house—Crimmins, as Irish as they came, who would argue with Ted about "busing the niggers"—where they laid low until they felt they could leave. But later that day, after canceling another appearance when word came that the protesters would be harassing him there, Ted told a group of Democratic town committeemen that he wasn't concerned about the effect busing would have on his Senate reelection chances the following fall. "I've taken a stand," he said. "I haven't changed it. We'll have to let the chips fall where they may." The schools had to be integrated.

And when the schools opened that September of 1975 for the new year, the violence continued, "eddied through the streets at night," as *Newsweek* put it, "as residents attacked the most available symbol of court-ordered busing"—when Ted wasn't available—the police, whom the white residents now saw as an occupation force. As *Newsweek* reported it, protesters tossed Molotov cocktails at the officers and spread an oil slick on a steep street to deter motorcycle cops from following them. One seventeen-year-old Southie Irish boy told *Newsweek* of the new legal order the Southie boys had established: "If you're going to hit a nigger, you might as well take his wallet too. That way the cops get you for assault or robbery—not for violating civil rights." (When Southerners used the reprehensible word, they pronounced it "nigra," almost as if to soften its ugliness, but in Southie, where the word was sneered, it was pronounced with both hard "g" sounds, its full ugliness unrelieved.) Meanwhile, black residents formed what they called neighborhood "internal security" units. But there was no security. Someone dynamited the Suffolk County Courthouse, injuring twenty-four, and police fielded thirty bomb threats shortly thereafter. One bomb spoke again to the rage that continued to boil against Ted: A firebomb on the night of September 8, almost exactly a year to the day of the City Hall Plaza rally, tore through John Kennedy's modest two-story birthplace on Beals Street in Brookline, leaving $100,000 in damage. The "bombing of the shrine," some locals called it. And on the sidewalk outside, in thick black paint, the perpetrator had spray-painted: BUS TEDDY.*

---

*That perpetrator, it turned out, was the notorious Boston mobster Whitey Bulger, who also set fire to a school near the home of Arthur Garrity. "He wanted to make a point," an associate told *The Boston Globe*. "He liked to say he was doing something active to fight busing. He was and is a racist." Shelley Murphy, "Bulger Linked to '70s Antibusing Attacks," April 22, 2001.

Teddy's people they had been, but Teddy's people they were no longer. "Teddy's no longer welcome here," said a Charlestown saloonkeeper named William Sullivan, at whose tavern, Sully's, John Kennedy had kicked off his first congressional campaign and where there was still a yellowed photo of him on the wall. "He couldn't chance coming in here now," Sullivan said of Ted. Ted had to travel the city, *his* city, with two Boston policemen—the only time he had had security except when Nixon assigned the Secret Service to him. He was an outsider. "They look down on people of color like me," said Pixie Palladino, "they" being the Kennedys, and "people of color" being her and the other Italians. After the bombings, Ted marched with Ed Brooke in a demonstration to restore peace to the streets. But there would be no peace.

Perhaps more than any other issue, busing had come to symbolize not only the imposition of liberal elitism on ordinary folks who had never had any great affinity for African Americans to begin with but also the end of liberalism's moral authority among the working class, who had once been the backbone of American liberalism. And Ted Kennedy, never a great defender of busing, had, as his nephew said, nevertheless come to symbolize it. He, like Bobby, had managed to straddle the white blue-collar and black communities and had offered the promise of some convergence of the segments of the underclass against the forces of wealth. This had been one of Bobby's greatest appeals and one of his greatest hopes. Ted had inherited both. Samuel Beer, who had been one of Ted's early mentors, had written to Ted back in 1968, after Bobby's death, of a conversation Beer had had with a Croatian construction worker in Chicago, who told him, "We're fucking tired of feeding niggers," and Beer had told Ted that the conservatives, clearly thinking of Nixon, were "bamboozling" the white working class with appeals to racial hatred but that Ted, now that Bobby was gone, was the only one who could keep the "old coalition as well as win the new ones." For a time, Ted, no doubt, thought so too; it was certainly one of the reasons he went to visit George Wallace, beyond the political expedience of it. But race was too divisive, the conservative appeals to race hatred too powerful, the revulsion against busing too all-consuming, for the coalition—a fragile one to begin with—to hold, and when Ted didn't denounce busing, when he couldn't reverse Garrity's busing plan, he became a traitor to his people. (Indeed, Louise Day Hicks, Pixie Palladino, and John Kerrigan were all Democrats.)

The wand—the wand had failed, and the onetime ethnic Democrats blamed Ted for not working his magic. They "seemed to think that he could stop busing but didn't," James King said. And on the other side, the "blacks and white liberals felt that if he came out stronger, there would be no trouble." King believed that "Ted saw this coming, knew that the old coalitions were breaking down." Joseph Kennedy II traced the divorce to that morning on City Hall Plaza when Ted was silenced, humiliated, harassed. "That had to do with the sense of abandonment of white America," he would say years later, "particularly in blue-collar, working-class neighborhoods. . . . This is a fight about whether or not blue-collar America gets the resources it needs to survive." And he said that Teddy walked into those "crosshairs" that day. "Reactionary populism," the scholar Ronald Formisano called it, noting the thin line that had always separated populism from reactionary politics: Since populism was based on grievance, those grievances could cut against the power elite, in which case the populism would have a liberal bent, or against competing groups, in which case it would have a conservative bent, though in busing, class resentments got entangled with race resentments. A thin line it was, and with busing, many crossed from progressive populism to conservatism. And to them, Ted himself had crossed over, from populism to elitism, from one who understood their grievances to one who felt they had to capitulate to a new moral order that they didn't want and didn't understand. Those blue-collar Irish, Ted's old people, had to bus their children, had to accept black children to their schools. The white liberals, the Ted Kennedys of the world, didn't. The "real issue," as John Kerrigan, the man who forbade Ted from speaking, put it, "is that those who can escape escape." Kerrigan wasn't wrong. The liberals, in their self-righteousness, were making those working-class white citizens do things that they themselves didn't do and might not have done if they were in the same position as those whites. The epithets were vile, the violence worse. The racism was real and unconscionable. But the failure of liberalism to address the grievances was unconscionable too. Ted understood all of this. "In their eyes, I had become just one more of those Boston elitists who didn't care about ordinary people and their children." But he felt he couldn't just turn his back on social justice either. Instead, the Democrats, most of whom supported school integration, lost their moral authority among those ordinary people as well as many of their voters.

J. Anthony Lukas, whose Pulitzer Prize–winning book *Common Ground* was an account of the Boston busing crisis, made the same observation as

tions that provided support for that journey. The Woodrow Wilson International Center for Scholars in Washington, D.C., gave me a public policy scholarship that allowed me to work in Washington and use the resources there. The Center also gave me the services of Nick Charles, a wonderful young man and able research assistant who shared my enthusiasm for this project and went above and beyond the call of duty to aid it. I shall always remember prowling the dark bowels of the National Archives with him and rummaging through boxes of materials, hoping we might find some gold nugget. Occasionally we did. I am also indebted to the Shorenstein Center on Media, Politics and Public Policy at Harvard University, which awarded me a fellowship. My four months at the Center were invigorating and productive. In addition, they allowed me to spend time in Boston, roaming Senator Kennedy's old stomping grounds. That debt extends to the entire staff, but especially to Alex Jones, the then director, who was unfailingly encouraging; to Thomas Patterson, who sharpened my arguments and taught me a thing or two about quantitative research; and to Alexi White, another brilliant young scholar who assisted me, enthused with me over discoveries, listened to me work out ideas and helped me with them, and generated the graphs and charts in the paper I wrote there on Edward Kennedy and his relationship to the press. Another debt goes to the C. V. Starr Center for the Study of the American Experience at Washington College in Chestertown, Maryland, where I was the Patrick Henry Writing Fellow, for which one of the perquisites was getting to live in Patrick Henry's house during the fellowship term. I owe special gratitude to Adam Goodheart, the Starr Center's director, and to Jenifer Emley, then the program coordinator, who was a great support, a patient listening post, and a kind and generous friend. The months I spent in Chestertown were rewarding ones, both in terms of work and friendship.

At the many institutions, too many to list, that I visited or with which I corresponded, I owe special debts to Stephen Plotkin at the John F. Kennedy Presidential Library, who was always more than helpful on my visits there; to Donald Ritchie, the former Senate historian, at the Senate Historical Office, who kindly answered many questions, directed me to sources, and took me on an unforgettable tour of the Capitol and to Senator Kennedy's hideaway off the Senate floor; to the entire staff of the National Archives who enabled me to examine the Senate records there and whose cooperation was very much appreciated; to Barbara Perry, Robert Martin, Marc Selverstone, and Brian Balogh at the Miller Center, who withstood many requests from me over the years, especially as I awaited the release of the Edward Kennedy oral histories, and who fielded many questions; to Randall Flaherty at the University of Virginia Law School; and to Francine Lane, Corrine Page, Meghan Pease, and Anne Jones at the Amagansett Free Library, who uncomplainingly and diligently filled my hundreds of requests for material over the decade during which I worked on this book.

I am also indebted to Robert Reeves, who, as the chairman of the Creative Writing and Literature Program and now the associate provost of Southampton Graduate Arts Program of the State University of New York at Stony Brook, where I have taught for a decade, has extended to me more kindnesses than I can possibly repay and who has been a steadfast friend. My colleagues at Stony Brook deserve thanks as well. And I thank my students, who have shared my enthusiasms as I teach them the works of my favorite writers—my instructions are simple: Read the best, steal from the best, and make it your own—for never allowing me stagnate.

Since, in some sense, biography is an ongoing, even collaborative process, I owe enormous gratitude to all those Edward Kennedy biographers who preceded me: among them, James MacGregor Burns, Peter Canellos, Lester David, Burton Hersh, Max Lerner, Murray Levin and T. A. Repak, Theo Lippman, Jr., and especially the late Adam Clymer, who made provision to place his notes and interviews at the John F. Kennedy Library where they are available to scholars and provide an invaluable source. I stood on the shoulders of all these men.

Among the inhabitants of my village were a great many friends without whom I could never have continued over the ten plus years I researched and wrote. The inestimable Bill Moyers is a national treasure, with whom I was fortunate enough to work for two years writing a column on his billmoyers.com website and for whom I have the highest admiration and deepest affection; one could do no better when writing a book on political morality than to think of Bill. My television and film manager Deborah Miller and her husband, Sandy Lakoff, the Dickson professor emeritus of political science at the University of California–San Diego, eagerly read the manuscript and provided feedback, and Sandy's eye kept me from errors of fact, while his wisdom kept me from errors of judgment; they are more than friends, and I cannot imagine having written this book without them. Deborah's colleague, Bob Bookman, who was generous enough to phone me years ago and offer his assistance in helping me secure film and television work to support my writing, has given me friendship and advocacy, and I am grateful for both. My dear friend Elizabeth Bassine read the early chapters of the book despite ongoing issues with her sight and encouraged me when I most needed encouragement. My friend Elaine Grove listened to me discuss the book over many hours on many dog walks and did so without the slightest hint of boredom, at least visibly. My friends Inda Eaton and Annemarie McCoy also listened, and Annemarie, a tech wizard, provided me with essential computer assistance when I needed to reconfigure my tens of thousands of notecards after the company that provided my notetaking software disappeared while I was in the middle of the project. Phil Rosenthal and Monica Horan, two wonderful people, were truly friends indeed at a time of need. Rich Bradley read the first part of the manuscript and offered suggestions. Bob Spitz, a celebrated biographer and good friend, offered commiseration, as only one who does this for a living can. Ian Lynch provided research assistance in the final stages and earned my absolute trust. I am grateful, too, to John Taylor Williams, who introduced me to Patrick Kennedy, and to Patrick for breaking the Kennedy *omerta* and agreeing to speak with me. Gratitude is also due all those who consented to be interviewed, despite the Kennedy disapprobation. Craig Hoffman, who has been a friend for well over thirty years, was always there.

In my literary family, I am fortunate to have the support of my agent Joy Harris, an indefatigable defender of her authors, who managed to keep me above water financially and otherwise, and whose confidence in me never flagged. Every author should be so lucky. And I was fortunate, too, to have the support of her associate, Adam Reed, who performed so many thankless tasks and did them so agreeably. My gratitude to both of them is boundless.

At Crown, my new publishing family, I was the recipient of a gift every author dreams about and too seldom receives: people who cared about the book as if it was their own. Christopher Brand designed the beautiful jacket. Fritz Metsch provided the elegant interior design. They made the book lovely. Dennis Ambrose, the production editor who shepherded the book from manuscript to printed text, brought a keen eye and a fine comb to the task. He made the book better. Lydia Morgan did everything else and then some.

And then there is Kevin Doughten. When John Glusman left Crown, the book was adopted by Rachel Klayman, who, thankfully, never once asked me why it was taking me so long and who supported me on those occasions when I needed support. When Rachel was diverted to other projects, the book was assigned to a new parent in Kevin. Kevin had not signed the book, nor had he been with me through the long research process. It was essentially a foundling, albeit a rather old foundling, placed on his doorstep. But from the moment he took it in, he bestowed upon the book the greatest attention and respect. He read it carefully, made astute suggestions, and was an unstinting champion of it. In addition, Kevin insisted that this very long book be published in two volumes rather than be amputated into one. He was a true collaborator and a friend. I cannot imagine a happier publishing experience than the one I had. That was Kevin's doing. Special doesn't begin to describe him.

Then my family. My daughters, Laurel and Tänne, my son-in-law Braden, whose legal accomplishments I have already extolled, my daughter-in-law, Shoshanna, and my granddaughter, Sadie, have provided me with incomparable pride, joy, and love. Words should never fail a writer. Here they do. I am blessed beyond words. And lastly Christina. Like Dilsey, she endured.

It goes without saying that no one acknowledged here is responsible for any errors of fact or judgment or infelicity of prose. Those deficiencies are mine alone. Those acknowledged are blameless for everything except the support and encouragement they provided a writer in need and one so deeply appreciative of them.

NOTES

ABBREVIATIONS

BG   *The Boston Globe*
EMK   Edward M. Kennedy
Int.   Interview
JPK   Joseph P. Kennedy
LAT   *Los Angeles Times*
Lib.   Library
Ltr.   Letter
NYT   *The New York Times*
WSJ   *The Wall Street Journal*
WP   *The Washington Post*

INTRODUCTION: THEY CAME

xiii **"embrace you in love":** http://www.capecodtimes.com/article/20090827/NEWS/908270313.
xiv   **"The last was first":** Ray Henry, *The Boston Globe*, "Kennedy Motorcade Departs for Boston," Aug. 27, 2009.
xiv   **Leaving Hyannis Port, entering Boston:** "Ted Kennedy Leaves Hyannis Port the Last Time," Aug. 27, 2009, https://www.youtube.com/watch?v=FMhPR3mdImM; "Mourning a Kennedy Brother Again," *The New York Times*, Aug. 30, 2009; "Kennedy Motorcade Departs for Boston," *Huffington Post*, August 27, 2009; "A Swelling Tide of Emotion," *BG*, Aug. 28, 2009; wbur.org/news/2009/08/26/kennedy-hyannisport.
xv   **"Shed a Little Light":** "Taylor Sings Tribute to Kennedy," http://archive.boston.com/ae/music/articles/2009/08/28/james_taylor_sings_tribute_to_senator_edward_kennedy/.
xv   **Red Sox:** "Red Sox Pay Tribute to Kennedy," AP, Aug. 26, 2009.
xvi   **It was a national mourning:** "Across U.S., Activists Hail Their Advocate," *BG*, Aug. 28, 2009; "Kennedy's Senate Desk Draped in Black," politcalticker.blogs.cnn.com/.
xvi   **"Esteemed by almost everyone":** E. J. Dionne Jr., "Compassionate Liberalism," *Commonweal*, Sept. 11, 2009.
xvi   **"manners and morals":** Matt Bai, "A Dynasty in Decline," *Newsweek*, June 23, 1997.
xvi   **"senior statesman":** Ted Sorensen, "The Kid Brother," *Time*, Aug. 26, 2009.
xvi   **"Elvis, Marilyn and Ringo. . . .":** **Steven** Stark, "The Cultural Meaning of the Kennedys," *The Atlantic*, Jan. 1994.
xvii **"part of American culture":** "The Kennedy Challenge," *Time*, Nov. 5, 1979.
xvii **"We needed to say goodbye":** "Hundreds Turn Out to Witness End of Era," *USA Today*, Aug. 31, 2009.
xvii **"most powerfully centered":** Tom Wicker, "The Importance of Being Kennedy," *NYT*, July 27, 1969.
xvii **"everything was safe":** "Mourning a Kennedy Brother, Again," NYT, August 27, 2009.
xviii **"He wants to know he mattered":** Melody Miller to author.

xviii "his name on **more legislation**": Robert Byrd interview, Clymer Papers, Series 2, Box 3, Folder B, JFK Library, Feb. 12, 1993.

xviii "**He's one of the most effective legislators**": Tom Daschle, quoted in "The Torchbearer," *People*, Aug. 16, 1999.

xviii "**it would be Ted Kennedy**": Paul Simon, *P. S.: The Autobiography of Paul Simon* (Chicago: Bonus Books, 1999), 2,003.

xviii "**my thirty-eight years in the Senate**": Kirk Victor, *Making Government Work* (Columbia: University of South Carolina Press, 2008), p. 85.

xviii "**he's productive and effective**": Robert Dole int., Miller Center, UVA, May 15, 2006.

xviii "**they'll find a spot for him somewhere**": Charles Pierce, "Kennedy Unbound," *Boston Globe Magazine*, Jan. 5, 2003.

xviii "**only one name comes up—Kennedy**": David Brooks, "The Prosaic Ted Kennedy," *NYT*, Aug. 26, 2009.

xviii "**the Calhouns, the Clays, and the Websters**": Doris Kearns Goodwin on MSNBC, May 20, 2008.

xviii "**ninth-child talent**": Martin Nolan, "Kennedy Dead at 77," *BG*, Aug. 26, 2009.

xviii "**What did Webster do?**": Edmund Reggie int., Miller Center, UVA, Dec. 16, 2008.

xviii "**more than most presidents**": Thomas Oliphant, "The Lion at Rest," *Democracy*, Winter 2010, 100.

xix "**associated in one way or another**": *CBS Evening News*, Aug. 26, 2009.

xx "**today if not for him**": Nick Littlefield int., Miller Center, UVA, Feb. 14, 2009.

xx "**mantra of pragmatism**": Robert Caro, *The Years of Lyndon Johnson: The Passage of Power* (New York: Knopf, 2012), xviii.

xx "**but prose**": Brooks.

xx "**The Brother Who Mattered Most**": Richard Lacayo, "The Brother Who Mattered Most," *Time*, Aug. 26, 2009.

xxi "**test of time**": Jeffrey Blattner int., Miller Center, UVA, March 30, 2007.

xxi "**To make gentler the human condition**": Thomas Rollins int., Miller Center, UVA, May 14, 2009.

xxi "**opposing them with any force**": James Carroll, "The End of the Dream," *The New Republic*, June 24, 1991.

xxii " 'we can light those beacon fires again' ": Lacayo.

xxiii "**wage has been raised again**": Littlefield int., Miller Center, UVA, May 3, 2008.

xxiii "**we felt happened to our family**": "Deep Into Night, Memories Carry Throngs to Wake," *BG*, Aug. 28, 2009.

xxiv **Letter to children**: Patrick Kennedy and Stephen Fried, *A Common Struggle: A Personal Journey Through the Past and Future of Mental Illness and Addiction* (New York: Blue Rider Press, 2015), 307.

xxiv **Memorial service**: "Kennedy Is Mourned with Tears and Laughter," *NYT*, Aug. 28, 2009; "Friends, Relatives Celebrate Kennedy's Life," *USA Today*, Aug. 28, 2009; John McCain, C-SPAN, Aug. 28, 2009; www.youtube.com/watch?v=eWrBPefWtbQ; "Vice President Joe Biden Remarks," *The Washington Post*, Aug. 26, 2009; www.youtube.com/watch?v=03jzJkSxLjU.ABC; "Kennedy Mourners Memorialize 'Soul of Democratic Party,' " *NYT*, Aug. 30, 2009.

xxvi **arranged a bone-marrow transplant in Boston**: "Deep Into Night, Memories Carry Throngs to Wake," *BG*, Aug. 28, 2009.

xxvi **a Bronze Star posthumously**: "Mourning a Kennedy Brother, Again," *NYT*, Aug. 30, 2009.

xxvi "**he talked to you man to man**": "Deep Into Night."

xxvi **Kennedy sponsored a friend of hers**: "Many Tell Stories of Advocate," *USA Today*, Aug. 28, 2009.

xxvi "**when a wedding was to be celebrated**": Kerry Kennedy, "Reflections on Senator Ted Kennedy," Robert F. Kennedy Center. rfkcenter.org/reflections-on-senator-ted-kennedy-5?lang=en&view =article [disabled].

xxvi "**that's not the norm**": Curran Raclin int., Miller Center, UVA, Nov. 10, 2009.

xxvi "**Lourdes of Capitol Hill**": "Why Kennedy Legend Lives On," *U.S. News & World Report*, July 23, 1979.

xxvii **slipping in quietly**: "A Final Visit to Storied Mission Church," *BG*, Aug. 27, 2009; "A New Mission Hill to Bow on World Stage," *BG*, Aug. 28, 2009; "The Senator's Last Mission," *BG*, Aug. 28, 2009.

xxviii **and not to yield**: "Kennedy Mourners Memorialize 'Soul of the Democratic Party,' " *NYT*, Aug. 30, 2009.

xxix **"we will be better prepared"**: "Remembrances," *NYT*, Aug. 29, 2009.

xxix **always room for everyone**: www.youtube.com/watch?v=MbfXTaT9sZ4.

xxix **Obama eulogy**: https://abcnews.go.com/Politics/TedKennedy/story?id=8441986.

xxxi **"at the end of the day"**: Patrick Kennedy int. by author.

xxxi **Burial service**: "Kennedy Mourners Memorialize 'Soul of Democratic Party.'"

xxxii Ltr. to **Pope Benedict XVI**: fratres.wordpress.com/2009/08/30/full-text-edward-m-kennedy -letter-to-pope-benedict-xvi/.

xxxiii **"Kennedy is overexposed"**: Kenneth Aunchincloss, "Family Ties that Bind," *Newsweek*, Dec. 13, 1982.

xxxiv **"is secrecy"**: Kennedy and Fried, 370.

xxxiv **"worst as well as the best"**: Lewis Lapham, "Edward Kennedy and the Romance of Death," *Harper's*, Dec. 1979.

xxxiv **"searching for home and peace"**: Steven Roberts, "Ted Kennedy: Haunted by the Past," *NYT Magazine*, Feb. 3, 1980.

CHAPTER ONE: THE YOUNGEST

3 **"skittish"**: Rose Fitzgerald Kennedy, *Times to Remember* (Garden City, N.Y.: Doubleday & Co., 1974), 124.

3 **he warned his wife**: James MacGregor Burns, *Edward Kennedy and the Camelot Legacy* (New York: W. W. Norton & Co., 1976), 33.

3 **reparation for Kennedy's torrid affair**: Doris Kearns Goodwin, *The Fitzgeralds and the Kennedys: An American Saga* (New York: Simon & Schuster, 1987), 426.

3 **before Joseph left alone for New York**: David Nasaw, *The Patriarch: The Remarkable Life and Turbulent Times of Joseph P. Kennedy* (New York: Penguin Books, 2013), 163.

4 **"he felt so sorry for me"**: *Ibid.*

4 **"bond between the two men"**: Goodwin, 334.

4 **"unfailing support for me"**: Rose Kennedy, 89.

4 **Joe sold them his Brookline, Massachusetts, house**: Nasaw, 63; Kate Clifford Larson, *Rosemary: The Hidden Kennedy Daughter* (Boston: Houghton Mifflin Harcourt, 2015), 39.

4 **"saw to it Joe wore his rubbers"**: "London Legman," *Time*, Sept. 18, 1939.

4 **called him a "valet"**: Richard Whalen, *The Founding Father: The Story of Joseph P. Kennedy*, (New York: New American Library, 1964), 149.

4 **"flunky"**: Burton Hersh, *The Education of Edward Kennedy: A Family Biography* (New York: William Morrow & Co., 1972), 25.

5 **"occasional babysitter"**: Amanda Smith, *Hostage to Fortune: The Letters of Joseph P. Kennedy* (New York: Viking, 2001), 9.

5 **Kennedy and Moore set up a real estate company**: Nasaw, 59–60.

5 **hide Wall Street transactions**: Whalen, 132.

5 **"get into difficulties"**: Barbara Perry, *Rose Kennedy: The Life and Times of a Political Matriarch* (New York: W. W. Norton & Co., 2013), 78.

5 **"clap"**: Robert Dallek, *An Unfinished Life: John F. Kennedy, 1917-1963* (Boston: Little, Brown & Co., 2003), 48.

5 **"Irish as a clay pipe"**: "London Legman."

5 **"cherished Eddie's convivial soul"**: Edward Kennedy, *True Compass* (New York: Twelve, 2009), 38.

5 **"infinite capacity to make friends"**: Goodwin, 434.

5 **"greatness of Joseph P. Kennedy"**: Nasaw, 180.

5 **Joe's "shadow"**: Gloria Swanson, *Swanson on Swanson: An Autobiography* (New York: Pocket Books, 1980), 357.

6 **the commission's subsidy structure**: Joe McCarthy, *The Remarkable Kennedys* (New York: The Dial Press, 1960), 65–66.

6 **"endearing"**: Patrick Kennedy int. by author.

6 **uncles included a Boston mayor and a doctor**: McCarthy, 37.

6 **series of sinecures**: Nasaw, 14.

6 **"pocket-sized welfare state"**: Whalen, 14-15.

7 **"Pixie-like"**: Dallek, 9.

7 **he studied the Boston Brahmins**: Goodwin, 39.

7 Fitzgerald enters politics: *Ibid.*, 61, 66, 72.
7 served as Honey Fitz's hostess: "The Kennedys," *American Experience*, prod. Elizabeth Deane, WGBH, 1992.
8 "a grandiosity that refused to accept limits": Max Lerner, *Ted and the Kennedy Legend: A Study in Character and Destiny* (New York: St. Martin's Press, 1980), 7.
8 "not likely to improve": Arthur Schlesinger Jr., *Robert Kennedy and His Times* (New York: Houghton Mifflin Co. 1978), 12.
9 indifferent student: Nasaw, 21–22.
9 "hard as rock": Goodwin, 210.
9 "siege against the world": *Ibid.*
9 bank presidency at the age of twenty-five: *Ibid.*, 254–255.
9 appointed assistant general manager: Whalen, 51–52.
10 Ford contracted to buy coal: Goodwin, 328–329.
10 using insider information: Whalen, 54.
10 relying on Columbia Trust: Nasaw, 71.
10 "That's the way I've operated": Lawrence O'Brien, *No Final Victories: A Life in Politics* (Garden City, N.Y.: Doubleday & Co., 1974), 27.
10 "to meet people like the Saltonstalls?": Whalen, 44.
10 It galled him: McCarthy, 34–35.
11 Harvard or Christian country clubs: Goodwin, 473.
11 "stick together": Nasaw, 103.
11 where he made his real fortune: *Ibid.*, 91–92.
11 named his company Somerset: Goodwin, 444.
11 "referred to him as an 'Irishman' ": *True Compass*, 47.
11 "They wouldn't have asked my daughters": McCarthy, 53.
12 Rose had to form her own charity group: Edward Kennedy int., Miller Center, UVA, Oct. 8, 2007.
12 ability to speak French: Stephen Birmingham, "The Upward Social Climb of America's Irish Rich," *New York*, Oct. 15, 1973, 65.
12 "going to accept us?": Whalen, 401.
12 "us against the rest": Larry Newman quoted in "The Kennedys," *American Experience*, prod. Elizabeth Deane, WGBH, 1992.
12 "they would have been big men": McCarthy, 22.
13 just as discriminatory: Edward Kennedy int., Miller Center, UVA, Apr. 3, 2007.
13 "Irish House": Evan Thomas, *Robert Kennedy: His Life* (New York: Simon & Schuster, 2000), 33.
13 Rose liked the way the lawn sloped to the water: Nasaw, 132.
13 $4.2 million in assets: *Ibid.*, 168–169.
13 "almost unshakable pessimism": *Ibid.*, xxi.
13 "like listening to nuns talk about sex": Charles Spaulding quoted in Schlesinger, 15.
13 put up a "wall": Edmund Reggie int., Miller Center, UVA, Aug. 5, 2008.
14 "the biggest people in America": Goodwin, 427.
14 sabotaged Kennedy's primary campaign: Nasaw, 27.
14 how to treat Irish Catholics respectfully: Goodwin, 318; Nasaw, 61.
14 Smith's vulgar, working-class style: Nasaw, 135.
15 "some prestige to my family": Schlesinger, 9.
15 "the strange idiosyncrasies of Boston": *Ibid.*, 6.
15 "self-perpetuating aristocracy": Rose Kennedy, 49–50.
16 "the family was his only interest": Edward Kennedy, *The Fruitful Bough* (self-published, 1965), 201.
16 "togetherness long before it became a slogan": McCarthy, 18.
16 "We would be brothers and sisters, unchanging forever": *True Compass*, 106.
16 "The Kennedys were all in love with one another": Schlesinger, 20.
16 "they all got married somewhat older": Edward Kennedy int., Miller Center, UVA, Dec. 1, 2006.
16 "really aristocratic": Laurence Leamer, *The Kennedy Women: The Saga of an American Family* (New York: Villard Books, 1994), 226.
16 "as if they were the sons of one": Henry Fairlie, *The Kennedy Promise: The Politics of Expectation* (Garden City, N.Y.: Doubleday & Co., 1973), 52.
16 "promenading up and down the foyer": Perry, 36–37.
16 full household staff: *Ibid.*, 45.

16 **the Secretary, the Cook, the Chauffeur:** Barbara Gibson and Ted Schwarz, *Rose Kennedy and Her Family: The Best and Worst of Their Lives and Times* (New York: Birch Lane Press, 1995), viii.

17 **"first Irish Brahmins":** McCarthy, 93.

17 **"I didn't have them":** Edward Kennedy int., Miller Center, UVA, Aug. 15, 2006.

17 **to love—to the Kennedys:** *Ibid.*, Nov. 29, 2006.

17 **"Stick with family":** Hugh Sidey, "The Dynasty: The Kennedys," *Time*, June 14, 1999.

17 **"win, win, win":** Whalen, 91.

17 **Joe sent him to his room:** Mary Jo Gargan quoted in Peter S. Canellos, *Last Lion: The Fall and Rise of Ted Kennedy* (New York: Simon & Schuster, 2009), 32.

17 **"We competed at games of wit":** *True Compass*, 22.

17 **"nothing in between":** Jack Newfield, *Robert Kennedy: A Memoir* (New York: E. P. Dutton & Co., 1969), 42.

17 **"out for blood":** McCarthy, 28–29.

18 **"the pleasures of coming in first":** Goodwin, 351.

18 **Rose cited fraternal rivalries:** Rose Kennedy, 285.

18 **raising the expectations of each:** Edward Kennedy, *The Fruitful Bough*, 201.

18 **"they're differing or fighting with one another":** *True Compass*, 67–68.

18 **"I never heard one gossip about another":** Rita Dallas and Jeanira Ratcliffe, *The Kennedy Case* (New York; G. P. Putnam's Sons, 1973), 64.

18 **"conscious work of art":** Lerner, 8.

18 **turn sideways to make them look thinner:** Perry, 11.

19 **toothbrushing:** *Ibid.*, 74–75.

19 **"drilled us in our catechism":** Rose Kennedy, 14.

19 **Rose drilled her own children:** Goodwin, 319; Edward Kennedy int., Miller Center, UVA, Nov. 29, 2006.

19 **"much a part of our identity":** Edward Kennedy int., Miller Center, UVA, Aug. 15, 2006.

19 **ordered him to attend a religious retreat:** *Rose Kennedy*, 162.

19 **"try harder to dedicate myself":** Goodwin, 182, 185.

19 **"the model of *perfection*":** Perry, 25.

20 **"Also say rosary in month of October":** Robert F. Kennedy Jr., *American Values: Lessons I Learned from My Family* (New York: Harper, 2018), 54.

20 **"as perfect as possible":** Perry, 50.

20 **"we were expected to do as well as we could":** William Peters, "Teddy Kennedy," *Redbook*, June 1962.

20 **"quite a little pressure":** Schlesinger, 17–18.

20 **"Tears accomplish nothing":** Rose Kennedy, 421.

20 **"bellyaching":** Lester David, *Ted Kennedy: Triumphs and Tragedies* (New York: Grosset & Dunlap, 1972), 42.

20 **"charm his way through life":** Edward Kennedy, *The Fruitful Bough*, 203.

20 **"play polo, no":** *Ibid.*, 204.

21 **"with that glare":** Hersh, 29; Peters.

21 **to win praise:** Edward Kennedy int., Miller Center, UVA, Nov. 29, 2006.

21 **"sense of understanding and love":** Edward Kennedy int. with Robert Coughlin, MS 82-5, Rose Kennedy Papers, JFK Lib.

21 **"never seemed far away":** Rose Kennedy, 80.

21 **"unqualified support":** Edward Kennedy, *The Fruitful Bough*, 201.

22 **"stopped a riot":** Richard Rhodes, "Things As They Are, Things That Never Were: The Last Kennedy,"*Audience*, Nov./Dec. 1971, 84.

22 **left Joe Kennedy in 1920:** Goodwin, 308–309.

22 **"its own language and its own traditions":** *Ibid.*, 320.

22 **Joe would tease her:** *Ibid.*, 396.

23 **"the only man I've ever kissed":** Robert Shriver III int., Miller Center, UVA, Jan. 29, 2010.

23 **"No more sex":** Goodwin, 392.

23 **vacationed without their children:** Perry, 13.

23 **"Gee, you're a great mother":** Goodwin, 353.

23 **respite from the children:** Dallek, 25.

23 **she took seventeen of these trips:** Perry, 83.

23 **"I would always just say, 'Yes, dear' ":** *True Compass*, 68.

23 "awakening of educational and intellectual pursuits": EMK int., Clymer Papers, Series 2, Box 5, EMK interviews 1992–1994 folder, JFK Lib., Oct. 29, 1994.
23 "taking skating lessons": Perry, 80.
23 "You're at the theater, so what do you do?": *Ibid.*, 49.
24 "I had no time to spend with you children": Leamer, 689.
24 "it cemented a special bond": *True Compass*, 65–66.
24 records kept meticulously: Medical Records, 1934–1943, Health cards, Box 28, Doris Kearns Goodwin Papers, JFK Lib.
24 "when they're young": John Henry Cutler, *Honey Fitz: Three Steps to the White House* (Indianapolis: Bobbs-Merrill, 1962), 243–244.
24 determined that she "pass" as normal: Larson, 22, 41, 73.
25 "very sore subject with the boss": Swanson, 393.
25 "star-studded adornments": Goodwin, 360.
25 "in every way I could do so": Rose Kennedy, 124.
25 "He would never get upset": Perry, 71.
25 "always had a 'sunny disposition'": Rose Kennedy, 486.
25 She rarely spanked Teddy: Mrs. Vincent Greene, quoted in David, 20.
25 "gentle and lovable": *Ibid.*, 21.
25 "Outgoing and friendly": Peters.
26 "you always had to hold him back": "Teddy and Kennedyism," *Time*, Sept. 28, 1962.
26 Ted would later joke: Smith, *Hostage to Fortune*, 97; Lloyd Grove, "The Liberal Element," *The Washington Post*, July 9, 1996.
26 "Ted never seemed to resent it": "Teddy and Kennedyism."
26 "the younger ones would come along": Thomas Morgan, "Teddy," *Esquire*, Apr. 1962.
26 sleeping on a massage table: Leamer, 458; Burns, 68.
26 the barest hint of irritation: Rose Kennedy, 127.
26 shunting him off to kindergarten at four: Letter, Julian Markham, principal, Bronxville School, to Rose, Apr. 21, 1937, Education 1936-1953, JPK Personal Papers, 1.2.1 Family: Subject files, EMK, Box 34, JFK Lib.
27 admitting that she shouldn't have done so: Goodwin, 638.
27 Ted was home only on holidays: Burns, 39.
27 enough time to neutralize Kennedy: Nasaw, 272-273.
28 had a large room to himself: *True Compass*, 51; David, 40–41; McCarthy, 71; Nasaw, 285.
28 until Rose forbade it: Rose Kennedy, 219.
28 St. Moritz and the French Riviera: Burns, 35.
28 she bought two hundred dresses: McCarthy, 71.
28 "adjusted quickly": "Nine Young U.S. Ambassadors," *Parents*, Sept. 1939.
28 "always bubbly and happy": Goodwin, 539.
28 "helluva long way from East Boston," Rose Kennedy, 27.
28 "loneliness I felt": *True Compass*, 55.
28 had found his own circle of friends: Nasaw, 297.
28 reading to him in Ted's room: *Ibid.*, 297.
29 get him ready for bed: Goodwin, 539.
29 Sometimes the role fit: Schlesinger, 61.
30 "very normal, cheerful little boy": Burns, 33, 35.
30 "world of strangers proved different": *True Compass*, 54.
30 "what a great man Chamberlain was": Rose Kennedy, 562.
30 "Did some shopping and got a report about Teddy": Perry, 116.
30 missing his birthday: *Ibid.*, 131.
30 The family kept the sofa: Edward Kennedy int., Adam Clymer Papers, Series 2, Box 5, EMK int., 1996–1999, JFK Lib., Oct. 9, 1995.
31 "I hope you will always be good and pious": *Ibid.*; Smith, 319–320.
31 "my dad was working very hard." *True Compass*, 17.
31 would only prolong war: Nasaw, 348–370; Goodwin, 471–569; McCarthy, 79.
31 "run the country without much reference": Nasaw, 315.
32 "can save the world": *Ibid.*, 431–432.
32 "make such a sacrifice worthwhile": Robert F. Kennedy Jr., 12–13; Schlesinger, 28.
32 take the children back to the United States: *True Compass*, 57.

32 **Britain's survival would only prolong:** Nasaw, 461.

33 **"as war does":** Ltr., JPK to Ted, Rose Kennedy Papers, Box 14, Edward M. Kennedy folder, JFK Lib., Sept. 11, 1940.

33 **"loves it there":** Rose Kennedy, 257.

33 **so did Ted's education:** Burns, 38.

33 **"smile in our midst":** Ltr., Martha Colleen to Rose, Education, 1936–1953, JPK Personal Papers, 1.2.1, Family: Subject files, Edward M. Kennedy, Box 34, JFK Lib., Jan. 7, 1940.

33 **"Democracy is all done":** Nasaw, 498.

33 **"lonely existence":** Edward Kennedy int., Miller Center, UVA, Nov. 29, 2006.

34 **"No foundation for fourth-grade work":** Burns, 38.

34 **park her youngest:** Elizabeth Shannon int., Miller Center, UVA, Apr. 28, 2009.

34 **"three different peer groups":** Edward Kennedy, *True Compass*, 61–62.

34 **Bronxville Country Day School:** Bill, Milton School, Education, 1936–1953, JPK Personal Papers, 1.2.1, Family: Subject files, EMK, Box 34, JFK Lib., Feb. 2, 1943.

34 **"nearly always a stranger":** *True Compass*, 61.

34 **"I was the subject of some teasing":** Edward M. Kennedy int., Adam Clymer Papers, Series 2, Box 5, EMK int., 1996–1999, JFK Lib., Oct,. 9, 1995.

34 **"The Plowdens are better than the Kennedys":** *Ibid.*

35 **dropped him on Ted's bed:** *True Compass*, 61–62.

35 **he didn't get on with the other students:** Burns, 36.

35 **"not exactly conducive":** *True Compass*, 63–65.

35 **"You're losing your mooring":** Edward Kennedy int., Miller Center, UVA, Nov, 29, 2006.

35 **They lived in resort communities:** Fox Butterfield, "Views of the Kennedy House," *The New York Times*, April 10, 1991.

35 **he felt homeless:** *True Compass*, 60.

35 **He described it lovingly:** *Ibid.*, 37, 39.

36 **"my Palm Beach trousseau":** Ltr., Rose to children, JPK, box 2, JFK Lib., Dec. 5, 1941; Larson, 173.

36 **"loss of stability":** Goodwin, 638.

36 **"bleak kind of period":** Edward Kennedy int., Miller Center. UVA, Nov. 29, 2006.

36 **Joe did make at least one appearance:** Daniel Blake Burns int., classmate Fessenden, Adam Clymer Papers, Series 2, Box 3, Folder B, JFK Lib., Feb. 17, 1995.

36 **one of only thirteen Catholics:** *Ibid.*

36 **"tension between Protestant and Catholic":** Edward Kennedy int., Miller Center, UVA, Apr. 3, 2007.

36 **other boys would stare at them:** Daniel Blake Burns int.

37 **"frownies":** Dallas, 51.

37 **"Teddy is as fat as ever":** Rose Kennedy, 259.

37 **"as healthy as it is possible to look":** *Ibid.*, 260.

37 **"like two boys instead of one":** Canellos, 26.

37 **" extra-large suits":** *Ibid.*, 264.

37 **"Teddy is such a fatty":** *Ibid.*

37 **"you can spare a few pounds":** Ltr., JPK to Teddy, Jan. 31, 1946, Smith, 624.

37 **"I think he has put on the ten pounds":** Gibson and Schwarz, 147.

37 **his son Teddy ate quickly:** Goodwin, 527.

37 **"Biscuits and Muffins":** Canellos, 14.

37 **"such a delightful, able youngster":** Hazel Brodbury to Rose, Education, 1936–1953, JPK Personal Papers, 1.2.1, Subject files, EMK, JFK Lib., June 13, 1942.

37 **"so get on your toes":** Ltr., JPK to EMK, Oct. 5, 1943, in Smith, 569.

38 **"his arithmetic teacher in the fall?":** Canellos, 27.

38 **he was paddled thirteen times:** *True Compass*, 72; Ted Kennedy int. with Robert Coughlin, Rose Kennedy Papers, MS 82-5, Int. for *Times to Remember*, JFK Lib., Nov. 13, 1972.

38 **a teacher's stash of candy:** Daniel Blake Burns int.

38 **"good and trustworthy friend":** Rose Kennedy, 134.

38 **"provoked him to mischief":** Gibson and Schwarz, 147.

38 **"he is a good salesman":** Ltr., JPK to Rose, Nov. 23, 1942, in Goodwin, 639; also in Nasaw, 547–548.

38 **He had his grandfather Honey Fitz:** *True Compass*, 82–83.

38 **he would take the subway to Boston:** *Ibid.*, 77.

39 **"he collected information":** Robert P. Fitzgerald Sr. int., Miller Center, UVA, June 18, 2009.
39 **he would circulate among the diners:** *True Compass,* 77; Ted Kennedy int. with Robert Coughlin; Edward Kennedy int., Miller Center, UVA, June 3, 2005.
39 **"He knew everyone":** *Ibid.,* Apr. 3, 2007.
39 **"He was outgoing and warm":** *Ibid.*
39 **framed and hung one in his house:** Edward Kennedy int., Miller Center, UVA, June 3, 2005.
39 **"Appoint one of your own, Honey Fitz!"** *Ibid.,* Apr. 3, 2007. Edward Kennedy int., Miller Center, UVA, April 3, 2007.
40 **"He knew people's problems":** Rose Kennedy, 334.
40 **"and Joe wasn't and that was it":** Perry, 107.
40 **"sort of an extra parent":** Edward Kennedy int., Miller Center, UVA, Feb. 27, 2006.
40 **inherited his political style from his grandfather:** *True Compass,* 78–79.
41 **on the wrong side of history:** Schlesinger, 32–33; Goodwin, 614.
41 **"worth something in some position":** Burns, 31–32.
41 **"careers rather than my own":** Nasaw, 542.
41 **he put his money in oil and real estate:** *Ibid.,* 529.
41 **"the kids felt it":** Goodwin, 636–637.
41 **"his parents needed what he had to give":** Canellos, 22.
42 **"always" absent:** Perry, 74.
42 **"inspiring and authoritarian figure":** Edward Kennedy int., Miller Center, UVA, Nov. 29, 2006.
42 **"to listen and to encourage us":** Edward Kennedy, *The Fruitful Bough,* 205.
42 **"second father," Teddy called Bobby:** David, 177.
42 **"to get Ted to make the extra effort":** Hersh, 43.
42 **"making sure I had something to do":** David, 177.
42 **"and that counted":** Rose Kennedy, 486.
42 **"golden child":** Canellos, 22.
42 **"He related to Teddy":** Arthur Schlesinger Jr., *Journals, 1952–2000,* Andrew Schlesinger and Stephen Schlesinger, eds. (New York: Penguin Press, 2007), 419–420.
43 **Joe made him pay back the money:** *Ibid.*
43 **sent them back to pick up the sailboat:** Peters.
43 **"hard work, buggy and hot":** Canellos, 23.
43 **Joe Kennedy, a "stern" disciplinarian:** Victoria Reggie int., Miller Center, UVA, Apr. 8, 2010.
43 **"tendency to cut corners":** Dallas, 316.
43 **"than we ever thought possible":** *Ibid., 316.*
44 **Ted talked about sports:** *Ibid.,* 318.
44 **Ted read comic books:** Canellos, 31.
44 **"when we failed to meet his standards":** Schlesinger, *Journals: 1952–2000,* 152.
44 **"critical and impatient":** "Different Children" diaries, RFKP, Box 5, JFK Lib.; Larson, 41.
44 **"conducting myself like them":** *True Compass,* 69.
45 **"which kind of life I wanted to lead":** *Ibid.,* 40.
45 **Rose wouldn't see her:** Larson, 146–147, 175, 178.
45 **"more loving even than other brothers and sisters":** Edward Kennedy int., Miller Center UVA, Nov. 29, 2006; Hersh, 190–192.
46 **"I was cool about it too":** Edward Kennedy int., Nov. 29, 2006.
46 **"same thing could happen to me":** Burton Hersh, *Edward Kennedy: An Intimate Biography* (New York: Counterpoint, 2010), 522.
46 **emaciated to skin and bones:** Nigel Hamilton, *JFK: Reckless Youth* (New York: Random House, 1992) 626–627.
46 **"clenching and unclenching his fists":** Chris Matthews, *Jack Kennedy: Elusive Hero* (New York: Simon & Schuster, 2011), 62.
46 **"must have rankled Joe Jr.":** Rose Kennedy, 285.
47 **killed instantly:** For a complete account of the mission see Jack Olsen, *Aphrodite: Desperate Mission* (New York: Putnam, 1970).
47 **"biggest explosion I ever saw":** David Burner and Thomas R. West, *The Torch Is Passed: The Kennedy Brothers and American Liberalism* (New York: Atheneum, 1984), 41.
47 **" 'particularly good to your mother' ":** Edward Kennedy, *The Fruitful Bough,* 206.
47 **"long, hard course toward renewal and hope":** *True Compass,* 86.

47 Jack spent time with Ted: Robert Shrum, quoted in Canellos, 23–24.

48 "find comfort, transcendence": *True Compass*, 89.

48 "extricate" her daughter: Paula Byrne, *Kick: The True Story of JFK's Sister and the Heir to Chatsworth* (New York: HarperCollins, 2016), 220.

48 a great deal of tension: Edward Kennedy int., Miller Center, UVA, Nov. 29, 2006.

49 "You're getting rather old now": Ltr., JPK to EMK, Jan. 31, 1946, in Smith, 624.

49 "too distant, too remote": Burns, 39.

49 "not to mind being alone": Newfield, 41–42.

49 two or three times a year: Peters.

49 "pain" of that period: Patrick Kennedy int. by author.

50 the basis for his politics: Canellos, 26.

50 thought Ted might like it: Peters.

50 Joe rescinded the offer: Edward Kennedy, *The Fruitful Bough.*

50 only to fall again: Burns, 42.

50 "Life for him was to act": Arthur Bliss Perry quoted in *ibid.*, 41.

50 called him a "plugger": *Ibid.*

50 "The favorite customer of the school's tutor": David, 53.

50 described as "dogged": Hersh, *The Education of Edward Kennedy*, 77.

50 touchdown against Milton's rival: Canellos, 32.

50 "absolutely fearless": Burns, 42.

50 He joined the debate team: Ltr., EMK to JPK, Rose Kennedy Papers, Box 14, EMK folder, JFK Lib., May 10, 1948.

50 according to his debate coach: Hersh, *The Education of Edward Kennedy*, 76–77.

50 only course in which he won honors: Burns, 42.

51 "just damn good company": Hersh, *The Education of Edward Kennedy*, 46.

51 "Ted was probably in the middle of it": Frank Cohouet int., Clymer Papers, Series 2, Box 3, Folder C, JFK Lib., March 23, 1995.

51 "Good-humored, fun sort of kid": David, 53.

51 "charming to grown-ups": Burns, 41.

51 practice smiling in the mirror: Burns, 41.

52 his first girlfriend: *True Compass*, 87.

52 "which couldn't please me more": Ltr., EMK to JPK, Rose Kennedy Papers, Box 14, EMK folder, JFK Lib., Apr. 25, 1948.

52 "bright dawn after the cheerlessness": *True Compass*, 88.

52 "It's rather nice not having to be a Kennedy": Byrne, 266.

53 threatened to leave Joe: *Ibid.*, 278.

53 to implore her daughter: *Ibid.*, 279.

53 None of the four passengers survived: *Ibid.*, 280–281.

53 "I remain the ninth and youngest child": *True Compass*, 19.

CHAPTER TWO: THE LEAST

54 thirty-sixth of fifty-six in his class: David Burner and Thomas R. West, *The Torch Is Passed: The Kennedy Brothers and Liberalism* (New York: Atheneum, 1984), 227.

54 seriously considered Stanford: James MacGregor Burns, *Edward Kennedy and the Camelot Legacy* (New York: W. W. Norton & Co., 1976), 43.

54 left her severely underweight: Eileen McNamara, *Eunice: The Kennedy Who Changed the World* (New York: Simon & Schuster, 2018), 52–53.

54 "dissuaded" from attending Stanford: William Peters, "Teddy Kennedy," *Redbook*, June 1962.

55 "Harvard and playing football": Edward Kennedy int., Series 2, Box 5, EMK interviews 1995, Clymer Papers, JFK Lib., Apr. 17, 1995.

55 "to finish his course there": Ltr., JPK to Delmar Leighton, Dean of Freshmen, Harvard College, Education, 1936–1953, JPK Personal Papers, 1.2.1, Subject files, EMK, Box 34, JFK Lib., July 31, 1950.

56 if it left a deeper impression: European Trip Diary 1950, JPK Personal Papers, 1.2.11, Family Subject files, EMK, JFK Lib.

57 **"He demanded it"**: Doris Kearns Goodwin, *The Fitzgeralds and the Kennedys: An American Saga* (New York: Simon & Schuster, 1987), 705.

57 **"I have prevailed on him to stay"**: Barbara Perry, *Rose Kennedy: The Life and Times of a Political Matriarch* (New York: W. W. Norton & Co., 2013), 188.

57 **"and all my brothers and sisters"**: Adam Clymer, *Edward Kennedy: A Biography* (New York: William Morrow & Co., 1999), 516.

57 **" 'I'm Honey Fitz from Boston' "**: Martha Bebinger, "Kennedy Remembered as the Senate's Hardest-Working Man," WBUR, August 26, 2009, wbur.org/2009/08/26/kennedy-tributes.

57 **"the emotions of ordinary people"**: Goodwin, 747–748.

58 **"bright line marker for the end of my childhood"**: Edward Kennedy, *True Compass* (New York: Twelve, 2009), 95.

58 **"You guys, shut up!"**: Peter Canellos, *Last Lion: The Fall and Rise of Ted Kennedy* (New York: Simon & Schuster, 2009), 45.

58 **"controlled everything Ted did"**: *Ibid.*

58 **"looking at those report cards"**: John Culver int., Miller Center, UVA, March 31, 2005.

58 **at least on weekdays**: Canellos, 45–46.

58 **" 'Who the hell does he think he is?' "**: Edward Kennedy, *The Fruitful Bough* (self-published, 1965), 205.

58 **of the class was Catholic**: John McGreevy, "Catholics, Catholicism and the Humanities Since World War II," in *The Humanities and the Dynamics of Inclusion Since World War II*, David Hollinger, ed. (Baltimore: Johns Hopkins, 2006), 192.

59 **"particularly hospitable place"**: *True Compass*, 95.

59 **"terrifically warm and wonderful"**: Edward Kennedy int., Series 2, Box 5, Edward M. Kennedy Interviews, 1995-1996 Folder, JFK Lib., April 17, 1995.

59 **"I wasn't all that happy"**: *Ibid.*

59 **"getting along with them"**: David Nasaw, *The Patriarch: The Remarkable Life and Turbulent Times of Joseph P. Kennedy* (New York: Penguin Books, 2013), 221.

59 **Joe Jr. followed that injunction**: Chris Matthews, *Jack Kennedy: Elusive Hero* (New York: Simon & Schuster, 2011), 27.

59 **"Lumbago Pass"**: Burton Hersh, *The Education of Edward Kennedy: A Family Biography* (New York: William Morrow & Co., 1972), 80.

60 **"the spirit to go with them"**: Rose Fitzgerald Kennedy, *Times to Remember* (Garden City, N.Y.: Doubleday & Co., 1974), 125.

60 **"He never shirked from any drill"**: Richard Clasby int., Miller Center, UVA, Oct. 11, 2005.

60 **"that's for darned sure"**: *Ibid.*

60 **stayed like that after practice**: John Culver int.

60 **gave it to the Salvation Army**: Richard Clasby int.

60 **" 'dinner in twenty-two minutes' "**: *Ibid.*

61 **permit him to do anything else**: John Culver int.

61 **"see the beam in Jack's eyes"**: Richard Clasby int.

61 **King of the Kennedys**: Lester David, *Ted Kennedy: Triumphs and Tragedies* (New York: Grosset & Dunlap, 1972), 249.

62 **"the beginning of the book"**: Ltr., EMK to JPK, Rose Kennedy Papers, Box 14, Edward M. Kennedy folder, JFK Lib., Dec. 12, 1946.

62 **"so far they have been going fairly well"**: Ltr., EMK to Paul [Murphy], Corr M—family, Box 33, JPK Papers, JFK Lib., Jan. 24, 1951.

62 **he thought of it as a kind of prank**: *True Compass*, 95–96; Edward Kennedy int., April 17, 1995; Melody Miller int., Miller Center, UVA, July 15, 2008.

63 **he and Frate were to be expelled**: Hersh, 81.

63 **"I've never had a failure in my life"**: Gloria Swanson, *Swanson on Swanson: An Autobiography* (New York: Pocket Books, 1980).

63 **"the longest and worst drive I ever had to make"**: *True Compass*, 96.

63 **"grew inside him as he got older"**: Burns, 44; Hersh, 81-82.

63 **"How do we help you?"**: Rose Kennedy, 141.

64 **"Outraged and upset"**: Edward Kennedy int., Miller Center, UVA, Nov. 29, 2006.

64 **"you're not one of them"**: *True Compass*, 96.

64 **"It was a difficult time"**: Edward Kennedy int., Nov. 29, 2006.

64 **"discipline and seriousness":** Arthur Schlesinger Jr., *Journals: 1952-2000*, Andrew Schlesinger and Stephen Schlesinger, eds. (New York: Penguin Press, 2007), 150.

64 **"constructive and responsible citizenship":** "Edward Kennedy Admits Ouster By Harvard," *The New York Times*, March 31, 1962.

64 **expulsion put an end to that:** Ltr., Katherine Donovan to L. Lepree, Campagnie Generale Transatlantique, EMK Misc, Box 34, JPK Papers, JFK Lib., Aug. 6, 1951.

64 **no guarantee of readmission:** Edward Kennedy int., Nov. 29, 2006.

64 **"brooding . . . sometimes for hours":** *National Enquirer*, Sept. 21, 1969.

65 **it would be too hard on their parents:** *True Compass*, 99.

65 **keep him out of the war:** Evan Thomas, *Robert Kennedy: His Life* (New York: Simon & Schuster, 2000), 40–41.

65 **he missed the deadline:** Ltr., Capt. D. V. Gladding to EMK, July 25, Corr re: Edward M. Kennedy, Box 33, JPK Papers, JFK Lib., July 25, 1950.

65 **opted for the shorter term:** Edward Kennedy int., Apr. 17, 1995.

65 **Ted would not be assigned to Korea:** Hersh, 82.

66 **never been around black people:** Edward Kennedy int., Miller Center, UVA, Apr. 3, 2007.

66 **"He probably could have been in the Olympics":** Canellos, 38–39.

66 **This was Ted Kennedy's new life:** Edward Kennedy int., Apr. 3, 2007.

67 **"for what they were and what they did:"** *Ibid.*

67 **He only made it up to Hyannis Port:** Edward Kennedy int., Apr. 17, 1995.

67 **"except my mother":** Canellos, 38–39.

67 **"All the guys would be looking":** *Ibid.*

67 **pressured his father for PT deployment:** Tel. Gen. McInerny, Ft. Holabird, to Ted, Corr M—family, Box 33, EMK Corr, JPK Papers, JFK Lib., Dec. 19, 1951.

68 **found out about his cheating:** Edward Kennedy int., Apr. 17, 1995.

68 **Ted went to Paris, Troy to Korea:** Burns, 45–46.

68 **"interesting assignment":** Nasaw, 649.

68 **He skied the Alps with his sisters:** Canellos, 39.

68 **"Teddy Dear":** *True Compass*, 102–103.

68 **"he is lucky as usual":** Canellos, 41–42.

69 **setting their own schedules and hours:** Edward Kennedy int., Apr. 3, 2007.

69 **"couple of very tough, bad fights":** Edward Kennedy int., Nov. 29, 2006.

69 **"A lot of diversity":** Edward Kennedy int., Apr. 17, 1995.

69 **"kinds of high emotions":** Hersh, 86.

69 **"I didn't want to make any more mistakes":** Edward Kennedy int., Nov. 29, 2006.

70 **"a time that I put behind me":** Edward Kennedy int., Apr. 17, 1995.

70 **"good use of these last two years":** Ltr., Delmar Leighton, Dean of Students, to JPK, Education 1936–1953, JPK Personal Papers, 1.2.1 Subject Files, EMK, Box 34, JFK Lib., May 6, 1953.

70 **Bobby was serving as assistant counsel:** John Culver int., Miller Center, UVA, March 31, 2005.

70 **coaching the boys in basketball:** Edward Kennedy int., Apr. 17, 1995; Edward Kennedy int., Apr. 3, 2007.

70 **the House of Mesomorphs:** *True Compass*, 106; David, 54.

70 **He went to the business library:** Hersh, 83.

70 **"worked, worked hard":** Edward Kennedy int., Apr. 17, 1995.

71 **"He was no aristocrat":** Hersh, 83.

71 **"what was necessary to remain":** David, 70; Burns, 49.

71 **"majored" in football:** Clymer, 20–21.

71 **"kind of player a coach appreciates":** Byron Roberts, "A Man Who Knew Kennedy When," *The Washington Post*, Sept. 17, 1962.

71 **"carefully avoiding the forearm":** Peters.

71 **"more open and outgoing":** *Ibid.*

72 **knocked out one of his teeth:** *True Compass*, 107–108.

72 **"like they signed your death warrant":** Edward Kennedy int., Apr. 17, 1995.

72 **scoring twice in the fourth quarter:** *NYT*, Nov. 21, 1954.

72 **"if only for your future":** Ltr., JPK to EMK, Sept. 3, 1955, in Smith, 671.

72 **Ted's taking public-speaking courses:** Peters.

72 **top half of his class:** Burns, 49.

72 **"zest for life":** Canellos, 43.
73 **the sheep evacuated everywhere:** *Ibid.;* David, 58; Hersh, 85.
73 **averaged fifty-six minutes a game:** EMK int., Clymer Papers, Series 2, Box 5, EMK interviews 1992–1994 folder, JFK Lib., Sept. 10, 1992.
73 **Jack took an interest in that and in him:** *Ibid.,* Oct,. 9, 1996.
73 **"when his fellow players think that":** Canellos, 37.
74 **Harvard's lone touchdown:** *NYT,* Nov. 20, 1955.
74 **two touchdowns:** Harvard Athletic Dept. records.
74 **invitation from the Green Bay Packers:** *True Compass,* 107–108.
74 **Joe eventually scotched the idea:** Canellos, 43; *Los Angeles Examiner,* July 9, 1954; Christopher Lawford, *Symptoms of Withdrawal: A Memoir of Snapshots and Redemptions* (New York: William Morrow & Co., 2005), 62.
74 **worked as a forest ranger:** Burns, 48.
74 **"attorney or defendant":** Clymer, 21.
75 **"legal training gives you perspective":** Peters.
75 **"the [Law School] Aptitude Test":** Arthur Schlesinger Jr., *Robert Kennedy and His Times* (Boston: Houghton Mifflin Co., 1978), 81.
75 **he always surrendered to his father:** Peters.
75 **Ted would be staying east:** Burns, 49.
75 **where he himself had spoken recently:** Edward Kennedy int., Series 2, EMK interviews, JFK Lib., Oct. 9, 1996.
75 **Ted was admitted:** Max Lerner, *Ted and the Kennedy Legend: A Study in Character and Destiny* (New York: St. Martin's Press, 1980), 48.
76 **" 'tenacious prime ministers' ":** Edward Kennedy int., Miller Center, UVA, Apr. 3, 2007, May 30, 2007; *True Compass,* 109–111; Ltr., EMK to JPK, Edward Kennedy, JPK Personal Papers, 1.1, Family: Family Corr., JFK Lib., Feb. 13, 1956.
77 **motives of their leaders:** Despatches, Fall 1956, Articles on North Africa Drafts, Series 1.2.10, Box 33, JPK Papers, JFK Lib.
77 **when the colonialists and the indigenous populations:** *True Compass,* 111.
78 **"the way he carried himself":** John Tunney int., Miller Center, UVA, May 3, 2007.
78 **"He had a warmth to him":** Canellos, 50.
78 **remained that way over the next three years:** John Tunney int., Clymer Papers, Series 2, Box 5, T folder, Interviews, JFK Lib., March 6, 1995.
78 **Tunney and Ted would argue heatedly:** John Tunney int., May 3, 2007.
78 **"one of the ones who failed":** *Ibid.*
78 **"we got through":** *Ibid.*
78 **developed an ulcer:** Hersh, 105.
78 **without having to take exams:** John Tunney int., May 3, 2007.
79 **"I think I notice a greater maturity":** Ltr., JPK to EMK, Rose Kennedy Papers, Box 55, Family Corr. Children (1955–1958), JFK Lib., July 26, 1957.
79 **"the great thoughts of Western civilization":** Canellos, 51.
79 **"to attract other people to him and to lead":** John Tunney int., Clymer Papers, JFK Lib., March 6, 1995.
79 **"incredible physical courage":** *Ibid.*
79 **holding a jerry-rigged parachute:** Clymer, 13.
79 **"kept doing it, egged on with great applause":** Rose Kennedy, 125–126.
79 **while traveling with Tunney:** William Honan, *Ted Kennedy: Profile of a Survivor* (New York: Quadrangle Books, 1972), 163.
79 **exulted over the story he would tell:** Canellos, 52; John Tunney int., Clymer Papers, Series 2, Box 5, T folder, JFK Lib., March 6, 1995.
80 **"tough schedule":** John Tunney int., March 6, 1995.
80 **retreat to their rooms once again:** John Tunney int., Miller Center, UVA, Oct. 12, 2009.
80 **His boat-sized car:** Laurence Leamer, *The Kennedy Women: The Saga of an American Family* (New York: Villard Books, 1994), 468.
80 **neither of them ever drank and drove:** Canellos, 53.
80 **$35 fine for speeding:** Hersh, 103–104; "Do Charlottesville Memories Worry Kennedy Campaign?" *Charlottesville Daily Progress,* Oct. 28, 1979.
80 **Ted would not graduate:** "Stain Kennedy's Past," *Cavalier Daily,* Nov. 19, 1979.

80 **Tunney once got into a fight:** *Ibid.*
80 **"went down in the annals":** Canellos, 53.
81 **"stopped worrying about 'catching up' ":** *True Compass*, 112.
81 **"studying all the time":** John Tunney int., March 6, 1995.
82 **"sacrilege among the Kennedys":** Hersh, 100.
82 **with a jar of Maalox:** Timothy Hanan int., Miller Center, UVA, May 7, 2009.
82 **Ted sent the professor a thank-you note:** "Do Charlottesville Memories Worry Kennedy Campaign?"
82 **"he didn't have the best grades":** David, 79.
82 **"no attempt to get around it:"** Burns, 52.
82 **this might just have been discretion:** Ted Carey quoted in Canellos, 46.
82 **"He had a twinkle in his eye for pretty girls":** *Ibid.*, 43.
83 **"for the oldest brother and not the youngest":** Ltr., JPK to EMK, Sept. 3, 1955, in Smith, 670.
83 **"darn good-looking":** Clymer, 23.
83 **"he was gorgeous":** Canellos, 55.
83 **"took me under her wing"** Rose Kennedy, 30–432; David, 46–47; Joan Kennedy int., Clymer Papers, Series 2, Box 4, K folder, JFK Lib., Jan. 18, 1996.
84 **if he would fill in for him:** *True Compass*, 117.
84 **she would get a demerit:** Rose Kennedy, 430–432.
84 **she took her over to meet Ted:** Lester David, *Joan: The Reluctant Kennedy* (New York: Funk & Wagnalls, 1974) 46–47.
84 **Murray introduced him to Joan:** *True Compass*, 117.
84 **"exquisitely beautiful young student":** *Ibid.*
84 **" 'This is it, this is the one' ":** Rose Kennedy, 430–432.
84 **phoned her the next night:** Leamer, 470.
84 **just as her evening date was arriving:** *Ibid;* Canellos, 56.
85 **conservative in both temperament and politics:** David, 17–18.
85 **politics was never a subject:** Peters.
85 **"A nice quiet kid":** Lester David, "Joan—The Reluctant Kennedy," *Good Housekeeping*, June 1972.
85 **"bottled up inside":** *Ibid.*
85 **"nobody asked me what I was going to do":** Carol Stocker, "Joan Kennedy: New Life, New Goals and a Sense of Excitement," *The Boston Globe*, June 2, 1984.
85 **braces on her teeth:** David, "Joan—The Reluctant Kennedy."
85 **homely and lonely:** David, *Joan—The Reluctant Kennedy*, 28.
85 **"some divinity must have shaped her ends":** *Ibid.*, 9.
85 **"comparing her to an Ingrid Bergman":** David, *Joan—The Reluctant Kennedy*, 39-40.
85 **queen of the Bermuda Chamber of Commerce:** *Ibid.*, 38.
85 **"She loved the nuns, her studies, her friends":** David, "Joan—The Reluctant Kennedy."
86 **"we remained pure, immaculate and innocent":** Stocker.
86 **"marriage mill":** Marcia Chellis, *Living With the Kennedys: The Joan Kennedy Story* (New York: Simon & Schuster, 1985), 31.
86 **boys and girls roomed separately:** Joan Kennedy int., Clymer Papers, Series 2, Box 4, K folder, JFK Lib., Jan. 18, 1996.
86 **"such patient, sweet encouragement":** Clymer, 23.
86 **they had several dates in Bronxville:** Joan Kennedy int., Jan. 18, 1996.
86 **she was seeing a Kennedy:** Leamer, 470–471.
86 **"as often as possible":** Rose Kennedy, 431.
86 **"we were on a fast track":** Canellos, 117.
86 **a passion they shared:** Leamer, 470–471.
86 **"very cozy":** Joan Kennedy int., Jan. 18, 1996.
86 **Ted got up and began calling:** *Ibid.*
87 **Joan's mother had led the children:** Canellos, 57.
87 **the reports were good:** Leamer, 470–471.
87 **"What do we do next?":** Rose Kennedy, 432.
87 **"I can't believe our luck":** Leamer, 470–471.
87 **conduct what Joan called an "interview":** Rose Kennedy, 432.
87 **wouldn't see Ted again until her engagement party:** Leamer, 473.
88 **"Lots of love":** Ltr., Joan Bennett to JPK, nd., JPK Personal Papers, 1.1 Family Corr, Box 5, JFK Lib.

88   **called Joan "Connie":** Canellos, 57.

88   **"that was that":** "Joan Kennedy's Worries," *People Weekly*, June 24, 1974.

88   **"skating rink":** David, *Ted Kennedy*, 74; Leamer, 473.

88   **"long-distance call to her in New York":** Lawrence O'Brien, *No Final Victories: A Life in Politics* (Garden City, N.Y.: Doubleday & Co., 1974), 53.

88   **they had only shared kisses:** Canellos, 56.

88   **"It was sort of romantic":** Leamer, 472.

88   **"he couldn't get me any other way":** Chellis, 34.

89   **dubbed her "the Dish":** David, *Ted Kennedy*, 74.

89   **confessed as much to a friend:** Leamer, 477.

89   **"out of the gossip columns":** Ltr., JPK to EMK, Rose Kennedy Papers, Box 55, Fam Corr., Children (1855–1958), JFK Lib., May 2, 1958.

89   **they should postpone the wedding:** Clymer, 24.

89   **she had no idea:** Joan Kennedy int., Jan. 18, 1996.

89   **"my son is being tossed over":** Mary Lou McCarthy, Kennedy cousin, quoted in Leamer, 474.

89   **he didn't have to be faithful:** Clymer, 24.

90   **"That was our honeymoon":** Canellos, 58; *True Compass*, 126.

91   **Nobody thought they would win:** John Tunney int., Miller Center, UVA, May 3, 2007; Hersh, 101.

91   **"Up early every morning":** Hersh, 101.

91   **Ted was "forceful":** John Tunney int., May 3, 2007.

91   **"projected a lot of vitality and dynamism":** Hersh, 101.

91   **"just speak to the trees":** John Tunney int., May 3, 2007.

91   **"how this team of Kennedy and Tunney were able to do it":** John Tunney int.

92   **"started to feel that he was the master":** Patrick Kennedy int. by author.

93   **Ted pounded his fist on the table:** Canellos, 52–53.

93   **"principal academic achievement in our lives":** John Tunney int., March 6, 1995.

93   **"to that time and among those of all time":** *True Compass*, 114–115.

93   **"able to excel at something in law school":** John Tunney int., March 6, 1995.

93   **"including your father!"** Canellos, 53.

CHAPTER THREE: THE SUCCESSION

94   **"Teddy will be the senator from Massachusetts":** Harold Martin, "The Amazing Kennedys," *The Saturday Evening Post*, Sept. 7, 1957.

94   **socialist political scientist Harold Laski:** Robert Dallek, *An Unfinished Life: John F. Kennedy 1917–1963* (Boston: Little, Brown), 41.

94   **"and that includes my sons":** Arthur Schlesinger Jr., *Robert Kennedy and His Times* (Boston: Houghton Mifflin Co., 1978), 20.

95   **"that's what they [the Kennedys] were":** John Aloysius Farrell int., Miller Center, UVA, July 13, 2006.

95   **"that has not been opposed as communistic":** Address to Democratic Businessmen's League of Mass., FDR Papers, Oct. 24, 1936, quoted in Schlesinger, 11.

95   **"half the country would be against it":** Ltr., JPK to Kathleen Kennedy Hartington, May 1, 1945, in Amanda Smith, ed., *Hostage to Fortune: The Letters of Joseph P. Kennedy* (New York: Viking, 2001), 615–616.

95   **donating $150,000 to Nixon's war chest:** Thomas P. O'Neill with William Novak, *Man of the House: The Life and Political Memoirs of Speaker Tip O'Neill* (New York: Random House, 1987), 81.

95   **"The strongest man in America":** Ltr., JPK to RFK, Aug. 15, 1954, in Amanda Smith, *Hostage to Fortune: The Letters of Joseph P. Kennedy* (New York: Viking, 2001), 664.

96   **"trying to ruin my son's career":** Chris Matthews, *Jack Kennedy: Elusive Hero* (New York: Simon & Schuster, 2011), 143.

96   **" 'all engines ahead full' ":** Hersh, 50.

96   **"I'm not comfortable with those people":** James MacGregor Burns, *John F. Kennedy: A Political Profile* (New York: Harcourt Brace, 1960), 134–135.

96   **he was "happy" Nixon had beaten Douglas:** Burner and West, 49–50.

96   **considered himself a liberal:** Dallek, 236.

97   **creating new social dynamics:** G. Calvin Mackenzie and Robert Weisbrot, *The Liberal Hour: Washington and the Politics of Change in the 1960s* (New York: The Penguin Press, 2008), 14.

98 **errand boy for the campaign:** Rose Fitzgerald Kennedy, *Times to Remember* (Garden City, N.Y.: Doubleday & Co., 1974), 313.

98 **he should take an interest in what happened:** Edward Kennedy int., Miller Center, UVA, Nov. 29, 2006.

99 **raced to Sumner Tunnel:** Theo Lippman, *Senator Ted Kennedy: The Career Behind the Image* (New York: W. W. Norton & Co., 1976), 12.

99 **"chief signature getter":** Peter Canellos, *Last Lion: The Fall and Rise of Ted Kennedy* (New York: Simon & Schuster, 2009), 59.

99 **working to get his brother:** Lawrence O'Brien, *No Final Victories: A Life in Politics* (Garden City, N.Y.: Doubleday & Co., 1974), 52.

99 **Like Honey Fitz, he loved people:** Hersh, 105.

99 **"I've never seen a congressman":** O'Neill, 87.

99 **"He was bent on a national constituency":** Clayton Fritchey, "Who Belongs to the Senate's Inner Club?" *Harper's,* May 1967, 108.

100 **the campaign had to tear up:** Edward Kennedy int., Miller Center, UVA, June 3, 2005.

100 **"I wanted an area of my own":** Hersh, 132.

101 **traveling through the West:** Hyman Raskin int., JFK Oral History Coll., JFK. Lib., May 8, 1964.

101 **"It was a one–two punch":** Edward Kennedy int., June 3, 2005.

101 **assured Jack that Ted had been working:** Edward Kennedy, "The Unforgettable Byron White," *Yale Law Journal,* Vol. 112, 973–9740; Edward Kennedy int., Clymer Papers, Series 2, Box 5, EMK interviews, 1996–1999, JFK Lib., Oct. 9, 1995.

101 **again in January 1960:** Preconvention Political files, New Mexico, EMK trip file, JFK Lib., Jan. 6, 1959–Dec. 23, 1959.

102 **Three days alone in that small plane:** Edward Kennedy int., Clymer Papers, Series 2, Box 5, Interviews 1995–1996, Oct. 9, 1995.

103 **"licking stamps and envelopes":** Max Lerner, *Ted and the Kennedy Legend: A Study in Character and Destiny* (New York: St. Martin's Press, 1980), 67; Adam Clymer, *Edward M. Kennedy: A Biography* (New York: William Morrow & Co., 1999), 27–28.

103 **he was bitten by a dog:** Robert Healy, *Boston Globe* reporter, int., Miller Center UVA, Aug. 10, 2005.

103 **"felt like an independent merchant":** Clymer, 27.

103 **remained with him long:** Edward Kennedy, *True Compass* (New York: Twelve, 2009), 144–146.

104 **"So back to the boondocks":** "Pride of the Clan," *Time,* July 11, 1960.

104 **"What's a hundred million":** Carl Solberg, *Hubert Humphrey: A Biography* (New York: W. W. Norton & Co., 1984), 210.

104 **"finest TV broadcast":** Theodore H. White, *The Making of the President 1960* (New York: Atheneum, 1961), 128.

104 **"Ted really took over' ":** David Nasaw, *The Patriarch: The Remarkable Life and Turbulent Times of Joseph P. Kennedy* (New York: The Penguin Press, 2012), 736.

105 **"If it comes down to it":** Hersh, 137–138.

105 **McCracken announced the vote:** David Broder int., Miller Center, UVA, Dec. 1, 2006; Scott Crass, "Vibrant Wyoming Democrats Put Kennedy Over Top in '60," http://themoderatevoice.com /vibrant-wyoming-democrats-put-kennedy-over-top-in-60/. While one account has Teno Roncalio making the announcement, Theodore White says that McCracken actually announced the vote, 203; so did Edward Kennedy, *True Compass,* 149–150.

105 **"a lot of servicemen":** Schlesinger, 64.

106 **"we hope more vigorous":** Abigail McCarthy, *Private Faces, Public Places* (Garden City, N.Y.: Doubleday & Co., 1972), 242.

106 **"most telegenic person in public life":** John Shaw, *JFK in the Senate: Pathway to the Presidency* (New York: St. Martin's Press, 2013), 173.

106 **"likely to be uncannily correct":** John F. Kennedy, "Television as I See It: A Force That Has Changed the Political Scene," *TV Guide,* Nov. 14, 1959.

106 **"that will be very exhausting":** David Halberstam, *The Best and the Brightest* (New York: Random House, 1972), 98.

107 **"would be brave enough":** Norman Mailer, "Superman Comes to the Supermarket," *Esquire,* Nov. 1960.

107 **"hardest-working man I've ever known":** Canellos, 63.

107 **four or five college campuses:** *True Compass,* 157.

107 **rode a bucking bronco:** Rose Kennedy, 364–365.

108 **he stumped the state:** John Tunney int., Clymer Papers, Series 2, Box 5, T folder, Interviews, JFK Lib., March 6, 1995.

108 **only thirteen nights:** Thomas Morgan, "Teddy," *Esquire*, April 1962.

108 **went to Acapulco to recuperate:** *True Compass*, 158.

108 **"Joan Kennedy—Too Beautiful to Use":** Joan Kennedy int., Clymer Papers, Series 2, Box 4, K folder, JFK Lib., Dec. 12, 1996; *True Compass*, 165.

108 **should he decide to seek state office:** Edward Kennedy int., Clymer Papers, Oct. 9, 1995.

109 **the weekly plane to Rhodesia:** Clymer, 31–32; Edward Kennedy int., Series 2, Box 5, EMK interviews, 1992–1994 folder, Clymer Papers, JFK Lib., Oct. 7, 1993. There is some discrepancy over how long Ted was gone. Clymer says fifteen days and nine nations. Thomas Morgan, in his *Esquire* piece, says five weeks and sixteen nations. Kennedy himself says four weeks (*True Compass*, 164). I have chosen his time frame.

109 **formerly been servants' quarters:** Joan Kennedy int., Clymer Papers, Dec. 12, 1996.

109 **"accommodate myself to my husband's schedule":** Lester David, *Joan—The Reluctant Kennedy* (New York: Funk & Wagnalls, 1974), 52.

109 **"I felt accepted as a little sister":** William Peters, "Teddy Kennedy," *Redbook*, June 1962.

110 **"looking at herself in comparison":** Doris Kearns Goodwin, *The Fitzgeralds and the Kennedys: An American Saga* (New York: Simon & Schuster, 1987), 771–772.

110 **"They think we're weird":** Canellos, 71–72.

110 **"attaining the greatest happiness":** Richard Reeves, *President Kennedy: Profile of Power* (New York: Simon & Schuster, 1993), 480.

110 **"basis of rigorous comparison":** Burns, 279–280.

111 **"The nation had settled into":** Rick Perlstein, *Before the Storm: Barry Goldwater and the Unmaking of the American Consensus* (New York: Hill & Wang, 2001), xi.

111 **"would not hear of that party again":** Paul Krugman, *The Conscience of a Liberal* (New York: W. W. Norton & Co., 2007), 58–59. For full letter, dated Nov. 8, 1954, see: http://teaching americanhistory.org/library/document/letter-to-edgar-newton-eisenhower/.

111 **a consensus that marginalized:** Godfrey Hodgson, *America in Our Time: From World War II to Nixon* (Garden City, N.Y.: Doubleday & Co., 1976), 72, 76.

111 **"end of ideology":** Daniel Bell, *The End of Ideology: On the Exhaustion of Political Ideas in the Fifties* (Cambridge: Harvard Univ. Press, 1962; rep. 1988).

111 **"smooth deal":** Karl Meyer, *The New America: Politics and Society in the Age of the Smooth Deal* (New York: Basic Books, 1961).

111 **simply "the American consensus":** Perlstein, xi.

111 **"the old pattern may not be too violent":** George Packer, "The New Liberalism," *The New Yorker*, Nov. 17, 2008.

111 **defeating the very purpose of them:** Reeves, 332.

111 **"We'd lose everything":** *Ibid.*, 452.

112 **stave off Republican charges:** *Ibid.*, 306–307.

112 **"Life is unfair":** *Ibid.*, 129, 491.

112 **"a source of national renewal":** Hubert H. Humphrey, *The Education of a Public Man: My Life and Politics* (Minneapolis: University of Minnesota Press, 1991), 177.

112 **"all dreams within grasp":** Schlesinger, 584.

112 **"he made no pretense about it,"** Rita Dallas and Jeanira Ratcliffe, *The Kennedy Case* (New York: G. P. Putnam's Sons, 1973) 139–140.

112 **calling his brother "the President":** *Ibid.*, 140–141.

113 **"largely in terms of politics":** Hersh, 101.

113 **Bobby never did:** *Ibid.*, 275.

113 **"splendid quests and triumphs":** *True Compass*, 172.

113 **"Hmmmmmm, still wet, I see":** Dallas, 139–140.

113 **Ted made Jack look good:** David, 22.

113 **because Jack suffered from inhibitions:** Rose Kennedy, 126.

113 **"not so grim as the headmaster":** *Ibid.*, 488–489.

114 **"what he could and should not do":** Canellos, 62.

114 **"far from extinct":** Arthur Schlesinger Jr., *Journals: 1952–2000*, Andrew Schlesinger and Stephen Schlesinger, eds. (New York: Penguin Press, 2007), 122.

114 **"just dying with pleasure":** Hersh, 141–142.

114 **"The only way I'll go to the Senate":** Reeves, 29; Hugh Sidey, "Brother on the Spot," in *The Kennedy Circle,* Lester Tanzer, ed. (Washington, D.C.: Robert B. Luce, Inc., 1961), 186.

114 **"see to it that Bobby gets the same chance":** Clark Clifford with Richard Holbrooke, *Counsel to the President: A Memoir* (New York: Random House, 1991), 336–337.

115 **rumors of his joining the Cabinet:** Dallek, 319.

115 **he was always an outsider:** Edward Kennedy int., Clymer Papers, Series 2, Box 5, EMK interviews, 1992–1994 folder, JFK Lib., Oct. 29, 1994.

115 **while a freshman at Harvard:** Edward Kennedy int., Series 2, Box 5, EMK interviews 1995–1996 folder, Clymer Papers, JFK Lib., Apr. 17, 1995.

115 **telling his family of the appeal:** *True Compass,* 106.

115 **jumping onto a pool table:** Canellos, 49.

115 **from their nightly political arguments:** *Ibid.,* 52.

115 **"And here's to 1962, *Senator* Kennedy":** Edward Kennedy, "The Spark Still Glows," *Parade,* Nov. 13, 1983.

115 **"godlike figures to me":** *True Compass,* 162.

115 **"sacrificed himself":** RFK int., II, 61–62, JFK Oral Hist. Program, Apr. 13, 1964, quoted in Schlesinger, 371.

116 **the opportunity of higher office:** Edward Kennedy int., Clymer Papers, Series 2, Box 5, EMK interviews, 1992–1994 folder, JFK Lib., Oct. 7, 1993.

116 **"shape his own identity":** Patrick Kennedy int. by author.

116 **New Mexico, a Democratic state:** Peters.

116 **"fallen in love" with Arizona:** Joan Kennedy int., Clymer Papers, JFK Lib., Dec. 12, 1996.

116 **"It passed through my head":** Edward Kennedy int., Miller Center, UVA, June 3, 2005.

116 **for his political future:** John Tunney int., Miller Center, UVA, May 3, 2007.

117 **"He predicted unparalleled success for Teddy":** Edward Kennedy, *The Fruitful Bough* (self-published, 1965), 220.

117 **"and you did that":** Canellos, 67.

117 **delegation of senators McGee, Church, and Moss:** Edward Kennedy int., Clymer Papers, Series 2, Box 5, Interviews, 1992–1994 folder, JFK Lib., Oct. 7, 1993.

117 **decision seemed to have been made:** Edward Kennedy int., Clymer Papers, Series 2, Box 5, EMK interviews, 1995–1996 folder, JFK Lib., Oct. 9, 1996.

117 **"you better be ready to grab it":** Goodwin, 776.

118 **worth seriously considering:** Edward Kennedy int., Clymer Papers, JFK Lib., Oct. 9, 1996.

118 **"overcoat touch the floor":** Milton Gwirtzman int., Miller Center, UVA, May 29, 2009.

118 **"Great Brink's Robbery,"** Edward Kennedy int., Miller Center, UVA, March 23, 2005.

118 **get his youngest brother involved:** Memo, M. A. Jones to DeLoach, 11/21/62, Part 1, 12, Edward Kennedy FBI file.

120 **cases they gave to new attorneys:** Edward Kennedy int., Clymer Papers, JFK Lib., Oct. 7, 1993; Edward Kennedy int., Miller Center, UVA, March 23, 2005. In *True Compass,* Kennedy says it took twenty-six minutes to acquit Hennessey (167–168).

120 **Ted annoyed his fellow attorneys:** Burns, 75.

120 **"Teddy's the hardest worker I've got":** Morgan.

120 **even if it damaged his own case:** Al Hutton, quoted in Hersh, 150.

120 **"getting with child":** James Doyle int., Clymer Papers, Series 2, Box 3, D folder, JFK Lib., Feb. 9, 1995.

121 **describe his African experience:** Edward Kennedy int., Miller Center, UVA, March 23, 2005.

121 **"what was going on there":** Dan Fenn int., Miller Center, UVA, Nov. 4, 2004.

121 **his father became his "co-conspirator":** *Ibid.*

121 **the right answer was Bobby or Teddy:** O'Neill with Novak, 81–82.

122 **the first time it wasn't Joe Jr. and Jack and Bobby:** Edward Kennedy int., Clymer Papers, JFK Lib., Oct. 7, 1993; Dallek, 497; *True Compass,* 170.

122 **Jack was keeping the seat:** Lester David, *Ted Kennedy: Triumphs and Tragedies* (New York: Grosset & Dunlap, 1972), 90.

122 **"enormously devoted to my brother":** Edward Kennedy int., Miller Center, UVA, March 23, 2005.

122 **"slap in the face":** Murray Levin, *Kennedy Campaigning: The System and the Style as Practiced by Senator Edward Kennedy* (Boston: Beacon Press, 1966), 3–4.

122 **proud of the appointment:** Milton Gwirtzman int., Miller Center, UVA, May 29, 2009.

123 **Ben Smith, family friend:** Edward Kennedy int., Miller Center, UVA, March 23, 2005.

123   **largely as an enforcer:** "Edward McCormack Was Speaker's Brother," *The Washington Post*, Nov. 19, 1963.

123   **"self-effacing as a bass drum":** Garrison Nelson, *John William McCormack: A Political Biography* (New York: Bloomsbury, 2017), 59.

124   **"calculated risk":** Levin, 8.

124   **nearly came to blows:** O'Brien, 47-49.

124   **would abandon the Senate race:** Nelson, 613.

124   **Ted insisted he would never do that:** O'Neill, 171–172.

125   **it should be his, not Ted's:** Ed McCormack int., Clymer Papers, Series 2, Box 4, M folder, JFK Lib., May 15, 1992.

125   **"I've got the delegates sewed up":** O'Neill, 171–172.

125   **at talks in Italian communities:** Edward Kennedy int., Miller Center, UVA, March 23, 2005.

125   **Tunney leapt at the chance:** John Tunney int., Miller Center, UVA, May 3, 2007.

125   **The FBI, following Ted's trip:** Edward Kennedy file, Part Five, and Memo, Legat Embassy, Mexico City, to Director, FBI file, July 20, 1961.

125   **so they could listen to Radio Havana:** *True Compass*, 177.

126   **"So you can see what I'm up against":** Ltr., EMK to JPK, RFK, Rose Kennedy Papers, Box 14, Edward M. Kennedy folder, JFK Lib., July 1961.

126   **he debated whether he could afford it:** Edward Kennedy int., Miller Center, UVA, March 23, 2005.

126   **"every single night":** *Ibid.*

126   **"the central part of his life":** *Ibid.*

127   **"with a score of girls":** "Off and Running," *Time*, Oct. 27, 1961.

127   **"which have really helped out":** Ltr., EMK to JPK, Rose Kennedy Papers, Box 14, EMK folder, JFK Lib., 1961.

127   **"more loyal than Jack Crimmins":** Robert Fitzgerald, Sr., int., Miller Center, UVA, June 18, 2009.

127   **Culver was loyal:** John Culver int., Miller Center, UVA, March 31, 2005.

128   **neutralizing opposition:** Ed Martin int., Miller Center, UVA, Apr. 20, 2005; Edward Kennedy int., Miller Center, UVA, March 23, 2005.

128   **to aid Teddy in the French areas:** Ltr., Rose Kennedy, 1961, Smith, 699.

128   **people willing to go to war:** Levin, 167–168.

129   **"I don't think we can afford to feed him":** Canellos, 73.

129   **looked like an "unmade bed":** Nance Lyons int., Miller Center, UVA, May 9, 2008.

129   **"more about the Massachusetts situation":** Hersh, 155.

129   **"any school I could":** Edward Kennedy int., Miller Center, UVA, March 23, 2005.

130   **"Kennedy in '62" on the clasp:** *Ibid.*

130   **European and Mideast Trip:** "Edward Kennedy Finds Friends of U.S. Among Belgian Students," Feb. 11, 1962, *NYT;* "Edward Kennedy in Israel," Feb. 12, 1962, *NYT;* "E. M. Kennedy Briefed," Feb. 16, 1962, *NYT;* "E.M. Kennedy in Poland," Feb. 18, 1962, *NYT;* "Edward Kennedy in Paris," Feb. 20, 1962, *NYT.*

130   **"they do not have apples every day":** Edward Kennedy int., Miller Center, UVA, March 23, 2005.

130   **setting off a diplomatic tempest:** "Reds Propagandize Ted Kennedy's Slip," *WP,* Feb. 26, 1962.

130   **"It's good to be home":** "Ted Kennedy Gets Gay Irish Welcome," *WP,* Feb. 26, 1962.

131   **so as not to be usurped:** "President's Youngest Brother and Political Rival Overseas," *The New York Times,* Feb. 16, 1962.

131   **"more sensitive about the dynasty charge":** Robert Ajemian, "He Did More Than Just Get Well," *Life,* Jan. 15, 1965.

131   **"Well, get back there and help":** Hersh, 159.

131   **O'Brien said he didn't have the talk:** O'Brien, 142.

131   **"he's the man to discuss it with":** Dallek, 497–498.

132   **"I'm not sure I would have supported the idea":** Hersh, 160.

132   **likely to help them, not hurt them:** Eunice Kennedy, quoted in Nasaw, 766.

132   **"not to pick any new arguments":** Theodore Sorensen, Miller Center, UVA, May 19, 2005.

132   **to break the news to him:** Milton Gwirtzman int., Miller Center, UVA, May 29, 2009.

132   **"practiced a lot more after that":** Edward Kennedy int., Clymer Papers, JFK Lib., Oct. 9, 1996.

132   **prepped Teddy, writing up answers:** Edward Kennedy int., Miller Center, UVA, March 23, 2005.

133   **said that was just where Ted ought to be:** *Ibid.*

133 **cannily refused to say:** "Edward Kennedy Hints Senate Bid," *NYT*, March 12, 1962; Canellos, 75; Burns, 75.

133 **"kid three years out of college":** "Edward Kennedy Announces," *WP*, March 15, 1962.

133 **"Competition is healthy":** "Edward Kennedy in Senate Race," *NYT*, March 15, 1962.

133 **"before they make the sacrifice":** "Fun and Acid for Teddy," *Time*, March 30, 1962.

133 **"everybody else in the family has":** James Reston, "Another Kennedy Reaches for the Brass Ring," *NYT*, March 11, 1962.

134 **"president should not become involved":** Edward Kennedy int., Miller Center, UVA, March 23, 2005; Burns, 77.

134 Ted was **"on his own":** Tom Wicker, "President Bars Aid for Brother," *NYT*, March 15, 1962.

134 **break the story themselves:** Clifford with Holbrooke, 368–371; "The Kennedys," *American Experience*, prod. Elizabeth Deane, WGBH, 1992.

134 **The cheating scandal negotiations:** Robert Healy int., Miller Center, UVA, Aug. 10, 2005; Robert Healy int., Clymer Papers, Series 2, Box 3, H folder, JFK Lib., July 9, 1994; Clymer, 36–37; David, *Ted Kennedy*, 64–65; Hersh, 158; McGeorge Bundy int., Clymer Papers, Series 2, Box 3, B folder, JFK Lib., Nov. 11, 1993.

136 **"I remember that being a long, long day":** Edward Kennedy int., Miller Center, UVA, March 23, 2005.

136 **he could get through this after all:** *Ibid.*

136 **message to the recalcitrant:** "Edward Kennedy Pays His Congressman a Visit," *NYT*, Feb. 2, 1962.

137 **"he really felt great":** Gerard Doherty int., Miller Center, UVA, Oct. 10, 2005.

137 **"by the intellectual community":** Hersh, 156.

137 **"virtually nonexistent":** Levin, 129; Clymer, 37.

137 **sought to provide free defense attorneys:** Anthony Lewis, *Gideon's Trumpet*, (New York: Random House, 1964), 154.

137 **"not a Harvard professor":** Samuel Beer int., Miller Center, UVA, Feb. 17, 2005.

137 **"bothered him the most":** Hersh, 175.

138 **"affront to the Senate":** "The Teddy Issue," *Time*, Aug. 24, 1962.

138 **"affront to political decency":** "Kennedy Turns to Debate Again," *NYT*, Aug. 26, 1962.

138 **Radcliffe announced its support:** "E. J. McCormack Backed," *NYT*, Apr. 19, 1962.

138 **"running against George Washington":** John Meroney, "A Conversation with Gore Vidal," *The Atlantic*, Oct. 2009.

138 **"he could barely complete a sentence":** Samuel Beer int., Clymer Papers, Series 2, Box 3, B folder, JFK Lib., July 2, 1993.

138 **not even the right answers:** Hersh, 169.

139 **Ted didn't budge:** Charles Haar int., Miller Center, UVA, Oct. 10, 2005.

139 **"he was virtually indefatigable":** *Ibid.*

139 **craft speeches expressly for him:** Milton Gwirtzman int., Miller Center, UVA, May 29, 2009.

139 **Wooing the academics:** Dan Fenn Jr. int., Miller Center, UVA, Nov. 4, 2004.

140 **"yank" Ted out:** Gerard Doherty int., Miller Center, UVA, Oct. 10, 2005; "Ted Kennedy Denies He's Quitting Race," *WP*, Apr. 28, 1962.

141 **polls showed Ted leading McCormack:** "President Involved in Massachusetts Race," *Los Angeles Times*, Apr. 9, 1962; Levin, 116.

141 **"we understand that he's going to do well":** Gerard Doherty int., Miller Center, UVA, Oct. 10, 2005.

142 **"turning point":** Canellos, 80–81.

142 **"kick-started the campaign":** Edward Kennedy int., Miller Center, UVA, March 23, 2005.

142 **he had a lot to learn about running:** Betty Taymor int., Miller Center, UVA, July 8, 2005.

142 **"wiggle my way into the car":** Gerard Doherty int., Miller Center, UVA, Oct. 10, 2005.

142 **as sophisticated as his older brother's:** Robert Fitzgerald, Sr., int., Miller Center, UVA, June 18, 2009.

CHAPTER FOUR: "IF HIS NAME WAS EDWARD MOORE . . . "

143   **"to lack entirely a sense of responsibility":** Doris Kearns Goodwin, *The Fitzgeralds and the Kennedys: An American Saga* (New York: Simon & Schuster, 1987), 462.

143   **"Sloppy in almost all of his organization":** *John Fitzgerald Kennedy: As We Remember Him*, Joan Meyers, ed. (New York: Atheneum, 1965), 14.

143   **was enigmatic:** Edward Kennedy, *True Compass* (New York: Twelve, 2009), 23.

143   **"He lived within himself":** Richard Rhodes, "Things As They Are, Things That Never Were: The Last Kennedy," *Audience*, Nov./Dec. 1971, 87.

143   **"remember everything about him":** Ted Sorensen, *Counselor: A Life at the Edge of History* (New York: HarperCollins, 2008), 102.

144   **"come up ready for a Newport ball":** Barbara Perry, *Rose Kennedy: The Life and Times of a Political Matriarch* (New York: W. W. Norton & Co., 2013), 218.

144   **"we had to shove Jack into the streets":** "He Did More Than Just Get Well," *Life*, Jan. 15, 1965.

144   **at least the younger Bobby was:** Sorensen, *Counselor,* 250; Theodore Sorensen, *The Kennedy Legacy* (New York: Macmillan, 1969), 36.

144   **"unsociable":** Ltr., Rose to children, Jan. 5,1942, quoted in Arthur Schlesinger Jr., *Robert Kennedy and His Times* (Boston: Houghton Mifflin, 1978), 41.

144   **"Bobby lived in a heaven-and-hell world:"** "The Kennedys," *American Experience*, prod. Elizabeth Deane, WGBH, 1992.

144   **"right and wrong, good and evil":** William vanden Heuvel and Milton Gwirtzman, *On His Own: RFK 1964–1968* (Garden City, N.Y.: Doubleday & Co., 1970), 22.

144   **called him "sanctimonious":** Barbara Gibson and Ted Schwarz, *Rose Kennedy and Her Family: The Best and Worst of Their Lives and Times* (New York: Birch Lane Press, 1995), 183.

144   **he was a "punk":** John Tunney int., Miler Center, UVA, May 3, 2007.

145   **infuriating Dever:** Goodwin, 763.

145   **"contempt for self-indulgence":** Thurston Clarke, *The Last Campaign: Robert F. Kennedy and 82 Days That Inspired America* (New York: Henry Holt & Co., 2008), 23.

145   **" 'Larry, I don't know how you stand it' ":** Lawrence O'Brien, *No Final Victories: A Life in Politics from John F. Kennedy to Watergate* (Garden City, N.Y.: Doubleday & Co., 1974), 30.

145   **"it's the touching him they never forget":** Clarke, 212.

145   **"looking into the soul of the earth":** Gladys Gifford int. by author.

145   **" 'Let's make it fun time' ":** Rita Dallas and Jeanira Ratcliffe, *The Kennedy Case* (New York: G. P. Putnam's Sons, 1973), 64.

145   **"affability of an Irish cop":** "The Ascent of Ted Kennedy," *Time*, Jan. 10, 1969.

145   **"Now I can't eat and I don't sing!":** Christopher Lawford, *Symptoms of Withdrawal: A Memoir of Snapshots and Redemption* (New York: William Morrow, 2005), 379.

145   **"Nothing formal about him":** Melissa Ludtke int. by author.

146   **"Stalwart and optimistic":** Rose Fitzgerald Kennedy, *Times to Remember* (Garden City, N.Y.: Doubleday & Co., 1974), 365.

146   **"I think that comes through":** Betty Taymor int., July 8, 2005, Miller Center, UVA.

146   **"He'd find something [to like] in all five":** Brock Brower, "The Incident at Dike Bridge," *Life*, Aug. 1, 1969.

146   **"Ted's all heart":** Mrs. Robert Healy int., Miller Center, UVA, Aug. 10, 2005.

146   **"The reincarnation of Honey Fitz":** Perry, 66.

146   **"the way he did Ted":** Burton Hersh, *The Education of Edward Kennedy: A Family Biography* (New York: William Morrow and Co., 1972), 46.

146   **"The most naturally gifted":** *Ibid.,* 106.

146   **"best street personality":** "He's Not the Same Old Ted," *Newsweek*, June 24, 1968.

147   **"in somebody that young":** Milton Gwirtzman int., Series 2, Box 3, folder G, Clymer Papers, JFK Lib., Apr. 3, 1993.

147   **"Can I buy it from you?":** Gerard Doherty int., Miller Center, UVA, Oct. 10, 2005.

147   **"shrewdness about human motivation":** Hersh, 128.

147   **"the big smile, the slap on the back":** *Ibid.,* 110.

147   **"designed by his maker":** Lester David, *Ted Kennedy: Triumphs and Tragedies* (New York: Grosset & Dunlap, 1972), 115.

147   **"don't let that last play upset you":** John Culver int., Miller Center, UVA, March 31, 2005.

148 "get the hell out of here!": Gerard Doherty int., Miller Center, UVA, Oct. 10, 2005.
148 workers wouldn't be insulted: Charles Tretter int., Miller Center, UVA, Aug. 8, 2005.
148 "He was really brought up well": Milton Gwirtzman int., Apr. 3, 1993.
148 stern, yes, cruel, never: Charles Tretter int., Miller Center, UVA, Aug. 8, 2005.
148 "They respect the power": Murray Levin, *Kennedy Campaigning: The System and Style as Practiced by Senator Edward Kennedy* (Boston: Beacon Press, 1966), 151.
149 "he was interested in them": Hersh, 108.
149 "his hand black with grease": "Teddy and Kennedyism," *Time*, Sept. 28, 1962.
149 "You didn't miss a thing": Edward Kennedy int., Miller Center, UVA, March 23, 2005.
149 gather around him naturally: Charles Haar int., Miller Center, UVA, Oct. 10, 2005.
150 "just had it": John Tunney int., Miller Center, UVA, May 3, 2007.
150 "a spontaneous reaction": Levin, 110.
150 "whipped the crowds into football fervor": "Teddy and Kennedyism."
150 "Teddy is a Hollywood star": Levin, 110.
150 "seems to have that attraction": *Ibid.*, 26.
150 "The schedules were unbelievable": Barbara Souliotis int., Miller Center, UVA, July 12, 2005.
150 at the factory gates: Milton Gwirtzman int., Miller Center, UVA, May 29, 2009.
150 as many as 450 an hour: Edward Kennedy int., Miller Center, UVA, June 3, 2005.
151 On another day: Edward Kennedy int., Miller Center, UVA, March 23, 2005.
151 celebrating one nationality or another: *Ibid.*
151 Or the "house parties": Levin, 156.
151 was paying the tab: Edward Kennedy int., Miller Center, UVA, March 23, 2005.
151 and they would talk: Milton Gwirtzman int., Miller Center, UVA, May 29, 2009.
151 "out on the hustings again": Edward Kennedy, *The Fruitful Bough* (self-published, 1965), 204.
151 "He was just strenuously strong": Ed Martin int., Miller Center, UVA, Apr. 20, 2005.
152 shaking hands with the bathers: Hersh, 173.
152 his athletic competitions: Milton Gwirtzman int., Series 2, Box 3, folder G, Clymer Papers, JFK Lib., Apr. 3, 1993 and Jan. 30, 1993.
152 "on his own merits as a candidate": Rose Kennedy, 428.
152 it would be beneath him: John Seigenthaler int., Clymer Papers, Series 2, Box 5, S folder, R-Edward Kennedy folder, JFK Lib., Sept. 27, 1995.
152 I want to join my brothers: David, 103.
153 25,000 new voters: Levin, 163–164.
153 "a vitality, a real spirit": Charles Tretter int., Miller Center, UVA, Aug. 8, 2005.
153 some apartment buildings even had: Levin, 175-177.
153 a negative piece about Knocko: Douglass Cater, "How Teddy Beat Eddie," *The Reporter*, July 5, 1962.
153 "Because we've got it": "The Teddy and Eddie Show," *The Boston Globe*, Sept. 13, 1962.
153 missing two weeks of campaigning: Levin, 137.
153 supported McCormack and wanted to work: *Ibid.*, 147.
153 "Did you ever shake his hand?": *Ibid.*, 91.
153 "The presence isn't there": *Ibid.*, 127.
154 made him look "shifty": Cater; Levin, 18.
154 something less than alacrity: Milton Gwirtzman int., Miller Center, UVA, May 29, 2009.
154 "like running against the Church": Levin, 8.
154 "whore's paradise": Hersh, 164.
154 the 1954 state convention: Burns, 79.
154 "uphill battle": Edward Kennedy int., Miller Center, UVA, March 23, 2005.
155 supporter in the community: Levin, 52–53.
155 sent Joan to meet with the wives: *Ibid.*
155 "including Edward McCormack": Murray Levin and T. A. Repak, *Edward Kennedy: The Myth of Leadership* (Boston: Houghton Mifflin Co., 1980), 19–20.
155 1,300 of the 1,800 delegates: Hersh, 166–167.
155 phoning those he hadn't visited: Levin, 54.
155 "like a Dutch uncle": "Ted Kennedy Proves Successful Vote-Getter," *BG*, June 10, 1962.
155 "He just made me feel good": Levin, 78.
155 "cast of characters plagiarized": Cater.
156 "very important symbolically": Edward Kennedy int., Miller Center, UVA, June 3, 2005.

156 proceeded to give a short speech: "Pressure, Pressure," *Time*, June 15, 1962.
156 "'do yourself a favor'": "Teddy and Kennedyism."
156 the person he would focus on: Levin, 54–55.
157 six aides with walkie-talkies: *Ibid.*
157 "tirelessly putting his team through dry runs": Cater.
157 shouting above the cacophony: *Ibid.*
157 Convention that had nominated his brother: "Ted Kennedy Proves Successful Vote-Getter."
157 Doherty's count was off: Gerard Doherty int., Miller Center, UVA, Oct. 10, 2005.
157 Martin knew the count was wrong: Ed Martin int., Miller Center, UVA, Apr. 20, 2005.
157 "as though it was his convention": "Ted Kennedy Proves Successful Vote-Getter."
157 discussing post office business: Levin, 62.
157 "to win the Senate at the cost": Cater.
158 "like a first cousin to me": "Pressure, Pressure."
158 "you know, for the convention": Edward Kennedy int., Miller Center, UVA, March 23, 2005.
158 "I'm handling the patronage": Paul Driscoll, "Jack Was Asking About You," *The New Republic*, June 4, 1962.
158 "Think of what he could do to us!": Levin, 75.
159 son's staff had to stop him: Canellos, 82.
159 "haranguing" delegates: "Pressure, Pressure."
159 "best perform the work that must be done": Levin, 66.
159 he should concede rather than be humiliated: "Pressure, Pressure."
159 "With all this enthusiasm": Levin, 67.
159 a supporter shouted, "In Washington": "Edward Kennedy Chosen by Party," *The New York Times*, June 9, 1962.
160 Navy shipmate, Paul "Red" Fay: Thomas P. O'Neill with William Novak, *Man of the House: The Life and Political Memoirs of Speaker Tip O'Neill* (New York: Random House, 1987), 171–172.
160 the president would do no such thing: Hersh, 165.
160 ten questions for each candidate: Levin, 182–185.
161 one day he said, "Let's do it": Ed Martin int., Miller Center, UVA, Apr. 20, 2005.
161 "swing in voter attitudes": Edward Kennedy int., Miller Center, UVA, March 23, 2005.
161 agreed to take the offensive: Levin, 188–189.
161 "Have no feah, we are heah": Schlesinger, 371.
162 "surprisingly relaxed and informed": Theodore Sorensen int., Miller Center, UVA, May 19, 2005; "Sorensen on Kennedy: The 'Kid Brother' Who Grew Up" *Time*, Aug. 26, 2009.
162 "he'll look like a fool": Schlesinger, 371.
162 refuse to swing back: John Seigenthaler int., Clymer Papers, Series 2, Box 5, S folder, R-Edward Kennedy folder, JFK Lib., Sept. 27, 1995.
162 "you'll come out okay": Levin, 187.
162 Before the debate: "Great Debate Ends Without a Handshake," and "Contraband in Southie," *BG*, Aug. 28, 1962.
163 Lon Chaney movie: Mary McGrory, "Did Ed Hand Ted the Sympathy Vote?" *BG*, Aug. 28, 1962.
163 more frequently, "Teddy": "Going for the Jugular," *Time*, Sept. 7, 1962; Hersh, 178; Levin, 193.
164 "'I disagree with you respectfully'": Gerard Doherty int., Miller Center, UVA, Oct. 10, 2005.
164 Gwirtzman called "vicious": Milton Gwirtzman int., Miller Center, UVA, May 29, 2009.
164 "the candidate whom you feel": "The Teddy and Eddie Show"; "Edward Kennedy Assailed in Debate," *NYT*, Aug. 28, 1962; Levin, 210–211.
164 "shaking" during his closing statement: "Edward Kennedy Assailed in Debate."
164 he turned white and bit his lip: Milton Gwirtzman int., May 29, 2009.
164 he had to forge ahead: Levin, 211.
165 "when he brought up Eddie Moore": Hersh, 182.
165 as he stormed off the stage: Gerard Doherty int., Miller Center, UVA, Oct. 10, 2005.
165 "shock therapy": Ed McCormack int., Series 2, Box 4, M folder, Clymer Papers, JFK Lib., May 15, 1992.
165 "shock the people into understanding": Levin, 212.
165 bring it back forcefully: David, 113.
165 "swung from the floor": C. R. Owens, "Which Style Will Sell?" *BG*, Aug. 28, 1962.
165 he looked "shaken": McGrory.
165 "wiped the floor with him": *Ibid.*

165 **McCormack had won the debate:** Ed Martin int., Apr. 20, 2005.

166 **"candidate had been slaughtered":** Levin, 214.

166 **"in front of the entire country":** Hersh, 182–183.

166 **no sense of how the debate had gone:** Edward Kennedy int., Series 2, Box 5, EMK interviews 1995–1996 folder, Clymer Papers, JFK Lib., Apr. 17, 1995.

166 **"somebody who's just gone through that":** Milton Gwirtzman int., Clymer Papers, JFK Lib., Apr. 3, 1993.

166 **"Make him feel good":** Richard Reeves, *President Kennedy: Profile of Power* (New York: Simon & Schuster, 1993), 324.

166 **began calling people randomly:** Edward Kennedy int., Series 2, Box 5, EMK interviews 1995, Clymer Papers, JFK Lib., Apr. 17, 1995.

167 **apologize for McCormack's remarks:** Milton Gwirtzman int., Miller Center, UVA, May 29, 2009.

167 **deathly was the feeling:** *True Compass*, 185-186.

167 **"dirty politician":** Milton Gwirtzman int., May 29, 2009.

167 **for him and against McCormack:** Edward Kennedy int., Series 2, Box 5, EMK interviews, 1995–1996 folder, Clymer Papers, JFK Lib., Apr. 17, 1995.

167 **"Hey, I'm with Kennedy too":** Ed Martin int., Apr. 20, 2005.

167 **"the race is over":** Canellos, 85.

167 **the way McCormack had treated Ted:** *Ibid.*

167 **to "lacerate" McCormack:** Levin, 214.

168 **had effectively put away McCormack:** Edward Kennedy int., Series 2, Box 5, EMK interviews 1995, Clymer Papers, JFK Lib., Apr. 17, 1995.

168 **"razor sharp and spontaneous and lively":** Edward Kennedy int., Miller Center, UVA, March 23, 2005.

168 **the debate was "gentlemanly":** Milton Gwirtzman int., Miller Center, UVA, May 29, 2009.

168 **"softer tones of a family lawyer":** "Kennedy and McCormack Renew Their Debate," NYT, Sept. 6, 1962.

168 **"its most vigorous champion":** Levin, 157–158.

168 **"then I don't want any part of politics":** "Teddy and Kennedyism."

168 **"I just feel it coming my way":** "Campaigns at End in Massachusetts," NYT, Sept. 18, 1962.

169 **won McCormack's own precinct:** "Teddy and Kennedyism."

169 **"going to be a good ballot":** Edward Kennedy int., Miller Center, UVA, March 23, 2005.

169 **"He's not feeling well":** *Ibid.*

169 **robbed him of his speech:** Rose Kennedy, 416–417.

169 **"It was almost more than I could bear":** *True Compass*, 178.

169 **"and usually succeeded":** Dallas, 140.

170 **"It was pitiful":** George Smathers int., Oral History Interviews, Senate Historical Office, Aug. 1–Oct. 24, 1989.

170 **"the dignity of the Senate":** "Little Brother Wins," NYT, Sept. 19, 1962.

170 **"whether there are too many Kennedys":** Reeves, 325.

170 **"I am Ted Kennedy's brother":** "The Third Kennedy," NYT, Sept. 23, 1962.

171 **had trumped everything else:** Burns, 93; "Teddy and Kennedyism."

171 **"the hottest political properties":** "Teddy and Kennedyism."

171 **the faculty of the Harvard Business School:** https://www.hbs.edu/faculty/Pages/profile.aspx ?facId=7116.

171 **Teddy was going to run:** George Lodge int., Miller Center, UVA, July 8, 2005.

172 **the sobriquet "peace candidate":** Russell Baker, "Edward Kennedy Called Safe Bet," NYT, Oct. 12, 1962.

172 **gaining any traction:** Edward Kennedy int., Clymer Papers, Series 2, EMK interviews, Series 2, Box 5, EMK interviews, 1995–1996 folder, JFK Lib., Oct. 9, 1996; Hendrik Hertzberg, "Ted and Harvard, 1962," *The New Yorker*, Aug. 27, 2009.

172 **"can still be beaten":** Baker.

172 **"qualified to be a U.S. senator":** "Teddy and Kennedyism."

172 **"Who can get the most out of":** "Ted Kennedy Gives an Answer to Eisenhower," LAT, Oct. 17, 1962.

172 **"Democratic voice to speak for Massachusetts":** *Ibid.*

173 **"I would like to run":** Stewart Alsop, "What Made Teddy Run?" *The Saturday Evening Post*, Oct. 27, 1962.

173 **Massachusetts needed a Republican senator:** Baker.

173 **his policy positions:** Burns, 85.

173 **The committee met in his office:** "Ted Kennedy Aids 'Refugee' Plans," *WP,* May 8, 1962.

173 **the manager should be fired:** George Lodge int., Miller Center, UVA, July 8, 2005.

173 **Jack Crimmins, who also dispensed:** *Ibid.;* Ed Martin int., Miller Center, UVA, Apr. 20, 2006; Milton Gwirtzman int., Clymer Papers, JFK Lib., Jan. 30, 1993.

173 **"knew how much a victory":** Rose Kennedy, 428.

174 **"it isn't difficult to get worked up":** Edward Kennedy int., Miller Center, UVA, March 23, 2005.

174 **"one of the happiest years of my life":** Canellos, 79.

174 **"after all, Teddy's my life":** "Joan's Shy But Not About Ted," *WP,* Nov. 9, 1962.

174 **"Do you think he would be happy":** David, *Joan: The Reluctant Kennedy* (New York: Funk & Wagnalls, 1974), 70.

174 **"Teddy wasn't just a smart-ass kid":** *Ibid.,* 63.

174 **"amazed and delighted":** Milton Gwirtzman int., May 29, 2009.

174 **peeling away liberal votes from Ted:** Baker.

174 **"somewhat supercilious":** Hersh, 170.

175 **scheduled for that evening:** Edward Kennedy int., Clymer Papers, Series 2, EMK interviews, JFK Lib., Oct. 9, 1996.

175 **apparently a nervous laugh:** Edward Kennedy int., Miller Center, UVA, March 23, 2005; George Lodge int., Miller Center, UVA, July 8, 2005.

175 **the situation was so delicate:** Ted Sorensen int., Miller Center, UVA, May 19, 2005; *True Compass,* 188–189.

175 **agreed to remove the missiles:** Edward Kennedy int., Miller Center, UVA, June 3, 2005.

176 **before they made their bid:** Edward Kennedy int., Miller Center, UVA, March 23, 2005.

176 **"Campaign fatigue":** Baker.

176 **as McCormack had on the last day:** Nan Robertson, "A Diligent Senator," *NYT,* July 26, 1969.

176 **"You'd never know he's running for anything":** Baker.

176 **"never forgot":** Hertzberg.

177 **endorsing a health-insurance plan for senior citizens:** "Kennedy to Cast Ballot in Boston," *NYT,* Nov. 6, 1962.

177 **staff had made 300,000 phone calls:** Theo Lippman, *Senator Ted Kennedy: The Career Behind the Image* (New York: W. W. Norton & Co., 1976), 18.

177 **that didn't seem accurate:** "Vote Expense Listed by Ted Kennedy," *NYT,* Nov. 24, 1962.

177 **closer to $1 million:** Levin, 237.

177 **"It wasn't so much a victory":** Robert Sherrill, *The Last Kennedy* (New York: The Dial Press, 1976), 41.

177 **"Ted ran a perfect campaign":** Hersh, 183.

178 **"you can smile":** Edward Kennedy int., Miller Center, UVA, Oct. 8, 2007.

178 **Lodge could have no control:** George Lodge int., Miller Center, UVA, July 8, 2005.

CHAPTER FIVE: THE LOWEST EXPECTATIONS

180 **"when we slumbered":** Arthur Schlesinger Jr., *The Politics of Hope* and *The Bitter Heritage,* rep. (Princeton, N.J.: Princeton Univ. Press, 2008), 105, 9.

180 **"what they were going to do."** Edward Kennedy int., Miller Center, UVA, June 3, 2005, and Aug. 7, 2007.

180 **"encrusted with floral":** *NY Herald,* Jan. 5, 1859.

180 **"where business really seems to be done":** "A Public Building," *Harper's New Monthly,* Jan. 1869, 204–210.

180 **become "tawdry":** "New Senate Chamber," *The New York Times,* Dec. 8, 1895.

180 **"the upper legislative chamber":** *Ibid.*

180 **"time that you are privileged to serve":** Edward Kennedy, *True Compass* (New York: Twelve, 2009), 482–483.

181 **"just because I had a rocker":** "Senator Ted Makes Maiden Speech," *The Washington Post,* Jan. 11, 1963.

181 **Bobby's wife, Ethel, and Rose:** "Proud Wives Take the Gallery as Senators Take the Floor," *WP,* Jan. 11, 1963.

181 **This could be a long process:** J. Stanley Kimmitt Oral History, Senate Historical Office, 2003, 57.

181 **where John Kennedy had sat:** Robert Albright, "Teddy Bears Down in Silent, Sure Fashion," *WP*, March 3, 1963.

181 **Ted got Jack's desk:** Michael O'Brien, *Philip Hart: The Conscience of the Senate* (East Lansing: Michigan State Univ. Press, 1995), 150.

182 **"knocked on doors":** Birch Bayh int. by author.

182 **considering the Labor and Judiciary:** Edward Kennedy int., Miller Center, UVA, Jan. 6, 2007.

183 **petition, did not complain:** Edward Kennedy int., Miller Center, UVA, March 23, 2005.

183 **to thwart civil rights legislation:** William Honan, *Ted Kennedy: Profile of a Survivor* (New York: Quadrangle Books, 1972), 144.

183 **"very foxy, shrewd individual":** Edward Kennedy int., Clymer Papers, Series 2, Box 5, EMK int., 1992–1994 folder, JFK Lib., Oct. 7, 1993.

184 **"just getting his committee assignment":** Edward Kennedy int., Miller Center, UVA, March 23, 2005, and Oct. 8, 2007.

184 **"Judiciary Committee, which I did":** James Eastland int., nd, James O. Eastland Collection, Univ. of Mississippi.

184 **"aristocratic waster" when he arrived:** "King of the Hill," *The Economist*, Jan. 12, 2002.

184 **"some of the cloakroom jokes":** Robert Sherrill, *The Last Kennedy* (New York: The Dial Press, 1976), 45.

184 **"goddamn it, there it is":** David Burke int., Miller Center, UVA, June 19, 2007.

184 **"Bonus Baby":** "Ted Kennedy Acquires Humility from Rebuff," *Los Angeles Times*, Aug. 11, 1963.

185 **those close to him didn't:** Theodore Sorensen int., Miller Center, UVA, Dec. 7, 2006.

185 **"a politician no one takes seriously":** Stewart Alsop, "What Made Teddy Run?" The *Saturday Evening Post*, Oct. 27, 1962.

185 **"playing with the babes":** Lee Fentress int., Miller Center, UVA, Oct. 16, 2009.

185 **"Senate does its best to ignore him":** Richard Rhodes, "Things As They Are, Things That Never Were: The Last Kennedy," *Audience*, Nov./Dec. 1971, 92.

185 **"always out for a good time":** Burton Hersh, *The Education of Edward Kennedy: A Family Biography* (New York: William Morrow & Co., 1972), 194.

185 **"I knew I had a lot to learn":** Edward Kennedy int., Miller Center, UVA, Nov. 29, 2006; Richard Reeves, "A Publicly Moral Man," *USA Today*, Aug. 27, 2009.

185 **virtual campaign of pirating":** "Ted Kennedy Defense Work 'Piracy' Flayed," *LAT*, Dec. 20, 1962.

185 **"Na-na-na. Shame on you":** Lee Fentress int., Miller Center, UVA, Oct. 16, 2009.

185 **"a freshman should be seen and not heard":** "Family Reunion," *Newsweek*, Jan. 19, 1963.

185 **"You can't show off":** Charles Tretter int., Miller Center, UVA, Aug. 8, 2005.

186 **other freshmen were scheduled:** "Kennedy Striving to Escape Limelight," *WP*, Dec. 31, 1962.

186 **supporting Jack's reelection:** "Ted Kennedy Raps Goldwater," *WP*, Nov. 17, 1963.

186 **single press conference:** "Teddy Bears Down in Silent, Sure Fashion," *WP*, March 3, 1963.

186 **she was occupied with the children:** "Senator Kennedy Grants First News Interview," *LAT*, Apr. 22, 1963.

186 **focused on fishing:** Hersh, 219.

186 **his brother's legislative program:** "Senator Kennedy Grants First News Interview."

186 **"something that is going to fall on its face":** Theo Lippman, *Senator Ted Kennedy: The Career Behind the Image* (New York: W. W. Norton & Co., 1976), 6.

186 **seven million, five rooms:** Rochelle Jones and Peter Woll, *The Private World of Congress* (New York: The Free Press, 1979), 188.

186 **The office:** Lippman, 5; Honan, 157; Lester David, *Ted Kennedy: Triumphs and Tragedies* (New York: Grosset & Dunlap, 1972), 36–37.

187 **"wise old fox":** Barbara Lahage int., Miller Center, UVA, May 8, 2008.

187 **"hit the ground running":** Barbara Souliotis int., Miller Center, UVA, July 12, 2005.

187 **formed his own law firm:** Milton Gwirtzman int., Miller Center, UVA, May 29, 2009.

187 **"den mother" to the other women:** Terri Haddad Robinson int., Miller Center, UVA, Aug. 25, 2009.

187 **knew nothing about press relations:** John Culver int., Miller Center, UVA, March 31, 2005.

188 **called Gwirtzman the next day:** Milton Gwirtzman int.

188 **"Jobs simply evolved":** Anne Strauss int., Miller Center, UVA, Apr. 10, 2008.

188 **"he'd keep people waiting":** Charles Tretter int., Miller Center, UVA, Aug. 8, 2005.

189 **He was helping Ted Kennedy:** *Ibid.*

189 **"worse by the time":** *Ibid.*

189 **thought the senator had typed:** Anne Strauss int. April 10, 2008.

189 **"Everyone loved working there":** Terri Haddad Robinson int., Miller Center, UVA, Aug. 25, 2009.

190 **the ones who ran the club:** George Packer, "The Empty Chamber," *The New Yorker*, Aug. 9, 2010, 44.

190 **average age:** Robert Byrd, *The Senate: 1789–1989, Volume Two*, Wendy Wolf, ed. (Washington, D.C.: Govt. Printing Office, 1993), 288.

190 **"difficult to secure the enactment":** Richard Reeves, *President Kennedy: Profile of Power* (New York: Simon & Schuster, 1993), 325.

190 **"keeping Washington at a distance":** G. Calvin Mackenzie and Robert Weisbrot, *The Liberal Hour: Washington and the Politics of Change in the 1960s* (New York: The Penguin Press, 2008), 62.

190 **"one for all and all for one":** Tom Wicker, "Winds of Change in the Senate," *NYT Magazine*, Sept. 12, 1965, 119.

190 **"but it doesn't sink":** Robert C. Byrd, *The Senate, 1789–1989: Addresses on the History of the United States Senate, Volume One*, Mary Sharon Hall, ed. (Washington, D.C.: U.S. Government Printing Office, 1988), 715.

191 **reported to the Senate floor:** Edward Kennedy int., Miller Center, UVA, June 3, 2005.

191 **one had to take a "pledge":** Edward Kennedy int., Miller Center, UVA, March 23, 2005.

191 **"He knew how a young person":** Milton Gwirtzman int., Miller Center, UVA, May 29, 2009.

191 **"how to make a contribution to it":** David, 119.

192 **"lot of old bulls here":** Edward Kennedy int., Clymer Papers, Series 2, Box 5, EMK interviews, 1992–1994 folder, JFK Lib., Oct. 7, 1993.

192 **"as if I had pointed a gun at him":** Joe McCarthy, *The Remarkable Kennedys* (New York: The Dial Press, 1960), 129.

192 **"advice they have for you":** Edward Kennedy int., Miller Center, UVA, March 23, 2005.

192 **"greater respect for as a senator":** John Culver int., Miller Center, UVA, March 31, 2005.

192 **"how they were related to the Senate":** Edward Kennedy int., Oct. 7, 1993.

192 **prayer breakfast or at lunch:** Edward Kennedy int., Miller Center, UVA, March 23, 2005.

192 **seldom went to one another's offices:** Robert Shrum, *No Excuses: Concessions of a Serial Campaigner* (New York: Simon & Schuster, 2007), 75.

193 **"and governor of Georgia":** "Ted Kennedy Acquires Humility from Rebuff."

193 **laughing over Russell's expert putdown:** John Culver int., March 31, 2005.

193 **to find out what they were saying:** Edward Kennedy int., Clymer Papers, Series 2, Box 5, EMK interviews, 1995–1996 folder, JFK Lib., Oct. 9, 1996.

193 **discuss the day's events:** Edward Kennedy int., March 23, 2005.

193 **he gained contacts and information:** *Ibid.*

193 **"four or five plates in the air":** Lester David, *Joan: The Reluctant Kennedy* (New York: Funk & Wagnalls, 1974), 93.

194 **until three in the morning:** Adam Clymer, *Edward M. Kennedy: A Biography* (New York: William Morrow and Co., 1999), 46.

194 **"just on the basis of stories":** Edward Kennedy int., Oct. 7, 1993.

194 **an issue that would become important:** Edward Kennedy int., March 23, 2005.

194 **"He kept his mouth shut":** Lippman, 5.

194 **his two committees, Justice and Labor:** Lippman 4; "Ted Kennedy Acquires Humility from Rebuff."

194 **"take the attention away":** Milton Gwirtzman int., Series 2, Box 3, folder G, Clymer Papers, JFK Lib., Apr. 3, 1993.

195 **"He enjoyed understanding":** John Culver int., Miller Center, UVA, June 5, 2007.

195 **a "terrific fellow":** Milton Gwirtzman int., Apr. 3, 1993; Lippman, 4.

195 **"one of the most attractive young men":** Joseph Tydings int., Clymer Papers, Series 2, Box 5, T folder, JFK Lib., June 15, 1993.

195 **Federal Reserve chairman, Arthur Burns:** Edward Kennedy int., Clymer Papers, Series 2, Box 5, EMK interviews, 1997–1999, JFK Lib., Apr. 12, 1996.

195 **"determined to be a good senator":** George McGovern, *Grassroots: The Autobiography of George McGovern* (New York: Random House, 1977), 91.

195 **"heard an unkind word":** "Ted Kennedy Acquires Humility from Rebuff."

195 **the poll tax, in which Ted:** *The Committee on the Judiciary: A Brief History* (Washington, D.C.: Senate Historical Center, 2007).

195 "complete control over every aspect": Chris Myers Asch, *The Senator and the Sharecropper* (New York: The New Press, 2008), 268.

196 "if they weren't going to do judges": Edward Kennedy int., March 23, 2005.

196 "That was very important to him": Edward Kennedy int., Clymer Papers, Series 2, Box 5, EMK interviews, 1992–1994 folder, JFK Lib., Oct. 7, 1993.

196 Eastland's "little drinking club": *True Compass*, 192.

196 return him to Washington on Mondays: Edward Kennedy int., Miller Center, UVA, Jan. 6, 2007.

197 legislation went to die: J. Todd Moye, *Let the People Decide: Black Freedom and White Resistance Movements in Sunflower County, Mississippi, 1945–1986* (Chapel Hill: Univ. of NC Press, 2004), 19.

197 at the time Woods was acquitted: Asch, 6–32; Moye, 9–10.

197 "My father completely controlled me": Asch, 38.

197 hung in Eastland's Senate office: *Ibid.*, 36.

197 "we gotta have help from Washington": Booth Mooney, *LBJ: An Irreverent Chronicle* (New York: Crowell, 1976), 50.

198 "Ted's a master of that": Honan, 146.

198 "There was a lot of chemistry then": Edward Kennedy int., Clymer Papers, JFK Lib., Oct. 7, 1993.

198 "It is beyond explanation": Lippman, 4.

198 "you're going to get it out": Edward Kennedy int., Miller Center, UVA, Jan. 6, 2007.

199 "inconceivable that Mansfield": Ross Baker, "Mike Mansfield and the Birth of the Modern Senate," in Baker, *First Among Equals: Outstanding Senate Leaders* (Washington, D.C.: Congressional Quarterly, 1991), 283–284.

199 both vying for the position: Byrd, 674–679.

200 "lolling on the beach": *Ibid.*, 678.

200 "a permissive young don": Lewis Gould, *The Most Exclusive Club: A History of the Modern United States Senate* (New York: Basic Books, 2005), 233.

200 chipped away the bulls' power: J. Stanley Kimmitt Oral History, Senate Historical Office, (2003), 64.

200 to pressure them: Francis R. Valeo, Sec. of Senate, Oral Hist. Interviews, Senate Historical Office.

200 "anti-Johnson": Robert Dove int. by author.

200 "guiding force in the Senate": Byrd, *The Senate, Volume One*, 680.

200 Mansfield did not punish: Meg Greenfield, "Uhuru Comes to the Senate," *The Reporter*, Sept. 23, 1965.

200 attacked him on the Senate floor: "Harsh Words Are Used in Senate," *NYT*, Nov. 8, 1963.

201 "and no title, political face lifter": Byrd, *The Senate, Volume One*, 681.

201 "bipartisan liberal institution": Packer.

201 preparing for his presidential run: James MacGregor Burns, *Edward Kennedy and the Camelot Legacy* (New York: W. W. Norton & Co., 1976), 281.

202 "that guy from Arizona, Carl Hayden": Milton Gwirtzman int., Clymer Papers, JFK Lib., Apr. 3, 1993.

202 folkways of the Senate: *True Compass*, 484–485.

202 "I might be able to make it here": Edward Kennedy int., Miller Center, UVA, March 23, 2005.

202 "for each other's ideas": "Sen. Kennedy Grants First News Interview."

202 "so we were very guarded": Terri Haddad Robinson int., Miller Center, UVA, Aug. 25, 2009.

202 "lackey for his brothers": Milton Gwirtzman int., Miller Center, UVA, May 29, 2009.

202 diplomatic relations with Red China: "Ted Kennedy Acquires Humility from Rebuff."

203 "Tough shit": Richard Reeves, *President Kennedy: A Profile of Power*, 461.

203 in the vestibule: Burton Hersh, *The Shadow President: Ted Kennedy in Opposition* (South Royalton, Vt.: Steerforth Press, 1997).

203 a silver humidor that John Culver: Lippman, 282.

203 "awful lot done in the Senate": *Ibid.*, 272.

203 fly up to Hyannis together: Edward Kennedy int., Miller Center, UVA, March 23, 2005; EMK int., Clymer Papers, JFK Lib., Oct. 9, 1996; EMK int., Miller Center, UVA, Nov. 29, 2006.

204 "too demanding for the president": Arthur Schlesinger Jr., *Journals: 1952–2000*, Andrew Schlesinger and Stephen Schlesinger, eds. (New York: Penguin Press, 2007), 419.

204 "perplexities he wished for a moment": Arthur Schlesinger Jr., *Robert Kennedy and His Times* (Boston: Houghton Mifflin Co., 1978), 599.

204 **Mansfield left the floor immediately:** Rein J. Vander Zee int., Senate Historical Office, Jan. 28, 1992.

205 **his brother, the president of the United States:** David, *Ted Kennedy*, 129; *True Compass*, 208–209; McGovern, 91–92.

205 **Ted went to Lyndon Johnson's office:** William Manchester, *The Death of a President: November 20, 1973–November 25, 1963* (Boston: Little, Brown, 1967), 198.

206 **she recognized Ted and relented:** Peter Canellos, *Last Lion: The Fall and Rise of Ted Kennedy* (New York: Simon & Schuster, 2009), 93.

207 **simply told Ted, "He's dead":** Rita Dallas and Jeanira Ratcliffe, *The Kennedy Case* (New York: G. P. Putnam's Sons, 1973), 18.

206 **"the world lurched apart from me":** *True Compass*, 209.

207 **"Let's go to the White House":** Manchester, 198–199.

207 **"You could know that he was dead":** Milton Gwirtzman int., Miller Center, UVA, May 29, 2009.

207 **described it as a quiet tableau:** *Ibid.*; Rose Fitzgerald Kennedy, *Times to Remember* (Garden City, N.Y.: Doubleday & Co., 1974), 445.

208 **and then returned to the White House:** Milton Gwirtzman int., May 29, 2009.

208 **"Send this one. Send that one.":** Anne Strauss int., Miller Center, UVA, Apr. 10, 2008.

208 **which the staff did:** Terri Haddad Robinson int., Miller Center, UVA, Aug. 25, 2009.

209 **"in a very manly fashion":** John Culver int., Miller Center, UVA, March 31, 2005.

209 **"Oh, what a weekend that was":** John Tunney int., Miller Center, UVA, May 3, 2007.

209 **returned to Ted's house:** *Ibid.*

210 **"Get me *Paris Match*":** Terri Haddad Robinson int.

210 **"Insupportable emotional shock":** Rose Kennedy, 458.

210 **thinking Ted "heartless":** Dallas, 254–255.

210 **"I just show up":** Reeves, *Kennedy*, 104.

210 **"taken a bolt of lightning":** "The Kennedys," *American Experience*, prod. Elizabeth Deane, WGBH, 1992.

211 **"displaced by novel contours":** Richard Goodwin, *Remembering America: A Voice from the Sixties* (Boston: Little, Brown, 1988), 446.

211 **"as though he had withdrawn":** Schlesinger, *Robert Kennedy*, 637.

211 **"bruised spiritually and emotionally":** "The Kennedys," *American Experience*.

211 **Edith Hamilton's *The Greek Way*:** Schlesinger, *Robert Kennedy*, 618.

211 **"and so are often afraid of happiness":** Norman Mailer, *Miami and the Siege of Chicago*, (New York: World Publishing Co., 1968), 200–201.

211 **"wise counsel, and constant friend":** *True Compass*, 24.

211 **"he would break down and cry":** David, *Ted Kennedy*, 135.

211 **keep his grief from "disabling" him:** *True Compass*, 212-213.

211 **for some undefined transgression:** Edward Kennedy int., Miller Center, UVA, Nov. 29, 2006.

212 **talked again in mid-November:** Burns, 102–103.

212 **"Now I have more of a part":** David, *Ted Kennedy*, 251.

212 **"surrogate," their "dream-self":** Garry Wills, *The Kennedy Imprisonment: A Meditation on Power* (Boston: Little, Brown, 2002), 149.

212 **"but what exactly did he accomplish?":** Sherrill, 30.

212 **"technology could be mastered":** Henry Fairlie, *The Kennedy Promise: The Politics of Expectation* (Garden City, N.Y.: Doubleday & Co., 1973), 13.

213 **"JFK gave us the world":** James Carroll, "The End of the Dream," *The New Republic*, June 24, 1991.

213 **"but within our powers":** Goodwin, 235, 237.

214 **"want to share the Kennedy dream":** Nicholas deB. Katzenbach, *Some of It Was Fun: Working With RFK and LBJ* (New York: W. W. Norton & Co., 2008), 146.

214 **did not dissipate the hate:** Jeff Shesol, *Mutual Contempt: Lyndon Johnson, Robert Kennedy and the Feud that Defined a Decade* (New York: W. W. Norton & Company, 1997), 54–55.

214 **"There are going to be a lot of changes":** Manchester, 378.

215 **"He knows all about politics":** Schlesinger, *Journals*, 215.

215 **"larger than life and out of size":** Mackenzie and Weisbrot, 93.

215 **"In a cactus, all the pricks are on the outside":** Gould, 231–232.

216 **"I don't like it much":** John Bartlow Martin int., II, 8-17, JFK Lib., May 1, 1964; Schlesinger, *Robert Kennedy*, 653.

216 **"basically an administrative or executive problem":** Reeves, *Kennedy*, 321.

216 **"responded to utilitarian concerns":** *Ibid.*, 189.

216 **didn't live to see presented:** Stanley Greenberg, *The Two Americas: Our Current Political Deadlock* (New York: St. Martin's Griffin, 2005), 40; Mackenzie and Weisbrot, 91.

216 **he accepted the Supreme Court's decision:** McCarthy, 173–174.

217 **"We didn't lay awake nights":** Harris Wofford, *Of Kennedys and Kings: Making Sense of the Sixties* (New York: Farrar, Straus and Giroux, 1980), 129.

216 **"a bunch of chimpanzees":** Robert Dallek, *An Unfinished Life: John F. Kennedy, 1917–1963* (Boston: Little, Brown, 2003), 494.

217 **Americans opposed the Riders** *Ibid.*, 388; Richard Reeves, *Kennedy*, 133.

217 **"stop and examine his conscience":** JFK Address on Civil Rights, June 11, 1963. https://www .jfklibrary.org/archives/other-resources/john-f-kennedy-speeches/civil-rights-radio-and-television -report-19630611.

217 **78 percent of white Americans would move out:** https://ropercenter.cornell.edu/public-opinion -on-civil-rights-reflections-on-the-civil-rights-act-of-1964. [disabled]

218 **"ultimately make a decision":** Schlesinger, *Robert Kennedy*, 348.

218 **"fly on the wall":** Edward Kennedy int., Clymer Papers, JFK Lib., Oct. 9, 1996.

218 **could not tolerate ridicule:** *True Compass*, 200–201; Edward Kennedy int., Miller Center, UVA, Apr. 3, 2007.

218 **Ted made sure he was there:** "Edward Kennedy Greets Negro," *NYT*, May 13, 1962.

218 **"fully baptized":** *True Compass*, 201.

219 **"This is why he can't ever be president":** Schlesinger, *Robert Kennedy*, 336–337.

219 **since Reconstruction:** See Robert Caro, *Master of the Senate* (New York: Alfred A. Knopf, 2002), for the story of Johnson's shepherding of the 1957 bill.

219 **"The president is the cannon":** "Johnson's Tapes: A Treasure Under Seal for 50 Years," *WP*, Feb. 5, 1982.

220 **"very important part of the Republicans":** Edward Kennedy int., Miller Center, UVA, Apr. 3, 2007.

220 **"complete blueprint for the totalitarian state":** Moye, 127.

220 **"Judiciary Committee purgatory":** Clay Risen, *The Bill of the Century: The Epic Battle for the Civil Rights Act* (New York: Bloomsbury Press, 2014), 174.

220 **Mansfield moved to have the bill:** *Ibid.*, 173–174.

221 **seventy-five days of debate:** For the full story of the law's passage, read Risen, who attributes the legislative victory to a host of forces, not just Lyndon Johnson.

221 **"substance of the discussion":** *True Compass*, 216–217.

221 **what he called his "maiden" speech:** Charles Whalen, *The Longest Debate: A Legislative History of the 1964 Civil Rights Act* (Cabin John, Md.: Seven Locks Press, 1984), 161.

223 **to congratulate him:** Edward Kennedy int., Miller Center, Apr. 3, 2007.

224 **"Who do you imagine wrote it for him?":** Hersh, *The Shadow President*, 6.

224 **they would call for a vote often:** Charles Whalen, 144.

224 **critical to any prospect:** Edward Kennedy int., Miller Center, UVA, March 23, 2005 and Apr. 3, 2007; Edward Kennedy int., Series 2, Box 5, EMK interviews, 1997–1999, Clymer Papers, JFK Lib., Apr. 12, 1996.

225 **"A Beatles reception":** David, *Ted Kennedy*, 140–141.

225 **"their tribe of Irishmen":** Edward Behr, "A Day of Joy and Sadness," *The Saturday Evening Post*, July 11–18, 1964.

225 **"There wasn't a dry eye":** William vanden Heuvel int., Miller Center, UVA, July 19, 2005.

226 **"any more spring days here":** Behr.

226 **to signify "Aye":** Risen, 228.

227 **"glad to hear it":** *Ibid.*, 235.

227 **both in the South and in the Senate:** Whalen, 211.

227 **It passed 73 to 27:** Whalen, 214–215; Risen, 237.

227 **"No army can withstand the strength":** Risen, 220. Dirksen's role in the passage was obviously enormous. Though conservative on most issues, he was progressive on civil rights. In fact, Republicans generally hadn't been opposed to civil rights; given the number of Southerners in the Democratic caucus, Republicans actually had a better voting record on civil rights than Democrats, though there were recalcitrant Republicans from rural states who invoked states' rights as

a way of slowing racial progress. Dirksen managed to steer some of them into voting for the bill. In identifying heroes for the passage of the act, Dirksen qualifies as one.

CHAPTER SIX: "DO A LITTLE SUFFERING"

228 **"those bums up there in Boston":** Garrison Nelson, *John William McCormack: A Political Biography* (New York: Bloomsbury, 2017), 513.
229 **"no matter how small the fight":** Robert Ajemian, "He Did More Than Just Get Well," *Life*, Jan. 15, 1965.
229 **"active in the party":** Tom Wicker, "1962 Is Key Year for Fortunes of Democrats in Massachusetts," *The New York Times*, May 31, 1962.
229 **"he is my leader":** Burton Hersh, *The Education of Edward Kennedy: A Family Biography* (New York: William Morrow & Co., 1972), 195.
229 **handpicking legislative candidates:** Robert Novak and Rowland Evans, "Teddy Faces Test at Home," *The Washington Post*, Feb. 5, 1965.
229 **"difference between night and day":** Robert Donovan, "Ted Kennedy Gaining in National Stature," *Los Angeles Times*, March 4, 1964.
230 **And he was in control now:** "Ted Kennedy Passing Peace Pipe," *WP*, Aug. 16, 1965.
230 **"not to nominate Joan":** Hersh, 96.
231 **"didn't appear afraid at all":** John Tunney int., Miller Center, UVA, Oct. 12, 2009.
231 **"Flying through a black void":** Lester David, *Ted Kennedy: Triumphs and Tragedies* (New York: Grosset & Dunlap, 1972), 145.
231 **"down in sort of a rocky bluff":** Edward Kennedy int., Miller Center, UVA, Nov. 29, 2006.
231 **"like a toboggan ride":** "Ted Kennedy Likens Crash to 'Toboggan,'" *LAT*, Oct. 20, 1964.
232 **"something was seriously wrong with me":** *Ibid.*; Edward Kennedy, *True Compass* (New York: Twelve, 2009), 219–221.
232 **"what seemed an extraordinarily long time":** "Ted Kennedy Likens Crash to 'Toboggan.'"
232 **where they called an ambulance:** Edward Kennedy int., Miller Center, UVA, Apr. 3, 2007.
233 **He asked about the condition:** Hersh, 199–200.
233 **"I felt the tide was going out":** Edward Kennedy int., Miller Center, UVA, Nov. 29, 2006.
233 **And then he passed out:** *Ibid.*
233 **taillight of the plane kept rotating:** Birch Bayh int. by author.
233 **were already arriving:** Ed Martin int., Miller Center, UVA, Apr. 20, 2005.
233 **informing Joan:** Lester David, *Joan: The Reluctant Kennedy* (New York: Funk & Wagnalls, 1974), 152-155; Hersh, 201; Don Dowd int., Miller Center, UVA, August 9, 2005.
234 **Jean Kennedy Smith rushed in:** Rose Fitzgerald Kennedy, *Times to Remember* (Garden City, N.Y.: Doubleday & Co., 1974), 148.
234 **"Is he dead?":** Birch Bayh int. by author.
234 **"Gun it":** Rita Dallas and Jeanira Ratcliffe, *The Kennedy Case* (New York: G. P. Putnam's Sons, 1973), 280–281.
234 **Johnson ordered specialists:** "Kennedy's Recovery Is Expected," *WP*, June 21, 1964.
234 **Ted in an oxygen tent:** William vanden Heuvel int., Series 2, Box 3, A-H folder, Clymer Papers, JFK Lib., Apr. 6, 1995.
234 **"I thought he was dying":** Ed Martin int. Miller Center, UVA, Apr. 20, 2005.
235 **doctors knew yet whether he was paralyzed:** William Shannon, "How Ted Kennedy Survived His Ordeal," *Good Housekeeping*, Apr. 1965.
235 **had doubts whether he would survive:** "Senator Kennedy Almost Recovered," *WP*, Dec. 13, 1964; "A Very Special Patient," *Time*, July 3, 1964.
235 **He expired at 6:15 A.M.:** "A Six-Hour Battle to Save Moss," Cooley Dickinson Hospital, June 28, 1964, cooley-dickinson.org/Main/EdwardMoss.aspx. [link disabled]
235 **"Hi, Joansie. Don't worry":** David, *Ted Kennedy*, 148.
235 **a speech he was set to deliver:** Hersh, 201.
235 **"Is it true you are ruthless?":** Rose Kennedy, 458.
235 **"He was looking forward":** Milton Gwirtzman int., Miller Center, UVA, Aug. 5, 2009.
235 **"deader than a mackerel":** "Fastened Seat Belt Saved Kennedy," *WP*, July 4, 1964.
236 **"Somebody up there doesn't like me":** Arthur Schlesinger Jr., *Robert Kennedy and His Times* (Boston: Houghton Mifflin, 1978), 654.

236 **Jack Kennedy's back:** Tracy Staedler, "How John F. Kennedy's Back Pain Affected His Life and Death," *Live Science*, July 11, 2017, www.livescience.com/59764-john-f-kennedy-back-pain -affected-life-and-death.html; Doris Kearns Goodwin, *The Fitzgeralds and the Kennedys: An American Saga* (New York: Simon & Schuster, 1987), 775–776.

237 **"It seemed over":** Chris Matthews, *Jack Kennedy: Elusive Hero* (New York: Simon & Schuster, 2011), 188.

237 **Ted first began painting:** Carey Parker int., Miller Center, UVA, Oct. 27, 2008.

237 **There would be no operation:** *True Compass*, 222; Dallas, 283–284; Shannon.

237 **"get a hot dog on the way":** Ltr., John Kraft to EMK, John F. Kraft (#148) Personal Papers, Series 1, Corr., Box 13, EMK, JFK Lib., July 13, 1964.

237 **never going to walk again:** Edward Kennedy int., Miller Center, UVA, Nov. 29, 2006.

237 **tended by three surgeons:** Dr. H. D. Adams, *The Knife that Saves: Memoirs of a Lahey Clinic Surgeon* (Boston: Francis A. Countway Library of Medicine, 1991), 308–309.

237 **six months after the accident:** "Edward Kennedy Won't Need Operation on His Back," *NYT*, Aug. 14, 1964.

237 **"They can't keep a good man down":** LBJ conversation with EMK, (WH6408.19), Miller Center, UVA, Aug. 13, 1964.

237 **lifting Ted:** Barbara Gibson and Ted Schwarz, *Rose Kennedy and Her Family: The Best and Worst of Their Lives and Times* (New York: Birch Lane Press, 1995), 245.

238 **"your own discursive dull recital":** "In Walks Ted as the 89th Gets Under Way," *Life*, Jan. 15, 1965; Ltr., Rose to EMK, Rose Kennedy Papers, Box 59, Fam. Corr: EMK, 1958–1972, JFK Lib., 1964.

238 **he couldn't fall asleep again:** David, *Ted Kennedy*, 152.

238 **"go forward and go forward:"** William vanden Heuvel int., Miller Center, UVA, July 19, 2005.

238 **never even turned it on:** Ajemian.

238 **Vitale would fetch the meals:** Charles Tretter int., Miller Center, UVA, Aug. 8, 2005.

239 **"amazingly brave, determined, and cheery":** Ted Sorensen, *Counselor: A Life at the Edge of History* (New York: HarperCollins, 2008), 257.

239 **Evangelist Billy Graham visited:** *BG*, Sept. 23, 1964.

239 **liked him "very much":** Ed Martin int., Miller Center, UVA, Apr. 20, 2005.

239 **leaving "confusion" in his wake:** *True Compass*, 223–224; "LBJ Comes to Hub to Chat With Ted," *BG*, Sept. 29, 1964; Adam Clymer, *Edward M. Kennedy: A Biography* (New York: William Morrow & Co., 1999), 62; Edward Martin int., Miller Center, UVA, Nov. 29, 2006.

239 **"Lots of pilot error":** Birch Bayh int. by author.

239 **memory to be tarnished:** Edward Kennedy int., Miller Center, UVA, Nov. 29, 2006.

240 **paintings to his family members:** "Ted Kennedy Doffs Toga to Don Smock," *WP*, June 10, 1965.

240 **listened incessantly to opera:** David, *Ted Kennedy*, 242.

240 **gave him a crash course:** James MacGregor Burns, *Edward Kennedy and the Camelot Legacy* (New York: W. W. Norton & Co., 1976), 122; John Tunney int., Clymer Papers, Series 2, Box 5, T folder, Interviews, JFK Lib., March 6, 1995. See also Ltr., Robert C. Wood to EMK, Robert C. Wood Personal Papers, Series 2, EMK Corr. (#312), Box 1, JFK Lib., Aug. 6, 1964, for a sense of the reading program.

240 **could only read a "bit":** John Kenneth Galbraith int., Clymer Papers, Series 2, Box 3, G folder, JFK Lib., Feb. 6, 1995.

241 **he didn't think he had to study:** Samuel Beer int., Miller Center, UVA, Feb. 17, 2005.

241 **reading and jotting those notes:** Ajemian.

241 **"Teddy's reading all the books":** Hersh, 202.

241 **remembered the important points:** Jeffrey Blattner int., Miller Center, UVA, March 30, 2007.

241 **"something surreal":** Charles Tretter int., Miller Center, UVA, Aug. 8, 2005.

241 **"sheer bedlam":** Dallas, 283.

242 **who would tell Martin how:** Ed Martin int., Miller Center, UVA, Apr. 20, 2005.

242 **"we even took more rooms":** Charles Tretter int.

242 **"so he wants me to tell you":** *Boston Herald*, Oct. 9, 1964, Oct. 12, 1964.

242 **movies of them visiting him:** "Mrs. Kennedy Campaigns for Her Sons," *WP*, Oct. 14, 1964.

242 **"delight was genuine":** Arthur Egan quoted in David, *Joan: The Reluctant Kennedy*, 74, 83.

242 **"I do it for Ted":** *Ibid.*, 85.

243 **she would return to Ted:** *Ibid.*, 158–159.

243 **"and why I think you should return":** "Mrs. Kennedy Campaigns for Her Sons," *WP*.

243   **"I'm glad it was a short one tonight":** Arthur Egan quoted in David, *Joan: The Reluctant Kennedy,* 83.

243   **"Joan won in 1964":** Hersh, 203.

243   **"composed of the same elements":** Robert Caro, *The Passage of Power* (New York: Alfred A. Knopf, 2012), 575.

244   **47 percent of Democrats:** Jeff Shesol, *Mutual Contempt: Lyndon Johnson, Robert Kennedy, and the Feud that Defined a Decade* (New York: W. W. Norton & Co., 1997), 193.

244   **"so many of you nice fellows":** *Ibid.,* 209.

244   **he was a "carpetbagger":** Arthur Schlesinger Jr., *Journals: 1952–2000,* Andrew Schlesinger and Stephen Schlesinger, eds. (New York: The Penguin Press, 2009), 211.

244   **to tour the district with his friend:** John Tunney int., Miller Center, UVA, May 3, 2007; John Tunney int., Clymer Papers, Series 2, JFK Lib., March 6, 1995.

245   **and done so successfully:** Robert Dallek, *An Unfinished Life: John F. Kennedy, 1917–1963* (Boston: Little, Brown, 2003), 689.

245   **to draft a plan to thwart:** Schlesinger, *Robert Kennedy,* 451.

245   **"in a pluralistic society":** "Extremism in Perspective," Sept. 26, 1964, Samuel Beer files, in Burns, 340.

246   **by "fanatics":** Rick Perlstein, *Nixonland: The Rise of a President and the Fracturing of America* (New York: Scribner, 2008), 13.

246   **"sanctity" of property:** https://www.washingtonpost.com/wp-srv/politics/daily/may98/gold waterspeech.htm.

246   **"to drive the politics out of politics":** Richard Hofstadter, *The Paranoid Style in American Politics and Other Essays* (New York: Alfred A. Knopf, 1965), 121.

247   **"'nigger, nigger, nigger!' ":** Frank Cormier, *LBJ: The Way He Was* (Garden City, N.Y.: Doubleday & Co., 1977), 125.

248   **"the country I grew up in":** Paul Krugman, *The Conscience of a Liberal* (New York: W. W. Norton & Co., 2007), 11.

248   **they talked about Ted's recovery:** John Tunney int., Clymer Papers, JFK Lib., March 6, 1995.

248   **"stood beside his son":** Dallas, 285.

248   **"take short evening walks":** "Sen. Kennedy Almost Recovered," *WP,* Dec. 13, 1964.

248   **"Very few people could recover":** "In Walks Ted as the 89th Gets Under Way."

248   **the dog jumped into Ted's lap:** Peter Canellos, *Last Lion: The Fall and Rise of Ted Kennedy* (New York: Simon & Schuster, 2009), 108–109.

249   **he returned to the hospital for his release:** Hersh, 208–209; *BG,* Dec. 16, 1964.

249   **and adjust his covers:** Dallas, 320–321.

249   **to stand fully erect again:** *True Compass,* 223.

249   **"spiritual rebirth":** Samuel Beer int., Miller Center, UVA, Feb. 17, 2005.

249   **Bobby in the aftermath of Jack's death:** Sorensen, 145.

250   **"We'd really sold Ted Kennedy to the academic elite":** Samuel Beer int., Miller Center, UVA, Feb. 17, 2005.

250   **"what I wanted to do with my life":** William Shannon, "How Ted Kennedy Survived His Ordeal," *Good Housekeeping,* Apr. 1965.

250   **"wanted something with more substance":** Hersh, 207.

250   **"set you on an even finer course":** Theodore Irwin, "The Ordeal and Comeback of Ted Kennedy," *Altoona Mirror,* Jan. 23, 1965.

250   **"an effective and hardworking senator":** Schlesinger, *Journals,* 236.

250   **"I'll take my chances with that":** LBJ conversation with EMK, (WH6406.19), Miller Center, UVA, June 29, 1964.

CHAPTER SEVEN: "A HEIGHTENED SENSE OF PURPOSE"

251   **with a silver-headed cane:** Edward Kennedy int., Clymer Papers, Series 2, Box 5, EMK interviews, 1995–1999, JFK Lib., Sept. 11, 1998.

251   **"grimace and a smile":** "Ted Kennedy Returns to Take His Senate Seat," *The Washington Post,* Jan. 4, 1965.

251   **Returning to the Senate:** Robert Ajemian, "He Did More Than Just Get Well," *Life,* Jan. 15, 1965.

252   **"It's awfully nice to look forward":** Dan Cordtz, "The Senate Revolution," *The Wall Street Journal,* Aug. 6, 1965.

252 "a richer life of mind and spirit?": http://michiganintheworld.history.lsa.umich.edu/environmentalism/files/original/ddc6f706fd1f0dc3ff4e68f5373552db.pdf.

252 no liberal dream undreamed: http://www.presidency.ucsb.edu/ws/?pid=26907.

252 74 percent of Republicans approved: Rick Perlstein, *Nixonland: The Rise of a President and the Fracturing of America* (New York: Scribner, 2008), 5.

253 "astonishing silence of the South": Meg Greenfield, "Uhuru Comes to the Senate," *The Reporter*, Sept. 23, 1965.

253 "unimpressed by the old rules": Cordtz.

253 "half to three-quarters": Clayton Fritchey, "Who Belongs to the Senate's Inner Club?" *Harper's*, May 1967.

253 "There is no club in the Senate anymore": Robert C. Byrd, *The Senate, 1789–1989: Addresses on the History of the United States Senate, Volume One*, Mary Sharon Hall, ed. (Washington, D.C.: U.S. Government Printing Office, 1988), 687.

253 "urban industrialized America": Tom Wicker, "The Winds of Change," *The New York Times Magazine*, Sept. 12, 1965.

254 they would socialize again at night: Edward Kennedy int., Miller Center, UVA, March 23, 2005.

254 military bands played: Edward Kennedy int., Miller Center, UVA, June 3, 2005.

254 "We passed everything in the next year or two": Byrd, 683.

255 few, very few, did: Edward Kennedy int., Miller Center, UVA, June 3, 2005.

255 "I like Teddy. He's good": Peter Canellos, *Last Lion: The Fall and Rise of Ted Kennedy* (New York: Simon & Schuster, 2009), 127.

255 " 'best politician in the whole family' ": Joseph Califano Jr., *Governing America: An Insider's Report from the White House and the Cabinet* (New York: Simon & Schuster, 1981), 90.

256 "I'm just a trustee": LBJ to EMK, LBJ Lib.—#2707, March 30, 1964; discoverlbj.org/item/tel-02707.

256 "he's also doing us a lot of good": LBJ to Steve Smith, May 11, 1964, in Guian McKee, *The Presidential Recordings: Lyndon B. Johnson* (New York: W. W. Norton & Co., 2007), 546.

256 "he's more popular than Jack or Lyndon": LBJ to Ann Gargan, May 11, 1964, in *Ibid.*, 549.

256 Ted Kennedy did not doubt Johnson's liberalism: "Sen. Kennedy Asks for Democratic California," *LAT*, Jan. 26, 1964.

256 "the loyalty and the affection": LBJ and EMK (WH6411.02), Miller Center, UVA, Nov. 4, 1964.

257 "somewhat affected by how I came into the Senate": Edward Kennedy int., Clymer Papers, Series 2, Box 5, EMK interviews, 1992–1994 folder, JFK Lib., Oct. 7, 1993.

257 "become identified": LBJ and EMK (WH6501.01), Miller Center, UVA, Jan. 9, 1965.

257 "I'll do my damnedest": LBJ and EMK (WH6503.04), Miller Center, UVA, March 8, 1965.

258 attempting to make him a Johnson man: Edward Kennedy int., Clymer Papers, Series 2, Box 5, EMK interviews, 1996–1999 folder, JFK Lib., Oct. 9, 1995.

258 "side with an outsider against another Kennedy": Edward Kennedy, *True Compass* (New York: Twelve, 2009), 228.

258 "Their favors are courted": "Two Senators Named Kennedy," *Newsweek*, Jan. 17, 1966.

258 "You could feel the electricity": Robert Dove int. by author.

258 "much more intimate professional life": John Culver int., Miller Center, UVA, June 5, 2007.

258 described as "shorthand": William vanden Heuvel and Milton Gwirtzman, *On His Own: RFK 1964–1968* (Garden City, N.Y.: Doubleday & Co., 1970), 189.

258 "wonderful place": Edward Kennedy int., Miller Center, UVA, March 23, 2005.

258 " 'Let's get the job done' ": Dun Gifford int., Miller Center, UVA, July 13, 2005.

259 "As long as necessary, Robbie": Vanden Heuvel and Gwirtzman.

259 He joked that he chose the left: Nancy Soderberg int., Miller Center, UVA, Oct. 9, 2008.

259 "fast-blossoming idealism": *True Compass*, 230.

259 "jump ahead to the solution": Burton Hersh, *The Education of Edward Kennedy: A Family Biography* (New York: William Morrow & Co., 1972), 365.

259 "that big fat Irish bastard": John Aloysius Farrell, *Tip O'Neill and the Democratic Century* (Boston: Little, Brown, 2001), 177.

260 "not a bad attribute in this chamber": "If the Torch Is Passed to Kennedy, Maybe It Will Light on Ted," *Buffalo Evening News*, 1968.

260 "pull a quip that would get a laugh": Hersh, 365.

260 "had a way of talking down to the rest of us": *Ibid.*, 119.

260 **"With big words?":** Theo Lippman, *Senator Ted Kennedy: The Career Behind the Image* (New York: W. W. Norton & Co., 1976), 33.

260 **"You're learning, Robbie":** Vanden Heuvel and Gwirtzman.

260 **"not just as United States senators":** Jack Newfield, *Robert Kennedy: A Memoir* (New York: E. P. Dutton & Co., 1969), 34.

260 **"He is respected but not loved":** "Two Senators Named Kennedy."

260 **"then I would have known how to vote":** Arthur Schlesinger Jr., *Robert Kennedy and His Times* (Boston: Houghton Mifflin Co., 1978), 680.

260 **"He was the alpha dog":** John Tunney int., Miller Center, UVA, May 3, 2007.

261 **"And Ted deferred to him":** Milton Gwirtzman int., Clymer Papers, Series 2, Box 3, folder G, Interviews, JFK Lib., Jan. 30, 1993.

261 **"I think Ted had a real fear of center stage":** Hersh, 260.

261 **"stay off the floor":** Lippman, 31.

261 **"Well, that's par for the course":** William Honan, *Ted Kennedy: Profile of a Survivor* (New York: Quadrangle Books, 1972), 132–133.

261 **"I know what state it's in":** Hersh, 216–217.

261 **Bobby climbed the mountain anyway:** Honan, 132.

261 **McNamara closed Brooklyn:** Edward Kennedy int., Oct. 7, 1993.

262 **listed the speaking engagements:** Robert Donovan, "Ted Kennedy Gaining in National Stature," *LAT,* March 4, 1964.

262 **"Bobby came in and upset everything":** Rita Dallas quoted in Canellos, 111.

262 **"people whose high regard":** David Burke int., Miller Center, UVA, June 19, 2007.

262 **took elocution lessons:** Milton Gwirtzman int., Series 2, Interviews, Box 5, G folder, Clymer Papers, JFK Lib., Apr. 3, 1993.

263 **"gracious gesture":** Charles Tretter int., Miller Center, UVA, Aug. 8, 2005.

263 **"It was like I settled for less":** David Burke int., Miller Center, UVA, June 19, 2007.

263 **"passed muster":** *Ibid.*

264 **now joined Ted's staff:** Dun Gifford int., July 13, 2005.

264 **Gifford made $26,000:** Gladys Gifford int. by author.

264 *How did I get into this situation?:* David Burke int., Miller Center, UVA, June 19, 2007.

264 **memo on every piece of legislation:** Meg Greenfield, "The Senior Senator Kennedy," *The Reporter,* Dec. 15, 1966.

265 **when he felt that Bobby was better prepared:** Lippman, 30–31.

265 **"they had just been destroyed":** David Burke int., Miller Center, UVA, June 19, 2007.

265 **"Toppers":** Lippman, 30.

265 **"had to do after an election":** Greenfield.

265 **"fills you with a heightened sense":** *True Compass,* 482-483.

266 **"'not a guide by which to live'":** Richard Rhodes, "Things As They Are, Things That Never Were: The Last Kennedy," *Audience,* Nov./Dec. 1971.

266 **"major legislation every month":** G. Calvin Mackenzie and Robert Weisbrot, *The Liberal Hour: Washington and the Politics of Change in the 1960s* (New York: The Penguin Press, 2008), 113.

266 **"rather sleepy subcommittee":** Edward Kennedy int., Miller Center, UVA, Oct. 8, 2007.

266 **Honey Fitz had argued:** Doris Kearns Goodwin, *The Fitzgeralds and the Kennedys: An American Saga* (New York: Simon & Schuster, 1987), 102.

266 **immigration law was passed in 1952:** Joyce Vialet, "Summary of Developments in Immigration Law," *Immigration and Nationality Law Review,* 1979–1980, 101–155.

267 **a premium on family reunification:** John F. Kennedy, *A Nation of Immigrants* (New York: Harper & Row, 1964). The book had originally been published by the Anti-Defamation League in 1958 and was in the process of being revised at the time of John Kennedy's death. It was commercially published posthumously.

267 **Azorean Refugee Act of 1958:** Daniel Marcos, *The Capelinhos Eruption: Window of Opportunity for 2008 Azorean Emigration* (Providence: Brown University, 2008).

267 **"This was something alive":** Edward Kennedy int., Miller Center, UVA, April 3, 2007.

267 **"assault on America's immigration system":** Jerry Kammer, "The Hart–Celler Immigration Act of 1965," *Center for Immigration Studies,* Sept. 30, 2015.

267 **"without basis in either logic or reason":** Vialet, 144–145.

268 **deputized Ted as the acting chairman:** Tom Gjelten, *A Nation of Nations: A Great American Immigration Story* (New York: Simon & Schuster, 2015), 110.

268   **the opening witness:** Edward Kennedy, "The Immigration Act of 1965," *Annals of the American Academy of Political and Social Science*, 367, Sept. 1966, 142.

268   **"based on the work a man could do":** https://millercenter.org/the-presidency/presidential-speeches/january-4-1965-state-union.

268   **Hart commended him for his work:** *Congressional Record*, 89th Congress, 1st Session, Vol. 1, 111, Jan. 15, 1965.

268   **"great scorching issue":** Hersh, 221–222.

269   **Ireland, England, and Germany:** "Immigration and Nationality Legislation of 1965," Box 132, Information Briefing folder, Refugee subcommittee, Legislative Archives, 89th Congress, National Archives.

269   **"especially advantageous":** See Kennedy, "The Immigration Act of 1965," *Center for Immigration Studies*, https://cis.org/Report/HartCeller-Immigration-Act-1965.

271   **proportions highly favorable to the desirable Northern Europeans:** Press release, Rep. Michael Feighan, 89th Congress, Senate Judiciary Comm., Subcommittee on Refugees, Immigration, Misc. issues, Box 132, Senate Records, Nat. Archives, June 1, 1965.

271   **national-origin quotas by another name:** Tom Gjelten, "The Unintended Consequences of a 50-Year-old Immigration Bill," *WP*, Sept. 25, 2015.

271   **Feighan's chain-migration priority:** "House Judiciary Panel Expected to Reach Accord on Immigration Bill," *NYT*, June 30, 1965.

271   **"Just shove it any way you can":** Gjelten, *A Nation of Nations*, 117.

272   **" 'It's just not fair' ":** David Burke int., Miller Center, UVA, June 19, 2007.

272   **"historically had the greatest influence":** Senate Subcommittee on Immigration and Naturalization of the Committee on the Judiciary, Immigration Hearings, 89th Congress, 1st Session, Washington, p. 67.

272   **to confirm a Mississippi judge:** Gjelten, *A Nation of Nations*, 128.

272   **pinning a shamrock on Ervin's:** William Shannon, "The Emergence of Senator Kennedy," *NYT Magazine*, Aug. 22, 1965.

273   **reintroduce it the following year:** Edward Kennedy int., Miller Center, UVA, Oct. 8, 2007.

273   **"moral principle" of the bill:** Gjelten, *A Nation of Nations*, 129.

273   **bill was approved on September 8:** "Immigration Bill Gains in Senate," *NYT*, Aug. 27, 1965.

273   **stack of fifty blue notecards:** "Two Senators Named Kennedy."

273   **" 'he's going to kill me' ":** David Burke int., Miller Center, UVA, Apr. 9, 2008.

273   **first bill to repeal:** Duane Tananbaum, *Herbert H. Lehman: A Political Biography* (Albany, N.Y.: SUNY Press, 2016), 418.

274   **which were given nonquota status:** *Congressional Record*, 89th Congress, 1st Session, 24225, Sept. 22, 1965; "Immigration Statement," Box 132, Immigration Hearings folder, Refugee subcommittee, Legislative Records, 89th Congress, 1st Session, National Archives, Sept. 17, 1965.

274   **Thurmond, who called for an overall reduction:** "Senate Starts Debate on Immigration Reform," *LAT*, Sept. 18, 1965.

274   **"exactly how many nigras":** Burton Hersh, *Edward Kennedy: An Intimate Biography* (Berkeley, Calif.: Counterpoint, 2010), 201.

274   **Thurmond's idea to impose:** Kennedy, "The Immigration Act of 1965."

274   **"the devotion which the senator":** *Congressional Record*, 89th Congress, 1st Session, 24784, Sept. 22, 1965.

274   **"perhaps the single most":** Otis Graham, "Tracing Liberal Woes to '65 Immigration Act," *Christian Science Monitor*, Dec. 28, 1995.

276   **"to right wrong, to do justice, to serve man":** "Transcript of the Johnson Address on Voting Rights," March 16, 1965, *NYT*.

277   **measured accomplishments:** Martin Nolan, "Kennedy Dead at 77," *The Boston Globe*, Aug. 26, 2009.

277   **"We just got to":** David Burke int., Miller Center, UVA, June 19, 2007.

277   **a signal moment:** "Joseph Rauh Jr., Groundbreaking Civil Liberties Lawyer, Dies at 81," *NYT*, Sept. 5, 1992.

278   **one of the organizers of the March:** http://repository.wustl.edu/concern/videos/rj430634r.

278   **hot issue, he said, was the poll tax:** David Burke int., Miller Center, UVA, June 19, 2007.

279   **"particularly worked up":** Edward Kennedy int., Miller Center, UVA, Apr. 3, 2007.

279   **a provision of the bill:** Birch Bayh int., Clymer Papers, Series 2, Box 3, B folder, JFK Lib., Feb. 3, 1995.

279   **a committee "filibuster":** Nicholas Katzenbach int., Miller Center, UVA, Nov. 29, 2005.

279   **he conferred with other experts:** Edward Kennedy int., Clymer Papers, JFK Lib., Oct. 7, 1993.

279   **one wouldn't have to wait:** Edward Kennedy int., Apr. 3, 2007.

280   **"That's how the poll-tax fight began":** Hersh, *The Education of Edward Kennedy,* 227–229.

280   **Ted rebutted:** *Congressional Record,* Senate, 89th Congress, 1st Session, 10081, May 11, 1965.

281   **"If you can tell the states":** Andrew Glass, "Poll Tax Beaten, But Ted Prevails," *BG,* May 12, 1965.

281   **Burke Marshall, a close friend:** "Ted Rocking Lyndon's Boat," *BG,* May 7, 1965.

281   **Ted was grandstanding:** Nicholas Katzenbach int., Nov. 29, 2005.

281   **finding it at the expense:** Nicholas Katzenbach int., Nov. 29, 2005.

281   **being condescending to Ted:** David Burke int., Miller Center, UVA, June 19, 2007.

282   **"any new senator ingratiate":** Shannon.

282   **a "fundamental problem":** *Ibid.*

283   **"gentlemanly ways":** "Bobby–Teddy Team Works for New Kennedy Era," *WP,* May 12, 1965.

283   **"his right hand clutching":** "Teddy's Triumph," *Newsweek,* May 24, 1965.

283   **Mansfield offered Ted a seat:** Roscoe Drummond, "Ted Kennedy Has Come of Age," *LAT,* May 6, 1965.

284   **decided to rush his own and Dirksen's bill:** *Ibid.*

284   **"many hours we spent":** Charles Haar int., Miller Center, UVA, Oct. 10, 2005.

285   **going over it "again and again":** David Burke int., Miller Center, UVA, Apr. 9, 2008.

285   **"If you can beat me, beat me":** Nicholas Katzenbach int., Nov. 29, 2005.

286   **"I will get right on it":** Recording, LBJ and Vance Hartke, #7600, LBJ Library, May 7, 1965.

286   **"We're running out of time":** LBJ and EMK (WH6505.07), Miller Center, UVA, May 11, 1965.

286   **it was probably unconstitutional:** Rowland Evans and Robert Novak, "Johnson Isn't Really Against Poll Tax Ban," *LAT,* May 18, 1965.

287   **"rare moment of high drama":** "Senate Rejects Poll-Tax Ban," *LAT,* May 16, 1965; "Bobby–Teddy Team Works for New Kennedy Era."

287   **"its effect is obviously discriminatory":** Edward Kennedy int., Miller Center, UVA, Apr. 3, 2007.

287   **to see if the president would need their votes:** "Senate Rejects Ban on Poll Tax," *NYT,* May 12, 1965.

287   **Ted "cheerfully":** "Bobby–Teddy Team Works for New Kennedy Era."

287   **"We felt he was too soft":** Drummond.

287   **"earned the right not to be called 'the kid' ":** Lippman, 44.

288   **"a radically new direction":** Robert Sherrill, *The Last Kennedy* (New York: The Dial Press, 1976), 48.

288   **his late brother had often failed":** "Bobby–Teddy Team Works for New Kennedy Era."

288   **"He almost—but not quite—persuaded me":** "Senate Rejects Poll-Tax Ban."

288   **"no scars":** Andrew Glass, "Ted Loses New Boy Look," *BG,* May 16, 1965.

288   **A "moral victory":** "Senate Reject Poll-Tax Ban."

288   **A "personal triumph":** "Senate Rejects Poll-Tax Ban in Voting Bill," May 12, 1965, *LAT.*

288   **"insult and blasphemy":** "Dr. King Denounces Action," *NYT,* May 12, 1965.

289   **"unable to awaken the South":** "Mansfield Gives Plan on Poll Tax," *NYT,* May 18, 1965.

290   **"his swiftly rising son":** Richard Goodwin, *Remembering America: A Voice from the Sixties* (Boston: Little, Brown, 1988), 24–25.

290   **was "way off base":** David Nasaw, *The Patriarch: The Remarkable Life and Turbulent Times of Joseph P. Kennedy* (New York: The Penguin Press, 2012), 768.

290   **he felt no compunction:** "Ted Kennedy in Toughest Political Fight of Career," *LAT,* Oct. 10, 1965.

290   **"You finished seventh":** Robert Healy int., Miller Center, UVA, Aug. 10, 2005. In an earlier interview with Adam Clymer, Healy remembered the location as California; Clymer Papers, Interviews, Series 2, Box 3, H folder, JFK Lib., July 9, 1994.

291   **"It ain't gonna happen:"** Robert Healy int., Aug. 10, 2005.

291   **the bean suppers with him:** Edward Kennedy int., Miller Center, UVA, Jan. 6, 2007.

291   **"Teddy's eyes and ears":** Gerard Doherty int., Miller Center, UVA, Oct. 10, 2005.

291   **"Frank raised my approval rating":** *True Compass,* 170.

291   **"God love you":** Milton Gwirtzman int., Miller Center, UVA, Aug. 5, 2009.

292   **"He was a sketch":** Milton Gwirtzman int., Miller Center, UVA, May 29, 2009.

292   **"always ridiculed":** Gerard Doherty int., Oct. 10, 2005.

292   **was not going to risk embarrassment:** David Burke int., Miller Center, UVA, June 19, 2007.

292 **"a matter of loyalty"**: *True Compass*, 234.
292 **he had a commitment**: Edward Kennedy int., Miller Center, UVA, Jan. 6, 2007.
292 **Morrissey had even said this publicly**: "JFK Promised Federal Judgeship," *WP*, Oct. 1, 1965.
293 **"Teddy is one of the most loyal people"**: Rita Dallas and Jeanira Ratcliffe, *The Kennedy Case* (New York: G. P. Putnam's Sons, 1973), 140.
293 **"he came back and told me"**: George Abrams int., Series 2, Box 3, folder A, Clymer Papers, JFK Lib., June 17, 1992.
293 **"Do you really want this?"**: Milton Gwirtzman int., Miller Center, UVA, May 29, 2009.
293 **"he is giving it a little extra push"**: Recording, LBJ, JPK, and EMK, LBJ Library, #8902, Sept. 24, 1965.
293 **Katzenbach himself was "pissed"**: Milton Gwirtzman int., Series 2, Box 3, Folder G. Clymer Papers, JFK Lib., April 3, 1993.
294 **as a way, Sullivan felt**: William Sullivan, *The Bureau: My Thirty Years in Hoover's FBI* (New York: W. W. Norton & Co., 1979), 59–60.
294 **given Morrissey's history**: David Burke int., June 19, 2007.
294 **"I'd withdraw it tomorrow"**: Recording, LBJ and Katzenbach, LBJ Library, #8906, Sept. 28, 1965.
295 **"They usually don't say much"**: "Ted Kennedy in Toughest Political Fight of Career."
295 **"To them a federal judgeship"**: Milton Gwirtzman int., Miller Center, UVA, May 29, 2009.
295 **"does not measure up"**: "Morrissey Called Unqualified," *BG*, Sept. 27, 1965.
295 **the chance to defend himself**: "Morrissey Furor Mounts," *BG*, Sept. 29,1965.
296 **"If the guy on top likes you"**: Milton Gwirtzman int., Miller Center, UVA, Apr. 3, 2009.
296 **"We'll do the best we can"**: George Abrams int.
296 **give the upstart a lesson**: *Ibid.*
297 **possibly charmed Dirksen**: David Burke int., June 19, 2007.
298 **at variance with Jenner's testimony**: "Bar Assn., Morrissey Conflict," *BG*, Oct. 13, 1965.
298 **Tydings "tore into him"**: George Abrams int.
298 **"embarrassing questions"**: "Panel Likely to Approve Morrissey," *WP*, Oct. 13, 1965.
298 **saying that Morrissey had lied**: Robert Healy int., Miller Center, UVA, Aug. 10, 2005.
299 **"no hard feelings"**: "From Pillory to Post," *Time*, Oct. 22, 1965.
299 **"all good conscience"**: Edward Kennedy int., Miller Center, UVA, Jan. 6, 2007.
299 **seven members declined to vote**: "Ted Vows to Push for Morrissey," *BG*, Oct. 16, 1965.
300 **promising to help fund-raise**: "Kennedy Bloc Strained," *WP*, Oct. 24, 1965.
300 **"Don't ask me why"**: "Morrissey's Atlanta Address Backed by Katzenbach," *BG*, Oct. 19, 1965.
300 **" 'he ain't going to blame himself' "**: Califano, 90.
300 **"There is no basis whatsoever to question"**: "Report by Katzenbach Backs Morrissey Story," *LAT*, Oct. 19, 1965.
300 **the FBI had several witnesses**: "Morrissey's Atlanta Address Backed by Katzenbach."
301 **to recommit the nomination**: "Dirksen Doubtful Morrissey Can Win," *BG*, Oct. 20, 1965.
301 **Johnson answered noncommittally**: Recording, LBJ and Dirksen, LBJ Library, #9026, Oct. 20, 1965.
301 **"I try to get everything"**: "Ted Yields," *BG*, Oct. 22, 1965.
301 **"Can't we keep you out of trouble, Teddy?"**: Edward Kennedy int., Miller Center, UVA, March 23, 2005.
301 **challenged him to make the charges**: Fred Graham, "Edward Kennedy Drops His Fight for Morrissey," *NYT*, Oct. 22, 1965.
302 **"That was one of the best friends I ever had"**: "Ted Yields."
302 **Morrissey was a victim**: "Profile in Brinkmanship," *Time*, Oct. 29, 1965.
303 **"tragedy for the man"**: Lester David, *Ted Kennedy: Triumphs and Tragedies* (New York: Grosset & Dunlap, 1972), 158–159.
303 **"Adam as only Adam can do"**: Milton Gwirtzman int., Miller Center, UVA, May 29, 2009.
304 **Morrissey's nomination was finally dead**: "Profile in Brinkmanship"; "Ted Yields."
304 **"If it's the right thing to do"**: Charles Ferris int., Clymer Papers, Series 2, Box 3, F folder, JFK Lib., Apr. 10, 1992.
304 **"and to take the heat"**: Milton Gwirtzman int., Clymer Papers, JFK Lib., Jan. 30, 1993.
304 **" 'I think we've fulfilled our commitment' "**: Milton Gwirtzman int., May 29, 2009.
305 **five or six votes short**: Edward Kennedy int., Miller Center, UVA, March 23, 2005.

305 "Ted Kennedy went all the way to the brink": "Profile in Brinkmanship."
305 "only the Senator's reputation": "Few in Morrissey Fight Emerged," *WP*, Oct. 25, 1965.
305 lost some of his confidence: Meg Greenfield, "The Senior Senator Kennedy," *The Reporter*, Dec. 15, 1966.
305 "surprise retreat": Graham.
305 "anything but beneficial": "Ted Yields."
305 "He did the right thing": David Burke int., June 19, 2007.
306 "It showed an indication of character": Francis Valeo int., Oral History Interviews, Senate Historical Office.
306 "the brink of embarrassment": "Profile in Brinkmanship."

CHAPTER EIGHT: A DYING WIND

307 Bobby Kennedy was the more furious: Joseph Tydings int., Clymer Papers, Series 2, Box 5, T folder, JFK Lib., June 15, 1993.
307 "as hard a jaw-biting": Edward Kennedy int., Miller Center, UVA, March 23, 2005.
308 Madame Nhu lobbied Ted: Edward Kennedy, *True Compass* (New York: Twelve, 2009), 205–206.
308 his first remarks on Vietnam: Adam Clymer, *Edward M. Kennedy: A Biography* (New York: William Morrow & Co., 1999), 49–50.
308 a 1954 conference in Geneva: Stanley Karnow, *Vietnam: A History* (New York: Penguin, 1997, revised), 264.
309 "'soft on communism' charges": Richard Reeves, *President Kennedy: Profile of Power* (New York: Simon & Schuster, 1993), 230.
309 "Too liberal to fight": Reeves, 351.
309 "manhood can be affirmed only": Arthur Schlesinger Jr., *Robert Kennedy and His Times* (Boston: Houghton Mifflin, 1978), 722, 431.
309 "Vietnam is the place": Reeves, 173; Karnow, 265.
309 he should never trust the military brass: Clymer, 52.
310 "one authentically humanist": G. Calvin Mackenzie and Robert Weisbrot, *The Liberal Hour: Washington and the Politics of Change in the 1960s* (New York: The Penguin Press, 2008), 286.
310 he criticized hard-liners: Robert Dallek, *An Unfinished Life: John F. Kennedy, 1917–1963* (Boston: Little, Brown, 2003), 455.
310 "show that we mean business": Karnow, 270.
310 "if they have it in the first place": Robert C. Byrd, *The Senate, 1789–1989: Addresses on the History of the United States Senate, Vol. One*, Mary Sharon Hall, ed. (Washington, D.C.: U.S. Government Printing Office, 1988), 691.
311 "That will never happen": Karnow, 266.
311 "make damned sure that I am reelected": Kenneth O'Donnell and David Powers, *Johnny, We Hardly Knew Ye: Memories of John F. Kennedy* (Boston: Little, Brown, 1972), 16.
311 "get the American people to reelect me": Reeves, 484.
311 "beginning to understand": Edward Kennedy int., Miller Center, UVA, May 30, 2007.
311 "be forced to escalate the war": Mackenzie and Weisbrot, 308.
311 "They'll forgive you for anything": Tel. conversation, LBJ and Richard Russell, June 11, 1964, in *Presidential Documents: Words That Shaped a Nation from Washington to Obama, Second Edition*, Thomas McInerney and Fred L. Israel, eds. (New York: Routledge, 2012), 295.
312 "stand up to the pressure": "Edward Kennedy Feels Brother Gave Impetus," *LAT*, Sept. 28, 1965.
312 "our words will not be good": *Issues and Answers*, Aug. 29, 1965, quoted in James MacGregor Burns, *Edward Kennedy and the Camelot Legacy* (New York: W. W. Norton & Co., 1976), 133.
312 he was soliciting experts: EMK to Marks, Subcommittee on Refugees, Box 51 [1965], folder 1965 & Before, Senate Records, National Archives, May 28, 1965.
312 how Ted found himself: George Abrams int., Clymer Papers, Series 2, Box 3, A folder, JFK Lib., Nov. 27, 1992.
312 "our foreign-policy vehicle": *Ibid.*
313 "very politically dangerous subject": *Ibid.*
313 "two sets of numbers": *Ibid.*
313 had given little or no thought: Clymer, 80.

313 **"impossible to move an administration"**: Abrams int., Clymer Papers.

313 **information about the refugees:** *Ibid.*

314 **"not the bigger picture":** *Ibid.*

314 **a "movable cocoon":** John Tunney int., Clymer Papers, JFK Lib., March 6, 1995; John Tunney int., Miller Center, UVA, May 3, 2007.

314 **Lee Kuan Yew:** Edward Kennedy int., Miller Center, UVA, May 30, 2007.

314 **"this will last a long time":** Clymer, 82.

315 **"happening to the . . . civilian population":** *Ibid.*

315 **the primary focus of the mission:** *Ibid.*, 81–82.

315 **"only political figure in Washington":** Neil Sheehan, *A Bright Shining Lie: John Paul Vann and America in Vietnam* (New York: Vintage, 1989), 620.

315 **"If we do not support freedom":** Clymer, 83.

315 **"Fissures began to show up":** John Tunney int., Series 2, Box 5, T folder, Clymer Papers, JFK Lib., March 6, 1995.

315 **the Americans now had replaced the French:** John Tunney int., Miller Center, UVA, May 3, 2007.

316 **Fall refuted nearly everything:** Edward Kennedy int., Series 2, Box 5, EMK interviews 1995, Clymer Papers, JFK Lib., Apr. 17, 1995.

316 **"what was going on below":** David Burke int., Miller Center, UVA, June 19, 2007.

317 **cautioned Ted not to believe:** William vanden Heuvel, Miller Center, UVA, July 19, 2005.

317 **"the beginning of my transition":** Edward Kennedy int., Miller Center, UVA, May 30, 2007.

318 *Look* **would be less than happy:** George Abrams int.

318 **volunteer, nonmilitary international force:** Edward M. Kennedy, "A Fresh Look at Vietnam," *Look*, Feb. 8, 1966.

318 **hawks might escalate the war:** "Two Senators Named Kennedy," *Newsweek*, Jan. 17, 1966.

318 **"say anything very tough":** Memo, Re: Phone Conversation with Ted Kennedy, Bundy to LBJ, Jan. 26, 1966, LBJ Lib., Jan. 26, 1966.

319 **certainly have voted with Johnson:** Tel. EMK and LBJ, #3967, June 30, 1964, https://www .discoverlbj.org/item/tel-03967; Karnow, 380–394. There is a great deal of controversy over what actually happened in the Gulf of Tonkin over those few days, though it is likely the American ships were baiting the North Vietnamese to attack.

319 **"putting a fox in a chicken coop":** Jack Newfield, *Robert Kennedy: A Memoir* (New York: E. P. Dutton & Co., 1969), 124–125.

319 **"Ho Chi Kennedy":** Schlesinger, 736–737.

319 **same opportunity for subversion:** "Ted Kennedy Asks 'Direct Contacts With Viet Cong,'" *LAT*, March 7, 1966.

320 **"quiet consultations":** Meg Greenfield, "The Senior Senator Kennedy," *The Reporter*, Dec. 15, 1966.

320 **out through the back door:** Edward Kennedy int., Miller Center, UVA, Apr. 3, 2007.

320 **the racism of the North:** William vanden Heuvel int., Miller Center, UVA, July 19, 2005.

321 **sparked Ted's curiosity:** Peter Canellos, *Last Lion: The Fall and Rise of Ted Kennedy* (New York: Simon & Schuster, 2009), 105.

321 **Ted was "very taken":** Dr. Jack Geiger int., Clymer Papers, Series 2, Box 3, G folder, JFK Lib., May 18, 1995; Martha Bebinger, "Kennedy's Forty Year Push for Universal Coverage," WBUR, Jan. 21, 2009.

321 **"hours on public transportation":** Edward Kennedy, "The Cause of My Life," *Newsweek*, July 27, 2009.

322 **"stars of that long, tense morning":** Dun Gifford int., Miller Center, UVA, July 15, 2005.

322 **"you can put the other two wherever":** Edward Kennedy int., Miller Center, UVA, March 28, 2008.

322 **"and he supported me":** Edward Kennedy int., Clymer Papers, Series 2, Box 5, EMK interviews, 1995–1996, JFK Lib., Oct. 9, 1995.

323 **"lessening degrees":** *True Compass*, 238.

323 **"definitively and precisely":** George Abrams int.

324 **let him air his grievances:** "Ted Kennedy Debates Viet War Hecklers," *LAT*, Oct. 28, 1966.

324 **saw the anger in those protesting:** Edward Kennedy int., Miller Center, UVA, June 17, 2005.

324 **while he opposed the war "totally":** Theo Lippman, *Senator Ted Kennedy: The Career Behind the Image* (New York: W. W. Norton & Co., 1976), 51.

324 **"the elders in the institution"**: John Herbers, "Edward Kennedy is Gaining Stature in the Senate," *NYT*, June 2, 1967.

324 **"seen as the future"**: Robert Dove int. by author.

324 **"tendency to be grimmer"**: Drew Pearson, "The Next President Kennedy?" *The Washington Post*, Nov. 11,1964.

325 **"future president of the United States"**: "75,000 Hail Ted Kennedy in Cleveland," *LAT*, Sept. 15, 1965.

325 **31 percent thought it should exercise**: Lloyd A. Free and Hadley Cantril, *The Political Beliefs of Americans: A Study of Public Opinion* (New Brunswick, N.J.: Rutgers Univ. Press, 1967), 19.

325 **only 32 percent thought entering the war**: https://www.cbsnews.com/news/cbs-news-poll-u-s -involvement-in-vietnam/.

326 **rendered by his Warren Court**: Alden Whitman, "Earl Warren, 83, Who Led High Court in Time of Vast Social Change, Is Dead," *NYT*, July 10, 1974.

327 **"sadly aware he was absorbing"**: "The Senate Revolution," *The Wall Street Journal*, Aug. 6, 1965.

328 **working with senator Howard Baker Jr.**: *True Compass*, 253–254.

328 **increase Republican representation**: Burton Hersh, *The Education of Edward Kennedy: A Family Biography* (New York: William Morrow & Co., 1972), 268.

328 **the partnership was struck**: Howard Baker int., Clymer Papers, Series 2, Box 3, B folder, JFK Lib., Jan. 13, 1994.

329 **the names of thirty senators**: "Kennedys Swing Passage of 1 Man, 1 Vote Now," *WP*, June 9, 1967.

329 **"doomed crusade"**: "Home for Ted," *Time*, Dec. 1, 1967.

330 **"anybody else in the Senate"**: Hersh, 269.

330 **middle of the Arab–Israeli War**: Herbers.

330 **would likely be ruled unconstitutional**: *Ibid.*

330 **he worked the phones**: *True Compass*, 253–254.

330 **an obvious attempt to obstruct**: "Conferees Delay Districting Date," *NYT*, Oct. 19, 1967.

331 **"unconstitutional, unconscionable"**: "Senate Rejects a Delay Until '72 of Redistricting," *NYT*, Nov. 9, 1967.

331 **"We think it worked out nicely"**: Hersh, 271.

331 **"He isn't a wise guy:"** "Home for Ted."

331 **"surely been underestimated"**: David Broder, "Apportionment Honors Due Senators Kennedy," *WP*, Nov. 14, 1967.

331 **"The center of our concerns"**: Karnow, 493.

332 **death and destruction on the nightly news**: https://alphahistory.com/vietnamwar/us-escalation -in-vietnam/.

332 **44 percent of Americans favored withdrawal**: https://ropercenter.cornell.edu/public-support -vietnam-1967/. [link disabled]

332 **protests against the war grew**: https://ropercenter.cornell.edu/public-support-vietnam-1967/. [link disabled]

332 **"has been a casualty"**: Clymer, 97.

333 **"Dr. Spock's outfit"**: Roche to LBJ, Marvin Watson Papers, Box 29, file: Roche, John—Memos, LBJ Lib., Feb. 17, 1967, cited in Joseph Palermo, "The Johnson Administration Responds to Sen. Edward M. Kennedy's Trip to South Vietnam," *Peace & Change*, Jan. 1998, 49.

333 **treatment was usually inadequate**: EMK to McNamara, Refugee Subcomm., 90th Congress, Box 65, Senate Records, National Archives, March 15, 1967.

333 **Ted would desist from publicizing:** "Vietnam to Get 3 U.S. Hospitals," *NYT*, Apr. 7, 1967.

334 **"the politics of inadvertence"**: John Aloysius Farrell, *Tip O'Neill and the Democratic Century* (Boston: Little, Brown, 2001), 230.

334 **he and his staff set up meetings**: George Abrams int.

334 **a much sunnier press release**: "More Health Aid for Saigon Urged," *NYT*, Sept. 22, 1967.

334 **decided to hold public hearings**: Lippman, 53.

335 **more than two million displaced**: "Vietnam's Refugees," *NYT*, Oct. 21, 1967.

335 **"critical to our success"**: "U.S. Agency Scores Two War Programs," *NYT*, Oct. 12, 1967.

335 **Bundy responded feebly**: "William Bundy Challenged on Vietcong Recruiting," *NYT*, Oct. 17, 1967.

335 **Ted didn't take more criticism**: Burns, 137.

336 **"That's really rather different"**: David Burke int., Miller Center, UVA, June 19, 2007.

337 **"the hearts of the people":** "The Hearts of the People," *Time*, Oct. 20, 1967.

337 **"vote of confidence and gratitude":** "Edward Kennedy Praises Johnson's Skill and 'Heart,'" *NYT*, Oct. 8, 1967.

337 **"bullet will never defeat":** *Congressional Record*, 90th Congress, 1st Session, Senate, 34190-34192, Nov. 29, 1967.

337 **"to use our men and resources":** "Edward Kennedy Urges Shift in Vietnam Policy," *NYT*, Nov. 1, 1967.

337 **" 'People getting hurt!' ":** Lippman, 56.

338 **"were poor and urban":** Edward Kennedy int., Clymer Papers, Series 2, Box 5, EMK interviews, 1995–1996 folder, JFK Lib., Oct. 9, 1996; Edward Kennedy int., Miller Center, UVA, June 17, 2005.

338 **drafting nineteen-year-olds first:** "His Proposal: Draft '19's' First," *WP*, Oct. 7, 1966.

338 **he submitted a resolution:** "Ted Kennedy Proposes Johnson Move on Draft," *LAT*, Feb. 24, 1967.

338 **"calls the signals":** "Gen. Hershey in Reversal Backs Draft Lottery," *NYT*, March 21, 1967.

339 **Congressional approval would be required:** "Johnson's Draft Lottery Plan Assailed in House," *NYT*, May 3, 1967; "House Group Backs Curb On Johnson Draft Lottery," *NYT*, May 19, 1967; "Draft Extension of 4 Years Voted," *NYT*, May 26, 1967.

339 **called instead for a one-year extension:** "Senate Approves Draft Bill," *NYT*, June 15, 1967.

339 **The bill passed 72 to 23:** Clymer, 90–91.

340 **"We're a Navy state and a Navy family":** *Ibid.*, 91.

340 **and the war continued:** White House meeting.

340 **"We are in danger of losing":** "Mood Indigo," *Time*, Dec. 15, 1967.

340 **"single most important reason":** File 3: Senator Kennedy's Visit to Paris, Vietnam: Notes—U.S.–North Vietnamese Peace Talks. Donated Historical Materials: John Gunther Dean, Country files, Box 16, Carter Papers.

341 **speech on the Senate floor on March 2:** *True Compass*, 249; Newfield, 133.

341 **"pass a protest vote":** "Bob Kennedy's Brother Backs Halt to Bombing," *LAT*, March 5, 1967.

341 **"It is not our mission to make Asia safe":** Robert Sherrill, *The Last Kennedy* (New York: The Dial Press, 1976), 52.

342 **"he ended up far more liberal":** Ted Sorensen, *Counselor: A Life at the Edge of History* (New York: HarperCollins, 2008), 254.

342 **"preoccupied with suffering and despair":** Newfield, 18.

342 **he would submit legislation:** Melody Miller int., Miller Center, UVA, July 15, 2008.

343 **"Safe Streets and Crime Control Acts":** Daniel Patrick Moynihan, "The Democrats, Kennedy, and the Murder of Dr. King," *Commentary*, May 1968.

343 **"improvement of the quality of American life":** Burns, 135–136.

343 **Bobby Kennedy didn't just want a cause:** RFK int., 10-11, JFK Oral History Program, Dec. 22, 1964, quoted in Schlesinger, 372.

343 **would do anything to be president:** *Ibid.*, 825.

344 **worried that the characterization:** Edward Kennedy int., Miller Center, UVA, June 17, 2005.

344 **"a lot of emotional things":** Thurston Clarke, *The Last Campaign: Robert F. Kennedy and 82 Days That Inspired America* (New York: Henry Holt & Co., 2008), 87.

344 **he was taking a very long time:** Edward Kennedy int., Clymer Papers, Series 2, Box 5, EMK interviews, 1995–1996 folder, JFK Lib., Apr. 12, 1996.

344 **thinking of asking Ted to run:** "Edward Kennedy Reported Weighed as Johnson Stand-In," *NYT*, Nov. 17, 1967.

345 **"varying degrees of intensity":** Edward Kennedy int., June 17, 2005.

345 **The consensus again was to move slowly:** *Ibid.*

346 **"he was deeply distressed":** George McGovern, *Grassroots: The Autobiography of George McGovern* (New York: Random House, 1977), 109–111.

346 **"there was meanness in his heart":** Thomas P. O'Neill with William Novak, *Man of the House: The Life and Political Memoirs of Speaker Tip O'Neill* (New York: Random House, 1987), 202.

346 **no better reason than that:** Hersh, 291.

346 **McCarthy meeting:** *True Compass*, 252; Edward Kennedy int., Miller Center, UVA, June 17, 2005.

347 **"He was just buffaloed, blinking":** Hersh, 294–295.

347 **McCarthy told Ted he had no choice:** *True Compass*, 252.

347 **"and I will do everything I can":** "Ted Kennedy Disavows Run as Favorite Son," *WP*, Dec. 5, 1967.

348 **the meeting lasted only seven minutes:** Abigail McCarthy, *Private Faces, Public Places* (Garden City, N.Y.: Doubleday & Co., 1972), 305–306.

348   **Bobby's deliberations:** *True Compass,* 252–253; Schlesinger, 832–833; Arthur Schlesinger Jr., *Journals: 1952–2000,* Andrew Schlesinger and Stephen Schlesinger, eds. (New York: Penguin Press, 2007), 268-269; William vanden Heuvel and Milton Gwirtzman, *On His Own: RFK 1964–1968* (Garden City, N.Y.: Doubleday & Co., 1970), 289–290.

348   **"overrun daily":** Palermo, 50–51.

349   **a sobbing plane spotter:** *True Compass,* 255–257.

350   **not notifying villagers:** William Honan, *Ted Kennedy: Profile of a Survivor* (New York: Quadrangle Books, 1972), 149–151.

350   **"really didn't give a damn":** William Knowlton int., Office of Secretary General Staff for the Army, LBJ Lib., March 21, 1975.

350   **"sticking your nose into something":** Edward Kennedy int., Clymer Papers, JFK Lib., Oct. 9, 1996; quoted in Lippman, 57.

351   **"I drank a great deal of liquor":** *True Compass,* 257.

351   **"An enormous impact":** David Burke int., Miller Center, UVA, June 19, 2007.

351   **issued a preemptive counter:** Tel. Bunker and Komer to Rusk, NSFCFVN, Box 102, file: Vietnam, Dec 1967–March 1968, Congressional Attitudes and Statements, LBJ Lib., Dec. 29, 1967; in Palermo, 51–52.

351   **Ted and David Burke were invited:** Palermo, 53–54.

352   **President wasn't pleased with Ted's message:** Ibid.

352   **"If we flop on this one":** Ibid.; *True Compass,* 257–258.

353   **"the government that rules them":** "Edward Kennedy Upbraids Saigon," *NYT,* Jan. 26, 1968.

353   **"victims of a war deliberately undertaken":** Palermo, 57–58, 62.

354   **"where a man has to span":** Ibid., 58–60.

354   **former general Maxwell Taylor:** Ibid., 61.

354   **called for a troop reduction:** *Face the Nation,* CBS, Jan. 28, 1968.

354   **they couldn't expect us to maintain:** "Ted Kennedy Assails S. Vietnam Corruption," *WP,* Feb. 6, 1968.

354   **he received an enthusiastic reception:** "Ted Kennedy Tests War Sentiment at Home," *WP,* Feb. 14, 1968.

CHAPTER NINE: ALL HELL FELL

355   **Johnson response to Ted:** Joseph Palermo, "The Johnson Administration Responds to Sen. Edward M. Kennedy's Trip to South Vietnam," *Peace & Change,* Jan. 1998, 54–56, 63–64. See also Memo: HHH to Rostow, LBJ Lib., Jan. 30, 1968.

356   **"exploded around the country":** Stanley Karnow, *Vietnam: A History* (New York: Penguin, 1997, revised), 536.

357   **a majority of Americans said they opposed it:** Godfrey Hodgson, *America in Our Time: From World War II to Nixon* (New York: Vintage, 1978), 357.

357   **"he didn't feel that he was going to win:"** *Face the Nation,* CBS, Jan. 28, 1968.

357   **"clear my mind in the sun":** Edward Kennedy int., Clymer Papers, Series 2, Box 5, EMK interviews, 1995–1996 folder, JFK Lib., Apr. 12, 1996. In *True Compass,* Ted says it was Bobby who called him. Dutton seems more likely.

357   **Ted got dressed immediately:** Edward Kennedy int., Miller Center, UVA, June 17, 2005.

358   **"bravery to discard the comfort of illusion":** http://teach.yauger.net/us/vietnam/rfkvietnam.pdf.

358   **"the strongest opponent of his moving":** Arthur Schlesinger Jr., *Journals: 1952–2000,* Andrew Schlesinger and Stephen Schlesinger, eds. (New York: Penguin Press, 2007), 276.

358   **"He really believed it":** David Burke int., Miller Center, UVA, June 19, 2007; Edward Kennedy int., Apr. 12, 1996.

358   **he approached George McGovern:** Thurston Clarke, *The Last Campaign: Robert F. Kennedy and 82 Days That Inspired America* (New York: Henry Holt & Co., 2008), 31.

358   **"if he'd given him the real reasons":** Dun Gifford int., Miller Center, UVA, July 13, 2005.

359   **"But he would have done it himself":** Richard Goodwin, *Remembering America: A Voice from the Sixties* (Boston: Little, Brown, 1988), 479–480; Adam Clymer, *Edward M. Kennedy: A Biography* (New York: William Morrow & Co., 1999), 106.

359   **he lived in the moment:** Edward Kennedy, *True Compass* (New York: Twelve, 2009), 288.

359   **"I don't have anyone to be for me":** Jack Newfield, *Robert Kennedy: A Memoir* (New York: E. P. Dutton & Co., 1969), 199.

359   "a kind of resignation": Fred Dutton int., Clymer Papers, Series 2, Box 3, D folder, JFK Lib., July 25, 1995.

359   he and Dutton strolled to Bobby's office: Newfield, 211–212; Hersh, 288.

360   suggested a "peace commission": Theodore Sorensen, *The Kennedy Legacy: A Peaceful Revolution for the 70's* (New York: The Macmillan Co., 1969), 135–138. For a very detailed and still different account, see Jules Witcover, *85 Days: The Last Campaign of Robert Kennedy* (New York: Putnam, 1969), 73–80.

360   calling it an abdication: Clark Clifford int. III, LBJ Lib., July 14, 1969.

360   "the peace commission idea was absurd": Hersh, 297.

361   "If Gene McCarthy talked about the cities": Edward Kennedy int. Apr. 12, 1996.

361   "I'm going to lose them": Joe Dolan int. with L. J. Hackman, 122, RFK Papers, Apr. 11, 1970, quoted in Schlesinger, *Robert Kennedy and His Times* (Boston: Houghton Mifflin, 1978), 844.

362   "He has made all the decisions already": Schlesinger, *Journals*, 280–281; Schlesinger, *Robert Kennedy*, 850; William vanden Heuvel int., Clymer Papers, Series 2, Box 3, H folder, JFK Lib., Apr. 6, 1995; Edward Kennedy int., Miller Center, UVA, June 17, 2005.

362   "hadn't foreclosed involvement, definitely": Newfield, 212.

362   he was going simply to tell McCarthy: Hersh, 295.

363   Clark took the idea to Goodwin: Blair Clark int., Clymer Papers, Series 2, Box 3, C folder, JFK Lib., Jan. 30, 1996.

363   whether or not he would get reimbursed: *Ibid.*

363   "a veneer of commercial-grade carpeting": Abigail McCarthy, *Private Faces, Public Places* (Garden City, N.Y.: Doubleday & Co., 1972), 366–374.

363   "I should have known": Edward Kennedy int., Apr. 12, 1996.

363   whom he referred to as "Bob": Schlesinger, *Robert Kennedy*, 855–856.

364   "pretty much in the catbird seat": Edward Kennedy int., Miller Center, UVA, June 17, 2005.

364   "glowering and Gene hardly awake": Blair Clark int., Jan. 30, 1996.

364   "really angry at Bobby": Willian vanden Heuvel int., Clymer Papers, Series 2, Box 3, H folder, JFK Lib., Apr. 6, 1995.

364   "Kennedys don't act that way:" Schlesinger, *Robert Kennedy*, 856.

364   "I just can't believe we are sitting around": *Ibid.*

365   "cut it as close as you can": *Ibid.*

365   "Well, we're going to be all right": David Burke int., Miller Center, UVA, Apr. 9, 2008.

365   "our right to moral leadership": http://www.4president.org/speeches/rfk1968announcement.htm.

365   "use up what capital you had": Hersh, 289.

367   "St. Patrick did not drive all the snakes": Garry Wills, *The Kennedy Imprisonment: A Meditation on Power* (Boston: Little, Brown, 2002), 102.

367   he didn't need him: *True Compass*, 266.

367   "Everyone's got to march to his own music": Clarke, 37.

367   "I had to play a different role": *Ibid.*, 65.

367   "we didn't pursue the subject": Lawrence O'Brien, *No Final Victories: A Life in Politics from John F. Kennedy to Watergate* (Garden City, N.Y.: Doubleday & Co., 1974), 223.

368   On that feeling, Bobby committed: Gerard Doherty int., Miller Center, UVA, Oct. 10, 2005.

369   O'Brien would leave shortly thereafter: Arthur Krim int. March 18, 1984, Addendum to Interview III, LBJ Lib., March 18, 1984, 8, 9, 11, 18–19.

369   Johnson called "just awful": *Ibid.*, 12.

369   Walter Cronkite broadcast: Douglas Brinkley, *Cronkite* (New York: HarperCollins, 2012), 377–378.

369   "take steps to disengage": Michael Cohen, "LBJ Drops Out of 1968 Presidential Race," OUP Blog, Apr. 2, 2016, https://blog.oup.com/2016/04/lbj-drops-out-1968/.

370   "The whole situation was unbearable": Doris Kearns, *Lyndon Johnson and the American Dream* (New York: Harper & Row, 1976), 343.

370   "I will not accept, the nomination of my party": http://www.historyplace.com/speeches/lbj-decision.htm.

371   asking them to hold their pledges: Hubert H. Humphrey, *The Education of a Public Man: My Life and Politics (1976)* Reprint (Minneapolis: Univ. of Minnesota Press, 1991), 268.

371   "What startling developments!": Clarke, 73–74.

371   it was Lyndon Johnson they disliked: Kearns, 338.

371   **Johnson's departure would not help:** William vanden Heuvel int., Miller Center, UVA, July 19, 2005.

371   **"I suppose I am dissatisfied":** Schlesinger, *Robert Kennedy*, 800.

372   **"It'll get worse":** Int. with Jean Stein, Jan. 22, 1970, quoted in *Ibid.*, 819.

372   **"perhaps the darkest moment":** Hodgson, 361–362.

372   **"Then they turn":** Schlesinger, *Robert Kennedy*, 878.

372   **"the last friend left":** Newfield, 251.

373   **"I'm afraid there are guns":** Clarke, 115.

373   **"This really isn't such a happy existence":** *Ibid.*, 205.

373   **downplaying the very reasons:** *Ibid.*, 141.

373   **this was not a productive strategy:** *Ibid.*, 150.

374   **"I don't think I'll pass that on":** Edward Kennedy int., Clymer Papers, JFK Lib., Apr. 12, 1996.

374   **"Teddy provided the atmosphere":** Hersh, 310.

374   **"hearing about the campaign":** Edward Kennedy int., April 12, 1996.

374   **"Indiana primary changed the balance":** James Doyle, quoted in Hersh, 304.

375   **"rolling mobs of teeny-boppers":** "How Bobby Kennedy Won the '68 Indiana Primary," *Newsweek*, May 19, 1968.

375   **"a prayer away from being dismembered":** *Ibid.*

375   **"response of passion to passion":** Theodore H. White, *The Making of the President 1968* (New York: Atheneum, 1969), 172.

376   **"I always thought that it was much better to win":** "How Bobby Kennedy Won the '68 Indiana Primary."

376   **Wallace had won in the primary four years earlier:** Newfield, 264.

376   **Kennedy won 60 percent of the rural vote:** Clarke, 223.

377   **"very unresponsive and quite antagonistic":** Edward Kennedy int., Apr. 12, 1996.

377   **"Humphrey was strongly endorsed":** Hersh, 320.

377   **but might lose "badly":** David Burke int., Miller Center, UVA, Apr. 9, 2008.

377   **Gallup poll in early June:** Michael A. Cohen, *American Maelstrom: The 1968 Election and the Politics of Division* (New York: Oxford Univ. Press, 2016), 147.

378   **"Bob seemed to be in color":** Steven Roberts, "Ted Kennedy: Haunted by the Past," *NYT Magazine*, Feb. 3, 1980.

378   **"and replace them with Negroes":** Newfield, 253.

378   **"what kind of men we are":** Clarke, 45–46.

379   **"he would embarrass his friends":** Schlesinger, *Robert Kennedy*, 45.

379   **"we've made some other contribution":** Clarke, 85.

379   **lead to economic redistribution:** "Why Do They Hate Him So?" *The Saturday Evening Post*, June 15, 1968.

379   **"a yearning on his part":** David Burke int., Miller Center, UVA, Apr. 9, 2008.

379   **because that is what Bobby needed:** Lester David, *Ted Kennedy: Triumphs and Tragedies* (New York: Grosset & Dunlap, 1972), 165.

380   **"One giant suburb":** Hersh, 323.

380   **Ted never set foot there:** Edward Kennedy int., Apr. 12, 1996.

380   **"Maybe the people don't want things changed":** Clarke, 237.

380   **"If we lose here":** "Robert Kennedy Shot, Killed in Los Angeles," *Newsweek*, June 16, 1968.

380   **shown Humphrey out in front:** https://news.gallup.com/vault/235283/gallup-vault-look-back-robert-kennedy.aspx.

381   **returned to the Fairmont:** David, 167–170.

381   **"he would have floated out of the room":** Clarke, 271.

381   **"and let's win there":** http://jfk.hood.edu/Collection/White%20Materials/White%20Assassination%20Clippings%20Folders/Kennedy%20Family%20Folders/Kennedy%20Robert%20F/RFK%200391.pdf.

382   **Ted had raced down the stairs:** Peter Canellos, *Last Lion: The Fall and Rise of Ted Kennedy* (New York: Simon & Schuster, 2009), 132–133.

382   **Burke and Phil Burton:** David Burke int., Miller Center, UVA, June 19, 2007. Burke told a different story to Burton Hersh. He said he had phoned Burton (Hersh, 330).

382   **"he set his jaw":** William Honan, *Ted Kennedy: Profile of a Survivor* (New York: Quadrangle Books, 1972), 127–128.

383 "Solicitous": John Seigenthaler int., Clymer Papers, Series 2, Box 5, R-Edward Kennedy, JFK Lib., Sept. 27, 1995.

383 "just barely controlling himself:" Dun Gifford int., Miller Center, UVA, July 13, 2005.

383 Bobby would survive only: Milton Gwirtzman int., Miller Center, UVA, Aug. 5, 2009.

383 the new "family burdens": Lester David, *Joan: The Reluctant Kennedy* (New York: Funk & Wagnalls, 1974), 171.

383 Ted and arrangements: David Burke int., Miller Center, UVA, June 19, 2007; David, *Ted Kennedy*, 170–171; Honan, 127–128; Hersh, 330.

383 "It was beyond grief and agony": "Fortune and Misfortune," *Time*, July 26, 1999; Canellos, 134.

384 the family stood there: Goodwin, 539.

384 "Never had I seen such anguish": John Tunney int., Miller Center, UVA, May 3, 2007; Patrick Kennedy int. by author.

384 manning telephones in a nearby suite: David Burke int., Miller Center, UVA, June 19, 2007.

384 "We also pray that divisiveness": Witcover, 283.

384 "history slipping through my fingers": Clarke, 9.

385 "We are down to one Kennedy": Tel. J. Edgar Hoover, 116, Edward Kennedy FBI file, June 6, 1968.

385 "'Don't look at him'": John Tunney int., Miller Center, UVA, May 3, 2007.

385 tell his children about the death: Joan Kennedy int., Clymer Papers, Series 2, Box 4, K folder, JFK Lib., Oct. 12, 1998.

385 "feel our way along": Johnson conversation with Ted Kennedy, #13113 (WH6806.01), Miller Center, UVA, June 6, 1968.

385 he would "carry on": Honan, 129–130.

386 Ted personally helped lift the casket: David, *Ted Kennedy*, 171.

386 Ted comforted the passengers: Dun Gifford int., Clymer Papers, Series 2, Box 3, G folder, JFK Lib., Feb. 2, 1996.

386 "He does not know whether": "Kennedy Widow, Brother Nap Beside Bier on Plane," *WP*, June 8, 1968.

386 "what Bobby meant to the country": Max Lerner, *Ted and the Kennedy Legend: A Study in Character and Destiny* (New York: St. Martin's Press, 1980), 86.

386 he said he wanted nothing to do with it: David, *Ted Kennedy*, 171.

386 he wrote it out of his feelings for Ted: Milton Gwirtzman int., Miller Center, UVA, Aug. 5, 2009.

387 cruised the streets: John Culver int., Miller Center, UVA, Sept. 22, 2009.

388 "'I dream things that never were and say why not'": http://www.nydailynews.com/news/politics/ted-kennedy-eulogy-brother-robert-st-patrick-cathedral-new-york-city-june-8-1968-article-1.394707.

388 "the sensed helplessness of citizens": Goodwin, 528.

388 "The only white politician left who could": Clarke, 5.

388 "last liberal politician who could communicate": Newfield, 83.

389 he had lost fifty-nine of seventy: William vanden Heuvel and Milton Gwirtzman, *On His Own: RFK 1964–1968* (Garden City, N.Y.: Doubleday & Co., 1970), 349.

389 "suburbanized": Newfield, 61–62.

389 only 31 percent thought that: Rick Perlstein, *Nixonland: The Rise of a President and the Fracturing of America* (New York: Scribner, 2008), 198.

390 "futile and pointless": O'Brien, 245.

390 "completely skeptical about any possibility": Schlesinger, *Journals*, 293.

390 "a generational broken heart": Barbara Mikulski int., Miller Center, UVA, Sept. 26, 2006.

390 "bleak despair": Clarke, 7.

390 "and now we have come to understand": Rose Fitzgerald Kennedy, *Times to Remember* (Garden City, N.Y.: Doubleday & Co., 1974), 471.

390 "our best political leaders were part of memory now": Newfield, 304.

390 "It was just over": "The Kennedys," *American Experience*, prod. Elizabeth Deane, WGBH, 1992.

391 "rendezvous with reality": Robert Sherrill, *The Last Kennedy* (New York: The Dial Press, 1976), 55.

391 "our public and private lives": "Kennedys Thank U.S. for Sympathy in Grief," *LAT*, June 16, 1968.

391 "When we were boys": Hersh, 331–332.

391 "They're like crossed fingers": Nancy Gager Clinch, *The Kennedy Neurosis: A Psychological Portrait* (New York: Grosset & Dunlap, 1973), 342.

391 **"That's all right. I have another brother":** *American Journey: The Times of Robert Kennedy,* Jean Stein and George Plimpton, eds. (New York: Harcourt Brace Jovanovich, 1970), 146–147.

392 **"He had no one to talk to":** Brock Brower, "The Incident at Dike Bridge," *Life,* Aug. 1, 1969.

392 **"I don't want sourpusses around here":** Edward Kennedy, *The Fruitful Bough* (self-published, 1965), 201.

392 **"To understand the profound authority":** *True Compass,* 41.

392 **"They never talked about the pain":** David Breasted, quoted in Ken Ringle, "Ted Kennedy's Strength in Sorrow," *The Washington Post,* July 21, 1999.

392 **steaks that Gargan had ordered:** Hersh, 334.

393 **because he had promised it to them:** Melody Miller int., Miller Center, UVA, July 15, 2008; "Edward Kennedy Against '68 Race," *The New York Times,* June 11, 1968.

393 **a foundation to support his work:** "Teddy Kennedy's Decision," *Newsweek,* Aug. 5, 1968.

393 **"They were angry":** Christopher Lawford, *Symptoms of Withdrawal: A Memoir of Snapshots and Redemption* (New York: William Morrow & Co., 2005), 107.

393 **"A lot of it is duty":** Charles Tretter int., Miller Center, UVA, Aug, 8, 2005.

393 **"least intellectual and introspective":** "The Mysteries of Chappaquiddick," *Time,* Aug. 1, 1969.

393 **"a care in the world":** Rita Dallas and Jeanira Ratcliffe, *The Kennedy Case* (New York: G. P. Putnam's Sons, 1973), 139.

393 **"most open of the Kennedys":** Christopher Lydon, "A Special Kind of Grief in Massachusetts," *NYT,* Aug. 3, 1969.

393 **"To Teddy, who has his own enemy within":** Patrick Kennedy int. by author.

393 **"deep reserve":** Lydon.

393 **"there was still a sadness":** Dallas, 139.

393 **"the sad one":** Mike Mansfield int., Clymer Papers, Series 2, Box 4, M folder, JFK Lib., Jan. 27, 1993.

393 **" 'Teddy's fighting mad' ":** "Teddy Kennedy's Decision."

394 **screaming, blasting music:** Dallas, 323.

393 **"kind of hibernation":** "The Ascent of Ted Kennedy," *Time,* Jan. 10, 1969.

393 **"almost like he didn't care":** Edmund Reggie int., Miller Center, UVA, Dec. 16, 2008.

394 **"just a sadness toward everything":** Gladys Gifford int. by author.

394 **"What am I doing here? All this stuff":** John Tunney int., Miller Center, UVA, May 3, 2007.

394 **destroyed Ted's sense of identity:** John Tunney int., Clymer Papers, JFK Lib., March 6, 1995.

394 **"shells of their former selves":** Patrick Kennedy int. by author.

394 **"he had a nervous breakdown":** Myra MacPherson, "Senator Kennedy: Alone with the Legacy," *WP,* June 4, 1978.

394 **"as if he's taken a little":** "He's Not the Same Old Ted," *Newsweek,* June 24, 1968.

394 **take long walks along the beach:** "Teddy Kennedy's Decision."

394 **"lost soul":** Dallas, 345.

395 **gray-stone jetty:** Brower.

395 **he wasn't up to facing anyone:** "Teddy Kennedy's Decision."

395 **"He tried valiantly":** Dallas, 322–323.

395 **"one after the other":** Anne Taylor Fleming, "The Kennedy Mystique," *NYT Magazine,* June 17, 1979.

395 **"inaccurate to say he wasn't drunk at all":** Hersh, 334.

395 **"it's me for the brass ring":** Fleming, 44.

395 **"blur in my memory":** *True Compass,* 273.

395 **details of those sailing expeditions:** Edmund Reggie int., Miller Center, UVA, Dec. 16, 2008.

396 **"It anchors you":** Mike Barnicle, "Of Memory and the Sea," *Time,* Aug. 27, 2009.

396 **"telling stories, whooping it up":** Dun Gifford int., Miller Center, UVA, July 13, 2005; Gifford int., Clymer Papers, Series 2, Box 3, G folder, JFK Lib., Feb. 2, 1996.

396 **Sometimes he would stop at a cove:** "Teddy Kennedy's Decision."

396 **Ted shaved it off first:** Warren Rogers, "Ted Kennedy Talks About His Past and Future," *Look,* March 4, 1969.

396 **Rose went occasionally, to calm him:** Dallas, 331.

396 **and he would lie on the deck:** "The Ascent of Ted Kennedy."

397 **"part of the natural order of things":** *True Compass,* 273–274.

397 **his wounds could heal:** Scott Stossel, "Knifed," *The Atlantic,* May 2004.

397 **Gifford would be stuck:** Dun Gifford int., Miller Center, UVA, July 13, 2005.

397 **"so wounded by Bobby's death":** William vanden Heuvel int., Miller Center, UVA, July 19, 2005.

397 **"determinedly buoyant"**: "Teddy Kennedy's Decision."

397 **"to come back and see them"**: Edward Kennedy int., Miller Center, UVA, Nov. 29, 2006.

397 **"one of those Maine harbors"**: Brower.

398 **"taken the father of ten children?"**: *True Compass*, 479.

398 **"but after Bobby . . ."**: Memo, James Wechsler, Re: Conversation with Ted Kennedy, nd., Kennedy, Edward M. 1968–1971 folder, Box 37, Joseph L. Rauh Jr. Papers, Lib. of Congress.

398 **"just breathtakingly lovely"**: Edward Kennedy int., Miller Center, UVA, Nov. 29, 2006.

398 **" 'Now what, Teddy?' "**: Dun Gifford int., Miller Center, UVA, July 13, 2005.

CHAPTER TEN: A FALLEN STANDARD

399 **"without aspiring to a higher goal"**: John Herbers, "Edward Kennedy: Problems and Challenges," *NYT*, June 16, 1968.

399 **"You gotta run for president"**: Milton Gwirtzman int., Clymer Papers, Series 2, Box 5, G folder, JFK Lib., Apr. 3, 1993; Milton Gwirtzman int., Miller Center, UVA, Aug. 5, 2009.

400 **"I hope it's not true"**: "Edward Kennedy Against '68 Race," *NYT*, June 11, 1968; "Humphrey Hints Kennedy Is Choice as Running Mate," *NYT*, July 19, 1968.

400 **a six-page memo**: Milton Gwirtzman int., April 3, 1993; Milton Gwirtzman int., Aug, 5, 2009.

400 **"begging him to run for vice president:"** "Teddy Kennedy's Decision," *Newsweek*, Aug. 5, 1968.

400 **same poll showed**: "Ted Kennedy Ticket Could Win," *WP*, June 24, 1968.

400 **A poll a month later**: "The Kennedy Effect," *Los Angeles Times*, July 29, 1968.

400 **Yet another Harris poll**: "Teddy Kennedy's Decision."

400 **"I hope the convention will draft him"**: "2 Governors Endorse Kennedy for No. 2 Spot," *Los Angeles Times*, July 22, 1968; "Teddy Kennedy's Decision."

400 **a "one-man" draft**: "Edward Kennedy to Be Nominated," *NYT*, July 14, 1968.

400 **"He realized that he was being sought"**: Rita Dallas and Jeanira Ratcliffe, *The Kennedy Case* (New York: G. P. Putnam's Sons, 1973), 315.

401 **demand concessions on Vietnam**: Richard Harwood, "Kennedy Quietly Ponders Future," *WP*, July 20, 1968.

401 **wary of antagonizing Johnson**: Gwirtzman int., Miller Center, UVA, Aug. 5, 2009.

401 **he said he would sit out the campaign**: "Teddy Kennedy's Decision."

401 **Mayor Daley said he had spoken to Ted**: "Daley Talks to Kennedy," *NYT*, July 26, 1968.

401 **"successful in the coming election"**: "Kennedy Bars Race," *NYT*, July 27, 1968.

402 **keep Bobby's flame alive**: Tom Wicker, "Kennedy Will Speak on War Next Week," *NYT*, Aug. 14, 1968.

402 **drafted most of it**: Ted Sorensen int., Clymer Papers, Series 2, Box 5, S folder, JFK Lib., June 17, 1996.

403 **"make gentle the life of this world"**: "Transcript of Address," *NYT*, Aug. 22, 1968; "No Safety in Hiding," *Newsweek*, Sept. 2, 1968.

403 **"the shock of his brother's death"**: John Herbers, "Kennedy's Party Role," *NYT*, Aug. 23, 1968.

403 **Ted was "drained"**: Burton Hersh, *The Education of Edward Kennedy: A Family Biography* (New York: William Morrow & Co., 1972), 341.

404 **"but I wasn't prepared to sign on"**: Edward Kennedy int., Miller Center, UVA, June 17, 2005.

404 **"inappropriate," they called it**: "Edward Kennedy Against '68 Race."

404 **McGovern announced his own candidacy**: George McGovern, *Grassroots: The Autobiography of George McGovern* (New York: Random House, 1977), 118.

404 **"expressed clear sympathy"**: "Kennedy's Party Role," *NYT*, Aug. 23, 1968.

405 **"No way was he going to get involved"**: John Aloysius Farrell, *Tip O'Neill and the Democratic Century* (Boston: Little, Brown, 2001), 256.

405 **"Ted [the old Ted] didn't do that"**: Hersh, 352.

405 **" 'What was it all about?' "**: *Ibid.*, 339.

405 **given the vagaries of life**: Edward Kennedy int., Clymer Papers, Series 2, Box 5, EMK interviews, 1995–1996 folder, JFK Lib., Oct. 9, 1996.

406 **" 'Let me just explore this' "**: Edward Kennedy int., Miller Center, UVA, June 17, 2005.

406 **"best information that was available"**: John Tunney int., Clymer Papers, Series 2, Box 5, T folder, JFK Lib., March 6, 1995.

406 **"I didn't go there for my health"**: John Tunney int., Miller Center, UVA, May 3, 2007.

406 **they weren't certain he wanted it:** Theodore Sorensen int., Miller Center, UVA, Dec. 7, 2006; Dun Gifford int., Clymer Papers, Series 2, Box 3, G folder, JFK Lib., Feb. 2, 1996.

407 **"They were in despair":** Hersh, 351.

407 **"about to erupt":** Milton Gwirtzman int., Miller Center, UVA, Aug. 5, 2009.

407 **"just stay away":** Milton Gwirtzman int., Series 2, Box 3, G folder, Clymer Papers, JFK Lib., Apr. 3, 1993.

407 **"madness was in the air":** David Burke int., Miller Center, UVA, Apr. 9, 2008.

408 **"All he had to say was yes":** Warren Rogers, "Ted Kennedy Talks About His Past and Future," *Look,* March 4, 1969.

408 **painted signs for Ted:** "Unruh Rejects Kennedy's 'No,' " *LAT,* Aug. 27, 1968; "Unruh Hints He May Nominate Ted Kennedy," *LAT,* Aug. 25, 1968.

408 **"No. I'm not going to do it":** William vanden Heuvel int., Clymer Papers, Series 2, Box 3, H folder, JFK Lib., Apr. 6, 1995; vanden Heuvel int., Miller Center, UVA, July 19, 2005.

409 **"wholly in the battle":** John Kenneth Galbraith, *A Life in Our Times* (New York: Houghton Mifflin, 1981), 499.

409 **"Let's keep in touch":** Richard Goodwin, "The Night McCarthy Turned to Kennedy," *Look,* Oct.15, 1968.

410 **Ted, Burke said, was almost jovial:** David Burke int., Miller Center, UVA, June 19, 2007.

410 **Smith told Seigenthaler to call Ted:** John Seigenthaler int., Clymer Papers, Series 2, Box 5, S folder, JFK Lib., Sept. 27, 1995.

410 **"Daley says we can just have it":** William Honan, *Ted Kennedy: Profile of a Survivor* (New York: Quadrangle Books, 1972), 126.

410 **"dicey situation":** Edward Kennedy int., Miller Center, UVA, June 17, 2005.

410 **"Not if Kennedy will take it":** Robert Shrum, *No Excuses: Concessions of a Serial Campaigner* (New York: Simon & Schuster, 2007), 76.

410 **McCarthy had told Smith:** Peter Maas, "Ted Kennedy—What Might Have Been," *New York,* Oct. 7, 1968.

410 **"typically mystical performance":** Rowland Evans and Robert Novak, "Lack of Support from McCarthy, Daley Caused Kennedy to Withdraw," *WP,* Aug. 29, 1968.

411 **"really upset":** Robert Healy int., Miller Center, UVA, Aug. 10, 2005.

412 **he had phoned McGovern:** McGovern, 124.

412 **"he wanted to preserve":** Lester Hyman int., Miller Center, UVA, Oct. 6, 2008.

412 **"Sheep without a shepherd":** Edward Kennedy int., Series 2, Box 5, EMK interviews 1995–1996 folder, Clymer Papers, JFK Lib., Oct. 9, 1996.

412 **met with a Johnson representative:** William vanden Heuvel int., Miller Center, UVA, July 19, 2005.

413 **until 4 P.M. the following afternoon:** Tom Wicker, "Democrats Delay Fight on the Vietnam Plank," *NYT,* Aug. 29, 1968.

414 **declare his availability:** William vanden Heuvel int., Miller Center, UVA, July 19, 2005.

414 **"knew he wasn't ready:** David Burke int., Miller Center, UVA, Apr. 9, 2008.

414 **trading on his brothers' names:** Rogers.

414 **"I simply could not summon the will":** *True Compass,* 272.

414 **It was to be Bobby's nomination:** Honan, 130–131.

415 **"we are not making this one happen:"** Arthur Schlesinger Jr., *Journals: 1952–2000,* Andrew Schlesinger and Stephen Schlesinger, eds. (New York: Penguin Press, 2007), 298.

415 **Ted once again refused:** Fred Dutton int., Clymer Papers, Series 2, Box 3, D folder, JFK Lib., July 25, 1995.

415 **Humphrey would try to draft him anyway:** "Teddy Kennedy's Decision."

416 **"slow him down or shut him up":** Scott Stossel, "Knifed," *The Atlantic,* May 2004, 106–112.

416 **"unfriendly act":** Max Kampelman, *Entering New Worlds: The Memoirs of a Private Man in Public Life* (New York: HarperCollins, 1991), 168.

416 **Ted went off sailing again:** Milton Gwirtzman int., Clymer Papers, JFK Lib., Apr. 3, 1993; Gwirtzman int., Miller Center, UVA, Aug. 5, 2009.

417 **"substance of America's moral rot":** Rick Perlstein, *Nixonland: The Rise of a President and the Fracturing of America* (New York: Scribner, 2008), 5.

418 **he called for a crackdown:** Richard Nixon, "What Has Happened to America?," *Reader's Digest,* Oct. 1967.

418 **hoisted the opposition:** "Kennedy Brothers Split Rights Bill Opposition," *LAT,* March 7, 1968.

419   **gun-control legislation:** "He's Not the Same Old Ted," *Newsweek*, June 24, 1968; "Limited Gun
      Law," *Time*, Sept. 27, 1968; Joseph Tydings int., Clymer Papers, Series 2, Box 5, T folder, JFK Lib.,
      June 15, 1993.
419   **His waist has begun to thicken:** "The Ascent of Ted Kennedy," *Time*, Jan. 10, 1969.
419   **then turn back, unable to enter:** Max Lerner, *Ted and the Kennedy Legend: A Study in Character and
      Destiny* (New York: St. Martin's Press, 1980), 95.
419   **His voting record after Bobby's death:** James MacGregor Burns, *Edward Kennedy and the Camelot
      Legacy* (New York: W. W. Norton & Co., 1976), 174.
419   **"expect him to do any campaigning this year":** John Herbers, "Enter a New Kennedy," *NYT*,
      Sept. 1, 1968.
419   **"Aaron Burr in this Republic":** "Humphrey Hints Kennedy Is Choice as Running Mate," *NYT*,
      July 19, 1968.
419   **"I'll be right on those issues":** Edward Kennedy int., Miller Center, UVA, June 17, 2005.
420   **he and Humphrey had driven down Tremont:** *Ibid.*
420   **death that he "shook":** Hubert H. Humphrey, *The Education of a Public Man: My Life and Politics*
      (Minneapolis: Univ. of Minnesota Press, 1991, reprint), xxi.
420   **"applauded mechanically":** "Kennedy Booed as He Backs Humphrey at Rally," *LAT*, Sept. 20,
      1968.
420   **"in a Humphrey administration":** "Kennedy Measures Praise for HHH," *WP*, Sept. 20, 1968.
420   **A Gallup poll in late September:** Lewis Chester, Godfrey Hodgson, Bruce Page, *An American Melo-
      drama: The Presidential Campaign of 1968* (New York: The Viking Press, 1969) 610.
421   **"carried a stench of disaster with him":** *Ibid.*, 644.
421   **"I'm going to fight":** Michael A. Cohen, *American Maelstrom: The 1968 Election and the Politics of
      Division* (New York: Oxford Univ. Press, 2016), 293.
421   **he wrote the draft himself:** Chester, Hodgson, Page, 648.
421   **"willing to stop the bombing":** http://www2.mnhs.org/library/findaids/00442/pdfa/00442-02
      747.pdf.
422   **"worked and prayed for peace":** Edward Kennedy int., Miller Center, UVA, June 17, 2005.
422   **"beaming":** Lawrence O'Brien, *No Final Victories: A Life in Politics from John F. Kennedy to Water-
      gate* (Garden City, N.Y.: Doubleday & Co., 1974), 261.
422   **"but obviously this will be":** Edward Kennedy int., Miller Center, UVA, June 17, 2005.
422   **shown on election eve:** O'Brien, 262.
422   **"building a bridge over the Potomac":** G. Calvin Mackenzie and Robert Weisbrot, *The Liberal
      Hour: Washington and the Politics of Change in the 1960s* (New York: The Penguin Press, 2008),
      349.
422   **"ablest demagogue of our time":** Cohen, 220.
422   **"Sieg heil!":** *Ibid.*, 239.
422   **"There are a lot of rednecks":** *Ibid.*, 222.
423   **"It must be repudiated":** "Kennedy Assails Wallace," *WP*, Oct. 25, 1968; "Kennedy Asks Vote
      Rejecting Wallace," *NYT*, Oct. 25, 1968.
424   **"a respite from anxiety and frustration":** Humphrey, xxiv.
425   **"This is the future of this party":** George Packer, "The Fall of Conservatism," *The New Yorker*,
      May 26, 2008.
425   **"lost the confidence":** Godfrey Hodgson, *America in Our Time: From World War II to Nixon* (NY:
      Vintage, 1978), 465.
426   **"and perhaps with greater ease":** Philip Converse, Warren Miller, Jerrold Rusk, and Arthur
      Wolfe, "Continuity and Change in American Politics: Parties and Issues in the 1968 Election,"
      American Political Science Review, Vol. 63, No. 4 (Dec. 1969), 1,089–1,090.
426   **sitting up there in his ivory tower:** Cohen, 221.
426   **"can't even park their bikes":** *Ibid.*, 222.
426   **rednecks in suburbia:** Chester, Hodgson, Page, 663–664. A study by pollster Fred Currier found
      that in Michigan, Wallace support came "particularly from the upper-income segment of the
      blue-collar class."
426   **Nixon's resentments:** Perlstein, 22–23, 29.
427   **"panic of the threatened soul":** Goodwin, 106.
427   **doubted there even was a sign:** William Safire, "The Way Forward," *NYT*, Sept. 2, 2007.
428   **"And getting your fifty-one percent":** Jeffrey Toobin, "The Dirty Trickster," *The New Yorker*, June 2,
      2008, 63.

428 "overpowering American understanding": Theodore H. White, *The Making of the President 1968* (New York: Atheneum, 1969), 416.

429 "if I slackened my drive": *True Compass*, 279.

429 "Bobby's assassination had devastated her": *Ibid.*, 281.

429 "a personal bid for power": Memo, James Wechsler, Re: Conversation with Ted Kennedy, nd, Kennedy, Edward M. 1968–1971 folder, Box 37, Joseph Rauh, Jr., Papers, Lib. of Congress.

429 "to work toward the goals": Rose Fitzgerald Kennedy, *Times to Remember* (Garden City, N.Y.: Doubleday & Co., 1974), 489.

429 "and at the same time to continue his own": Peter Canellos, *Last Lion: The Fall and Rise of Ted Kennedy* (New York: Simon & Schuster, 2009), 136.

429 "supporting their causes": Ted Sorensen, *Counselor: Life at the Edge of History* (New York: HarperCollins, 2008), 257.

429 "surrogate father": Robert Fitzgerald Sr., int., Miller Center, UVA, June 18, 2009.

430 "concern for the forgotten American": Theo Lippman, *Senator Ted Kennedy: The Career Behind the Image* (New York: W. W. Norton & Co., 1976), 281.

430 "in very personal terms": Brock Brower, "The Incident at Dike Bridge," *Life*, Aug. 1, 1969.

430 "meteor getting ready to take off": Robert Bates, quoted in Canellos, 146.

430 "You made our misfortunes yours": "The Distant Horizon," *Time*, Dec. 20, 1968.

430 "But it is in our conscience": Adam Clymer, *Edward M. Kennedy: A Biography* (New York: William Morrow, 1999), 130.

431 pressure the State Department: *True Compass*, 299; Robert C. Byrd, *Child of the Appalachian Coalfields* (Morgantown: West Virginia Univ. Press, 2005), 251.

431 "I had no idea what it would be": Dun Gifford int., Clymer Papers, Series 2, Box 3, G folder, JFK Lib., Feb. 2, 1996.

431 "have some influence with": Honan, 113–114.

431 "so difficult to break through": Lippman, 273.

431 "bombastic": J. Stanley Kimmitt Oral History, Senate Historical Office, 2003, 77–78.

431 "get him out of here": Robert Dove int. by author.

431 He had tied up the Senate: "Teddy Cracks the Whip," *Newsweek*, Jan. 13, 1969.

432 "black with rage": D. Mervin, "United States Senate Norms and the Majority Whip Election of 1969," 9/3: 321-333, *Journal of American Studies*, Dec. 1975, 325.

432 the only senator to visit: Honan, 170.

432 Mansfield appointed four junior senators: Ross Baker, "Mike Mansfield and the Birth of the Modern Senate," in *First Among Equals: Outstanding Senate Leaders of the Twentieth Century*, Richard Baker and Roger Davidson, eds. (Washington, D.C.: Congressional Quarterly, 1991), 280–281.

432 ignored the Democratic Policy Committee: Walter Oleszek, "Party Whips in the Senate," 33/4: 955–979 *Journal of Politics*, Nov. 1971, 960; Robert C. Byrd, *The Senate, 1789–1989: Addresses on the History of the United States Senate*, Mary Sharon Hall, ed. (Washington, D.C.: U.S. Govt. Printing Office, 1988), 199.

433 "it was such a strange role": David Burke int., Miller Center, UVA, June 19, 2007.

433 "best speechwriters and legislative assistants": Garry Wills, *The Kennedy Imprisonment: A Meditation on Power* (Boston: Little, Brown, 2002), 212.

433 "reviewing his presentation": "Kennedy Victory," *U.S. News & World Report*, Jan. 13, 1969.

433 "pushed Edward Kennedy as much as he could": Robert Dove int.

433 "I just arrived there": Edward Kennedy int., Miller Center, UVA, Jan. 6, 2007.

433 "I saw an opening": Edward Kennedy int., Miller Center, UVA, Oct. 14, 2005.

433 "threatened with the new administration": Edward Kennedy int., Clymer Papers, Series 2, Box 5, EMK interviews, 1995–1996 folder, JFK Lib., Apr. 17, 1995.

433 "constructive impact": *Ibid.*

433 he had decided to challenge Long: "Sen. Kennedy to Fight Long for Whip Job," *WP*, Dec. 31,1968.

434 "was what it was all about": David Burke int., Miller Center, UVA, June 19, 2007.

434 "designs on the White House": Honan, 137.

434 "generalist rather than a specialist": Lippman, 114.

434 "earned his stripes the hard way": Honan, 138.

434 "And he knew that": Dun Gifford int., Clymer Papers, Series 2, Box 3, G folder, JFK Lib., Feb. 2, 1996.

435 **"only one who was and is a Senate man":** "Mansfield Rules Out Kennedy in 1972," July 27, 1969, *NYT*, July 27, 1969; "Kennedy Defeats Long," *WP*, Jan. 4, 1969.

435 **"I had to think about other things":** "Teddy Cracks the Whip."

435 **"running out of gas":** *True Compass*, 280; "Teddy Cracks the Whip."

435 **he began to think about the whip possibility:** Honan, 138.

435 **consistent with his carelessness:** Anne Strauss, Miller Center, UVA, April 10, 2008.

435 **"Do. I urge you to":** "The Ascent of Ted Kennedy."

435 **he hardly did any skiing:** "Ted Kennedy Talks About His Past and Future."

436 **"Why not?":** "The Ascent of Ted Kennedy."

436 **"but it is the only way":** *Ibid.*

436 **"run against Russell Long fo'?":** Honan, 135.

436 **"I will put no stone in your path":** Charles Ferris int., Clymer Papers, Series 2, Box 3, F folder, JFK Lib., Apr. 10, 1992; Theo Lippman quotes a Russell aide who claims to have been with Russell when the call came in, and Russell told Ted that he would not "raise a hand against you." (*Senator Ted Kennedy: The Career Behind the Image*, 114.)

436 **Long was surprised by Ted's news:** Rogers.

436 **he flew to the Sugar Bowl:** "Teddy Cracks the Whip."

436 **he was saying that he would:** "The Ascent of Ted Kennedy."

436 **He made so many calls:** "Teddy Cracks the Whip."

437 **"did so on their own":** "The Ascent of Ted Kennedy."

437 **"a good thing to do":** Lippman, 113.

437 **"took on a life of its own":** Charles Ferris int., Clymer Papers, JFK Lib., Apr. 10, 1992.

437 **"coming up roses":** David Burke int., Miller Center, UVA, June 19, 2007.

437 **"Kennedy would have the votes":** LBJ and HHH phone conversation, Dec. 30,1968, www .discoverlbj.org/item/tel-13831.

438 **"vote against a Kennedy":** J. Stanley Kimmitt Oral History.

438 **"I'm afraid he's been busy":** LBJ and EMK phone conversation, WH6812.03, Miller Center, UVA, Dec. 30, 1968.

439 **"outgunned in the United States":** "The Ascent of Ted Kennedy."

439 **"you would do just this":** Rauh to EMK, Box 37, Kennedy, Edward M. folder, Joseph Rauh, Jr., Papers, Lib of Congress, Jan. 6, 1969.

439 **"in the upcoming Congress":** "The Ascent of Ted Kennedy."

439 **"able opponent ready for him":** "Kennedy Victory."

439 **he laughed:** "Teddy Cracks the Whip."

439 **visit the grave sites:** Martin Nolan, "Kennedy Dead at 77," *BG*, Aug. 26, 2009.

CHAPTER ELEVEN: A SHADOW PRESIDENT

440 **"that sort of thing":** William Honan, *Ted Kennedy: Profile of a Survivor* (New York: Quadrangle Books, 1972), 113; Edward Kennedy, *True Compass* (New York: Twelve, 2009), 313.

440 **chatting with Nixon:** Edward Kennedy int., Clymer Papers, Series 2, Box 5, EMK interviews 1997–1999 folder, JFK Lib., June 2, 1997.

441 **"Well, this is a strange room, isn't it?":** Arthur Schlesinger Jr., *Journals: 1952–2000*, Andrew Schlesinger and Stephen Schlesinger, eds. (New York: Penguin Press, 2007), 307.

441 **"I'm not a personality kid":** Christopher Matthews, *Kennedy & Nixon: The Rivalry that Shaped Postwar America* (New York: Simon & Schuster, 1996), 282.

441 **"have become the forgotten Americans":** Transcript, *The New York Times*, Aug. 9, 1968.

442 **"and there she'll die":** Richard Goodwin, *Remembering America: A Voice from the Sixties* (Boston: Little, Brown, 1988), 426.

442 **Johnson later agreed:** Joseph Califano Jr., *Governing America: An Insider's Report from the White House and the Cabinet* (New York: Simon & Schuster, 1981), 91–92.

442 **how far the Democrats had fallen:** Don Oberdorfer, *Senator Mansfield: The Extraordinary Life of a Great American Statesman and Diplomat* (Washington, D.C.: Smithsonian Books, 2003), 353–354.

442 **"at Mansfield's elbow":** "Kennedy: Colorful Workhorse," *The Washington Post*, Feb. 1, 1969.

443 **"last survivor":** Max Lerner, *Ted and the Kennedy Legend: A Study in Character and Destiny* (New York: St. Martin's Press, 1980), 139.

443 **"years into the future":** Robert C. Byrd, *Child of the Appalachian Coalfields* (Morgantown: West Virginia Univ. Press, 2005), 247.

443 **"prospects are clearly enhanced":** "The Ascent of Ted Kennedy," *Time*, Jan. 10, 1969.

443 **over if he accepted:** Dan Rather and Gary Paul Gates, *The Palace Guard* (New York: Harper & Row, 1974), 39.

444 **affected counties in South Carolina:** "Hunger: An Underdeveloped Country," *Time*, Feb. 28, 1969.

444 **didn't even know who the present whip was:** William Honan, "Is Teddy, As They Say, Ready?" *NYT Magazine*, Feb. 23, 1969.

445 **"the country as I see them":** Honan, *Ted Kennedy*, 155.

445 **ask questions and monitor debates:** "Liberal Democrats Seek Stronger Senate Voice," June 15, 1969.

445 **"geographical and philosophical":** Honan, *Ted Kennedy*, 159–160.

446 **Ted met with David Burke:** Theo Lippman, *Senator Ted Kennedy: The Career Behind the Image* (NY: W.W. Norton & Co., 1976), 118.

446 **"issues, not telephone calls":** Burton Hersh, *The Education of Edward Kennedy: A Family Biography* (New York: William Morrow & Co., 1972), 364.

446 **"platform into the law":** "Is Teddy, As They Say, Ready?"

447 **he invited experts to his office:** Lippman, 118.

447 **"can make that work":** Samuel Beer int., Miller Center, UVA, Feb. 17, 2005.

447 **"just waiting to take over":** Rather and Gates, 167.

448 **"you wanted to work for you":** David Burke int., Miller Center, UVA, June 19, 2007.

448 **"Democratic nominee for president":** Robert Bates int., Miller Center, UVA, May 8, 2007.

448 **"It was Kennedy for president":** Carey Parker int., Miller Center, UVA, Sept. 22, 2008.

448 **"work for any other senator":** Burke int.

449 **"he is no flashing rabbit":** "Is Teddy, As They Say, Ready?"

449 **"sort of pick up on":** Edward Kennedy int., Miller Center, UVA, Nov. 29, 2006.

450 **"Robert was promoting":** Robert Bates int., Miller Center, UVA, May 8, 2007.

450 **more willing to take risks:** Hersh, 366.

450 **"kind of what-the-hell attitude":** Brock Brower, "The Incident at Dike Bridge," *Life*, Aug. 1, 1969.

450 **to book a plane for him immediately:** *Ibid.*

451 **"can no longer be tolerated":** "Kennedy Greets Grape Strike March at Calexico," *Los Angeles Times*, May 19, 1969.

451 **"those beyond affluence's pale":** "Ted's Troubles in the Tundra," *Time*, Apr. 18, 1969.

451 **plea for Bobby's assassin:** "A Plea for Mercy," *Time*, May 30, 1969.

451 **"cause for the taking of another life":** "Death for Sirhan Set," *NYT*, May 22, 1969.

451 **"a lot of time on Indian matters":** Thomas Susman int., Miller Center, UVA, May 23, 2007.

451 **drove him three hours to the destination:** *Ibid.*

452 **"certainly more than any other Easterner":** Lippman, 94.

452 **probably the inspiration for me:** Edward Kennedy int., Miller Center, UVA, June 17, 2005.

452 **"deferments for students on a moral basis?":** Thurston Clarke, *The Last Campaign: Robert F. Kennedy and 82 Days that Inspired America* (New York: Henry Holt & Co., 2008), 87.

452 **Johnson himself harbored some concerns:** "The ABM, Through Thick and Thin," *Time*, Feb. 28, 1969.

453 **Ted had begun reaching out:** Carey Parker int., Miller Center, UVA, Nov. 10, 2008.

454 **"very big fight":** Dun Gifford int., Clymer Papers, Series 2, Box 3, G folder, JFK Lib., Feb. 2, 1996.

454 **"we must win":** H. R. Haldeman, *The Haldeman Diaries: Inside the Nixon White House* (New York: G. P. Putnam's Sons, 1994), entry Apr. 8, 1969, 48.

455 **"way out there on a limb":** Dun Gifford int., Clymer Papers, JFK Lib., Feb. 2, 1996.

455 **president of the Ford Motor Company:** "Goldberg and Harriman Lead ABM Opponents," *LAT*, Apr. 18, 1969.

455 **"changing his mind almost every day":** Honan, *Ted Kennedy*, 32.

456 **testified against the ABM:** "Kennedy Report Finds Safeguard Unreliable," *LAT*, May 7, 1969.

456 **"should have been asked before in Congress":** Carey Parker int., Miller Center, UVA, Nov. 11, 2008.

456 **"Awakening the country":** *Ibid.*

456 **Ted Kennedy's real triumph:** J. P. Ruina, "ABM: An Evaluation of the Decision to Deploy an Anti-Ballistic System," *NYT Book Review*, June 29, 1969.

456 **as a result of Ted's effort:** Lippman, 193.

456 **"changed the tone of the defense debate":** Carey Parker int., Miller Center, UVA, Nov. 10, 2008.

457 **"It dominated everything else":** Memo, James Wechsler, Re: Conversation with Ted Kennedy, nd., Kennedy, Edward M. 1968–1971 folder, Box 37, Joseph L. Rauh, Jr., Papers, Lib. of Congress.

457 **"precipitate":** Rick Perlstein, *Nixonland: The Rise of a President and the Fracturing of America* (New York: Scribner, 2008), 387–388.

457 **"gallant victory":** James Willbanks, "Hell on Hamburger Hill," *Vietnam Magazine*, May 8, 2009, http://www.historynet.com/hell-on-hamburger-hill.htm.

458 **"It caused an uproar":** David Burke int., Miller Center, UVA, Apr. 9, 2008.

458 **"It just did":** Dun Gifford int., Miller Center, UVA, July 13, 2005.

459 **"false sense of military pride":** http://www.tedkennedy.org/ownwords/event/vietnam.html.

459 **"cruelty and savagery":** Perlstein, 388; "Kennedy Again Blasts 'Senseless' War Acts," *WP,* May 31, 1969.

459 **"And for what?":** "Dirksen, Mansfield Clash Over Kennedy," *LAT,* June 3, 1969.

460 **"He is moving":** James Reston, "Edward Kennedy's Challenge to President Nixon," *NYT,* May 21, 1969.

460 **"position of political preeminence":** Warren Weaver Jr., "The Republicans and Some Democrats Have a Kennedy Problem," *NYT,* June 8, 1969.

460 **tabbed Ted as the most admired:** Perlstein, 388.

460 **"Draft Kennedy" groups were forming:** Edward Kennedy int., Miller Center, UVA, Oct. 14, 2005.

461 **"he'd blow hot and cold":** Milton Gwirtzman int., Series 2, Box 3, folder G, Clymer Papers, JFK Lib., Apr. 3, 1993.

461 **"life and fate came together":** William vanden Heuvel int., Miller Center, UVA, July 19, 2005.

461 **"obscure":** *True Compass,* 314.

462 **seating of the new Senate:** Charles Ludlam Oral History, 2004, Senate Historical Office, 10.

462 **John Kennedy did not attend:** David Mervin, "United States Senate Norms and the Majority Whip Election of 1969," *Journal of American Studies,* 93, Dec. 1975, 321–333.

462 **"subcommittee chairman's primary concern":** Robert Caro, *Master of the Senate* (New York: Alfred A. Knopf, 2002), 1028.

462 **"for administrative oversight":** *True Compass,* 314.

463 **"how full his plate was already":** Carey Parker int., Miller Center, UVA, Oct. 6, 2008.

463 **ten in the subcommittee office:** Rochelle Jones and Peter Woll, *The Private World of Congress* (New York: The Free Press, 1979), 181.

463 **"base of operations":** *True Compass,* 314.

463 **"fire brigade for liberal causes":** Lippman, 154.

463 **"from one conflagration to another":** Martha Derthick and Paul Quirk, *The Politics of Deregulation* (Washington, D.C.: The Brookings Institution, 1985), 40–41.

464 **"'we don't get to do anything'":** Stan Jones int., Miller Center, UVA, Sept. 14, 2007.

464 **That's how Ted did it:** Mark Schneider int., Miller Center, UVA, Feb. 2, 2009.

464 **accuse him of "harassment":** "Ted's Troubles in the Tundra."

465 **this was the road to greatness:** Rather and Gates, 82–84.

465 **announced a force reduction:** Brower.

465 **"there's no doubt anymore":** Warren Weaver Jr., "By His Deeds . . ." *Esquire,* Feb. 1, 1972.

466 **"a personal kind of conflict":** Brower.

466 **the administration also curbed:** Weaver.

466 **Nixon lived in terror of a Kennedy restoration:** Matthews, 19.

466 **"What did I pick up from Democrats?":** Robert Healy int., Miller Center, UVA, Aug. 10, 2005.

466 **"other kinds of activities":** Edward Kennedy int., Miller Center, UVA, May 8, 2006.

467 **Ehrlichman suggested that the president:** Perlstein, 388.

467 **"colonialism":** "GOP Senators Quit Kennedy's Tour of Alaska," *LAT,* April 11, 1969.

467 **"to confirm preconceived conclusions":** "Angry Republicans Quit Kennedy's Alaskan Tour," *WP,* Apr. 11, 1969.

468 **"just tired of a one-man show":** "Ted's Troubles in the Tundra."

468 **"This isn't Air Force One yet":** Brower.

468 **"look at people who have money":** Walter Mondale int., Miller Center, UVA, March 20, 2006.

468 **"Murphy":** Brower.

468 **"the natives of Alaska":** Walter Mondale int., Miller Center, UVA, March 20, 2006.

468 "First time I used it": Brower; "The Mysteries of Chappaquiddick," *Time*, Aug. 1, 1969.

468 "First one to find the northern lights": Burton Hersh, *Edward Kennedy: An Intimate Biography* (Berkeley: Counterpoint, 2010), 339.

468 "the way they shot Bobby's": *Ibid.*, 340.

468 "Eskimo Power!": Hays Gorey int., "The Kennedys," *American Experience*, prod. Elizabeth Deane, WGBH, 1992; Brower.

469 "enjoyer": Brower.

469 "the demands of his public image": "The Mysteries of Chappaquiddick."

469 "T.M.B.S.": Brower.

469 "trying to figure things out": *Ibid.*

469 "something terrible will happen": Lester Hyman int., Miller Center, UVA, Oct. 6, 2008.

469 "a personal burden in so many ways": William vanden Heuvel int., Miller Center, UVA, July 19, 2005.

470 "if you want to know the truth": John Tunney int., Miller Center, UVA, May 3, 2007, Oct. 12, 2009.

470 "I never quite thought that it was . . .": Edward Kennedy int., Miller Center, UVA, Nov. 29, 2006.

470 "all these things are just predetermined": *True Compass*, 286–287.

CHAPTER TWELVE: "THE WRONG SIDE OF DESTINY"

471 "I've never been so tired in my life": Edward Kennedy, *True Compass* (New York: Twelve, 2009), 288.

471 then jetted out right after: *Ibid.*, 288.

471 Arriving at Chappaquiddick: Charles Tretter int., Miller Center, UVA, Aug. 8, 2005.

472 "freshen up": *True Compass*, 290; John Barron, "Chappaquiddick: The Still-Unanswered Questions," *Reader's Digest*, Feb. 1980.

472 the "boiler-room girls": Gladys Gifford int. by author.

472 "maybe that was good": Nance Lyons int., Miller Center, UVA, May 7, 2008.

473 "to tell war stories": Melody Miller int., Miller Center, UVA, Oct. 7, 2008.

473 told him it would mean a lot: *True Compass*, 288.

473 "He felt in some ways a charity case": Melody Miller int., Oct. 7, 2008.

473 "You were kind of a fairy": Leo Damore, *Senatorial Privilege: The Chappaquiddick Cover-Up* (Washington, D.C.: Regnery Gateway, 1988), 65.

473 "He was a gofer": Gladys Gifford int. by author.

473 "they never seemed to appreciate him": Barbara Gibson and Ted Schwartz, *Rose Kennedy and Her Family: The Best and Worst of Their Lives and Times* (New York: Birch Lane Press, 1995), 174.

474 "who was consulted like Steve Smith": Melody Miller int., Miller Center, UVA, Oct. 7, 2008.

474 "An extremely likable man": Rita Dallas and Jeanira Ratcliffe, *The Kennedy Case* (New York: G. P. Putnam's Sons, 1973), 330–331.

474 Gargan who served as host: Lester David, *Ted Kennedy: Triumphs and Tragedies* (New York: Grosset & Dunlap, 1972), 189–190; "Kennedy to Face Charge in Crash for Leaving Site," *The New York Times*, July 21, 1969.

474 "of putting on a party": Charles Tretter int., Miller Center, UVA, Aug. 8, 2005.

474 "people in for the evening": "Kennedy's License Suspended by State," *The Washington Post*, July 24, 1969.

474 "Some people were bored to death with it": Damore, 75.

474 "very little scotch": *The Inquest into the Death of Mary Jo Kopechne* (New York: EVR Production and Lincoln Graphic Arts, 1970), 49.

474 another that he poured himself at nine: *Ibid.*, 7.

475 "He was not having a helluva good time": Burton Hersh, *The Education of Edward Kennedy: A Family Biography* (New York: William Morrow & Co., 1972), 392.

475 she said she wanted to leave: *True Compass*, 290.

475 she had had too much sun: "Chappaquiddick Revisited," *WP*, Feb. 22, 1976.

475 later got "agitated": Hersh, 393; Esther Newberg testimony, *Inquest*, 58; "Sheriff's Version Among Many Conflicts with Kennedy Story," *The Boston Globe*, Oct. 29, 1974.

475 "real straight arrow": Gladys Gifford int. by author.

475 Mary Jo background: "Victim Drawn to Politics," *NYT*, July 20, 1969; Jane Farrell, "Memories of Mary Jo," *Ladies' Home Journal*, July 25, 1989.

476 "Just you and the president": David, 191–192.

476 **then joined a consulting firm:** "Victim Drawn to Politics."

476 **she once stayed up all night:** "Grief, Fear, Doubt, Panic—And Guilt," Newsweek, Aug. 4, 1969.

476 **"sleeper":** "The Mysteries of Chappaquiddick," *Time*, Aug. 1, 1969.

476 **she vacationed with her parents:** Farrell.

476 **her friends were concerned:** Melody Miller int., Miller Center, UVA, Oct. 7, 2008.

476 **defrauded her:** Memo, Carmen DeLoach to Clyde Tolson, Re: Edward Kennedy, 125, Part 3, FBI file, Oct. 17, 1969.

476 **"the virgin":** Melody Miller int., Miller Center, UVA, Oct. 7, 2008.

477 **he frequently got lost driving:** Dallas, 88.

477 **"automatically wind up in the water":** "The Mysteries of Chappaquiddick."

477 **"Perilous even in broad daylight":** Arthur Schlesinger Jr., *Journals: 1952–2000*, Andrew Schlesinger and Stephen Schlesinger, eds. (New York: Penguin Press, 2007), 311.

477 **"that bridge was ridiculous":** Charles Tretter int., Miller Center, UVA, Aug. 8, 2005.

477 **"Something was bound to happen there":** Brock Brower, "The Incident at Dike Bridge," *Life*, Aug. 1, 1969.

478 **"impossible to even hold it back":** Inquest, 7–8.

478 **for another fifteen or twenty minutes:** *Ibid.*, 8.

478 **Ted's account of period after accident:** *Ibid.*, 14.

480 **"Perhaps I could wish it all away":** True Compass, 292.

480 **"sobbing":** Inquest, 45.

480 **Ted's reaction:** *Ibid.*, 8–9, 44, 34–35.

480 **"Rosencrantz and Guildenstern of this dark evening":** John Gregory Dunne, "On the Matter of Chappaquiddick," *New West*, Dec. 3, 1979.

480 **"I will take care of the accident":** Inquest, 36.

481 **Ted returned to his room:** *Ibid.*, 10.

481 **"to call Mrs. Kopechne":** *Ibid.*, 10–11.

481 **"just a nightmare":** *Ibid.*, 47.

481 **seeking Smith's phone number:** Shaun Considine, "Helga Wagner Sells 'She Shells,'" *People*, Sept. 8, 1980.

482 **"would be involved in a myriad of details":** Inquest, 37, 11.

482 **remove her corpse:** "Kennedy to Face Charge in Crash for Leaving Site"; "Woman Passenger Killed, Kennedy Escapes in Crash," *NYT*, July 20, 1969; Brower.

483 **Gargan or Markham told the man:** "Kennedy Took Sharp Turn on Obscure Road," *WP*, July 22, 1969.

483 **"Oh, yeah. We just heard about it":** "Grief, Fear, Doubt, Panic—and Guilt."

483 **to report what had happened:** Barron.

483 **"Miss Mary":** "Kennedy to Face Charge in Crash for Leaving Site."

483 **"I just can't do it":** "Kennedy Calls His Conduct 'Irrational and Inexcusable,'" *BG*, Oct. 27, 1974.

484 **"turning it off and it's all over":** "Kopechne Family: 'Our World Fell Apart,'" *WP*, July 30, 1969.

484 **Bob Carroll, who also piloted the plane:** Peter Canellos, *Last Lion: The Fall and Rise of Ted Kennedy* (New York: Simon & Schuster, 2009), 161.

484 **"state of semi-shock":** Robert Sherill, *The Last Kennedy* (New York: The Dial Press, 1976), 68.

484 **"the death of the young woman":** Rose Fitzgerald Kennedy, *Times to Remember* (Garden City, N.Y.: Doubleday & Co., 1974), 491–492.

484 **Joe Kennedy reached for his son's hand:** Dallas, 338–339.

484 **"you could almost feel his pain":** David, 208.

484 **"blockage":** Hersh, 408–409.

484 **he didn't want people to think:** Dallas, 341.

484 **"acute cervical strain":** Inquest, 90–92.

484 **"rage and horror and anger":** "The Kennedys," *American Experience*, prod. Elizabeth Deane, WGBH, 1992.

485 **she specifically cited Moore:** Laurence Leamer, *The Kennedy Women: The Saga of an American Family* (New York: Villard Books, 1994), 651–652.

485 **later disinheriting him:** Gibson and Schwarz, 263–264.

485 **"narrow brush with death":** "Teddy Escapes, Woman Drowns," *Chicago Tribune*, July 20, 1969.

485 **"prominence in American political life":** "Woman Passenger Killed, Kennedy Escapes in Crash."

485 **"none has been so tragedy-ridden":** "Kennedy Successes Haunted by Tragedy," *WP*, July 26, 1969.

485 **"Ted Kennedy and his nationwide constituency"**: "Wrong Turn at the Bridge," *Time*, July 25, 1969.

485 TEDDY ESCAPES: *New York Daily News*, July 20, 1969.

485 **"defect in the senator's character"**: "The Kennedy Episode," *Chicago Tribune*, July 22, 1969.

486 **"more than they did the war"**: "The Mysteries of Chappaquiddick."

486 **any statement could affect**: Hersh, 409.

486 **"I immediately contacted police"**: "Woman Passenger Killed, Kennedy Escapes in Crash."

486 **"how he could come out of this"**: William vanden Heuvel int., Miller Center, UVA, July 19, 2005.

486 **"I think they disserved him"**: Lester Hyman int., Miller Center, UVA, Oct. 6, 2008.

487 **A "caravan of stars"**: David Burke int., Miller Center, UVA, June 19, 2007.

487 **"Where's Teddy? Where's my brother?"**: Leamer, 648.

487 **"They weren't dragooned"**: David Burke int., Miller Center, UVA, June 19, 2007.

487 **"Your best friend is in terrible trouble"**: John Tunney int., Miller Center, UVA, Oct. 12, 2009.

488 **"he should tell what his reasons were"**: Milton Gwirtzman int., Miller Center, UVA, May 29, 2009.

487 **"The Cuban Missile Crisis all over again"**: Robert Sherrill, *The Last Kennedy* (New York: The Dial Press, 1976), 101.

488 **"he was suddenly self-assured"**: Dallas, 341, 339.

488 **"Nobody could decide what to do"**: Hersh, 411.

488 **Ted was likely to get a light sentence**: E. J. Rooney, "Kennedy Called Brain Trust to Advise Him," *LAT*, July 29, 1969.

489 **"Many cross streams"**: Hersh, 411.

489 **"stupor, more alone"**: Dallas, 339.

489 **"grave damage politically"**: *WP*, July 24, 1969.

489 **"That's too much"**: "Kennedy's Political Future Is Seen as Dim," *Chicago Tribune*, July 24, 1969.

489 ***"Res ipsa loquitu"***: "Democrats Urge Kennedy to Speak," *NYT*, July 25, 1969.

489 **"There goes the presidency"**: Canellos, 162.

489 **"going to be the duke of Windsor?"**: Milton Gwirtzman int., Clymer Papers, Series 2, Box 3, G folder, JFK Lib., Apr. 3, 1993.

490 **"never know how close it was"**: Schlesinger, *Journals*, 312.

490 **"he wasn't going to tell it to me?"**: John Tunney int., Miller Center, UVA, Oct. 12, 2009.

490 **"He thought she had gotten away"**: Milton Gwirtzman int., Miller Center, UVA, May 29, 2009.

490 **"obviously felt very sorry"**: Theodore Sorensen int., Miller Center, UVA, Dec. 7, 2006.

490 **"It was not the high point"**: Ted Sorensen, *Counselor: A Life at the Edge of History* (New York: HarperCollins, 2008), 257.

491 **"screwing somebody outside of marriage"**: Hersh, 411.

491 **Gwirtzman's major contribution**: Canellos, 169.

491 **Ted desired to say this**: Adam Clymer, *Edward M. Kennedy: A Biography* (New York: William Morrow, 1999), 151.

491 **insisted that the passage be struck**: Milton Gwirtzman int., Miller Center, UVA, May 29, 2009.

491 **thought it should have been simpler**: Ted Sorensen int., Miller Center, UVA, Dec. 7, 2006; Dun Gifford int., Clymer Papers, Series 2, Box 3, G folder, JFK Lib., Feb. 2, 1996.

491 **arranged for the funeral home**: Dun Gifford int., Miller Center, UVA, July 13, 2005.

492 **"The worst part of it for me"**: *Ibid.*

492 **"didn't want to be negative about Ted"**: Gladys Gifford int. by author.

492 **because Ted had asked him to**: William vanden Heuvel int., Miller Center, UVA, July 19, 2005.

492 **"Like a man in a catatonic trance"**: Schlesinger, *Journals*, 311.

492 **"he was so emotional"**: "Kopechne Family: 'Our World Fell Apart.' "

492 **"I was working automatically"**: "Kopechne Family: 'Our World Fell Apart.' "

492 **Ted had offered to cover the funeral**: Barron.

492 **seven hundred spectators had collected**: "3 Kennedys Attend Funeral for Drowned Secretary," *NYT*, July 23, 1969.

493 **"that was before the Revolutionary War"**: "Kopechne Family: 'Our World Fell Apart.' "

493 **"I saw him! I saw him!"**: "Accident Victim Buried," *WP*, July 23, 1969.

493 **across from the Kopechnes**: "Grief, Fear, Doubt, Panic—And Guilt."

493 **"above the slag heaps"**: "3 Kennedys Attend Funeral."

493   **"talking to my sister":** "Kopechne Family: 'Our World Fell Apart.' "

493   **"we can't help thinking":** "The Kopechnes: Awaiting Answers," *Time*, Aug. 22, 1969.

493   **"down but determined":** Hersh, 411.

493   **"hardly able to respond or function":** Dallas, 341.

495   **"Dad, I've done the best that I can":** *Ibid.*, 342.

495   **"And it was not believed":** William Honan, *Ted Kennedy: Profile of a Survivor* (New York: Quad-rangle Books, 1972), 81.

495   **Mauldin drew Ted looking into a mirror:** James MacGregor Burns, *Edward Kennedy and the Camelot Legacy* (New York: W. W. Norton & Co., 1976), 168.

495   **"A Checkers speech with class":** "Grief, Fear, Doubt, Panic—And Guilt."

496   **"startled him out of his rather casual ways":** "Senator Kennedy's Impossible Question," *NYT*, July 27, 1969.

496   **"still-unanswered questions":** "Editorial Comment on Kennedy Speech," *NYT*, July 27, 1969.

496   **found it "unsatisfactory":** "Still a Tragedy and a Mystery," *NYT*, July 27, 1969.

496   **"aura can ever be won back":** "Editorial Comment on Kennedy Speech."

497   **a Republican would win Ted's senate seat:** "Murphy Foresees GOP Winning Kennedy Seat," *LAT*, Sept. 23, 1969.

497   **"and I don't think I got it":** "Senator's Statement Regarded as First Step," *WP*, July 26, 1969.

497   **"Stay with us":** "Senators Hoping Kennedy Stays On," *NYT*, July 26, 1969.

497   **"if he should resign":** "Thousands Back Kennedy," *WP*, July 27, 1969.

497   **So did Speaker John McCormack:** "Humphrey Asks Kennedy Not to Step Down," *NYT*, July 29, 1969.

497   **"My God, what an ill-starred family":** Francis Valeo, Oral History Interviews, Senate Historical Office.

497   **Daley promised to support him:** "Most Back Kennedy in Mass Poll," *WP*, July 29, 1969.

497   **"hope he decides to stay on as senator":** "Mother of the Victim Opposes Autopsy and Backs Senator," *NYT*, July 26, 1969.

497   **poll showed 84 percent of Massachusetts voters:** "84% of Those Voters Polled in Bay State Back Kennedy," *NYT*, July 29, 1969.

497   **Two-thirds wanted him to run for president:** "Most Back Kennedy in Mass Poll."

497   **they ran 100 to 1 in Ted's favor:** "Grief, Fear, Doubt, Panic—And Guilt"; "Thousands Back Kennedy."

497   **"We're with you":** "Ted Greeted by Supporters' Cheers," *Chicago Tribune*, July 28, 1969.

498   **44 percent believed he hadn't told the truth:** "Public Reaction: Charitable, Skeptical," *Time*, Aug. 8, 1969.

498   **"the boy-come-of-age":** "William Weaver Jr., "By His Deeds . . ." *Esquire*, Feb. 1, 1972.

498   **he assumed Ted was drunk:** H. R. Haldeman, *The Haldeman Diaries: Inside the Nixon White House* (New York: G. P. Putnam's Sons, 1994), 72.

499   **"it was in the papers that afternoon!":** Lippman, 199.

499   **"too many reporters want to win a Pulitzer Prize":** Rick Perlstein, *Nixonland: The Rise of a President and the Fracturing of America* (New York: Scribner, 2008), 397.

499   **a malice born of resentment:** Richard Nixon, *The Memoirs of Richard Nixon* (New York: Grosset & Dunlap, 1978), 542–543.

500   **"inaccuracy of Kennedy's story":** Tony Ulasewicz with Stuart McKeever, *The President's Private Eye: The Journey of Detective Tony U. from the N.Y.P.D. to the Nixon White House* (Westport, Conn.: Macsam, 1990), 192, 217.

500   **Anderson would later say:** Jack Anderson, "Kennedy Seen as Real Target of Break-In," *WP*, June 6, 1974.

500   **"we may be able to develop some useful information":** Memo, Jack Caulfield to John Ehrlichman, Re: Chappaquiddick Inquiry, Folder 308-A, Stanley, Box 20, White House Special Files: Staff Member and Office Files: John D. Ehrlichman, Nixon Lib., July 31, 1969.

500   **concerned that the White House switchboard might be tapped:** Haldeman, 72–75.

501   **Ehrlichman authorized wiretaps:** "Tap Reportedly Put on Kopechne Phone," *NYT*, July 7, 1973.

501   **"to get it properly exploited":** John Ehrlichman, *Witness to Power: The Nixon Years* (New York: Simon & Schuster, 1982), 292.

501   **asked the FBI to "discreetly" determine:** Memo, D. J. Brennan Jr. to W. C. Sullivan, Part 3, page 131, Edward Kennedy, FBI file, Oct. 22, 1969.

501 **"At an Appropriate Time":** Ulasewicz, 219.

501 **"guys that ought to be able to find it out":** Haldeman quoted in Christopher Matthews, *Kennedy & Nixon: The Rivalry that Shaped Postwar America* (New York: Simon & Schuster, 1996), 284.

501 **she had taken hormone shots:** Joan Braden, "Joan Kennedy Tells Her Own Story," *McCall's,* Aug. 1978.

501 **"give Patrick a little brother or sister":** Canellos, 234.

501 **left for Europe:** Leamer, 651.

502 **"Nothing ever seemed the same after that":** Marcia Chellis, *Living with the Kennedys: The Joan Kennedy Story* (New York: Simon & Schuster, 1985), 86.

502 **"choosing politics over our baby":** Canellos, 176.

502 **"After that I just thought":** Braden.

502 **Joan operated in denial:** David, *Ted Kennedy,* 211.

502 **"on my high horse for the first time in my life":** Lester David, *Joan: The Reluctant Kennedy* (New York: Funk & Wagnalls, 1974), 182.

502 **"Ted and I were brought closer together":** Lester David, "Joan—The Reluctant Kennedy," *Good Housekeeping,* June 1972.

502 **"difficult time with her":** Edward Kennedy int., Miller Center, UVA, Nov. 29, 2006.

502 **committed to a sanitarium:** Leamer, 651.

503 **"then she had a tough period":** Edward Kennedy int., Miller Center, UVA, Nov. 29, 2006.

503 **"looking like a ruined man":** "The Mysteries of Chappaquiddick."

503 **"beyond anything this court can impose":** Jack Olsen, *The Bridge at Chappaquiddick* (Boston: Little, Brown, 1970), 240.

503 **showed no signs of inebriation:** "Kennedy to Face Charge in Crash for Leaving Site."

503 **"A Roman holiday":** Richard Harwood, "Kennedy Probe: 'A Roman Holiday' " *WP,* July 2, 1969.

503 **agreed with Harwood's characterization:** Sherrill, 77–80.

503 **"I don't know— Never":** Hersh, 413.

504 **felt that the Kennedys had ignored him:** "Inquest Is Sought in Kennedy Case," *NYT,* Aug. 1, 1969.

504 **"I don't need your brother":** "Take-Charge Jurist to Run Mass Inquest," *WP,* Sept. 2, 1969.

504 **"unsupported by any medical facts":** "Autopsy Denied in Kopechne Case," *NYT,* Dec. 11, 1969.

504 **requested a postponement:** "Kopechne Inquest Put Off," *NYT,* September 3, 1969.

505 **backed up and drove down Dike Road:** *Inquest,* 73.

505 **"came out of a courthouse door":** James Reston, "Edgartown, Mass.: The Strange Case of Senator Edward Kennedy," *NYT,* Jan. 7, 1970.

505 **"You are just looking for Mickey Mouse charges":** George Lardner, Jr., "Chappaquiddick 1989," *WP,* July 16, 1989.

506 **"as far as some people are concerned":** "Chappaquiddick: Suspicions Renewed," *Time,* May 11, 1970.

506 **red bowties and soft fedoras:** "Conductor of Inquest," *NYT,* Jan. 6, 1970.

506 **"to exercise due care":** *Inquest,* 123–126.

506 **contemplating leaving public life:** Honan, 5.

506 **writing, teaching, or traveling:** "Kennedy Statement Rejects Findings," *NYT,* April 30, 1970.

506 **required him by statute:** Fred Graham, "Questions Are Raised by Judge's Report on Inquest," *NYT,* May 1, 1970.

507 **he had seen him drunk in that period:** "The Mysteries of Chappaquiddick."

507 **"we knew that was absurd":** Melody Miller int., Miller Center, UVA, 7, 2008.

508 **"the most sinister thing":** Hersh, 396.

508 **he had changed his story three times:** "Kennedy Feels Chappaquiddick Would Not Rule Out Presidency," *NYT,* July 18, 1979; "Chappaquiddick Revisited," *WP,* Feb. 22,1976.

508 **driving at least thirty miles per hour:** Barron.

508 **"when looked at with automobile headlights":** Olsen, 287; "Kennedy to Face Charge in Crash for Leaving Site."

509 **because he was dazed:** "Kennedy Calls His Conduct 'Irrational and Inexcusable.' "

509 **"profound state of shock":** William vanden Heuvel int., Miller Center, UVA, Dec. 7, 2006.

509 **channel was entirely swimmable:** "Kennedy's Week of Tragedy," *NYT,* July 27, 1969.

509 **And he was exhausted:** "Thousands Back Kennedy."

509 **"not unusual for a person who had suffered":** "The Mysteries of Chappaquiddick."

509 **and then drove her off the bridge:** R. B. Cutler, *You the Jury . . . In Re: Chappaquiddick* (Danvers, Mass.: Betts & Mirror Press, 1973); Zad Rust, *Teddy Bare* (Belmont, Mass.: Western Islands Press, 1971); Kenneth Kappel, *Chappaquiddick Revealed: What Really Happened* (New York: Shapolsky Publishers, 1989).

510 **said that Ted had changed clothes to go swimming:** Anonymous to Richard Kleindeinst, Part 3, 139-140, EMK, FBI file, Dec. 22, 1969; "Memories of Mary Jo." The Keough hypothesis, based, in part, on the fact that her handbag was found in the car, is also the subject of a book: Donald Frederick Nelson, *Chappaquiddick Tragedy: Kennedy's Second Passenger Revealed* (Gretna, La.: Pelican Publishing, 2016). Keough said that she left her purse in the car when she and Tretter went to Edgartown to get a radio, which is entirely plausible.

510 **"nil":** "The Recurring Doubts About Chappaquiddick," *McCall's*, Nov. 1975.

510 **"at least disorient them thoroughly":** Olsen, 125.

510 **Mary Jo could have survived:** "Frustrated Grand Jurors Say It Was No Accident Ted Kennedy Got Off Easy," *People*, July 24, 1989.

510 **"pristine":** Dun Gifford int., Miller Center, UVA, July 13, 2005.

510 **without Ted knowing about it:** Olsen, 266–268.

511 **"the accident that killed Mary Jo Kopechne":** Damore, 66.

511 **"I'm a fool in the eyes of my own children":** *Ibid.*, 423.

511 **"You've got to do what I've been saying right along":** *Ibid.*, 81, 90–93, 200–201.

511 **"we'll both be criticized for it":** Olsen, 142.

512 **impossible to prove given the condition of the bridge:** James E. T. Lange and Katherine DeWitt Jr., *Chappaquiddick: The Real Story* (New York: St. Martin's Press, 1992). Of all the numerous books that purport to tell what happened that night, this evenhanded, nonsensational book is the best. It concludes that Kennedy told the truth about the accident.

512 **"girl was lying at the bottom of the pond":** Richard Harwood, "Recirculation of Testimony Damaging to Senator Kennedy," *WP*, Sept. 3, 1969.

512 **"a moment of panic or trauma":** Dunne.

512 **"as a result of Bobby's death":** Gladys Gifford int. by author.

512 **"there is nothing to catch him out in":** Garry Wills, *The Kennedy Imprisonment: A Meditation on Power* (Boston: Little, Brown, 2002), 56.

513 **"what happened was an accident":** Canellos, 164.

513 **"I don't think he ever lied to me":** Dun Gifford int., Miller Center, UVA, July 13, 2005.

513 **"he was telling me the truth":** John Tunney int., Miller Center, UVA, May 3, 2007.

513 **"unwarranted and unjustified":** "Kennedy Calls His Conduct 'Irrational and Inexcusable.' "

513 **"those who had already made up their minds":** *True Compass*, 289.

513 **John Tunney thought his friend:** John Tunney int., Miller Center, UVA, Oct. 12, 2009.

513 **"at the hands of a merciless fate":** Doris Kearns Goodwin, *The Fitzgeralds and the Kennedys: An American Saga* (New York: Simon & Schuster, 1987), xv.

513 **"end of the Kennedy era":** Perlstein, 400.

513 **"effectively ended all of the activities":** Edward Kennedy int., Miller Center, UVA, Oct. 14, 2005.

513 **Ted had run ten points better against Nixon:** "Poll Finds Kennedy Trails Two Democrats," *NYT*, Aug. 19, 1969.

514 **Nixon held a fourteen-point lead over him:** "Sen. Kennedy Fails to Regain Support," *WP*, Nov. 23, 1969; "Ted's Crumbling Position," *Time*, Nov. 7, 1969.

514 **"but I wouldn't let that Teddy drive it":** "The Mysteries of Chappaquiddick."

514 **"Our shock at what happened":** David Broder, "Politicians, Pundits Played God with Edward Kennedy," *WP*, July 29, 1969.

514 **"It was going to be different":** Canellos, 161.

514 **"Kennedys began their descent":** "Chappaquiddick's Echoes," *The New Yorker*, July 25, 1994.

514 **"that shaped his action":** Max Lerner, *Ted and the Kennedy Legend: A Study in Character and Destiny* (New York: St. Martin's Press, 1980), 120.

515 **"Kennedy's were probed":** "Chappaquiddick Echoes."

515 **"soaring made him look ridiculous":** Charles Pierce, "Kennedy Unbound After 40 Years in U.S. Senate," *Boston Globe Magazine*, Jan. 5, 2003.

516 **"the parameters of his leadership":** Walter Mondale int., Miller Center, UVA, March 20, 2006.

516 **"party left groping for a center":** Marquis Childs, "Miserable, Tragic Accident May End the Kennedy Era," *WP*, Aug. 1, 1969.

516 **"serious blow to our party and country":** Califano, 243.
516 **$90,904, which he paid himself:** Dunne.
516 **"lift this heavy, heavy burden from my heart?":** Dun Gifford int., Clymer Papers, Feb. 2, 1996; Farrell.
516 **sobbing on Marty Nolan's shoulder:** Martin Nolan int., Miller Center, UVA, Sept. 14, 2006.
517 **"all about Chappaquiddick":** "Following the Letters to the Law," *WP*, Aug. 16, 1991.
517 **"It is with me every day":** "Remembering Ted Kennedy," *National Journal*, Sept. 5, 2009.
517 **"I will for the rest of my life":** "Kennedy Calls His Conduct 'Irrational and Inexcusable.'"
517 **"haunts me every day of my life":** *True Compass*, 288.
517 **she never discussed it with him:** Leamer, 646.
517 **he fell into silence:** Patrick Kennedy and Stephen Fried, *A Common Struggle: A Personal Journey Through the Past and Future of Mental Illness and Addiction* (New York: Blue Rider Press, 2015), 41.
517 **Joyce Carol Oates would write a novella:** Joyce Carol Oates, *Black Water* (New York: E. P. Dutton, 1992).
517 **2018 film titled *Chappaquiddick*:** *Chappaquiddick*, John Curran, dir., 2017.
518 **"something quite different from that":** John Tunney int., Miller Center, UVA, Oct. 12, 2009.
518 **"continuation of involvement in public life":** "Kennedy Feels Chappaquiddick Would Not Rule Out Presidency."
518 **"I am a different person":** "Kennedy Says Chappaquiddick Changed His Life," *LAT*, Dec. 2, 1979.
518 **"What agonies of remorse has he reserved for himself?":** Christopher Lydon, "A Special Kind of Grief in Massachusetts," *NYT*, Aug. 3, 1969.

CHAPTER THIRTEEN: STARTING FROM SCRATCH

519 **headed to Majority Leader Mike Mansfield's desk:** "Kennedy: 'I'm Glad to Be Back,'" *WP*, Aug. 1, 1969; "Kennedy Back in Senate," *LAT*, Aug. 1, 1969.
519 **"This is where you belong":** Mike Mansfield int., Clymer Papers, Series 2, Box 4, M folder, JFK Lib., Jan. 27, 1993.
519 **and would not run for president:** "Kennedy to Seek Reelection," *LAT*, July 31, 1969.
519 **other senators approached him:** "Kennedy Back in Senate," *NYT*, Aug. 1, 1969.
519 **"terse and solemn":** "Kennedy Back in Senate"; William Weaver Jr., "By His Deeds . . ." *Esquire*, Feb. 1, 1972; Max Lerner, "Is the Kennedy Mystique in the Process of Collapse?" *LAT*, Aug. 8, 1969.
520 **"I always wondered what he would have said":** Lester Hyman int., Miller Center, UVA, Oct. 6. 2008.
520 **another long talk:** Michael O'Brien, *Philip Hart: The Conscience of the Senate* (East Lansing: Michigan State Univ. Press, 1995), 151.
520 **Drew Pearson on effectiveness:** "Kennedy's Effectiveness Impaired," *WP*, Aug. 5, 1969.
520 **"hallmark of his entire distinguished career":** Lerner; Burton Hersh, *The Education of Edward Kennedy: A Family Biography* (New York: William Morrow & Co., 1972), 419.
520 **"his usual well-founded sense":** Weaver.
521 **"more softly, more slowly":** Sylvia Wright, "The Revival of Ted Kennedy," *Life*, Oct. 3, 1969.
521 **"if they will just go on and on and on":** William Honan, *Ted Kennedy: Profile of a Survivor* (New York: Quadrangle Books, 1972), 93.
521 **"instead of a state of almost disbelief":** Edward Kennedy int., Miller Center, UVA, Nov. 29, 2006.
521 **his spirits revived only:** Arthur Schlesinger Jr., *Journals: 1952–2000*, Andrew Schlesinger and Stephen Schlesinger, eds. (New York: Penguin Press, 2007), 313–314.
521 **He avoided looking people in the eye:** "The Anguish of Ted Kennedy," *Time*, Aug. 29, 1969.
521 **"and he'll snap out of it":** Honan, 92.
522 **"his mind is elsewhere":** *Ibid.*
522 **"a damn thing either he or you could do about it":** Lester David, *Ted Kennedy: Triumphs and Tragedies* (New York: Grosset & Dunlap, 1972), 212.
522 **"This was a summer I was anxious to have end":** Wright.
522 **"It was painful":** Walter Mondale int., Miller Center, UVA, March 20, 2006.
522 **"untenable quality in politics: pity":** Robert Sherrill, *The Last Kennedy* (New York: The Dial Press, 1976), 215.

522 "They just needed him less": Hersh, 417.

522 "Now he's . . . just another man": *Ibid.*, 418.

522 "He can never moralize again": David, *Ted Kennedy*, 217.

522 "start all over again from scratch": Honan, 112.

523 "manic gaiety": Wright.

523 one of his associates in New York: Nance Lyons int., Miller Center, UVA, May 9, 2008.

524 left, too, their faith betrayed: David Burke int. by author, Miller Center, UVA, Apr. 9, 2008.

524 "So that's what I did": Edward Kennedy int., Miller Center, UVA, Nov. 29, 2006.

524 "a flawed record at best": Weaver.

525 he couldn't speak to what Ted was feeling inwardly: Carey Parker int., Miller Center, UVA, Oct. 6, 2008.

525 "Would that just be okay?": Wright.

525 called him "aggressive": "Kennedy Renews Role as Vigorous Crusader," *LAT*, Sept. 21, 1969.

525 "walked by with his eyes on the floor": "Back from Chappaquiddick," *Time*, Oct. 10, 1969.

525 "iron went into Edward Kennedy's soul": Hersh, 383.

525 so that he could be a more effective whip: Adam Clymer, *Edward M. Kennedy: A Biography* (New York: William Morrow, 1999), 156.

525 "allowed him to become a more serious legislator": Peter Canellos, *Last Lion: The Fall and Rise of Ted Kennedy* (New York: Simon & Schuster, 2009), 176–177.

525 "turned him into a superior senator": Sherrill, 227.

526 "dictate the future of young American lives?": "Vietnam: Trying to Buy Time," Time, Sept. 26, 1969.

526 "gestured almost playfully": Wright.

526 "he's still a voice to be listened to": "Kennedy Renews Role as Vigorous Crusader."

527 "gall" to defend Ted: Memo, Nofziger to Harlow, Re: Counteracting Senator Kennedy, Folder: Vietnam, Box 14, White House Central Files: Staff Member and Office Files: Bryce Harlow, Nixon Lib., Sept. 22, 1969.

527 "powerfully to blunt this attack": Memo, Nixon to Haldeman, Sept. 22, 1969, in *From: The President: Richard Nixon's Secret Files*, Bruce Oudes, ed. (New York: Harper & Row 1989), 44–45.

528 told Ted that he had voted for him: Edward Kennedy int., Clymer Papers, Series 2, Box 5, EMK interviews, 1995–1996 folder, JFK Lib., Apr. 17, 1995.

528 "cumulatively": "Haynsworth Talks of Vending Business," *NYT*, Sept. 17, 1969.

528 "completely frank with the [Judiciary] committee": Wright.

528 "contemporary man of the times": Edward Kennedy int., Miller Center, UVA, Jan. 6, 2007; Wright.

528 "bottom really fell out for him fast": Edward Kennedy int., Miller Center, UVA, Jan. 6, 2007.

529 "Carswell May Make Some People Long for Haynsworth": *NYT*, Jan. 25, 1970.

529 "implement the Southern strategy": Richard Harris, *Decision* (New York: E. P. Dutton & Co., 1971), 11.

529 "No one was jumping up to lead it": Canellos, 178–179.

530 "stemwinder": Harris, 36–37, 22–24.

530 "left no fingerprints": Thomas Oliphant int. by author.

530 Flug wrote a memo: Harris, 37.

530 "Monday Morning Meetings," they were called: *Ibid.*, 79.

530 while he was United States attorney: Edward Kennedy, *True Compass* (New York: Twelve, 2009), 318.

530 "most slender credentials": "Words on Carswell," *NYT*, Feb. 8, 1970.

530 "entitled to a little bit of representation": https://library.cqpress.com/cqalmanac/document.php?id=cqal70-1292761.

531 "principles of white supremacy": Harris, 15–16.

531 only three senators—not including Ted: "Words on Carswell."

531 telephoned in his vote: "Kennedy, Ill With Pneumonia, Telephones in His Vote," *NYT*, Feb. 17, 1970.

531 "I smell blood": Harris, 58–59.

531 made Ted even more hostile: *Ibid.*

531 "unfettered by Senate review?": Clymer, 160–161.

531 the Republicans do the same with Carswell: Harris, 119–120.

532   **"Not a fingerprint":** Oliphant int. by author.

532   **"I never relished the thought of defeating":** Edward Kennedy int., Miller Center, UVA, Jan. 6, 2007.

532   **"It's too good to believe":** Harris, 202.

532   **"Have to declare war":** H. R. Haldeman, *The Haldeman Diaries: Inside the Nixon White House* (New York: G. P. Putnam's Sons, 1994), 148.

533   **"You have just made a political contribution":** Christopher Lawford, *Symptoms of Withdrawal: A Memoir of Snapshots and Redemption* (New York: William Morrow, 2005), 81.

533   **"very difficult time from then on":** Edward Kennedy int., Miller Center, UVA, Nov. 29, 2006.

533   **"We have to report to Dad":** Robert Shriver III int., Miller Center, UVA, Jan. 29, 2010.

533   **"Well, as my dad always says":** Victoria Kennedy int., Miller Center, UVA, April 8, 2010.

533   **more forgiving with him than with Jack and Bobby:** David, *Ted Kennedy*, 29.

533   **"for he seemed to be lonelier":** Rita Dallas and Jeanira Ratcliffe, *The Kennedy Case* (New York: G. P. Putnam's Sons, 1973), 337–338.

534   **then slid into his hand:** *Ibid.*, 345–346.

534   **sleeping bag underneath the casket:** Matthew Storin, quoted in Canellos, 177.

534   **"pain of that burden was almost unbearable":** *True Compass*, 293.

534   **"You'll see a tremendous change in Teddy":** Hersh, 32.

535   **"crowds that still point and mutter as he goes by":** James Reston, "Edgartown, Mass.": The Strange Case of Senator Edward Kennedy," *NYT*, Jan. 7, 1970.

535   **"they love you when you're down":** Martin Nolan, "Humor, Mischief, and a Sense of Fun," *BG*, Aug. 27, 2009.

535   **"like an actor going onstage":** Reston.

535   **"So, uh, your family, ah, likes . . . meat?":** "How Ted Kennedy Found Himself," *Time*, Aug. 26, 2009.

535   **"insufferable":** "The Non-Candidacy of Edward Moore Kennedy," *Time*, Nov. 29, 1971.

535   **"I haven't seen that in any other Kennedy":** *Ibid.*

536   **"what polio was for FDR":** John Gregory Dunne, "On the Matter of Chappaquiddick," *New West*, Dec. 3, 1979.

536   **"as long as I have a voice in the Senate":** Robert Scheer, "Ted Kennedy Cites Lasting Legacy of the New Frontier," *LAT*, Nov. 21, 1983.

536   **"I'd like to be their voice, their senator":** David, 253.

537   **"My greatest passion":** Edward Kennedy int., Clymer Papers, Series 2, Box 5, EMK interviews, 1992–1994 folder, JFK Lib., Feb. 1992.

537   **"But it's not just being a senator":** Stephen Breyer int., Miller Center, UVA, June 17, 2008.

537   **"he is a publicly moral man":** Richard Reeves, "A Publicly Moral Man," *USA Today*, Aug. 27, 2009.

538   **Ted's widow would say, was "complicated":** Victoria Kennedy int., Miller Center, UVA, Apr. 8, 2010.

538   **"And to whomsoever much is given":** "Rose Kennedy at 85," *People*, Sept. 22, 1975.

538   **"just being politically successful:"** John Tunney int., Clymer Papers, Series 2, Interviews, JFK Lib., March 6, 1995.

539   **"to act on behalf of one's fellow human beings":** *True Compass*, 29.

539   **"our ultimate and eternal reward":** Edward Kennedy int., Miller Center, UVA, Nov. 29, 2006.

539   **"Irish versus the Yankees":** Doris Kearns Goodwin, *The Fitzgeralds and the Kennedys: An American Saga* (New York: Simon & Schuster, 1987), 365.

539   **"No Irish Need Apply":** Thomas P. O'Neill with William Novak, *Man of the House: The Life and Political Memoirs of Speaker Tip O'Neill* (New York: Random House, 1987), 122.

539   **the photograph that hung on a wall:** Edward Kennedy int., Miller Center, UVA, Oct. 8, 2007.

539   **the people with whom Ted Kennedy identified:** Edward Kennedy int., Miller Center, UVA, May 31, 2007.

539   **"He was emotional about these things":** Patrick Kennedy int. by author.

540   **"Rosemary enriched the humanity of all of us":** *True Compass*, 25; Edward Kennedy int., Clymer Papers, Sept. 10, 1992.

540   **"prejudices of his fellow Americans":** Richard Reeves, *President Kennedy: Profile of Power* (New York: Simon & Schuster, 1993), 62.

540   **the families huddled in their apartments:** Joe McCarthy, *The Remarkable Kennedys* (New York: The Dial Press, 1960), 43–44.

540 **"man who was connected to the world's pain"**: "The Kennedys," *American Experience*, prod. Elizabeth Deane, WGBH, 1992.

540 **"you can look and see the pain"**: Canellos, 322.

541 **"it seems to me I just try"**: Warren Rogers, "Ted Kennedy Talks About His Past and Future," *Look*, March 4, 1969.

541 **"have given him a sympathy with human frailty"**: Samuel Beer int., Miller Center, UVA, Feb. 17, 2005.

541 **"he's just not worthy"**: Patrick Kennedy int. by author.

541 He had a **"losing-side consciousness"**: Jack Newfield, "The Senate's Fighting Liberal," *The Nation*, March 7, 2002.

541 He had little sense of entitlement: Victoria Kennedy int., Miller Center, UVA, Apr. 8, 2010.

541 insisted on flying coach: Tad Devine int. by author.

541 **"It's more familial"**: Margaret Spellings int., Miller Center, UVA, Aug. 27, 2008.

541 **"Focusing on other people always"**: Stephen Breyer int., Miller Center, UVA, June 17, 2008.

541 **"one of the oldest and fattest ladies"**: Ltr., Dance instructor [no name] to Ted, nd, Rose Kennedy Papers, Box 59, Family Corr., EMK 1973–1977, JFK Lib.

542 **"spending $50,000 a year on incidentals?"**: Edward McLaughlin, quoted in Hersh, 49.

542 **"day that the scales fell from my eyes"**: Thomas Rollins int., Miller Center, UVA, Apr. 22, 2009.

542 **"What is its impact on distributional equity?"**: Rashi Fein int., Miller Center, UVA, March 21, 2007.

542 **"problems, in one form or another"**: Burton Hersh, *The Shadow President: Ted Kennedy in Opposition* (South Royalton, Vt.: Steerforth Press, 1997), 43.

542 **"individual stories"**: Patrick Kennedy int. by author.

542 for each item on their résumé: Mark Leibovich, "The Kennedy Factor," *WP*, July 13, 2004.

543 **"touched" by the lives of people**: Barbara Mikulski int., Miller Center, UVA, Sept. 26, 2006.

543 **"genuinely liked and cared about people"**: Albert Hunt, "Ted Kennedy Forged Legacy with Joyful Magic," Aug. 27, 2009, bloomberg.com.

543 **"that made them believe that they could"**: Melody Miller int., Miller Center, UVA, July 15, 2008.

543 **"and will not let them rest"**: Arthur Schlesinger Jr., *Robert Kennedy and His Times* (Boston: Houghton Mifflin, 1978), 778.

543 McLean home: "Ted Kennedy to Build New Home in McLean," *WP*, May 19, 1967; David.

543 **"Cape Cod on the Potomac"**: Rogers.

544 large pink-and-white master bedroom: "Touring the Kennedys' House on the Potomac," *NYT*, May 10, 1970; Lester David, "Joan—The Reluctant Kennedy," *Good Housekeeping*, June 1972.

544 And, inside, a picture-perfect family: Melody Miller int., Miller Center, UVA, July 15, 2008.

544 visiting Bobby's children twice a week at Hickory Hill: "The Non-Candidacy of Edward Moore Kennedy"; John Tunney int., Miller Center, UVA, Oct. 12, 2009; Melody Miller int., Miller Center, UVA, July 15, 2008.

544 **"his children were his life"**: Melissa Leudtke int. by author.

544 Ted engaged a photographer to film the family: Patrick Kennedy and Stephen Fried, *A Common Struggle: A Personal Journey Through the Past and Future of Mental Illness and Addiction* (New York: Blue Rider Press, 2015), 37.

544 **"the three Kennedy youngsters' birthday parties"**: "The Non-Candidate's Wife," *Time*, Nov. 29, 1971.

545 **"this is a marriage that will just be perfect"**: Laurence Leamer, *The Kennedy Women: The Saga of an American Family* (New York: Villard Books, 1994), 474.

545 **" 'family' virtually defined my entire consciousness"**: *True Compass*, 183.

545 **"get to know themselves and each other"**: Ibid.

545 **"put their wives on a pedestal but don't talk to them"**: Marcia Chellis, *Living with the Kennedys: The Joan Kennedy Story* (New York: Simon & Schuster, 1985), 151–152.

545 **"real mismatch"**: Penelope McMillan, "The Troubled Marriage of Joan and Ted Kennedy," *McCall's*, Nov. 1975.

545 **"while I was public, political, and on the go"**: *True Compass*, 183.

545 Ted should have married her sister: Lloyd Shearer, "Joan Kennedy—Coming into Her Own," *WP*, April 18, 1971.

545 But she felt she lost herself doing so: William Peters, "Teddy Kennedy," *Redbook*, June 1962; David, "Joan—The Reluctant Kennedy."

545 **"I'd rather take long walks"**: "A Second Chance," *People*, Aug. 7, 1978.

545 **while Bobby's wife, Ethel, had baby after baby:** Joan Kennedy int.,Clymer Papers, Series 2, Box 4, K folder, JFK Lib., Oct. 12, 1998; Joan Braden, "Joan Kennedy Tells Her Own Story," *McCall's*, Aug. 1978.

545 **playing her piano, while Ted worked:** Lester David, *Joan: The Reluctant Kennedy* (New York: Funk & Wagnalls, 1974), 95.

546 **"then I'd just drop it":** Braden.

546 **"Is this all?":** Betty Friedan, *The Feminine Mystique* (New York: W. W. Norton & Co., 1963), 15.

546 **starting from scratch after Patrick's birth:** Kennedy and Fried, 33.

546 **"And that was before I was a Kennedy":** Melody Miller int., Miller Center, UVA, July 15, 2008.

546 **"did you expect the photographer?":** Myra MacPherson, *The Power Lovers: An Intimate Look at Politics and Marriage* (New York: G. P. Putnam's Sons, 1975), 69.

546 **"Now I feel a little ridiculous":** David, "Joan: The Reluctant Kennedy"; Joan Kennedy int., Clymer Papers.

546 **"I had a pretty good figure":** David, *Joan*, 193.

546 **she said, "Vulnerable":** Myra MacPherson, "Closing Scenes from a Kennedy Marriage," *WP*, Jan. 22, 1981.

546 **" 'Don't let your emotions out' ":** *Ibid.*

547 **"It's sort of like coming out of the shadows":** Shearer.

547 **"how to show their affection":** "Joan Kennedy: Life Without Ted," *Ladies' Home Journal*, Apr. 1981.

547 **"Toodles":** Goodwin, 200, 247.

547 **"thought this was part of his charm":** Garry Wills, *The Kennedy Imprisonment: A Meditation on Power* (Boston: Little, Brown, 2002), 18–19.

547 **"other women, was a Kennedy achievement":** *Ibid.*, 24.

547 **separated for three hundred days out of each year:** David Nasaw, *The Patriarch: The Remarkable Life and Turbulent Times of Joseph P. Kennedy* (New York: Penguin Books, 2013), 241.

547 **"his idea of manliness":** Quoted in David E. Koskoff Papers, JFK Lib.

547 **"one of the ways of showing power":** Leamer, 463.

547 **"she was really dumbfounded":** Ltr., Rose to daughters, nd, Box 3, Rose Kennedy Papers, JFK Lib.

548 **"nearly destroyed everything they had":** Goodwin, 426.

548 **"form of being successful at something":** Robert Dallek, *An Unfinished Life: John F. Kennedy, 1917–1963* (Boston: Little, Brown, 2003), 46.

548 **the FBI was keeping a file on:** "Hoover's Kennedy File," *Newsweek*, Dec. 29, 1975.

548 **"I can't help it":** "The Kennedys," *American Experience*, prod. Elizabeth Deane, WGBH, 1992.

548 **"Yes, and he still is":** Gene Tierney with Mickey Herkowitz, *Self-Portrait* (New York: Wyden Books, 1979), 206.

548 **He didn't return immediately:** Goodwin, 785.

548 **"beautiful women at Cape Cod" with his "oldest brother":** Barbara Perry, *Rose Kennedy: The Life and Times of a Political Matriarch* (New York: W. W. Norton & Co., 2013), 217.

549 **"and all three have managed well":** Rose Fitzgerald Kennedy, *Times to Remember* (Garden City, N.Y.: Doubleday & Co., 1974), 44.

549 **"Women chase after politicians":** Joan Kennedy int., Clymer Papers, Jan. 18, 1996.

549 **"But he just has this addiction":** Canellos, 119.

550 **" 'I might as well have a drink' ":** Braden.

550 **"That's when I truly became an alcoholic":** Leamer, 651.

550 **"maybe I drank because there was another mistress":** *Ibid.*, 701.

550 **"He wouldn't even kiss women supporters":** Betty Taymor int., Miller Center, UVA, July 8, 2005.

550 **if they saw him with a pretty girl:** Melody Miller int., Miller Center, UVA, July 15, 2008.

550 **"David had a strong moral sense":** Canellos, 119.

550 **Ted told her, "Convince me":** Edward Kennedy int., Clymer Papers, JFK Lib., Oct. 9, 1996; Nance Lyons int., Miller Center, UVA, May 9, 2008.

551 **"to keep a bull from charging a red flag":** Richard Burke with William and Marilyn Hoffer, *The Senator: My Ten Years with Ted Kennedy* (New York: St. Martin's Press, 1992), 133.

551 **the source said he still didn't reform:** James MacGregor Burns, *Edward Kennedy and the Camelot Legacy* (New York: W. W. Norton & Co., 1976), 335.

551 **"got the women up one staircase and down the other":** Chellis, 202.

551 **"He just doesn't care":** *Ibid.*

551 **he wound up in the library:** Burke, 42.

551 **he had a weekend tryst with Margaret Trudeau:** "Kennedy Out Late in Paris," *LAT,* Nov. 30, 1970; Burke, 71.

552 **Holmby Hills residence of a famous singer:** Maxine Cheshire, "Amanda in Idaho for Divorce," *LAT,* Aug. 10, 1972; Joyce Haber, "Teddy Says No—But the Heat Goes On," *LAT,* Aug. 15, 1972.

552 **"I heard you. It's okay":** "Memories of JFK in Palm Beach," *Palm Beach Daily News,* Nov. 22, 2013.

552 **began a jewelry business there:** Shaun Considine, "Helga Wagner Sells 'She Shells,'" *People,* Sept. 8, 1980.

552 **"problem that was gnawing at me":** Edward Kennedy int., Miller Center, UVA., Nov. 29, 2006.

553 **"ugly, ugly alcoholism":** Patrick Kennedy int. by author.

553 **ordered Ted to get her home:** Barbara Gibson and Ted Schwarz, *Rose Kennedy and Her Family: The Best and Worst of Their Lives and Times* (New York: Birch Lane Press, 1995), 193, 275.

553 **"say I was good?":** David, *Joan,* 119.

553 **Eunice knew Ted was cheating:** Leamer, 676.

553 **" 'They must think we're some kind of kooks' ":** Braden.

553 **"No one paid attention to me":** "Joan Kennedy: Life Without Ted."

553 **"to drown my sorrows":** "A Second Chance."

553 **She became a family ghost:** Kennedy and Fried, 32.

553 **"and don't tell Ted":** Lester Hyman int., Miller Center, UVA, Oct. 6, 2008.

553 **"just immediately crumple into a chair":** John Seigenthaler int., Clymer Papers, Series 2, Box 5, S folder, JFK Lib., Sept. 27, 1995.

554 **with mayonnaise in her hair:** Gibson and Schwarz, 275.

554 **"to see what he was up against":** Hersh, *The Shadow President,* 21.

554 **"She just doesn't seem to give a damn":** David, *Joan,* 229.

554 **"she had drunk too much, alas, and was forlorn":** Schlesinger, *Journals,* 376.

554 **"large pots":** Melissa Luedtke int. by author.

554 **"He had a bit of a hollow leg":** Gladys Gifford int. by author.

554 **"See you at eight":** Melissa Ludtke int. by author.

554 **"He just got funnier and funnier":** Gladys Gifford int. by author.

555 **"He was always crystal clear":** Edmund Reggie int., Miller Center, UVA, Dec. 16, 2008.

555 **he preferred a Heineken beer:** "The Non-Candidacy of Edward Moore Kennedy."

555 **" 'Here she goes again' ":** Kennedy and Fried, 39.

555 **"to be likened to my mother":** Patrick Kennedy int. by author.

555 **"might be expected to turn at any moment":** Gibson and Schwarz, 194.

555 **discouraged her from going to the psychiatrist:** Patrick Kennedy int. by author.

555 **"Let's get Sister Hargrove on the phone":** Burke and Hoffer, 119.

555 **"The family pathology was secrecy":** Kennedy and Fried, 370.

555 **"How the h-e-l-l did I make it through?":** Sally Jacobs, "Prime Time with Joan Kennedy," *BG,* July 9, 2000.

555 **"of horror and shame and tragedy and trauma":** Patrick Kennedy int. by author.

556 **"I just saw things getting worse":** Edward Kennedy int., Miller Center, UVA, May 31, 2007.

556 **not in favor of federal enforcement:** Haldeman, 142.

556 **Nixon again said he supported voting rights:** Rick Perlstein, *Nixonland: The Rise of a President and the Fracturing of America* (New York: Scribner, 2008), 464.

557 **but Congress overrode the veto:** Edward Kennedy int., Miller Center, UVA, Apr. 3, 2007; Mark Schneider int., Miller Center, UVA, Feb. 2, 2009; Clymer, 183.

557 **But he did not lead the process to do so:** Burns, 183.

557 **" 'harshness of the historic process' ":** Theo Lippman, *Senator Ted Kennedy: The Career Behind the Image* (New York: W. W. Norton, 1976), 71–72.

557 **"name-calling by men in high office":** "Kennedy Assays Means of Reform," *NYT,* March 4, 1970.

558 **"act in a way meaningful to someone":** Honan, 96–97.

559 **its passage was no certainty:** Carey Parker int., Miller Center, UVA, Sept. 22, 2008; Edward Kennedy int., Miller Center, UVA, Apr. 3, 2007.

559 **if the Senate sent it one:** Senate Aide A int., Clymer Papers, Series 2, Box 5, Unnamed sources folder, JFK Lib., Jan. 3, 1997.

559 **got ahold of one of the memos:** *Ibid.;* John Finney, "Kennedy Mapping Vote-at-18 Move," *NYT,* Feb. 22, 1970.

560 **which also meant that Ted was out:** Lippman, 90–91.

560 **" 'Gimme your amendment' ":** Carey Parker int., Miller Center, UVA, Oct. 27, 2008.

560   **he slammed down the receiver:** Charles Ferris int., Clymer Papers, Series 2, Box 3, F folder, JFK Lib., Apr. 10, 1992.

560   **Ted didn't have the suasion to get the bill passed:** Honan, 107.

560   **laying out the legal groundwork:** http://www.tedkennedy.org/page/-/legacy/pdf/kennedy-speech -1970-voting-age.pdf.

561   **"He could not have vetoed the voting rights legislation":** Carey Parker int., Miller Center, UVA, Sept. 22, 2008.

561   **"and I used them all":** Edward Kennedy int., Miller Center, UVA, Apr. 3, 2007.

561   **"fastest ratification of a constitutional amendment":** Carey Parker int., Miller Center, UVA, Sept. 22, 2008.

561   **"in terms of the sanctity to vote":** Edward Kennedy int., Miller Center, UVA, Apr. 3, 2007.

562   **"who can defeat him is Henry Cabot Lodge":** Memo, Chotiner to Colson, May 1, 1970; Oudes, 123.

562   **"because it just isn't in him":** R. W. Apple, "Kennedy Is Running Hard Against His '64 Vote Total," *NYT*, Aug. 26, 1970.

562   **28 percent shortly after the accident:** *NYT*, June 16, 1970.

562   **three-quarters of Massachusetts residents approved:** *Ibid.*

562   **"so why should I change now?":** Apple.

563   **that he run again as a birthday present:** Sparks, "Rose Kennedy's Determined Coaching Kept Ted in Ball Game," *Hartford Courant*, July 12, 1970.

563   **"I expect it to be gone forever":** Honan, 95.

563   **"what you stand for, and how they see you":** Apple.

563   **"to raise the issue":** "Kennedy Presses Despite a Sure Victory," *NYT*, Oct. 31, 1970.

563   **"it was exhausting":** Paul Kirk Jr. int., Miller Center, UVA, Nov. 23, 2005.

564   **was finished for the day:** *Ibid.*

564   **"those things he's been through":** Honan, 92.

564   **admitted he didn't care who won:** *Ibid.*

564   **"Well—check with me before you do that":** Hersh, *The Education of Edward Kennedy*, 450–451.

564   **A Gallup poll three weeks later:** "Kennedy's Popularity High Among Democrats," *WP*, Nov. 26, 1970.

565   **"would be more at a disadvantage":** David Burke int., Miller Center, UVA, June 19, 2007.

565   **Burke flew back empty-handed:** *Ibid.*

565   **willing to provide a list of POWs:** Report to Sen. Edward Kennedy, Re: American Prisoners of War, Dec. 22, 1970, John Nolan. Comm. on Judiciary Subcommittee on Refugees, General Corr. Re: POWs and MIAs, Box 3, Senate Records, National Archives.

566   **Ted contacted John Nolan:** "Legends in the Law: John Nolan," *Washington Lawyer*, May 2003.

566   **invited Ted to come to Paris:** Report to Sen. Edward Kennedy, Re: American Prisoners of War.

566   **"Chappaquiddickized":** Sherrill, 218.

566   **"like a legislative concierge":** David Burke int., Miller Center, UVA, June 19, 2007.

566   **"minding the store":** Lippman, 113.

567   **"holding hands with all these members and their staffs":** Paul Kirk int., Miller Center, UVA, Nov. 23, 2005.

567   **"he's been going at it maybe two-thirds of the way":** Hersh, *The Education of Edward Kennedy*, 452.

567   **Ted seldom showed up:** Mike Mansfield int., Clymer Papers, Series 2, Box 4, M folder, JFK Lib., Jan. 27, 1993.

567   **when he did run legislation:** J. Stanley Kimmitt Oral History, Senate Historical Office, 2003, 78–79.

567   **call it up, and withdraw it:** William Hildenbrand Oral History, Senate Historical Office, 1985, 133.

567   **Dirty work:** Robert C. Byrd, *The Senate, 1789–1989: Addresses on the History of the United States Senate,* Mary Sharon Hall, ed. (Washington, D.C.: U.S. Govt. Printing Office, 1988), 199.

567   **"Uriah Heep":** Charles Ferris int., Clymer Papers, Series 2, Box 3, F folder, JFK Lib., Apr. 10, 1992.

567   **"the lord and the serf":** J. Stanley Kimmitt Oral History Senate Historical Office, 2003.

567   **"there almost every day and undertook any chore":** Mansfield int., Clymer Papers, JFK Lib., Jan. 27, 1993.

568   **his law degree from American University:** Robert C. Byrd, *Child of the Appalachian Coalfields* (Morgantown: West Virginia Univ. Press, 2005).

568 **"I have only had to work all my life"**: George Smathers Oral History Interviews, Senate Historical Office, Aug. 1–Oct. 24, 1989.

568 **"Well, if I did know, I wouldn't tell you"**: Robert Byrd int., Clymer Papers, Series 2, Box 3, B folder, JFK Lib., Feb. 12, 1993.

568 **whether he should take Ted on**: "Attempt to Unseat Kennedy as Whip Is Weighed," *WP*, Nov. 15, 1970.

568 **which Johnson happily did**: Byrd, *Child of the Appalachian Coalfields*, 297.

568 **while Byrd continued campaigning**: "Senate and House Warmings," *WP*, Jan. 22, 1971.

569 **"furiously ambitious"**: Francis Valeo, Oral History Interviews, Senate Historical Office.

569 **"He had an edge from that point on"**: Edward Kennedy int., Miller Center, UVA, Jan. 6, 2007; Ted told a slightly different version on Oct. 14, 2005, saying that he had called Fulbright to inform him of the offer, then spoke to him again the next week; Fulbright said that the committee would be meeting that afternoon to determine a course of action. And that is when Ted told him that Nolan had already secured the list. In yet another interview, with Adam Clymer, on April 17, 1995, Ted said that Fulbright told him he had gotten the list and was dealing with it and resented Ted taking any action.

569 **"Chappaquiddick got him"**: Walter Mondale int., Miller Center, UVA, March 20, 2006.

570 **convincing four freshman senators to support him**: Robert Dove int. by author; *True Compass*, 296.

570 **had spelled his name "Bird"**: Edward Kennedy int., Clymer Papers, JFK Lib., Apr. 17, 1995.

570 **"I believe you. I know you voted for me"**: Melody Miller int., Miller Center, UVA, July 15, 2008.

570 **Jackson had benefited substantially from his brothers' support**: Shelby Scates, *Warren G. Magnuson and the Shaping of Twentieth-Century America* (Seattle: Univ. of Washington Press, 1997), 279–280.

570 **"we should have known"**: Weaver.

570 **"It's hard to lie to another member"**: William Hildenbrand Oral History, Senate Historical Office, 1985, 91.

570 **"Kennedys didn't mark you down unless they had you"**: Weaver.

570 **"don't touch me, they don't get to me"**: Honan, 5.

570 **"The Kennedys have known personal tragedy before"**: Richard Reeves, "Teddy or Not," *New York*, Apr. 22, 1974.

571 **"want to be a senator even more"**: Carey Parker int., Miller Center, UVA, Oct. 27, 2008.

571 **"you don't deserve to win"**: Byrd, *Child of the Appalachian Coalfields*, 297.

571 **"Let's go on"**: Lippman, 124.

571 **"with considerable strength"**: Haldeman, 237.

571 **"Games," Ted called them**: Edward Kennedy int., Miller Center, UVA, Oct. 14, 2005.

571 **He said he reread the Constitution**: *True Compass*, 296–297.

571 **"one of the best things that ever happened to me"**: Robert Byrd int., Clymer Papers, JFK Lib., Feb. 12, 1993.

572 **"discouraged or downhearted to carry out that role"**: Ltr., Joseph Rauh Jr. to EMK, Rauh Papers, Box 37, Kennedy, Edward M. folder, Lib. of Congress, Feb. 5, 1971.

CHAPTER FOURTEEN: "PEOPLE DO NOT WANT TO BE IMPROVED"

573 **"It was just a constant hum"**: Milton Gwirtzman int., Clymer Papers, Series 2, Box 3, folder G, JFK Lib., Apr. 3, 1993.

573 **"black militant uproars"**: Joseph Alsop, "His Revised Judgment of Nixon Gives Kennedy Pause as to '72," *WP*, Apr. 28, 1969.

574 **Ted might still run**: Robert Novak and Rowland Evans, "The Kennedy Camp Stirs," *WP*, Dec. 20, 1970.

574 **"Gethsemane face"**: Warren Rogers Jr., "Kennedy's Comeback: Will He or Won't He?" *Look*, Aug. 10, 1971.

574 **"I could tell instantly"**: Fred Dutton int., Clymer Papers, Series 2, Box 3, D folder, JFK Lib., July 25, 1995.

574 **"Not next year or in six months"**: Memo, James Wechsler, Re: Conversation with Ted Kennedy, nd, Kennedy, Edward M., Box 37, 1968–1971 folder, Joseph Rauh Papers, Lib. of Congress.

575 **"maybe more than I"**: *Ibid.*

575 **"much more radical domestic programs":** *Ibid.*

575 **"will fester and grow":** Joseph Califano Jr., *Inside: A Public and Private Life* (New York: Public Affairs, 2004), 243.

575 **"For the Kennedys, the die is cast":** Memo, James Wechsler.

576 **But what she really feared was the vulnerability:** Lester David, "Joan—The Reluctant Kennedy," *Good Housekeeping*, June 1972.

576 **"I have to force myself":** Sparks, "Rose Kennedy's Determined Coaching Kept Ted in Ball Game," *Hartford Courant*, July 12, 1970.

576 **"shitstorm coming":** Patrick Kennedy int. by author.

576 **"a madman or person who was psychotic":** John Tunney int., Miller Center, UVA, Oct. 12, 2009.

576 **"We plan the best funerals":** David.

576 **Will come when it will come:** William Honan, *Ted Kennedy: Profile of a Survivor* (New York: Quadrangle Books, 1972), 165.

577 **"no end to the Kennedys":** Dan Rather and Gary Paul Gates, *The Palace Guard* (New York: Harper & Row, 1974), 167.

577 **"Information would be our first line of defense":** Richard Nixon, *The Memoirs of Richard Nixon* (New York: Grosset & Dunlap, 1978), 357.

577 **"big pictures of Kennedy":** Rick Perlstein, *Nixonland: The Rise of a President and the Fracturing of America* (New York: Scribner, 2008), 461.

578 **"Operation O'Brien":** H. R. Haldeman, *The Haldeman Diaries: Inside the Nixon White House* (New York: G. P. Putnam's Sons, 1994), 134.

578 **"ammunition factory":** Memo, Colson to President, Re: Memorandum for the President's File, Box 21, CD, Nixon Lib., July 15, 1970.

578 **"everyone in America running to vote for Teddy":** Alexander Butterfield int. by Timothy Naftali, Nixon Lib., June 12, 2008.

578 **"so effectively in previous campaigns":** Nixon, 496.

579 **"What's she trying to prove?":** Nixon Tapes on EMK, Apr. 9, 1971, Nixontapes.org/emk.html.

579 **"use another Dem as front":** "Archives Show Nixon's Targeting of Foes," *LAT*, Dec. 3, 2008. The entry is dated June 23, 1971.

579 **"in-depth background research":** Memo, Strachan to Haldeman, Nixon Lib., Apr. 15, 1971.

580 **"Keep after him, see?":** Nixon Tapes on EMK, May 28,1971, nixontapes.org/emk.html; Haldeman, *The Haldeman Diaries*, entry May 28, 1971, 293.

580 **"that we can't let be forgotten":** Haldeman, *The Haldeman Diaries*, entry June 9, 1971, 297.

580 **Such were the preoccupations of the president:** Haldeman Notes, EMK, WHSF, SMOF, H. R. Haldeman. Nixon Lib., June 23, 1971.

580 **"all the Kennedy haters at the White House":** Rather and Gates, 280.

580 **"hit man":** H. R. Haldeman with Joseph DiMona, *The Ends of Power* (New York: Times Books, 1978), 5.

580 **He would run over his own grandmother:** Charles Colson, *Born Again* (Old Tappan, N.J.: Chosen Books, 1976), 79.

580 **"Ruthless," he called himself:** *Ibid.*

580 **"I might have attacked him physically":** Rather and Gates, 286.

580 **photographs "leaked" to the press:** Charles Colson int., Nixon Lib. Aug. 17, 2007; Haldeman, *The Haldeman Diaries*, entry Dec. 5, 1970, 215.

580 **"Teddy Kennedy question":** Haldeman, *The Haldeman Diaries*, entry Dec. 19, 1970, 222.

580 **Hunt wore a red wig:** Jack Anderson, "Colson Role in Chappaquiddick Quiz," *WP*, June 18, 1973; "Hunt Testifies About Probe of Kennedy," *WP*, June 29, 1973.

581 **"We ought to persecute them":** Nixon Tapes on EMK, Sept. 8, 1971, nixontapes.org/emk.html.

581 **a stake in a Toyota auto dealership:** Memo, Allen to Haldeman, Subj., EMK, Nixon Lib., Oct. 14, 1971, nixonlibrary.gov/virtuallibrary/documents/nixondonated.php?print=yes.

581 **"not terribly attractive":** Strachan Notes, EMK, Daily Notes, Box 327, WHSF, SMOF, H. R. Haldeman, Nixon Lib., Dec. 17, 1971.

581 **"or under fear of extortion":** John Dean, *Blind Ambition: The White House Years* (New York: Simon & Schuster, 1976), 78.

581 **not delivering the State of the Union:** Haldeman, *The Haldeman Diaries*, Jan 18, 1969–Apr. 30, 1973, National Archives, Nov. 1, 1971.

581 **"to bring down the shining Kennedy name":** Garry Wills, *The Kennedy Imprisonment: A Meditation on Power* (Boston: Little Brown, 2002), 192.

582 **"to be more centrist than conservative"**: Rather and Gates, 166.

583 **Nixon knew he was onto something**: Nixon, 490–491.

583 **"toryhood of change"**: Perlstein, 277.

583 **"feel they should take to the streets"**: Robert Sherrill, *The Last Kennedy* (New York: The Dial Press, 1976), 220.

584 **"panders to their prejudices"**: Honan, 30.

584 **"leadership and vision of the Democratic party"**: Ibid., 46–55.

584 **"and that is at top speed"**: "Teddy: Will He or Won't He?" *Newsweek*, Nov. 15, 1971.

584 **"three or four balls in the air at all times"**: Theo Lippman, *Senator Ted Kennedy: The Career Behind the Image* (New York: W. W. Norton & Co., 1976), 127.

585 **"Long live Kennedy"**: "Kennedy's Searing Trip Through Pakistani Grief," *Life*, Aug. 27, 1971.

585 **a tent of elderly people dying**: Tape One of EMK Trip to India, EMK Notes, Senate Judiciary Comm., Subcomm. on Refugees, 1972–1977, South Asia, Bangladesh Investigation, Box 37, Senate Records, National Archives.

585 **"because we are Hindus"**: "Pakistan Withdraws OK for Kennedy Visit," *LAT*, Aug. 11, 1971.

585 **"blood money"**: "Kennedy's Searing Trip Through Pakistani Grief."

585 **announced a special committee on refugees**: Honan, 24–26.

585 **the bones lay bleached in the sun**: "Kennedy Sees Sheik, Visits Mass Graves," *LAT*, Feb. 15, 1972.

585 **focused attention on their plight**: "Kennedys Mobbed by Dacca Students," *WP*, Feb. 15, 1972.

586 **forced the administration's hand**: Edward Kennedy int., Clymer Papers, Series 2, Box 5, EMK interviews, 1995–1996 folder, JFK Lib., Oct. 9, 1996; Lippman, 176–177.

586 **called his staff "irresponsible"**: Lippman, 60.

586 **"announced in 1972 instead of 1971?"**: Nixon Conversation, 005-002, Miller Center, UVA, June 10, 1971.

587 **Nixon phoned Humphrey to thank him**: Ibid.; "Humphrey Challenges Kennedy's Nixon Blast," *LAT*, June 10, 1971.

587 **until Nixon found it politically expedient**: Rod Gramer, *Fighting the Odds: The Life of Senator Frank Church* (Pullman: Washington State Univ. Press, 1994), 337–339.

587 **"threatened with service in the war"**: Lippman, 83.

588 **Ted compared amnesty for Vietnam resisters**: "Kennedy Unit Plans Quiz on Draft Amnesty," *LAT*, Feb. 7, 1972; Lippman, 84–85.

588 **prevented him from getting a visa**: Jimmy Carter int., Clymer Papers, Series 2, Box 3, C folder, JFK Lib., May 15, 1998. Carter said Bill Haddad had told him this.

588 **He received a standing ovation**: "Kennedy Critical of Nixon Policies," *NYT*, Oct. 20, 1971.

588 **"appearing to say just the opposite"**: Colson to Buchanan, Oct. 14, 1971, in *From: The President: Richard Nixon's Secret Files*, Bruce Oudes, ed. (New York: Harper & Row, 1989), 328.

588 **"what needs to be done, what's right"**: Honan, 33.

589 **poll showed Muskie leading him**: "Sen. Kennedy Tops Survey of Democrats," *WP*, May 17, 1971; "Muskie Ahead of Kennedy In a Survey," *NYT*, Nov. 15, 1971.

589 **"seesaw polls"**: "Survey Shows Kennedy Lags," *WP*, July 18, 1971; "Seesaw Polls," *Time*, Oct. 4, 1971.

589 **"the most difficult candidate the president could face?"**: Memo, Buchanan to Nixon, Sept. 25, 1971, in Oudes, 324.

589 **"Consciously, he does not want to run"**: "What is Kennedy Up To?," *U.S. News & World Report*, May 24, 1971.

590 **"broken promises" speech**: "The Non-Candidacy of Edward Moore Kennedy," *Time*, Nov. 29, 1971.

590 **a sign either of Ted's high spirits**: Honan, 29.

590 **"It was astounding and a little frightening"**: "The Non-Candidacy of Edward Moore Kennedy."

590 **"I intend to fulfill my responsibilities"**: Honan, 58–59.

590 **"why did he bring his wife way the hell up here?"**: Ibid., 19–20.

590 **"he might not be able to keep them all up"**: Ibid., 59.

590 **"I would like to do it on my own someday"**: "Kennedy's Long-Range Future."

591 **led Muskie again 32 percent to 25 percent**: "Kennedy Pulls Away in Final Gallup Poll," *LAT*, Dec. 26, 1971.

591 **"I'd just be a senator from Massachusetts"**: "The Non-Candidacy of Edward Moore Kennedy."

591 **"prepared to see many advantages if he is not asked"**: Arthur Schlesinger Jr., *Journals: 1952–2000*, Andrew Schlesinger and Stephen Schlesinger, eds. (New York: Penguin Press, 2007), 344–345.

591 **"abdication by the federal government"**: David Broder, "Kennedy Says Nixon Sacrifices Vietnamese," *LAT*, Jan. 19, 1972.

591 **"carried out with the lives of men, women, and children"**: Rick Perlstein, 648.

591 **"futile military gesture taken in desperation"**: Richard Nixon, 606.

592 **"the whole thing may well be lost"**: Haldeman, *The Haldeman Diaries*, entry May 1, 1972, 450.

592 **The exclusion carried, 78 to 4:** Lester David, *Ted Kennedy: Triumphs and Tragedies* (New York: Grosset & Dunlap, 1972).

592 **Dong heartily endorsed:** Memo, Dale DeHaan to EMK, Re: POWs and MIAs, W. Sohier pickup, Senate Judiciary Comm., Subcomm. on Refugees, Gen. Corr: POWs and MIAs, Box 3, Senate Records, Nat. Archives, July 26, 1972.

592 **to discuss the propriety of a visit:** Edward Kennedy int., Miller Center, UVA, May 30, 2007.

593 **would take more to defeat Richard Nixon:** Notes of Meeting, Paris, W. Sohier pickup, Senate Judiciary Committee, Sub. On Refugees, Gen Corr.: POWs and MIAs, Box 3, Senate Records, National Archives, July 31, 1972.

593 **"our prisoners must remain in Hanoi":** Statement on Brooke Amendment, nd, Kennedy Statements, Comm. on Judiciary, Refugee Subcomm., Box 3, Senate Records, National Archives, Aug. 2, 1972.

593 **why the campaign swing?:** James MacGregor Burns, *Edward Kennedy and the Camelot Legacy* (New York: W. W. Norton & Co., 1976), 195.

593 **"much to contend with":** Honan, 174.

594 **"hopes to be a compromise candidate this July":** "Kennedy's Intentions," *NYT*, Apr. 29, 1972.

594 **"for the asking":** George McGovern, *Grassroots: The Autobiography of George McGovern* (New York: Random House, 1977), 156.

594 **"George Romney of the Democratic Party":** "Nixon v. Kennedy in '72?" *Time*, Nov. 23, 1970.

594 **"Kennedy is bound to go":** "Nixon Picks Kennedy," *WP*, March 27, 1972.

594 **paid for by cash payments from Colson:** Haldeman, 616.

594 **"public thinks he is a candidate":** "Senate Quietly Votes Protection for Kennedy," *LAT*, Apr. 22, 1972.

595 **chair the committee on delegate selection:** McGovern, 135–137.

595 **didn't deign to attend a single session:** *Ibid.*, 141.

595 **"pseudo-influence of the ADA":** JPK to Frank Coniff, Aug. 5, 1953, in *Hostage to Fortune: The Letters of Joseph P. Kennedy*, Amanda Smith, ed. (New York: Viking, 2001), 663.

596 **"Democratic presidential nominee in 1972":** McGovern, 158.

596 **the splash that killing Nixon would have:** Arthur Bremer, *An Assassin's Diary* (New York: Harper Magazine Press, 1973), 105.

596 **visited him in the hospital:** "Gov. Wallace, Sen. Kennedy Talk Politics," *WP*, Sept. 23, 1972.

597 **"most liberal member of the Senate—including McGovern":** Honan, 29.

597 **Ted told Broder that he wouldn't run:** "Mass. Senator Spurns Race," *WP*, March 16, 1972.

597 **"general agreement that he's going to be the candidate":** Haldeman, *The Haldeman Diaries*, entry Apr. 5, 1972, 435–436.

598 **"I would have to reconsider my position":** "Kennedy Insists on Marching to a Different Tune," *LAT*, June 23, 1972.

598 **"I liked him and I thought he was courageous":** Edward Kennedy int., Clymer Papers, Oct. 9, 1995.

598 **if McGovern didn't need it:** Richard Bergholz, "Kennedy Will Do All He Can to Help McGovern," *LAT*, May 23, 1972.

598 **Ted said he didn't remember any such meeting:** Robert Novak, "Meany, Kennedy Confer," *WP*, June 16,1972; Edward Kennedy int., Clymer Papers, JFK Lib., Oct. 9, 1995.

598 **Ted Kennedy was the plan:** Norman Mailer, *St. George and the Godfather* (New York: New American Library, paperback, 1972), 27–28.

598 **he would not be following the convention:** "Democrats Can Heal Breach, Kennedy Says," *LAT*, July 7, 1972.

598 **"Which would position you better to be president?":** Milton Gwirtzman int., Clymer Papers, Apr. 3, 1993.

599 **"feeling he [Ted] didn't want to raise those issues":** Quoted in Peter Canellos, *Last Lion: The Fall and Rise of Ted Kennedy* (New York: Simon & Schuster, 2009), 186.

599 **he knew Ted felt a duty to the party:** McGovern, 193.

599 **Ted said he might accept the nomination:** "Kennedy Would Consider Second Spot," *LAT,* June 15, 1972.

599 **Ted Sorensen had drafted a memo:** Edward Kennedy, *True Compass* (New York: Twelve, 2009), 294.

599 **family obligations would prevent him:** McGovern, 193.

599 **"and I think he felt that he just couldn't handle it":** John Tunney int., Miller Center, UVA, May 3, 2007.

599 **Ted told reporters he had declined the nomination:** McGovern, 193.

599 **McGovern had run down a list:** *True Compass,* 330.

600 **Shriver was in Moscow at the time:** Edward Kennedy int., Miller Center, UVA, Oct. 14, 2005. Ted bases this in part on Pierre Salinger, who was involved in the selection process.

600 **"reservedly resistant":** McGovern, 224.

600 **called back a short time later:** *Ibid.,* 197–198.

601 **"I am still 10,000 percent in the Kennedy corner":** Eagleton to EMK, Rose Kennedy Papers, Box 59, Fam. Corr., EMK, 1958–1972, JFK Lib., July 31, 1972.

601 **he first approached Mike Mansfield:** Don Oberdorfer, *Senator Mansfield: The Extraordinary Life of a Great American Statesman and Diplomat* (Washington, D.C.: Smithsonian Books, 2003), 431.

601 **"Bad for us":** Haldeman, *The Haldeman Diaries,* entry July 25, 1972, 486.

601 **"his involvement with the socialite":** *Ibid.,* entry Aug. 4, 1972, 490.

602 **"That's pretty arrogant":** Nixon Tapes on EMK, Aug. 2, 1972, Nixontapes.org/emk.html.

602 **"This would be very useful":** Nixon Tapes on EMK, Sept. 7, 1972, Nixontapes.org/emk.html.

602 **"Let the son of a bitch squeal":** Nixon Tapes: Nixon, Haldeman, Ehrlichman, Bull, Tape 772, #6, National Archives, Sept. 1, 1972.

602 **"He can't say no to the Secret Service":** "Nixon Ordered Spy Placed in Kennedy's Secret Service Detail," *WP,* Feb. 8, 1977.

602 **"ordered a sailboat ready":** "Uncle Teddy Goes to Sea," *BG,* Aug. 3, 1972.

603 **And now it was finally over:** McGovern, 222.

603 **Ted said he relayed this information to Shriver:** *True Compass,* 330–331.

603 **"we'll have to change our tactics a little":** Haldeman, *The Haldeman Diaries,* entry July 11, 1972, 481.

604 **would eventually exceed that of Lyndon Johnson:** Stanley Greenberg, *The Two Americas: Our Current Political Deadlock* (New York: St. Martin's Griffin, 2005), 51.

604 **expansion further empowered the executive:** Theodore Lowi, *The End of the Republican Era* (Norman: Univ of Oklahoma Press, 1995), 58.

604 **"in conservative rhetoric":** Daniel Patrick Moynihan, *Coping: Essays on the Practice of Government* (New York: Random House, 1973), 23.

604 **"in a brutal, vicious attack on the opposition":** Haldeman, *The Haldeman Diaries,* entry Apr. 21, 1972, 443.

605 **"our mood has to be harder on this":** *Ibid.,* entry Sept. 20, 1972, 506–507.

605 **"alienate many of the 'hawks'":** McGovern, 129.

605 **"to cast their foes as anti-American":** E. J. Dionne, *Why Americans Hate Politics* (New York: Simon & Schuster, 1991), 44.

605 **Americans felt more negatively toward "Vietnam War Protesters":** Godfrey Hodgson, *America in Our Time: From World War II to Nixon* (New York: Vintage paperback, 1978), 393.

605 **"we would have far the larger half":** George Packer, "The Fall of Conservatism," *The New Yorker,* May 26, 2008, 48.

606 **"Not blacks, not Jews":** Haldeman, *The Haldeman Diaries,* entry Sept. 1, 1972, 507.

606 **"unyoung, unpoor, and unblack":** Dionne, 200.

606 **"Patriotic themes to counter an economic depression":** Perlstein, 498–499.

606 **"they won't have sufficient resources":** "The Non-Candidacy of Edward Moore Kennedy."

607 **He said Wallace:** Burns, 301.

607 **In truth, McGovern had moderated:** "Issues Fade—Party's Getting Rough," *NYT,* Oct. 8, 1972.

607 **"great Democratic president—George McGovern":** Robert Shrum, *No Excuses: Concessions of a Serial Campaigner* (New York: Simon & Schuster, 2007), 49–50.

608 **"his secret plan to end the war":** "Kennedy Gets Crowds for McGovern in Pa." *WP,* Sept. 14, 1972.

608 **"We'll take it either way":** "Kennedy Charisma Enlivens a Four-Day Run of McGovern," *WP,* Sept. 16, 1972.

608   **"But that's just the way we feel here in Pittsburgh":** Jules Witcover, "McGovern and Kennedy Sharing Spotlight," *LAT,* Sept. 14,1972.

608   **"there is the crush of eager crowds":** "Keeper of the Flame," *WP,* Oct. 22, 1972.

608   **"wistfulness that went beyond the tumult":** Julie Baumgold, "Teddy at the Tiller," *New York,* Oct. 9, 1972.

608   **"could deceive so many Americans for so long":** McGovern, 47.

609   **"one even Democrats came to avoid":** Tom Daschle with Michael D'Orso, *Like No Other Time: The 107th Congress and the Two Years that Changed America* (New York: Crown Publishers, 2003).

609   **By one poll, 36 percent of Democrats:** Hodgson, 427.

609   **"separate and irreconcilable groups of Americans":** Perlstein, 46.

610   **"is power by any means":** Haldeman, *The Haldeman Diaries,* entry July 19, 1972, 483–484.

610   **as it had been Nixon's rhetoric:** Hodgson, 422.

610   **"change in the entire American political structure":** Haldeman, *The Haldeman Diaries,* entry Apr. 22, 1972, 444.

610   **"from drug addicts and welfare mothers":** Hodgson, 422.

611   **an October poll indicated:** George Gallup, "Democratic Loss Laid to Nominee," *WP,* Nov. 12, 1972.

611   **"manipulate the race issue for party advantage":** Schlesinger, *Journals,* 365.

611   **"embourgeoisement":** Everett Carll Ladd Jr., "Liberalism Upside Down: The Inversion of the New Deal Order," *Political Science Quarterly,* Vol. 91, No. 4, Winter 1976–1977, 597.

612   **"serious sense of injustice and resentment":** Burns, 300.

612   **"ideological corner from which he cannot escape":** "Sen. Kennedy's Move to the Center," *LAT,* Apr. 12, 1973.

612   **"suddenly make all things right":** David, *Ted Kennedy,* 232.

612   **"Kennedy was being touted for 1976":** "Edward Kennedy Now the Hope," *Time,* Nov. 20, 1972.

612   **"He's got a fine future":** *Ibid.*

CHAPTER FIFTEEN: "AWESOME POWER WITH NO DISCIPLINE"

613   **"confident that we can close ranks":** "Sen. Kennedy Extends Olive Branch to Nixon," *LAT,* Dec. 12, 1972.

613   **"we've got to do our planning on that basis":** H. R. Haldeman, *The Haldeman Diaries: Inside the Nixon White House,* entry Oct. 16, 1972 (New York: G. P. Putnam's Sons, 1994), 521.

613   **"the whole McGovern argument thing":** Haldeman, entry Feb. 28, 1973, 583. Ibid.

614   **"who worship him and hate him":** *Ibid.,* entry Jan. 16, 1973, 570.

614   **"imperial presidency":** Arthur Schlesinger Jr., *The Imperial Presidency* (Boston: Houghton Mifflin, 1973).

614   **"how the Senate does":** Richard Reeves, *President Nixon: Alone in the White House* (New York: Simon & Schuster, 2001), 576.

615   **"piecemeal" and "unnecessary":** "Kennedy Battles Nixon's Vetoes," *NYT,* March 1, 1973.

616   **"relatively unheard of for a senator":** Carey Parker int., Miller Center, UVA, Oct. 27, 2008; "Kennedy in Court to Fight Veto of His Medical Plan," *LAT,* March 1, 1973.

616   **"spring, Christmas, or Thanksgiving recess":** "Kennedy Battles Nixon's Vetoes."

616   **no president had ever used a pocket veto:** "Kennedy in Court to Fight Veto of His Medical Plan."

616   **"and I feel better about doing that than the other":** "Kennedy Battles Nixon's Vetoes."

617   **it was the Senate's:** Carey Parker int., Miller Center, UVA, Oct. 27, 2008.

617   **Ted followed up with a trip of his own:** George Abrams int., Clymer Papers, Series 2, Box 3, folder A, JFK Lib., Nov. 27, 1992.

617   **"This was all opposed by the Nixon administration":** Mark Schneider, Miller Center, UVA, Feb. 2, 2009.

618   **signed new contracts with Pinochet:** *Ibid.*

618   **he applied pressure of his own:** Press Release, Comm. on Judiciary Subcomm. on Refugees, 1972–1977, Corr: Soviet Jewry, Box 4, Senate Records, National Archives, May 6, 1973. (See also Press Release, March 4, 1971, to see how long Ted had been working on this issue.)

618   **"the world would be really different now":** Memo, James Wechsler, Re: Conversation with Ted Kennedy, nd, Box 37, Kennedy, Edward M. folder, Joseph L. Rauh Papers, Lib. of Congress.

618   **"go down in infamy in American history":** Rod Gramer, *Fighting the Odds: The Life of Senator Frank Church* (Pullman: Washington State Univ. Press, 1994), 405–406.

619 **"none of us should have to bear that stain":** *Congressional Record,* 12563-12564, June 29, 1973, quoted in James MacGregor Burns, *Edward Kennedy and the Camelot Legacy* (New York: W. W. Norton & Co., 1976), 227.

619 **"including medical facilities, schools, housing":** Ltr., DeHaan to EMK, Senate Judiciary Comm., Subcomm. on Refugees, Vietnam Study Mission, Box 55, Senate Records, National Archives, Apr. 2, 1973; DeHaan Diary, Box 55, Diary of Dale DeHaan folder, Senate Records, National Archives.

619 **Ted wrote more letters:** Ltrs., EMK to Hannah, July 13, 1973, and June 28, 1973; EMK to Rogers, June 7, 1973; EMK to Parker, Dec. 10, 1973; EMK to Richardson, Feb. 2, 1973; EMK to Kissinger, March 13, 1973; Kissinger to EMK, March 25, 1973, Senate Judiciary Comm., Subcomm. on Refugees, Boxes 64 & 65, Senate Records, National Archives.

620 **"Kennedy wouldn't be able to criticize us":** Theo Lippman, *Senator Ted Kennedy: The Career Behind the Image* (New York: W. W. Norton & Co., 1976), 61.

620 **Having cooked up numerous dirty tricks:** Fred Emery, *Watergate: The Corruption of American Politics and the Fall of Richard Nixon* (New York: Times Books, 1994), 107.

620 **Having ordered his associates:** Murray Chotiner to John Mitchell, Re: Chapman's Friend Reports, Box 303, Press Reports (Chapman's Friend Reports), White House Special Files, Staff Member and Office Files, H. R. Haldeman, Nixon Lib., Nov. 8, 1971. Chapman's friend was a journalist hired to infiltrate Democratic campaigns. Two journalists served this function: Seymour Friedin and then Lucianne Cummings Goldberg, who would later play a prominent role in revealing the relationship between President Bill Clinton and intern Monica Lewinsky. (See George Lardner Jr., "Goldberg a Veteran at Recording Gossip," *WP,* Feb. 4, 1998.)

620 **having his operatives fabricate cables:** Emery, 71–72.

620 **henchmen try to plant left-wing literature:** *Ibid.,* 116.

621 **"wild man":** J. Anthony Lukas, *Nightmare: The Underside of the Nixon Years* (New York: Viking Press, 1976), 94.

621 **"not for us to get something on him":** G. Gordon Liddy, *Will: The Autobiography of G. Gordon Liddy* (New York: St. Martin's Press, 1980), 325.

621 **an alleged relationship between Ted, McGovern:** Lippman, 201.

621 **it was Ted's relationship to O'Brien:** "Kennedy Seen as Real Target of Break-In," *WP,* June 6, 1974.

621 **"real cloak-and-dagger stuff":** Lukas, 220.

622 **Hunt was not just a security official:** Chris Matthews, "How Kennedy Brought Down Nixon," *Daily Beast,* Sept. 13, 2009; Bob Woodward and Carl Bernstein, "Hunt Tried to Recruit Agent to Probe Senator Kennedy's Life," *WP,* Feb. 10, 1973.

622 **"ruin him for '76":** "Nixon Ordered Spy Placed in Sen. Kennedy's Secret Service Detail," *WP,* Feb. 8, 1997.

622 **"doing more damage than the Watergate bugging itself":** Woodward and Bernstein, "Gray Seen Destroying Hunt's Files," *WP,* Apr. 27, 1973.

623 **in exchange for Nixon terminating the actions:** "The Extraordinary I.T.T. Affair," *NYT,* Dec. 16, 1973.

623 **"Kleindienst is a damn fool":** John Dean, *Blind Ambition: The White House Years* (New York: Simon & Schuster, 1976), 52.

623 **Ted questioned Kleindienst:** Thomas Susman int., Miller Center, UVA, May 23, 2007.

623 **"He was lying":** Edward Kennedy, *True Compass* (New York: Twelve, 2009), 325.

624 **"gulped from her oxygen mask":** *Ibid.,* 326–327.

624 **"she would collapse or die or whatever":** Edward Kennedy int., Miller Center, UVA, May 8, 2006.

624 **interviewed on the *60 Minutes*:** "Mrs. Beard Defies Her Doctors," *NYT,* Apr. 3, 1972.

624 **made a deal with Mitchell:** Dean, 53.

624 **"Let the chips fall":** Nixon conversation, 005-113, Miller Center, UVA, 006–113, July 2, 1971.

625 **"Hot ammunition to discredit O'Brien":** H. R. Haldeman with Joseph DiMona, *The Ends of Power* (New York: Times Books, 1978), 19.

625 **or other Republican financial shenanigans:** Stanley Kutler, *The Wars of Watergate* (New York: Alfred A. Knopf, 1990), 203–204.

625 **"round the clock":** Thomas Susman int., Miller Center, UVA, May 23, 2007.

625 **"ferocious arguments":** John Tunney int., Miller Center, UVA, May 3, 2007.

626 **"We knew immediately that was high-level stuff":** Lippman, 203.

626 **"at the dirty tricks during the election":** Thomas Susman int., Miller Center, UVA, May 23, 2007.

626   "Nobody else was kind of involved in it": Edward Kennedy int., Clymer Papers, Series 2, Box 5, EMK interviews, 1995–1996 folder, JFK Lib., Apr. 12, 1996.

626   **Ford managed to convince several Democrats:** Edward Kennedy int., Miller Center, UVA, May 8, 2006.

626   **"preliminary inquiry":** "Kennedy Is Backed on Subpoenas," *NYT,* Oct. 15, 1972.

627   **"They're thugs":** Bob Woodward and Carl Bernstein, *All the President's Men* (New York: Simon & Schuster, 1974), 247.

627   **"nickel-and-dime stuff":** *Ibid.*

627   **"part of the file in the Watergate [investigation]":** John Tunney int., Miller Center, UVA, May 3, 2007.

627   **"handing out subpoenas like traffic summonses":** Lukas, 377.

627   **"week to ten days ahead of the press":** Edward Kennedy int., Clymer Papers, Apr. 12, 1996.

628   **"Kennedy will tear me to shreds":** Woodward and Bernstein, *All the President's Men,* 202.

628   **"You win the Congress, you take control of the committees":** Matthews.

628   **he approached Majority Leader Mike Mansfield:** Edward Kennedy int., Clymer Papers, Apr. 12, 1996.

628   **"and to everyone else":** Francis Valeo, Oral History Interviews, Senate Historical Office.

629   **was not entirely sidelined:** Mike Mansfield int., Clymer Papers, Series 2, Box 4, M folder, JFK Lib., Jan. 27, 1993.

629   **"I think we would have had a different outcome":** Edward Kennedy int., Miller Center, UVA, May 8, 2006; Edward Kennedy int., Clymer Papers, JFK Lib., Apr. 12, 1996.

630   **"jump-started":** *True Compass,* 333.

630   **dogged old investigator:** Edward Kennedy int., Clymer Papers, JFK Lib., Apr. 12, 1996.

630   **continued to work on Watergate:** Lippman, 206.

630   **"regardless of which party was in the White House":** Richard Burke with William and Marilyn Hoffer, *The Senator: My Ten Years with Ted Kennedy* (New York: St. Martin's Press, 1992), 28.

630   **"Just more clever":** Feb. 28, 1973, http://www.nixontapeaudio.org/chron5/865-014a.mp3.

631   **"regarding the Ervin investigation":** Haldeman, *The Haldeman Diaries,* entry Feb. 9, 1973, 577.

631   **"other controversies in foreign and domestic policy":** "Watergate Puts U.S. on Trial," *LAT,* May 5, 1973.

632   **Ted suggested that Califano write:** Joseph Califano Jr., *Inside: A Public and Private Life* (New York: Public Affairs, 2004), 285.

632   **"extraordinary impropriety":** Edward Kennedy int., Miller Center, UVA, May 8, 2006; Edward Kennedy int., Clymer Papers, JFK Lib., Apr. 12, 1996.

632   **"to be a man of unshakable integrity":** Elliot Richardson, *The Creative Balance: Government, Politics, and the Individual in America's Third Century* (New York: Holt, Rinehart and Winston, 1976), 37.

632   **"in an unbiased way":** Richard Nixon, *The Memoirs of Richard Nixon* (New York: Grosset & Dunlap, 1978), 910–911.

633   **"within eighteen minutes of his swearing in":** Theodore H. White, *Breach of Faith: The Fall of Richard Nixon* (New York: Atheneum, 1975), 253.

633   **Nixon believed that Kennedy was somehow manipulating:** Haldeman, The *Haldeman Diaries,* entry March 27, 1973, 612.

633   **"thirty minutes that ensnared Nixon":** Emery, 368.

633   **"inherent" power as president:** *Ibid.,* 372.

634   **"find Teddy Kennedy a hard product to sell":** "Are There Any Leaders Left to Take Us To?" *NYT,* Sept. 13, 1973.

634   **43 percent of Americans still doubted:** "Integrity of Kennedy Doubted," *NYT,* Oct. 16, 1973.

634   **"man of Chappaquiddick leading an impeachment battle":** "Kennedy Makes a Move," *NYT,* Sept. 16, 1973.

635   **he should not be confirmed otherwise:** "Kennedy Seeks Ford Pledge on Tapes," *NYT,* Oct. 18, 1973.

635   **Ted's withering cross-examination:** Edward Kennedy int., Miller Center, UVA, May 8, 2006.

635   **"partisan viper we had planted in our bosom":** Nixon, 929.

635   **called the "Harvards":** Lukas, 459.

635   **encircled by those Harvards:** White, 251–252.

637   **"get rid of Cox":** Richardson, 38.

638 **his conversations on Friday:** Edward Kennedy int., Clymer Papers, JFK Lib., Apr. 12, 1996.

638 **Nixon in his memoirs said he didn't:** Nixon, 934.

638 **"Saturday Night Massacre was born in Kennedy's office":** Chris Matthews, *Kennedy & Nixon: The Rivalry that Shaped Postwar America* (New York: Simon & Schuster, 1996), 333.

638 **Now the deed seemed to be done:** Much of this narrative is woven from several accounts: Emery, Chapters 16 & 17; Kutler, Chapter 15; Lukas, Chapters 11 & 13.

639 **"What can senators do?":** Milton Gwirtzman int., Miller Center, UVA, May 29, 2009.

639 **they did not have to give up their files:** Milton Gwirtzman int., Series 2, Box 3, folder G, Clymer Papers, Apr. 3, 1993.

639 **"no regard for a man of conscience":** "Richard Nixon Stumbles to the Brink," *Time*, Oct. 29, 1973.

639 **Americans did not want Nixon to be impeached:** "Gallup Poll Finds 55% of Americans Oppose Impeachment," *BG*, Oct. 30, 1973.

639 **decided to invite Cox to testify:** *Ibid.*

640 **"I'm glad to hear":** "Cox Calls Independence 'Crucial' for Prosecutor," *NYT*, Oct. 30, 1973.

640 **"Partisan bickering":** "Senate Panel's Hearings on Dismissal of Cox Fall into Partisan Bickering," *NYT*, Nov. 1, 1973.

CHAPTER SIXTEEN: S.3

641 **"Don't be a gadfly":** George Packer, "The Empty Chamber," *The New Yorker*, Aug. 9, 2010.

641 **"extraordinary discomfort":** Edward Kennedy int., Miller Center, UVA, March 23, 2005, and March 28, 2008; Edward Kennedy int., Series 2, Box 5, EMK interviews 1995, Clymer Papers, 1995–1996 folder, JFK Lib., Apr. 17, 1995.

641 **while he was a student at Milton:** Edward Kennedy int., Miller Center, UVA, June 3, 2005.

641 **"cornerstone of my interest in health matters":** Edward Kennedy, *True Compass* (New York: Twelve, 2009), 171.

642 **who suffered from kidney disease:** Gerard Doherty int., Miller Center, UVA, Oct. 10, 2005.

642 **Ted and Herbert Adams:** Herbert Adams, *The Knife that Saves: Memoirs of a Lahey Clinic Surgeon* (Boston: Francis A. Countway Library of Medicine, 1991), 309.

642 **first foray into health-care legislation:** David Burke int., Miller Center, UVA, June 19, 2007.

642 **"I realized that access to health care was a moral issue":** *True Compass*, 225.

642 **Committee of 100:** "Insurance for the Nation's Health," *Time*, May 11, 1970.

643 **attacks on Reuther:** Victor Reuther, *The Brothers Reuther and the Story of the UAW: A Memoir* (Boston: Houghton Mifflin, 1976), 276–278.

643 **Reuther as social visionary:** Jill Quadagno, *One Nation Uninsured: Why the U.S. Has No National Health Insurance* (New York: Oxford Univ. Press, 2005), 110–112.

643 **asked how Medicare was coming:** Max Fine int., Miller Center, UVA, May 25, 2007.

643 **win passage:** *Ibid.*

643 **The referendum failed:** Alan Derickson, *Health Security for All: Dreams of Universal Health Care in America* (Baltimore: Johns Hopkins Univ. Press, 2005), 8–9; Paul Starr, "Public Health Then and Now," *American Journal of Public Health*, Jan. 1982, 78–88.

644 **any hope for national health insurance:** Derickson, 80–87.

644 **Failures of health insurance:** Sven Steinmo and Jon Watts, "It's the Institutions, Stupid!: Why Comprehensive National Health Insurance Always Fails in America," *Journal of American Health Politics, Policy and Law*, Vol. 20, No. 2, 1995, 329–372; "Insurance for the Nation's Health," *Time*, May 11, 1970.

644 **government-funded insurance:** Derickson, 110–114.

644 **forcing hospitals to integrate:** Paul Krugman, *The Conscience of a Liberal* (New York: W. W. Norton & Co., 2007), 67.

644 **"Socialized medicine is the keystone":** Colin Gordon, *Dead on Arrival: The Politics of Health Care in Twentieth-Century America* (Princeton, N.J.: Princeton Univ. Press, 2003), 143–145.

644 **joined with the AMA to prevent it:** Derickson, 109–110.

644 **"American political institutions are structurally biased":** Steinmo and Watts, 329–330.

645 **"He was enormously persuasive":** Edward Kennedy int., Series 2, Box 5, EMK interviews, Clymer Papers, 1995–1996 folder, JFK Lib., Apr. 17, 1995; Edward Kennedy int., Series 2, Box 5, EMK interviews, 1996–1999, Clymer Papers, 1995–1996 folder, JFK Lib., Apr. 12, 1996.

645 **take the Health and Scientific Research Subcommittee chair:** Edward Kennedy int., Clymer Papers, JFK Lib., Apr. 17, 1995; Edward Kennedy int., Clymer Papers, JFK Lib., Apr. 12, 1996.

646 **the face and the voice for government-financed:** Max Fine int., Series 2, Box 3 F folder, Clymer Papers, JFK Lib., June 9, 1995.

646 **the final drafting of the bill began:** Max Fine int. by author; Edward Kennedy int., Series 2, Box 5, EMK interviews, 1997–1999 folder, Clymer Papers, JFK Lib., March 27, 1998.

647 **"hard-line conservative":** Carey Parker int., Miller Center, UVA, Sept. 22, 2008.

647 **"government takeover":** Max Fine int. by author.

647 **"We had a lot of things going":** *Ibid.*

647 **"he had put it together":** Rashi Fein int., Miller Center, UVA, March 21, 2007.

648 **"I gather you're not interested":** Max Fine int., Miller Center, UVA, May 25, 2007.

648 **"Boy, this Chappaquiddick thing":** Max Fine int. by author.

648 **from the Committee of 100:** Max Fine int., Miller Center, UVA, May 25, 2007.

648 **"It picked up later, but it wasn't the same":** Max Fine int. by author.

648 **help obliterate the stain:** Peter Canellos, *Last Lion: The Fall and Rise of Ted Kennedy* (New York: Simon & Schuster, 2009), 177.

648 **"push the issue as a member":** Carey Parker int., Miller Center, UVA, Sept. 22, 2008.

649 **he was now a lame duck:** "Conservative Beats Yarborough," *NYT,* May 3, 1970.

649 **"a living memorial to Walter Reuther":** "Reuther Is Lauded at Lasker Lunch," *NYT,* May 15, 1970.

649 **William Saxbe and John Sherman Cooper:** "National Health Insurance Proposed by 15 Senators," *NYT,* Aug. 28, 1970.

649 **"spate of media attention":** Frank Campion, *The AMA and U.S. Health Policy Since 1940* (Chicago Review Press, 1984), 314–315.

650 **"legislative quackery":** "Meany Vows Aid for Health Plan," *NYT,* Sept. 25, 1970.

650 **"get the credit for what he proposed":** Ltr., Ehrlichman to Morgan, Box 36, File IS:1, White House Special Files (confidential files), WHSF, Nixon Papers, National Archives, Dec. 17, 1969, and Ehrlichman to Nixon, IS:1, Nov. 10, 1970, in Gordon, 273.

650 **"windfall of billions of dollars":** Quadagno, 114–115.

651 **it had to have his name on it:** Max Fine int. by author.

652 **"Kennedy gets all the press":** Joseph Califano Jr., *Governing America: An Insider's Report from the White House and the Cabinet* (New York: Simon & Schuster, 1981), 93.

652 **"bring Long and Kennedy [to] each other's throats":** Ltr., Ehrlichman to Morgan, Dec. 17, 1969, in Gordon, 273.

652 **"A lot of his future course":** Carey Parker int., Miller Center, UVA, Oct. 6, 2008.

652 **"*My* committee":** Carey Parker int., Miller Center, UVA, Sept. 22, 2008.

652 **"He controls the entire majority staff":** Theo Lippman, *Senator Ted Kennedy: The Career Behind the Image* (New York: W. W. Norton & Co., 1976), 233.

652 **"Mr. Health Care in the Senate":** Carey Parker int., Miller Center, UVA, Oct. 6, 2008.

652 **a "major push":** LeRoy Goldman int., Miller Center, UVA, May 5, 2007.

652 **four or five years:** Memo, James Wechsler, Re: Conversation with Ted Kennedy, nd, Joseph Rauh Jr., Papers, Box 37, Kennedy, Edward M., 1968–1971 folder, Lib. of Congress.

652 **"steep mountain":** LeRoy Goldman int., Miller Center, UVA, May 5, 2007.

652 **" 'This is our goal' ":** Carey Parker int., Miller Center, UVA, Sept. 22, 2008.

653 **LeRoy Goldman:** LeRoy Goldman int. by author.

654 **"You could do something like that":** Stan Jones int., Miller Center, UVA, March 9, 2007.

654 **Jones organizing hearings:** *Ibid.*

654 **"People who were less secure":** Philip Caper int., Miller Center, UVA, March 20, 2007.

654 **"contrivance that we created":** LeRoy Goldman int., Miller Center, UVA, May 5, 2007.

655 **Ted wanted to make a presidential run of his own:** Stan Jones int., Miller Center, UVA, March 9, 2007.

655 **"arouse the kind of human-interest coverage":** Memo, James Wechsler, Re: Conversation with Ted Kennedy.

655 **"horror stories":** Philip Caper int., Miller Center, UVA, March 20, 2007.

655 **"health crisis in America":** LeRoy Goldman int. by author.

655 **"Thank you, Senator Dominick":** *Ibid.*

655 **"The bedrock of it":** LeRoy Goldman int. by author, health data https://www2.census.gov/prod2/statcomp/documents/CT1970p1-03.pdf.

656 **A widow named Betty Roche:** Health Care Crisis in America, Hearings, Senate Subcomm. on Health of the Comm. on Labor and Public Welfare, 92nd Congress, Part 7, Apr. 14, 1971, 1,667–1,668.

656 **"We played the game of the establishment":** *Ibid.*, 1,586.

656 **"They die":** *Ibid.*, 1555–1557.

657 **"It seems they don't treat you":** *Ibid.*, 1,704.

657 **then there was Isabel Rodriguez:** *Ibid.*, 1,706–1,707.

658 **Its subsidies would replace Medicaid:** Stuart Altman and David Shactman, *Power, Politics, and Universal Health Care: The Inside Story of a Century-Long Battle* (Amherst, N.Y.: Prometheus Books, 2011), 42–44; *The CBS Evening News*, Feb. 18, 1971.

658 **"stretching present Medicaid money":** Health Options 1971, Box IS:1, WHSF, Nixon Papers, July 13, 1970, in Gordon, 32.

658 **"It was a way of having a placeholder":** LeRoy Goldman int., Miller Center, UVA, May 5, 2007.

659 **"demagogic ploy":** Gordon, 32; "Insurance for the Nation's Health"; "Kennedy's Health Care Plan Too Costly," *LAT*, June 23, 1971.

659 **"add momentum to a national dialogue":** "Kennedy Health Bill Ahead of Its Time," *LAT*, May 1, 1971.

659 **European and Middle Eastern trip:** Philip Caper int., Miller Center, UVA, March 20, 2007.

659 **"only two industrialized nations":** LeRoy Goldman int., Miller Center, UVA, May 5, 2007.

659 **"If they can do this, why can't we?":** Philip Caper int., Miller Center, UVA, March 20, 2007.

660 **Origins of National Cancer Act:** Vincent DeVita Jr. and Elizabeth DeVita-Raeburn, *The Death of Cancer* (New York: Farrar, Straus and Giroux, 2015), 131–135.

660 **consider it an "honor":** Richard Rettig, *Cancer Crusade: The Story of the National Cancer Act of 1971* (Princeton, N.J.: Princeton Univ. Press, 1977), 121.

660 **the new agency the "Conquest of Cancer Agency":** "The Politics of Cancer," *Time*, July 5, 1971.

661 **"three focal points":** LeRoy Goldman int., Miller Center, UVA, May 5, 2007.

661 **"Goldman–Cutler Show":** *Ibid.*

661 **"If we are going to spend the money":** Memo, Nixon to Ehrlichman, Apr. 28, 1971, in *From: The President: Richard Nixon's Secret Files*, Bruce Oudes, ed. (New York: Harper & Row, 1989), 244.

662 **Hearings:** Rettig, 143–162; "A New Government Cancer Agency Is Opposed at Hearing," *NYT*, March 10, 1971.

662 **advice columnist Ann Landers:** *Ibid.*, 170–172.

662 **"presidential guidance may hasten the day":** *Ibid.*, 178–181; "President Vows to Lead a Drive Against Cancer," *NYT*, May 12, 1971.

663 **barely able to contain his rage:** "War on Cancer," *NYT*, May 31, 1971; LeRoy Goldman int., Miller Center, UVA, May 5, 2007.

663 **But Benno Schmidt was not:** Remarks of Benno Schmidt at meeting of President's Cancer Panel, National Cancer Institute, Dec. 9, 1986.

664 **"Jack, you don't understand":** Edward Kennedy int., Miller Center, UVA, March 23, 2005.

664 **"Maybe we ought to just recess":** Rettig, 185–186.

664 **"then you are not as smart":** Remarks of Benno Schmidt, National Cancer Institute, Dec. 9, 1986.

665 **"And, Peter, why don't *you* report the bill?":** LeRoy Goldman int., Miller Center, UVA, May 5, 2007.

665 **"hadn't been interested in it":** Edward Kennedy int., Miller Center, UVA, March 28, 2008.

665 **" 'strike all [the language] after the enacting clause' ":** LeRoy Goldman int., Miller Center, UVA, May 5, 2007.

666 **a "brick wall":** Edward Kennedy int., Clymer Papers, JFK Lib., Apr. 12, 1996.

666 **appointing the new administrator as well:** LeRoy Goldman int., Miller Center, UVA, May 5, 2007.

666 **"a chilling insight into American politics":** *Ibid.*

667 **HMOs, the brainchild:** Altman and Shactman, 35–36; Quadagno, 115.

667 **he had included it in his 1971 health-care plan:** James Morone, *The Heart of Power: Health and Politics in the Oval Office* (Berkeley: Univ. of California Press, 2009), 226–230.

667 **to flag as the election approached:** Philip Caper int., Miller Center, UVA, March 20, 2007.

667 **"My best sense is that he was very much afraid":** Stuart Altman int., *Frontline*, PBS, Nov. 13, 2009.

668 **Ted, who was "incredulous":** Morone, 242–243.

669 **"is a one-man blockade":** Kay Collett Goss, *Mr. Chairman: The Life and Legacy of Wilbur D. Mills* (Little Rock, Ark.: Parkhurst Brothers, 2012).

669　Cohen called their agreement "historic": "Kennedy, Mills Unite on Total Health Plan," *WP*, Aug. 18, 1972.

669　"and then the staffs would sort of work those up": Edward Kennedy int., Clymer Papers, JFK Lib., Apr. 12, 1996.

670　wanted to land a spot on the Democratic ticket: LeRoy Goldman int., Miller Center, UVA, May 5, 2007; Stan Jones int., Miller Center, UVA, March 9, 2007; Stan Jones int., Clymer Papers, Series 2, Box 4, I-J folder, Clymer Papers, JFK Lib., Nov. 11, 1993.

670　arrive at a compromise bill: "Kennedy, Mills Eye Joint Health Bill," *WP*, Sept. 30, 1972.

670　he had made no real effort to pass one of his own: Morone, 234.

671　"I willed myself not to think of the possibilities": *True Compass*, 306.

671　the surgery was delayed until the following Saturday: *Ibid.*, 305–307.

671　"We wanted his life to be as normal as possible": *Ibid.*

672　"Teddy wanted to have him out": Lee Fentress int., Miller Center, UVA, Oct. 16, 2009.

672　Ted said, he had finally phoned Joan: *True Compass*, 307.

672　his father never subsequently discussed: Lester David, *Joan: The Reluctant Kennedy* (New York: Funk & Wagnalls, 1974); *The Oprah Winfrey Show*, Nov. 25, 2009.

672　finally elicited a laugh from Ted Jr.: Arthur Schlesinger Jr., *Journals: 1952–2000*, Andrew Schlesinger and Stephen Schlesinger, eds. (New York: Penguin Press, 2007), 376; Ltr., Eunice Shriver to Nixon, Nov. 16, 1973, in Oudes, 606.

673　"And how proud he would be of me": Kathleen Kennedy Townsend int., Nov. 3, 1997, Series 2, Box 5, T folder, Clymer Papers, JFK Lib., Nov. 3, 1997.

673　"their fingers pressed to their closed eyes": "Tragedy Dims Happy Occasion," *WP*, Nov. 18, 1973.

673　"one's mind went back through the sad years": Schlesinger, 376.

673　"During that period, his devotion to his son": Philip Caper int., Miller Center, UVA, March 20, 2007.

673　"It was the most important thing in his life": "Kennedy, His Children, and Cancer," *BG*, May 25, 2008.

673　he wondered if he had done enough: Stewart Auerbach int., Clymer Papers, Series 2, Box 3, A folder, Clymer Papers, JFK Lib., May 18, 1997.

673　held a four-hour discussion: Canellos, 189.

674　"get him into his classroom on Monday mornings": *True Compass*, 310.

674　"intensively" for the next couple of days: Edward Kennedy int., Miller Center, UVA, March 28, 2008.

674　fever, chills, and terrible pain: "Ready for Teddy?" *Newsweek*, June 2, 1975.

674　a "little bit better" by Saturday night: Edward Kennedy int., Miller Center, UVA, Oct. 14, 2005.

674　"But unless you get every last cell": Burton Hersh, *The Shadow President: Ted Kennedy in Opposition* (South Royalton, Vt.: Steerforth Press, 1997), 18.

674　until Ted himself could take the night shift: Richard Burke with William and Marilyn Hoffer, *The Senator: My Ten Years with Ted Kennedy* (New York: St. Martin's Press, 1992), 51–52.

674　"I can't tell whether it would have been so": Hersh, 18.

674　the old Kennedy stoicism: Laurence Leamer, *The Kennedy Women: The Saga of an American Family* (New York: Villard Books, 1994), 675–676.

674　"He should be kept entertained": Patrick Kennedy and Steven Fried, *A Common Struggle: A Personal Journey Through the Past and Future of Mental Illness and Addiction* (New York: Blue Rider Press, 2015), 42; Leamer, 675–676.

675　accusing her of not wanting their son to have fun: Joan Kennedy int., Clymer Papers, Series 2, Box 4, K folder, Clymer Papers, JFK Lib., Oct. 12, 1998.

675　"He was a Kennedy": Leamer, 676.

675　admitted that his Senate work suffered: Edward Kennedy int., Miller Center, UVA, Aug. 7, 2007.

675　even running away: Hersh, 19.

675　"I needed some relief": Penelope McMillan, "The Troubled Marriage of Joan and Ted Kennedy," *McCall's*, Nov. 1975.

675　"They just didn't know": Canellos, 190.

676　Joan was suffering from "emotional problems": Kennedy and Fried, 43; "Joan Kennedy Reported in Psychiatric Hospital," *LAT*, June 1, 1974.

676　"She just needed a rest": "Joan Kennedy's Worries," *People Weekly*, June 24, 1974.

676　The friend was right: "People," *Time*, June 17, 1974.

676　she was clearly in crisis: "Joan Kennedy's Worries."

676 unable to remember how to turn on the stove: Burke, 21.
676 so he could be at her side: "Joan Kennedy Cited as Drunken Driver," Oct. 10, 1974, *LAT*.
676 he and Joan always arrived separately: Burke and Hoffer, 53.
677 "being put through this kind of system": Edward Kennedy int., Miller Center, UVA, March 28, 2008.
677 reluctant to use his personal tragedies: Edward Kennedy int., Series 2, Box 5, EMK int. 1992–1994 folder, Clymer Papers, JFK Lib., Feb. 1992.
677 "personal overlay": Edward Kennedy int., Miller Center, UVA, Aug. 7, 2007.
677 asked Altman to do the spade work: Stuart Altman int., *Frontline*, PBS, Nov. 13, 2009.
677 "it might even save Nixon from impeachment": Edward Kennedy int., Miller Center, UVA, March 28, 2008.
678 "You simply can't fight something with nothing": Morone, 236–238; Altman and Shactman, 34–35.
679 "We can beat Kennedy anyway": Gergen to Haid, Re: Health Insurance Message, Folder: Feb Chron—David Gergen, Box 6, White House Central Files, David Gergen, Chronological File, Nixon Lib., Feb. 6, 1974.
679 "Health Security [Act] as a standard": Gordon, 34–35; Brindle to Glasser, Box 105, Part II, UAS-SSD Records, Feb. 15, 1974; Fine to EMK, Box 110, Part II, Series VI, UAW-SSD Records, Dec. 21, 1973.
679 Mills even questioned now why Weinberger: Stuart Altman int., Clymer Papers, Series 2, Box 3, A folder, Clymer Papers, JFK Lib., Sept. 17, 1993.
679 threatened to propose a new committee: Steinmo and Watts.
680 Long looked at it and turned it down: Edward Berkowitz, *Robert Ball and the Politics of Social Security* (Madison: Univ. of Wisconsin Press, 2003), 222–230.
680 "It's bullshit, basically": Altman and Shactman, 57.
681 President Nixon was "very pleased": Berkowitz, 230.
681 "we have reached the stage": Memo, Vern Loen through Max Friedersdorf to Bill Timmons, Re: Comprehensive Health Insurance Plan, Folder: National Health Insurance, Box 45, White House Central Files, Staff Member and Other files, William Timmons, Subject files, Nixon Lib., Apr. 24, 1974.
681 "A new spirit of compromise is in the air": Paul Starr, "Public Health, Then and Now," *American Journal of Public Health*, Jan. 1982, 85.
681 "I saw this as a way of sort of expanding our base": Edward Kennedy int., Clymer Papers, JFK Lib., Apr. 12, 1996.
681 called Kennedy–Mills II "socialist": David Dranove, *The Economic Evolution of American Health Care: From Marcus Welby to Managed Care* (Princeton, N.J.: Princeton Univ. Press, 2000), 30.
681 essentially administrators of the plan: Stan Jones int., Miller Center, UVA, Sept. 14, 2007.
682 "go and say, 'Join my union'": Edward Kennedy int., Miller Center, UVA, March 28, 2008.
682 "precious few of the latter": LeRoy Goldman int., Miller Center, UVA, May 5, 2007.
682 "that was a very big deal": Rashi Fein int., Miller Center, UVA, March 21, 2007.
683 "What are you going to do about him?": LeRoy Goldman int., Miller Center, UVA, May 5, 2007; Stan Jones int., Miller Center, UVA, March 9, 2007; Altman and Shactman, 55–56.
683 certain of a Democratic president: "Labor Hardens Opposition to Compromise Health Bill," *WP*, May 18, 1974.
683 "election is not going to change anything": Altman and Shactman, 55–56; Stan Jones int., Miller Center, UVA, March 9, 2007.
683 But the leaders sat in stony, boiling silence: Stan Jones int., Miller Center, UVA, March 9, 2007.
683 "the liberal leader whom his peers trusted": Thomas Oliphant, "The Lion at Rest," *Democracy*, Winter 2010, 104.
683 opened the door and motioned them out: Altman and Shactman, 56.
684 "yelling and cheering": Stan Jones int., Miller Center, UVA, March 9, 2007.
685 seem proactive on cancer: LeRoy Goldman int., Miller Center, UVA, May 5, 2007.
685 When the House reconvened: Fred Emery, *Watergate: The Corruption of American Politics and the Fall of Richard Nixon* (New York: Times Books, 1994), 404.
686 He had lived in fear of Ted Kennedy: Altman and Shactman, 35.
686 Laird had suggested a pay-or-play system: Edward Kennedy int., Miller Center, UVA, March 28, 2008.
686 it not exceed a certain cost: Stan Jones int., Miller Center, UVA, March 9, 2007.

687   "and they're ready to crucify me out there": Ibid.

687   "were designed to divert attention from Watergate stuff": Caspar Weinberger int., Clymer Papers, Series 2, Box 5, V-Z folder, Clymer Papers, JFK Lib., Jan. 8, 1997.

687   Ted watched his departure from the Senate cloakroom: One Nixon diehard, a former White House fellow named Geoff Shepard, attributes Nixon's downfall to an intricate, devious, and cleverly stage-managed scheme by Ted Kennedy and his "clan" to set up a Kennedy presidency. His book, which requires an enormous suspension of disbelief, is titled *The Secret Plot to Make Ted Kennedy President* (New York: Sentinel, 2008); *True Compass*, 343.

687   they would find a way to make good use: Philip Caper int., Miller Center, UVA, March 20, 2007.

688   "there's no point in bringing it up": Stan Jones int., Miller Center, UVA, March 9, 2007.

688   too close to bring the bill: Rick Mayes, *Universal Coverage: The Elusive Quest for National Health Insurance* (Ann Arbor: Univ. of Michigan Press, 2004), 93–94.

688   a major concession, especially from Corman: *Ibid.*

688   "a bill that will get through the House": "House Panel Rift Appears to Doom Health Cost Bill," *NYT*, Aug. 22, 1974.

688   Wilbur Mills arrest: "Mills Admits Being Present During Tidal Basin Scuffle," *WP*, Oct. 11, 1974.

689   "opposed to any kind of national health insurance": Philip Caper int., Miller Center, UVA, March 20, 2007.

689   "You didn't have a prayer": Stan Jones int., Miller Center, UVA, Sept. 14, 2007.

689   really serious about it: Caspar Weinberger int., Clymer Papers, JFK Lib., Jan. 8, 1997.

689   " 'we won't compromise' ": Stan Jones int., Miller Center, UVA, March 9, 2007.

689   "pressing and pushing for it": Edward Kennedy int., Clymer Papers, JFK Lib., Apr. 12, 1996.

689   "I didn't support the Nixon plan": Michael Myers, "Obama's Deal," *Frontline*, PBS, Dec. 15, 2009.

CHAPTER SEVENTEEN: "OUR LONG NATIONAL NIGHTMARE IS OVER"

690   the "very model of a father": James Cannon, *Gerald R. Ford: An Honorable Life* (Ann Arbor: Univ. of Michigan Press, 2013), 43.

690   Ford had something Nixon never had: For the fullest account of Ford's early life, see Cannon, Chapter 4.

691   "There were fewer people mad at Ford": Charles Goodell, quoted in Richard Reeves, *A Ford, Not a Lincoln* (New York: Harcourt Brace Jovanovich, 1975), 6.

691   A "team player," he called himself: *Ibid.*, 7.

691   Carl Albert had been the one: Cannon, 129.

691   "I don't think he's missed a beat": "A Sure Touch in Ford's Second Week," *Time*, Sept. 2, 1974.

692   Senate passing campaign reform: "Senate Votes Spending Election Reform," *NYT*, July 31, 1973.

693   "taxation without representation": "Senate Bars Move Weakening Public Financing," *NYT*, March 29, 1974.

693   the Senate be publicly financed: Adam Clymer, *Edward M. Kennedy: A Biography* (New York: William Morrow, 1999), 221–222.

693   Thus were the incumbents spared: For an extensive treatment of the legislative battle, see Theo Lippman, *Senator Ted Kennedy: The Career Behind the Image* (New York: W. W. Norton & Co., 1976), 128–142.

694   the "most important bill of the year": "The Price of Independence," *NYT*, Aug. 4, 1974.

694   almost certainly would have vetoed: "Campaign-Spending Bill's Key Provision Doesn't Apply," *NYT*, Oct. 6, 1974.

694   "most extensive reform of federal campaign-financing": "Bill to Reform Campaign Funds Signed by Ford," *NYT*, Oct. 16, 1974.

694   which was not seriously at all: "Freedom of Information at 40," *National Security Archive*, July 4, 2006, https://nsarchive2.gwu.edu//NSAEBB/NSAEBB194/index.htm.

695   "fair amount of time": Thomas Susman int., Miller Center, UVA, May 23, 2007. Also: Thomas Susman int. by author.

695   "without a reasonable basis in law": "Veto Battle 30 Years Ago Set Freedom of Information Norms," Nov. 23, 2004, *National Security Archive*, https://nsarchive2.gwu.edu//NSAEBB/NSAEBB142/index.htm.

695   to assist the bureau: Memo, J. J. McDermott to Jenkins, Re: Freedom of Information Legislation, June 7, 1974, https://nsarchive2.gwu.edu//NSAEBB/NSAEBB142/Susman%201.pdf.

695 "as bad as possible": Memo, J. J. McDermott to Jenkins, June 17, 1974, https://nsarchive2.gwu
.edu//NSAEBB/NSAEBB142/Susman%20I.pdf.

695 more than willing to bottle it up: *Ibid.*

696 "stonewalled": Thomas Susman in "Access Reports," 25th Anniversary Retrospective of FOIA,
1991, https://nsarchive2.gwu.edu//NSAEBB/NSAEBB142/Stalled%20Negotiations%20-%20
Access%20Reports%20Recollections%20-%20Tom%20Susman.pdf.

697 Ted Kennedy had won another major victory: "Veto Battle 30 Years Ago Set Freedom of Information Norms."

697 "and Kennedy did that": Thomas Susman int., Miller Center, UVA, May 23, 2007.

698 53 percent of Americans opposed it: "Americans Grew to Accept Nixon's Pardon," Gallup, May 21,
2001, https://news.gallup.com/poll/3157/americans-grew-accept-nixons-pardon.aspx.

698 71 percent of Americans suspected some quid pro quo: Donald Rumsfeld, "How the Nixon Pardon Tore the Ford Administration Apart," *Politico*, May 20, 2018, https://www.politico.eu/article/
how-richard-nixon-pardon-tore-gerald-ford-administration-apart-watergate/.

698 Ford's favorability rating plummeted: John Lawrence, *The Class of '74: Congress After Watergate
and the Roots of Partisanship* (Baltimore: Johns Hopkins Univ. Press, 2018), 52.

698 "Yes! Yes! Yes! Yes!": *Ibid.*, 50.

699 he would be reintroducing S.3: "Labor Again Pushes Health Insurance Bill," *LAT*, Dec. 26, 1974.

699 "JACKIE'S NEW LOVE": "Ready for Teddy?" *Newsweek*, June 2, 1975.

700 "low point of economic policymaking": Alan Greenspan, *The Age of Turbulence* (New York: Penguin Press, 2007), 66.

700 it was the president who wasn't: Jimmy Breslin, "What Does Ford Stand For? For Status Quo,"
Los Angeles Times, July 15, 1975.

700 gave Democrats an opportunity: Lippman, 185–188.

701 "They chose prison or exile": Senate Subcomm. on Administrative Practice and Procedure,
Hearings on Selective Service System Procedures and Administrative Possibilities for Amnesty,
Feb. 28, March 1, 1974, 179.

701 "mercy, healing, and leniency built into it": "Kennedy Hits VFW Amnesty Position," *LAT*, Aug.
22, 1974.

701 clemency board that Ford had created: "By Almost Any Standard, the Amnesty Plan Isn't Working," *NYT*, Oct. 17, 1974.

701 "over the same old war": "And Still the War . . ." *Newsweek*, Feb. 10, 1975.

702 Ted wound up voting against it: Lippman, 62.

702 reaffirmed our belief in human rights: "Kennedy Disagrees with Ford's Vietnam Proposals," *LAT*,
Apr. 12, 1975.

702 "more aggressive and more active": Clymer, 558.

703 joined with Senator Alan Cranston: Lippman, 193–195.

703 "substantive debate": Mark Schneider int., Miller Center, UVA, Feb. 4, 2009.

703 won the release of some political prisoners: *Ibid.*

704 "large step to the right": Sean Wilentz, *The Age of Reagan: A History 1974–2008* (New York: HarperCollins, 2008), 63–64.

704 it would remove him from Ford's campaign: Cannon, 383.

704 asserting control over his staff: Robert Hartmann, *Palace Politics: An Inside Account of the Ford
Years* (New York: McGraw-Hill, 1980), 365–379.

704 "prove himself as a national leader": *Ibid.*, 379.

705 two or three conversations: Milton Gwirtzman int., Clymer Papers, Series 2, Box 3, folder G, JFK
Lib., Apr. 3, 1993.

705 sent Ted a private memo: Edward Kennedy int., Miller Center, UVA, Oct. 14, 2005.

705 he could campaign in such a way: Milton Gwirtzman int., Clymer Papers, Apr. 3, 1993.

705 "but not as good as the presidency": *Ibid.*

706 "American electorate in 1976": Memo, Sorensen to EMK et al., Theodore Sorensen Personal Papers, Series 19: The Democratic Party, Box 118, JFK Lib., March 9, 1973.

707 "blue-collar guys swilling beer?": Melody Miller, Miller Center, UVA, Oct. 7, 2008.

707 "maybe liberals should": "Sen. Kennedy's Move to the Center," *WP*, Apr. 12, 1973.

707 all of whom advised him to accept: Lippman, 106.

707 "No other family in the U.S.": "George and Teddy Harmonize," *Time*, July 6, 1973.

707 "We are no more entitled": William Safire, "A Cap over the Wall," *NYT*, July 5, 1973.

708 "I have great love and admiration for the man": "Kennedy Censured by SCLC," *NYT*, Aug. 18, 1973.

708 "confuse him with Oliver Wendell Holmes": "Senator Kennedy in Alabama," *WP*, July 8, 1973.

708 "it took a Kennedy to open up the competition": Safire.

709 acknowledging that in going to Alabama: Tom Wicker, "Ted &," *NYT*, July 6, 1973.

709 stage a debate with the arguments: Milton Gwirtzman int., Clymer Papers, JFK Lib., Apr. 3, 1993.

709 German leaders eagerly sought: "Kennedy Sees Shift in Alliance," *WP*, April 9, 1974.

709 "because I want to make an impact": Joseph Kraft, "Senator Kennedy's Travels," *WP*, Apr. 7, 1974.

709 "broaden the options for the Democratic party": *Ibid.*

710 "Hell, I spend half my time": Richard Reeves, "Teddy or Not," *New York*, Apr. 22, 1974.

710 "getting into a car in New York City": "Aide to Kennedy Denies He Ruled Out 1976 Race," *LAT*, Apr. 26, 1974.

710 "I'm not going to change my views": "Of Kennedy, A Degree of Seven Veils," *BG*, Oct. 5, 1973.

710 "I can't stay out of this kind of bully pulpit": James MacGregor Burns, *Edward Kennedy and the Camelot Legacy* (New York: W. W. Norton & Co., 1976), 322.

710 "played on it": Edward Kennedy int., Miller Center, UVA, Aug. 7, 2007.

711 "quite different in mood": Edward Kennedy, *True Compass* (New York: Twelve, 2009), 343–344.

711 "trim" or "cut back on": Milton Gwirtzman int., Clymer Papers, JFK Lib., Apr. 3, 1993.

711 "any prospect of success": Arthur Schlesinger Jr., *Journals: 1952–2000*, Andrew Schlesinger and Stephen Schlesinger, eds. (New York: Penguin Press, 2007), 376.

712 "Just down from trees": Evan Thomas, *Being Nixon: A Man Divided* (New York: Random House, 2015), 257.

712 "'I'm your *only* senator'": Philip Caper int., Miller Center, UVA, March 20, 2007.

712 Lead poisoning: Robert Bates int., Miller Center, UVA, May 8, 2007.

713 soothe the fears of anxious white voters: Robert Bates int., Miller Center, UVA, May 8, 2007.

714 "one of those things that he felt he had to do": Paul Kirk int., Miller Center, UVA, June 20, 2007.

714 "control their own people": Milton Gwirtzman int., Clymer Papers, JFK Lib., Apr. 3, 1993.

714 no other candidate with more than 9 percent: "Kennedy Creates a Free-for-All," *Time*, Oct. 7, 1974.

714 he had promises of financial support: Milton Gwirtzman int., Clymer Papers, JFK Lib., Apr. 3, 1993.

714 "give up a part of himself": Burns, 269.

714 "unwilling to take the personal risk": Milton Gwirtzman int., Clymer Papers, Apr. 3, 1993.

715 already been thoroughly litigated: "The Memory that Would Not Fade," *Time*, Oct. 7, 1974.

715 "It was just the wrong time": Edward Kennedy int., Miller Center, UVA, Oct. 14, 2005.

715 "domestic problems of great magnitude": Betty Taymor int., Miller Center, UVA, July 8, 2005.

716 "she's not even expected": Penelope McMillan, "The Troubled Marriage of Joan and Ted Kennedy," *McCall's*, Nov. 1975.

716 "independently living by wives": Milton Gwirtzman int., Clymer Papers, JFK Lib., Apr. 3, 1993.

716 her anxiety about his safety: "Ted Kennedy Gives Firm 'No' to Presidential Race," *Chicago Tribune*, Sept. 24, 1974.

717 "And I thought rather than sort of wait": Edward Kennedy int., Clymer Papers, Series 2, Box 5, EMK interviews, 1995–1996 folder, JFK Lib., Apr. 12, 1996.

717 "best opportunity" to be president: Carey Parker int., Miller Center, UVA, Oct. 13, 2008.

717 "a very complicated kind of decision": Edward Kennedy int., Clymer Papers, JFK Lib., Apr. 12, 1996.

717 "in solitude": "Kennedy Creates a Free-for-All."

717 "shifts according to the time of day": Schlesinger, 410.

717 Ted rejected them: "Kennedy Creates a Free-for-All."

717 "To the tips of my fingers": Stephen Wermiel and S. J. Micchia, "It's Firm and Final," *BG*, Sept. 24, 1974.

718 declined Ted's invitation to campaign for him: Tom Wicker, "Kennedy Frees Democrats," *NYT*, Sept. 24, 1974.

718 "My primary responsibilities are at home": "Ted Kennedy Gives Firm 'No' to Presidential Race."

718 "the last hope was gone": Robert Healy, "It was the Kennedys' Last Hurrah," *BG*, Sept. 24, 1974.

718 "spare his family further apprehension": "Sen. Kennedy's Difficult Decision," *LAT*, Sept. 24, 1974.

719 **"some of the Kennedy allure had been lost"**: "Kennedy Creates a Free-for-All."
720 **"segregative intent"**: J. Anthony Lukas, *Common Ground: A Turbulent Decade in the Lives of Three American Families* (New York: Vintage, paperback, 1986), 235–27.
720 **he was opposed to busing**: Burns, 139.
721 **Judge Wendell Arthur Garrity Jr.**: Lukas, 225–231.
722 **an indication of how politically radioactive**: Lippman, 104–105.
722 **"cruel hypocrisy"**: "Nixon Appeals to Prejudice on Busing," *LAT*, Feb. 20, 1972.
722 **Nixon had advocated for desegregation**: Thomas, 261.
722 **"We had this conference"**: Edward Kennedy int., Miller Center, UVA, May 31, 2007.
722 **busing plans**: "From Schools to the Streets," *Time*, Oct. 21, 1974.
723 **disagreement with Garrity's decision**: Ronald Formisano, *Boston Against Busing: Race, Class, and Ethnicity in the 1960s and 1970s* (Chapel Hill: Univ. of N.C. Press, 1991), 2.
723 **invitation to disaster**: "From Schools to the Streets."
723 **A "punitive" decision**: Formisano, 9.
723 **If violence ensued**: Lukas, 238–240. Lukas's is the most detailed account of the Boston busing imbroglio.
723 **"appeal to the fears and emotions"**: Lippman, 107.
724 **"A sad day for the country"**: "Conference Over Busing," *NYT*, July 10, 1974.
724 **ensure a student's constitutional rights**: "Conferees Limit Courts on Busing," July 23, 1974, *NYT*.
724 **"They think he can wave a magic wand"**: Burns, 243.
725 **And he met, too, with a new organization**: Edward Kennedy int., Miller Center, UVA, May 31, 2007.
725 **"I think with probably marginal kinds of effect"**: *Ibid.*
726 **"And, to you, Senator Kennedy, they would listen"**: Mike Barnicle, "The Minority of Children," *BG*, Sept. 8, 1974; Lukas, 260–261.
726 **"Don't go"**: Michael O'Brien, *Philip Hart: The Conscience of the Senate* (East Lansing: Mich. State Univ. Press, 1995), 188.
726 **Prior to the rally**: Joseph Kennedy II int., Clymer Papers, Series 2, Box 4, K folder, JFK Lib., Jan. 10, 1995.
727 **"I was coming over there with a group"**: Edward Kennedy int., Miller Center, UVA, May 31, 2007.
727 **"off he went . . . right into the middle of that crowd"**: Joseph Kennedy II int., Clymer Papers, Jan. 10, 1995.
727 **"They had thrown out a challenge"**: Lukas, 261.
727 IMPEACH KENNEDY: Bob Sales, "Sen. Kennedy Jeered from Stage at Rally," *BG*, Sept. 10, 1974.
727 **"You're not going to speak"**: Ken Botwright, "A Rally for Parents and Pupils—Not Kennedy," *BG*, Sept. 10, 1974.
728 **"Now let me say what I need to say"**: Mark Schneider int., Miller Center, UVA, Feb. 2, 2009.
728 **the snarling crowd**: 261; Formisano, 76–77. Lukas, 261.
728 **"A sense of palpable fear"**: Robert Bates int., Clymer Papers, Series 2, Box 3, B folder, JFK Lib., Sept. 21, 1994.
728 **"I was afraid they were going to hurt him"**: Ed Martin int., Miller Center, UVA, Apr. 20, 2005.
728 **"crowds like these are always cowards"**: Edward Kennedy int., Miller Center, UVA, May 31, 2007.
728 **When Ted got to within thirty yards**: *Ibid.*
728 *How will it be if the United States senator*: Paul Kirk int., Miller Center, UVA, June 20, 2007.
729 **"They'd pat us on the backs"**: Pat Ranese quoted in Formisano, 77.
729 **"Why didn't I know about this?"**: Mark Schneider int., Miller Center, UVA, Feb. 2, 2009.
729 **"visibly shaken"**: Sales.
729 **there couldn't be two rules**: Clymer, 223–224.
729 **"the focus of the anti-busing movement"**: Joseph Kennedy II int., Clymer Papers, Jan. 10, 1995.
729 **hurting the black students inside those buses**: Lukas, 241.
729 **"Bring your ass over here!"**: Burns, 204.
729 **"scared to death"**: Robert Bates int., Miller Center, UVA, May 8, 2007.
729 **The whole city was taut**: "From Schools to the Streets"; Lukas, 241.
730 **could wrangle them now**: Lukas, 243.
730 **"quality education"**: Sales.
730 **reached out to the aggrieved parents**: Edward Kennedy int., Miller Center, UVA, May 31, 2007.
731 **"What about forced busing?"**: Formisano, 181.
731 **"top of her lungs"**: Edward Kennedy int., Miller Center, UVA, May 31, 2007.

731 "Hounding him like a banshee": Formisano, 181.

731 "We could see the beer on the trucks": Barbara Souliotis int., Miller Center, UVA, July 12, 2005.

732 the angry mob threw rocks at its windows: *True Compass*, 350–351.

732 but they lost it: Edward Kennedy int., Miller Center, UVA, June 3, 2005.

732 "irritated" and "bedraggled": "Kennedy Jostled by Busing Foes," *NYT*, Apr. 7, 1975.

733 "busing the niggers": "Senator Kennedy: Alone with the Legacy," *WP*, June 4, 1978.

733 "We'll have to let the chips fall where they may": "Kennedy Position Firm," *NYT*, Apr. 7, 1975.

733 "That way the cops get you for assault or robbery": "Mean Streets of Boston," *Newsweek*, Sept. 22, 1975.

733 police fielded thirty bomb threats: "Hoover's Kennedy File," *Newsweek*, Dec. 29, 1975.

734 "He couldn't chance coming in here now": "Mean Streets of Boston."

734 the only time he had had security: Barbara Souliotis int., Miller Center, UVA, July 12, 2005.

734 "They look down on people of color like me": Formisano, 183.

734 "old coalition as well as win the new ones": Lukas, 262–263.

735 "Ted saw this coming": Burns, 243.

735 Teddy walked into those "crosshairs" that day: Joseph Kennedy II int., Clymer Papers, JFK Lib., Jan. 10, 1995.

735 "Reactionary populism": Formisano, 5.

735 "those who can escape escape": *Ibid.*, 177.

735 "I had become just one more of those Boston elitists": *True Compass*, 348.

736 "something had happened that day": Lukas, 262.

BIBLIOGRAPHY

A NOTE ON SOURCES

The bibliography that follows is necessarily a highly selected one because the literature of the Kennedys is so vast that a complete bibliography would be a book unto itself, and it would take anyone decades to read through, listen to, or view all the material listed. That list would include not only the hundreds of books written about the Kennedys, arguably America's most famous family—books from those seriously minded like Doris Kearns Goodwin's *The Fitzgeralds and the Kennedys* to the salacious like *Teddy Bare*—but also thousands of magazine articles and tens of thousands of newspaper articles, as well as archival material, letters, interviews and oral histories, audio recordings, legal records, public addresses, and documentary films. I have tried my best to read or view as many of these as I could—I pored through five decades of the *The Boston Globe, The New York Times, The Washington Post,* and *The Los Angeles Times,* just to mention the newspapers alone that I referenced, not including many others that I read more selectively—and it took me roughly ten years to do so. Nor was that all of it. Even before examining Kennedy material, I spent months, during my tenure as a public policy scholar at the Woodrow Wilson International Center for Scholars in Washington, examining books and articles on liberalism and conservatism that would provide me with the largest possible context to understand the shifting winds of American politics over the course of Edward Kennedy's career. I have not cited all of those books in the bibliography, though one can find most of them in the endnotes. Neither have I cited every magazine or newspaper article in the bibliography, which would have made it many pages longer than it is, though one can also find many of those articles in the endnotes.

And there was another obstacle. To the challenge of going through the immense amount of material on the Kennedys generally and on Edward Kennedy specifically in his forty-seven years in the Senate was added an equally difficult challenge. The Kennedys, understandably, are secretive, as I state several times in this biography. They and those around them function in a kind of *omerta*. Though this is not an official or authorized biography—I wouldn't write such a book—when I first embarked on this project, as a matter of courtesy, I wrote Senator Kennedy to tell him what I intended to do, and he replied with a short but very Kennedy-esque note saying that while he had begun work on his own memoir and was looking forward to it, he also encouraged my "own venture (or adventure!)." In subsequent months, his office cooperated with me. But then Senator Kennedy was diagnosed with his brain tumor, which, of course, ended both our personal contact and my contact with his office. Still, when I wrote a letter to Mrs. Kennedy after the diagnosis, expressing my concern, I received a lovely handwritten note from her in which she said that her husband was "doing well and looking forward to giving you a lot more material for your book."

Mindful to respect the family's privacy in the year that he wrestled with cancer, it was only well after the senator's death that I made preliminary contact with friends, colleagues, and staff requesting interviews. No sooner had I done so than I received a letter from Robert Barnett, the noted attorney who represented the senator and Mrs. Kennedy in the negotiations for his memoir, asking me to desist. Though Barnett apologized to me when I sent him copies of my correspondence with the senator, his wife, and his office, he still insisted that, at Vicki's instruction, I not contact anyone. (A Kennedy associate told me that Mrs. Kennedy was trying to protect the senator's memoir, *True Compass*, from any book that might compete with it. I have no way of knowing if that was accurate or not.) A number of people I interviewed offered to approach Mrs. Kennedy for me, and I was happy for them to do so. But if they did, I never heard from them or from her. I chalked this up, rightly or wrongly, to the notorious Kennedy secrecy. A "really private man," Ted Jr. has said of his father, and "protective." Indeed, the family famously sued author William Manchester for his book on John Kennedy's assassination, *The Death of a President*—a book that they themselves had commissioned. Eventually, with the passage of time and Barnett's proscription notwithstanding, I was able to speak with many individuals who worked with the senator or who worked for him or had known him. The family, however, remained off limits. I spoke with Edward Kennedy, Jr., several times in the hope that I could persuade him to go on the record with an interview, which are the only kinds of interviews I conduct. I could not. He always hedged. In the end, only one family member spoke with me: the senator's son Patrick. He gave me a lengthy and illuminating interview, something it is unlikely any other Kennedy would have provided, and one for which I am deeply grateful.

Fortunately, Senator Kennedy had arranged for an oral history of his life, which contained not only two dozen long interviews (many of them several hours) with the senator, but also contained hundreds of interviews with family members (including his wife, Vicki), staff, colleagues, friends, supporters, advisers, and intimates of all sorts. I read every one of these when they were finally made available by the Miller Center at the University of Virginia, which organized the oral history project. They were an essential trove of information and I use them extensively in the book. Moreover, *New York Times* Washington correspondent Adam Clymer had written an earlier biography of Senator Kennedy, *Edward M. Kennedy: A Biography*, with the senator's cooperation. Under Kennedy's imprimatur, Clymer, a first-rate reporter, also interviewed dozens of the senator's intimates. Clymer made those interviews available at the John F. Kennedy Presidential Library, where I read all of them as well. They, too, are essential sources and fill many of the gaps I wished my own interviews to have filled had the family permitted.

It had been my fondest desire to examine the senator's extensive office files, the boxes of which, if laid end to end, would run a mile long. Those files had only just begun to be opened at the time this book was being written, and even then, they were being slowly processed, as is customary. Doubtless they will not be available in full to scholars for many years to come, and doubtless some future biographer, a decade or two from now, will pore over them and find new nuggets of information and quite possibly revelation. However much it pains me to say that I was not able to conduct an exhaustive search of every last document pertaining to the senator's life, that is the nature of biography. The process is always ongoing. Similarly, though I did have access to the Senate Records in the National Archives, most of which are only very lightly cataloged by session and committee, there is a twenty-year moratorium on their release, which meant that I had no access to the committee records of the last nineteen years of the senator's time in office. That pains me too.

Despite these lacunae, I like to feel that the material I did have allowed me to paint a detailed, honest, and accurate portrait of the senator, though what I said in the notes to my biography of Walt Disney also applies to Edward Kennedy. This is a big and important life—an overwhelmingly large life. I have done my best with the information available to me to examine it. I also drew conclusions about it that are mine and mine alone, which is another part of the biographical enterprise. Other biographers will likely come to different conclusions. For biographers, lives are made to be studied and then restudied, considered and then reconsidered. This life will be reconsidered too. And consequently, the bibliography that follows will need to be extended and amended in years and decades to come as scholars continue to debate the role that Edward Kennedy played in the nation's politics and governance.

BOOKS

Adams, Herbert D. *The Knife that Saves: Memoirs of a Lahey Clinic Surgeon.* Boston: Francis A. Countway Library of Medicine, 1991.

Altman, Stuart, and David Shactman. *Power, Politics and Universal Health Care: The Inside Story of a Century-long Battle.* Amherst, N.Y.: Prometheus, 2011.

Ambrose, Stephen. *Nixon: The Triumph of a Politician.* Vol. 2. New York: Simon & Schuster, 1990.

Asch, Chris Myers. *The Senator and the Sharecropper: The Freedom Struggles of James O. Eastland and Fannie Lou Hamer.* New York: New Press, 2008.

Ashby, LeRoy, and Rod Gramer. *Fighting the Odds: The Life of Senator Frank Church.* Pullman: Washington State University Press, 1994.

Baker, Richard A., and Roger H. Davidson. *First Among Equals: Outstanding Senate Leaders of the Twentieth Century.* Washington, D.C.: Congressional Quarterly, 1991.

Bell, Daniel. *The End of Ideology: On the Exhaustion of Political Ideas in the Fifties.* Cambridge, Mass.: Harvard University Press, 1988.

Berkowitz, Edward. *Robert Ball and the Politics of Social Security.* Madison: University of Wisconsin Press, 2003.

Beschloss, Michael. *Kennedy and Roosevelt: The Uneasy Alliance.* New York: W. W. Norton & Co., 1980.

Blumenthal, David, and James Morone. *The Heart of Power: Health and Politics in the Oval Office.* Berkeley: University of California Press, 2009.

Branch, Taylor. *Parting the Waters: America in the King Years 1954–1963.* New York: Simon & Schuster, 1989.

———. *Pillar of Fire: America in the King Years 1963–1965.* New York: Simon & Schuster, 1998.

Bremer, Arthur. *An Assassin's Diary.* New York: Harper's Magazine Press, 1973.

Brinkley, Douglas. *Cronkite.* New York: HarperCollins, 2012.

Burke, Richard, with Marilyn and William Hoffer. *The Senator: My Ten Years with Ted Kennedy.* New York: St. Martin's Press, 1992.

Burner, David, and Thomas R. West. *The Torch is Passed: The Kennedy Brothers and American Liberalism.* New York: Atheneum, 1984.

Burns, James M. *Edward Kennedy and the Camelot Legacy.* New York: W.W. Norton, 1976.

———. *John F. Kennedy: A Political Profile.* New York: Harcourt, Brace, 1960.

Byrd, Robert. *Child of the Appalachian Coalfields.* Morgantown: West Virginia University Press, 2005.

———. *The Senate: 1789–1989: Addresses on the History of the United States Senate.* Vol. 1. Edited by Mary Sharon Hall. Washington, D.C.: Government Printing Office, 1988.

———. *The Senate: 1789–1989.* Vol. 2. Edited by Wendy Wolff. Washington, D.C.: Government Printing Office, 1993.

Byrne, Paula. *Kick: The True Story of JFK's Sister and the Heir to Chatsworth.* New York: HarperCollins, 2016.

Califano, Joseph, Jr. *Governing America: An Insider's Report from the White House and the Cabinet.* New York: Simon & Schuster, 1981.

————. *Inside: A Public and Private Life*. New York: PublicAffairs, 2004.

Campion, Frank. *The AMA and U.S. Health Policy Since 1940*. Chicago: Chicago Review Press, 1984.

Canellos, Peter S. *Last Lion: The Fall and Rise of Ted Kennedy*. New York: Simon & Schuster, 2009.

Cannon, James. *Gerald R. Ford: An Honorable Life*. Ann Arbor: University of Michigan Press, 2013.

Caro, Robert. *Master of the Senate*. New York: Alfred A. Knopf, 2002.

————. *The Passage of Power*. New York: Alfred A. Knopf, 2012.

Chellis, Marcia. *Living with the Kennedys: The Joan Kennedy Story*. New York: Simon & Schuster, 1985.

Chester, Lewis, Godfrey Hodgson, and Bruce Page. *An American Melodrama: The Presidential Campaign of 1968*. New York: Viking Press, 1969.

Clarke, Thurston. *The Last Campaign: Robert F. Kennedy and 82 Days That Inspired America*. New York: Henry Holt, 2008.

Clifford, Clark, with Richard Holbrooke. *Counsel to the President: A Memoir*. New York: Random House, 1991.

Clinch, Nancy Gager. *The Kennedy Neurosis: A Psychological Portrait of an American Dynasty*. New York: Grosset & Dunlap, 1973.

Clymer, Adam. *Edward M. Kennedy: A Biography*. New York: William Morrow, 1999.

Cohen, Michael A. *American Maelstrom: The 1968 Election and the Politics of Division*. New York: Oxford University Press, 2016.

Collier, Peter, and David Horowitz. *The Kennedys: An American Drama*. San Francisco: Encounter Books, 2002.

Colson, Charles. *Born Again*. Old Tappan, N.J.: Chosen Books, 1976.

The Committee on the Judiciary: A Brief History. Washington, D.C.: Senate Historical Center, 2007.

Cormier, Frank. *LBJ: The Way He Was*. Garden City, N.Y.: Doubleday, 1977.

Cutler, John H. *Honey Fitz: Three Steps to the White House*. Indianapolis, Ind.: Bobbs-Merrill, 1962.

Cutler, R. B. *You the Jury . . . In Re: Chappaquiddick*. Danvers, Mass.: Betts & Mirror Press, 1973.

Dallas, Rita, and Jeanira Ratcliffe. *The Kennedy Case*. New York: G.P. Putnam's Sons, 1973.

Dallek, Robert. *An Unfinished Life: John F. Kennedy, 1917–1963*. Boston: Little, Brown, 2003.

Damore, Leo. *Senatorial Privilege: The Chappaquiddick Cover-up*. Washington, D.C.: Regnery Gateway, 1988.

Daniels, Roger. *Guarding the Golden Door*. New York: Hill & Wang, 2004.

Daschle, Thomas, and Michael D'Orso. *Like No Other Time: The 107th Congress and the Two Years That Changed America*. New York: Crown, 2003.

David, Lester. *Joan: The Reluctant Kennedy*. New York: Funk & Wagnalls, 1974.

————. *Ted Kennedy: Triumphs and Tragedies*. New York: Grosset & Dunlap, 1972.

Dean, John. *Blind Ambition: The White House Years*. New York: Simon & Schuster, 1976.

Derickson, Alan. *A Health Security for All: Dreams of Universal Health Care in America*. Baltimore, Md.: Johns Hopkins University Press, 2005.

Derthick, Martha, and Paul Quirk. *The Politics of Deregulation*. Washington, D.C.: Brookings Institution, 1985.

DeVita, Vincent, Jr., and Elizabeth DeVita-Raeburn. *The Death of Cancer: After Fifty Years on the Front Lines of Medicine, a Pioneering Oncologist Reveals Why the War on Cancer is Winnable—And How We Can Get There*. New York: Farrar, Straus & Giroux, 2015.

Dionne, E. J., Jr. *Why Americans Hate Politics*. New York: Simon & Schuster, 1991.

Doherty, Gerard. *They Were My Friends—Jack, Bob and Ted: My Life In and Out of Politics*. Wareham, Mass.: Omni, 2017.

Dranove, David. *The Economic Evolution of American Health Care: From Marcus Welby to Managed Care*. Princeton, N.J.: Princeton University Press, 2000.

Ehrlichman, John. *Witness to Power: The Nixon Years*. New York: Simon & Schuster, 1982.

Emery, Fred. *Watergate: The Corruption of American Politics and the Fall of Richard Nixon*. New York: Times Books, 1994.

Fairlie, Henry. *The Kennedy Promise: The Politics of Expectation*. Garden City, N.Y.: Doubleday, 1973.

Farrell, John Aloysius. *Richard Nixon: The Life*. New York: Doubleday, 2017.

————. *Tip O'Neill and the Democratic Century*. Boston: Little, Brown, 2001.

Formisano, Ronald. *Boston Against Busing: Race, Class, and Ethnicity*. Chapel Hill: University of North Carolina Press, 1991.

Free, Lloyd A., and Hadley Cantril. *The Political Beliefs of Americans: A Study in Public Opinion*. New Brunswick, N.J.: Rutgers University Press, 1967.

Friedan, Betty. *The Feminine Mystique*. New York: W.W. Norton, 1963.

Galbraith, John Kenneth. *A Life in Our Times.* New York: Houghton Mifflin, 1981.

Germany, Kent B., Robert David Johnson, Guian A. McKee, David Shreve, Ernest May, and Timothy Naftali, eds. *The Presidential Recordings: Lyndon B. Johnson.* New York: W.W. Norton, 2007.

Gibson, Barbara, and Ted Schwarz. *Rose Kennedy and Her Family: The Best and Worst of Their Lives and Times.* New York: Birch Lane Press, 1995.

Gjelton, Tom. *A Nation of Nations: A Great American Immigration Story.* New York: Simon & Schuster, 2015.

Goodwin, Doris K. *The Fitzgeralds and the Kennedys: An American Saga.* New York: Simon & Schuster, 1987.

————. *Lyndon Johnson and the American Dream.* New York: Harper & Row, 1976.

Goodwin, Richard. *Remembering America: A Voice from the Sixties.* Boston: Little, Brown, 1988.

Gordon, Colin. *Dead on Arrival: The Politics of Health Care in Twentieth-Century America.* Princeton, N.J.: Princeton University Press, 2003.

Goss, Kay Collet. *Mr. Chairman: The Life and Legacy of Wilbur D. Mills.* Little Rock, Ark.: Parkhurst Brothers, 2012.

Gould, Lewis. *The Most Exclusive Club: A History of the Modern Senate.* New York: Basic Books, 2005.

Greenberg, Stanley. *The Two Americas: Our Current Political Deadlock.* New York: St. Martin's Griffin, 2005.

Greenspan, Alan. *The Age of Turbulence.* New York: Penguin Press, 2007.

Halberstam, David. *The Best and the Brightest.* New York: Random House, 1972.

Haldeman, H. R. *The Haldeman Diaries: Inside the Nixon White House.* New York: G.P. Putnam's Sons, 1994.

Haldeman, H. R., with Joseph DiMona. *The Ends of Power.* New York: Times Books, 1978.

Hamilton, Nigel. *JFK: Reckless Youth.* New York: Random House, 1992.

Harris, Richard. *Decision.* New York: E.P. Dutton, 1971.

Hartmann, Robert. *Palace Politics: An Inside Account of the Ford Years.* New York: McGraw- Hill, 1980.

Hersh, Burton. *The Education of Edward Kennedy: A Family Biography.* New York: William Morrow, 1972.

————. *Edward Kennedy: An Intimate Biography.* Berkeley, Calif.: Counterpoint, 2010.

————. *The Shadow President: Ted Kennedy in Opposition.* South Royalton, Vt.: Steerforth Press, 1997.

Hodgson, Godfrey. *America in Our Time: From World War II to Nixon.* New York: Vintage Books, 1978.

Hofstadter, Richard. *The Paranoid Style in American Politics and Other Essays.* New York: Alfred A. Knopf, 1965.

Hollinger, David, ed. *The Humanities and the Dynamics of Inclusion Since World War II.* Baltimore, Md.: Johns Hopkins University Press, 2006.

Hollings, Ernest F., and Kirk Victor. *Making Government Work.* Columbia: University of South Carolina Press, 2008.

Honan, William. *Ted Kennedy: Profile of a Survivor.* New York: Quadrangle, 1972.

Humphrey, Hubert H. *The Education of a Public Man: My Life and Politics.* Minneapolis: University of Minnesota Press, 1991.

The Inquest (into the Death of Mary Jo Kopechne). New York: EVR Production & Lincoln Graphic Arts, 1970.

Jones, Rochelle. *The Private World of Congress.* New York: Free Press, 1979.

Kampelman, Max. *Entering New Worlds: The Memoirs of a Private Man in Public Life.* New York: Harper-Collins, 1991.

Kappel, Kenneth. *Chappaquiddick Revealed: What Really Happened?* New York: Shapolsky, 1989.

Karnow, Stanley. *Vietnam: A History.* New York: Penguin, 1997.

Katzenbach, Nicholas deB. *Some of It Was Fun: Working with RFK and LBJ.* New York: W.W. Norton, 2008.

Kennedy, Edward. *The Fruitful Bough.* Edited by Milton Gwirtzman. Self-published, 1965.

————. *True Compass.* New York: Twelve, 2009.

Kennedy, John F. *A Nation of Immigrants.* New York: Harper & Row, 1964.

Kennedy, Patrick, and Stephen Fried. *A Common Struggle: A Personal Journey Through the Past and the Future of Mental Illness and Addiction.* New York: Blue Rider Press, 2015.

Kennedy, Robert F., Jr. *American Values: Lessons I Learned from My Family.* New York: Harper, 2018.

Kennedy, Rose F. *Times to Remember.* Garden City, N.Y.: Doubleday, 1974.

Krugman, Paul. *The Conscience of a Liberal.* New York: W.W. Norton, 2007.

Kutler, Stanley. *The Wars of Watergate.* New York: Alfred A. Knopf, 1990.

Lange, James E. T., and Katherine DeWitt, Jr. *Chappaquiddick: The Real Story.* New York: St. Martin's Press, 1992.

Larson, Kate C. *Rosemary: The Hidden Kennedy Daughter.* Boston: Houghton Mifflin Harcourt, 2015.

Lawford, Christopher. *Symptoms of Withdrawal: A Memoir of Snapshots and Redemptions.* New York: William Morrow, 2005.

Lawrence, John. *The Class of '74: Congress After Watergate and the Roots of Partisanship.* Baltimore, Md.: Johns Hopkins University Press, 2018.

Leamer, Laurence. *The Kennedy Women: The Saga of an American Family.* New York: Villard, 1994.

Lerner, Max. *Ted and the Kennedy Legend: A Study in Character and Destiny.* New York: St. Martin's Press, 1980.

Levin, Murray. *Kennedy Campaigning: The System and Style as Practiced by Senator Edward Kennedy.* Boston: Beacon Press, 1966.

Levin, Murray, and T. A. Repak. *Edward Kennedy: The Myth of Leadership.* Boston: Houghton Mifflin, 1980.

Lewis, Anthony. *Gideon's Trumpet.* New York: Random House, 1964.

Liddy, G. Gordon. *Will: The Autobiography of G. Gordon Liddy.* New York: St. Martin's Press, 1980.

Lippman, Theo, Jr. *Senator Ted Kennedy: The Career Behind the Image.* New York: W.W. Norton, 1976.

Lowi, Theodore. *The End of the Republican Era.* Norman: University of Oklahoma Press, 1995.

Lukas, J. Anthony. *Common Ground: A Turbulent Decade in the Lives of Three American Families.* New York: Vintage Books, 1986.

———. *Nightmare: The Underside of the Nixon Years.* New York: Viking Press, 1976.

Lupo, Alan. *Liberty's Chosen Home: The Politics of Violence in Boston.* Boston: Little, Brown,1977.

Mackenzie, G. Calvin, and Robert Weisbrot. *The Liberal Hour: Washington and the Politics of Change in the 1960s.* New York: Penguin, 2008.

MacPherson, Myra. *The Power Lovers: An Intimate Look at Politics and Marriage.* New York: Charles Putnam's Sons, 1975.

Mailer, Norman. *Miami and the Siege of Chicago.* New York: Plume, 1986.

———. *St. George and the Godfather.* New York: New American Library, 1972.

Manchester, William. *The Death of a President: November 20—November 25, 1963.* Boston: Little, Brown, 1967.

Marcos, Daniel. *The Capelinhos Eruption: Window of Opportunity for Azorean Emigration.* Providence, R.I.: Gávea-Brown, 2008.

Matthews, Chris. *Jack Kennedy: Elusive Hero.* New York: Simon & Schuster, 2011.

———. *Kennedy and Nixon: The Rivalry that Shaped Postwar America.* New York: Simon & Schuster, 1996.

Mayes, Rick. *Universal Coverage: The Elusive Quest for National Health Insurance.* Ann Arbor: University of Michigan Press, 2007.

McCarthy, Abigail. *Private Faces, Public Places.* Garden City, N.Y.: Doubleday, 1972.

McCarthy, Joseph. *The Remarkable Kennedys.* New York: Dial Press, 1960.

McGovern, George. *Grassroots: The Autobiography of George McGovern.* New York: Random House, 1977.

McInerney, Thomas, and Fred L. Israel, eds. *Presidential Documents: Words That Shaped a Nation from Washington to Obama.* 2nd ed. New York: Routledge, 2013.

McNamara, Eileen. *Eunice: The Kennedy Who Changed the World.* New York: Simon & Schuster, 2018.

Meyer, Karl. *The New America: Politics and Society in the Age of the Smooth Deal.* New York: Basic Books, 1961.

Meyers, Joan, ed. *John Fitzgerald Kennedy—As We Remember Him.* New York: Atheneum, 1965.

Mooney, Booth. *LBJ: An Irreverent Chronicle.* New York: Crowell, 1976.

Moye, J. Todd. *Let the People Decide: Black Freedom and White Resistance Movements in Sunflower County, Mississippi, 1945–1986.* Chapel Hill: University of North Carolina Press, 2004.

Moynihan, Daniel Patrick. *Coping: Essays on the Practice of Government.* New York: Random House, 1973.

Nasaw, David. *The Patriarch: The Remarkable Life and Turbulent Times of Joseph P. Kennedy.* New York: Penguin, 2012.

Nelson, Donald Frederick. *Chappaquiddick Tragedy: Kennedy's Second Passenger Revealed.* Gretna, La.: Pelican , 2016.

Nelson, Garrison. *John William McCormack: A Political Biography.* New York: Bloomsbury, 2017.

Newfield, Jack. *Robert Kennedy: A Memoir.* New York: E.P. Dutton, 1969.

Nixon, Richard. *The Memoirs of Richard Nixon.* New York: Grosset & Dunlap, 1978.

Oates, Joyce Carol. *Black Water.* New York: E.P. Dutton, 1992.

Oberdorfer, Don. *Senator Mansfield: The Extraordinary Life of a Great American Statesman and Diplomat.* Washington, D.C.: Smithsonian Books, 2003.

O'Brien, Lawrence. *No Final Victories: A Life in Politics—from John F. Kennedy to Watergate.* Garden City, N.Y.: Doubleday, 1974.

O'Brien, Michael. *Philip Hart: The Conscience of the Senate.* East Lansing: Michigan State University Press, 1995.

O'Donnell, Kenneth, and David Powers. *Johnny, We Hardly Knew Ye: Memories of John Fitzgerald Kennedy.* Boston: Little, Brown, 1972.

Olsen, Jack. *Aphrodite: Desperate Mission.* New York: G.P. Putnam's Sons, 1970.

———. *The Bridge at Chappaquiddick.* Boston: Little, Brown, 1970.

O'Neill, Thomas P., and William Novak. *Man of the House: The Life and Political Memoirs of Speaker Tip O'Neill.* New York: Random House, 1987.

Oudes, Bruce, ed. *From: The President, Richard Nixon's Secret Files.* New York: Harper & Row, 1989.

Perlstein, Rick. *Before the Storm: Barry Goldwater and the Unmaking of the American Consensus.* New York: Hill & Wang, 2001.

———. *Nixonland: The Rise of a President and the Fracturing of America.* New York: Charles Scribner's Sons, 2008.

Perry, Barbara. *Rose Kennedy: The Life and Times of a Political Matriarch.* New York: W.W. Norton, 2013.

Quadagno, Jill. *One Nation Uninsured: Why the U.S. Had No National Health Insurance.* New York: Oxford University Press, 2005.

Rather, Dan, and Gary Paul Gates. *The Palace Guard.* New York: Harper & Row, 1974.

Reeves, Richard. *A Ford, Not a Lincoln.* New York: Harcourt Brace Jovanovich, 1975.

———. *President Kennedy: Profile of Power.* New York: Simon & Schuster, 1993.

———. *Richard Nixon: Alone in the White House.* New York: Simon & Schuster, 2001.

Rettig, Richard. *Cancer Crusade: The Story of the National Cancer Act of 1971.* Princeton, N.J.: Princeton University Press, 1977.

Reuther, Victor. *The Brothers Reuther and the Story of the UAW: A Memoir.* Boston: Houghton Mifflin Harcourt, 1976.

Richardson, Elliot. *The Creative Balance: Government, Politics, and the Individual in America's Third Century.* New York: Holt, Rinehart & Winston, 1976.

Risen, Clay. *The Bill of the Century: The Epic Battle for the Civil Rights Act.* New York: Bloomsbury, 2014.

Rust, Zad. *Teddy Bare: The Last of the Kennedy Clan.* Belmont, Mass.: Western Islands Press, 1971.

Scates, Shelby. *Warren G. Magnuson and the Shaping of Twentieth-Century America.* Seattle: University of Washington Press, 1997.

Schaap, Dick. *R.F.K.* New York: New American Library, 1968.

Schapsmeier, Edward, and Frederick Schapsmeier. *Dirksen of Illinois: Senatorial Statesman.* Champaign: University of Illinois Press 1985.

Schlesinger, Arthur, Jr. *The Imperial Presidency.* Boston: Houghton Mifflin Harcourt, 1973.

———. *Journals, 1952–2000.* Edited by Andrew Schlesinger and Stephen Schlesinger. New York: Penguin, 2007.

———. *The Politics of Hope and the Bitter Heritage: American Liberalism in the 1960s.* Princeton, N.J.: Princeton University Press, 2008.

———. *Robert Kennedy and His Times.* Boston: Houghton Mifflin Harcourt, 1978.

———. *A Thousand Days: John F. Kennedy in the White House* Boston: Houghton Mifflin, 1965.

Shaw, John. *JFK in the Senate: Pathway to the Presidency.* New York: St. Martin's Press, 2013.

Sheehan, Neil. *A Bright Shining Lie: John Paul Vann and America in Vietnam.* New York: Vintage Books, 1988.

Shepard, Geoff. *The Secret Plot to Make Ted Kennedy President.* New York: Sentinel, 2008.

Sherrill, Robert. *The Last Kennedy.* New York: Dial Press, 1976.

Shesol, Jeff. *Mutual Contempt: Lyndon Johnson, Robert Kennedy, and the Feud that Defined a Decade.* New York: W.W. Norton, 1997.

Shrum, Robert. *No Excuses: Concessions of a Serial Campaigner.* New York: Simon & Schuster, 2007.

Simon, Paul. *PS: The Autobiography of Paul Simon.* New York: Bonus Books, 1999.

Smith, Amanda, ed. *Hostage to Fortune: The Letters of Joseph P. Kennedy.* New York: Viking Press, 2001.

Smith, Jeffrey. *Bad Blood: Lyndon B. Johnson, Robert F. Kennedy, and the Tumultuous 1960s.* Bloomington, Ind.: AuthorHouse, 2010.

Solberg, Carl. *Hubert Humphrey: A Biography.* New York: W.W. Norton, 1984.

Sorensen, Theodore. *Counselor: A Life at the Edge of History.* New York: HarperCollins, 2008.
———. *Kennedy.* New York: Harper & Row, 1965.
———. *The Kennedy Legacy: A Peaceful Revolution for the Seventies.* New York: Macmillan, 1969.
Stein, Jean. *American Journey: The Times of Robert Kennedy.* Edited by George Plimpton. New York: Harcourt Brace Jovanovich, 1970.
Sullivan, William. *The Bureau: My Thirty Years in Hoover's FBI.* New York: W.W. Norton, 1979.
Swanson, Gloria. *Swanson on Swanson: An Autobiography.* New York: Pocket Books, 1980.
Tananbaum, Duane. *Herbert H. Lehman: A Political Biography.* Albany: SUNY Press, 2016.
Tanzer, Lester, ed. *The Kennedy Circle.* Washington, D.C.: Robert B. Luce, 1961.
Thomas, Evan. *Being Nixon: A Man Divided.* New York: Random House, 2015.
———. *Robert Kennedy: His Life.* New York: Simon & Schuster, 2000.
Tierney, Gene, and Mickey Herskowitz. *Self-Portrait.* New York: Wyden Books, 1979.
Ulasewicz, Tony, and Stuart McKeever. *The President's Private Eye: The Journey of Detective Tony U. from the N.Y.P.D. to the Nixon White House.* Westport, Conn.: MACSAM, 1990.
vanden Heuvel, William, and Milton Gwirtzman. *On His Own: RFK 1964–1968.* Garden City, N.Y.: Doubleday, 1970.
Warner, Jack L. *My First Hundred Years in Hollywood.* New York: Random House, 1964.
Whalen, Charles, and Barbara Whalen. *The Longest Debate: A Legislative History of the 1964 Civil Rights Act.* Cabin John, Md.: Seven Locks Press, 1985.
Whalen, Richard. *The Founding Father: The Story of Joseph P. Kennedy.* New York: New American Library, 1964.
White, Theodore H. *Breach of Faith: The Fall of Richard Nixon.* New York: Atheneum, 1975.
———. *The Making of the President, 1960.* New York: Atheneum, 1961.
———. *The Making of the President, 1968.* New York: Atheneum, 1969.
Wilentz, Sean. *The Age of Reagan: A History, 1974–2008.* New York: HarperCollins, 2008.
Wills, Garry. *The Kennedy Imprisonment: A Meditation on Power.* Boston: Houghton Mifflin Harcourt, 1981.
Witcover, Jules. *85 Days: The Last Campaign of Robert Kennedy.* New York: HarperCollins, 2016.
Wofford, Harris. *Of Kennedys and Kings: Making Sense of the Sixties.* New York: Farrar, Straus & Giroux, 1980.
Woodward, Bob, and Carl Bernstein. *All the President's Men.* New York: Simon & Schuster, 1974.

INTERVIEWS AND ORAL HISTORIES

Adam Clymer Personal Papers, JFK Library

Abrams, George, int., Series 2, Box 3, Folder A. June 17, 1992.

Abrams, George, int. Series 2, Box 3, Folder A. November 27, 1992.

Altman, Stuart, int. Series 2, Box 3, Folder A. September 17, 1993.

Auerbach, Stewart, int. Series 2, Box 3, Folder A. May 18, 1997.

Baker, Howard, int. Series 2, Box 3, Folder B. January 13, 1994.

Bates, Robert, int. Series 2, Box 2. September 21, 1994.

Bayh, Birch, int. Series 2, Box 3, Folder B. February 3, 1995.

Beer, Samuel, int. Series 2, Box 3, Folder B. July 2, 1993.

Bundy, McGeorge, int. Series 2, Box 3, Folder B. November 11, 1993.

Burns, Daniel B., int. Series 2, Box 3, Folder B. February 17, 1995.

Byrd, Robert, int. Series 2, Box 3, Folder B. February 12, 1993.

Carter, Jimmy, int. Series 2, Box 3, Folder C. May 15, 1998.

Clark, Blair, int. Series 2, Box 3, Folder C. January 30, 1996.

Cohouet, Frank, int. Series 2, Box 3, Folder C. March 23, 1995.

Doyle, James, int. Series 2, Box 3, Folder D. February 9, 1995.

Dutton, Fred, int. Series 2, Box 3, Folder D. July 25, 1995.

Ferris, Charles, int. Series 2, Box 3, Folder F. April 10, 1992.

Fine, Max, int. Series 2, Box 3, Folder F. June 9, 1995.

Galbraith, John Kenneth, int. Series 2, Box 3, Folder G. February 6, 1995.

Geiger, Jack, int. Series 2, Box 3, Folder G. May 18, 1995.

Gifford, Kilvert Dun, int. Series 2, Box 3, Folder G. February 2, 1996.

Gwirtzman, Milton, int. Series 2, Box 3, Folder G. January 30, 1993.

Gwirtzman, Milton, int. Series 2, Box 3, Folder G. April 3, 1993.

Healy, Robert, int. Series 2, Box 3, Folder H. July 9, 1994.

Jones, Stan, int. Series 2, Box 4, I-J Folder. November 11, 1993.

Kennedy, Edward, int. Series 2, Box 5, Edward M. Kennedy Interviews, 1992–1994 Folder. February 1992

Kennedy, Edward, int. Series 2, Box 5, Edward M. Kennedy Interviews, 1992–1994 Folder. September 10, 1992.

Kennedy, Edward, int. Series 2, Box 5, Edward M. Kennedy Interviews, 1992–1994 Folder. October 7, 1993.

Kennedy, Edward, int. Series 2, Box 5, Edward M. Kennedy Interviews, 1992–1994 Folder. October 29, 1994.

Kennedy, Edward, int. Series 2, Box 5, Edward M. Kennedy Interviews, 1995–1996 Folder. April 17, 1995.

Kennedy, Edward, int. Series 2, Box 5, Edward M. Kennedy Interviews, 1995–1996 Folder. October 9, 1995.

Kennedy, Edward, int. Series 2, Box 5, Edward M. Kennedy Interviews, 1995–1996 Folder. April 12, 1996.

Kennedy, Edward, int. Series 2, Box 5, Edward M. Kennedy Interviews, 1995–1996 Folder. October 9, 1996.

Kennedy, Edward, int. Series 2, Box 5, Edward M. Kennedy Interviews, 1997–1999 Folder. June 2, 1997.

Kennedy, Edward, int. Series 2, Box 5, Edward M.

Kennedy Interviews, 1997–1999 Folder. March 27, 1998.

Kennedy, Edward, int. Series 2, Box 5, Edward M. Kennedy Interviews, 1997–1999 Folder. September 11, 1998.

Kennedy, Joan, int. Series 2, Box 4, Folder K. January 18, 1996.

Kennedy, Joan, int. Series 2, Box 4, Folder K. December 12, 1996.

Kennedy, Joan, int. Series 2, Box 4, Folder K. October 12, 1998.

Kennedy, Joseph, II, int. Series 2, Box 4, Folder K. January 10, 1995.

Mansfield, Mike, int. Series 2, Box 4, Folder M. January 27, 1993.

McCormack, Ed, int. Series 2, Box 4, Folder M. May 15, 1992.

Senate Aide A, int. Series 2, Box 5, Unnamed Sources Folder. January 3, 1997.

Seigenthaler, John, int. Series 2, Box 5, R-Edward Kennedy Folder. September 27, 1995.

Sorensen, Theodore, int. Series 2, Box 5, Folder S. June 17, 1996.

Townsend, Kathleen Kennedy, int. Series 2, Box 5, Folder T. November 3, 1997.

Tunney, John, int. Series 2, Box 5. Folder T. March 6, 1995.

Tydings, Joseph, int., Series 2, Box 5, Folder T. June 15, 1993.

vanden Heuvel, William, int., Series 2, Box 3, Folder A-H. April 6, 1995.

Weinberger, Caspar, int., Series 2, Box 5, Folder V-Z. January 8, 1997.

James O. Eastland Collection, University of Mississippi

Eastland, James, int. , n.d. (recording)

John F. Kennedy Oral History Collection, JFK Library

Kennedy, Robert F. , int., April 13, 1964.

Raskin, Hyman, int., May 8, 1964.

LBJ Presidential Library

Clifford, Clark, int., July 14, 1969.

Knowlton, William, int., Office of Secretary General Staff for the Army. March 21, 1975.

Krim, Arthur, int., Addendum to Interview III. March 18, 1984.

Miller Center, University of Virginia

Barnes, Melody, int., August 16, 2006.

Bates, Robert, int., May 8, 2007.

Beer, Samuel, int., February 17, 2005.

Blattner, Jeffrey, int., March 30, 2007.

Breyer, Stephen, int., June 17, 2008.

Broder, David, int., December 1, 2006.

Burke, David, int., June 19, 2007.

Burke, David, int., April 9, 2008.

Caper, Philip, int., March 20, 2007.

Clasby, Richard, int., October 11, 2005.

Culver, John, int., June 5, 2007.

Culver, John, int., March 31, 2005.

Culver, John, int., September 22, 2009.

Doherty, Gerard, int., October 10, 2005.

Dole, Robert, int., May 15, 2006.

Dowd, Don, int., August 9, 2005.

Farrell, John A. , int. July 13, 2006.

Fein, Rashi, int., March 21, 2007.

Fenn, Dan, int., November 4, 2004.

Fentress, Lee, int., October 16, 2009.

Ferris, Charles, int., June 29, 2006.

Fine, Max, int., May 25, 2007.

Fitzgerald, Robert P., Sr. , int., June 18, 2009.
Gifford, Kilvert Dun, int., July 13, 2005.
Gifford, Kilvert Dun, int., July 15, 2005.
Goldman, LeRoy, int., May 5, 2007.
Gwirtzman, Milton, int., April 3, 2009.
Gwirtzman, Milton, int., May 29, 2009.
Gwirtzman, Milton, int., August 5, 2009.
Haar, Charles, int., October 10, 2005.
Hanan, Timothy, int., May 7, 2009.
Healy, Robert, int., August 10, 2005.
Healy, Mrs. Robert, int., August 10, 2005.
Hyman, Lester, int., October 6, 2008.
Jones, Stan, int., March 9, 2007.
Jones, Stan, int., September 14, 2007.
Katzenbach, Nicholas, int., November 29, 2005.
Kennedy, Kara, Patrick Kennedy, Edward
    Kennedy, Jr., int., December 9, 2009.
Kennedy, Edward, int., March 23, 2005.
Kennedy, Edward, int., June 3, 2005.
Kennedy, Edward, int., June 17, 2005.
Kennedy, Edward, int., October 14, 2005.
Kennedy, Edward, int., February 27, 2006.
Kennedy, Edward, int., May 8, 2006.
Kennedy, Edward, int., August 15, 2006.
Kennedy, Edward, int., November 29, 2006.
Kennedy, Edward, int., December 1, 2006.
Kennedy, Edward, int., January 6, 2007.
Kennedy, Edward, int., April 3, 2007.
Kennedy, Edward, int., May 30, 2007.
Kennedy, Edward, int., May 31, 2007.
Kennedy, Edward, int., August 7, 2007.
Kennedy, Edward, int., October 8, 2007.
Kennedy, Edward ,int., March 28, 2008.
Kennedy, Victoria, int., April 8, 2010.
Kirk, Paul, Jr., int., November 23, 2005.
Kirk, Paul, Jr., int., June 20, 2007.
Lahage, Barbara, int., May 8, 2008.
Littlefield, Nick, int., May 3, 2008.
Littlefield, Nick, int., February 14, 2009.
Lodge, George, int., July 8, 2005.
Lyons, Nance, int., May 7, 2008.

Lyons, Nance, int., May 9, 2008.
Martin, Edward, int., April 20, 2005.
Mikulski, Barbara, int., September 26, 2006.
Miller, Melody, int., July 15, 2008.
Miller, Melody, int., October 7, 2008.
Mondale, Walter, int., March 20, 2006.
Mongan, James, int., May 9, 2007.
Nolan, Martin, int., September 14, 2006.
Parker, Carey, int., September 22, 2008.
Parker, Carey, int., October 6, 2008.
Parker, Carey, int., October 13, 2008.
Parker, Carey, int., October 27, 2008.
Parker, Carey, int., November 10, 2008.
Parker, Carey, int., November 11, 2008.
Raclin, Curran, int., November 10, 2009.
Reggie, Victoria, int., April 8, 2010.
Reggie, Edmund, int., August 5, 2008.
Reggie, Edmund, int., December 16, 2008.
Robinson, Terri Haddad, int., August 25, 2009.
Rollins, Thomas, int., April 22, 2009.
Rollins, Thomas, int., May 14, 2009.
Schlesinger, Jr., Arthur, int., July 20, 2005.
Schneider, Mark, int., February 2, 2009.
Schneider, Mark, int., February 4, 2009.
Seigenthaler, John, int., June 5, 2007.
Shannon, Elizabeth, int.. April 28, 2009.
Shriver, Robert, III, int., January 29, 2010.
Soderberg, Nancy, int., October 9, 2008.
Sorensen, Theodore, int., May 19, 2005.
Sorensen, Theodore, int., December 7, 2006.
Souliotis, Barbara, int., July 12, 2005.
Spellings, Margaret, int., August 27, 2008.
Strauss, Anne, int., April 10, 2008.
Susman, Thomas, int., May 23, 2007.
Taymor, Betty, int., July 8, 2005.
Tretter, Charles, int., August 8, 2005.
Tunney, John, int., May 3, 2007.
Tunney, John, int., October 12, 2009.
vanden Heuvel, William, int., July 19, 2005.
vanden Heuvel, William, int., December 7,
    2006.

Richard Nixon Presidential Library

Butterfield, Alexander, int. by Timothy Naftali,
    June 12, 2008.

Colson, Charles, int., August 17, 2007.

Rose Fitzgerald Kennedy Personal Papers, JFK Library

Kennedy, Edward, int. by Robert Coughlin.
    MS 82-5.

Senate Historical Office

Hildenbrand, William, int., Oral History. 1985.
Kimmitt, J. Stanley, int., 2003.
Ludlam, Charles, Oral History. 2004.
Smathers, George, int., Oral History Interviews.
    August 1–October 24, 1989.

Valeo, Francis R., Secretary of the Senate, int.,
    Oral History Interviews. n.d.
Vander Zee, Rein J., int., January 28, 1992.

ARCHIVES, PRESIDENTIAL LIBRARIES, AND COLLECTIONS

Jimmy Carter Presidential Library.
Gerald Ford Presidential Library.
Doris Kearns Goodwin Papers, JFK Library.
Edward Kennedy, FBI Files
Lyndon Baines Johnson Presidential Library.
John F. Kennedy Presidential Library.
Joseph P. Kennedy Personal Papers, JFK Library.
Robert F. Kennedy Personal Papers, JFK Library.

Rose Fitzgerald Kennedy Personal Papers,
　JFK Library.
John F. Kraft Personal Papers. JFK Library.
Richard Nixon Presidential Library.
Joseph L. Rauh Papers, Library of Congress.
Senate Records, National Archives.
Theodore Sorensen Personal Papers,
　JFK Library.
Robert C. Wood Personal Papers, JFK Library.

RECORDINGS

Johnson, Lyndon B. Conversation with
　Edward Kennedy. June 29, 1964.
　WH6406.19. Miller Center, UVA.
Johnson, Lyndon B. Conversation with Edward
　Kennedy. August 13, 1964. WH6408.19.
　Miller Center, UVA.
Johnson, Lyndon B. Conversation with Edward
　Kennedy. November 4, 1964. WH6411.02.
　Miller Center, UVA.
Johnson, Lyndon B. Conversation with Edward
　Kennedy. January 9, 1965. WH6501.01.
　Miller Center, UVA.
Johnson, Lyndon B. Conversation with
　Edward Kennedy. March 8, 1965.
　WH6503.04. Miller Center, UVA.

Johnson, Lyndon B. Conversation with Edward
　Kennedy. May 11, 1965. WH6505.07. Miller
　Center, UVA.
Johnson, Lyndon B. Conversation with Edward
　Kennedy. June 6, 1968. WH6806.01,
　#13113. Miller Center, UVA.
Johnson, Lyndon B. Conversation with Edward
　Kennedy. December 30, 1968. WH6812.03.
　Miller Center, UVA
Nixon Conversation. June 10,1971. 005-002.
　Miller Center, UVA.
Nixon Conversation. July 2, 1971. 006-113.
　Miller Center, UVA.

ACADEMIC JOURNAL ARTICLES AND THINK TANK REPORTS

"A Creeping Doubt: Public Support for Vietnam in 1967." *Roper Center for Public Opinion Research* (August 16, 2017).https://ropercenter.cornell.edu/blog/creeping-doubt-public-support-vietnam-1967
"A Six-Hour Battle to Save Moss." *Cooley Dickinson Hospital (*June 28, 1964). cooley-dickinson.org/Main/EdwardMoss.aspx.
Converse, Philip, Warren Miller, Jerrold Rusk, and Arthur Wolfe. "Continuity and Change in American Politics: Parties and Issues in the 1968 Election." *American Political Science Review* 63, no. 4 (December 1969): 1083–105.
Gabler, Neal. "The Press and Edward Kennedy: A Case Study of Journalistic Behavior," Shorenstein Center, Harvard University, 2015.
Kalk, Bruce. "The Carswell Affair: The Politics of the Supreme Court in the Nixon Administration." *American Journal of Legal History* 42, no. 3 (July 1998): 261–87.
Kammer, Jerry. "The Hart-Celler Immigration Act of 1965." *Center for Immigration Studies*. September 30, 2015. https://cis.org/Report/HartCeller-Immigration-Act-1965.
Kennedy, Edward. "The Immigration Act of 1965." *Annals of the American Academy of Political and Social Science* 367 (September 1966): 137–49.
Kennedy, Edward. "The Unforgettable Byron White." *Yale Law Journal* 112 (2003): 973–74.
Ladd, Everett Carll, Jr. "Liberalism Upside Down: The Inversion of the New Deal Order." *Political Science Quarterly* 91, no. 4 (Winter 1976–77).
"Legends of the Law: John Nolan." *Washington Lawyer* (May 2003).
Mervin, David. "United States Senate Norms and the Majority Whip Election of 1969." *Journal of American Studies* 9, no. 3 (December 1975): 321–33.
Oleszek, Walter. "Party Whips in the Senate." *Journal of Politics* 33, no. 4 (November 1971): 955–79.
Oliphant, Thomas. "The Lion at Rest." *Democracy* (Winter 2010).
Palermo, Joseph. "The Johnson Administration Responds to Sen. Edward Kennedy." *Peace and Change* (January 1998).

"Public Opinion on Civil Rights: Reflections on the Civil Rights Act of 1964 Blog." *Roper Center for Public Opinion Research* (July 2, 2014). https://ropercenter.cornell.edu/blog/public-opinion -civil-rights-reflections-civil-rights-act-1964-blog.

Starr, Paul. "Public Health, Then and Now." *American Journal of Public Health* (January 1982): 78–88.

Steinmo, Sven, and Jon Watts. "It's the Institutions, Stupid!: Why Comprehensive National Health Insurance Always Fails in America." *Journal of American Health Politics, Policy and Law* 20, no. 2 (1995): 329–72.

Vialet, Joyce. "Summary of Developments in Immigration Law." *Immigration and Nationality Law Review* 3 (1979–80): 101–55.

MAJOR MAGAZINE ARTICLES

Ajemian, Robert. "He Did More Than Just Get Well." *Life*, January 15, 1965.

Alsop, Steward. "What Made Teddy Run?" *Saturday Evening Post*, October 27, 1962.

"The Ascent of Ted Kennedy." *Time*, January 20, 1969.

Barron, John. "Chappaquiddick: The Still Unanswered Questions." *Reader's Digest*, February 1980.

Behr, Edward. "A Day of Joy and Sadness." *Saturday Evening Post*, July 11–18, 1964.

Birmingham, Steven. "The Upward Social Climb of America's Irish Rich." *New York Magazine*, October 15, 1973.

Braden, Joan. "Joan Kennedy Tells Her Own Story." *McCall's*, August 1978.

Brower, Brock. "The Incident at Dyke Bridge." *Life*, August 1, 1969.

Carroll, James. "The End of the Dream." *New Republic*, June 24, 1991.

Cater, Douglas. "How Teddy Beat Eddie." *Reporter*, July 5, 1962.

David, Lester. "Joan—The Reluctant Kennedy." *Good Housekeeping*, June 1972.

Dunne, John Gregory. "On the Matter of Chappaquiddick." *New West*, December 3, 1979.

Farrell, Jane. "Memories of Mary Jo." *Ladies' Home Journal*, July 1989.

Fleming, Anne Taylor. "The Kennedy Mystique." *New York Times Magazine*, June 17, 1979.

Goodwin, Richard. "The Night McCarthy Turned to Kennedy." *Look*, October 15, 1968.

Greenfield, Meg. "The Senior Senator Kennedy." *Reporter*, December 15, 1966.

———. "Uhuru Comes to the Senate." *Reporter*, September 23, 1965.

"Grief, Fear, Doubt, Panic—And Guilt." *Newsweek*, August 4, 1969.

Hertzberg, Hendrik. "Ted and Harvard, 1962." *New Yorker*, August 27, 2009.

"He's Not the Same Old Ted." *Newsweek*, June 24, 1968.

Honan, William. "Is Teddy, As They Say, Ready?" *New York Times Magazine*, February 23, 1969.

"How Bobby Kennedy Won the Indiana Primary." *Newsweek*, May 19, 1968.

"In Walks Ted as the 89th Gets Under Way." *Life*, January 15, 1965.

"Joan Kennedy's Worries." *People Weekly*, June 24, 1974.

Kennedy, Edward. "The Cause of My Life." *Newsweek*, July 27, 2009.

———. "A Fresh Look at Vietnam." *Look*, February 8, 1966.

———. "The Spark Still Glows." *Parade*, November 13, 1983.

Kennedy, John F. "How TV Revolutionized Politics." *TV Guide*, November 14, 1959.

Lapham, Lewis. "Edward Kennedy and the Romance of Death." *Harper's Magazine*, December 1979.

Maas, Peter. "Ted Kennedy—What Might Have Been." *New York*, October 7, 1968.

Mailer, Norman. "Superman Comes to the Supermarket." *Esquire*, November 1960.

McMillan, Penelope. "The Troubled Marriage of Joan and Ted Kennedy." *McCall's*, November 1975.

Meroney, John. "A Conversation with Gore Vidal." *Atlantic*, October 2009.

Morgan, Thomas. "Teddy." *Esquire*, April 1962.

"The Mysteries of Chappaquiddick." *Time*, August 1, 1969.

Nixon, Richard. "What Has Happened to America?" *Reader's Digest*, October 1967.

"The Non-Candidacy of Edward Moore Kennedy." *Time*, November 29, 1971.

Packer, George. "The Empty Chamber." *New Yorker*, August 9, 2010.

———. "The Fall of Conservatism." *New Yorker*, May 26, 2008.

———. "The New Liberalism." *New Yorker*, November 17, 2008.

Peters, William. "Teddy Kennedy." *Redbook*, June 1962.

Pierce, Charles. "Kennedy Unbound After 40 Years in US Senate." *Boston Globe Magazine*, January 5, 2003.

"Pressure, Pressure." *Time*, June 15, 1962.

"Profile in Brinksmanship." *Time*, October 29, 1965.

Rhodes, Richard. "Things as They Are, Things That Never Were: The Last Kennedy." *Audience*, November–December 1971.

Roberts, Steven. "Ted Kennedy: Haunted by the Past." *New York Times Magazine*, February 3, 1980.

Rogers, Warren. "Kennedy's Comeback: Will He or Won't He?" *Look*, August 10, 1971.

———. "Ted Kennedy Talks About His Past and Future." *Look*, March 4, 1969.

Shannon, William. "The Emergence of Senator Kennedy." *New York Times Magazine*, August 22, 1965.

———. "How Ted Kennedy Survived His Ordeal." *Good Housekeeping*, April 1965.

"Teddy and Kennedyism." *Time*, September 28, 1962.

"Teddy Cracks the Whip." *Newsweek*, January 13, 1969.

"Teddy Kennedy's Decision." *Newsweek*, August 5, 1968.

"Two Senators Named Kennedy." *Newsweek*, January 17, 1966.

Weaver, Warren, Jr. "By His Deeds . . ." *Esquire*, February 1972.

Wicker, Tom. "Winds of Change in the Senate." *New York Times Magazine*, September 12, 1965.

Wright, Sylvia. "The Revival of Ted Kennedy." *Life*, October 3, 1969.

MAJOR NEWSPAPER ARTICLES

Baker, Russell. "Edward Kennedy Called Safe Bet." *New York Times*, October 12, 1962.

Barry, Dan. "Kennedy Mourners Memorialize 'Soul of the Democratic Party.' " *New York Times*, August 30, 2009.

"Bobby-Teddy Team Works for New Kennedy Era." *Washington Post*, May 12, 1965.

"Edward Kennedy Against '68 Race." *New York Times*, June 11, 1968.

Herbers, John. "Edward Kennedy Is Gaining Stature in the Senate." *New York Times*, June 2, 1967.

———. "Kennedy's Party Role." *New York Times*, August 23, 1968.

Lydon, Christopher. "A Special Kind of Grief in Massachusetts." *New York Times*, August 3, 1969.

McGrory, Mary. "Did Ed Hand Ted the Sympathy Vote?" *Boston Globe*, August 28, 1962.

Nolan, Martin. "Kennedy Dead at 77." *Boston Globe*, August 26, 2009.

Reeves, Richard. "A Publicly Moral Man." *USA Today*, August 27, 2009.

Reston, James. "Edgartown, Mass.: The Strange Case of Senator Edward Kennedy." *New York Times*, January 7, 1970.

Sales, Bob. "Senator Kennedy Jeered from Stage at Rally." *Boston Globe*, September 10, 1974.

Stocker, Carol. "Joan Kennedy: New Life, New Goals and a Sense of Excitement." *Boston Globe*, June 2, 1984.

"Ted Kennedy Acquires Humility from Rebuff." *Los Angeles Times*, August 11, 1963.

"Ted Kennedy Proves Successful Vote-Getter." *Boston Globe*, June 10, 1962.

SPEECHES AND EVENTS

Biden, Joe. "Edward Kennedy Memorial Service—(Part 1)." Boston, August 28, 2009. PoliticsNews-Politics. YouTube video, 10:35. https://www.youtube.com/watch?v=o3jzJkSxLjU.

Goldwater, Barry. "Acceptance Speech." San Francisco, July 16, 1964. https://www.washingtonpost.com/wp-srv/politics/daily/may98/goldwaterspeech.htm.

Humphrey, Hubert H. "Address to the Nation on Vietnam and American Foreign Policy." Salt Lake City, September 30, 1968. http://www2.mnhs.org/library/findaids/00442/pdfa/00442-02747.pdf.

Johnson, Lyndon B. "Voting Rights Act Address." Washington, D.C., March 15, 1965. https://www.greatamericandocuments.com/speeches/lbj-voting-rights/.

———. "President Lyndon B. Johnson Decides Not to Seek Re-election." Washington, D.C., March 31, 1968. http://www.historyplace.com/speeches/lbj-decision.htm.

Kennedy, Edward. "First Floor Speech." U.S. Senate, April 8, 1964. www.tedkennedy.org/ownwords/event/civil_rights.

———. "Hamburger Hill Speech." U.S. Senate, May 20, 1969. http://www.tedkennedy.org/ownwords/event/vietnam.html.

———. "Senator Kennedy Testifies on Reducing the Voting Age to 18 by Statute." Washington, D.C., March 9, 1970. http://www.tedkennedy.org/page/-/legacy/pdf/kennedy-speech-1970-voting-age.pdf.

———. "Ted Kennedy's Eulogy of Brother Robert." St. Patrick's Cathedral, New York, June 8, 1968.

http://www.nydailynews.com/news/politics/ted-kennedy-eulogy-brother-robert-st-patrick
-cathedral-new-york-city-june-8-1968-article-1.394707.

Kennedy, Patrick. "Kennedy's Funeral: Patrick Remembers," Boston, August 29, 2009. YouTube
video, 7:51, https://www.youtube.com/watch?v=MbfXTaT9sZ4.

Kennedy, Robert F. "Announcement of Candidacy for President." Washington, D.C., March 16, 1968.
http://www.4president.org/speeches/rfk1968announcement.htm.

———. "Primary Victory Speech." Los Angeles, June 5, 1968. http://jfk.hood.edu/Collection/White%20
Materials/White%20Assassination%20Clippings%20Folders/Kennedy%20Family%20Folders/
Kennedy%20Robert%20F/RFK%200391.pdf.

———. "Unwinnable War Speech (1968)." Chicago, February 8, 1968. http://teach.yauger.net/us/
vietnam/rfkvietnam.pdf.

McCain, John. "McCain Remembers Teddy." Boston, August 28, 2009. YouTube video, 6:28.
https://www.youtube.com/watch?v=7_KN7d6mts4.

"Nation Remembers Ted Kennedy." August 29, 2009. http://www.cnn.com/2009/POLITICS/08/29/
ted.kennedy.videos/index.html.

Obama, Barack. "Eulogy Delivered at Sen. Ted Kennedy Funeral." Boston, August 29, 2009.
https://abcnews.go.com/Politics/TedKennedy/story?id=8441986.

Schmidt, Benno. "Remarks at Meeting of President's Cancer Panel." National Cancer Institute, December 9, 1986.

CONGRESSIONAL HEARINGS

U.S. Congress. Senate. Subcommittee on Administrative Practice and Procedure. Hearings on Selective
Service System Procedures and Administrative Possibilities for Amnesty. 93rd Congress, 2nd session, 1974.

U.S. Congress. Senate. Subcommittee on Health of the Committee on Labor and Public Welfare. Health
Care Crisis in America. 92nd Congress, 1st session, 1971.

U.S. Congress. Senate. Subcommittee on Immigration and Naturalization of the Committee on the
Judiciary. Immigration Hearings. 89th Congress, 1st session, 1965.

OTHER MEDIA AND SOURCES

Bebinger, Martha. "Kennedy Remembered as Senate's Hardest-Working Man." WBUR, August 26,
2009. wbur.org/2009/08/26/kennedy-tributes.

Carroll, Joseph. "Americans Grew to Accept Nixon's Pardon." Gallup, May 21, 2001. https://news
.gallup.com/poll/3157/americans-grew-accept-nixons-pardon.aspx.

Cohen, Michael A. "LBJ Drops Out of 1968 Presidential Race." Oxford University Press Blog, April 2,
2016. https://blog.oup.com/2016/04/lbj-drops-out-1968/.

Curran, John, dir. Chappaquiddick. Century City, Los Angeles: Entertainment Studios, 2018.

Deane, Elizabeth, prod. "The Kennedys," American Experience. WGBH, 1992.

Kennedy, Victoria Reggie. Interview by Oprah Winfrey. Oprah Winfrey Show, November 25, 2009.

Kirk, Michael, prod. "Obama's Deal." Frontline. PBS, April 13, 2010.

Llewellyn, Jennifer, Jim Southey, and Steve Thompson. "U.S. Escalation in Vietnam." Alpha History,
June 22, 2019. https://alphahistory.com/vietnamwar/us-escalation-in-vietnam/.

Rauh, Joseph. Interview by Eyes on the Prize. October 31, 1985. Washington University in St. Louis
video, 40:20. http://repository.wustl.edu/concern/videos/rj430634r.

Saad, Lydia. "Gallup Vault: A Look Back at Robert Kennedy." Gallup, June 5, 2018. https://news
.gallup.com/vault/235283/gallup-vault-look-back-robert-kennedy.aspx.

Staedter, Tracy. "How John F. Kennedy's Back Pain Affected His Life and Death." Live Science, July 11,
2017. www.livescience.com/59764-john-f-kennedy-back-pain-affected-life-and-death.html.

"U.S. Involvement in Vietnam." CBS News, January 28, 2018. https://www.cbsnews.com/news/cbs
-news-poll-u-s-involvement-in-vietnam/.

INDEX

Key to abbreviations:
Lyndon Baines Johnson = LBJ
Edward Moore Kennedy = EMK
John F. Kennedy = JFK
Joseph Kennedy, Sr. = JPK
Robert F. Kennedy = RFK
Franklin Delano Roosevelt = FDR

ABC News, 312
   EMK's Senate run and, 140–41
Abel, I. W., 595
Abernathy, Ralph, 708
Abrams, Creighton, 591–92
Abrams, George, 264, 293, 295, 296, 298,
   312–13, 323, 334, 617
   EMK's *Look* piece on Vietnam and, 317–18
Acheson, Dean, 310
Adams, Eddie, 356
Adams, Gerry, xxvii
Adams, Herbert D., 237, 248, 642
Adams, John, 6
Adams, Rich, xxvi
Adenauer, Konrad, 225
Aeschylus, 372
AFL–CIO (American Federation of Labor–
   Congress of Industrial Organization), 286,
   377
   Carswell nomination and, 529
   EMK and Hart at Detroit convention,
   presidential hopes and (1974), 717–18
   national health insurance and, 645, 650, 651,
   682–83
   See also Meany, George
African Americans
   Civil Rights Act of 1964 passed, 227
   Democratic Party and, 247
   EMK and forced busing, 719–36
   EMK and the March on Washington, 218, 712
   EMK and sickle cell anemia research, 712
   EMK's bill to treat lead-based paint poisoning,
   712–13
   EMK's commitment to, 173, 450
   EMK's first African American staff member,
   448

   EMK's poll tax fight, 194, 276–89, 331, 346,
   449
   EMK's standing among, 288, 400, 707, 708,
   712, 713
   JFK and, 112, 217, 227, 712
   LBJ and, 227, 252, 342–43
   Moynihan's report on the "Negro family," 464
   Nixon's attitude toward helping, 556
   presidential campaign (1968) and, 400
   Republican Party and, 325, 712
   RFK and, 217, 342, 712
   Voting Rights Act of 1965 passed, 289
   voting rights and, 252, 276–77, 278, 280
   white supremacy and, 197, 226
   See also civil rights
Agnew, Spiro, 520, 634–35, 636, 637, 691
Ahlbum, Jon, 482
Aiken, George, 497, 706
Albert, Carl, 271, 413, 635, 691
Albert Lasker Medical Journalism Awards, EMK
   speech on national health care, 649
Aldrin, Edwin "Buzz," 485
Alexander, Lamar, 328
Algeria, 76
Ali, Muhammad, 674
Allen, James, 693
Allen, Richard, 580
Alsop, Joseph, 31–32, 573, 594
Alsop, Stewart, 147, 176, 185, 557
   "Why Do They Hate Him So?," 379
Altman, Stuart, 667, 677, 686
American Association for Labor Legislation,
   643
*American Dilemma, An: The Negro Problem and
   Modern Democracy* (Myrdal), 659
American Enterprise Institute, 578

American Medical Association (AMA), 644, 670
  cancer legislation and, 662
  Kennedy-Mills-Weinberger plan and, 688
  national health care plan (Medicredit), 649,
    650, 681, 688, 689
American Presidency, The (Rossiter), 614
American Public Health Association, 642
Americans for Democratic Action (ADA), 529,
    595, 606–7
  EMK's speech on Vietnam, 341, 343
Americans With Disabilities Act, xix
Anderson, Clinton, 251
Anderson, Jack, 500, 621, 622–23, 622n, 625,
    626
Anderson, Wendell, 607
Andy Williams Show, The (TV show), 546–47
anti-ballistic missile system (ABM)
  Chayes–Wiesner report, 455
  EMK fight against, 452–56, 519–20, 524
  National Citizens Committee Concerned
    About Deployment of the ABM, 455
Antonelli, Theresa, xxx
Apple, Johnny, 562, 563
Arena, Dominick, 482, 483, 503, 508, 508n, 511
Arkansas, 173, 668
  Fort Chaffee, 67
  segregationists group, Hyannis Port cook and,
    218
  See also McClellan, John; Mills, Wilbur
Arlington Cemetery
  EMK visiting his brothers' graves, 439
  JFK's permanent plot in, 336, 543
  RFK's burial in, 388
arms control, 117, 158, 453–54
  EMK's ABM system fight and, 452–56,
    519–20, 524
Armstrong, Neil, 485
Arredondo, Carlos and Melida, xxvi
Arthur Little consulting firm, 510n
Ashbrook, John, 722
Association of American Medical Colleges,
    662
Astor, Vincent, 16
Atlanta Constitution
  editorial on EMK immorality and
    Chappaquiddick, 496
Attlee, Clement, 1st Earl Attlee, 76
Auchincloss, Kenneth, xxxiii
Auerbach, Stuart, 673
Azorean Refugee Act of 1958, 267

Bachelet, Michelle, 617
Bailey, John, 104
Baker, Bobby, 104, 200
Baker, Howard, Jr., 328, 330, 331, 630
Baker, Russell, 172, 176
Ball, George, 311, 332
Ball, Robert, 680

Baltimore Sun
  on EMK and Chappaquiddick, 496
Bangladesh, 585–86
Barker, Bernard, 621
Barkley, Alben, 438
Barnicle, Mike, 726
Bartlett, Charles, 185, 311, 401
Bashista, Joanne, 232–33
Bashista, Walter, 232–33
Bates, Robert
  black issues and, 448, 450, 712, 713
  Boston violence over forced school busing
    and, 726–27, 728, 729
  on Chappaquiddick's impact on EMK, 525, 648
  as EMK's first black staff member, 448
Baumgold, Julie, 608
Bayh, Birch, 435, 445, 559, 560
  Carswell nomination and, 529–30, 531
  Electoral College amendment and, 529
  EMK's plane crash and, 230–34, 239
  as freshman senator with EMK, 181, 182, 193,
    228
  Haynsworth nomination and, 528
  Joan Kennedy campaigning for, 243
  Nixon targeting, 532
  Voting Rights Act and, 279
  Watergate investigation and, 631, 640
Bayh, Marvella, 193, 230
  EMK and plane crash, 230–33
Beall, J. Glenn, Jr., 652
Beard, Dita, 623–24
Beatrix, Crown Princess, 244
Beaverbrook, Lord (Max Aitken), 90, 96
Beck, Józef, 130
Bedford Stuyvesant Restoration Corporation, 378
Beer, Samuel
  as EMK advisor, 138, 140, 447, 734
  on EMK as Senate majority whip and "shadow
    president," 447
  on EMK's pain, 541
  as EMK's tutor after plane crash, 240, 241,
    249–50
  on how EMK learned, 647
Bell, Daniel, 111
Bellino, Carmine, 630
Bellmon, Henry, 467
Bellotti, Francis, 230
Benedict XVI, Pope, xxxii
Ben-Gurion, David, 130
Bennett, Candy (sister-in-law), 85, 206, 545
Bennett, Harry, Jr. (father-in-law), 85, 89
Bennett, Harry, Sr., 84–85
Bennett, Tony, xxvii
Bentsen, Lloyd, 649, 660
Bergen, Candice, 580
Berkshire Eagle
  on EMK as a prince, 150
Berlin, Germany, 130

Bernstein, Carl, 621–22, 627, 628, 632–33
Biafra, 430–31
Bickel, Alexander, 527
Biddle, Anthony, 68
Biden, Joseph "Joe"
  advice to EMK, 641
  EMK's kindness to, xxv
Biemiller, Andrew, 529, 682
Billings, LeMoyne, 51, 52, 57, 114, 146, 548
  Chappaquiddick incident and, 487
Birmingham, Ala., 217, 276
  church bombing, 226
  protests, 217
Black, Hugo, 561
Blackmun, Harry, 532
Black Water (Oates), 517
Blanchard, James, 698
Blattner, Jeffrey, xx–xxi, 241
Bloom, Lillian, 656
Blumenthal Sacred Heart School, Holland, 19
Bo, Mai Van, 566
Bobst, Elmer, 662, 664
Boggs, Hale, 413
Boland, Edward, 313, 345, 346, 405
Bolling, Richard, 679
Book of Wisdom 3:1–9, xxviii
Bork, Robert, 638
Boston, Mass.
  anti-Catholic bias and, 9, 11, 12, 12–13, 14,
    39, 539
  Basilica of Our Lady of Perpetual Help, xxvi,
    xxvii
  Boston Common, xv
  Brahmins and Yankee pride in, 7, 9, 10, 12, 15,
    95, 439
  Catholic-Protestant hostility in, 8–9, 539
  Collins as mayor, 230
  Columbia Point Health Center, 321, 642
  Cunard shipping and, 8
  Curley as mayor, 4, 123
  Democratic Irish establishment, 6
  EMK and Joan's home, Charles River Square,
    119, 133, 166, 172, 203
  EMK and school busing, Irish-black tensions,
    EMK's loss of Irish support, xv, xxxi,
    719–36, 733n
  EMK faces anti-busing mobs, 727–28, 731–33,
    735
  EMK's apartment, Bowdoin St., 126, 127, 142,
    160, 562
  EMK's funeral and motorcade, xiv, xv,
    xxiii–xxvi, xxx, xxxi
  EMK's popularity in, 535
  EMK's relationship with, 724–25
  EMK's Senate office in, xv, 724
  EMK's Senate run (1961) and, 117, 121, 123,
    124, 126, 128, 129, 134–35, 136–37, 157,
    159, 161, 164, 168–69
  EMK's speech to World Affairs Council on
    Vietnam, 352–53, 354
  Faneuil Hall, xv, 724
  Fitzgerald as mayor, 4, 7, 39
  Irish Catholic population, 8
  Irish cultural inheritance in, 8
  Irish immigration to, 8
  JFK library, xv, xvii, xxii, xxiv, xxvi
  John F. Kennedy Federal Building, 724
  JPK moves from, 12
  Kennedy family history and, 724
  Locke-Ober restaurant, 128
  mayor, Thomas Menino, xv
  McCormacks and Democratic politics, 123
  McCormacks vs. Kennedys in, 124
  Morgan v. Hennigan, 721
  Peters as mayor, 4
  Restore Our Alienated Rights (ROAR), 725,
    729, 731
  Rose Fitzgerald Kennedy Greenway, xv
  School Committee, 721, 722, 725
  "shanty Irish" and "lace-curtain Irish," 9, 721
  Sully's tavern, 734
  VAULT group, 539
  White as mayor, 119, 600
Boston Children's Hospital, 674, 677
Boston Globe
  Barnicle's "open letter" to EMK, 726
  on Carswell nomination, 530, 531–32
  on Chappaquiddick incident, 483–84, 497,
    515, 516, 517, 715
  on EMK and the Democratic ticket (1968), 411
  on EMK as a negotiator, 683
  on EMK as vice presidential pick (1972), 599
  EMK refuses presidential run (1974), 718
  on EMK's cheating scandal, 134–36
  EMK's funeral and, xv
  on EMK's liberalism, 710–11
  on EMK's recovery following Chappaquiddick,
    535
  on EMK's Senate address on the civil rights
    bill, 223
  on EMK's Senate reelection (1970), 562
  on EMK's Senate run (1961), 129, 157
  EMK's series on Latin America in, 125
  Healy and Nixon, 466
  Healy as executive editor, 291
  on JFK and Morrissey, 290, 290n
  on JFK campaign "tea," 95
  JFK leaks EMK's run for the Senate, 117
  JPK interview, "Democracy is all done," 33
  on Morrissey judicial appointment, 298, 299,
    300
  "A Swelling Tide of Emotion," xvi
Boston Herald (*Boston Herald Traveler*), 127, 161
  EMK's Senate run and, 126, 128, 153
Boston Latin School, 6–7, 9
Boston Red Sox, xv

Boston University
   EMK as trustee, 125–26
   Law School, 123
   Medical Center, EMK speech at, 648
Bourguiba, Habib, 76
Boyle, William, 504, 505, 506, 508, 512, 562
Braden, Tom, 513
Brandeis, Louis, 300
Brandt, Willy, 130, 709
Branigin, Roger, 368, 373, 376
Brasfield, Brad, 529
Brazil, 617, 618
Bremer, Arthur, 596, 620
Breslin, Jimmy, 372, 403, 700
Brewer, Basil, 126
Breyer, Stephen, xxvii, 537, 541
Brezhnev, Leonid, 638, 700
Bridge at Chappaquiddick, The (Olsen), 621
Bridgewater State Teachers College
   EMK's commencement address, 716
Brinkley, David, 388
Broder, David, 331, 514, 535, 597, 608
Bronxville, N.Y.
   EMK and, 35–36
   EMK's devastation at home's sale, 36
   EMK's wife Joan and, 84, 102
   Kennedy estate in, 12, 29, 30–31, 35, 41, 84
   St. Joseph's Roman Catholic Church, 85, 88
Brooke, Edward, 530, 593, 725, 734
Brookings Institution, 578
Brookline, Mass., 4, 12
   Edward Devotion School, 24
   JFK's birthplace, firebombing of, 733, 733n
Brooks, David, xviii, xx
Brower, Brock, 468, 477
Brown, Edmund, Jr., 718
Brown v. Board of Education, 217, 284, 527, 659, 719, 720, 724
Bruno, Jerry, 361
Buchanan, Pat, 424–25, 588, 589, 605, 610, 632–33
Buchwald, Art, 597–98, 602
Bulger, Billy, 128
Bulger, Whitey, 733n
Bundy, McGeorge, 135, 318, 369
Bundy, William, 313, 335
Bunker, Ellsworth, 350, 353–54, 355
Burden, Amanda, 551–52, 601
Burdick, Quentin, 183
Burger, Warren, 528
Burke, Beatrice, 482, 523–24
Burke, David, 403
   California primary (1968) and, 380–81
   Chappaquiddick incident and, 480, 482, 484, 487, 489, 491, 492
   departure from EMK's staff, 523–24
   EMK and Democratic ticket (1968), 406–7, 408, 409–10, 414

   EMK and foreign policy, 336
   EMK and lowering the voting age, 559, 560
   EMK and the Vietnam War, 316, 337
   EMK as majority whip and, 446, 566, 570
   EMK's back problems and, 273
   EMK's decisiveness after RFK's death, 450
   EMK's grief for RFK and, 403
   EMK's immigration bill, 271–72
   EMK's *Look* piece on Vietnam and, 317–18
   EMK's Morrissey appointment and, 294, 297, 305
   EMK's poll tax fight and, 277–81, 285
   EMK's presidential ambitions, 379
   EMK's presidential prospects (1976) and, 705, 706, 717, 718
   EMK's running for Senate majority whip and, 433, 434, 437, 444
   EMK's second Vietnam fact-finding trip and, 348–51
   EMK's Senate reelection 1970 and, 563
   on EMK's Senate staff, 261, 262, 263–65
   EMK's staff enlargement and, 448
   EMK's Vietnam debriefing meeting with LBJ and, 351–52
   EMK's womanizing and, 550
   RFK's assassination and, 381–82, 383
   RFK's eulogy and, 386
   RFK's presidential candidacy and, 345, 365, 373, 377
   Vietnam negotiations and, 592–93
   Vietnam War and, 458, 565
Burke, Richard, 676
Burke, William "Onions," 124, 228–29
Burley, Nancy, 52
Burns, Arthur, 195
Burns, James MacGregor, 140, 201, 551, 593, 612, 714, 724
   on "Camelot decision-making," 110
Burns, John, 5–6
Burton, Phillip, 382
Butterfield, Alexander, 578, 633, 692
Byrd, Harry, 220
Byrd, Robert, xxx, 184, 260, 445, 635
   background, 567–68
   on EMK, xviii
   Senate majority whip position and, 567–71, 652
Byrne, Garrett, 118, 120

Cain, Virginia, xiv
Califano, Joseph, Jr., 300, 442, 516, 575, 631–32
California
   delegates, DNC (1968) and "draft Ted," 408
   presidential primary (1968), 380–81
   RFK assassination, 381–85
Calley, William, 589
campaign-finance reform, 692
Campion, Frank, 649
Camus, Albert, 375, 396

Canellos, Peter, 206
Cannon, Howard, 635
Cannon, Lou, 612, 707
Caper, Philip, 654, 655, 656, 671, 672, 673, 712
Cardozo, Benjamin, 277
Carey, Ted, 73
Caro, Robert, xx, xxxv–xxxvi, 462
Caroline (plane), 234, 249, 264
Carroll, James
  "The End of the Dream," xxi, 213
Carswell, G. Harrold, 529–32, 711
Carter, Jimmy, 516
Carter, Tim Lee, 666
Case, Clifford, 618
Case, Harold, 125–26
Cassini, Oleg, 547
Castro, Fidel, 269, 308, 621, 703
Caulfield, Jack, 499, 500, 532
Cavanaugh, Father John, 64, 88
CBS
  national health care documentary, 649
  RFK's presidential candidacy and, 362
  Schieffer on EMK's social legislation, xix
Celebrezze, Anthony, 158
Celler, Emanuel, 269, 270, 271, 327, 328, 329,
    559, 560
Chamberlain, Neville, 30, 31
Chambers, Whittaker, 604n
Chappaquiddick (film), 517–18
Chappaquiddick incident, xvii, xxviii, xxxi, xxxv,
    471–518, 471n
  account of accident and aftermath, 476–83,
    481n
  alcohol consumption and, 474–75
  court hearing on, 503
  depictions of EMK afterward, 517–18
  Dike Bridge, 471, 477, 508, 512
  district attorney's reopening of investigation,
    503–4
  EMK and moral absolution, 490, 491, 516,
    525–26, 648
  EMK as changed afterwards, 524–25, 527,
    532, 535–36
  EMK's aging, weight loss, and, 498, 503, 519,
    520–21, 525
  EMK's fatigue and, 471, 473
  EMK's friends and advisors gather after,
    486–89
  EMK's grief over, 480, 483, 486, 516–17
  EMK's injuries, 484, 486, 489
  EMK's legal status, 486, 488, 489, 506–7
  EMK's physical and mental state, 479–80,
    481, 483, 484, 489, 490, 491, 493–94, 495,
    508–9
  EMK's presidential prospects and, 486, 489,
    491, 513, 589, 599, 608, 634, 714–15,
    718–19
  EMK's recovery following, 535
  EMK's Senate seat and, 489–90
  EMK's statement about, 490–91, 493–97
  EMK's vehicle, 471, 475, 482, 500
  gathering of "boiler-room girls" and, 472–73,
    474
  inquest testimony, doubts, and theories,
    504–13, 508n
  Joan's miscarriage and, 501–2
  Kennedy image and, 543
  Kopechne and, 475–80, 482, 489, 490,
    491–93
  likeliest explanation, 511–13
  long-lasting consequences of, 513–18, 551
  loss of moral authority and, 522, 524, 543,
    582, 634, 647, 651
  media coverage, 485, 486, 495–96, 503, 512,
    513, 516–17, 519
  "The Memory That Would Not Fade," 715
  Nixon response and investigation, 498–501
  Nixon's wiretaps and, 501
  politicians' reaction to, 496–97
  Poucha Pond, 471, 476–77, 478, 479, 482,
    499, 508
  public's response to, 497–98, 513
  ugly speculation and, 494, 496
Chavez, Cesar, 362
  EMK marching with, 450–51
Chayes, Abram, 453, 454
Cheney, Dick, 704
Chicago, Ill.
  anti-war protests at DNC (1968), 404, 407, 409
  Democratic National Convention (1968),
    404–16
  La Salle Hotel, 408
  Sherman House Hotel, 408
  Standard Club, 406
  See also Daley, Richard J.
Chicago Tribune
  calls RFK "Ho Chi Kennedy," 319
  Chappaquiddick incident and, 485
Chile, 617
China, 202, 309, 459
  Nixon and, 588, 703, 708
Choate School, Wallingford, Conn., 143
Chotiner, Murray, 562, 578
Christian Science Monitor
  on Chappaquiddick incident, 496
Christopher, Warren, 632
Church, Frank, 108, 117, 445, 587, 617, 618
Churchill, Winston, xxi–xxii
CIA (Central Intelligence Agency), 314, 509,
    604n, 695, 704
  Bay of Pigs and, 135, 308
  Evans as former operative, 188, 263
  Hunt as former operative, 580, 621, 622n
Citadel (White), 191
civil rights
  barriers to legislation, 198

civil rights (*cont'd*):
    Birmingham, Ala. church bombing, 226
    Birmingham, Ala. protests, 217
    blue-collar whites and, 425, 723
    Brown v. Board of Education and, 217, 284,
       527, 659, 719, 720, 724
    Carswell judicial nomination and, 530–31
    Democratic National Convention (1948) and,
       277–78
    Democratic National Convention (1964),
       black delegation seated and, 278
    Democratic Party and, 424, 605
    desegregating public accommodations, 201
    EMK, turning point for, 218
    EMK and, 173, 320, 327
    EMK and Civil Rights Act of 1991, xix
    EMK and forced school busing, xv, xxxi, 719–36
    EMK and Voting Rights Act amendments,
       xviii–xix, 558–61
    EMK and Voting Rights Act and poll tax fight,
       276–89, 328, 329, 346, 439, 449
    Freedom Riders, 217, 226
    Humphrey and, 376–77, 389
    integration and, 217
    JFK and, xxxiv, 204, 216–19, 712
    JFK's civil rights bill, 194, 217–18, 219
    JFK's moral authority and, 275
    JFK's presidency and, 112, 213
    Kennedy family and, xxiii
    LBJ and, xxxiv, 218–19, 247
    liberalism and, 389
    March on Washington, 218, 243, 278, 712
    Nixon and, 591, 603
    one man, one vote and "gerrymandering"
       problem, 327
    Republicans and, 771n227
    RFK and, 217, 218, 712, 377
    school integration, xv, 719–23
    urban riots (1967) and, 340
    U.S. Senate and, 191
    Wallace at the school house door and, 217
    "white backlash," 325
Civil Rights Act of 1957, 190, 218, 219, 220
Civil Rights Act of 1960, 190
Civil Rights Act of 1964, xxxv, 194, 199, 217–27,
    245, 253, 276, 320, 325, 426, 444, 711,
    712, 772n227
    EMK and passage of, 224–27
    EMK's Senate speech, 221–23, 275
    equal employment provision, 221
    filibuster and, 221, 221n, 226
    as honoring JFK's memory, 223, 225, 226
    LBJ and, xxxv, 223, 224, 226
    as victory for morality, 227
Civil Rights Act of 1991, xix
Clancy, Hal, 126, 127, 128, 161
Clark, Blair, 363, 364
Clark, Joseph, 338

Clark, Robert, 487
Clark, Robert, III, 487
Clarke, Thurston, 371
Clasby, Richard "Dick," 60–61, 73, 82, 89, 113,
    115, 533
Clay, Henry, xv
Clifford, Clark, 114, 185, 360, 639
Clymer, Adam, 86, 308, 339, 491, 598, 809n569
Cohen, Wilbur, 669
Colby, William, 704
Cold War, 97, 308, 309
    LBJ and, 311
Cole, Ken, 664
Cole, Vicki Lynne, 584
Coles, Robert, 344, 672
College of the Holy Cross, 402
Collins, John, 230
Collins, Michael, 485
Colson, Charles, 562, 604, 622n, 623, 624
    EMK targeted by, 580, 588, 594, 621
    Nixon's dirty tricks and, 581, 620, 666
Columbia Trust Company, 6, 9, 10, 540
Committee for National Health Insurance
    (Committee of 100), 642, 643, 645, 646n,
    647, 679
    Chappaquiddick incident, impact on EMK's
       moral authority and, 648
Common Cause, 692
Common Ground (Lukas), 735
communism, 97
    Chile and, 617
    containment and, 417
    Democrats and perception of being soft on,
       308, 309, 310, 320
    "domino theory," 311
    EMK's view on colonialism and, 77
    immigration policy and, 267, 270
    Indochina and Vietnam, 308, 311
    JPK, McCarthy, and, 95
    Vietnam and, 311, 326, 331
    U.S. foreign policy and, 111
    "Who Lost China?," 309, 459
Connally, John, 610, 634, 635, 691
Connors, Bill, 731
conservatism, xxxi, 85, 97, 110, 155, 214, 221,
    244, 247, 252, 296, 309, 373, 375, 417, 506,
    510, 527, 562, 578, 610, 631, 652, 703, 706,
    722, 734, 735
    Bentsen and, 649
    blue-collar Democrats and, 609
    delegitimizing liberalism, xxii
    Dirksen and, 771n227
    Ford and, 635, 703
    JPK, Joe, Jr. and, 537
    media and, xxxv, 126, 128, 368, 485, 557
    nation's shift to, xxi, xxii, xxiii, xxxv, 424,
       443
    Nixon and, 465, 582, 604, 607, 647, 698

postwar, 428
  Senate and, 190, 196, 201, 252, 266, 270,
    278, 280, 322, 327, 445
Consolidated Omnibus Budget Reconciliation
    Act of 1985, xix
Conyers, John, 328
Cook, Howard, 689
Cooley Dickinson Hospital, Northampton,
    Mass., 233–37
Coolidge, Calvin, 14
Cooper, John Sherman, 453, 520, 587, 649
Cooper, Ted, 686
Corbin, Paul, 399
Cordaro, Phil, 125
Corman, James, 645, 650–51, 688
Corriden, Thomas, 234
Council of Economic Advisers, 111
Cowan, Paul, 389
Cox, Archibald, 558–59
  firing of, 636–38
  Senate testimony of, 639–40
  as Watergate special prosecutor, 632–33,
    635–36
Cox, William Harold, 217
Cranston, Alan, 445, 597, 659, 703
Cranwell School, Lenox, Mass., 49
Crimmins, Jack, 127, 147, 173, 233, 234, 563–64,
    718, 731, 733
  Chappaquiddick incident and, 471, 472, 474,
    475, 477
Cronkite, Walter, 362, 600
  Vietnam War and, 369
Cuba, 125, 269, 588, 703
  Bay of Pigs invasion, 308
  refugees and, 584
Cuban Missile Crisis, 174–76, 178, 179, 309
Culver, John, xxv, 49–50, 263, 345, 429
  Chappaquiddick incident and, 487
  as congressman, 307
  on EMK and football, 60
  on EMK and RFK in the Senate, 258
  on EMK's childhood unhappiness, 50
  EMK's grief for RFK and, 387
  as EMK's Harvard roommate and friend, 49,
    58, 70
  EMK's Senate run and, 127, 138, 147
  on EMK's Senate staff, 187–88, 193, 195
  gift to EMK, 203
  JFK and, 60–61
  JFK's assassination and, 209
  loyalty and, 127
  Vietnam fact-finding mission and, 307,
    313
Cunard, Samuel, 8
Curley, James Michael, 4, 123
Curtis, Carl, 260
Cushing, Richard Cardinal, 118, 222, 289
Cutler, Jay, 661, 665

Daley, Richard J., 101, 359–60, 400, 401, 424
  anti-war protests at DNC (1968) and, 407
  Chappaquiddick incident and, 497
  DNC floor fight (1968) and, 413
  EMK and Democratic ticket (1968), 407–8,
    410, 412, 413–14
Daley, William "Bill," 410
Dallas, Rita
  Chappaquiddick incident and, 477, 484, 488,
    489, 493, 533–34
  on EMK after RFK's death, 394–95, 400
  on EMK and JFK, 112, 113
  on EMK and JPK's stroke, 169, 533
  on EMK's personality, 145, 249, 393
  on EMK's plane crash, 248, 249
  on Gargan, 474, 488
  on the Kennedys, 110
  on the Kennedy's reaction to JFK's death, 207,
    210
Dallek, Robert, 115, 217
Damore, Leo, 510–11
Daschle, Tom, xviii, 609, 610
Dash, Sam, 630, 635
David, Lester, 165, 205n, 211, 212, 233, 242,
    380, 382, 484, 521, 545, 546, 575
Davis–Bacon Act of 1931, 542
Dean, John, 501, 581
  Watergate scandal and, 622, 630, 633
Death of a President, The (Manchester), 205n,
    206–7
DeBakey, Michael, 648
de Gaulle, Charles, 225, 340, 551, 580
DeHaan, Dale, 313, 617, 619
DeLoach, Cartha, 294
Democratic Party
  in Boston, 6
  Chappaquiddick incident's consequences for,
    515–16, 582, 595–96, 634
  civil rights and, 277
  Daley–Rizzo Democrats, 424
  divisions within, 605
  election results (1972), 611
  EMK after Chappaquiddick and, 526, 583
  EMK as presumptive presidential nominee
    (1972), 443, 447, 449, 460–61, 513
  EMK campaigning for candidates, 256, 323,
    337, 564
  EMK campaigning for Humphrey, 419–20,
    422–23
  EMK campaigning for McGovern, 607–8
  EMK heading, 450
  EMK's National Convention address (1980),
    xv
  EMK vice president offer (1968), 399–400,
    403–4, 405, 415–16
  FDR coalition in, 179
  JPK and cash for support, 104
  Kennedys loyalty to, 14

Democratic Party (*cont'd*):
LBJ and, 215–16
LBJ's re-nomination challenged, 341, 343,
345–48, 357–70
LBJ's withdrawal from election and, xxxv,
370–71, 424
liberalism and, xxi, xxxiv, xxxv–xxxvi, 439
loss of Catholic voters, 179
loss of Southern voters, 179
midterms (1958), 97, 110
midterms (1962), 179
midterms (1966), 325
midterms (1970), 582–83
midterms (1974), 698, 718
moral authority and, 332, 698–99, 708
National Convention (1948), 220, 277–78,
376–77
National Convention (1960), 104–5, 106, 346
National Convention (1964), 278
National Convention (1968), 404–16
National Convention (1968), Vietnam peace
plank, 411–12, 413, 415
National Convention (1972), 594, 598–601
New Deal coalition, 376, 378, 424, 606
Nixon Democrats, 609
Nixon's presidency, impact on, 441–42
as the party of high taxes and anti-
Americanism, 609
presidential election (1960), 100–108
presidential election (1968), 345, 347, 357–81,
399–403
presidential election (1968), "Draft Ted" and,
404–15
presidential election (1968), RFK's campaign,
xxxiv, 343–48, 357–81, 388
presidential election (1972), 564–65, 573, 583,
589–608
RFK's assassination, 399–403
segregationists in, 247
soft on communism charge, 308, 309, 310,
320
Southern voters and, 708–9
Stevenson Democrats, 97
Vietnam War and split in, 346, 402, 404,
411–12, 415, 595, 605
Wallace Democrats, 424
See also liberalism; *specific people*
Dempsey, Jack, 77
Dent, Harry, 529
de Valera, Éamon, 225
de Valera, Sinéad, 225
Dever, Paul, 17, 127, 145
Diem, Ngo Dinh, 308
Nixon's fake documents on JFK and, 620, 622,
624
Dillard, Hardy Cross, 78
Dillon, C. Douglas, 111, 203, 397
Dingell, John, Sr., 644

Dinis, Edmund, 503–4, 505–6
Dionne, E. J., Jr., "A Swelling Tide of Emotion,"
xvi
Dirksen, Everett, 190, 196, 205, 259, 273, 277,
464
Baker as son-in-law, 328, 331
Civil Rights Act of 1964 and, 221, 223, 224,
226, 227, 771n227
EMK's Vietnam War opposition countered,
459
Morrissey judicial appointment and, 296–97,
298, 299, 300, 301–2, 304, 305
one man, one vote and redistricting fight, 327,
328–29, 330, 331
quoting Victor Hugo, 227
as Senate minority leader, 190, 196, 296–97,
327, 441
Voting Rights Act of 1965 and, 278, 280–81,
283–84, 288, 289, 329
DiSalle, Michael, 400, 405, 408
Disraeli, Benjamin, 464
Dixon, Bertha, 656–57
Dixon, Paul Rand, 463, 525
Docking, Robert, 261, 368–69
Dodd, Chris, xxiv–xxv
Dodd, Thomas, 200, 432
Doherty, Gerard, 99, 128–29, 135–37, 174, 186,
261, 292, 406, 718
"boiler-room girls" and, 142
directing EMK's Senate run, 140–42, 147,
160, 291
EMK, health care issues, and, 320–21
EMK's Senate run debates and, 164, 165
as Massachusetts Democratic Party chair, 229
RFK's presidential candidacy and, 368, 373,
374
tuberculosis and, 320, 641–42
Dolan, Joe, 476
Dole, Robert, xviii, 531, 586
Domingo, Plácido, xxviii
Dominick, Peter, 655, 662, 664, 665
Donahue, Maurice, 140
Dong, Pham Vanh, 592
Donovan, James, 566
Donovan, Robert, 229, 262
Dougherty, Bill, 404, 599
Doughton, Robert, 668
Douglas, Helen Gahagan, 95, 96
Douglas, Paul, 223, 324, 325, 326, 327
Dove, Robert, 200, 258, 324, 431, 433, 570
Dowd, Don, 128, 174, 233, 718
Dowd, Phoebe, 233
Dowling, Eddie, 5
Downey, Morton, 14, 83
draft reform, 338–40, 449, 452, 558, 587, 592,
701
end of college deferments, 452, 452n
Drayne, Dick, 373, 469, 516, 550, 710, 718, 732

Dubinsky, David, 684
Dunne, John Gregory, 480, 536
Dunphy, Chris, 552
Durbin, Richard, 540
Dutton, Fred, 357, 359, 360, 406, 415, 574, 599

Eagleton, Thomas, 600–601
Eastland, James, 183, 191, 436, 438, 530, 624
    Civil Rights Act of 1964 and, 220
    EMK's relationship with, 195–98
    EMK tested by, assigned subcommittees,
        183–84
    Immigration and Nationality Act and, 266,
        268, 272, 274, 279
    as Judiciary Committee chair, 461–62, 695
    one man, one vote and redistricting fight,
        329
    racism, white supremacy, and, 196–98
    Voting Rights Act of 1965 and, 279, 280n
    Watergate investigation and, 626–27, 628,
        639, 640
Eastland, Oliver, 197
Eastland, Woods, 197
Eccles, Marriner, 455
Edelman, Marian Wright, 529
Edelman, Peter, 359
education issues, xix, xxiii, xxxii, 570, 645, 652
    Elementary and Secondary Education Act,
        275
    federal aid to parochial schools, 139, 271
    Great Society and, 252, 275
    Higher Education Act, 275
    Nixon and, 604
    RFK, EMK, and Native American education,
        451, 467, 594
    school integration and busing, 724–34
Ehrlichman, John, 467, 499, 501, 580, 581, 602,
    650, 652, 658–59, 661, 677, 712
    Watergate scandal and, 622, 633
Eisenhower, Dwight, 111, 129, 172, 213, 454
    Vietnam War and, 308
Eisenhower, Edgar, 111
Ellender, Allen, 289
Ellsberg, Daniel, 588
Ellwood, Paul, 667
Emerson, Ralph Waldo, 6
"End of the Dream, The" (Carroll), xxi, 213
Enemy Within, The (RFK), 393
England
    air blitz on London, 32–33
    ambassador's residence, 27–28
    appeasement, Munich Agreement, 30, 31
    EMK in, 27–30, 32
    JFK memorial at Runnymede, 225
    JPK as U.S. ambassador to, 6, 27–33
    resistance to Hitler, 32
Engle, Clair, 226
Enthoven, Alain, 240, 647

environmental protection, 275
Environmental Protection Agency, 603
Ervin, Sam, 193, 196, 272, 329
    immigration reform and, 272–73, 274
    one man, one vote and, 329, 330
    Voting Rights Act and, 279, 280n
    Watergate investigation and, 626, 629–31,
        635, 677, 685
Esquire magazine
    on EMK's resilience, 524
    on Nixon's "Kennedy desk," 465
    "Superman Comes to the Supermarket," 107,
        213
Evans, Bill, 142, 188, 263, 292
Evans, Roland, 229, 631
Evers, Charles, 372
Evers, Medgar, 372

Face the Nation (TV show), EMK and his Vietnam
    War position, 354, 355, 357
Fairlie, Henry, 212, 213
Falk, Isidore "Ig," 643, 648, 649, 655, 689
Fall, Bernard, 315–17, 317n
Family and Medical Leave Act, xix
Family Practice Medicine Act, 614–15
Farber, Sidney, 126, 641
    Cancer Crusade, 641, 660
Farenthold, Frances "Sissy," 600
Farrar, John, 482, 508, 509, 510
Fauntroy, Walter, 373
Fay, Paul "Red," 96, 160
Federal Bureau of Investigation (FBI), 125, 206,
    236, 239, 299, 300, 385
    file on JFK, 548
    FOIA bill and, 695
    Liddy as former agent, 621
    Nixon's use of against EMK, 501, 509–10
    Watergate investigation and, 622, 638–39
Federal Cigarette Labeling and Advertising Act,
    275
Feighan, Michael, 270–71, 272
Fein, Rashi, 647, 654, 682
Feldman, Myer, 132, 245
Fenn, Dan, Jr., 139
Fentress, Andrew, 671
Fentress, Lee, 414n, 671–72, 672n
Ferguson, Clarence, 279
Ferris, Charles, 304, 437, 560, 560n
Fessenden School, West Newton, Mass., 36,
    37–38, 42, 43, 49
Field, Mervin, xvii
Finch, Robert, 667
Fine, Max, 643, 645, 646, 646n, 648, 649, 651,
    679
Fingold, George, 123
Finney, John, 559
Firicano, Franca, xxvi
Fisk Tire Factory, Chicopee, Mass., 149

Fitzgerald, John "Honey Fitz" (grandfather), 4, 7, 63–65, 171, 222
  anti-Catholic bias and, 39, 539
  as Boston Irish politician, 7, 229
  at the Breakers Hotel, Palm Beach, 57
  daughter Rose and, 7, 8, 22
  death of, 57
  EMK's political, psychological, and moral education by, 38–41, 43, 57–58, 149, 266, 539–40
  EMK's relationship with, 211
  gift for friendship and, 77
  house in Hull, Mass., 12–13
  JFK's political career and, 57
  outgoing personality, 7, 39, 51, 90
  as Patrick Kennedy's political rival, 14
  political career, 7, 64
  populism and, 7
  in U.S. Congress, 117, 266
  womanizing of, 547, 549
Fitzgerald, Mary Josephine "Josie" Hannon (grandmother), 176–77
Fitzgerald, Robert (cousin), 127, 382, 429–30
Fitzpatrick, Teresa, 188, 671
Fitzwilliam, Peter, 52
Flug, Jim
  AdPrac and, 463, 626
  Carswell nomination and, 529–32
  as EMK's Judiciary aide, 328, 385, 448, 529, 550, 559, 573–74, 623
  lowering the voting age and, 559
  one man, one vote issue, 329–30, 331
  Watergate investigation and, 626, 627, 630, 632, 638
Fong, Hiram, 196
Food for Peace program, 186
food stamps, 444, 464
Ford, Cristina, 601–2
Ford, Gerald, 626, 635, 685, 687, 714
  anti-busing position, 724
  "awarded" the presidency, 691
  background, 690–91
  campaign-finance reform and, 694, 697
  clemency for draft resisters, 701
  fear of leaks and, 696
  FOIA amendments and, 696
  foreign policy and, 703
  Halloween Massacre, 703–4
  inaugural address, 691–92
  likeability and, 690, 691, 704
  national health insurance and, 688–89, 697
  in the Navy, World War II, 691
  nuclear-arms limitation agreement, 700
  pardoning of Nixon by, 697–98
  presidential race, 1976 and, 714
  racial questions and, 711
  A Time to Heal, 703
  U.S. economy and, 699–700

as vice president, 635, 691
  Vietnam War and, 702
  Whip Inflation Now (WIN), 700
Ford, Henry, 10
Ford, Henry, III, 601
Formisano, Ronald, 735
Forrest, Nathan Bedford, 197
Fortas, Abe, 527, 528, 529
Fort Dix, N.J., 65–66, 69
Fortune magazine
  full issue on national health care, 649
Foster, Theodore and Dwight, 251
Foxe, Fanne, 688
Frankfurter, Felix, 277
Frate, Bill, 62, 63, 135
Freedom of Information Act (FOIA), xix, 694
Frei, Emil, III, 673
Freund, Paul, 279, 284
Friedin, Seymour, 815n620
Fritchey, Clayton, 99, 253
Frost, David, 367
Frost, Robert, 309
  "The Road Not Taken," xv
Fruitful Bough, The (EMK), 239
Fulbright, J. William, 569, 809n569
Fullerton, Bill, 669, 680, 686, 687, 688, 689
Furcolo, Foster, 122, 158, 290

Galbraith, John Kenneth, 240, 249, 362, 409, 487, 501, 571, 600n
Gans, Curtis, 363
Gargan, Ann (cousin), 22, 41, 256, 293, 383, 533, 534
Gargan, Joe (nephew), 472
Gargan, Joey (cousin), 42, 43, 47, 64
  background, 473–74
  on campaign team, 128
  Chappaquiddick incident and, 471, 472, 473, 474, 479–80, 481, 482, 483, 485, 488, 495, 508, 509, 511
  as EMK's companion, 473, 533–34
  EMK's Senate reelection (1970) and, 563
  European trip with EMK (1950), 55–56
  life at Hyannis Port, after RFK's assassination, 392, 396
Gargan, Mary Agnes Fitzgerald (aunt), 473
Gargan, Mary Jo (cousin), 42, 43
Garrity, Wendell Arthur, Jr., 721–23, 725, 729, 730, 733n, 734
Gates, Gary Paul, 580
Geiger, Jack, 321
Georgetown University Hospital, 671, 674
Gergen, David, 678–79
Germany, 31, 32, 55, 56, 68–69, 130, 225, 269
Gibbs School, London, 30
GI bills, 202
Gibson, Barbara, 473
Gibson, Count, Jr., 321

Gierek, Edward, 676
Gifford, Dun, 472, 718
    Chappaquiddick incident and, 489, 491–92,
        493, 510, 513, 514, 516
    on EMK as majority whip, 434
    EMK's grief for RFK and, 383, 396, 397, 398
    EMK's invoking morality and, 365
    on EMK's staff, 258, 264, 321, 322, 339–40,
        373, 406, 431, 450
    EMK's opposing the Vietnam War, 324, 458
    Nixon-EMK ABM fight and, 453, 454, 455
    on RFK, 258, 321–22, 358
Gifford, Gladys, 145, 472, 473, 475, 512, 554
Ginsberg, Allen, 372
Gladstone, William, 465
Goldberg, Arthur, 320, 455
Goldberg, Lucianne Cummings, 815n620
Goldman, LeRoy, 652, 653–55, 658–62, 664–65,
    665n, 667–69, 682, 684–86
Goldwater, Barry, 212, 245–47, 251, 252, 417,
    560n, 633
Good, Frederick, 4
Good Samaritan Hospital, Los Angeles, Ca., 383
Goodwin, Doris Kearns, xviii, 4, 14, 369, 539
    on EMK's childhood, 36
    on the infidelity of the Kennedys, 547–48
    on JPK at Harvard, 9
    on JPK providing competitive not moral
        guidance, 18
    LBJ on JFK's legislative program, 276
    on Rose's unhappiness in marriage, 22
Goodwin, Richard, 147, 211, 213, 214, 243,
    289–90, 345, 384, 486n
    Chappaquiddick incident and, 487, 488, 491,
        495
    "Draft Kennedy" (1968) and, 409
    on Nixon, 427
    RFK's presidential candidacy and, 358–59,
        359n, 362, 363, 364, 381, 388
    Vietnam War speech, 333–34
Gould, Jack, 106
Graham, Billy, 239
Graham, Fred, 506
Grant, Jared, 509
Graul, Rita, 727, 730–31
Graves, W. B.
    Intergovernmental Relations in the United States,
        241
Gray, Patrick, 622
Great Depression, 11, 13–14, 245, 441, 584
    modern liberalism and, xxxv, 275, 389,
        611–12
Greece, 130, 393, 501
Greek Way, The (Hamilton), 211
Green Bay Packers, 74
Greenfield, Meg, 253, 305
Greenspan, Alan, 700
Grier, Roosevelt, 381

Griffin, Robert, 531
Griffiths, Martha, 651, 688
Griswold, Anne, xiii
Griswold, Erwin, 297
gun-control legislation, 419, 430
    Gun Control Act of 1968, 524
Gurney, Edward, 531, 624, 640, 724, 725
Guthman, Ed, 214, 383
Gwirtzman, Milton, 71, 202
    Chappaquiddick incident and, 486, 486n,
        487–88, 490–91, 494, 497
    on EMK and the Democratic ticket (1968),
        399, 400, 401, 406, 407, 416
    on EMK and the presidential race (1972), 573
    EMK on racial justice and, 714
    EMK's domestic problems and, 716
    on EMK's interactions in the Senate, 191, 195
    on EMK's manners, 148
    EMK's plane crash and, 235, 240
    on EMK's political skills, 147
    EMK's presidential prospects and, 460–61,
        704–5, 709, 711
    EMK's Senate run and, 151, 152, 154–55, 164,
        166, 167, 168, 174
    as EMK's Senate staffer and speechwriter, 139,
        140, 187–88, 221, 263, 287
    on EMK's wife Joan, 174
    on EMK's womanizing, 550
    JFK's assassination and, 206–7, 208
    memo on EMK as vice presidential pick, 598
    Morrissey judicial appointment and, 291, 292,
        293, 295, 296, 303, 304
    on RFK, 144, 260–61
    RFK's assassination and, 383
    RFK's eulogy and, 386–88
    RFK's presidential candidacy and, 361, 389
    Watergate investigation and, 638, 639

Haar, Charles, 138–39, 149, 240, 271, 279, 284
Haber, Joyce, 551–52
Hackett, David, 108, 210, 379, 383, 472
Hague Academy of International Law, 78–79
Haig, Alexander, 637, 638, 678
Halberstam, David, 425
Haldeman, H. R., 454, 498, 500, 527, 532, 571,
    577, 580, 601, 604, 605, 609–10, 613
    "awesome power with no discipline," 613
    Nixon's dirty tricks and, 620
    Watergate scandal and, 628, 631, 633
Hall, Arthur, 50
Hamilton, Charles, 160
Hamilton, Edith, The Greek Way, 211
Hammond, George, 237
Hanan, Timothy, 82
Hannah, John, 619
Hardin, Clifford, 444
Hargrove, Sister Katherine, 555
Harlow, Bryce, 526

Harper's magazine
    Fritchey on JFK in Congress, 99
    Fritchey on the liberal Senate, 253
    Lapham on EMK, xxxiv
Harper's Monthly
    describing the Senate chamber (1895), 180
Harriman, W. Averell, 314, 333, 455, 565–66, 592
Harris, Fred, 416, 595
Harris, Louis, 441
Harris, Richard, 529, 531, 532
Harris, Thomas, 529
Harrison, Pat, 438
Hart, Phil, 181, 196, 223–24, 299, 313, 624, 635,
        640, 692, 717–18, 726
    ABM system fight and, 453, 520
    campaign-finance reform, 692
    Carswell judicial nomination and, 529, 531
    as "the conscience of the Senate," 520
    EMK and Hart-Celler immigration bill,
        268–69, 270
    as EMK role model, 277
    FOIA amendments and, 695
    Haynsworth appointment opposed, 528
    in a new Senate generation of liberals, 97
    Voting Rights Act and, 279, 281, 286, 288–89
    Watergate investigation and, 631, 637, 638,
        639, 696
Hartford Courant
    on EMK's failure at Chappaquiddick, 496
Hartigan, William, 157
Hartington, William "Billy," Marquess of
        Hartington, 47
Hartke, Vance, 285, 286
Harvard Crimson, 172, 176
Harvard University
    anti-Catholic bias at, 9, 58–59, 73
    Claverly Hall, 9
    EMK and, 54–64, 70–74
    EMK and football, 59–61, 71–74
    EMK's cheating scandal, 62–65, 134–36, 249,
        485
    EMK's friends and associates at, 49, 58–61
    EMK's Senate run and, 137, 138
    EMK's summer jobs and, 74
    EMK's unhappiness at, 59
    Fitzgerald at, 7
    football at, 54–55, 59–61
    Hasty Pudding Club, 72–73
    Joe, Jr. at, 59
    JPK and, 6, 9, 54, 58–59
    JPK's "negligible incident," 9
    RFK and, 50, 54–55
    ROTC at, 65
    Winthrop House, 70
    Young Democratic Club, 138
Harvard University Law School, 33
    EMK speaking against the war at, 583–84
Harwood, Richard, 503

Hatch, Orrin, xviii, xxv
Hatcher, Richard, 373
Hayden, Carl, 202, 226
Hayden, Stone & Co. brokerage, 10
Haynsworth, Clement, 92, 527, 528–29
Hays, Wayne, 693
health care, xix, xxiii, xxxii, xxxiii, 204, 641–70
    cancer care costs, 676–77
    community health centers, 321, 449, 642
    costs of, 1965–70, 655
    EMK and issues of, 320–22
    EMK's interest in, roots of, 641–42
    Farber's Cancer Crusade and, 641, 660
    Health Insurance Portability and
        Accountability Act, xix
    HMOs and, 666–67
    labor unions and, 644
    Medicare and, 275
    National Cancer Act, S.34, 660–66, 685
    Nixon's cancer bill, 663
    State Children's Health Insurance Program,
        xix
    uninsured Americans, 656
    Wagner–Dingell bill, 644
    See also Medicare
health care, national health insurance, 213,
        641, 642, 649–59, 667–70
    Chappaquiddick incident, impact on EMK's
        moral authority and, 648, 651, 652
    Comprehensive Health Insurance Plan
        (CHIP), 678–80
    Corman and, 645, 651
    costs of, 659, 670, 678
    EMK introduces Reuther's bill, 649–53
    EMK's Europe and the Middle East health care
        tour (1971), 659
    EMK's Senate bill, Health Security Act, S.3,
        655–59, 678, 679, 680, 682, 699
    EMK studying issue, 647
    Kennedy–Mills II plan, 680, 681, 682, 683,
        684–85
    Kennedy-Mills-Weinberger plan, 687–88
    Long–Ribicoff plan, 680
    media attention, 649
    "Medicare for All," 643, 648, 679
    Mills and, 667–70
    Nixon and, 650, 658, 678–80, 684
    obstacles to, 644, 646
    Republican opposition, 689
    Reuther and, 642–43, 646, 646n, 647, 648,
        649, 652, 655, 682
    Senate Finance Committee and, 652, 655
    Senate hearings on, 654–55, 656–58
    single-payer plan, 643, 651, 679, 680, 681,
        683, 687, 688, 689
Healy, Robert "Bob," 117, 134–36, 290, 291, 411,
        718
    on EMK vs. JFK, 146

Morrissey judicial appointment and, 298, 778n290

Nixon and, 466

Hearst, William Randolph, 14

Heinz, Teresa, xiii

Heller, Walter, 111

Hemingway, Ernest, 77

Hennessy, Luella, 28, 29, 32, 36, 41, 211, 501

Henningan, James, 721

Herbers, John, 324, 399, 403

Hersh, Burton, 185, 186, 233, 268, 280, 329, 347, 360, 362, 374, 395, 447, 450, 468

Chappaquiddick incident and, 475, 488, 489, 493, 503, 508

on EMK after Chappaquiddick, 522

on EMK and Joan's alcoholism, 554

EMK's empathy with the individual, 542

on presidential race 1972 and EMK, 564

on Ted, Jr.'s cancer, 674

Hershey, Lewis, 338

Hertzberg, Hendrik, 176

Hesburgh, Theodore, 600

Hession, Mark, xxviii

Hewitt, Dick, 482–83, 509

Hicks, Louise Day, 725, 727–28, 730, 731, 734

Hildenbrand, William, 570

Hill, Lister, 182

Hilsman, Roger, 334

Hiss, Alger, 604, 604n, 636

Hitler, Adolf, 30

Ho Chi Minh, 319, 592

Hodges, Luther, 217

Hodgson, Godfrey, 610

Hoffa, Jimmy, 374

Hofstadter, Richard, 246

Hogan, Daniel, 230

Holbert, Luther, 197

Holborn, Fred, 72, 76

Holcombe, Arthur, 70, 71, 96

Holland, Spessard, 205, 274

Hollings, Ernest, xviii, 597

Holloway, Kernel, 50

Hollywood, Calif., 10–11

JPK as film mogul in, 10

Holmes, Oliver Wendell, Sr., 708

Homestead Resort, Hot Springs, Va., 3

Honan, William, 431, 445, 449, 455, 495, 506, 563, 564, 588, 590, 593

on EMK after Chappaquiddick, 521–22, 570

Hooton, Claude, 72, 74, 107, 130, 206, 519

Chappaquiddick incident and, 487, 497

Hoover, Herbert, 14, 26

Hoover, J. Edgar, 385, 509, 622

file on JFK's womanizing, 548

Howe, Mark DeWolfe, 137, 240, 279, 284

Hruska, Roman, 196, 530

Hughes, Charles Evans, 12, 171–72

Hughes, Howard, 624–25

Hughes, H. Stuart, 171–72, 174, 308

Hughes, Richard, 400

Hugo, Victor, 227

Hume, Brit, 625

Humphrey, Hubert, 75, 102, 103, 104, 112, 156, 199, 213, 300, 371, 460, 497, 513, 580

advice to EMK, 641

Civil Rights Act of 1964 and, 226, 227, 228

civil rights and, 217, 220, 376–77, 389

Democratic National Convention speech (1948), 220

EMK and, 223

EMK campaigning for (1968), 420, 422–23

EMK offered 1968 vice presidential slot, 399–400, 403–4, 405, 415

EMK's running for Senate majority whip and, 437

as LBJ's heir apparent, 373

as LBJ's vice president, 244, 373

Muskie as vice presidential pick (1968), 416

Nixon and, 586–87, 587n

presidential race (1968) and, 376–77, 379, 390, 401, 408, 411–12, 419–24, 426, 577, 587n, 594

presidential race (1972) and, 596, 597, 598–601, 603

RFK's assassination and, 383, 384, 390, 391

as Senate majority whip, 200, 204, 434, 436, 567

as senator, 444, 702

Vietnam refugees and, 701–2

Vietnam War and, 319, 355, 403–4, 412, 420–22, 424

Voting Rights Act of 1965 and, 284, 285, 286–87, 288

Hunt, Al, 543

Hunt, E. Howard, 580, 621, 622, 622n, 624

Hunter, Robert, 703

Huntley–Brinkley Report (TV show), 505

Long on EMK as Nixon opponent, 439

Hyannis Port, Kennedy home, xiii–xiv, 13, 17, 35, 234

called the "Irish House," 13

"Draft Kennedy" (1968) and, 405, 406, 408, 409–10

EMK, Chappaquiddick incident, and, 484–85

EMK and JFK at, summer (1963), 203–4

EMK and sailing at, xxv, xxix, 17, 19, 26, 41, 43, 47–48, 121, 168, 395–96, 398, 414, 416, 598

EMK decides not to seek presidency in 1976 and, 717

EMK's football friends at, 60–61

EMK's friends and advisors gather after Chappaquiddick, 486–89

EMK's political events at, 151

EMK's Senate run and, 121, 139, 161–62, 168

EMK's wife Joan and, 86, 87, 109–10

Hyannis Port, Kennedy home (*cont'd*):
   football at, 59, 144
   JFK and, 13, 17, 60–61
   JFK's assassination and, 207, 210
   JPK at, 14, 41–45, 121, 127, 533
   Kennedy family at (1942), 41
   "King of the Raft" and, 61
   life at, post-RFK assassination, 392, 397
   O'Donnell brothers visiting, 55
   sauna and Gene Tunney, 77
   videotaped address to America after RFK's
      assassination from, 391
Hyannis Port, Mass.
   EMK's funeral in, xiii–xvii
   John F. Kennedy Museum, xiv
   St. Francis Xavier Church, 497
Hyatt, George, 671, 672
Hyman, Lester, 405, 406, 412, 469, 486, 520, 553

Ickes, Harold, 31
immigration, xxx
   Azorean Refugee Act of 1958, 267
   "chain migration," 271, 272
   EMK and, xxx, xxxii, 266
   EMK and Immigration and Nationality Act of
      1965, xix, 269–75, 270n, 277, 279, 289,
      325, 327
   JFK and, xxxiv, 213, 216, 266–68
   LBJ and, xxxiv, 268
   Massachusetts and, 222
   Northern European bias, 266, 269, 271–72
   reform, 201
India
   EMK visit on Bangladesh (1972), 585–86
   EMK visit on Pakistani refugees (1971),
      584–85
Indiana, 653
   presidential primary (1968), 373–76, 389
   presidential primary (1972), 596
   RFK's Indianapolis "tame the savageness of
      man" speech on the night of King
      assassination, 22, 372, 403, 713
   RFK's Notre Dame speech, 379
   See also Bayh, Birch; Goldman, LeRoy
Indiana University, 510n
Inouye, Daniel, 181
Intergovernmental Relations in the United States
   (Graves), 241
International Ladies' Garment Workers Union
   (ILGWU)
   EMK's appearance, Miami (1974), 683–84
   "Ted for President," 684
International Telephone and Telegraph (ITT),
   622–23, 625
Iona College, 583
Ireland, 138
   EMK in (1964), 225–26
   EMK in (1970), 559, 560

   EMK's speech on tolerance and violence, 557,
      559, 583
   EMK trip to County Wexford (1962), 130
   immigration from, 8–9
   JFK's birthday observed, 225–26
   Shannon as ambassador, 250
Israel, 130, 138
Issues and Answers (TV show)
   EMK on, Vietnam discussed, 312
Italy, 55, 125, 138
   EMK trip (1961), 125, 301

Jackson, Henry "Scoop," 435, 443, 569, 570,
   700, 709
Jackson, Jesse, 707
Jackson, Susan, xvii
Javits, Jacob, 195, 304, 660, 661, 663–64
Jaworski, Leon, 685
Jenner, Albert, Jr., 295, 297, 298, 300
John F. Kennedy Library, Boston, xv, xvii, xxiii,
   xxvi, 225, 243, 317
   EMK raising funds for, 225
   Stephen Smith Hall, xxiii, xxiv
John F. Kennedy Museum, Hyannis Port, Mass.,
   xiv
Johnson, Hiram, 446
Johnson, Lady Bird, 234
Johnson, Lyndon Baines (LBJ), xx, xxii, 144,
   190, 214–16, 225, 595, 654, 721
   background, 199, 219
   Byrd and, 568
   Chappaquiddick incident and, 488, 499n
   character and personality, 215, 368
   Civil Rights Act of 1964 and, xxxv, 223, 224,
      226, 444
   civil rights and, 199, 218, 219, 247
   commencement address, U. Michigan,
      252
   as Committee on Equal Employment
      Opportunity head, 219
   dog Yuki, 352
   draft reform bill and, 338–39
   Economic Opportunity Act, 245
   EMK and, xxxiv, 179, 332, 333, 336, 337, 347,
      348, 351, 353, 354, 355, 434
   EMK's friendship with, 239, 242, 250, 255–57,
      258, 336, 385, 430
   EMK's plane crash and, 234, 237, 239
   EMK's running for Senate majority whip and,
      437–38
   enmity toward the Kennedys, 215
   FOIA and, 694
   Great Society, 252, 275, 321, 325, 331, 332,
      342–43, 389, 425, 428, 465, 612, 644,
      646
   the "Harvards" and, 427, 635
   Humphrey as heir apparent, 373
   Humphrey as vice president, 244

immigration issues and Immigration and
Nationality Act of 1965, xxxiv, 268, 269,
271, 270–74
JFK's assassination and, 205
JFK's presidential run (1959–60) and,
100–101, 102, 104–5
Kennedy family and, 255–56, 257
Kerner Commission and, 556
Kosygin meeting, 348
legislative program of, 253–58, 275, 276
liberalism and, 214, 216, 256, 424
Medicare and, 444, 643, 651, 670
moral authority and, 219, 275–76, 331
Morrissey judicial appointment and, 293–94,
300, 301, 304–5
opponents of second term, 341, 343, 345–48,
357–70
overpromising by, 425
presidential election (1964), 244–47, 252
refusal to run for reelection, xxxv, 368–71,
424
RFK and, xxxiv, 214–16, 239, 244, 255,
257–58, 259, 341, 342, 343–44, 368, 370
RFK's assassination and, 384, 385, 391, 430
as Senate majority whip, 432, 434
as senator, 192, 196, 199–200, 201, 214, 215,
219, 257, 278, 336, 444, 462, 463
State of the Union Address (1965), 252, 268
State of the Union Address (1966), 331, 342
State of the Union Address (1967), 342–43
as vice president, 182, 199, 214, 215, 219
Vietnam War and, xxxiv, 254–55, 307, 311–13,
318, 319, 322–24, 331–32, 341, 351,
353–57, 360, 369, 371, 403, 415, 421, 424
Voting Rights Act of 1965 and, 276, 280, 281,
283, 285, 329
war on poverty, 245
Jones, Jim, 385
Jones, Stan, 654, 655, 666, 667, 669, 680, 684,
686–87, 688, 689
Jones, Thomas, 616
Jordan, Lloyd, 71, 72
Jordan, Vernon, 707
Julius Caesar (Shakespeare), 576

Kaiser, John, 656
Kalmbach, Herbert, 627
Kampelman, Max, 104
Kansas City Star, 496
Kaplan, Sumner, 167
Karamanlis, Konstantinos, 130
Karnow, Stanley, 356
Katzenbach, Nicholas, 214, 224, 234, 235, 277,
278, 280, 285, 286, 288
Morrissey judicial appointment and, 293, 299,
300–301
Kaysen, Carl, 240, 571
Keating, Kenneth, 185, 244

Kefauver, Estes, 77
Kelley, Clarence, 638–39
Kempton, Murray, 211, 366–67, 541
Kennedy, Caroline (niece), xiii, xxiv, xxv, 23
EMK and her wedding, xxx
Kennedy, Edward Moore "Ted"
birth of, 3, 25
burial, Arlington Cemetery, xxx–xxxii
cancer diagnosis, xxvii
Chappaquiddick incident, xvii, xxviii, xxxi,
xxxv, 471–518, 471n
children born, 102, 181
daughter's cancer diagnosis, xxvii
father's death, 534–35
father's relationship with, 13, 15–16, 28–29,
38, 42–45, 49, 53, 58, 72, 74, 75, 78, 79, 93,
94, 122, 169–70, 249, 533–34 (*see also*
Kennedy, Joseph P., Sr.)
father's stroke, 169–70
funeral, xiii–xvii, xxiii–xxxiii
grandfather Fitzgerald and, 38–41, 43, 57–58,
149, 211, 266, 374, 539–40
Harvard cheating scandal, 62–65, 134–36,
249, 485
JFK as godfather for, 26
JFK's assassination and, 204–12, 205n, 207n,
461
JFK's relationship with, 112–14, 146, 180,
182, 203–4, 211–12, 262 (*see also* Kennedy,
John. F.)
Joe, Jr. and, 26, 47
as Kennedy family paterfamilias, surrogate
father, 672–73, 675, 717
marries Joan Bennett, 89
marries Victoria Reggie, xxv
McLean, Va., home, 391, 403, 439, 543–44
mother's relationship with, 23–24, 29, 30, 35,
68 (*see also* Kennedy, Rose Fitzgerald)
naming of, 4, 6
picking up his brothers' fallen standard, xvii,
394, 399–403, 412, 415, 429, 439, 443,
449–50, 456–57, 459, 461, 536
plane crash, 230–40, 249–50, 251, 265, 453,
540, 641
posthumous tributes, xx
premise of his political career, xxviii
RFK relationship with, 28–29, 42, 50, 73,
74, 92, 93, 120, 251, 258, 260–63, 367,
374–75, 391–93 (*see also* Kennedy,
Robert F.)
RFK's assassination, 381–88, 391–98, 405,
406, 429, 443, 451, 461, 467–70, 472
RFK's funeral, eulogy, 386–88
RFK's legacy and, 429, 430–31, 449, 515
sister Kathleen's death and, 52
sister Rosemary and, 540
son Ted's cancer, xxviii–xxix, 641–75, 677,
683, 716–17

Kennedy, Edward Moore "Ted" (*cont'd*):
  Squaw Island, Mass. home, 151, 242, 392,
    414, 472, 487, 718
—**characteristics and defining traits**,
    xxiv–xxix, xxxi, xxxii, xxxiii, xxxv
  charisma of, 79, 146, 149, 153, 176
  childhood pain as basis for politics of, 50
  as competitive, 17, 238, 261, 265
  desire to serve and, 538–43
  drinking by, xxxi, 395, 419, 429, 468–70, 496,
    507, 538, 554–55
  empathy of, 41, 67, 98, 174, 221, 288, 306,
    312, 427, 541, 543, 676
  energy of, 60, 91, 150–52, 155, 419, 468
  expectations, living up to or surpassing, xxxiv,
    18, 107, 161, 184, 195, 199, 201, 212, 224,
    239, 251, 282, 331, 395, 434
  faith of, devoutness, xxvii–xxviii, xxxii, xxxiii,
    208, 211, 384, 525–26, 538–39, 541
  family as abiding metaphor for, 21–22
  fatalism of, xxxiv, 394, 470, 575, 576, 591, 717
  favorite poem, xxviii
  favorite prayer, 541
  favorite song, xxvi
  Fitzgerald heritage dominant in, 43, 44, 58,
    81, 90, 146, 149
  flying and pilot's license, 101, 231
  friendships, gift for friendship, and, 49, 69–70,
    74, 77–78, 107, 108, 248, 258, 263, 307, 395
    (*see also* Hooton, Claude; Tunney, John
    Varick; *specific people*)
  Hooton on his "zest for life," 73
  humility of, xxix, 184, 541
  identity as a "Senate man," 202, 203, 257,
    285, 324, 336, 431, 434, 435, 615
  as irrepressible, 81, 238
  Lampham on character of, xxxiv
  as a liberal, xxi, xxxiv, xxxv, 133, 264, 266,
    322, 343, 366, 433, 443–45, 515, 536,
    538–43, 571–72, 710–11, 714
  losing possessions, carelessness, 435
  "losing-side consciousness" of, 541
  magnanimity of, 178, 230
  manners, civility of, 148
  mantra of, 146
  "ninth-child talent," xviii, 191, 272
  opera loved by, 240
  as outsider, 427
  pain, living with, connection to, 210, 238,
    249, 263, 394, 395, 397, 401, 429, 467, 469,
    470, 484, 494, 522, 534, 540–41, 554, 696
  painting by, 237, 240
  personality, 25–26, 28, 29, 38, 39, 51, 58, 62,
    72–73, 78, 82, 113, 114, 145, 146, 147, 238,
    374, 465, 515
  personality, differing from his brothers,
    143–46, 147, 306, 336, 393, 435, 469,
    541–42

  political instincts and gifts, 146–48, 153–54,
    182, 229–30, 288
  public speaking and, 90–91, 262
  public vs. private image, xxxiv, 393, 469
  reckless daring of, 79, 103, 107, 107n, 113–14,
    231, 429, 496
  Roberts on character of, xxxiv
  sailing and, xxv, xxix, 17, 19, 26, 43, 47–48,
    121, 168, 395–97, 398, 414, 416, 471, 498,
    521, 533, 598, 718
  self-doubt and, 78, 106, 119, 131, 147, 262,
    393
  sympathy for the underdog, 302–3, 306, 542
  temperament, 132, 251
  tenacity and, 60, 91, 248, 274, 287
  view of the world, 542
  womanizing of, xxxi, 82–83, 88, 89, 395, 467,
    496, 538, 547–49, 550–52, 554, 581, 601–2
  work ethic, xxix, 60, 70, 91, 99, 101, 119, 120,
    130, 150–52, 155
—**childhood and early adulthood**
  academic struggles, 37–38, 44, 49, 54, 62, 71
  appearance as a young man, 51–52, 59–61,
    66, 71, 82, 83
  Army service and lessons learned, 64–70
  birth of, as an afterthought, 3–4, 27, 43
  in Bronxville, N.Y., 33, 35–36
  childhood illnesses, 24, 35, 37
  as chubby, "Biscuits and Muffins," 26, 36–37,
    50, 51, 52, 61
  dating and marrying Joan Bennett, 83–84,
    86–90
  discovering girls, 52
  discovering himself, 51–52
  emotional support and, 21
  Europe trips (1950, 1957), 55–56, 78–79
  family competitiveness and, 17
  family expectations of, 20, 54, 55, 57
  family rules and, 20–21
  father as U.S. ambassador and, 27–30, 32
  father's conversation with, on a serious or
    nonserious life, 44–45, 64
  at Fesseneden School, 36–38, 42, 43, 49
  future in politics, 75, 76
  girlfriends, 52, 68, 82–83
  as "golden child," 42
  grandfather Fitzgerald and shaping of, 38–41,
    43, 51, 58, 146, 149, 539–40
  grandfather Fitzgerald's death and, 57, 58
  Harvard and, 54–65, 71–74
  Hyannis Port and, 60
  investiture of Pope Pius and, 30
  as Irish Catholic in Protestant schools, 36,
    58–59, 78
  Irish heritage and family, 3–28
  JFK's advice to, 44
  lack of permanency in school or homes, 27,
    28, 29–30, 33, 34–35, 49

law school as a way into politics, 74–75,
77–82
life as the youngest child, 26–27
London blitz, father's letter about, 32–33
maturing of, 70–74, 76–77, 249
at Milton Academy and transformation,
50–52, 54, 62, 72
moral education lacking, 19, 21, 41, 63, 83
North African trip (1956), 76–77
in Palm Beach, 33, 35, 36
at Portsmouth Priory, R.I., 34–35
as prankster, jester at school, 38, 58, 62,
72–73
race, understanding of, and, 69
reading comic books, 44
religious instruction, 19
rich kid's prerogatives and, 67–68
at Riverdale Country School, 35
role in the family, 29, 33, 41, 53
scars left by his childhood, 49–50
Settlement House volunteerism, 70
teasing of, 26
unhappiness and loneliness of, 29–30, 33–34,
35, 36, 37, 38, 49, 59
at Virginia Law School, 75, 77–82, 528
World War II and, 32, 33
as youngest Kennedy, 3, 6, 26, 29, 31
—early career, campaigning for JFK, and
entering politics
desire to distance himself from his father,
116–17
detractors and opponents, 136–38, 140, 282
doubts and, 131–32
entering politics, charity work as
campaigning, 126
entering politics, deciding on what to run for,
115–17
entering politics, Morrissey and, 120–21, 125,
126, 128, 146, 291
fact-finding trip (as Senate race preparation),
West Africa (1960), 108–9, 117, 121,
758n109
fact-finding trips (as Senate race preparation),
Ireland, Europe, Middle East trip (1961–62),
125, 130, 138
father's financing of Senate campaign, 152,
153
family and marriage, toll on, 108–9
first political address, 115
Haar as adviser to, 138–39, 149
Harvard cheating scandal, impact of, 134–36
JFK and his father directing his political
future, 94, 100, 108–9, 115–18, 120, 121,
131, 133–34
JFK and his Senate run, 129, 131–35, 138,
140–42, 146, 153, 177
JFK as president and hero worship of, 112–14,
180, 211

JFK's advice to take an interest in elected
office, 98
JFK's political campaigns, working on, 57, 88,
90, 98–100, 126, 147, 149, 379
JFK's presidential race, campaigning with,
100–108, 107n
Kennedy "secretaries" and, 128
legal career, Massachusetts assistant district
attorney, 118–21, 125, 138
liberal education of, 120
liberalism and, 133
"magic with crowds," 149–50
Martin as press secretary, 127–28, 157, 160,
165–66, 167
meeting with leftists, 125
Meet the Press appearance, 131–32
network for campaigns, 128
politicking in Boston, 121
retail politics and, 146
RFK and his Senate run, 125, 126, 128, 130,
139, 140, 141–42, 162, 168
Senate campaign, "boiler-room girls" and,
142
Senate campaign, cost, 177
Senate campaign, deciding, preparing,
assembling a team, 117–18, 120, 121–42
Senate campaign, energy of, campaigning
schedule, 150–52, 155
Senate campaign, Gwirtzman as
speechwriter, 139
Senate campaign, issues and promises,
139–40
Senate campaign, organization created, 142,
153, 156–57
Senate campaign, tie clasp handouts, 129–30
Senate general election, against George Cabot
Lodge, 171–78
Senate primary campaign, buying off delegate
charges, 157–58
Senate primary campaign, Massachusetts
Democratic Party convention and, 154–59
Senate primary campaign against
McCormack, 143–70
winning as vindication for, 169
—presidential ambitions, campaigns, xxxiii,
324–25, 336
address at the 1980 Democratic Convention,
xv
appearance at ILGWU, Miami (1974) and,
683–84
assassination fears and, 451, 599, 705
Chappaquiddick incident, impact of, 486, 489,
491, 513, 524, 525, 589, 595–96, 599, 608,
634, 714–15, 718–19
funding and, 714
liberalism and, 710–11, 714
Nixon's fears of an EMK presidential
candidacy, 576–82, 602, 612

—**presidential ambitions, campaigns**
(*cont'd*):
perceived as future presidential candidate
(1968), 433
political reemergence after Chappaquiddick,
583–84
polling of voters for 1972 race, 611
polling of voters for 1976 race, 714
pollster Field's characterization of EMK's
presidential run, xvii
popularity of, xvii, xxxvi, 150, 590, 684
presidential nomination attempted (1968),
404–15
presidential race (1972), as presumptive
nominee, 443, 447, 449, 460–61, 513
presidential race (1972) reconsideration and,
573–76, 583, 589–99
presidential race (1976), 607, 608, 612, 692,
704–16
presidential race (1976), decision not to run,
717–19, 729
presidential race (1976), obstacles to , 710,
716–17
racial questions and, 711
RFK's assassination and 1968 election,
399–403
RFK's presidential candidacy and, 379
Secret Service protection for (1972), 594, 597,
602
stump speech "forgotten promises" (1971),
584, 590
targeting Nixon (1971), 583–84
vice presidential slot offered to (1968),
399–400, 403–4, 405, 410, 415–16
vice presidential slot offered to (1972),
598–600, 602–3, 603n
Wallace and, 706–9
—**Senate years**
ABM system fight, 452–56, 519–20, 524
as AdPrac chair, 461–63, 464, 465, 525, 587,
626, 628, 654, 695
African Americans and, 450–51, 712–13,
719–23
age at election to, xxi
Alaska trip (1969) and drinking, 467–70, 496,
497
approach to getting results through
friendships, compromise, negotiation,
xxii–xxiii, xxx, 258–59, 272, 274, 282, 288,
322, 324, 339–40, 436, 613
approach to legislation, typical, 681
arrival in Washington and learning the ropes,
179–203
Biafra civil war and, 430–31
Brazil and Chile human rights violations
addressed by, 617
called a "plodder," 449, 460, 515
called "Teddy," 184–85

campaign-finance reform and, 692–94
Carswell judicial nomination opposed,
529–32
as champion of the underprivileged, 444,
450–51, 464, 465, 536–37, 564, 658
Chappaquiddick incident, impact on status
and performance in, 496–97, 519–26, 530,
532, 551, 557–61, 560n, 565–66, 569, 648,
651, 652
civil rights and, xv, xxxi, xxxii, 191, 218,
221–23, 226, 320, 327, 450–51
Civil Rights Subcommittee and, 183–84
contemplation and study (1970), 571
daily schedule at, 254
death penalty opposition, xxxii, 451
defense establishment opposed by, 454, 456,
457, 569 (*see also* ABM system fight, *above*)
Democratic opposition to Nixon and, 446–50
Democrats' opinions of, 184, 185
draft reform bill and, 338–40, 449, 452, 465,
558–61, 587, 592, 701
Eastland's relationship with, 183–84, 195–98
education issues and, xix, xxiii, xxxii, 139,
271, 451, 467, 570, 594, 645, 652
enemies of, 569
Europe fact-finding trips (1964, 1974), 225,
709
expert input sought by, 453
Fair Housing Act and, 713
Family Practice Medicine Act, and pocket veto
lawsuit, 614–17
fighting for his constituents, 202–3
first appearance as presiding officer, 186
first bills, 186
first major Senate address, 221–23
first public address after RFK's death, 401–3
first public speech as a senator, 181
fishing bills, 186, 194, 277
FOIA amendments and, 695–97
foreign policy and, 336–37, 617–20, 702, 709
freshman year, 189–203, 204, 222
Georgetown brownstone residence, 188, 194
gun-control legislation, 419, 430, 524
Haynsworth judicial appointment opposed,
527, 528
health care and Health Security Act, S.3 (as
Mr. Health Care), xix, xxiii, xxxii, xxxiii,
320–22, 641–70, 676–85, 699
as Health Subcommittee of the Labor
Committee chair, 589, 652–55, 661
immigration issues and the Immigration and
Nationality Act of 1965, xxx, xxxii, 266,
268–74, 270n, 277, 289, 327, 449
Immigration Subcommittee and, 183, 266,
272–73
independence from White House positions,
202–3
Indian Education Subcommittee and, 467

India visits (1971, 1972), 584–86
influencing Nixon's policy decisions, 464–65, 603–4, 619–20, 650, 661, 678
Ireland visit (1970), 557, 559, 560, 583
JFK and his committee assignments, 182, 183
JFK and the summer of 1963, 203–4
JFK's advice to, 192–93
JFK's keeping tabs on, 185, 193
JFK's legislative program and, 186, 190, 447
Judiciary Committee and, 183, 184, 191, 195–96, 220, 224, 266, 272, 279, 283, 284, 295, 296, 299, 304, 328, 329, 445, 528, 531, 622, 624, 626, 629, 631–32, 635, 695, 705
Judiciary Committee hearings on Kleindienst and, 622–23, 625
Labor Committee and, xix–xx, 182, 194, 254, 255, 259, 265, 338, 646, 648, 650, 651, 654, 664
last visit to chambers, xxv
LBJ and, 239, 242, 250, 255–58, 332, 333, 336, 337, 347, 348, 351–52, 354, 385, 430, 434
LBJ's legislative agenda and, 253–58
lead-based paint poisoning bill and, 712–13
legislative achievements, xvii–xx, xxxii–xxxiii
legislative agenda, 264, 266, 274, 449–50
liberal coalition created by, 445–46
liberalism and, xxi–xxii, xxxiv, xxxv, xxxvi, 264, 266, 322, 343, 433, 444–45, 536, 538–43, 571
love for the Senate, 201–3
lowering the voting age and, 558–61, 560n
low expectations of, underestimation of, 184–85, 195, 224, 238–39, 282, 331, 434
majority whip position and, 431–39, 444, 445–50, 793n436
majority whip position lost, 566–72, 652, 809n569
making his legislative mark, 282, 287
March on Washington and, 218, 712
Meals on Wheels and, xix, 556–57
media attention, hearings used for, 463–64
Middle East peace and visits, 617, 699
minimum wage and, xxiii
minority hiring and, 719
morality, moral authority, in positions and, 221, 225, 227, 274, 365, 366, 522, 524, 526, 536, 537, 582, 634, 659, 735
moral leadership and, 288, 354, 403, 709
Morrissey judicial appointment fight and, 289–306, 307, 331
National Cancer Act, S.34 (War on Cancer) and, 660–66
as national figure, 262, 439, 460
Native American issues and, 451–52, 459, 465
as Nixon opponent and "shadow president,"

440–46, 447, 453, 455, 456, 460–61, 463, 465, 470, 515, 578
as Nixon rival and antagonist, 573, 583–89, 614–20
Nixon targeting of, 576–82, 627, 631
Nutrition and Human Needs Subcommittee, food stamp issue, 443–44, 464
oath of office by, 179
office of, called "Lourdes of Capitol Hill," xxvi
office of, location, furnishings, decor, 186–87
one man, one vote and redistricting fight, 326–31, 449
Pakistan trip, 465
plane crash and transformation, heightened sense of purpose, 265–306, 312, 320
place crash recovery, tutorials and studies during recuperation, 240–41, 249–50, 263, 279, 453
plane crash recovery, working from the hospital, 241–43, 263
pneumonia of (1970), 531, 566
police life insurance issue, 465
political views moving leftward, 588, 589
popularity of, 251, 288, 289, 332, 339
racial justice and, 713–14
reelection, 1964 and, 203–4, 228, 242–43
reelection, 1964, Massachusetts State Democratic Convention endorsement for Senate, 228
reelection, 1970 and, 519, 561–65
reelection, 1976 and, 733
Refugee Subcommittee and, 312–13, 463, 465, 584, 587, 617, 701–2
Republican partners and, 661
Republicans' opinions of, 184
reputation and image, 185–95
respect, earning, 223, 287–89, 296, 305–6, 320, 322, 324, 331
return after RFK's assassination, demeanor and voting record, 419, 429–39
reverence for the office, 180
reversing Civilian Aeronautics Board ruling, 277
RFK as presidential candidate and, 343–48, 357–81, 359n
RFK as senator from New York serving with, 258–63, 265, 266, 306
RFK's death and change in, 450
RFK's legacy and, 449–50
Russian trip and plight of Soviet Jews, 618, 709
school integration and busing issue, 719–23
school integration and busing issue, Boston and violent resistance, 724–34
sickle cell anemia research, 712, 719
social justice and, 536, 735
Soviet relations and, 618

—**Senate years** (*cont'd*):
staff and inner circle, xix, xx–xxi, xxiii, 186–89, 191, 262–65, 447–48, 462–63, 522–24, 537, 653–54
state politics and, 229–30
transparency in government and, 697
Vietnam War and, xxxii–xxxiii, 307–8, 311–18, 322–24, 326, 331–37, 341, 347–54, 347n, 403–4, 456–60, 526–27, 557–58, 565–66, 583–84, 586–87, 591–93, 618–19
Vietnam War and amnesty for draft resisters, 587, 701
Voting Rights Act of 1965 and poll tax fight, 276–89, 328, 329, 346, 439, 449
Watergate investigation and, 620–40, 654
women's rights, women constituents and, 550–51
as workhorse, 186, 194
years of service in, xv, xxxiv
—**writings**
Boston Globe series on Latin America, 125
The Fruitful Bough, 239
travel diaries and notebooks, 55–56, 76, 125
True Compass, 207n
Kennedy, Ethel Skakel (sister-in-law), xiii, xxiv, 83, 87, 108, 545, 632
at EMK's first major Senate address, 221
at EMK's Senate speech for Morrissey, 303
at EMK's Senate swearing in, 181
JPK's death and, 534
Kopechne's funeral and, 493
RFK's assassination and, 384, 386, 394
RFK's presidential candidacy and, 362, 365, 381
sailing with EMK, 396
Kennedy, George, 508n
Kennedy, Jacqueline Bouvier "Jackie" (sister-in-law), xxx, 79–80, 83, 87, 394
Chappaquiddick incident and, 487
on EMK's marriage and wife Joan, 109–10, 553
on EMK's womanizing, 549
father-in-law's death and, 534
JFK's assassination and, 208, 209
JFK's birthday observed, 225
Kennedy family and, 110
miscarriage of, 548
Onassis and, 393
presidency as "Camelot" and, 212
quotation follow Medgar Evers funeral, 372
RFK and, 211
RFK's assassination and, 384, 386
sailing with EMK, 396
will of, appointing EMK as guardian of her children, 204n
Kennedy, Joan Bennett (wife), 108, 659, 699, 709
alcoholism and sanitariums, 501–2, 549–50, 551, 552–56, 675–76, 716, 718

background and family, 84–85
birth of children, 102, 181
blond beauty of, 85, 546
Boston townhouse, Charles River Square and, 119, 166, 203
Catholicism of, 85
Chappaquiddick incident and, 501
character and personality, 85–86, 242
as chaste, 88–89
depression of, 502
early days of marriage, 92, 109–10, 545
EMK in the Senate and, 179, 181, 186, 193–94, 254
EMK's absences from family, 108
EMK's dating and wedding of, 83–84, 86–90
at EMK's first major Senate address, 221, 223
on EMK's grief for RFK, 395
EMK's incompatibility with, 545
EMK's infidelity and, 89, 547–49, 550–52, 554
EMK's plane crash, recovery, and, 233–34, 235, 241, 242–43
at EMK's pocket veto argument, 616
EMK's political future and, 116
on EMK's presidential ambitions, 575–76
EMK's presidential prospects (1972) and, 590
EMK's presidential prospects (1976) and, 716
EMK's press conference on not running (1976) and, 718
EMK's priorities vs., 108–9
EMK's reelection (1964), campaigning, 242–43
EMK's relationship with, 545–46, 549–50, 552, 554, 555, 671, 676, 716
EMK's sailing with, 396
EMK's Senate run and, 159, 167, 174
at EMK's Senate speech for Morrissey, 303
engagement ring, 88
feelings of inadequacy, insecurity, unhappiness, 545–47, 549
Georgetown home, 188, 194
honeymoon, 90
Hyannis Port and, 86, 87, 109–10
Italy trip (1961), 125
JFK dubs "The Dish," 89
JFK's assassination and, 206, 209
JFK's gift to, for campaigning, 108
Kennedy family and, 83, 87, 90, 109–10
Kopechne's funeral and, 492–93
married life of, 543–56
McLean, Va., home, 391, 543–44, 546
miscarriages, 226, 501–2, 545
Montego Bay vacation (1970), 568
musical talent of, 547
relationship with Jackie Kennedy, 553
relationship with Joe Kennedy, 87–88, 89, 90

relationship with Rose Kennedy, 86, 87, 88, 553
RFK's assassination and, 383, 384–85, 429
Senate Ladies and, 193
son Patrick, pregnancy with, 391
son Ted, Jr.'s cancer and, 671, 672, 674–75, 676, 716
Squaw Island, Mass. home, 472, 501
Stowe, Vt., ski trip, 86
Kennedy, John F. (JFK, brother)
advice to EMK, 44
anti-communism and, 96, 309, 310, 311
Arlington grave site, 336, 543
assassination of, xvi, 204–12, 461
awakening a new American optimism, 180
Azorean Refugee Act of 1958, 267
back problems and health issues, 46, 99, 113, 236–37, 249, 641
Bay of Pigs and, 308
"the best and brightest" and, 425
Billings and, 114
British memorial at Runnymede, 225
campaign speech on fealty to America over the Catholic Church, 104
Catholic voters and, 103
character and personality, evolution of, 113, 119, 143–44
character and personality, vs. his brothers, 144–46, 147, 541–42
charisma of, 378
childhood, 23, 44
at Choate, 143
civil rights and, 112, 213, 216–19, 537, 712
civil rights bill, 194, 217–18, 219, 223, 225, 226–27
confidence of, 106
congressional race (1946), 57, 95, 96, 98, 118, 126, 289–90, 734
as congressman, 99
critics of, 212–13
Cuban Missile Crisis, 174–76, 179
defense spending and, 111–12, 308–9
domestic policy, 111
EMK, sailing, and, 47
EMK and the summer of 1963, 203–4
EMK as a senator and, 181, 185, 192, 193, 203
EMK as campaign manager (1958), 98
EMK as comic relief, 114
EMK as paterfamilias, surrogate father for his children, 675
EMK loved by, 146, 182, 204, 262
EMK picking up his fallen standard, xvii, xxxiii, 402, 429, 439, 536
EMK's advice on Algeria and, 76–77
EMK's cheating scandal and, 64
EMK's fulfilling his legacy, 212
as EMK's godfather, 26

EMK's health, strength, and, 61, 73, 74, 113, 146
EMK's hero worship of, 112–14, 180, 211
EMK's last times with, 211–12
EMK's political future and, 75–76, 98, 120
EMK's pranks and, 73
EMK's Senate committee assignments and, 182, 183
EMK's Senate race and, 129, 131–35, 138, 140–42, 146, 153, 166, 170, 175
EMK's Senate win and advice to, 177–78
EMK's wedding and, 89
EMK's working on political campaigns, 57, 88, 90, 98–108, 147, 149, 379
fatalistic mantra, 146
father's influence on, 44, 94, 132
father's stroke and, 169–70
frailty of, 60–61, 146
funeral of, xiv, xxvii, 208–9
gifts to family for campaigning, 108
grandfather Fitzgerald's impact on his political career, 57–58
Harvard football and, 59
heroism in the Pacific, 46, 309
at Hyannis Port compound, 13, 41, 60–61
immigration reform and, xxxiv, 213, 216, 266–68
impact on the nation, 213
independent judgments of, vs. his father's, 132
JPK and political career, 56–57, 74, 96
Judge Wendell Arthur Garrity, Jr. and, 721
judicial appointments, 217
King and, 711n
legislative program of, 186, 190, 201, 204, 214, 245
liberalism and, 96, 97, 110, 213, 216
Mailer on, 107, 213, 144
marriage to Jacqueline Bouvier, 87
McCarthy and, 96, 97
media and, 134
Medicare and, 216, 537, 643, 645
as mediocre student, 37
moonshot and, 485
moral authority and, 98, 227, 274
moral courage and, 217–18
Morrissey and, 289–91, 292
naming of, 6
A Nation of Immigrants, 267, 776n267
New Frontier and, 367, 515
Nixon debates, 162
Nuclear Test-Ban Treaty, 444
political beliefs, 96–97, 110–11
political change in, 537–38
popularity of, 179
presidency of, 110–12, 252
presidency of, as "Camelot," 212
presidential ambitions, 94, 97, 98, 99, 100, 573

Kennedy, John F. (JFK, brother) (cont'd):
  presidential library, 225
  presidential race (1959–60), 17, 100–108, 117,
    757n105
  presidential race, JPK's cash payouts, 104
  Profiles in Courage, 239–40, 495
  PT-109 tie clasps, 129–30, 287
  public speaking and, 90
  public's perception of, 112
  reelection and, 186, 204, 217
  Reeves's description of, 540
  relationship with his father, 46, 97
  Republican Party swing to the right and, 245
  reputation for indolence, 99
  retail politics and, 145
  RFK as attorney general, 114–15
  RFK compared with, 29
  RFK running his campaigns, 98, 144–45
  RFK's relationship with, 113, 204, 210
  rocking chair and, 181
  sailing and, 471
  self-confidence of, 241
  Senate race (1952), 98, 129, 145, 171
  Senate race (1958), 97, 98–99, 149
  as senator, 70, 75, 97, 98, 99, 192, 201, 259,
    462
  sensitivity to the poor, 98
  sister Rosemary and, 24
  taking Joe Jr.'s place in Kennedy family, 56–57
  television and, 106
  using family by, 108
  vacated Senate seat of, and Ben Smith,
    122–23
  vacated Senate seat of, and Eddie McCormack,
    124
  vice presidential nomination fight (1956) and,
    77, 228–29
  Vietnam and, 308, 309–10, 311, 319
  womanizing of, 5, 82, 83, 89, 395, 547–48
  World War II and U.S. Navy, 33, 46
Kennedy, Joseph, II (nephew), xxiv, 726, 727,
    735, 736
Kennedy, Joseph P., Jr. (brother)
  conservatism and, 537
  as eldest, chosen one in the family, 47
  EMK and, 37
  in Germany (1934), Hitler and, 31
  Harvard football and, 59
  Harvard Law School and, 33, 74
  at Hyannis Port compound, 41
  as mediocre student, 37
  naming of, 6
  sister Kick and, 47
  sister Rosemary and, 24
  studying with Harold Laski, 94
  World War II and fatal mission, 46–47, 208,
    750n47
  World War II and U.S. Navy, 33

Kennedy, Joseph P., Sr. (father), 3
  absences from home and family, 22, 41
  allegiance to Irish Catholics, 95
  anti-Catholic bias and, 9, 11, 12–13, 14, 15,
    539
  anti-Semitism and, 11, 31, 97
  as athlete, 59
  background, 6–7, 9
  in banking, 9–10
  bootlegger myth, 11
  Boston Globe interview "Democracy is all
    done," 33
  Bronxville, N.Y. estate, 12, 36, 41
  career, social status, and stigma of being
    Irish, 10, 15
  childhood home, 6
  closest friend, Edward Moore, 4–6
  Clover Club speech (1937), 15
  Columbia Trust Company and, 6, 9, 10, 540
  competitive not moral guidance by, 18
  conservatism and, 537
  controlling his children's lives, 41, 56–57,
    74–75, 87, 88–90, 94–110, 114–17, 118,
    534
  courting and marrying Rose Fitzgerald, 7–8
  daughter Rosemary and, 25
  death of, 533
  Democratic Party and, 595
  dynasty building by, 114–17, 131, 171, 172
  EMK, Chappaquiddick incident, and, 484,
    494, 495, 533
  EMK and choice between serious or
    nonserious life, 44–45, 64
  EMK on, 11
  EMK's birth and, 3, 4
  EMK's campaign, financing of, 152, 153
  EMK's cheating scandal and, 63–65, 64n
  EMK's football prowess and, 73–74
  EMK's future and, 74, 75, 76, 100, 108
  EMK's moot court competition win and, 93
  EMK's oath of office and, 179
  EMK's plane crash and, 237, 248
  EMK's pranks and, 73
  EMK's relationship with, 28–29, 38, 42–45,
    49, 53, 58, 61, 72, 75, 78, 79, 122, 169–70,
    249, 396, 533–34
  EMK's Senate run and, 118, 121–42, 168
  EMK's wife Joan and, 87–88
  family as principal interest in life, 15–22, 32
  family dinners and, 44
  family image and, 18
  FDR and, 5, 14–15, 27, 30, 31, 95
  Fenway Building Trust real estate company, 5
  financial conservatism of, 11
  focus on his children's careers, 41
  French Riviera and, 28
  Great Depression and, 11, 13–14
  Harvard University and, 6, 9, 54, 58–59

health issues and strokes, 169–70, 173, 532–33, 641

his "siege against the world," 9, 11, 15

home on Beals Street, 4

Hyannis Port during the war years and, 41–45

Hyannis Port house and, 13, 14

isolationism and, 111

JFK and, 46

JFK's assassination and, 207–8

JFK's campaign, cash payouts and, 104

JFK's campaigns and, 98

JFK's presidential race (1959–60) and, 100–108

Joe, Jr.'s death, reaction to, 47, 53

learning to "stick together," 11

leaves Boston for New York, 12

liberalism and, 95, 96

loyalty and, 127, 292

as Maritime Commission head, 5–6, 27

married life of, 22, 23

McCarthy and, 95

Morris Electric Company and, 10

Morrissey and, 289–90, 291–92

movie industry and, 5, 10

Nixon and, 95

in Palm Beach, 3, 4, 35, 90, 100, 169, 249, 552

parenting by, 17, 18, 20–22, 63–65, 82, 83, 87, 88, 106

pessimism of, 13

political beliefs, 94–96, 97

political careers of his sons and, 94–110, 130, 132, 405

Pope Pius and, 30–31

power, politics, and, 13–15, 94

presidential ambitions, 31, 94

pretensions and, 40

pulling strings for his children, 46, 67–68, 118–19

Republican Party and, 14

RFK's assassination and, 391

RFK's relationship with, 29, 42

Riverdale, N.Y. mansion, 12

Rosemary's lobotomy and institutionalization of, 45

rules for his family, 20–21, 90, 209

as Securities and Exchange Commission chairman, 5, 27

self-image, as aristocrat, 16

slogans of, 117, 405, 415

Somerset liquor distribution company, 11

standards set for his children, 44, 82

Swanson affair and, 3, 25, 63

Tunney and, 77

as U.S. Ambassador to the Court of St. James, 6, 27–33

as vindictive, 158

"wall" between family and business, 13

wealth of, 10, 11, 14, 15

on winning, 17–18, 82, 92

womanizing of, 22, 23, 395, 547–48

World War I and Fore River shipping plant, 9–10

World War II and, 31–32, 41–42

Kennedy, Kara (daughter), xxiv, xxviii, 102, 181, 242, 501, 544, 675, 699

cancer diagnosis, xxvii

EMK's posthumous letter to, xxiv

Kennedy, Kathleen "Kick" (sister), 26, 29, 57, 95

death of, 52–53, 208

engagement to Peter Fitzwilliam and mother's outrage, 53

marriage to Hartington and ostracism by parents, 47

war death of husband, Billy, 47

at the *Washington Times-Herald*, 47

World War II and, 33, 47

Kennedy, Kathleen (niece), EMK and wedding of, 672–73

Kennedy, Kerry (niece), xxvi

Kennedy, Patricia "Pat" (sister), 32, 33

Kennedy, Patrick Joseph "P.J." (grandfather), 6, 8, 14

Kennedy, Patrick (son), 501, 534, 539, 544

asthma of, 641

Chappaquiddick incident and, 517

on EMK and Joan's drinking, 555

on EMK and Joan's marriage, 92

on EMK's childhood unhappiness, 49–50

on EMK's connection to the pain of others, 541

on EMK's empathy with the individual, 542

on EMK's fatalism, 576

EMK's funeral and, xiii, xiv, xxiv

on EMK's grief for RFK, 394

EMK's posthumous letter to, xxiv

on his father's desire to go west, 117

on his mother's alcoholism, 553

illnesses and addictions, xxix

on Kennedy family's emotional repression, 392, 555–56

speaking at his father's funeral, xxix

Kennedy, Robert F., Jr. (nephew), 20, 500

on his grandfather, 32

Kennedy, Robert F. (RFK, brother), xiii, 403

ABM system opposed, 453

in Acapulco post-1960 election, 108

Aeschylus quoted by, 372

assassination of, xvi, 381–88, 424, 451, 461

birth of, 3

"boiler-room girls" and, 472–73, 476, 493, 581

brain trust for, 344–45, 348, 359, 361, 364, 368, 371, 393, 401

challenging his father's prejudices, 97–98

as champion of the underprivileged, 734

Kennedy, Robert F. (RFK, brother) (*cont'd*):
  character and personality, 259, 260, 262, 324, 345, 374
  character and personality, vs. his brothers, 144–46, 147, 306, 322
  Civil Rights Act of 1964 and, 226
  civil rights and, 217, 218, 712
  coalition building by, 376, 378, 425
  competitiveness, 261, 265
  critics and opponents, 366–67, 379
  crowds greeting, charisma and, 375, 378
  Cuban Missile Crisis, 175
  educational inconstancy of, effects of, 49
  education as issue for, 645
  EMK, draft reform bill, and, 338
  EMK and eulogy for, 386–88
  EMK as paterfamilias, surrogate father for his children, 544, 672–73, 675
  EMK picking up his fallen standard, xvii, 401, 402–3, 412, 415, 429, 439, 443, 449–50, 456–57, 459, 461, 536
  EMK's childhood and, 28, 42, 50
  EMK's concern for his safety, 358, 377
  EMK's grief for, 391–98, 405, 406, 429
  EMK's one man, one vote fight and, 328, 330
  EMK's plane crash and, 234, 235, 236
  EMK's relationship with, 73, 74, 92, 93, 120, 251, 258, 260–63, 367, 374–75, 391–92, 393
  EMK's school, Milton Academy and, 50
  on EMK's Senate address on the civil rights bill, 224
  EMK's Senate race and, 125, 126, 128, 130, 139, 140, 141–42, 162, 168
  EMK's weight and, 37
  The Enemy Within, 393
  epigraph of commonplace book, 543
  as face of American liberalism, 243
  as faithful to Ethel, 547, 548
  fatalism of, 372, 373
  father as U.S. ambassador in England and, 28, 30
  father's political ambitions for, 94
  father's relationship with, 29, 42
  father's stroke and, 169
  friendship with George Cabot Lodge, 171
  funeral of, xiv, xvi, xxvii
  grudge against Tydings, 307
  at Harvard, 50
  at Harvard, football and, 54–55
  as a hater, 214, 215, 307
  Hickory Hill, McLean, Va., home, 194, 205, 357, 364, 391, 450, 544, 671
  Hickory Hill seminars, 194
  Hyannis Port and, 17
  idealism of, 243, 259, 360, 379
  Immigration and Nationality Act of 1965 and, 272, 273

  as impulsive, 359
  Jackie and, 211
  JFK compared with, 29
  JFK's assassination and, 205–6, 207, 207n, 208–9, 210–11, 243, 540
  as JFK's attorney general, 114–15, 172, 281, 566
  JFK's legacy and, 215, 243–44
  JFK's political campaigns and, 98, 373
  JFK's presidency and, 113
  JFK's presidential race (1959–60) and, 100–108
  JFK's relationship with, 113, 204, 210
  King assassination and, 372
  law school and, 74, 75, 82, 92, 93
  LBJ and, xxxiv, 214–16, 243–44, 255, 256, 257–58, 259, 341, 342
  LBJ's withdrawal from the 1968 election and, 370–71
  lesson of JFK's death, 266
  liberalism and, xxxiv, 214, 243, 265–66, 341–42, 343, 361, 378, 389, 417
  as living memorial to JFK, 341–42, 344, 367
  marriage to Ethel Skakel, 87
  McCarthy and, 96, 328, 537
  as mediocre student, 37
  memorials and honors, 393, 430
  moral authority and, 365–66, 371–72, 373, 375–76, 378–79, 387, 389, 404, 452, 515, 538
  Morrissey and, 291, 300, 301–2, 304
  national moral redemption and, 417, 423
  Native Americans and, 451
  in Naval Reserve, 50, 65
  political change in, 537–38
  politics personalized by, 465–66
  at Portsmouth Priory, 34
  poverty issues and, 321–22
  presidential ambitions, 260, 261, 324, 335, 573
  presidential campaign (1968) and, xxxiv, 343–48, 357–81, 388
  primary mission in politics, 243, 265–66, 378, 388, 417
  as protector of the poor, 98, 342, 450–51, 536, 540
  public speaking and, 90, 262
  Rackets Committee investigations, 374, 393, 537
  retail politics and, 145
  as runt of the Kennedy litter, 98
  as "ruthless," 144–45, 235, 343, 344, 630
  as sanctimonious, 366
  Senate race in New York (1964), 244, 247
  Senate Special Subcommittee on Indian Education, 451, 463
  Senate staff, 262–63, 392–93

as senator from New York, 251, 255, 258–63, 265, 266, 272, 273, 287, 322, 324
"tame the savageness of man" speech on the night of King assassination, 22, 372, 403, 713
toughness of, 29
transformation of, 243, 249, 259, 265–66, 341–42, 378, 540
Vietnam War and, 314, 319, 322, 324, 332, 334, 336, 340, 341–42, 357–58, 404, 452, 456, 459
Voting Rights Act of 1965 and, 277, 285–86
wedding of, 89
women and, 84
Kennedy, Rose Fitzgerald (mother)
absences from home and family, 23, 30, 34, 144
Ace of Clubs formed by, 12
aesthetic values of, 18–19, 20
background and status, 6, 15
birth of Jean, 3
birth of RFK, 3
at Blumenthal convent school, Holland, 19
Bronxville, N.Y. estate, 12, 36
as class conscious, 16
courtship and marriage, 7–8
daughter Kathleen's engagement to Fitzwilliam opposed, 52–53
daughter Kathleen's marriage to Hartington opposed by, 47
daughter Rosemary and, 24
daughter Rosemary's lobotomy and institutionalization, 45
Democratic Party and, 14
EMK, Chappaquiddick incident, and, 484–85, 489, 517, 533
on EMK and a "ninth-child talent," xviii, 191
on EMK and JFK, 113–14
EMK as youngest child, and unplanned for, 3, 25
on EMK going to law school, 74–75
EMK's campaigning and, 151, 152
EMK's childhood and, 30
on EMK's dedication to JFK and RFK, 429
EMK's grief for RFK and, 396
EMK's oath of office and, 179
on EMK's personality, 146
EMK's plane crash injuries and, 238
EMK's presidential prospects (1976) and, 717
on EMK's reckless courage, 79
EMK's Senate race and, 128, 173
EMK's Senate reelection (1964), and, 243
EMK's Senate reelection (1970) and, 563
on EMK's size, 60
EMK's swearing in, 181
EMK's wife Joan and, 86, 87, 88, 553
on expectations for her children, 44
faith of, devoutness, xxxii, 19, 53, 397–98, 538
family image and, 18–19, 20

father denies her going to Wellesley, 19
as father's hostess for political events, 7
funeral of, xiv–xv
household staff of, 16–17
husband as U.S. ambassador to England and, 28
husband's health issues and, 169
husband's infidelity, 3, 22, 23, 547, 548–49
on JFK, 144
JFK's assassination and, 207, 209, 210
Luke 12:48 and, 538
married life of, 3, 4, 22, 23, 547
New York apartment of, 516
Palm Beach and, 16, 33, 35, 36
parenting by, 19–20, 23–26, 30, 33, 35, 44, 641
perfection and, 19–20, 24–25
pretensions and, 40
prudishness of, 22–23
relationship of her husband and Eddie Moore, 4, 5
on RFK, 144, 366
RFK's assassination and, 383, 391, 397–98
in Riverdale, N.Y. mansion, 12
St. Stephen's Church and, xiv–xv
spiritual values of, 19
vanity of, 37
warning to her daughters-in-law, 549
wealth of, 16–17
Kennedy, Rosemary (sister), 24–25, 28, 33, 53, 540, 641
EMK and, 45–46, 540
lobotomy and institutionalization of, 45
as mentally challenged, 24, 45–46
World War II, in England, 32
Kennedy, Ted (Edward), Jr. (son), xxiv, 242, 501, 544
birth of, 181
cancer and amputation, xxviii, 641–75, 676
EMK prioritizing his recovery, 673, 677, 683, 716–17
EMK's posthumous letter to, xxiv
on his father, xxxi
Nixon's call to, 672
speaking at his father's funeral, xxviii–xxix
Kennedy, Victoria "Vicki" (wife)
EMK's funeral and, xxiv
wedding of, xxv
Kennedy family
achievement and, 21
aesthetics and, 20, 21, 23, 54, 88, 89, 106, 148, 392
as America's royalty, 107
anti-Catholic bias and, 11–12, 539
arrogance, rudeness of, 541
blood ties and, 415–16, 473
Bobby as runt of the litter, 98
as Boston Irish royalty, 6, 16

Kennedy family (*cont'd*):
brand of, xxii, 171, 379, 405, 464
in Bronxville, N.Y., 12, 29, 30–31
Chappaquiddick incident and end of an era, 513–18
children not taught about business, 17
clannishness, 109–10
as class conscious, 16
Columbia Trust Company and, 6, 9, 10
competitiveness of, 17–18, 24, 45, 59, 82, 392
desire to serve and, 538
Edgartown Regatta and, 471
EMK, Chappaquiddick incident, and, 484
EMK, football, and physical ability, 61
EMK as ninth and youngest child, 3, 29, 31, 44, 53, 191, 260, 336, 465
EMK as paterfamilias, surrogate father, 672–73, 675, 717
EMK's family responsibilities, 392–93, 395, 397, 398, 399, 429–30
EMK's funeral and, xxiv
EMK's presidential prospects (1976) and, 717
EMK's role in, 29, 33, 41, 53
EMK's status in, 6, 64, 71, 393
EMK teased by, 37
emotional trauma as weakness in, 49
energy of, 60
expectations of, xxxiv, 18, 20, 44, 54, 57, 78, 161, 395
fate and, 513
Fitzgerald's way versus Kennedy's, 39–41
football and, 59, 71, 73, 110, 113, 144
Harvard University and, 54, 55
home and family as sacrosanct, 17, 21, 717
home in Bronxville, N.Y., 4
Hyannis Port compound and, 13
image and, xxxiv, 18, 20, 21, 43, 46, 53, 87, 106, 109, 543, 553, 555
infidelity of men in, 547
JFK's assassination and, 208, 209
JFK's political campaigns and, 100–108
Joe, Jr. lost in combat, World War II, 47
Joe, Jr.'s place in, 47
JPK and family dinners, 44
JPK controlling choices for his children, 41, 56–57, 74–75, 87, 89, 94–110, 114–17, 118
JPK's absences and, 22, 41
JPK seeking power and prestige for, 15
JPK's lesson about precedence of family, 15–16, 17, 18, 21–22
JPK's rules, 90, 392
Kathleen lost in a plane crash, 52–53
Kathleen ostracized, 47
known to the public by first names, xvi–xvii
as "lace-curtain" or "high Irish," 9, 12, 13, 124
lack of permanent residence, 35
lack of sibling enmity or jealousy, 18

LBJ and, 255–56, 257
learning that the best defense is to "stick together," 11, 16, 17
Luke 12:48 quoted to, 21, 40, 538
money not discussed in, 13
moral education lacking, 18, 19, 21
move from Boston to New York (1927), 12
as nation's soap opera, xvi
parental rules for, 20–21
pathology of secrecy in, xxxiv, 45–46
place in the America century, xvi
political and cultural meaning of, xvii
as a political dynasty, 114–17, 131, 171, 172, 184
primogeniture in, 260
pursuit of perfection and, 19–20, 21, 24–25, 46
reshaping of American politics by, 107
RFK's presidential candidacy and, 375
rituals of loss, 208
role of each child in, 29
Rosemary lost (to lobotomy), 45
the sea and sailing, as balm for grief, 47–48, 395–97
secrecy and, 555
as Shakespearean tragedy, xvi
social progress, liberalism, and, 515, 537
solidarity of, 126
spiritual values of, 19
stoicism of, 238, 249, 383, 392, 555–56, 674–75
tenacity and, 73
traditions of, 4
as vindictive, 158, 177–78
wealth of, 60
winning and, 436
womanizing of, 82
World War II and disintegration of, 33, 35, 45–48
yacht, the *Ten of Us,* 3
Kent, Frank, Jr., 547
Kent State University, Ohio, 557, 583, 588
Keough, Rosemary, 472, 475, 510
Kern, John Worth, 432
Kerner Commission, 556
Kerrigan, John, 727, 734, 735
Kerry, John, xiii, xxv, 586
Khrushchev, Nikita, 308
Kilmuir, Lord, 92
Kimmitt, J. Stanley, 181, 431, 567
King, Coretta Scott, 383, 386
King, Ed, 233
King, Jim, 149, 243, 244, 500, 535, 724, 731–32, 735
King, Martin Luther, Jr., xv, 226, 376, 711n
assassination of, 372, 424
Cicero, Ill. march, 320
EMK and, 320

EMK's poll tax fight and, 288, 288n
"I Have a Dream" speech, 218
March on Washington and, 218
RFK's " tame the savageness of man" speech
on the night of his assassination, 22, 372,
403, 713
Kintner, Robert, 32
Kirk, Paul, Jr.
EMK's campaigning and, 563, 567
EMK's presidential possibility for 1976 and,
705, 706, 713
on EMK's Senate staff, 448, 460, 705, 718,
726, 727
Kissinger, Henry, 212, 500, 501, 588, 601, 604,
606, 617–18, 700, 703
Klein, Joe, 535
Kleindienst, Richard, 509–10, 618
ITT payoff and, 622, 623, 625, 626, 640
resignation of, 632
Knowlton, William, 350
Komer, Robert, 350, 353, 355
Kopechne, Gwen, 475, 483–84, 492–93, 497,
516, 715
Kopechne, Joe, 475, 483–84, 492, 493, 516, 715
Kopechne, Mary Jo
account of Chappaquiddick accident and
aftermath, 476–83, 490
asks EMK for ride back to Edgartown, 475
"bachelor's ball" dinner, 472
background, 475–76
body recovered, 482, 489
character, as "real straight arrow," 475–76,
507
district attorney's reopening of investigation
and, 504
EMK's moral duties for, 491
EMK notifying her parents, 483–84
EMK's payment to her family, 516
EMK's transfer of her body, 491–92
evidence of any romantic link to EMK absent,
507
gathering of "boiler-room girls" on
Chappaquiddick and, 472, 475
Kielty Funeral Home, Plymouth, Pa., and
funeral, 492
media coverage and, 485
Nixon's investigation and, 501
RFK's presidential campaign and, 472–73, 476
Korean War, 55, 56, 65, 67, 68
Kornitzer, Bela, 125
Kosygin, Alexei, 348
Kraft, Joseph, 215
Krock, Arthur, 17
Ky, Nguyen Cao, 314

labor unions, 245, 368, 377, 378, 529, 595, 596
decline of unionized blue-collar jobs, 611
EMK for president and, 684

national health insurance and, 650, 682,
683–85
negotiated employment-based health plans,
644, 682
Lacayo, Richard, xxii
Ladd, Everett Carll, Jr., 611
Lahage, Barbara, 187
Lahey Clinic, Burlington, Mass., 237, 248,
383
EMK as trustee, 642
Laird, Melvin, 453, 677, 686, 689, 691
Lamar, Henry, 71
Landers, Ann, 662
Lapham, Lewis, xxxiv
LaRosa, Raymond, 248, 474, 479
Lasker, Albert, 660
Lasker, Mary, 660, 661, 662, 663
Laski, Harold, 94, 537
Lauder, Polly, 77
Lavidor, Elise, xvii
Lawford, Christopher (nephew), 533
Lawford, Patricia Kennedy (sister), 84, 92
Chappaquiddick incident and, 487
at EMK's oath of office, 179
EMK's plane crash and, 234
at EMK's Senate swearing in, 181
father's death and, 534
RFK's assassination and, 383, 384
Lawford, Peter (brother-in-law), 84, 238
Lawrence, David, 101
Lawrence Park West Country Day School, 33
Leamer, Laurence, 86, 87, 544–45, 550
Legislative Reorganization Act, 432
Lehman, Herbert, 273
Leighton, Delmar, 70
Leland, Leslie, 505
Lenzner, Terry, 635
Lerner, Max, 75, 443
Ted and the Kennedy Legend, 514
Levin, Murray, 150, 153, 156
Lewis, Anthony, 343, 593–94
Lewis, Bill, 129
Lewis, John, 381, 384
liberalism
accomplishments of 89th Congress and, 252,
325, 343
backlash against, 389, 556
Bentsen's victory and end of in Texas, 649
boost in 1974 midterms, 698
Boston anti-busing violence and, 725, 734
change, speed of, and, 428
Chappaquiddick incident's consequences for,
515
civil rights and, 97, 216
decline of, reasons for, xxxv–xxxvi, 326, 343,
366, 608–9, 611–12
Democratic Party and, xxi, xxxiv, xxxv–xxxvi,
439

liberalism (*cont'd*):
 as dying wind, 307
 elitism and, 710, 734, 735
 EMK and, xxi, xxxiv, xxxv, 264, 266, 322, 343,
  366, 433, 443–45, 515, 536, 538, 543,
  571–72
 EMK's liberal education, 120
 EMK's motivations for championing
  liberalism, 538–43
 EMK's presidential prospects (1976) and,
  710–11, 714
 EMK's Senate run and, 133
 failure of, 735
 FDR and, 95
 FDR's definition of a liberal, 111
 fear of perception of weakness, 309, 311
 Goldwater's attack on, 246
 health care issues and, 320
 Humphrey's defeat and, 424
 immigration issues and, 267, 275
 Irish Catholic Democrats and, 95
 JFK and, 96, 97, 110, 213, 216
 JFK's assassination and, 275, 428
 JFK's death and moral moment, 713
 JFK's legislative program and, 186, 190, 201,
  204, 214
 JFK's moral authority and, 98, 227, 274
 JFK's moral courage and, 217–18
 JPK and, 95, 96
 LBJ and, 214, 216, 256
 LBJ's election and, 424
 LBJ's Great Society and, 252, 275, 322, 325,
  389, 428
 "limousine liberal" and elitism, 607
 "lost the confidence of the majority," 425
 moral authority and, xxxv–xxxvi, 213, 247,
  275, 332, 365–66, 389, 403, 404, 417, 428,
  515, 537, 698–99, 708, 734, 735
 morality in politics and, xxxvi, 97, 201, 219,
  331
 national health insurance and, 646
 Nixon's threat to, 417, 443, 582, 604–6,
  608–12, 613–14
 post–New Deal liberal consensus, 111, 201,
  245, 246, 378, 417, 424, 425, 515, 609, 610
 postwar economic boom and, 97
 presidential election (1972), Nixon's landslide
  victory, and, 608–9, 612
 racial issues, white rage, and, 734
 RFK and, xxxiv, 214, 243, 265–66, 341–42,
  343, 361, 365–66, 378, 389, 417
 RFK's moral authority and, 365–66, 371–72,
  373, 375–76, 378–79, 387, 389, 404, 452,
  515, 538
 rightward turn in politics and, xxxv, 710
 U.S. Congress, Democratic majority and
  (1965), 252
 U.S. Senate and, 190–91, 201, 217

 Vietnam War harmful to, 322, 325–26,
  342–43, 358, 389
 Warren Court and, 527–28
 working class as backbone, 734
Library Services Act, 204
Liddy, G. Gordon, 621, 625
Life magazine, 468
 on Chappaquiddick incident, 477
 on EMK after Chappaquiddick, 520–21
 on EMK's return to the Senate, 251
 on EMK visit to India (1971), 585
Lincoln, Abraham, funeral train, xiv
Lincoln, Evelyn, 114, 132
Lindsay, John, 469, 562, 607
Linh, Tran Ngoc, 315
Lippman, Theo, 437, 451, 499, 586, 619, 626,
  692, 693, 793n436
Littlefield, Nick, xxiii, xxv
 EMK's funeral and singing "Love Changes
  Everything," xxv
 EMK's legislative legacy and, xix–xx, xxiii
 as EMK's staff director, chief counsel on the
  Labor Committee, xix
Loan, Nguyen Ngoc, 356
Lodge, George Cabot, 171–78, 241
 debating EMK, 174–75
Lodge, Henry Cabot, 171
Lodge, Henry Cabot, Jr., 129, 171, 313, 353, 562
Loen, Vernon, 681
Long, Huey, 431
Long, Russell, 260, 408, 418, 431, 436, 670
 alcoholism of, 431, 436, 439, 469, 555
 EMK's challenge to majority whip position,
  431–39, 569, 793n436
 as Finance Committee chairman, 431, 438,
  652, 653, 655, 667, 680
 health insurance and, 681
 oil interests and, 435, 436, 444
 political positions of, 444
 as Senate majority whip, 431–32, 433, 435,
  438, 567
Look, Christopher, 504–5, 508, 510
Look magazine
 EMK's piece on Vietnam, 317–18
 "Kennedy's Comeback: Will He or Won't
  He?," 574
Lorain County Medical Society, 648
Los Angeles Times, 229, 262, 288
 Cannon on EMK's politics, 612
 Chappaquiddick incident and, 497, 715
 on EMK after Chappaquiddick, 525
 on EMK and anti-war protesters, 324
 EMK refuses to run in 1976 and, 718
 on EMK's crowds, 608
 EMK's presidential prospects (1972) and, 590
Louisiana, 593
 presidential election (1968) and, 408
 See also Boggs, Hale; Long, Russell

Lowenstein, Allard, 343, 385, 399, 559
Lucey, Patrick, 323–24, 600
Ludtke, Melissa, 146, 554
Lukas, J. Anthony, 727, 729, 735–36
    Common Ground, 735
Luke 12:48, 21, 40, 538
Lynch, John "Pat," 124
Lyons, Mary Ellen, 472
Lyons, Nance, 472, 473, 511, 523, 550–51

Ma, Yo-Yo, xxviii
Maas, Peter, 410–11
MacArthur, Douglas, 277
Macdonald, Torbert, 59
MacLeish, Archibald, 138
Macmillan, Harold, 140, 225
Magnuson, Warren, 558, 559–60, 560n, 569,
    570
Magruder, Jeb, 579
Maguire, Dick, 134
Maguire, Joseph, 66, 67
Mahern, Louis, 371
Mailer, Norman, 144, 211, 598
    "Superman Comes to the Supermarket," 107,
    213
Maine
    EMK's grief for RFK and sailing, 397–98,
    414
    Muskie as senator, 416
    Tunney's home in, 397, 406
Malm, Mrs. Pierre, 482, 508
Manac'h, Étienne, 340
Manatos, Mike, 283
Manchester, William
    The Death of a President, 205n, 206–7
Manchester Union-Leader, Nixon's dirty tricks
    against Muskie and, 594
Manhattanville College of the Sacred Heart,
    Purchase, N.Y., 83, 555
    EMK's wife Joan at, 84–86
    Kennedy girls Eunice and Jean at, 83, 84
    Kennedy gymnasium at, 84
    Rose Kennedy and, 84, 87
Mankiewicz, Frank, 383–85, 513, 599, 705
Mansfield, Mike, 181, 182, 192, 199, 204, 253,
    304, 571, 635, 693
    background, 199
    Carswell judicial nomination and, 531
    Chappaquiddick incident and, 497, 519, 521
    Civil Rights Act of 1964 and, 220–21
    defense appropriations and, 456
    draft reform bill and, 339
    EMK as majority whip and, 442–43, 444, 446,
    567, 569
    on EMK as "the sad one," 393
    EMK earns respect of, 305
    EMK provided Secret Service protection by,
    594

EMK running for senate majority whip and,
    433, 438
    on EMK vs. his brothers, 434–35
    LBJ and, 199–200, 369
    lowering the voting age and, 559–60, 561
    Nixon's presidency and, 442
    presidential race (1972) and, 601
    as Senate majority leader, 181, 182, 199–201,
    215, 431, 432, 433, 436, 461
    Vietnam War and, 310–11, 369, 459, 587
    Voting Rights Act of 1965 and, 278, 280,
    280n, 283–84, 286, 288, 289, 329
    Watergate investigation and, 628–29
March on Washington, 218, 243, 278, 712
Marcos, Imelda, 546
Maria Pia, Princess, 551, 580
Markham, Paul, 479, 481, 482, 483, 495, 509,
    511
Marsh, Jerry, 188, 263
Marshall, Burke, 224, 281, 361, 407, 488, 639,
    706
    Chappaquiddick incident and, 480, 481, 482,
    483, 484, 486, 487
Marshall, E. G., 647, 648
Marshall, Thurgood, 279, 284
Martha's Vineyard, Mass., 471
    Chappaquiddick island and, 471
    Edgartown, resentment of the Kennedys in,
    505
    Edgartown Regatta, 471, 472
    EMK arrives in, July 18, 1969, 471
    Shiretown Inn, 472, 474, 480–81, 481n, 507,
    511
    See also Chappaquiddick incident
Martin, Ed, 127, 471, 541, 706, 718, 726, 727
    EMK's plane crash and, 230, 233, 234, 239,
    248
    EMK's Senate run and, 127–28, 157, 160,
    165–66, 167
    on EMK's Senate staff, 241–42, 244
Martin, John Bartlow, 216, 390
Massachusetts, 228
    ABM site proposed for, 453
    Brooke as first black senator, 530
    civil rights in, 218, 223
    EMK and Chappaquiddick, public's response,
    497–98, 513
    EMK as senator and, 186, 194, 195, 202–3,
    216, 222, 229, 257, 268, 277, 293
    EMK campaigning for Humphrey (1968), 420,
    422–23
    EMK's first public address after RFK's death,
    401–3, 420
    EMK's promise to investigate corruption in,
    139–40, 164, 228, 229
    EMK's Senate reelection (1964), 247
    EMK's Senate reelection (1970), 519,
    561–65

Massachusetts (*cont'd*):
  EMK's speeches against the Vietnam War in,
    352–53, 354
  EMK's statement on Chappaquiddick incident
    and, 494
  immigration and, 216, 222, 268
  political corruption in, 154, 157, 228
  presidential election (1964) and, 247
  "Racial Imbalance Act," 720, 721, 723
  Saltonstall as senator, 295, 299
  See also Boston, Mass.; *specific places*
Massachusetts Democratic Party, 520
  conservatism of, 155
  corruption in, 139, 229
  EMK endorsed for Senate (1964), 228
  EMK's primary race against McCormack and,
    141, 142, 154–55, 169, 228
  EMK's taking over of, 229
  JFK's presidential ambitions (1956) and,
    228–29
  presidential candidate (1968) and, 346–47,
    347n
Mathias, Charles, 639, 700
Matthew 25:31–32A, 34–40, xxviii
Mauldin, Bill, 495
McCain, John, xxv
McCall's magazine
  "The Troubled Marriage of Joan and Ted
    Kennedy," 716
McCarron, Richard, 487, 503
McCarthy, Abigail, 363, 364
McCarthy, Eugene, 97, 181, 285, 345–46, 376
  EMK and, 346
  EMK's meeting on RFK's decision to run,
    363–65, 364n
  enmity toward RFK, 286
  "meanness in his heart," 346
  presidential race (1968) and, 346–48, 357,
    360–61, 362, 366, 367, 368, 376, 389, 401,
    404, 408–11, 411n, 416
  RFK's assassination and, 384
  RFK's presidential candidacy and, 362–64,
    364n, 365, 366, 376
  Vietnam War and, 411
McCarthy, John, 562
McCarthy, Joseph, 95, 96, 97, 277, 310, 328, 428,
    537
McCarthy, Mary, 363
McClellan, John, 193, 196, 695
McCloskey, Robert, 70–71
McClure, Stewart, 254
McCormack, Edward, Jr. "Eddie," 123, 137, 265,
    504, 600
  announces candidacy for Senate, 133
  background and family, 123
  "Billy Boy" anti-Ted song, 152
  debating EMK, 149, 160–68
  on EMK as a politician, 147

EMK's win and relationship with, 177–78, 230
Massachusetts Democratic Party convention
    and, 154–59
as primary opponent, EMK's Senate run,
    123–31, 133, 135, 136, 138, 140, 141, 142,
    149, 152–69
resentment of the Kennedys, 124, 152
supporters, 136–37
McCormack, Edward, Sr. "Knocko," 123, 148,
    153, 157–58, 159, 169
McCormack, Emilie, 160
McCormack, John, 124, 130, 160, 192, 228, 438,
    497, 539
  championing minorities, 539
  EMK in the Senate and, 229
  JFK in the Senate and, 192
  Morrissey judicial appointment and, 297
  as Speaker of the House, 123, 297, 438, 497,
    559, 560
McCracken, Tracy, 105, 757n105
McDermott, Tom, xxvi
McGee, Gale, 105, 108, 117
McGovern, George, 181, 195, 205, 250, 358, 435,
    445, 575, 605, 621, 705
  Democratic National Convention (1972) and,
    594, 598–601
  election results (1972), 608, 611
  EMK campaigning for, 607
  leftwing positions of, 607
  Nixon targeting of, 631
  presidential race (1968) and, 345–46, 404,
    408, 412
  presidential race (1972) and, 593–608, 670
  vice presidential pick (1972), 598–603
  Vietnam War and, 411, 412, 457, 459
McGrory, Mary, 163, 165, 287, 347–48
McIntyre, Joe, 187, 188, 262–63, 497
McIntyre, Thomas, 181
McKinley, William, 105
McLaren, Richard, 622, 623
McLean, Va.
  EMK's home on Chain Bridge Road, 391, 403,
    439, 543–44, 546
  Hickory Hill, RFK's home, 194, 205, 357, 364,
    391, 450, 544, 671
McMillan, Leslie, xxiii
McNamara, Robert, 254, 261, 323, 352, 452,
    487
McPherson, Harry, 200
Meany, George, 377, 596, 598, 649–50, 687–88
Medicaid, 644, 658
Medicare, xxiii, xxxiv, 201, 216, 266, 275, 325,
    444, 643, 644, 645, 651, 669, 670
Meet the Press (TV show)
  EMK on, 132–33, 175, 255, 319
  McCormack on, 123–24
  RFK on, 371–72
Memphis, Tenn., EMK speaking in, 450

Menino, Thomas, xv
Mental Health Parity Act, xix
Mercouri, Melina, 130
Meserve, Robert, 291, 297
Metcalf, Lee, 181, 345
Meyer, Karl, 111
"Middle America and the Emerging Republican
  Majority" (Phillips), 583
Mikulski, Barbara, 390, 543
Miller, Arjay, 455
Miller, Jack, 274
Miller, Melody, 342, 473–74, 476, 507, 543, 544,
  570
Miller, William, 172
Mills, Wilbur, 598, 600, 659, 679, 683, 706
  background, 668
  EMK's health insurance plan and, 667–70,
    687
  political ambitions of, 667–68, 669, 670
  quashes health care bill, 688
  stripper-drunk driving scandal, 688
Milton Academy, Milton, Mass.
  EMK and, 50–52
  EMK and honors in public speaking, 50, 72
  EMK and sports at, 50, 52, 59
  EMK called "The Politician" and "Smilin' Ed,"
    51
  EMK's academic struggles at, 62
  EMK's graduation, 54
  EMK's tutor at, 50
  headmaster's assessment of EMK, 50
  RFK and, 210
  RFK's intervention and EMK's attendance, 50
Milton Academy for Girls, Milton, Mass., 52
Mira (rented yawl), 396, 414
Mitchell, Brian Stokes, xxv
Mitchell, Clarence, 285, 529
Mitchell, John, 588, 622, 624, 626
Mitterand, François, 340, 366
Mizner, Addison, 35
Model Cities Program, 275
Mohammed V, sultan of Morocco, 76
Mohbat, Joseph, 373, 470
Moley, Raymond, 5
Mondale, Walter, 437, 445, 468, 569, 600, 667,
  700
  Chappaquiddick incident and, 515–16
Moore, Edward "Eddie," 12, 164, 165, 166–67,
  485
  as EMK's namesake, 4
  FDR whistle-stop tour and (1932), 14
  JPK as U.S. ambassador to England and,
    27–28, 32
  JPK's business dealings, personal affairs, and,
    5
  as JPK's closest friend, 4, 5–6
  as procurer of women, 5
  as Rosemary's godfather, 24, 25

  sociability of, 5
  World War II and home for Rosemary and, 33
Moore, Mary, 4, 14, 166–67
Morgan, Edward, 652
Morgan, J. P., 27
Morgan, Tallulah, 721
Morgenthau, Hans, 138
Morgenthau, Henry, 27
Moro, Aldo, 225
Morocco, 76
Morrissey, Francis X. "Frank," 721
  background, 292, 303
  called a "personal factotum," 289–90, 292
  EMK and federal judicial appointment fight,
    289–306, 290n, 331, 531, 778n290
  EMK's Senate run and, 120–21, 125, 126, 128,
    140, 146, 292, 293
  JFK and, 118, 289–91, 292
  JPK, as invalid, and, 289–92
  as victim of class prejudice, 302–3
Morse, Wayne, 204, 255
Morton, Rogers, 465
Morton, Thruston, 260
Moss, Edward "Ed," 108, 117, 188, 230, 244,
  474
  death in plane crash, 231, 232, 233, 235, 236,
    248
Moss, Katie, 235, 236, 248
Motor Vehicle Air Pollution Control Act, 275
Mount Kennedy, Yukon, 261
Moursund, A. W., 311
Moyers, Bill, 294, 415
Moynihan, Daniel Patrick, 342–43, 377, 604
  Nixon and, 464–65
  report on the "Negro family," 464
Murphy, George, 467–68, 496–97
Murphy, Paul, 62
Murray, Margot, 84, 86
Music, Olga and Ned, xxiii
Muskeget Island, Mass., 398
Muskie, Edmund, 97, 181, 416, 435, 438, 445,
  460, 497, 519, 532, 577, 580
  FOIA amendments and, 694, 696
  Nixon's dirty tricks against, 589, 594, 596,
    620
  presidential race (1972) and, 513, 564, 574,
    583, 589, 594, 596, 600n
Mussolini, Benito, 56
Myrdal, Alva, 659
Myrdal, Gunnar, 659
  An American Dilemma: The Negro Problem and
    Modern Democracy, 659

NAACP (National Association for the
    Advancement of Colored People), 285
  Boston busing class action, Morgan v.
    Hennigan, 721
  Carswell judicial nomination and, 529

Nader, Ralph, 260, 623
    Congress Project, 463
Nagel, Michelle, xxvi
Napolitan, Joe, 166
Nasaw, David, 5, 11, 14
Nashville *Tennesseean*, Seigenthaler as editor,
    152
National Cancer Act, 660–66, 685
National Cancer Institute, 660–61, 662, 664,
    666
National Council of Churches, 286
National Foundation on the Arts and
    Humanities Act, 275
National Institutes of Health (NIH), 653, 654,
    660, 661, 662–63
National Press Club, 591
National Service Corps, 186
Nation of Immigrants, A (JFK), 267, 776n267
Native Americans, 451–52, 459, 465
NBC, 386, 439, 505
    Brinkley on RFK, 388
    What Price Health? 649
Nelson, Gaylord, 181, 261, 599–600, 664, 666
Nelson, Verlin, 529
New Bedford *Standard-Times*
    on Chappaquiddick incident, 503
    EMK and editor Brewer, 126
Newberg, Esther, 472
Newbrand, Robert, 602
New Democratic Coalition, 459
New England Baptist Hospital
    EMK leaves, 248–49
    EMK recovering at, 238–41
    EMK running his Senate office from, 241–42
    EMK transferred to, 237
Newfield, Jack, 342, 372, 378, 384, 389, 597
    benediction for RFK, 390
New Hampshire
    presidential primary (1968), 359, 360, 361,
        362–63, 368, 371, 390
    presidential primary (1972), 594, 596
New Republic, The
    "The End of the Dream," xxi, 213
    Osborne on Ford's Halloween Massacre, 704
    Pincus on EMK's health care focus, 642
    Strout on Wallace as demagogue, 422
Newsday, editor Moyers and Humphrey's vice
    presidential pick, 415
Newsweek
    on anti-busing violence in Boston, 733
    Auchincloss on EMK's character, xxxiii
    on EMK, after RFK's assassination, 393–94,
        397
    on EMK and the Democratic ticket (1968),
        400
    on EMK and RFK in the Senate, 258
    EMK as a freshman senator and, 185
    on EMK's agony after RFK's death, 469

on EMK's political reemergence, 584
    EMK's poll tax fight and, 283
    on EMK's repaired reputation after
        Chappaquiddick, 699
    JFK on pressures on EMK, 57
    on RFK as a senator, 260
    on RFK phenomenon, 375
Newton, Huey, 380
New York City, 86, 499, 500, 710
    EMK and the Stork Club, 82
    Rose Kennedy's Central Park South
        apartment, 516
    Steve Smith's apartment, 361
    Wallace speaking at Madison Square Garden,
        423
New York Daily News
    Chappaquiddick incident and, 485
New Yorker
    Buchanan interview, 424
    on Carswell judicial nomination, 529
    Chappaquiddick incident and, 514, 515
    Roger Stone on politics in, 428
New York Herald Tribune
    Morrissey judicial appointment and, 295
New York magazine
    Baumgold on EMK's popularity, 608
    EMK's presidential prospects (1976) and,
        709–10
    Maas on EMK and Democratic ticket (1968),
        410–11
New York Post, Wechsler as editor, 309, 398, 429,
    456, 574, 618, 652
New York Times, 282
    Califano op-ed on Watergate, 632
    "Carswell May Make Some People Long for
        Haynsworth," 529
    Chappaquiddick incident and, 485, 489, 496,
        505, 506, 508, 509, 518
    editorial against EMK's cancer bill, 663
    "Edward Kennedy's Challenge to President
        Nixon," 450
    EMK and lowering the voting age, 559, 561
    on EMK and Vietnam, 315
    on EMK and Vietnam War hearings, 335
    on EMK as Nixon's primary antagonist, 460
    on EMK campaign-finance bill, 694
    EMK on the Senate as a forum for change, 431
    on EMK's future, after RFK's death, 399–400
    EMK's plane crash and, 237
    on EMK's poll tax fight and, 288
    on EMK's popularity vs. RFK's, 324
    EMK's recovery following Chappaquiddick,
        535
    EMK's Senate run and, 170, 172
    EMK's Senate run and youth of, 133
    EMK's Senate run debates and, 168
    on forced school busing, 724
    Goldwater op-ed in Nixon's defense, 633–34

Gould on JFK's being telegenic, 106
Krock as columnist, and the Kennedys, 17
leak of Kleindienst phone call to, 640
leaping "Ed Kennedy" and, 74
Lewis on EMK's presidential prospects (1972)
    and, 593–94
on Mills blocking Medicare, 669
Morrissey judicial appointment and, 305
"Poll Finds Kennedy Is Losing Esteem," 562
on RFK's charisma, 378
RFK's presidential ambitions and, 343
on the Senate chamber, 180
Wicker column on JFK, 386, 388
Wicker on EMK and Wallace, 708
Wicker on Nixon impeachment, 634
Wicker on the Senate as progressive, 253
New York Times Magazine
    Honan on EMK's senatorial leadership, 449
    Roberts on EMK, xxxiv
    Shannon's EMK profile, 284
    Sherrill on Chappaquiddick, 715
Nhu, Madame (Tran Le Xuan), 308
Nicholson, Jack, xxvii
Niebuhr, Reinhold, 138
Nixon, Donald, 625
Nixon, Julie, 579
Nixon, Pat, 546
Nixon, Richard, xxxv, 96, 213, 345, 654
    Agnew resignation and, 634–35
    appeal to law and order, 372, 403, 417–18
    "awesome power with no discipline," 613,
        614, 617, 630, 633, 640
    background, 426–27
    backlash against liberalism and, 556
    busing opposed by, 722, 723, 724
    campaign contributions (1972), 692
    cancer agency and war on cancer, 661–62
    Carswell defeat, desire for revenge, 532
    Carswell judicial nomination, 529–32, 711
    Chappaquiddick incident, response to,
        498–501, 514–15
    character and personality, 440–41, 499
    "Checkers speech," 495
    China and, 588, 703, 708
    civil rights and, 556, 591
    code words and, 711, 712
    dirty tricks and, 465–67, 501, 578–79, 581,
        589, 594, 596, 620, 621, 622, 624–25, 627,
        666, 694, 815n620
    a divided America and, 427, 428
    draft reform and, 465
    EMK after Chappaquiddick and, 526–27
    EMK as rival, 573, 587–88, 589, 597, 601–2,
        661, 662–63, 667
    EMK as "shadow president," 447, 453, 455,
        456, 460–61, 463, 465, 470, 499, 578
    EMK influencing policy of, 464–65, 603–4,
        619–20, 650, 661, 678

EMK opposes ABM system and, 452–56,
    519–20
EMK's legislation blocked by, 466
EMK's liberalism and, xxxv, 441
on EMK's loss of majority whip position, 571
EMK's relationship with, 440, 441, 613
EMK's Senate reelection (1970) and, 562
EMK's son's cancer and, 672
EMK targeted by, 576–82, 602, 612, 621, 627,
    631, 666
employer-mandated insurance system and
    CHIP vs. EMK's national health insurance,
    647, 650, 658, 670, 677–80, 684, 686–87
"enemies list," 690
Environmental Protection Agency and, 603
executive power and "imperial presidency,"
    614–15, 617, 628
FBI file on JFK and, 548
food stamp cuts and, 444
Ford as vice president, 635, 691
"forgotten Americans" and, 441
Haynsworth judicial nomination, 527–29
Hiss case and, 604, 604n
impact on American politics, 428
impeachment and, 634, 635, 638, 639, 641,
    677, 685
Independent Conservative party idea, 610
IRS investigations of opponents, 580, 620
ITT payoff and, 622–23, 624, 625, 626
JPK and, 95
Justice Department and, 448
Kennedys, his obsession with, 466, 498–99,
    577, 580, 624
landslide victory (1972), 608–9
LBJ's Great Society and, 442
as liberalism foe, 417, 443, 538, 582, 604–6,
    608–12, 613–14
lowering the voting age and, 559, 561
moral authority as suspect, 515
Moynihan and, 464–65
National Cancer Act and, 666, 685
Occupational Safety and Health Act, 603
Oval Office tapes and, 633, 634, 635, 636, 637,
    638–39, 672, 685–86, 692
Pakistani refugees and, 585
paranoia of, 465–67, 577, 580, 612, 620
pardon of, by Ford, 697–98
Pinochet government and, 617–18
pocket veto and EMK's lawsuit, 614–17
political career of, 441
politics of fear and, 583
politics personalized by, 466
presidential race (1960) and, 106, 107, 108,
    171
presidential race (1968) and, 348, 352, 400,
    403, 416–24, 577
presidential race (1972) and, 576–78, 582,
    590, 603–8

Nixon, Richard (*cont'd*):
  racial questions and, 605–6, 711–12, 711n
  Rehnquist nomination, 588
  resentments of, 426–27, 428, 441, 499, 583, 589, 614, 690
  resignation of, 687, 692, 693, 821n687
  "the Saturday Night Massacre," 638, 703
  as senator, 441
  Silent Majority and, 427, 441, 542, 607, 642
  social programs and, 464–65, 603–4, 642
  Soviet Union détente, 638, 708
  speechwriters for, 424–25, 427
  State of the Union Address (1970), 577
  State of the Union Address (1974), 678
  Supplemental Security Income and, 603
  tax reform, 520
  as vice president, 440
  Vietnam War and, 348, 417, 442, 456, 465, 526–27, 558, 586–87, 587n, 591–93, 618–19
  view of the world, 542
  voting rights and, 558
  Watergate and, xxxv, 620–40
  "What Has Happened to America?," 417–18
No Child Left Behind, xix
Nofziger, Lyn, 526–27, 589
Nol, Lon, 701
Nolan, John, 566, 569, 638, 809n569
Nolan, Martin, 516, 535, 570, 599, 710
North Atlantic Assembly, 702
Notre Dame (University of), 64, 64n
Novak, Robert, 229, 631

Oates, Joyce Carol
  Black Water, 517
Obama, Barack
  EMK and, xxix
  EMK's letter to the pope and, xxxii–xxxiii
  eulogy for EMK by, xxix–xxx, xxxi
O'Brien, Lawrence "Larry," 228
  EMK's presidential race (1972) and, 575
  EMK's Senate race and, 117–18, 124, 131, 140, 141, 142, 166
  Humphrey's presidential campaign and, 422
  JFK's Senate campaign (1958) and, 98, 99
  LBJ and, 351, 352, 369
  Nixon targets, 578, 624–25
  Nixon wiretapping of, 621, 622, 624
  RFK and, 145, 367, 369, 390
O'Byrne, Mother Elizabeth, 87
Occupational Safety and Health Act, 603
O'Connell, Tom, 727–28
O'Connor, Carroll, 647
O'Donnel, Cleo, 55
O'Donnell, Kenny, 55, 59, 62, 98, 228, 234, 237, 298, 345, 359, 416
  Chappaquiddick incident and, 487
  EMK's Senate run and, 117–18, 131, 135, 140, 141, 154–55, 159–60, 162

O'Donnell, Warren, 62
Office of Economic Opportunity, 321, 448
Oglesby, Carl, 310
Older Americans Act of 1965, 556–57
  Meals on Wheels and, xix, 556–57
Oliphant, Thomas, 530, 531–32, 683
Olsen, Jack, 510
  The Bridge at Chappaquiddick, 621
Onassis, Aristotle, 393
O'Neill, Thomas "Tip," 99, 124, 136, 159, 194, 313, 346
  on EMK, 405
  RFK's contempt for, 259
  Vietnam War and, 333–34
Onek, Joe, 463
Oregon
  presidential primary (1968), 380, 401
  presidential primary (1972), 596
  See also Packwood, Robert
Ormandy, Eugene, 77
Osborne, John, 704
Oswald, Lee Harvey, 239
Owens, Wayne, 446, 447, 567, 569

Pace, Courtney, 183
Packer, George, 424
Packwood, Robert, 590, 678
Paley, Babe, 551
Paley, William, 551
Palladino, Elvira "Pixie," 731, 734
Palm Beach, Fla.
  Bath and Tennis Club, 144
  EMK and his grandfather Fitzgerald in, 57
  EMK and Joan at, 90
  EMK in (1964), 249
  EMK meets Helga Wagner in, 552
  JFK in, 117
  JPK buys vacation home in, 35
  JPK in, 3, 4, 35, 90, 100, 169, 249, 552
  Kennedy home in, 3
  Kennedys wintering in, 33, 35
  nephew accused of rape and, xxxi
  wealthiest Americans in, 16
Palm Beach Private School, 33, 34, 49
"Panis Angelicus" (Franck), xxviii
Parker, Andrew, 92
Parker, Carey, 525
  ABM system fight and, 455, 456
  campaign-finance reform and, 693
  on EMK's Senate staff and, 448, 463, 570–71, 584, 615, 616, 717–18
  national health insurance and, 646–47, 652
  Voting Rights Act amendments and, 558–59, 560, 560n, 561
Parker, Daniel, 619
Parks, Jeanus, 279
Parmeter, Adrian, 467
Pastore, John, 444

Patman, Wright, 626
Peachey, Russell, 481n, 507
Pearson, Drew, 324, 520
Pell, Claiborne, 264, 646, 652
Pellikaan, Tom, 205
Pelosi, Nancy, xxvii
Percy, Charles, 400, 556
Perlstein, Rick, 110, 417, 426, 606, 609
Perry, Arthur Bliss, 50, 63
Peters, Andrew James, 4
Peterson, Donald, 413
Petrie, Don, 415
Philadelphia Eagles, 176
Philadelphia Inquirer
    Chappaquiddick incident and, 715
Phillips, Kevin
    "Middle America and the Emerging
        Republican Majority," 583
Phillips, Wendell, 721
Photoplay magazine
    "The Party's Over," 514
Pierce, Charles, 515
Pincus, Walter, 642
Pine Manor Junior College, 82
Pinochet, Augusto, 617
Pius XII, Pope
    investiture of, 30
    Kennedy family and, 30–31
plane crash (1964), 230–51
    account of the accident, 230–33
    heightened sense of purpose after, 453
    injuries, recuperation, 233–40
    LBJ's response, 234, 236, 237, 239
    permanent disability, 248, 251, 283, 287, 516,
        540
    pilot's error and, 239
    senatorial duties during hospitalization, 241–42
    suffering and personal transformation, 249–50,
        251, 265
    tutorial sessions and studying during rehab,
        240–41, 641
Plank, John, 125, 140
Poland, 130
Pollak, Louis, 530
Pompidou, Georges, 225
Poppen, James, 237, 383
populism, 7, 8, 428, 431, 708, 735
Portsmouth Priory, R.I., 34, 42
    EMK as social outcast at, 34–35
Powell, Adam Clayton, Jr., 322
Powers, Dave, 113, 132–33
Presidential Election Campaign Fund Act of
    1966, 431–32
Procaccino, Mario, 607
Profiles in Courage (JFK), 239–40, 495
progressivism
    EMK and, xvii, 465, 522
    Humphrey and, 420

immigration reform and, 270
national health insurance and, 642–43
Senate bulls blocking legislation and, 190,
    214, 252
Senate turning toward, 253
Proxmire, William, 497, 532
Psalm 72, xxviii

Queen Kelly (film), 63
Quinn, Luke, 660

Raclin, Caroline (stepdaughter), xxviii
Raclin, Curran (stepson), xxvi, xxviii
Radcliffe College, 138
Rahman, Sheik Mujibur, 585
Railsback, Thomas, 559
Rampton, Calvin, 590
Randolph, A. Philip, 218
Randolph, Jennings, 203, 558, 561
Raskin, Hyman, 101
Rauh, Joseph, 277–78, 279, 285, 286, 345, 439,
    529, 530, 571–72
Rayburn, Sam, 190, 192, 668
Reader's Digest, 417, 508
Reagan, Ronald, 400, 563–64, 586, 609, 704
    as governor of California, 325
Real Majority, The (Wattenberg and Scammon),
    582, 583, 606
Reardon, Timothy, 59
Reed, Stanley, 92
Reedy, George, 144
Reeves, Richard, 110, 210, 308–9, 537, 540,
    709–10
Rehnquist, William, 588
Reid, Herbert O., 279
Reilly, John, 153
Reporter, The, 253, 305
Republican Party
    anti-school busing and, 722, 723
    black voters and, 325
    blue-collar whites and, 609, 611
    civil rights and, 771n227
    community health centers and, 321
    conservatism and, 417
    EMK's opposition in, xxii, xxiii
    Goldwater and right wing of, 245–46
    LBJ's Great Society and, 252
    in Massachusetts, 14
    midterms (1958), 97
    midterms (1970), 582–83
    midterms (1974), 698
    national health insurance and, 644, 646
    Nixon Watergate scandal and, 685
    post–New Deal liberal consensus, 245,
        246
    presidential campaign (1968) and, 343,
        348, 417–24
    presidential campaign (1972), 586

Republican Party (*cont'd*):
presidential election (1964) and, 245–47
South as Republican, xxi, xxxv, 328, 424–25, 529, 712
as Vietnam hawks, 319–20
See also conservatism; Nixon, Richard
Reston, James, 133, 308, 309, 450, 535
Chappaquiddick incident and, 487, 495–96, 505
on Dike Bridge as treacherous, 477
Rettig, Richard, 664
Reuther, Walter, 245, 368, 377, 390, 682
death of, 649
EMK recruited for national health care campaign, 644–45
national health insurance and, 642–43, 646, 646n, 647, 648, 649, 652, 655, 682
Rhodes, John, 681, 689
Rhodes, Richard, 143, 265–66
profile of EMK, 22
Ribicoff, Abraham, 181, 600, 680
Richardson, Elliot, 619, 632, 635–36, 664
refusal to fire Cox, 637, 638
Riedel, Richard Langham, 205, 205n
Riley, Mike, 371
Risen, Clay, 221n
Ritchie, Donald, 201
Riverdale, N.Y.
Kennedy mansion in, 12, 13
Riverdale Country School, 24, 35, 37
Rivers, Mendel, 339
Rizzo, Frank, 424
"Road Not Taken, The" (Frost), xv
Roberts, Steven, 378
Robertson, Reuben, 623
Robertson, Willis, 193, 202
Robinson, Joseph, 438, 668
Robinson, Terri Haddad, 187, 189, 208, 209–10
Roche, Betty, 656
Roche, John, 333
Rockefeller, Nelson, 400, 589, 703, 704
Rodriguez, Isabel, 657–58
Rogers, Warren, Jr., 574
Rogers, William, 465, 585, 618, 619
Romney, George, 594
Romney, Mitt, xxiv
Roncalio, Teno, 757n105
Roosevelt, Eleanor, 85
Roosevelt, Franklin D. (FDR), 78, 390–91
Barkley and, 438
death of, JPK on, 95
"forgotten Americans" and, 441
JPK and, 5, 15, 30, 31, 32, 95
JPK and whistle-stop tour (1932), 5, 14
JPK as British ambassador, 27–33
JPK as supporter, 14–15
liberalism and, 95

national health insurance and, 643–44
New Deal, 95, 111, 252, 275, 646
as N.Y. governor, 14
polio and, 98, 249, 536
presidential race (1940), 32
Roosevelt, Franklin D., Jr., 104
Roosevelt, James, 27
Roosevelt, Theodore, 105
Rosenbloom, Carroll, 176
Rossiter, Clinton
The American Presidency, 614
Rostow, Walt, 355, 384
Rowley, James, 602
Royko, Mike, 516–17
Ruckelshaus, William, 638
Rumsfeld, Donald, 696, 704
Rusk, Dean, 313, 320, 351, 355
Russell, Bill, xxvii
Russell, Richard, 259, 442, 443, 569–70
Civil Rights Act of 1964 and, 227
EMK and, 192–93, 194, 195, 251, 253
EMK's running for Senate majority whip and, 436, 438
LBJ and, 196
national draft and, 338–40
as Senate bull, 192, 445
as Vietnam hawk, 311
Rustin, Bayard, 218
Ryan, Elizabeth "Toodles," 547
Ryan White Comprehensive AIDS Resources Emergency (CARE) Act, xix

Safire, William, 427, 499, 708
St. Aiden's, Brookline, Mass., 19
St. Moritz, France, Kennedy family in, 28
St. Patrick's Cathedral, N.Y.C., xxvii, 386
St. Stephen's Church, Boston, xiv–xv
Salinger, Pierre, 344–45, 382, 383, 384n, 386
Saltonstall, Leverett, 181, 295, 299
Sampson, Arthur, 615–16
Samuelson, Paul, 111
Sargent, Francis, 720
Sarnoff, David, 41
Satkewich, Charles, xvii
Saturday Evening Post
promoting JFK's presidential aspirations, 94
Saxbe, William, 468, 649
Scammon, Richard
The Real Majority, 582, 583, 606
Schauer, Robert, 232
Schieffer, Bob, xix
Schlesinger, Arthur, Jr., 8, 44, 111, 112, 135, 138, 204, 214, 309, 345, 390, 441, 611, 614, 673, 711
Chappaquiddick incident and, 477, 487, 489–90
on EMK after Chappaquiddick, 521, 522, 535–36

EMK and the Democratic ticket (1968), 414–15

EMK and RFK's presidential run, 358

EMK's presidential prospects (1972) and, 591

EMK's presidential prospects (1976) and, 711, 717

EMK's transformation and, 250

JFK's administration and, 179–80

on Joan Kennedy's drinking, 554

RFK and, 243–44, 348

RFK's presidential candidacy and, 361–62, 363, 364

on Ted, Jr.'s cancer, 672

Schlesinger, Arthur, Sr., 138

Schlesinger, James, 703

Schmidt, Benno, 663, 664

Schneider, Mark, 617, 702, 703

Schumacher, David, 364n, 411

Scott, Hugh, 196, 299, 614, 692

Seale, Bobby, 713

Secret Plot to Make Ted Kennedy President, The (Shepard), 822n687

Segal, Bernard, 297

Segretti, Donald, 627, 628

Seigenthaler, John, 152, 162, 210, 211, 382, 383, 406, 410, 553, 706

Selma, Ala., 276

Senior Citizens Hospital Insurance Act, 186

Sequoia (presidential yacht), 203

Shannon, William, 250, 282, 284

Shapiro, Sam, 400

Sharbutt, Jay, 457

Shaw, George Bernard, 77

Sheehan, Neil, 315

Sheehy, Gail, 145

Shepard, Geoff, *The Secret Plot to Make Ted Kennedy President*, 822n687

Sheridan, Walter, 236

Sherrill, Robert, 287–88, 522, 525, 715

Shields, Mark, 437

Shorenstein, Walter, 718

Shriver, Eunice Kennedy (sister)

Chappaquiddick incident and, 487, 491

death of, xiii

on EMK and JFK, 113

on EMK as a child, 25–26

on EMK's childhood and lack of stability, 49

at EMK's oath of office and, 179

at EMK's pocket veto argument and, 616

at EMK's Senate speech for Morrissey and, 303

at EMK's swearing in, 181

on family competitiveness, 17

on family expectations, 20

father as U.S. ambassador in England and, 28

father's death and, 534

on her mother, 23–24

JFK's assassination and, 207–8, 209

Joan Kennedy and, 553

RFK's assassination and, 383, 384–85

South American trip with her mother, 34

at Stanford, 54

Shriver, Robert (nephew), 22–23, 533

Shriver, Sargent (brother-in-law), xiii, 207, 233, 257–58, 415–16, 534, 600

as McGovern's vice presidential pick, 603

Shriver, Timothy (nephew), xxxiv, 555

Shrum, Robert, 410

Silver Hill sanitarium, New Canaan, Conn., 676

Simon, Paul, xviii

Simpson, Alan, 517

Simpson, Milward, 181

Sirhan, Sirhan, 451

Sirica, John, 636, 685

60 Minutes (TV show), 624

Skakel, George, Jr., 83

Skinner, B. F., 583

Sloane Street School for Boys, London, 29–30

Smathers, George, 170, 199, 476, 548, 568

Smith, Alfred E. "Al," 14

Smith, Benjamin A., 122–23, 132, 137, 139, 179

EMK and Senate office of, 186

EMK and Senate staff of, 187

Smith, Howard, 190

Smith, Jean Kennedy (sister), xiii, 16, 29

birth of, 3

calls EMK "Biscuits and Muffins," 37

Chappaquiddick incident and, 487

on EMK as the "enjoyer," 469

on EMK's grief for RFK, 392

at EMK's oath of office and, 179

on EMK's personality, 146

EMK's plane crash and, 234

at EMK's pocket veto argument and, 616

at EMK's swearing in, 181

on EMK's womanizing, 548

father's death and, 534

on her childhood, 24, 26

introduces Joan to EMK, 83–84

RFK's assassination and, 383, 384

World War II and leaving England, 32

Smith, Margaret Chase, 532

Smith, Stephen (brother-in-law), xxiii, 83, 345, 474, 534

Chappaquiddick incident and, 481, 482, 487, 490, 503

EMK and the Democratic ticket (1968), 401, 405–6, 409, 411, 413–14

EMK as senator and, 256

EMK's presidential prospects (1976) and, 705–6, 718

EMK's Senate run and, 128, 142, 157, 160, 161, 168–69

at EMK's swearing in, 181

RFK's assassination and, 381–82, 383, 384

Smith, Stephen (brother-in-law) (*cont'd*):
    RFK's presidential candidacy and, 361, 405
    Shriver and, 415–16
Social Security Act Amendments of 1965, 275
Sohier, Walter, 592
Sorensen, Theodore, xvi, 132, 175, 249, 345,
    348, 383
    Chappaquiddick incident and, 487, 489,
      490–91, 494
    EMK and Democratic ticket (1968), 401, 406,
      407
    EMK's first public address after RFK's death,
      402
    on EMK's injuries, bravery, 239
    on EMK's personality, 146
    EMK's presidential prospects (1976) and,
      705–6
    EMK's Senate run and, 132
    EMK's Senate run debates and, 161–62, 164
    on JFK as enigmatic, 143–44
    on JFK's political ideas, 98
    JFK's presidential run (1959–60) and, 100,
      101
    memo on EMK as vice presidential pick, 599,
      602
    national commission on Vietnam proposed,
      359, 360
    on RFK, 144, 341–42
    RFK's presidential candidacy and, 359, 360,
      364, 381
Souliotis, Barbara, 150, 187, 731, 732
South Christian Leadership Conference (SCLC),
    708
South Dakota
    EMK in, 593
    McGovern and, 607
    primary race (1968) and, 381, 404
    See also McGovern, George
South End Settlement House, Boston, 70
Soviet Union
    Cold War and, 97
    EMK and, 618
    EMK and plight of Soviet Jews, 618, 709
    LBJ and Kosygin meeting, 348
    Nixon and, 703, 708
    nuclear-arms limitation agreement, 700
Spain, 393, 397, 481, 482
Sparkman, John, 438
Spaulding, Josiah, 562, 564
Spellman, Francis Cardinal, 88
Spinella, Michael, 301
Spivak, Lawrence, 133
Spock, Benjamin, 333
Squaw Island, Mass., Kennedy home on, 151,
    242, 392, 414, 472, 487, 501, 718
Stahura, Walter, 73–74
Stalcup, Margaret, 187
Stanford University, 54, 75, 116

Steele, Walter, 488
Stein, Herbert, 606
Stennis, John, 251, 432, 436, 438, 452, 456, 592,
    637, 685
Stevens, Ted, 468
Stevenson, Adlai, 96, 101, 104–5, 213, 228, 309,
    343, 346
Stewart, John, 200
Stewart, Potter, 448
Stokes, Anson, 222
Stone, Galen, 10
Stone, I. F., 334
Stone, Roger, 428
Stossel, Scott, 415
Stowe, Vt., 185
    ski trip of EMK while dating Joan, 86
Strachan, Gordon, 580
Strauss, Anne, 188, 189
Strout, Richard, 422
Students for a Democratic Society, 310, 573
Sullivan, William, 294, 734
Sun Valley, Idaho
    EMK and family vacationing in, 435, 436
"Superman Comes to the Supermarket"(Mailer),
    107, 213
Supplemental Security Income, 603
Susman, Thomas, 451, 463, 623, 626, 627
    FOIA amendment and, 695–96, 697
Swanson, Gloria, 3, 5, 25, 63, 547
Swearingen, John, 578
Symington, Stuart, 102, 195, 251

Taft, Robert, xv
Taiwan, 588
Talmadge, Herman, 652, 653, 655, 706
Tannenbaum, Susan, 472
Taylor, James, xv
    "Shed a Little Light," xv
Taylor, Maxwell, 310, 311, 313, 314, 354
Taylor, William, 136
Taymor, Betty, 131, 142, 146, 550, 715
Teacher Corps, 275
Ted and the Kennedy Legend (Lerner), 514
Tennyson, Alfred Lord
    "Ulysses," xxviii, xxxiv
Thang, Ton Duc, 565
Thieu, Nguyen Van, 314, 350, 353, 526
Thimmesch, Nick, 590
Tho, Le Duc, 592
Thomas, April, xiii
Thurmond, Strom, 274, 550, 639, 640
Tierney, Gene, 548
Time magazine, 468
    "The Brother Who Mattered Most," xx
    Chappaquiddick incident and, 485–86, 493,
      521
    on the Democratic Party's future, 612
    on EMK after Chappaquiddick, 525

on EMK after RFK's death, 469
on EMK and Joan's marriage, 544
on EMK and RFK's legacy, 430
EMK as presumptive 1972 presidential
    nominee, 443
on EMK at Worcester textile plant, 149
EMK on the mood of the country (1971), 606
on EMK refusing to run in 1976, 718–19
on EMK's appeal to women, 150
on EMK's image, 393
on EMK's one man, one vote fight and, 329,
    331
EMK's posthumous tributes in, xxii
EMK's presidential polling (1972), 589, 591
EMK's presidential prospects (1976) and, 717
on EMK's resilience, 524
EMK's running for Senate majority whip and,
    435
EMK's Senate race and, 127, 133, 156, 171
EMK stands in for JFK on campaign trail,
    103–4
EMK's Vietnam War opposition, 526
on Ford presidency, 691
Joan Kennedy's alcoholism and, 676
on JPK and Eddie Moore, 4, 5
on the Kennedy brand, 171
"The Memory That Would Not Fade," 715
Morrissey judicial appointment and, 305, 306
Rose on EMK as ninth child, 26
"Ted's Crumbling Position," 514
Time to Heal, A (Ford), 703
Timmons, Bill, 681
Tobin, James, 111
Tobin, Maurice J., 289, 292
Toohey, Ed, 140
Tower, John, 681
Tretter, Charles, 148, 165, 188–89, 193, 241,
    263, 393, 406
    Chappaquiddick incident and, 471, 474, 475
Trinh, Nguyen Duy, 619
Troy, Matthew, 68
Trudeau, Margaret, 551
Trudeau, Pierre, 551
True Compass (EMK), 207n
Truman, Harry, 310, 459, 653
    national health insurance and, 644
Tunney, Gene, 77, 78
Tunney, John Varick, 77–78, 248, 258, 431, 435,
    436, 625, 716
    on basis of EMK's desire to serve, 538
    Chappaquiddick incident and, 487, 490, 518
    EMK and, rent a house, hire a housekeeper,
        79–81
    EMK and Democratic ticket (1968), 406
    EMK and flying incident, 231
    on EMK and RFK in the Senate, 260
    on EMK as gifted politician, 147
    EMK as senator and, 203

on EMK's agony after RFK's death, 469–70
on EMK's charisma and courage, 79
on EMK's fatalism, 576
on EMK's grief for RFK, 394, 397
on EMK's idolizing JFK, 112–13
EMK's Latin America trip (1961) and, 125
on EMK's "magic with crowds," 149–50
EMK's marital problems and, 599
on EMK's political ambitions, 115
on EMK's prioritizing his son's cancer, 673
EMK's vice presidential offer (1972) and, 602,
    603n
at Hague Academy of International Law, with
    EMK, 78–79
as Irish Catholic, 78
JFK's assassination and, 209
job offers following moot court win, 93
kinship with EMK, 78
moot court competition, with EMK, 91–93
politics of, 78
on RFK, 144
RFK's assassination and, 384, 385
RFK's eulogy and, 386
running for Congress (1964), 244
at University of Virginia Law School, 77–80
Vietnam fact-finding mission and, 307, 313,
    314, 315–16
Vietnam War, anti-war position, 317, 334
Tunney, Mieke, 244, 716
TV Guide
    JFK on influence of television on politics, 106
Tydings, Joseph, 195, 279, 298, 299, 307, 313,
    315, 419, 435
    Carswell judicial nomination and, 529–30,
        531
Tyler, Harold, Jr., 632

UAW (United Auto Workers), 377, 643, 645, 650,
    651
    Carswell nomination and, 529
    national health insurance and, 682, 688
    See also Reuther, Walter
Udall, Mo, 438
Ulasewicz, Tony, 499, 501, 532
"Ulysses" (Tennyson), xxviii, xxxiv
Umberto, King, 551
United States
    "the American consensus," xxi
    anti-Semitism in, 11
    anti-war protests, 323–24, 333, 341, 605, 631
    Chappaquiddick incident and consequences
        for America, 514–15
    citizen-politicians favored over career
        politicians, 170–71
    Civil Rights Act of 1964 and victory for
        morality, 227
    demographic shifts (1970s), 611
    89th Congress and redefining America, 325

United States (*cont'd*):
  election results (1972) and, 608
  EMK and change in politics, 170
  EMK and his family address the nation after
    RFK assassination, 391
  first manned moon landing, 485, 499, 500
  globalism and, 111
  health-care crisis, 655–56
  individualism in, 246
  JFK's assassination and, xxxv, 204–5, 209,
    212, 213
  JFK's assassination and liberalism in, 275
  JFK's impact on, 213
  JFK's presidency and, 110–12, 212
  King assassination and rioting, 372
  liberalism's decline in, xxi–xxii
  moral authority and, 366
  national health insurance and, 641–55
  New Dealism and, xxi
  Nixon and division in, 427, 428
  Nixon as polarizing figure, 609
  personal character issue in politics, 515
  pessimism of 1971, 584
  post–New Deal liberal consensus, 111, 201,
    245, 246, 378, 417, 424, 425, 515, 609, 610
  presidential election (1964), as plebiscite,
    244–47
  presidential election (1968), American
    division, and Nixon's win, 416–24
  progressivism in, xvii (*see also* progressivism)
  racial animosity in, 320
  RFK's assassination and, xxxv, 381–88
  RFK's presidential candidacy and reuniting of,
    376, 388–89
  rightward turn in politics, 710, 714
  Schlesinger forecasts "new mood in politics,"
    180
  shift from liberalism to conservatism, xxxv
  Silent Majority and, 427, 441, 542, 607, 642
  urban riots (1967), 340, 417, 556
  Vietnam War as divisive, 331–32, 340, 348
  World War II and, 41
  See also civil rights; health care; national
    health insurance; *specific national issues*
University of Michigan
  LBJ commencement address, 252
University of Utah College of Law, 590
University of Virginia Law School
  EMK and moot court competition, 90–93, 528
  EMK and Tunney at Hague Academy of
    International Law, 78–79
  EMK and Tunney rent a house, hire a
    housekeeper, 79–80
  EMK attending, 77–82, 90
  EMK's academic struggles at, 82, 90
  EMK's admission to, 75
  EMK's excellent at arguing a case, 90–93
  EMK's friends and associates at, 77–78

  EMK's scrapes, partying, and reckless driving,
    80–81
  EMK's ulcer and, 78, 82
  EMK tagged "Cadillac Ed," 80
  RFK at, 75, 82
Unruh, Jesse, 116–17, 368, 381, 406, 408
Urban Mass Transportation Act, 186
U.S. Agency for International Development
  (USAID), 313, 334
U.S. Army
  EMK assigned to Paris, France and football
    team, Germany, 68–69
  EMK at Fort Dix, 65–66, 69
  EMK enlistment, 64–65
  EMK's discharge from, 69
  EMK's life, lessons, and maturation in, 65–70
  rich kid's prerogatives and, 67–68
U.S. Department of Justice
  Civil Rights Act of 1964 and, 226
  RFK as attorney general, 114–15, 172, 226
U.S. economy
  downturn after Nixon, 699
  inflation (1974), 699
  minimum wage, xix, xxiii
  postwar boom, 97
  tax cuts to stimulate, 111
  unemployment (1974), 699
U.S. House of Representatives
  Armed Services Committee, 338, 339
  Banking Committee and ITT investigation,
    626
  campaign-finance reform, 693–94
  Democratic majority (1965), 252
  election (1972) and, 611
  EMK's community health centers and, 322
  Fitzgerald in, 7
  FOIA amendment, 694
  Hart–Celler Act, 269, 270, 270n
  House Rules Committee, 190
  immigration issues, 267
  JFK in, 99
  JFK's congressional race (1946), 57, 95, 96, 98
  Judiciary Committee, 559
  Judiciary Committee, Nixon impeachment
    and, 685
  lowering the voting age and, 559, 560, 560n
  midterms (1962) and Democrats, 179
  midterms (1966), 325
  Nixon impeachment and, 639
  one man, one vote bill, 326–27, 329, 330
  Rayburn as Speaker, 190
  resolution on the Vietnam War, 618
  Ways and Means Committee, 659, 667,
    668–69, 670, 681, 683, 688
U.S. Military Academy at West Point, 64n
U.S. News & World Report
  EMK's presidential prospects (1972), 589
  on EMK's star power, 433

U.S. Senate, xxxiv, 302–3
  ABM system fight, 452–56, 520, 524
  Administrative Practice and Procedure
    (AdPrac) Subcommittee, 461–63, 464, 465
  Afro-Asian Subcommittee, 462
  alcoholism of members, 431, 432
  Appropriations Committee, 445
  Armed Services Committee, 445, 452, 456
  Armed Services Committee, Preparedness
    Subcommittee, 462, 463
  average age of members, 190
  Azorean Refugee Act of 1958, 267
  as a "bipartisan liberal institution," 201
  Brooke as only black senator, 530
  Carswell judicial confirmation hearings and,
    529–32
  chamber of, history and description, 180
  chemistry between members and, 272
  Civil Rights Act of 1964 and, 219–27, 221n,
    245, 253
  civil rights and, 97, 198, 418
  as a club, 189–90, 202, 253
  committee assignments, 182, 445
  conservative Republicans and, 253
  defense appropriations and, 456, 457
  Democratic majority (1965), 252–53
  Democratic opposition to Nixon, 446
  desks, status of member and, 181, 202
  dining room, 192
  Dirksen as Minority Leader, 190, 296–97, 327,
    441
  Economic Opportunity Act, 245
  election (1972) and, 611
  Elementary and Secondary Education Act
    extension, 723–24
  EMK and AdPrac, 461–63, 464, 465, 525, 587,
    626, 627, 654, 695
  EMK and draft reform bill, 338–40, 449, 452,
    558, 587, 592, 701
  EMK and Judiciary Committee, 183, 184, 191,
    195–96, 220, 224, 266, 272, 279, 283, 284,
    295, 296, 299, 304, 328, 329, 445, 528,
    531, 622, 624, 626, 629, 631–32, 635, 695,
    705
  EMK and Labor Committee, xix–xx, 182, 194,
    254, 255, 259, 265, 338, 646, 648, 650, 651,
    654, 664
  EMK and lowering the voting age, 558–61
  EMK and Meals on Wheels, xix, 556–57
  EMK and one man, one vote redistricting
    fight, 326–31, 449
  EMK and RFK both serving in, 251, 258–63,
    265, 266, 272, 287, 306, 418
  EMK and RFK's legacy in, 449–50
  EMK as a "Senate man," 202, 203, 257, 285,
    324, 336, 431, 434, 435, 615
  EMK as moral leader, 288
  EMK as national figure, 262
  EMK as president's brother, 191
  EMK begins first term, 179, 180
  EMK respected by colleagues, 223, 287–89,
    320, 331, 339–40
  EMK returns, post-plane crash, 251
  EMK's ascendance in, 446, 453
  EMK's committee assignments, 182
  EMK's death, honoring, xv
  EMK's desk, 181–82
  EMK's election to, xx, 177–78
  EMK's enemies in, 569
  EMK's first bills, 186
  EMK's freshman class in, 181, 182
  EMK's freshman year, 189–203, 204
  EMK's heightened sense of purpose, 265–306,
    312, 320
  EMK's last visit, xxv
  EMK's legislative achievements, xvii–xxi
  EMK's legislative package, 449–50, 461
  EMK's liberal coalition, 445
  EMK's love for, 201–3, 431
  EMK's majority whip position, 431–39,
    442–43, 444, 445–46
  EMK's majority whip position lost (1970),
    566–72
  EMK's office called "Lourdes of Capitol Hill,"
    xxvi
  EMK's plane crash and recovery, working
    from the hospital, 230–43
  EMK's poll tax fight, 276–89, 331, 346, 449
  EMK's popularity in, 251, 288, 324, 332, 339,
    436
  EMK's return after Chappaquiddick, and
    starting from scratch, 519–26, 532
  EMK's return after RFK's assassination, 419,
    429–39
  EMK's run for, 121–42
  EMK's Vietnam War opposition, 456–60,
    526–27
  EMK's years of service in, xv, xxxiv
  Fair Housing Act, 713
  family picnics and, 254
  Family Practice Medicine Act, and pocket veto
    lawsuit, 614–17
  Finance Committee, 191, 220, 431, 438, 536,
    652, 655, 680, 683
  FOIA amendments, 694–97
  folkways of, 202
  Foreign Relations Committee, 569
  Great Society legislation, 275
  Gun Control Act of 1968, 524
  gun-control legislation, 419
  gym, 192
  Haynsworth confirmation hearings,
    528–29
  health care legislation and, 320–22
  Health Security Act, S.3, 655, 678, 679, 680,
    682, 699

U.S. Senate (*cont'd*):
Health Subcommittee on Children and Families, 589
HEW's cancer bill, S.1828, 662, 664–65
Humphrey as majority whip, 434, 436, 444
Immigration and Nationality Act of 1965, 269–74, 449
immigration issues, 266, 268–74
Indian Education Subcommittee, 451, 463, 467
JFK and, xxxiv, 97, 99, 119, 192, 201, 462
JFK's legislative program and, 186, 190, 201, 447
Judiciary Committee, 183–84, 191, 194, 195–96, 220, 224, 272, 278, 283, 295, 328, 445, 461, 528, 530, 559, 622, 695
Judiciary Committee, Watergate special prosecutor and, 632
Labor and Welfare Committee, 182, 194, 254, 255, 265, 338, 451, 646, 649–50, 651
Labor's Health Subcommittee, 645, 646, 649, 651–53, 660, 661
LBJ and, xx, xxii, xxxiv, 199–200, 201, 214, 215, 419, 444, 462, 463
LBJ as majority leader, 278
LBJ as majority whip, 432
LBJ's legislative agenda and, 253–58, 276
liberalism and, xxxiv, 97, 217, 253, 444–45
liberals in, 190–91, 445
longest serving senator, 202
Mansfield as majority leader, 181, 182, 199–201, 215, 278, 339, 431, 432, 436, 461
McCarthy's Investigations Subcommittee, 96, 328, 537
Medicare and, 266, 444
midterms (1958) and Democrats, 97, 110
midterms (1962) and Democrats, 179
midterms (1966), 325
"minnows and whales" in, 190, 201
National Cancer Act, S.34, 660–66, 685
national health insurance hearings, 654–55
Nixon as senator, 441
Nixon's presidency and, 442–46
Nixon's tax reform bill, 520, 524
Nutrition and Human Needs Subcommittee, 443–44, 464
office allocation and, 186
Old Senate Office Building, 192, 193
operation of, legislating by, 259
Oval Office tapes and, 633, 634, 635, 636, 637, 638–39, 672, 685–86, 692
post–New Deal liberal consensus, 201
poverty programs, 266
Public Health Service Act amendment, 655
Rackets Committee, 537
Refugee Subcommittee, 312–13, 463, 465, 584, 587, 617
relaxed schedule at, 253–54

reorganization of 1946, subcommittees and, 462
RFK as senator from New York, 251, 255, 258–61, 272, 287, 324, 418–19
RFK's staff, EMK finding jobs for, 392–93
Rules Committee, 635, 693
Scott–Kennedy campaign-finance bill, 692–94
Select Subcommittee (Watergate investigation), 628–31, 654, 677
Southern states' senators (bulls), 190, 198–201, 213, 214, 215, 219–20, 226, 227, 251, 253, 259–60, 267, 272, 289, 329, 330, 331, 436, 444–45, 455, 532, 653
Special Committee on Aging, 557
staffing for, 187
Subcommittee on Constitutional Rights, 626
three-year sunset provisions, 653
traditions of, 202
Vietnam War resolution ending war funding, 618
Vietnam War troop withdrawal and, 593
Voting Rights Act extension, 713
Voting Rights Act of 1965, 266, 276–89
War Powers Act amendment, 617
Ways and Means Committee, 536
Wednesday prayer breakfasts, 192, 193
whip's job and perks, 432, 444, 446, 566
whip's rooms in the Capitol, 446–47
women's rights, 550–51
U.S. Supreme Court
Baker v. Carr, 326, 327, 328, 527
Blackmun joins, 532
Brown v. Board of Education, 217, 284, 527, 659, 719, 720, 724
Carswell nomination, 529–32, 711
Colegrove v. Green, 326
Engel v. Vitale, 527
Gideon v. Wainwright, 527
Griswold v. Connecticut, 527
Haynsworth nomination, 527–29
Keyes v. School District No. 1, Denver, 720
Loving v. Virginia, 527
Miranda v. Arizona, 527
poll tax deliberations, 284
Rehnquist nomination, 588
Reynolds v. Sims, 527
Swann v. Charlotte-Mecklenburg, 719
Warren Court as engine for liberal transformation, 527–28
Wesberry v. Sanders, 326, 527
U Thant, 391, 431

Valeo, Francis, 305–6, 497, 569, 602, 628
vanden Heuvel, William, 144, 225, 234, 238, 317, 345, 363, 364, 371, 389, 397, 405, 408
Chappaquiddick incident and, 486, 492, 509
on EMK's agony after RFK's death, 469

on EMK's assassination theory, 461
presidential election (1968) and, 408, 412–13, 414, 414n
Vander Zee, Rein J., 204
Vanocur, Sander, 386, 390
Victura (EMK's sailboat), 396, 472
Vietnam War, 254–55, 307–26, 331–37, 347–48
  "all hell fell," 390
  amnesty for draft resisters, 587–88, 701
  CIA and, 314
  civilian massacre, 589
  collapse of the South Vietnamese government, 701, 702
  costs of, 325
  Diem government, 308, 310
  as divisive issue, 340, 348
  domino theory and, 311–12
  Eisenhower and, 308
  EMK and civilian casualties, 333, 334, 335, 348–49, 350–51, 587
  EMK and public hearings on, 334–35, 337
  EMK and refugees, 312–13, 315, 318, 320, 322, 332–33, 335, 587, 701–2
  EMK breaks from LBJ and, 341, 352–54, 403–4
  EMK's concern for American soldiers, 337–38
  EMK sends delegation to North Vietnam, 619
  EMK's fact-finding missions, 307–8, 313–15, 316, 348–51
  EMK's opposition to Nixon's policy, 456–60, 465, 526–27, 557–58, 583, 586, 591–93, 618–19
  EMK's transformation from hawk to dove, 316–18, 322–24, 326, 351, 586
  EMK wooed by North Vietnamese and POW list (1970), 565–66, 569
  Ford and, 701–2
  France and, 340–41
  Geneva Accords and, 310
  Great Society ended by, 340, 342–43
  Gulf of Tonkin resolution, 319, 781n319
  "Hamburger Hill," 457–58, 465
  hawks, doves, and, 310, 605
  Humphrey and, 319, 355, 403–4, 412, 420–22, 424
  impact on the U.S., 355–58, 424
  JFK and, 308, 309, 311
  JFK's portrait hung in homes, 350
  Kent State shootings and, 557, 583
  LBJ and, xxxiv, 254–55, 307, 311–12, 313, 318, 319, 322–24, 331–32, 341, 351, 355–57, 360, 369, 421, 424
  liberalism impacted by, 322, 325–26, 342–43, 358, 389
  midterm elections (1966) and, 325
  New Left and, 605
  Nixon and, 348, 417, 424, 442, 589
  Nixon's bombing of Cambodia and Laos, 558, 618–19
  Paris peace talks, 411
  peace accords (1973), 700
  Republican hawks and, 319–20
  RFK and, 314, 319, 322, 324, 332, 334, 336, 340–41, 357–58, 402, 404, 452, 456, 459
  Tet Offensive, 355–57, 452n, 457, 459
  USAID report on civilian suffering, 334–35
  U.S. casualties, 332
  U.S. military "advisors" and, 310, 311
  U.S. peace movement and protests, 332, 335, 336, 341, 344, 357, 583, 605
  U.S. soldiers as poor and urban, 452, 452n
  U.S. troops in, 332
Village Voice
  Cowan on RFK as liberal, 389
Vineyard Gazette, Martha's Vineyard, 487
Volpe, John, 123, 242
Voting Rights Act of 1965, xix, 266, 276–82, 320, 327, 426, 556, 558, 711
  lowering the voting age and amending, xviii–xix, 558–61
Voutselas, Angelique, 241, 487, 718

Waddy, Joseph, 616
Wade, Richard, 373
Wagner, Helga, 481–82, 552
Wagner, Robert, 643–44
Waldrop, Frank, 33
Walinsky, Adam, 269, 303, 386
Wallace, George, 217, 376, 427, 428, 607, 620, 711, 714
  assassination attempt on, 594, 596, 598, 706
  Audie Murphy Patriotism Award, 706
  EMK speaks at Wallace hosted event, 706–9, 734
  EMK visits, 596–97
  presidential race (1968) and, 400, 420, 422, 424, 425, 426, 596, 791n426
  presidential race (1972) and, 596, 597
Wallace, Mike, 412
Wall Street Journal
  on Dirksen, 327
  on the liberal Senate, 253
Walsh, David, 187
Walter, Francis, 267, 270
Wanamaker, Rodman, 35
Waring, Lloyd, 126
Warnecke, John Carl, 543
Warner, Jack, 11
War Powers Act, 617
Warren, Earl, 326
Washington, D.C.
  Cathedral of St. Matthew the Apostle, xxvii
  EMK's funeral motorcade and, xxx
  mourning EMK in, xv

Washington Post, 288, 508, 509
  Califano as attorney for, 631
  Chappaquiddick incident and, 485, 489, 503
  on EMK and Wallace, 708
  on EMK's crowds, 608
  on EMK's one man, one vote fight and, 331
  on EMK's poll tax speech, 287
  on Goldwater, 245–46
  Morrissey judicial appointment and, 295, 298, 300, 305
  on national health care, 681
  Woodward-Bernstein investigation and, 621–22, 627, 628, 632–33
Washington Times-Herald
  Kick Kennedy at, 47, 48
  Waldrop as editor, 33
Watergate scandal, 620–40, 692
  break-in of Democratic National Committee headquarters, 620–21, 625n
  Committee for the Reelection of the President (CREEP) and, 620, 621, 622
  Cox as special prosecutor, 632–33, 635–36
  EMK begins investigation of, 626–29
  impeachment of Nixon and, 634, 635, 638, 639, 677, 685
  Jaworski as special prosecutor, 685
  Nixon firing of Cox, 636–38, 639
  Oval Office tapes and, 633, 634, 635, 636, 637, 638–39, 672, 685–86, 692
  personal morality and, 715
  "the Plumbers" and, 622
  "the Saturday Night Massacre," 638, 685, 703
  Senate Select Committee and, 628–31
  transparency in government and, 694
  Woodward-Bernstein investigation and, 621–22, 627, 628, 633
Water Quality Act, 275
Watson, Marvin, 351, 371
Watson, Tom, 397
Watt, Robert, 484
Wattenberg, Ben, 612
  The Real Majority, 582, 583, 606
Weaver, Warren, Jr., 460, 465, 524
Webster, Daniel, xv, xviii, 203
  EMK's desk and, xv
Wechsler, James, 309, 398, 429, 456–57, 574–75, 652, 655
Weinberger, Caspar, 677–78, 679, 681, 686–87, 689
Wellesley College, 19
Wertheimer, Fred, 692–93
Westmoreland, William, 314, 350, 353, 356, 369
West Virginia
  Morgantown federal rehabilitation center, 430
  presidential campaign (1960), 108
  primary race (1960), 102, 103–4, 122, 430
  See also Byrd, Robert C.

"What Has Happened to America?" (Nixon), 417–18
Wheeler, Earle, 355
"When Irish Eyes Are Smiling" (song), xxvi, 673
White, Byron, 101
White, Kevin, 119, 600, 600n
White, Theodore H., 212, 375, 428, 635, 757n105
White, William
  Citadel, 191
Whitmore, Howard, Jr., 242
Wicker, Tom, 168, 229
  big Democratic donors backing Jackson, 718
  on EMK and Chappaquiddick, xvii
  on EMK and Wallace, 708
  on EMK calling for Nixon impeachment, 634
  on JFK's assassination, 386, 388
  on the liberal Senate, 253
  on Southern power in the Senate, 190
Wiesner, Jerome, 240, 453, 454, 456
Wilkins, Roy, 390
Williams, Andy, 383
Williams, Harrison, 646
Willkie, Wendell, 78
Wills, Garry, 212, 213, 433, 512–13, 547, 581–82
Wilson, Woodrow, 171, 172
Wirtz, Willard, 219, 254
Wisconsin
  presidential primary (1960), 721
  presidential primary (1972), 596
Witcover, Jules, 608
Wofford, Harris, 217
Women's National Press Club, 181, 186
women's rights, 550–51
  Equal Rights Amendment, 550–51
Wood, Robert, 137, 140, 240, 250
Woodcock, Leonard, 600, 651, 688
Woods, Rose Mary, 637, 672
Woodward, Bob, 621–22, 628, 632–33
Wordsworth, William, xxix
World War II
  German invasion of Poland, 32
  Germany-Soviet nonaggression pact, 32
  impact on Europe, EMK witnesses, 56
  Japanese attack on Pearl Harbor, 41
  JFK's heroism in the Pacific, 46
  Joe, Jr.'s death in, 46–47
  JPK and, 31–32, 94
  Munich Agreement, 30
  U.S. enters, 41
Wright, Charles Alan, 633, 685
Wright, Sylvia, 367, 468, 520–21, 522–23, 526
Wyman, Eugene, 613
Wyzanski, Charles, Jr., 295

Yarborough, Ralph, 259, 260, 451, 646, 648–49, 652, 653, 660
Yew, Lee Kuan, 314
Young, Andrew, 707
Young, Whitney, 455
Youth Employment Act, 186

Zacharias, Jerrold, 240
Zais, Melvin, 457
Zedong, Mao, 601
Ziegler, Ron, 601
Zimny, Ed, 230, 231, 232, 233, 239

ABOUT THE AUTHOR

NEAL GABLER is the author of five books, including three biographies: *An Empire of Their Own,* which won the *Los Angeles Times* Book Prize; *Winchell,* which was named *Time* magazine's nonfiction book of the year and was nominated for the National Book Critics Circle Award; and *Walt Disney,* which won him his second *Los Angeles Times* Book Prize and was named biography of the year by *USA Today.* He has been the recipient of a Guggenheim Fellowship, a Shorenstein Fellowship from Harvard, and a Woodrow Wilson Public Policy scholarship, and was the chief nonfiction judge of the National Book Awards.